ADVERTISING MANAGEMENT

Fifth Edition

Rajeev Batra
University of Michigan

John G. Myers
University of California at Berkeley

David A. Aaker
University of California at Berkeley

Prentice Hall
Upper Saddle River, New Jersey 07458

Batra, Rajeev.
　　Advertising management / Rajeev Batra, John G. Myers, David A.
Aaker. — 5th ed.
　　　　p.　　cm.
　　Aaker's name appears First on 4th ed.
　　Includes bibliographical references and index.
　　ISBN 0-13-305715-1
　　　1. Advertising—Management.　　I. Myers, John G.,
II. Aaker, David A.　　III. Title.
HF5823.A13　　1995
659.1—dc20　　　　　　　　　　　　95–25901
　　　　　　　　　　　　　　　　　　CIP

Acquisitions Editor: *Dave Borkowsky*
Editorial Supervision/Production: *Americomp*
Production Coordinator: *Lynne Breitfeller*
Associate Managing Editor: *Carol Burgett*
Manufacturing Buyer: *Vincent Scelta*
Marketing Manager: *John Chillingworth*
Assistant Editor: *Melissa Steffens*
Editorial Assistant: *Theresa Festa*
Interior Design: *Maria Lange*
Cover Designer: *Lorraine Castellano*
Design Director: *Pat Wosczyk*

Cover Art: Ed Honowitz/Tony Stone Images

The chapter opening quotation on page 173 from the book *How To Advertise*, copyright ©
1976 by Kenneth Roman and Jane Maas is reprinted with special permission from St.
Martin's Press, Inc. and the Julian Bach Literary Agency, Inc., New York, NY. The chapter
opening quotation on page 316 from Sidney Levy is reprinted by permission of the
Harvard Business Review. Excerpt from "Symbols for Sale" by Sidney J. Levy (July-
August 1959). Copyright © 1959 by the President and Fellows of Harvard College; all
rights reserved. The chapter opening quotation on pages 219, 316, 414, and 500 from
David Ogilvy are excerpts reprinted with permission of Atheneum Publishers, an imprint of
Macmillan Publishing Company from *Confessions of an Advertising Man* by David Ogilvy,
copyright © 1963, 1987 David Ogilvy Trustee. The chapter opening quotation on page
345 is from *Personal Influence* by Elihu Katz and Paul F. Lazarsfeld. Copyright © 1955 by
The Free Press; copyright renewed 1983 by Patrica Kendall Lazarsfeld and Elihu Katz.
The chapter opening quotation on page 658 by Bauer and Greyser is reprinted by permis-
sion and is from Raymond A. Bauer and Stephen A. Greyser, "Advertising in America: The
Consumer View," Boston: Division of Research, Harvard Business School, 1968.

 © 1996 by Prentice Hall, Inc.
A Simon and Schuster Company
Upper Saddle River, New Jersey 07458

Printed in the United States of America
10　9　8　7　6　5　4　3　2　1

ISBN 0-13-305715-1

Prentice-Hall International (UK) Limited, *London*
Prentice Hall of Australia Pty. Limited, *Sydney*
Prentice-Hall Canada Inc., *Toronto*
Prentice-Hall Hispanoamericana, S. A., *Mexico*
Prentice-Hall of India Private Limited, *New Delhi*
Prentice-Hall of Japan, Inc. *Toyko*
Simon & Schuster Asia Pte. Ltd., *Singapore*
Editora Prentice-Hall do Brazil, Ltda., *Rio de Janeiro*

CONTENTS

Chapter 6   **Segmentation and Positioning**   **173**

Part III   **Message Strategy**

Chapter 7   **Attention and Comprehension**   **219**

Chapter 8   **Understanding Benefit-Based Attitudes**   **249**

PREFACE

Advertising is a fascinating subject—"the most fun you can have with your pants on," as Jerry Della Femina once said. Yet it is also perhaps the aspect of marketing where it is most difficult to know for sure what "works," and thus to improve the productivity with which budgets are spent. This book is written with the objective of giving students and practitioners alike the framework and knowledge with which to make more effective advertising decisions, and to communicate some of the excitement and vitality that characterizes the advertising business. Towards this end, the book tries to pull together what we currently know about how advertising "works," and to draw lessons from that knowledge for better advertising decision-making.

CHANGES IN THE FIFTH EDITION . . . .

This fifth edition of *Advertising Management* has been extensively updated. We have not only updated the research foundations of the book but have taken special care to add many more examples and case histories and to make the presentation more application-oriented. One way in which we have made the book more contemporary is by adding new readings at the ends of chapters or sections, taken from leading business and advertising publications. Together with the revised text, they provide an exciting picture of the rapidly changing place of advertising and ad agencies in the total context of marketing communications.

In keeping with this new perspective on how advertising fits into the bigger marketing communications picture, there is now a new chapter on integrated marketing communications, covering that topic as well as sales promotions, direct marketing, public relations, and other communications tools. There is also an entirely new chapter on global advertising, in keeping with the increasing interest in managing a brand's global communications program in a way to optimally balance cost efficiencies with local marketing needs.

Other major changes include more material on brand equity, advertising production, and client-agency relationships; greater discussion of successful copywriting techniques; updated information on copy-testing services; and a new appendix on media data sources. A major resequencing of chapters has led to the placing of the chapters entitled "How Advertising Works" and "Attention and Comprehension," earlier in the book.

It goes without saying that all the research covered in this book has been significantly updated, and some older, less relevant material has either been pruned or dropped entirely. We have also tried harder to draw out implications from the research discussed for actual advertising decision making, rather than merely summarizing the state of academic knowledge on each topic.

ORIENTATION AND TARGET AUDIENCE . . . .

Despite these substantial changes, the basic thrust of the book remains at it was earlier. The overriding objective is again to provide an approach to the management of advertising that is sophisticated, thoughtful, and state-of-the-art, while being practical and relevant to real-world advertising planning, decision making, and control. The book again draws on and attempts to integrate three related disciplines: the behavioral sciences, marketing and advertising research, and management science.

While we do mention the industry rules-of-thumb and "received wisdom" at appropriate points, our orientation is clearly one of understanding and applying relevant research. We continue to believe that too many advertising decisions are made wastefully and inappropriately and that the application of relevant research can contribute substantially to reducing such waste. Having said that, we recognize that advertising is both a science and an art—and while we cannot teach the art of it, we can at least attempt to develop an appreciation for it, in our chapters on the creative and production processes.

This book is intended for users and potential users of advertising, as well as for those who are preparing for a career in advertising. Previous editions have been used successfully in both undergraduate and graduate courses in advertising, advertising management, communications management, and management of promotions. It has also been used as the basis for training in various leading advertising agencies and marketing organizations. No previous knowledge is assumed, although some familiarity with elementary principles of marketing will, of course, be helpful.

ORGANIZATION AND CONTENT . . . .

The book is divided into six parts. Part I describes the field of advertising, and the institutions through which advertising "flows," positions advertising within the organization, and introduces advertising planning and decision making. Part II focuses on setting advertising objectives within the broader context of integrated marketing communications, and presents a review of existing knowledge on "how advertising works" as well as the concepts of segmentation and positioning. Part III examines the interrelated aspects of message strategy: building awareness and communication copy points, changing benefit-based attitudes, associating feelings with the brand, developing brand personality and equity, leveraging group influences, and precipitating action. Part IV discusses tactical issues, those related to actual message execution: choosing among various creative approaches, writing and evaluating actual copy, testing copy for effectiveness and diagnostics, and producing and implementing advertising—including the topic of how clients and agencies can work together more effectively. Part V moves on to media strategy (setting budgets) and media tactics (allocating budgets). Part VI then returns the reader to the broader environment, looking at the regulatory constraints and social impact, as well as the global marketing context.

ACKNOWLEDGMENTS . . . .

We would like to thank the many people who helped significantly to improve this fifth edition of the book, including the publishers and media data companies that allowed us to reproduce articles and source materials, and the advertisers who (usually) graciously acquiesced to our request to use their ads. There are too many of them to acknowledge individually, but each source is acknowledged in the text at the point of usage. Thanks also to Harlan Spotts and David Schmittlein for suggesting improvements. They join the many reviewers who helped us on previous editions, including Boris Becker, John Deighton, Julie Edell, David Furse, Sharan Jagpal, Betsy Gelb, Ewald Grether, Stephen Greyser, Manoj Hastak, Hal Kassarjian, Trudy Kehret-Ward, Dean Krugman, James Krum, Rich Lutz, Andy Mitchell, William Mindak, Francesco Nicosia, Tom O'Guinn, Michael Ray, Allan Shocker, Camille Schuster, Doug Stayman, Debra Stephens, Bill Wilkie, and Terrance Witkowski. We also thank Prashanth Unnikrishnan for help on the Instructor's Manual and ancillary materials. Finally, we owe much to Lynne Breitfeller of Prentice-Hall, and to Susan Hayes for accommodating our design preferences and for seeing the book through production in the way we wanted it.

To all these people and others whose efforts and contributions now escape our memory, we offer our thanks. Our faculty colleagues and students at Berkeley and Michigan have been a constant source of inspiration and encouragement. Finally, we thank our wives and families for their support and understanding. The book is dedicated to them.

Rajeev Batra
John G. Myers
David A. Aaker

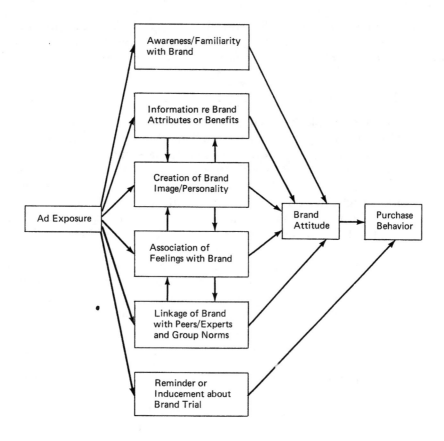

In this book, advertising is seen as influencing consumer attitudes and purchase behaviors in a variety of interlinked ways. An ad exposure can increase brand familiarity, communicate brand attributes and benefits, develop an image and personality for the brand, associate specific feelings with the brand, link the brand to reference groups such as peers and experts, and directly induce action.

PART I

INTRODUCTION

1 THE FIELD OF ADVERTISING MANAGEMENT

> The trade of advertising is now so near to perfection
> that it is not easy to propose any improvements.
> (Samuel Johnson, 1760)

> The competent advertising man must understand
> psychology. The more he knows about it the better.
> He must learn that certain effects lead to certain
> reactions, and use that knowledge to increase
> results and avoid mistakes. Human nature is the
> same today as in the time of Caesar. So the
> principles of psychology are fixed and enduring. We
> learn, for instance, that curiosity is one of the
> strongest of human incentives.
> (Claude Hopkins, Scientific Advertising, 1926)

The field of advertising management is made up of a system of interacting organizations and institutions, all of which play a role in the advertising process. At the core of this system are advertisers, the organizations that provide the financial resources that support advertising. Advertisers are private or public sector organizations that use mass media to accomplish an organizational objective. It is the decision to invest resources in purchasing time or space in such mass media as television, radio, newspapers, or magazines that basically distinguishes advertisers from nonadvertisers. Advertisers make use of mass media. Nonadvertisers do not.

Advertising management is heavily focused on the analysis, planning, control, and decision-making activities of this core institution—the advertiser. The advertiser provides the overall managerial direction and financial support for the development of advertising and the purchase of media time and space, even though many other institutions are involved in the process. A focal point is the development of an advertising program or plan for the advertiser. In cases where several different kinds of products or services are offered by the advertising organization, a separate program may be developed for each. The resulting advertisement is usually aired or placed several times, and the resulting schedule of exposures is referred to as an *advertising campaign*. The development and management of an advertising campaign associated with an advertiser's brand, product, or service is thus a major point of departure for advertising management.

In developing and managing an advertising campaign, the advertiser basically deals with numerous institutions, as Figure 1–1 illustrates. The advertising agency, the media, and the research suppliers are three supporting or *facilitating* institutions external to the advertiser's own organization. The agency and the research suppliers assist the advertiser in analyzing opportunities, creating and testing advertising ideas, and buying media time and space; the media, of course, supply the means by which to advertise. Others are, in effect, *control* institutions that interact with and affect the advertiser's decision-making activities in numerous ways. Government and competition are the two most important external control institutions. Most advertisers are affected by a wide range of government regulations concerning their products, services, and advertising. Direct or indirect competitors are usually present and serve as a major external control. What competitors do and how they react is thus an important part of advertising management.

The markets or consumers the advertiser is attempting to reach through advertising can be thought of as yet another kind of external institution that both facilitates and controls advertising. The concepts of *markets* and *consumers* will be used interchangeably to refer to any classification of individuals, organizations, or groups the advertiser is attempting to reach or "get a message to." Examples could be homemakers; electronic engineers; automobile dealers; voters; hospital patients; government officials; or other industrial, retail, government, or nonprofit organizations. Without an existing or potential target for advertising messages, the rationale for advertising would not exist. The consumer is a controlling force, mainly through a whole range of behavioral possibilities, such as viewing or not viewing, buying or not buying, voting or not voting, and so on. It is the consumer, in this broad sense, to whom advertising campaigns are directed, for whom media

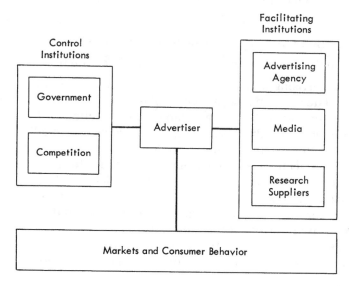

Figure 1–1.   Major institutions involved in the field of advertising management.

are used and advertising agencies create copy, and on whom advertising research is done. The identification and understanding of markets and consumer behavior is thus also a vital part of advertising management.

In this chapter, background information is presented on advertisers and on the three major facilitating institutions: advertising agencies, the media, and research suppliers. A discussion of several perspectives on the subject of advertising, including the one adopted in this book, follows. The balance of the book, from the perspectives of Figure 1–1, deals, in one way or another, with advertising planning and decision making in the context of markets, competition, and governmental constraints.

THE ADVERTISER . . . .

The advertiser is the core institution of the field of advertising management, and expenditures of advertisers provide the basis for estimates of the size of the advertising industry. Annual expenditures by all advertisers in all media (newspapers, magazines, business papers, television, radio, direct mail, outdoor billboards, and so on) were estimated to be $138 billion in 1993.[1] One estimate is that by the year 2000, annual advertising expenditures in the U.S. will reach $320 billion and will exceed $780 billion worldwide.[2] It has been estimated that the level of annual advertising expenditures in the U.S. has remained stable at about 2.1 to 2.2 percent of gross national product (GNP) for about the last fifty years.[3]

The *Standard Directory of Advertisers*[4] lists 17,000 companies engaged in advertising in a typical year. Most are small, private, or nonprofit organizations utilizing broadcast or print media on a local basis in the immediate region or metropolitan area in which they are located. Even this large figure excludes public service advertisements (PSAs),[5] nonpaid advertisements by nonprofit organizations, and classified advertisements in local newspapers purchased by private citizens. Advertisers utilizing local media, although large in number, do not account for the majority of advertising expenditures. In 1993, for example, local advertising that largely reflects media use by small advertisers accounted for about 42 percent of all advertising expenditures, whereas national advertising, reflecting large-scale users, accounted for the remaining 58 percent.[6]

Small- and large-scale advertisers can be distinguished according to the degree to which they use the facilitating institutions shown in Figure 1–1. Private citizens and many local small-scale advertisers, for example, buy media time or space directly and do not use an advertising agency or the services of a research supplier. The typical large national advertisers will have one or more advertising agencies under contract and will buy numerous types of research services, as well as conduct research on their own. In general, they make full use of the system shown in Figure 1–1, whereas small-scale advertisers, for budgetary reasons, use only parts of the system. Although many of the case examples, models, and research techniques and results presented in this book focus on the full system, and are thus most directly applicable to large-scale advertisers, the underlying principles involved are equally applicable to any advertiser, large or small, profit or nonprofit, and so on.

Advertisers differ according to the markets they serve, the goods and services they produce, and the media they use. In the private sector, advertisers can be distinguished according to whether they are predominantly *consumer, industrial,* or *retail* advertisers. Consumer advertisers are those mainly involved in the manufacture of durable or nondurable goods and services for consumer markets. Industrial advertisers predominantly manufacture and market products for industrial markets, and retailers often advertise locally to attract store patronage. Many large firms, such as General Motors, Kraft General Foods, and Sears, Roebuck service more than one market, which makes attempts to classify advertisers on this basis less meaningful. The media-use distinctions, however, are comparatively clear-cut. Retail advertisers, particularly at the local level, use newspaper advertising extensively. Consumer goods and services advertisers make heavy use of television, radio, and consumer magazines. Industrial advertisers generally make heavy use of trade magazines, business papers, direct mail, and trade shows. The audience for industrial advertising is made up of professionals who are often more willing and able to accept and process detailed information than is an audience made up of members of households.

About 52 percent of all national advertiser expenditures is accounted for by ninety-nine private corporations and the federal government.[7] After a recession-based slump in overall advertising expenditures in 1990 and 1991, the industry rebounded in 1992 and 1993. Table 1–1 shows expenditures for thirty-one product and service categories in 1993, which accounted for a total of over $48 billion. The highest-spending industries were retail, automotive, business and consumer services, entertainment and amusements, foods, toiletries and cosmetics, drugs and remedies, travel, hotels, and resorts, direct response companies, and candy, snacks, and soft drinks. As can be seen, industrial categories spend relatively less on advertising.

The top 10 national advertisers for 1989 and 1993 are shown in Table 1–2. In 1993, they accounted for over $12.2 billion of advertising investment, or more than 31 percent of all expenditures of the leading 100 national advertisers, which were $37.9 billion. Notice that with some exceptions, the same companies tend to appear in the top 10. Procter & Gamble once again regained its position as the nation's leading advertiser, with expenditures of almost $2.4 billion. Philip Morris (including its subsidiary, Kraft General Foods) was the nation's second largest advertiser in 1993, with expenditures of over $1.8 billion (outside the United States, Unilever and Nestlé are the other biggest spenders).[8] These are huge consumer packaged-goods companies, and their brands have huge budgets. Business-to-business marketing companies spend heavily in trade papers and business magazines. Although their advertising expenditures are much less than consumer companies, the expenditures are nevertheless significant. In 1993, for example, the top 5 and their expenditures in millions of dollars were IBM ($96.7), AT&T ($51.2), Microsoft ($45.5), Hewlett-Packard ($44.9), and Digital Equipment Corp. ($44.5)[9].

In many instances, advertising management is done by a brand manager who is responsible for managing all marketing-related aspects of the brand. His or her job has been likened to the president's position in a small company because the amount of money involved in advertising individual brands runs into the millions

Table 1–1. Product and Service Categories Represented by Top 100 Advertisers, 1993 (millions of dollars)

Rank	Category	Expenditures
1	Retail	8,082.3
2	Automotive	7,754.5
3	Business & consumer services	5,259.4
4	Entertainment & amusements	3,749.9
5	Foods	3,442.8
6	Toiletries & cosmetics	2,608.4
7	Drugs & remedies	2,294.7
8	Travel, hotels & resorts	2,030.5
9	Direct response companies	1,404.8
10	Candy, snacks & soft drinks	1,286.7
11	Insurance & real estate	1,242.3
12	Apparel	1,090.5
13	Sporting goods, toys & games	990.9
14	Publishing & media	806.6
15	Computers, office equipment	799.8
16	Beer & wine	779.0
17	Household equipment & supplies	696.7
18	Soaps, cleansers & polishes	668.4
19	Electronic equipment	432.4
20	Jewelry & cameras	353.4
21	Cigarettes	340.2
22	Building materials	336.9
23	Gasoline, lubricants & fuels	309.9
24	Household furnishings	301.8
25	Horticulture & farming	229.4
26	Liquor	218.4
27	Pets & pet foods	195.0
28	Freight	148.7
29	Industrial materials	124.0
30	Business propositions	46.6
31	Airplanes (not travel)	18.1
32	Other	308.3
	Total	48,351.2

Reprinted with permission from Advertising Age, *September 28, 1994. © Crain Communications, Inc. All rights reserved.*

Table 1–2. Top Ten National Advertisers in 1989 and 1993 (millions of dollars)

Rank	1989 Category	1989 Expenditures	Rank	1993 Category	1993 Expenditures
1	Philip Morris	2,072.0	1	Procter & Gamble	2,397.5
2	Procter & Gamble	1,779.3	2	Philip Morris	1,844.3
3	Sears, Roebuck	1,432.1	3	General Motors	1,539.2
4	General Motors	1,363.8	4	Sears, Roebuck	1,310.7
5	Grand Metro PIC	823.3	5	Pepsico	1,038.9
6	Pepsico	786.1	6	Ford	958.3
7	McDonald's	774.4	7	AT&T	812.1
8	Eastman Kodak	718.8	8	Nestle	793.7
9	RJR Nabisco	703.5	9	Johnson & Johnson	762.5
10	Kellogg	611.6	10	Chrysler	761.6
		11,064.9			12,218.8

Reprinted with permission from Advertising Age, September 26, 1990 and September 28, 1994. © Crain Communications, Inc. All rights reserved.

of dollars. Table 1–3 shows the advertising expenditures of leading brands in various product categories in 1993. In pain relievers, for example, over $91 million was spent on Advil advertising. Nike spent over $132 million, and $75.6 million was spent on advertising for Marlboro cigarettes. Other leading brands in their categories (Folgers coffee, Crest toothpaste, Kleenex, Tylenol pain reliever, and so on), had very large advertising budgets. Shown at the left are brands and companies whose expenditures exceeded $100 million, ranging from AT&T with $511.1 million to Budweiser beer with $113.2 million. The brand managers in charge of Miller beer and Coca-Cola products were responsible for about $217 and $133 million of advertising expenditures, respectively, in 1993. Leading brands in the less-than-$50-million category are shown at the right. Managers of leading brands such as those given in these examples are in charge of significant human and financial resources and have jobs that are not unlike the presidents of similarly-sized corporations.

Since consumer products are bought by virtually every household, most of their budgets are spent on television advertising: over 71 percent of Philip Morris's advertising and almost 83 percent of Procter & Gamble's total measured media budget went into television (national, spot, cable, and syndicated).[10] In contrast, a manufacturer of durable goods will typically be more inclined toward print media than will a manufacturer of packaged goods, because a durable product is more complex and requires longer and more detailed copy. Print advertising, especially newspapers, are also more used by retail advertisers. Sears, Roebuck, the fourth largest advertiser in 1993, spent millions of dollars in newspaper advertising. Whereas national advertising for retailers such as department stores or food chains is the exception, local advertising is vital for these advertisers. Much local retail advertising features item and price listings, but some retailers take a broader view and emphasize store image. John Wanamaker, a retail executive in the early 1900s, was among the first to focus on store image, using such headlines as "The quality is remembered long after the price is forgotten."

Nonprofit organizations, such as schools, colleges, churches, hospitals, and libraries, are increasingly making use of local advertising. They have many of the same problems as business firms. They must identify the groups they serve, determine their needs, develop products and services to satisfy those needs, and communicate with their constituencies. This communication can often be done most effectively by advertising. National advertising is also increasing among nonprofit organizations, particularly for fund-raising or behavior-change efforts by the major medical associations and such groups as the Boy Scouts, Girl Scouts, and the United Way. One of the most dramatic advertising stories of the early 1990s was the use of advertising and mass media by government and nonprofit groups to reduce cigarette consumption in the United States. Consumers were bombarded with a constant stream of antismoking messages which, combined with legislation which banned smoking in many public places, significantly reduced smoking behavior. The federal government was the thirty-eighth largest national advertiser in 1993, spending $304.4 million, a decline from $342.4 million in 1992. The largest governmental advertising effort was for the U.S. Postal Service ($78.6 million), followed by the military, Amtrak, HUD, and Veterans Affairs.[11]

An interesting, unusual form of advertising, called *advocacy advertising*, be-

Table 1-3. Advertising Expenditures of Some Leading Brands in 1993 (millions of dollars)

Over $100 Million		$50 to $100		Less Than $50 Million	
AT & T	511.1	Advil	91.7	M& M Candy	27.9
McDonald's	410.5	American Airlines	91.1	Pampers	27.2
Kelloggs Cereals	382.4	Crest	91.0	Cheerios	21.4
Chevrolet	317.7	Levis	75.8	Pert Plus	29.5
Ford	276.6	Marlboro	75.6	Mennen	20.6
Toyota	258.2	Apple Computer and Software	67.1	Vicks	26.6
Hasbro Toys	217.3	Folgers	65.2	Stouffers	38.0
Miller Beer	216.7	Campbell Soups	62.2	Gillette Razors	34.4
VISA	193.9	Kleenex	61.2	Monistat 7	36.3
Kraft Foods	158.5	Tide	60.8	Dove	21.3
Tylenol	143.8	Kodak Single-Use	54.5	Noxzema	14.0
Coca-Cola	132.9	Purina	53.6	Doritos	15.0
NIKE	132.5	Alka-Selzter	52.1	Nyquil	41.4
Cadillac	122.0	Oil of Olay	51.1	Hanes	37.4
Pepsi	119.3			Clairol	48.2
L'Oreal Cosmetics	118.1			Clorox	46.5
Wrigley's Gum	117.7			Yoplait	11.7
Budweiser	113.2				

gan about 1973. Business institutions using this type of advertising take a public position on controversial issues of social importance, aggressively state and defend their own viewpoints, and criticize those of their opponents. Professional groups, like lawyers, are now legally allowed to advertise their services and thus became yet another type of advertiser.

There are thus dozens of different types of advertisers and an equally large number of forms of advertising, including national, local, consumer, industrial, service, comparative, cooperative, corrective, advocacy, counter, and public service advertising. Each is discussed in various sections of this book.

The Role of the Brand Manager

As mentioned earlier, the brand manager, for many large advertisers, both industrial and consumer, is a central figure in the development and management of advertising. The brand manager, either directly or through a staff advertising manager, makes the advertising policy decisions and interacts with the advertising agency. He or she is responsible for all marketing aspects of the brand and, internally, draws upon the full range of line and staff resources of the corporation. This includes such departments as sales, new product planning, marketing research, and so on. In many cases, the advertising budget is the most significant expenditure associated with marketing the brand. The brand manager usually represents the interests of just one corporation brand and oversees the development of the advertising and marketing program for it. Table 1–3 shows advertising expenditures of some leading brands in 1993.

In recent years, some large client companies have moved away from traditional brand management organizational structures. Many companies that market multiple brands within the same product category have introduced a higher-level post of "category manager," a person who is responsible for supervising and coordinating the brand managers for individual brands and making sure that competition between the company's own brands does not become unproductive. In Procter & Gamble, for instance, brand managers for Tide and Cheer and other detergents report (through another organizational layer called ad managers) to the category manager for laundry products. The category managers are charged with overseeing personnel, sales, product development, advertising and promotion of their respective categories.[12] In an effort to cut costs, Procter & Gamble and other companies have also recently begun to reduce the number of organizational layers in their brand management structures.

The brand manager role is particularly important in the study of advertising management, even though it is not the only one for which the materials in this book are relevant. Basically, the concepts, models, and decision aids presented here are completely general, even though they are often presented from the viewpoint of a brand manager in a consumer packaged-goods organization. It should also be emphasized that they apply when the object of the advertisement is other than a packaged consumer product; it may be a service, a political candidate, or a government program. The same concepts apply when the target of the advertising is other than a consumer; for example, an organization, an industrial buyer, a voter, or a client of an organization.

A product or a specific version of a product—a brand—is thus a major reference point for the study of advertising management. We use the term "product" or the term "object" in a general sense throughout the book to refer to the reference point for advertising. It can be something tangible like Green Giant peas, a service like Allstate Insurance, or even an idea like "Just Say No" in an antidrug campaign. As noted, the organizational role most often used to identify the manager of day-to-day advertising operations in a great number of cases is that of the brand manager.

FACILITATING INSTITUTIONS . . . .

All advertisers, by definition, use some form of media to accomplish organizational objectives. Where significant amounts of media expenditures are involved, the advertiser will also use the services of an advertising agency and one or more research suppliers. Together, these three types of institutions make up the primary facilitating institutions of advertising management. In this section, we present an overview of the role, nature, and scope of these three institutions. Much of the organizational dynamics of advertising management is best understood by observing the role of the facilitating institutions in relation to the advertiser, as shown in Figure 1–2.

First, note that the advertising agency is represented in a position "between" the advertiser and the media. A major role of the advertising agency is the purchase of media time and space. The agency, on the one hand, is interacting with the advertiser and, on the other, with one or more media organizations. A second point to note is the role of research. Although not shown explicitly in Figure 1–2, most large firms, at each of the levels of advertiser, agency, and media, will have their own internal research departments, and each will also be purchasing research data externally from some outside research supplier. The research input to the system is a vital aspect on which many of the formal models, theories, and decision aids presented in this book are based.

Another insight from Figure 1–2 is that a typical advertising campaign evolves from the activities of a project or planning group composed of representatives of the advertiser, the agency, and one or more research suppliers. Basically, many meetings of this group will take place over the course of campaign development. Oral presentations of creative ideas and media plans will be made by the agency representatives. Similarly, research suppliers will make oral presentations on the

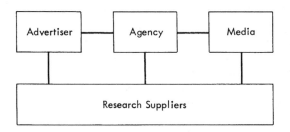

Figure 1–2.   Role of facilitating institutions.

results of a consumer survey, a copy test, and so on. Much written and telephone communication also takes place during this process.

In the previous section, it was suggested that the brand manager was the major representative of the advertiser's interests. The analogous positions at each of the three facilitating institution levels are the account executive for the agency, the media representative for media, and the project supervisor for research suppliers. Each level of the system is also represented by a professional trade association. For example, the Association of National Advertisers (ANA) represents advertiser interests; the American Association of Advertising Agencies (AAAA) serves the agency component; and associations like the National Association of Broadcasters (NAB), the American Newspaper Publishers Association (ANPA), the Magazine Publishers Association (MPA), the Direct Marketing Association (DMA), and the Outdoor Advertising Association of America (OAAA) serve the major media. The Advertising Research Foundation (ARF) is heavily concerned with the research aspects of the system.

The Advertising Agency

A unique aspect of advertising is the advertising agency, which, in most cases, makes the creative and media decisions. It also often supplies supportive market research and is even involved in the total marketing plan. In some advertiser-agency relationships, the agency acts quite autonomously in its area of expertise; in others, the advertiser remains involved in the creative and media decisions as the campaign progresses.

The first advertising agent, Volney B. Palmer, established an office in Philadelphia in 1841.[13] He was essentially an agent of the newspapers. For 25 percent of the cost, he sold space to advertisers in the various 1,400 newspapers throughout the country. He made no effort to help advertisers prepare copy, and the service he performed was really one of media selection. His knowledge of and access to the various newspapers were worth something to an advertiser.

Although the nature of an agency has changed considerably since Palmer's day, the fixed-commission method of compensation is still the one used most often. The basic compensation for most agencies is a fixed percentage of advertising billings, 15 percent, which they receive from the media in which the advertisements are placed. On "noncommissionable" (nonmedia) services (such as preparing brochures and collateral materials), an agency usually marks up the supplier's invoice cost by 17.65 percent so that it still keeps 15 percent of the total cost to the client company (of every $100 paid by the client, if the agency keeps $15 and pays $85 to its supplier, it is keeping 17.65 percent of the $85). The fixed-commission system has been criticized because it encourages the agency to recommend higher media budgets than may be appropriate, may not relate to the actual amount of work the agency does for the client, and is not linked to the success of the advertising campaign. Thus, many client companies (including IBM, General Foods, R. J. Reynolds, Nestlé/Carnation, and the German detergent giant Henkel) now either pay their agencies a fixed, negotiated dollar fee or some combination of commission and fee.[14] Many companies now also link the compensation to campaign performance, paying the agency a bonus (or a higher commission rate) if the campaign exceeds agreed-upon communication goals.[15] The subject of how the success or failure of ad campaigns ought to be evaluated is discussed at length in Chapter 3, and agency compensation is discussed in Chapter 14.

By the turn of the century, agencies started to focus their attention on the creation of advertising for clients. Probably the first agency with a reputation for creative work was Lord and Thomas, which was blessed with two remarkable copywriters, John E. Kennedy and Claude Hopkins. Kennedy believed that advertising was "salesmanship in print" and always tried to provide a reason why people should buy the advertised goods. One of Kennedy's first tasks when he joined Lord and Thomas in 1898 was to re-create an advertisement for a new washer that had relied on the headline "Are you chained to the washtub?" appearing over a figure of a worn, disgruntled housewife shackled to a washtub.[16] Kennedy's advertisement showed a woman relaxing in a rocking chair while turning the crank of a washer. The copy emphasized the work of the ball bearings and the time and chapped hands the machine would save. The cost of the resulting inquiries decreased from $20 each to a few pennies.

Claude Hopkins, who joined Lord and Thomas in 1907, was regarded by many as the greatest creator of advertising who ever practiced the art. One year, soon after joining the firm, he made nearly $200,000 just writing copy.[17] He was particularly good at understanding the consumer and at integrating the advertising into the total marketing effort. His first account was Campbell's Pork & Beans.[18] He discovered, using his own research, that 94 percent of American housewives baked their own beans. Yet the advertisers of the day were focusing on the relative advantages of their own brands compared to competitors'. Hopkins's campaign argued against home baking, reminding housewives of the sixteen hours involved in preparing the beans and the probability of ending up with crisp beans on top and mushy beans below. His "primary demand" appeal (getting people to buy the product—any brand) was enormously successful. In response to the competitive reaction, he boldly ran advertisements challenging consumers to "Try Our Rivals Too." He also secured distribution among restaurants and then advertised to the consumers the fact that restaurants had selected the Campbell brand. Hopkins knew the importance of developing an advertising program that was based on consumer desires. In his words, "Argue anything for your own advantage and people will resist to the limit. But seem unselfishly to consider your customers' desires and they will naturally flock to you."[19]

Hopkins also took on the task of advertising the company's evaporated milk, a new product for Campbell.[20] In introducing the brand, Hopkins used a technique on which he often relied. He offered to buy housewives a 10-cent can as an indication of his confidence in the brand. In a single newspaper advertisement that ran in New York for one day only, he inserted a coupon that could be redeemed at a retail store for one can of milk. His idea proved to be brilliant. It provided incentives for people to try the product without tarnishing its image, as a 50-cents-off coupon might have done. More important, it encouraged retailers to stock the brand to satisfy customer demands and to share in the profit represented by the offer. Entering a New York market dominated by another brand, the technique gained for Campbell 97 percent distribution practically overnight. More than 1.46 million customers redeemed the coupon featured in the single New York advertisement. The $175,000 cost of the program was recovered in less than nine months, and Campbell captured the New York market.

The agencies grew in size and influence through the years as they demonstrated an ability to create effective advertising. Lord and Thomas grew from less than $1 million in billings in 1898 to more than $6 million in 1910 and to $14 million in 1924.[21] In 1993, Foote, Cone & Belding, the successor to Lord and Thomas, had worldwide billings of more than $5.33 billion.

Table 1–4 shows the top ten advertising organizations and agency brands in 1993.[22] Because of mergers and acquisitions, many of the largest and well-known agencies are now part of large advertising organizations or groups such as the WPP Group, the Interpublic Group, and the Omnicom Group. In Table 1–4, billings represent media costs, whereas income is the money retained by the agency, generally around 15 percent of billings. The largest agency organization in 1993 was the WPP Group, headquartered in London, England, followed by Interpublic and Omnicom. WPP had billings of about $18.5 billion in that year, an enormous number when you think of this as the amount of money spent on advertising and marketing activities being managed by this one group. Saatchi and Saatchi is another huge British advertising organization headquartered in London, England; in 1995, it changed its name to The Cordiant Group.

Notice in Table 1–4 that the top-ten list of advertising organizations is made up of companies from several different countries and is no longer dominated by U.S. agencies and "Madison Avenue." Using the top-ten criterion, the United States, Britain, Japan, and France are the countries that dominate advertising worldwide. The competition from European and Asian manufacturing companies is, as might be expected, quite well reflected in the top-ten advertising organizations. Note that significant volume in all but the two Japanese agencies represented in the top ten is generated in the United States. The three largest groups derive from 32 percent to 47 percent of total billings from the U.S. In contrast, the two Japanese agencies, Dentsu and Hakuhodo generate only about 1 percent of their volume in the U.S.

Many of the "megagroups" that now exist in advertising are the result of a wave of acquisitions and mergers in the advertising agency business during the 1980s. The WPP group acquired (among many others) the Ogilvy & Mather and J. Walter Thompson advertising agency groups.[23] In addition to its advertising agency group holdings, WPP Group also owns direct marketing agencies, sales promotion agencies, public relations firms, marketing research companies, and specialized companies concentrating on health, entertainment, recruitment, and Yellow Pages advertising. Other leading agency megagroups are Saatchi and Saatchi (which owns that agency, plus Backer Spielvogel Bates), the Interpublic Group (which owns McCann-Erickson, Lintas-Campbell-Ewald, Ammirati and Puris/Lintas, and Lowe and Partners/SMS), and Omnicom (which owns BBDO and DDB Needham). (Changes in ownership and name occur all the time, and those presented here may well be out-of-date by the time you read them.)

There are several reasons for this wave of acquisitions and growth and the consequent building of worldwide agency networks. First, most client companies

Table 1–4. Top Ten Advertising Organizations and Agency Brands, 1993 (millions of dollars)

Rank[a]	Advertising Organization	World Billings	Gross World Income	Agency Brands	World Billings	Gross World Income
1	WPP Group, London	18,485.3	2,633.6	Dentsu Inc.	10,377.6	1,340.9
2	Interpublic Group, New York	13,967.3	2,078.5	Mccann-Erickson Worldwide	6,556.0	982.9
3	Omnicom Group, New York	13,839.1	1,876.0	J. Walter Thompson	5,805.8	835.9
4	Dentsu Inc., Tokyo	10,846.3	1,403.2	Euro RSCG Worldwide	4,938.6	704.6
5	Saatchi & Saatchi Co., London	10,809.6	1,355.1	BBDO Worldwide	5,003.5	688.2
6	Young & Rubicam, New York	7,559.0	1,008.9	Hakuhodo Inc.	4,938.0	667.8
7	Euro RSCG, Neuilly, France	6,508.9	864.8	Grey Advertising	4,438.5	660.6
8	Grey Advertising, New York	5,171.8	765.7	Lintas Worldwide	4,172.9	626.8
9	Hakuhodo, Tokyo	4,938.0	667.8	Leo Burnett Co.	4,223.5	622.4
10	Foote, Cone & Belding, Chicago	5,336.0	633.7	DDB Needham Worldwide	4,542.6	604.1

Reprinted with permission from Advertising Age, April 13, 1994. © Crain Communications, Inc. All rights reserved.

[a]*Based on worldwide gross income.*

are themselves merging, and growing substantially outside the United States, thus demanding larger agency office networks worldwide. Procter & Gamble, for example, already gets 40 percent of its business from outside the United States, a figure expected to grow to 60 percent by 2000. This focus on non–U.S. markets is due, in part, to the fact that population—and, thus, market size—is growing more rapidly outside than within the United States and the fact that the effect of advertising on sales is also greater outside the United States.[24] Such globalization is often accompanied by the growth of "global brands" that employ similar ad campaigns worldwide. The campaigns for Marlboro cigarettes and Dewar's Scotch whisky, for example, are very similar in concept around the world.[25] Not all brands and ad campaigns can be so standardized, however, and the reader is cautioned to be somewhat critical of the concept of "global marketing."[26] Chapter 20 discusses this subject in detail.

When companies grow worldwide, the agencies that hope to have a client's business worldwide (or not at all) must therefore create worldwide servicing networks, by owning overseas agencies or creating partnerships with them. McCann-Erickson, for example, now has 144 agencies in 67 countries and used to service Coca-Cola in almost all of these markets. It even has a global account director for Coca-Cola in New York, responsible for the agency's work on that account worldwide. In 1989, almost 39 percent of McCann-Erickson's total billings came from Europe, 13 percent from Asia and the Pacific, and 10 percent from Latin America. It should be noted that in addition to the client-derived "demand" for overseas growth, another reason for the agencies' overseas expansion is simply that advertising spending rates are higher overseas than in the United States, since the per capita base levels are usually lower overseas. The volume of total advertising spending outside the United States now roughly equals that in the United States.[27]

The second major reason for the creation of these megagroups is the realization that ad agencies and media advertising are only one part of a client's total communications and marketing mix, which also includes sales promotions, public relations, direct marketing, marketing to minorities, and so on. Chapter 3 discusses this idea of using "integrated marketing communications." Since many of these other elements of the mix are, in fact, growing faster than advertising (with advertising dollars often being moved to sales promotions or direct marketing), it makes sense for companies to offer clients not simply media advertising capabilities but these other capabilities as well. The claim is that a client's total communications needs can be better coordinated and served if the client has all these different needs serviced by units of the same megagroup, an idea expressed by phrases such as "complete orchestration" or "the whole egg." Not many client companies appear to have bought into this claim, however, and it appears in hindsight that many of these agency megagroups might have overdiversified, leading to financial strains. The Saatchi and Saatchi group, for instance, which pioneered this concept, had to sell off many of its holdings in 1989 and 1990. A schematic of the diversified agency megagroup WPP appears in Figure 1–3.

The third reason for the creation of agency holding groups that own several agency networks is to avoid account conflict. A client will almost never give an account to an agency that also services a competitor. It is hoped, however, that if the

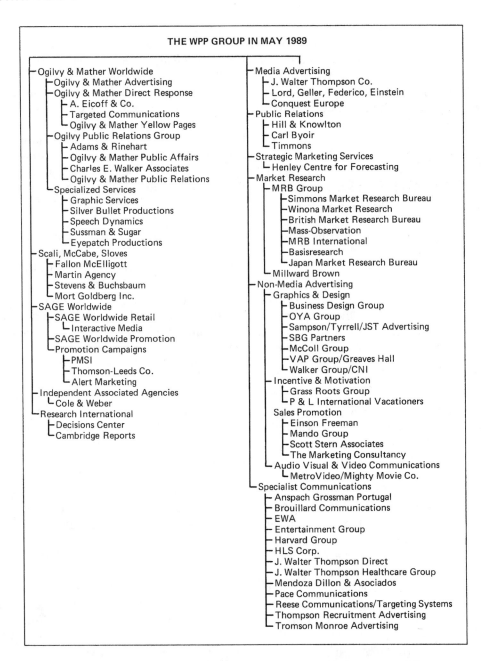

THE WPP GROUP IN MAY 1989

- Ogilvy & Mather Worldwide
  - Ogilvy & Mather Advertising
  - Ogilvy & Mather Direct Response
    - A. Eicoff & Co.
    - Targeted Communications
    - Ogilvy & Mather Yellow Pages
  - Ogilvy Public Relations Group
    - Adams & Rinehart
    - Ogilvy & Mather Public Affairs
    - Charles E. Walker Associates
    - Ogilvy & Mather Public Relations
  - Specialized Services
    - Graphic Services
    - Silver Bullet Productions
    - Speech Dynamics
    - Sussman & Sugar
    - Eyepatch Productions
- Scali, McCabe, Sloves
  - Fallon McElligott
  - Martin Agency
  - Stevens & Buchsbaum
  - Mort Goldberg Inc.
- SAGE Worldwide
  - SAGE Worldwide Retail
    - Interactive Media
  - SAGE Worldwide Promotion
  - Promotion Campaigns
    - PMSI
    - Thomson-Leeds Co.
    - Alert Marketing
- Independent Associated Agencies
  - Cole & Weber
- Research International
  - Decisions Center
  - Cambridge Reports

- Media Advertising
  - J. Walter Thompson Co.
  - Lord, Geller, Federico, Einstein
  - Conquest Europe
- Public Relations
  - Hill & Knowlton
  - Carl Byoir
  - Timmons
- Strategic Marketing Services
  - Henley Centre for Forecasting
- Market Research
  - MRB Group
    - Simmons Market Research Bureau
    - Winona Market Research
    - British Market Research Bureau
    - Mass-Observation
    - MRB International
    - Basisresearch
    - Japan Market Research Bureau
  - Millward Brown
- Non-Media Advertising
  - Graphics & Design
    - Business Design Group
    - OYA Group
    - Sampson/Tyrrell/JST Advertising
    - SBG Partners
    - McColl Group
    - VAP Group/Greaves Hall
    - Walker Group/CNI
  - Incentive & Motivation
    - Grass Roots Group
    - P & L International Vacationers
  - Sales Promotion
    - Einson Freeman
    - Mando Group
    - Scott Stern Associates
    - The Marketing Consultancy
  - Audio Visual & Video Communications
    - MetroVideo/Mighty Movie Co.
- Specialist Communications
  - Anspach Grossman Portugal
  - Brouillard Communications
  - EWA
  - Entertainment Group
  - Harvard Group
  - HLS Corp.
  - J. Walter Thompson Direct
  - J. Walter Thompson Healthcare Group
  - Mendoza Dillon & Asociados
  - Pace Communications
  - Reese Communications/Targeting Systems
  - Thompson Recruitment Advertising
  - Tromson Monroe Advertising

Figure 1–3.   The different parts of the WPP agency megagroup in May 1989.

competitor's account is at one of a megagroup's agencies, a potential client will still consider the group's other agency networks, since the different agency networks are supposedly run autonomously.

Obviously, clients do not pick agencies on the basis of size and servicing capabilities alone. Creative reputations also matter a great deal. A survey of agency reputations was conducted for *Advertising Age* by SRI Research Center in the last quarter of 1984.[28] A random sample of 300 advertising directors of companies with revenues over $25 million per year selling to the top twenty U.S. markets was interviewed. Six attributes of the agency were identified as most important: (1) creativity, (2) account executives, (3) media, (4) top management, (5) marketing, and (6) research. J. Walter Thompson ranked first on five of the attributes, a reputation distinguished by its across-the-board strength. Ogilvy & Mather, Chiat/Day (now part of Omnicom) and Doyle Dane Bernbach (now part of DDB Needham) were perceived as strongest on creativity.

This survey also identified factors considered most important in assessing the strengths of an agency and those on which agencies were perceived as weak. Figure 1–4 shows the results. Creative talent and knowing the client's business were the two most important "necessary strengths" of an advertising agency. Quality of people was also very important. Not knowing client business, inadequate cost estimating, lack of creativity, poor account executives, and misrepresentation were most frequently mentioned as weak spots.

Recent Trends

Some of the key trends have already been mentioned or will be discussed below: the growth of global brands and global agency networks; the shift of marketing dollars away from mass advertising and into sales promotions and direct marketing; the desire for more integrated marketing communications; new developments in the media environment; the change in agency compensation levels and arrangements, and so on.[29]

Possibly the biggest change, however, has been the perception among some leading advertisers that the traditional advertising agency business has not been providing the "creative spark" that some advertisers need. Some advertisers, notably Coca-Cola, have thus begun to "diversify" their sources of creative talent and ideas. In the case of Coca-Cola, many of its ads for the flagship Coca-Cola Classic brand now come not from their long-time ad agency, McCann-Erickson, but instead from a Hollywood talent agency, Creative Artists Agency (CAA). In addition, the Coca-Cola agency has diversified its agency roster by giving assignments to several of the "hot," perceivedly more creative agencies, including Chiat/Day, Fallon McElligot, and Wieden and Kennedy.

Relatedly, more and more large clients are separating the job of media buying from their many different ad agencies and passing that on to the new independent media buying services, consolidating it (often on a media-by-media basis) with one particular agency, or even setting up their own media buying operations. As is discussed below, this leads to greater negotiating clout with the media owners, thus lower media costs.

As a result, many agencies are scrambling to "reinvent" or "reengineer" them-

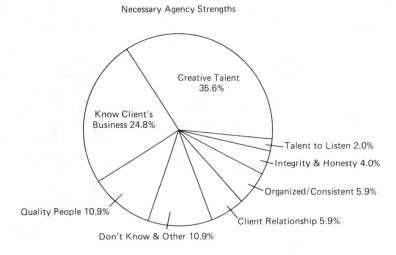

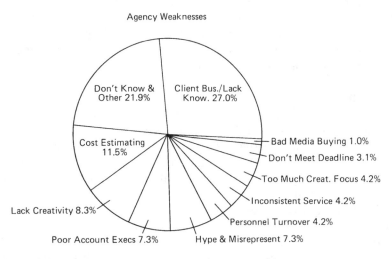

Figure 1–4.   Advertising agency strengths and weaknesses.

Reprinted with permission from the March 28, 1985 issue of Advertising Age. *Copyright 1985 by Crain Communications, Inc. All rights reserved.*

selves. As a case in point, the Interpublic Group (the owner of McCann-Erickson, which has part of the Coca-Cola account) has recently (a) acquired several smaller, creative agencies, such as Ammirati and Puris/Lintas and merged them into its networks, (b) "spun off" smaller "creative boutiques" under its umbrella, and (c) acquired Western International Media, one of the leading independent media buying services. In addition, this agency group, like many others, is exploring how best to use the newer media options, including interactive media, for its clients.[30]

Many of these trends, and others, are discussed further in the two readings at the end of this part of the book (after Chapter 2).

Agency Organization

A modern agency employs three different types of people in addition to those handling administration. The first is the creative services group, which includes copywriters, artists, and people concerned with advertising production. This group develops the advertising campaign, prepares the theme, and creates the actual advertisements. The second is the marketing services group, whose responsibility includes media and market research. This group contains the technical specialists—the psychologists who direct market research efforts and the operations researchers who develop the media buying models. The final major group is the client services group, which includes account executives. An account executive is, in many respects, an agency's counterpart to a client's brand manager. An account executive is responsible for contact with the client. One of his or her important functions is to understand and perhaps contribute to the development of the client's advertising objective and then to communicate it to the creative services and marketing service groups. As the advertising campaign is developed, the account executive obtains advice and decisions from the client as they are needed. In addition to these operating groups, there is usually a review board consisting of key agency people who review all campaigns generated within the agency.

In recent years, several agencies have embraced another organizational innovation called "account planning," first developed in the United Kingdom. An account planner is a specialist in consumer attitudes and motivations who relies on qualitative in-depth research and who works with the account and creative teams in ensuring that the campaign is built with a deep and thorough understanding of the consumer's point of view. In the United States, the Chiat/Day agency, which is well known for its creativity, has championed this approach. It is more frequently used (and talked about) by smaller agencies, who wish to show that their creative leaps are also strategically sound. Many of the largest agencies do not have an explicit account planning function, although some of the same work is performed by research specialists who work closely with the account; these people are often called "consumer insights" specialists.[31]

The Full-Service Agency and Alternatives

The dominant type of agency provides a full spectrum of services, including market research, new product introduction plans, creative services, and media purchases, and is termed a *full-service agency*. Alternatives to the full-service agency for large advertisers have recently appeared. Basically, these involve the replacement of the large agency with smaller specialized organizations, perhaps supplemented by a greater in-house client involvement in the process. It is stimulated by the development of organizations that specialize in media purchases (such as Western International Media, or Vitt Media International, which keep about a 3 percent commission) and others that provide only creative services—the "creative boutiques." The perceived need to make advertising and media dollars work harder—by negotiating bigger media discounts by consolidating media buying and by using smaller agencies that are sometimes perceived to be more creative than the larger ones—have led to these developments. Several client companies and advertising agencies have set up subsidiaries through which media buys are consolidated, and thus made more cheaply, while medium-sized advertising agencies often turn to external media buying companies to benefit from the negotiating clout of these companies.[32]

Magnavox is a firm that has had experience with à la carte buying of advertising services. A Magnavox executive explained the reasoning behind the move, pointing out that the new wave of à la carte advertisers seems to be eliminating many costs related to agency middleman functions, such as account management and marketing and research processors. Along with the elimination of the full-service agency's overhead factors, this probably reduces the 15 percent commission that the agency normally collects by at least one-third. The advertiser should be able to obtain the needed services for the remaining 10 percent and, if it does some of the media buying internally, for print, it can come in under 10 percent. The 15 percent agency commission on ad production, research, and other functions that an agency buys outside is also saved.[33]

The American Association of Advertising Agencies has set forth a position paper in which it presents the case for the full-service agency, arguing against "piecemealing." They identified ten advantages of a full-service agency, including centralization of responsibility and accountability, simplified coordination and administration of a client's total advertising program, greater objectivity, sales-oriented creative work, synergistic experience, a stronger pool of talent, and a better working climate.

The Media

The amount of money spent on advertising in the various media from 1935 to 1993 is shown in Table 1–5. Through the years, the largest media category has been newspapers, which carried about 23 percent of all advertising placed in 1993, measured in terms of total client expenditures of $32.03 billion. The second-largest medium in 1993 was television, which was nonexistent until 1945, with $30.6 billion. Direct mail was the third-largest medium, with expenditures of about $27 billion. Thus, direct mail, a medium with low visibility in many respects, garnered almost three times as much advertising revenue as did radio ($9.5 billion). Direct mail has dramatically increased its share of media expenditures in recent years, rising from 14 percent of all media expenditures in 1980 to 19.7 percent in 1993. In contrast, newspapers during the same period dropped from 28.5 percent to 23.2 percent. Television increased in media share from 20.7 percent to 22.2 percent, whereas magazine share dropped from 5.9 percent to 5.3 percent. The strength of direct mail is its potential for pinpointing an audience and its capacity to present large quantities of advertising. It is a rapidly growing medium, and we discuss it in detail in Chapter 3. Business papers are primarily the trade magazines used by industrial advertisers and others who target their advertising to nonconsumer audiences.

Media developments have dramatically influenced the thrust of advertising through the years. Perhaps the most significant contribution to advertising was the development of the printing press by Guttenberg in 1438. Forty years later, in 1478, William Caxton printed the first English language advertisement, a handbill for a book of rules for the clergy at Easter.[34] The printing press, of course, made

Table 1-5.   Estimated Advertising Expenditures in Major Media, 1935–1993 (millions of dollars)

	1935	1945	1955	1960	1965	1970	1975	1980	1984	1989	1993
Newspapers	761	919	3,077	3,681	4,426	5,704	8,442	15,615	23,744	32,368	32,025
National	148	203	712	778	784	891	1,221	2,335	3,007	3,720	3,620
Local	613	716	2,365	2,903	3,642	4,813	7,221	13,280	20,737	28,648	28,405
Magazines	130	344	691	909	1,161	1,292	1,465	3,225	4,932	6,716	7,357
Business Papers	51	204	446	609	671	740	919	1,695	2,270	2,763	3,260
Television	—	—	1,035	1,627	2,515	3,596	5,263	11,330	19,874	26,891	30,584
National[a]	—	—	810	1,347	2,129	2,892	3,929	8,365	14,819	18,949	22,149
Local	—	—	225	280	386	704	1,334	2,965	5,055	7,942	8,435
Radio	113	424	545	693	917	1,308	1,980	3,690	5,813	8,323	9,457
National	78	290	218	265	335	427	519	935	1,513	2,023	2,115
Local	35	134	327	428	582	881	1,461	2,755	4,300	6,300	7,342
Direct mail	282	290	1,299	1,830	2,324	2,766	4,124	7,655	13,800	21,945	27,266
Outdoor	31	72	192	203	180	234	335	610	872	1,111	1,090
Miscellaneous	342	555	1,793	2,342	2,985	3,848	5,571	10,795	16,775	23,813	27,04T
Total national	890	1,740	5,380	7,305	9,340	11,350	15,340	30,435	49,590	68,990	80,010
Total local	830	1,100	3,770	4,655	5,910	8,200	12,820	24,315	38,490	54,940	58,070
Grand total	1,720	2,840	9,150	11,960	15,250	19,550	28,160	54,750	88,080	123,930	138,080

Reprinted with permission from Advertising Age, April 30, 1980, Part 4, February 16, 1981, May 4, 1985, May 14, 1990, and May 2, 1994. © Crain Communications, Inc. All rights reserved.

[a]*The following is the breakdown for television, giving the expenditures for network, cable (national and nonnetwork), syndication, and national and local spot television for 1993:*

Network	*10,209*
Cable (national)	*1,970*
Syndication	*1,576*
Spot (national)	*7,800*
Spot (local)	*8,435*
Cable (nonnetwork)	*594*
Total	*30,584*

possible newspapers and magazines, the print media on which most advertising still relies.

The first important medium was newspapers. The earliest agencies, in the mid-nineteenth century, were essentially agents for newspapers. They provided a classic wholesaling function for the newspapers, each of which was too small by itself to sell space directly to the national advertisers. To a large extent, newspapers, particularly the smaller ones, still employ agents to sell their space to national advertisers, although these agents are now organizations distinct from agencies. However, the newspaper is really the domain of the local merchant. More than 80 percent of newspaper advertising is placed at the local level, and the most important newspaper advertisers are local retailers. There were about 1,640 daily newspapers in the country in 1990, reaching 63 percent of all adults (and a higher percentage of those highly educated and with high incomes). The highest-circulation newspapers are *The Wall Street Journal* (1.9 million weekday circulation) and *USA Today* (1.3 million).[35]

For all the attention that television, cable, and the new multimedia forms of audio-visual communications have received, it is nevertheless interesting that total television advertising (including network, cable, spot, and syndication) in 1993 was still exceeded by total newspaper advertising (see Table 1–5). Furthermore, although the total share of newspaper advertising has declined since the advent of television, the decline has only amounted to a few percentage points. In 1993, about 23 percent of all advertising expenditures went into newspapers, and most of this went into local newspapers. Local newspaper advertising expenditures in 1993 were $28.4 billion, down slightly from 1989, when they were $28.6 billion. The strength of newspapers comes from their dominant role in local advertising, especially by retailers such as department stores and automobile companies.

During the last decades of the 1800s, magazines began to assume increasing importance. In that period, Lord and Thomas concentrated on religious and agricultural periodicals, becoming the exclusive agent for many of them. After the Civil War, a young space salesman, J. Walter Thompson, decided to focus on the general magazine field, particularly the just-emerging area of women's magazines.[36] He provided advertisers with a list of several dozen from which they could choose. His choice of emphasis partly explains the phenomenal early success of the agency that still bears his name.

Until television arrived, magazines were the largest national advertising medium. With the advent of television, the magazine industry—and particularly the mass-circulation magazines—began to feel the heavy pressure of competition. With the failure of such classic magazines as *The Saturday Evening Post*, *Look*, and, finally, *Life*, many began to question the long-term future of the magazine industry. Actually, magazines have considerable strength and vitality, despite these visible setbacks. The year that the *Post* stopped publishing, 20 other magazines also merged or closed their doors, but more than 100 new ones appeared.[37] In 1950, magazine circulation was 140.2 per 100 population; twenty years later, it was 170.5 per 100 population and was still growing.[38]

The character of magazine publishing is changing, however. Despite the continued success of the *Reader's Digest* and *TV Guide*, whose circulations were each more than 16 million in 1990, it is a fact that magazines are becoming more specialized.[39] (In 1990, the highest-circulation magazine was actually *Modern Maturity*, with 20 million.) Magazines today are aiming at special-interest groups and are often regional in scope. In 1990, there were about 2,100 consumer and farm magazines and about 4,900 business magazines.[40] (Note that media people usually refer to magazines as "books.") As a result of magazine specialization, the audience is often more specialized and is therefore desirable to an advertiser who is attempting to reach more specific audiences.

Magazines are innovating and attempting to capitalize on their physical contact with the audience to make their advertisements more effective.[41] Perfumed ink was used as early as 1957 for Baker's coconut in a *Better Homes & Gardens* advertisement. Since then, it has been used in advertisements for perfume, cologne, vodka, and soap. Recordings, such as Remington's "Music to Shave By," are included in advertisements. They are particularly effective in business advertisements that have a lengthy, detailed story to tell. Actual product samples have appeared in advertisements for Band-Aids, candy, facial tissues, and computer software. Catalogs and other booklets have been included in magazine advertisements. These and other innovations reflect the willingness of magazines to build on their strengths.

Radio emerged in 1922 as an exciting, new advertising medium. Its coverage of the 1922 World Series established it dramatically as a unique communication medium. The 1930s and 1940s were the golden years of radio. Without the competition of television, the network programs—from the soap operas to the major evening shows that starred such luminaries as Jack Benny, Eddie Cantor, Fred Allen, and Bing Crosby—caught and held the attention of the American people. With the advent of television, however, radio went into the doldrums. But in the 1960s, radio started to make a comeback, finding a useful niche for itself by providing entertainment, news, and companionship, particularly for those in a car or otherwise occupied outside the home. It seemed to serve a purpose in a mobile and restless society. Radio's revitalization has been achieved by such programming innovations as talk shows, the all-news format, and hard-rock programs, and by such technological innovations as transistors and the "Walkman," which makes radios highly portable for people of all ages. Like magazines, radio has become more specialized as stations try to serve well-defined segments of the population. It has been particularly successful in developing a youth appeal. Like newspapers, it is a good medium for local advertisers, who provide radio with more than 60 percent of its advertising. In 1990, there were over 5,000 AM and 5,000 FM stations, plus about 1,700 noncommercial FM stations, and although individual radio stations only command, on average, a 1 percent share of local listenership, radio networks enable advertisers to reach 8 to 9 percent of all U.S. adults at any one time and up to 75 to 80 percent of all U.S. adults cumulatively in a week.[42]

Television, delayed by World War II, began in the mid-1940s. In 1948, Milton Berle premiered his show, which was to dominate the ratings during the early years of commercial television. During the first decade of television, the advertiser usually sponsored and was identified with an entire program. This differs from the present practice of having several advertisers share a program. Advertisers were naturally attracted to this new medium because it provided an opportunity for presenting live demonstrations to large audiences. Television grew rapidly during the 1950s and 1960s. The number of homes with television sets in the top fifty markets increased from 6 million in 1950 to 30 million in 1960 and to 40 million in 1970.[43] Today, about 92 million of the 94 million U.S. homes can be reached by television, through the approximately 200 affiliates of each of the big three broadcast networks, the Fox network, and major cable channels like ESPN, CNN, WTBS, USA, Nickelodeon, MTV, and TNN. Each of these cable channels is now available in approximately 50 million TV homes.

The installation of fiber-optic cable to households throughout the United States and many parts of the world promises to speed the development of the so-called information highway with many important implications for the media industry. Some of the likely developments during the 1990s will be the addition of many more kinds of interactive services in which consumers can play games, order products, do their banking, and search libraries and databases. Whether the television set, an elaborate telephone, or a computer workstation becomes the dominant entry vehicle remains to be seen. All these functions may well be integrated into one comprehensive communications unit. Also, this new vision promises consumers hundreds of cable television channels, on-line access via Internet to computer networks throughout the world, movies that will be provided instantly on demand, and dozens of other services. Much of the merger activity among telephone, entertainment, cable, and computer companies that took place during the early 1990s and continues today is motivated by a desire to take advantage of these new media environments.

The advent of cable television, pay television, video recorders, and video-discs promises to bring to television the same level of specialized audiences that magazines now deliver. In 1993, cable TV was in approximately 62 percent of U.S. homes with television. One consequence of these new technologies are the relative decline of the three major television networks (ABC, CBS, and NBC), which have lost audience share to cable channels and independents in homes with cable TV; from 91 percent in 1978, the network share declined to 62 percent in 1990.[44] Another development has been the widespread use of remote control devices to "zap" commercials by switching TV channels whenever ads appear. These new technologies have thus moved us to the era of the "invited commercial," because viewers with the capability of bypassing commercials will only tend to watch commercials that are exceptionally entertaining, informative, or involving. Reaching this audience will require very different approaches to advertising creation and testing. These consequences are discussed later in this book at appropriate points.

Through other developing media technologies, including the ability to specifically "address" each cable TV home from the cable "head," the capability of offering programs to small special interest audiences is slowly emerging. Further, these "addressable" cable systems are beginning to be tied into systems that, using grocery store checkout-lane scanner data, can create consumer databases that bring together data on what every household saw in terms of advertising and then purchased in local stores. Clearly, these technologies might someday make possible some very sophisticated targeting of consumers, for it may be possible for advertisers to schedule ad exposures to only those consumers considered most important from either a retention or switching assessment. Also rapidly emerging are new developments in direct-to-home satellite transmission, with the ultimate prospect of reaching world audiences using visual approaches that are not tied to any particular language.

Like the top advertisers and top advertising agencies, there are top media companies. An important characteristic of the media industry is that most of the leading companies are diversified and are large multinational conglomerates spanning all forms of media. Many of them also have significant revenues generated from nonmedia sources as well. These worldwide media giants include Time Warner which owns, among others, magazines such as *People* and *Sports Illustrated*, Home Box Office and Warner Amex Cable, Warner books and Warner records, Time-Life Books, and the Warner Brothers movie studio. Other companies include the Germany-based Bertelsmann, Italy's Fininvest, Canada's Thompson, Australia's News Corporation (which owns *TV Guide* and Fox broadcasting in the United States), France's Hachette, and the United Kingdom's Maxwell Corporation.

Table 1–6 shows the top-ten leading media companies in the United States in 1993. The biggest company was Time Warner, with $5.72 billion in U.S. media revenues in 1993. Notice that the three big broadcast networks (ABC, CBS and GE's NBC) are represented in the top ten. To understand the media history, it is important to appreciate that newspapers still dominate all other media in terms of revenue. Among the top-ten media companies in 1993, for example, four own mostly newspapers (Gannett, Advance Publications, Times Mirror, and Knight-Ridder). The importance of magazines is reflected in the top group by Time Warner, publisher of *Time*, *Fortune*, *Life*, *Money*, *People*, and *Sports Illustrated*. The largest cable television companies in 1993 were Time Warner and Tele-Communications, Inc., which reported about $3.6 billion and $4.2 billion in cable TV revenue, respectively.

Various types of sales promotions can also be considered by the advertiser and represent yet another kind of media. The sales promotion industry has grown rapidly in recent years, faster than advertising expenditures. In 1983, about 37 percent of the total advertising and promotion budgets of packaged-goods companies was spent on advertising, another 37 percent on trade promotions, and 26 percent on consumer promotions. By 1993, the advertising share was down to 25 percent trade promotions were up to 47 percent, and consumer promotions were up to 28 percent.[45] Like the major media, each form of promotional activity is represented by a professional trade association. Thus, the Promotion Marketing Association of America (PMAA) and the National Premium Sales Executive Association (NPSEA) focus on premiums, promotions, contests, couponing, sampling, price-offs, and cash refunds; the Point-of-Purchase Advertising Institute (POPAI) covers point-of-purchase and aisle display materials; the Specialty Advertising Association International (SAAI) is concerned with specialty advertising, such as imprinted

Table 1-6. Top Ten Media Companies, 1993

Rank	Company	1993 Media Revenues (Millions)						1992–1993 % Change
		Total	News-Paper	Maga-zine	Broad-Cast	Cable TV	Other	
1	Time Warner, New York	5,719.4		2,070.4		3,649.0		2.9
2	Capital Cities/ABC, New York	5,512.3	568.7	328.3	3,882.3	733.0		10.0
3	Tele-Communications Inc., Denver	4,153.0				4,153.0		16.2
4	CBS Inc., New York	3,510.1			3,510.1			0.2
5	Gannett Co., Arlington, VA	3,472.0	2,844.0		397.2		230.8	5.2
6	Advance Publications, Newark, N.J.	3,266.0	1,800.0	970.0		496.0		2.4
7	General Electric, Fairfield, Conn.	3,102.0			3,008.0	94.0		-7.8
8	Times Mirror Co., Los Angeles	2,681.9	1,980.7	230.8		470.4		-1.5
9	News Corp., Sydney	2,651.8	138.8	600.0	1,426.0		487.0	7.5
10	Knight-Ridder, Miami	2,068.6	2,068.6					3.6
	Total	36,137.1	9,400.8	4,199.5	12,223.6	9,595.4	717.8	

business cards and gifts; and the Trade Show Bureau (TSB) with trade shows. Direct mail, represented by the Direct Marketing Association, is also often included in this category.

A major trend in the media industry for the 1990s is the so-called information highway built with fiber-optic cable and connecting millions of households and businesses throughout the United States and other parts of the industrialized world. Dozens of multimedia services are being developed, to take advantage of the new information age, from home movies on demand to bill paying, home banking, and in-home shopping. Interactive media, with which consumers can request movies and do their shopping and banking from home computers or television sets, is also evolving. Advertising will play a major role in these developments and they, in turn, will undoubtedly shape advertising in new and different ways.

Another trend is toward consolidation and new competitive forms in the media, telephone, computer, entertainment, and electronic industries. Barriers to competition between traditional telephone companies and cable companies are breaking down and some rather hasty mergers and acquisitions have taken place.

Research Suppliers

The final type of facilitating institution is made up of companies that supply research services to advertisers, advertising agencies, and the media. Currently, there are more than 500 firms in the United States[46] that supply all kinds of research information for advertising-planning purposes and for specific decisions, such as copy and media decisions.

The first advertising researchers developed methods for assessing the effectiveness of print advertising. From these early beginnings, research companies have sprung up to provide a wide variety of services to advertisers, ranging from consumer surveys and panels to copy testing, audience measurement, and many others.[47] The progress of the field of advertising research closely parallels the development of each of the major media. The Audit Bureau of Circulations (ABC) was one of the earliest firms to develop the first audits of newspaper circulation in 1914. The notion of auditing circulation quickly spread to magazines, and Daniel Starch, a professor at Harvard University, developed the recognition method for measuring magazine readership in 1919. Later, in 1932, Starch founded the firm of Daniel Starch and Staff, which is still one of the largest firms that supply research on print advertising. It is now called Starch INRA Hooper.

Radio research, and broadcast ratings in general, first began in the 1920s, when Archibald Crossley started the Crossley Radio Ratings. The industry expanded greatly during the 1930s and 1940s, as politicians and advertisers realized the potential of radio for reaching national audiences. Frank Stanton, later to become president of CBS, began his career in radio research and, with Paul Lazarsfeld and others, initiated an office of radio research at Princeton University. Lazarsfeld later moved this office to Columbia University to form the Bureau of Applied Social Research.

Television research became one of the numerous specialties of the A. C. Nielsen Company, and this company is particularly well known for its television program rating services. A. C. Nielsen, Sr., who founded the company in Chicago, began by developing auditing services of the movement of products through retail stores. This service is an important part of the current range of research services supplied by this company, with revenues in 1993 of $1.05 billion. Nielsen's other major service focuses on media research and had revenues of about $204 million in 1993. The company was acquired by Dun & Bradstreet in 1984 and is currently part of D&B Marketing Information Services, Cham, Switzerland, a subsidiary of D&B, Westport, Connecticut. A. C. Nielsen has long been known as the largest research supplier in the United States, with five to six times the research revenues of its closest competitors.

In a similar way to the internationalization of client, agency, and media firms, research suppliers are increasingly international companies with offices in many countries around the world. D&B Marketing Information Services, the parent of A. C. Nielsen, derived 61 percent of its research revenues outside of the United States in 1993.[48] Table 1–7 shows the largest U.S. research companies in 1993 and their research revenues. As can be seen, D&B Marketing Information Services, which includes IMS International (a company specializing in research for the pharmaceutical industry), as well as A. C. Nielsen, heads the list with total research revenues of over $1.868 billion. Information Resources Inc. (IRI), which has grown very rapidly and is best known for its supermarket scanner services, was in second place, followed by Arbitron, Walsh International, and Westat. Most of the firms shown on the list provide data for advertising planning, implementation, and control purposes. D&B, IRI, and Arbitron, offer syndicated services to which advertisers subscribe on an ongoing basis. Others, such as Market Facts, provide custom services tailored to the individual client's specific needs.

Some companies tend to specialize in either copy testing (ad testing is commonly called copy testing even though it is the whole advertisement that is usually tested, not just the copy) or audience measurement and provide information most useful for copy and media decision making. In broadcast, ASI Market Research, ARS, McCollum Spielman Worldwide, and the Gallup Organization are well known for their copy-testing services. Among the better known copy-testing services for print advertisements are those of Starch INRA Hooper. Concerning audience measurement, D&B (A. C. Nielsen) is the most prominent in broadcast. Simmons Market Research Bureau is one of the leaders in print audience measurement. Dozens of specialized services, such as Scarborough and CMR (CMR monitors advertiser spending rates), are available for media planners. In print, ABC provides basic circulation and other data for magazines and newspapers, and BPA provides similar information for business, technical, and trade papers. SRDS (Standard Rate and Data Service), Simmons, and MRI (Mediamark Research, Inc.) provide very useful information on all media. Information Resources is an example of a firm that uses supermarket checkout scanner data to evaluate advertising and other marketing effects. Their service, called BehaviorScan, has grown rapidly and has now attracted competing companies.

Market research is a significant industry in the United States and is the source of much of the information used in advertising management. Throughout the book, we will show how research information enters at various stages of ad-

Table 1-7. Top Ten Research Companies, 1993[a]

Rank 1993	Rank 1992	Company	Research Revenues (Millions)	% Change From 1992	Research Revenues From Outside U.S. (Millions)
1	1/2	D&B Marketing Information Services	$1,868.3	–1.2%	$1,139.7 est
2	3	Information Resources, Inc.	334.5	21.1	50.2
3	4	The Arbitron Co.	172.0	–3.4	
4	6	Walsh International/PMSI	115.4	32.1	39.7
5	5	Westat, Inc.	113.1	–0.5	
6	7	Maritz Marketing Research Inc.	74.4	6.7	
7	8	The NPD Group	66.0	15.6	15.7
8	10	NFO Research Inc.	51.9	10.2	
9	11	Elrick & Lavidge Inc.	47.1	0.6	
10	12	Market Facts Inc.	45.6	12.0	
		Total	$2,888.3	9.4%	$1,245.3

Adapted from Jack J. Honomichl, "The Honomichl 50," Marketing News, 28, no. 12 (June 6, 1994), H4. Published by the American Marketing Association.

[a]*For some companies, total revenues that include nonresearch activities are significantly higher than those shown in the table. Percent change from 1992 has been adjusted so as not to include revenue gains from acquisition.*

vertising management and discuss specific services in more detail. Here it is important to gain an initial impression of the diversity and range of such services and to appreciate the importance of their role in advertising management.[49]

PERSPECTIVES ON ADVERTISING . . . .

There is an extensive literature on advertising, made up of books, monographs, reports, journal articles, and speeches, most of which have been written since the turn of the century. David A. Revzan of the University of California lists more than 450 books on the subject of advertising written between 1900 and 1969.[50] There are at least six advertising handbooks, eight histories, and several biographical accounts of advertising people. Among recent such assessments are Stephen Fox's *The Mirror Makers* and Eric Clark's *The Want Makers.*[51]

In addition to handbooks and historical perspectives, advertising has been approached through a variety of paths and traditions. These different paths partly reflect the perspectives of such various disciplines as economics, psychology, social philosophy, and management. They also reflect the needs of the audiences to which they are addressed. Although many of the paths cross and some are ill defined, it is possible and useful to identify some of the main tracks that have been followed through the years.

Several books with an economic perspective, including Roland Vaile's *Economics of Advertising*, were published in the 1920s.[52] The depression of the 1930s increased public concern with the role advertising plays in our competitive economic system. Critics argued that advertising inhibits competition. In this environment, Harvard professor Neil Borden published a classic study of the economic effects of advertising.[53] The evaluation of advertising as an economic force in society has continued to receive attention over the years. A recent book in this tradition is Julian Simon's *Issues in the Economics of Advertising.*[54] The economic perspective tends to deal with aggregate statistics of firms and industries and is concerned with public policy implications.

The writings of sociologists, religious leaders, philosophers, and politicians are also extensive, many reflecting critical views of advertising. Thus, in 1932, Arthur Kallet and F. J. Schlink published *100,000,000 Guinea Pigs*, followed by such works as A. S. J. Basker's *Advertising Reconsidered* in 1935, H. K. Kenner's *The Fight for Truth in Advertising* in 1936, Blake Clarke's *The Advertising Smoke Screen* in 1944, F. P. Bishop's *The Ethics of Advertising* in 1949, and later works like Vance Packard's *The Hidden Persuaders*, Francis X. Quin's *Ethics, Advertising and Responsibility*, and Sidney Margolius's *The Innocent Consumer vs. the Exploiters.*[55] Advertising is a controversial subject about which scholars, intellectuals, and businesspeople tend to form strong and often contradictory opinions.[56]

Another approach to advertising, descriptive in nature, typifies the introductory texts covering the principles of advertising that have appeared from the early 1900s to the present time. They describe such institutions of advertising as advertising agencies and the various media, often from an historical perspective. The relative importance and the operation of these institutions is of central interest. Books of this type often also describe in some detail the physical process of creating advertising—the selection of type faces, the production process, and other practical particulars. The descriptive approach generally focuses on what advertising is in a macro sense and how it works at a detailed level. A good example is William Wells, John Burnett, and Sandra Moriarty, *Advertising Principles and Practice*.[57]

Behavioral approaches to advertising can be traced to Walter Dill Scott's 1913 book, *The Psychology of Advertising*.[58] Since then, there has been a steady stream of books firmly tied to the behavioral disciplines, such as D. Lucan and C. E. Benson's *Psychology for Advertisers* in 1930 and, more recently, Edgar Crane's *Marketing Communications*.[59] This approach is largely concerned with the analysis of the communication process, using behavioral science theory and empirical findings. The interest in motivation research in the 1950s and consumer buyer behavior in the 1960s provided impetus to this area of thought. During the past decade, in particular, an enormous amount of progress has been made in using theories and models from psychology, social psychology, and sociology to help understand buyer behavior, the communication process, and the link between the two.

The research tradition in advertising parallels the development of the various media research services discussed earlier. It has also done much to motivate academic work on basic advertising research and studies of advertising effectiveness.

The managerial tradition is really more recent in origin. Perhaps the first book truly devoted to the subject of advertising management was a case book by Neil Borden and Martin Marshall, *Advertising Management: Text and Cases*, published in 1950 and revised in 1959.[60] This book, and the others that followed, approached the subject from the viewpoint of a manager faced with the tasks of preparing an advertising budget, deciding how to allocate funds to different media, and choosing among alternative copy strategies. These books were thus decision-oriented and provided a contrast to the principles approach, in which the nature and role of advertising institutions and advertising techniques tended to be the point of emphasis.

Still another approach to advertising, even more recent in origin, is the model-building perspective originating from the fields of operations research and statistics. Although it had early predecessors, it really began in the late 1950s with the development of decision models concerned with allocating the media budget.

The Approach of This Book

This book, like others, will touch on all these traditions, although its main thrust is really to blend the last four. The managerial perspective will largely motivate the book. The focus is on decision making, specifically those decisions that generate an advertising campaign. The book involves an attempt to analyze and structure systematically the various decision areas within advertising and to present material that shows promise of helping decision makers generate better alternatives and improve their decision-making process.

In doing this, the book will draw heavily on the models and theories that have originated from the behavioral disciplines and the more quantitative models that have emerged from operations research and statistics and the research techniques and approaches that underlie each. Our goal will be to extend and organize these models in such a way as to reveal their potential utility to decision makers.

SUMMARY . . . .

There are four major advertising institutions with which the reader should be familiar: the advertiser, the advertising agency, the media, and the research suppliers. There is a wide variety of advertisers. Those who are classified as national advertisers spend the largest share of advertising dollars. The balance is spent by local advertisers. Advertisers can also be distinguished by the product type with which they are involved: consumer packaged goods, consumer durables, retail stores, or industrial products, for example.

In most cases, an advertising agency actually creates the advertisements and makes the media-allocation decisions. For this service, it receives from the various media 15 percent of the advertising billings it places. During the 1980s, advertising agencies underwent a wave of acquisitions and mergers leading to the creation of huge megagroups. Reasons for this trend include the high number of mergers in client firms, the rise in other communications mix activities like promotions and direct mail, and the need to reduce client conflict.

Media developments have dramatically influenced the thrust of advertising through the years. The printing press made possible newspapers and magazines, the major media before the advent of the broadcast media, television and radio. Radio in 1922 and television in 1948 provided a new dimension to advertising and sparked a period of growth. Despite the competition of the broadcast media, newspapers continue to be the largest medium, with more than $32 billion in advertising revenues in 1993. Television was second with about $30.6 billion, followed by direct mail advertising's over $27 billion. The rapid expansion of cable television and the new computer networks that will make up the "information highway," as well as the capacity of interactivity between sender and receiver promises to bring television the same level of specialized audiences that magazines now deliver. Increased competition from cable has also cut deeply into market shares of the major broadcast television networks. The marriage of computer and television technologies, and the explosion of acquisitions and mergers in these and related telephone, entertainment, and electronic industries are profoundly affecting our views of what is meant by print and broadcast media and the roles that they will play in the next century.

Modern advertising management is heavily involved with research, and a sizable industry of research supplier firms has grown up to serve the needs of advertisers, agencies, and the media. Today, over $1 billion is spent annually on marketing and advertising research and specialized services associated with each of the major media.

Since the 1900s, hundreds of books on advertising have been published, most of which can be categorized into different writing traditions. Some are historical and others descriptive in their orientation; still others represent the perspectives of economists, social philosophers, managers, behavioral scientists, and quantitative model builders. As with past editions, this edition of *Advertising Management* is motivated by the managerial perspective, the creative tasks, and media decisions that generate new advertising campaigns or guide the management of ongoing campaigns. The book also draws heavily on research and models that have their origins in both the behavioral and quantitative disciplines. A major purpose is to integrate these two model-building traditions to enhance their power and relevance to advertising decision makers.

DISCUSSION QUESTIONS . . . .

1. Advertisers are defined as organizations that make use of mass media, whereas nonadvertisers do not. Are there any exceptions to this definition? In what other ways might advertisers and nonadvertisers be distinguished?
2. How will the role of advertising differ when the product involved is a consumer packaged product instead of a consumer durable? How will it differ for a retailer and an industrial advertiser? What part of the marketing program will advertising be assigned to in each case?
3. What similarities and differences would there be between the development of an advertising campaign for the Ford Foundation or the Forestry Service and Procter & Gamble or General Motors?
4. Consider the major institutions of advertising management given in Figure 1–1. Are there others that should be included? Write a brief statement explaining the primary roles of each institution.
5. Do you believe that a company like Procter & Gamble should develop its own in-house agency, thereby keeping the 15 percent commission it would otherwise pay an agency?
6. What are some consequences of the significant number of advertising agency mergers in the 1980s? Discuss and give examples to support your arguments.
7. Examine Table 1–5 for media trends. Why did outdoor media decline between 1955 and 1965? What is its likely future now? Why did total advertising expenditures increase so dramatically in 1950 and again in 1955 and 1984? Why did radio decline in 1955?
8. Consumers will soon be able to purchase prerecorded videodiscs and engage in two-way communications via cable television systems. What are some of the implications of these developments for advertisers?
9. Critics of advertising often wonder why certain advertisements are used. Outline the major research studies and research supplier services that would be involved in developing a major national campaign.
10. Consider the different perspectives on advertising. For each, try to determine what would be regarded as the key issues. What types of experimental evidence would be of the greatest interest to each?
11. What are some advertising issues associated with global branding? Discuss the pros and cons of family branding from a global, international perspective.
12. If you were to select an advertising agency to develop and implement a campaign for a new Honda sports car, what agency attributes would you consider most important?

NOTES. . . . .

1. *Advertising Age*, September 29, 1993, p. 1.
2. Robert J. Coen, "Vast U.S. and Worldwide Ad Expenditures," *Advertising Age*, November 13, 1980, p. 10.
3. Seymour Banks, "Cross-national Analysis of Advertising Expenditures: 1968–1979," *Journal of Advertising Research*, (April/May 1986), pp. 11–24.
4. *Standard Directory of Advertisers* (Skokie, IL: National Register Publishing Company). This directory, one of the so-called Red Books, is published annually by National Register, a subsidiary of Standard Rate and Data Service, and is a very useful reference to information on advertisers. A companion volume is *Standard Directory of Advertising Agencies*. Another useful reference to all aspects of the advertising industry is "Twentieth Century Advertising and the Economy of Abundance," *Advertising Age*, April 30, 1980.
5. The term PSA generally refers to advertisements sponsored by the Advertising Council, Washington, DC, for federal government and other nonprofit organizations. There are, however, significant numbers of public service announcements donated by media at the local level. None of this national or local advertising activity enters into estimates of the size of the advertising industry given here.
6. *Advertising Age*, May 2, 1994, p. 4.
7. *Advertising Age*, September 26, 1990, p. 8.
8. *Advertising Age*, December 4, 1989, p. S-2.
9. *Business Marketing*, October, 1994, p. 33.
10. *Advertising Age*, September 28, 1994, p. 66.
11. *Advertising Age*, September 28, 1994, p. 71.
12. *Advertising Age*, September 25, 1989, p. 6.
13. Maurice J. Mandell, *Advertising* (Englewood Cliffs, NJ: Prentice Hall, 1968), p. 24.
14. *Advertising Age*, May 1, 1989, p. 20.
15. *Business Week*, July 4, 1988, p. 66.
16. Albert Lasker, *The Lasker Story* (Chicago: Chicago Advertising Publications, 1963), pp. 29–31.
17. Claude C. Hopkins, *My Life in Advertising* (Chicago: Chicago Advertising Publications, 1966), p. 172.
18. Ibid., pp. 101–105.
19. Ibid., p. 102.
20. Ibid., pp. 106, 111.
21. Lasker, *The Lasker Story*, p. 38.
22. *Advertising Age*, April 13, 1994, p. 12.
23. *Advertising Age*, May 22, 1989, p. 72.
24. John U. Farley, "Are There Truly International Products—and Prime Prospects for Them?" *Journal of Advertising Research*, October/November 1986, pp. 17–20.
25. *Advertising Age*, August 14, 1989.
26. Kamran Kashani, "Beware the Pitfalls of Global Marketing," *Harvard Business Review*, September/October 1989, pp. 91. For a discussion, see Chapter 20 of this book.
27. *Advertising Age*, March 6, 1989, p. 4.
28. *Advertising Age*, March 28, 1985.
29. *Business Week*, September 23, 1991, pp. 66–71.
30. For some general background, see *Fortune*, November 15, 1993, pp. 147–164.
31. *Advertising Age*, December 11, 1989, p. 28.
32. *Advertising Age*, August 6, 1990, p. 6.
33. "Advertising That Comes à La Carte," *Business Week*, May 1, 1971, p. 46.
34. Mandell, *Advertising*, p. 24.
35. *Leo Burnett Media Costs and Coverage Guide*, 1990.
36. *Advertising Age*, December 7, 1964, p. 32.

37. *Advertising Age*, October 20, 1969, p. 50.
38. *Advertising Age*, April 30, 1980, p. 270.
39. Ibid.
40. *Leo Burnett Cost Guide*, 1990.
41. *Advertising Age*, October 20, 1969, p. 184.
42. *Leo Burnett Cost Guide*, 1990.
43. Ibid., p. 66.
44. *Advertising Age*, April 24, 1989, p. 2; for the more recent statistics, see Chapter 17 of this book.
45. Donnelley Marketing Inc., *The 16th Annual Survey of Promotional Practices*, 1994.
46. For information on the marketing and advertising research supplier industry, see *Bradford's Directory of Marketing Research Agencies and Management Consultants in the U.S. and the World* (biennial) (Fairfax, VA) and *International Directory of Marketing Research Houses and Services*, published by the New York Chapter of the American Marketing Association. Other useful information is contained in the Roster of the American Marketing Association. Recent marketing research texts also provide useful listings. See Donald R. Lehmann, *Marketing Research and Analysis* (Homewood, IL: Richard D. Irwin, 1979), pp. 138–148 and 161–171, and John G. Myers, William F. Massey, and Stephen A. Greyser, *Marketing Research and Knowledge Development* (Englewood Cliffs, NJ: Prentice Hall, 1980), pp. 101–166.
47. See *Advertising Age*, April 24, 1978.
48. Jack J. Honomichl, "The Honomichl 50," *Marketing News* 28, no. 12 (June 6, 1994), H4.
49. See *Advertising Age*, March 17, 1984, pp. M–17ff.
50. David A. Revzan, *Marketing Bibliographies*, Parts I and II (Berkeley: University of California Press, 1959), Supplement 1 published 1963; Supplement 2 published 1970.
51. Stephen Fox, *The Mirror Makers* (New York: Vintage Books, 1985); Eric Clark, *The Want Makers* (New York: Penguin Books, 1988).
52. Roland S. Vaile, *The Economics of Advertising* (New York: Ronald Press, 1927).
53. Neil H. Borden, *The Economic Effects of Advertising* (Homewood, IL: Irwin, 1942).
54. Julian L. Simon, *Issues in the Economics of Advertising* (Urbana: University of Illinois Press, 1970).
55. Arthur Kallet and F. J. Schlink, *100,000,000 Guinea Pigs* (New York: Vanguard Press, 1932); A. S. J. Basker, *Advertising Reconsidered* (London: P. S. King and Son, 1935); H. K. Kenner, *The Fight for Truth in Advertising* (New York: Roundtable Press, 1936): Blake Clarke, *The Advertising Smoke Screen* (New York: Harper & Row, 1944); F. P. Bishop, *The Ethics of Advertising* (London: Robert Hale, 1949); Vance Packard, *The Hidden Persuaders* (New York: David McKay, 1957); Francis X. Quin, *Ethics, Advertising and Responsibility* (Rome, NY: Canterbury Press, 1963); and Sidney Margolius, *The Innocent Consumers vs. The Exploiters* (New York: Trident Press, 1967).
56. For a business perspective, see Francesco M. Nicosia, *Advertising, Management and Society: A Business Point of View* (New York: McGraw-Hill, 1974).
57. William Wells, John Burnett and Sandra Moriarty, *Advertising Principles and Practice*, 3rd ed. (Englewood Cliffs, NJ: Prentice Hall, 1994).
58. Walter Dill Scott, *The Psychology of Advertising* (Boston: Small Maynard, 1913).
59. D. Lucas and C. E. Benson, *Psychology for Advertisers* (New York: Harper & Bros., 1930), and Edgar Crane, *Marketing Communications*, 2nd ed. (New York: Wiley, 1972).
60. Neil H. Borden and Martin V. Marshall, *Advertising Management: Text and Cases*, rev. ed. (Homewood, IL: Irwin, 1959).

2 ADVERTISING PLANNING AND DECISION MAKING

> Plans are nothing, planning is everything.
> (Dwight D. Eisenhower)

If you are planning a career as a brand or product manager in a large corporation or perhaps a career as an accountant executive in an advertising agency, or if you think you will probably join a small firm or start a business of your own, you need to learn how to develop and write advertising and marketing plans. President Eisenhower may have been right when he put the emphasis on the process of planning rather than on the plan itself, but it most cases you will be responsible for developing a written plan and defending that plan in front of your peers and senior executives of a corporation or nonprofit organization. And, if you want to stay employed in one of those well-paid positions, you must learn decision making—how to identify strategic choices, how to choose the best alternative from among those available in a given situation, and how to implement strategic and tactical decisions. This book should increase your learning and skills in all of these facets of the subject of advertising management.

Chapter 1 presented a broad view of the field. Recall that the advertiser component is the core of the system. Many of the perspectives in this chapter and the balance of the book reflect the advertiser viewpoint. The major activities of advertising management are planning and decision making. In most instances, the advertising or brand manager will be involved in the development, implementation, and overall management of an advertising plan. The development of an advertising plan essentially requires the generation and specification of alternatives. The alternatives can be various levels of expenditure, different kinds of objectives or strategy possibilities, and numerous kinds of options associated with copy creation and media choices. The essence of planning is thus to find out what the feasible alternatives are and reduce them to a set on which decisions can be made. Decision making involves choosing from among the alternatives. A complete advertising plan reflects the results of the planning and decision-making process and the decisions that have been made in a particular product-market situation.

This chapter presents a framework for advertising planning and decision making. It is an elaboration of the advertising system model given in Chapter 1 and expands the advertiser component. It also provides an overview of the structure and contents of the book.

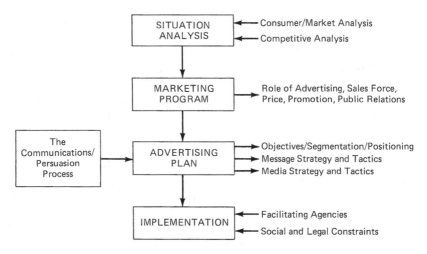

Figure 2–1.   **Framework for advertising planning and decision making.**

PLANNING FRAMEWORK . . . .

The major internal and external factors involved in advertising planning and decision making are shown in Figure 2–1. Internally, situation analysis, the marketing program, and the advertising plan are key considerations. As suggested in the diagram, the three legs of advertising planning concern: (1) objective setting and target market identification, (2) message strategy and tactics, and (3) media strategy and tactics. The advertising plan should flow from the overall marketing program. Any advertising plan is best thought of as part of an overall marketing plan which should be developed following a situation analysis of the organization's particular situation. Situational analysis implies research and research is vital to planning and decision making. Once developed, an advertising plan is implemented and becomes an advertising campaign, carried out in the context of social, legal, and global factors and with the aid of various types of facilitating agencies.

The balance of this chapter addresses each of these considerations. First, situation analysis is explained and discussed. Then a brief review of a marketing plan is presented. This is followed by sections on facilitating agencies and a discussion of the role of social, legal, and global factors.

MARKETING STRATEGY AND SITUATION
ANALYSIS . . . .

The planning and decision-making process begins with a thorough analysis of the situation the advertiser faces and the development of marketing strategy. Marketing strategy includes the long-run vision and objectives of the company as well as an articulation of the specific strategic position it will aim to occupy in the marketplace in the years ahead. The company's strategic position might be either one in which it is the low-price leader, seeking growth through offering prices that are consistently lower than competitors, or one in which it focuses on offering differentiated products that offer high quality and reliability.[1] The development of marketing strategy thus should begin with situation analysis, and a comprehensive examination and analysis of all important external and internal factors operating in a particular situation. This includes assessing the strengths, weaknesses, threats, and opportunities, so-called "SWOT analysis," of the company involved. In many cases, it means that new research studies will be undertaken as well as relying on company history and experience.

AT&T, for example, developed a new strategy for its long-distance telephone services that was based on five years of research.[2] The research encompassed market segmentation studies, concept testing, and a large-scale field experiment. The field experiment focused on testing a new advertising campaign called "Cost of Visit." An existing "Reach Out" campaign, although successful, did not appear to get through to a large group of people who had reasons to call but were limiting their calls because of cost. Research based on annual surveys of 3,000 residential telephone users showed that most did not know the cost of a long-distance call or that it was possible to make less expensive calls during off-peak periods. Five copy alternatives were subsequently developed and tested, from which "Cost of Visit" was chosen. This campaign was credited with persuading customers to call during times that were both cheaper for them and more profitable for AT&T and, overall, this campaign was more effective than the "Reach Out" campaign. One estimate was that by switching $30 million in advertising from "Reach Out" to "Cost of Visit," an incremental gain in revenue of $22 million would result in the first year and would top $100 million over five years.

This example highlights a "situation" in which advertising was undoubtedly a major factor, extensive research was done to study the situation, and large sums of money were involved in both research and advertising. A complete situation analysis will cover all marketing components and will involve finding answers to dozens of questions about the nature and extent of demand, competition, environmental factors, product, costs, distribution, and the skills and financial resources of the firm. Table 2–1 provides a list of topics and relevant questions that need to be answered for each topic.

Situation analysis invariably involves research of some kind. For advertising planning and decision making, the principal thrust of research efforts is on market analysis or, more broadly, the analysis of consumer motivation and behavior with respect to the product, service, idea, or object to be advertised. It is this kind of research that is most important in advertising, and many of the research approaches, techniques, models, and results presented throughout this book pertain to it. Situation analysis can be based on conventional wisdom, managerial experience, or the creative team's inherent imaginative abilities, but current market and environmental conditions—what the situation is now—can only be adequately assessed by research. Such research flows from the company and its agency's research efforts, secondary data sources, and/or is purchased from research suppliers. Several good planning guides are available on situation analysis.[3] Suffice it to say that situation analysis is generally the foundation for any well-developed marketing program and the cornerstone for an advertising plan.

Table 2–1.   Topics and Questions Involved in Situation Analysis

A. Nature of demand
  1. How do buyers (consumer and industrial) currently go about buying existing products or services?
     Describe the main types of behavior patterns and attacks.
     A. Number of stores shopped or industrial sources considered
     B. Degree of overt information seeking
     C. Degree of brand awareness and loyalty
     D. Location of product category decision—home or point of sale
     E. Location of brand decision—home or point of sale
     F. Sources of product information and current awareness and knowledge levels
     G. Who makes the purchase—male, female, adult, child, purchasing agent, buying committee, and so on?
     H. Who influences the decision maker?
     I. Individual or group decision (computer versus candy bar)
     J. Duration of the decision process (repeat, infrequent, or new purchase situation)
     K. Buyer's interest, personal involvement, or excitement regarding the purchase (hairpins versus trip to caribbean)
     L. Risk or uncertainty of negative pruchase outcome—high, medium, or low (specialized machinery versus hacksaw blades, pencils versus hair coloring)
     M. Functional versus psychological considerations (electric drill versus new dress)
     N. Time of consumption (gum versus dining room furniture)
  2. Can the market be meaningfully segmented or broken into several homogeneous groups with respect to "what they want" and "how they buy"?
     Criteria:
     A. Age
     B. Family life cycle
     C. Geographic location
     D. Heavy versus light users
     E. Nature of the buying process
     F. Product usage
B. Extent of demand
  1. What is the size of the market (units and dollars) now, and what will the future hold?
  2. What are the current market shares, and what are the selective demand trends (units and dollars)?
  3. Is it best to analyze the market on an aggregate or on a segmented basis?

Table 2–1. (Continued)

C. Nature of competition

  1. What is the present and future structure of competition?

    A. Number of competitors (5 versus 2,000)

    B. Market shares

    C. Financial resources

    D. Marketing resources and skills

    E. Production resources and skills

  2. What are the current marketing programs of established competitors? why are they successful or unsuccessful?

  3. Is there an opportunity for another competitor? why?

  4. What are the anticipated retaliatory moves of competitors? can they neutralize different marketing programs we might develop?

D. Environmental climate

  1. What are the relevant social, political, economic, and technological trends?

  2. How do you evaluate these trends? do they represent opportunities or problems?

E. Stage of product life cycle

  1. In what stage of the life cycle is the product category?

    A. What is the chronological age of the product category? (Younger more favorable than older?)

    B. What is the state of the consumers' knowledge of the product category?

  2. What market characteristics support your stage-of-life-cycle evaluation?

F. Cost structure of the industry

  1. What is the amount and composition of the marginal or additional cost of supplying increased output?

G. Skills of the firm

  1. Do we have the skills and experience to perform the functions necessary to be in the business?

    A. Marketing skills
    B. Production skills
    C. Management skills
    D. Financial skills
    E. R&D skills

  2. How do our skills compare with those of competitors?

    A. Production fit

    B. Marketing fit

    C. And so on

Table 2–1.   (Continued)

H. Financial resources of the firm
   1. Do we have the funds to support an effective marketing program?
   2. Where are the funds coming from, and when will they be available?

Source: Adapted from an unpublished note by Professor James R. Taylor of the University of Michigan. Used with permission.

In many cases, a situation analysis is undertaken from the perspective of the total company or product line and will involve finding answers to dozens of questions, including questions about the history of the product, distribution, pricing, packaging, consumer analysis, and competition. While there are many parts to a good situation analysis, two key components are the nature and structure of consumer demand and the nature of competition.

Consumer and Market Analysis

A situation analysis often begins by looking at the aggregate market for the product, service, or cause being advertised: the size of the market, its growth rate, seasonality, geographical distribution; the possible existence of different segments; and trends in all of these aggregate market characteristics. See section B in Table 2–1 for sample questions.

It is vitally important, however, that the *reasons* for these aggregate statistics and market trends be understood. The analyst needs to examine and understand the attitudes and behaviors of consumers as individuals (or, in some cases, as decision-making groups). See section A in Table 2–1. Who makes the purchase decision? What benefits are they seeking from the product category? Why are they satisfied or dissatisfied with particular brands? Key aspects of such consumer research and analysis are examined in Chapter 4 (Setting Goals and Objectives), Chapter 5 (How Advertising Works), and in Chapter 6 (Segmentation and Positioning).

Competitive Analysis

Advertising planning and decision making are heavily affected by competition and the competitive situation the advertiser faces. Competition is such a pervasive factor that it will occur as a consideration in all phases of the advertising planning and decision-making process and the various topics treated in much of the balance of this book. A type of market structure analysis that involves the development of perceptual maps of a market, for example, attempts to locate the relative perceptual positions of competitive brands. This topic is covered in detail in Chapter 6.

Situation analysis should usually include an analysis of what current share the brand now has (if it is an established brand), what shares its competitors have, trends in these shares, reasons for these trends, what share of a market is possible for the brand, and from which competitors an increase in share will come. The planner also has to be aware of the relative strengths and weaknesses—financial, production, and marketing—of the different competing companies, and the history of competitive moves and objectives in the product category. If we spend advertising dollars communicating the fact that our brand has a desired benefit, will certain competitors begin claiming the same benefit, thus eliminating any competitive advantage we may hope to get?

Opportunities for marketing and advertising can also be uncovered using competitive analysis. Is there a "hole" in the market not now being filled by a competitive offering? In other terms, is there a bundle of attributes that a consumer segment desires that some competitor has not yet targeted against? Much research shows that companies that are the first to launch brands that meet unmet needs often have a "pioneering advantage" that later competing entries find difficult to fight.[4]

These types of questions need to be asked and answered not only in the initial stages of developing an advertising plan but through the years in which old campaigns are evaluated and improved. Many companies have initiated their own tracking systems for monitoring competitive advertising that monitor the content of the advertising, how much money is being spent, and the media in which competitive ads appear. We discuss some secondary sources of such competitive information in Chapter 17, since such competitive spending information is often a useful input into the budgeting decision. A chapter is not devoted to competition in this book. It is important to look at competition as a precursor to the planning process and to appreciate that the development of plans and decision making with respect to objectives, budgets, copy, and media all must take into account the competitive factor.

THE MARKETING PLAN. . . . .

Advertising planning and decision making take place in the context of an overall marketing plan. The marketing plan includes planning, implementation, and control functions for the total corporation or a particular decision-making unit or product line. The marketing plan will include a statement of marketing objectives and will spell out particular strategies and tactics to reach those objectives. The marketing objectives should identify the segments to be served by the organization and how it is going to serve them. The needs and wants of consumers on which the firm will concentrate, such as the needs of working men and women for easily prepared meals, are identified and analyzed in a marketing plan.

There are several marketing tools that can be used to help an organization achieve its marketing objectives. Most people are familiar with the "4 Ps"—the marketing mix which includes product, price, place, and promotion. A marketing plan formulates the strategy and tactics for each of these. The marketing plan should be based on the specific problems or opportunities uncovered for the brand by the situation analysis. It should serve as a response to those problems or opportunities through the allocation of the marketing budget and the development of specific plans for various components of the marketing mix. A discussion of how to create a good marketing plan can be found in any marketing textbook and is thus not repeated here.

The effectiveness of the various elements of the marketing mix with respect to the problems or opportunities should be the factor that determines what share each receives of the total marketing budget. Conceptually, the budget should be divided so that the marginal value of an extra dollar will be the same in all components of the mix: dollars should be shifted to the areas that will produce the greatest incremental sales volume. In evaluating the advertising budget, therefore, it is important to keep in mind that incremental amounts of money put into advertising must be more useful than the same amounts put into distribution or product refinement, or even reduced prices. Chapter 16 is devoted to a discussion of the media budget and how the optimal budget level can be determined.

Once this budgetary allocation has been decided, integration of the elements of both the marketing mix and the communication mix is vital to the development of successful marketing and advertising plans. Chapter 3 (Integrated Marketing Communications) focuses on this issue and discusses complementary communications tools such as direct marketing, sales promotion and other action-oriented advertising, public relations, and so on.

THE COMMUNICATION AND PERSUASION PROCESS . . . .

The most important factor to be considered in planning advertising, in addition to the marketing plan, is an understanding of the communication and persuasion process. Although much has been researched and written about the effects of advertising and how it works, it is important to appreciate that this is a subject about which there are few definitive answers. There are perhaps as many theories about how advertising "works" as there are people who work in advertising, and it is impossible to discuss them all here. Some of these theories will appear in later chapters, but we will present two well-known ones here. An appreciation for the processes by which advertising works is of great value in designing advertising plans—plans that maximize the advertisement's impact on the consumer.

Advertising Communication System

Figure 2–2 shows one simple model of the advertising communication system. Advertising communication always involves a perception process and four of the elements shown in the model: the source, a message, a communication channel, and a receiver. In addition, the receiver will sometimes become a source of information by talking to friends or associates. This type of communication is termed *word-of-mouth* communication, and it involves social interactions between two or more people and the important ideas of group *influence* and the *diffusion of information*.

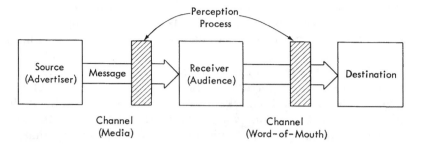

Figure 2–2.   Model of the advertising communication system.

These ideas are discussed in Chapter 11 (Group Influence and Word-of-Mouth Advertising).

Source

The *source* of a message in the advertising communication system is the point of which the message originates. There are many types of "sources" in the context of advertising, such as the company offering the product, the particular brand, or the spokesperson used. A model on source factors is developed in Chapter 12 (Creative Approaches) to show the various dimensions of source effects, such as credibility and attractiveness. They are of obvious importance in deciding how best, and through whom, to communicate the advertising message.

Message

The *message* refers to both the content and execution of the advertisement. It is the totality of what is perceived by the receiver of the message. The message can be executed in a great variety of ways and can include, for example, the use of humor and fear, as discussed in Chapter 9 (Associating Feelings with the Brand). In later chapters, specific types of television commercials will be discussed and can also be considered ways to think about the advertising message.

Channel

The message is transmitted through some *channel* from the source to the receiver. The channel in an advertising communication system consists of one or more kinds of media, such as radio, television, newspapers, magazines, billboards, point-of-purchase displays, and so on. The impact of the communication can be different for different media. For example, an advertisement exposure in *Vogue* can have an effect quite different from exposure to the same advertisement in *Good Housekeeping*. In Chapter 17 (Media Tactics: Allocating Media Budgets), this channel effect will be considered in more detail. Word-of-mouth communication, as mentioned above, represents another channel that is of special interest because it can sometimes play a key role in an advertising campaign. It should be noted that any communication system has a channel capacity. There is only so much information that can be moved through it and only so much that a receiver will be motivated to receive and capable of processing. For example, there is a physical limit to the number of advertisements that can be shown on prime time. Shortages of available advertising time can be a real problem.

Receiver

The *receiver* in an advertising communication system is also called the target audience. Thus, the receiver can be described in terms of audience segmentation variables, lifestyle, benefits sought, demographics, and so on. Of particular interest might be the receiver's involvement in the product and the extent to which he or she is willing to search for and/or process information. It is the characteristics of the receiver—the demographic, psychological, and social characteristics—that provide the basis for understanding communications, persuasion, and market processes.

Destination

The communication model in Figure 2–2 does not stop at the receiver but allows for the possibility that the initial receiver might engage in word-of-mouth communication to the ultimate destination of the message. The receiver then becomes an interim source and the destination becomes another receiver. As mentioned earlier, word-of-mouth communication resulting from advertising can be a critical part of a campaign. The reality is that for some products the absence of word-of-mouth communication can be fatal. It is only the word-of-mouth communication that has the credibility, comprehensiveness, and impact to affect the ultimate behavior of a portion of the audience. Furthermore, advertising can actually stimulate word-of-mouth activity. Even when it cannot stimulate it, a knowledge of its appropriateness and power can be very helpful.

Note that an advertising message can have a variety of effects upon the receiver. It can

- Create awareness
- Communicate information about attributes and benefits
- Develop or change an image or personality
- Associate a brand with feelings and emotions
- Create group norms
- Precipitate behavior

Advertising Exposure Model

Figure 2–3 presents another model of the communication and persuasion process that shows the various processes that can occur after consumers are exposed to an advertisement. First, exposure to the advertisement can create awareness about the brand, leading to a feeling of familiarity with it. Second, information about the brand's benefits and the attributes on which the benefits are based can register with the consumer can also result from exposure to the ad. Third, advertisements can also generate feelings in an audience that they begin to associate with the brand or its consumption. Fourth, through the choice of the spokesperson and various executional devices, the advertisement can lead to the creation of an image for the brand, often called "brand personality." Fifth, the advertisement

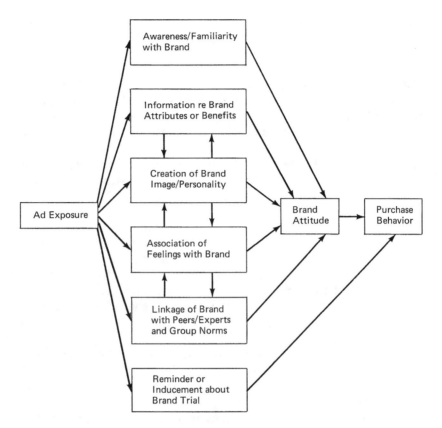

Figure 2–3.   A model of the communication/persuasion process.

can create the impression that the brand is favored by the consumer's peers, or experts—individuals and groups the consumer likes to emulate. This is often how products and brands are presented as being fashionable. These five effects can create a favorable liking, or attitude, toward the brand, which in turn should lead to purchasing action. Sometimes the advertiser will attempt to spur purchasing action directly by providing a reminder or by attacking reasons why the consumer may be postponing that action.

These two models help us to understand how and why consumers acquire, process, and use advertising information. It is also important at the planning stage to develop a good understanding of where advertising fits into the total pool of information and influence sources to which a consumer is exposed. Understanding information processing invariably leads to the need for understanding a wide range of other important psychological constructs, such as perception, learning, attitude formation and change, source effects, brand personality and image, cognitive and affective response, and social factors such as group influence. Chapters 5 through 10 are devoted to these topics. With this background in the communication and persuasion process behind us, let us return to the steps involved in the creation of the advertising plan.

THE ADVERTISING PLAN. . . . .

As depicted in the flow diagram of Figure 2–1, the advertising plan should only be developed once the overall marketing plan has been created and the role of advertising within it has been assessed. Advertising planning and decision making focus on three crucial tasks: objectives and target selection, message strategy and tactics, and media strategy and tactics. Every advertising plan will, at a minimum, reflect planning, decisions, and commitments concerning each of these three major components. The broad purpose of advertising management is to develop, implement, and control an advertising plan. Planning as a process involves the generation and specification of alternatives. Decision making concerns the choice of the best alternative. Which strategy alternatives are feasible in a given situation? Which one should be adopted? What media mix will be most effective? These are some of the questions every advertising manager must address.

In an established-brand situation, analysis will involve a retrospective look at what has been done in the past and whether basic changes in the current plan are called for. In new product situations, the manager may be essentially starting from scratch, and each aspect of the plan will require basic new thinking, significant amounts of new research information, and the development of entirely new advertising objectives and new copy and media strategies.

Alternatives with respect to objectives and the target market must first be carefully evaluated and specified. Then copy alternatives must be developed and analyzed with respect to both content (message strategy) and execution (message tactics). The decisions made at this stage take the form of the advertising campaign adopted in the particular situation. Finally, media alternatives need careful specification and analysis and decisions must be made on how much money to spend (media strategy) and where to allocate it (media tactics). In each case, planning and decision making are involved.

Objectives and Target Selection

The pivotal aspect of any management plan is the development of *operational objectives.* An operational objective is one that provides useful criteria for decision making, generates standards to measure performance, and serves as a meaningful communication device. Objectives in advertising can be couched in many ways and still fulfill the functions of an operational objective. It is sometimes possible to develop objectives in terms of sales goals. Such goals are desirable because they appear to provide a readily accessible and absolute indication of advertising performance. However, because other marketing variables and competitors' actions can have an important impact on sales, it is often necessary to establish objectives in terms of intervening variables such as brand awareness, image, and attitude. The link between such intervening variables and advertising is more direct. Thus a significant increase in brand awareness can usually be identified with advertising. There are simply few other possible causes. To justify the use of intervening variables, a link must be established between them and subsequent sales. Much of Chapters 4, 5, and 6 of this book will deal with the nature of that link.

An important part of the objective is the development of a precise, disciplined description of the target audience. It is often tempting to direct advertising at a broad audience; the implicit argument is that everyone is a potential customer. The risk is that a campaign directed at too wide an audience will have to have such a broad appeal that it will be of little interest to anyone and thus be ineffective. It is best to consider directing the advertising to more selected groups for which it is easier to develop relevant, stimulating copy. An advertiser need not be restricted to one objective and one campaign. It is quite possible to develop several campaigns, each directed at different segments of the market, or to develop one campaign based on multiple objectives. Chapter 6 looks at different ways of segmenting markets and ways to "position" brands to attract specific segments.

Message Strategy and Tactics

The actual development of an advertising campaign involves several distinct steps. First, the advertising manager must decide what the advertising is meant to communicate—by way of benefits, feelings, brand personality, or action content. We call this *message strategy* and devote five chapters in Part III to it. Once the content of the campaign has been decided, decisions must be made on the best and most effective ways to communicate that content. These executional decisions, such as the choice of a spokesperson, the use of humor or fear or other tones, and the selection of particular copy, visuals, and layout, are what we call *message tactics.* Part IV of the book discusses these tactics, as well as other aspects of implementation, such as copy testing, advertising production, and the process of client-agency interaction.

Message Strategy

One of the first strategic objectives has to be the design of an advertisement that gains attention, for without that nothing else is possible. In Part III (Message Strategy), we review in Chapter 7 (Attention and Comprehension) theories of attention, comprehension, and perception processes and discuss how advertisements can be created that capture and retain a consumer's attention. How can attention best be captured in an age in which thousands of advertisements compete for attention and in which consumers can flip television channels with a mere flick of a remote control device? Chapter 8 (Understanding Benefit-Based Attitudes) then examines theories of benefit-based attitudes. Much of the material draws on recent work of consumer behavior researchers in this area, particularly in extending our understanding of learning, attitudes, and attitude change. It focuses on how decisions can be made about which attributes and benefits to emphasize in the advertising.

Chapter 9 focuses on theories and research that contribute to our understanding of advertising that is explicitly designed to generate emotional responses in the audience, such as warmth, excitement, pride, and so on, and to "transform" the brand by associating these feelings with it. How should advertisers choose which emotions to evoke, and how can they tell when they have been successful?

Chapter 10 (Brand Equity, Image, and Personality) examines such questions as: What is brand equity? How can it be measured? What personality dimensions or traits can brands acquire through advertising? What are the situations when brand personality is more important in driving purchase? What is the importance of brand personality in creating long-term "goodwill" for a brand? Most importantly, how can advertising and other marketing mix elements create such a brand image?[5]

Next, Chapter 11 (Group Influence and Word-of-Mouth Advertising) looks at the processes of group influence and word-of-mouth advertising and examines how advertising can help shape group norms and fashions. In what advertising situations is group influence likely to play a major role? It is often useful to conduct a *personal influence audit*, explained in this chapter as part of a general situation analysis.[6]

Message Tactics

In Part IV (Message Tactics), we begin with Chapter 12 (Creative Approaches). The pros and cons of different kinds of spokespersons and the kinds of advertising situations in which they may be most appropriate are presented and discussed. Chapter 12 also examines other decisions on "tone and format," such as the use of fear, humor, comparative advertising, and devices to increase distraction.

The content and tone must eventually be translated into specific advertisements. Throughout the process, decisions have to be made concerning which different copy approaches, scripts, and final advertisements will be used. Chapter 13 (The Art of Copywriting) examines some of the existing knowledge on the principles of good copywriting for each of the major media (print, television, radio, outdoor), and presents capsule portraits of some of the creative geniuses that have graced the advertising business.

Assessments of what makes for "good" copy are not merely subjective, of course, and several kinds of research-based tests can be used, in the laboratory or in the field, to enable a creative team to check the evolving campaign continually against its objectives. These are discussed in Chapter 14 (Advertising Copy Testing and Diagnosis).

Concluding Part IV, Chapter 15 (Production and Implementation) examines how advertisements actually get created, produced, and implemented and describes the client-agency relationship through which this happens. Here, we also present some wisdom on how clients and agencies can best work together to create the most effective advertising.

Media Strategy and Tactics

Whereas message strategy generally concerns decisions about how much to allocate to creating and testing advertising copy, media strategy concerns decisions on how many media dollars to spend on an advertising campaign. Media tactics comprise the decisions about which specific media (television, radio, magazines, etc.) or media vehicles (David Letterman's *Tonight Show*, *Reader's Digest*, etc.) to use. Both media strategy and tactical issues are covered in Part V.

Media Strategy

The advertising budget decision, covered in Chapter 16 (Media Strategy: Setting Media Budgets), is closely tied in with the objectives and target selection decisions discussed in Chapters 3, 4, and 5. Although there are many rules of thumb often used to decide how much money to spend on advertising, the soundest rules involve beginning with a detailed specification of what a corporation is attempting to accomplish with advertising, and the resources necessary. It is only when the job to be done is well specified that the amount and nature of the effort—the amount of money to be invested in advertising—can be really determined. In Chapter 16, we will examine some of the traditional approaches to the advertising budget decision and contrast them with approaches we recommend.

Media Tactics

Chapter 17 (Media Tactics: Allocating Media Budgets) discusses criteria that apply in the allocation of an advertising budget across media types and within each media type. The media-allocation decision and media planning represent one of the few areas in advertising in which the use of mathematical techniques and computer programs is well accepted. These will be discussed, as will other factors that need to be taken into consideration. One such factor is the type of vehicle audience and how well it matches the target audience of the campaign. Another is the ability of the vehicle to enhance the advertising impact, perhaps by creating a compatible mood or setting.

The type and nature of research information required to support media models differs somewhat from the perspectives of research in the case of copy decisions. A media planner is interested in questions concerning the reach and frequency of media alternatives, the effects of various vehicles, and matters involving learning and decay rates over the life of a campaign. Media research is thus a special topic that is treated, along with the sources of media data, in Part V.

The decisions made in the media area and in the other areas of objectives and copy constitute the final advertising plan. What we want to stress is that advertising plans must all take these three major factors (objectives and target groups, message strategy and tactics, and media strategy and tactics) into consideration and that advertising plans will differ according to the decisions made in each area. The internal differences between advertising plans stem largely from differences in the external factors and the environmental situations that face advertisers. These external factors shape the advertising plan in many ways, and it is vital that they be analyzed in depth as the planning process proceeds.

FACILITATING AGENCIES . . . .

Another external factor identified in Figure 2–1 involves the agencies that facilitate advertising and provide the means to advertise. Recall that the nature and role of these types of agencies and institutions were reviewed in Chapter 1. From a situation-analysis viewpoint, the advertiser basically needs to know what kinds of facilitating agencies exist and the nature of the services they can provide. From a planning viewpoint, much local advertising, for example, is done without the services of an advertising agency or a research supplier. A national advertiser, on the other hand, may have under contract many different agencies and research suppliers, each serving one or more brands in a product line made up of several products.

Many advertising decisions involve choices among facilitating agency alternatives. What advertising agency should be chosen? What media should be used? What copy-testing supplier will be best for our particular situation? Concerning the question of agency selection, for example, Cagley and Roberts[7] found that the "people factor" tends to dominate in agency selection. Characteristics such as the quality of personnel, reputation, integrity, mutual understanding, interpersonal compatibility, and synergism were very important. The study involved a mail questionnaire sent to 125 companies and ratings on twenty-five attributes ranging from "critically important" to "not important." Consideration of the facilitating agency factor is woven throughout many parts of the book, with special focus in Chapter 15 on client-agency relations. In addition, the question of choosing a copy-testing research supplier is treated at length in Chapter 14, and the question of what media and what media research services to use are the topics of Chapters 16 and 17.

SOCIAL, LEGAL, AND GLOBAL FACTORS . . . .

The final external factor in the planning framework concerns environmental factors—social, legal, and global. In developing specific advertisements, there are certain legal constraints that must be considered. Deceptive advertising is forbidden by law. However, the determination of what is deceptive is often difficult, partly because different people can have different perceptions of the same advertisements. In guarding against deception, all types of perceptions must be considered. Furthermore, the letter and the spirit of the law on deceptive advertising is evolving rapidly. It is no small task to keep abreast of these developments. One solution is to create bland advertising that is vague and contains little specific information. However, such an approach can result not only in ineffective advertising, but it can lessen the social value of advertising by reducing the amount of useful information that it provides to society. Thus, an advertiser who attempts to provide specific, relevant information must be well aware of what constitutes deception in a legal and ethical sense and of other aspects of advertising regulation. These topics are covered in detail in Chapter 18 (Advertising Regulation).

Even more difficult considerations for people involved in the advertising effort are broad social and economic issues. Does advertising raise prices or inhibit competition? Also, issues such as the appropriateness of the use of sex or fear appeals are being examined. It has been suggested that women and minority groups are exploited in advertising by casting them in highly stereotyped roles. Another concern is that advertising, especially when it is more irritating than entertaining, is an intrusion into an already excessively polluted environment. A whole set of rules is emerging to cover advertising directed at children, and advertising of products such as alcohol and cigarettes, and the use of environmental and health claims in advertising. These and other similar concerns, particularly those that affect copy and creative strategy, are developed more fully in Chapter 19 (Advertising and Society).

Most large corporations and advertising agencies are now multinationals and global in their perspectives and organization. Chapter 20 (Global Marketing and Advertising) addresses some of the issues, benefits, and costs of global marketing and advertising. This is the last chapter in the book, and it provides a fitting end to understanding modern advertising and advertising management in the world of the 1990s.

SUMMARY. . . . .

The predominant perspective of advertising management is that of the advertiser or brand manager in the advertiser component of the overall system. The broad purpose of the manager is to develop, implement, and control an advertising plan. His or her major activities involve planning and decision making.

Planning concerns the generation and specification of alternatives, and decision making concerns the choice process. Which alternative should be chosen? Which message or media strategy is best in a particular situation? What copy theme should be used? What media mix will be most effective? The advertising plan is developed in the context of the company's total marketing program which flows from situation analysis and an assessment of the consumer/market and competitive situation the company is in. Externally, the manager needs to engage in situation analysis with respect to the market conditions that are operating at the time and to assess the consumer/market, competitive, facilitating agency, and social, legal, and global factors that will affect decision making and the development of the plan. Internally, analysis should focus on the overall marketing program and how advertising will interact with the various components of the program. It is vital that the advertising plan be developed so as to mesh with and support the various components of the marketing and communications mix such as personal selling, pricing, public relations, and promotion. The advertising manager also needs to know the major areas of his or her planning and decision-making responsibilities. There are three areas of major importance: objective and target selection considerations, message strategy and tactics, and media strategy and tactics. Planning and decision making are required from each perspective, and the final advertising plan will reflect the various decisions made in each area. Figure 2–1 organized these factors into a planning and decision-making framework for advertising management that is driven by the need for advertising managers to have an in-depth understanding of communication and persuasion processes.

Two views of communication and persuasion processes were presented in this chapter (Figures 2–2 and 2–3), and later chapters will develop others. Cognitive and affective, or feeling, processes that occur between exposure to advertisements and ultimate buying or consuming behavior are primary points of focus. Exposure can lead to increased awareness of and familiarity with the brand, added information on brand attributes and benefits, creation of a brand image or personality, association of feeling with the brand, linkages of brands with peers and experts, and/or reminders and inducements to try or continue using the brand. All can affect brand attitude and ultimately purchase behavior.

Implementation of advertising plans is done with the assistance of many different kinds of external organizations such as production houses, broadcast and print media, advertising agencies, and research supplier companies. These are the "facilitating agencies" that help in bringing advertising into being. Also, implementation takes place in an environment of major social, economic, legal, and global forces. These, too, must be understood to develop effective advertising and engage in effective advertising management.

DISCUSSION QUESTIONS . . . .

1. What are the basic differences between planning and decision making in advertising management? How does an advertising plan differ from an overall marketing plan? How do advertising decisions differ from other types of marketing decisions?

2. Outline the major components and considerations that you would include in your advertising plan if you were the brand manager of a brand of gasoline, a major credit card, or a new electronic device for use in business computers. In what ways would the plans differ? In what ways would they be similar?

3. An important internal component to be considered is the overall marketing plan. Provide additional examples of how advertising interacts with the elements of the marketing plan.

4. Using the model in Figure 2–3, explain your reactions to a recent television advertisement.

5. Give an example of how a competitive situation would affect the development of an advertising plan for a museum, an airline company, and a telephone product.

6. Suppose in your assessment of the current advertising plan for your product you decided that the execution of the advertising campaign was fundamentally weak. Which of the facilitating agencies would you look to as a possible source of the problem? Discuss some of the considerations in switching sources in this case.

7. Advertising plans rest on three central planning and decision making considerations. Name them and give examples of each.

8. Explain the meaning of the term "message strategy." Give an example of three alternative messages strategies that might be adopted for a brand of peanut butter. Choose one of the strategies and defend your position.

9. It has been said that an advertising manager lives in an environment of considerable uncertainty. Explain this statement. Do you agree? What are the chief avenues open to reduce uncertainty?

10. It was stated in this chapter that it is often difficult to decide what is deception in advertising and what is not. Do you agree? What rules or principles should an advertiser use in deciding whether or not a message is likely to be considered "deceptive"?

NOTES. . . . .

1. There has been much interest and new work in the area of business and marketing strategy in recent years. See David A. Aaker, *Strategic Market Management*, 3rd ed. (New York: Wiley, 1992); David A. Aaker, *Managing Brand Equity* (New York: The Free Press, 1991); and Michael E. Porter, *Competitive Strategy* (New York: The Free Press, 1980).
2. Alan P. Kuritsky, John D. C. Little, Alvin J. Silk, and Emily S. Bassman, " The Development, Testing, and Execution of New Marketing Strategy at AT&T Long Lines," *Interfaces* 12 (December 1982) 22–37.
3. See "Outline for Developing an Advertising Plan," in Don E. Schultz and Dennis G. Martin, *Strategic Advertising Campaigns* (Chicago: Crain Books, 1979), pp. 13–16. For a parallel approach which is specific to advertising called "advertising opportunity analysis," see Edward M. Tauber, "Point of View: How to Get Advertising Strategy from Research," *Journal of Advertising Research* 20 (October 1980), 67–72. For a book on marketing planning, see William A. Cohen, *The Marketing Plan* (New York: Wiley, 1995).
4. Gregory S. Carpenter and Kent Nakamoto, "Consumer Preference Formation and Pioneering Advantage," *Journal of Marketing Research* 16 (August 1989), 285–298.
5. John G. Myers, *Consumer Image and Attitude* (Berkeley, CA: Institute of Business and Economic Research, 1968).
6. A personal influence audit can be usefully done in conducting a situation analysis. See Chapter 9 for procedures involved in conducting a personal influence audit.
7. James W. Cagley and C. Richard Roberts, "Criteria for Advertising Agency Selection: An Objective Appraisal," *Journal of Advertising Research* 24 (April/May 1984), 27–31.

READINGS . . . .

#1—WHAT HAPPENED TO ADVERTISING?[a] . . . . .

Mark Landler, Walechia Konrad, Zachary Schiller, and Lois Therrien

Madison Avenue was always a street that had just one side: sunny. The ad game, after all, is about optimism and the power of positive thinking. Advertising legend David Ogilvy regularly exhorted his top lieutenants to "encourage exuberance" and "get rid of sad dogs who spread gloom."

Well, welcome to Madison Avenue, 1991: It's the gloomiest kennel you ever saw. This once-buoyant business is suffering through the deepest and most prolonged ad drought in 20 years. Advertising has muddled through its share of recessions. But this downturn has sent an unusual shiver through the industry. The gloom has even reached Château de Touffou, the 12th century French castle where Ogilvy now lives in retirement. The advertising world, says the 80-year-old adman, is haunted by "a pervasive atmosphere of fear."

BIG COMEDOWN . . . .

What's causing the fear is the suspicion among ad executives—and many of the publishers and broadcasters who depend on ad sales for much of their revenues—that the current hard times are only a foretaste of much slower growth to come. It's a stunning comedown for a business that had grown accustomed to a seemingly limitless boom. From 1976 through 1988, total U.S.

ad spending consistently grew faster than the economy as a whole. In 1981 and 1982, when the U.S. economy caught a nasty cold, the ad biz didn't even sneeze. Instead, it recorded eye-popping growth rates of 12.8% and 10.2%, respectively.

New product categories, from personal computers to compact-disk players, were sprouting everywhere. All of them required lots of advertising. Airline deregulation prompted carriers to launch ad-intensive fare wars. The breakup of American Telephone & Telegraph Co. created seven Baby Bells that had to make names for themselves. Financial-services advertising stampeded along with the bull market.

For the mass media, it was a seller's market. The three TV networks demanded and got double-digit ad rate hikes every year. As ad revenues soared, the agencies reaped millions from their standard 15% commissions on media billings. Such heady growth spurred empire-building: Rupert Murdoch and Robert Maxwell built multinational media conglomerates. Maurice and Charles Saatchi snapped up ad agencies in Britain and the U.S., while three great American agencies—BBDO Worldwide, Doyle, Dane, Bernbach, and Needham Harper Worldwide—combined to form conglomerate Omnicom Group Inc.

Then the party stopped. Even before the recession, the industry began lagging behind gross national product growth (chart). As consumer spending slowed and corporate profits withered, marketers put the brakes on ad expenditures. Total ad spending grew just 5% in 1989 and 3.8% in 1990—well below nominal GNP growth. It could grow as little as 3% this year, according to Robert J. Coen, the industry's top forecaster. Coen, a senior vice-president at agency McCann-Erickson, has already downgraded his bellwether estimate twice.

And those aggregate statistics, which and spending on local ads, cable television, and direct mail, don't reflect the much sharper downturn in advertising in the big mass media, such as TV networks and national publications. Network ad spending fell 7.1% in the first half of 1991 from the same period last year, according to the Television Bureau of Advertising. And revenues at the 170 magazines tracked by Publishers Information Bureau fell nearly 5% in the first half of 1991. Newspapers have also seen their growth contract sharply, pressed by the wave of retailer bankruptcies and plummeting real-estate and help-wanted classified ads. Total newspaper ad spending fell 7% in the first half of 1991, says the Newspaper Advertising Bureau.

Now, advertising and media executives are searching fruitlessly for signs that clients are ratcheting up spending. "I don't know whether we've reached bottom," says Allen Rosenshine, chairman of BBDO. "At best, there's a wait-and-see attitude among clients." As Rosenshine and his colleagues gird for a bleak winter, many of them are asking: Why did a relatively mild recession trigger a depression in advertising?

Loyalty Gap

To many marketers, the reason is as simple as it is scary: The recession has laid bare forces that are giving advertising a permanently diminished role in the selling of goods and services. Cynical consumers are wearying of the constant barrage of marketing messages. They're becoming less receptive to the blandishments of Madison Avenue. And their loyalty to brands has eroded as they see more products as commodities distinguished only by price.

At the same time that consumers have changed, technology and the proliferation of media are transforming the science of marketing to them. Now, companies increasingly can aim their messages to carefully pinpointed consumers through direct mail. General Motors Corp., for example, is rolling out its new Cadillac Seville with a mailing offering a videocassette to 170,000 young and affluent consumers. Or they can advertise on one of the new and sharply targeted media. To reach young children, Levi Strauss & Co. used to advertise mostly during Saturday morning cartoons on the networks. Now, the company also advertises on MTV and a new music channel on cable called Video Jukebox Network.

Then, too, there is a shift in philosophy at many major marketers. Leveraged buyouts, such as the $30 billion deal to take RJR Nabisco private, have left many giant consumer-goods companies saddled with huge levels of debt. And megamergers, such as Grand Metropolitan's purchase of Pillsbury and Philip Morris' acquisitions of both Kraft and General Foods, have led to a harsher bottom-line approach. So in category after category, brand managers are scram-

bling to boost quarterly sales instead of investing in image advertising to nurture brands for the long haul. To pump sales, they're shifting marketing dollars from ads into promotions such as coupons, contests, or sweepstakes. And because most promotions are placed locally, companies are shifting dollars from national to local media. Many marketing experts believe that such strategies—carried to an extreme—run the risk of damaging valuable brand franchises that enable marketers to price their products at a premium.

"SOBERED UP" . . . .

To be sure, some marketers believe advertising spending will come back as soon as corporate profits rebound. Advertising, they point out, is one of the easiest expenses to cut when profits fall, since the savings go straight to the bottom line. Unlike interest expenses or capital costs, advertising is "easy to get to from a budget-cutting point of view," says James C. Reilly, general manager for U.S. marketing at IBM.

And it's true that ad spending often moves in concert with a company's profits. IBM, Adolph Coors, and Chrysler all saw their profits fall in the first quarter of 1991. And all three pared their advertising budgets, according to market researcher Leading National Advertisers. Profits at Philip Morris Cos., on the other hand, rose 22% in the same period. And the company boosted its ad spending for Kraft Miracle Whip, Maxwell House Coffee, and other brands by an average of 5.1%

For most marketers, however, there's a more fundamental shift taking place: They no longer regard advertising as the sine qua non *of their marketing efforts. As a result, say many companies, while ad spending will turn up with the recovery, it will probably never again outperform the overall economy as it did in the boom years. "I absolutely, unequivocally do not see a time when advertising budgets will grow like they did in the halcyon days," says Philip Guarascio, executive director of advertising strategies at GM. The marketing chief at one of the largest national advertisers puts it more bluntly: "The recession has sobered everybody up," he says, "and if agencies think we're all going to start drinking from the same bottle again, they're kidding themselves."*

Madison Avenue is already feeling the postbinge blues. After years of ramping up, it now faces a wrenching readjustment. Pretax profits at WPP Group PLC, the world's largest ad holding company, plummeted 65% in the first half of 1991. Ogilvy & Mather Worldwide Inc., a WPP subsidiary, has let almost 10% of its staff go, while Ayer, Inc., the nation's oldest ad agency, recently laid off 60 staffers. In agency hallways, beleaguered employees murmur as much about pink slips as about their newest commercial.

The downturn has had a ripple effect on the media. The decline in ad spending has pummeled the profits of newspapers, magazines, and broadcasting companies. Worse, as their column inches, ad pages, and commercial time go begging, publishers and broadcasters have had to cut rates—eroding margins even further. Publications such as 7 Days *and* The National *have failed. The squeeze has forced media giants such as* The New York Times, *Time Warner, CBS, and McGraw-Hill, publisher of* Business Week, *to cut costs by buying out contracts of senior employees or laying off staffers. With new rivals such as cable and Fox Broadcasting Co., some media industry observers even wonder if the pinched ad economy can still support three TV networks.*

It's enough to make media executives pine for the simpler days of the '50s, when GM promoted cars by having Dinah Shore sing, "See the USA in your Chevrolet." GM still mounts big TV campaigns, of course: Its Heartbeat of America pitch is a well-supported successor to that vintage Chevy campaign. But now, says Guarascio, "We're looking at a whole bag of marketing options: event sponsoring, direct marketing, public relations, you name it."

SATURATION POINT . . . .

Guarascio and other marketers recognize how much has changed since the 1950s. For one thing, consumers don't pay attention to advertising the way they used to. The average U.S. adult is already bombarded with 3,000 marketing messages a day. So it's well-nigh impossible to get any one pitch noticed or remembered amid all the clamor. "One of our real concerns is that we have an inability to stand out," says Robert Watson, director of advertising services at AT&T.

With good reason: Market researcher Video Storyboard Tests say viewer retention of television commercials has slipped dramatically in the past six years. In 1986, 64% of those surveyed could name a TV commercial they had seen in the previous four weeks. In 1990, just 48% could.

Worse, even when consumers do notice an ad, they're less interested in the brand message it conveys. Consumers once clung to brands: There were Crest households and Colgate households, families that washed with Ivory and ones that showered with Dove. And the characters Madison Avenue dreamed up to pitch brands became pop-culture icons—the likes of Star-Kist's Charlie the Tuna, Philip Morris' Marlboro Man, Procter & Gamble's Mr. Clean, or the Pillsbury doughboy.

Now, many Americans, brought up on a steady diet of commercials, view advertising with cynicism or indifference. With less money to shop, they're far more apt to buy on price. And they're a lot less likely to be smitten by Tony the Tiger or the Campbell Kids. A survey by ad agency DDB Needham Worldwide Inc. found that 62% of consumers polled in 1990 say they buy only well-known brands, compared with 77% in 1975. A recent Grey Advertising Inc. study says 61% of consumers regard brand names as an assurance of quality—a drop of six percentage points since July, 1989. In the same study, 66% say they're trading down to lower-priced brands.

But even if consumers remained staunchly brand-loyal, marketers would be less willing to blanket them with media advertising. To be sure of reaching the right audience, companies once had no choice but to use general advertising campaigns, which reach nearly everybody. Now, computerized market research is letting them collect detailed information on their customers—not just the approximations offered by demographics, but the specifics of names and addresses. Marketers such as American Express Co. and Philip Morris have assembled vast data bases identifying their customers and their buying habits. With such information, companies now believe it's as important to reach the right people as it is to reach lots of people.

Increasingly, direct marketing is the vehicle of choice. Junk mailed used to be the sales tool for fairly specialized products and their services—credit cards or magazine subscriptions. Now, marketers of mass consumer products ranging from cars to coffee are turning from the TV box to the mailbox. Chrysler Corp., for example, recently mailed a videocassette promoting the changes in its 1991 minivan to 400,000 current minivan owners. It included a coupon for a Rand McNally road atlas redeemable at any Chrysler dealer. McCann-Erickson's Coen figures national direct-mail spending will grow 6.5%, to $24.8 billion, in 1991, while ad spending on network television will creep up just 1.5%, to $9.5 billion.

Even such traditional TV advertisers as Kraft General Foods Group are shifting to direct marketing. Kraft uses individual mailings, a newsletter, and a toll-free telephone to sell its Gavelia Kaffe, a premium Swedish coffee, to baby boomers and older consumers.

Direct mail has its problems. Consumers are also weary of being flooded by junk mail. And the vast data bases of marketers have prompted fears that they could invade the privacy of consumers.

SLICED THIN . . . .

The woes of the traditional mass media are being sharpened by the proliferation of new competing media outlets. CBS, NBC, and ABC once commanded a 93% share of U.S. homes watching television. Now, they have just over 60%. The rest are watching Bart Simpson on Fox or a baseball game on cable TV, which now reaches 59% of homes. Or they're watching a movie on a rented videotape. Or a boxing match on pay-per-view television.

Some new media target even thinner slices of the population. Want to reach air travelers? Turner Broadcasting System Inc. recently began testing a channel that will beam news from Cable News Network and commercials to TV monitors in airport waiting lounges. GM, AT&T, and American Express have signed up as charter advertisers. How about grocery shoppers? Turner is also rolling out a channel to be viewed at supermarket checkouts. Both services beat mass media on one important count: The advertisers know who their messages are reaching.

Packaged-goods companies such as Nestlé are also relying more on targeted media. Camillo Pagano, Nestlé's worldwide market chief, figures that in the past two years, the giant Swiss company has shifted roughly 20% of its advertising budget into alternative media. Pagano wouldn't give details, but he says Nestlé will use a variety of these media in a new venture with Coca-Cola Co. to sell cold canned coffee and tea under the Nescafé and Nestea brand names. Says Pagano: "There's no question in our mind that the key point is more targeting of the consumer."

Nestlé and other marketers are spurred by a growing desire to measure the effectiveness of their advertising. Media entrepreneur Chris Whittle says marketers can get more bang for their buck by using his targeted media. His products include Special Reports Family Network, a group of publications and a TV channel distributed to doctors' waiting rooms, and Channel One, a satellite service that beams 12 minutes of programming and commercials each day into school classrooms. Whittle says a 30-second commercial on Channel One reaches 40 times more teens than one on MTV.

Ad executives are unimpressed by such claims: "These methods may be effective," says Philip H. Geier, chairman of Interpublic Group of Cos., "but they are only adjuncts to mass media." Still, Whittle has persuaded Quaker Oats Co., Procter & Gamble Co., and Burger King Corp. to buy commercials on Channel One. "There are still people who believe in a core buy: three networks and a dose of women's magazines," says Whittle. "But a lot of people understand that's not the way things work anymore."

There's no denying that marketers want more accountability. Struggling to meet financial goals in markets that often grow no faster than the population as a whole, packaged-goods companies have been riding herd on their brand managers to produce quarterly sales results. The impact of image-building advertising on sales can often be tough to see. Not so with price discounts or coupons, which give sales a quick, easily measured kick. "People are saying: 'I can't wait for advertising to work. I've got to turn these dollars around more quickly,'" says Don E. Schultz, a professor of advertising at Northwestern University.

In addition to luring consumers, manufacturers must satisfy the demands of an increasingly powerful retail trade. Scanning devices at the checkout counter enable supermarkets to see which products sell and allocate shelf space accordingly. To hold on to a coveted place on the shelf, marketers must ante up dollars in the form of various "slotting fees," trade discounts, subsidies for the retailer's own advertising, or payments for in-store displays. These fees have ballooned because the explosion of new products has made shelf space that much more precious. And paying for them all cuts down on the amount of money available for traditional brand advertising.

That has hit advertising like a kidney punch. Companies now spend 70% of their marketing budget on promotions, leaving just 30% for ads, according to researcher Donnelley Marketing. Ten years ago, advertising got 43%, vs. 57% for promotions. Ad execs and marketers grouse that trade promotions are a form of extortion and that too many coupons dilute a brand. But with the pressure for sales and the power of retailers only growing, few predict that advertising will ever regain its share.

LOCAL TIE-INS . . . .

Promotions also hurt mass media because they siphon dollars from national to local marketing efforts. Burger King now spends half its ad budget on local tie-ins to build traffic in its franchises. Burger King Chief Executive Barry J. Gibbons says that because of the greater choice of media, network TV advertising will become less important. "The networks are efficient," says Gibbons, "but dollar-for-dollar, they're not as effective."

Even some brand advertising now carries promotional components. Not long ago, the Super Bowl telecast provided a huge audience for some of the year's flashiest new ads—for example, Apple Computer Inc.'s atmospheric anti-IBM commercial that paid homage to George Orwell's 1984. Now, the telecast has become a platform for fevered promotions and sweep-

stakes. The Bud Bowl, which invites consumers to guess the score of a mock football game for prizes, competes with noisy promos for the soft-drink companies.

The highly praised Diet Pepsi ads starring Ray Charles and his bluesy rendition of You've Got the Right One Baby, Uh-huh *represent one of the best brand-image campaigns of 1991. But the commercials also invited viewers to send in videos featuring their own rendition of the jingle. A few are chosen for use in future Diet Pepsi commercials, and those viewers will win cash prizes. Pepsi also just ended the Summer Chill Out campaign, a slickly produced series of ads that gave away discounts, cash prizes, and 130 new cars. So what's wrong with that? Again, the money to run sweepstakes and promotions comes at the expense of airing more ads.*

Media advertising is not going away, of course. Campbell Soup Co. plans to boost its ad budget 30% next year. Some of that money will go to revive its fabled Campbell Kids campaign. Herbert M. Baum, president of Campbell North America, hopes the new Kids will win younger consumers over to its red-and-white soup cans. "We missed a generation or two of kids," he says. Another big marketer, P&G, has also bolstered its U.S. ad spending. And most advertisers acknowledge that mass media can't be beat as a low-cost way to reach huge audiences. "The networks are still the Main Street of advertising," says Peter S. Sealey, senior vice-president and head of global marketing at Coca-Cola.

"BLOODY FOOLS" . . . .

Sealey and other marketers also recognize that advertising is still the most effective method to nurture a brand's image over the long haul. The risk in cutting advertising support is that the brand will erode: Mars Inc. surpassed venerable Hershey Foods Corp. as the nation's largest chocolate maker because it spent more to advertise M&Ms and its other brands than Hershey did. "Brands can take short-term cuts in ad spending," says Roy J. Bostock, chairman of D'Arcy Masius Benton & Bowles. "But there's a time bomb waiting to go off."

What's more, marketers have an interest in maintaining strong brand franchises because it enables them to price their products at a premium. In doing so, America's big consumer marketers have been able to roll up comfortable profit margins.

So there's no question ad spending will recover to some degree. But with companies racing to reach consumers in so many new ways, Madison Avenue is struggling to adjust: Since agencies now draw most of their commissions from placing media ads, they're rushing to develop the faster-growing disciplines such as promotions and direct mail. They're also looking overseas: The deregulation of media in Western Europe has fueled faster ad spending growth in many of those markets.

As the industry adjusts to these new realities, it may actually be returning to the fundamentals of its business. Advertising, after all, does work in some fashion, even if its workings are often mysterious. But when the good times were rolling, many ad agencies hurried to see who could produce ever more lavish, ever more "creative" advertising. Clients complained that their shops were interested only in grabbing awards or raking in millions from agency mergers.

Perhaps these hard times will help the business relearn a valuable lesson, says David Ogilvy: "Maybe we'll stop being such bloody fools and get down to our business, which is selling products for clients." He should know. He began his career as a door-to-door salesman, and the verity he learned then applies to the hard truths taking hold today: "No sale, no commission. No commission, no eat."

THE MEDIA GET THE MESSAGE—AND IT'S GRIM .

Each summer, its a cat-and-mouse game. The Big Three networks post big rate hikes and purr quietly as advertisers scamper to lock up precious commercial time for the coming season. But this year, the mice are having all the fun. Advertisers are having little trouble finding available time. Best of all, they're getting discounts of up to 25%. Battered by a yearlong advertising downturn that feels more like depression than recession, CBS Inc. and NBC Inc. are offering these sweet deals because they have little choice. Their fear: If they don't catch the advertisers now, they may have to offer more expensive bait later.

Many magazine publishers are caving in to pressure, too. Until recently, most didn't budge from their published rate card. Now, although most won't admit it, publishers are offering their advertisers premiums or outright discounts. "There's a school of thought that says: 'If you can say you've got the most pages, you're in good shape,'" observes Reginald K. Brack Jr., chairman of Time Warner Publishing.

YESTERDAY'S DARLINGS . . . .

But rather than shield the traditional mass media from a decline in advertising spending, such stopgap measures have only worsened the pain. Now, not only are media companies selling less advertising, but they're also earning less for what they do sell.

The effect on profits has been devastating. Profits of media companies are especially sensitive to fluctuations in ad revenue because they have high fixed costs involving staff, production, and distribution. Since the cost of adding ad pages or commercial time is fairly small, any incremental gain in ad revenue produces a much bigger jump in profits. Likewise, any loss of ads slashes profits disproportionately. Selling time at a discount, for example, will badly hurt CBS, which already reported a 67% decline in profits in the first half of 1991. Still, CBS's troubles are nothing compared to Financial News Network Inc. or Family Media Inc., publisher of Discover *and* Health *magazines. Both have shut down.*

The wave of failures has also come because of a glut in the business. For most of the 1980s, the media were everybody's favorite boom industry. All three networks were gobbled up by profit-hungry corporations. Rupert Murdoch paid $3 billion for TV Guide. *publishers flooded the shelves with hundreds of new magazines every year. And why not? The industry rolled up annual increases in ad rates of 8% to 10%. Now all the new players have vastly overbuilt the business—and the industry is in a shakeout.*

Then there are structural changes in the ad marketplace that are reducing the number of traditional mass media advertisers. Airlines, banks, savings and loan associations, movie studios, and retailers are consolidating into fewer players, so each industry will spend less on advertising. The turmoil in the retail industry, for example, has sharply reduced the volume of newspaper advertising. In New York City, the liquidation of B. Altman & Co. and Gimbels hurt papers such as The New York Times. *The* Times, *which saw its ad linage plunge 18.5% in the first half of 1991, says it doesn't expect its advertising to return to mid-1980s levels.*

Magazines, meanwhile, are struggling as tobacco merchants, one of their key supporters, continue to retreat from advertising. Cigarette makers are reducing print advertising as they concentrate on promotions and direct marketing. Cigarette ad spending in magazines dropped 8.6% in the first half of 1991, according to Publishers Information Bureau.

The media have coped with lower profits by slashing costs. The Big Three networks have laid off scores of staffers and closed bureaus from Johannesburg to St. Louis. Newspapers and magazines are thinning their ranks through early retirement or layoffs.

The media are also striving to alter their approach. Traditionally, magazines relied on advertising for more than half of their revenues. But many publishers are now raising subscriptions and newsstand prices. And most new magazines make the bulk of their revenue from subscription fees, according to Samir A. Husni, a professor at the University of Mississippi who tracks magazine growth.

Still, most media are scrambling to look more attractive to advertisers. CBS is selling packages of ads on several of its marquee sports events such as Major League Baseball, which were once sold separately at high prices.

The print media are dividing their readership into thinner slices for niche-minded marketers. Time, Newsweek, *and four other magazines are using special ink-jet printing technology to allow General Motors Corp.'s Buick Div. to personalize ads for its readers. "There is a sea change in what advertisers are demanding," says Thomas Rider, president of American Express Publishing Corp. "They want targeting and micromarketing."*

Multimedia companies are seeking an advantage by offering marketers advertising opportunities across several media. Time Warner has signed up Chrysler Corp. and Mazda Inc. to advertise in Time's magazines and in electronic media such as Warner's home videocassettes. In return, they get more attractive ad rates.

The networks, meanwhile, are extolling themselves as the last redoubt for mass marketers. With the proliferation of media, they say, nobody can match the broad reach of the Big Three. Daniel B. Burke, CEO of Capital Cities/ABC Inc., points out that even with declining audience share, each network still commands 20% of the viewing audience every night. Cable networks, by contrast, rarely reach more than 2% apiece. "If you look at what we're turning into," says Burke, "it's still an enviable, wonderful thing."

Such confidence led Burke to take a big gamble this year: ABC charged marketers significantly more per rating point than CBS or NBC. Burke believes advertising spending will recover in early 1992. And if it does, ABC will have more time left to sell.

Other entrepreneurs share Burke's confidence. Walt Disney Co., for example, just bought Discover. Kohlberg, Kravis, Roberts & Co. paid $650 million to buy nine magazines from Murdoch. And Fidelity Investments has snapped up several regional papers near Boston. "The recession will end," says Burke. "It always does." Now if only advertisers would agree.

READINGS . . . .

#2—DO YOU NEED YOUR AD AGENCY?[b] . . . .

Patricia Sellers

Do you need your ad agency?

If you buy Coca-Cola's audacious new views on marketing, maybe not. Ever since Michael Ovitz, the Hollywood talent agent, last fall snatched the advertising business of the most famous global brand from the world's largest ad agency, McCann-Erickson Worldwide, the earth has been shaking beneath Madison Avenue. The latest quake: In early October, Coca-Cola pulled its huge Diet Coke account, an estimated $65 million in the U.S. alone, from another ad giant, Lintas. Observes M. Douglas Ivester, Coca-Cola's executive vice president and master of these maneuverings: "An ad agency person, of course, is saying, 'This breaks my paradigm. And it makes my head hurt to even think about it.' "

The pain in the paradigm is caused by impatient viewers who are zapping ads even as the media marketplace gets more turbulent by the day. Brand equity, that commercial karma between consumers and products, is eroding universally. As a result, connecting with consumers today requires more ads more often—but without more cost—produced and delivered in new, unusual ways.

Yet the agencies have been devising big, expensive, cookie-cutter campaigns for these increasingly fickle audiences in much the same way that top-heavy, vertically integrated, multi-layered manufacturers used to produce automobiles no one would buy—and at cost plus a 15% commission, no less. Now, just like manufacturing, the advertising industry is undergoing seismic change.

Big, bureaucratic agencies are delayering their managements, unbundling their services, and "boutiquing." Lintas even concocted an in-house agencyette called L_2 to appease malcontent client IBM. No go. IBM unplugged its $55 million personal computer account in late October, switching to tiny Merkley Newman Harty in the U.S. and DDB Needham in Europe.

Needham last August spun off creative star Andy Berlin into his own agency to keep Volkswagen of America's $40 million account from driving away.

Brand owners, including MasterCard International and Reebok, are stepping to lesser-known ad firms like Ammirati & Puris or to a few oddly configured large ones such as Leo Burnett, where the creed essentially is "We don't act big." Nestlé and MCI alighted on Messner Vetere Berger McNamee Schmetterer/Euro RSCG, a gang of street-smart, highly productive ad-makers who set up shop in 1986. Says partner and co-founder Bob Schmetterer, 49: "We thought there was something tragically wrong with the traditional agency structure. The industry had gone astray from the central thing clients need—giving insight and creative ways to sell."

The weirdest new architecture of all: Chiat/Day, which is eliminating offices and desks and giving employees lockers for their belongings. Enigmatic Chairman Jay Chiat, 62, America's most celebrated ad-man a decade ago, says his "virtual agency" should foster creative thinking and collaboration. It had better. Chiat/Day has lost a ton of business.

Coca-Cola isn't finished making mischief, either. The company is moving Diet Coke to Lowe & Partners, a limber midsize agency that shares a parent, Interpublic Group, with Lintas and McCann. But the soft-drink giant plans to tap anyone, anywhere for ideas. So for the first time since 1955, Coke is going outside the Interpublic agencies for major ad ideas. The recruits so far are highly creative: little Fallon McElligott in Minneapolis, Nike's agency Weiden & Kennedy in Portland, Oregon, and probably even deskless Chiat/Day. Jeff Goodby, a ponytailed partner at fast-growing Goodby Berlin & Silverstein in San Francisco, observes all the commotion with glee. "It's kind of like deregulation," he says. "The rules are gone."

The rule of the Eighties was "Consolidate and integrate": Merger-created mega-agencies like Saatchi & Saatchi and WPP Group combined diverse services such as product design, corporate identity, public relations, and consulting under one roof, on the notion that these specialties could be peddled to global corporations. The whole egg, Young & Rubicam called it.

Most clients saw little reason to one-stop shop, and the egg began to rot. Advertising conglomerates got stuck with unprofitable divisions and loads of debt. The stock of Saatchi (including Saatchi & Saatchi Advertising, Backer Spielvogel Bates, CME KHBB, and Rowland Worldwide public relations) is trading around $7, vs. a high of $17.38 in 1991. The company, with billings of $11.8 billion, is expected to show earnings this year for the first time since 1988. WPP (Ogilvy & Mather, J. Walter Thompson, Hill & Knowlton PR) sells at $3, vs. $24 three years ago. The company barely makes a profit, and CEO Martin Sorrell is selling assets to raise cash.

Though the conglomerates have cracked, operating profit margins in advertising have stayed around 10%, according to Morgan Anderson & Co., a New York consulting firm that helps companies like MasterCard and Sears Roebuck work with their ad agencies. The pill that has kept Madison Avenue looking fit is an age-old compensation system, the 15% commission. Think about it: Your agency receives 15 cents in revenues for every dollar it spends in the media. That's akin to your salespeople getting paid based on how much they spend instead of how much they sell.

Thanks largely to the 15% commission, the price of placing an ad on network prime-time TV doubled in a decade, yet delivered 25% fewer viewers. No wonder cost-conscious companies such as H. J. Heinz, RJR Nabisco, and BMW rebelled, slicing the 15%. Today less than one-third of major U.S. advertisers pay full commission, and an increasing number prefer set fees. Leo Burnett Chairman Rick Fizdale, 54, whose agency got rich on the commish, is now publicly speaking against it. Says he: "It's incenting us to do the wrong thing, to recommend network TV and national magazines and radio when other forms of communication like direct marketing or public relations might do the job better."

What marketers must do, amid the change and confusion, is align with new and improved partners that cost less, work faster, are fully adaptable to the broadly expanding needs of their clients. And are highly creative, of course. Some agencies are up to the task already. Typically they are untraditional, versatile organizations, delivering surprising sorts of service.

Messner Vetere Berger McNamee Schmetterer/Euro RSCG is one of those thriving. The midsize agency has the most muddled name in the ad trade. But the people who run the firm aren't muddled about their mission: Concentrate on clients' business. They create the ads for

MCI, Nasdaq, Volvo, Nestlé's Stouffer frozen foods group, and A&W Brands, among others—mostly scrappy underdogs in highly competitive, unsteady categories.

Schmetterer, former chief operating officer of Scali McCabe Sloves, and the other founders, who left New York's Ally & Gargano agency in 1986, have established a company in Manhattan's arty SoHo district that's informal, flexible, responsive. Almost all 300 employees work on advertising. Everyone has at least one computer, some hooked into clients' offices. There are no secretaries, though the 11 partners share four assistants. To encourage cooperation, they also share offices.

So creative director Ron Berger 43, has his stark black and chrome desk at one end, facing the elegant blond-wood furniture of Louise McNamee, 43.

Titles are rare, but McNamee is president, pursuer of new business, and—like her partners—supervisor of a few clients' accounts. She arrived last year when her ex-partner, famously irreverent adman Jerry Della Femina, trotted off to run trendy restaurants and reinvent himself as Jerry Inc. Thereupon Della Femina/McNamee merged with Messner Vetere.

"If we need balance, I'm here to provide it," McNamee jokes, referring mainly to her liberal Democratic leanings within a Republican fort. Founders Berger, Tom Messner, and Barry Vetere all belonged to the ad hoc ad "Tuesday Teams" that helped put Reagan and Bush in the White House.

The political grounding here, remarkably, contributes to good work for clients. Consider MCI. The No. 2 long-distance company was losing market share before Messner Vetere won the ad account three years ago. The agency came up with a frankly political premise: "People don't buy a phone company. They elect one," as Berger puts it. Messner Vetere, which employs conservative political strategist Roger Ailes as a consultant, steered MCI into political-style overnight polling to gauge the company's momentum as a candidate would. They also turned to confrontational ads.

"MCI used to be the Michael Dukakis of the telecommunications industry," says Berger. Meaning: When AT&T attacked MCI in its ads (as Bush bashed Dukakis), Wells Rich Greene, MCI's previous agency, wasn't keen on a client's firing back at a rival that outspends it 5 to 1. Messner Vetere counterattacked. "No wonder they want you back," says one ad, with charts that show AT&T's falling market share.

The admakers' toughest trick was combining a cocky stance and a cozy image, which they decided MCI should have since a warm likability is one thing AT&T sorely lacks. Messner, 49, an eccentric, instinctive copywriter, argued for MCI to brand its service offerings. So, much as Procter & Gamble labels soap, he thought up the name "Friends and Family" for a new program that the client had intended to call "MCI to MCI." This is the plan that gives discounts to customers who sign up a "calling circle" of other MCI subscribers.

An unremitting flow of fresh ads has helped MCI grab over 19% of the combined consumer and business market, up from less than 13% in 1990 according to the company. The gain amounts to more than $3.6 billion in additional revenues. Says Angela Dunlap, 36, president of MCI's $5 billion consumer markets division, of the agency's strength: "They're very in tune with the fact that the world is changing fast, and you have to act differently."

With many big agencies behaving like factories these days, midsize firms such as Messner Vetere and Ammirati & Puris are acquiring fans and expanding rapidly. Says Lee Anne Morgan of Morgan Anderson: "Midsize agencies tend to serve clients best. They usually offer a very good, solid balance between strategic and left-brain thinking and creative right-brain thinking."

Ammirati & Puris's founders are Ralph Ammirati, 63, a shy, owlish art director, and Martin Puris, 54, an eloquent and affable copywriter who 19 years ago penned the line "the ultimate driving machine" for the agency's first major client, BMW. You know the firm's work today for Compaq Computer, RCA, UPS, Four Seasons Hotels, and Nikon, to name a few. It's intelligent, witty, and print-heavy because the bosses love the written word. They demand that clients' senior management become deeply involved in ad strategy, and occasionally they fire clients—this year Cadbury-Schweppes soft drinks—that they think don't invest wisely. Reasons Puris, the businessman of the duo: "Great clients make great agencies. Dopey clients will take you down with them."

For Aetna Life Insurance, Ammirati took the radical approach that less is more. Mary Herrmann, an account service manager who is Puris's wife, recently advised the company not to increase its ad budget. Instead, Ammirati has changed the message, switching from folksy ("Aetna, I'm glad I met 'ya!") to edgy and adult—on TV, stark black and white messages with background voices pointing up issues like drunken driving, AIDS, and drug abuse. Why the attitude adjustment? Says Elizabeth Krupnick, the insurer's senior vice president who oversees advertising: "Aetna's a professional company confronting serious issues."

Yet the ads are extremely inexpensive to produce—around $40,000 for a 30-second spot, one-tenth of what most major brands pay. More important, while insurance commercials are zapped more than any other type, Aetna's actually get watched. Aetna's consumer survey shows that awareness of its advertising is up 29% since Ammirati's campaign began. "Most advertising fails before it's written," says Puris. "Strategies are weak and the claims are superficial, like 'This is the best car or the best deal.' "

The agency positioned new client MasterCard as "Smart Money," zeroing in on utility, not grand aspirations, in a market where the other biggies, American Express and Visa, promote luxury and prestige. MasterCard also bumped its ad spending to $60 million from $40 million in 1991, which clearly helped pull the card out of a 14-year rut of flat or declining market share. But James Desrosier, the company's vice president for advertising, says he is certain that Ammirati's work has contributed significantly. Consumer perception of MasterCard's broad acceptance by merchants—its most important selling feature—is way up. This year MasterCard is the fastest-growing card in the U.S., with sales up more than 20% from last year.

MasterCard preceded Diet Coke out of the arms of Lintas. The agency was unable to stop the card's slide. Don't blame the whole thing on Lintas. Unstable management within MasterCard stifled growth too. But Desrosier says Lintas's ad talent didn't flow to the customer. "Big agencies lose sight of the fact that they operate primarily to serve clients," he says.

That's how Coca-Cola views large agencies lately too. In fact, when you talk to both sides of the severed Coke-McCann partnership, you wonder how it remained intact for 38 years.

On the 21st floor of McCann's New York headquarters, where senior management resides, you don't see any advertising on the walls. Is this a bank, or what? CEO Robert James, an avid sailor who decorates his office in a nautical motif, won't talk about Coca-Cola (which still uses McCann for media buying and select ads). But asked whether client or agency should be "custodian of a brand" and decide its strategy, James replies firmly, "The agency."

Ivester's testy response: "No way." The Coke executive says in Atlanta, "Our shareholders hold us responsible for our trademark. There's no way our shareholders can hold a third party responsible."

While Ivester, 46, loves signs and stadium displays—what Coke calls presence marketing— James, 57, denigrates it. McCann's chief says this about such ad formats: "They're brand-reminder vehicles, not selling propositions." While Coke sees more of these alternative media, McCann derives about 95% of its total revenues from traditional venues like TV, radio, and magazines. James's boss, Interpublic Group CEO Philip Geier, Jr., 58, says that's fine because client spending in conventional media should accelerate soon. Ivester and most other marketers disagree.

"How big can we get before we get bad?" was always the mantra of Jay Chiat, who dreaded the evil effects of size on creativity. There's one agency that has both, simply because management focuses on the latter. Just about every creative leader in the industry—Puris and Chiat, to name two—says that BBDO, the world's fifth-largest ad firm, delivers the most imaginative ads most consistently.

Until recently at least, its Pepsi commercials regularly flogged Coke's. The agency also has told you that Apple Computer delivers "the power to be your best," that Gillette is "the best a man can get," and that General Electric "brings good things to life."

Unlike almost any other large agency, BBDO has copywriters in charge. Chairman Allen Rosenshine, 54, is an impatient man who despises the industry's habit of heaping awards on itself. Vice chairman Phil Dusenberry, 57, is BBDO's creative chief, and his philosophy—that an ad must tell a story and lift the spirit—pervades the work.

Though tiny, with a whisper of a voice, Dusenberry is tenacious and almost impossible to *satisfy. Some insiders joke that BBDO stands for "Bring it Back and Do It Over." Dusenberry pays his creative people exceedingly well: up to 50% above other agency salaries, so a clever copywriter in her late 20s can earn more than $200,000 a year. Notes Dusenberry: "Account people rule the roost at most big agencies. Here, creative rules."*

Says Bruce Crawford, 64, the urbane chairman of Omnicom, the parent: "There's nothing wrong with being a giant agency network as long as you decentralize. BBDO has not been sullied because it's been allowed to stick with its knitting, creating, great advertising."

For marketers such as Philip Morris, United Airlines, and Sony—which want lots of services as well as lots of service—the agency of choice is Chicago-based Leo Burnett. James Cantalupo, president of McDonald's International, says, "They overservice us. And in the difficult economy these days, that goes a long way."

Integrated marketing works here because Burnett, unlike other large agencies, PR, and direct marketing as separate profit centers. That means you won't find some eager manager who's supposed to be busy on your account pitching services à la carte to other prospects. Such soliciting is forbidden. Yet, observes veteran ad executive Alvin Achenbaum, now a New York marketing consultant, "Burnett gets its tentacles into clients like an octopus." Half its U.S. clients have stuck with the agency at least 20 years.

Burnett staffers receive cross training in various marketing disciplines, so copywriters on the Hallmark account write junk—er, direct—mail and in-store promotion posters too. Burnett operates just one full-service office in the U.S., on Chicago's Wacker Drive, America's largest agency under one roof. Founder Leo Burnett wanted it that way because he insisted on seeing every ad. He resisted international expansion until his death in 1971, but now Burnett has 55 offices in 49 countries, deriving half its billings abroad.

In September that network drew Reebok, which is turning abroad to foment growth and seeks to blare its ad messages through an array of media formats. Stunning the ad industry, Reebok untied itself from Chiat/Day, which is weak internationally, and handed its $140 million worldwide account to Burnett without even screening other agencies. Says Fizdale, Burnett's cerebral, chatty chairman: "This is the first time we've ever won a client globally. We've always started with clients regionally. This shows that our global system works."

In October, on the heels of the Reebok win, CEO William Lynch, 51, realigned Burnett's management to make sure senior execs really are working tightly with particular clients. Sound familiar? Fizdale, who thrives on fixing knotty problems, got plugged into Burnett's most troubled accounts: Oldsmobile and Miller Lite. Fizdale figures, "The advertising industry won't survive unless agencies make every move right. We have to prove our relevance."

And so must the industry. Ad agencies are needed more than ever to rebuild bruised brands and guide marketers into an interactive, multimedia future where connecting with the consumer will be more complicated than ever. Trailblazers the agencies are not. Ironically, the industry was born and grew because its members are said to understand what the consuming public needs and wants, but these professional communicators don't seem to be communicating with their own customers.

At the very least, advertisers must become the stewards of their brands. They need to scrutinize constantly whether their ad partners are delivering the important goods: insight and creative ways to sell. Everything else is overhead.

HOW CAA BOTTLED COCA-COLA. . . . .

"We are dead."

John Bergin, McCann-Erickson's former vice chairman, slipped a note with those blunt words on it to an associate as the two watched Michael Ovitz's Creative Artists Agency make a dazzling pitch that would cost McCann the Coke account.

In fact, the handwriting was already on the wall. A secret and unorthodox Coca-Cola study begun in 1989 on the future of marketing preordained the stunning move. Called Project Balance, the study tapped ten unconventional thinkers—business consultants like Peter Drucker, Harvard marketing expert Ted Levitt, and research whiz Arthur Nielsen—for their views on reaching consumers in this media-saturated age. Management felt some urgency: Sales of Coke's main brand were barely increasing in the U.S., and Pepsi's ads consistently scored higher.

The group's first report, published in 1990, posed a provocative premise: "A brand advertised in a normal way, with normal media, is likely to develop a normal image, and not something special." So the experts advised: Don't be normal.

McCann-Erickson was a normal agency. So believed Donald Keough, Coke's president and longtime marketing guru who retired last April. Keough, 67, told FORTUNE in February that traditional agencies tend to approach advertising as if they're "delivering coal"—shoveling money into network TV because it's easy money for the agency.

Keough, who had known Ovitz since the days Coke owned Columbia Pictures, was intrigued by CAA's pipeline into pop culture and by Hollywood's "raw creativity." A partnership was born in 1991.

Enter Peter Sealey. One of the more insightful contributors to Project Balance, Sealey, 53, had been a McCann adman, a Coke executive, and then head of domestic marketing at Columbia Pictures. Keough made him director of Coca-Cola's global marketing. Sealey set up a skunkworks: himself, staffers Ogden Tabb and Elizabeth Rue, in Atlanta; and CAA's duo of Shelly Hochron, a former Columbia movie marketer, and Len Fink, who had worked at Chiat/Day.

Brainstorming from spring 1992 through October, the Coke-CAA team devised over 100 ideas for the 1993 global campaign, then winnowed the list to about 50. "We didn't do any formal research. None. Zero," says Hochron.

Presentation day last October at "the Tower," Coke's headquarters, turned into defenestration day for McCann. The agency proposed the usual half-dozen platform ads positioning Coke as a ubiquitous product, for all people. The CAA show, introduced by Ovitz, was a whirlwind 60 minutes in which the 50 ideas were pitched in many styles for many audiences.

Seeing the Coke side so elated, Bergin passed his note to McCann vice chairman Marcio Moreira. Coke management selected 24 ideas from CAA, including those computer-generated polar bears. The McCann gang sold two.

Unveiled last winter, the new campaign was praised as innovative, sexy, playful, and breathtaking. But was it advertising? Entertainment gymnastics, industry critics carped. Consumers recently rated the ads tops among all campaigns.

Sealey went on to brag publicly that Coke's new advertising not only was far cheaper to produce but constituted a breakthrough for Coke as well. "It's no longer one sight, one sound, one sell," he crowed. Maybe he should have kept quiet. He clashed with Keough's successor, Douglas Ivester, a quiet, methodical ex-accountant who is most likely Coke's future CEO. Ivester canned Sealey last summer, although he remains a consultant.

Sealey's replacement is Sergio Zyman, 48, a temperamental former Coke marketer who crushed any notion that the company would return to the Madison Avenue fold. A week into the job, Zyman rejected McCann's ideas for the 1994 global campaign.

CAA is set to do Coke Classic's entire 1994 campaign. Meanwhile, Ovitz and Bill Gates of Microsoft are meeting quietly. Apple Computer has retained Ovitz as a marketing consultant. And Nike recently hired CAA to help with sports marketing events for TV. At Interpublic, McCann's parent, CEO Philip Geier, Jr., is busily realigning McCann's management. He wants another crack at Coke. America's most powerful adman says, "We've got to do a better job."

PART

II

OBJECTIVE

SETTING AND

MARKET

POSITIONING

3 INTEGRATED MARKETING COMMUNICATIONS

"Integrated Marketing Communications is a concept
of marketing communications planning that
recognizes the added value of a comprehensive plan
that evaluates the strategic roles of a variety of
communications disciplines—for example, general
advertising, direct response, sales promotion, and
public relations—and combines these disciplines to
provide clarity, consistency, and maximum
communications' impact (through the seamless
integration of discrete messages)."
(Modified from the definition used by the American Association
of Advertising Agencies)

When Southwest Airlines started flights out of its new Baltimore hub in September 1993, they knew they had to familiarize East Coast travelers, unaware of what Southwest stood foor, with the no-frills, low-fare, high-frequency service that it offered. Five weeks before the first flight, they staged a public relations event: Southwest Airlines Chairman Herb Kelleher and the Maryland Governor jointly announced Southwest's entry into Baltimore, and Kelleher handed the Governor a flotation device, calling it a "lifesaver" from high fares for the people of Baltimore. Another public relations event followed: to launch the $49 fare to Cleveland, Southwest flew 49 elementary schoolchildren free to the Cleveland Zoo. Next, the company sent a direct mail piece to frequent short-haul travelers in the Baltimore area, offering a special promotion to join Southwest's frequent-flier program. Another consumer promotion followed that featured employees handing out fliers and peanuts at Baltimore street corners, promoting the airline's low "Just Peanuts" fares. And, only then did TV and print ads kick in. This combination of public relations, direct mail, sales promotions, and advertising led to a company record for advance bookings—90,000 passengers bought advance tickets even before service began.[1]

This case is an excellent example of an increasingly popular approach—called *integrated marketing communications,* or IMC for short—to combining and integrating different elements of the communication mix. We will discuss what IMC is and how to implement it in detail later in this chapter. The key idea behind IMC, however, is simply that advertising has various strengths and weaknesses and that it thus has to be combined with the other elements of the *communications mix*—for example, direct marketing, consumer and trade promotions, publicity and public relations, and event and sports marketing, and others—in an integrated and consistent way.

In addition, these different elements of the communications mix have to be used in a way that the strengths of one are used to offset the weakness of another. For instance, one of advertising's weaknesses is its frequent failure to induce immediate action. Very often advertising can create high awareness and favorable attitudes, but it cannot create the final "push" needed to get the inquiry, trial, or sale. When such a situation appears, a marketer must use direct marketing, or sales promotions, to get the necessary action, possibly after an advertising campaign.

In this chapter, we will first discuss some of the strengths and weaknesses of advertising, in the context of the other communications tools available to the marketer. We will then review some of these other communications tools: direct marketing, sales promotions, and public relations and publicity. (Using the sales force to close a sale is another element, but for a discussion of that we defer to books on sales force management.) We will also discuss some other specialized forms of advertising that attempt to create actual behavioral change, such as retail advertising, co-op advertising, and industrial advertising that aims to generate sales leads. Then we will return to the concept of IMC to understand both the key ideas involved and the tactical issues involved in implementing it.

THE ROLE OF ADVERTISING WITHIN THE MARKETING PROGRAM. . . . .

Advertising planning and decision making take place in the context of an overall marketing program, as just discussed in Chapter 2. Obviously, there are several marketing tools that can be used to help an organization achieve its marketing objectives. Its product or service can be developed or refined. A distribution network can help match an organization's output with its clientele. Pricing strategy is another marketing decision variable. The most appropriate way to improve the sales of a brand may not involve promotion or advertising at all, but may involve more extensive distribution, better relationships with the trade, a lower price, or simply better product quality.

A brand manager needs to spend considerable time pinpointing the exact source of a brand's poor sales before deciding that the core problem is inadequate or poor advertising or promotion. For instance, if research data indicate that consumers are trying the brand but are not repurchasing it, it may well be that the firm's advertising is successful (since consumers are trying the brand) but that the brand's product quality needs attention (since people who try the brand do not repurchase it). The marketing plan thus should be based on the specific problems or opportunities uncovered for the brand by the kind of situation analysis discussed in Chapter 2.

In addition to placing the advertising plan in this total context, the brand manager must also take care to develop a marketing program in which the component parts work in a coordinated, synergistic manner instead of at cross-purposes. For instance, when a firm develops a prestige product with a premium price, it is important that the advertising reinforce that idea of high quality and prestige. This can be done by associating the product with prestigious people, situations, or events. If the advertising objectives are written to encourage the use of advertising copy and advertising media incompatible with a prestige image, the whole marketing program may be jeopardized. Alternatively, when a firm offers a low-priced product, the job of advertising might be to stress the price differential by using hard-hitting copy.

As another example, the role of advertising will also depend on the distribution channel selected. If door-to-door selling is employed, advertising may be used only to introduce the salesperson, or it may not be used at all. If wholesalers, retailers, or other middlemen are employed, different advertising strategies are available. The advertising and selling effort may be primarily directed to either the consumer or the trade. In the former case, the intent would then be to have consumer interest "pull" the merchandise through the distribution channel; in the latter case, distributor margins would get the emphasis, consumer advertising would be less, and the intent would be to "push" it through the channel. Generally, the nature and significance of advertising will differ according to whether the company is stressing a push or pull strategy and whether its distribution strategy is intensive (the use of many outlets to maximize customer convenience), exclusive (the use of a few outlets to maximize retailer interest), or selective (intermediate arrangements).

THE ROLE OF ADVERTISING WITHIN THE "COMMUNICATIONS MIX" . . . .

Once it has been determined that a key problem or opportunity for the brand involves its communication with consumers, it should not be immediately concluded that more money needs to be spent on advertising. Advertising is only one part of the communications mix: a firm can also communicate with its consumers through the sales force, through publicity or public relations, and through various consumer and trade promotions.

Within this mix, advertising has various strengths and weaknesses. Unlike the high cost of a sales call, which by some estimates now exceeds $225 per call once all relevant costs are considered,[2] advertising is a much cheaper way to reach target consumers (often pennies per exposure), since it uses mass media. And, again, unlike sales calls, advertising can use complex visual and emotional devices to increase the persuasiveness of the message. However, salespeople can often communicate more complex information (often necessary in industrial or big-ticket purchases) better than advertising can, can tailor the nature of the message much more closely to the message recipient, and are much more likely to "close" the sale by getting an order. Thus, direct marketing may be needed to target certain prospects with a more customized message, provide them with detailed information, and induce them to act. Direct marketing will be introduced below.

Advertising is notorious for this inability to actually get the sale: while the effects of advertising in increasing brand awareness and favorable attitudes for the brand are easily documented, effects on sales are harder to find (some reasons for this are discussed in Chapter 4). It is thus often useful, after advertising creates awareness of a brand, to supplement advertising with sales promotions (both consumer promotions and trade promotions), which are often more effective in actually getting consumers to try the brand. Such sales promotions may be especially required if research shows, during the situation analysis, that target consumers are aware of the brand and think it has the features they are looking for but have not gotten around to trying it. Sales promotions are outlined below.

Finally, advertising is also weak in another respect: it is widely perceived as biased. Many consumers often do not trust advertising and are skeptical about its claims. In such situations, it is often useful for a marketer to try to communicate his message to consumers through media that are perceived as more credible and unbiased, such as editorial endorsements obtained through publicity and public relations (PR) campaigns. Such PR programs are introduced below.

Thus, an integral part of the advertising planning and decision-making process is an assessment of the role that advertising is meant to play—as one part of a firm's communications mix and as one part of the total marketing mix. Once this perspective has been gained, the brand manager must design a marketing and communications plan in which the different elements complement each other in increasing the sales for the brand. Although this book deals mostly with advertising management, we cannot emphasize enough that an advertising plan can only be developed in the context of a total marketing and communications plan for the brand.

To help place advertising in the context of this total communications mix, we will now discuss the other nonadvertising elements (direct marketing, sales promotions, and public relations) as well as some more specialized, action-oriented types of advertising. Then, we will address some of the conceptual, strategic, and tactical issues involved in integrating all these elements.

DIRECT OR DATABASE MARKETING. . . . .

Direct marketing includes not just *direct mail*, but also *telemarketing* and *direct response* advertising on TV and radio and other media, in which the ad aims to generate an action response (such as calling a toll-free number). Direct marketing has two key advantages that differentiate it from regular, mass advertising: (1) the ability to target specific, individual consumers (not just demographically described segments) with an *offer* that is tailored to that consumer and (2) the ability to directly measure response. For example, the *script* used by a telemarketer can be tailored to what is known about the person being called. The response (or lack of it) can then be entered into a computerized database so that the next marketing effort aimed at this individual can be customized to whatever the direct marketer knows about this specific individual.

Unlike traditional mass media advertising, the goal of most direct marketing efforts is not simply to build awareness or change preference, but to generate an action: either an order or request for more information, a visit to a dealer or a store, and so on. This need to generate action is another distinguishing element of direct marketing and has implications for its creative requirements, which we will discuss further below.

These features of action orientation, targetability, customization ability, and measurability have led to the tremendous growth in direct marketing over the past decade and have led to the current popularity of so-called *database marketing*.[3] While the first catalog in the United States was offered as far back as 1744 by Benjamin Franklin, today about 4,000 catalogs go through the mails each year in the U.S., and almost 100 million Americans shop every year by mail or telephone, spending over $50 billion.[4] By one estimate, Americans today receive 62 billion pieces of direct mail and 18 million telemarketing calls per year!

To share in this growth, all the major ad agency groups now own direct marketing units. The leading direct marketing agencies in the United States include Ogilvy and Mather Direct (New York), Wunderman Cato Johnson (a division of Young and Rubicam, in New York), Rapp Collins Marcoa (a part of the Omnicom group, and based in New York), Kobs and Draft Worldwide (Chicago), and Bronner Slosberg Humphrey (Boston).[5]

This explosion in direct marketing has occurred because more and more traditional "mass market" advertisers have taken to combining direct marketing efforts with their regular advertising efforts, in an effort to not only sharpen their ability to win new customers (by mailing more targeted offers to prospects) but also to retain the loyalty of existing customers, to *cross-sell* new products and services to these existing customers, and to increase the amount or frequency of usage.[6] As some examples of such databases, consider these: Pizza Hut now has a database of 10 million pizza eaters in the country; Kraft General Foods has one on 25 million of its customers; Seagram knows the names and addresses of over 10 million liquor buyers, and Marriott Hotels and Resorts has one on 4 million of its regular guests.

Uses and Examples

As an example of the first goal mentioned above that an advertiser may have—*customer acquisition*—a magazine advertisement for a new General Motors car may feature a coupon inviting the reader to write in for a free copy of a book that will help him make a better automobile-buying decision. The coupon collects not just the reader's name, address, and telephone number, but also information on his present car and how soon he expects to buy his next car. The coupon-sending customer is then sent further collateral materials (such as brochures and catalogs) on the car, with an invitation to test-drive the car at a local dealership. The dealership will also be sent that coupon information on the reader so that the dealer can follow up with a telephone sales call (called *outbound telemarketing*). Other ways of building up databases might involve inducing customers who use a grocery coupon to also write in their name and address, as part of a sweepstakes entry. (The easiest way, of course, is simply to rent a mailing list, which is discussed below.)

Obviously, this marketing effort may or may not result in a sale. Whatever the response or lack of it, all the information now known about the consumer and his response is entered into a computer database, and this database is subsequently utilized to target certain individuals for further mailings or telemarketing efforts. For example, if the car in the example above is a luxury Cadillac model, a mailing for it may be sent to those known to own a competing model of luxury car such as BMW or Lexus (using a mailing list obtained from automobile registration data). Every subsequent response (or nonresponse) that can be directly tracked and attributed to a specific mailing piece or phone call is entered into this database, and the cycle of targeting and measuring response continues.

As an example of the second goal—*customer retention,* or *loyalty building*—a company such as DuPont Automotive might send all its present customers a regular newsletter on its new research and new products to build up its relationship with these customers. In many businesses, a key 20 percent or so of customers account for 80 percent or so of volume, so building relationships with these key customers is obviously vital. To enhance customer satisfaction, a company might offer a toll-free telephone number for service questions, customer enquiries, or product complaints. (Such a telephone service is an example of *inbound telemarketing.*) An airline might send all its frequent-flyer program members a newsletter with special loyalty-building offers. A credit card might use an *envelope stuffer* mailing to induce its present customers to charge even more. Many of these *loyalty programs* offer free gifts or incentives to a company's best customers: American Express offers the top 5 percent of its cardmembers special restaurant and travel offers that vary by the zip code in which the card member lives.[7]

Such mailings can be used not only to strengthen relationships and build loyalty, but also to accomplish the third and fourth goals—*cross-selling* products or *increasing the usage rate.* Thus, a large financial services company such as American Express might attempt to sell new insurance or financial planning services to its charge card membership base, or a large foods company like Kraft General Foods might try to get a customer of one low-fat product to try its other low-fat products (by mailing them coupons or samples). As an example of direct marketing to increase the usage rate, or amount of repeat consumption, an automobile dealership or repair facility (such as Goodyear Auto Service) may track the mileage of the cars brought in for service and send mailed reminders to these customers to bring their cars in for service at regularly scheduled intervals.

Because of the high cost of personal sales calls, companies also often use direct marketing in after-market sales (e.g., selling copier supplies to people who bought copiers and whose names and addresses and phone numbers are now in a database), and in generating sales inquiries that can then be followed up by telephone and personal sales calls. The use of databases also allows companies to use direct marketing to target mailings of coupons and samples to only high-opportunity individuals and households. The traditional users of direct marketing have always been magazines and newspapers (who use it to sell subscriptions), the marketers of insurance-by-mail, the record and book clubs (in what are called the *negative option continuity programs,* through which customers are sent something every few weeks till they say no), and, of course, the catalog retailers (such as Spiegel's, Lands' End, etc.).

Targeting

The targeting ability of direct marketing can be greatly enhanced by a systematic development of the direct marketer's database. Someone who knows your address and, thus, your postal zip code or census block group, can obtain information from database companies about various characteristics (such as the median income, average age, etc.), of the zip code in which you live, based on the average for the geodemographic *cluster* in which you live (such clusters are discussed in Chapter 6). This information is then used to assess whether you are a likely prospect for a particular product, on the assumption that your individual profile is similar to the average data available for your zip code. The average profile of people living in some of Donnelley's "Clusterplus" forty-seven clusters are provided in Figure 3–1; every household can be classified into one of these clusters based on its zip code.

In addition, data are also available that apply to consumers as individuals: lifestyle (hobby and activity) information supplied on product warranty registration cards can be purchased, as can driving license and automobile registration data (in most states). Any other source to whom consumers reveal their incomes or age or anything else may also sell this information to the large database companies (such as Donnelley, Metromail, Polk, etc.) that maintain household databases on almost every household in the United States. Databases on business establishments are maintained by companies like Dun & Bradstreet, containing information on the businesses' sales, number of employees, and nature of business (using the Standard Industrial Classification, or SIC, code).

Companies can also acquire names from their databases in other creative ways: a company making diapers, like Kimberly-Clark, may acquire the names of all those expectant mothers who take a childbirth class before delivery—or from newspaper birth announcements after the delivery. Many packaged goods companies attempt to "capture" the names and addresses of users by obtaining them from sweepstakes entries, from those sending in mail-in offers for promotional premiums and gifts, from those who cash in rebates or writing in response to free sample offers, or from those who include a sweepstakes entry form as part of a regular grocery coupon that is redeemed in a store. The consumer who writes in a name and address on the redeemed coupon thus not only receives the coupon's promised cents-off but also enters a sweepstakes. Retailers build up lists of customers by obtaining names and addresses as part of the regular sales process. Obviously, the availability of such information on consumers raises all kinds of concerns about privacy.[8]

Cluster code

01	Highest SESI, highest income, prime real estate areas, highest education level, professionally employed, low mobility, homeowners, children in private schools
02	Very high household income, new homes and condominiums, prime real estate areas, highly mobile, high education level, professionally employed, homeowners, families with children
03	High income, high home values, new homes, highly mobile, younger, high education level, professionally employed, homeowners, married couples, high incidence of children, larger families
04	High income, high home values, high education level, professionally employed, married couples, larger families, highest incidence of teenagers, homeowners, homes built in 60's
05	High income, high home values, high education level, professionally employed, low mobility, homeowners, homes built in 50's and 60's
06	Highest incidence of children, large families, new homes, highly mobile, younger, married couples, above average income and education, homeowners
07	Apartments and condominiums, high rent, above average income, high education level, professionally employed, mobile, singles, few children, urban areas
08	Above average income, above average education, older, fewer children, white collar workers
09	Above average income, average education, households with two or more workers, homes built in 60's and 70's
10	High education level, average income, professionally employed, younger, mobile, apartment dwellers, above average rents
11	Above average income, average education, families with children, high incidence of teenagers, homeowners, homes built in 60's, small towns
12	Highly mobile, young, working couples, young children, new homes, above average income and education, white collar workers
13	Older, fewer children, above average income, average education, white collar workers, homeowners, homes built in 50's, very low mobility, small towns
14	Retirees, condominiums and apartments, few children, above average income and education, professionally employed, high home values and rents, urban areas
15	Older, very low mobility, fewer children, above average income and education, white collar workers, old housing, urban areas
16	Working couples, very low mobility, above average income, average education, homeowners, homes built in 50's, urban areas
17	Very young, below average income, high education level, professionally employed, highly mobile, singles, few children, apartment dwellers, high rent areas
18	High incidence of children, larger families, above average income, average education, working couples, homeowners

Source: Donnelley Marketing Information Services.

Figure 3–1.   Demographic characteristics of selected ClusterPLUS^{SM} neighborhood clusters.

Source: Donnelley Marketing Information Services.

Measuring and Improving Response

Typically, the direct marketing companies compute response on a response-rate-per-thousand-mailings basis, abbreviated as *OPM* (orders per thousand). They can tell which mailing to which a customer responded by using code numbers (called *key codes*) on the response coupons that uniquely identify a mailing package. Companies continually test different mailing packages to see which ones "pull" best. Thus, different mailing pieces may be sent to random samples of 10,000 to 25,000 individuals, with the mailing peices varying systematically in the size and color scheme of the envelope, the copy in the sales letter, the size and illustrations in the brochure, and the price and payment terms. The objective in such tests is to see which of these many new *test packages* yields a response rate or order rate greater than the mailing piece being used currently, called the *control package.*

Response rates—which can be very low, often just 1 to 2 percent of the packages mailed—are a function of many factors. First, of course, there is the product being offered, at a certain price and payment term, and with or without a *premium*, or free gift. These are collectively called the *offer.* Response rates are higher if the product is unique and not available in regular retail channels, if the price is credibly low, and if the payment terms are easy, and so on. Second, there are the quality and responsiveness of the names in the mailing lists that the direct marketer is renting, through a *list broker* or *list compiler* (perhaps paying $100 for every thousand names mailed). Are the people on the list really interested in this product or service? Third, of course, is the quality of the creative message: the letter, the brochure, the envelope, and so on. Even with such low response rates, and even with production and mailing costs of 50 to 60 cents per mailing piece, a mailing can still be profitable if the gross profit per response is high. Conversely, if the gross profit per sale is low, and/or if the target marget is reached more efficiently by mass media than through targeted direct marketing, mass marketing and advertising may make more economic sense than a direct marketing program.

Direct marketers also spend large sums of money building analytical models of the responses to their mailings. For example, a logit or logistic regression model might be estimated on a previous mailing, which can be used to forecast which of the prospects for an upcoming mailing are most likely to respond to it, and the mailing can be limited to only the most likely responders. Such models to a company's existing customers often model the likelihood of response as a function of how long it has been since that customer's last order (called *recency*), how many times that customer has purchased in the past (called *frequency*), and how much money that customer has spent with the company in the past (called *monetary value*). Such RFM models (for the first letters of these three concepts) are very often used by traditional catalog direct marketers, but newer and more sophisticated modeling methods—some even using artificial intelligence techniques called *neural nets*—are often superior to such RFM models.

In building a direct marketing business, a direct marketer is concerned not just with maximizing the response rates to a mailing (called the *front-end* of the business), but also the (*back-end*) profitability of the customers acquired. For example, a book club can very easily boost response rates to a mailing by giving away more books free of charge, and requiring no commitment from the new member to buy any more books ever. Such a *soft offer* would obviously boost response rates! However, the members acquired through such a mailing may well not end up buying many books over the lifetimes of their memberships with the book club and may thus be relatively unprofitable to acquire. In contrast, a *hard offer* that offers fewer free books and requires bigger and longer commitments to buy a certain number of books may well result in a lower overall response, but more profitable members long-term. A direct marketer is concerned not just with immediate pay-off but with the *lifetime value* of its customers.

Mailing List Rental and Processing

Mailings or telemarketing campaigns can obviously be made to a company's list of existing or past customers, called its *house list.* For mailings to prospects, however, *outside lists* usually have to be rented. Mailing lists are usually rented on a per-use basis, rather than bought and sold. Compliance with rental conditions is monitored by inserting *dummy* or *decoy* names into the list to which the renting mailer will unknowingly send mailings, which can be tracked for frequency of use.

Such outside lists are of two primary kinds. A *response list* is a list of the customers of another business. Such a list will obviously contain a name and complete address, but may also contain information on the recency, frequency, and monetary value of the name on the list (these terms were defined above). If these are customers who ordered from that business very recently, the list may be called a *hotline list* (and command a higher price). In contrast, a *compiled list* is a list together from directories and other sources, and is usually cheaper to rent, since it is unknown how likely the people on the list will be to respond to the mailing.

Such outside lists are usually rented through a *list broker*, who represents the people who own or compile the lists (for a commission, of course). List brokers offer access to a huge number of lists—over 40,000 by one count, including every conceivable occupation and profession. Lists are rented on a *per-thousand-names* basis, with the charge varying on the desirability of the list (it may cost $100 per thousand names, for instance). Since a renter may end up renting several hundred small lists, the multiple lists used are first merged and purged of duplicate names, and payment is usually made on a net basis, after deleting duplicate names. This *merge/purge* is done by computer bureaus. The actual mailing of the mailing pieces, using the mailing labels or names supplied by the list broker, is done through *lettershops.*

Creative Guidelines

Good direct mail pieces are built on an intuitive understanding of the psychology of inducing action. Think about the state of mind of a consumer opening a direct-mail solicitation. He or she has doubts about the quality of the product, since it cannot be physically inspected. There is no salesperson to answer questions and overcome objections. And, there is the very human tendency to postpone things: even if the consumer feels vaguely interested, there will typically be a reaction of "I'll get around to this later, not now."

What good direct marketing copywriters have discovered—and this is wisdom that even non–direct marketers can benefit from—is that direct-mail copy that gets action tries hard (1) to use testimonials and guarantees to develop confidence; (2) to use as much information as is necessary in the letter to clarify doubts, overcome objections, and increase the reader's level of desire for the product; (3) to make it easy for the consumer to take action, by having easy-to-use response cards or toll-free telephone numbers; (4) to "involve" the reader, through devices such as peel-off stamps and scratch-off numbers; and (5) to express urgency about the need for immediate response, by saying that the offer or free premium is good "for a limited time," expires by a certain date, and so on. In direct marketing, as in all marketing, the key barrier to getting consumers to act is sheer inertia, and ads that target such inertia directly are most likely to obtain action.

Figure 3–2 shows an advertisement from a very successful mail-order campaign. Although the advertisement is not a one-time effort but part of a continuing campaign, its primary goal is intended to precipitate immediate response and its effectiveness can be properly measured by this response. Direct marketing advertising has long been recognized as being perhaps the only area in advertising in which immediate sales are a reliable indication of advertising performance. As a result, advertising professionals look to the experience of mail-order advertisers to learn what works and what doesn't.

SALES PROMOTIONS . . . .

Sales promotions are of two broad types: *consumer promotions*, such as coupons, sampling, premiums, sweepstakes, low-cost financing deals, and rebates; and *trade promotions*, such as slotting allowances, allowances for featuring the product in retail advertising, display and merchandising allowances, and the like. They are used to get consumers to try or to repurchase the brand and to get the retail trade to carry and to "push" the brand.

Additionally, promotions are also used by manufacturers to "discriminate" between different segments of consumers—for example, only those consumers who have the time to clip coupons will clip and use them and obtain a lower price for themselves, while those consumers who are time-pressed won't use coupons (and will end up paying a higher price). Finally, retailers use promotions to clear their inventory of slow-moving, out-of-season, or shelf-unstable products (those products, such as fresh produce, that will spoil if they are not sold quickly). Retailers thus run their own promotions aimed at consumers, such as price cuts, displays, frequent shopper programs, and so on.

While this is a book about advertising management, and while sales promotion is a distinct area of research and management—with its own textbooks[9]—it is necessary for us to spend some time discussing sales promotions. There are three reasons for doing so.

First, sales promotions are a key element in inducing trial or repurchase in many communications programs in which advertising creates awareness and favorable attitudes but fails to spur action. One of the reasons they spur action—compared to simple price cuts—is that they are typically run for a limited duration,

Figure 3–2.   A successful mail-order advertisement.

Courtesy of Book-of-the-Month Club, Inc.

which means that the consumer must act quickly, before the promotion ends. Other reasons they spur action is simply that many consumers feel they get value for their money if they buy "a good deal" (they are "smart shoppers"). In fact, many consumers automatically assume that if a brand is being promoted it must be a good deal (which is not always true!). By one estimate, 80 percent of U.S. households use coupons, 75 percent of the appliances bought in the U.S. are bought on deal, and 70 percent of the packaged goods sold to retailers are sold with a trade promotion. Thus, it is important to understand the complementary roles of advertising and sales promotion in order to conduct situation analyses properly and to set communications, advertising, and sales promotion goals.

Second, according to a 1993 survey of promotional practices in seventy leading companies, sales promotions constitute about 73 percent of marketing expenditures (about 27 percent is spent on consumer promotions, 46 percent on trade promotions), whereas advertising constitutes about 27 percent.[10] The share of the marketing dollar spent on trade promotions has risen rapidly in recent years, in large part due to the growing power of ever-larger retail chains. For instance, America's largest retail chain, Walmart, now accounts for 10 to 15 percent of the sales of many of America's largest packaged goods companies! Some of the power of retail chains also comes from their access to accurate checkout scanner data, which reveals which brands are moving fast off the retail shelves (and which are not) and to their ownership of the precious retail shelf-space "real estate" that the manufacturing companies covet (and are willing to pay for). Other reasons for the growth in promotional spending are the trend to more local and regional marketing programs and the greater price competition posed to national brands by store-label (*private label*) brands.

Clearly, since advertising expenditures take place in this total promotional context and not in isolation, it is essential that the advertising manager have a good understanding of sales promotions as well. While the implementation details of sales promotions and advertising are handled by different individuals in most marketing organizations, brand managers usually are responsible for both areas. In order to be able to offer "integrated" sales promotion services, many of the major advertising agency groups own one or more sales promotion companies (such as Alcone Sims O'Brien, owned by Omnicom, or Lintas: Marketing Communications, owned by Interpublic), although many of the leading firms in this area are still independent.[11]

Finally, advertising and sales promotions operate together in their impact on the consumer. When designed and run in tandem, they yield powerful synergies that magnify their individual effects. For example, a coupon offer in a Sunday newspaper *free-standing insert* (FSI) can have a higher redemption rate if theme ads for that brand are run concurrently. On the other hand, if advertising and sales promotion efforts are designed and run in isolation, they can lead to effects that hurt each other—poorly designed promotions, in particular, can quickly erode the long-term image of the brand that advertising has worked hard to build up over several years. This longer-term *brand equity dilution* effect of promotions is probably greater for brands in highly involving image and "feeling" product areas, because promotions might "cheapen" a brand's image. Brands in product categories in which choices are based on "economic," price-minimizing criteria are not as vulnerable to brand equity dilution.[12] Even if the brand's image is not hurt, most promotions end up only drawing volume from existing users who would have bought anyway, so that the promotion may end up costing the company more money than it brings in.

It is therefore essential that the advertising manager understand the need for this interaction between advertising and sales promotions. The thrust of this section thus will be to explore this interaction. Before we do that, however, we will briefly describe several different types of sales promotions, stressing those aspects that relate in some way to the advertising program.

Consumer Promotions

Consumer promotions are designed to offer consumers an incentive (such as a lower price or a free or low-cost premium or gift) to try a brand for the first time, to switch back to it, or to repurchase it. The different types of consumer promotions vary in their trial versus repurchase orientation, as will be pointed out below. A few consumer promotions, such as sweepstakes and premiums, can be designed with a view to enhancing the key imagery equities of the brand.

Coupons

Coupons are perhaps the most frequently used consumer promotion—over 300 billion coupons were distributed in the United States through print media in the early 1990s, but only about 3 percent were redeemed.[13] Although over 75 percent of all coupons are currently distributed through newspaper FSIs,[14] coupons distributed through direct mail are more targeted than are those distributed through print media (newspapers and magazines) and thus have much higher redemption rates (about 9 to 10 percent in direct mail versus about 2 to 3 percent in newspapers). Whereas coupons that are in or on the pack are specifically designed to build repeat purchase and loyalty, those that are carried in other products consumed by a similar target market (such as coupons for a baby shampoo carried in a diaper product) are designed to attract new customers. These latter coupons are called *cross-ruff* coupons. Coupons (or cash checks) are often offered as straight price *rebates* for durable products, such as cars or appliances, and are sometimes offered as *refunds,* mailed to consumers who send in proof of purchase. (Manufacturers often hope that many consumers who buy products because of a mail-in rebate never in fact mail-in the rebate, and this is often the case!)

From an advertising perspective, it is important in couponing to design the coupon ad in such a way that it builds on, and reinforces the positioning and key benefits developed in theme advertising, rather than having a different theme (or no theme at all, other than the price incentive). Similarly, a rebate offer might be creatively designed to highlight a brand strength—for instance, an offer to pay for a car's gas consumption or maintenance expenses in its first year might better highlight the car's gas economy or repair record than a simple rebate check. In addition, of course, the coupon must be designed so it is easy to clip, shows the package prominently, has the appropriate legal copy, and so on.

From a media standpoint, another key objective in couponing is to make sure it really gets new users instead of merely going to existing users who would have bought it anyway. The easiest way to deliver coupons, to gain mass reach, is to use newspapers. However, it has been estimated that only one-third of coupon usage, from such mass-distributed coupons (such as those in Sunday newspaper FSIs), comes from new users. As a result, many more companies are either mailing coupons via direct mail to those known to be nonusers, or using new in-store services (such as Catalina Marketing's Checkout Coupon service) which prints a coupon for a brand at the point-of-sale to someone who has just bought a competing brand. The coupon is "triggered" by the scanned purchase of the competing product.

This synergy can work the other way as well: coupons or other promotional offers can be used to increase the effectiveness of an ad by increasing readership. Apple Computer supported the introduction of its Macintosh with a "Test Drive a Macintosh" promotion, which allowed customers to leave computer showrooms with $2,400 worth of equipment.[15] The budget was $10 million, of which $8 million went to advertising and the rest supported such activities as in-store displays and carrying the inventory costs. Around 200,000 Macintoshes were test driven, at a cost of only $5 each.

Sampling

Giving people *free samples* or *trial packs* (door to door, at street corners, in stores or shopping malls, or through the mail) is another promotional technique and is an excellent (but expensive) way to get consumers to try a product. Chesebrough-Pond's, for instance, distributed 80,000 full-size samples of its new products, plus coupons and literature, in five shopping malls. A new product launch could include a small sample mass-mailed to possibly half of the nation's households. Alternatively, for an existing product, small trial packs could be mailed to households known—as part of a databased marketing effort—to be current users of a competitive product. New and creative avenues for in-store sampling include sampling children's products in toys stores such as Toys R Us, sampling products aimed at teenagers in college bookstores, and so on. In such sampling programs, care must be taken to provide enough product quantity to convince the trier that this is indeed a better product, while simultaneously minimizing product, packaging, and mailing expenses.

Figure 3–3 shows an ad for Lipton's new teas that ask consumers to write in for trial tea bags. It is often appropriate to do such sampling for new brands, after running an introductory flight of ads to build awareness and favorable attitudes (so that consumers who receive the free sample already know about it and are predisposed to try it). It may often be more cost effective to do such sampling than to run additional advertising for such new brands, after that introductory advertising. When feasible, the advertising could feature an in-store coupon for a free trial pack or a toll-free phone number to call for one.

Figure 3–3.   Sampling via trial packs: Lipton Teas.

Courtesy of Thomas J. Lipton Company.

Price Packs

Price packs (packs that offer a lower than usual price, or greater than usual quantity) are another kind of consumer promotion that can both attract switching and reinforce loyalty. Here again, it may be more supportive of the brand's advertised image to offer "extra" product volume than to simply lower price. For some products (such as tea, coffee, detergents, etc.), it may be possible to offer the "extra" volume in a special container (such as a glass carafe or plastic dispensing unit) that reinforces some aspect of the brand's image.

Premiums and Gifts

The same kind of thinking can be used to select *premiums* that are offered to consumers (these are "free" products that are provided in the pack or mailed if multiple proofs of purchase are sent in, either at no cost or at below-retail prices. If the latter, they are called *self-liquidating premiums* because the company recovers its out-of-pocket costs). An intelligently selected premium can be used to reinforce a brand image: Mueslix cereal from Kellogg, from instance, which built its initial advertising campaign around a European heritage, offered consumers a packet of European currency notes if they sent in the required number of proofs of purchase. In-pack premiums (such as toy characters in children's cereals) can also be designed to build a brand's image. The cigarette brand Marlboro offers loyal consumers—those who collect enough boxtops—merchandise with an outdoorsy, Western, cowboy theme that reinforces the brand's classic imagery. Since such premiums typically require multiple proofs of purchase, they are designed most often to build repeat purchase and customer loyalty.

Sweepstakes

Sweepstakes are another kind of consumer promotion, and these offer the greatest potential to reinforce a brand's advertising platform. McDonald's, for instance, ran a sweepstakes promotion at the same time that its ads were featuring a "McDonald's menu song" in which consumers had to play a plastic record to find out if they had won—with the record featuring the same menu song. Benson & Hedges cigarettes, around the time it launched a 100-mm-length version, ran a sweepstakes in which consumers had to pick which one of a hundred minicontests they wanted to enter, in which each of these minicontests had as their prize 100 units of something (such as 100 pints of ice cream).

Subsidized Financing

This incentive is frequently used in the promotional programs for many durable products, including automobiles. Since these products are often purchased by consumers on monthly installment plans, the consumer is more concerned with the monthly payment amount, including the monthly interest payment, than the total amount paid. Companies therefore attempt to lower this monthly amount by offering a subsidized interest rate, often through a captive financing subsidiary (such as General Motors Acceptance Corporation, in the case of General Motors).

The key thought in the foregoing discussion on consumer promotions is that promotions are needed to move the consumer along to making the needed "action" step, or needed to build loyalty and promote repurchase, after advertising has done its job in creating awareness and preference. However, promotions can sometimes hurt a brand's image by cheapening it, but this is not necessary if the promotion is designed with a view to working with and strengthening the brand's advertised image.

Trade Promotions

Trade promotions are financial incentives given to the trade to stock the product, to buy in larger quantities, to move merchandise from the warehouse onto the retail shelf, to display the brand in end-aisle displays, or to feature the brand in local retailer advertising (such as on "best food days"—Wednesdays or Thursdays), including offering retailer coupons, and so on. Another purpose served by trade promotions is that they give the manufacturer some degree of control over the final price charged to the end-consumer: if the price to the retailer is cut, it should lead to (at least slightly) lower prices for the consumer. Cooperative advertising is discussed later in this chapter, but many of the other types of trade allowances are discussed briefly below.

These trade promotions often have the objective of "buying" retail shelf space and getting additional retailer "push" by loading the retailer with extra inventory or of giving the retailer a temporarily lower price in the hope that some of the price cut is passed on to the consumer. Unfortunately, retailers have begun to keep back for themselves much of the price incentive they are expected to pass on to the consumer (the *pass-through* percentage is often only about 50 percent). In addition, many retailers often *forward buy* more deal-promoted product volume than they can sell at that time, either using the extra volume for nonpromoted future time periods, or "diverting" that volume to other dealers at a slight mark-up. As a consequence of these practices, trade promotions have begun to account for a very large percentage (20 to 30 percent) of retailers' total profits.

Because of these problems, manufacturers have recently begun to cut back on these promotions, often by substituting a lower *everyday low price* (EDLP) for a sometimes-high, sometimes-low (*high-low*) price and promotion policy. Since cutting back on trade promotions will obviously hurt retailers' profits, manufacturers have begun to compensate for these cuts by also trying to hold down the costs that retailers incur in warehousing, transporting, and stocking that manufacturer's products through processes called *efficient consumer response.* The hope is that the retailers' *direct product profitability* (DPP) on these manufacturers' brands does not suffer.

In addition, many companies have begun to offer advice to retailers on how to maximize their dollar return from each section of the store, by showing them how to allocate their retail shelf space optimally among the different brands, using *planograms.* This approach is called *category management,* and has led to many manufacturers developing closer relationships with each retail chain so that they can understand the retailer's needs better, often on a store-by-store or market-by-market basis.

Some of the types of trade promotions frequently used by manufacturers are described briefly below.

Off-Invoice or Buying Allowances

These incentives are the simplest form of trade promotion and are nothing more than a price cut of a certain percentage applied to the volume bought by a retailer during the promotional period (e.g., 5 percent may be taken off the invoice, hence the name). No retailer performance (such as displays, feature ads in retail store circulars, etc.) is required. As mentioned, retailers often purchase more than they can sell during such promotional periods to have enough stock to last them to the next promotional period, a practice called *bridge buying* or *forward buying.* A variant of such promotions is the offer of *free goods*, such as one unit free per dozen purchased. This has the advantage of requiring the retailer to actually sell the free good before the gains from the promotion are financially realized, putting greater "push" pressure on the retailer.

Count-Recount Allowances

Under this type of trade promotion, the discount is applied not to the quantity the retailer buys from the manufacturer during the promotional period, but only to that quantity that is moved from the retailer's warehouses into the retailer's stores. As a consequence, the retailer is given a greater incentive to pass the price cut on to the consumer so that the product "moves" from the store into consumers' hands.

Billback Allowances

These allowances are paid by the manufacturer to the retailer on a per-case basis only if certain performance criteria are met. While they have the advantage of "pay-for-performance," they have the disadvantage of requiring sales force and administrative time to monitor compliance.[16] The kinds of "performance" expected from the retailer could include in-store displays, feature ads in the retailer's circulars, and so on.

Display Allowances

These allowances are incentives to the trade to display the product prominently, in an end-of-aisle or store-window display. These have been found to be very effective, because many time-pressed consumers simply pick up those brands that are made salient by such displays, assuming they are on sale (which is not always the case). Stores like such allowances because they are a good source of revenue (a grocery chain might charge $200 per week per store for a display). For durable goods, such displays are often a very valuable tool to educate both the consumer and the retail salespeople about the special features of the product.

In-Ad Grocer Coupon

This type of payment by the manufacturer is made to the retailer in return for which the retailer features a coupon for that brand in the retailer's weekly adver-

tising circulars. The coupon is redeemable only in that retailer's store. The manufacturer pays the coupon face value, plus handling costs.

Slotting or Facing Allowances

These allowances are one-time fees paid by the manufacturer to the retailer to get
a new brand on the retailer's shelf, paid to compensate the retailer for the brand
removed to make space for this new brand and for associated inventory and administrative costs—and the risk—involved with the new brand. These fees may
cost manufacturers anywhere from $10,000 to $100,000 per item per chain.[17]

Trade Inventory Financing or Delayed Billing

These financial incentives are used most often in durable goods industries, such as
appliances or automobiles. The manufacturer lowers the cost to the retailer to purchase products to stock on the retail floor or in inventory, either by offering a
reduced-rate financing facility, by delaying billing, or both.

Sweepstakes, Contests, and *Spiffs.*

These are incentives used to reward retail salespeople who meet their sales quotas for the manufacturer's goods, usually for durable goods, paid for by the manufacturers of those products. Ideally, these are timed to run concurrently with
consumer promotions.

There is emerging consensus that, in addition to the several negative consequences already discussed earlier, these trade promotions also have the potential
to erode a brand's franchise and image. They do this by reducing the amount spent
on advertising and in increasing the extent to which the consumers buy the brand
in the supermarket because it is "on deal" that week, rather than because of its advertised image. This leads to an increase in the perception that the brand is a commodity, or parity product, rather than something with unique added values (the
subject of Chapters 9 through 11). Here, again, the smart advertiser must strive to
focus these trade deals on advertising-enhancing activities (such as thematically
linked displays or thematically consistent retailer advertising).

In the longer run, of course, only an advertiser with a strong brand consumer
franchise—built up through consistent advertising—will have the market clout to
withstand retailer pressure to provide higher and higher trade allowances. Strong
brands with demonstrated "sell-through" (advertising-induced consumer demand) will not have to give as much to the retailer (although the trade will often
"push" stronger brands of their own accord) and will thus end up as more profitable brands.

Thus far we have discussed the interaction between advertising and promotions mainly in terms of the content of both. Another form of interaction pertains
to their timing: consumers are more likely to notice the advertising for a brand and
the promotions for it if both are run concurrently rather than in separate time periods. Such a coordinated campaign is more likely to break through the clutter.
This is likely to enhance the effectiveness of both the advertising campaign
(through higher readership or viewership) and of the promotional program
(through greater coupon redemption or in-store sales from special displays).

OTHER ACTION-ORIENTED COMMUNICATIONS . .

Retail Advertising

Another example of advertising that has direct, action objectives is the advertising of retailers, or *retail advertising*. What are the advertising practices of successful retailers? The best retail advertisements are those that provide the consumer with a lot of specific information, so that the consumer can see immediately that he or she must indeed visit the store. It is not enough, therefore, to say (for example) that the shirts on sale are available in various colors and sizes; it is much more action-inducing to list the exact colors, sizes, and prices. Any piece of missing information could hinder action. It is also important to create a sense of immediate availability and urgency, by stressing that this availability (and these prices) are "for a limited time only."

While there is probably little carryover effect of advertising of a specific storewide sale, retail advertisers are very particular that every retail ad fit and enhance the specific long-term image of the store. Every ad from Bloomingdale's, Lord & Taylor, and so on is carefully tuned to the particular character—the "look and feel"—that the store has carefully developed over the years. (See Figure 3–4).

For durable products, such as large appliances and automobiles, an appropriate behavioral objective for advertising might be to entice customers to visit a dealer's showroom. For large-ticket consumer items, the final phases of the selling process are usually best handled by a person-to-person sales effort, with advertising used appropriately to draw people to the showroom. In such situations, "traffic-building" advertising becomes key, and (once again) the advertising must try to create a strong sense of desire, curiosity, and urgency to get the reader or viewer to make that store visit.

Cooperative Advertising

A situation closely related to retail advertising is that of *cooperative advertising*, in which a manufacturer offers retailers an advertising program for the latter to run.[18] The program may include suggested advertising formats, materials to be used to create actual advertisements, and money to pay a portion (often, half) of the cost. It also often includes requests or requirements that the retailer stock certain merchandise quantities and perhaps use certain displays. By some estimates, almost one-half of retail advertising is some form of co-op advertising.

There are three types of co-op advertising: (1) *vertical* (when an *upstream* manufacturer or service provider, such as Royal Cruise Lines, pays for a *downstream* retailer's ads, such as a travel agent's ads); (2) *horizontal* (when local dealers in a geographical area pool money, as in automobiles or fast-food chains); and (3) *ingredient producer co-op* (when the *producer* of an ingredient, such as Nutrasweet, pays part of an ad run by the *user* product, such as Diet Coke). Recent estimates have put the amount of co-op advertising in the U.S. at about $10 billion per year, of which about two-thirds are spent through newspapers.[19] Co-op ads thus consitute a large portion of newspaper advertising revenue, and newspapers

Fuchsia? Fabulous!

Exclusively ours, the most brilliant idea around.
Fuchsia lampshade lit by a garland of silk flowers unfurled
to the sun. By Eric Javits, in fine Milan straw, one size, **150.00**

Meet designer Eric Javits
and enjoy informal modeling of his collection.
Main Floor, Fifth Avenue, tomorrow, March 22nd, noon to 2 pm.

Figure 3–4.   A retail ad.
Courtesy of Lord and Taylor.

have set up set up organizations (such as the Newspaper Co-op network, and the Newspaper Advertising Cooperative Network) to alert local retailers to manufacturer co-op programs they may not be fully utilizing.

The intent of cooperative advertising, in part, is often to stimulate short-term sales. The advertising is well suited to this task because it is usually specific as to the product, the place at which it can be purchased, and the price. However, co-op advertising also has other longer-term objectives: namely, to reinforce the brand image of the original manufacturer or service provider and to maintain the manufacturing company's leverage with the retail trade. The former is especially important because retail store buyers and salespeople often favor products that come with large allowances, to the extent that a product not having the expected co-op amount can find itself losing distribution.

The latter implies that the manufacturer needs to monitor and control co-op advertising content carefully, to ensure that it is consistent with the national ad campaign. Weak control over the creative content and media placement of co-op ads run by small retailers can contribute to a lack of consistency in the image of the brand and even the creation of negative associations with the brand, potentially hurting the brand's equity (see Chapter 10). Such creative control can be obtained by providing the local retailer with *advertising slicks* created by the manufacturer's agency, which can then be customized by the local retailer while still being consistent with the national campaign for the brand.

Given the pressures from the retail trade (and from one's own sales force) to maintain and even increase co-op advertising allowances, a marketer is often tempted to allocate more money into co-op advertising at the expense of national advertising. In deciding how much money to allocate to co-op advertising, the marketer needs to determine if the product will really benefit from being associated with a store's image. Such benefits are typically higher for the case of fashion goods, hi-fi stereo equipment, and so on, which are expensive and image-driven products about which consumers seek retail information and endorsements; these benefits are lower for inexpensive, frequently purchased products (such as toothpaste or shampoo) about which the consumer does not seek retail advice. The key question is: What are the relative roles of national advertising and store advertising in influencing consumer brand choice processes?

In addition to looking at consumer decision processes, the advertising planner must also be concerned with the need to acquire or expand distribution; a high need typically compels higher co-op allowances. Further, legal and administrative requirements must be met. For example, co-op allowances have to be offered on an "equally available to all" basis unless it can be demonstrated that certain stores (to whom proportionately higher allowances are being offered) will lead to a greater gain in new customers to the manufacturer.[20] A co-op program is likely to yield greater benefits to the manufacturing company if the program is tightly monitored (e.g., limited to certain slow-moving sizes of products rather than all sizes). The administrative burdens of a co-op program also need to be remembered: claims need to be documented and compliance checked before payments are made, and this can be a tremendous headache if hundreds of retail accounts are involved. Software packages exist to streamline this process.[21]

Reminder, Point-of-Purchase, and Specialty Advertising

Sometimes the primary role of advertising is to act as a reminder to buy and use the brand. The brand may be established and have a relatively solid, stable image. *Reminder advertising* then serves to stimulate immediate purchase and/or use to counter the inroads of competition. A good example is the Budweiser advertisement shown in Figure 3–5. Other examples of reminder advertising are the "shelf talkers" or other *point-of-purchase* (P-O-P) materials placed in stores at or near the place where the brand is on display. Such P-O-P materials often feature the package, price, and a key selling idea.

Reminder advertising can work in several ways. First, it can enhance the top-of-mind awareness of the brand, thus increasing the probability that the brand gets included on the shopping list or gets purchased as an impulse item. A media plan that aims to enhance or maintain top-of-mind awareness through reminder ads might utilize shorter ads (such as fifteen-second commercials) with a high level of frequency or use media such as outdoor billboards or transit that are suited to such reminder advertising. Second, it can reinforce the key elements of the na-

Figure 3–5. **A reminder advertisement.**
Courtesy of Anheuser-Busch, Inc.

tional campaign at the point-of-purchase. It has been shown in research by Kevin Keller that if there is a match between the type of information used in the P-O-P material and in an ad for the brand seen previously, the consumer is more likely to recall the information in the ad successfully, and this leads to more favorable judgments about the brand involved.[22]

In addition, it is often useful in such situations to use items of *specialty advertising,* useful products given free to consumers that have the manufacturer's name and related information on them. Specialty advertising items go beyond the usual calendars, ball-point pens, coasters, and Rolodex cards to all kinds of creative, high-quality products (such as a refrigerator magnet for Domino's Pizza that reminds a hungry but time-starved consumer which phone number to call for quick, home-delivered pizza). Manufactured by *supplier* companies, such specialty advertising items are not usually handled by traditional advertising agencies but by organizations called specialty distributors or specialty advertising agencies.[23]

In addition to maintaining top-of-mind awareness for a particular brand, reminder advertising can also increase the motivation for the use of the product class as a whole. In this context, the advertising may tend to simply increase the purchase and use of the product class and thus work to the advantage of the leading brand. Thus, reminder advertising for Royal Crown Cola may tend to increase purchases of other colas, to the advantage of Coke and Pepsi. Similarly, Campbell's Soup is the soup brand that is in the best position to conduct reminder advertising.

In-Store Advertising and Merchandising

In-store advertising is a rapidly growing area of advertising, in large part because of the increasing realization among marketers that most consumer decisions about which brand to buy are made after the consumer enters the store and scans the brands on the aisles.[24] As a result, a variety of new in-store media have become available to the advertiser, such as electronically scrolling ads in the aisles, ads on TVs near the checkout lanes, ads in radio programs played in-store while the consumer shops, on-aisle coupon dispensers, even ads on shopping carts equipped with special video screens. While some of these new services have shown rapid sales growth, others have had to shut down after an experimental run, in part because of the difficulty in measuring results. Actmedia, Catalina, Advanced Promotion Technologies, and VideOcart are some of the companies that are very visible in this rapidly growing area.[25]

Another frequently neglected type of in-store communication is the *merchandising environment,* by which we mean the displays, signs, and positioning of the brand in that particular store. Creative and attention-getting displays in the store serve to do much more than stock the product: they can greatly add to a sense of excitement about the product and lead to much greater involvement by the consumer in that product. An example would be the in-store "computers" used by cosmetics companies such as Noxell that lets consumers make their own color matches. Service establishments, such as banks like Citibank or fast-food restaurants like McDonald's, are constantly experimenting with better branch displays and signage to increase cross-selling opportunities as well as to create the particular kind of image and ambience that are so vital to creating a service company's brand image and equity (see Chapter 10).

Industrial Marketing: Sales Leads

Industrial (business-to-business) marketing is similar to the marketing of durables in that advertising can rarely be expected to make the sales. Rather, a salesperson is usually required to supply information and to handle the details of the transaction. Advertising, in this case, can provide the engineer or buyers with the opportunity to express interest in the product by returning a card which is a request for additional information. These inquiries or leads are then typically *qualified* by a telemarketing callback to determine if an in-person sales call is necessary and cost effective. Often this telemarketing call can itself lead to a sale. Once qualified, the salesperson then follows up these leads by calling on the prospect, discussing his or her requirements, and trying to "close" the sale. Thus, for industrial advertising, a useful objective is to generate such inquiries or leads. Figure 3–6 shows a rather dramatic industrial advertisement for Savin copiers. The reader can get specific information by calling the toll-free number in the ad.

PUBLIC RELATIONS . . . .

Because consumers are exposed to so much advertising these days, they often try hard to avoid it—and are very skeptical of it when they do get exposed it. To reach these hard-to-reach consumers and to convey messages to them in a manner that is more credible partly because it is more subtly delivered, more and more companies today are devoting a portion of their communication budgets to the use of *public relations* (PR) for marketing purposes. Some of the different ways in which this is done are reviewed below, but what most of them have in common is the delivery of a message about the brand not through paid, explicit advertising, but rather through an implied or explicit endorsement of a credible third-party media source, such as the editorial content of a newspaper or magazine, or by associating themselves with a sports or cultural event, or a charitable organization.

Public relations is usually regarded of as a way to build a corporation's public image before stakeholders such as government, shareholders, employees, and so on, and as a way to counteract negative publicity (such as the scare about Tylenol after it was involved in cyanide murders in 1982). While these *corporate reputation* and *crisis communications* uses of public relations are still very important, it is being used more and more in the form of *marketing public relations*.[26] Budgets for such uses of public relations are rising—one estimate puts the total annual amount of PR spending in the U.S. at about $8 billion. Most leading PR agency groups today own one or more PR firms, including two of the biggest: the WPP Group owns Hill & Knowlton, and Young & Rubicam owns Burson-Marsteller.

The following are examples of public relations used as an essential element in marketing.

The original Savin 750

THIS COPIER OUTLASTED 52 VPs, 14 SR VPs, 4 CFOs, AND ONE S.O.B.

Ah yes, the ever-changing faces at the office. Some with titles they're not even aware of. But nobody ever talks behind a Savin copier's back. They're so dependable they've been known to last twenty years. Perhaps the only reason you'd replace your old Savin copier is to get your hands on the full range capability of a new one. Take the new Savin 9710. It has all the features you

© 1991 Savin Corporation

need in this don't-give-me-any-problems-I-have-to-have-it-now-or-the-S.O.B.-will-fire-me business world. Like high speed and high volume performance, with a 3700-sheet paper capacity. Seven

The new Savin 9710

preset enlargement/reduction modes, automatic copying from unburst computer forms, simple guidance display, and a Job Card System that makes those tedious copying jobs duck soup. So here are two suggestions. Pray that the S.O.B. doesn't resurface at your next job. And call Savin today at 1-800-52-SAVIN.

savin.
WE MIND YOUR BUSINESS.

Figure 3–6. **An industrial ad seeking inquiries and leads.**

Courtesy of Savin Corporation.

News Stories and Media Editorial Coverage

Cabbage Patch Dolls became a toy craze in 1985 after being featured in a *Newsweek* cover story, appearing in network and local TV and radio broadcasts, and after first lady Nancy Reagan was shown worldwide giving them to two Korean children hospitalized for heart treatment. New products of various kinds—from Ford cars like the Taurus, to fat substitutes like Simplesse—achieved very high levels of brand awareness even before advertising for them broke because of favorable news coverage. To convey an image of industry leadership, many industrial marketers try hard to have trade magazines carry articles by-lined by their top executives.

Event and Sports Marketing

Ed Bernays, considered the father of modern public relations, pulled off a huge publicity coup for General Electric by orchestrating the celebrations for the fiftieth anniversary of Edison's invention of the the light bulb, in which then-President Herbert Hoover—and millions of others—switched on their electric lights after an NBC announcer gave the signal. Budweiser sponsored the concert tour of the Rolling Stones, Pepsi that of Michael Jackson, both gaining tremendous visibility. Fast food (and other) companies often run tie-in promotions with movies. Cigarette companies sponsor sports events, like Virginia Slims Tennis and Winston Cup NASCAR racing. Most athletes at most major sports events today are paid to wear the logos of sponsoring companies.

The sponsorship of big events and sports competitions—such as the Statue of Liberty Centennial, or the L'eggs 10K Mini Marathon for women—is a multi-billion-dollar business involving its own specialist firms. Obviously, the key issue here is the "fit" between the event being sponsored and the desired positioning and image of the sponsoring brand or company.

Cause-Related Marketing

Pampers diapers are distributed free at mobile baby care centers at state and county fairs across the country, gaining not only trial but much goodwill for the brand. American Express asks cardmembers to "charge against hunger," donating a few cents from every card use to hunger-fighting organizations. Hall's cough suppressant tablets are distributed free in many concert halls. Phillip Morris, IBM, and AT&T have sponsored major art exhibitions at the Metropolitan Museum of Art in New York and at other museums. Local McDonald's restaurants take the lead in raising funds for Ronald McDonald children's charities and Houses. Campbell Soup gives elementary schools free equipment in return for collected labels for its products.

Product Placement

Sales of Reese's Pieces candy soared after they were shown in the hit movie *E.T.* When Ray-Ban provided actor Tom Cruise sunglasses to wear in the movie *Top Gun*, sales reportedly rose 30 to 40 percent. Auto makers provide cars for free for use in Hollywood TV shows. Almost 75 percent of local TV stations are reported to make use of video news releases, including those on the making of commercials.[27] A study by *Advertising Age* found 1,035 instances of "product plugs" in a single day of programming on the four major networks.[28] Again, specialist companies exist that, for the necessary fee, will "place" your product in movies and TV shows.

Contests

Pillsbury's bake-off recipe contests lead to big sales increases after they are held annually and have made Pillsbury synonymous with baking. Pepto-Bismol sponsors a chili-cooking contest. Combat roach killer sponsors a contest for the World's Largest Roach.

In all of these cases of marketing public relations, the benefit to the brand is not only that the message is delivered through (or in the context of) a perceivedly neutral, objective, and trustworthy organization or institution, but also that it is relatively cheap. Unlike ad budgets, which can run into the hundreds of millions of dollars, most public relations programs cost well under $1 million. The downside of this cheapness and credibility, of course, is the lack of control: you can hope the media will present your story the way you want, but you have no way of ensuring that is what will happen. Public relations payoffs are also hard to quantify. Most companies simply attempt to add up the seconds or minutes of free media exposure for their brand names or logos and then value that exposure at advertising rate equivalents. A few companies actually test for increases in brand awareness, attitudes, or sales in markets with versus without the PR campaign.[29]

Obviously, the standard way to try to get PR coverage is to send out news releases to the media or to hold a news conference. These are more likely to be used by the media if they contain something that is genuinely newsworthy in the context of the publications that are targeted. Ask yourself: If I were the journalist receiving this news release, would I consider it news that my readers should see? Following this logic, Quaker Oats sponsored and publicized research about the health benefits of eating oats, which was picked up by most media because they thought most readers would in fact benefit from that information. Other ways include the creation of events such as McDonald's sale of its 50 billionth hamburger or the opening of its restaurants in Moscow and Beijing, or the contests described above.

INTEGRATING THE DIFFERENT ELEMENTS. . . . . .

Thus far in this chapter, we have discussed some of the other communication elements that a communications manager can and should use in addition to advertising. It should be clear that a huge variety of these communication elements exist, and the purpose of this chapter was merely to introduce you to what they were and to refer you to sources for further information. Obviously, the best communication programs manage to use many of these elements in ways that reinforce each other. The Southwest Airlines case noted at the beginning of this chapter illustrates such mutual reinforcement of these elements and is an example what is today being called *integrated marketing communications* (IMC).

What Is Integrated Marketing Communications?

Despite the increasing use of the term "integrated marketing communications" by both practitioners and academics in recent years, there is little agreement on what the term actually means. According to one recent review,[30] at least two related ideas are involved:

One-Voice Marketing Communications

As consumers increasingly begin to be addressed by the same marketer in a variety of different ways—through image-building advertising, public relations, direct marketing, sales promotions, point-of-sale material, collateral material (e.g., brochures and catalogs), and sales force calls—there is the obvious need to ensure a consistency of positioning, message, and tone across these different media. As discussed in Chapter 10 of the book, such consistency is a vital element of brand-building. Ideally, these different communications would all begin from the same vision of what the consumer was supposed to be hearing from the marketer so that they all operate seamlessly, reaching the consumer with one voice. At the very least, this implies that the different marketing communications elements—mass media advertising, direct marketing, sales promotions, package graphics, point-of-sale material, events, trade shows, employee communications, and public relations—need to be created in a tightly coordinated manner by the many different agencies and organizations (the PR firm, direct response agency, sales promotion firm, ad agency, client company) that work on the different elements.

Integrated Communications

A marketer's consumer communications need to not only raise brand awareness, or create or change brand preference and image, or to get sales trial or repurchase, but to do all of the above at the same time. Increasing image without getting a sales result is not good enough and getting short-term sales (e.g. via sales promotion) at the expense of a brand's long-term image is also courting disaster. Thus, it is argued that all marketing communication materials, paticularly ads, should attempt to *simultaneously* achieve targeted communication goals (e.g., raising attitudes or building image) *and* lead to some behavioral action (e.g. trial or repurchase).

Why IMC Has Grown

As should be apparent from the two conceptualizations of IMC above, the need for IMC has grown in parallel with the trend to allocate marketing communication budgets away from their mainstay of mass media advertising. As reviewed in Chapter 1, both consumer goods and industrial goods marketers have moved increasingly large proportions of marketing resources into direct marketing and sales promotions. The amounts of money being spent in direct marketing and in sales promotions have thus grown dramatically.[31] These trends in spending patterns have occurred for various reasons, including the increased splintering and fragmentation of consumer media, the increasing segmentation of consumer tastes and preferences, the easier access to consumer databases and computational resources, the increased pressure on marketers to maintain the momentum of short-term sales, the increased power of the retail trade, the recognition of the importance of reinforcing consumer loyalty and repurchase via relationship marketing, and so on. At the same time, marketers have also been forced to recognize the vital importance of building and increasing a brand's image-based equity (see Chapter 10).[32]

Thus, marketers now must accomodate more complex and multiple communication objectives simultaneously, must spread their marketing communications resources over a much wider array of techniques and media, and usually must implement these multiple communications programs through a larger number of vendors or agencies. The multiplicity of markets and media and objectives and organizations can very easily lead to a fragmentation and dilution of message consistency and impact, unless steps are taken to integrate these various communications efforts.

Impact of IMC on Advertising Practice

Two major studies of the attitudes toward, and use of, IMC were conducted in 1991 in the United States, by researchers from Northwestern University and the University of Colorado.[33] In both, almost 80 percent of the respondents surveyed (marketing and advertising managers from client firms) said the concept of IMC was valuable to them by potentially providing greater consistency to their communications, reducing media waste. Their expectation was that the use of IMC would increase, provided that the key barrier to its use—turf battles and egos within their companies and in outside agencies—could be overcome. There was disagreement, however, on who should do the integrating. While marketing managers from larger, higher-expertise companies (surveyed in the Northwestern study) felt that the companies themselves should do the integrating, managers from smaller companies (in the Colorado survey) felt that such integration was the responsibility of the outside agencies. Clearly, how best to organize for IMC is a key issue in implementing it, and we will return to it below. Meanwhile, both clients and agencies have clearly become conscious of the need for IMC, and many companies and agencies have begun programs to train their managers to take a more integrated approach to marketing communications.

IMC Strategies and Tactics

According to Thomas Duncan, a company that thinks it is doing IMC should begin by conducting an audit: check to see the real degree to which it is coordinating its various communications activities and the real degree to which it is sending out messages that are integrated and consistent. Most companies that do this find they are actually doing less IMC than they first thought.[34] There are many barriers to doing real IMC, among them a lack of appreciation for its value (especially among top management), a lack of skills and training, and organizational structures and systems that create territorialism. We will discuss organizational issues further below, and providing skills and training (and an appreciation of its value) are obvious prerequisites to implementing IMC. But is there anything more to IMC than the commonsensical idea that all communications to the consumer about a particular brand should be "synergized," which is hardly a novel or earthshaking idea?

There is no clear answer to this last question, and only a few interesting implementation-oriented ideas have emerged. Most of these borrow heavily from the concepts of database or direct marketing, discussed earlier in this chapter. Don Schultz and colleagues, for instance, have suggested that marketers should build a comprehensive database of customers and prospects and then think through what different time and place opportunities exist for the company to contact each segment of customers (such as loyals, switchers, new prospects, etc.), what medium or communications mode, with what message and tonality, and for what overall marketing objectives. An overall communications strategy must then be developed that guides the integration of the different communications tactics. Each communications *contact* with the target must then not only deliver the intended message, but also solicit a response, which is then added to the database for further analysis.[35]

For example, the following sequence of questions should help develop an integrated marketing communications program:

1. What is the target customer's information gathering, decision, and shopping process?
2. Who or what are all the media, institutions (e.g., retailers), and people or influencers (e.g., pharmacists) with which the target customer comes in contact? In what sequence do these contacts occur? What communications opportunities do these contacts create for us?
3. For all these people, what attitudes and/or behaviors do we want to affect?
4. Therefore, for each communication opportunity, what are our communications needs? What quantitative goals?
5. For each communications opportunity, given what we need to accomplish, what is the best program(s) to accomplish it—advertising, direct mail, public relations, sales promotion, or other?
6. Given this choice and sequence of programs, how should the budget be allocated?
7. Who is to be responsible for implementing which part?
8. How will we measure the degree of success of each part?

The key to ensuring the desired integration and consistency in these various contacts is having organizational arrangements that facilitate rather than impede such integration, and we now turn to discussing these.

Organizing for IMC

Obviously, the easiest way to organize for IMC is to have just one outside communications *supplier,* such as an ad agency, and to have centralized responsibility for all brand communications within the client company, at either a brand/product manager or marketing vice president level. In terms of outside suppliers, ad agencies are more likely to have the expertise to perform multiple communication tasks (advertising, direct marketing, sales promotions, public relations) than standalone single-function suppliers (such as public relations, direct marketing, or sales promotion firms). Indeed, large ad agencies have for long claimed an ability to orchestrate all of a client's communications efforts if they were all done by that agency and its affiliates and have used this claim to solicit all of a client's communications budget, not just the ad budget. Such orchestration should obviously be better for the consistency of message and tone necessary for brand building. Agencies also claim that if they handled all of a client's communication needs the client would have greater control, because overall responsibility for all those efforts would lie with one account supervisor at the agency rather than being dispersed. The agency would also supposedly be more responsive to the client's needs if it handled all these communications because the client's total billings with that agency would now be a larger percentage of the agency's revenue.

However, many clients have balked from giving their lead ad agency these multiple responsibilities because of a perception that a single ad agency might not have the best sets of skills in all these different areas, so that the client might get better expertise by mixing and matching skills from several specialized communications suppliers, instead of relying on "one-stop" shopping, while relying on the client organization staff itself to perform the necessary integration (especially among larger client firms).[36] Some even argue that an ad agency will never get the best talent in the nonadvertising communications areas simply because such people will always be "second-class citizens" in ad agencies. Consolidating all of a client's business at one agency also potentially reduces the motivating effect of having several suppliers compete with each other to come up with the best communications ideas for that client. In addition, most ad agencies themselves have had trouble integrating the different functions, especially if the functions are organized as affiliate companies or departments instead of being organized as people with different resources and skills working as part of one integrated account team. Many clients are thus skeptical that the different functions will be better integrated if they are combined under a single agency umbrella, instead of being at multiple unaffiliated suppliers, although they do believe the potential for miscommunication would be reduced.[37]

It is not entirely clear, however, that the many people involved in communications programs at the client organization themselves perform the integration of which they believe they are capable. The sales force, trade account management, public relations, sales promotion, direct marketing and other staffs within client companies sometimes run programs that are not adequately coordinated with the mass media programs typically managed by brand or advertising managers and with each other.[38] Many organizations such as IBM are experimenting with cross-functional teams as a solution.[39] At McDonald's, the various departments involved in a marketing project are all represented on a strategy review board led by a project manager, so they have input into the decisions and know what actions are to be taken by whom.[40] It is obviously important to train everyone involved in the concept of integrated marketing, in the skills necessary to make it work, and to create a shared vision in them about what is to be communicated, with what tonality and with what effect.

Ad agencies too often have problems in properly incentivizing the use of a truly integrated approach by their account staff: if PR, direct mail, sales promotions, and mass media advertising are structured as separate profit centers, the managers of these divisions battle for budgets instead of doing what is best for the client. Again, cross-functional account teams led by one "communications director"—who could be a direct marketing specialist, not necessarily the ad agency account manager—appear to be a superior organizational arrangement when combined with a financial structure that measures total account billings, not billings by function. It thus appears that the key needs in organizing for better IMC are (1) better communication and common goal-sharing among the various client personnel themselves and (2) better integration of the various functions within the major ad agencies that offer all or most of these different communications functions.

SUMMARY . . . .

Advertising has many strengths (reaching mass audiences, creating awareness, building preference, etc.), but it also has major weaknesses (targeting individual consumers, making them believe a message, and pushing them to action). Thus, its use has to be combined with that of other communications elements (such as direct marketing, sales promotions, and public relations). And, this usage of all these elements has to be integrated in terms of its message, tone, and effect.

Direct marketing is one communications approach that aims to evoke action. Its distinctive features are the ability to target small segments of consumers, to measure response to different offers, and to build customer databases. Direct marketing ads try to get consumers to respond immediately by building confidence, providing information, making it easy to order, involving consumers in the order process, and creating a sense of urgency that can overcome the natural tendency to inertia.

Sales promotions can be designed to create trial purchases, to stimulate short-term sales, to enhance purchase volume or brand loyalty, or to affect the brand image. Consumer promotional devices include coupons, samples, price packs, premiums, and sweepstakes. Trade promotions attempt to obtain or maintain shelf space, build retail inventory, get retail "push," and lower retail prices. More money is spent on sales promotions than on advertising, and it is essential that sales promotion efforts be coordinated with advertising efforts, to maximize the effectiveness of each and to ensure that the sales promotions do not dilute the long-term image of the brand.

Retail ads aim both to build the store's image and to create immediate sales, through building store traffic. Co-op ads, paid for by both the retailer and the manufacturer, are another important form of retail advertising. Reminder advertising seeks to maintain high top-of-mind awareness, through high frequency and other visibility-enhancing means. In-store ads try to increase brand salience at the point-of-purchase. Industrial ads seek to generate leads and inquiries that can then be followed up through sales calls.

Public relations as a part of marketing tries to increase the credibility of a marketer's communications by appearing subtly in a third-party editorial vehicle.

Techniques include news and editorial mentions, event and sponsorships, product placement, contests, and cause-related marketing. Genuine newsworthiness makes for easier placement. Such PR events are relatively cheap to create but harder to control.

The emerging discipline and philosophy of integrated marketing communications tries to make all these elements work with one voice and in mutually reinforcing ways. A detailed IMC plan for every brand and situation need to be thought through. The key problems issues in implementing it are those of training and organization, both internal and external.

DISCUSSION QUESTIONS . . . .

1. Provide examples of current advertising campaigns that seem to be directed at generating behavioral response. Are they attempting to communicate information and/or change attitudes or are they concerned solely with behavior? Write a reasonable objective for each campaign that is operational. How would you measure results against that objective?

2. Consider the American Airlines frequent-flyer program, a free sample program for a new soap, a 25-percent-off price offered to retailers by a cereal brand, and two promotions that recently affected your purchasing. What were the objectives of these promotions? What role does advertising play in these promotions? What impact will these promotions have in the long-term? How would you measure that impact?

3. Compare the advantages and disadvantages of the different consumer promotions techniques with respect to alternative objectives of (a) getting trial from new consumers, (b) holding (retaining) present customers, and (c) building brand image.

4. Examine a direct-mail promotional piece you (or somebody you know) has recently received. Look at every element of the package, and discuss its role in promoting consumer action.

5. Select an ad (or public service announcement) that has recently been attempting to change a consumer behavior and discuss its strengths and weaknesses. Why is it usually so difficult for such messages to succeed in such objectives? How could such messages be better designed?

6. Select two retailer's ads from different product categories that you have recently seen and discuss their strengths and weaknesses with respect to (a) building store image and (b) increasing sales in the short term. If you were a manufacturer being pressured to increase co-op advertising allowances in these two cases, in which one is it more beneficial to you to do so? Why?

7. Identify a sales promotion that has recently been run that you think works to enhance the brand image and one that serves to hurt brand image. Justify your selections.

8. Pick a brand, any brand. Develop an integrated marketing plan for it that includes advertising, direct marketing, sales promotions, and direct marketing. Discuss exactly why each element is being used, for what objectives, and in

what sequence. Show how each element contributes to the overall brand image and positioning you seek.

NOTES. . . . .

1. Jennifer Lawrence, "Integrated Mix Makes Expansion Fly," *Advertising Age*, November 8, 1993, p. S-10–S-12.
2. The median cost per call was $225, according to *Sales and Marketing Management*, February 26, 1989, p.75.
3. For a discussion of database marketing issues, see Lisa Petrison, Robert C. Blattberg, and Paul Wang, "Database Marketing: Past, Present, and Future," *Journal of Direct Marketing*, 7 Summer 1993, no. 3, 27-44.
4. For these and other statistics, see the "Catalog Review" supplement to *The New York Times*, March 27, 1994.
5. See *Advertising Age*, July 12, 1993, Special Report on Direct Response
6. For information on databased direct marketing, consult David Shepard Associates, Inc., *The New Direct Marketing: How to Implement a Profit-Driven Database Marketing Strategy* (Homewood, IL: Dow Jones–Irwin, 1990). For more general information on direct marketing, see Robert Stone, *Successful Direct Marketing Methods*, 4th ed. (Lincolnwood, IL: National Textbook Company, NTC Business Books, 1988).
7. *Advertising Age*, May 24, 1993, p. 13.
8. For a discussion, see Glen J. Nowak and Joseph Phelps, "Understanding Privacy Concerns," *Journal of Direct Marketing*, 6, no. 4 (Autumn 1992), pp. 28–39.
9. See, for example, Robert C. Blattberg and Scott A. Neslin, *Sales Promotions: Concepts, Methods, and Strategies* (Englewood Cliffs, NJ: Prentice Hall, 1990); John A. Quelch, *Sales Promotion Management* (Englewood Cliffs, NJ: Prentice Hall, 1989); Don E. Schultz and William A. Robinson, *Sales Promotion Management* (Chicago: Crain Books, 1982); John C. Totten and Martin P. Block, *Analyzing Sales Promotions: Text and Cases* (Chicago: Commerce Communications, 1987); and Stanley M. Ulanoff, ed., *Handbook of Sales Promotion* (New York: McGraw-Hill, 1985).
10. Progressive Grocer, 72, no. 10 (October 1993), p. 69.
11. *Advertising Age* has special reports on sales promotion agency revenues; for example, May 17, 1993.
12. Blattberg and Neslin, *Sales Promotions*, p. 474.
13. *Advertising Age*, various issues.
14. *Advertising Age*, April 3, 1989, p. 38.
15. William A. Robinson and Kevin Brown, "Best Promotions of 1984: Back to Basics," *Advertising Age*, March 11, 1985, p. 42.
16. *Food and Beverage Marketing*, Nov 1, 1992, p. 30.
17. *Food and Beverage Marketing*, May 1991, p. 30.
18. Robert F. Young, "Cooperative Advertising, Its Uses and Effectiveness: Some Preliminary Hypotheses," Marketing Science Institute Working Paper, 1979.
19. *Sales and Marketing Management*, May 1992, p. 40.
20. Isadore Barmash, "FTC Plans Rule Change on Co-op Ads," *The New York Times*, February 21, 1989.
21. *Sales and Marketing Management*, May 1986, p. 90.
22. Kevin L. Keller, "Cue Compatibility and Framing in Advertising," *Journal of Marketing Research,* 2 (Februuary 1991), 42-57.
23. For details, see George L. Herpel and Steve Slack, *Specialty Advertising: New Dimensions in Creative Marketing* (Irving, TX: Specialty Advertising Association International,) and Charles S. Madden and Marjorie J. Caballero-Cooper, "Expectations of Users of Specialty Advertising," *Journal of Advertising Research*, July/August 1992, p. 45.
24. *Marketing News*, May 14, 1990.

25. See, for example, *Business Week*, March 29, 1993, p. 60, and *Advertising Age*, July 19, 1993, p. 31.
26. This phrase, and many of the examples that follow, are taken from Thomas L. Harris, *The Marketers Guide to Public Relations* (New York: John Wiley, 1993). The interested reader is strongly encouraged to read this book.
27. See, for example, the *The Wall Street Journal*, September 24, 1993, p. B1.
28. *Advertising Age*, July 12, 1993, p. 21.
29. *Advertising Age,* Special Report on Event Marketing, June 21, 1993.
30. Glen J. Novak and Joseph Phelps, "Conceptualizing the Integrated Marketing Communications' Phenomenon: An Examination of Its Impact on Advertising Practices and Its Implications for Advertising Research," *Journal of Current Issues and Research in Advertising*, 16, no. 1 (Spring 1994), 49–66.
31. See Novak and Phelps for some recent statistics on growth rates and spending estimates.
32. Many of these trends are discussed in detail in Tom Duncan, Clarke Caywood, and Doug Newsom, "Preparing Advertising and Public Relations Students for the Communications Industry in the 21st Century," Report on the Task Force on Integrated Communications, December 1993.
33. Clarke Caywood, Don Schultz, and Paul Wang, "Integrated Marketing Communications: A Survey of National Consumer Goods Advertisers," Department of Integrated Advertising/Marketing Communications, Northwestern University, June 1991, and Thomas R. Duncan and Stephen E. Everett, "Client Perceptions of Integrated Marketing Communications," *Journal of Advertising Research,* 33 no. 3 (May/June 1993), 30–39.
34. Tom Duncan, "Is your Marketing Program Coordinated?" *Advertising Age*, January 24, 1994, p. 26.
35. Don E. Schultz, Stanley I. Tannenbaum, and Robert F. Lauterborn, *Integrated Marketing Communications* (Chicago: NTC Business Books, 1993).
36. Adrienne Ward Fawcett, "Marketers Convinced: Its Time Has Arrived," *Advertising Age*, November 8, 1993, p. S-1.
37. See the Caywood, Schultz, and Wang report, op. cit., for more details on these client perceptions.
38. Tom Duncan, "Is Your Marketing Program Coordinated?" *Advertising Age*, January 24, 1994, p. 26.
39. Wayne McCullough, "Organizational Issues in Integrating Marketing Communications: The Relationship Between Structure and Functioning," Marketing Science Institute Report 94-109, July 1994, Conference Summary on "Marketing Communications Today and Tomorrow."
40. Roy T. Bergold, "Integrated Marketing and the McLean Deluxe," in "Integrated Marketing Communications," Northwestern University, Medill School of Journalism, June 1991.

4 SETTING ADVERTISING OBJECTIVES

> For an advertisement to be effective it must be noticed, read, comprehended, believed, and acted upon.
> (Daniel Starch, 1923)
>
> For one who has no objective, nothing is relevant.
> (Confucius)

The luxury car Porsche saw its annual sales in the U.S. market plummet in the early 1990s. Sales dropped from 30,471 cars in 1986 to 4,115 cars in 1992. In January 1993, they fired their ad agency, Fallon McElligott, which had had the account since September 1987.[1] Should they have done so? Was bad advertising responsible for their drop in sales? (Hint: there was a major economic recession around that time.) Can *any* ad campaign be evaluated on the basis of sales results alone?

If clients wish to compensate their agencies based in part on how well their ad campaigns perform, just how should they measure the success or failure of these ad campaigns?

The AIM mutual fund companies ran two sets of ads in late 1993. One showed a man who should have been living a happy retired life working, instead, as an elevator operator. It argued that people even years away from retirement should be saving aggressively for retirement, because otherwise they would be facing the situation of the man in the ad. The other ad simply showed why the AIM mutual fund in question had a superior performance record, citing third-party statistics and rankings. It argued that investors' funds should go to the AIM fund instead of competitive funds. Which ad made more sense for them? (Hint: the AIM mutual fund organization has relatively low awareness and distribution, compared to giants like Fidelity, Vanguard, etc.). When should *any* company try to increase overall "category demand," instead of merely attempting to increase its market-share?

Answers to questions like these are the subject of this chapter. How should one measure the effectiveness of ad campaigns? And, if ad budgets are getting smaller than they used to be, how can a manager increase an ad campaign's effectiveness, by setting goals and objectives that are strategically correct, achievable, and measurable?

It should be obvious that it is vitally important to understand clearly what kinds of objectives can be set for an ad campaign, and how a choice can be made among them. Without good objectives, it is nearly impossible to guide and control decision making. This chapter will therefore discuss a manager's options regarding objectives, and some characteristics of "good" objectives, at a conceptual level. We will then continue in the next chapter with a discussion of how different advertising situations call for different objectives to be targeted.

FUNCTION OF OBJECTIVES. . . . .

Objectives serve several functions in modern management. One function is to operate as communication and coordination devices. They provide a vehicle by which the client, the agency account executive, and the creative team communicate. They also serve to coordinate the efforts of such groups as copywriters, radio specialists, media buyers, and research specialists.

A second function of objectives is to provide a criterion for decision making. If two alternative campaigns are generated, one must be selected. Rather than relying on an executive's esthetic judgment (or on that of his or her spouse), he or she should be able to turn to the objective and select the criterion that will most readily achieve it.

A related function of an objective is to evaluate results. This function implies that there needs to be a measure such as market share or brand awareness associated with the objective. At the end of the campaign, that preselected measure is employed to evaluate the success of the campaign—such success is increasingly how advertising agencies are getting compensated, as was pointed out in Chapter 1.

Sales As an Objective

Advertising objectives, like organizational objectives, should be operational. They should be effective criteria for decision making and should provide standards with which results can be compared. Furthermore, they should be effective communication tools, providing a line between strategic and tactical decisions.

A convenient and enticing advertising objective involves a construct like immediate sales or market share. The measure is usually readily available to "evaluate" the results of a campaign. There are clearly some situations—mail-order advertising and some retail advertising, for example—when immediate sales are a good operational objective, and others in which they can play a role in guiding the advertising campaign. Chapter 3 discussed in more detail such situations in which sales or market share make useful objectives.

However, objectives that involve an increase in immediate sales are not operational in many cases for two reasons: (1) advertising is only one of many factors influencing sales, and it is difficult to isolate its contribution to those sales; and (2) the contributory role of advertising often occurs primarily over the long run.

Advertising is only one of the many forces that influence sales, as Figure 4–1 illustrates. The other forces include price, distribution, the sales force, packaging, product features, competitive actions, and changing buyer needs and tastes. It is extremely difficult to isolate the effect of advertising. For instance, suppose a car company runs a campaign for a new model, but not many cars get sold. While the

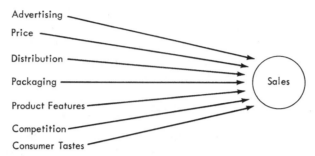

Figure 4–1.   Some of the factors influencing sales.

problem may indeed lie with the campaign, it might also be the case that the campaign did in fact draw potential buyers to the dealerships, but that something else (the car's quality, price, or poorly trained sales people) was the reason why they didn't end up buying.

It is clearly unfair, in this situation, to gauge the success of the ads themselves by the number of cars sold. Such a situation did actually occur with Nissan's new luxury car, the Infiniti, when it was launched. Many people thought the campaign failed because not too many cars were sold in the initial months. But in fact the campaign did generate a huge number of inquiries for catalogs, and led to many dealer visits. It was at the dealership that many prospects decided not to buy the car—but this was hardly the fault of the advertising![2]

Some people therefore argue that evaluating advertising only by its impact on sales is like attributing all the success (or failure) of a football team to the quarterback. The fact is that many other elements can affect the team's record—other plays, the competition, and the bounce of the ball. The implication is that the effect of the quarterback's performance should be measured by the things he alone can influence, such as how he throws the ball, how he calls the plays, and how he hands off. If, in a real-world situation, all factors remained constant except for advertising (for example, if competitive activity were static), then it would be feasible to rely exclusively on sales to measure advertising effectiveness. Such a situation is, in reality, infeasible, though for packaged nondurable goods it is often possible to run sophisticated field experiments using grocery scanner data that yield fairly accurate estimates of the effect of current advertising on short-term sales (see Chapter 16). For the most part, we must start dealing with response variables that are associated more directly with the advertising stimulus.

The second reason involves the long-term effect of advertising on sales. If we believe that advertising generates a substantial lagged effect on sales, then the impact of an advertising campaign may not be known for certain until an unacceptable length of time has passed. For example, an important contribution of a six-month campaign might be its impact twelve months hence. Research has estimated that, at least for frequently purchased nondurable goods, the effect of an advertising exposure can take up to nine months to get dissipated.[3] As Figure 4–2 illustrates, advertising might attract buyers who will be loyal customers for sev-

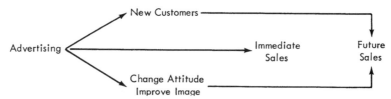

Figure 4–2.   Long-run impact of advertising.

eral years, or it might start the development of positive attitudes or brand equity that will culminate in a purchase much later. To determine this effect from sales data, even in a scanner panel field experiment, it may be necessary to wait far beyond the end of the six-month campaign. Two problems are created. First, the difficulty of isolating the sales change caused by advertising becomes more severe as the time between the advertising expenditure and the sales response increases. Yet decisions must be made immediately and cannot wait for such data. Second, for more timely and accurate information, variables that respond more quickly to advertising input must be sought.

Thus, advertising objectives that emphasize sales are usually not very operational because they provide little practical guidance for decision makers. No one argues the desirability of a sales increase, but which campaign will (or did) generate such an increase? If an objective does not contribute useful criteria on which to base subsequent decisions, it cannot fulfill its basic functions.

Toward Operational Objectives

If immediate sales do not form the basis of operational objectives in most situations. how does one proceed? The answer lies in part in three sets of questions. Addressing these questions in a careful, systematic way will often yield useful and effective objectives.

1. **Who is the target segment?**
2. **What is the ultimate behavior within that segment that advertising is attempting to precipitate, reinforce, change, or influence?**
3. **What is the process that will lead to the desired behavior and what role can advertising play in the process? Is it necessary to create awareness, communicate information about the brand, create an image or attitude, build long-term brand equity and associations, or associate feelings or a type of user personality with a brand?**

The first step is to identify the target audience. Usually, but not always, the target is the end-consumer. Exceptions arise when a company wants to recognize and motivate its employees (such as life insurance agents, or the sales force), induce intermediate distribution channels to stock and push a product, or increase favorability among stakeholders such as financial stock analysts, government regulators, stockholders, and so on. We will not deal with such cases here, for they are fairly obvious in their implications. When the ultimate concern is with end-consumers, the specification of the target audience (e.g., upscale buyers of stereo equipment) should be a part of the marketing objectives. However, the segmentation description may need to be refined in the advertising context, that is, those upscale buyers of stereo equipment who have no present awareness of Bose speakers, among whom we wish to create such awareness. We deal with this targeting decision in detail in the next chapter.

The second step involves the analysis of the ultimate desired behavior such as trial purchases of new customers, maintenance of loyalty of existing customers, creation of a more positive use experience, reduction of time between purchases, increasing the use-up rate, or the decision to visit a retailer.

A part of the analysis of targeting and objective-setting should be an estimate of the long-term impact on the organization of such a behavior. What exactly is the value of the desired behavior? For example, the value of attracting a new customer to try a brand will depend upon the likelihood that the customer will like the brand and rebuy it. Companies often call this the *lifetime value of a customer* and attempt to compute it. Does this lifetime value exceed the acquisition cost of a new customer? How might different kinds of objectives affect this acquisition cost? Which segment has the greatest difference between its lifetime value and its acquisition cost? Based on this analysis, what kind of behavioral change in what kind of target segment will give us the highest return on our marketing investment?

The third step then involves an analysis of the communication and decision process that will lead to the desired behavior in the targeted segment. Operationally, this usually involves using advertising-response measures that intervene between the incidence of the stimulus (advertising) and the ultimate behavioral response (certain purchase decisions) that is the focus of the advertising. Such response measures are called intervening variables and refer to a wide range of mental constructs such as awareness, brand knowledge, emotional feelings, and attitude. Thus, it might be that the key variable in inducing a new customer to try your brand is to inculcate high levels of brand awareness. The best way to maintain loyalty could be to strengthen an attitude. Even though the end goal is behavioral, the operational objective guiding decision making will often be specified in terms of one or more of such intervening variables. The determination of which intervening variables provide the best link to the desired behavior and which can be influenced economically by advertising is, of course, a challenge.

We start with the analysis of the desired behavior. After then turning to the advertising response variables, we will finally discuss the recommended procedures and theoretical frameworks to set advertising objectives.

BEHAVIORAL DYNAMICS . . . .

An understanding of market dynamics is necessary to an analysis of the ultimate behavior on which advertising should focus. An increase in sales or, more generally, an increase in product use (if the advertiser were a library or hospital or credit card company, a sales measure would be inappropriate) can basically come from various sources: from new customers attracted to the brand for the first time; by increasing the loyalty of existing customers, and by inducing existing customers to use more of the product class, either by increased usage or in new situations.

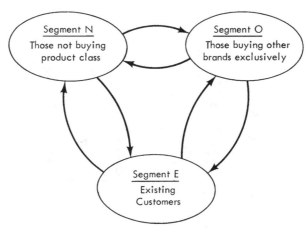

Figure 4–3.   Customer types.

New Customers from Other Brands

Figure 4–3 shows a market divided into three segments. Segment E includes those who now buy our brand, brand A. Some members of segment E will buy only our brand, but many will probably also buy others because they are either somewhat indifferent about a few brands or because they prefer other brands for some applications and our brand for others. They all buy our brand to some extent. Segment O contains those who buy other brands to the exclusion of ours. Some members of segment O will be loyal to another brand, and others will switch among other brands, but none is a buyer of our brand. Segment N members are not buyers of any brand in the product set. They get along without coffee, computers, lathes, or whatever product is involved.

The focus here is on increasing the size of segment E. One approach is to attract members of segment O to get them to try our brand. In Figure 4–4, the Diners Club card is directing its campaign primarily to members of segment O (American Express cardholders). Such an effort may be difficult if the other brands are performing satisfactorily. It is therefore best to try to find out which existing users of the competing brand are the most dissatisfied with it and target these "switchable" consumers. For instance, if some segment of American Express cardholders value some feature such as frequent user rewards for which Diners Club can claim superiority, that segment might be most cost-efficient as a conversion target for Diners Club. It would pay to target those American Express cardholders in particular, rather than all of them.

Alternatively, one should try to acquire those customers of the competing brand who are the most likely to grow their sales volume in the years to come (such as companies with rapid sales growth), and/or are the most profitable (because they require the least servicing, for instance).[4] For many product categories, about 20 percent of the customers (heavy users) are likely to account for over 50 percent of the sales volume and profits and are clearly worth focusing on as new

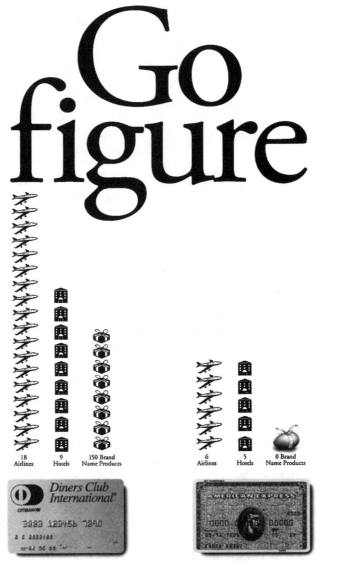

Figure 4–4.   An advertisement aimed at users of a competitive brand.

Courtesy of Citcorp Diners Club.

brand users. We discuss such a heavy user strategy in the next chapter. The customer's propensity to buy on deal is another key variable: such customers make you less money. Campbell Soup found that 4 percent of soup consumers, who paid more per purchase and bought less often on discount, were the most profitable to target, yielding a $3.38 return on a marketing dollar.[5] One could also try to target those customers who are the most likely to influence others to switch too. Nike, for example, specifically tries to get coaches of athletic teams to wear its athletic shoes because of the visibility and impact that has on other athletes and fans.

New Customers from Other Categories

Another approach is to attract people from segment N, those not now using the product class. Pepsi might conclude that it is easier to get young coffee drinkers to switch from coffee to Pepsi for their morning drink (they actually tested a higher-caffeine version called Pepsi A.M.), than it is to get Coke drinkers to switch to Pepsi. An example of such an approach is the Dannon Yogurt ad shown in Figure 4–5. The intent of that advertisement is to attract those using sour cream as a baked potato topping to a different type of topping that they are not currently using. Such an approach, called a *primary demand* approach, might be particularly worthwhile to a large firm that already serves most of those buying the product class (such as Dannon Yogurt). The firm in the industry that has the highest market share, the largest distribution, the biggest sales force, and the highest awareness is the one most likely to get the sale from a customer just entering the product category. On the other hand, such a strategy makes much less sense for a smaller firm that runs the risk that the segment N member who is induced to try the product class may buy from a larger competitor.

For example, a smaller cellular phone manufacturer (like Oki) might waste its money if it ran ads telling people why cellular phones in general were useful for personal or business reasons. A consumer seeing those ads might decide that, yes, they need a cellular phone, but might then end up buying the better-known Motorola or NEC brands. The smaller firm should therefore be content to let these larger firms attract people from segment N (see Figure 4–6 for a category-expanding NEC ad) and confine itself to trying to obtain its new customers from segment O (called a *secondary demand* strategy). Such an ad would focus not on why cellular phones were useful but why Oki phones were better than Motorola or NEC (and other) competitive brands. The value of a segment O member will depend, of course, on how large a product-class buyer she or he ultimately becomes and on the share of these purchases eventually obtained by the advertiser.

Increasing *Share of Requirements* (SOR)

Other customers may repeatedly switch among our brand and others. In many product categories, customers have more than one preferred brand, and they allocate their total category requirements over these few brands based, in part, on temporary price discounts, habits, and so on. They have a "repertoire" of preferred brands, not just one brand. It may be possible in such situations to convince customers like these to become more loyal.[6] For example, a consumer might use

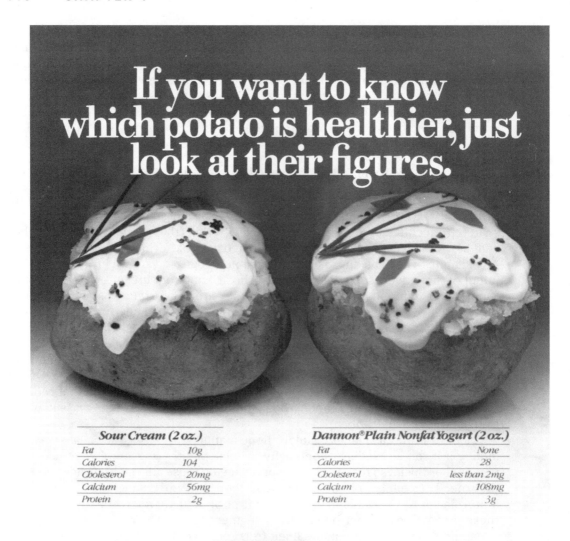

Figure 4–5.   An advertisement attempting to attract users from another product category.

Courtesy of Dannon Yogurt, Inc.

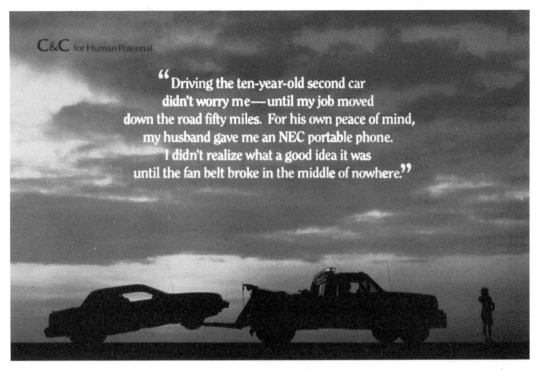

Figure 4–6.   An advertisement increasing primary demand.

Courtesy of the NEC Corporation.

three different brands of bar soap in a month or charge purchases to one of three different credit cards in a month. It thus makes sense for a particular card to try to increase its "share-of-wallet." A credit card company such as Citibank mightrun a sweepstakes promotion that states: "every time you charge your purchases to our card, you are automatically entered into our sweepstakes. So make our card the one you use." The advertising task here is not one of getting a new user but of increasing that existing user's *share of requirements* going to that particular brand.

If there are real brand advantages of which the target consumers may be unaware, such a task might be feasible. If, however, they are firmly convinced that several brands are equal, the effort may be difficult and costly. The cost of generating the desired behavioral response must be balanced with its worth in terms of future purchase.

Increasing Brand Loyalty, Reducing Attrition and Price Elasticity

A defensive strategy is also possible. We are not the only ones advertising: all our competitors are, all the time, trying to steal our customers away from us or trying to increase their own share of requirements. It is very important, therefore, to recognize the effect that advertising has on reinforcing a present customer's existing preference for our brand (though actual experience with our product probably is the bigger determinant of brand satisfaction and loyalty).[7] Some research by Gerald Tellis about the effects of advertising suggests that the bulk of the effect is not gaining new triers but on reinforcing the loyalty of existing users.[8]

Efforts could be thus be made to reduce the flow from segment E to segment O if we find that our brand suffers from a particularly high attrition rate (i.e., a low repurchase rate). The goal would be to reduce the likelihood that a member of segment E would be tempted to try another brand and would, as a result, eventually stop using our brand. A large firm may also be concerned about customers moving from segment E to segment N. Existing users of the product could drop out of the market altogether. Coffee drinkers may switch to drinking some other beverage, something which concerns category leaders Maxwell House and Folgers.

The members of segment E, the existing customers, will, in general, also be buying from competitors. Figure 4–7 shows the brand switching that could occur among existing customers. Some existing customers will be extremely loyal, buy-

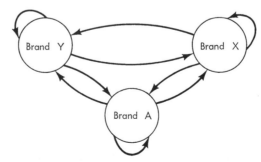

Figure 4–7.   **Brand switching among existing customers.**

ing from competitors only rarely if at all. For such customers, the goal would be to maintain their loyalty and repurchase rates, thus reducing the likelihood that they would begin sharing their purchases with other brands and perhaps ultimately move to segment O. Advertising might attempt to remind them of the important features of the brand or to reinforce the use experience.

Further, certain consumer promotions, such as premiums requiring multiple proofs of purchases, might also be used. The Campbell's advertisement shown in Figure 4–8 may be in this category. It provides the opportunity for a user to express loyalty by obtaining a mug that in turn will help to reinforce the usage experience. Other communications strategies, such as "frequent shopper/buyer" programs, might also be implemented using database marketing techniques (see Chapter 3). They would try to reduce attrition or "churn" in the customer base by creating "switching costs" for the customer.

A related behavioral objective to that of increasing loyalty might be to decrease a consumer's price sensitivity. A company would hope that by creating more loyal consumers it is able to charge a higher price (or reduce the need for discounts) and thus increase its contribution margin. However, the evidence on the ability of advertising to actually decrease an existing user's price elasticity or sensitivity is mixed. One viewpoint suggests that high advertising levels must be leading to nonprice competition and decreasing price elasticities. It has also been argued, however, that higher levels of advertising might actually increase the extent to which consumers do comparison shopping and compare prices, and thus actually increase, rather than decrease, price elasticity. Both types of empirical results have been reported.[9]

Increasing Usage

It is also possible to increase the usage of existing customers in the product class. This is especially true for market leader brands in the food and beverage product categories, such as Bisquick or Campbell Soup, or for leaders in other *consumable* categories such as Kodak film or Energizer batteries. In essence, the goal would be to increase the amount consumed per usage occasion, or to suggest new usage occasions and opportunities. Campbell Soup, for example, with a 75 percent market share in a slow-growing category, now needs to increase the share of soups among all meal occasions, thus increasing its total usage quantity.[10] The effect of increasing usage would be to reduce the time between purchases. Figure 4–9 shows a typical distribution of interpurchase times among existing customers. The effort would involve sliding the area under the curve to the left.

As mentioned, several approaches are available. Product use could be expanded by inducing people to use the product more frequently. Or, a new use application could be suggested. For example, Scotch tape could be used for decorative as well as conventional purposes, or the use of chewing gum as a cigarette substitute might be suggested as a new application, as in Figure 4–10. It may be possible to get existing customers to use the product in the familiar way but more frequently. Here the aim would usually be to do more than just induce an extra purchase; we would want to actually change long-term behavioral patterns so

Figure 4–8.   Maintaining brand loyalty.

Courtesy of Campbell Soup Company.

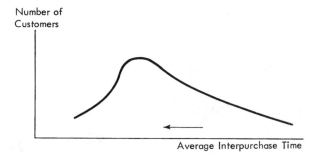

Figure 4–9.   Interpurchase time of existing customers.

that the increased usage, at least for some customers, would continue over time. The value of advertising will then be represented by the increased usage. If the increased usage extends over a long time period, it will obviously be of greater value. As before, however, the value must be balanced against the cost involved. Ads that have this kind of objective need special copy testing approaches, since most copy tests measure an ad's ability to create shifts in brand preference, rather than its ability to increase usage sucessfully.[11]

Behavioral or Action Objectives

An analysis of market dynamics can lead to behavioral measures that by themselves can provide the basis for operational objectives. If the advertising's target is new customers, the goal may be to get new customers to try a brand for the first time. The results would be measured by the number of new customers attracted. Such an estimate could be obtained from a consumer panel or by a count of a cents-off coupon if that were a part of the advertising effort. The number of new triers, of course, is quite different from short-run sales. The quantity of sales in the short run represented by new customers is usually minuscule and will be swamped by the behavioral patterns of regular customers (segment E).

An example of an ad trying to generate action—leads or inquiries—is the Allied Van Lines ad in Figure 4–11. Clearly, the hope is that people who are about to move will be interested in the free booklet and will call the toll-free telephone number, thus identifying themselves as prospects for a sales call.

ADVERTISING RESPONSE VARIABLES INTERVENING BETWEEN ADVERTISING AND ACTION . . . .

Usually advertising is not well suited to directly precipitate action. Rather, it is better at conducting some communication, association, or persuasion task that will hopefully result in the desired action being precipitated. A communication results in the audience members learning something new or gaining an improved understanding or memory of some fact; for example, Jell-O comes in a low-calorie form.

Figure 4–10.   An advertisement attempting to suggest new uses.

Courtesy of the Wm. Wrigley Jr. Company.

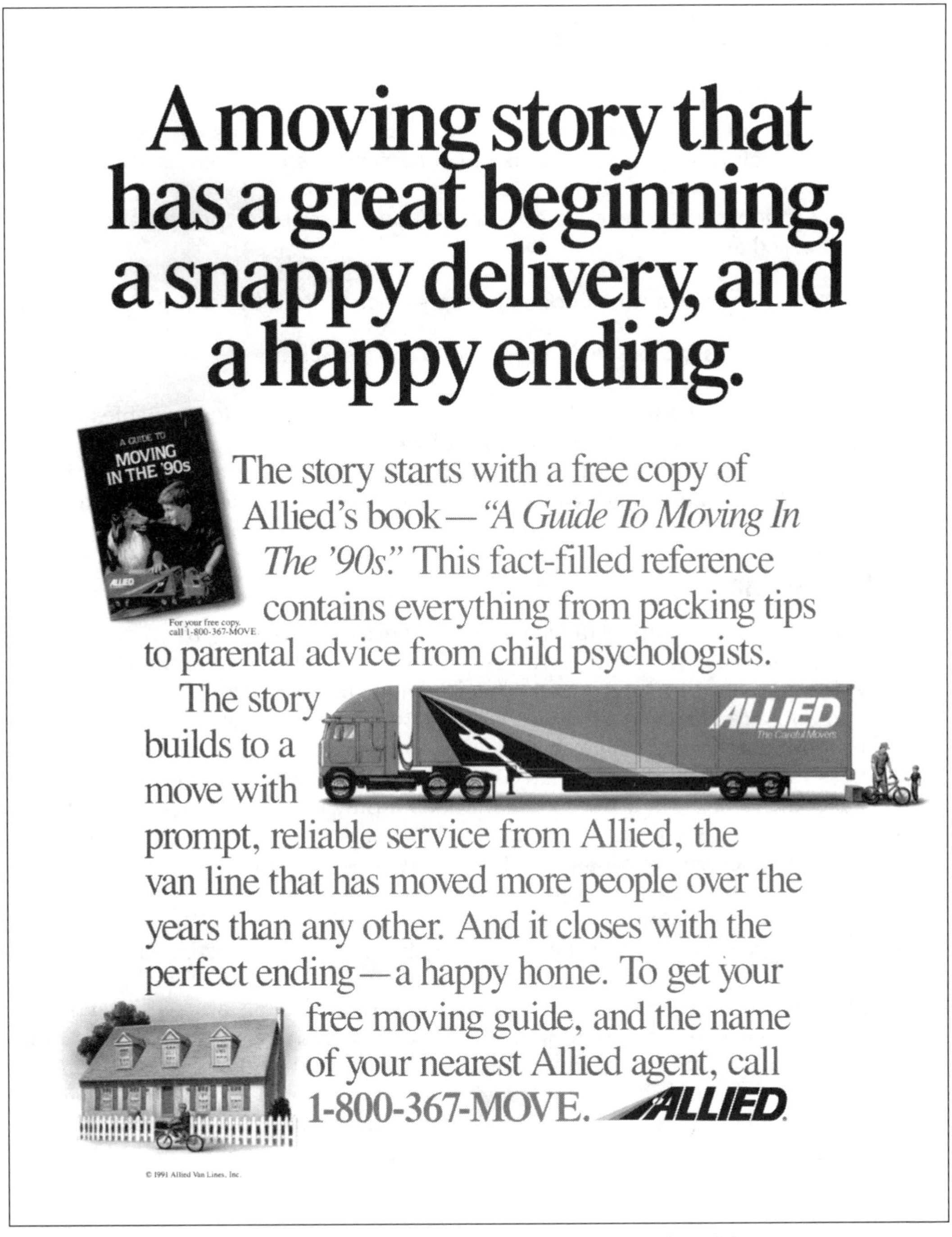
A moving story that has a great beginning, a snappy delivery, and a happy ending.
A GUIDE TO MOVING IN THE '90s
For your free copy. call 1-800-367-MOVE
The story starts with a free copy of Allied's book—"A Guide To Moving In The '90s." This fact-filled reference contains everything from packing tips to parental advice from child psychologists.
The story builds to a move with prompt, reliable service from Allied, the van line that has moved more people over the years than any other. And it closes with the perfect ending—a happy home. To get your free moving guide, and the name of your nearest Allied agent, call 1-800-367-MOVE.
ALLIED
The Careful Movers
ALLIED
© 1991 Allied Van Lines, Inc.

Figure 4–11. An advertisement aimed at attracting sales inquiries.

Used with permission of Allied Van Lines, Inc.

Associations link a brand to concepts such as types of people, use situations, or feelings; for example, driving a Pontiac creates an exciting feeling. Persuasion involves creating or changing an attitude toward an object; for example, an attitude expressed as "I rather like that brand."

The identification and selection of the best advertising response variable upon which to base objectives is difficult. Nevertheless, there is still great payoff to proceed in this direction.

To identify and use advertising response variables, the key questions to be addressed are

1. **What communication, association, or persuasion task will be likely to precipitate the desired action?**
2. **How can this task best be conceptualized and measured?**

In asking the first question, there is a set of intervening variables that is frequently useful. This set includes brand awareness, brand comprehension, brand image or personality, brand attitude, the perception that an important reference group values that brand, and the association of desired feelings with a brand or use experience.

Brand Awareness

A basic communication task in which advertising excels is to create awareness. Awareness can be particularly needed when the goal is to stimulate a trial purchase perhaps of a new brand. The model is shown as Model A in Table 4–1. Advertising creates awareness in the new brand, and the awareness will create the trial purchase, after which the brand is on its own to gain acceptance. The awareness measure could be based on a telephone survey in which people are if they have heard of the new brand and perhaps if they know what type of product is involved ("Yes, I've heard of Arizona Iced Tea; it is a new iced tea"). The percentage answering correctly would be the awareness measure. Different measures of awareness are possible: top-of-mind awareness (first brand mentioned, without any prompting), other unaided mention, or aided awareness.

Awareness may also be an advertising response measure that could be instrumental at generating loyalty such as postulated in Model B in Table 4–1. Some low-involvement products, such as gum, soap, or beer, are purchased without much thought or consideration. The choice is often based upon which brand is most familiar. One role of advertising is to get a brand to be more prominent in people's minds so that it is the choice in those no-thought choices. The goal in such situations could be to improve top-of-mind awareness, since this should indicate maximum familiarity.

Brand Comprehension

Another communication task for which advertising is well suited is to communicate facts about the brand, in particular about its attributes. An audience's perceptions of these attributes, in turn, influence its *brand comprehension*. Thus,

Table 4–1. Intervening and Behavioral Variables

Model	Advertising variable	Intervening variables	Behavioral variables
A	Advertising	→ Brand Awareness	→ Trial Purchase
B	Advertising	→ Brand Awareness	→ Loyalty
C	Advertising	→ Brand Awareness → Knowledge of Brand Attributes	→ Trial Purchase
D	Advertising	→ Knowledge of New Application	→ Increase Usage
E	Advertising		→ Sales Leads
F	Advertising	→ Knowledge About Company	→ Sales Via Personal Selling
G	Advertising	→ Associate Brand with User Type	→ Loyalty
H	Advertising	→ Brand Attitude	→ Loyalty
I	Advertising	→ Associate Feelings and Brand Use	→ Loyalty
J	Advertising	→ Brand Awareness → Knowledge of Brand Attributes → Brand Attitude	→ Trial Purchase
K	Advertising	→ Knowledge of Brand Attributes → Brand Attitude	→ Trial Purchase

when IBM launched its OS/2 operating system software for personal computers, its key task was to communicate exactly why it was better than the existing Microsoft Windows software. Model C in Table 4–1 shows a new brand context in which trial purchase is not only dependent on brand awareness but also on learning about a key brand attribute. The perception of that brand on that attribute could be measured by asking respondents to indicate their relative or agreement or disagreement as to whether the brand has that attribute, as follows:

Agree Strongly $+3 + 2 + 1$ 0 $-1 - 2 - 3$ Disagree Strongly

In Model D in Table 4-1, the behavioral goal is to increase usage. The brand comprehension intervening variable is to communicate knowledge of a new application. Such a campaign was run by Arm & Hammer baking soda, which wanted to get people to use its product to deodorize refrigerators.[12] The percentage of households that reported having used the product in this application went from 1 percent to 57 percent in just fourteen months. Later campaigns suggested its use as a sink, freezer, and cat-litter deodorizer.

In an industrial context, a goal might be to get organizations to purchase the advertised product. However, a realistic appraisal might indicate that a personal selling effort will play the key role in precipitating the decision. The role of advertising might then be to support the sales force by creating inquiries or by communicating information about the company as suggested by Models E and F in Table 4–1. McGraw-Hill's advertisement, shown in Figure 4–12, dramatically illustrates the role that advertising can play in supporting the sales effort. It is useful to note that communication is not expected to play any significant direct role in precipitating purchase decisions. Thus, it would not be reasonable to measure its impact in terms of purchase decisions. Rather, it is linked causally with the reception that the salesperson receives, particularly on early visits.

Brand Image and Personality

Brand image and personality refer especially to types of associations that the brand develops with a type of person or even another product. Thus, Charlie perfume, discussed in Chapter 6, was a perfume designed around a very specific type of female lifestyle. It is represented as Model G in Table 4–1. Apple computers compete in the personal computer marketplace by being positioned as a "friendlier" computer. Chapter 10 will explore in more detail the nature of a brand personality objective and a procedure for generating image objective alternatives and for selecting among them.

Brand Attitude

A *brand attitude* represents the like-dislike feeling toward a brand. Model H in Table 4–1 shows a case in which loyalty is predicated on increasing the attitude toward the object.

Attitude can be measured in a variety of ways, as will be discussed in Chapter 8. One approach is to measure it based on brand comprehension, which, as was

Figure 4–12.   Advertising's role in supporting the personal selling effort.
Courtesy of McGraw-Hill Publications Company.

stated earlier, is derived from perceptions of the brand with respect to specific attributes and characteristics. Another is to use the like-dislike dimensions as with this scale:

$$\text{Dislike} \quad -3 - 2 - 1 \quad 0 \quad +1 + 2 + 3 \quad \text{Like}$$

Still another alternative is to measure it based on behavioral intentions—that is, the percentage of customers who say they awill "definitely" or "probably" buy this brand. Chapter 8 will cover attitudes and their use in advertising objectives in detail. It will also include the role that brand comprehension has in creating and changing attitudes.

Associating Feelings with Brands or Use Experiences

Sometimes the advertising objective can be to create feelings of warmth, energy, fun, anticipation, fear, or concern and associate those feelings with the brand and the use experience. Model I in Table 4–1 could represent a gum brand that is attempting to associate feelings of togetherness and happiness with its use.

There are well-developed models, concepts, and measures that guide our use of image and attitude objectives. In contrast, the role of feelings is much less mature and far less is known about how they work or even if they do work. Chapter 9 will present some emerging ideas about the feeling response to advertising. It suggests that in addition to measuring how audience members feel when being exposed to a commercial it might be useful to measure how they liked the commercial and their impressions of their use experience with the brand. The concept is that if feeling advertising (at least positive-feeling advertising) is effective, it will probably result in advertising that is liked, and, therefore, it should impact upon the use experience.

More Complex Models and Multiple Objectives

In many contexts, there are two or more advertising responses that are needed for a desired behavior to occur. For example, Model J in Table 4–1 shows a trial purchase model that suggested that awareness can lead to trial purchase directly or through the creation of attribute knowledge and brand attitude. There are thus two routes to precipitating trial. Model K shows another multiple construct model, one in which there is no sequence implied. Two tasks are required but one need not precede the other.

When the advertising campaign can focus upon a single, well-defined objective, the communication task is made easier. When several objectives are introduced, there is always the danger that the campaign will become a compromise that will be ineffective with respect to all objectives. Copywriting wisdom suggests that simplicity in ad advertisement is vital: an ad that tries to say too much loses focus and becomes ineffective (we will discuss principles of good copywriting in Chapter 13).

In addition, research has shown that advertising that tries to maximize effectiveness with regard to one objective very often fails to be effective on other objectives. For instance, an advertisement that is very successful in attracting attention (for example, by creating anxiety or fear) may fail to persuade (because people may get defensive in the face of such anxiety). As another example, an advertisement using a famous spokesperson may get a lot of people to pay attention, but fewer copy points may get communicated because people who watch the ad may pay more attention to (and get distracted by) the spokesperson, thus paying less attention to the message content of the ad. This aspect of advertising response has been named the *compensation principle* by the psychologist William McGuire, who implies that single advertisements must therefore not aim at more than one objective, and that different and complementary advertisements must be created (as part of a total campaign) if there is more than one objective.[13]

Thus, when it is appropriate and necessary to deal with multiple objectives, these multiple objectives could require more than one advertising message, sequenced as part of an *advertising campaign*, although such a need may not be determined until after the creative process has begun.

Multiple objectives could involve more than one target audience. For example, a computer company might need to gain awareness among one segment and to communicate the existence of a new product to another. Or there might be two communication tasks for the same target segment. For example, an industrial chemical company might need to generate sales leads for its salespeople and to establish an image of a solid company of substance.

SPECIFYING THE TARGET SEGMENT . . . .

A basic question in the objective-setting process is the identity of the *target segment*. To whom is the advertising to be addressed? The target audience can be defined in many ways, and Chapter 6 provides a detailed discussion of segmentation and segmentation variables. The process of objective setting is intimately connected with that of selecting a target segment and may involve subsegments that are relevant to the communication task. For example, in the case of marketing a product line to small banks, it might be appropriate to communicate cost savings for a computer model to bank presidents, software reliability to bank administrative personnel, and to ignore loan officers. Although the general marketing strategy would include all professionals in small banks, the advertising objectives could appropriately refine this group into subgroups.

The behavioral measures discussed in this chapter such as usage and loyalty can also be used to define target segments. A target thus could be the heavy user, the nonuser, the loyal user of our brand, or the group loyal to another brand. In Chapter 6, benefit segmentation will be explored in a context in which a target segment is defined by the benefits sought from a product. For example, a target segment might be those who are particularly concerned with the cost of operating a computer, whereas another segment might be interested primarily in the computer's speed.

The advertising response measures just presented can be particularly useful segmentation variables in the advertising context. Thus, segments can often be identified that are unaware of the brand, do not know or are not convinced that it has a key attribute, or have not yet developed a positive attitude. One or more of these segments can then be selected as the primary target. Such a segmentation choice can make the advertising more effective since a campaign designed to create awareness will tend to be very different from one designed to communicate a product attribute.

THE DAGMAR APPROACH . . . .

The approach to setting advertising objectives just outlined will be expanded on in the next seven chapters and in the balance of the book. Research findings, constructs, and measurement tools will be developed that will serve to make the approach effective and operational. In this section of this chapter, the historical foundations for our approach to setting advertising objectives will be presented. It provides a rationale and basis for the introduction of advertising response measures in advertising objectives and for the concept of measuring such objectives over time.

There are several reasons for this diversion. First, the historical roots of the approach are not only interesting but provide a deeper understanding of thrust and scope. Second, they provide suggestions on implementation that are still useful and valid.

In 1961, Russell H. Colley wrote a book under the sponsorship of the Association of National Advertisers called *Defining Advertising Goals for Measured Advertising Results.*[14] The book introduced what has become known as the *DAGMAR approach* to advertising planning and included a precise method for selecting and quantifying goals and for using those goals to measure performance. The performance measurement feature had great appeal to managers of the 1960s, who were frustrated by the available methods for controlling advertising efforts and impatient with embryonic methods of developing sales-response models.

The DAGMAR approach can be summarized in its succinct statement "defining an advertising goal." An *advertising goal* is a specific communication task, to be accomplished among a defined audience, in a given period of time. Note that a communication task is involved as opposed to a marketing task and that the goal is specific, involving an unambiguously defined task, among a defined audience, in a given time period.

A Communication Task

An advertising objective involves a *communication task*, something that advertising, by itself, can reasonably hope to accomplish. It is recognized that advertising is mass, paid communication that is intended to create awareness, impart information, develop attitudes, or induce action.

In the DAGMAR approach, the communication task is based on a specific model of the communication process, as illustrated in Figure 4–13. The model suggests that there is a series of mental steps through which a brand or objects must climb to gain acceptance. An individual starts at some point by being unaware of a brand's presence in the market. The initial communication task of the brand is to

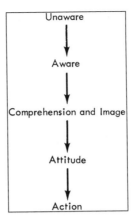

Figure 4–13.   A hierarchy of effects model of the communications process.

increase consumer awareness of the brand—to advance the brand one step up the hierarchy.

The second step of the communication process is brand comprehension and involves the audience member learning something about the brand. What are its specific characteristics and appeals, including associated imagery and feelings? In what way does it differ from its competitors? Whom is it supposed to benefit? The third step is the attitude (or conviction) step and intervenes between comprehension and final action. The action phase involves some overt move on the part of the buyer, such as trying a brand for the first time, visiting a showroom, or requesting information.

A communication model such as the DAGMAR model, which implies that the audience member will sequentially pass through a set of steps, is termed a *hierarchy-of-effects model*. A host of hierarchy models have been proposed. The *AIDA model*, developed in the 1920s, suggested that an effective personal sales presentation should attract **A**ttention, gain **I**nterest, create a **D**esire, and precipitate **A**ction. The *new adopter hierarchy model*, conceived by rural sociologists, postulated five stages: awareness, interest, evaluation, trial, and adoption.

Another hierarchy model is particularly interesting because of its close ties with social psychological theory. Developed by Robert Lavidge and Gary Steiner,[15] it includes six stages: awareness, knowledge, liking, preference, conviction, and purchase. They divided this hierarchy into the three components corresponding to a social psychologist's concept of an attitude system. The first stage, consisting of the awareness and knowledge levels, is comparable to the cognitive, or knowledge, component of attitude. The affective component of an attitude, the like-dislike aspect, is represented in the Lavidge and Steiner hierarchy by the liking and preference levels. The remaining attitude component is the conative component, the action or motivation element, represented by the conviction and purchase levels, the final two levels in the hierarchy.

A Specific Task

We have mentioned that the DAGMAR approach emphasizes the communication task of advertising not the marketing objectives of the firm. The second important concept of the DAGMAR approach is that the advertising goal be specific. It should be a written, measurable task involving a starting point, a defined audience, and a fixed time period.

Measurement Procedure

The DAGMAR approach needs to be made specific when actual goals are formulated. When brand comprehension is involved, for example, it is necessary to indicate exactly what appeal or image is to be communicated. Furthermore, the specification should include a description of the measurement procedure. If a high-protein cereal were trying to increase brand comprehension among a target audience, managers could well decide to promote its protein content. However, merely mentioning its protein content is inadequate and open to different interpretations. Is the cereal to be perceived as one containing a full day's supply as a protection against illness or as one that supplies more energy than other cereals? If a survey includes the request, "Rank the following cereals as to protein content," then brand comprehension could be quantified to mean the percentage who rated it first.

Benchmark

President Lincoln has been quoted as saying, "If we could first know where we are and whither we are tending, we could better judge what to do and how to do it."[16] A basic aspect of establishing a goal and selecting a campaign to reach it is to know the starting conditions. Without a benchmark, it is most difficult to determine the optimal goal. The selection of an awareness-oriented goal might be a mistake if awareness is already high. Without a benchmark measure, such a circumstance could not be ascertained quantitatively. In addition, benchmarks can suggest how a certain goal can best be reached. For example, it would be useful to know whether the existing image needs to be changed, reinforced, diffused, or sharpened. A benchmark is also a prerequisite to the ultimate measurement of results, an essential part of any planning program and of the DAGMAR approach in particular. Despite the obvious value of having benchmarks before goals are set, this is often not done. In fact, the key to the DAGMAR approach is probably the generation of well-conceived benchmarks before advertising goals are determined. With such measures, the rest of the approach flows rather naturally.

Target Audience

A key tenet of the DAGMAR approach was that the target audience be well defined. If the goal was to increase awareness, for example, it was essential to know the target audience precisely. Perhaps the goal was to increase awareness among the heavy user segment from 25 percent to 60 percent in a certain time period. The benchmark measure could not be developed without a specification of the target segment. Further, the campaign execution will normally depend on the identity of the target segment. The heavy user group will likely respond differently from a segment defined by a lifestyle profile.

Time Period

The objective should involve a particular time period, such as six months or one year. With a time period specified, a survey to generate a set of measures can be planned and anticipated. All parties involved will understand that the results will be available for evaluating the campaign, which could lead to a contraction, expansion, or change in the current effort. The length of the time period must fit into various constraints involving the planning cycle of both a company and an agency. However, the appropriate time necessary to generate the kind of cognitive response desired should also be considered.

Written Goals

Finally, goals should be committed to paper. Under the discipline of writing clearly, basic shortcomings and misunderstandings become exposed, and it becomes easy to determine whether the goal contains the crucial aspects of the DAGMAR approach.

Suppose that the product of interest were an economy-priced bourbon. It has a bad quality image despite the fact that blind taste tests indicated that it does not have any real quality problems. An objective might be developed with respect to a scale ranging from –5 to +5 (inadequate taste to adequate taste). An admissible objective would be to increase the percentage of male bourbon drinkers in the United States who give a nonnegative rating on the scale from 5 to 25 percent in a twelve-month period. Notice that this objective is measurable and has a starting point, a definite audience, and a fixed time period.

The DAGMAR Checklist

An aid to those implementing the DAGMAR approach is a checklist of promotional tasks, partially reproduced as Table 4–2. The suggestion was to rate each of the promotional tasks in terms of its relative importance in the context of the product situation involved. The intent was to stimulate ideas or decision alternatives, often the most difficult and crucial part of the decision process.

Following are two examples of the DAGMAR approach as presented in Colley's book. It is left to the reader to examine these examples critically to see if they satisfy the requirements of the approach as it has been presented here.

Overseas Airline Service[17]—A DAGMAR Case Study

The company was one of the smaller of several dozen airlines competing for American overseas airline passengers. It was recognized at the outset that it was impossible to compete with the giant airlines in advertising volume. The small budget would not permit the size of space, frequency, and media breadth used by the major airlines.

The copy and media strategy decided on was, therefore, to concentrate on a particular segment of the audience, with highly distinctive copy and art beamed at

Table 4–2.   **Partial Checklist of Promotional Tasks**[a]

To what extent does the advertising aim at closing an immediate sale?

1.   Perform the complete selling function (take the product through all the necessary steps toward a sale).

2.   Close sales to prospects already partly sold through Past advertising efforts ("ask for the order" or "clincher" advertising).

3.   Announce a special reason for "buying now" (price, premium, etc.).

4.   *Remind* people to buy.

5.   Tie in with some special buying event.

6.   Simulate impulse sales.

Does the advertising aim at near-term sales by moving the prospect, step by step, closer to the sale (so that when confronted with a buying situation, the customer will ask for, reach for, or accept the advertised brand)?

7.   Create awareness of existence of the product or brand.

8.   Create *brand image* or favorable emotional disposition toward the brand.

9.   Implant information or attitude regarding benefits and superior features of brand.

10.   Combat or offset competitive claims.

11.   Correct false impressions, misinformation, and other obstacles to sales.

12.   Build familiarity and easy recognition of package or trademark.

Does the advertising aim at building a long-range consumer franchise?

13.   Build confidence in company and brand, which is expected to pay off in years to come.

14.   Build consumer demand that places company in stronger position in relation to Its distribution (not at the "mercy of the marketplace")

15.   Place advertiser in position to select preferred distributors and dealers.

16.   Secure universal distribution.

17.   Establish a "reputation platform" for launching new brands or product lines.

18.   Establish brand recognition and acceptance that will enable the company to open up new markets (geographic, price, age, sex).

Table 4–2. Partial Checklist of Promotional Tasks[a] (Continued)

How important are supplementary benefits of end-use advertising?

19. Aid salespeople in opening new accounts.

20. Aid salespeople in getting larger orders from wholesalers and retailers.

21. Aid salespeople in getting preferred display space.

22. Give salespeople an entree.

23. Build morale of company sales force.

24. impress the trade.

Source: Russell H. Colley, Defining Advertising Goals for Measured Advertising Results (New York: Association of National Advertisers, 1961), pp. 61–68.

[a]*The complete list included fifty-two items.*

this particular audience. The audience was experienced, sophisticated world travelers. The message was the image of an airline that caters to a distinctive, discriminating, travel-wise audience. Experience and judgment indicated that selling to the seasoned traveler was a wise strategy. Not only does he or she make a more frequent customer, but his or her advice is sought and habits are emulated by the "first trippers."

Art and copy, in a highly distinctive style, were directed at attracting the attention and interest of the more experienced and sophisticated world travelers. In fact, a new name was coined and used extensively in the advertising to refer to such a person (TRAVOIR-FAIRE). Instead of featuring the more commonplace tourist attractions in the countries served, the advertising featured off-the-beaten-path scenes and unusual objects of art and interest. Whereas mass-appeal airlines were featuring hardware (make and speed of their jet service), advertising of the subject airline treated the make and speed of the airliner in a subtle manner and emphasized instead distinctive items of decor, comfort, cuisine, and service.

In addition to the usual reports of opinion on advertising effectiveness that come through inquiries and comments made to ticket and travel agents, the company conducted an inexpensive attitude survey. Travel agents in selected cities furnished names and addresses of overseas travelers (two or more trips). Questionnaires were sent out by mail periodically to a representative sample of several hundred such persons. Questions were directed toward determining the following information:

Awareness: What airlines can you name that offer all-jet service to_____?

Image: Which of these airlines would you rate as outstanding on the following? (A checklist of characteristics and features was included.)

Preference: On your next overseas trip, which of these airlines would you seriously consider? Why?

An unusually high return of questionnaires was received because of the offer of a free booklet of high interest to international travelers. Survey costs were small (several hundred dollars for each semiannual survey).

The results shown in the accompanying table indicate a steadily rising awareness, a growing image as portrayed in the advertising, and an increase in preference. This was ample indication that advertising had succeeded in conveying the intended message to the selected audience.

Survey Results (Percent)

	Before advertising campaign	End of six month	End of one year
Awareness (have heard of company	38	46	52
Image (luxury all-jet overseas service)	9	17	24
Preference (would seriously consider for next trip)	13	15	21

Electrical Appliances[18]—A DAGMAR Case Study

The following case example concerned electrical appliances but serves to illustrate the advertising dynamics of other consumer durables such as automobiles or furniture.

The market was 26 million homemakers who are logical prospects. A logical prospect is defined as an owner of an appliance three years old or more, plus new households formed by marriage and new home construction.

Marketing Objective

The marketing objective was to get sales action now and sell carloads of appliances this season, thus reducing substantial dealer and manufacturer inventories.

Advertising Objective

The advertising objective was to induce immediate action. The brand name and product advantages are already well known through consistent and effective advertising.

Advertising's task, at this particular stage, was to persuade homemakers to visit dealers' showrooms and see a demonstration. A special ice cube tray was offered as an added inducement.

Specific Advertising Goal

The specific advertising goal was to persuade 400,000 homemakers to visit 10,000 dealers in four weeks, yielding an average of forty prospects who will physically cross the threshold of each dealer's showroom.

Results were measured in several different dimensions. The medium used was sponsorship of special audience telecasts. The results: two telecasts drew a combined audience of 84 million people. Approximately 18 percent, or 15 million people, could play back the commercial messages. Nearly one-half million took immediate action by walking into a dealer's showroom and purchasing the special offer. Advertising accomplished its assigned task by inducing consumers to visit the dealer's showroom. It is true that dealers sold a large volume of appliances during the special promotion. But advertising cannot claim all the credit since it was only one factor in the consummation of the sale. However, further research indicated that 44 percent of the people who bought a refrigerator gave advertising as the major factor in choice of brand.

Challenges to the DAGMAR Approach

The DAGMAR approach had enormous visibility and influence. It really changed the way that advertising objectives were created and the way that advertising results were measured. It introduced the concept of communication objectives like awareness, comprehension, image, and attitude. The point was made that such goals are more appropriate for advertising than is some measure like sales which can have multiple causes. In introducing communication objectives, behavioral science constructs and models such as attitude models were drawn upon. The DAGMAR approach also focused attention upon measurement encouraging people to create objectives so specific and operational that they can be measured. In doing so, it provided the potential to improve the communication between the creative teams and the advertising clients.

A measure of the significance of an idea is the degree of both theoretical and empirical controversy that it precipitates. By this measure the DAGMAR approach has been most significant. There have been six different kinds of challenges to the DAGMAR model.

Sales Goal

First, some purists believe that only a sales measure is relevant. As pointed out by Michael Halbert, one of the pioneering group at DuPont engaged in the use of experimental-design approaches to measure advertising effect,[19]

> *When a study using one of the goals just mentioned [e.g., increase awareness] is published and reported at a meeting, I sometimes get the unsocial urge to question the author with, "So what?" If he has shown that advertising does, in fact, increase brand name awareness or favorable attitude toward the company, on what grounds does this increase a justifiable use of the company's funds? The answer usually given is that more people will buy a product if they are aware of it or if they have a favorable attitude. But why leave this critical piece of inference out of the design of the original research?*

For example, if awareness does not affect sales, why bother to measure it? If it does have a close relationship, why not measure sales directly? This argument has gained strength in recent years since it is now possible to measure advertising effects on short-term sales for packaged goods with great precision through controlled experiments utilizing scanner data panels (see Chapter 16). However, as mentioned before, even these tests cannot typically yield unambiguous estimates of the long-term effects of advertising.

A second version of this criticism is that if sales effects measures are flawed, the use of intermediate objectives has serious flaws too. For instance, any use of an intermediate objective, as suggested by the DAGMAR model, involves the assumption that the relationship between sales and that intermediate objective is positive and monotonic (i.e., as one goes up the other does too), and that this relationship applies equally strongly (i.e., with equal "slopes") to all consumer segments being targeted or being compared for relative ad effects. These assumptions may not hold true in all situations.[20]

Practicability

A second objection focuses on the many implementation difficulties inherent in the DAGMAR approach. In particular, the checklist falls short of providing sufficient details to implement the approach. As Leo Bogart has observed, Colley provides broad outlines much like the dragonfly that, after showing a hippopotamus the relationship between wing movement and flying, was asked exactly how to do it and replied, "I'll give you the broad idea and you work out the details."[21] A level in the hierarchy to be attacked must be selected, and a campaign to influence those at that level must be developed. Neither of these tasks is easy.

Measurement Problems

The third problem is measurement. What should we really measure when we speak of attitude, awareness, or brand comprehension? Substantial conceptual and measurement problems underlie all these constructs.

Noise in the System

A fourth problem is noise that exists in the hierarchy model, just as it does in the other, more simple, response models involving immediate sales. We have argued that there are many causal factors other than advertising that determine sales. In a more complex model, it can be argued that there are many causal factors besides advertising that determine awareness. For example, variables such as competitive promotion or unplanned publicity can affect an awareness campaign.

Inhibiting the Great Idea

The "great creative idea" is a dream or hope of many advertisers (see discussion in Chapter 13). The DAGMAR model is basically a rational, planned approach that, among other things, provides guidance to creative people. The problem is that if it does in fact have any influence on their work, it must also necessarily inhibit their efforts. When the creative approach of copywriters and art directors is inhibited, there is less likelihood that they will come up with a great idea and an increased probability of a pedestrian advertising campaign resulting. Of course, there might also be a lesser probability of a spectacularly ineffective advertising campaign.

Anthony Morgan, an agency research director, argues that the hierarchy model, which he terms the "HEAR-UNDERSTAND-DO" model, inhibits great advertising by emphasizing tests of recall, communication, and persuasion.[22] He gives two examples. First, a campaign with all music and warm human visuals which everyone loved failed to meet the "company standard" for the day-after recall test (where on the day after ad exposure viewers are asked to recall specific copy points—discussed in Chapter 14). A potentially great campaign was clearly being evaluated by the wrong criteria. A more appropriate model for this campaign might have been "SENSE-FEEL-RELATE." Chapter 9 will expand on this concept.

The second example is the Campbell's Soup "Soup Is Good Food" campaign created to arrest a ten-year decline in per capita consumption of Campbell's Red & White line of soups. The campaign objectives were to communicate news, to change the perception of soup, and to increase consumption. The first commercials received the lowest persuasion scores (from a test measuring the impact of commercial exposure on attitudes and intentions) that any Campbell's commercial had ever scored. However, the campaign, which stimulated three years of sales increases, was designed not to have much initial impact but to withstand enormous repetitions and to work over time. The testing was simply inappropriate. The implication is that it can be dangerous to rely on testing based on the hierarchical model (or any other single conceptualization). Rather, conceptual and research flexibility needs to be employed.

Hierarchy Model of Communication Effect

The sixth type of argument against the DAGMAR approach attacks the basic hierarchy model which postulates a set of sequential steps of awareness, comprehension, and attitude leading to action. The counterargument is that other models may hold in various contexts and that it is naive to apply the DAGMAR hierarchy models in all situations. For example, action can precede attitude formation and even comprehension with an impulse purchase of a low-involvement product. At this point there is general agreement that, indeed, the appropriate model will depend upon the situation and a key problem in many contexts is in fact to determine what that model is. We discuss such alternative models and their situational applicability in the Chapter 5. However, the basic thrust of DAGMAR-the use of advertising response measures as the basis of objectives and the focus on measurement-does not depend upon the DAGMAR hierarchy model, so this issue is not really that crucial as it may have once appeared.

We now turn to implementation of the DAGMAR approach, using two applied examples.

Applied Example One: The Leo Burnett Program (CAPP)

CAPP, an acronym for *continuous advertising planning program*, was developed by the Leo Burnett advertising agency. As reported by John Maloney,[23] one of its architects, it is based on still another hierarchy-of-effect model consisting of unawareness, awareness, acceptance, preference, brand bought last, and brand satisfaction. Termed *the consumer demand profile*, it is shown graphically in Figure 4–14.

Here, the acceptance level implies that the brand is acceptable to an individual; it meets his or her minimum requirements. Brand preference indicates the percentage of total product-class users who rate the brand, on a four-point scale, higher than any other brand. A unique element of the CAPP hierarchy is brand sat-

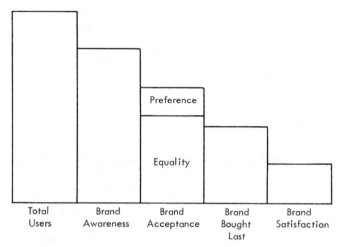

Figure 4–14.   Consumer demand profile.
Source: John C. Maloney, "Attitude Measurement and Formation," paper presented at the Test Market Design and Measurement Workshop, American Marketing Association. Chicago, April 21, 1966.

isfaction, which is meant to reflect the performance of the brand after purchase and repeat buying.

A cross-sectional sample of 1,000 households, interviewed on a monthly basis, provided the data base. Information was obtained from each household on their media habits and their location on the CAPP hierarchy with respect to the brands of interest. Monthly data provide a sensitive indicator of the response to the advertising campaign. Clearly, such time-series information has much greater and more timely interpretative power than measures restricted to immediately before and immediately after a campaign. If a substantial change is to be generated in a hierarchy measure, progress should be observed along the way and an appropriate campaign developed accordingly.

Which Hierarchy Level?
How can knowledge of the CAPP hierarchy profile and its trends be helpful in determining what level to attack? Maloney suggested an examination of the hierarchy patterns. The adjacent levels in the hierarchy were of particular interest. For example, if there were a small number of people who were aware of the brand (relative to the number of total users), then a worthwhile target could be to increase awareness. If a substantial number of people had accepted the brand, but only a few preferred it, perhaps it would be necessary to sharpen up the brand image in some respect. On the other hand, if there were a high degree of acceptance but a very low level of brand bought last, then it might become necessary to stimulate a trial purchase. If brand satisfaction is low compared to brand bought last, then perhaps there is a basic problem with the brand itself, and some very specific questions should be asked about its capacity to satisfy customer wants and needs.

Essentially, the proposal is to consider the ratio of the size of adjacent levels, for example, the number of those who bought the brand last divided by the number who indicated brand satisfaction. A good level to consider as an objective is one for which this ratio involving the next lower level is high. This decision rule reflects the fact that it is usually worthwhile to concentrate on large segments and ignore smaller ones. It identifies that segment that contains large numbers of potential movers.

Naturally, it would be desirable to refine this decision rule by providing numerical guidelines. To do so, the profile histories associated with other brands in the product class would have to be considered to provide a frame of reference. The ultimate goal should be to expand the decision rule into a decision model that would make Maloney's suggestion explicit. Such a model will be developed, but in the context of our second applied example.

Applied Example Two: The General Motors Approach

Another major application of the DAGMAR model was the General Motors approach, as reported by Gail Smith.[24] Although General Motors reportedly does not use this approach currently,[25] believing that the effects of advertising and other marketing elements (such as word of mouth, dealer experience, news reports) are impossible to disentangle for even these intermediate nonsales effects, it nonetheless serves as an excellent example of the kind of analysis that the DAGMAR approach makes possible.

The data base for this effort consisted of six matched, cross-sectional surveys taken in September, October, December, January, March, and June. In the automobile industry, the impact of advertising effort is much more important in the fall than in the summer; therefore, the measurement schedule was adjusted accordingly. Seven types of information, shown in Table 4–3, were obtained in each survey. They included a hierarchy measure, product image, message registration, market behavior, product inventory, demographics, and media consumption.

The hierarchy used by General Motors consisted of *awareness*, *buying class*, *consideration class*, and *first choice*. A brand is in a respondent's buying class if she or he considers it similar to or competitive with the brands she or he would actively consider when entering the market. Consideration class consists of those brands the respondent will favorably consider the next time he or she enters the market. Both of these measures were obtained through open-ended questions. The first choice is the one brand the respondent would select if a choice were made at the time the questionnaire was administered.

The image section consisted of thirty-five semantic differential questions measuring such dimensions as styling, prestige, and trade-in value. The message registration section measured the impact of the advertising. Did the slogans and the product attributes that were part of the advertising message get through to the audience? This information, in conjunction with the media consumption data, is, of course, interesting in itself. It provides the possibility of measuring the relative message impact of the various media. The market behavior section includes shopping behavior, purchases, and intentions. These kinds of constructs represent the ultimate payoff, and we shall attempt to use them to quantify the decision about which level to attack. The product inventory and demographic sections provided information that permits cross-classification on the data, a basic approach to evaluating segmentation strategies. For example, the answers from young owners of foreign cars might be compared with responses from young owners of American cars.

Which Hierarchy Level?

The existence of such cross-sectional information provides a firm basis for the DAGMAR approach. However, to provide sensitive measures of the economic value of goal accomplishment, it is desirable to measure the same respondent at several

Table 4–3. **General Content of the Questionaire Used to Establish Advertising Goals for General Motors Products.**

I. Preferences levels by brand, by series of brand
   Awareness
   "Buying class"
   "Consideration class"
II. Product image
III. Message registration
   Specific product attributes
   Slogans
   Story line
IV. Market behavior
   Shopping behavior, dealer visits
   Purchases
   Intentions
V. Product inventory
   Content and condition
VI. Demographics
VII. media consumption
   Television: by hours per week, by selected programs
   Magazines: by hours per week, by selected magazines
   Radio: by hours per week, by time slot
   Newspapers: by hours per week, by type

Source: Gail Smith, "How GM Measures Ad Effectiveness," in Keith K. Cox, ed., Readings in Market Research (New York: Appleton-Century-Crofts, 1967), p.172.

points in time. Accordingly, General Motors questioned a subsample of the respondents in each survey twelve months later. One purpose was to obtain a measure of the accuracy of answers regarding planned shopping behavior, dealer visits, and so forth. Table 4–4 summarizes such information for a car, here called Watusi, which was developed by General Motors for the youth market.

The first column of Table 4–4 shows the sample proportion in each hierarchy level. The second indicates the probability that the respondent will visit a dealer. The third, the probability of a Watusi purchase, potentially provides the basis for an economic judgment about which level in the hierarchy would be the most profitable to attack. The table indicates that, if a respondent gave Watusi as a first choice, his or her probability of buying would be 0.56, whereas if the Watusi was only in the consideration class, the purchase probability would be 0.22. Thus, if someone who moves up to the first-choice hierarchy level behaves like those already there, the latter's purchase probability would increase by

$$0.56 - 0.22 = 0.34$$

To determine the relative value of a campaign directed at those in the consideration class hierarchy level, it would also be necessary to weigh (1) the number of people in the consideration class hierarchy level, and (2) the cost and

Table 4–4.   Value of Preference Levels in Terms of Probability and Dealer Visitation and Purchase.

Hierarchy Level		Preference Level Proportion	Probability will visit Watusi dealer	Probability will buy Watusi
5	Watusi first choice	0.05	0.840	0.560
4	Watusi in consideration class	0.07	0.620	0.220
3	Watusi in buying class	0.08	0.400	0.090
2	Aware of Watusi	0.14	0.240	0.050
1	Not aware of Watusi	0.66	0.015	0.004
	Total	1.00		

Source: Gail Smith, "How GM Measures Ad Effectiveness," in Keith K. Cox, ed., Readings in Market Research *(New York: Appleton-Century-Crofts, 1967), p. 175.*

effectiveness of an advertising campaign designed to move them to the first-choice hierarchy level.

Moving People up the Hierarchy

How can advertising go about moving people from one hierarchy level to another? This problem will be addressed in later chapters of the book. However, it is useful to consider here the General Motors approach, which was based upon a thirty-five question semantic differential. Brand image profiles for all people on each level were obtained and an average secured for each level. Table 4–5 shows such average profiles for those in the consideration class and the buying class. These average profiles are then compared and significant differences between them are noted.

In Table 4–5, the largest difference is the image dimension labeled *trade-in value*. Thus, it seems reasonable to work on this particular dimension to move the image of those in the buying class toward the image of those in the consideration class. The assumption is that, if an image can be so changed for an individual, he or she will change classes so that the new image will match the average image of

Table 4–5.   Ratings of Watusi, by Item, by Those Considering Watusi to Be in Their Buying Class (on scale of 1–100)

	But will not give it favorable consideration	But Will give it favorable consideration	Difference
Smooth riding	88	91	3
Styling	76	89	13
Overall comfort	81	87	6
Handling	83	86	3
Spacious interior	85	85	0
Luxurious interior	79	85	6
Quality of workmanship	80	83	3
Advanced engineering	77	83	6
prestige	73	82	9
Value for the money	76	79	3
Trade-in value	59	77	18
Cost of upkeep and maintenance	63	67	4
Gas economy	58	58	0

Source: Gail Smith, "How GM Measures Ad Effectiveness," in Keith K. Cox, ed., Readings in Market Research (New York: Appleton-Century-Crofts, 1967), p.176.

"his or her class." Perhaps this is an extreme assumption. It places undue stress on the average. Nevertheless, this approach does have appeal.

To implement these hypothetical conclusions properly, it is necessary to reach those in the level of interest, in this case, the buying class. The survey information reported in Table 4-3 includes a media-consumption section. Using these data, it may be possible to identify media vehicles that will be effective in reaching those in the buying class. Furthermore, it may be possible to reach those in that class who have a low impression of the trade-in value of the Watusi automobile. Thus, to the extent that vehicles can be so identified, the cost of changing the image of the average profile is minimized.

SUMMARY. . . . .

Operational objectives provide criteria for decision making, standards against which to evaluate performance, and serve as a communication tool. Short-run sales usually do not provide the basis for operational objectives for two reasons: (1) advertising is usually only one of many factors influencing sales, and (2) the impact of advertising often occurs primarily over the long run.

The development of more operational objectives involves three considerations. First, the behavioral decisions or actions that advertising is attempting to influence need to be analyzed. The relevant behavior could be visiting a retailer, trying a new brand, increasing usage levels, increasing share-of-requirements, maintaining existing brand loyalties, or donating money to a charity. Second, the communication and decision process that precedes and influences that behavior should be examined. This process will usually involve constructs like awareness, image, or attitude. Third, the specification of the target segment needs to be specified. Segment defining variables that are often useful include usage, benefits sought, awareness level, brand perceptions, and life-style.

This approach to setting objectives is a refinement and extension of an approach developed over a decade ago and known as the DAGMAR approach. This approach defines an advertising goal as a specific communication task to be accomplished among a defined audience in a given time period. Thus, a communication task is involved, as opposed to a marketing task, based on a hierarchy model of the communication process involving awareness, comprehension, attitude, and action. The goal is specific, with a definite measure, a starting point, a defined audience, and a fixed time period.

By introducing behavioral science theory into advertising management, the DAGMAR model provides the framework for the development of more operational objectives. However, it has been challenged through the years on several fronts. Some critics believe that the only appropriate measure of advertising is sales. Another objection is that it is difficult to select a hierarchy level on which to base objectives and to know how to move people up the hierarchy. Others believe that the approach is limited by measurement problems and noise in the system. By providing guidance to operating people, the DAGMAR approach is said to inhibit the development of "the great idea."

Another criticism is that a single hierarchy model of the communication process is not appropriate, and that different hierarchies may be relevant in different kinds of situations. A crucial question in many advertising campaigns therefore is to determine which intervening variable is most important in leading to sales in different situations, and consequently needs to be the focus of the campaign. Here, research conducted over the last thirty years on "how advertising works" needs to be examined (see Chapter 5). In addition, the advertiser also needs to determine those hierarchy levels that have not yet been reached by large numbers of potential customers. An extension of this approach is to consider not only the size of the segment but the difficulty and, therefore, cost of moving them up the hierarchy, as weall as the likelihood of their eventually making the desired decision (e.g., to buy an automobile) once they have moved up.

DISCUSSION QUESTIONS

1. What are operational objectives? Consider various organizations. By research or by speculation, determine their objectives. Are they operational? Is profit maximization an operational business objective? Is sales maximization an operational advertising objective? Under what circumstances might it be?
2. Evaluate the judgment of a brand manager of Budweiser beer who decides that the goal of his advertising should be to remind people of the brand.
3. Why might advertising have an impact many years after it appears?
4. Distinguish between a communication objective and a marketing objective.
5. What is the difference between brand image or personality, brand comprehension, and brand attitude?
6. How would you go about selecting which advertising response variable on which to base an advertising objective?
7. If awareness does not affect sales, why bother to measure it? If it does have a close relationship to sales, why not measure sales directly? Comment.
8. What is the "great idea" concept? Identify some campaigns that would qualify. Attempt to specify a set of DAGMAR objectives that might apply. Is the DAGMAR approach inconsistent with the hope of obtaining a truly brilliant creative advertising campaign?
9. Consider the CAPP data of Figure 4–14. Suppose that brand acceptance was 50 percent but brand preference was only 3 percent. What would be your diagnosis if you were a brand manager for a cereal? For an appliance? What if the brand awareness were 90 percent but brand acceptance were only 30 percent?
10. In the Watusi example, it was suggested that the trade-in value would be a good appeal to use. What were the assumptions that underlie that conclusion? Given Table 4–5, under what conditions would it be worthwhile to focus on the "spacious interior"?
11. Two case studies were presented in the chapter, Overseas Airline Service and Electrical Appliances. Two more are presented with the appendix, Regional

Brand of Beer and Cranberries. For each of the four consider the following questions:

a. Were the principles of the DAGMAR approach followed to the letter?

b. What objectives would you establish for the upcoming period?

NOTES. . . . .

1. *The New York Times*, January 18, 1993, p. C11.
2. *The New York Times*, January 10, 1990, p. C6.
3. D. G. Clarke, "Econometric Measurement of the Duration of Advertising Effect on Sales," *Journal of Marketing Research*, 13 (November 1986), 345–357.
4. Adrian J. Slywotzky and Benson P. Shapiro, "Leveraging to Beat the Odds: The New Marketing Mind-Set," *Harvard Business Review*, Sept.–Oct. 1993, pp. 97–107.
5. Bickley Townsend, "Market Research that Matters," *American Demographics*, August 1992, pp. 58–60.
6. Josh McQueen, "The Different Ways Ads Work," *Journal of Advertising Research*, Aug./Sept. 1990, RC-13–RC-16.
7. Colin McDonald, "The Key is to Understand Consumer Response," *Journal of Advertising Research*, 33, no. 5 (Sept./Oct. 1993), 63–69; A. S. C. Ehrenberg, "Repetitive Advertising and the Consumer," *Journal of Advertising Research*, April 1974.
8. Gerald Tellis, "Advertising Exposure, Loyalty, and Brand Purchase: A Two-Stage Model of Choice," *Journal of Marketing Research*, 25 (May 1988), 134–144.
9. See, for example, Vinay Kanetkar, Charles B. Weinberg, and Doyle L. Weiss, "Price Sensitivity and Television Advertising Exposures: Some Empirical Findings," *Marketing Science*, 11, no. 4 (Fall 1992), 359–371, for a review.
10. "Cambell turns up heat on soup," *Advertising Age*, July 5, 1993, p. 1.
11. Brian Wansink and Michael L. Ray, "Estimating an Advertisement's Impact on One's Consumption of A Brand," *Journal of Advertising Research*, 32, no. 3 (May/June 1992), 9–16.
12. Jack J. Honomichl, "The Ongoing Saga of 'Mother Baking Soda,'" *Advertising Age*, September 20, 1982, pp. M2–M3.
13. William J. McGuire, "An Information Processing Model of Advertising Effectiveness," in H. L. Davis and A. J. Silk (eds.), *Behavioral and Management Science in Marketing* (New York: Ronald Press, 1978), pp. 156–180.
14. Russell H. Colley, *Defining Advertising Goals for Measured Advertising Results* (New York: Association of National Advertisers, 1961).
15. Robert J. Lavidge and Gary A. Steiner, "A Model for Predictive Measurements of Advertising Effectiveness," *Journal of Marketing*, 25 (October 1961), 59–62.
16. Colley, *Defining Advertising Goals*, p. 31.
17. Ibid., p. 83.
18. Ibid., p. 73.
19. Michael Halbert, "What Do We Buy with an Advertising Dollar?" Speech presented at the Ninth Annual Seminar in Marketing Management, Miani University, Oxford, Ohio, May 1961.
20. Robert J. Schreiber and Valentine Appel, "Advertising Evaluation Using Surrogate Measures for Sales," *Journal of Advertising Research* (December 1990/January 1991), pp. 27–31.
21. Leo Bogart, *Strategy in Advertising* (New York: Harcourt Brace Jovanovich, 1967).
22. Anthony L. Morgan, "Who's Killing the Great Advertising Campaigns of America?" *Journal of Advertising Research*, 24 (December 1984/January 1985), 33–37.
23. John C. Maloney, "Attitude Measurement and Formation." Paper presented at the Test Market Design and Measurement Workshop, American Marketing Association, Chicago, April 21, 1966.

24. Gail Smith, "How GM Measures Ad Effectiveness," in Keith K. Cox, ed., *Readings in Market Research* (New York: Appleton-Century-Crofts, 1967).

25. Andy Hardy, "GM's New Philosophy for Developing and Assessing Effective Advertising." Paper presented at a conference of the Marketing Science Institute, June 8, 1988.

APPENDIX: ADDITIONAL CASE STUDIES . . . .

Regional Brand of Beer

The subject brand of beer has been the largest selling brand in its headquarters market for generations. The company has gradually expanded distribution into contiguous markets and now distributes in over a dozen states. Company policy was to avoid entering a new market until it is ready to go all out on advertising and distribution. During the first year in a new market, advertising expense, as a percentage of sales, runs three or four times the normal expenditure in an established market. It may take two or three years to reach the break-even point.

When first entering a new market, brand awareness is low. It is necessary to match or outspend the largest selling brand in order to capture a share of the consumer's attention and gradually woo him or her to try the brand. Management believed that anyone who is not prepared to enter competitive combat, quantitatively and qualitatively, is wasting money trying to open up new markets in this industry.

The advertising objective was to attain deep and incessant exposure. The goal was to establish an 80 percent level of brand identity among moderate to heavy beer drinkers in the market area within six months and to maintain that level thereafter. Through a series of simple unaided and aided recall tests, consumers were asked to identify various brands of beer sold and advertised in the market area. Experience in past market introductions had shown that the brand had always succeeded in getting a firm foothold in a market in which an 80 percent brand-awareness level had been established. Once the brand name was established through "investment" advertising, expenditures as a percentage of the sales dollar returned to a normal level.

Cranberries

A hypothetical trade association was made up of growers of cranberries that included many small producers who cannot afford to advertise individually. Consumption of cranberries is highly seasonal, traditionally during the Thanksgiving and Christmas seasons. A poor season, because of weather or other conditions, threatened to wipe out many producers who depended on this single crop for their livelihood. Land was unsuitable for crop diversification. Hence, the salvation of many growers was found in better marketing. Broad marketing objectives were (1) to increase consumption of cranberries and (2) to diversify use of cranberries so that marketing activities were not crowded into one short season.

MARKETING STRATEGY. The marketing strategy was to develop new uses of product and create consumer demand through advertising, publicity, and promotion. The first step was to engage food technologists and home economists to develop delectable new recipes. The result was an exciting new product, cranberry bread, was developed and tested.

ADVERTISING GOALS.   The company intends to spread the word among homemakers that cranberry bread is delicious, easy to bake, and a culinary accomplishment that will bring praise to the cook by all who taste it. Specifically, these one-year goals were set:

Awareness (have heard about cranberry bread): 50 percent of market
Favorable attitude (would like to bake it): 25 percent of market
Action (have baked it): 10 percent of market

Since advertising funds of cranberry growers were very limited, it was necessary to get participation and tie-in advertising of others who would benefit, such as flour millers and nut growers. With advertising as the pivotal force, retailers were willing to devote display space, food editors treated the new item editorially, and manufacturers of flour and other products were persuaded to include recipes on packages.

Proof of advertising performance was needed to convince all the cooperating groups of the success of the initial effort and of the advantages of continued support. The sales volume of cranberries was not, by itself, a suitable index of advertising effectiveness. The entire crop is always disposed of, if necessary, at distress prices. Furthermore, price received is not a reliable index since abundance of crops is governed by weather and other factors. Hence, measurement of the effectiveness of advertising alone was needed. Measurement was accomplished through a simple consumer panel survey to determine the percentage of homemakers who had heard about, wanted to try, or had actually baked the product. Results clearly indicated success of the first year's campaign and the desirability of continued promotional efforts, with emphasis on converting those who know about the product to repetitive users.

DIAGNOSTIC CASE* . . . .

The following data have been collected in five samples.

Measure	Case 1	Case 2	Case 3	Case 4	Case 5
Brand awareness	30%	80%	80%	80%	80%
Favorable attitude toward brand	25	25	45	45	10
Purchased brand once	23	23	23	35	35
Repeat purchase	20	20	20	30	8

In case 1, 30 percent of all respondents were aware of the brand being examined. Twenty-five percent indicated that they had a favorable attitude toward the brand. All of these people were ones who were aware of the brand. Twenty-three percent of all respondents purchased the brand, and all of these were from among those who were favorable toward it. Finally 20 percent purchased the brand more than once.

For each of the five cases described, identify the problem, if any, and indicate your course of action to remedy the problem.

*Source: Professor Brian Sternthal, J. L. Kellogg Graduate School of Management, Northwestern University. Reproduced by permission.

5 HOW ADVERTISING WORKS: SOME RESEARCH RESULTS

> "Because you see," says Bloom, "for an advertisement you must have repetition. That's the whole secret."
> (from *Ulysses*, by James Joyce)

> "Just the place for a Snark! I have said it thrice: What I tell you three times is true."
> (from *The Hunting of the Snark*, by Lewis Carroll)

The graveyard of ad campaigns is littered with cases where the campaign failed because the agency and/or the advertiser chose the wrong advertising objective. In the automotive field, for example, Isuzu created an attention-getting and memorable character called Joe Isuzu, who drew attention with his clearly labeled lies about Isuzu cars, but the ads didn't sell too many Isuzu cars. The campaign was eventually changed and the agency fired.[1] Similarly, Subaru fired Weiden and Kennedy in July 1993 after its high-profile campaign for that agency also failed to sell many cars.[2]

While there are always multiple reasons for such a failure, it would seem that in this case, one contributing factor was the fact that the ads succeeded admirably in creating high recall but were weaker on the persuasion (attitude changing) dimension. Consumers remembered Joe Isuzu but not why Isuzu cars were the ones worth checking out at a dealership. Since consumers are likely to buy their cars rather carefully based on a careful assessment of features and benefits, rather than merely on the basis of which car ad campaigns come to mind first, this was most likely a major strategic blunder.

Obviously, therefore, it would have been worth the agency's time to spend some time thinking more carefully about what exactly their goals and objectives ought to have been—what kind of communication effect they needed to achieve. Chapter 3 discussed, in general terms, the process of setting operational and measurable objectives, be they ones of awareness, or attitude change, and so on. This chapter moves on to the issue of choosing among the alternative goals and objectives: exactly which kind of communication effect should the ad attempt to achieve?

As outlined in Figure 2–3 of Chapter 2, advertising can affect consumers in various ways, and the mechanism—or "route" of effect—sought in any particular situation needs to be clearly specified and understood before an ad can actually be created. Should the element influenced by advertising be changes in attitudes, awareness, brand personality, the social norms concerning the brand, or the feelings associated with it? Or, should it simply be the inducement of some kind of action? Should certain kinds of thoughts be evoked in the consumer's mind?

Questions like these can be answered better once we have an understanding of how advertising "works" in different types of situations. Because of the visibility of advertising and because it touches all our lives, everyone has a pet theory of how advertising has its (supposedly strong and pernicious) effects. It is said that every person is an expert in two fields—the field in which he or she is really an expert, and in advertising. However, while our common sense and intuition may indeed be accurate, they may also be wrong, and so it is useful to review what scientific research has revealed—or suggests—about how advertising really works. Such research results can help us challenge and reassess the validity of the many myths and pieces of conventional wisdom that populate the advertising business and guide us to better advertising decision making.

Such research-based insights can change our very basic understanding of how consumers process advertising. For example, while discussing objective setting earlier in Chapter 4, we relied primarily on a single hierarchy of response model in which awareness preceded attitudes, which, in turn, led to buying action. Taken literally, this hierarchy would suggest that advertisers should always first create advertising to increase awareness, follow up with a campaign to change attitudes, and subsequently aim to induce trial action. Is this always true? If not, what implications might it have for how we design ads?

As we indicated in Chapter 4, the choice of which objective to set for one's advertising campaigns is, in fact, not as simple as the DAGMAR hierarchy implies, and different hierarchies might indeed be relevant in different situations. A tremendous amount of research exists on which hierarchy level should be the target of advertising for what kinds of brands and consumer segments and marketing situations, and it is clearly in the advertiser's interest to become familiar with this research so that the choice of advertising objective can be made in a more informed manner.

In this chapter, therefore, we discuss what research has to tell us about what kind of effect an ad should try to create, in what kind of situation. To do this, we review several streams of research that bear on the question of how advertising "works," discussing these research results in the order of their historical development. The following chapters in the book discuss more specific guidance on *how* ads can be used to change attitudes, create awareness, associate feelings with the brand, and so on. Before we get to that, however, we need to understand *when* each of these *target variables* becomes more important. The objective in reviewing these different research streams is to create such understanding.

RESEARCH STREAM ONE: FOCUS ON EXPOSURE, SALIENCE, AND FAMILIARITY. . . . .

Some ads have very low information content and yet seem to be effective at affecting attitudes, particularly with repetition (as James Joyce aptly observed in the opening quote for this chapter). Why? Some answers will be provided in Chapter 16, when repetition is discussed. However, one explanation considered here is that repeated exposure to an advertised brand can, by itself, create a liking for it.

The most extreme and controversial version of this *mere exposure effect* was initially offered in the late 1960s by a prominent psychologist, R. B. Zajonc, who hypothesized that preference is created simply from repeated exposure, with no associated cognitive activity.[3] In one study, for example, researchers presented subjects with a series of polygons, at different levels of repetition.[4] They then exposed the subjects to pairs of polygons, asking which one they had seen previously and which one was new, and which they preferred. The previously exposed polygons were preferred even though there was no recognition above chance levels as to which they had actually seen previously. This implies that the exposure effect occurred at some preconscious level, and not simply because subjects preferred those polygons they thought they had seen earlier.

Other research has also shown that aspects of advertisements (such as whether they are dominated by pictures or text) can make us like or dislike these advertisements through effects at this *preattentive* level, without our being aware of these effects.[5] There is continuing academic debate about the extent to which these preattentive effects are *cognitive* or *affective*, with no clear resolution.[6]

Clearly, one must be careful in jumping from research on polygons to making decisions about advertising processing, because advertisements (unlike polygons) contain meaningful information and can therefore be cognitively processed. Nevertheless, these studies suggest that advertising repetition may in some situations itself lead to preference, even if consumers don't absorb information on product benefits, and so on. It is therefore clear that keeping brand awareness at a high level should often be considered as a possible advertising objective.

Such *brand salience* or *top-of-mind awareness* is especially important when the advertising is aimed not so much at getting new customers, but at making existing customers buy a particular brand even more frequently, by increasing the proportion of times they select this brand instead of other brands in the category (its share-of-requirements, discussed earlier in Chapter 4). A. S. C. Ehrenberg, Gerald Tellis, and others have emphasized that, for most mature brands, advertising serves mostly to reinforce (rather than create) brand preference, in the face of competitive advertising, and that one way of reinforcing it is to have high levels of *reminder advertising,* that use frequent repetition.[7]

A related view of the exposure effect suggests that repeated exposure creates a conscious sense of *familiarity* with the brand, which then causes liking. The concept here is that familiar, known objects are evaluated more highly than are unknown objects with associated uncertainty. Perhaps uncertainty creates a tension, which is undesirable. Or, familiarity may create positive feelings of comfort, security, ownership, or intimacy. As the advertising researcher H. E. Krugman has pointed out, a product is often preferred not because it is indeed better but because of "the pleasure of its recognition . . . sheer familiarity."[8]

This familiarity model would explain why people develop positive attitudes toward brands and advertisements that are recognizable, even if these people cannot provide any facts about the brands. Although the *familiarity model*, like the *mere exposure model*, may not involve any in-depth cognitive activity (this is a topic for much academic debate), there is evidence proving that people can actually perceive objects faster if they are familiar with them, a phenomenon called *perceptual fluency*. Such perceptual fluency is believed to lead to the feeling of familiarity people experience when they encounter these previously repeated objects.[9]

Again, this evidence suggests that creating such familiarity, through awareness-building advertising (as well as extensive distribution, etc.) should be a more important advertising objective in situations when consumers are unlikely to extract much meaningful, "hard" information from advertisements.

Recently, Scott A. Hawkins and Stephen J. Hoch found that when consumers processed ads under low-involvement conditions (described in more detail below) they began to believe statements about a brand to be more true simply as a function of how often those statements were repeated to them in advertising. In other words, those assertions were felt to be "more true" simply because they were repeated more frequently. These effects emerged even though the consumers were not processing the ad information evaluatively.[10]

Relatedly, research by Amna Kirmani and Peter Wright also suggests that consumers sometimes use the perceived amount of advertising (judged by ad size, ad frequency, etc.) they see for a brand as an indicator of the brand's quality and of the advertiser's willingness to back that high quality with a high degree of marketing effort. The implication here is that building a sense of familiarity may be especially important if the company is new and needs to overcome doubts about its reliability. Such a *signalling* effect, however, works only as long as the consumer cannot find some other justification or explanation for the high spending level, such as a belief that the company is spending so much because it is desperate to move merchandise; such negative beliefs may arise especially when the perceived level of ad spending appears excessive to consumers.[11]

Implications for Managers

Together, the research reviewed above seems to suggest that a high level of ad repetition is especially important when consumers don't process ads with a view to extracting much information from them. When ads are likely to be processed in such a shallow manner, a high level of ad repetition can lead to brand preference simply because that brand is now top-of-mind, feels familiar and comfortable, is preconsciously liked, is perceived to be more believable, and feels safer and more trusted.

RESEARCH STREAM TWO: LOW-INVOLVEMENT LEARNING . . . .

In the DAGMAR hierarchy discussed in Chapter 4, comprehension of advertising content leads to attitude change. An alternative view is Krugman's classic model of television advertising, *low-involvement learning*, first offered in 1965.[12] Krugman, who at that time was an advertising manager with General Electric, observed that when products are advertised on television, consumers have little opportunity to think deeply about them because TV ads cannot be slowed down or stopped to be viewed at the consumer's pace. In contrast, a consumer can linger over and return to a print ad that he or she likes, thus relating more cognitively to the ad. If people don't learn much information from TV ads, then just how do TV ads have their effect?

In a study comparing consumer thoughts in response to TV ads versus print ads, Krugman found that TV ads yielded fewer responses linking the ad to a person's own life. Krugman observed, however, that despite their apparent inability to communicate much information, TV ads nonetheless did appear to increase brand preference, after repetition. He reasoned that perhaps repeated TV ads led to a gradual perceptual change in the consumer about what the brand represented. Thus, a brand might be considered primarily "modern" instead of being primarily "reliable. However, repeated exposure to an advertising message can alter the viewer's frame of reference and now give reliability the primary role in organizing the concept of the brand.

This subtle change in cognitive structure provides the potential to see a brand differently and can trigger a behavioral event such as an in-store purchase of the brand. This act of buying, or trial, event can then subsequently generate an attitude change or adjustment that is more consistent with the shift in perceptual structure. Thus, in low-involvement situations, product adoption can be characterized in Krugman's terms as occurring through gradual shifts in perceptual structure, aided by repetitive advertising in a low-involvement medium such as television, activated by behavioral choice situations, and followed at some time by a change in attitude.

Further work on such low-involvement learning was reported by Michael L. Ray and colleagues in a series of repetition studies done at Stanford University in the early 1970s.[13] In essence, they argued that when the products involved were of low risk and low interest (and thus of low involvement) to the consumer, and when the ads involved were television ads, advertising did not lead to an information-based attitude change, which then led to trial. Instead, the ads appeared to lead to trial simply because of greater top-of-mind awareness; this trial then led to attitude change. In short, in low-involvement situations the sequence of advertising effects was not

cognitive (product features) → attitudinal → behavioral (which they called the *high-involvement* hierarchy, and resembles the DAGMAR hierarchy)

but instead

cognitive (awareness) → behavioral → attitudinal

In recent years, substantial additional research has been done on the concept of involvement and its importance in determining the way in which advertising shapes consumer attitudes and behaviors. While some researchers now equate involvement with the amount of attention paid to the brand information in the advertisement, others measure it by the extent to which the message is personally relevant to the consumer, or the degree to which the consumer's thoughts, while viewing the ad, concern the brand instead of the way the ad is made.[14] Regardless of these conceptual differences, there is substantial agreement that the degree to which the consumer is "involved" is of critical importance in determining which part of the advertisement will shape the consumer's final attitude toward the brand. Later in this chapter we discuss one such view, the *elaboration likelihood model*.

It is also commonly agreed that consumers are more highly involved when they consider the message content more relevant (high motivation), when they have the knowledge and experience to think about that message content (high ability), and when the environment in which that message content is presented does not interfere with such thinking (high opportunity).[15] The *motivational involvement* factor is determined both by the individual's intrinsic level of interest in the product category (*enduring involvement*), as well as more temporary factors, such as how close the consumer is to a purchase in that product category and the degree of perceived risk in making a purchase in that category (*situational involvement*).[16]

Involvement is not, of course, the only variable that determines the extent to which the consumer will process the message attribute information in the ad: there are many others, including the kind of benefit the consumer is seeking from the product category. When the benefit is primarily sensory or image and ego enhancement, for example, the advertising might need to focus more on evoking the right kinds of emotions or imagery, rather than providing factual message content.[17] We discuss these situations in Chapters 9, 10, and 11.

Implications for Managers

For advertising managers seeking to make decisions about objectives, the overall implication of this research on involvement is that when advertisers are in a high-involvement situation, with the consumer seeking rational or problem-solving benefits, the advertisers ought to have as their objectives the communication of product benefits through message content, for only that can lead to the attitude change necessary for behavioral effects. Low-involvement situations, however, should lead to the targeting of greater awareness as a primary objective, rather than the communication of attitude-enhancing arguments about why the brand is better. Research by Wayne D. Hoyer and Steven P. Brown has shown that when subjects prefer to economize on time and effort in making a brand choice, they give great weight to the fact that they are previously aware of a brand instead of probing quality differences in detail.[18]

RESEARCH STREAM THREE: CENTRAL VERSUS PERIPHERAL ROUTES TO PERSUASION AND THE ELABORATION LIKELIHOOD MODEL . . .

In the preceding section on involvement, we said that considerable research has highlighted the crucial role played by involvement in determining which aspect of the ad has the biggest effect on consumer preference for the brand. One model of advertising that focuses on the role of such involvement is the *elaboration likelihood model*, or ELM.

According to the ELM, developed by psychologists Richard E. Petty and John T. Cacioppo, a basic dimension of information processing and attitude change is the depth or amount of information processing. At one extreme, the consumer can consciously and diligently consider the information provided in the ad in forming attitudes toward the advertised brand. Here, attitudes are changed or formed by careful consideration, thinking, and integration of information relevant to the product or object of the advertising. Using our previous terminology, the consumer is highly involved in processing the advertisement. This type of persuasion process is termed the *central route* to attitude change.[19] (There may also be different types of such central processing or cognitive elaboration, varying in whether the consumer focuses on differences between pieces of information, or the similarities among them,[20] but we will ignore these fine distinctions here.)

In contrast to such central processing, there also exists what Petty and Cacioppo term the *peripheral route* to attitude change. In the peripheral route, attitudes are formed and changed without active thinking about the brand's attributes and its pros and cons. Rather, the persuasive impact occurs by associating the brand with positive or negative aspects or executional cues in the ad that really are (or should not be) central to the worth of the brand. For example, rather than expressly considering the strength of the arguments presented in an advertisement, an audience member may use cognitive "shortcuts" and accept the conclusion that the brand is superior because

- **There were numerous arguments offered, even if they were not really strong and logical.**
- **The endorser seemed to be an expert, or was attractive and likable.**
- **The consumer liked the way the ad was made, the music in it, and so on.**

Conversely, a conclusion may be rejected not because of the logic of the argument but because of some surrounding cues. For example,

- **The position advocated may have been too extreme.**
- **The endorser may have been suspect.**
- **The magazine in which the ad appears was not respected.**

Attitudes resulting from central processing should be relatively strong and enduring, resistant to change, and predict behavior better than attitudes framed by the peripheral route. Such an observation makes sense particularly if the extreme cases are considered. If a person reaches a conclusion after conscious thought and deliberation, that conclusion should be firmer than if he or she merely based attitudes on peripheral cues. Scott B. MacKenzie and Richard A. Spreng did find that attitudes formed centrally, because of higher motivation, predicted purchase intentions more strongly.[21] However, attitudes formed peripherally can still end up determining choice, especially if the "central" information available to the consumer doesn't really help in selection (e.g., when the alternative brands are highly similar, or when no brand is clearly dominant).[22]

Obviously, an advertiser setting objectives needs to predict whether, in a given context, the central route is feasible—whether audience members will actually exert the effort involved to process an advertisement with strong arguments deeply. If this is unlikely, and the consumer is more likely to form attitudes peripherally, then the advertiser is better off creating an ad with likable or credible spokespeople, rather than relying on strong, logical arguments.

Which Route?

Petty and Cacioppo have proposed the framework in Figure 5–1, which predicts when the audience member will cognitively *elaborate* and follow the central route. Two factors identified in the ELM as significant are an audience member's motivation to process information and *ability* to process information (note that their definition of *ability* also includes what we called *opportunity* earlier). Consumers are most likely to process centrally when both motivation and ability are high; when either is low, peripheral processing is more likely. These motivation and ability factors are now discussed in greater detail.

Motivation to Process Information

Central processing requires first the motivation to process information, because information processing requires effort. Unless there is some reason to expend the

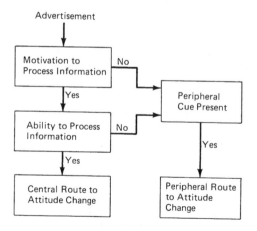

Figure 5–1.   The ELM model of attitude change.

energy or pay the price, the "hard" information in the ad will not be processed. Such effort will not be expended unless the consumer is involved with the product and associated purchase decision and unless the information in the advertisement is both relevant and important.

For an advertisement to be relevant, the consumer should, at a minimum, be a user or potential user of the product. A confirmed user of drip coffee will be unlikely to want to process information about instant coffee. There may also be situational factors: the choice of a wine for a special occasion, or a gift, will be more important than if a routine use occasion was involved. Such motivational involvement can also be dependent on the ad itself: comparative ads, for instance, get consumers more motivated to process ads centrally, compared with noncomparative ads.[23]

Ability (and Opportunity) to Process Information

In addition to being motivated to process information centrally, the consumer must also have the ability and capacity to process information. There is no point in attempting to communicate information or make an argument that the target audience simply cannot process without a level of effort that is unacceptably high.

For example, someone not familiar with the vocabulary and refinements of stereo systems or high-end personal computers may lack the knowledge and experience to process a highly technical presentation of such equipment. Durairaj Maheswaran and Brian Sternthal found that novices in a product category will not process ad information described in terms of technical attributes, rather than benefits, even when they are highly motivated to process such information, because they are simply unable to process the ad at that technical level. Novices did process the ad if the message dealt with benefits, rather than attributes, and if they were given some reason (motivation) to think about the message. Product category experts, however, required no such external motivation, because they already were interested in the category and were able to process the more technical attribute information.[24]

Media environment affects ability and opportunity as well: someone listening to a short radio ad in a cluttered and distracting listening environment may simply not have the opportunity to think about what is being said.

An ELM Experiment

A print ad for disposable razors was used to illustrate and test the ELM model.[25] Respondents were shown a booklet of ten ads. Half of these respondents (high motivation) were told that they would be able to select a brand of razor as a gift and that the product would soon be available in their geographical area. The other half (low motivation) were told they would select a free toothpaste and that the products in the booklet were being tested in another area. Half of each group were shown ads with strong arguments, such as "in direct comparison tests, the Edge blade gave twice as many close shaves as its nearest competitor." The other half received weak arguments such as "designed with the bathroom in mind." Finally,

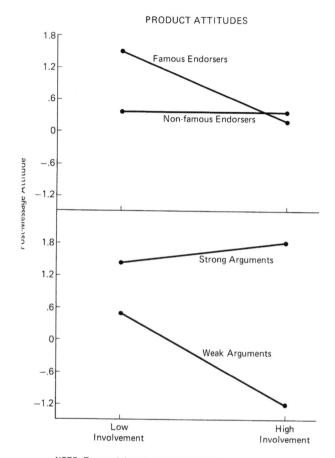

PRODUCT ATTITUDES

NOTE: Top panel shows interactive effect of involvement and endorser status on attitudes toward Edge razors. Bottom panel shows interactive effect of involvement and argument quality on attitudes toward Edge razors.

Figure 5–2.   Product attitudes.

Source: Richard E. Petty, John T. Cacioppo, and David Schumann, "Central and Peripheral Routes to Advertising Effectiveness: The Moderating Role of Involvement," Journal of Consumer Research, *10, September 1983, p. 142. Published by The University of Chicago.*

the endorser was either a celebrity (a professional athlete) or an "average" citizen of Bakersfield, California.

Figure 5–2 summarizes the results. The ELM model would predict that the celebrity status of the product endorsers would have a greater impact on product attitudes under low- rather than high-motivation conditions because, being a peripheral cue, it would be used more in the former situation. In fact, the famous endorser did enhance attitude impact only under the low-motivation condition, where the peripheral route would be employed. Further, the impact of a strong argument was considerably greater in the high-motivation condition, where central processing would tend to occur, than in the low-motivation condition of peripheral processing.

The ELM model is a useful conceptualization of attitude change, but it is not perfect. For example, if the product is one involving sensory or pleasure benefits (such as a shampoo), audience members may process cues such as endorser attractiveness centrally rather than peripherally. Remember also that processing does not have be either central or peripheral in mutual exclusion, but could consist of a blend of both. (Indeed, there is a similar model by Shelly Chaiken called the *systematic/heuristic* model that explicitly suggests a continuum of processing rather than an either/or dichotomy.)[26]

Implications for Managers

From the advertising planning point of view, the key implication of this research stream is that the motivation and ability of the target audience are key criteria in objective setting. If motivation and ability are both high and central processing is most likely, it makes sense to try to focus on changing attitudes through strong "reasons why" the brand is better. Thus, an ad selling expensive office copiers might not be best served by using a celebrity endorser, which would be a peripheral cue.

But if either motivation or ability are low and peripheral processing is more likely, the objective should be to create a likable feeling for the brand through the choice of the spokesperson and/or executional elements, rather than through the strength and quality of the arguments about the brand. Thus, because consumers don't really know much about the differences between brands, it makes sense for a scotch whisky to use an endorser (see Figure 5–3).

Some of the various consumer, brand, product category, ad execution, and ad medium factors that shape the amount of motivation and ability to think deeply (i.e., more cognitive elaboration) about an ad's message content are as follows:

- *Ad medium.* The more control the consumer has over the pace of presentation, the more likely is the processing to be central. For example, print ads can lead to more cognitive elaboration than faster-paced TV or radio ads. *Thus, broadcast media are more likely to lead to peripherally created attitudes.*
- *Involvement or motivation.* Consumers more interested and involved with the content of the ad (e.g., the product category itself) will generate more total cognitive elaboration and form attitudes centrally. *If consumers don't care much about what you're saying, their attitudes will be formed peripherally.*
- *The knowledge level of the subjects.* More knowledgeable people will be able to generate more message-related thoughts than will less knowledgeable people and will form attitudes centrally. *If consumers don't know much about what you're saying, their attitudes will be formed peripherally.*
- *Comprehension.* If the consumer cannot comprehend the product information in the ad, either because their knowledge level is low or because the time allowed to process the ad is too limited, they will tend to process the ad more in terms of the source and other peripheral cues, instead of in terms of the message arguments.[27]
- *Distraction.* If either the environment for the ad or something in the ad itself, distracts the consumer, fewer message-related thoughts are produced, reducing central processing.
- *Emotion.* If the ad evokes a positive emotion that puts the consumer in a good mood, the consumer is often less willing to spend the energy thinking about the ad content and

Figure 5–3.   Low consumer knowledge situations call for peripheral cues.
Courtesy of Schiefflelin and Somerset Co., New York.

thus generates fewer total cognitive thoughts and forms attitudes peripherally rather than centrally.

- *Need for cognition.* Some individuals are simply more interested in thinking about things (i.e., they have a higher need for cognition), and they usually generate more message-related thoughts. Thus their attitudes are more centrally based.[28]

RESEARCH STREAM FOUR: THE COGNITIVE RESPONSE MODEL . . . .

To recapitulate, research streams one through three have established that:

- In low-involvement situations, it may be more appropriate to create ads that raise awareness and change brand attitudes through executional liking and credibility, while
- In high-involvement situations, it may be better for ads to provide strong "reasons why" the brand is superior.

Ways to accomplish the former strategy can be thought of intuitively—using attractive or credible endorsers, creating likable advertising, repeating ads frequently, and so on. But exactly how do we get strong message-oriented advertising to change attitudes in the high involvement, central route?

It is natural to assume that when advertisements change consumer attitudes in such high-involvement, central processing situations, it is because consumers *learn* the content of the advertisement and that this learning then leads to changes in attitude toward the brand. If this were true, then advertisers should attempt to design ads that maximize this consumer learning of message content. It would also make sense to test the effectiveness of these advertisements by measuring how much of their content was actually learned by consumers exposed to them, by asking consumers what they remembered from the ad.

Research in the late 1960s and early 1970s showed, however, that there was only a weak relationship between what a consumer could recall about the content of a message and that consumer's attitude toward the brand in the message.[29] Instead, what appeared to be really important in determining attitudes was the nature of the thoughts that went through the consumer's head as the ad was shown, as the consumer evaluated the incoming information in the context of past knowledge and attitudes. These thoughts that the consumer has when viewing an ad are called *cognitive responses*.

Research into cognitive responses usually involves asking audience members during the ad exposure or just after it to write down all the thoughts that occurred to him or her during the exposure. A variety of types of cognitive responses are potentially relevant in such analysis. A *counterargument* (CA) occurs when the audience member argues against the message argument presented by the ad. For example, Northwest Airlines ran a newspaper ad in 1993 showing an open can of sardines and the headline, "Wouldn't you really rather be sitting in First Class instead?" (Figure 5–4.) One can imagine readers who cannot afford to fly (or don't believe in flying) first class arguing furiously with the assertion that regular coach seats pack travelers together like sardines! A *support argument* (SA) is a cognitive

FLY FIRST CLASS FOR THE PRICE OF FULL-FARE COACH ON NORTHWEST CONNECTING FLIGHTS.

Don't let other airlines put the squeeze on your business travels. As one of the new ways we're helping business travelers feel more comfortable, we're offering a free upgrade to First Class when you reserve a full-fare coach ticket to anywhere Northwest flies in the U.S. on a qualifying connecting flight. Or you'll receive double miles in the WorldPerks℠ free travel program for each segment in which First Class is not available. This offer is good for travel through December 31, 1993, and other restrictions may apply, so call your travel agent, visit your Northwest City Ticket Office or call Northwest today at **1-800-225-2525.**

General Conditions: Offer excludes Northwest Airlink. Travel in First Class using the full coach fare is valid in most domestic markets when the itinerary involves either a stop or change of planes. Passenger must travel in First Class if seats are available. Reservations in First Class are required; seats are limited. These fares may not be used in conjunction with certain certificates, coupon discounts, upgrades, bonus or promotional offers/tickets. Other restrictions may apply. © 1993 Northwest Airlines

♻ *Northwest recycles enough paper to save 40,000 trees a year.*

Figure 5–4.   Will this ad evoke SAs or CAs?

Courtesy of Northwest Airlines.

response that affirms the argument made by an ad (e.g. "I could use a product that could provide whiter clothes"). Both CAs and SAs could take several forms.

Obviously, the impact on attitude of cognitive responses will depend on the nature of the cognitive responses evoked by the ad. The basic predictive model is that the number of SAs will be positively associated with changes in beliefs, attitudes, and behavioral intentions and that the number of CAs will be negatively correlated. This predictive model has been generally (although not always) supported in dozens of studies in advertising and psychology, especially in high-involvement situations.[30] In situations in which consumers watching the ad are not particularly interested in deciding whether or not they like the brand (because they are not highly involved), their later attitudes about the brand are more significantly influenced by the execution-related responses they have (e.g., "the ad seems phony"), than by SAs or CAs about the message content of the ad.

Consumers can also have various other thoughts when they view ads, some possibly related to their own lives and experiences, with their minds going off "on tangents" based on something they see or hear in the ad. While some of these idiosyncratic thoughts can add richness and personal meaning to how they see the advertised brand,[31] others of these thoughts can possibly distract them from learning the message(s) the advertiser intended them to learn. Such distraction effects are discussed in the chapters on communication (Chapter 11) and in Chapter 12.

Implications for Managers

It seems safe to conclude that when trying to create or change attitudes, especially in high-involvement situations, it is desirable to stimulate SAs and minimize CAs. It also seems safe to conclude that when measuring the effectiveness of an ad, one must look not only at what was learned from the ad, but, more importantly, one must examine exactly what the consumer was thinking when he or she saw the ad. Finally, it seems important that while aspects of the ad's execution be put there to attract attention or increase likability, care must be taken that they not distract the consumer from the key points the ad needed to make in the first place.

How SAs and CAs Can Be "Managed"

We said earlier that to create favorable attitudes we need our ads to raise the number of SAs and reduce the number of CAs. The research to date has provided some clues as to what can affect the ratio or *nature* (positive versus negative) of the SAs and CAs that consumers have when processing ads.[32]

- *Repetition.* Studies have found that the number of CAs fall and then rise with repetition, while SAs do the reverse. As a result, the net positive balance (SAs minus CAs) is often highest at intermediate levels of repetition levels—so that this repetition level is the point at which attitudes are usually at their highest level. *It is thus important, when repeating ads, not to repeat them too often so that they begin to evoke negative responses.* Such "wearout" is discussed in Chapter 16.
- *Discrepancy from the previously held position or belief.* If the currently held position or belief matches the communication, SAs are likely, but as the discrepancy increases, so will the number of CAs. *So, don't expect to have a hostile audience won over easily.*

- *Strength of argument.* If the argument being made by the ad has some logic and strength to it, SAs are generated; if it is a weak argument, CAs are generated. *Implication: Unless you have a strong message, discourage central processing. There is an old advertising saying: If you have nothing to say, sing it!*
- *Nature of emotion being felt.* If people are put in a positive mood, either by the ad or by something else while they process the ad, they are more likely to generate SAs and less likely to generate CAs. *If you don't have a strong message, create an ad that puts people in a good mood while you tell them your story.*

Obviously, it is an advertiser's interest to increase the number of SAs generated, especially when advertising to an hostile audience. Thus, when advertising to people who have a negative prior attitude about the brand, it may help to use distraction or to create positive moods—perhaps through using humor—because these might help reduce the number of CAs produced. Thus Dr. Scholl, makers of products to fight foot odor, uses humor in its ads to get its point across.

RESEARCH STREAM FIVE: THE RELATIONSHIP BETWEEN RECALL AND PERSUASION . . . . .

It was stated above that recall of message content does not have a very strong relationship to persuasion overall because what matters more in determining persuasion is what people themselves thought when they saw your ad, rather than their memory or recall of what you told them in your ad. This general conclusion must be qualified by several factors.

Recall does indeed relate to persuasion (and thus is an appropriate advertising objective) when the consumer is in a low-involvement situation and is therefore not evaluating the brand at the time the advertisement is seen (because the consumer does not see the need for such an on-the-spot evaluation). Consequently, when such a low-involvement consumer eventually needs to pick a brand (later in time), he or she has to search in memory for facts to use in that choice decision—and brands that they can recall more about stand a better chance of being selected. In fact, increasing a brand's likelihood of being recalled at a later choice occasion can by itself itself increase the likelihood of it being considered for choice (entering the *consideration set*) and being chosen, regardless of any effects on the brand's evaluation.[33] (What matters, however, is not the sheer amount of material that can be recalled about the brand, but rather what the recalled material implies about the brand's quality and whether it is believable.[34]) These findings about the relationship between recall and persuasion in low-involvement situations fit in quite nicely with what we reviewed in the very first research stream discussed in this chapter.

The relationship between recall and persuasion gets more complicated in high-involvement situations. Another way to think about whether or not recall should be an advertising objective in such situations is to remember that recall is a necessary but not sufficient condition for persuasion. That is, if someone does not remember the ad, they cannot possibly remember what was in it and are unlikely to develop a preference for the advertised brand. But just because they remember what you said about your brand doesn't mean you convinced them, if they were looking for some other benefit altogether.

Research by David W. Stewart and his colleagues has established that recall of the ad is necessary for comprehension of ad content, and comprehension of ad content is necessary for persuasion—but such persuasion also requires, in addition to recall and comprehension, message content that sets the brand apart as being superior to competition.[35] This, of course, is what the DAGMAR hierarchy model we discussed earlier has long maintained: awareness is necessary for comprehension, and comprehension for persuasion, but awareness by itself is not sufficient to create persuasion (though awareness may be especially crucial in low-involvement situations). At least in high-involvement situations, the ad must not only create awareness and recall, but must also have message content to which the consumer reacts favorably, by generating favorable cognitive responses.

Another reason why recall may be unrelated to persuasion may simply be that whatever does get recalled about a brand at the time the consumer is about to choose a brand is simply not very relevant or helpful in that later brand selection decision. John G. Lynch, Jr., and his colleagues have pointed out that for some piece of information to be used by a consumer in selecting a brand, it must be both (1) available and accessible in memory and (2) considered more diagnostic (useful) in that brand choice decision than other remembered information.[36] Thus, even if some pieces of information (such as pictures of brand attributes) are remembered later, they may not get used (and thus have little impact on persuasion) if they are considered less helpful in brand selection than some other pieces of information available to the consumer later that the consumer considers more useful in making a choice.[37]

This means that advertisers really have two hurdles to cross. First, they must try to place into the consumer's memory those brand-differentiating features that the consumer is likely to actually *use* in making a choice and that prove the brand is *superior*. Second, these attributes must be *easily recallable* by the consumer— they should be easily *accessible* in that consumer's memory. Ways to make this information more accessible and recallable include more frequent repetition,[38] and reminder material at the point-of-purchase that *cues* the consumer to what was said by the ad when it was seen in the past.[39]

Implications for Managers:

The key ideas here are that in low-involvement situations, the simple fact that your brand is remembered may matter more than exactly what is remembered about your brand, so recall is very important and may itself lead to choice. In high-involvement situations, however, the consumer must not only be able to recall something about your brand, but what they recall must be something they consider useful in choosing a brand, and it must set your brand apart as being competitively superior. Thus, in high-involvement situations, expecting some piece of ad copy that gets high recall scores to be also necessarily very persuasive is illogical. While recall of the right material is a valid goal, recall and persuasion should be thought of as separate advertising goals in such cases, which might well call for different kinds of advertising creative executions and will require independent measures of effectiveness. We will return to this issue in Chapter 14.

SUMMARY. . . . .

Five research streams on "how advertising works" were reviewed. The first dealt with the effects of ad exposure and ad-created brand familiarity. The most extreme version of the mere exposure effect hypothesizes that liking can be created simply from exposure, with no cognitive activity at all. Such a phenomenon has been demonstrated for nonsense syllables and could provide insights as to how repetition affects the impact of advertising. The familiarity model suggests that people like objects with which they are familiar and that advertising leads to such familiarity.

Second, low-involvement learning research postulates that television advertising, operating under low involvement and perceptual defenses, creates changes in perceptual structure that can trigger a behavioral act, which, in turn, affects attitude. Related research develops this low-involvement hierarchy (behavior change preceding real attitude change) for certain types of products and contrasts it with the high-involvement DAGMAR hierarchy reviewed earlier (in which behavior follows attitude change).

The third stream of research covered the elaboration likelihood model. Here, the central route to persuasion describes an active, conscious, in-depth processing of information and adjustment of attitudes. In the peripheral route, in contrast, peripheral cues such as the credibility of the source influence attitudes, with little active thinking about the object. The central route will be employed only when the audience member is motivated to process information and has the ability to do so. For motivation to be present, the audience member needs to be involved with the product, and the information in the ad needs to be relevant and important. A problem is to determine exactly what will be processed as a peripheral cue and exactly how it will affect attitudes.

Fourth, in high-involvement situations, during or just after being exposed to a communication, the audience can engage in cognitive responses such as counterarguing or support arguing. In the cognitive response model, this activity is assumed to affect attitudes. By this model, advertising can increase its effectiveness by encouraging support arguing and by inhibiting counterarguing.

Finally, it was shown that the while recall was a necessary condition for persuasion in high involvement conditions, it was not a sufficient condition. Material about the brand not only has to be easily recallable by the consumer at the time the choice is being made, but the recalled material must also be considered useful by the consumer in making a choice in order to have an impact, and it must show the brand to be competitively superior. In low-involvement situations, however, brand recall itself is often a major determinant of choice, or at least of entry into the final consideration set of brands being considered for choice.

In sum, these research streams suggest that when consumers are highly involved in a purchase and are knowledgeable about the product category, they are likely to process ad claims about the brand carefully and use their reactions to these claims (called cognitive responses) to determine their brand attitudes. This was called the central route to forming and changing attitudes. When consumers lack the motivation and ability to process such brand information, however, their attitudes toward the brand are based more on their liking of the ad's peripheral aspects, such as the endorser or music, or on their ability to recall the brand name and their sense of familiarity with the brand.

It is therefore crucial, in deciding which intermediate variable to target in an ad, to consider carefully the nature of the consumer's motivation and ability.

DISCUSSION QUESTIONS

1. In proposing that liking can occur without any cognitive activity, Zajonc suggests that the acquisition of tastes for very hot spices in Mexico (spices that others would dislike intensely) need not involve any rational decision or cognitive activity but might involve parental reinforcement, social conformity pressures, identification with a group machismo, and so on. Do you agree that no cognitive activity is involved in the development of such tastes?

2. Subliminal advertising is that in which a message such as "Drink Coke" is flashed during a movie so fast that it is not visible but still influences behavior. Such stimuli have been shown to activate drives such as hunger, but the consensus among advertisers is that it simply does not work in the advertising context. Relate subliminal advertising to the exposure effect.

3. Do people first form beliefs and then attitudes, or the reverse? Do people change attitudes before changing behavior?

4. What other types of cognitive responses are there besides support arguments and counterarguments? How could they be useful in predicting and managing response to advertising?

5. Why might the number of CAs start high, then recede, and then increase with repetition? What else might you predict about cognitive response during repetition?

6. Contrast the central and the peripheral routes to persuasion. Categorize the other approaches covered in the chapter as to whether they follow the central or peripheral route.

7. Bring in a print ad that provides as example of a peripheral cue and another that offers an example of a central cue.

8. Provide an example of a case in which a reader of a print ad would not be motivated to process information and an example in which a reader would not be able to process the information in the ad.

9. Under what circumstances is the "standard" (DAGMAR) hierarchy model most likely to hold? When will awareness precede and contribute to brand comprehension? When will brand comprehension precede and contribute to attitude? When will attitude change cause behavioral change? In particular, consider various product classes, various usage histories, and various decision processes.

10. When is maximizing advertising recall a valid advertising objective? When is maximizing the likability of the advertising itself (through the use of a likable endorser, likable music, or humor) most appropriate? When are these two strategies not appropriate? Can you think of ads that represent examples of appropriate and inappropriate strategies?

NOTES. . . . .

1. *Advertising Age*, January 22, 1990, p. 49.
2. *The Wall Street Journal*, July 27, 1993, p. B1.
3. R. B. Zajonc, "Attitudinal Effects of Mere Exposure," *Journal of Personality and Social Psychology*, Monograph, 9 (2, Part 2), 1968, 1–28; R. B. Zajonc, "Feeling and Thinking: Preferences Need No Inferences," *American Psychologist*, 35 (1980), 151–175; and R. B. Zajonc and H. Markus, "Affective and Cognitive Factors in Preferences," *Journal of Consumer Research*, 9 (September 1982), 123–131.
4. William R. Kunst-Wilson and Robert B. Zajonc, "Affective Discrimination of Stimuli That Can Not Be Recognized," *Science*, 207 (February 1980), 557–558.
5. Chris Janiszewski, "Preconscious Processing Effects: The Independence of Attitude Formation and Conscious Thought," *Journal of Consumer Research*, 15 (September 1988), 199–209.
6. See, for instance, the debate in the September 1990 issue of the *Journal of Consumer Research* (vol. 17) on the "Logic of Mere Exposure."
7. A. S. C. Ehrenberg, "Repetitive Advertising and the Consumer," *Journal of Advertising Research* (April 1974); Gerald Tellis, "Advertising Exposure, Loyalty, and Brand Purchase: A Two-Stage Model of Choice," *Journal of Marketing Research*, 25 (May 1988), 134–144.
8. H. E. Krugman, "The Learning of Consumer Likes, Preferences and Choices," in F. M. Bass, C. W. King, and E. A. Pessemier (eds.), *Applications of the Sciences in Marketing Management* (New York: Wiley, 1968).
9. Larry Jacoby, "Perceptual Enhancement: Persistent Effects of an Experience," *Journal of Experimental Psychology: Learning, Memory and Cognition*, 9 (March 1983), 21–38.
10. Scott A. Hawkins and Stephen J. Hoch, "Low-Involvement Learning: Memory without Evaluation," *Journal of Consumer Research*, 19 (September 1992), 212–225.
11. Amna Kirmani and Peter Wright, "Money Talks: Perceived Advertising Expense and Expected Product Quality," *Journal of Consumer Research*, 16 (December 1989), 344–353; see also Amna Kirmani, "The Effect of Perceived Advertising Costs on Brand Perceptions," *Journal of Consumer Research*, 17 (September 1990), 160–171.
12. Herbert E. Krugman, "The Impact of Television Advertising: Learning Without Involvement," *Public Opinion Quarterly*, 29 (1965), 353.
13. Michael L. Ray et al., "Marketing Communication and the Hierarchy of Effects," in P. Clarke (ed.), *New Models for Communications Research* (Beverly Hills, CA: Sage Publications, 1973).
14. See, for example, Rajeev Batra and Michael L. Ray, "Operationalizing Involvement as Depth and Quality of Message Response," in R. P. Bagozzi and Alice M. Tybout, eds., *Advances in Consumer Research*, vol. 10, (Ann Arbor, MI: Association for Consumer Research, 1983), pp. 309–313; Meryl Paula Gardner, Andrew A. Mitchell, and J. Edward Russo, "Low Involvement Strategies for Processing Advertisements," *Journal of Advertising*, 12, no. 2 (1985), 4–13; Anthony G. Greenwald and Clark Leavitt, "Audience Involvement in Advertising: Four Levels," *Journal of Consumer Research*, 11 (June 1984), 551–592; Andrew A. Mitchell, "The Dimensions of Advertising Involvement," in Kent Monroe, ed., *Advances in Consumer Research*, vol. 7 (Ann Arbor, MI: Association for Consumer Research, 1981), pp. 25–30; Judith Lynne Zaichkowsky, "Measuring the Involvement Construct," *Journal of Consumer Research*, 12, no. 3 (1985), 341–352; Darrel D.

Muehling, Russell N. Laczniak and J. Craig Andrews, "Defining, Operationalizing, and Using Involvement in Advertising Research: A Review," *Journal of Current Issues and Research in Advertising*, 15, no. 1 (Spring 1993), 21–58.

15. Rajeev Batra and Michael L. Ray, "How Advertising Works at Contact," in L. F. Alwitt and A. A. Mitchell, eds., *Psychological Processes and Advertising Effects* (Hillsdale, NJ: Erlbaum, 1985), pp. 13–44; Deborah J. MacInnis and Bernard J. Jaworski, "Information Processing from Advertisements: Toward an Integrative Framework," *Journal of Marketing*, 53 (October 1989), 1–23.

16. Marsha L. Richins, Peter H. Bloch, and Edward F. McQuarrie, "How Enduring and Situational Involvement Combine to Create Involvement Responses," *Journal of Consumer Psychology*, 1, no. 2 (1992), pp. 143–153.

17. See, for example, Deborah J. MacInnis and Bernard J. Jaworski, "Information Processing from Advertisements: Toward an Integrative Framework," *Journal of Marketing*, 53 (October 1989), 1–23; Richard Vaughn, "How Advertising Works: A Planning Model Revisited," *Journal of Advertising Research* (February/March 1986), 57–66.

18. Wayne D. Hoyer and Steven P. Brown, "Effects of Brand Awareness on Choice for a Common, Repeat-Purchase Product," *Journal of Consumer Research*, 17 (September 1990), 141–148.

19. See Richard E. Petty and John T. Cacioppo, "Central and Peripheral Routes to Persuasion: Application to Advertising," in Larry Percy and Arch Woodside, eds., *Advertising and Consumer Psychology* (Lexington, MA: Lexington Books, 1983), pp. 3–23; and Richard E. Petty, Hohn T. Cacioppo, and David Schumann, "Central and Peripheral Routes to Advertising Effectiveness: The Moderating Role of Involvement," *Journal of Consumer Research*, 10 (September 1983), 135–146.

20. Joan Meyers-Levy, "Elaborating on Elaboration: The Distinction between Relational and Item-Specific Elaboration," *Journal of Consumer Research*, 18 (December 1991), 358–366.

21. Scott B. MacKenzie and Richard A. Spreng, "How Does Motivation Moderate the Impact of Central and Peripheral Processing on Brand Attitudes and Intentions?" *Journal of Consumer Research*, 18 (March 1992), 519–529.

22. Paul W. Miniard, Deepak Sirdeshmukh, and Daniel E. Innis, "Peripheral Persuasion and Brand Choice," *Journal of Consumer Research*, 19 (September 1992), 226–239.

23. Cornelia Dröge, "Shaping the Route to Attitude Change: Central Versus Peripheral Processing Through Comparative Versus Noncomparative Advertising," *Journal of Marketing Research*, 26 (May 1989), 193–204; Darrel J. Muehling, Jeffrey J. Stoltman, and Sanford Grossbart, "The Impact of Comparative Advertising on Message Involvement," *Journal of Advertising*, 19 no. 4 (1990), pp. 41–50.

24. Durairaj Maheswaran and Brian Sternthal, "The Effects of Knowledge, Motivation, and Type of Message on Ad Processing and Product Judgments," *Journal of Consumer Research*, 19 (June 1990), 66–73.

25. Petty, Cacioppo, and Schumann, "Central and Peripheral Routes to Advertising Effectiveness."

26. Shelly Chaiken, "Heuristic versus Systematic Information Processing and the Sse of Source versus Message Cues in Persuasion," *Journal of Personality and Social Psychology*, 39, no. 5 (1980) 752–766.

27. S. Ratneshwar and Shelly Chaiken, "Comprehension's Role in Persuasion: The Case of Its Moderating Effect on the Persuasive Impact of Source Cues," *Journal of Consumer Research*, 18 (June 1991), 52–62.

28. Curtis P. Haugtvedt, Richard E. Petty, and John T. Cacioppo, "Need for Cognition and Advertising: Understanding the Role of Personality Variables in Consumer Behavior," *Journal of Consumer Psychology*, 1, no. 3 (1992), 239–260.

29. Anthony G. Greenwald, "Cognitive Learning, Cognitive Responses to Persuasion, and Attitude Change," in A. G. Greenwald et al., eds., *Psychological Foundations of Attitudes*, (New York: Academic Press, 1968), pp. 147–170; Peter L. Wright, "The Cognitive Responses Mediating the Acceptance of Advertising," *Journal of Marketing Research*, 10 (February 1973), 53–62.

30. See a review by Peter Wright, "Message-Evoked Thoughts: Persuasion Research Using Thought Verbalizations," *Journal of Consumer Research*, 7 (September 1980), 151–175. See also Manoj Hastak and Jerry C. Olson, "Assessing the Role of Brand-Related Cognitive Responses as Mediators of Communication Effects on Cognitive Structure," *Journal of Consumer Research*, 15 (March 1989), 444–456.

31. David G. Mick and Claus Buhl, "A Meaning-based Model of Advertising Experiences," *Journal of Consumer Research*, 19 (December 1992), 317–338.

32. Ibid., pp. 166–171; Richard E. Petty and John T. Cacioppo, *Communication and Persuasion* (New York: Springer, 1986); Rajeev Batra and Douglas M. Stayman, "The Role of Mood in Advertising Effectiveness," *Journal of Consumer Research*, 17 (September 1988), 203–214.

33. Prakash Nedungadi, "Recall and Consumer Consideration Sets: Influencing Choice without Altering Brand Evaluations," *Journal of Consumer Research*, 17 (December 1990), 263–276.

34. Amitava Chattopadhyay and Joseph W. Alba, "The Situational Importance of Recall and Inference in Consumer Decision-Making," *Journal of Consumer Research*, 15 (June 1988), 1–12.

35. David W. Stewart, "The Moderating Role of Recall, Comprehension, and Brand Differentiation on the Persuasiveness of Television Advertising," *Journal of Advertising Research* (April/May 1986), 43–46; David W. Stewart and Scott Koslow, "Executional Factors and Advertising Effectiveness: A Replication," *Journal of Advertising*, 18, no. 3 (1989), 21–32.

36. John G. Lynch, Jr., Howard Marmorstein, and Michael F. Weigold, "Choices From Sets Including Remembered Brands: Use of Recalled Attributes and Prior Overall Evaluations," *Journal of Consumer Research*, 15 (September 1988), 169–184.

37. Carolyn L. Costley and Merrie Brucks, "Selective Recall and Information Use in Consumer Preferences," *Journal of Consumer Research*, 18 (March 1992), 464–474.

38. Ida E. Berger and Andrew A. Mitchell, "The Effect of Advertising on Attitude Accessability, Attitude Confidence, and the Attitude-Behavior Relationship," *Journal of Consumer Research*, 16 (December 1989), 269–279.

39. Kevin L. Keller, "Memory Factors in Advertising: The Effect of Advertising Retrieval Cues on Brand Evaluations," *Journal of Consumer Research*, 14 (December 1987), 316–333.

6 SEGMENTATION AND POSITIONING

> Before you look at advertising, review the strategy
> . . . your target audience, your consumer benefit, or
> promise, and the support for that promise. . . . The
> results of your advertising depend less on how your
> advertising is written than on how your product or
> service is positioned-how you want the consumer to
> think about it. . . . Just as in war, the strategy is half
> the battle. The other half is the advertising itself.
> (Kenneth Roman and Jane Maas, heads of two ad agencies, in
> *How to Advertise*)

Many marketers believe that, at least in the United States, "micromarketing" is replacing "mass marketing" in the 1990s. The U.S. market for many products for many products is slowly breaking up along regional and demographic lines—an ethnic market here, a suburban market there, a "Generation X" market here, an elderly market there.[1] As the rate of growth in overall households slows, finding unit growth means seeking out those segments that show higher-than-average growth rates. This may mean tailoring products and ad campaigns at Hispanic and African American consumers, or single-person households, or teenagers watching MTV.

Campbell Soup, for instance, has different soup flavors in Texas and California than in the rest of the country, and Spanish-language radio campaigns in specific markets to push V-8 juice to Hispanics. Where there were once Oreos, now there are Fudge-Covered Oreos, Oreo Double Stufs, and Oreo Big Stufs. Procter and Gamble has six different ad campaigns aimed at Crest toothpaste buyers—including kids, African Americans, and Hispanics. And, such micromarketing means going at these smaller consumer groups through much more finely targeted, fragmented media: not national ads on the four major TV networks, but distinctly localised ads on several hundred spot and cable TV channels, through direct mail, and on nontraditional media like store shopping carts and on videocassettes.

Clearly, most brands today cannot afford to just be one image and one selling message to one huge homogenous market out there. It is more important than ever to target specific customer groups, with specific messages. The present chapter examines this target-selection decision and considers the two most important concepts involved, segmentation and positioning. Deciding which consumers the advertising campaign should be aimed at is a critical outcome of the situation analysis process, detailed in Chapter 2. It involves considerations of market size and trends, the process of consumer decision making, the benefits specific consumer segments seek from the product category, how consumers perceive the different brands in the category, and so on.

Based on this analysis, the advertising decision maker has to decide which groups of consumers, or market segments, are most likely to be responsive to the competitive strengths of the brand being advertised. Since the competitive strengths of the brand can depend on how the brand is advertised, this identification of high-potential market segments is usually accompanied by the process of deciding exactly which aspect of the brand should dominate the advertising. What image or overall perception of the brand should consumers be left with, and what "position" must the brand occupy in their minds?

We discuss market segmentation first, followed by positioning strategy.

SEGMENTATION STRATEGY. . . . .

The term *market segmentation* was not coined until the latter part of the 1950s. Since then, however, it has had a major impact on marketing and advertising theory and practice. It is based on the rather trivial observation that all potential customers are not identical and that a firm should therefore either develop different marketing programs for different subgroups of the population or develop one program tailored to just a single subgroup. The fact that consumers differ and a single marketing program directed to all of them is not always the best strategy may seem rather obvious. Yet it is the essence of market segmentation that has the potential to improve dramatically the management of a wide variety of organizations.

Market segmentation strategy involves the development and pursuit of marketing programs directed at subgroups of the population that an organization or firm could potentially serve. A variety of marketing tools can be utilized to implement a segmentation strategy. Products and services can be developed and positioned for particular segments of the population. Distribution channels can be selected to reach certain groups. A pricing strategy can be designed to attract particular types of buyers. An advertising program can be created to appeal to certain types of consumers. Although the emphasis in this book is on the advertising plan, a segmentation strategy is not limited to any one element of the marketing program.

In some situations, the marketing program may involve subsegments. A strategic program may require a particular segmentation scheme. In implementing the accompanying advertising campaign, a more detailed breakdown of the market may be required. Suppose that an organization has decided to focus on the clothing needs of the style-conscious upper class and has selected retail outlets and product lines that will attract members of this group. In developing the advertising plan, it may be useful to divide this upper-class segment further on the basis of age, thus creating two subsegments—the young, upper-class woman and those who are older—each of which will tend to be exposed to different media and will be attracted by different appeals.

An example of the use of subsegments can also be drawn from the area of industrial marketing, which deals with the problems of marketing to organizations. Suppose that a new, small computer for use by small firms was to be developed and marketed. The market could be divided into banks, food stores, and other business categories. Assume that it was decided to develop one marketing program especially for small banks and a second program for individual food retailers. This would be a market-segmentation strategy. As the program directed at the banks evolved, it might be useful to develop subsegments: the decision makers in the bank might be divided into the officers and the data processing personnel. Thus, two advertising campaigns would accompany the direct sales programs. The one directed at the officers might explain the economic advantages of the new computer and would run in magazines that bank presidents tend to read. The other would be more specialized in content and would explain the technical aspects and potential advantages of the computer to the data processing people. Such a campaign would appear in magazines favored by data processing managers.

Concentration versus Differentiation Strategy

There are two different types of segmentation strategies. The first is the strategy of *concentration* in which the organization focuses on only one subgroup and develops a marketing program directed to it. The second is the strategy of *differentiation* in which two or more population subgroups are identified and marketing programs are developed for each. If segmentation is not employed and a single marketing program is developed and applied to all groups, the resulting marketing strategy is termed *undifferentiation*, or *aggregation.*

If a strategy of concentration is pursued and a very large segment is the target, the approach is similar to one of undifferentiation in that an effort is made to reach a broad market. Such a strategy is enticing. Marketing decision makers often attempt to determine who the frequent users of the product are and then use that information to identify the target segment for a strategy of concentration. The problem is that competitors follow the same logic. They, too, have identified the segment with the "large" potential and are directing their efforts at it. As a result, the attractive segment might have several brands fighting for it, whereas there might be a smaller segment that no brand is attempting to serve. This phenomenon is very common and is called the majority fallacy.[2] The segment with the biggest potential is not always the most profitable, once the costs of fighting many competitors is considered! It may be much more profitable to attempt to gain a small segment heretofore ignored, even if it represents only 5 percent of the market, than to fight ten other brands for a share of a large segment that represents 70 percent of the market. It is obviously costly to do direct battle with large, established competitors in a broadly based market segment.

A concentration strategy focusing on a smaller segment is particularly useful to a small firm that enters a market dominated by several larger ones. This is sometimes called a *niche* strategy. It may, in fact, be suicidal for the small company to compete with the larger ones for the large segment. However, if the small firm will concede the business represented by the large segment and discipline itself to direct its effort to a small segment with specialized needs, it may do very well. Furthermore, assuming that the smaller segment cannot really support two firms, the probability of losing the market to a competitor may then be rather small, since potential competitors will tend to avoid making an effort to secure a footing in this segment.

There are many examples of a concentration strategy. Midas Muffler does not attempt to satisfy the general service needs of car owners but concentrates instead on just servicing mufflers, a small part of total service needs. Successful computer companies, such as Cray or Tandem, have not tried to attack IBM head-on: they have concentrated on specific segments (large-size research applications and transaction processing, respectively). A boat manufacturer may specialize in one particular type of boat oriented to only a small segment of the entire boat market.

Under a strategy of differentiation, an organization does not restrict its efforts to a single segment but rather develops several marketing programs, each tailored to individual segments. These programs could differ with respect to the product lines. Perhaps the classic case of a differentiated marketing program involving product lines is the General Motors organization. Early in the company's life, General Motors decided to develop a prestige product line (Cadillacs), an economy line (Chevrolets), and several others to fill the gap between the two. The company thus covered the whole market but divided it into segments and developed a line for each segment. A differentiated segmentation strategy could, however, involve just the advertising campaign. The advertising could emphasize one brand attribute to one segment and a different brand advantage to another. Thus, a bicycle manufacturer might stress the recreational uses of its bicycle in the United States and its transportation value in Europe, where it is more frequently used for that purpose.

Segmentation is not always the optimal approach. It may be that a single product and appeal will be equally effective for everyone. Naturally, this type of strategy requires substantial resources. The Coca-Cola Company could be considered to be pursuing an undifferentiated marketing segmentation strategy with Coca-Cola. The product name, package, and advertising are designed to appeal to virtually everyone, as Figure 6–1 illustrates. It could be argued, however, that the Coca-Cola Company, too, has moved away from a pure strategy of undifferentiation, with Diet Coke, different flavors (e.g., Cherry Coke, New Coke or Coke II), caffeine-free versions, and new brands aimed at new segments (e.g. Fruitopia, OK Cola, etc.). Such a move is partly a natural evolution. As a product class gains maturity, consumer needs often become more specialized and a segmentation strategy is a natural response of manufacturers to these needs.

Developing a Segmentation Strategy

The development of a segmentation strategy can take place in two ways, described in the paragraphs that follow. In each, the objective is to identify a group of consumers that (1) are not being served well presently by competition, and are therefore likely to try our brand; (2) are large enough, or growing in size; and (3) are most likely to respond positively to the benefits offered by our brand.

Figure 6–1.   An advertisement directed at a wide audience.
Courtesy of The Coca-Cola Co.

In the first approach to segmentation, one can attempt to segment a market on an *a priori* basis, assuming that differences must exist among, for example, older versus younger consumers, or heavy versus light users. Here, the basis on which the market might be segmented is determined before any data on the marketplace are actually examined. The data are then analyzed one variable at a time; for example, we might seek to "profile" male buyers versus female buyers, or consumers in different age groups, or heavy buyers of the product category versus medium and light buyers, or buyers who live in New York versus those who live in California.

A related strategy of a priori segmentation is to identify which subgroups in the population are growing most rapidly (for example, the number of dual-income couples and single-parent households is expected to grow rapidly in the 1990s), and then aim at them.[3] The logic here is that since these segments are only now becoming large, they are probably not being served adequately by our competitors at the moment and represent an untapped opportunity.

Some bases for a priori segmentation are discussed shortly, before we discuss the second kind of segmentation, called *empirical segmentation.* In this second approach, the segments are created directly on the basis of the differences in the benefits they seek or the lifestyles they pursue, and demographic differences are then sought across these segments.

Age

A very basic but useful a priori demographic segmenting variable is *age*. People often seek different features or benefits depending upon their age (and, relatedly, their family life-cycle stage). Consequently, people in different age groups often differ in which brands they prefer within a product category, and it is sometimes possible to target particular brands at particular age groups. Researchers have found that a person's "cognitive age" is a much better predictor of purchase patterns than "actual" (chronological) age. For instance, a forty-year-old man may still feel as if he was in his thirties, in terms of interests and activities.[4]

In making such targeting decisions, it pays to also know which age group in the population is likely to show significant growth. As one example, the forty-five-to fifty-four-year-old age category is expected to grow rapidly between 1990 and the year 2000, as the 77 million "baby boomers" (those born between 1946 and 1964) move into that age category. It is useful to learn as much as possible about prospective target segments. What kinds of products and services will your target age group want to buy, what kinds of features will they seek, what kinds of advertising appeals and personalities will they be most responsive to? Some advertisers believe the "aging boomers" will respond more to "middle-age," conservative values, and display home-oriented, "nesting" or "cocooning" behaviors. And, as the under-thirty-five post-boomer or so-called "Generation X" consumers become major buying influences in many categories, some advertisers believe this segment is especially skeptical of "hype," and requires more no-nonsense, fact-filled, value-themed advertising.[5] As an example, see the Chrysler Neon ad in Figure 6–2. Such information is often collected through customized market research surveys, as well as through syndicated data sources (two of which are discussed later below).

Obviously, segments of different age groups often need different advertising approaches, both in terms of message and execution. Some advertisers argue that today's teenagers, used to rapidly-edited music videos, also need ads with such quick-cut, "jazzy" shots to have any hope of appearing "cool."[6] Both young children (under age five), and elderly (over sixty-five) consumers have special needs in the way information is communicated to them, because of differences in the way they process information compared to other consumers.[7]

Gender

Much research suggests that men and women process information from ads differently. For instance, it has been shown that women process more detailed information than do men, possibly because they are more attuned to paying attention to external cues than men are.[8] (Obviously, these are gross generalizations!). The woman manager who headed Nike's marketing campaigns to grow its womens' markets agrees, and claims that women are more discerning buyers than men, and that they research many products and weigh several factors before they buy. According to her, women—unlike men—find ads using celebrity endorsements to be unpersuasive because they "don't like being preached at." In her experience, women are responsive instead to ads that portray women as powerful, capable people who hate being told they can't do things simply because they are women. A Nike campaign empathetic to these feelings was apparently very successful.[9]

Income

Another useful a priori demographic variable is *income*. Not surprisingly, higher-income households tend to be less price-sensitive, placing a higher value on buying higher-quality merchandise. Because of the growth in dual-income households, there has been a dramatic growth in the proportion of total spending in the economy coming from such households, implying that the market for high-end products and services should increase substantially. While two-earner couples were only 29 percent of all married couples in 1960, by 1990 they formed 52 percent, and this is expected to rise to 57 percent by the year 2000. By one estimate, the number of households of thirty-five to fifty-year-olds earning more than $50,000 per annum will triple between 1990 and 2000.[10]

Geographic Location

Geographic location can often provide the basis for an effective a priori segmentation strategy. A firm with modest resources can dominate, if it so chooses, a small geographic area. Its distribution within the limited area can be intense. Local media such as newspapers or spot television can be employed, and it is possible to buy space in regional editions of major national magazines. The classic example of a concentration strategy is the local or regional organization that restricts itself geographically and attempts to tailor its marketing program to the needs of the people in that area. A local brewery or potato chip marketer may compete with national brands, but only in a limited geographic area. In response, national marketers (such as Frito-Lay) are increasingly developing specific advertising and marketing programs for specific regions of the country, often using a regionalized marketing organization. This helps the companies develop programs better tailored to regional differences: in snack foods, for instance, Frito-Lay found it faced competition from local tortilla products in the western United States, from pretzel manufacturers in the East, and from popcorn in Boston.[11]

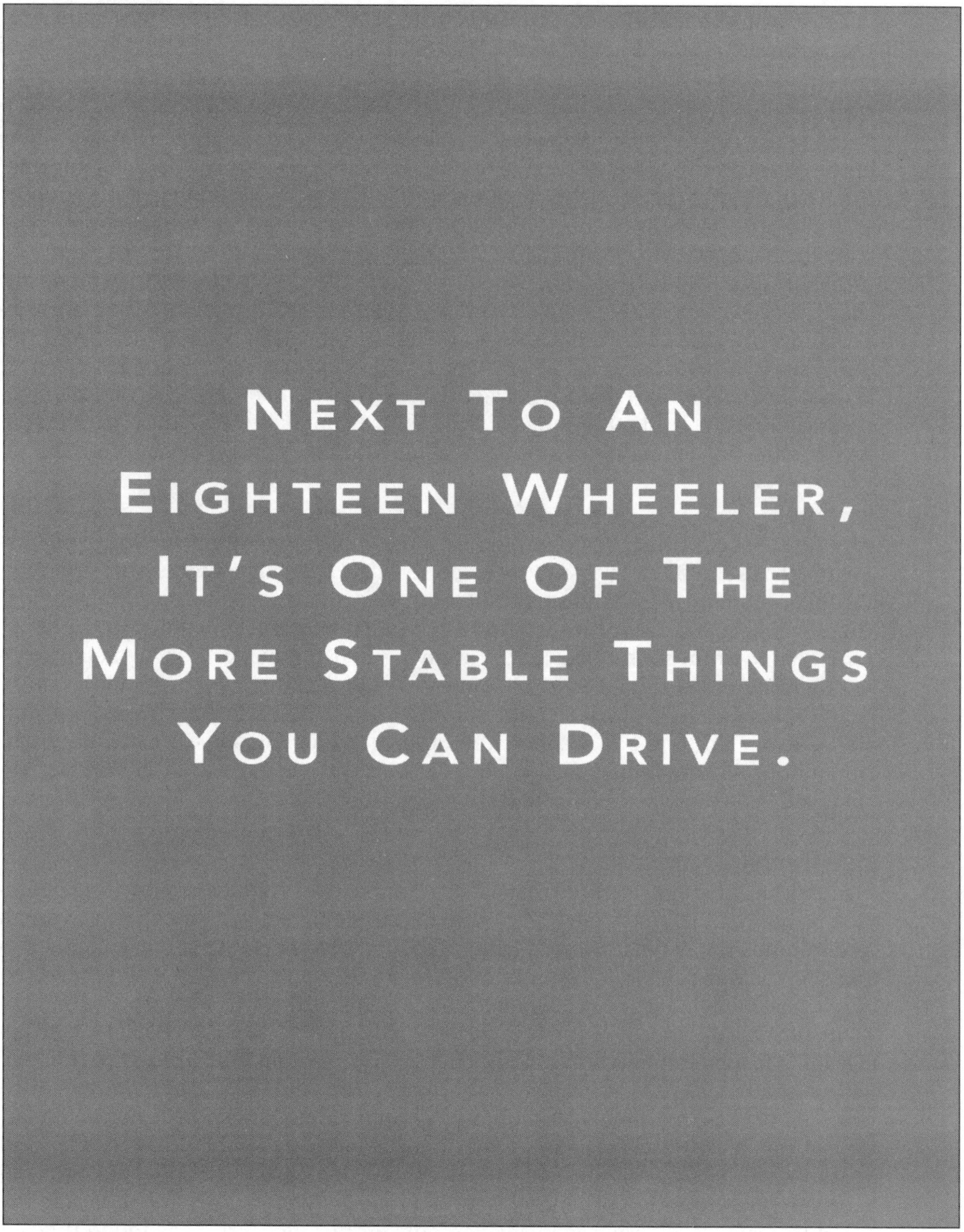

NEXT TO AN EIGHTEEN WHEELER, IT'S ONE OF THE MORE STABLE THINGS YOU CAN DRIVE.

Figure 6–2.   An ad aimed at "Generation X."
Courtesy of the Dodge and Plymouth Divisions of Chrysler Corporation.

Driving next to a big rig can be more than a little intimidating. But there's a way around that. It's called Neon. And it's *Automobile Magazine*'s "Automobile of the Year."

We pushed Neon's wheels out to the corners and moved the leading edge of the windshield forward to give it the remarkable stability that comes with an aerodynamic, cab-forward design.

We also gave it a four-wheel independent suspension. Special tires developed with Formula One racing technology. And plenty of passing power in

Hi.

the form of a responsive, 132 horsepower, sixteen-valve engine. Because while we wanted you to like the new Neon...we didn't want you to be blown away.

$8,975 F O R S T A R T E R S. $12,500 N I C E L Y L O A D E D.
ONLY FROM PLYMOUTH AND DODGE
1-800-NEW NEON

 OFFICIAL SPONSOR OF THE 1994
U.S. OLYMPIC TEAM 36 USC 380   MSRPs exclude tax & destination charge.   Always wear your seat belt.

Figure 6–2. *(continued)*

Many advertisers often target markets geographically after developing indices for the per capita consumption of their brands in each market region, relative to the national average. For example, if their sales in Pittsburgh are 2 ounces per capita per year, while the national average is 1 ounce per capita per year, then the index (called *brand development index*, or *BDI*) is 200. A similar index is created for consumption of the product category overall, for all brands combined. This index is called the *category development index*, or *CDI*. It is then possible to examine a market's BDI and CDI and decide how much advertising attention needs to be given to each market. For instance, a market with a high CDI but low BDI would be a high-opportunity market, calling for high advertising spending, while a low-CDI but high-BDI market probably cannot be developed much further and should only receive maintenance-level budgets.

In recent years, it has become increasingly possible to learn something about a company's target consumers simply by knowing the postal zip code in which they live. Census-based demographic data on households, as well as lifestyle data (collected through warranty registration cards) and automobile registration data, have been analyzed by various companies to yield "average profiles" for households in different segments, or groups, of zip codes. (These data are actually analyzed by finer classifications called *census block groups*, and the groups are called *clusters*.) In these analysis schemes, zip codes are placed into a common cluster if they have similar profiles on these variables, even if they are geographically far apart. Thus, a zip code of an affluent suburb of Chicago might be classified as belonging to the same cluster as the zip code of an affluent town in Long Island, New York, because they are very similar to each in terms of their scores on these variables. An advertiser can examine these scores of each zip-based cluster and identify which ones are most likely to respond to an advertising or direct marketing effort. Direct marketing, and these "neighborhood clusters," were discussed in Chapter 3.

Usage

A natural and powerful a priori segmentation variable is product-class *usage*. Who are the heavy users of the product or service? In many product categories, the heavy users (who are usually 20 to 30 percent of the users) account for almost 70 to 80 percent of the volume consumed: this is sometimes called the "80:20" rule. It is obviously extremely valuable for a brand to have most of its users from the heavy-user category, for that should lead to a disproportionately higher share of units sold.

One segmentation scheme might thus involve heavy users, light users, and nonusers. This particular segmentation scheme is likely to be useful wherever the focus is on building up the market. Each person is classified according to usage, and a program is developed to increase the usage level. The segments defined by usage usually require quite different marketing programs. So a program tailored to one of these segments can generate a substantially greater response than would a marketing program common to all segments. Of course, designing and implementing several marketing programs is costlier than developing one, but the resulting market response will often be significant enough to make it worthwhile.

How does one identify the demographics of these usage segments? One standard method is to use a syndicated data source such as the Simmons *Selected Markets and the Media Reaching Them*, from Simmons Market Research Bureau, or similar data from Mediamark Research, Inc. (MRI). Both these data services interview many thousands of consumers every year on the quantity of their consumption of hundreds of products and services, and the extent to which they buy the different brands available. These consumers are then classified as heavy, medium, or light users of each category and each major brand, based on certain cutoff levels (for example, someone who reports consuming more than 300 cans of soft drinks per year might be classified as a heavy user). The demographic and geographic profiles of these usage segments are then provided in tables, as are media data, using index numbers relative to the national average. One can scan the column of index numbers and find out if, for example, heavy users of ready-to-eat cereals tend to come disproportionately from certain age or income groups, or certain geographical regions. A sample page from a Simmons volume is provided in Table 6–1.

A somewhat different aspect of usage segmentation is the possibility that consumers may seek different benefits from the same product (e.g., soft drinks) depending on the nature of the usage-occasion (e.g., social use versus food-enhancement). Different ad campaigns to address these different occasion-based segments are therefore also possible.[12]

Brand Loyalty

When a brand such as Tide is competing in a well-defined product class such as detergents, it is useful to consider *brand loyalty* as a basis for a priori segmentation. Loyalty data are also available from Simmons or similar services, or from customized research. The users of Tide can then be divided into those who are loyal buyers of the brand and those who are not. The nonloyal buyer tends to buy several brands, selecting, for example, the least expensive or the most convenient at the moment. Here, the objective is to increase the proportion of this user's detergent purchases that are Tide, its "share-of-requirements". This can be done either by giving coupons in or on the pack, good on the next purchase (see Chapter 3 on consumer sales promotions), or by creating advertising that serves to reinforce the loyalty of such purchasers.[13]

Similarly, nonusers of Tide can be divided into those who are loyal to other brands and those who buy several other brands. It is usually not easy to increase usage by turning nonloyal buyers into loyal buyers, since this tendency toward brand loyalty, with respect to a certain product class, has likely become ingrained over many years. The highest potential lies with the nonusers. The nonuser who is not loyal to another brand needs to be enticed to try the brand and thus to expand the *evoked set,* the group of brands he or she buys, to include the brand of interest. A special in-store display or a cents-off coupon might accomplish this task.

Buyers who are loyal to another brand will be very difficult and very costly to attract to a trial purchase. However, once attracted, there is an excellent chance of their becoming loyal buyers of the brand, since their tendency toward loyalty is not likely to change. Obviously, however, a special display or a cents-off coupon is

Table 6–1. Portions of Cold Breakfast Cereal: Usage in last 7 days (Female Homemakers)

	Total U.S. '000	All Users A '000	B % Down	C Across %	D Indx	Heavy Users Ten or More A '000	B % Down	C Across %	D Indx	Medium Users Five–Nine A '000	B % Down	C Across %	D Indx	Light Users Four or Less A '000	B % Down	C Across %	D Indx
Total Female Homemakers	86361	75496	100.0	87.4	100	21818	100.0	25.3	100	30219	100.0	35.0	100	23458	100.0	27.2	100
18-24	7911	6803	9.0	86.0	98	1650	7.6	20.9	83	2732	9.0	34.5	99	2421	10.2	30.6	113
25-34	20745	18318	24.3	88.3	101	6164	28.3	29.7	118	6950	22.9	33.5	95	5224	22.3	25.2	93
35-44	17764	15797	20.9	88.9	102	5953	27.3	33.5	133	5562	18.4	31.3	89	4282	18.3	24.1	89
45-54	12326	10650	14.1	86.2	99	3044	14.0	24.7	98	4318	14.3	35.0	100	3268	13.9	26.5	98
55-64	10847	9545	12.6	88.0	101	2081	9.5	19.2	76	4014	13.3	37.0	106	3451	14.7	31.8	117
65 or Older	16765	14402	19.1	85.9	98	2927	13.4	17.5	69	6663	22.0	39.7	114	4812	20.5	28.7	106
18-34	28656	25121	33.3	87.7	100	7814	35.8	27.3	108	9663	32.0	33.7	96	7645	32.6	26.7	98
18-49	53038	46487	61.6	87.6	100	15297	70.1	28.8	114	17606	58.3	33.2	95	13585	57.9	25.6	94
25-54	50837	44746	59.3	88.0	101	15161	69.5	29.8	118	16810	55.6	33.1	94	12774	54.5	25.1	93
35-49	24383	21366	28.3	87.6	100	7483	34.3	30.7	121	7943	26.3	32.6	93	5940	25.3	24.4	90
50 or Older	33322	29008	38.4	87.1	100	6522	29.9	19.6	77	12613	41.7	37.9	106	9873	42.1	29.6	109
Graduated college	14461	12652	16.8	87.5	100	4117	18.9	28.5	113	4393	14.5	30.4	87	4142	17.7	28.6	105
ATTENDED COLLEGE	15754	13704	18.3	87.0	100	3853	17.7	24.5	97	5461	18.1	34.7	99	4389	18.7	27.9	103
Graduated high school	36201	31843	42.2	88.0	101	9734	44.6	26.9	106	12931	42.8	35.7	102	9178	39.1	25.4	93
Did not graduate high school	19944	17297	22.9	86.7	99	4115	18.9	20.6	82	7434	24.6	37.3	107	5749	24.5	28.8	106
Employed	49122	42748	56.6	87.0	100	12767	58.5	26.0	103	16586	54.9	33.8	96	13396	57.1	27.3	100
Employed full-time	41357	35974	47.7	87.0	100	10162	46.6	24.6	97	14055	46.5	34.0	97	11756	50.1	28.4	105
Employed part-time	7765	6775	9.0	87.3	100	2605	11.9	33.5	133	2531	8.4	32.6	93	1639	7.0	21.1	78
Not employed	37238	32747	43.4	87.9	101	9051	41.5	24.3	96	13634	45.1	36.6	105	10062	42.9	27.0	99
Professional/Manager	13838	12127	16.1	87.6	100	3919	18.0	28.3	112	4278	14.2	30.9	88	3930	16.8	28.4	105
Tech/Clerical/Sales	22113	19271	25.5	87.1	100	5750	26.4	26.0	103	7502	24.8	33.9	97	6019	25.7	27.2	100
Precision/Craft	1208	1064	1.4	88.1	101	**264	1.2	21.9	87	*544	1.8	45.0	129	**256	1.1	21.2	78
Other employed	11963	10287	13.6	86.0	98	2835	13.0	23.7	94	4262	14.1	35.6	102	3191	13.6	26.7	98
Single	11628	9637	12.8	82.9	95	1911	8.8	16.4	65	3816	12.6	32.8	94	3910	16.7	33.6	124
Married	53109	47310	62.7	89.1	102	15906	72.9	29.9	119	18815	62.3	35.4	101	12589	53.7	23.7	87
Divorced/Separated/Widowed	21624	18549	24.6	85.8	98	4002	18.3	18.5	73	7588	25.1	35.1	100	6959	29.7	32.2	118
Parents	32364	29575	39.2	91.4	105	12491	57.3	38.6	153	10267	34.0	31.7	91	6817	29.1	21.1	78
White	74071	65082	86.2	87.9	101	19504	89.4	26.3	104	25495	84.4	34.4	98	20082	85.6	27.1	100
Black	10120	8539	11.3	84.4	97	1905	8.7	18.8	75	3899	12.9	38.5	110	2735	11.7	27.0	99
OTHER	2170	1875	2.5	86.4	99	*409	1.9	18.8	75	825	2.7	38.0	109	*641	2.7	29.5	109
NORTHEAST–CENSUS	18325	16065	21.3	87.7	100	4059	18.6	22.2	88	7039	23.3	38.4	110	4967	21.2	27.1	100
Midwest	21483	19206	25.4	89.4	102	6844	31.4	31.9	126	6851	22.7	31.9	91	5511	23.5	25.7	94
South	29926	25776	34.1	86.1	99	6903	31.6	23.1	91	10279	34.0	34.3	98	8595	36.6	28.7	106
West	16626	14448	19.1	86.9	99	4012	18.4	24.1	96	6051	20.0	36.4	104	4386	18.7	26.4	97
Northeast-Mktg.	18809	16536	21.9	87.9	101	4228	19.4	22.5	89	7192	23.8	38.2	109	5116	21.8	27.2	100
East Central	12604	11075	14.7	87.9	101	3453	15.8	27.4	108	3906	12.9	31.0	89	3717	15.8	29.5	109
West Central	14706	13293	17.6	90.4	103	4894	22.4	33.3	132	4835	16.0	32.9	94	3565	15.2	24.2	89
South	25698	22096	29.3	86.0	98	5772	26.5	22.5	89	8939	29.6	34.8	99	7585	31.5	28.7	106
Pacific	14543	12495	16.6	85.9	98	3472	15.9	23.9	94	5348	17.7	36.8	105	3675	15.7	25.3	93

County size A	35301	30313	40.2	85.9	98	9057	41.5	25.7	102	12548	41.5	35.5	102	8708	37.1	24.7	91
County size B	25652	22545	29.9	87.9	101	6219	28.5	24.2	96	8766	29.0	34.2	98	7559	32.2	29.5	106
County size C	13413	11950	15.8	89.1	103	3398	15.6	25.3	100	4791	15.9	35.7	102	3761	16.0	28.0	103
County size D	11994	10688	14.2	89.1	102	3144	14.4	26.2	104	4114	13.6	34.3	98	3430	14.6	28.6	105
Metro Central City	27494	23929	31.7	87.0	100	6244	28.6	22.7	90	10152	33.6	36.9	106	7532	32.1	27.4	101
Metro Suburban	39058	33847	44.8	86.7	99	10644	48.9	27.3	108	13049	43.2	33.4	95	10134	43.2	25.9	96
Non Metro	19809	17720	23.5	89.5	102	4910	22.5	24.8	98	7018	23.2	35.4	101	5792	24.7	29.2	108
Top 5 ADI's	19248	16726	22.2	86.9	99	4565	20.9	23.7	94	7038	23.3	36.6	104	5124	21.8	26.6	98
Top 10 ADI's	26751	23086	30.6	86.3	99	6390	29.3	23.9	95	9814	32.5	36.7	105	6882	29.3	25.7	95
Top 20 ADI's	39079	33488	44.6	85.7	98	9717	44.5	24.9	98	13879	45.9	35.5	101	9892	42.2	25.3	93
Hshld inc. $60,000 or more	12765	11139	14.8	87.3	100	4088	18.7	32.0	127	3906	12.9	30.6	87	3145	13.4	24.6	91
$50,000 or more	19492	16929	22.4	86.9	99	5913	27.1	30.3	120	6352	21.0	32.6	93	4663	19.9	23.9	88
$40,000 or more	28802	25201	33.4	87.5	100	8362	38.3	29.0	115	9615	31.8	33.4	95	7224	30.8	25.1	92
$30,000 or more	41434	36284	48.1	87.6	100	12433	57.0	30.0	119	13748	45.5	33.2	95	10104	43.1	24.4	90
$30,000–$39,999	12633	11083	14.7	87.7	100	4071	18.7	32.2	128	4132	13.7	32.7	93	2879	12.3	22.8	84
$20,000–$29,999	14613	12934	17.1	88.5	101	3764	17.3	25.8	102	5210	17.2	35.7	102	3959	16.9	27.1	100
$10,000–$19,000	16772	14688	19.5	87.6	100	3084	14.1	18.4	73	6403	21.2	38.2	109	5201	22.2	31.0	114
Under $10,000	13542	11589	15.4	85.6	98	2537	11.6	18.7	74	4859	16.1	35.9	103	4194	17.9	31.0	114
Household of 1 person	13686	11102	14.7	81.1	93	1110	5.1	8.1	32	4640	15.4	33.9	97	5351	22.8	39.1	144
2 PEOPLE	29863	25572	33.9	85.6	98	4942	22.7	16.5	66	11319	37.5	37.9	108	9311	39.7	31.2	115
3 OR 4 PEOPLE	32539	29414	39.0	90.4	103	10738	49.2	33.0	131	11275	37.3	34.7	99	7401	31.6	22.7	84
5 OR MORE PEOPLE	10273	9407	12.5	91.6	105	5029	23.0	49.0	194	2985	9.9	29.1	83	1394	5.9	13.6	50
NO CHILD IN HSHLD	51214	43284	57.3	84.5	97	8509	39.0	16.6	66	18751	62.0	36.6	105	16043	68.4	31.3	115
CHILD(REN) UNDER 2 YRS	7771	7187	9.5	92.5	106	2696	12.4	34.7	137	2343	7.8	30.2	86	2148	9.2	27.6	102
2–5 YEARS	12431	11478	15.2	92.3	106	5245	24.0	42.2	167	3969	13.1	31.9	91	2264	9.7	18.2	67
6–11 YEARS	16564	15212	20.1	91.8	105	7166	32.8	43.3	171	5299	17.5	32.0	91	2748	11.7	16.6	61
12–17 YEARS	14864	13581	18.0	91.4	105	5676	26.0	38.2	151	4901	16.2	33.0	94	3005	12.8	20.2	74
RESIDENCE OWNED	58684	51791	68.6	88.3	101	15854	72.7	27.0	107	20477	67.8	34.9	100	15460	65.9	26.3	97
VALUE: $70,000 OR MORE	29899	26565	35.2	88.8	102	8883	40.7	29.7	118	10121	33.5	33.9	97	7561	32.2	25.3	93
VALUE: UNDER $70,000	28785	25226	33.4	87.6	100	6971	32.0	24.2	96	10356	34.3	36.0	103	7900	33.7	27.4	101

*Projection relatively unstable because of sample base—use with caution

**Number of cases too small for reliability—shown for consistency only

unlikely to attract the buyer who is loyal to another brand. He or she must be presented with a solid reason to change. If such a reason does exist, there is still the problem of communication, as the loyal buyer of one brand is not seeking information and, in fact, tends to avoid advertising for other brands. Thus, there is a trade-off. On the one hand, the loyal buyer of another brand is an appealing prospect because if converted she or he will generate sales dividends for several years. On the other hand, the loyal buyer is difficult and costly to attract.

Attitudes and Benefits

Attitudes, preferences, and many related psychological constructs such as motivations, perceptions, beliefs, product benefits, and so on, can also be used to segment markets through the second empirical segmentation approach. Consumers differ in the "need" for which they buy the same product, so the fact that buyers will tend to place different degrees of importance on the benefits obtained from that type of product leads logically to the fact that they represent different segments. For example, in 1993, General Motors decided to segment the vehicle market not on the basis of physical size and shape (compact car, pickup, etc.) but rather on the basis of the need being satisfied (functional transportation, fun/excitement, etc.).[14]

The idea of segmenting on the basis of important attributes has been termed *benefit segmentation* by Russell Haley.[15] He illustrated the perspective several years ago by an analysis of the toothpaste market at that time. Four segments were hypothesized, as shown in Table 6–2. The first is the Sensory segment, which values flavor and the appearance of the package. This segment tends to be represented by children characterized by high self-involvement and hedonistic lifestyle. Colgate and Stripe did well in this segment (Aim should, too, as should all gels). This segment should have high importance weights on flavor and appearance and tend to prefer brands whose product and advertising strategies have emphasized these dimensions.

The second segment, termed the Sociables, contained those who are interested in the brightness of their teeth. They are largely young people in their teens or early twenties who lead active lives and are very social. They have a relatively large percentage of smokers in their midst. Macleans, Plus White, and Ultra Brite are big sellers in this segment. The recent baking soda toothpastes would also attract this segment.

The benefit sought by the third segment was that of decay prevention. A high proportion of this segment has large families who tend to be heavy toothpaste users. In general, they have a conservative lifestyle and show concern for health and dental hygiene. Crest is disproportionately favored by this segment, which is termed the Worriers.

The fourth segment, the Independent segment, was made up of people oriented toward price and value. It tends to include men who are heavy toothpaste users. They probably are concerned with obtaining good value in all their purchases and tend to be attracted to whatever brand is on sale.

The value of benefit segmentation for advertising is seen by considering the different advertising approaches that will be appropriate for each segment. The

Table 6–2. Toothpaste Market Segment Description

Characteristics	Sensory Segment	Sociables	Worriers	Independent Segment
Principal benefit sought	Flavor, product appearance	Brightness of teeth	Decay prevention	Price
Demographic strengths	Children	Teens, young people	Large families	Men
Special behavioral characteristics	Users of spearmint-flavored toothpaste	Smokers	Heavy users	Heavy Users
Brands Disproportionately favored	Colgate, Stripe	Macleans, Plus White, Ultra Brite	Crest	Brand on Sale
Personality characteristics	High self-involvement	High sociability	High health	High autonomy
Lifestyle characteristics	Hedonistic	Active	Conservative	Value-oriented

Source: Adapted from Russell I. Haley, "Benefit Segmentation: A Decision-Oriented Research Tool," Journal of Marketing, 32, July 1968, p. 33.

copy should probably be light for the Sociable or Sensory segments but more serious for the others. The setting could also be adjusted; the focus should probably be on the product for the Sensory group, on a social situation for the Sociable segment, and perhaps on a laboratory demonstration for the Independent segment. Similarly, the media to be used can be selected with the particular target segment in mind. Television might be more appropriate for the Sociables and the Sensory segment, where there is less need to communicate hard information. A serious rational argument, possibly supported by clinical evidence, might appeal to the Independent group, assuming that such an argument can demonstrate value. A long print advertisement, therefore, might be appropriate for this segment.

As another example of benefit segmentation, the NPD Research Company identified four segments of food and beverage consumers in 1989 through an analysis of data: the traditional taste group, who liked butter, sweets, fried foods, and fast foods; the health maintainers, who place a premium on health, nutrition, and dieting considerations; the busy urbanites, who value convenience and eating out; and the moderates, who flip around a lot.[16]

Earlier, we mentioned that there were two broad approaches to segmentation, one of which we called *a priori*. Note that benefit segmentation is an example of the second kind, called *empirical segmentation*. While a priori segmentation begins by picking a variable such as income or frequency of usage and then checks if people at different levels of these segmenting variables also differ in terms of the benefits they seek or the brands they buy in the product category, empirical segmentation works the other way around. In benefit segmentation, for instance, we begin by asking people what benefits they seek in the product category; we then group them into segments based on the similarity of the benefits they seek (often using a multivariate statistical technique called cluster analysis), and we then see what makes these segments (created only on the basis of benefit importance ratings) different, in terms of demographics, and so on. It is important, in generating market segments through such cluster analysis, to make sure that the segments that emerge from the data are reliable and valid or robust, through conducting the appropriate statistical tests.[17]

Lifestyle and culture segments are also usually created through this second, empirical approach: we group people into clusters based on their similarity of personalities, opinions, activities, interests, and so on, and then see how these lifestyle segments differ on demographics and brand usage.

Lifestyle or Psychographics

A person's pattern of interests, opinions, and activities combine to represent his or her *lifestyle*. A knowledge of lifestyle can provide a very rich and meaningful picture of a person. It can indicate whether the person is interested in outdoor sports, shopping, culture, or reading. It can include information concerning attitudes and personality traits. Lifestyle also can be used to define a segment empirically; this is often called *psychographic* (as opposed to demographic) segmentation.

Lifestyle is particularly useful as a segmentation variable in categories where the user's self-image is important, such as fragrance; we therefore discuss it in some detail in Chapter 10. As an example of lifestyle segmentation in fragrances, Revlon's Charlie cosmetic line was targeted at a lifestyle segment profiled as follows:

- Is irreverent and unpretentious.
- Doesn't mind being a little outrageous or flamboyant.
- Breaks all the rules.
- Has her integrity based on her own standards.
- Can be tough; believes rules are secondary.
- Is a pacesetter, not a follower.
- Is very relaxed about sex.
- Is bored with typical fragrance advertising.
- Mixes Gucci and blue jeans; insists on individual taste, individual judgment.
- Has a sense of self and sense of commitment.

Various typologies of consumers exist that use personalities, values, lifestyles, and attitudes as variables, among them VALS and the more recent VALS 2, values and lifestyles typologies created by SRI, Inc.[18] In its first version, VALS focused on the distinction between *inner-directed consumers*, driven by their convictions, passions, and need for self-expression, and *outer-directed consumers*, driven by their responses to signals from other people. Using this distinction, it grouped people into nine categories (called Survivors, Sustainers, Belongers, Emulators, Achievers, I-Am-Mes, Experientials, Societally Conscious, and Integrateds). VALS 2 uses the additional classifying dimension of the "resources" people have (education, income, etc.) to create eight categories (called Fulfilleds, Believers, Achievers, Strivers, Experiencers, Makers, Strugglers, and Actualizers). (See Figure 6–3.)

Culture and Ethnic Subculture

Cultural segmentation is obviously important when global firms attempt to develop a segmentation strategy with the world as a market. Given the increasing importance of global marketing (see Chapters 1 and 20), and the need to gain economies of scale in marketing expenditures, firms often try to develop common advertising themes or executions for countries that have similar cultural attitudes and values.

VALS 1	VALS 2
Integrateds	Actualizers
Inner-Directed Consumers	Principle-Oriented Consumers
• Societally Conscious	• Fulfilleds
• Experientials	• Believers
• I-Am-Me's	
	Status-Oriented Consumers
Outer-Directed Consumers	
	• Achievers
• Achievers	• Strivers
• Emulators	
• Belongers	Action-Oriented Consumers
	• Experiencers
Need-Driven Consumers	• Makers
• Sustainers	
• Survivors	Strugglers

Figure 6–3.   The VALS 1 and VALS 2 values and lifestyles typologies.

Source: Advertising Age, *February 13, 1989, p. 24. Copyright by Crain Communications, Inc. All rights reserved. Used with permission.*

Differences across cultures can affect product acceptance and advertising campaigns, and there are many "war stories" of ad campaigns which worked fine in some countries but were disasters in others where they were inappropriately extended, because certain cultural nuances were missed. Again, countries are often based into cultural segments on the basis of an empirical segmentation strategy, using techniques such as cluster analysis. Chapter 20 has details.

Cultural differences are also very important within certain countries such as the United States, where different ethnic groups often have their own *subculture*. While generalizations are obviously never entirely correct, some research shows that in the United States Hispanics show higher brand loyalty, Asian Americans are more likely to shop on the basis of price, and African Americans' brand loyalty falls in-between the other two groups.[19] Among American Hispanics, those of Mexican origin (in California and Texas) differ from those of Cuban origin (in Florida), who differ from those of Puerto Rican origin (living in New York). Figure 6–4 shows an ad aimed at the Hispanic segment.

Reaching Target Segments

There are two ways by which markets can be reached: controlled coverage and customer self-selection.[20]

In the controlled-coverage approach, the objective is to reach desired target segments and to avoid reaching those who are not in the target segments. Suppose that a segment is defined as "better golfers," and it is determined that they usually read *Golf Digest.* Suppose, further, that there are few readers of *Golf Digest* who are not in the target segment. Then an advertising campaign in *Golf Digest* would be an efficient way to communicate with the target segment. Another way might be to use direct marketing techniques to mail a message to people who are subscribers of *Golf Digest*, renting their names from the magazine or a list broker (see Chapter 3). As was discussed in Chapter 3, many companies are now creating immense computerized databases on their actual and potential customers, enabling them to execute extremely targeted direct marketing programs. This technique is often called *database marketing.*

Customer self-selection is an alternative approach. Here the advertising program is directed to a mass audience of which the target segment may be only a small part. Those in the target segment are attracted to the marketing effort since it is tailored to them. Those not in the target group will probably avoid exposure, not because the program is unavailable to them, but because they either consciously or unconsciously choose to avoid it. For example, although ski equipment has a rather narrow appeal, a firm may run an advertisement about it in a mass circulation magazine. The target segment, all skiers, will be attracted to the advertisement if it is well done, but nonskiers will probably not be tempted to read it.

POSITIONING STRATEGIES . . . .

Just as segmentation involves the decision to aim at a certain group of customers but not others, our next concept—*positioning*—involves a decision to stress only certain aspects of our brand, and not others. The key idea in positioning strategy is that the consumer must have a clear idea of what your brand stands for in the product category, and that a brand cannot be sharply and distinctly positioned if it tries to be everything to everyone. Such positioning is achieved mostly through a brand's marketing communications, although its distribution, pricing, packaging, and actual product features also can play major roles. It is often said that positioning is not what you do to the product, but what you do to the consumer's mind, through various communications. Many products in the over-the-counter drug market, for instance, have identical formulas but are promoted for different symptoms, by using different names, packaging, product forms, and advertising.[21] The strategic objective must be to have segmentation and positioning strategies that fit together: a brand must be positioned in a way that is maximally effective in attracting the desired target segment.

A brand's position is the set of associations the consumer has with the brand. These may cover physical attributes, or lifestyle, or use occasion, or user image, or stores that carry it. A brand's position develops over years, through advertising and publicity and word of mouth and usage experience, and can be sharp or diffuse, depending on the consistency of that brand's advertising over the years.

A brand's position in a consumer's mind is a relative concept, in that it refers to a comparative assessment by the consumer of how this brand is similar to or different from the other brands that compete with it. Think of every consumer as having a mental map of the product category. The location of your brand in that map, relative to that of your competitors, is your position, and the locations of all the brands in that map are determined by the associations that the consumer makes with each brand. If all this sounds rather abstract, several examples are provided here which should clarify the concept.

A positioning strategy is vital to provide focus to the development of an advertising campaign. The strategy can be conceived and implemented in a variety of ways that derive from the attributes, competition, specific applications, the types of consumers involved, or the characteristics of the product class. Each represents a different approach to developing a positioning strategy, even though all of them have the ultimate objective of either developing or reinforcing a particular image for the brand in the mind of the audience. Seven approaches to positioning strategy will be presented: (1) using product characteristics or customer benefits, (2) the price-quality approach, (3) the use or applications approach, (4) the product-user approach, (5) the product-class approach, (6) the cultural symbol approach, and (7) the competitor approach.

Using Product Characteristics or Customer Benefits

Probably the most-used positioning strategy is to associate an object with a *product characteristic* or *customer benefit*. Imported automobiles illustrate the variety of product characteristics that can be employed and their power in image creation. Honda and Toyota have emphasized economy and reliability and have become the leaders in the number of units sold. Volvo has stressed safety and durability, showing commercials of "crash tests" and telling of the long average life of its cars, although in 1993 it began to emphasize other attributes as well, because by then

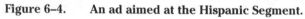

Figure 6–4.   An ad aimed at the Hispanic Segment.

Courtesy of McDonald's Corporation. Used with permission.

Figure 6–4. *(continued)*

almost every auto maker stressed safety features.[22] In the 1980s, BMW attempted to put forth an image of performance in terms of handling and engineering efficiency. The tag line used by BMW was "the ultimate driving machine." BMW advertisements showed the cars demonstrating their performance capabilities at a German racetrack. By the early 1990s, BMW, too, felt the need to show itself as a "value" car, in keeping with the trend away from luxury consumption.

Sometimes a new product can be positioned with respect to a product characteristic that competitors have ignored. Brands of paper towels had emphasized absorbency until Viva was successfully introduced stressing durability. Viva demonstrations showed its product's durability and supported the claim that Viva "keeps on working."

Sometimes a product will attempt to position itself along two or more product characteristics simultaneously. In the toothpaste market, Crest became the leader decades ago by positioning itself as a cavity fighter, a position that was established by an endorsement by the American Dental Association. However, several other successful entries have positioned themselves along two product characteristics. Aim, introduced as a good-tasting, cavity fighter, achieved a share of more than 10 percent. Aqua-fresh was introduced by Beecham as a gel paste that offers both cavity-fighting and breath-freshening benefits. Lever 2000 soap combined the moisturizing and deodorizing benefits usually found in two different soaps.[23] Sometimes different models of a product may be positioned towards different segments by highlighting different attributes: the two Timex watches in Figure 6–5 are an example.

It is always tempting to try to position along several product characteristics as it is frustrating to have some good product characteristics that are not communicated. However, advertising objectives that involve too many product characteristics can be most difficult to implement. The result can often be a fuzzy, confused image, which usually hurts a brand.

Myers and Shocker[24] have made a distinction between physical characteristics, pseudophysical characteristics, and benefits, all of which can be used in positioning. Physical characteristics are the most objective and can be measured on some physical scale such as temperature, color intensity, sweetness, thickness, distance, dollars, acidity, saltiness, strength of fragrance, weight, and so on. Pseudophysical characteristics, in contrast, reflect physical properties that are not easily measured. Examples are spiciness, smoky taste, tartness, type of fragrance (smells like a . . .), greasiness, creaminess, and shininess. Benefits refer to advantages that promote the well-being of the consumer or user. Ginger ale can be positioned as a product that "quenches thirst." Thirst quenching is a benefit and provides the basis for this type of positioning strategy. Other examples are the following: does not harm the skin, satisfies hunger, is easy to combine with other ingredients, stimulates, is convenient, and so on.

Positioning by Price and Quality

The *price-quality* product characteristic is so useful and pervasive that it is appropriate to consider it separately. In many product categories, there exist brands

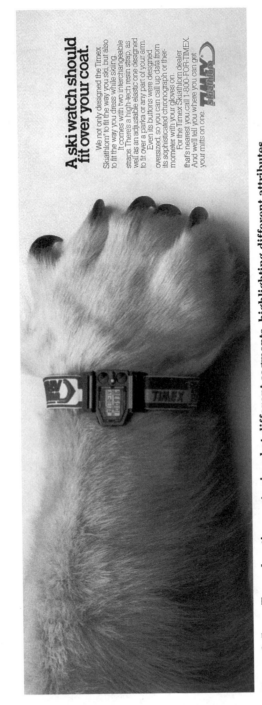

A ski watch should fit over your coat.

We not only designed the Timex Skiathlon® to fit the way you ski, but also to fit the way you dress while skiing.

It comes with two interchangeable straps. There's a high-tech resin strap, as well as an adjustable elastic one designed to fit over a parka or any part of your arm.

Even its buttons were designed oversized, so you can call up data from its sophisticated chronograph or thermometer with your gloves on.

For the Timex Skiathlon dealer that's nearest you, call 1-800-FOR-TIMEX. And we'll tell you where you can get your mitts on one.

TIMEX®

Figure 6–5. Two advertisements aimed at different segments, highlighting different attributes.

Reprint permission granted by Timex Corporation.

Figure 6–5. *(continued)*

that deliberately attempt to offer more in terms of service, features, or performance. Manufacturers of such brands charge more, partly to cover higher costs and partly to help communicate the fact that they are of higher quality. Conversely, in the same product class there are usually other brands that appeal on the basis of price, although they might also try to be perceived as having comparable or at least adequate quality. In many product categories, the price-quality issue is so important that it needs to be considered in any positioning decision.

For example, in general merchandise stores, the department stores are at the top end. Neiman-Marcus, Bloomingdale's, and Saks Fifth Avenue are near the top, followed by Macy's, Robinson's, Bullock's, Rich's, Filene's, Dayton's, Hudson's, and so on. Stores like Sears, Montgomery Ward, and J. C. Penney are positioned below the department stores, but above the discount stores like Target, K Mart, and Wal-mart. It is usually very difficult to compete successfully using both quality and price: Sears is just one advertiser that has faced the very tricky positioning task of retaining the image of low price while communicating a quality message. There is always the risk that the quality message will blunt the basic "low-price" position or that people will infer that if the prices are low, the quality must be low, too.

Positioning by Use or Application

Another way to communicate an image is to associate the product with a *use*, or *application*. Campbell's Soup for many years positioned itself as a lunch-time product and used noontime radio extensively. AT&T associated long-distance calling with communicating with loved ones in its "Reach out and touch someone" campaign.

Products can, of course, have multiple positioning strategies, although increasing the number involves obvious difficulties and risks. Often a positioning-by-use strategy represents a second or third position for the brand, a position that deliberately attempts to expand the brand's market. Thus, Gatorade, a summer beverage for athletes who need to replace body fluids, has attempted to develop a positioning strategy for the winter months. The concept is to use Gatorade when flu attacks and the doctor says to drink plenty of fluids. Similarly, Quaker Oats has attempted to position its product as a natural whole-grain ingredient for recipes in addition to its breakfast food niche. Arm & Hammer baking soda has successfully extended its fresh/clean positioning in pushing usage as an odor-destroying agent in refrigerators (as the storyboard shown in Figure 6–6 illustrates), and has recently been quite successful with its baking-soda toothpaste.

Positioning by Product User

Another positioning approach is to associate a product with a *user* or a class of users. Michael Jordan, for example, was used by products as diverse as Nike, Gatorade, and McDonald's. Many cosmetic companies have used a model or personality to position their product. Makers of casual clothing such as jeans have introduced "designer labels" such as Calvin Klein or Jordache to develop a fashion image. The expectation is that the model or personality will influence the product's image by reflecting the characteristics and image of the model or personality com-

Product: ARM & HAMMER BAKING SODA
Length: 30 SECONDS   DATE: 5/30/80
Title: "THREE BOXES"
Commercial No.: ZCTB 4035

1. HARRY: (ON) Louise! Three boxes of Arm & Hammer Baking Soda?

2. LOUISE: (ON) Makes the house smell fresher, saves money.

3. Box one is our carpet deodorizer. No cover-up perfume, and costs less.

4. HARRY: (ON) I like it.

5. LOUISE: (ON) Box two keeps the litter box fresher.

6. First baking soda – then litter.

7. HARRY: (ON) I like it.

8. LOUISE: (ON) Box three deodorizes our refrigerator...

9. (VO) better than the new gadgets and costs less.

10. (ON) Three boxes make the house fresher – and save money.

11. HARRY: (ON) I like it. I like it. BOTH: (ON) I like it.

12. ANNCR: (VO) Arm & Hammer Baking Soda.

Figure 6–6.   **Positioning by application.**

Photographs courtesy of Arm & Hammer Division, Church & Dwight Co., Inc.

municated as a product user. This strategy is discussed in more detail in Chapters 10 and 11.

Johnson & Johnson repositioned its shampoo from one used for babies to one used by people who wash their hair frequently and therefore need a mild shampoo. This repositioning resulted in a market share that moved from 3 percent to 14 percent for Johnson & Johnson.

In 1970, Miller High Life was the "champagne of bottled beers" and had an image of a beer suitable for women to drink. In fact, it was purchased primarily by upper-class socioeconomic groups.[25] Philip Morris then purchased Miller and moved the product out of the champagne bucket into the lunch bucket, repositioning it as a beer for the blue-collar working man who is the heavy beer drinker. The long-running campaign showed working men reaching the end of a hard day, designated as "Miller time," relaxing with a Miller beer. This campaign, which ran virtually unchanged for about fifteen years, was extremely successful, although Miller's market share has since then dropped considerably as they have unsuccessfully tried to find an equally successful replacement campaign.

Miller's Lite beer, introduced in 1975, used a similar positioning strategy. It was positioned as a beer for the heavy beer drinker (called "Six Pack Joe" in the industry), who wants to drink a lot but dislikes that filled-up feeling. Thus, Miller's used convincing beer-drinking personalities such as Dick Butkus and Mickey Spillane to communicate the fact that this beer was not as filling. In contrast, previous efforts by others to introduce low-calorie beers were dismal failures, partly because they emphasized the low-calorie aspect. One even claimed its beer had fewer calories than skim milk, and another featured a trim light beer personality. Of course, not every beer needs to go after the heavy users: some other light beers, such as Coors Light, have in fact tried to attract single women, depicting a very different kind of user than that shown in most beer advertising (see Figure 6–7).

Positioning by Product Class

Some products need to make critical positioning decisions that involve *product-class* associations. For example, Maxim freeze-dried coffee, the first one in the market, needed to position itself with respect to regular and instant coffee. Some margarines position themselves with respect to butter. Dried milk makers came out with instant breakfast positioned as a breakfast substitute and a virtually identical product positioned as a dietary meal substitute. The toilet soap Dove positioned itself apart from the soap category as a cleansing cream product, for women with dry skin.

The soft drink 7-Up was for a long time positioned as a beverage that had a "fresh clean taste" that was "thirst quenching." However, research uncovered the fact that most people did not regard 7-Up as a soft drink but rather as a mixer beverage; therefore, the brand tended to attract only light soft-drink users. The positioning strategy was then developed to position 7-Up as a "mainline" soft drink, as a logical alternative to the "colas" but with a better taste. The successful "Uncola" campaign was the result.

Positioning by Cultural Symbols

Many advertisers use deeply entrenched *cultural symbols* to differentiate their brand from competitors. The essential task is to identify something that is very meaningful to people that other competitors are not using and associate the brand with that symbol. The Wells Fargo Bank, for example, uses a stagecoach pulled by a team of horses and very nostalgic background music to position itself as the bank that opened up the west. Advertising is filled with examples of this kind of positioning strategy. Marlboro cigarettes chose the American cowboy as the central focus to help differentiate its brand from competitors and developed the Marlboro Man. The Green Giant symbol was so successful that the packing company involved was renamed the Green Giant Company. Pillsbury's "doughboy" and dozens of other examples illustrate this type of positioning strategy.

Positioning by Competitor

In most positioning strategies, an explicit or implicit frame of reference is one or more *competitors*. In some cases the reference competitor(s) can be the dominant aspect of the positioning strategy. It is useful to consider positioning with respect

Figure 6–7.   Positioning beer at light users: Coors Light.

Courtesy of Coors Brewing Company.

to a competitor for two reasons. First, the competitor may have a firm, well-crystallized image developed over many years. The competitor's image can be used as a bridge to help communicate another image referenced to it. If someone wants to know where a particular address is, it is easier to say it is next to the Bank of America building than to describe the various streets to take to get there. Second, sometimes it is not important how good customers think you are; it is just important that they believe you are better than (or perhaps as good as) a given competitor.

Perhaps the most famous positioning strategy of this type was the Avis "We're number two, we try harder" campaign. The message was that the Hertz company was so big that they did not need to work hard. The strategy was to position Avis with Hertz as major car-rental options, and therefore to position Avis away from National, which at the time was a close third to Avis. See Figure 6–8 for a classic ad from the Avis campaign.

Positioning with respect to a competitor can be an excellent way to create a position with respect to a product characteristic, especially price and quality. Thus, products that are difficult to evaluate, like liquor products, will often use an established competitor to help the positioning task. For example, Sabroso, a coffee liqueur, positioned itself with the established brand, Kahlua, with respect to quality and also with respect to the type of liqueur. Its print advertisement showed the two bottles side by side and used the head, "Two great imported coffee liqueurs. One with a great price."

Positioning with respect to a competitor can be accomplished by comparative advertising, advertising in which a competitor is explicitly named and compared on one or more product characteristics. Subaru has recently used this approach to position some of their cars as being comparable in safety to Volvo, which has consistently stressed its safety qualities and is thus closely identified with safety. As Figure 6–9 illustrates, by comparing Subaru to a competitor that has a well-defined safety image, such as a Volvo, the communication task becomes easier for Subaru.

DETERMINING THE POSITIONING STRATEGY . . . .

What should be our positioning strategy? The identification and selection of a positioning strategy can be difficult and complex. However, it becomes more manageable if it is supported by marketing research and decomposed into a six-step process.

1. **Identify the competitors.**
2. **Determine how the competitors are perceived and evaluated.**
3. **Determine the competitors' positions.**
4. **Analyze the customers.**
5. **Select the position.**
6. **Monitor the position.**

In each of these steps one can employ marketing research techniques to provide needed information. Sometimes the marketing research approach provides a conceptualization that can be helpful even if the research is not conducted.

Avis is only No.2 in rent a cars. So why go with us?

We try harder.

(When you're not the biggest, you have to.)

We just can't afford dirty ash-trays. Or half-empty gas tanks. Or worn wipers. Or unwashed cars. Or low tires. Or anything less than seat-adjusters that adjust. Heaters that heat. Defrosters that defrost.

Obviously, the thing we try hardest for is just to be nice. To start you out right with a new car, like a lively, super-torque Ford, and a pleasant smile. To know, say, where you get a good pastrami sandwich in Duluth.

Why?

Because we can't afford to take you for granted.

Go with us next time.

The line at our counter is shorter.

© 1963 AVIS, INC.

Figure 6–8.   Positioning by competitor: Avis Rent-a-Car.
Courtesy of Avis, Inc.

Volvo Has Built A Reputation For Surviving Accidents. Subaru Has Built A Reputation For Avoiding Them.

The Volvo 240 has done a fine job of surviving accidents. And we, at Subaru, have always admired that.

So we gave the new Subaru Legacy unibody construction like the Volvo 240.

But at Subaru, we think there's something even better than surviving accidents. And that's not getting into them in the first place.

So unlike the 240, the Subaru Legacy offers an optional anti-lock braking system (ABS). A feature that pumps your brakes automatically for maximum maneuverability and gives you much greater steering control during heavy braking.

Unlike the 240, the Subaru Legacy

is available with full-time four wheel drive. A more civilized form of four wheel drive giving you greater traction on smooth high speed highways as well as on washboard dirt roads.

And unlike most cars in the world, the Subaru Legacy comes with both four wheel disc brakes and independent suspension.

At Subaru, we know that even cars not involved in accidents can eventually come apart. So every Subaru is put together to stay together through conditions which drive other cars into the ground. Of course, we can't guarantee how long every one of our cars will last. But we do know 93% of all Subaru cars registered in America

since 1979 are still on the road.*

And the new Subaru Legacy may even surpass that record for durability. A Subaru Legacy has broken the FIA World Speed/Endurance record by running 19 days at an average speed of 138.8 mph for more than 62,000 miles.**

So you see, it wasn't just accidents the Subaru Legacy was designed to avoid. But junk yards as well.

*R.L. Polk & Co. Statistics, July 1, 1988. **Validated by the Federation Internationale De L'Automobile.

Subaru Legacy™

We Built Our Reputation By Building A Better Car.

Figure 6–9.   **Positioning by competitor: Subaru cars.**

Courtesy of Subaru of America, Inc.

The first four steps or exercises provide a useful background. The final steps address the evaluation and measurement follow-up. Each step will be discussed in turn.

Identifying the Competitors

A first step is to identify the competition. This step is not as simple as it might seem. Pepsi might define its competitors as follows:

1. **Other cola drinks.**
2. **Nondiet soft drinks.**
3. **All soft drinks.**
4. **Nonalcoholic beverages.**
5. **All beverages except water.**

In most cases, there will be a primary group of competitors and one or more secondary competitors, and it will be useful to identify both categories. Thus, Coke will compete primarily with other colas, but other nondiet soft drinks and diet colas could be important as secondary competitors. As another example, the flower-delivery service Teleflora will compete primarily with other flower-delivery services such as FTD, but also secondarily with other gifts such as boxed chocolates. *Time* magazine may compete more with the TV news shows and channels than with *Newsweek*. Such secondary competition is of special concern to brands that are market leaders in their categories, for they are the ones that need to be most considered with issues of category (*primary*) demand.

A knowledge of various ways to identify such groupings will be of conceptual as well as practical value. One approach is to determine from buyers of a product which other products they considered. For example, a sample of cola drinkers might be asked what other beverages they might have consumed instead. Or, the respondent could be asked what brand would have been purchased had that particular cola brand been out of stock. The resulting analysis will identify the primary and secondary groups of competitive products. Instead of customers, retailers or buyers knowledgeable about customers could provide the information.

Another approach is the development of associations of products with use situations.[26] A respondent might be asked to keep a diary or to recall the use contexts for Pepsi. One might be with an afternoon snack. The respondent could then be asked to name all the beverages that would be appropriate to drink with an afternoon snack. For each beverage so identified, the respondent could be asked to identify appropriate use contexts so that the list of use contexts was more complete. This process would continue for perhaps twenty or thirty respondents until a large list of use contexts and beverages resulted. Another group of respondents would then be asked to make a judgment, perhaps on a seven-point scale, as to how appropriate each beverage would be for each use situation. Then, groups of beverages could be clustered based on their similarity of appropriate use situations. Thus, if Pepsi was regarded as appropriate with snacks, it would compete primarily with other beverages regarded as appropriate for snack occasions. If it was not regarded as appropriate for use with meals, it would be less competitive with beverages deemed more appropriate for meals.

These two approaches suggest a conceptual basis for identifying competitors even when marketing research is not employed. The concept of alternatives from which customers choose and the concept of appropriateness to a use context can be used to understand the competitive environment. A management team or a group of experts, such as retailers or buyers who have an understanding of the customer, could employ one or both of these conceptual bases to identify competitive groupings.

Determining How the Competitors Are Perceived and Evaluated

To determine how competitor products are perceived, it is necessary to choose an appropriate set of product attributes for the comparison. The term *attributes* includes not only product characteristics and customer benefits but also product associations such as product uses or product users. Thus for beer, a relevant attribute could be the association of a brand with outdoor picnics as opposed to a nice restaurant. Another could be the association with athletes.

In any product category there are usually a host of attribute possibilities. Further, some can be difficult to specify. Consider the taste attribute of beer. Taste testers in a *Consumer Reports* study considered the taste attribute but also the related attributes of smell, strength, and fullness. However, the strength of a beer is probably related to both its taste and its aroma characteristics, and perhaps also to its alcoholic content. Likewise, the notion of fullness is highly interrelated with the other attributes. Fullness can refer to the degree to which the drinker is left with a "full feeling" after consuming beer, to the visual color and texture of the product, and to a wide variety of other possible attributes.

The task is to identify potentially relevant attributes, to remove redundancies from the list, and then to select those that are most useful and relevant in describing brand images.

One approach to the generation of an attribute list is the Kelly repertory grid. The respondent is first given a deck of cards containing brand names from which all unfamiliar brands are culled. Three cards are then selected randomly from those remaining. The respondent is asked to identify the two brands that are most similar and to describe why those two brands are similar to each other and different from the third. The respondent is then asked to rate the remaining brands on the basis of the attributes thus identified. This procedure is repeated several times for each respondent. As a variant, respondents could be asked to select a preference between two brands and then asked why one brand was selected over the other.

Such a technique will often generate a rather long list of attributes, sometimes as many as several hundred and usually well over forty. The next step is to remove the redundancy from the list. In most cases there will be a set of words or phrases that will essentially mean the same thing. Such redundancies can be identified using logic and judgment.

Another approach is to remove redundancy through a statistical technique called factor analysis.[27] Respondents are asked to rate each of the objects with respect to each attribute. For example, they might be asked to rate Budweiser on a seven-point scale as to the degree it is full bodied. Correlations between attributes are then calculated, and factor analysis essentially groups the attributes on the basis of those correlations.

After a list of nonredundant attributes is obtained, the next task is to select those that are the most meaningful and important to the customer's image of the competitive objects. The selected attributes should be those that are important and relevant to the customer in making distinctions between brands and in making purchasing decisions. One study found that the relevant attribute list for toothpaste was considered to include prevention of decay, taste, whitening capability, color, and attractiveness of the product and its packaging, and price.[28] Chapter 8 will discuss several approaches for selecting the most useful and meaningful attributes.

Determining the Competitors' Positions

Another useful exercise is to determine how competitors (including our own entry) are positioned. The primary focus of interest is how they are positioned with respect to the relevant attributes. What is the customer's image of the various competitors? We are also interested in how they are positioned with respect to each other. Which competitors are perceived as similar and which as different? Such judgments can be made subjectively. However, it is also possible to use research to help answer such questions empirically. Such research is termed multidimensional scaling because its goal is to scale objects on several dimensions (or attributes). Multidimensional scaling can be based upon either attribute data or nonattribute data. Approaches based on attribute data will be considered first.

Attribute-Based Multidimensional Scaling

The most direct way to determine images is simply to ask a sample of the target segment to scale the various objects on the attribute dimensions. One approach is to use a seven-point agree-or-disagree scale. For example, the respondent could be asked to express his or her agreement or disagreement with statements regarding the Ford Escort: With respect to its class I would consider the Ford Escort to be

Sporty.
Roomy.
Economical.
Good handling.

Alternatively, perceptions of a brand's users or use contexts could be used to determine the brand image: I would expect the typical Escort owner to be

Older.
Wealthy.
Independent.
Intelligent.

The Escort is most appropriate for

Short neighborhood trips.
Commuting.
Cross-country trips.

Another approach, the *semantic differential*, was used by W. A. Mindak to obtain the image of three beer brands.[29] The resulting profiles are shown in Figure 6–10. Notice that the image is not only obtained with respect to nine product attributes but also with respect to ten customer characteristics. Several observations emerge. Brand X is especially strong on the refreshing dimensions. Brand Z is weak across the board. The consumer profiles are really similar, which, in this case, was regarded as good news for the makers of brand X, who deliberately tried to appeal to a broad segment.

Non-Attribute-Based Multidimensional Scaling

Attribute-based approaches have several conceptual disadvantages. A complete, valid, and relevant attribute list is not easy to generate. Furthermore, an object may be perceived or evaluated as a total whole that is not really decomposable in terms of attributes. These disadvantages lead us to the use of nonattribute data, such as similarity data. *Singular!*

Similarity measures simply reflect the perceived similarity of two objects in the eyes of the respondents. For example, each respondent may be asked to rate the degree of similarity of each pair of objects. Thus, the respondent does not have an attribute list that implicitly suggests criteria to be included or excluded. The result, when averaged over all respondents, is a similarity rating for each object pair. A *multidimensional scaling program,* then, attempts to locate objects in a two- or three- (or more if necessary) dimensional space. Such a space is again termed a perceptual map. The program attempts to construct the perceptual map such that the two objects with the highest similarity are separated by the shortest distance, the object pair with the second highest similarity is separated by the second shortest distance, and so on. Of course, the programs will rarely be able to accomplish this goal, but many different perceptual maps are tried to get as close as possible.

In a study of car images several years ago,[30] between-object similarities were obtained for six cars and an "ideal car." The resulting perceptual map is shown in Figure 6–11. The disadvantage of the similarity-based approach is that the interpretation of the dimensions does not have the attributes as a guide. Thus, in Figure 6–11 one horizontal axis might be determined "prestige" and the other horizontal axis "size," but there are no attributes on which to base these judgments. Attribute data can be collected separately and correlated with the dimensions found in Figure 6–11, but it would be a distinctly separate analysis. The underlying perceptual map, of course, would still be based upon the similarity data. In addition to the use of similarity data, methods have recently been developed that can extract positioning maps from purchase data of members of longitudinal purchase panels, based on the patterns of brand switching for individual households, as well as in

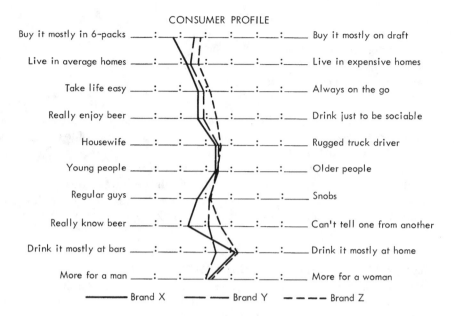

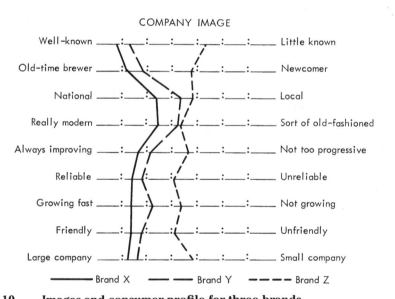

Figure 6–10.   Images and consumer profile for three brands.

Source: W. A. Mindak, "Fitting the Semantic Differential to the Marketing Problem," Journal of Marketing, *25, April 1961, pp. 31-32. Published by American Marketing Association.*

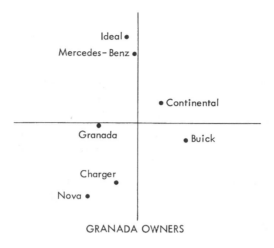

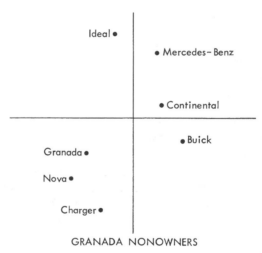

Figure 6–11.   Similarity-based perceptual map.

Source: Robert E. Wilkes, "Product Positioning by Multidimensional Scaling," Journal of Advertising Research, *17, August 1977, p. 16.*

other ways. These are not discussed here, and the interested reader is referred to marketing research texts and journals for more information.[31]

Analyzing the Customers

The ultimate positioning decision specifies where in the perceptual map the brand should be positioned. Making that decision obviously requires knowing which areas in the map will be attractive to the customers. In most cases, customers will differ markedly as to the area in the perceptual map they prefer even if their perceptions of brands are similar. Thus, the task is usually to identify segments or clusters of customers based on their preferred locations in the perceptual maps. The decision will then involve selecting the segment or segments as well as the target position.

One approach to segmentation involves identifying which attributes or customer benefits are most important and then identifying groups of customers who value similar attributes or benefits. In Chapter 8, methods to identify important attributes or benefits will be discussed. Another approach uses the concept of an "ideal object." An ideal object, also discussed in Chapter 8, is an object the customer would prefer over all others, including objects that can be conceptualized but do not actually exist.[32] It is a combination of all the customer's preferred attribute levels. Customers who have similar ideal objects will form relevant segments.

It is often important to consider customers' preference for attributes in the context for the use context.[33] Preferences may be very sensitive to use context. In one study, focus groups (structured discussions involving eight to ten people) and judgment were used to identify nine relevant use contexts for coffee:[34]

1. **To start the day.**
2. **Between meals.**
3. **Between meals with others.**
4. **With lunch.**
5. **With supper.**
6. **Dinner with guests.**
7. **In the evening.**
8. **To keep awake in the evening.**
9. **On weekends.**

In this study, there were differences across use occasion (Hill's Brothers had a 7 percent share of breakfast use but only a 1.5 percent share of the remainder of the day). The major differences were found between A.M. coffee drinkers and P.M.. coffee drinkers.

MAKING THE POSITIONING DECISION . . . .

The four steps or exercises just discussed should be conducted prior to making the actual positioning decision, as the results will nearly always contribute to the decision. The exercises can be done subjectively by the involved managers if necessary. Although marketing research will be more definitive, if research is not feasible or justifiable, the process should still be pursued. However, even with that background, it is still not possible to generate a cookbook solution to the positioning question. However, some guidelines or checkpoints can be offered.

1. *An economic analysis should guide the decision.* As was noted in Chapter 4, the success of any objective basically depends on two factors: the potential market size times the penetration probability. Unless both of these factors are favorable, success will be unlikely.

The market segment size, right now or very soon, should be worthwhile. If new buyers are to be attracted to the product class, a reasonable assessment should be made of the potential size and share of that growth area. Demographic trends are obviously very useful in making such forecasts: the recent growth in single-person households, for example, has led to special campaigns from cruise lines, food companies, and so on, aimed at the singles market.[35] Additionally, various other kinds of data sources (such as syndicated survey reports by Yankelovich, Roper, etc.)[36] are used by marketers to keep track of lifestyle and attitudinal trends among consumers so that they can find fast-growth areas. For instance, such services alerted marketers to the trend among consumers to seek flavorful foods and beverages in the early 1990s, leading Seagrams to bring out flavored alcoholic drinks, Heinz to launch salsa-flavored ketchup, and so on. However, some surveys (such as annual lifestyle and behavior data collected by ad agency DDB Needham) have shown that alleged shifts in consumer values and attitudes do not always translate into equivalent changes in buying patterns, so caution must always be applied in interpreting data about such trends.[37]

If categories are not growing, and share gains are sought from other brands within the category, those brands should have a large enough market share to justify the effort. Research must show that there exists a good reason why users of these targeted brands might switch. The "penetration probability" must indicate that there is indeed a competitive weakness to attack, or a competitive advantage to exploit, that will lead to the intended share gain.

2. *Positioning usually implies a segmentation commitment.* Positioning usually means that an overt decision is being made to ignore parts of the market and to concentrate only on certain segments. Such an approach requires commitment and discipline, because it is not easy to turn your back on potential buyers. Yet the effect of generating a distinct, meaningful position is to focus on the target segments and not be constrained by the reaction of other segments.

There is always the possibility of deciding to engage in a strategy of *undifferentiation*—that of attempting to reach all segments. In that case, it might be reasonable to consider deliberately generating a *diffuse image*, or an image that will mean different things to different people. Such an approach is risky and difficult to implement and usually would only be used by a large brand with a very strong market position. The implementation could involve projecting a range of advantages while avoiding being identified with any one. Alternatively, there could be a conscious effort to avoid being explicit about any particular feature. Pictures of bottles of Coca-Cola superimposed with the words "It's the real thing," or Budweiser's claim that "Bud is the king of beers," or "Somebody still cares about quality" illustrate these strategies.

It is possible to "oversegment" the market, and aim at too specialized a market. Some recent research shows that communicating several differentiating features for a brand in one ad (rather than few, spread over several ads), can lead to the perception of the brand being so different from the others in the category that it is seen as a *specialty* or *subtype,* as being almost a different product than the *standard* or *reference* product.[38]

3. *If the advertising is working, stick with it.* An advertiser will often get tired of

a positioning strategy and the advertising used to implement it and will consider making a change. However, the personality or image of a brand, like that of a person, evolves over many years, and the value of consistency through time cannot be overestimated. Some of the very successful, big-budget campaigns have run for ten, twenty, or even thirty years. Larry Light, while the executive vice president of BBDO, a major New York advertising agency, said that the "biggest mistake marketers make is to change the personality of their advertising year after year. They end up with a schizophrenic personality at worst, or no personality at best."[39] Burger King, for example, which has had many different advertising campaigns in the last ten years, has been accused of weakening its positioning in the marketplace by this too-rapid change.[40] See Figure 6–12.

4. *Don't try to be something you are not.* It is tempting but naive, and usually fatal, to decide on a positioning strategy that exploits a market need or opportunity but assumes that your product is something it is not. Before positioning a product, it is important to determine the position of the various competitors. One approach is to scale the competitors on the various identified attributes. The fourth step involves customer analysis. What segmentation variables seem most relevant? What about benefit segmentation?

Consider Hamburger Helper, introduced in 1970 as an add-to-meat product that would generate a good-tasting, economical, skillet dinner. It did well during the early 1970s, when meat prices were high, but in later years, homemakers switched back to more exotic, expensive foods. Reacting to the resulting drop in sales, a decision was made to make Hamburger Helper more exotic by positioning it as a base for casseroles. However, the product—at least in the consumers' minds—could not deliver. The consumers continued to view it as an economical, reliable convenience food; furthermore, they felt that they did not need help in making casseroles.

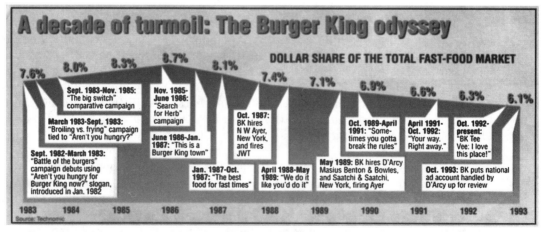

Figure 6–12.   Changes in Burger King campaigns over the years.

5. *Consider symbols.* A symbol or set of symbols can have strong associations that should be considered when making positioning decisions. Symbols like the Marlboro Man or the Jolly Green Giant can help implement a campaign, of course, but there can be existing symbols already developed by the brand or organization that can be used. Their availability can affect the positioning decision. For example, Wells Fargo bank has used the Wells Fargo stagecoach with all its associations for many years. The role of symbols in creating a brand personality is discussed further in Chapter 10.

A positioning objective, like any advertising objective, should be operational, in that it should be measurable. To evaluate the advertising and to generate diagnostic information about future advertising strategies, it is necessary to monitor the position over time. A variety of techniques can be employed to make this measurement; typically, test ads are shown to one group of consumers, but not to another, and differences in their positioning maps are then compared. Techniques have also been developed which can relate changes in brand purchasing histories, obtained from households that are members of longitudinal panels, to the advertising and other marketing mix elements aimed at those household panel members.[41] These methods allow managers to test different ad executions to see which ones are most likely to succeed in repositioning brands in desired directions on positioning maps, and, subsequently, to track changes in brand positioning over time.

SUMMARY. . . . .

A key advertising objective is identifying the target market segments. A concentration strategy involves the selection of a single segment, whereas a differentiation strategy will have several segments, perhaps each having a separate advertising goal. Among the ways to identify segments that might be worthwhile and attractive is by describing them by age, income, geographic location, ethnicity, product usage, or brand loyalty. Segments can also be created by grouping customer in segments that want the same product benefits or share the same lifestyle or culture.

There are a variety of positioning strategies available to the advertiser. An object can be positioned as follows:

1. **By product characteristics or customer benefit (Crest is a cavity fighter).**
2. **By price and quality (Sears is a "value" store).**
3. **By use or application (Gatorade is for flu attacks).**
4. **By product user (Miller is for the blue-collar, heavy beer drinker).**
5. **By product class (7-Up is a soft drink like the colas, not a mixer).**
6. **By cultural symbol (the Marlboro cowboy).**
7. **By competitor (Avis positions itself with Hertz).**

Four steps should precede the selection of a positioning strategy. In the first, an effort should be made to identify the competitors. In the second step, the attributes used to perceive and evaluate competitors are determined. The third step involves the determination of the position of the various competitors. The fourth step involves customer analysis. What segmentation variables seem most relevant? What about benefit segmentation?

The positioning decision should involve an economic analysis of the potential target segments and the probability of affecting their behavior with advertising. Other factors include realizing that positioning involves a segmentation commitment, sticking to a strategy that is working, being sure that the product matches the positioning strategy, and consideration of available symbols that may contribute to image formation. Finally, marketers should consider the evaluation stage, when the position is monitored.

DISCUSSION QUESTIONS

1. Some argue that usage is the most useful segmentation variable. Others believe that the benefit provided by the product or service is the most useful. Still others will refute both statements. What is your position? Why?
2. Distinguish between controlled coverage and customer self-selection. Which approach would likely be most effective for the manufacturer of an expensive sports car?
3. Develop segmentation strategies for the following:
   a. Wristwatch company.
   b. Manufacturer of electronic calculators.
   c. College.
   d. Police department.
   e. Pleasure-boat company.
   f. Large retail hardware store.
   g. Church.
   h. Hair spray.
4. Select six television and ten print advertisements. How are the products positioned?
5. Can you expand the list of seven positioning strategies mentioned in the text?
6. Obtain two examples of each of the positioning strategies discussed in the chapter.
7. Consider the following beer brands: Lowenbrau, Miller Lite, Miller Genuine Draft, Coors, Coors Light, Bud, Bud Light, Michelob Dry, Schlitz Malt, Heineken, and Beck's.
   a. In each case, write down what you think is the image the general public holds of that brand. Confine your answers to a few statements or phrases.
   b. Generate an attribute list for beer, using the Kelly repertory grid approach. Revise your answer to part (a).
   c. Identify the competitors of the listed brands of beer by asking consumers or potential consumers of that object what they would select if that object were not available.
   d. Determine the use situations relevant to beer, and for three use situations list other products that might be appropriate.
8. Consider all possible pairs of the following brands of soft drinks: 7-Up, Pepsi, Diet 7-Up, Diet Pepsi, Coke, Orange Crush, Diet Coke, and your ideal brand.

    a. Rank the brand pairs in terms of their similarity. Was the task a reasonable one? Are you comfortable with all your rankings?

    b. Pick several sets of three brands, identify the two most similar brands in the set, and explain why you regard them as the most similar. Using the Kelly repertory grid technique, generate a list of attributes relevant to this product class. Scale each of the attributes in terns of how important they are to you in your choice of a soft drink.

    c. How would you say each of these brands is "positioned"?

9. What would be the characteristics of an ideal brand of toothpaste for you? How might the concept of an ideal brand be related to benefit segmentation? What brand did you buy last? Why? How would your ideal brand differ from this brand?

10. Suppose Anheuser-Busch is interested in entering the soft drink market. They have developed a new drink called Chelsea, which is a carbonated apple-juice drink that contains 0.5 percent alcohol. It is packaged in a glass bottle partially wrapped in foil, like some of the labels used on premium beers. What are the positioning alternatives open to Chelsea? How would you go about selecting the optimal one?

NOTES. . . . .

1. "Marketing's New Look," *Business Week*, January 26, 1987, pp. 64–69; "Stalking the New Consumer," *Business Week*, August 28, 1989, pp. 54–62.
2. See Alfred A. Kuehn and Ralph L. Day, "Strategy of Product Quality," *Harvard Business Review*, 40 (November/December 1962), 100–110.
3. Most of the demographic figures mentioned here come from different issues of *American Demographics*, which the interested advertising planner is urged to follow.
4. Nancy Stephens, "Cognitive Age: A Useful Concept for Advertising?" *Journal of Advertising*, 20, no. 4 (December 1991), 37–48.
5. *Advertising Age*, August 9, 1993, p. 8;
6. *Advertising Age*, August 30, 1993, p. 12.
7. For discussions of these needs see Laura A. Peracchio, "Young Children's Processing of a Televised Narrative: Is a Picture Really Worth a Thousand Words," *Journal of Consumer Research*, 20 (September 1993), pp. 281–293, and Catherine Cole and Siva K. Balasubramaniam, "Age Differences in Consumers' Search for Information: Public Policy Implications," *Journal of Consumer Research*, 20 (June 1993), 157–169.
8. Joan Meyers-Levy and Brian Sternthal, "Gender Differences in the Use of Message Cues and Judgments," *Journal of Marketing Research*, 28 (February 1991), 84–96.
9. *Working Woman*, June 1993, pp. 23–25.
10. For some statistics, see *The Wall Street Journal*, October 13, 1993, p. A1.
11. "Frito-Lay Packs $90m Ad Punch," *Advertising Age*, December 18, 1989, p. 18.
12. Joel S. Dubow, "Occasion-based vs. User-based Benefit Segmentation," *Journal of Advertising Research*, 32, no 1 (March–April 1992), 11–18.
13. A. S. C. Ehrenberg, "Repetitive Advertising and the Consumer," *Journal of Advertising Research* (April 1974).
14. *The Wall Street Journal*, October 26, 1993, p. A7.
15. Russell I. Haley, "Benefit Segmentation: a Decision-Oriented Research Tool," *Journal of Marketing*, 32 (July 1968), 30–35.
16. "Research Finds Fickle Consumers," *Advertising Age*, June 26, 1989, p. 31.
17. Russell I. Haley and Philip J. Weingarden, "Running Reliable Attitude Segmentation Studies," *Journal of Advertising Research* (December 1986/January 1987), 51–55.

18. Arnold Mitchell, *The Nine American Lifestyles* (New York: Macmillan, 1983), and *Advertising Age*, February 13, 1989, p. 24. For a review of earlier research on psychographics, see William D. Wells, "Psychographics: A Critical Review," *Journal of Marketing Research*, 12 (May 1975), 196–213.
19. *Advertising Age*, February 15, 1993, p. 6.
20. These concepts are developed in the context of a normative mathematical model in Ronald E. Frank, William F. Massy, and Yoram Wind, *Market Segmentation* (Englewood Cliffs, NJ: Prentice Hall, 1972), especially in Chapter 8.
21. *The Wall Street Journal*, February 1, 1991, p. B1.
22. *Advertising Age*, September 20, 1993, p. 52.
23. *Business Week*, January 27, 1992, p. 84.
24. James H. Myers and Allan D. Shocker, "Toward a Taxonomy of Product Attributes." Working paper (Los Angeles: University of Southern California, June 1978), p. 3.
25. "Miller's Fast Growth Upsets the Beer Industry," *Business Week*, November 8, 1976.
26. George S. Day, Allan D. Shocker, and Rajendra K. Srivastava, "Customer-Oriented Approaches to Identifying Product Markets," *Journal of Marketing*, 43 (Fall 1979), 8–19.
27. David A. Aaker and George S. Day, *Marketing Research* (New York: Wiley, 1989).
28. Russell J. Haley, "Benefit Segmentation: A Decision Oriented Research Tool," *Journal of Marketing* (July 1968), 30–35.
29. W. A. Mindak, "Fitting the Semantic Differential to the Marketing Problem," *Journal of Marketing*, 25 (April 1961), 28–33.
30. Robert E. Wilkes, "Product Positioning by Multidimensional Scaling," *Journal of Advertising Research*, 17 (August 1977), 15–18.
31. See, for example, Steven M. Shugan, "Estimating Brand Positioning Maps Using Supermarket Scanning Data," *Journal of Marketing Research*, 24, no. 1 (1987), 1–18, and Hotaka Katahira, "Perceptual Mapping Using Ordered Logit Analysis," *Marketing Science*, 9, no. 1 (Winter 1990), 1–17.
32. In Figure 4–7, an ideal point is shown as a point on the map. However, if an attribute-based multidimensional scaling was involved and a scale such as "inexpensive to buy-expensive to buy" were employed, the respondent would prefer to be as far to the right as possible. In that case, the "ideal point" would actually appear in the perceptual map as an ideal direction or vector instead of as a point.
33. Rajendra K. Srivastava, Robert P. Leone, and Allan D. Schocker, "Market Structure Analysis: Hierarchical Clustering of Products Based on Substitution in Use," *Journal of Marketing*, 45 (Summer 1981), pp. 38–48.
34. Glen L. Urban, Philip L. Johnson, and John R. Hauser, "Testing Competitive Market Structures," *Marketing Science*, 3 (Spring 1984), 83–112.
35. *Advertising Age*, July 20, 1992, p. 2.
36. *Marketing News*, January 6, 1992, p. 6.
37. *Advertising Age*, September 24, 1990, p. 24.
38. Mita Sujan and James R. Bettman, "The Effects of Brand Positioning Strategies on Consumers' Brand and Category Perceptions: Some Insights from Schema Research," *Journal of Consumer Research*, 26 (November 1989), 454–467.
39. "Style Is Substance for Ad Success: Light," *Advertising Age*, August 27, 1979, p. 3.
40. *Advertising Age*, October 25, 1993, p. 3; *Business Week*, November 15, 1993, p. 62.
41. William R. Dillon, Teresa Domzal, and Thomas J. Madden, "Evaluating Alternative Product Positioning Strategies," *Journal of Advertising Research* (August/September 1986), 29–35; Russell S. Winer and William L. Moore, "Evaluating the Effects of Marketing-Mix Variables on Brand Positioning," *Journal of Advertising Research* (February/March 1989), 39–45.

PART III

MESSAGE STRATEGY

7 ATTENTION AND COMPREHENSION

I advise you to include the brand name in your headline. If you don't, 80 percent of the readers (who don't read your body copy) will never know what product you are advertising. If you are advertising a kind of product only bought by a small group of people, put a word in your headline that will flag them down, such as asthma, bedwetters, women over 35.
(David Ogilvy)

The advertiser must provide vivid incentives if he is to gain the favorable attention of a person whose senses have been dulled by fatigue or relaxation.
(Darrell Lucas and Steuart Britt, *Advertising Psychology and Research*)

Researchers have attempted to measure the number of advertisements that each consumer is potentially exposed to every day, and these estimates range from at least several hundred to a couple of thousands.[1] Between 1967 and 1981, the average number of network TV commercials per day rose from 1,856 to 4,079, and by 1989 this number had risen further to 6,180. The rates of increase in non-network TV commercials was even greater. These increases occurred both because more TV minutes per hour were devoted to commercials, and because more—and shorter—TV commercials ran in each commercial minute. While sixty-second TV commercials constituted 77 percent of all network commercials in 1965, they made up only 2 percent of the total in 1989, by which time thirty-second ads formed 57 percent of the total and fifteen-second spots formed 38 percent of the total.[2]

With this increasing amount of clutter, and with more households zapping ads through their TV remote controls, it is becoming increasingly difficult for ads to gain the attention of consumers. And, because channel-switching and ad-avoidance means consumers are viewing fewer seconds of ever-smaller commercials with ever-reducing attention, even ads that do get watched communicate less of the intended information. Studies have found that ads are fully or partly mis-comprehended between 20 to 30 percent of the time.[3]

Clearly, regardless of whether an ad is aiming at boosting recall, changing brand attitudes, or inducing purchase action, there are two important prerequisites for *any* effect to occur. First, an individual must be exposed to it and pay some attention to it. As the hierarchies of effect (discussed in Chapters 4 and 5) pointed out, gaining a consumer's attention is usually the first step in creating effective advertising. Getting such attention is rarely enough by itself, but an ad that fails to get attention is unlikely to achieve anything else. One might say that getting (and holding) a consumer's attention is a necessary but not sufficient condition in creating effective advertising. In the second step, a consumer who does pay attention to an ad must interpret and comprehend it in the way the advertiser intended it to be interpreted. The communication must not be misinterpreted or miscomprehended; if this does happen, the ad is unlikely to lead to the kind of attitude change that the advertiser seeks.

Each of these steps of attention and comprehension represents, in some sense, a perceptual barrier through which many advertisements fail to pass. Some advertisements are not successful at stimulating sense organs in the recipient to a minimal threshold level of interest or awareness. Other advertisements have their meaning distorted by the recipient in such a way that the effect of the advertisement is quite different from what the advertiser intended.

Perception has been defined as "the process by which an individual maintains contact with his environment"[4] and elsewhere as "the process whereby an individual receives stimuli through the various senses and interprets them."[5] *Stimuli* here can refer to sets of advertisements (such as a campaign), to a single advertisement, or to a portion of an advertisement. The process, as conceptualized in Figure 7–1, includes two stages—attention and interpretation (or comprehension). Both play a role in helping an individual cope with the infinite quantity of accessi-

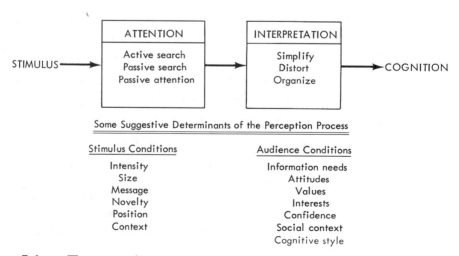

Figure 7–1.   **The perception process.**

ble stimuli, a quantity that would otherwise be impossible to process. The first stage is the attention filter. The second stage in perception is the interpretation process. An individual organizes the stimulus content into his or her own models of reality, models that may be very different from those of other individuals or of the sender. In doing so, the person often simplifies, distorts, organizes, and even "creates" stimuli.[6]

Given this background on the perceptual process, it is clearly helpful to develop some understanding of these psychological processes, so that ads can be designed to maximize their attention-getting ability and their ability to correctly communicate the targeted copy-points. In the balance of the chapter we will consider, in turn, attention and comprehension.

ATTENTION . . . .

Attention can be viewed as an information filter—a screening mechanism that controls the quantity and nature of information any individual receives. Getting a consumer's attention is not easy. An individual, overtly or accidentally, avoids exposure to stimuli. The advertising environment is truly "cluttered"; most major magazines, for example, have almost one-half of their pages carrying advertisements, the other half carrying editorial matter.

Amid all this advertising "noise," it is not easy to create an ad that stands out enough to get noticed, processed, and remembered. The effectiveness of ads is reduced not only by the higher levels of clutter in general, but even more significantly by the proximity of ads for competing brands from the same product category. A recent study by Robert Kent found that 20 to 30 percent of the TV ads per hour per network were for the same product category.[7] As one might expect, research by Raymond Burke and Thomas Srull does show that consumer memory for a particular brand's ad does get hurt—less brand information is remembered—if the consumer sees that ad in the midst of competitive advertising, and especially if the consumer is not processing the ad with a view to possible purchase.[8]

The situation is made worse in the broadcast media, especially television. Viewers have always had the freedom to do other things while a program is being shown, including leaving the room mentally or physically, but the use of remote control devices has made channel-switching endemic. Television advertisers today have to cope with the phenomena of *zapping* (switching across programs using a remote control device) and *zipping* (fast-forwarding through ads when viewing prerecorded programs on a videocassette recorder).

Combating Clutter, Zapping and Zipping

Clutter

As discussed above, a major problem facing advertisers today is the difficulty of gaining attention in the face of the increase in advertising clutter. Research by Peter Webb and Michael Ray has clearly shown that higher levels of clutter hurt the performance of individual ads—the more the clutter, the lower are average levels of ad recall, for instance.[9] For an average commercial, another study showed the following drop in the correct brand recall of the last commercial seen between 1965 and 1981:

Year	Percent
1965	18
1974	12
1981	7

A recent study by Tom Brown and Michael Rothschild showed, however, that while increased clutter may decrease ad effectiveness as gauged by unaided recall measures, the effects are reduced if the attention-getting power of the ad is measured instead by unaided recall or by recognition. Further, even for unaided recall, they found that increasing clutter further from today's already high levels did not appear to hurt ad effectiveness very much, and they speculate that the effects of clutter on such recall may be near its maximum.[10]

How can you fight clutter? Research shows that the effects of increased clutter do not affect all ads equally. Webb found that ads placed either at the beginning or the end of a commercial break ("pod") were less affected than were ads in the middle of such breaks. This suggests that advertisers ought to negotiate the first or last position in a pod. High-involvement ads were also less affected than lower-involvement ads, suggesting that ads that evoke greater inherent involvement (or succeed in creating enough "borrowed interest") might suffer less from clutter.[11] In the print medium, several advertisers have tried to fight clutter by using devices as varied as three-dimensional pop-ups to musical microchips in their magazine ads. These ads can cost millions of dollars apiece, but they do succeed in getting nearly 100 percent readership.[12] Whether this translates into attitudinal or sales effects, of course, is another matter altogether.

Zapping

Only a few years ago, the major concern of television advertisers was to inhibit viewers from leaving the room during the commercials. Now there is a much more serious problem—commercials can get zapped without leaving the room.[13] A viewer can turn off the sound or change channels with a remote control tuner (zapping) or run fast-forward on a prerecorded program (zipping). Households with remote controls for their TV sets zap ads 60 percent more than do those without remotes—and such remotes are now in more than 50 percent of all U.S. TV homes, and there are more of them every day.[14]

Using scanner data, Fred Zufryden, James Pedrick and Avu Sankaralingam found that, in addition to the presence of remotes, zapping also to be higher among households with cable TV, and with multiple people at home, households with children under eighteen living at home, households with college-educated adults, and households where VCRs are used. Interestingly, they reported TV channel switching to occur more during TV programs than during ads, and they found the strange result that TV ads appeared to affect sales more strongly if they were zapped than if they were not! They suggest that perhaps consumers are forced to pay more attention to ads they are zapping—ads not being zapped might just be completely ignored![15]

Meanwhile, according to proprietary studies by the scanner data company Information Resources, Inc. (IRI), zapping tends to be higher for the first ad in a commercial break, and higher among more media-savvy younger consumers, especially those who have higher incomes and male. Other surveys also point out that younger adults zap ads more often than older adults, and men more than women. Zappers are less likely to plan their TV viewing and more likely to flip TV channels till they find something they like (sometimes called "channel grazing").[16]

The obvious approach to combating zapping (and zipping and clutter) is to create commercials that are so interesting that viewers will prefer to watch them rather than zap or zip them.[17] Research shows that zapping tends to occur most strongly during the first five seconds of a commercial, so that it is crucial to sustain the consumer's interest during these first few seconds. In sustaining the viewer's interest, advertisers can make use of all the principles that we will discuss further below—offer information that is useful, create ads that are complex and interesting, create ads that "fit" with prior expectations and attitudes, and so on.

In making such ads, the "interesting" and "novel" elements appear to be more important than the "useful information" aspects, at least for casual, low-involvement viewers. Indeed, a recent study by T. J. Olney, Morris Holbrook, and Rajeev Batra found that viewers' tendency to zip and zap commercials was reduced to the extent they found the commercials pleasurable—but increased for ads that were simply useful and utilitarian.[18] A study by the McCann-Erickson agency also found that zapping was reduced for ads that were more entertaining.[19] Having said that, it must also be pointed out that getting and gaining attention is not everything: the executional elements that are used for these purposes must not detract and distract from the real, eventual purpose of the ad, such as changing attitudes.

Ideally, ads should be so interesting that viewers would look for or wait for commercials to come on! Perhaps the most spectacular commercial of recent times was a spot for the Apple Macintosh computer. Called "1984," it aired only once during the Super Bowl. A young woman is shown throwing a sledgehammer through a giant TV screen featuring Big Brother. The tag line was: "Apple computer will introduce Macintosh and you'll see why 1984 won't be like 1984." The ad was enormously successful at generating interest in the computer. Apple's "Lemmings" commercial, aired at the 1985 Super Bowl, however, was less successful.[20]

Zipping

A study found that consumers playing back prerecorded programs on their video-cassette recorders tend to zip through ads over 60 percent of the time.[21] Another study looking at consumers zipping through videotaped programs and ads also found that while most consumers zipping through ads whipped through all ads indiscriminately, trying to avoid all of them, zipping rates were lowest for the first commercial in the first pod and highest for the commercials in the last pod.[22] So while it appears far more difficult to fight zipping than zapping, early pod placement might offer some hope. Other advertisers combat zipping by developing commercials that use visual elements (such as brand logos or package shots) that will be visible even if the viewer is fast-forwarding through the ad. Patricia Stout and Benedicta Burda found that such a "brand dominance" strategy does appear to inhibit the reducing effects of zipping on attitude toward the ad, brand beliefs, and purchase intentions.[23]

Creating Ads That Attract Attention

The attention filter operates at various levels of effort and consciousness. At one extreme is the process of *active search* wherein a receiver actually seeks information. He or she might solicit opinions of friends or search through magazines not normally read. Another level could be termed *passive search.* A receiver searches for information only from sources to which he or she is exposed during the normal course of events. The final level might be called *passive attention.* Here a receiver has little immediate need for the information and makes no conscious effort to obtain it, but some information may nevertheless enter the system.

At all three levels, it is appropriate to discuss why a person obtains information so that ads can be designed to maximize attention. There are, of course, as many reasons as there are situations and individuals. However, it is instructive to examine four general motives for attending to informative stimuli. A first motive is to obtain information that will have a high level of utility for a person. In an advertising context, an individual will obtain product information that will help make better purchase decisions. Second, people may be motivated to expose themselves to information that supports their opinions—supportive exposure—and to avoid "discrepant" information. Third, there is a desire to be exposed to information that stimulates. Finally, people are motivated to find stimuli that are interesting to them. These motives will be examined in turn.

Information of Practical Value

It might seem more than slightly redundant to mention that advertising does, in fact, inform and that people do use such information in making decisions. Although advertising practitioners and behavioral scientists search for subtle and often-disguised explanations for why some advertisements register and others do not, it is too easy to overlook the obvious and principal role of advertising as a mechanism for informing. Indeed, psychologists cite studies that demonstrate that people do expose themselves to information that has practical value to them. By now, the reader should not require such evidence. Clearly, there is a practical need for product information and effective advertisements tend to fulfill this need.

The Shell Company advertisement shown in Figure 7–2 is an example of an advertisement that offers to the reader some practical information, the availability of one of its "answer series" booklets. A measure of the success of the campaign was the fact that 600 million of these booklets were distributed during the first three years of the campaign. Clearly, the offered information was regarded as useful. Incidentally, the Shell campaign was effective in affecting the Shell image as a company that provides useful information for consumers.[24]

Figure 7–2. An advertisement offering practical information.

Courtesy of Shell Oil Company.

Many advertising copywriters have noted that in their experience many of the advertisements that do well in attracting attention (as evidenced, for example, by coupon returns) have headlines that promise free, useful information. A very successful headline format, for instance, is "How to . . . ," used in the context of the problem that the consumer is trying to solve with the purchase of this particular product. A consumer in the market for a refrigerator, for example, will very likely notice and read an advertisement that offers, in the headline, information on "How to select the best refrigerator for your needs."[25]

Robert Burnkrant applies a general theory of motivation that the behavioral tendency to process information is based upon three factors.[26] The first is the need for information about some topic. Obviously, audience members will have more information need for some products than others. For example, products that are costly, complex, or somewhat unknown because they are new or for some other reason will have associated with them an information need. The second is the expectancy (probability) that processing a particular ad will lead to relevant information exposure. The third would be a measure of the value of that particular as a source of relevant information: the goodness or badness of the message as an information source. This structure provides an approach to determine the extent to which a person might be motivated to process information from a particular ad.

Long Copy

An advertisement with short copy can be informative. A new brand or model in an established product class with strikingly different features may require no copy at all. However, in many situations a truly informative advertisement requires rather long copy (see our discussion of direct marketing copy in Chapter 3). The use of long copy and, consequently, the development of advertising with high informative content is inhibited by a widely accepted "rule" of the advertising business. This rule stipulates that copy must be short and punchy to be read. The concept is that readers will turn away from formidable lengthy copy.

Although such a rule may indeed apply for some products in some situations, it is by no means universally true. If a reader has a real use for the information and the information is well packaged, she or he can be induced to read long copy. Furthermore, it is often a small sacrifice to lose readership among those who do not need the information and thus are not motivated to read it. David Ogilvy makes the case for long copy, illustrating his point by his own print advertising.

> How long should your copy be? It depends on the product. If you are advertising chewing gum, there isn't much to tell, so make your copy short. If, on the other hand, you are advertising a product which has a great many different qualities to recommend it, write long copy: the more you tell, the more you sell.
>
> There is a universal belief in lay circles that people won't read long copy. Nothing could be farther from the truth. Claude Hopkins (a great copywriter in the first part of the century) once wrote five pages of solid text for Schlitz beer. In a few months, Schlitz moved up from fifth place to first. I once wrote a page of solid text for Good Luck Margarine, with most gratifying results.

Research shows that readership falls off rapidly up to 50 words of copy, but drops very little between 50 and 500 words. In my first Rolls-Royce advertisement I used 719 words—piling up one fascinating fact on another. In the last paragraph I wrote, "People who feel diffident about driving a Rolls-Royce can buy a Bentley." Judging from the number of motorists who picked up the word "diffident" and bandied it about, I concluded that the advertisement was thoroughly read. In the next one I used 1,400 words.

In my first advertisement for Puerto Rico's Operation Bootstrap, I used 961 words. Fourteen thousand readers clipped the coupon from this advertisement and scores of them later established factories in Puerto Rico. . . . We have even been able to get people to read long copy about gasoline. One of our Shell advertisements contained 617 words, and 22 percent of male readers read more than half of them.[27]

Infomercials

One way in which advertisers are trying to communicate large amounts of information to consumers in the television medium is the use of *infomercials*. These are long programs, usually thirty minutes in length, that go into depth about the features of the product. Many advertisers including Apple computers, Kodak (for its photo-CD product), etc. have begun to use infomercials, which previously were associated with less reputable direct response campaigns for shoddy merchandise appearing on late night television programs. Because of the increasing respectability and use of infomercials in the mid-1990s, some very established marketing clients have begun to use them, and large agency networks such as Interpublic have acquired or started infomercial-producing divisions.

Active Search

There are situations in which buyers will not obtain adequate information for decision making from sources to which they are normally exposed. In such cases, they may actively seek out information from advertising in special interest magazines, by soliciting opinions from others, or by reading technical reports.

Active search generates exposures that are extremely important because of the salience of the information to the receiver. Such exposures will be more likely to affect product knowledge and attitude structure than those not associated with effort. Furthermore, the receiver is apt to be close to a purchase and the chances of forgetting the message are therefore lower. Active search is more likely to occur when risk and uncertainty are high—with major purchases, products involving relatively high involvement, and products that are new. The need for information will be highest for new products and lowest for brands with which a buyer is very familiar. As buyers develop brand loyalty, for example, their need for product information will be reduced. Evans found that automobile buyers who repurchased the same make are less likely to shop than are those who switched from one make to another.[28] The active search for information is likely to be highest among those consumers who already have some knowledge and expertise about the product category—prior knowledge facilitates comprehension of additional information.

Those with lesser knowledge may seek less "hard" information, process it less analytically, and rely more on friends and salespeople for advice.[29]

Future Reference

A purchase need not necessarily be imminent for a person to collect product information. It is reasonable to acquire such information for future use, using processes we have described as passive search or passive attention. It costs time and effort to engage in active search, but such costs can be avoided or reduced if an individual keeps informed about a product class. For example, young men or women may keep informed about personal computers, to prepare themselves for the time when they make a purchase. Of course, there will likely be other motivations as well. John Howard and Jagdish Sheth mention the need "to be a well-informed buyer in fulfilling a social role, in maintaining a social position. One is valued according to how much one knows with regard to the availability and value of products."[30]

Information That Supports: The Consistency Theories

A natural and intuitively appealing hypothesis is that people have a psychological preference for supportive information. It follows that they therefore tend to avoid nonsupportive or discrepant information. This latter tendency is illustrated by a line attributed to comedian Dick Gregory: "I have been reading so much about cigarettes and cancer that I quit reading." The term selective exposure has been applied to these twin drives.

Selective exposure can be explained by the *consistency theories,* such as dissonance theory, which suggest that people have a cognitive drive to develop consistent cognitions and behaviors about objects. *Dissonance theory* predicts that cognitive dissonance, the existence of conflicting cognitive elements, is discomforting and that people will try to reduce it. One mechanism for reducing dissonance is selective exposure—to obtain supportive information and to avoid discrepant information.

Efforts to confirm the selective exposure hypothesis in psychology have not been definitive. In part, this has been due to the difficulty of disentangling selective exposure from the other motives to process information, particularly information utility and interest factors. However, the evidence in contexts more relevant to advertising is much more positive.

D. Ehrlich and other psychologists showed recent car buyers eight envelopes allegedly containing advertisements for different makes of cars. Over 80 percent of the respondents chose the advertisements for their own cars—advertisements that would presumably be supportive.[31] J. F. Engel interviewed two matched samples, one of which had purchased a new Chevrolet (a later replication used Volkswagens) a short time before (from one day to two weeks). New car owners seemed to have greater recall and interest in Chevrolet advertising.[32] Judson Mills found that, after controlling for differences in product desirability, a positive interest for advertisements of chosen products existed although there was no negative interest in advertisements for rejected products.[33] Using sophisticated statistical techniques on awareness data from a study of repeated magazine ads, Rajeev Batra and Wilried Vanhonacker also found evidence that ad awareness was higher for those who already seemed to have higher brand attitudes.[34]

Involuntary Exposure

Selective exposure should tend to increase when an individual's position is threatened by involuntary exposure to nonsupportive information. Consider a person who has a stable attitude and is loyal to one or several automobile models. Suppose that he or she is told of a rumored government report suggesting that one of the models he or she prefers has a characteristic that makes it tend to develop transmission difficulties. The person might then be sensitive to information that would support his or her position—that the model is actually quite reliable. An advertiser might therefore stand ready to respond immediately to any negative information his or her customers are likely to receive. Such a campaign would capitalize on selectivity and could be very effective. Its target would be existing customers, even loyal buyers, instead of those not now buying the brand. Oldsmobile ran such an ad in 1992, when rumors were floating that General Motors might shut down that division, to reassure existing buyers that it would indeed stay in business.

Combating Selective Exposure

How does an advertiser combat selective exposure—be it overt or de facto? He or she can use rewards, contests, or premiums to get people to read the material. Users of direct-mail advertisements have had great success with using contests to break through the selective-exposure barrier. An alternative is to not even try to reach certain segments directly, but to try to do it indirectly by a two-step flow of information, that is, reach opinion leaders and then rely on word of mouth to reach others (see Chapter 11).

Information That Stimulates: The Complexity Theories

There is a set of theories termed *complexity theories* that consistently makes inconsistent predictions than the consistency theories. The most dramatic position among the complexity theorists is Salvatore Maddi's variety theory. Its essence is that novelty, unexpectedness, change, and complexity are pursued because they are inherently satisfying. The definition of novelty and unexpectedness must stress the difference between existing cognitive content and current or future perceptions, and, hence, the experience of variety is very likely to also be the experience of inconsistency.[35]

Maddi's theory rests on the very reasonable assumption that people get bored and are motivated to reduce that boredom by seeking stimuli that are novel, unusual, and different. People are curious about the world around them, and this curiosity will influence exposure patterns. In particular, they may be motivated to seek out information that does not support their positions. A similar position is advocated by Berlyne,[36] who suggests that stimuli attract attention because of their *physical* properties (such as brightness, color and size) and their *collative* properties (such as complexity, novelty, motion, etc.).

The complexity theories have empirical support of their own.[37] Studies of exploratory behavior have found that when a new element is introduced into the environment, individuals will attempt to learn about it. In that respect, the use of the journalistic sense for what is news and how it can be dramatized can be useful to copywriters. David Ogilvy suggested as much when he advised copywriters to inject news into their headlines. He wrote that "the two most powerful words you can use in a headline are free and new. You can seldom use free but you can always use new—if you try hard enough."[38] Other studies have indicated that variety in the form of small degrees of novelty and unexpectedness is pleasurable, whereas completely predictable events become boring. Another empirical conclusion is that variety is not only pursued and enjoyed, but is actually necessary to normal living.

It is useful to search for generalizations relating descriptors of the ad, such as size and shape, to attention. If, as Daniel Berlyne argues, stimuli attract attention because of their physical and collative properties, what ad characteristics will attract attention?

Ad Characteristics

Many characteristics contribute to the ability of an advertisement to attract attention.

The size and intensity of an ad will often influence attention. Advertisement readership will increase with advertisement size, although not linearly. Research using Starch measures of advertising readership (discussed in Chapter 14) has found that readership scores of full-page ads using four colors are about 85 percent higher than are scores of half-page ads using four colors.[39]

A "loud" ad stimulus will be more likely to be perceived than one of less intensity. Color presentations will usually attract more attention than will those in black and white: Starch concludes that the use of four colors generates about 50 percent more readership than black and white for one-page and two-page ads. Position can also influence attention. The left side of the page and the upper half get slightly more readership because of people's reading habits. Starch has concluded that ads on the back of a magazine will attract about 65 percent more readers than those toward the middle. Ads on the inside front and back covers will attract about 30 percent more readers.

Research has also highlighted the attention-getting properties of "vivid" information—information that is concrete rather than abstract, imagery provoking, emotionally interesting, containing a great deal of detail and specificity about objects, actions, outcomes, and situational context. It has been suggested that advertising phrased in concrete, detailed, and specific terms will attract more attention (and be more influential in shaping product quality judgments) than will copy phrased in abstract and general terms.[40] It is important, however, for the message itself to be vivid, not simply the presentation of it, and for the consumer to process the information in terms of its imagery: vivid but irrelevant information may get initial attention but may not get processed and have no impact on subsequent attitudes.[41]

Several studies have also investigated the impact of an ad's collative properties on the amount of attention given to them. Morris Holbrook and Donald Lehmann found that ads rated as surprising, incongruous, or funny were more likely to have been read,[42] and Bruce Morrison and Marvin Dainoff found that the visual complexity of magazine ads was positively related to the time that readers spent looking at these ads.[43]

Forestalling Ad Wearout via Pool-Outs

It certainly seems obvious that advertising should avoid being predictable, especially in situations wherein selectivity can easily operate to screen out advertisements. One special case of this problem is when an advertiser chooses to repeat an ad with high frequency at the same target market, over the course of some time period. Since consumers have already seen that same ad execution, they will stop paying attention to it. This is called the problem of ad "wear-out," and to reduce its impact it is a good idea to repeat not that same identical ad execution, but slight variations of it, through using what are called "pool-outs."

Research by H. Rao Unnava and Robert Burnkrant has shown that while variations or pool-outs get more attention than the same execution repeated again, the pool-outs get an extra bonus if they are sufficiently distinct from each other: such variations can then lead to the creation of multiple associations in the viewer's mind about the brand, facilitating the retrieval of the brand name in memory, leading to higher subsequent brand name recall.[44] Additionally, David Schumann, Richard Petty, and D. Scott Clemons have shown that the nature of the variation employed needs to be different in high versus low involvement situations. Since high involvement consumers process an ad message in terms of its central arguments (see Chapter 5), repeated ads aimed at them need to vary not just cosmetic elements (such as illustration, font, endorser, etc.), but the core arguments being used. In contrast, ads aimed at less involved consumers should vary just these cosmetic elements, because that is how such consumers process the ad and that is therefore what they are likely to get bored with.[45]

Adaptation-Level Theory, Distinctiveness, and Incongruency

H. Helson has developed an *adaptation-level theory* that is relevant to this discussion.[46] He suggests that it is not only the focal stimuli that determine perception, but also the contextual stimuli (background) and residual stimuli (past experience). The individual learns to associate a stimulus set with a reference point, or adaptation level. Attention is then created when an object deviates markedly from that level. For example, if a person has a hand in hot water for a period of time, the hand will adapt to that temperature and other water will be perceived relative to it. Thus, a dish of warm water could be perceived as cold, relative to an individual's adaptation level.

Helson studied the adaptation-level construct in various contexts, among them light intensity, colors, and lifting tasks. He found empirically that a weighted average of the logarithm of the various stimuli involved provided a reliable predictor for the adaptation level. The inclusion of the logarithm suggests that a very intense stimulus may not dominate the adaptation level to the exclusion of the others. "Weber's Law," named after a nineteenth-century researcher, also suggests that the degree to which a stimulus will be regarded as different will depend not on the absolute stimulus change but on the percentage of change from some point of reference.

These concepts suggest that ads that are sufficiently different from an audience's adaptation level and expectations will attract attention, pointing out the importance of *distinctiveness*. It is extremely important for ads to stand out from what the consumer considers to be "expected" for "typical" ads of that product category. For example, while a humorous ad may usually attract attention if it is surrounded by more conventional copy approaches, if many humorous ads are used by competing brands in that category, the ability of any one of them to attract attention would be reduced. On the other hand, if past experience has suggested to consumers that most comparable advertising avoided humor in its copy, then one using humor may attract attention even if it is not otherwise unusual. Various studies, including one by J. Craig Andrews, Syed Akhter, Srini Durvasula, and Darrel Muehling, have found that ads that are distinctive beat nondistinctive ads on various measures of effectiveness, including attitudes and intentions, in low-involvement conditions (the effects did not appear for high-involvement ads, presumably because consumers would pay attention to the ads regardless of their executional distinctiveness).[47] An example of a campaign that was sufficiently different to be distinctive would be the Nike campaign for its football shoes, starring Dennis Hopper as a crazy football fanatic collecting and even sniffing shoes of his football heroes—indeed, many people found it to be distinctive enough to be disturbing and offensive.[48]

Within an advertisement, the illustration or copy may similarly stand out from the balance of the advertisement if it is sufficiently unusual or unexpected. This suggests that ads that have some elements (headlines, visuals, etc.) that somehow are *incongruent* with each other might be especially effective in attracting attention and stimulating elaborative processing. Susan Heckler and Terry Childers point out that ad elements can be incongruent either because they are unexpected (having a low probability of naturally appearing together, because they don't both fit into the theme of the ad), or because they appear to be irrelevant to the point the ad is trying to make. Their study suggests that the best ads (in terms of recall and elaboration of information) use ad elements that are unexpected but still relevant, in that they do contribute to the theme or message of the ad. Simply using irrelevant elements in ad doesn't appear to pay off.[49]

Based on the theories of psychologist George Mandler, it has also been suggested that it is better to use ad elements (such as headlines and visuals) that are moderately inconsistent with each other, rather than very consistent with each other (so that ad is almost processed automatically, without much thought) or extremely inconsistent (so that the inconsistency cannot be resolved by the reader, leading to frustration).[50] Edward McQuarrie and David Mick suggest that consumers perceive moderate inconsistencies in ads as clever and enjoy deciphering their meaning, leading to enhanced ad liking.[51] An example of the use of moderate inconsistency in advertising was the NYNEX campaign for its yellow pages advertising, which was designed to show the variety of small establishments that advertised there. Each ad used a pun on the directory listing of some kind of establishment or service, and there was an inconsistency between the opening visuals (for example, U.S. marine riflemen doing a drill march in the manner of a rock band) and the actual category of service establishments then revealed (e.g., rock drills).

A Reconciliation

How does one reconcile consistency and complexity theories, two intuitively plausible but conflicting positions? One approach is to assume that tendencies toward consistency and variety both exist. The one that will dominate will depend on the personality and the situation involved.[52] Assume that there is a level of activation at which an individual is comfortable and effective. When the activation level is lower than desired, the individual will pursue variety to increase it. When it is high, she or he will be motivated to reduce stimulation and seek harmony such as is predicted by consistency theories. Obviously, there will be differences across people in terms of the optimal activation level. The situation will also determine behavior. If a high level of activation is required for optimal task performance, variety seeking will emerge. Thus, if a person is embarking on a major purchase, he or she may require a variety of information; if it is a routine purchase, such a drive will not tend to emerge.

Information That Interests

People tend to notice information that is interesting to them. In turn, they are interested in subjects with which they are involved. They are essentially interested in themselves and in various extensions of themselves. Elihu Katz summarizes and interprets some relevant empirical findings:

> *Apart from the quest for support and for utility, mere interest would seem to be an important factor in selectivity. The desire to see one's self-reflection is part of this. So is the desire to keep watch over things in which one has invested one's ego. Thus moviegoers identify with screen stars of similar age and sex: one reads in the newspaper about an event in which one personally participated; one reads advertisements for the product one purchased; political partisans immerse themselves in political communications regardless of its source; smokers choose to read material supporting the smoking-lung cancer relationship no less than material disclaiming the relationship, and much more avidly than nonsmokers; after one has been introduced to a celebrity, one notices (or "follows") his name in print even more frequently.*[53]

The relationship of interest to attention can be seen by noting the difference in advertisement readership across product classes. A study in the early 1950s of nearly 8,000 one-page advertisements in *Post* and *Life* was conducted by Starch, a service that regularly reports advertising readership. It revealed that automobile advertisement readership by men, according to one of their measures, was five times as high as that for women's clothes and about twice as high as for toilet goods, insurance, and building materials. For women, the highest categories were motion pictures and women's clothing, which had twice the readership of advertisements for travel and men's clothing and four times that for liquor and machinery.[54]

Russell Haley offers several case studies to support his opinion that people are more apt to look at and remember things in which they are interested than things in which they are not.[55] He further hypothesized that people are interested in information concerning benefits that they feel are important in a product. He thus applies benefit segmentation to the task of penetrating the attention barrier. In one on-air television test, the interest in the benefit offered in the commercial was measured for each of five segments, as was the attention level achieved by the commercial. The results showed a nice relationship between interest and attention:

Segment	Interest	Attention
1	17	43
2	12	35
3	12	23
4	10	25
5	8	27

In another study reported by Haley, the target segment was preoccupied with their children's welfare. A child-oriented test advertisement received an attention level over five times that of each of the five other advertisements.

A most effective approach for gaining attention would be to run an advertisement about the person or persons to whom it is directed, mentioning him by name and discussing his activities. Max Hart (of Hart, Schaffner & Marx) reportedly scoffed at his advertising manager, George L. Dyer, when the latter offered to bet him $10 that he could compose a newspaper page of solid type that Hart would read word for word. Dyer said, "I don't have to write a line of it to prove my point. I'll only tell you the headline: THIS PAGE IS ALL ABOUT MAX HART."[56]

Such an approach is usually impossible (except in direct marketing mail pieces, where the letter and envelope can often be "personalized" by laser printing the recipient's name), but advertisements can be developed with which people can readily identify. For instance, an insurance company ran a series of advertisements in which agents were presented in a most personal way. Their hobbies and lifestyles were discussed in a manner that made it easy for readers to identify with them. Such advertisements, of course, were sure to have an enormous impact on the company's agents, who could easily picture themselves in them. A firm's own employees or its retailers are often an important audience, even if not the primary one.

Another approach is to present a communication involving topical issues—those in which the audience is likely to be heavily involved. Thus, in the late 1980s and early 1990s, many companies began tying their advertising appeals to various aspects of the highly topical issues of ecology and recycling. As long as the copy is handled properly, the resulting association will very likely be positive. "News value" can also be created by the advertiser, as was done by Taster's Choice Instant Coffee, which ran an ad campaign much like a soap opera miniserial, with TV viewers following each episode of the amorous goings-on between two apartment neighbors who met when she ran out of Taster's Choice for a dinner party and wanted to borrow some from him. Yet another approach is to address the lack of interest head-on and challenge it. When CIGNA insurance ran ads announcing its change in logo in 1993, the ad said "Was. (showed old logo), Is. (new logo), Who Cares? (copy giving reason for the change)." Obviously, a creative agency could come up with hundreds of other ways to create interest.

FROM ATTENTION TO RECALL. . . . .

As we said in Chapter 5, the recall of an ad's content is a necessary but not sufficient condition for persuasion. Recall is typically a more important ad objective in low involvement situations, because consumers may not go through a great degree of thinking about which brand to buy. In high-involvement situations, consumers typically use more brand-attribute information in deciding which brand is better for them, so persuasion becomes very important—but recall of the brand, and the attributes of the brand, is obviously still necessary, because the actual brand choice will likely occur at some point in time after the ad was seen. In both kinds of situations, therefore, an ad has not only to attract attention, but also to communicate the brand name and the brand benefits in a memorable way.

How can an ad create higher levels of brand name and copy point recall? Obviously, several complementary methods are possible. One is higher levels of advertising repetition, enabling a high level of competitive *share of voice*. This can be made possible by higher ad budgets (see Chapter 16) or by focusing on frequency rather than reach in one's media plan, perhaps by using smaller ad units (fifteen-second TV spots instead of thirty-second spots) or by utilizing cheaper media (such as radio or outdoor). These issues are discussed in Chapter 17.

Another obvious method is to utilize more distinctive creative material in the ad. Ads that are novel and distinctive not only get noticed more, they also get remembered more. In addition, ads can use higher levels of repetition (of the brand name and of the key selling message) *within* each ad. High-recall TV and radio ads, for instance, often repeat each of these three times or more within each commercial. Ads can also use memorable slogans or jingles that help get the consumer repeat the brand name and/or key selling idea to themselves long after they see the ad. These and other ideas are discussed more fully in the chapters on creative tactics (Chapters 12 and 13).

Finally, since the actual brand choice will be made most likely in an in-store environment far away from and much later than the actual advertising exposure, it is very helpful to try to use in-store cues that will help the consumer to remember the brand name and the brand's benefits at the moment when in-store choices are made. As we discussed more fully in Chapter 3, the advertiser can thus reproduce some key ad element on the packaging of the brand itself, on in-store point-of-purchase material, or in other forms of in-store advertising media, such as shopping cart advertising. These and other devices help the consumer recognize the brand and its message in the store, so they don't have to be recalled entirely from memory. They thus make the key advertising theme more retrievable and accessible in the consumer's mind at the time of choice, thus increasing the likelihood that the advertised brand will be chosen.

ATTENTION VERSUS COMPREHENSION. . . . .

The approaches discussed to make an ad more attention-getting could be said to "borrow interest" for the "real" material in the ad, from the various executional devices discussed, to increase attention for the entire ad. In doing so, an advertiser should be concerned not to attract attention in a manner that diverts interest from the important points of the message. In particular, it is not useful to attract an individual with a highly interesting subject if the brand and its message get lost in the process. For example, sexually attractive models tend to generate high interest among some audience segments, but they can also divert a reader from the message. A study by Jessica Severn, George Belch and Michael Belch found that sexually explicit ad stimuli can lead to the generation of thoughts that deal much more with the ad execution than with the message about the brand, so that while ad and brand name recall might go up, copy point recall tends to go down.[57]

These trade-offs arise not only with the use of sex in advertising, but with many other executional devices as well, including the use of humor, of endorsers, and so on. Thus, it appears that a portion of the advertisement can dominate a reader's perception to the detriment of the communication impact if that portion that dominates is not related to the advertisement objective. The deleterious effects of such distracting executional elements were also highlighted in a recent study of the copy test scores of 750 television commercials by ASI Market Research, Inc.[58] This analysis showed, first, that certain camera and sound techniques that detract from clarity of communication—such as camera techniques that interfere with clear framing, logical flow, and smoothness of motion, or sound effects and music that make it difficult for the words of the copy to be clearly heard—decrease attention to the ad. Second, the extent to which the viewer links the ad to the brand name, in memory, is dependent on how early and how often the brand name is mentioned. It seems clear that when an ad is being scripted, priority must be given to communicating the brand name and the key copy points, and attention-getting executional elements must not be allowed to interfere with the consumer's ability to pay attention to, understand, and remember these vital brand-related elements.

In sum, it cannot be emphasized enough that the task of the advertiser is not merely to create ads that evoke attention, vital enough as that is, but also to ensure that adequate *copy point communication* occurs. The comprehension of an ad's positioning, through its copy points, has a real and measurable impact on advertising response: most researchers today agree that good comprehension is vital for persuasion to occur. David Stewart and David Furse have demonstrated that the understanding of a brand's differentiating qualities is the most important factor in an ad's persuasion scores (referenced in Chapter 5's discussion of recall versus persuasion). Indeed, research has shown that if consumers fail to comprehend the arguments in an ad about why the brand is better, they will turn instead to the "peripheral" aspects of the ad (such as the expertise of the endorser) in forming their attitudes toward the brand. On the other hand, if comprehension does occur, this allows attitudes to be formed in a more "systematic" or "central" manner, and factors such as the source's expertise become less important. We therefore turn now to discussing some factors that help determine how successfully an ad conveys its desired copy points.

INTERPRETATION AND COMPREHENSION . . . . . .

We turn now to our second perceptual step, the interpretation and comprehension of stimuli. Here, there are two kinds of comprehension one could be concerned about. The first is objective comprehension: did the reader of the ad interpret it and comprehend it just the way the advertiser intended? This is what is being measured in copy test scales of copy point communication: how many consumers took away from the ad the message we wanted to give them. A second approach to comprehension is to ask how much subjective comprehension occurred. Did the ad reader think only about the explicit ad content, or did they they go beyond that and make some inferences about message content that weren't explicitly part of the ad? Did they go "deeper" and embellish the ad content in some way, using their own general knowledge about the way the world works? Did they go even "deeper," and somehow relate the ad's content to their own lives and own experiences and fantasies? David Mick has argued that the deeper the level of such subjective comprehension, the more effective the ad will be in credibility, in being liked, in persuasion, and in recall.[59]

The tenets of Gestalt psychology, which we will discuss below, are useful in understanding the psychological processes in both kinds of comprehension, because they tell us how and why someone could interpret the ad in ways possibly different from those intended.[60] The German word *gestalt* is roughly translated into configuration, or whole, or pattern. The Gestalt view is that it is necessary to consider the organized whole, the system of elementary events, since the whole has a meaning distinct from its individual parts. Gestalt psychologists enunciated two principles. The first is the concept of the organized whole, or gestalt. Stimuli are perceived not as a set of elements, but as a whole. When a person looks at a landscape, she or he does not see many blades of grass, several trees, white clouds, and a stream, but, rather, a field or total configuration. This total has a meaning of its own that is not necessarily deducible from its individual components. The second concept is that an individual has cognitive drive toward an orderly cognitive configuration or psychological field. An individual desires to make the psychological field as good as possible. A good field or gestalt is simple, familiar, regular, meaningful, consistent, and complete. The modern consistency theories, such as dissonance theory, so useful in attitude research, are outgrowths of this second tenet, which was developed in the study of the perceptual process.

In the following section, the first and basic principle of Gestalt psychology will be discussed and illustrated in an advertising context. The emergence of the organized whole from a limited set of stimuli is demonstrated by a set of classic experiments. The importance of interrelationships among stimuli is brought out. An implication of the Gestalt view is that a brand must be considered as an organized whole and not simply as the sum of independent attributes. Another is that the context is important. After these implications are considered, we turn to the concept of a cognitive drive toward a "good" Gestalt and to some determinants of perceptual organization.

The Organized Whole

S. E. Asch conducted a classic set of experiments, reported in 1946, that demonstrated how individuals form organized wholes and the importance of interactions among component parts.[61] A group was read a list of personal characteristics and asked to write a brief impression of the person described by the list. The list contained seven attributes: intelligent, skillful, industrious, warm, determined, practical, and cautious. A second group, with the same instructions, was read the same list except that the word "warm" was replaced by the word "cold." The difference in the two groups' perceptions was striking. The warm person was perceived to be happier, better natured, more sociable, more altruistic, more humorous, and more imaginative. Further experiments indicated that when polite versus blunt was used instead of warm versus cold, the differences became relatively minor. And, Asch determined that the first few terms established a context in which later terms were evaluated. Perception was affected by the order in which the terms were presented.

Asch generated several conclusions from these experiments. Even when the stimuli are incomplete, people seem to strive to form a complete impression of a person or object. Thus, advertising copy does not necessarily have to tell the whole story; an individual will naturally fill in the gaps. The studies indicated that stimuli are seen in interaction. The intelligence of a warm person is perceived differently from that of a cold person. Because of such interaction effects, the total impact of an advertising campaign needs to be considered. An appeal or an advertisement that may prove effective by itself may not be effective in the context of the whole campaign. Furthermore, the studies suggested that some attributes (warm-cold) are more central to the conceptual process than others (polite-blunt). Finally, the experiments indicated that the first few traits formed a set or context within which others are interpreted. Thus, an advertiser should be very concerned with first impressions. Generating trial with a big giveaway program may project a sleezy image from which a brand may never recover.

Principles of Perceptual Organization

An important tenet of Gestalt psychology is that there is a cognitive drive to obtain a good Gestalt or configuration, one that is simple, familiar, regular, meaningful, consistent, and complete. The human mind is not above making minor or even major distortions of the stimuli to accomplish this purpose. The following principles are related to this cognitive drive.

Closure

If we see a symbol that would be a square except that a small segment of one side is missing, our minds will fill in this gap and a square will be perceived. This process is called closure. In the Asch experiment, in which rather strong perceptions in individuals were obtained from a short list of attributes, closure was occurring. A detailed picture of an individual emerged from a sketchy list of cues.

An advertiser can use the closure process to make a campaign more efficient. A 60-second commercial can, for example, be run several times so that the content has been learned by a worthwhile percentage of the target audience. To combat forgetting, a shorter spot—maybe only 5 or 10 seconds long-could be used. Or, a radio campaign could be used to supplement a television campaign. Research by Julie Edell and Kevin Keller has shown that a viewer of the short TV spot, or a listener of the radio spot, will tend to visualize the omitted material.[62] Thus, the material contained in the sixty-second commercial will have been transmitted in a much shorter time. Furthermore, the risk of boring the viewer with repeated showings is reduced.

Another use of the closure concept is leaving a well-known jingle uncompleted. Those exposed will have a strong cognitive drive to effect closure by mentally completing the jingle. For example, Salem cigarettes mounted a campaign in which they presented "You can take Salem out of the country but you can't . . ." The audience then had to provide the familiar ending "take the country out of Salem." The Hathaway shirt advertisements showing the man in a dress shirt and eye patch ran without any mention of Hathaway. Again, the audience was expected via the closure process to insert the manufacturer's name. The ad for J&B scotch whisky shown in Figure 7–3 invites the reader to use closure to fill in the brand's initials. Activating the closure process in this manner can get the reader involved, even to the extent of stimulating effort on his or her part. Such involvement often enhances learning. Research by Frank Kardes and others has shown that forcing consumers to make their own inferences from an ad (rather than having the ad itself draw that conclusion explicitly) leads to consumer attitudes that are more accessible from memory and more stable over time because such inferences require cognitive effort.[63] Such inference-based accessible attitudes should then be more likely to have an impact on behavior.

Closely related to closure is the process of interpreting an ambiguous stimulus. Again, the interesting part of the process is the participant's involvement. The hope is that ambiguity will stimulate sufficient interest to sustain the cognitive activity necessary to "figure it out." There are several ways in which an advertisement can be made "ambiguous." Consider, for example, an advertisement made up of three principal elements—a picture, some written material, and the brand name. Ambiguity can be introduced into any of these components (and may be a way to highlight or emphasize a component) or into the relationship among components. The picture, for example, could be made ambiguous by leaving out parts of it or us-

Figure 7–3.   Seeking closure: J&B Scotch whisky.

Copyright by The Paddington Corporation. Reprinted by permission.

ing some form of abstract art. The written material could contain innuendo or indirect meanings. For example, "Does she or doesn't she?" and "I'm Sylvia—fly me to Miami" contain other associations besides those of hair coloring and air travel. Even the brand or company name could be made relatively or completely "ambiguous," as in the Hathaway shirt example. The object of ambiguity can be to tease an individual's curiosity, to draw attention to the advertisement, to initiate consideration and thinking, or to motivate an individual to learn. There are, of course, dangers in making an advertisement itself or any component thereof too ambiguous, just as moderate incongruity is better than extreme incongruity.

Assimilation-Contrast

Another principle of perceptual psychology is called *assimilation-contrast*. Cognitively, an individual will seek to maximize or minimize the differences among stimuli. Assimilation and contrast operate in cases in which stimuli are neither very similar nor very different. In these cases, an individual will tend to perceive them as being "more" similar than they really are (*assimilation*) or to exaggerate the differences (*contrast*) cognitively. Both tendencies are related to the cognitive drive to simplify stimuli. The perception process is made easier if one sees only similarities or dissimilarities, eliminating the "in-betweens."

An advertiser can take advantage of the assimilation principle in many ways. It provides a rationale for family or umbrella brands like Kellogg's, Betty Crocker, or Westinghouse. The hope is that buyers will tend to generalize their past experiences with the brand to a new product (a cereal, a cake mix, or a dishwasher) that carries the brand or company name. This tendency to assimilate a new product into a family brand will be enhanced by the use of advertising styles that have come to be associated with the family brand. Many advertisers (such as Microsoft, Compaq, Apple) thus strive for a common "look and feel" for all their ads.

The assimilation principle can also be used to advantage by the use of analogies, such as a luxury car trying to link itself with some other symbol of luxury (such as a Faberge egg). Joan Meyers-Levy and Brian Sternthal point out that assimilation can be expected to occur either if a consumer only uses low effort in processing the ad and focuses on the similarity between the two items being linked together, or when the two advertised objects display high overlap. If the consumer processes the ad much more deeply, however, and if the two items display low overlap, the differences between the two objects are more likely to be focused on, and a contrast effect is more likely to emerge.[64]

Assimilation can also work to an advertiser's disadvantage. Thus, a new product variation may be perceived as the same as the old one unless efforts are made to guard against this reaction. Also, advertisements for similar products, like menthol cigarettes, that tend to use similar appeals run the danger of being assimilated. As a result, a smaller brand may not get much mileage out of its advertising since the audience may not distinguish it from its more widely known competitor. In such situations, it is sometimes necessary to use dramatic means as UPS Overnight Delivery Service does in Figure 7–4, trying to distinguish itself from its more widely known rival, Federal Express. Another example of assimilation working to an advertiser's disadvantage would be the Eveready battery ads using a pink

Figure 7–4.   Fighting assimilation: UPS Overnight Delivery.

Courtesy of United Parcel Service of America, Inc.

bunny, which won praise for their humor but were often misidentified by consumers as being ads for other battery brands.

Miscomprehension of Advertising

If consumers can "naturally" misinterpret communications through the drive for closure and through such assimilation-contrast processes, then it could be argued that some of the advertising accused of being deliberately deceptive (see Chapter 18) is not intended to be so, but gets misinterpreted "naturally." To see what proportion of televised and written communications were miscomprehended, the Educational Foundation of the American Association of Advertising Agencies conducted two studies a few years ago. The first study covered television communications, and was conducted in 1979. Sixty thirty-second televised communications—including ads, public service communications, and editorial content—were tested for miscomprehension among nearly 2,700 consumers.[65] The study found that somewhere between 28 to 30 percent of the communications (ads or other content) were miscomprehended, as measured by a particular series of true-false questions. While this percentage should not be accepted uncritically, since it comes from one study using one particular research method, it does show the wide extent to which consumers can read unintended meanings into communications.

The second study was conducted a few years later and covered print (magazine) ads and editorial content.[66] Some 1,350 consumers were asked questions about fifty-four full-page magazine ads and another fifty-four editorial pages. This time, roughly 20 percent of the material was miscomprehended, with another 15 percent being not understood (the consumers said they "didn't know" when asked about 15 percent of the information). In both studies, miscomprehension was higher among older, less educated consumers. Taken together, these studies clearly point to the importance of creating ads that not only get attention, but also communicate clearly and unambiguously the key copy points that are intended to be gotten across. An example of miscomprehension hurting a brand is the case of the new soft-drink Crystal Pepsi. Unlike Pepsi, this drink had a lighter taste, but this fact was not made clear in the launch advertising, which used a playful line "You've never seen a taste like this." This line apparently wasn't comprehended by consumers to mean the taste was very different from Pepsi, so many people expected it to taste just like Pepsi (because of the similarity in names) and were disappointed when it didn't. The company therefore eventually dropped "Pepsi" from the name, and ran new ads that were much more direct about the "new citrus cola" taste of Crystal.[67]

SUMMARY

A successful advertising message must, first of all, be able to attract attention. The ad that fails to get attention is unlikely to achieve anything else. It must also be interpreted in the way that the advertiser intended. Perception is the process of attending to and interpreting stimuli. The first stage is the attention filter, and the second is the interpretation process. Each exists as a potential perceptual barrier through which an advertisement must pass if it is to influence the viewer, listener, or reader. Getting attention is not easy, particularly in television where viewers can do other things while a program is showing. Zipping (fast-forwarding through ads when viewing prerecorded programs on a videocassette recorder) and zapping (switching across programs using a remote control device) has made the problem of getting and holding viewer attention particularly difficult. Zipping and zapping can be reduced by creating commercials that are very interesting or entertaining. The perception process includes both attention and interpretation and is influenced by stimulus characteristics such as copy size, intensity, and message, and by audience variables such as needs, attitudes, values, and interests.

To understand the attention filter, it is instructive to determine why people attend to advertisements. One motivation is to secure information that has practical value to them in making decisions. In some circumstances people will engage in active search for information. A second motivation is selective exposure, obtaining information that supports attitudes or purchase decisions and avoiding nonsupportive information. A third motivation is to obtain variety and combat boredom. Adaptation-level theory postulates that individuals learn to associate a stimulus with a reference point or adaptation level. Attention is created when an object differs significantly from what it is supposed to be like. Weber's law addresses the question of how different a stimulus has to be from the adaptation level to be perceived as different. Finally, people are attracted to advertisements that are interesting.

Two concepts from Gestalt psychology help us to understand the interpretation process. The first is that stimuli are perceived as a whole. What is important in an advertisement interpretation is the total impression that it leaves. The second is that an individual has a cognitive drive toward an orderly cognitive configuration. Closure is an example of the cognitive drive toward a familiar, regular, and meaningful configuration. If a subject realizes that something is missing from a picture, his or her mind will add it. Assimilation-contrast, another example of this cognitive drive, is used by the audience member to remove ambiguity from a stimulus. A host of audience conditions can influence interpretation, among them needs, values, brand preferences, social situation, cognitive styles, and cognitive needs. Studies of miscomprehension in advertising have shown that from 20 percent to 30 percent of ads and other content are misinterpreted. It is vital that ads are created not only to gain attention, but also to communicate key copy points clearly and unambiguously and minimize miscomprehension.

DISCUSSION QUESTIONS

1. For each of the following products, indicate under what circumstances, if any, an audience member would engage in active search, passive search, or passive attention.
   a. Automobiles.
   b. Toothpaste.
   c. Sugar.
   d. Cement mixers.

e. Business forms.

f. Greeting cards.

g. Computers.

2. Under what conditions are people likely to read long copy?

3. Consider five advertisements you have read recently. Why did you read them? What was your motivation? Does your motivation fit into one of the four categories listed in the chapter? Should other categories be added?

4. In one study, it was found that recent car purchasers tended to read advertisements for the brand they bought. How do you explain this finding? Are there explanations in addition to those of consistency theory?

5. Pick out a print and a television advertisement that you feel is informative and one of each that you feel is not informative and explain your choices. Do you feel that television advertising in general is informative?

6. What are the factors that determine when a person will seek consistency and when a person will seek complexity? Suppose that you are advertising toothpaste and have identified one segment in one category and another segment in the other. How do you decide upon which segment to focus? How would the advertising campaigns for the two segments differ?

7. How should a copy team go about balancing the need to attract attention and gain advertisement readership with the need to generate a certain kind of impact? Be specific. What procedures should be followed? Can these procedures be embedded in a formal decision model?

8. What is adaptation-level theory in the advertising context? How could one measure the environment of the advertisement quantitatively?

9. How have advertisers attempted to minimize zipping and zapping? Which, in your opinion, is the more serious of the two problems? Estimate the economic impact of zapping for a brand of coffee with an annual advertising budget of $52 million.

10. Recall advertisements that use the concept of closure. Were they, in your opinion, more effective because of it? Why? What is the difference between closure and contrast?

11. Give an example of an advertisement that will motivate assimilation for some and that will activate a contrast mechanism for others.

12. What is meant by the *collative* property of an ad? What effect might it have on attention and interpretation?

NOTES. . . . .

1. Steuart H. Britt, Stephen C. Adams, and Allan S. Miller, "How Many Advertising Exposures per Day?" *Journal of Advertising Research*, 12 (December 1972), 3–9.

2. Cathy J. Cobb-Walgren, "The Changing Commercial Climate," *Journal of Current Issues and Research in Advertising* (1990) 343–368.

3. Jacob Jacoby and Wayne D. Hoyer, "The Comprehension/Miscomprehension of Print Communication: Selected Findings," *Journal of Consumer Research*, 15, no. 4 (1989), 434–443.

4. James J. Gibson, "Perception as a Function of Stimulation," in Sigmund Koch, ed., *Psychology: A Study of a Science* (New York: McGraw-Hill, 1959), p. 457.

5. David T. Kollat, Roger D. Blackwell, and James F. Engel, *Research in Consumer Behavior* (New York: Holt, Rinehart and Winston, 1970), p. 48.

6. By creation, we refer in part to the closure process, which will be discussed later in this chapter.

7. Robert J. Kent, "Competitive versus Noncompetitive Clutter in Television Advertising," *Journal of Advertising Research*, 33, no. 2 (March–April 1993), 40–45.

8. Raymond R. Burke and Thomas K. Srull, "Competitive Interference and Consumer Memory for Advertising," *Journal of Consumer Research*, 15 (June 1988), 55–68.

9. Peter H. Webb and Michael L. Ray, "Effects of TV Clutter," *Journal of Advertising Research*, 19 (June 1979), 7–12.

10. Tom J. Brown and Michael L. Rothschild, "Reassessing the Impact of Television Advertising Clutter," *Journal of Consumer Research*, 20 (June 1993), 138–146.

11. Peter Webb, "Consumer Initial Processing in a Difficult Media Environment," *Journal of Consumer Research*, 6 (December 1979), 225–236.

12. *Business Week*, November 23, 1987, p. 38.

13. Felix Kessler, "In Search of Zap-Proof Commercials," *Fortune*, January 21, 1985, pp. 68–70.

14. Barry M. Kaplan, "Zapping-The Real Issue Is Communication," *Journal of Advertising Research* (April/May 1985).

15. Fred S. Zufryden, James H. Pedrick, and Avu Sankaralingam, "Zapping and Its Impact on Purchase Behavior," *Journal of Advertising Research*, 33, no. 1 (January/February 1993), 58–66.

16. Carrie Heeter and Bradley S. Greenberg, "Profiling the Zappers," *Journal of Advertising Research*, 25 (April/May, 1985), 15–19.

17. Mark Lacter, "TV Commercial Industry Fights Back," *San Francisco Chronicle*, February 11, 1983, p. 59.

18. T. J. Olney, Morris Holbrook, and Rajeev Batra, "Consumer Responses to Advertising: The Effects of Ad Content, Emotions, and Attitude on Viewing Time," *Journal of Consumer Research*, March 1991.

19. John McSherry, "The Current Scope of Channel Switching," *Marketing and Media Decisions*, June 1985.

20. Joseph M. Winski, "Apple Fails to Register," *Advertising Age*, January 28, 1985, pp. 1, 98.

21. *Advertising Age*, October 26, 1986.

22. John J. Cronin and Nancy E. Menelly, "Discrimination Vs. Avoidance: 'Zipping' of Television Commercials," *Journal of Advertising*, 21, no. 2 (June 1992), 1–7.

23. Patricia A. Stout and Benedicta L. Burda, "Zipped Commercials: Are they Effective?" *Journal of Advertising*, 18, no. 4 (1989), 23–32.

24. David A. Aaker, "Developing Corporate Consumer Information Programs," *Business Horizons*, October 1981.

25. John Caples, *Making Advertising Pay* (New York: Dover Publications, 1966), and *Tested Advertising Methods* (Englewood Cliffs, NJ: Prentice Hall, 1974).

26. Robert E. Burnkrant, "A Motivational Model of Information Processing Intensity," *Journal of Consumer Research*, 3 (June 1976), 21–30.

27. David Ogilvy, *Confessions of an Advertising Man* (New York: Atheneum, 1964), pp. 108–110.

28. Franklin B. Evans, "Psychological and Objective Factors in the Prediction of Brand Choice: Ford Versus Chevrolet," *Journal of Business*, 32 (October 1959), 363.

29. Joseph W. Alba and J. Wesley Hutchinson, "Dimensions of Consumer Expertise," *Journal of Consumer Research*, 13 (March 1987), 418–419.

30. John A. Howard and Jagdish N. Sheth, *The Theory of Buyer Behavior* (New York: Wiley, 1969), pp. 164–165.

31. D. Ehrlich et al., "Post-decision Exposure to Relevant Information," *Journal of Abnormal and Social Psychology*, 54 (1957), 98–102.

32. J. F. Engel, "Are Automobile Purchasers Dissonant Consumers?" *Journal of Marketing*, 27 (1963) 55–58.

33. Judson Mills, "Avoidance of Dissonant Information," *Journal of Personality and Social Psychology*, 2 (1965), 589–593.
34. Rajeev Batra and Wilried R. Vanhonacker, "Falsifying Laboratory Results Through Field Tests: A Time-Series Methodology and Some Results," *Journal of Business Research*, 16 (1988), 281–300.
35. Salvatore R. Maddi, "The Pursuit of Consistency and Variety," in R. P. Abelson et al., eds., *Theories of Cognitive Consistency* (Chicago: Rand McNally, 1968).
36. Daniel E. Berlyne, *Conflict, Arousal, and Curiosity* (New York: McGraw-Hill, 1960).
37. A wide variety of relevant studies are reported in D. W. Fiske and S. R. Maddi, eds., *Functions of Varied Experience* (Homewood, IL: Dorsey Press, 1961).
38. Ogilvy, *Confessions of an Advertising Man*, p. 105.
39. These and subsequent Starch results are taken from Daniel Starch, *Measuring Advertising Readership and Results* (New York: McGraw-Hill, 1966).
40. Scott B. MacKenzie, "The Role of Attention in Mediating the Effect of Advertising on Attribute Importance," *Journal of Consumer Research*, 13 (September 1986), 174–195.
41. Ann L. McGill and Punam Anand, "The Effect of Vivid Attributes on the Evaluation of Alternatives: The Role of Differential Attention and Cognitive Elaboration," *Journal of Consumer Research*, 16 (September 1989), 188–196.
42. Morris B. Holbrook and Donald R. Lehmann, "From Versus Content in Predicting Starch Scores," *Journal of Advertising Research*, 20 (August 1980), 53–62.
43. Bruce J. Morrison and Marvin J. Dainoff, "Advertisement Complexity and Looking Time," *Journal of Marketing Research*, 9 (November 1972), 396–400.
44. H. Rao Unnava and Robert E. Burnkrant, "Effects of Repeating Varied Ad Executions on Brand Name Memory," *Journal of Market Research*, 28 (November 1991), 406–416.
45. David W. Schumann, Pichard E. Petty and D. Scott Clemons, "Predicting the Effectiveness of Different Strategies of Advertising Variation: A Test of the Repetition-Variation Hypothesis," *Journal of Consumer Research*, 17 (September 1990), 192–202.
46. H. Helson, "Adaption Level Theory," in *Psychology: A Study of a Science: 1, Sensory Perception and Physiological Formulations* (New York: McGraw-Hill, 1959).
47. J. Craig Andrews, Syed H. Akhter, Srinivas Durvasala, and Darrel D. Muehling, "The Effects of Advertising Distinctiveness and Message Content Involvement on Cognitive and Affective Responses to Advertising," *Journal of Current Issues and Research in Advertising*, 14, no. 1 (Spring 1992), 45–58.
48. *The Wall Street Journal*, Dec 16, 1993, p. B7.
49. Susan E. Heckler and Terry L. Childers, "The Role of Expectancy and Relevancy in Memory for Verbal and Visual Information: What Is Incongruency?" *Journal of Consumer Research*, 18 (March 1992), 475–492.
50. George Mandler, *Mind and Body* (New York: W. W. Norton), 1984.
51. Edward F. McQuarrie and David G. Mick, "On Resonance: A Critical Pluralistic Inquiry into Advertising Rhetoric," *Journal of Consumer Research*, 19 (Sept. 1992), 180–197.
52. Developed in Fiske and Maddi, *Functions of Varied Experience*.
53. Elihu Katz, "On Reopening the Question of Selectivity in Exposure to Mass Communications," in Abelson et al., *Theories of Cognitive Consistency*, p. 793.
54. Starch, *Measuring Advertising Readership and Results*, p. 89.
55. Russell I. Haley, "Beyond Benefit Segmentation," *Journal of Advertising Research*, 4 (November 1971), 3–8.
56. This anecdote was reported by Ogilvy, *Confessions of an Advertising Man*, p. 6.
57. Jessica Severn, George E. Belch, and Michael A. Belch, "The Effects of Sexual and Nonsexual Advertising Appeals and Information Level on Cognitive Processing and Communication Effectiveness," *Journal of Advertising*, 19, no. 1 (1990), 14–22.
58. David Walker and Michael F. von Gonten, "Explaining Related Recall Outcomes: New Answers from a Better Model," *Journal of Advertising Research* (June/July 1989), 11–21.
59. David G. Mick, "Levels of Subjective Comprehension in Advertising Processing and their Relations to Ad Perceptions, Attitudes, and Memory," *Journal of Consumer Research*, 18 (March 1992), 411–424.

60. For an excellent introduction to Gestalt and other theories in social psychology, see Morton Deutsch and Robert M. Krauss, *Theories in Social Psychology* (New York: Basic Books, 1965).

61. S. E. Asch, "Forming Impressions of Personality," *Journal of Abnormal and Social Psychology*, 41 (1946), 258–290.

62. Julie A. Edell and Kevin L. Keller, "The Information Processing of Coordinated Media Campaigns," *Journal of Marketing Research*, 26 (May 1989), 149–163.

63. Frank Kardes, "Spontaneous Inference Processes in Advertising: The Effects of Conclusion Omission and Involvement on Persuasion," *Journal of Consumer Research,* 15 (September 1988), 225–233.

64. Joan Meyers-Levy and Brian Sternthal, "A Two-Factor Explanation of Assimilation and Contrast Effects," *Journal of Marketing Research*, 30 (August 1993), 359–368.

65. Jacob Jacoby and Wayne D. Hoyer, "Viewer Miscomprehension of Televised Communication: Selected Findings," *Journal of Marketing*, 46, no. 4 (1982), 12–26.

66. Jacob Jacoby and Wayne D. Hoyer, "The Comprehension/Miscomprehension of Print Communication: Selected Findings," *Journal of Consumer Research*, 15, no. 4 (1989), 434–443.

67. *The Wall Street Journal*, April 30, 1993, p. B1.

8 UNDERSTANDING BENEFIT-BASED ATTITUDES

> Said a tiger to a lion as they drank beside a pool,
> "Tell me, why do you roar like a fool?"
> "That's not foolish," replied the lion with a twinkle in
> his eyes. "They call me king of all the beasts
> because I advertise."
> A rabbit heard them talking and ran home like a
> streak. He thought he would try the lion's plan, but
> his roar was a squeak. A fox came to investigate—
> and had his lunch in the woods.
> The moral: When you advertise, be sure you've got
> the goods!
> (Fable)

Once the target market for an advertising campaign has been identified, and communication and positioning objectives set, the advertising manager needs to make decisions about the content of the advertising message, or what we call *message strategy*. For example, what should be the basic thrust or message of the TV commercials or magazine ads that will make up the ad campaign for the brand in question?

Here—based in part upon the kinds of research reviewed in Chapter 5—the manager must decide if the message needs to focus on communicating product benefits (and, if so, exactly what benefits), developing or reinforcing a brand image or personality (and, if so, what specific personality), evoking and associating specific feelings and emotions with the brand, or making the brand appear fashionable by creating social and group influences. These topics are covered in the remaining chapters that constitute Part III of this book. Creating buying action is another possible objective, and the tools for doing that (such as direct marketing, cooperative advertising, or sales promotions) were discussed earlier in Chapter 3.

This chapter focuses on the question of which benefits need to be communicated in order to change consumer attitudes toward the brand. Until we provide a better definition later in this chapter, a product benefit can be thought of as a positive payoff to the consumer from a certain product attribute, and we will use the terms *attribute* and *benefit* interchangeably. In general, advertisers want to accent the positive and focus advertising on those attributes that are perceived as advantages of the product (either in an absolute "good-for-you" sense, or relative to competitor products). Sometimes it is advantageous to focus part of the advertising message on negative attributes of your product. *Refutational advertising* (Volkswagen is a "lemon") employs this technique. The point is that to analyze the question of which *benefits* to communicate, we really need to know which *attributes* are considered in making the brand-choice decision and which of them are most important in the targeted product-market situation.

And, in order to know whether a particular positioning strategy will really work, we need to know whether the product *attributes* and images are linked to overall attitudes in the consumer's mind. Do his or her perceptions, feelings, and beliefs about the attributes of a brand really influence the decision process? All these are questions about attitude and market structure.

The chapter therefore begins with a brief overview of the attitude construct and various approaches to measuring attitude. This is followed by a section on how to identify the important attributes and benefits in a given product-market situation. Then some well-known models of attitude are presented, and some of the things to look out for in using the models are noted. The use of the attitude construct for segmentation and market planning rounds out the chapter.

ATTITUDE LEVELS AND COMPONENTS . . . .

Attitude is a central concept in the entire field of social psychology, and theories and methods associated with its explanation and measurement have largely evolved from the work of social psychologists and psychometricians. Gordon W. Allport, for example, has stated that "Attitude is probably the most distinctive and indispensable concept in American social psychology. No other term appears more frequently in experimental and theoretical literature."[1]

The most widely held view of the structure of an attitude is that it is made up of three closely interrelated components: *cognitive* (awareness, comprehension, knowledge), *affective* (evaluation, liking, preference), and *conative* (action tendencies such as intentions, trial, or purchase). Attention is usually focused on the middle (affective) component, assessing the degree of positive or negative feelings for an object. The underlying assumption is that this overall liking component is based on the cognitive component (beliefs and knowledge about the brand) and then leads to the intention to try (or lack of it).[2] In other words, we buy something because we like it, and we like it because we cognitively evaluate its benefits to us as good.

There have recently been arguments that people often develop overall attitudinal liking for objects without first cognitively evaluating them as good, with such overall attitudes being based purely on emotions and feelings rather than some rational, cognitive belief- or benefit-based evaluation.[3] This might be especially true in situations in which consumers lack the interest or knowledge (motivation and ability) to really think about the merits of competing brands: the kind of "low-elaboration likelihood" situation we discussed in Chapter 5. We will discuss such feeling-based attitudes in Chapter 9, when we focus on creating feelings through advertising.

For the moment, let us suppose that we are in the kind of high-involvement situation where consumers actually base their overall attitudes toward competing brands on the basis of an evaluation (either thorough, or more casual) of the benefits offered by these different brands. In such situations, we must know how to measure overall attitude and to understand the basis on which it is formed, in order to develop an advertising campaign that strives to increase the favorability of attitudes toward our brand.

Attitude can be measured directly by asking a respondent to indicate whether he or she likes or dislikes a brand or by attempting a direct assessment of the degree of like or dislike on a positive-negative scale. While this is useful, it does not give us "diagnostics": it does not tell us *why* a brand is liked or disliked. To get this information, we can rely on the attitude models that assume that this overall liking is based on a cognitive evaluation of underlying attributes or benefits of the brand, and get consumer ratings of the brand on those underlying aspects. For example, a consumer could be asked to judge a brand on the basis of several attributes or characteristics according to whether it was positive or negative on each, and the mean of her or his scores taken as the attitude measure. Such measures are called *multiattribute evaluations of the brand* because they are based on the evaluation of underlying attributes that is assumed to underlie the directly measured overall attitude.

Direct Measures of Overall Attitude

The simplest way to measure overall attitude toward an object (brand, store, product class, or whatever) is to ask a respondent whether he or she likes or dislikes it. There are no explicit attribute criteria given on which the evaluation is made. Respondents are simply asked to answer "yes" or "no," and the responses are used to determine the brand attitude.

If interest centers on attempting to capture the degree of attitude, the question can be put in the form of a scale. For example, a respondent could be asked to express how much she or he liked a brand on a scale ranging from "very much" (1) to "very little" (7). Other terms could be used, such as "excellent-poor" or "good-bad." George S. Day,[4] a Wharton professor, for example, suggested the seven-point scale shown in Figure 8–1 as being particularly appropriate for durable products. He points out how segments of the scale might be used to identify whether the object is preferred and whether or not it is likely to be considered if a purchase situation developed.

An important question is whether attitudes are related to brand choice and market behavior. Obviously, of course, the attitudes have to be measured in the way that is most specifically relevant to the behavior being predicted.[5] Even if measured correctly, positive attitudes toward a brand will not always result in purchase behavior. A person can have a positive attitude for a brand and yet not be willing or able to buy it. Many teenagers have strong positive attitudes for a Porsche, but few are likely to be purchasers. Furthermore, situational events at the time of purchase and/or "impulsive" behavior can throw off short-run sales predictions made on the basis of attitude measures taken some time previous to the

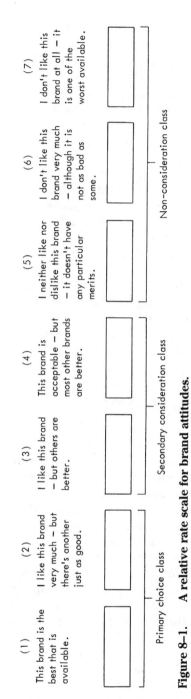

Figure 8-1. A relative rate scale for brand attitudes.

Source: George S. Day, Buyer Attitudes and Brand Choice Behavior (New York: Free Press, 1970), p. 160.

purchase occasion. As a third example, a consumer may end up buying a brand even if he or she does not have a favorable attitude, if the consumer feels that other people such as experts or a peer group like it, recommend it, or will be impressed by it. (These kinds of group norm effects are discussed in Chapter 11.)

However, if these types of cases are basically exceptions and are not dominant in the market or segment of interest, a strong relationship between attitude and purchase behavior should emerge. Alvin Achenbaum[6] has demonstrated that attitude and usage levels are associated in several consumer product categories. Figure 8–2 shows the attitude-usage relationship for a brand of cigarettes, deodorant, gasoline, laxative, and a dental product. For each of the four brands, the percentage using the brand is strongly related to the attitude toward it.[7]

According to some recent research, the relationship between attitudes and purchase behaviors gets stronger as the consumer gets more "direct" information about the brand (such as that obtained through actual trial): the consumer then feels more certain and confident about the attitude, and is more likely to use it in making purchase decisions.[8] Information about a brand obtained through advertising is relatively less "direct." Repeated advertising exposure, however, can increase how much information the consumer has about the brand, which can

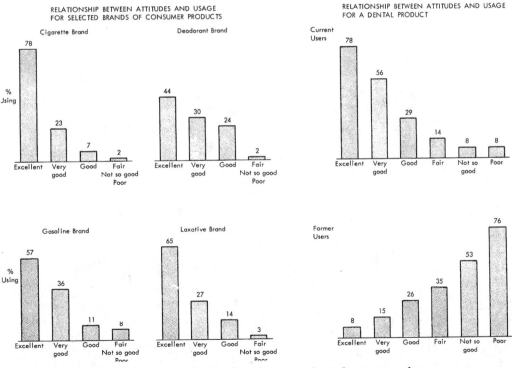

Figure 8–2.   Attitude-usage relationships in several product categories.

Source: Reprinted from Alvin A. Achenbaum, "Knowledge Is a Thing Called Measurement," in Lee Adler and Irving Crespi, eds., Attitude Research at Sea *(1966), p. 113, published by American Marketing Association.*

increase the confidence with which attitudes are held and thus increase their impact on behavior.[9]

Overall Attitude As an Objective

Overall attitudes are used for objective setting, strategic decision making, and evaluating performance in advertising. A range of attitudes can be identified for a brand that has been on the market for a short period. Figure 8–3 suggests that seven attitude segments might be identified for the brand, ranging from segment 1, holding strong negative attitudes, through segment 4, holding neither positive nor negative attitudes, to segment 7, holding strong positive attitudes. The tails of the distribution represent attitude extremes. The majority fall in the middle segments, holding slight tendencies in either direction or no *predisposition* one way or another with respect to the brand. These segments represent alternative targets for an advertising campaign.

Segment 7 might represent a small group of relatively heavy users who have become satisfied with the brand and are strongly loyal to it. Attitude in this case could be a measure of brand loyalty. We would expect this group to express strong positive feelings to back up their behavior and purchasing patterns.

Segment 4, on the other hand, could hold no attitude for our brand for at least two reasons. First, it represents people who do not yet know that our brand exists. They have not learned of it from our advertising, from friends, or by any chance use experience. Such people have not yet entered the *awareness* stage (this is the situation for new brands). Second, some people in this segment could be aware of the brand but be so uninvolved in purchasing with respect to the product class that no meaningful direction of predisposition exists. They could purchase it on one occasion but just as easily choose another brand on another occasion. Another representation of such consumers is to say that they see no meaningful differences in the brand choices available: their choice process is essentially random with respect to this product class, although it may not be with respect to others.

Segment 1 represents a small group of buyers who probably confine their

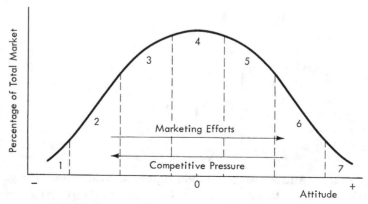

Figure 8–3.   Attitude segments for a hypothetical brand.

purchases to other competitive brands in the class, and reject ours. In other words, our brand is not in their *consideration class* or *evoked set* of alternatives from which they make a choice, even though they are aware of it. Their negative attitudes could be based on a host of reasons, many of which are sustained by our competitors.

In any of these situations, an argument can be made for continuing to engage in advertising to sustain or change attitudes for two fundamental reasons. First, attitudes decay over time, and go below the threshold needed for active consideration. Just as a good friend can be forgotten when not around, so a good brand can be forgotten unless effort is expended to keep its name before the public. The rate of decay and the number of insertions necessary to sustain the threshold level are questions to be examined later, in Chapter 17. The second reason is that in most market situations competitors are constantly attempting to create favorable attitudes for their brands at the expense of our own. As shown by the opposing arrow in Figure 8–3, there is a constant force operating in the opposite direction to our marketing efforts, a force that attempts to pull our customers away.

Importance of the Attributes That Underlie Overall Attitudes

Although an advertiser can glean much useful information from knowing the market's attitude for his or her brand, it is equally or more important to know what lies behind those attitudes. Basically, what are the strengths and weaknesses of the brand and what are the important criteria or attributes on which decision making is based? Particularly significant is the identification of the one or the few attributes used by consumers to choose between brands that are relatively similar or, as some would say, "functionally equivalent."

In most cases, copy development will focus on one or a few attributes. Competition for the consumer's attention is usually so intense that it is only possible to get one or a few ideas across, and it thus becomes crucial to identify the attribute (or the few attributes) that are most important in consumer decision making. Should a toothpaste manufacturer, for example, focus on decay prevention, bright teeth, fresh breath, or perhaps the taste of the product? Would a university be better off stressing the international reputation of its faculty, the physical environment in which it resides, or some exceptional aspect of its teaching or research programs?

Many of the questions reviewed in the last chapter concerning which positioning strategy to adopt can be reduced to "which attribute(s) is most important in a given purchasing or choice situation?" More precisely, these questions are ones of identifying the attributes that are most important in attitude formation and change and ultimately in the purchase-choice decision itself. Every product, service, or choice situation has associated with it a set of attributes on which the choices are made. In the case of choosing between Coke and Pepsi, for example, taste is likely to be very important.

Attributes can be examined at different levels. James Myers and Allan Shocker[10] have made a distinction between physical characteristics, pseudophysical characteristics, and benefits, all of which can be used in positioning and attribute selection. Physical characteristics are the most objective and can be measured on some physical scale such as temperature, color intensity, sweetness, thickness, distance, dollars, acidity, saltiness, strength of fragrance, weight, and so on. Pseudophysical characteristics, in contrast, reflect physical properties which are not easily measured. Examples are spiciness, smokey taste, tartness, type of fragrance (smells like a . . .), greasiness, creaminess, and shininess. Benefits refer to advantages that promote the well-being of the consumer or user. Psychological benefits can usually be classified at the benefits or pseudophysical level.

MEANS-ENDS AND LADDERING ANALYSIS. . . . . .

Another useful way of distinguishing between the different levels of attributes is through the *means-end chain model*.[11] This model focuses on the connection between product attributes, consumer consequences, and personal values, through a process called "laddering":

> product attributes → consumer consequences → personal values

In this model, values represent the desired end states. They can have an external orientation ("feeling important" or "feeling accepted"), or they can relate to how one views oneself ("self-esteem," "happiness," "security," "neatness," "accomplishment"). Product attributes and consumer consequences represent the means that can be used to achieve the desired ends. Product attributes include measurable physical characteristics such as "miles per gallon" or "cooking speed" and subjective characteristics such as "tastes good," "strong flavor," or "stylish." Consumer consequences are any result occurring to the consumer. Consequences can be functional ("saves money" or "don't have to wash your hair every day") or can affect self-perceptions ("having more friends," "having fun," or "being more attractive").

The means-end chain model suggests that it is the associational network involving attributes, consequences, and values that really represent needs to be understood in developing message content. Effective advertising should thus address all levels and not just be concerned with the product attributes. The major positive consumer consequences should be communicated verbally or visually, and the value level should provide the driving force behind the advertising.

One approach to eliciting a means-end chain can be illustrated using an airline example.[12] The process begins with a repertory grid exercise in which consumers are asked to state how two airlines out of a set of three are similar and how they differ. Suppose the attribute "has wide-bodied aircraft" emerges from this exercise. Consumers are then asked why an attribute such as "wide bodies" is preferred. One response might be "physical comfort." The consumer is then asked why "physical comfort" is desired. The answer could be to "get more done." Another "why" question yields a value, "feel better about self." Similarly, the "ground service" attribute leads to "save time," "reduce tension," "in control," and "feeling secure."

A campaign based on the ground service attribute would then address the consequences ("save time," "reduce tension," and "in control") and value ("feeling secure") dimensions. A mother needing personal service might be presented traveling with children. The theme is being "in control," being able to cope with the situation. The result is a feeling of security. The creative group will, of course, have knowledge of the total means-end structures as they develop the campaign. An example of a means-ends chain for the airline category is presented in Figure 8–4. An ad that illustrates the means-ends distinction is that for Sharp's nonalcoholic beer

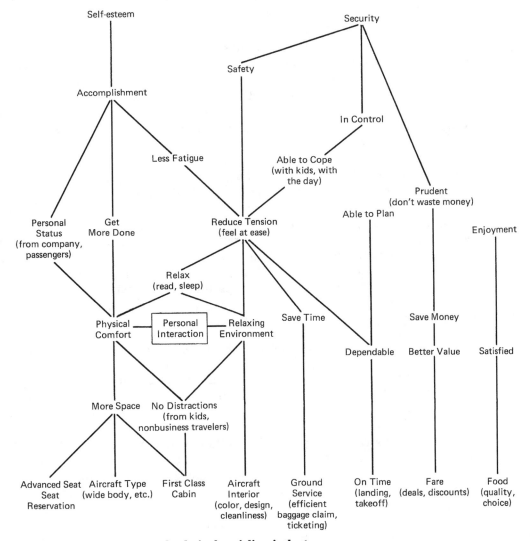

Figure 8–4.   Means-ends chain for airline industry.

Source: Thomas S. Reynolds and Jonathan Gutman, "Advertising Is Image Management," Journal of Advertising Research, 15, February/March 1984, p. 34. © 1984 by the Advertising Research Foundation.

in Figure 8–5: here the "means" is nonalcoholic beer, but the "end" is "keeping your edge" for the next bowling game.

IDENTIFYING IMPORTANT ATTRIBUTES OR BENEFITS . . . .

A great many methods, approaches, and techniques have been developed to identify and determine the relative importance of the set of attributes on which brands are perceived and evaluated. In some cases, the relevant set of attributes will be known from past experience with the product category or past research with similar brands. In others, the first task will be to conduct research designed to reveal the attribute set itself. Once this set has been found, other procedures for developing specific measures or importance weights on each attribute can be used.

Suppose an advertiser faces a situation in which very little is known about how buyers choose among alternatives. How can the relevant attribute set be identified? Procedures such as focus groups, in-depth consumer interviews, or the Kelly repertory grid[13] can be used. Jacob Jacoby and others[14] developed an extension of the repertory grid that uses an information display board. Analysis procedures have been developed that allow the ordering of the attributes identified in this way on the basis of their importance.[15]

Once the set of attributes has been identified, the problem of identifying which of them are more or less important can be addressed. In particular, the advertiser needs a specific measure of the importance of each attribute in the set. Various forms of attribute rating and ranking instruments can be used to obtain judgments about the attributes themselves. And, methods called *conjoint analysis,* which give respondents levels of each attribute to consider, are employed. Examples of these various approaches are presented in the next sections.

Rating, Ranking, and Conjoint Analysis

Attributes or benefits, rather than brands or objects, can be the focus of research, and procedures similar to those used for measuring overall attitude given earlier applied to measure their importance. The most straightforward ranking approach is simply to ask consumers to rank a list of attributes in order of importance. This is much like voting data in political elections, and the attributes that receive the most "votes" are considered to be the most important.

The most straightforward rating method, which has the advantage of ease of understanding and administration, is to present the attributes as a list with a very important–very unimportant scale alongside each. The consumer simply checks the appropriate scale position in each case according to how important the particular attribute is in the purchase decision. A modification of this procedure is to use a Likert scale. In this case, statements such as "It would be very important for me to know whether the next tire I purchased was steel-belted or nylon-belted" are developed. The respondents are asked to record the degree to which they agree or disagree with each such statement.

The direct rating and ranking methods, particularly those which ask in a

Figure 8–5.   An advertisement showing the brand as a means to an end.

Courtesy of Miller Brewing Company.

straightforward way the degree of importance of each attribute, are comparatively inexpensive and easy to administer. The argument is that if some attributes are included that are unimportant, this will simply show up in the final data analysis. A problem, of course, is that consumers are prone to want "everything" and tend to reflect these desires by rating everything as important. Most products are, in effect, trade-offs of desirable attributes, and the direct methods tend not to uncover these trade-offs. What the advertiser really wants to know is the degree to which consumers are willing to trade off one desirable feature in favor of another.

Another problem with the direct methods is that they do not specify what really is meant by "more" or "less" of an attribute. The respondent is presented with the attribute only, and not levels of the attribute. Much interest has thus been generated in methods designed to recover importance weights from data generated by presenting respondents with combinations of attribute levels. As a group, these procedures are known as *conjoint analysis*, or *conjoint measurement*. The goal of conjoint analysis is to derive importance weights of the attributes and attribute levels; this is similar to that of the ranking-rating methods, but the procedures differ in how the data are collected and analyzed. In all versions of the technique, the consumer is asked to make trade-offs between various attributes, all of which may be seen as desirable.

Figure 8–6 gives an example of a stimulus card used in conjoint analysis for a study of automobile tires in which five attributes—brand, tread life, sidewall, price, and type of belting—were involved. Various computer analysis routines can be used to derive importance weights from the data collected. Figure 8–7 shows

I. Trade-Off Approach

BRAND	TREAD LIFE		
	30,000 Miles	40,000 Miles	50,000 Miles
Goodyear	8	4	1*
Goodrich	12	9	5
Michelin	11	7	3
Brand X	10	6	2

1* Denotes best-liked combination

II. Full-Profile Approach

Brand: Brand X
Tread Life: 50,000 Miles
Sidewall: White on Black
Price: $55
Type of Belt: Steel Belted Radial

Respondent Rating?

7

Least Liked								Most Liked
1	2	3	4	5	6	7	8	9

Scale Board

Figure 8–6. Examples of stimulus cards used in trade-off and full-profile approaches of conjoint analysis.

Source: Patrick J. Robinson, "Applications of Conjoint Analysis to Pricing Problems," in David B. Montgomery and Dick R. Wittink, eds., Market Measurement and Analysis *(Cambridge, MA: Marketing Science Institute, 1980), p. 185.*

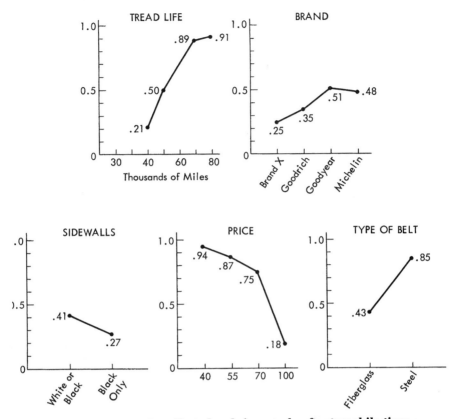

Figure 8–7.   Importance of attribute levels in a study of automobile tires.

Source: Patrick J. Robinson, "Application of Conjoint Analysis," in David B. Montgomery and Dick R. Wittink, eds., Market Measurement and Analysis *(Cambridge, MA: Marketing Science Institute, 1980), p. 186.*

that in this study, for example, respondents valued long tread wear (80,000 miles) and low price ($40) very highly in comparison with whether sidewalls were a particular color or even the tire brand. Also, as can be seen, whether the tire is steel-belted or fiberglass appears to make a significant difference. Respondents value steel-belted much more than fiberglass.

The overall importance of each attribute can also be derived from such data. Figure 8–8 shows the results in this study. As can be seen, price and tread life are the most important attributes in the set of five attributes tested, whereas type of belt, brand, and sidewalls follow in that order.

A significant advantage of conjoint measurement is that new combinations of attributes, and, hence, judgments about the relative attractiveness of new "products" can be derived from the data. By knowing how important each level of an attribute is, the researcher can combine various levels and derive the overall value of the new combination. Some recent developments in the area of conjoint analysis are presented in an appendix to this chapter.

Ranking, rating, and conjoint analysis procedures are most useful for deriving

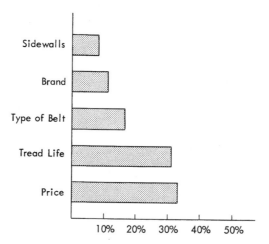

Figure 8–8.   Overall attribute importance in the automobile tires study.

Source: Patrick J. Robinson, "Applications of Conjoint Analysis," in David B. Montgomery and Dick R. Wittink, eds., Market Measurement and Analysis *(Cambridge, MA: Marketing Science Institute, 1980), p. 186.*

importance weights for a set of attributes as well as for providing the advertiser with many additional insights into feasible brand and product combinations. Whether such attributes do in fact determine attitudes and ultimate brand purchases is the subject of the next section.

Leverage and Determinant Attributes

Do the attributes identified by consumers as being important really make a difference when it comes to overall brand attitudes, preferences, and choices?

An attribute that has high *leverage* is one that has a high degree of influence on overall attitude. Its influence may derive from its importance to individuals in their attitude structure, the attribute weight. However, its influence may not be totally reflected by the importance weight. It is not unlikely that one attribute affects another in a cognitive structure. Thus, a communication that affects perception or belief along one attribute might have a significant indirect effect on other attributes and thus on the attitude structure. For example, an attribute like styling may have high leverage not only because the consumer values it highly (and by itself) with respect to a product class, but also because it may affect evaluations on other attributes like performance and convenience. Thus, a change in brand perception on the styling dimension may affect perception with respect to performance and convenience, and, therefore, have a stronger influence on attitude than might at first be suspected. If styling is, for some reason, the foundation for performance and convenience, a change in either of the latter may not have a similar effect on styling.[16]

One approach to measuring leverage might be to measure the strength of the cognitive link between one attribute and others. An attribute that is independent and not "connected" to other attributes might be considered to have no influence beyond that represented by its importance weights. Another attribute that seemed closely intertwined with other attributes (tends to have strong cognitive association) might have more leverage than is reflected by its importance weights.

Another more direct approach to measuring leverage might be to alter systematically the perception of a brand on a dimension and observe the change on the overall attitude scale. Attributes that had the greatest impact on overall attitude would be those with the highest leverage. Yet another approach is to obtain evaluative beliefs on a set of attributes and correlate these with brand attitude scores or buying intentions. The attributes with the highest correlations are considered to have the highest amount of leverage and are called *determinant attributes*.

James Myers and Mark Alpert[17] examined correlations of five attributes of a snack mix with a measure of overall attitude and buying intention. The new snack food was placed in 200 homes in the Los Angeles area, and homemakers were asked to serve it to families and friends. After serving, they were asked to rate the snack food in terms of color, appearance, taste, strength of flavor, and spiciness. Overall opinion (attitude) and buying intention measures were also obtained. The correlations (a number between −1 and +1 that indicates the degree of association) between these scales are given in Table 8–1. Of the five product attributes, taste has a much higher positive correlation with buying intention. Not only was taste by far the best predictor of buying intention, but it was a better predictor than overall attitude. Taste is obviously important in judging a snack food, but it may not be a useful criterion for distinguishing one brand of snack food from another.[18]

The Grey Advertising Agency has applied a similar conceptual approach by using different data collection and analysis procedures in well over twenty studies of attitudes and product usage over an eight-year period. Those attribute dimensions that correlate most highly with overall attitude are considered to be those with the highest leverage. Achenbaum,[19] in describing the Grey approach, points out that in many practical situations, it has provided information useful for prod-

Table 8–1. Correlation Matrix of Product Ratings for Snack Mix.

	1	2	3	4	5	6	7
1. Overall opinion		0.325	0.209	0.782	−0.324	−0.313	0.609
2. Color			0.498	0.308	−0.045	−0.099	0.189
3. Appearance				0.260	0.006	−0.133	0.036
4. Taste					−0.172	−0.161	0.617
5. Strength of flavor						0.759	−0.092
6. Spiciness							−0.084
7. Buying intention							

Source: James H. Myers, "Finding Determinant Buying Attitudes," Journal of Advertising Research, *10, December 1970, p. 11. © 1970 by the Advertising Research Foundation.*

uct development and packaging, as well as for advertising. In general, it is a diagnostic tool for understanding why particular attitude states exist. He points out that certain factors, such as safety, although relevant, rarely had competitive leverage among the major brands rated. Presumably most consumers consider the major brands to be safe to use although this may not be the case with some of the less well-known brands.

USING MULTIATTRIBUTE ATTITUDE MODELS . . . .

There are dozens of models and theories about the connection between perception and preference or attributes and attitudes.[20] In this section, the basic principles underlying each of these model classes are presented and assessed, and examples are given of their application to advertising.

Evaluative Belief Models of Cognitive Structure

A *cognitive structure model* assumes that a person forms an attitude toward an object by developing beliefs about that object and then combining those beliefs into a general overall attitude toward the object. The most commonly used cognitive structure model in advertising is the *evaluative belief model,* in which the attitude is the sum of the evaluative beliefs about how well each brand scores on each attribute, weighted by the importance of that attribute:

$$A_o = \Sigma \, w_d a_{od}$$

where

A_o = attitude of an individual or segment toward object o

a_{od} = evaluation of an individual or segment toward object o with respect to attribute or dimension d, the evaluative belief

w_d = measure of the relative importance or weight of attribute d to the individual or segment.

Suppose that A_o represents the attitude for a particular model of automobile, a Ford Escort, for example, and three characteristics—size, miles per gallon, and price—are most important to a particular segment. A study of the segment revealed the following set of weights and evaluative beliefs:

$$A_o = w_1 \, a_{o1} + w_2 a_{o2} + w_3 a_{o3}$$
$$= 2(-2) + 5(+1) + 3(+1)$$
$$= +4$$

Using Cognitive Structure Models for Message Strategy

How could advertising improve the attitude toward the Escort? Clearly, the objective is to increase the total sum of the (weights times beliefs). There are three routes to increasing this sum. The first is to change the weights. Advertising might attempt to decrease the importance of the size factor, for example, either by explicitly downplaying it or by ignoring it altogether and emphasizing good gas mileage instead. Second, the segment could be enticed to include new attributes, such as reliability, in their appraisal. Third, their evaluative beliefs could be altered by advertising. For example, a comparative advertisement could show that the Escort gets better mileage than its nearest competitors, and at the same time, costs less. This would raise the beliefs for the Escort and lower those for its competitors.

Examples of ads trying to increase the weights on attributes on which the brand is strong are Figure 8–9 (in which Subaru tries to make its all-wheel drive advantage more important) and Figure 8–10 (in which Fleischmann's margarine tries to raise the weight on its "no water added" attribute).

It should be obvious from the assumptions of this model that ads should not attempt to play up those brand features that are either not unique to the brand (i.e., the brand has no competitive superiority on these beliefs), or where the brand's belief superiority is not on highly rated attributes. Yet this does happen more often than you might imagine!

Model Assumptions

The model just discussed includes several explicit assumptions that may not always hold. For example, it assumes that there are a limited number of known attributes with known weights. In some circumstances, a consumer may not be aware of all the attributes used. A consumer, for example, may rationalize the purchase of a small sporty convertible on the basis of gas mileage but actually buy it because of a subconscious drive to lead an exciting life. Further, the model assumes that the weighted evaluative beliefs are added when there could be interactions present. A person may want some combination of attributes and will not value the object highly unless the desired set of attributes is included.

Another assumption is that a person first obtains belief information and then uses that information to alter attitudes. However, the process could actually work the opposite way. In one clever study, the psychologists Richard Nisbett and Timothy Wilson had subjects observe an interview with a person with a European accent.[21] For one group the person spoke in an agreeable and enthusiastic manner, whereas for another group, the same person appeared autocratic and distrustful. The students then rated the person's likability and three other attributes that were the same for both groups: physical appearance, mannerism, and accent. Subjects in the "warm" condition found these attributes attractive, whereas subjects in the "cold" condition found them irritating. Further, subjects in both conditions were certain that their liking of the teacher did not influence the attribute ratings, but rather, the reverse was true.

Ideal-Point Models

There are dozens of other attitude models that are elaborations of the basic evaluative belief model. Some, such as *ideal-point models*, rely on different approaches to data collection and an assumption that a particular combination of levels on each attribute can be found that represents a person's or total market's "ideal" combination. These models involve the perceptual mapping and multidimensional scaling procedures that were reviewed in Chapter 6.[22] The obvious message strat-

WHY BUY A CAR WITH SMART BRAKES AND DUMB WHEELS?

Buying a car with anti-lock brakes is a smart move. But what about when you're not braking? What happens when you're just driving? Or cornering? Or tackling a slippery hill? That's when you need a Subaru with the all-road, all weather traction of All-Wheel Drive.

a tricky turn. It's what makes a Subaru with All-Wheel Drive truly beautiful.

AWD MEETS ABS.

All-Wheel Drive provides extra

the Legacy a safety combination that you can't get on any other car in its class. Perhaps that's why Subaru sells more all-wheel drive cars in America than all other carmakers combined.[**]

The New All-Wheel Drive Legacy₂
LS Station Wagon

ACTIVE SAFETY
THE BEAUTY OF ALL-WHEEL DRIVE.

Unlike passive safety features like seat belts and air bags,[*] Subaru All-Wheel Drive is always working to help keep you out of trouble.

Under normal driving conditions, the system continuously delivers power to all four wheels. But should there be a loss of traction, power is instantly redirected to whichever wheels have the best grip. That way, you're always ready for an emergency swerve. A sudden storm. Even

traction to get you moving. But Subaru All-Wheel Drive also helps you stop.

During heavy braking situations, the All-Wheel Drive system actually assists the Anti-lock Braking System. With power available to all four wheels all the time, Subaru All-Wheel Drive can help control speed and works to bring you to a safe, controlled stop. This cooperation between All-Wheel Drive and anti-lock brakes gives

A SMALL PRICE TO PAY FOR
A SMART VALUE.

All-Wheel Drive isn't like **Tight Corner** standard four-wheel drive. It's automatic and low maintenance. It gets better mileage than a front-wheel drive Honda Accord **Snowy Road** Wagon or Toyota Camry.[†] And an All-Wheel Drive Legacy starts at $15,999.[††] **Wet Road**

So call 1-800-WANT-AWD or visit your dealer to test-drive an All-Wheel Drive Subaru. It's **Rough Road** the smartest thing on four wheels.

SUBARU.
The Beauty of All-Wheel Drive.™

Always wear seat belts. [*]Based on P. L. Polk & Company Registration Statistics for year-end 1993. [†]Based on comparison of EPA city fuel

economy estimates for 1995 Legacy, 1994 Honda Accord Wagon and 1994 Toyota Camry. [††]Suggested retail price of Legacy Brighton AWD M/T Station Wagon not including inland transportation, taxes, license and title fees. Dealer's actual price may vary. Pictured is AWD Legacy LS Wagon. MSRP is $21,455. Certain items shown are optional equipment available at an additional charge.

Figure 8–9.   Trying to increase an importance weight: Subaru.

Courtesy of Subaru of America, Inc.

Figure 8–10. Trying to increase an importance weight: Fleischmann's.

Courtesy of Nabisco, Inc.

egy implications of these models is to make the advertised brand seem perceptually closer to the ideal brand by using the positioning tactics discussed in Chapter 6.

Noncompensatory Models

The evaluative belief models we discussed are examples of *compensatory models.* A low rating on one dimension can be compensated for by a high rating on another dimension. There are also a set of *noncompensatory models* that might be better in certain situations. Three such models are the conjunctive, disjunctive, and lexicographic.

The *conjunctive model* emphasizes low ratings on the various attributes. An object will be deemed acceptable if it meets a minimum standard (a minimum attribute level) on each attribute. This process has been shown to operate in supermarket buying decisions. In one study,[23] new grocery products were considered for stocking by buyers only if they rated at least average in quality, company reputation, sales representation, and category volume and were less than 110 percent of the cost of the closest substitute. If they failed to meet any of these criteria, they were excluded. Similarly, one can imagine that a student buying a personal computer might have minimum requirements in terms of memory, chip speed, and so on. An advertiser must, in such situations, ensure that the ad's content does not make any "errors of omission" and present information about all the key attributes. For example, if target consumers want to buy PCs with at least 8 megabytes of RAM, they may ignore ads for brands that only offer 4 megabytes as standard, even if these computers can later be upgraded to more memory. It might make more sense to offer and advertise the PC with the desired minimum level of memory.

The *disjunctive model;* stresses high ratings. It regards objects as positive only when they have been rated outstanding on one or more of the relevant attributes. For instance, ready-to-eat breakfast cereals have many attributes (such as taste, nutritional content, etc.), but there may some eaters of such cereals who care most about the cereal not getting soggy in milk. Thus a cereal advertiser advertising to them needs to ensure that advertising focuses on the "stays crispy" benefit. The *lexicographic model* assumes that an individual will evaluate the brand on the most salient attribute. If two or more brands "tie" on this attribute, the evaluation will shift to the second most salient attribute. The process will continue until a brand is selected.

Research shows that some of these noncompensatory models (e.g., the lexicographic one) are often used when the consumer is not really very involved or is under time pressure to make a choice, so that choosing the very best brand is not the prime concern, just a brand that "is good enough." It is also quite possible that an individual in some contexts may use more than one model. He or she could, for example, use a conjunctive model to determine a set of brands to consider and then use a compensatory model to make the final decision. Clearly, the existence of such multimodel decision processes makes model evaluation more difficult.

Category Evaluation Models

The implicit assumption of cognitive structure models is that products are made up of discrete attributes and the decision makers combine these attributes to form an overall product attitude. A very different approach is *category-based evaluation*, which is based on the premise that people often divide the world into categories. In evaluating a new stimulus, it is placed into a category, and the attitude toward that category is retrieved from memory and applied to the stimulus. Reactions toward an individual can result from matching up that individual to a person category and applying the established attitudes toward that category.

For the category-based evaluation approach to operate, consumers develop a set of expectations about the product category. This expectation can be represented by either a typical example of the category, a *prototype*, or by a good example of the category, an *exemplar*.[24] To implement an advertising strategy based on the category-based model, the advertising should focus on positioning the brand with respect to some category exemplar. There would be no effort to communicate explicitly at the attribute level. One example is the humorous advertising for Parkay margarine which has a voice coming out of a box saying "butter." The advertising serves to position margarine with butter.

Another good example are the ads for the Yugo, the boxy Yugoslavian car that was introduced into the U.S. market at a base price under $5,000. The goal was to communicate that it was not only small and inexpensive but also dependable and reliable. The solution was to associate it with the Volkswagen Beetle. A TV commercial opened with a Beetle sitting in a white one-car garage with a voice-over saying: "The beloved Beetle. Once the lowest-priced car in America. Dependable. Basic transportation. But homely. And then it went away. Leaving an emptiness in the hearts of America." A Yugo print ad is shown in Figure 8–11. (Yugo has since left the U.S. market.)

SEGMENTATION USING ATTITUDE STRUCTURE ..

When the attitude is specified for a group rather than an individual, the attribute values are themselves averaged over those in the group. In such averaging, an implicit assumption is that the group is not excessively heterogeneous so that this average is representative of the total group, rather than only a small portion. As suggested in the section in Chapter 4 on segmentation, it is unlikely that all attributes are equally important to all people. In fact, it is much more likely that while consumer perceptions of how well the different brands perform on the different attributes are similar across consumers, their ratings of the relative importance of different attributes in brand selection will likely be different. Thus, while all consumers may agree that the Honda Civic car is very good in terms of fuel economy and that Volvos are very highly rated on safety, these consumers will probably differ in the relative importance they place on fuel economy or safety in their choice of a car.

It is therefore usually inadvisable simply to look at the average importance

Figure 8–11.   Positioning a brand with respect to a category.

Courtesy of Yugo-America.

ratings for attributes in any market. Instead, these differences across consumers in the importance placed on different product category attributes should be used to create segments for advertising campaigns and marketing strategy. In Chapter 6, for instance, we saw an example of benefit segmentation, where toothpaste users were placed into segments of the sensory consumers (highly valuing the attributes of flavor and appearance), sociables (highly valuing the brightness benefit), worriers (highly valuing decay prevention), and so on. The typical way to create these segments, as we discussed, was to collect research data from individual consumers on their attribute importance ratings, then to use cluster analysis techniques to create benefit segments, and then to compare, profile, the different segments in terms of their demographics, brand preferences, and media habits so that only appropriate segments could be targeted and messages created just for them.

Another example should illustrate this process (see Table 8–2 for some "made-up" data to illustrate the example). Suppose you were the advertising manager for AT&T's residential long-distance service. It is possible that research might show that AT&T was widely perceived as being the higher-quality telephone service, with better reliability, better customer service, and better operator assistance than its competitors (such as MCI). On the other hand, MCI might be rated higher on price (i.e., perceived as the lower-priced service). These perceptions might be pretty much the same for all consumers. However, consumers might differ in the importance placed on these attributes. One segment might want simply the lower-priced service, placing a greater weight on the price attribute than on quality, customer service, and operator assistance (let us call this the "price segment"). A second segment might place higher ratings on quality, customer service, and operator assistance, and lower value on cheaper prices (the "quality segment").

If this is what the research data showed, then it would make sense for AT&T to target the quality segment, because this segment places greater value on the attributes that AT&T is strong on, so that AT&T is at a greater competitive advantage in this segment. (Conversely, MCI might decide that it makes more sense to target the price segment.) Research would show who the quality segment is (for example, older and more affluent consumers, heavy readers of business magazines), and so AT&T could then develop advertisements for them demonstrating AT&T's superiority on these quality attributes and place them in appropriate media.

In the longer run, however, AT&T might also try to convert the price segment, by aiming campaigns at them that AT&T is not in fact more expensive in price (trying to change brand attribute adequacy perceptions), or by trying to convince them that they ought to place a greater weight on quality than on price (thus increasing consumer importance weights for an attribute that AT&T is competitively strong on). Conversely, MCI might in the longer run try to convert the quality segment by showing it was as good (or better) on quality as AT&T, or by increasing the importance weight on price.

As a different strategy, of course, AT&T (as the market leader, with close to 65 percent of the market), might try to increase total primary demand for residential

Table 8–2. Possible Analysis of Attitude Segments for Long-Distance Telephone Residential Market.

Attribute	"Price segment"			"Quality segment"		
	Importance weight[a]	Ratings of[b] AT&T	MCI	Importance Weight[a]	Ratings of[b] AT&T	MCI
Reliability	3.4	6.3	5.5	5.9	6.4	5.3
Customer service	4.6	6.5	5.1	6.3	6.7	4.9
Operator assistance	4.4	6.2	4.6	5.8	6.5	4.5
Price	6.2	5.5	6.5	4.6	5.7	6.2

[a]7 = most important, 1 = least important
[b]7 = rated better, 1 = rated worse.

long-distance phone calls. As discussed in Chapter 4, this strategy makes more sense for the market leader than for a small-share brand.

SUMMARY. . . . .

Once the target market has been identified and communication and positioning objectives set, decisions must be made about the content of the advertising message. This is called message strategy. Should the message focus on communicating product benefits, on developing/reinforcing brand image or personality, on evoking specific feelings and emotions, or on developing group associations? This chapter has focused on the benefits question. Benefits are the characteristics or attributes of a product that consumers perceive positively. In order to decide which and how many of them to focus on in an advertising campaign, we must understand attitude structure and processes of attitude formation and change. Attitude is a central concept in social psychology and has become, perhaps, the most significant focus of study in the fields of advertising management and consumer behavior. The most well-accepted view is that attitude is made up of three interrelated components called cognitive, affective, and conative. There are numerous approaches to attitude measurement, but they can be broadly classified into those that involve direct overall measures and those that involve derived multiattribute measures.

Direct measures involve questioning or observations of respondent behavior in which no explicit attribute criterion concerning the product is provided. Derived measures, on the other hand, rely on deriving overall attitude from a combination of subject response to attributes of the product. Attitude models generally refer to models which use attributes and derived measures to determine attitude. Such models provide useful diagnostic information, not generated in the direct case.

A market can be segmented on the basis of varying degrees of attitude-positive, neutral, and negative-held by customers or potential customers of a brand. Advertising objectives can then be cast in attitude terms with respect to specific segments or the market as a whole. In general, the two broad classes of objectives from this viewpoint are to attempt changes in the market from some negative or neutral to some positive position, or to sustain and to maintain a positive attitude and avoid attitude decay. Competition in this context is a force attempting to shift attitudes in the opposite direction.

Although knowing the overall market attitude for his or her brand is very useful for the advertiser, it is equally significant to identify the reasons for the attitude. In other terms, the advertiser needs to know what attributes, beliefs, and benefits are most important in the product-market situation, and in particular which of them are determinant in brand choice. The means-end chain model is useful in explaining the links between product attributes, consumer consequences, and personal values. Identify the relevant set of attributes is crucial to the analysis. Several procedures for doing this have been developed. Specific importance weights on each attribute can be derived by rating, ranking, and conjoint analysis methods. Conjoint analysis has undergone rapid development and is now widely used in industry. Leverage and determinant attribute research show how attributes that appear to have the greatest leverage in affecting an attitude structure or are most closely related to brand choice and behavior can be identified.

Attributes, benefits, and beliefs and their relation to overall attitudes have been formally studied in the context of evaluative belief attitude models. It is possible to focus on the two central constructs of an attitude model, evaluative beliefs and importance weights, and perform a segmentation analysis useful for diagnostic purposes. Each construct provides a criterion for classifying consumers into different market segments that have important strategy implications.

DISCUSSION QUESTIONS

1. Discuss the strategy implications of a bimodal (two-humped) distribution of brand attitude rather than the distribution shown in Figure 8–3.
2. Day recommends the following seven-point scale for obtaining direct measures of brand attitude:
    a. This brand is the best that is available.
    b. I like this brand very much, but there's another just as good.
    c. I like this brand, but other brands are better.
    d. This brand is acceptable, but most other brands are better.
    e. I neither like nor dislike this brand—it doesn't have any particular merits.
    f. I don't like this brand very much, although it is not as bad as some.
    g. I don't like this brand at all—it is one of the worst available.
    Administer this scale to twenty to thirty friends using five to ten brands in an appropriate product class. What are the shapes of the resulting distributions? What explanation could you offer for the shapes?
3. Discuss ways in which you could assess the strength (sometimes called the "valence") of an attitude. Is it true that a highly valenced attitude is always more stable than a weak one?
4. Compare and contrast the several methods used for identifying important attributes.
5. What fundamental assumption about belief-attitude relations underlies the "leverage" approaches to assessing the relative worth of alternative attributes? Why might an attribute be regarded as important but have low leverage? How might leverage be determined?
6. Explain the concepts of benefit, belief, attribute, and cognition.
7. Use the means-end chain model to explain the associational network that needs to be understood in developing message content for buying
    a. an automobile
    b. an expensive wristwatch
    c. shampoo
8. Collect data on attribute beliefs and weights for a Macintosh personal computer. Explain the alternative strategies Apple could use to advertise the Mac based on these data.
9. Suppose other research showed that personal computers were usually purchased based on noncompensatory evaluations. What does noncompensatory

mean in this context. Be specific and give examples. How would this affect message strategy for the Mac?

10. Assume the following information is available to you concerning the locations of four cereal brands on the two benefits of sweetness and crunchiness:

Brand	Sweetness	Crunchiness
A	2	−3
B	−1	2
C	4	5
D	3	2

Calculate the segment's attitude for each brand using the benefits information only. Rank the brands on this basis. Suppose that the importance weight for sweetness was found to be 0.80 and for crunchiness, 0.20. Recalculate attitude for each brand using the weighted belief model in the chapter. How would this change the rankings? Now suppose attitudes were formed using a conjunctive model in which the minimal desired sweetness level was 2. How would this change the rankings? What about a disjunctive model where only crunchiness mattered? Assume that you are the manager of brand B. Discuss the implications of these results for product and advertising strategy.

11. Think of a product category to which you can meaningfully relate, perhaps something you have contemplated buying. What comes to mind first as you contemplate the purchase: the attributes and benefits you would like to have satisfied, or the brands that are available to satisfy them? Will all people tend to follow this processing sequence? If so, why? If not, why not?

12. Write down the attributes that are meaningful to you and assign importance weights to each for jogging shoes or sneakers. Compare your results with two or three friends doing the same exercise. What problems occur in developing "importance weights" in this fashion?

NOTES . . . .

1. Gordon W. Allport, "Attitudes," in C. Murchison, ed., *Handbook of Social Psychology*, (Worcester, MA: Clark University Press, 1935). Reprinted in Martin Fishbein, ed., Readings in Attitude Theory and Measurement (New York: Wiley, 1967), p. 3.

2. Martin Fishbein and Icek Ajzen, *Belief, Attitude, Intention and Behavior: An Introduction to Theory and Research* (Reading, MA: Addison-Wesley, 1975).

3. Robert B. Zajonc, "Feeling and Thinking: Preferences Lead to Inferences," *American Psychologist*, 35 (1980), 151–175.

4. George S. Day, *Buyer Attitudes and Brand Choice Behavior* (New York: Free Press, 1970), p. 160.

5. Izek Ajzen and Martin Fishbein, "Attitude Behavior Relations: A Theoretical Analysis and Review of Empirical Research," *Psychological Bulletin*, 84, no. 5 (1977), 888–918.

6. Alvin A. Achenbaum, "Knowledge Is a Thing Called Measurement," in Lee Adler and Irving Crespi, eds., *Attitude Research at Sea* (Chicago: American Marketing Association, 1966), p. 126.

7. Ibid., p. 114.

8. Russell H. Fazio and Mark P. Zanna, "On the Predictive Validity of Attitudes: The Roles of Direct Experience and Confidence," *Journal of Personality*, 46, no. 2 (1978), 228–243; and Robert E. Smith and William R. Swinyard, "Attitude-Behavior Consistency: The Impact of Product Trial vs. Advertising," *Journal of Marketing Research*, 20, no. 3 (1983) 257–267.

9. Ida E. Berger and Andrew Mitchell, "The Effect of Advertising on Attitude Accessibility, Attitude Confidence and the Attitude-Behavior Relationship," *Journal of Consumer Research*, 16 (December 1989), 269–279.

10. James H. Myers and Allan D. Shocker, "Toward a Taxonomy of Product Attributes." Working paper (Los Angeles: University of Southern California, June 1978), p. 3.

11. Thomas J. Reynolds and Jonathan Gutman, "Advertising Is Image Management," *Journal of Advertising Research*, 25 (February/March 1984), 29–37; and Jonathan Gutman, "A Means-End Chain Model Based on Consumer Categorization Processes," *Journal of Marketing*, 46 (Spring 1983), 60–73. See also S. Young and Be. Feigin, "Using the Benefit Chain for Improved Strategy Formulation," *Journal of Marketing*, 39 (July 1975), 72–74.

12. Reynolds and Gutman, "Advertising Is Image Management," p. 32.

13. W. A. K. Frost and R. L. Braine, "The Application of the Repertory Grid Technique to Problems in Market Research," *Commentary*, 9 (July 1967), 161–175; and G. A. Kelly, *Psychology of Personal Constructs*, vols. I and II (New York: W. W. Norton, 1955).

14. Jacob Jacoby, George J. Szybillo, and J. Busato-Schach, "Information-Acquisition Behavior in Brand Choice Situations," *Journal of Consumer Research*, 3 (March 1977), 209–216.

15. John A. Quelch, "Behavioral Measurement of the Relative Importance of Product Attributes: Process Methodology and Pilot Application." Working paper 180R (London, Canada: School of Business Administration, University of Western Ontario, 1978).

16. John G. Myers and Francesco M. Nicosia, *Cognitive Structures, Latent Class Models, and the Leverage Index*. Paper presented at the Annual Meetings of the American Association for Public Opinion Research, Western Division, Santa Barbara, California, May 1968.

17. James H. Myers and Mark I. Alpert, "Determinant Buying Attitudes: Meaning and Measurement," *Journal of Marketing*, 32 (October 1968), 13–20.

18. Mark I. Alpert, "Identification of Determinant Attitudes: A Comparison of Methods," *Journal of Marketing Research*, 8 (May 1971), 184–191.

19. Achenbaum, "Knowledge Is a Thing Called Measurement."

20. In economics, for example, a long tradition of utility theory and associated models exists that essentially deals with this question. In social psychology, they are often referred to as evaluative belief models of cognitive structure to emphasize that attitudes are the product of both evaluations of the attributes and beliefs about how much of the attributes are possessed by the attitude object, as present in the consumer's cognitive understanding of the product category and brand. Paralleling the development of evaluative belief models and procedures has been a class of models that depend on deriving the attitude measure from a knowledge of the consumer's *ideal point*. Brands or objects that are closest to the ideal point in a positioning (multidimensional scaling) map are considered most preferred, and those farthest away, least preferred. The focus is first on locating the ideal point, and then deriving attitudes for each object as a function of the distance from this point.

21. Richard E. Nisbett and Timothy D. Wilson, "Telling More than We Can Know: Verbal Reports on Mental Processes," *Psychological Review*, 84 (May 1977), 231–259.

22. For some classic papers on the foundations of the work in advertising, see Ledyard R. Tucker, "Intra-individual and Inter-individual Multidimensionality," in H. Gulliksen and S. Messick, eds., *Psychological Scaling: Theory and Applications* (New York: Wiley, 1960); C. H. Coombs, "Psychological Scaling Without a Unit of Measurement," *Psychological Re-*

view, 57 (1950), 148–158; and J. F. Bennett and W. L. Hays, "Multidimensional Unfolding: Determining the Dimensionality of Ranked Preference Data," *Psychometrika*, 25 (1960), 27–43.

23. David B. Montgomery, "New Product Distribution: An Analysis of Supermarket Buyer Decisions," *Journal of Marketing Research*, 12 (August 1975), 255–264.
24. Eleanor Rosch and Barbara B. Lloyd, *Cognition and Categorization* (Hillsdale, NJ: Erlbaum, 1978).
25. Jordan L. Louviere, *Analyzing Decision Making: Metric Conjoint Analysis* (Beverley Hills, CA: Sage, 1988).
26. P. Cattin and D. R. Wittink, "Commercial Use of Conjoint Analysis: A Survey," *Journal of Marketing*, 46 (Summer 1982), 44–53.
27. D. R. Wittink and P. Cattin, "Commerical Use of Conjoint Analysis: An Update," *Journal of Marketing*, 53 (July 1989), 91–96.
28. D. R. Wittink, Marco Vriens, and Wim Burhenne, "Commercial Use of Conjoint Analysis in Europe: Results and Critical Reflections," *International Journal of Research in Marketing* (1993).
29. R. M. Johnson, "Comment on 'Adaptive Conjoint Analysis: Some Caveats and Suggestions'," *Journal of Marketing Research*, 28 (May 1991), 223–225.
30. Paul E. Green and V. Srinivasan, "Conjoint Analysis in Marketing: New Developments With Implications for Research and Practice," *Journal of Marketing*, (October 1990), 3–19.
31. Dick R. Wittink, Lakshman Krishnamurthi, and Julia B. Nutter, "Comparing Derived Importance Weights Across Attributes," *Journal of Consumer Research*, 8 (March 1982), 471–474.
32. Dick R. Wittink, Joel Huber, Peter Zandan, and Richard Johnson, *The Number of Levels Effect in Conjoint: Where Does It Come From, and Can It Be Eliminated?* (Ketchum, ID: Sawtooth Software Conference Proceedings, 1992).

APPENDIX: NEW DEVELOPMENTS IN CONJOINT ANALYSIS . . . .

Conjoint analysis has become well known and widely used in marketing and advertising research. Some marketing research companies such as Sawtooth Software and Bretton Clark have specialized in the techniques whereas other full-service marketing research firms such as Elrick and Lavidge have offered conjoint analysis as one of their service offerings. Some lesser-known methods focus on estimating preference functions at the aggregate or segment level [25] One of the most popular applications is in new product development. Conjoint analysis is useful in identifying attribute importance weights, part-worth utilities of attribute levels, and in simulations of various combinations of potential new products in a product category. P. Cattin and D. R. Wittink [26] found that almost three out of every four applications involved new product concept identification as one of the purposes. Pricing and market segmentation were also often mentioned as reasons for conjoint projects. Wittink and Cattin [27] provide similar data in an updated paper.

In yet another study, D. R. Wittink, Marco Vriens, and Wim Burhenne [28] surveyed European companies located throughout Europe, mostly in Germany and Britain. The authors found that the diffusion of conjoint analysis in Europe has been especially strong in recent years, particularly so in Germany and Britain. It is interesting that pricing was the most frequently mentioned use and that market segmentation was also ranked higher than in the United States. In contrast, use for competitive analysis was about twice as frequently mentioned in the United States. The personal interview was the most frequently used method of data collection in both Europe and the United States. The computer-interactive method called Adaptive Conjoint Analysis[29] (ACA) was a close second in Europe and has become much more widely used in the U.S. Concerning stimulus presentation, ACA is the most frequently used in Europe, followed by full-profile and tradeoff matrix formats. The vast majority of applications involve verbal descriptions for the presentation of stimuli. Rating scales also dominant as the most popular method of measuring response. Concerning estimation procedures, the authors found that OLS (Ordinary Least Squares) because it is easier to apply and commonly avaliable was used more often than the nonmetric procedures such as MONANOVA and LINMAP. Sample sizes ranged from as low as 30 to as high as 1,000 (the average was 268). As can be seen from these studies, conjoint is expanding in use in both the United States and Europe and is becoming a standard part of the arsenal of marketing and advertising research techniques.

Paul Green and V. Srinivasan[30] provide a relatively recent review of conjoint analysis. Their review updates an earlier 1978 review and addresses topics such as which type of preference model to use, data collection methods, stimulus set construction, stimulus presentation, measurement scales for the dependent variable, and estimation methods. The authors note that a relatively new data collection method called TMT (telephone-mail-telephone) has been developed. Respondents are recruited by telephone screening and the main interview materials (questionnaires, stimulus cards, incentive gifts, and other items) are mailed shortly afterwards. An appointment is scheduled for collecting all data by telephone and the conjoint exercise usually reserved for interviewer-interviewee interaction at the time of the followup call. The procedure can reduce selection bias, can include visual stimulus materials, completion rates are usually high, and there is no missing data problem.

An interesting problem in conjoint which has received a significant amount of research attention is called the attribute levels problem. D. R. Wittink, Lakshman Krishnamurthi, and Julia Nutter[31] and in several follow-up studies by Wittink and his colleagues found that the relative importance of an attribute increases as the number of levels on which it is defined increases, even though the minimum and maximum values for the attribute are held fixed. For example, the relative importance of price went up by 7 percentage points when two more intermediate levels were added to the three levels used for price. In their review, Green and Srinivasan suggest that the addition of intermediate levels to an attribute makes the respondent pay more attention to that attribute, thereby increasing its apparent importance in determining overall preferences. D. R. Wittink, Joel Huber, Peter Zandan, and Richard Johnson[32] argue that the source of the level effect is algorithmic rather than behavioral; it occurs more because of the algebra involved than because respondents give more attention to attributes with greater numbers of levels.

9 ASSOCIATING FEELINGS WITH THE BRAND

> Advertising that works is advertising that makes
> somebody feel something. . . . All advertising has
> some emotion. Some advertising is all emotion.
> (Hal Riney, Hal Riney & Associates)

> People do not buy from clowns.
> (Claude Hopkins, 1923)

Why do emotional, warmth-creating ads seem to work so well for Kodak film, but then seem to fail when Kodak introduced its hi-tech, new Photo CD product to consumers? Should beer ads focus more on feelings of fun, or on how their types of barley lead to better taste? Should Frigidaire appliance ads show a mother and baby going to the refrigerator for the night's feeding, or quote performance statistics? Is it always better to have ads that use likable humor?

To answer these questions, we need to understand the mechanisms through which ad-evoked feelings can shape consumers' attitudes towards brands. In Chapter 8, our discussion of message strategy focused on the thinking or cognitive response to advertising. The consumer processed information which potentially could change beliefs, attitudes, and behavior. This response often involves a logical, rational, thinking process. Advertising that attempts predominately to communicate or inform and thus activate the thinking process is termed "thinking" advertising.

In this chapter, however, we will focus on advertising which works by creating feelings that can ultimately influence attitudes and/or behavior. Thus, a commercial could portray active teenagers playing volleyball at the beach and enjoying 7-Up. A feeling of energy, vitality, fun, and belonging could be created that gets associated with the brand and thereby affects brand attitudes and behavior. Since these feeling responses usually are considered positive (liked) or negative (disliked), they are also termed affective responses. These specific feeling or affective responses (such as happiness, or warmth, or sadness) evoked by an ad are quite distinct from a consumer's overall rating of how likable or enjoyable or interesting the ad is, though they obviously will help determine such overall ratings of the ad's characteristics.[1]

The term *"feeling" advertising* is used here to describe advertising for which audience feeling response is of primary importance, and usually (but not always) little or no information content is involved. It usually is very much execution focused, as opposed to message focused, and relies on the establishment of a feeling, emotion, or mood and the association of this feeling, emotion, or mood with the brand. The association of such a feeling with the brand has been labeled a process of "emotional bonding" by some advertising agencies. Some of these feelings can also lead to brand imagery and personality, which we discuss in the next chapter. These associated feelings can also change the "symbolic or cultural meaning" that consumers associate with the brand: Kodak film, for instance, is now seen not just as a high-quality photographic film, but also as a part of American life, a part of families' warm experiences.

It should be clear that all commercials, even the most logical and informative, can develop feeling or affective responses. Similarly, some argue that even the most emotional commercials, seemingly without information content, can evoke some type of thinking and cognitive activity. Thus, there is a spectrum between pure "feeling" and pure "thinking" advertising according to the relative importance of the thinking response as opposed to the affective or feeling response. In fact, the Lowe and Partners/SMS agency believes that an effective advertisement should communicate at both the rational and emotional levels, using what they term the "emotional hard sell."[2] The idea is that it is necessary to arouse an emotional response, but the advertising also needs a rational hook—the tangible end benefits that the product will fulfill.

WHEN ARE FEELINGS MORE IMPORTANT? . . . . .

The Role of Involvement and Life-Cycle Stage

The role of feelings in advertising is most important when consumers don't have (or don't care to have) deeply considered attitudes towards brands. Michael Ray and Rajeev Batra have suggested that attitudes toward a brand have two components, an evaluative component that is influenced by beliefs about the brand and a brand-specific "liking" component that cannot be explained by knowledge about beliefs.[3] This "liking" component is presumed to be based on the attitude toward the ad as well as by exposure effects. The relative importance or "percentage contribution" of "liking" will be high when the amount of brand attribute information and associated processing effort are low. This suggests that feelings are probably more important in shaping brand attitudes in low-involvement situations.

Chris Allen, Karen Machleit, and Susan Kleine have also shown that specific feelings or emotions can have an effect on a consumer's behavior that go beyond the effects of a consumer's attitude toward the brand or behavior in situations where consumers don't really have well-thought out attitudes (for instance, towards the act of donating blood, which is often done out of habit or out of a desire to please others). In such situations when attitudes aren't well formed, the feelings that consumers associate with a brand or behavior can be especially important in determining whether they will actually choose that brand or perform that behavior.[4]

Consistent with these views, humor—as one example of feeling-evoking appeals—has not tended to be appropriate for high-involvement situations. As will be discussed when we look at the overall model of how feelings work in advertising, when ads evoke positive feelings it can sometimes reduce the total amount of thinking that consumers go through about the reasons stated in the ad why that brand is better. Such reductions in total thinking also occur when a feeling-oriented ad evokes what have been called "autobiographical memories." Thus, if a brand really has strong reasons why it should be preferred, and it is to the advantage of that brand to get the consumer to think about those reasons, then evoking positive feelings which reduce those kinds of thoughts doesn't make much sense. (See also our comments about the potentially harmful effects of "distractor thoughts" in Chapters 7 and 12).

Several advertising case-histories are consistent with the reasoning just presented. Federal Express Corporation dropped its lighthearted, humorous campaigns in favor of more serious, technology-based arguments (such as spare jets and backup computers, used to increase reliability), when competition intensified in the overnight package delivery business intensified in 1989.[5] The use of the Peanuts characters by Met Life (see Figure 9–1) to create a warm, likable feeling for the insurance company (and its agents) did not succeed in communicating its unique products and performance record.[6] Alka-Selzer's famous and well liked "I can't believe I ate the whole thing" humor ads did not stop the brand from losing sales when consumers decided they wanted antacid products with different formulations.[7] A series of field studies promoting audience attendance at social and business events found that a humorous promotion succeeded in improving attendance for a social event, but not for a business event.[8]

Similar reasoning would suggest that ads evoking feelings are most likely to be needed when consumers have a low level of intrinsic interest in the product category or brand, so that they are not forming deeply considered attitudes. This is most likely to happen in the mature stages of a product category's life cycle. In contrast, when a product category is new, and consumer interest in it is high, consumers might seek more "hard" product information (partly to educate themselves about the category or brand). Having feeling-oriented ads then might serve to reduce the amount of positive product information the consumer is looking for (because ads that evoke feelings reduce a consumer's ability and desire to "think"), and this might not be an advisable strategy. Thus, when Kodak launched its new Photo-CD product in late 1992, they initially ran warm, fuzzy ads for it (just like typical ads for Kodak film) but then discovered they needed more informative ads instead. By early 1993, they had switched to thirty-minute infomercials.[9]

The FCB and Rossiter-Percy Grids

However, consumer involvement in the product category (the consumer's need for information to choose the "best" brand) is only part of the story. According to the Foote, Cone & Belding (FCB) advertising agency, product categories (and different segments of product categories) can be classified into four categories, based on whether they are high or low in involvement and on whether they are "thinking" or "feeling" products. Thus "feeling" products can be either high-involvement (as in

Figure 9–1. Creating a warm, likable feeling: MetLife.

Courtesy of Metropolitan Life Insurance Company and United Feature Syndicate, Inc.

the case of cosmetics, jewelry, and fashion clothing) or low-involvement (e.g., beer, cigarettes, and candy, "life's little pleasures"). On the thinking products side, high-involvement products are illustrated by big-ticket items such as cars, appliances, and insurance, while low-involvement products are represented by paper towels, household cleaners, and gasoline. (See Figure 9–2.) Obviously, different sub-segments of product categories (such as cosmetic shampoos and medicated shampoos) can fall into different parts of the grid, and consumers can vary in where they would place different brands or categories. This "grid" has been extensively researched by FCB in many countries, and the firm recommends that feeling advertising is most appropriate for products and services that fall on the feeling side of the grid.[10] Other researchers have also found distinctions similar to FCB's thinking-feeling classification, such as Rajeev Batra and Olli Ahtola's classification of products into "utilitarian" versus "hedonic."[11]

John Rossiter and Larry Percy have recently offered an improvement on the FCB grid, with the notable expansion of the FCB think-versus-feel dichotomy into one with many more "motives" why consumers might wish to buy brands in different product categories. (See Figure 9–3.) They then show how ads can be designed to address each buying motive.

For instance, a "thinking" product could be purchased for one of several different "informational motives" that all have to with the consumer's desire to reduce certain negative feelings. Here, a product might be purchased either to remove a problem (in which case ads can show anger turning into relief through using that brand), for problem avoidance (show how fear changes to relaxation), or because of incomplete satisfaction with a prior purchase (show disappointment giving way to optimism), and so on.

On the "feeling" side, where various "transformational motives" can apply, consumers seek to increase certain positive feelings. Thus, something being bought for sensory gratification might be advertised emotionally by showing dullness changing to elation; something being bought for a sense of achievement or mastery needs to show how boredom can be changed to excitement through that brand purchase; and a product bought for social approval needs to show how the consumer's apprehension about social approval can be changed into feeling flattered.[12]

In the Rossiter-Percy model, the grid again has four cells, with low and high involvement being crossed with informational or transformational motives. In their view, ads in the low-involvement–informational quadrant need to focus on one or two key benefits, perhaps exaggerating them enough to provoke a trial purchase, and use a simple problem-solution format, without being concerned about likability. (Examples: Wisk's "ring around the collar" ads, or Charmin's original "Mr. Whipple.") Ads in the high-involvement–informational quadrant need convincing and logical brand claims, perhaps using refutational or comparative formats (we discuss these in Chapter 12). Ads in the low-involvement–transformational cell need a unique and authentic emotional benefit, delivered through a frequently repeated likable ad, that might use the "drama" format we will discuss later in this chapter.

Both the FCB and Rossiter-Percy models would thus predict that beer ads try-

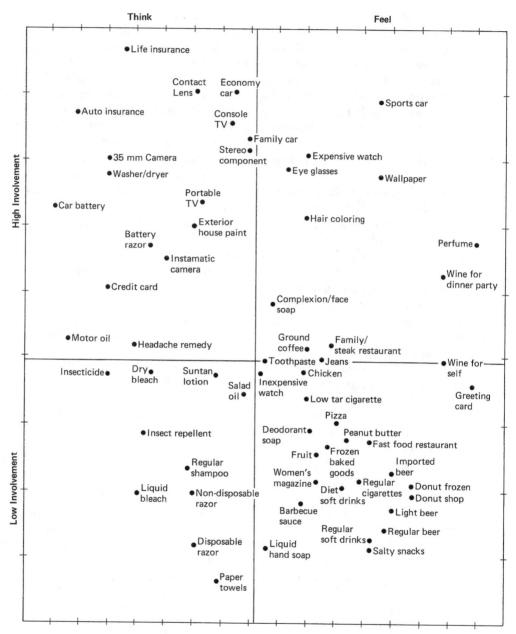

Figure 9–2.   FCB grid for 60 products.

Source: Modified from Ratchford, "New Insights About the FCB Grid," Journal of Advertising Research,
August/September 1987, p. 31. © 1987 by the Advertising Research Foundation.

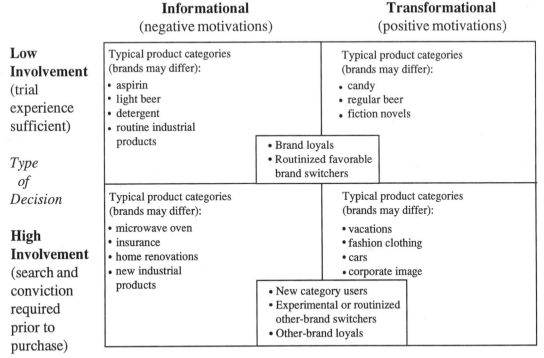

	Informational (negative motivations)	Transformational (positive motivations)
Low Involvement (trial experience sufficient) *Type of Decision*	Typical product categories (brands may differ): • aspirin • light beer • detergent • routine industrial products	Typical product categories (brands may differ): • candy • regular beer • fiction novels
	• Brand loyals • Routinized favorable brand switchers	
High Involvement (search and conviction required prior to purchase)	Typical product categories (brands may differ): • microwave oven • insurance • home renovations • new industrial products	Typical product categories (brands may differ): • vacations • fashion clothing • cars • corporate image
	• New category users • Experimental or routinized other-brand switchers • Other-brand loyals	

Figure 9–3.   The Rossiter-Percy grid.

Modified from Rossiter, Percy, and Donovan, "A Better Advertising Planning Grid," Journal of Advertising Research (October/November 1991), pp. 11–21. © 1991 by the Advertising Research Foundation.

ing a logical brand claim (such as ads in 1992 for Miller Reserve saying "Taste what barley does for a beer") would fail, as would attempts to sell washing machines or refrigerators using warmth (such as the 1993 ads for Kitchen-Aid refrigerators that said the refrigerators were "designed from a blueprint designed by Mother Nature").[13]

In the fourth high-involvement–transformational cell, the Rossiter-Percy model suggests that an ad has to not simply be liked but also create a feeling of lifestyle identification from the consumer, with some supportive "hard information" thrown in. Again, high repetition may be needed here. Other researchers have also suggested that ads for this fourth cell require appeals that show how the brand can reflect or reinforce the deeper life-values that the target consumer sees as part of his or her "self."[14] Thus, the ad here has to not only be likable but must create a brand image or personality that captures some deeper and richer meanings the consumer is attempting to get closer to by buying brands that have managed to associate themselves with those cultural, symbolic meanings. We discuss such advertising strategies in more detail in the next chapter, on Brand Equity, Image, and Personality (Chapter 10).

MODELING THE FEELING RESPONSE TO ADVERTISING . . . .

In Chapter 8 we have discussed a variety of models and approaches that were most relevant to understanding the thinking response to advertising. Most of these models are relatively well developed and accepted. In contrast, remarkably little is known about the *feeling*, or *affective*, *response* to advertising and how it works. Models of feeling advertising are just beginning to emerge and are incomplete. But even these limited models can help us better understand the situations when emotional advertising is most appropriate.

Emerging models of feeling or affective response tend to introduce one or more of four constructs. The first are the feelings that are engendered by the advertisement, feelings such as warmth, excitement, fear, and amusement. The second is the attitude toward the advertisement, the degree to which an audience member likes or enjoys the advertisement. The third is the transformation of the use experience, whereby attributes that may be intangible are effectively added to the brand. The fourth is the process, usually considered the classical conditioning process, by which the feelings, the attitude toward the advertisement, or the transformed use experience get associated with the brand.

Figure 9–4 provides one model of how feeling or affective response works.[15]

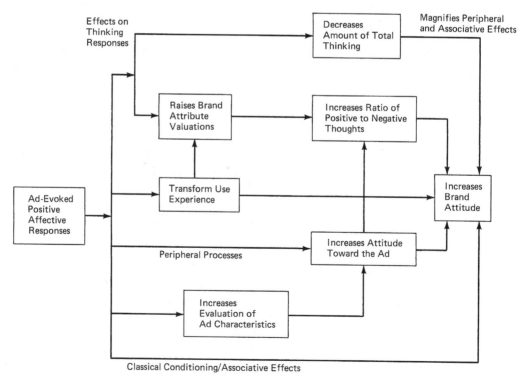

Figure 9–4.   A model of the feeling response to advertising.

The advertisement exposure can first have a thinking response, which usually involves factual learning, discussed at length in Chapter 8. The second (simultaneously felt) response is the affective response, the feelings that are created or aroused by the advertising. Feelings can be positive, such as feeling warm, cheerful, happy, energetic, active, or giving. Or, they could be negative, such as feeling afraid, depressed, guilty, anxious, or irritated. Feelings consist of both moods and emotions; moods are usually not as extreme or pronounced as emotions, although they have been described as mild emotions. We will use the terms *moods*, *feelings*, and *emotions* interchangeably.

Feelings are shown in Figure 9–4 as having four possible types of impact.

First, they can affect the amount and nature of the thinking response. Positive feelings may promote positive thoughts, leading to an increase in the ratio of support to counterarguments evoked by an ad. This is partly because people in good moods want to stay in good moods, and thus evaluate neutral or positive brand attribute arguments in the ad more positively than they otherwise would. It is also partly because when an ad puts people in a good mood they automatically think about other positive feelings that are stored in memory, which again gives a positive bias to evaluative thoughts about the ad. (Research by Barbara Kahn and Alice Isen has also found that such increases in the amount of "positive thinking" can also lead to people feeling generally more exploratory about things, and indulging in more variety-seeking behaviors among brands, as long as these brands are all considered safe and enjoyable.[16])

In addition to thinking more positive thoughts, however, people in good moods also sometimes think fewer total thoughts than they otherwise would, because thinking is effortful and can reduce their good mood. While the relative increase in the ratio of support to counterarguments serves to increase brand attitudes, the decrease in the number of total thoughts can serve to make brand attitudes based more on peripheral cues and attitude to the ad (discussed shortly), than on central message arguments.

Second, feelings can also work by "transforming" the use experience. The theory is as follows. After many exposures to a McDonald's commercial (to pick one example) showing a happy, family scene, a family's felt experience at McDonald's will actually be different because of the exposure to the advertising. The advertising exposures make their visit to McDonald's feel warmer and happier than it would otherwise be. Their McDonald's experience is transformed into one more closely matching that shown in the advertising. This transformation has the effect of adding a "warm and happy" attribute to an assessment of McDonald's, thus creating a "new belief" about McDonald's. This raises brand attitudes toward McDonald's. The effect is not simply one of increasing brand attitudes, however: as discussed earlier with Kodak film, the transformational effect can also add layers of rich meaning to what a brand begins to stand for in the consumer's mind.

Third, Figure 9–4 shows that feelings can also work by creating a positive attitude toward the advertisement (1) directly, through the kinds of "peripheral" mechanisms discussed in Chapter 5 and (2) indirectly, through increasing the favorability of evaluation of the ad's characteristics. For example, ads for Kodak film are usually extremely warm commercials. These warm feelings themselves lead to a liking for these ads, but they additionally lead to a more favorable assessment of the way the ad was made (its executional characteristics). Thus the Kodak ads tend to be well liked for both these reasons. The model suggests that this attitude toward the advertisement then becomes directly associated with or transferred to the brand.

The fourth and final way in which these ad-evoked feelings can become directly associated with the brand is through processes such as classical conditioning or other associative mechanisms. The result of this association could be an effect on the brand attitude or brand choice or both. The feelings of warmth that the audience experienced when being exposed to the Kodak commercials could, over time and with multiple exposures, become associated with Kodak film, and this association could directly affect the attitude toward the brand and purchase behavior. This impact would occur simply because of the association formed between the feeling and the brand through many repetitions.

This model shows a fairly complex network of effects, and certain aspects of feeling-oriented ads can thus have fairly complex consequences. For instance, likable music in an an ad that has strong ties to emotion-laden experiences can evoke positive feelings that get linked to the brand, which is good in low-involvement situations in which the consumer isn't really carefully picking a brand, but these can also distract consumers from processing information in the ad on why the brand is better—which can hurt ad effectiveness in high-involvement situations.[17]

The Association Process

Note the important role that the associative processes play in the model. In particular, the positive feelings or positive attitudes toward the advertisement or the transformed use experience created by the advertisement need to be associated with the brand. Advertising history is full of examples of campaigns that have been extremely entertaining and well liked but had no impact in part because the ads did not get associated with the brand. Audience viewers could recall much of the ad but not the brand advertised. It is thus obviously crucial to make sure an association gets made between the brand (its name and/or logo) and the feelings evoked by the ad. The association is enhanced when the brand is made the hero of the ad and when some kind of unique link is suggested between the brand and the feeling.

Creating such associations is vital because the brand choice is obviously going to be made at some point much later than the point when the ad gets seen (as we pointed out in Chapter 5). Thus, it is of little use for an ad to evoke some feelings when the ad gets seen, if these feelings fail to be connected to the brand name and fail to be "felt" again, or remembered, by the consumer when the brand is later being evaluated for purchase. Fortunately, Douglas Stayman and Rajeev Batra have shown that a consumer who feels certain feelings when a brand name is mentioned can remember those feelings much later, when the brand name is being thought about. In other words, ad-evoked feelings and brand names can and do become linked and associated in consumers' minds.[18] Obviously, some types of advertising do this more successfully than others, and this chapter will discuss how to create such successful feeling-oriented ads.

Theory and research from psychology can provide insights into how this association is created. One such theory, the exposure effect, was discussed in Chapter 5. Some other ways in which such associations can be created, as depicted in the components of the Figure 9–4 model, will now be explored.

TRANSFORMATIONAL ADVERTISING: TRANSFORMING THE USE EXPERIENCE . . . .

As Figure 9-4 pointed out, one way in which feeling-oriented advertising succeeds in associating feelings with brands is *transformational advertising*, a concept associated with Dr. William Wells of DDB Needham. Such advertising involves developing associations with the brand or brand use such that the experience of using the brand is transformed or changed into something quite different.[19] An example might be advertising for Marlboro cigarettes, which leads to a Marlboro smoker experiencing feelings of independence, masculinity, ruggedness, and so on—presumably being felt by the Marlboro cowboy.

Transformational advertising involves two types of associations. Creating and maintaining both are crucial to its success. The first are the associations of certain feelings with the use experience. It may be desired to associate feelings with the use experience (e.g., the use of Grandma's Cookies generates "motherly" feelings) or the type of user (e.g., active, stylish people wear Levi's jeans). The second kind of association is the association between the use experience or user (that now has those feelings "attached" to it) and the brand.

Christopher Puto and William Wells note that through these two kinds of associations, transformational advertising contains the following characteristics:[20]

1. It must make the experience of using the product richer, warmer, more exciting, and/or more enjoyable than that obtained solely from an objective description of the advertised brand.
2. It must connect the experience of the advertisement so tightly with the experience of using the brand that consumers cannot remember the brand without recalling the experience generated by the advertisement.

The association of feelings with the use experience and/or the brand may be created through a story vignette, through the use of "drama advertising" techniques, or through specific ad elements such as specific kinds of music.

Drama Advertising

Drama advertising dramatizes a situation involving the use experience and the brand, and draws in the viewer into the action it portrays (contrasted with the more usual "lecture" form, which makes straightforward arguments about why the brand is better). For example, an ad for McDonald's might show a father taking a son out to McDonald's because the son now has a younger baby brother and is feeling neglected. The father talks to his son at McDonald's and tells him that he is now the "big brother" on whose help the father is going to be counting on as they both teach the baby brother how to grow up. The feelings in this situation are very warm and believable and are felt spontaneously by the viewer without anyone "telling" the viewer to feel them.

A good drama has both a plot and distinct characters. When a drama is successful, the audience becomes "lost" in the story and experiences the concerns and feelings of the characters.[21] If the dramatized action in the ad naturally and spontaneously evokes memories from the consumer's own lives, so-called "autobiographical memories," the feelings linked to those memories can also add to the affective charge of the ad, often raising ad evaluations.[22]

Specific ad elements such as music can also be used to assist in the transformational effects being discussed here and to add desired "meanings" to the brand. As Linda Scott points out, several ads in the Levi's 501 ad campaign center around the color and word "blue," and use blues music. Such blues music (originally a black musical form), she argues, is particularly liked by white working-class urban youth because it is linked to their feelings of alienation, their exclusion from mature roles, and their consequent adoption of hedonistic approaches to life. Thus the choice of such music in Levi's jeans ads can help associate Levi's jeans, too, with these feelings of alienation and transform what Levi's jeans stand for (e.g., they are more than just garments; they are symbols of a lifestyle).[23]

When and How to Use Transformational Advertising

Effective transformational advertising should be positive. It should make the experience richer, warmer, and more enjoyable. An implication is that transformational advertising may be inappropriate for some products. It will be difficult to turn scrubbing the floor, cleaning the oven, or taking a laxative into a fun, upbeat experience. However, transformational advertising has been used to mitigate an unpleasant experience. For example, some of the transformational airline advertising has probably helped some face the anxieties of flying.

Conversely, there are some situations when transformational advertising is more likely to work. Steven Hoch and Young-Won Ha have suggested and shown that advertising is more capable of influencing consumers' perceptions about the quality of products—and, by implication, the nature of their usage experiences—when these consumers are less able to make quality judgments for themselves (situations that they label "ambiguous").[24] For instance, if I walk into a fast-food establishment that is clearly and unambiguously filthy, it will be more difficult for advertising to transform that into a warm and enjoyable experience. Transformational advertising is more likely to work when a consumer cannot make quality judgments for himself or herself and needs advertising to help interpret the product or use experience because the situation is open to multiple interpretations. This is more likely in service situations, situations when sensory experiences are involved (fragrances, liquor, food, etc.), and when consumer expertise and knowledge are minimal.

Transformational advertising must also ring true. It will not be effective if it is disconfirmed by real-life experiences with the product. No amount of "ride the friendly rails" would transform the experience of riding dirtier sections of the New York subway. This does not mean that the ad must be *literally* true; most people watching an ad for Keebler don't believe in elves, but they do accept that elves would behave as depicted in those ads, if elves did in fact exist. This property of "ringing true" (even if not literally true) has been called *verisimilitude* and is discussed further later in this chapter.

Requirements for Successful Transformational Advertising

To achieve such transformational associations, it is necessary to

- **Have a substantial media budget.**
- **Maintain consistency over time.**
- **Closely connect the brand with the advertising.**

Adequate Budget
Informational advertising can sometimes work with a single exposure. However, transformational feeling advertising requires heavy repetition to build the associations. The link between the advertiser and the use experience requires constant re-inforcement. If Marlboro were to stop advertising, someone else could "occupy Marlboro Country." Thus, a media budget and schedule delivering frequent exposure are necessary. Further, advertising testing must also adjust to the reality that the advertising impact is based on many exposures. Thus, single-exposure tests will probably understate the impact and may actually have little relevance in the evaluation of a commercial's ultimate performance in a transformational campaign.

Consistency
To obtain and retain the desired associations, transformational advertising must be consistent over time. The thrust of the campaign cannot be allowed to change frequently. It might be desirable or even necessary to be consistent for decades. That does not mean that the advertising needs to be repetitive (variations on a theme, rather than the same identical execution, could be used). It simply means that it needs to be cohesive, supporting the same associations.

Links to the Brand
The advertising needs to connect the use experience that is being created to the brand so tightly that people cannot recall one without thinking of the other. What will be ineffective is to establish the right use experience but not the association with the brand. Wells notes that a series of soap ads used the lines.[25]

- "New blouse?" "No, new bleach."
- "New dress?" "No, new bleach."
- "New shirt?" "No, new bleach."

Almost everyone remembered the line but almost no one remembered the advertiser.

WHAT AFFECTS THE INTENSITY OF FEELINGS? . .

Whether part of a transformational ad or not, the intensity of feelings or emotions precipitated by the advertising will depend on many factors. Although research is still preliminary, it seems likely that an advertisement attempting to generate an emotional response should be believable and engender empathy.[26]

Believability

If a person is to share an emotional experience vicariously or to be stimulated to relive a prior emotional experience, it may be necessary for there to be literal believability. If the scene is not realistic, if it could not happen in real life, it will be more difficult to generate a meaningful emotional response.

For any emotional response to occur, it seems evident that the advertisement must have *verisimilitude*—the appearance of truth or the depiction of realism, as in the theater or literature. The scene may not be literally true, but the commercial generates a willing suspension of disbelief. It has a ring of truth—if paper towels could speak, they would speak that way. There is no distracting thought that the scene is phony, contrived, or silly. For example, the introduction of a mouthwash solution to a social situation might be so contrived as to disrupt the verisimilitude and prevent the desired emotion from emerging. Thus, believability can act as a block to and/or an enhancer of an emotional response.

Empathy

If empathy is high and thus the understanding of another's situation is deeper, the emotional response should be more likely and more intense. Empathy will tend to be higher if the characters in the commercial are similar to the audience member and the settings are familiar. It will also tend to be higher when the audience member has had an experience identical or similar to that shown in the advertisement. The expectation is that a prior experience should make it easier to experience another's feelings vicariously. If a viewer has experienced the exultation of winning a tennis championship, he or she may be more likely to share vicariously the emotions of a commercial character who is clearly experiencing such emotions. Patricia Stout and John Leckenby have argued that what good feeling-oriented ads do is not only to describe or display certain feelings but to get consumers to *empathize* with those feelings and even, best of all, to *experience* those feelings vicariously.[27]

As discussed earlier, one way to increase the amount of consumer empathy (and also the amount of verisimilitude, discussed earlier), is to make an advertisement that uses a "drama" form, that depicts a situation and draws in the viewer into the action it portrays (contrasted with the more usual "lecture" form, which makes straightforward arguments about why the brand is better). When a drama is successful, the audience becomes "lost" in the story and experiences the concerns and feelings of the characters.[28] A drama's appeal is processed empathically; it succeeds if the viewer is in fact pulled into the story.

Interestingly, it also appears from research that consumers exhibit more intense emotional reactions if the ad shows actual situations that differ from desired imagined situations by only a little, rather than a great amount. For instance, more intense emotional responses might occur to an ad soliciting organ donations if the ad tells of a stoic child who died because a liver became available for a transplant one week (rather than one year) too late. Such shorter "temporal distance" apparently amplifies feelings of regret, the level of empathy, and so on. It was also found, however, that these effects of temporal distance only occur, and only have an effect on persuasion, when the consumer operates at a low level of involvement. That is because short temporal distance apparently evokes more intense feelings because it gets consumers to think more deeply about "what might have been." Since high-involvement consumers are already thinking such thoughts, no extra effects emerge with them.[29]

ATTITUDE TOWARD THE ADVERTISEMENT . . . . .

Perhaps the simplest explanation of how a feeling advertisement works is that people like it or dislike it *as an ad*, and this attitude gets transformed to or associated with the brand in the ad. There is thus the potential for a direct causal link between the attitude toward an advertisement and attitude and behavior toward a brand. As noted in Figure 9–4, feelings engendered by an ad can create or influence an attitude toward the ad directly, as well as indirectly, through assessments of the quality of the ad's executional characteristics. In fact, some researchers believe that attitude to the ad really has two different components: an affective one, reflecting the direct effect of the feelings evoked by the ad, and a second, more cognitive, one, reflecting how well made and useful the ad (and the information in it) is considered to be.[30]

Andrew Mitchell and Jerry Olson, and Terence Shimp, demonstrated in academic studies that the attitude toward an ad (liking for the ad) provided an impact on brand attitudes over and above any ability of the ad to communicate attribute information.[31] Several ad industry studies, notably one for the Advertising Research Foundation directed by Russell Haley, have also confirmed the importance of ad likability in creating brand persuasion effects, although it is only one of several ad-related factors that determine an ad's persuasion score.[32] Other studies have found that attitude toward an ad affects brand choice as well.[33] It is not clear whether this direct effect of ad liking persists over time, or whether it is short-lived; both kinds of conclusions have been reported. In fact, it has even been suggested that if a likable ad draws so much attention to itself that brand attributes in the ad are not processed by the consumer, after a time lag, the ad liking would have decayed and the consumer would have weaker attitudes to the brand than if the ad had not taken away attention from brand attributes in the first place![34]

McCollum-Spielman, a copy-testing company, suggests that ad disliking has more of an effect than ad liking on brand liking and that the effects of ad liking are more important for mood ads than for hard-sell (information-based) ads.[35] Research has also uncovered other conditions that determine whether the effects of ad liking on brand attitudes will be high or low. According to a recent review of several studies by Brown and Stayman, the effects are greater for novel and unfamiliar brands than for well-known ones, and for products that are not consumer nondurables.[36] Not surprisingly, the effects of ad liking on brand liking are also greatly reduced when actual brand trial has occurred.[37]

A considerable amount of research has been conducted on the mechanisms through which the thoughts and feelings evoked by an ad lead to a favorable attitude to the ad, and how (and under what conditions) the attitude to the ad leads to favorable brand attitudes. According to researchers Scott MacKenzie, Richard Lutz, and George Belch, attitude to the ad is influenced by the cognitions (thoughts and feelings) that the ad viewer has about the ad; this ad attitude then affects brand attitudes, which then affects the intention to buy or not buy the brand. In addition, however, the attitude toward the ad also affects the viewer's cognitions that relate to the brand, which, of course, also affect attitude to the brand. In other words, attitude toward the ad affects attitude toward the brand both directly, and indirectly (through shaping brand cognitions).[38] If we like an ad we are predisposed to being less critical about what the ad is saying about the brand. This is similar to the top portion of Figure 9–4, where we said that positive feelings evoked by an ad can lead to more positive (and fewer negative) thoughts about the brand. This model has received support in several follow-up studies.

Researchers have also tested if the attitude to the ad has a greater effect on brand attitudes under low-involvement conditions. Intuitively, just as the elaboration likelihood model (ELM) suggests a greater effect of peripheral cues on brand attitudes under low-involvement conditions, one would expect a greater effect of attitude to the ad on brand attitudes under low-involvement conditions (since the feelings that play a major role in shaping attitude to the ad are clearly peripheral in nature). Yet the research on this question has not always shown this relationship; it seems instead that attitude to the ad is often a contributor to brand attitudes under both high- and low-involvement conditions.[39]

Why this is so is not totally clear, but it seems that the different components of attitude to the ad (evaluation of the pleasure from it, and its usefulness), taken together, require both central and peripheral processing, so that it becomes an important variable under *both* high- and low-involvement conditions.[40] In other words, while the feelings on which we are focusing in this chapter are a major contributor to the attitude to the ad, they are not the only factors leading to it: a more cognitive, "central," appraisal of how useful the ad is, how informative it is, and how well made it is also plays a major role. Feelings may be the most important determinant of ad liking under low-involvement conditions, but both feelings (or other "peripheral" aspects of the ad) and the ad's usefulness (and other "central" aspects) jointly shape overall ad liking in high-involvement conditions.[41]

In any event, it is clearly important, in understanding how an ad ultimately affects brand attitude, to see what kind of attitude people develop toward the ad itself. If the feelings that the ad creates are positive, and if the way the ad is made (and the information in it) are evaluated favorably, then the ad should elicit a favorable attitude toward itself. Again, it is very important to remember than an can be liked either because it is entertaining or because it is considered useful, or both.[42] We need to understand more clearly how ad liking is created.

What Makes an Ad More Likable?

According to a recent model,[43] the attitude to the ad is influenced by the feelings evoked by the ad and the mood of the ad viewer; the ad viewer's attitude toward all ads in general; his or her attitude toward this advertiser, in general; his or her perceptions of the executional characteristics of the ad; and his or her perceptions of the credibility and believability of the ad. Obviously, one of the key factors shaping attitude to the ad is the nature of the execution, and that is where we shall focus here.

Different ads can lead to the same overall level of attitude to the ad by following very different executional strategies. For example, three equally liked commercials (i.e., having the same levels of attitude to the ad), one using slapstick humor, another employing serious informative copy, and a third with warm, sentimental copy, may impact the consumer in completely different ways, as could two equally disliked commercials, one that is considered boring and the other irritating. There has been a fair amount of research attempting to determine what it is that makes some commercials liked and how the liking level is affected by repetition.

One study by David Aaker and Donald Bruzzone found that the ads with higher irritation levels (and thus lower likability) tended to portray an unbelievable situation, a "putdown" person, a threatened relationship, graphic physical discomfort, tension, an unattractive or unsympathetic character, a suggestive scene, poor casting, or a sensitive product with a product-focused message. Irritation levels were lowered when the commercial included or conveyed a happy mood, a warm mood, a credible spokesman, humor, or useful information.[44]

According to an exhaustive review of the literature by Darrel Muehling and Michelle McCann, studies have found attitudes to the ad to be higher if the ad

- Is more credible.
- Evokes positive, likable feelings.
- Uses humor.
- Uses relevant or liked music, sex appeal, or other such executional devices.
- Uses likable and attractive celebrities.
- Uses endorsers of the same race as the target market.
- Doesn't have excessively high levels of fear (if using fear appeals, discussed below).
- Is for a brand the consumer already likes.
- Contains useful information, but not too much too make it boring.
- Is interesting and (reasonably) complex.

- Contains information that is itself liked (e.g., about a special deal).
- Is placed in a media environment that itself is liked.

Other research has shown that older and/or more educated consumers are less likely to like ads.[45]

Recall Effects of the Attitude toward an Advertisement

A positive attitude toward an advertisement, in addition to creating higher levels of attitude to the brand, can also affect advertising impact in a variety of other ways, such as improving the recall of the advertised material.[46] Remember from Chapter 5 that recall and attitudes are different goals, achieved through different information processing mechanisms. A well-liked ad, not surprisingly, is also remembered longer (though some standard recall copy tests actually show feeling ads performing more poorly on recall measures than they should, a point discussed later in our copy-testing chapter, Chapter 14). Interestingly, there is an argument that even disliked commercials can be effective in terms of recall and that, in fact, it is much better to be disliked than to be ignored. That is, both liked and disliked ads are supposed to be better on recall than are neutral ads.

There is no shortage of anecdotal evidence that irritating commercials have been effective. The classic example is the strong Rosser Reeves campaigns of past decades featuring his Unique Selling Propositions for Anacin, in which a hammer hitting a head was shown again and again and again. There are two explanations as to why a disliked ad can be effective in leading to brand preference via creating high recall.[47] First, in some contexts, attention to the ad, and processing of the information in it, could be increased without the negative feeling reaction being transferred to the product. Second, brand familiarity is created, which, particularly for low-involvement products that are bought on the basis of awareness rather than attitudes, may lead to increased brand choice. These effects are most likely to take place if, over time, the negative ad becomes disassociated from the brand (termed the *sleeper effect*). Thus, the impact of the ad-created negative feelings on the attitude to the brand declines over time, while the brand's awareness and familiarity remain high.

THE ROLE OF CLASSICAL CONDITIONING . . . .

One explanation as to why the liking for the ad gets transferred onto the attitude toward the brand draws on the theory of classical conditioning, which is based on Pavlov's work in the 1920s. Pavlov exposed a neutral stimulus, a metronome, termed a *conditioned stimulus* (*CS*), to a hungry dog. The conditioned stimulus was followed by another stimulus, the *unconditioned stimulus* (*US*), namely, food. The food automatically evoked a response, called the *unconditioned response* (*UR*), namely, salivation. As a result of the pairing of the two stimuli, the metronome (CS) and the food (US), the dog eventually salivated even when only the metronome stimulus was present, a response which is called the *conditioned response* (*CR*)—the dog became conditioned to it. Diagrammatically,

UNCONDITIONED STIMULUS (US) → UNCONDITIONED RESPONSE (UR)
Food   Salivation
Commercial   Positive attitude or feelings

CONDITIONED STIMULUS (CS) ——→ CONDITIONED RESPONSE (CR)
Metronome   Salivation
Brand or brand use   Positive attitude or feelings

Notice that there is no reinforcement present. The conditioned response does not occur because the subject has been rewarded or reinforced. It simply occurs as a result of the fact that the conditioned and unconditioned stimuli are related systematically in time (i.e., one always follows, precedes, or occurs simultaneously with the other), and the two thus became associated.

In our context, there could be an ad with actors and a scene that represents the unconditioned stimulus. The positive attitude toward the ad or the positive feelings are the unconditioned response. The idea is to pair the brand or use of the brand, which is the neutral or conditioned stimulus, with the ad content, the unconditioned stimuli. The goal is to have the unconditioned response become the conditioned response—that is, the brand or use of the brand should precipitate the same positive attitude or feelings that the ad did. Research by Janiszewski and Warlop has also shown that, in addition to leading to this transfer of feelings, classical conditioning procedures can also have an affect on attention levels for the CS: the conditioned brand starts getting attention more quickly than if it was not conditioned.[48]

There is a good deal of controversy as to whether this classical conditioning model can be used to explain the use of advertising, particularly feeling advertising, to create positive attitudes. Four influential studies addressing this very point are described in the paragraphs that follow.

Recent Conditioning Experiments

In a controversial experiment, Gorn argued that background music (UC) could be associated with a colored pen (CS).[49] Two hundred students heard music played while watching a slide containing a print ad with little information for an inexpensive pen costing 49 cents. Half the group heard a known "liked" one-minute segment of music from a popular musical. The ad showed a beige pen for half of this group and a light blue pen for the other half. The other half heard classical Indian music, known to be disliked by these students. All subjects later were invited to select one of the two colored pens. A total of 79 percent picked the color associated with the liked music. When asked why, 62 percent said they had a reason. Most said they had a color preference and no one mentioned the music. However, while Gorn's study suggests that conditioning processes do work in advertising, with just one exposure, two subsequent studies failed to get results similar to Gorn's, and it is not really clear whether Gorn's results were actually due to conditioning, or to some other processes.[50]

Another study, by Calvin Bierley and others, exposed 100 subjects to four sets of three colored arbitrary geometric stimuli.[51] In the first two sets, red stimuli were always followed by well-liked music, and yellow was never followed by this music. In the second set, the colors were changed. In the third, continuous music was in the background, and, in the fourth, no music was present. The preference for a stimulus was higher when it predicted music than when it did not for both colors.

In another study, Werner Kroeber-Riel paired a model brand name with emotion-loaded pictures in slide advertisements.[52] The pictures conveyed emotional events concerned with eroticism, social happiness, and exotic landscapes. A day after the conditioning the name alone aroused significant emotional reactions. Importantly, the conditioning worked only after thirty five-second exposures (twenty was inadequate), and only if the stronger of two emotional scenes was used.

In a fourth set of studies, Terence Shimp, Elnora Stuart, and Randall Engle performed twenty-one conditioning experiments using ads for various brands of colas. They found that effects were strongest for unknown and moderately known brands and occurred only when subjects became aware of the contingency (relationship) between the conditioned and the unconditioned stimuli.[53]

Some Relevant Classical Conditioning Findings

There has been an enormous amount of classical conditioning research conducted over the past five decades, and many of the findings have relevance to advertising. Research has consistently shown that for conditioning effects to emerge, you need (1) multiple exposures; (2) the CS consistently preceding the US in time, so that the consumer becomes aware that the two are associated—that one follows the other; (3) a CS and a US that somehow "fit" or "belong" together; (4) CSs that are novel and unfamiliar, such as brands that are new; and (5) USs that are biologically or symbolically salient (i.e., they "stand out").[54] Typically, conditioning effects cannot emerge with single exposures, or if the US is an already familiar stimulus (such as a well-known piece of music, unless the music is being used in a very novel way or a different context).

In addition, consider the following relevant phenomena:

Acquisition

The strength of the conditioned response increases as a function of the number of pairings of the US and the CS. However, each pairing results in a smaller increase in strength than the previous one until, after many pairings, the strength of the CR does not increase meaningfully. Thus, advertisers should plan to use enough repetitions to create the necessary associations. The speed of acquisition of the CR will depend on the salience of the US—how interesting and important it is to the audience. Therefore, it is important to involve strong US (the advertisement should make an impact), and the CS (the brand or its use) needs to be prominent and strongly linked to the US.

Extinction

Classical conditioned behavior will disappear if the relationship between the US and the CS is broken because, for example, a new advertising campaign does not maintain the same US. Suppose that a jingle (US) which generates a positive, upbeat feeling (UR), has been associated with a soft drink (CS). If the soft drink advertising is presented without the jingle, the CR will also disappear. Note that extinction is different from forgetting. The jingle may still be recalled, but the association will not be there.

Generalization

Generalization occurs when a new conditioned stimulus (CS_2) resembles the original conditioned stimulus (CS_1) and thus generates the same conditioned response. The color preferences generated in the experiment by Bierley and others generalized to colored shapes different from those used in the experiment. Thus, product extensions such as new varieties of a breakfast cereal might be presented in such a way as to create generalization.

SPECIFIC FEELINGS EXPERIENCED BY AUDIENCE MEMBERS . . . .

Undoubtedly, there are countless numbers of feelings and combinations of feelings that could potentially be precipitated by advertising. The fact is that we not only know little about how such feelings affect the persuasion process, but we do not even really know which feelings are the most relevant. There do exist many lists of feelings, emotions, and moods that may be helpful.

The psychologist Robert Plutchik, for example, developed a list of forty emotion words, including[55]

Defiant	Adventurous	Disgusted
Surprised	Inquisitive	Expectant
Enthusiastic	Affectionate	Curious
Receptive	Shy	Hopeless
Unhappy	Perplexed	Hesitant
Afraid	Bewildered	Annoyed
Hesitant	Sad	Cheerful
Joyful	Elated	Hostile

Any of these could be important to a given advertisement. Sadness would be aroused by a commercial showing an older woman reflecting on the loss of a mate or by an advertisement attempting to gain support for resources for a famine stricken country such as Somalia by portraying an undernourished child. Enthusiasm and joy might be created by commercials showing people playing volleyball at a beach with upbeat, active music in the background. A political ad might try to raise hostility toward the opponent.

Some ads can create a feeling of confidence. Other ads can create feelings of elegance. A perfume ad showed a sophisticated woman preparing for a ball. A BMW ad showed a stylish, elegant woman slowly entering a car. Both ads surely engendered feelings of elegance, style, and class for some audience members. The Lufthansa ad in Figure 9–5 shows yet another feeling, that of serenity. A quiet, warm day out in the country is the feeling evoked by the L. L. Bean ad in Figure 9–6.

Figure 9–5. Evoking a feeling of serenity: Lufthansa.

Courtesy of Lufthansa Airlines.

When I was growing up, you rode a 10-speed, took long road trips, and pedaled furiously all day. Now, it's more relaxed. The kids and I take it slow, poking around these old dirt roads. It's real quiet and the air smells fresh and clean. We've even snuck up on a deer now and then. Plus, it's nice to get out and do something special with my children. Just the three of us.

L. L. Bean.
For the outdoors inside each of us.

For 78 years, L. L. Bean has offered durable, practical products for men and women who love the outdoors. Our catalog includes active and casual apparel, footwear, equipment and accessories. All fully guaranteed and honestly priced. If you'd like a copy, please call 1-800-543-9089 anytime.

L.L.Bean®
FREEPORT, MAINE

© L. L. Bean, 1990

Figure 9–6. Evoking feelings of outdoors, "with nature" relaxation: L. L. Bean.

Courtesy of L. L. Bean.

Clearly, many of the feelings evoked by ads are not technically called emotions; some theorists call them *quasi-emotions* that may be of interest in these respective product categories.

There has by now been substantial research on the different types of feelings that can be and are created in advertising and on how different kinds of ad content can lead to different kinds of feelings. Rajeev Batra and Morris Holbrook, for instance, have identified twenty different types of distinct feelings that ads can create and have shown how to measure them validly and reliably. They point out that other researchers, such as the psychologist Carroll Izard, have developed classification schemes that contain even fewer types of emotions, while psychologist James Russell has argued that all feelings fall into one of four cells in a grid defined by two axes, "pleasant-unpleasant" (or positive-negative) and "low-to-high arousal." Thus, while anger is unpleasant and highly arousing, fear is unpleasant but less arousing, and while joy is positive and high arousal, a feeling of relaxation is positive but low arousal. Similar dimensions (axes) have been found using feeling-evoking ads, by researchers Julie Edell and Marian Burke, and by Holbrook and Batra.[56]

Based on such research, some advertising agencies consciously decide which kinds of feelings they need to create in particular situations and then design ads that have appropriate content and executional elements (such as the type of music, visual editing, and celebrity used). The ads can then be copy-tested to see if the targeted feelings are indeed being created, and if feelings that are not sought are inadvertently emerging. Some of the methods used to target and copy-test feeling responses are discussed later in Chapter 14. For instance, BBDO uses a card deck of people's faces, each of which displays a distinct emotional state. McCann-Erickson uses a list of emotional adjectives, as does Ayer.

Among the feelings that have been studied in the advertising context in some depth are warmth, humor, and fear.

Warmth in Advertising

When audiences are asked to describe advertisements, one dimension that is used can be interpreted as *perceived warmth.* The Aaker and Bruzzone study found a warmth dimension associated with commercials that utilized sentimental/family/kids/friends-feelings/feel-good-about-yourself creative approaches.[57] Wells and others included adjectives such as gentle, tender, soothing, serene, and lovely in a dimension they termed *sensuousness.*[58] Mary Jane Schlinger found an "empathy factor" associated with commercials involving affectionate couples, warm relationships, mother-child interactions, attractive products, vacation settings, or appealing characters such as Pillsbury's soft and cuddly doughboy.[59]

The warmth construct emerging from these dissimilar studies, although certainly complex, has some consistent characteristics and associations. It has been defined by Aaker, Stayman, and Hagerty to be "a positive, mild, transitory emotion involving physiological response and precipitated by experiencing directly or vicariously a love, family or friendship relationship."[60] A detached expression of love or friendship without concurrent involvement and physiological arousal would not generate warmth. On the other hand, a relationship experience in which the involvement, depth of feeling, and physiological arousal were extremely high would be too intense to be warm. Warmth is thus positioned as moderate in terms of involvement, depth of feeling, and physiological arousal. It is short-term in duration—capable of being created or changed in seconds or minutes rather than hours or days. A notable aspect of the definition is the suggestion that the direct or vicarious experience of a love, family, or friendship relationship is involved. Further, this relationship involves emotions such as love, pride, acceptance, joy, sentimentality, tenderness, or happiness.

In the advertising context, warmth can be experienced vicariously when one or more characters in a commercial are experiencing warmth. For example, a happy dinner scene in a Löwenbräu commercial that features a proud father and a son who just passed his bar exam shows feelings of warmth in both characters. The viewer could become involved enough to share the emotional experience vicariously with one or perhaps both. An advertisement could also involve a relationship between the audience member and a character in the commercial. The commercial character might be the object of pride or love. For example, an audience member might be proud of an elderly person seen accomplishing a difficult task or an athlete winning an Olympic gold medal. Finally, a viewer might be reminded of a prior warm experience by a commercial and be stimulated to relive it. For example, a Christmas scene could recall warm family moments.

Humor in Advertising

Humor is obviously not a feeling by itself, but it can evoke feelings such as surgency, energy, cheer, joy, and happiness. The potential then exists for the feelings engendered by this humor to become associated with the brand, thereby affecting the attitude toward the brand and perhaps its image/beliefs as well. Humorous ads form almost 25 percent of prime-time TV ads in the U.S.[61] As noted previously, humor appeals—because of the feelings of amusement and pleasure they evoke—can potentially affect information processing in a variety of ways, such as attracting attention, improving memory of the brand name, creating a good mood, and distracting the audience from counterarguing.

However, while humor can assist ads in some ways (such as gaining attention and creating likability), it can hurt the effectiveness of the ad in other ways (such as possibly interfering with copy-point communication), so it must be used with great care. According to a recent comprehensive review of studies on ads using humor, Marc Weinberger and Charles Gulas conclude that using humor in ads usually increases attention to the ad and the liking of the ad but does not appear to add to (and may sometimes hurt) message comprehension and ad persuasion. Further, ads that use "related" humor do better than ads that use "unrelated humor," and humor appears to work best for low-involvement and feeling-oriented products.[62]

In recent years, as the amount of advertising clutter has increased dramatically, the ability of humorous ads to gain attention has become even more valuable. Advertising testing results have confirmed that humorous ads have higher recall.[63] Cliff Freeman, who was part of the creative team for Little Caesar's "Pizza, Pizza" campaign and Wendy's "Where's the Beef" campaign, says "Humor is a great way to bound out of the starting gate. When you make people laugh and they feel good after seeing the commercial, they like the association with the product."[64] Some research has shown, however, that humor works only when it seen as coming from a brand that is already liked; Amitava Chattopadhyay and Kunal Basu found that if consumers have a negative prior evaluation of the sponsoring brand, a humorous ad can actually be less effective, not more so, than a nonhumorous ad.[65]

On the negative side, one of the difficulties in working with humor is that what strikes one person as humorous, another will simply consider silly and irritating. Thus, it is particularly important with humor to have a good concept of the target audience. Further, the tendency for humor to irritate undoubtedly will increase with repetition. Since feeling advertising requires repetition to build associations, the tendency for some in the audience to become irritated is enhanced. The use of many executions for the same campaign will reduce the problem. The pizza chain Little Caesar's, which has been running humorous ads from 1987 to 1993, has run more than thirty-five different ads in these years. Similarly, the Eveready Energizer bunny campaign has had a huge number of variations.[66]

Another problem is that humor, although often very successful in attracting attention to and creating liking for the ad, can sometimes hurt the comprehension of the main intended copy point. For instance, the Joe Isuzu ads for Isuzu cars led to high recall for that dishonest car salesman but not about the reasons why Isuzu cars were allegedly superior.[67] However, if communicated, that copy point may be accepted more easily (perhaps because the humor distracts the consumer from generating counterarguments). It has also been found that the use of humor can enhance the appeal of an endorser who has to make an otherwise dull appeal.[68]

Even a casual observer of humor in advertising will note that there are very different types. For example, some humorous advertising is very warm, such as a charming old couple teasing one another. Other humor efforts are very sophisticated and clever, such as a series in which James Garner bantered with Mariette Hartley about Polaroid. Then there is the heavy slapstick commercials such as those for Dorito Corn Chips, in which characters are knocked over by the sound of a loud crunch. Consider also the boisterous, silly commercials for Miller Lite Beer.

Psycholinguists such as Victor Raskin have developed theories that help explain why some kinds of ads are humorous and others are not. Humor can be created through the use of puns, understatement, jokes, ludicrous executional elements, satire, irony, and so on. The essence of humor is usually the creation of a text and story that can be interpreted at two levels that are opposite to each other (such as one "real" and the other "unreal") and the use of a punchline to switch you from one of these two contrasting ways to another. Dana Alden and Wayne Hoyer, who use Raskin's framework, found that ads that employed a contrast between the two levels of "everyday life" and the "unexpected (but still possible)" were more successful than those employing a contrast between "everyday life" and the "impossible." Recall our earlier point that humor "related" to the product is better than "unrelated" humor. Some authors have developed a taxonomy of humorous message ads.[69] Clearly, each of these approaches will involve different sets of feelings.

The use of humor is definitely culture-bound: tastes for different kinds of humor vary across cultures, and the acceptability of humor as an advertising creative approach also varies. British ads, for instance, use more humor than do U.S. ads, although in both countries it was used most with low-involvement/feeling products and least with high involvement/feeling and thinking products.[70] In addition, British humor does not always play well in the United States. A U.S. campaign for Kronenbourg beer that used a heavy dose of British humor was disliked by the managers of the French parent firm.[71] The campaign would have been killed had it not been so successful. Sales increased 22.5 percent during the year, while sales for total imported beers were up only 14 percent. One radio spot (featuring John Cleese of the Monty Python group) described the brew's slogan "better, not bitter" as the "current No.1 advertising disaster" and that the beer is a "terrific beer that doesn't taste as if it had a dead rat in it."[72] Later spots begged the audience to try the beer, as "it is the leading bottle of beer in the whole of Europe—it's not going to kill you."[73]

Fear and Anxiety in Advertising

Fear or anxiety about some threat, a very different type of feeling than warmth or humor, has been used in a variety of advertising contexts.[74] Such ads have even been humorously called "slice-of-death" ads, to contrast them with the usual format called "slice-of-life" (see Chapter 12). The most obvious are those involving a product designed to protect a person from loss of property (Allstate or Liberty Mutual automobile or home insurance, American Express travelers checks, First Alert Smoke Alarms) or health (NAPA auto parts, Prestone antifreeze, Mercedes and Volvo ads, Michelin tire campaigns). Public service advertising for seat belts and against smoking, AIDS, and drug abuse have all focused on the fear of losing one's life.

There are also more subtle fears associated with social and psychological motivations—the loss of friends, status, or job or a sense of failure to be a good parent or homemaker. Such fears are relevant to personal-care products (mouthwash, toothpaste) and homemaking products (foods and appliances). Some psychologists feel that ads using such appeals are more effective today than in years past because people today are more afraid of external threats than they used to be—the level of anxiety is higher.[75]

Fear appeals engender the emotional response of fear as well as related feelings such as fright, disgust, and discomfort. However, one well-accepted view of fear appeals, the *parallel response model* of the psychologist Howard Leventhal, suggests that a cognitive response, the belief that harm is likely to occur, is evoked in addition to the emotional response.[76] Both responses need to be considered in attempting to predict the reaction of audience members. The audience reaction preferred by the advertiser is to have the audience comply with the communication and change attitudes or behavior accordingly. But the audience may instead engage in defensive processes such as to deny vulnerability, counterargue, become irritated at something in the ad, or ignore it.

For the preferred "comply" reaction to occur, the fear needs to be at just the right level. According to a model by psychologist Robert Thayer, fear increases tension, which stimulates feelings of being active and energetic—up to a threshold point, after which the tension creates dysfunctional feelings of jitteriness and anxiety.[77] Thus, if the level of fear in the ad is too low, the emotional response will not be forthcoming and the ad will not be successful at creating attention and interest in the basic problem. For instance, antidrug ads seem to have changed attitudes among casual users or nonusers, but had almost no effect among hard-core users. If the level of fear is too high, the audience member will attempt to activate some defense mechanism to avoid facing the problem. Analyses of antidrug advertising has found, for instance, that viewers seeing strong fear appeals often tend to tune out the message or deny that it is relevant to them.[78]

Clearly, the level needs to be sensitive to the target audience. Strong fear appeals for campaigns such as antismoking should probably be directed at teens who do not now smoke. If they were directed at smokers already concerned, a strong appeal may result in an avoidance strategy. For low-involvement products such as mouthwash, the problem may be to generate a strong enough appeal to break through the perceptual filter. It is helpful to test the ads in advance to make sure the level of fear being depicted is not too high and that it is still likable (and yet gets people to do what you want them to do). It should also be noted that some studies have not found support for this idea that too much fear can backfire, but have instead have found that more fear is even better. It is never clear, obviously, whether these studies actually tested really high levels of fear.[79]

Equally important to the fear level is to provide an acceptable solution to the problem, one that the audience member feels that he or she is capable of pursuing. Without some reassurance that the solution is feasible, the audience member will tend to "turn off" the message. Thus, there needs to be a cognitive element in addition to the fear-arousing emotional element.

According to a recent theory called *protection motivation theory*, a fear ad needs four elements to be successful: the ad must convince the target that (1) the depicted threat is very likely, (2) that it will have severe consequences, (3) that the advocated behavioral change or action will lead to a removal of the threat, and (4) that the target consumer can if fact carry out the advocated behavior. For example, an antidrug ad aimed at teenagers must show that drug consumption will very likely lead to addiction; that such addiction will create severe biological, financial, and social consequences, possibly even death; that it is possible to not take drugs, even when faced with peer pressure; and that the target consumer has that capability to fight peer pressure. The "threat is likely and strong" information should precede the "here's how you can cope with it" information.[80]

Several pointers have been suggested with respect to tactical ways to make fear or anxiety ads more effective. One is to depict as the object or target of the threat not the person seeing the ad, but instead some family member or friend close to the ad viewer. For imagine, imagine you were advertising Prestone antifreeze or NAPA auto parts with the threat that any other brand might get your car to break down in some dangerous situation. You could show a male driver of the car in that threatened situation, since men presumably buy most auto parts. But the ad might be more effective if the man sees an ad in which you show his spouse or young child instead being in that threatened situation (which is what Prestone actually used).[81] It also helps to use real people, instead of dummies or drawings.

Another pointer is to be aware that fear appeals often have the effect of communicating need for that category rather than than brand. For instance, someone seeing an American Express travelers check ad might decide that yes, travelers checks need to be bought before going on vacation, but the need to buy American Express travelers checks in particular might be less clearly felt. This implies that fear appeals are probably less useful for brands that are not product category leaders, for they might simply create demand for the category leader with higher awareness and distribution levels. Another implication is that it is important to show how your brand in particular is better in getting rid of the depicted threat.

Figure 9–7 shows the use of fear and anxiety in the computer industry by Intel, to get personal computer buyers to buy Pentium-class computers instead of those with the 486 chip.

SUMMARY . . . .

In addition to communicating information, advertising can generate feelings such as warmth, happiness, and fear. Such feelings can become associated with the brand and can influence attitudes and behavior toward the brand in four ways.

First, ads that put people in positive moods can increase the number of positive thoughts about the brand and reduce the number of negative thoughts. This can enhance brand attitudes. People in positive ad-induced moods also tend to do less thinking about the intrinsic quality of the brand, and tend to form brand attitudes based more on ad likability (the peripheral route of attitude formation).

Second, transformational advertising transforms the use experience by associating feelings with it. It makes the experience richer, warmer, more exciting, and/or more enjoyable. For transformational advertising to work, it must be positive and ring true and the associations (between the feelings and the use experience and between the brand and the use experience) must be created and maintained with heavy repetition.

Third, research has shown that a positive attitude toward the advertisement itself can affect the brand over and above any communication effect. Ads can be liked for one (or both) of two basic reasons: they are enjoyable, and they are informative and useful. When a feeling-based ad leads to a more positive attitude toward the ad, it can lead to more positive brand attitudes, and also to more positive thoughts about brand attributes.

Fourth, classical conditioning provides another way in which feeling responses become associated with the brand. The feeling response (UR) is associated with the commercial (US). The commercial is then associated with the brand (CS). Finally, exposure to the brand even without the commercial stimulates the same feeling response (CR). The strength of the association between the feeling and the brand or brand use will depend on several factors, such as the number of repetitions, the time since the last exposure, and how close the brand is linked to the commercial.

There are many feelings and combinations of feelings that have potential rel-

386-based PCs   486-base

Let's say comp

Some computers have nine lives left. Others don't. That's why if you're buying a PC today, you should only be considering Pentium™ processor-based PCs.

The reason is simple. A more po PC lasts longer, since it will still hav plenty of horsepower when tomorro applications come along. And most Pentium processor-based systems al include the latest PC technology —

Figure 9–7.   Evoking anxiety: Intel.
Courtesy of Intel Corporation.

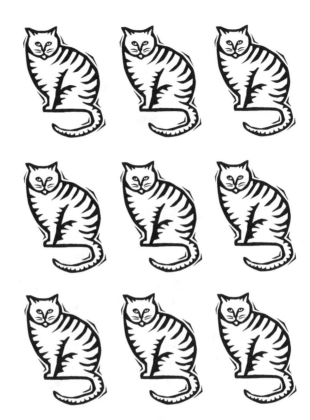

Pentium™ processor-based PCs

s have nine lives.

PCI local bus for high-speed graphics and Plug and Play technology for easy expansion in the years to come.

That, plus the fact that these PCs are now so affordable, makes this a great time to buy a Pentium processor-based PC. Especially when

you'll be getting a system that performs so well. Today. And several lives from now. For more information call 1-800-626-6788, Ext. 213.

Figure 9–7.   **(continued)**

evance to advertising, including warmth, humor, and fear or anxiety. Warmth is precipitated by experiencing directly or vicariously a love, family, or friendship relationship. A fear appeal in a context such as insurance advertising creates an emotional response and also a cognitive awareness of a problem. The ad should attempt to generate the optimal level of emotional response and provide a feasible solution to the problem. With humor, care is needed to ensure that some people are not irritated instead of entertained, especially after several repetitions.

Regardless of the specific type of feeling being evoked, advertisers must be careful to make the evoked feeling "ring true." It must also be used in situations in which it is more effective, such as when the evoked feeling is appropriate to the product category's character ("thinking" versus "feeling" benefits), and during the appropriate stage of the product life cycle (with mature brands, now less involving to consumers, being the most appropriate).

DISCUSSION QUESTIONS

1. Identify a feeling television commercial or print advertisement. Analyze exactly how it works. What feelings might be engendered by it? How will those feelings help the brand? Did the ad do well in creating an association between the brand and the feelings? How would you change the ad?

2. Analyze Figure 9–4. How would you change the model? What characteristics of the ad will affect the feeling response? To what extent is it important to have cognitive empathy—that is, the audience understanding the characters or literal believability?

3. What characteristics of the audience will be relevant in predicting the feeling response of the ad? What characteristics of the context in which the exposure is embedded will affect the emotional response?

4. Using an example of an actual commercial, explain to a friend how classical conditioning works.

5. What implications for advertising do you see for the classical conditioning experiments that were reported? What problems do you see in applying them to the "real" world? Do the first two indicate that you do not need many repetitions?

6. What are some ads that you liked? Why? What makes an ad well liked?

7. Under what circumstances will an ad be effective even if it is disliked?

8. What is *transformational advertising*? How does it work? What are some examples? When should it be used? "If Marlboro ever left Marlboro Country (stopped the Marlboro Country campaign), someone else could move right in." Comment.

9. A transformational ad must "ring true." Must it have literal believability? You should not use transformation advertising for avoidance products such as oven cleaners. Do you agree?

10. What is warmth in advertising? Must a social relationship be involved? Can a sunset generate a feeling of warmth? Give some examples of warm advertising. How did the "warmth" help? Would a warm ad be more effective if it followed a

humorous ad, a warm ad, or an irritating ad? Why? What would you predict would be the response to a warm ad over repetition?

11. How does humor work in advertising? Give some examples. What about fear? What other feelings can you identify as being present in advertising?

12. The chapter discusses of believability, both literal and verisimilitude. What is *verisimilitude*? Give some examples from current advertising. In your example, what emotional response is likely?

13. Classify products such as cars, jewelry, cigarettes, food, candy, house furnishings, and motorcycles as to whether they should use thinking or feeling advertising. Within each class divide them into high- and low-involvement products.

14. There is a saying in the advertising business, "When you have nothing to say, sing it," meaning that feeling-based advertising is most appropriate for brands that have no real point of difference over the competition. Does the research reviewed in this chapter support this saying?

NOTES. . . . .

1. Patricia A. Stout and Roland T. Rust, "Emotional Feelings and Evaluative Dimensions of Advertising: Are They Related?" *Journal of Advertising*, 22 no. 1 (March 1993), 61–71.
2. Stuart J. Agres, "Cognitive and Emotional Elements in Persuasion and Advertising." Working paper, The Marschalk Company, undated.
3. Michael L. Ray and Rajeev Batra, "Emotion and Persuasion in Advertising: What We Do and Don't Know About Affect," in Richard P. Bagozzi and Alice M. Tybout, eds., *Advances in Consumer Research*, vol. 10 (Ann Arbor, MI: Association for Consumer Research, 1983), pp. 543–547.
4. Chris T. Allen, Karen A. Machleit, and Susan S. Kleine, "A Comparison of Attitudes and Emotions as Predictors of Behavior at Diverse Levels of Behavioral Experience," *Journal of Consumer Research*, 18 (March 1992), 493–504.
5. *Advertising Age*, August 7, 1989, p. 58.
6. *Adweek's Marketing Week*, November 13, 1989, pp. 2–3.
7. *The New York Times*, January 26, 1990, Business section.
8. Cliff Scott, David M. Klein, Jennings Bryant, "Consumer Response to Humor in Advertising: A Series of Field Studies Using Behavioral Observation," *Journal of Consumer Research*, 16 (March 1990), 498–501.
9. "Kodak's next Photo-CD sales trick: Infomercial," *Advertising Age*, March 8, 1993, p. 3.
10. Richard Vaughn, "How Advertising Works: A Planning Model Revisited," *Journal of Advertising Research*, 26, no. 1 (Feb./Mar. 1986), 57–66, and Brian T. Ratchford, "New Insights About the FCB Grid," *Journal of Advertising Research*, 27, no. 4 (1987), 24–38.
11. Rajeev Batra and Olli T. Ahtola, "Measuring the Hedonic and Utilitarian Sources of Consumer Attitudes," *Marketing Letters*, 2, no. 2 (1990), 159–170; Ayn E. Crowley, Eric R. Spangenberg, and Kevin R. Hughes, "Measuring the Hedonic Dimensions of Attitudes Toward Product Categories," *Marketing Letters*, 3, no. 3 (1992), 239–249.
12. John R. Rossiter, Larry Percy, and Robert J. Donovan, "A Better Advertising Planning Grid," *Journal of Advertising Research* (Oct./Nov. 1991), 11–21; Larry Percy and John R. Rossiter, "A Model of Brand Awareness and Brand Attitude Strategies," *Psychology and Marketing*, 9, no. 4, (July/August 1992), 263–274.
13. "Beer Companies Shift Their Focus to, of All Things, Taste," *The New York Times*, Oct 15, 1992, p. C19; "Appliance Ads Get 'Warm, Fuzzy,' " *Advertising Age*, May 3, 1993, p. 44.
14. J. S. Johar and M. Joseph Sirgy, "Value-Expressive Versus Utilitarian Advertising Appeals: When and How to Use Which Appeal," *Journal of Advertising*, 20, no. 3 (September 1991), 23–34.

15. For tests of portions of this model, see Rajeev Batra and Michael L. Ray, "Affective Responses Mediating Acceptance of Advertising," *Journal of Consumer Research*, 13 (1986), 234–249; Morris Holbrook and Rajeev Batra, "Assessing the Role of Emotions as Mediators of Consumer Responses to Advertising," *Journal of Consumer Research*, 14 (December 1987), 404–419; Marian Chapman Burke and Julie A. Edell, "The Impact of Feelings on Ad-Based Affect and Cognition," *Journal of Marketing Research*, 26 (February 1989), 69–83; Rajeev Batra and Douglas M. Stayman, "The Role of Mood in Advertising Effectiveness," *Journal of Consumer Research*, 17 (September 1990), 203–214; and Scott MacKenzie, Richard Lutz, and George Belch, "The Role of Attitude Toward the Ad as a Mediator of Advertising Effectiveness: A Test of Competing Explanations," *Journal of Marketing Research*, 23 (May 1986), 130–143.

16. Barbara E. Kahn and Alice M. Isen, "The Influence of Positive Affect on Variety Seeking among Safe, Enjoyable Products," *Journal of Consumer Research*, 20 (September 1993), 257–270.

17. Deborah J. MacInnis and C. Whan Park, "The Differential Role of Characteristics of Music on High- and Low-Involvement Consumers' Processing of Ads," *Journal of Consumer Research*, 18 (September 1991), 161–173.

18. Douglas M. Stayman and Rajeev Batra, "Encoding and Retrieval of Ad Affect in Memory," *Journal of Marketing Research*, 28 (May 1991), 232–239.

19. William D. Wells, "How Advertising Works," Unpublished paper, 1980, and Christopher P. Puto and William D. Wells, "Informational and Transformational Advertising: The Differential Effects of Time," in Thomas C. Kinnear, ed., *Advances in Consumer Research*, vol. 11 (Ann Arbor, MI: Association for Consumer Research, 1983), pp. 638–643.

20. Puto and Wells, p. 638.

21. John Deighton, Daniel Romer, and Josh McQueen, "Using Drama to Persuade," *Journal of Consumer Research*, 16 (December 1989), 335–343.

22. Hans Baumgartner, Mita Sujan, and James R. Bettman, "Autobiographical Memories, Affect, and Consumer Information Processing," *Journal of Consumer Psychology*, 1, no. 1 (1992), 53–82.

23. Linda M. Scott, "Understanding Jingles and Needledrop: A Rhetorical Approach to Music in Advertising," *Journal of Consumer Research*, 17 (September 1990), 223–236.

24. Steven J. Hoch and Young-Won Ha, "Consumer Learning and the Ambiguity of Product Experience," *Journal of Consumer Research*, 13 (October 1986), 221–233.

25. Puto and Wells.

26. David A. Aaker and Douglas M. Stayman, "What Mediates the Emotional Response to Advertising? The Case of Warmth," in Pat Caferata and Alice Tybout, eds., *Proceedings of the 1985 Advertising and Consumer Psychology Conference*, Chicago, 1986.

27. Patricia Stout and John D. Leckenby, "The Nature of Emotional Response to Advertising: A Further Examination," *Journal of Advertising*, 17, no. 4 (1988), 53–57.

28. John Deighton, Daniel Romer, and Josh McQueen, "Using Drama to Persuade," *Journal of Consumer Research*, 16 (December 1989), 335–343.

29. Joan Meyers-Levy and Durairaj Maheswaran, "When Timing Matters: The Influence of Temporal Distance on Consumers' Affective and Persuasive Responses," *Journal of Consumer Research*, 19 (December 1992), 424–433.

30. Terence A. Shimp, "Attitude Toward the Ad as a Mediator of Consumer Brand Choice," *Journal of Advertising*, 10, no. 2 (1981), 9–15, and Thomas A. Madden, Chris T. Allen, and Jacqueline L. Twible, "Attitude Toward the Ad: An Assessment of Diverse Measurement Indices Under Different Processing 'Sets,'" *Journal of Marketing Research*, 28 (August 1988), 242–252.

31. Andrew A. Mitchell and Jerry C. Olson, "Are Product Attribute Beliefs the Only Mediator of Advertising Effects on Brand Attitude?" *Journal of Marketing Research*, 18 (August 1982), 318–332. See also Meryl Paula Gardner, "Does Attitude Toward the Ad Affect Brand Attitude Under a Brand Evaluation 'Set'?" *Journal of Marketing Research*, 22 (May 1985), 192–198, and Richard J. Lutz, Scott B. MacKenzie, and George Belch, "Attitude To-

ward the Ad as a Mediator of Advertising Effectiveness: Determinants and Consequences," in Richard Bagozzi and Alice Tybout, eds., *Advances in Consumer Research*, vol. 10 (Ann Arbor, MI: Association for Consumer Research, 1983), pp. 532–539; the article by Shimp is referenced above.

32. Russell I. Haley and Allan L. Baldinger, "The ARF Copy Research Validity Project," *Journal of Advertising Research*, 31 (April/May 1991), 11–31.
33. Gabriel Biehal, Debra Stephens, and Eleanora Curlo, "Attitude Toward the Ad and Brand Choice," *Journal of Advertising*, 21, no. 3 (September 1992), 19–36.
34. See Amitava Chattopadhyay and Prakash Nedungadi, "Does Attitude toward the Ad Endure? The Moderating Effects of Attention and Delay," *Journal of Consumer Research*, 19 (June 1992), 26–33, and Darrel D. Muehling and Russell N. Laczniak, "Advertising's Immediate and Brand Attitudes: Considerations Across Message-Involvement Levels," *Journal of Advertising*, 17, no. 4 (1988), 23–34.
35. "Does Commercial Liking Matter?" *Topline*, McCollum-Spielman Worldwide, no. 36 (February 1992).
36. Steven P. Brown and Douglas M. Stayman, "Antecedents and Consequences of Attitude Toward the Ad: A Meta-Analysis," *Journal of Consumer Research*, 19 (June 1992), 34–51.
37. Robert E. Smith, "Integrating Information from Advertising and Trial: Processes and Effects on Consumer Response to Product Information," *Journal of Marketing Research*, 30 (May 1993), 204–219.
38. Scott MacKenzie, Richard Lutz, and George Belch, "The Role of Attitude Toward the Ad as a Mediator of Advertising Effectiveness: A Test of Competing Explanations," *Journal of Marketing Research*, 23 (May 1986), 130–143.
39. For a review, see Pamela M. Homer, "The Mediating Role of Attitude Toward the Ad: Some Additional Evidence," *Journal of Marketing Research*, 27 (February 1990), 78–85.
40. Scott B. MacKenzie and Richard J. Lutz, "An Empirical Examination of the Structural Antecedents of Attitude Toward the Ad in an Advertising Pretesting Context," *Journal of Marketing*, 53 (April 1989), 48–65.
41. Paul W. Mimiard, Sunil Bhatla, and Randall L. Rose, "On the Formation and Relationship of Ad and Brand Attitudes: An Experimental and Causal Analysis," *Journal of Marketing Research*, 27 (August 1990), 290–303.
42. William F. Greene, "What Drives Commercial Liking?" *Journal of Advertising Research*, 32, no. 2 (March/April 1992), 65–68.
43. Ibid.
44. David A. Aaker and Donald E. Bruzzone, "What Causes Irritation in Television Advertising?" *Journal of Marketing*, 45 (Summer 1985), 47–57.
45. Darrel D. Muehling and Michelle McCann, "Attitude Toward the Ad: A Review," *Journal of Current Issues and Research in Advertising*," 15, no. 2 (Fall 1993), 25–58.
46. Michael L. Ray and Rajeev Batra, "Emotion and Persuasion in Advertising: What We Do and Don't Know About Affect," in Richard P. Bagozzi and Alice M. Tybout, eds., *Advances in Consumer Research*, vol. 10 (Ann Arbor, MI: Association for Consumer Research, 1983), pp. 543–547.
47. Alvin J. Silk and Terrence G. Vavra, "The Influence of Advertising's Affective Qualities on Consumer Responses," in G. D. Hughes and M. L. Ray, eds., *Consumer Information Processing* (Chapel Hill: University of North Carolina Press, 1974), pp. 157–186.
48. Chris Janiszewski and Luk Warlop, "The Influence of Classical Conditioning Procedures on Subsequent Attention to the Conditioned Brand," *Journal of Consumer Research*, 20 (September 1993), 171–189.
49. Gerald J. Gorn, "The Effects of Music in Advertising on Choice Behavior: A Classical Conditioning Approach," *Journal of Marketing*, 1 (Winter 1982), 94–101.
50. Chris T. Allen and Thomas J. Madden, "A Closer Look at Classical Conditioning," *Journal of Consumer Research*, 12 (December 1985), 311–315, and James J. Kellaris and Anthony D. Cox, "The Effects of Background Music in Advertising: A Reassessment," *Journal of Consumer Research*, 16 (June 1989), 113–118.

51. Calvin Bierley, Frances K. McSweeney, and Renee Vannieukerk, "Classical Conditioning of Preferences for Stimuli," *Journal of Consumer Research*, 12 (December 1985), 316–323.

52. Werner Kroeber-Riel, "Emotional Product Differentiation by Classical Conditioning," in Thomas C. Kinnear, ed., *Advances in Consumer Research*, vol. 11 (Ann Arbor, MI: Association for Consumer Research, 1983), pp. 538–543.

53. Terence A. Shimp, Elnora W. Stuart, and Randall W. Engle, "A Program of Classical Conditioning Experiments Testing Variations in the Conditioned Stimulus and Context," *Journal of Consumer Research*, 18 (June 1991), 1–12.

54. Terence A. Shimp, "Neo-Pavlovian Conditioning and Its Implications for Consumer Theory and Research," in T. S. Robertson and H. H. Kassarjian, eds., *Handbook of Consumer Behavior* (Englewood Cliffs, NJ: Prentice-Hall, 1991).

55. Robert Plutchik, "A General Psychoevolutionary Theory of Emotion," in Robert Plutchik and Henry Kellerman, eds., *Emotion: Theory, Research, and Experience* (New York: Academic Press, 1980), p. 18.

56. Rajeev Batra and Morris B. Holbrook, "Developing a Typology of Affective Responses to Advertising," *Psychology and Marketing*, 7 (Spring 1990), 11–25; Marian C. Burke and Julie A. Edell, "The Impact of Feelings on Ad-Based Affect and Cognition," *Journal of Marketing Research*, 26 (February 1989), 69–83; and Morris B. Holbrook and Rajeev Batra, "Assessing the Role of Emotions as Mediators of Consumer Responses to Advertising," *Journal of Consumer Research*, 14 (December 1987), 404–420.

57. David A. Aaker and Donald E. Bruzzone, "Viewer Perceptions of Prime-Time Television Advertising," *Journal of Advertising Research* (October 1981), 15–23.

58. William D. Wells, Clark Leavitt, and Maureen McConville, "A Reaction Profile for TV Commercials," *Journal of Advertising Research* (December 1971), 11–15.

59. Mary Jane Schlinger, "A Profile of Responses to Commercials," *Journal of Advertising Research*, 19, no. 2 (1979), 37–46.

60. David A. Aaker, Douglas M. Stayman, and Michael R. Hagerty, "Warmth in Advertising: Measurement, Impact, and Sequence Effects," *Journal of Consumer Research*, 12 (March 1986), 365–381.

61. Marc G. Weinberger and Charles S. Gulas, "The Impact of Humor in Advertising: A Review," *Journal of Advertising*, 21, no. 4 (December 1992), 35–59.

62. Marc G. Weinberger and Charles S. Gulas, cited earlier.

63. *The New York Times*, August 19, 1990, p. F5.

64. *The New York Times*, November 2, 1993, p. B3.

65. Amitava Chattopadhyay and Kunal Basu, "Hunmor in Advertising: The Moderating Role of Prior Brand Evaluation," *Journal of Marketing Research*, 27 (November 1990), 466–476.

66. *The New York Times*, November 2, 1993, p. B3.

67. *The New York Times*, November 2, 1993, p. B3.

68. For a review of the relevant literature on humor, see Brian Sternthal and C. Samuel Craig, "Humor in Advertising," *Journal of Marketing*, 37 (October 1973), 12–18; and Dana L. Alden and Wayne D. Hoyer, "An Examination of Cognitive Factors Related to Humourousness in Television Advertising," *Journal of Advertising*, 1993, 22(2), 29–37.

69. Paul Surgi Speck, "The Humorous Message Taxonomy: A Framework for the Study of Humorous Ads," *Journal of Current Issues and Research in Advertising* (1990), 1–44.

70. Marc G. Weinberger and Harlan E. Spotts, "Humor in U. S. vs. U. K. Commercials: A Comparison," *Journal of Advertising*, 18, no. 2 (1989), 39–44.

71. "Dry Humor Is Building a Thirst for Kronenbourg," *Business Week*, March 11, 1985, p. 120.

72. Ibid.

73. Ibid.

74. Michael L. Ray and William L. Wilkie, "Fear: The Potential of an Appeal Neglected by Marketing," *Journal of Marketing*, 32 (January 1970), 54–62.

75. "Marketers Exploit People's Fears of Everything," *The Wall Street Journal*, November 15, 1993, p. B1.

76. T. John Rosen, Nathaniel S. Terry, and Howard Leventhal, "The Role of Esteem and Coping in Response to a Threat Communication," *Journal of Research in Personality*, 16 (Spring 1983), 90–110.
77. Tony L. Henthorne, Michael S. LaTour, and Rajan Natarajan, "Fear Appeals in Print Advertising: An Analysis of Arousal and Ad Response," *Journal of Advertising*, 22, no. 2 (June 1993), 59–69.
78. "Speaking Softly of Life's Dangers," *The New York Times*, February 16, 1990, p. C1.
79. James T. Strong and Khalid M. Dubas, "The Optimal Level of Fear In Advertising: An Empirical Study," *Journal of Current Issues and Research in Advertising*, 15, no. 2 (Fall 1993), 93–99.
80. Ronald W. Rogers, "Cognitive and Physiological Processes in Fear Appeals and Attitude Change: A Revised Theory of Protection Motivation." in J. Cacioppo and R. Petty, eds., *Social Psychophysiology* (New York: Guildford, 1983); John F. Tanner, James B. Hunt, and David R. Eppright, "The Protection Motivation Model: A Normative Model of Fear Appeals," *Journal of Marketing*, 55 (July 1991), 36–45.
81. "Buy Our Brands Or You Die," *Ad Week's Marketing Week*, December 18, 1989, pp. 36–37.

10 BRAND EQUITY, IMAGE, AND PERSONALITY

> Modern goods are recognized as essentially
> psychological things which are symbolic of personal
> attributes and goals and of social patterns and
> strivings . . . all commercial objects have a symbolic
> character, and making a purchase involves an
> assessment—implicit or explicit—of this symbolism,
> to decide whether or not it fits.
> (Sidney Levy, in *Symbols for Sale*)

> We hold that every advertisement must be
> considered as a contribution to the complex symbol
> which is the brand image, as part of the long term
> investment in the reputation of the brand.
> (David Ogilvy, in *Confessions of an Advertising Man*)

Much of the growth of the giant consumer product corporations in the 1980s was achieved by a strategy of acquiring valuable brand names from other companies, often at huge prices that vastly exceeded the valuation of the plants and machinery (the so-called "hard assets") that went with these transactions. As examples, think of the acquisitions by Philip Morris of Kraft for four times book value, or by Nestlé of Rowntree for five times book value.[1] In each of these transactions, the price paid exceeded the book value of the physical assets because of the value of the brand names acquired in the transaction. A brand name that is well known and well liked by consumers thus has greater *equity* and is worth more.

Not surprisingly, companies have become very interested in using advertising and other elements of the marketing mix to build up this equity in their brands. They realize that good advertising doesn't simply "make a sale" of a product or service. As the quote above from Ogilvy points out, every ad also helps make a brand what it is in the minds of the consumer. This imagery, or personality, of a brand then partly determines the price premium that their brands can command from consumers. And, it is this imagery, plus the distribution and other resources of the brand, that determines the value of the brand as an asset that is bought and sold among companies.

When a brand lacks such equity, a consumer would much rather buy a cheaper-priced store or private-labeled brand instead of it, or a cheaper national-brand competitor. Various surveys of consumers, such as those by Roper or DDB Needham, have shown declining brand loyalty to national brands in recent years. Some of this has been caused by the sheer proliferation of brands and the increasing functional parity among them. As a result, private- or store-label brands have rapidly grown their share of many product category sales (often to 15 to 20 percent).

The marketers of big brands have recently begun to "fight back," in part by putting more money into equity-building advertising. When a brand does have strong equity, it has a strong competitive advantage, one that can last for decades. Some of the strongest brands of decades ago are still the market leaders today, such as Kodak film, Wrigley's chewing gum, Campbell soup, Ivory soap, Gillette razors and blades, Nabisco crackers, and Coca-Cola.[2]

This chapter is about creating such equity-building advertising. Thus far, we have discussed how advertising can make consumers more favorable to the brand by communicating information regarding product attributes or benefits (Chapter 8) or by associating certain highly valued feelings with the brand (Chapter 9). Here, we will try to understand exactly what determines a brand's equity and see how advertising can be used to build such equity. We will focus especially on how advertising can be used in the development of a *personality* for the brand.

This chapter is divided into five major sections. First, we discuss the meaning of brand equity. We then look at one part of brand equity, the personality and other associations of the brand. Third, we discuss reasons why such brand personality associations matter, both to the consumer and to the marketer. Fourth, we discuss the types of advertising situations when brand personality associations are more likely to be important in consumer brand-selection decisions. In the final section, we discuss how brand personality associations can be created or enhanced through advertising—how they can be researched, targeted, and executed.

BRAND EQUITY . . . .

A brand can have high *equity,* or value as a tradeable asset, for many reasons. According to David Aaker, brands have equity because they have high awareness; many loyal consumers; a high reputation for perceived quality; proprietary brand assets such as access to scarce distribution channels or to patents; or the kind of brand associations (such as personality associations) on which we will focus this chapter.[3] A schematic version of David Aaker's brand equity framework appears in Figure 10–1. As can be seen in the figure, this equity of the brand is "captured" in the name and symbol of the brand.

Consumers prefer high-equity brands because they find it easier to interpret what benefits the brand offers, feel more confident of it, and get more satisfaction from using it. Because of such consumer preference, the brand can charge a higher price, command more loyalty, and run more efficient marketing programs (e.g., it can spend less on retailer incentives, and it costs less to launch brand extensions). The brand can therefore command a higher asset value.

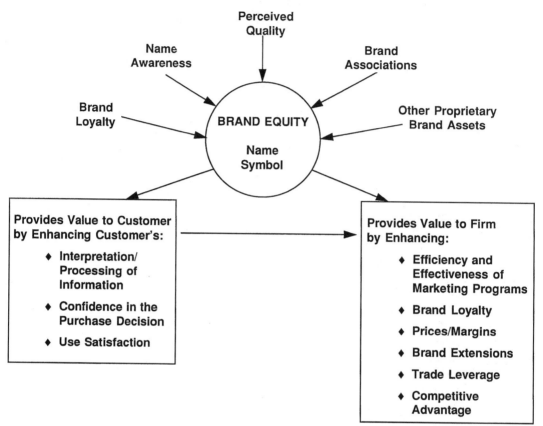

Figure 10–1.   Brand equity: an overview.

From David A. Aaker, Managing Brand Equity *(New York: Free Press, 1991), p. 17. Reproduced by permission.*

Notice that Aaker's framework defines a brand has having equity not only with consumers (through high awareness and strong associations), but also with the distribution trade and in terms of patented technology or other proprietary assets. For example, one reason why Coca-Cola is often ranked as the world's top brand[4] is its incredible worldwide distribution (the company states it wants to be "within an arm's reach of desire" anywhere).

If you focus only on the brand's relationship with its customers, however, Kevin Keller has argued that a brand has equity if the knowledge that the customer has about the brand—in terms of greater familiarity with it, and more favorable, strong, congruent, unique, and leverageable associations with it—leads to greater consumer preference.[5] Keller's framework appears in Figure 10–2. Note that these

Dimensions of Brand Knowledge

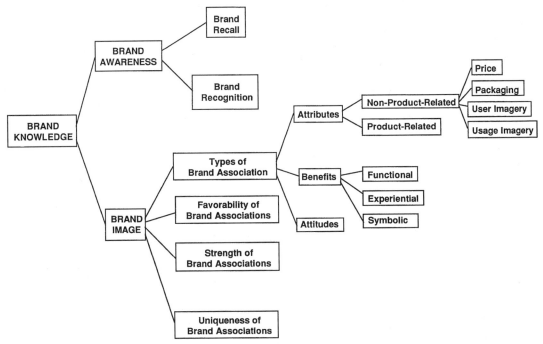

Figure 10–2.   Consumer knowledge about a brand.

Adapted from Kevin Lane Keller, "Conceptualizing, Measuring, and Managing Customer-Based Brand Equity," Journal of Marketing, *57, no. 1 (1993), p. 7. Published by the American Marketing Association.*

associations can be about the brand's attributes, or benefits (functional, experiential, and symbolic), or attitudes toward it.

Both of these frameworks point out that one of advertising's tasks in increasing a brand's equity is to increase consumers' awareness of it and familiarity with it. Since we have discussed strategies and tactics to build awareness and familiarity at various other points in this book (e.g., Chapters 7), we will not focus on that here. But we do need to spend much more time on the nature of the *associations* that advertising creates with the brand. These associations are what most people think of when they talk about a brand's *image*. Remember that a brand is not a physical entity but instead what the consumer thinks and feels and visualizes when he or she sees the brand's symbol or name.

Stronger brands have more "shape and substance": they evoke richer, stronger, and more consistent favorable meanings and associations. Further detail on these associated meanings has been offered by Alex Biel (see Figure 10–3).[6] He points out these associations can be "hard," dealing with tangible/functional attributes, such as speed, price, and so on. In addition, they could be "soft," such as Apple computer being youthful, Prudential Insurance being stable, and so on. They

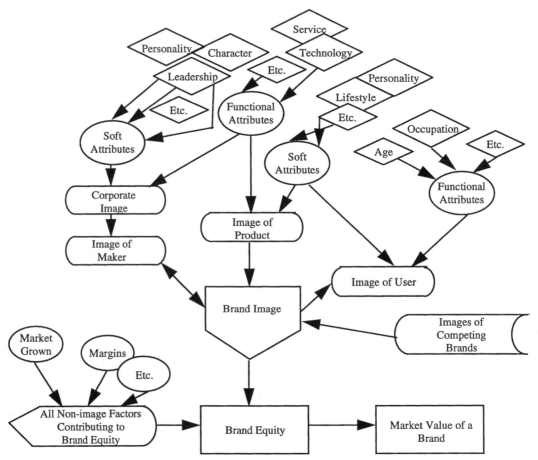

Figure 10–3.   Types of Brand Associations.

Modified from Alex Beil, "Converting Image into Equity," Journal of Advertising Research *(November/ December 1992), p. RC-9. © 1992 by the Advertising Research Foundation.*

could be derived from the image of the maker (corporate image), of the product it-self, or of the user. In the arena of global marketing, some of them may arise from the associations with the "country-of-origin" (see Chapter 20). For example, Coca-Cola, Levi's, and Marlboro may owe some of their worldwide success to the fact that they are seen as icons of core American values and lifestyles.

Combined, these associations lead to a brand having an imputed "personal-ity," one that advertising helps create. It is to these "brand personality associa-tions" that we now turn.

BRAND PERSONALITY ASSOCIATIONS . . . .

Joseph Plummer, former research director of Young & Rubicam, indicates that there are three components to a brand image: attributes, consequences, and brand personality.[7] It is perhaps more inclusive to think of a brand's image as encompassing *all* the associations that a consumer has for that brand: all the thoughts, feelings, and imagery—even colors, sounds and smells—that are mentally linked to that brand in the consumer's memory. Thus, McDonald's could be linked to a character such as Ronald McDonald, an image of a "typical user" as being a young teenager or a small child (rather than a middle-aged adult), a feeling of having fun, a product characteristic such as service, a colored symbol such as yellow golden arches, a lifestyle such as harried and being into "junk food," an object such as a car, or an activity such as going to a movie theater next to McDonald's, and the smell of french fries.

In previous chapters we have discussed at length how advertising can influence some of these associations: those with attributes or benefits (Chapter 8) and those with feelings (Chapter 9). Here we will turn to those associations within the overall brand image that are typically called *brand personality*, which include (but are not limited to) associations with particular characters, symbols, endorsers, lifestyles, and types of users. Together, such brand personality associations create a composite image of a brand that is not very different from the image that we have of other people: they make us think of a brand as if it were a person. Just as a person will have certain characteristics that define his or her personality, so can a brand. And, just as we "relate" to other people, consumers "have relationships" to brands: a consumer might relate very intensely to one brand (such as Harley-Davidson owners tattooing the motorcycle's logo on their bodies), while another brand (such as an upscale retailer) might be perceived as telling that consumer "you're not in my class."[8]

When we think of a person, what do we think of? First, of course, there are the obvious demographic descriptors: gender (male or female), age (young or old), and income or social class (poor, middle class, or rich). Similarly, a brand can often be thought of as masculine or feminine, modern or old-fashioned, and everyday blue-collar or elegantly upper-class.[9] Such a characterization is often made not just of particular brands but of certain product categories or segments of them: thus, wine could be thought of as more upper class than beer, regardless of the specific wine in question (although there will, of course, be gradations among wines themselves on this dimension). In thinking about the personalities of retail stores, for instance, one is quite likely to find the differences in perceived social class as dominating: a Saks Fifth Avenue or Neiman-Marcus, for instance, has a markedly more upscale store personality than a Walmart or a K Mart. Apart from the quality and high prices of the merchandise, such a store personality is also created through layout and architecture, symbols and colors used in advertising and design elements, and the quality and character and uniforms of the sales personnel.[10] Indeed, it is these elements that serve to "tangibilize" the image or personality of any service business, such as a store like Target, an airline like United, or an overnight delivery service like Federal Express.

Brand personality, just like human personality, goes beyond demographic descriptors, however. People typically characterize each other on hundreds of personality trait adjectives. Thus we may describe someone as being warm, stupid, mean-spirited, aggressive, and so on. Psychologists who have studied personality descriptions typically subscribe to a "trait" approach to studying and measuring human personality and believe that every person can be calibrated on the extent to which he or she possesses certain traits (such as being aggressive, warm, etc.). This approach is widely attributed to the psychologists Gordon Allport, H. J. Eysenck, and Raymond Cattell, who developed it from the late 1930s to the early 1960s. While people could potentially be measured on infinite trait adjectives, personality researchers have reduced the various adjectives to "the big five" basic underlying dimensions or factors:

1. **Extraversion/introversion** (example adjectives: adventurous–cautious, sociable–reclusive).
2. **Agreeableness** (examples: good-natured–irritable;gentle–headstrong).
3. **Conscientiousness** (examples: responsible–undependable; tidy–careless).
4. **Emotional stability** (composed–excitable; calm–anxious).
5. **Culture** (artistically sensitive–insensitive; intellectual–unreflective; refined–crude; imaginative–simple).[11]

Similarly, a brand could be characterized as adventurous, headstrong, undependable, excitable, and somewhat crude. In very recent research, Jennifer Aaker has developed an inventory of forty-five brand personality descriptors, which comprehensively cover five brand personality factors she uncovered, called "Sincerity," "Excitement," "Competence," "Sophistication," and "Ruggedness."[12]

As will be elaborated on shortly, a brand could acquire such a personality profile through advertising-created associations with certain types of users (the kinds of people depicted as using it) or the kinds of people used to endorse it in the advertising. Of course, other sources of such associations might be more important than advertising, including direct observations of typical users, the packaging, culturally ingrained stereotypes, word-of-mouth, and news media reports or publicity. Indeed, these avenues should be considered in tandem with advertising as ways of developing or enhancing brand personalities (developing group or peer norms are discussed in the next chapter).

In addition to being characterized on these personality traits, brand personalities—like human personalities—imply associated feelings. Thus, just as we can think of someone (or some brand) as being adventurous and excitable, we are likely also to associate with this person (or brand) feelings of surgency, excitement, or fun (for example, Pepsi). Alternatively, the act of buying or consuming some other brand might carry with it associated feelings of security and calmness (such as eating Ritz Crackers) or back-slapping folksiness (such as Bartles and Jaymes wine coolers). Eating Pepperidge Farm cookies or drinking Campbell's soup is likely to evoke warm, "homey" feelings because of the years of consistent advertising that used such imagery.

Further, a brand's personality also creates an association of that brand with certain important life values. A *value* has been defined by M. Rokeach as a "centrally held, enduring belief which guides actions and judgments across specific situations and beyond immediate goals to more ultimate end-states of existence."[13] Examples of values are the pursuit of an exciting life, the search for self-respect, the need to be intellectual, the desire for self-expression, and so on.[14] Individuals differ in the extent to which they hold different values as central to their lives: while one person may highly value the pursuit of fun and excitement, another may be more concerned with self-expression or security. A brand that acquires a distinctive personality may get strongly associated with a certain value and strongly attract people who attach great importance to that value. For example, Pontiac cars have positioned themselves as "building excitement," and are likely to attract that value segment. The value preferences of a key target segment ought to be researched and used in the development of a personality for a brand: if young adults who are heavy consumers of beer rank "fun and excitement" as their highest value, then the development of a "party animal" brand personality for Bud Light beer (using the celebrated spokesanimal Spuds Mackenzie) seems a logical advertising strategy.

Finally, what often matters more than the specific personality attributed to a brand is the question of whether a brand has any clear personality at all. The associations with a brand need not only to be positive and rich, but they also need to be clear and consistent, in order to be strong and distinctive. A brand that over the years acquires a distinctive, well-known personality becomes like an "old friend"; consumers feel familiar and comfortable with it, it offers a sense of security and reassurance, and most consumers would rather pick it up rather than a newer brand from which they feel more psychologically distant. One of the reasons that market-leading brands tend to stay that way (for example, Tide detergent) is that they acquire this "good friend" personality. However, such a personality can also become a liability, if the brand slowly becomes perceived as being old fashioned and out of step with the times, and consumers (at least a sizable segment of them) begin to prefer a more contemporary, new and different brand. It becomes vital in such situations to "contemporize" and "freshen" the brand personality over the years.

For example, research on Betty Crocker, involving more than 3,000 women, found that in general, Betty Crocker was viewed as a company that is

Honest and dependable.
Friendly and concerned about consumers.
A specialist in baked goods.

but

Out of date.
Old and traditional.
A manufacturer of "old standby" products.
Not particularly contemporary or innovative.

The conclusion was that the Betty Crocker image needed to be strengthened to become more modern and innovative and less old and stodgy.[15] As a result of such research, the depicted face of Betty Crocker, the fictional advice-giving spokeswoman for General Mills, has been changed six times over the past sixty years.[16]

Figure 10–4 shows how Betty Crocker looked in 1936, 1955, 1965, 1968, 1972, 1980, and 1989.

This concept of brand personality, of a "brand as a person," is used by various advertising agencies and marketing client companies. It has proved especially valuable in studies of corporate image.[17]

WHY ARE BRAND PERSONALITY ASSOCIATIONS IMPORTANT? . . . .

This question can be answered from two perspectives: that of the advertiser and that of the consumer.

Importance to Marketers

For the advertiser, the development and reinforcement of a personality for a brand serves to differentiate the brand from competition. At a time when many brands are at or near parity in terms of technology (or are perceived to be so by consumers), the only difference between brands is often the personality that is associated with them. By creating a favorable and liked brand personality, a marketer can set his brand apart, which often enables the marketer to gain market share and/or to charge a higher price (or, at minimum, to avoid losing share to competitive brands that charge lower prices or run frequent consumer or trade promotions). Further, a brand personality is often unique and nonpreemptible: while competitors can match your brand's features and price, they usually cannot duplicate your brand personality (and, if they try to do so, they may simply end up giving your brand free advertising).

There are other, longer-term advantages to building a distinctive brand personality. If advertising is not simply to be a short-term expense but a longer-term investment, a brand's advertising should not merely lead to immediate sales but should also lead to the long-term enhancement of the brand's "equity" or "goodwill." As discussed in the chapter-opening discussion of brand equity, companies that create advertising that enhance such brand equity treat the value of a brand (or brand name) as an asset, much like a bank deposit. Advertising that creates or reinforces a brand's personality serves to increase the asset value of that brand; advertising that lacks such character serves to depreciate this asset value.

Why care about this hard-to-quantify asset value? There are several reasons. First, of course, is the fact that the brand acquires a higher sale price if it is ever sold to another company. This was discussed at the beginning of the chapter. In some countries, such as Britain, the asset value of a brand can also be included on the firm's balance sheet, so it also has major financial implications (on debt-equity ratios, depreciation and amortization, taxation, etc.).

Second, a brand's asset value can command such high prices because of what it gives the company that owns it: access to a distribution network, with shelf facings in the stores; high consumer awareness and loyalty, leading to a stream of repurchases (and therefore income) in the years to come; and economies in terms of marketing expenses, especially in the costs of launching new brands. If a com-

Figure 10–4.   Updating a brand's personality: Betty Crocker.

Used with the permission of General Mills, Inc.

pany owns a well-known brand name, it can leverage it by using that same name on a new product, instead of having to create an entirely new brand name from scratch.

Brand Extensions

Such *brand extensions*, bearing an already-known brand name, do not require the huge budgets (reportedly in excess of $100 million) otherwise required to launch a new brand name. Companies use line extensions not only to reduce the costs of launch, but also to boost acceptance and trial, because a well-known name on the new product should presumably reduce the level of risk to the consumer—and to the retail trade.

Over 90 percent of new packaged goods launched in the United States are such brand extensions—but most of them still fail anyway.[18] One reason is that the new product might not "fit" very well with some of the associations of the "mother brand." Thus, Clorox, identified with bleach, did not work as a brand name on the new Clorox detergent extension, because consumers thought it might be "too strong" and damage clothes.

Another reason is that even if the old brand name "fits" well, it may lack the leverage or distinctiveness to be a competitive strength: the line-extension may simply be seen as a "me-too" entry by consumers. The irony is that when brand names have unique and strong, highly leverageable, associations (such as Hershey's with chocolate), it may reduce the "fit" of that name with other concepts (Hershey's strawberry syrup, for example, may "fit" less well).[19] Companies must also be concerned that the line extension does not hurt the associations of the original brand (what would Hershey's strawberry syrup do to Hershey's original "chocolateyness"?).

Importance to Consumers

Brand personality is important to the *consumer* for a rather different set of reasons. Knowingly or unknowingly, consumers regard their possessions as part of themselves; people acquire or reinforce their sense of self—their identities—in part through the goods they buy and what these material goods symbolize, both to themselves and to others they come into contact with and care about. Brands encapsulate social meaning (such as masculinity, or intelligence, or sophistication), so by acquiring specific brands we also acquire for ourselves the meanings that they symbolize. The process by which brands acquire symbolic meaning and serve to "transfer" it to consumers has been explained by the cultural anthropologist Grant McCracken[20] and is discussed further in the next chapter.

As a consequence of these symbolic associations that brands have, what is "me" depends, in part, on what is "mine." We define who we are not only by our physical bodies and our occupations, but also by our possessions (such as the brand of watch we wear). That is why a loss of material possessions—such as in a robbery or a natural disaster—leaves us feeling as if a "part of us" is gone. Of course, the extent to which we "invest our selves" in products and brands varies:

more, for example, in automobiles and clothing, less (perhaps) in the brand of paper towel we buy.[21]

It is also plausible to suggest that as traditional institutions in society—such as the family, and religion—decline in importance, more and more individuals in society define their self-worth in terms of material possessions and their symbolic associations, their "social value." Further, in such an "outer-directed" society our sense of belonging to peer and other groups can depend significantly on a sense (and display) of shared brand ownership. We use our possessions not only to define ourselves as individuals, but also to define which groups we belong to—and do not belong to.

As part of this *self-defining* process, consumers select those brands that have a brand personality that is congruent with their own self-concept. That is, a consumer who does not think of himself as "flashy" is likely to feel uncomfortable in a car that is extremely attention grabbing and different from the norm; there is a lack of congruency in such a situation.[22] In one study, it was found that automobile consumers sought out cars whose product image was similar to their own image, on various personality attributes (such as exciting/dull).[23] Importantly, there is some evidence that the type of congruency that is important in such brand choice is not that between a brand's personality and a consumer's actual personality but rather that between a brand's personality and a consumer's "ideal" or "aspirational" personality, although the evidence on this is not unequivocal.[24]

WHEN ARE BRAND PERSONALITY ASSOCIATIONS MORE IMPORTANT? . . . .

It was mentioned earlier that, to the extent that consumers select brands because of the congruity between their self-image and the brand's personality, this self-definition rationale would be stronger in some product categories than in others. Specifically, we said that consumers are more likely to "invest their sense of self" in product categories such as automobiles and clothing than in paper towels. As would make sense intuitively, researchers have argued that such image congruence is of greater importance in those situations in which the product is "socially conspicuous," which certainly characterizes automobiles and clothing.[25]

This makes sense because our sense of self is supposed to grow out of the reactions of significant others; the symbolic aspects of brand and product choice should thus matter more when others can see us choose or use them. Put another way, brand personality should be a more important determinant of brand choice in situations in which the *social signaling value* of that brand or product category is greater. This also applies when different consumption occasions for the same product are involved: drinking a beer at home by oneself is not socially conspicuous, but drinking a beer at home in front of guests—and drinking beer in a bar—are certainly more "socially conspicuous" situations, in which self-definition and brand personality become more important.

Another factor contributing to this signaling value, in addition to social conspicuousness, is the relative scarcity of the product category—luxury goods, being relatively more scarce, tell people more about the user's affluence and/or taste than do products that are more commonly available. A fur coat would not be as socially symbolic if everyone in sight were wearing one.

A third factor that research has shown as relevant is the extent to which the good is "ambiguous" regarding its inherent quality level.[26] If a consumer is not enough of an expert in a product or service category to clearly determine for himself or herself that the brand is of superior quality, then the consumer is more likely to rely on the image created through advertising to make that determination (and is more likely to believe what the advertising says). Brand personality is more likely to sway consumer purchases in such instances. Thus, ambiguous purchasing occasions may arise in the purchase of high-tech products, sensory (food, drink, fragrance) products, and consumer service situations. Brand personality (sometimes created through the transformational advertising discussed in the last chapter) is more likely to be important in such situations.

Finally, while we have only discussed differences in product categories until now, it has also been found that certain types of individuals are also more susceptible to brand personality symbolism. These are individuals who are always more conscious of how they appear to other people, how they are being evaluated by others, and who are constantly modifying their own personalities to appear more likable to others. Psychologists call such people *high self-monitors* and have shown that such people are more sensitive to imagery advertising appeals than are *low self-monitors*.[27]

IMPLEMENTING A BRAND PERSONALITY STRATEGY

There are three steps to implementing a brand personality strategy through advertising: researching the symbolic associations that currently exist with the product category and competitive brands; deciding which brand personality is going to be of greatest value with the target consumer segment; and executing the desired brand personality strategy (creating, enhancing, or modifying the brand's personality associations). These are discussed in the paragraphs that follow.

Researching Brand Personality Associations

There are various ways to learn about the brand personalities that consumers associate with the different brands in a product category, as well as with the product category itself. Some are more direct and quantitative, whereas others are more indirect and qualitative.

Among the quantitative techniques available, perhaps the simplest is to use have consumers rate a brand, and/or users of that brand, on various personality adjectives. Thus, a consumer might rate Pepsi, and/or a user of Pepsi, as being relatively high on scales for the adjectives of being competitive, aggressive, and so on. Different brands in a product category could then be "profiled" (compared) on these personality adjective scales.

In one study conducted by Young & Rubicam, respondents were asked to indicate which of a set of fifty personality-related words and phrases they would use to describe each of a set of brands.[28] A total of 39 percent said that Holiday Inn was "cheerful," whereas only 6 percent said that Bird's Eye was "cheerful." Holiday Inn was also described as friendly, ordinary, practical, modern, reliable, and honest, while Oil of Olay was described as gentle, sophisticated, mature, exotic, mysterious, and down-to-earth.

While easy to do, this method of buying scales and adjectives suffers from at least two disadvantages: the list of specific personality scales used might be incomplete (or some of them might be irrelevant), and consumers may be unable or unwilling to give their true opinions about a brand's personality through such "direct" elicitation techniques. The qualitative, projective techniques which we will discuss next attempt to get over this second limitation. The hope is that they will be more able to get at some of these "unconscious" (or difficult-to-articulate) personality perceptions that a consumer may have about a brand. For example, if a reason for using designer jeans is that consumers feel more socially accepted when they wear them because others wear them too, this is less likely to emerge in direct methods—where a logical, functional rationalization may be provided instead—but may well appear in these qualitative methods.

One way to obtain qualitative insight into the personality associations with the typical users of the product is to use *photo sorts*. Consumers are given photographs of individuals, are asked to pick which ones they think use particular brands, and then are asked to describe these individuals. In a twist on this technique, conducted when instant coffee was somewhat new, two groups of consumers were shown a seven-item shopping list. Maxwell House drip-grind coffee appeared on one group's list, and Nescafé instant coffee was on the companion list. Consumers were asked to describe the type of housewife who would use each type of list. The profiles of the two women were very different. The instant coffee buyer was perceived as being lazy, a bad homemaker, and slovenly, whereas the woman buying the drip-grind coffee was industrious, a good homemaker, and orderly.[29]

Another of these qualitative methods is the use of free associations: the subject is given a stimulus word (such as the brand name or advertising slogan) and then asked to provide the first set of words that come to mind. For example, years ago, Bell Telephone found that its slogan "The system is the solution" triggered negative "big brother is watching you" reactions among some people. Such a test for McDonald's yielded strong associations with Big Macs, golden arches, Ronald McDonald, and the notions of everywhere, familiar, greasy, clean, cheap, kids, and so on. Since such free-association tasks can yield a huge number of associations, consumers can be then asked (for each key association) how well it fits the brand (on a scale of "fits extremely well" to "fits not well at all"). Coders can then rate such free associations on their favorableness, uniqueness, frequency (implying strength), consistency and cohesiveness, and so on.

A variant of word association is sentence completion. The respondent is asked to complete a partial sentence: "People like the Mazda Miata because . . . ," or "Burger King is . . . ," and so on. Again, the respondent is encouraged to respond with the first thought that comes to mind.[30]

Another approach is to have consumers interpret a scene presented visually in which the product or brand is playing a role. For example, a consumer could be given one of two scenes: a break after a day hike on the mountains or a small evening barbecue with close friends. In each, the beer served was either Coors or Löwenbräu. Consumers were asked to project themselves into the scene and indicate on a five-point scale the extent to which they feel "warm," "friendly," "healthy," and "wholesome." The study was designed to test whether the advertising of Coors and Löwenbräu had established associations with the use context—Coors with hiking, wholesome, and health and Löwenbräu with a barbecue-type setting, friends, and warmth. The results showed that Coors was evaluated higher in the mountain setting and Löwenbräu in the barbecue setting, as expected, but that the other associations were not sensitive to the setting. For example, in the hiking context, Coors was higher on the "warm" and "friendly" dimensions as well as on "healthy" and "wholesome."[31]

Other projective techniques are also used. Ernest Dichter, the father of motivational research, routinely used a *psychodrama technique* where he asked people to act out a product. "You are Ivory soap. How old are you? Are you masculine or feminine? What type of personality do you have? What magazines do you read?"[32] McCann-Erickson has respondents draw figures of typical brand users.[33] In one case, they asked fifty people to draw figures of two brands of cake mix, Pillsbury and Duncan Hines. Pillsbury users were consistently portrayed as apron-clad, grandmotherly types. In contrast, Duncan Hines' purchasers were shown as slender, contemporary women.

Finally, another frequently used qualitative approach is to ask consumers to relate brands to other kinds of objects such as animals, cars, people, magazines, trees, movies, or books. For example, if this brand were a car, what type of car might it be? In one study, Young & Rubicam found that Oil of Olay was associated with mink, France, secretary, silk, swimming, and *Vogue* magazine. Kentucky Fried Chicken, in contrast, was associated with Puerto Rico, a zebra (recall the stripes on a KFC bucket!), a housewife dressed in denim, camping, and *TV Guide*. Clearly, the result of such techniques is a rich description of the product that suggests associations to develop and ones to avoid.

While the techniques above relate to a deeper understanding of the brand's *values* (i.e., associations), companies often seek a financially oriented measure of the brand's equity, or *value*. This may be needed either when the brand is being sold as an asset, or if a marketplace value of it is sought for balance-sheet valuation purposes, or simply because tracking it over time helps give managers a longer-term incentive and helps measure the success of marketing programs.

Many measures exist for these purposes, and are beyond the scope of this chapter.[34] One measure is the kind of royalty or licensing revenue that would accrue to the brand if it were licensed to another company. Another is the market price of the brand as an asset if it were to be sold. One developed by London's Interbrand Group involves judgments about the brand's degree of market leadership, and so on, which are then used to estimate a "price-earnings" ratio to be applied to the forecasted stream of net earnings attributable to the brand for the next several years. Obviously, it is very hard to decide exactly what constitutes the earnings attritibutable to the brand itself, since very often the brand is inseparable from related assets like factories, distribution access, sales offices, and so forth.

Some of the more realistic of these techniques test the extent to which a consumer is willing to "trade-off" the tested brand (either "as is" or reinforced with the marketing program being tested, such as a new ad campaign or new package) against competitive brands, at stated prices, to estimate the "price premium" the tested brand commands.[35] For instance, a conjoint analysis test (see Chapter 8) might test the extra value of a stated attribute or feature configuration with and without the brand nasme being valued. This "price premium per unit" can then be applied to the forecasted sales unit volume to get at the "dollar premium" of the brand alone.

Targeting a Brand Personality

The personality scale ratings or associations obtained through the methods just described can next be compared to the target consumer's ratings of his or her own personality, both actual and aspired-to, and inferences can be drawn on which aspects of a brand's personality need to be reinforced or changed through advertising. Clearly, this process of selecting a *target* brand personality requires a good sense of judgment, for one must choose a personality that corresponds to the "ideal" personality for a brand in that category, given the relevant use setting and context and keeping in mind the personality strengths and weaknesses of competitive brands.

It also goes without saying that the targeted personality must be consistent with the functional or psychological benefit that the brand is promising: if a bank is advertising good service, the personality must obviously be one of friendly, but efficient, service. Nike has very successfully associated the emotions of competition, determination, achievement, fun, and winning with its brand, figuring that its target market of real and aspiring athletes identifies most with them.[36] Calvin Klein has successfully identified the core value of "sexiness" as being essential for its lines of fragrances and intimate clothing and has attempted to create such associations through its black-and-white, often sexually suggestive ads.

In this judgmental process it is often useful first to identify the demographics of the target segment: are they women, or teenagers, or blue-collar men? One can then use research (and commonsense observation) to see what life values and personality traits to which the target segment is likely to aspire. For instance, research has shown that women are more likely than men to identify warm relationships with others and a sense of belonging as their most important value, whereas men are more likely to value a sense of accomplishment and fun-enjoyment-excitement.[37] Fun-enjoyment-excitement are also typically valued more by younger consumers, while security as a value increases with age.[38] Teenagers have always identified with rebelliousness and anti-establishment values, a value to which Pepsi has very successfully catered in attracting the teen market that forms an important portion of the heavy-users segment of the soft-drink market.

One can typically (through custom or syndicated research) profile one's target segment in terms of desired values and then try to develop a brand personality that will appeal most to the target segment—and create competitive differentiation. For example, Merrill Lynch tried to create a personality of being aggressive and independent in its financial recommendations ("a breed apart") to try to appeal to the target segment that did above-average stock trading, which, research showed, tended to be made up of independent-minded "Achievers."[39] Absolut vodka tried to develop a hip, contemporary, witty, and intelligent personality, knowing those were values to which its target market of affluent, college-educated trendsetters responded.[40] (See the Absolut vodka ad in Figure 10–9).

In targeting this brand personality, it is extremely important to be aware of social trends—how certain values become more or less important with time—and aware of how brands can acquire personalities that seem contemporary to one generation but old-fashioned and inappropriate to later, succeeding, generations. For instance, Cadillac's luxury image is very appealing to a cohort of older Americans but appears somehow less interesting and less exciting to a generation of younger (but also affluent) consumers, who would rather spend their luxury dollars buying BMWs. It is extremely important that advertisers track, over time, both the imagery that surrounds their brands as well as the possibly changing appeal of that imagery.

Executing a Brand Personality Strategy

Once a brand personality has been researched and targeted, advertising must be developed that creates, reinforces, or changes that target personality. While the following discussion is limited to the role of advertising in such brand personality development, it is extremely important to note that every element of the marketing and communication mix plays a role—especially corporate reputation and image, the brand name, brand packaging and iconography, pricing, sales promotions, and distribution. (For instance, the iced tea brand Arizona iced tea has a strong "desert-strength refreshment" image, created by the associations evoked by its name and southwestern-themed packaging.) Further, the extent to which a brand personality gets successfully created depends significantly on the extent to which these different forces operate synergistically. Expensive-looking advertising is not going to work if the product is priced at $1.99 and is distributed through every cheap neighborhood store.

Key advertising elements that contribute to a brand's personality are the following:

Endorser

The choice of an endorser is often crucial, because the personality of the endorser can get transferred to the brand with enough repetition. Anthropologist Grant McCracken has argued convicingly that endorsers can possess very strong symbolic properties, which then get transferred to the brand they endorse.[41] (This use of endorsers is discussed further in Chapter 12.) For example, Bill Cosby has done much to give Jell-O its warm personality, while Bruce Willis contributed substantially to the "party animal" image of Seagram wine coolers. David Ogilvy created a very strong image for Hathaway shirts by using a spokesperson wearing an eye patch (Figure 10–5). Nike athletic shoes has gained tremendous personality definition by its use of basketball star Michael Jordan, tennis star Andre Agassi, and so

The man in the Hathaway shirt

AMERICAN MEN are beginning to realize that it is ridiculous to buy good suits and then spoil the effect by wearing an ordinary, mass-produced shirt. Hence the growing popularity of HATHAWAY shirts, which are in a class by themselves.

HATHAWAY shirts *wear* infinitely longer—a matter of years. They make you look younger and more distinguished, because of the subtle way HATHAWAY cut collars. The whole shirt is tailored more *generously*, and is therefore more *comfortable*. The tails are longer, and stay in your trousers. The buttons are mother-of-pearl. Even the stitching has an ante-bellum elegance about it.

Above all, HATHAWAY make their shirts of remarkable *fabrics*, collected from the four corners of the earth—Viyella and Aertex from England, woolen taffeta from Scotland, Sea Island cotton from the West Indies, hand-woven madras from India, broadcloth from Manchester, linen batiste from Paris, hand-blocked silks from England, exclusive cottons from the best weavers in America. You will get a great deal of quiet satisfaction out of wearing shirts which are in such impeccable taste.

HATHAWAY shirts are made by a small company of dedicated craftsmen in the little town of Waterville, Maine. They have been at it, man and boy, for one hundred and fifteen years.

At better stores everywhere, or write C. F. HATHAWAY, Waterville, Maine, for the name of your nearest store. In New York, telephone MU 9-4157. Prices from $5.50 to $25.00.

Figure 10–5.   Brand personality via a sophisticated, mysterious endorser: Hathaway shirts.

Courtesy of C. F. Hathaway, Inc.

on. (See the Reading on Nike at the end of this Part of the book.) The endorser need not be real, or even human: the Marlboro cowboys; or the spokesdog Spuds Mackenzie, who gave Bud Light beer the personality of fun-loving abandon that made it so appealing to its heavy-drinking young male target segment (Figure 10–6). Where the characters are not real, the casting becomes vital: the people chosen to play a role need to be exactly right.

User Imagery

The kind of brand user portrayed in the ad can also be very important. The American Express card creates a very specific user image, for instance, in its photographic portrait campaign featuring celebrity cardholders (Figure 10–7), as does Dewar's Scotch whisky with its profiles of successful (but not necessarily well-known) drinkers. Rolling Stone magazine recently tried to change the perception of who its readers were by its depiction of "perceived" versus "real" readers (Figure 10–8). Again, the portrayed users can be fictional, as in the case of Calvin Klein jeans or fragrances.

Figure 10–6.   **Brand personality via a "party animal": Spuds MacKenzie for Bud Light Beer.**

Courtesy of Anheuser-Busch, Inc.

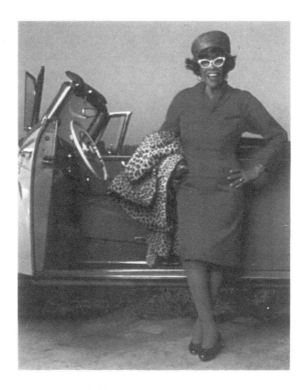

Ella Fitzgerald.   Cardmember since 1961.

Membership has its privileges.℠

Don't leave home without it.®
Call 1-800-THE CARD to apply.

Figure 10–7.   Brand personality via upscale user imagery: American Express.
Courtesy of American Express.

Perception.

Figure 10–8.   Brand personality via depiction of "actual" users: *Rolling Stone* magazine.

Courtesy of Rolling Stone magazine. © 1987, 88 by Straight Arrow Publishers, Inc., All Rights Reserved. Reprinted by Permission.

Reality.

To a new generation of Rolling Stone readers, pigs live on farms. You'll find the cops living in
Beverly Hills or on Hill Street, now heralded instead of hated. If you're looking for an 18 to 34 year old market
that is taking active part instead of active protest, you'll have a riot in the pages of Rolling Stone.

Figure 10–8.   (continued)

Executional Elements

Elements such as the choice (in broadcast ads) of music, visual direction, pace and nature of editing, color schemes used, and (in print ads) of color, layout, typography can all contribute substantially to a brand's personality. Some campaigns that have used the choice of executional elements to convey a personality of intelligence and wit include the recent print campaign for Absolut vodka (Figure 10–9), the TV campaigns for Honda cars (Figure 10–10), and the long-running bucolic black-and white campaign for Jack Daniels whisky (Figure 10–11).

Symbols

A very useful executional element is the use of an idiosyncratic brand symbol, such as Wells Fargo's stagecoach, McDonald's golden arches, Merrill Lynch's bull, or Prudential's rock. The best synbols have very appropriate associations, such as the trustworthiness and reliability imagery of Wells Fargo's stagecoach. If your brand doesn't have such a symbol, consider creating one, to give it identity and personality. Examples here include the Jolly Green Giant, Charlie the Tuna, the Keebler elves, the Pillsbury doughboy, the controversial "Joe Camel" character for Camel cigarettes, and so on.

Consistency

In addition to the content of the advertising, one other basic advertising principle is very important in executing a brand personality strategy. It is the principle of predictability and consistency. Just as in any positioning strategy, a brand personality can only develop successfully if the important symbolic aspects of the brand—such as those just described—remain consistent over time. Brands that change these elements risk diluting their personalities, or end up having no brand personality at all. Finally, decisions about other marketing elements—especially pricing, promotions, distribution, and line extensions—must always support and reinforce a brand's basic personality, not reduce its character. More and more companies are giving specific managers the explicit responsibility to guard the brand's associations, for it is those that constitute the essence of the brand in question.

SUMMARY . . . .

Building brand equity has become increasingly important to companies. Brand equity is derived from many things, including a reputation for quality and high brand awareness, but a key element is the associations that are evoked in the consumer by the brand name, symbol, and packaging. These associations can be "hard" or functional, as well as "soft" or symbolic. Together, these give the brand a "personality."

Thus, just as people have individual personalities, brands too can develop personality-like associations—if the advertising for these brands identifies and develops a consistent image that is reinforced over time. Through such a personality, brands can be seen as young or old, masculine or feminine, aggressive or introverted, or sophisticated or blue collar and in a variety of different ways. Just as with people, the brands we know can come to symbolize certain important life values and certain associated emotional characteristics.

Figure 10–9.   Brand personality via intelligent, witty ads: Absolut Vodka.

Courtesy of Carillon Importers, Ltd.

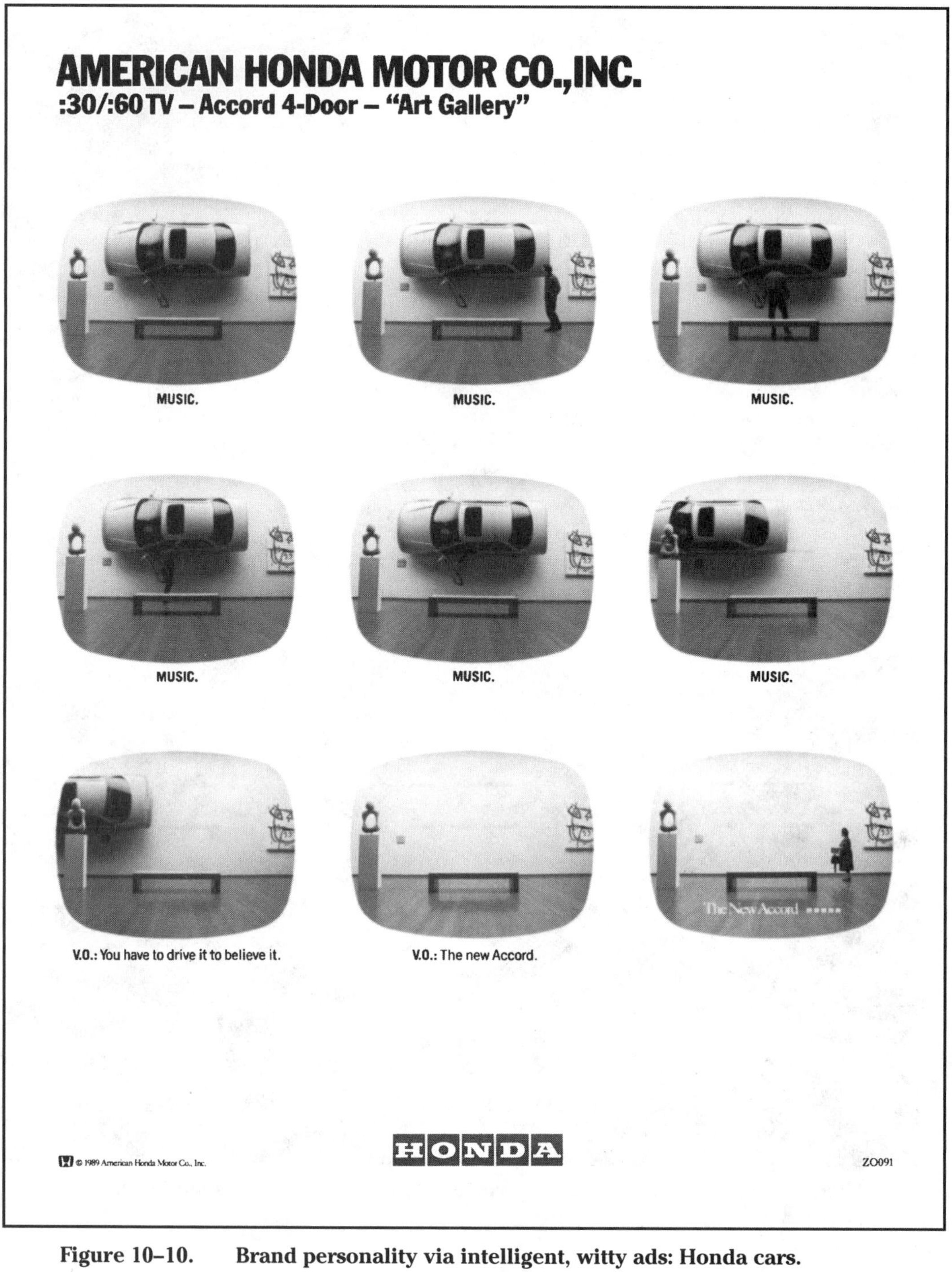

Figure 10–10.   Brand personality via intelligent, witty ads: Honda cars.

Courtesy of Honda of America, Inc.

Come visit us some day in Lynchburg. (It's especially pretty right now.)

LEAVES ARE FALLING ON ANOTHER year here in Lynchburg, Tennessee, home of Jack Daniel's Tennessee Whiskey.

We've been busier than ever this year making Jack Daniel's for friends all over the world. And, so say our barrelmen, the pace won't slacken till Christmas. But no matter how much whiskey we take from the barrel, we can promise you this: every drop is aged and mellowed to the oldtime rareness you like. Just as it was last year here in Lynchburg. And every day of every year since 1866.

SMOOTH SIPPIN'
TENNESSEE WHISKEY

Tennessee Whiskey • 40-43% alcohol by volume (80-86 proof) • Distilled and Bottled by Jack Daniel Distillery, Lem Motlow, Proprietor, Route 1, Lynchburg (Pop 361), Tennessee 37352
Placed in the National Register of Historic Places by the United States Government.

Figure 10–11.   Brand personality via executional elements.

Courtesy of Jack Daniel Distillery.

Brand personalities matter because consumers are attracted to brands that possesses personalities with which they themselves identify, or seek. Consumers often use their choice of brands to tell themselves, and other people they care about, what kinds of individuals they really are (or want to be seen as). To the companies that market these brands, a brand with a strong brand personality represents brand equity that can be capitalized on in marketing efforts (such as launching brand extensions much more economically than would otherwise be the case), and also represents brand goodwill that has intrinsic financial value.

While a brand personality can always add a defining character to a brand, it is especially important in leading to sales and market share in product categories that are expensive, purchased or consumed in socially conspicuous situations, and help a consumer calibrate product quality in otherwise ambiguous situations. Certain people, called high self-monitors, are especially swayed by a brand's personality.

Implementing a brand personality situation first calls for defining the target consumer segment and understanding what kind of brand personality to which they are most likely to be responsive, and how they currently rate different brands on different personality characteristics. A variety of quantitative and qualitative techniques can be used at this stage. Once a target personality has been defined for the brand, the appropriate personality can be created through the choice of an endorser or spokescharacter, portrayal of matching user lifestyles and imagery, the use of appropriate executional elements and actors, and so on. It is important that the personality sought be maintained both over time and across different elements of the communication and marketing mix.

DISCUSSION QUESTIONS

1. Select ten brands with which you are familiar, and describe the brand personality associations you think each has. Then analyze just how the advertising and other marketing mix elements for these brands have contributed to the development of a brand personality.
2. List five product or service categories in which you think consumers select brands based in large measure on their brand personality. Then think through what, if anything, these categories have in common and relate your thoughts to the research presented in the chapter on when brand personality becomes more important.
3. Select any one product or service category, and analyze the brand personality of the different competitors in it. Identify the specific elements of the advertising that have contributed to the development of this personality over time. For brands where you fail to find a clear or distinct brand personality, ask yourself why none has developed thus far.
4. Suppose you were a new entrant into the market you analyzed in question 3. How might you select a target brand personality for your new brand?
5. How might you create advertising to develop that brand personality?
6. Discuss the pros and cons of the different research techniques used to study the brand personalities of competing brands. Select one that you prefer and explain why.

7. Identify a target segment of consumers that you have some interest marketing to, and discuss the kinds of brand personalities they might be most responsive to.

8. Certain brand personality dimensions were listed in the chapter, based on the research of trait personality psychologists. Expand this list to a more comprehensive one that is more applicable in marketing contexts, using your intuition and observations about brand marketing strategies.

9. What is meant by an *ambiguous* product category? Why is this concept important in planning and working with a brand's personality?

10. In addition to advertising, what other elements of the communication and marketing mix can contribute to a brand's personality? Discuss three cases in which a brand appears to have successfully integrated these elements in developing and enhancing a brand personality and three cases in which it has not.

11. Can you think of brands where the brand personality appeals to one age cohort or generation, but not to another? Does this matter to these brands' long-term sales potentials? If it is a problem, why did it emerge? What can be done now to eliminate this problem?

NOTES. . . . .

1. *The Economist*, September 7, 1991, p. 67.
2. "What's in a Name?" *Business Week*, July 8, 1991, p. 66.
3. See David Aaker, *Managing Brand Equity* (New York: Free Press, 1991).
4. Stewart Owen, "The Landor ImagePower Survey: A Global Assessment of Brand Strength," in David A. Aaker and Alexander L. Biel, eds., *Brand Equity and Advertising* (Hillsdale, NJ: Erlbaum, 1993), pp. 11–30.
5. Kevin L. Keller, "Conceptualizing, Measuring, and Managing Customer-Based Brand Equity," *Journal of Marketing*, 57 (January 1993), 1–22.
6. Alexander L. Biel, "Converting Image into Equity," in David A. Aaker and Alexander L. Biel, eds., *Brand Equity and Advertising*, (Hillsdale, NJ: Erlbaum, 1993), pp. 67–82.
7. Joseph T. Plummer, "Brand Personality: A Strategic Concept for Multinational Advertising." Paper presented to the AMA 1985 Winter Marketing Educators Conference, Phoenix, Arizona, February 1985.
8. See Max Blackston, "Beyond Brand Personality: Building Brand Relationships," in David A. Aaker and Alexander L. Biel, eds., *Brand Equity and Advertising* (Hillsdale, NJ: Erlbaum, 1993), pp. 113–124.
9. Sidney J. Levy, "Symbols for Sale," *Harvard Business Review* (July/August 1959), 117–124.
10. Pierre Martineau, "The Personality of the Retail Store," *Harvard Business Review* (January/February 1958), 47–55.
11. For a fuller discussion, see Walter Mischel, *Introduction to Personality* (New York: Holt, Rinehart and Winston, 1986), on which this discussion is based.
12. Jennifer L. Aaker, "Measuring Brand Personality." Working Paper, Graduate School of Business, Stanford University Graduate School of Business, October 1994.
13. M. Rokeach, *The Nature of Human Values* (New York: Free Press, 1975); Donald E. Vinson, Jerome E. Scott, and Lawrence M. Lamont, "The Role of Values in Marketing and Consumer Behavior," *Journal of Marketing* (April 1977), 44–50.
14. Sharon E. Beatty, Lynn R. Kahle, Pamela Homer, and Shekhar Misra, "Alternative Measurement Approaches to Consumer Values: The List of Values and the Rokeach Value Survey," *Psychology and Marketing*, 2, no. 3 (1985), 181–200.

15. Keith Reinhard, "How We Make Advertising." Paper presented to the Federal Trade Commission, May 11, 1979, pp. 22–25.
16. Hal Morgan, *Symbols of America* (New York: Penguin Books, 1987), p. 126.
17. Aaron Spector, "Basic Dimensions of Corporate Image," *Journal of Marketing*, 25, no. 6 (October 1961), pp. 47–51.
18. "What's in a Name?" *Business Week*, July 8, 1991, p. 66.
19. Edward M. Tauber, "Fit and Leverage in Brand Extensions," in David A. Aaker and Alexander L. Biel, eds., in *Brand Equity and Advertising* (Hillsdale, NJ: Erlbaum, 1993), pp. 313–318.
20. Grant McCracken, *Culture and Consumption* (Bloomington: Indiana University Press, 1988), chap. 5.
21. For a wonderful exposition of this concept, see Russell W. Belk, "Possessions and the Extended Self," *Journal of Consumer Research*, 15, no. 2 (September 1988), 139–168.
22. M. Joseph Sirgy, "Self-Concept in Consumer Behavior: A Critical Review," *Journal of Consumer Research*, 9 (December 1982), 287–300.
23. A. E. Birdwell, "A Study of Influence of Image Congruency on Consumer Choice," *Journal of Business*, 41 (January 1968), 76–88.
24. Sirgy, "Self-Concept in Consumer Behavior," p. 288.
25. Ibid., p. 295.
26. John Deighton, "The Interaction of Advertising and Evidence," *Journal of Consumer Research*, 11 (December 1984), 763–770, and Stephen J. Hoch and Young-Won Ha, "Consumer Learning: Advertising and the Ambiguity of Product Experience," *Journal of Consumer Research*, 13 (September 1986), 221–233.
27. Mark Snyder and Kenneth G. DeBono, "Appeals to Image and Claims about Quality," *Journal of Personality and Social Psychology*, 49, no. 3 (1985), 586–597.
28. Joseph T. Plummer, "How Personality Makes a Difference," *Journal of Advertising Research*, 24 (December 1984/January 1985), 27–31.
29. Mason Haire, "Projective Techniques in Marketing Research," *Journal of Marketing* (April 1950), 649–656.
30. Joseph S. Newman, *Motivation Research and Marketing Management* (Boston: Harvard University Press, 1957), p. 143.
31. David A. Aaker and Douglas M. Stayman, "Implementing the Concept of Transformational Advertising," *Psychology and Marketing*, forthcoming.
32. Rena Bartos, "Ernest Dichter: Motive Interpreter," *Journal of Advertising Research* (February/March 1986), 15–20.
33. Annetta Miller and Dody Tsiantar, "Psyching out Consumers," *Newsweek*, February 27, 1989, pp. 46–47.
34. See, for example, *Financial World*, September 1, 1992; John Murphy, ed., *Brand Valuation: Establishing a True and Fair View* (London: The Interbrand Group, 1989); and Patrick Barwise et al., *Accounting for Brands* (London: London Business School and the Institute for Chartered Accountants, 1989).
35. See the article by Max Blackston in *Brandweek*, June 28, 1993, p. 22.
36. See "High Performance Marketing: An Interview with Nike's Phil Knight," *Harvard Business Review* (July–August 1992), 90–101.
37. Lynn R. Kahle, ed., *Social Values and Social Change: Adaptation to Life in America* (New York, Praeger, 1983), p. 75.
38. Ibid, pp. 82–91. See also Lynn R. Kahle, Basil Poulos, and Ajay Sukhdial, "Changes in Social Values in the United States During the Past Decade," *Journal of Advertising Research* (February/March 1988), 35–44.
39. *Advertising Age,* November 9, 1981, p. 82.
40. See the Darden Graduate Business School (University of Virginia) case UVA-M-366, *Absolut Vodka*, for details.
41. Grant McCracken, "Who is the Celebrity Endorser? Cultural Foundations of the Endorsement Process," *Journal of Consumer Research*, 16 (December 1989), 310–321.

11 GROUP INFLUENCE AND WORD-OF-MOUTH ADVERTISING

> What we shall call opinion leadership, if we may call it leadership at all, is leadership at its simplest. . . . It is not leadership on the high level of a Churchill, nor of a local politico, nor even a social elite. It is quite the opposite extreme; it is almost invisible, certainly inconspicuous form of leadership at the person-to-person level of ordinary, intimate, informal, everyday contact.
>
> (Katz and Lazarsfeld, 1955)

> You can't explain much in 60 seconds, but when you show Michael Jordan, you don't have to. People already know a lot about him. It's that simple.
>
> (Phil Knight, CEO of Nike)

Advertising relies heavily on group influence and often uses appeals to a consumer's needs for group identification, belongingness, and adherence to social and community norms. Whether the advertiser's objective is awareness, knowledge, persuasion, or purchasing, social needs and group influence are powerful motivations that can often be relied upon to accomplish the objective. For example, television commercials that use "slice-of-life" appeals often show one person demonstrating product benefits to another. This is an example of television simulating a personal influence process. Slice-of-life advertising has been shown to be very effective and continues to be used extensively by large consumer package companies such as Procter and Gamble. Dental hygiene products such as toothpastes and mouthwashes, deodorants, perfumes, cosmetics, clothing, and dozens of other products rely heavily on group influence and social appeals. In addition to the pressures of complying with social norms (bad breath and body odor are commonly frowned on in the United States), we wear clothing that is socially acceptable and consistent with what is currently fashionable, buy cars that will impress relatives and neighbors, and engage in a wide variety of behaviors designed to impress or attract other people. All of these examples are evidence of group and personal influence at work and are the subject of this chapter.

Paramount Pictures' movie "Forrest Gump" generated over $100 million in revenue in three weeks, one of the fastest climbs in history. Although advertising played a role, word-of-mouth advertising was much more important in this case.[1] Worth-of-mouth advertising is a form of personal influence in which information is passed along or diffused through a social system from one person to the next. It is particularly interesting because, unlike regular advertising in mass media, word-of-mouth advertising is not directly paid for by the advertiser nor under his or her direct control. In many product markets, however, it is very important and the advertiser should and can attempt to influence the extent and nature of diffusion and word-of-mouth advertising. This chapter also addresses this important subject. We begin with some background ideas on reference group influence.

THE CONCEPT OF REFERENCE GROUPS . . . .

V. Parker Lessig and C. Whan Park define a reference group as actual or imaginary institutions, individuals or groups having significant relevance on the target individual's evaluations, aspirations, or behavior.[2] Such reference groups could be those (1) used as standards of comparison for self-appraisal (the "Jones's' " we try to keep up with), (2) those considered to be informative experts, or (3) those used as a source of norms, standards, and attitudes (such as athletes like Michael Jordan). They need not be the groups in which the individual participates, although they sometimes are, but can be large social groupings—social class, ethnic group, subculture, and so on—that the individual is a member of, aspires to being a member of, or otherwise exerts influence on the individual.

The important feature of the reference group concept is that an individual does not have to be a member of the group for the influence to occur. Thus, a student's behaviors and lifestyle can be heavily determined by emulation of the people in a group to which he or she aspires to belong. An occasional jogger (a so-called "weekend athlete") might aspire to belong to a group of serious athletes and might place tremendous weight on the fact that a Michael Jordan or a Bo Jackson endorses Nike running shoes. The key point is that the relationship between the target individual and the reference group should be motivationally and psychologically significant.[3]

Various studies have demonstrated that such reference groups do in fact have an impact on consumer behavior. Martin Fishbein has extended the basic evaluative belief attitude models reviewed in Chapter 8 to include an explicit measure of this type of personal influence, referred to as the *subjective norms* associated with the choice object.[4] In this *extended behavioral intention model,* total behavioral intentions toward buying a brand can be thought of as based on both the target consumer's own attitude toward buying it as well as a subjective norm. The consumer's *own* attitude is based on an assessment of the consumer's importance ratings of the attributes of the product, weighted by the consumer's perception of the extent to which the brand adequately possesses those attributes (as discussed in Chapter 8). In a similar fashion, the subjective norm is expected to be based on the consumer's beliefs about what the reference group is expected to like, weighted by the consumer's motivation to comply with that perceived expectation from the reference group. Michael Ryan has shown that while this formulation is theoretically elegant there are several difficulties in applying it in practice.[5]

NATURE OF REFERENCE GROUP INFLUENCES ON BRAND CHOICE . . . .

One way to think of different kinds of reference group influence is to make a distinction between influences that are (1) external and explicit and (2) internal and implicit. By *external*, we mean the likelihood that decision making involves explicit social interactions such as a situation in which two or more people (for example, a husband, wife, and children) are involved. The consumer might seek to include friends and neighbors in the decision-making process or otherwise refer to the product in the course of conversations and social interactions. An industrial buyer might seek advice or information from associates. This is often called *word-of-mouth advertising* to distinguish this kind of communication from *mass communication advertising.*

Internal personal influence refers to the likelihood that decision making is affected by mental processes that involve people or groups. Thus, for example, many products are purchased as gifts for someone else where no interaction takes place with the intended recipient. Others are purchased primarily for their symbolic role. They may symbolize a particular social class position or status. Still others, particularly in the clothing and fashion industry, are heavily influenced by the decision maker's judgment of "what other people might think" or "how I will look to the Jones's" and so on. Many products are purchased so as to be "first with the latest thing." In all these instances, personal influence is operating but may involve little or no explicit social interaction or specific conversation between the consumer and someone else.

Another key distinction often made by researchers is that between reference group influence that is (1) informational and (2) normative.[6] *Informational reference group effects* pertains to situations in which low-knowledge consumers seek information from other people—friends, or salespeople, or media personalities—that they consider experts in the product category. Our discussion of the expertise and credibility of endorsers in Chapter 12 pertains to such situations. The second kind of influence, *normative influence,* refers to situations in which consumers identify with a group to enhance their self-image and ego or comply with a group's norms to gain rewards or to avoid punishments.

Why do reference groups have such influence, informative or normative? There are several explanations. For one, individual consumers are placed in various social roles throughout their lives.[7] Some of these roles are ones we voluntarily seek out and acquire (e.g., that of a successful businessperson); others are ascribed to us by society (e.g., age and sex roles). When consumers "play" a role, they use consumer goods to symbolize that role and to perform adequately in it. For example, someone playing the role of an athlete has to own (and show others that he/she owns) the right sports equipment, a gourmet cook has to own a food processor, a "hip" teenager may have to have purple-colored punky hair; and a new parent may proudly display a "child in car" bumper sticker on the family car. Since we are not all brought up knowing how to perform these roles, we look to others—to reference groups, actual or depicted in media—to learn how that role is played. When we are uncertain about what to do in a social situation, we turn to others for guidance. Media stereotypes, direct contact and instruction, and advertising are all important here, and advertising can use this influence to link the brand in question to the successful performance of a certain role. For instance, Nike can imply in its ads that a serious athlete always wears Nike running shoes. As consumers actually acquire that role, they are likely to deviate from the media-depicted stereotype and modify it in ways that individualize themselves. Further, not all consumers accept the stereotypic role description to begin with, so advertising needs to use role depiction with care (for example, sex roles for men and women are changing rapidly in our times, and depicting what the "right" role is for women society is obviously fraught with considerable danger).

A second explanation for the importance of reference groups in our social lives is that we are members of several different groups (political, religious, ethnic, occupational, etc.), and we use consumer goods to help us define what groups we belong to and differentiate ourselves from the groups we don't belong to. This group influence may owe its power to the fact that if we don't do what the group does it may reject us (for example, a "nerdy" appearance may lead to rejection from a "hip" teenage group). Alternatively, it may be because we identify deeply with the group (for example, a consumer may drive an imported car because he identifies strongly with the "smart and sophisticated" crowd). Finally, the influence may simply be internalized and subconscious, to the extent that the group's values become considered "personal" values—for example, a strongly proenvironmental shopper may not even consider himself part of a proenvironmental group, though those values in essence define what that group is.

Whatever the nature of the influence, the essential point is that every group has its norms or standards and values, and the kinds of consumer goods and services that group members do and do not form a key part of these norms (for example, the kinds of clothes we wear, the types of food we buy, the liquor we drink). These norms are communicated within the group through role models-members of the group who have greater than average influence either because they are seen as experts, or because they are seen as powerful or especially attractive, or because they are very similar to the average group member. What advertising can do is to communicate that purchase and consumption of the consumer good or service being advertised is an integral part of the norms of a group that the target consumer seeks to belong to and to communicate this through an explicit or implicit endorsement from (or association with) a role model. For example, in the soft drink-industry, susceptible teenagers—who are target consumers because they are the heavy users—are told that to "belong" with other teenagers, they should drink Pepsi or Coke (as the case may be), and this message is communicated by showing Michael Jackson drinking Pepsi, George Michael drinking Coke, and so on.

FACTORS INFLUENCING THE DEGREE OF GROUP INFLUENCE. . . . .

It is well known that the degree to which such social influence processes operate is affected by the nature of the product, service, or idea in question, as well as the characteristics of the consumer and of the decision-making process. An advertiser considering the use of advertising to create social or group influence needs to evaluate the extent to which these factors increase the role of social and group influences in a particular situation.

Individual Differences in Susceptibility

Consumers differ with respect to the extent of their susceptibility to social and group influence.[8] Some people are simply more "persuadable" than others, more extroverted, more likely to engage in social interactions, and more affected in their decisions by the opinions of friends, neighbors, role models, and so on. This heterogeneity can be found within any particular market target. Research by William Bearden, Richard Netemeyer, and Jesse Teel has shown that there is a difference between susceptibility to informational reference group influence and that to normative influence. It has been found by C. Whan Park and Parker Lessig[9] that younger consumers are more susceptible to reference group influence. This could be because they tend to have lower product category knowledge (and thus reduced self-confidence in brand choice), or have more social contacts and greater social visibility, or are undergoing more intense identity-seeking and socialization processes.

Decision-Making Unit

The purchase of a package of gum, a breath mint, or numerous other types of consumer products, particularly in the "impulse" category, is predominantly an individual-oriented decision. The decision-making unit (DMU) tends to be one individual, and such purchases are unlikely to involve a group decision. In contrast, many major family purchase decisions, such as that of a home or an automobile or a vacation spot, are group decisions. Such family decision making obviously involves personal influence, and the advertiser should make a determination of the existing and potential uses of the product in the consumption system of the family and the likely relative influence of various family members. Does the wife tend to carry most weight in choosing a brand for this product? The husband? Are children likely to be a significant influence? Similarly, a large number of industrial product decisions are group decisions, in which the person who finally uses is usually not the one who places the order or even the one who influences or finally approves the decision. At least two, and often several, people will be involved, and it is a better understanding of this group decision-making process that advertisers in these product categories must acquire.

An implicit personal influence process takes place in many other purchase decisions. Many purchases that appear to be made for the self are in fact being made with some other individual or reference group in mind. Thus, the home-maker, for example, in buying provisions for the household, is often more concerned with what others in the household will want, use, and eat than with his or her own personal consumption. The distinction between the "consumer" and the "customer" in each situation must be clearly understood. The consumer of men's socks is in the majority of cases men. The customer for men's socks, however, is often a woman. All products given as gifts fall into this category, and it is of fundamental importance to assess the nature of the thing being advertised from this viewpoint.

Nature of the Product Category

Are there certain kinds of product categories in which reference group influence is likely to be stronger? Although there are no definitive conclusions, researchers have found that personal influence will be more likely to operate in situations in which large rather than small amounts of money are involved, when the decision *is riskier*, when the product is not easily testable, and when the consumer *is more involved* in the choice.[10] Thus, consumers are likely to seek out and acquire information of all kinds, including the advice and opinion of friends, family, and experts, where the financial and emotional investment is high. Where risk and high involvement are present, personal influence will also be likely to occur at the decision and postdecision stages of the process. Thus a salesperson plays a more important role with some products than with others, and the opinion of friends may be actively sought out after the decision has been made. These conditions are most likely for products such as large appliances, television sets, home computers, automobiles, and furniture.

Another key attribute of product categories high in reference group influence is that they are generally "socially conspicuous." The product must be conspicuous in the most obvious sense that it can be seen and identified by others, and it must be conspicuous in the sense of standing out and being noticed. No matter how visible a product is, if virtually everyone owns it, it is not conspicuous in the second sense. Thus such conspicuousness has two aspects: relative scarcity (such as the purchase of luxury goods) and public visibility, where ownership or consumption can be seen by others.[11] Such product categories, where the reference group can see what the consumer has bought or is consuming, are sometimes nicknamed *badge products* or *wardrobe products*, for obvious reasons. Examples are clothing, footwear, automobiles, watches, and jewelry. William Bearden and Michael Etzel[12] report on a study in which consumer perceptions of reference group influence on product and brand decisions were examined. A panel made up of 645 members and a follow-up study of 151 respondents classified products such as golf clubs, automobiles, trash compactors, blankets and mattresses. In general, respondents correctly classified products into categories such as luxury or necessity and public or private and the associated degrees of potential group influence.

Nature of the Consumption or Purchasing Situation

The *situation* for which the purchase is made is another factor that has been intensively studied and shown to affect product attitudes and choice. Personal influence is often the major distinguishing characteristic between one situation and the next. Purchasing beer or wine to drink by oneself can differ from purchasing these products for an important social occasion (as in a bar or in a party at home with guests). Clearly, one's sensitivity to what the reference group feels is likely to be much greater in the first situation. The advertiser must appreciate that his or her product may be locked into a particular situational use for which personal influence will operate to a greater or lesser degree.

INFORMATIONAL INFLUENCE: WORD-OF-MOUTH AND DIFFUSION PROCESSES . . . .

Chapter 12 later in this book will explore the ways in which endorsers can serve as credible experts in convincing consumers that an advertised brand is worth buying, which is one way in which reference groups can have an informational influence. Another way in which informational influences operate is through the operation of *word-of-mouth processes*, in which a potential consumer relies on the opinion of another to decide on brand adoption; adoption through such mechanisms is part of what has been called the *diffusion process*. Diffusion and personal influence are important topics for an advertiser for several reasons.[13] First, great advertising campaigns and many apparently worthwhile products have floundered because of a failure to stimulate diffusion and word-of-mouth communication to support the product or service advertised. Some campaigns, on the other hand, have achieved great success, primarily because of the word-of-mouth communication that they stimulated. Second, there are significant reasons why, in many product categories, the relative influence of face-to-face communications greatly surpasses the influence of advertising in stimulating or determining brand choice. Third, segmentation strategies must take into account the fact that a target segment may have an important influence on the attitudes and behaviors of other groups not included within it. Next, we discuss several characteristics that increase the likelihood of success of word-of-mouth communications.

Motivational Characteristics

What motivates people to talk to others about a product or ad campaign? Ernest Dichter[14] argued that for talking to take place, there must exist some material interest: there must be satisfaction or reward associated with the behavior. In other words, a speaker will choose products, listeners, and words that are most likely to serve basic needs and goals. In a study of product talking and listening behavior, he found that talking motivations tended to fall into four categories, each associated with various kinds of involvement.

The first is *product involvement*. People have a tendency to want to talk about distinctly pleasurable or unpleasurable things. Talk can serve to relive the pleasure the speaker has obtained and dissipate the excitement aroused by the use of a product or the experience of having shopped for and purchased it. Talk can confirm ownership of it for the speaker in many subtle ways.

The second is *self-involvement.* The speaker essentially seeks confirmation of the wisdom of the decision from his or her peers and as a way to reduce dissonance. Self-confirmation behavior is engaged in to gain attention, show connoisseurship, and enhance feelings of being first with something, having inside information, suggesting status, spreading the gospel, seeking confirmation of one's own judgment, and asserting superiority. The point is that a product or advertising object can be the central focus of conversations engaged in for these kinds of goals and motivations.

The third is *other involvement* in which the major motivation is the need and intent to help other persons and share with and enjoy the benefits of the product. Products can serve to express sentiments of neighborliness, care, friendship, and love. The fourth motivation for speaking about products is called *message involvement* and derives from the nature of advertising itself. Advertising, for many reasons, can stimulate word-of-mouth communications and often itself becomes the focus of such conversations.

Opinion Leadership

Who are the kinds of people who have the most impact on others in such informational and word-of-mouth processes? The concept of the opinion leader is relevant here, and it has been a central focus for much empirical research in sociology and marketing.[15] It is interesting to recall that Katz and Lazarsfeld first defined the concept as "leadership at its simplest," "almost invisible," at the "person-to-person level of ordinary, intimate, informal, everyday contact."[16]

In their pioneering study, four types of opinion leaders were identified: marketing, fashion, movie, and public affairs leaders. Marketing opinion leaders were found to be married women with comparatively large families, gregarious, and not concentrated at any particular social-status level. In contrast to the influence of immediate family members (for example, husband and child), the authors stressed the importance of extrafamilial influence in many consumer product situations.

Since the publication of this study, a great deal of other research attention has been devoted to the concept of opinion leadership, both in marketing and in other disciplines. John Myers,[17] for example, found in the case of the adoption of new frozen-food products, in which the new products were given to "positive" and "negative" opinion leaders, that group opinions toward the new products tended to follow those of the opinion leader in both positive and negative cases.

One of the first questions that needs to be asked is whether opinion leadership is a general or a specific phenomenon. It is not at all clear that an opinion leader in one product class (e.g., fashionable clothes) also tends to be an opinion leader in another (e.g., personal computer equipment). From an advertiser's viewpoint, another important question is the degree to which opinion leaders are differentially responsive to advertising appeals. Without the establishment of this fact, many of the basic postulates of a two-step flow of mass communications break down. It is ultimately a question of the connection, or lack of connection, between the formal mass media channel and the informal channels of interpersonal communication and influence. Do individuals play different roles in introducing advertising communications into a social network?

In an important book on the subject, Everett Rogers[18] argued that at the time of introduction of an innovation, the population can be divided into five groups (segments) made up of *innovators, opinion leaders, early majority, late majority*, and *laggards*. He further argued that the distribution of these groups approximated a normal curve: the early and late majority groups would tend to be much larger than those at the tails, innovators and laggards. Second, he redefined the process of diffusion and adoption as involving five stages: *awareness, interest, evaluation, trial,* and *adoption*. The argument is that all people go through this process on the way to adoption (or rejection) of an innovation. Mass media and impersonal sources of influence tend to be most important at the early stages of awareness and interest, and word-of-mouth and personal influence tend to be most important in the later stages of evaluation, trial, and adoption.

Researchers have focused attention on the degree to which the five types of market segments exist during new product introductions. The results are mixed and depend heavily on the nature of the new product and the competitive and other conditions at the time of entry. The concept of *innovator* has received particular attention. It is useful to consider the innovator concept for several reasons. First, it can be a useful segmentation variable. An advertiser may want to reach an innovator if a new product is involved simply because innovators may represent the most attractive segment, especially at the onset. Second, an innovator may, by example, influence others. Noninnovators tend to wait until innovators have acted. Therefore, it is reasonable to look first at the innovator segment. Finally, much research has gone into describing innovators in marketing. Since there is evidence of an overlap between innovators and opinion leaders, this research should also be relevant to those who would attempt to identify opinion leaders.

Motivations for Listening to Opinion Leaders

Thus far we have talked about the nature of the people who are at the sending end of the word-of-mouth communications. But what about the listeners—who are they more likely to be? Motivations for listening also require that the listener receive some satisfaction or reward from the interaction. Dichter[19] found two conditions particularly important: (1) that the person who recommends something is interested in the listener and his or her well-being and (2) that the speaker's experience with and knowledge about the product are convincing. Obviously, basic questions of the trust the listener-receiver has in the speaker-sender are involved and the credibility of the source of the communications. Seven kinds of sources were found to be particularly important and potentially successful in their influence attempts: commercial authorities, celebrities, connoisseurs, sharers of interest, intimates, people of goodwill, and bearers of tangible evidence. A discussion of the dimensions of source credibility will be found in Chapter 12.

Recent Studies and Models of Diffusion of Innovations

In some recent research, Gatignon and Robertson[20] point out that advertising can have its greatest influence on product and brand diffusion when the level of cognitive processing is low, whereas personal influence will be greatest when there is a large amount of cognitive activity. Personal influence and mass media are complementary and personal influence is more important under conditions of information-seeking and less important under conditions of information-giving.

One important determinant of the speed of diffusion (for example, how quickly a new product is accepted by a market segment) is the compatibility of the innovation with the norms and values of the social system. And, the more homogenous the social system, the faster will be the diffusion rate and the higher will be the maximum penetration. There has been a new surge of interest in building formal models of new product diffusion.[21] Interesting questions that have received significant research attention are whether it is advantageous to preannounce a new product, and whether it is an advantage to be first in the market with a new product, so-called pioneering advantage. Jehoshua Eliashberg and Thomas Robertson[22] found that firms preannounce in about 50 percent of the cases. They present an interesting model of conditions under which the firm should or should not preannounce. In general, it depends on competitive and consumer behavior conditions. For example, if market share is low or if there are high customer switching costs, they it is worthwhile to preannounce. And, it is generally true that there are advantages to being the pioneer in a market such as the potential for erecting barriers to later entrants, building consumer preference and loyalty for your brand, and so on.

Vijay Mahajan, Eitan Muller, and Rajendra Srivastava[23] in an imaginative extension of the classic Bass and Rogers models, show that the five adopter categories defined by Rogers (Innovators, Early Adopters, Early Majority, Late Majority, and Laggards) can be derived from a knowledge of the inflection points in the Bass model. Rogers proposed, based on basic statistical parameters of the normal distribution that the typical innovation would have the following population distribution in each category:

Innovators	2.5%
Early Adopters	13.5%
Early Majority	34.0%
Late Majority	34.0%
Laggards	16.0%

Mahajan and others studied the timing and size of these categories for eleven consumer durable products based on modifications of the Bass model. As expected, there were significant differences in timing and category size across each of the products, but also a high degree of correspondence with the original normal distribution based on Rogers model. Table 11–1 shows the data for the eleven products and five diffusion categories.

Note in Table 11–1 that the size of the Innovators and Early Adopters groups

Table 11–1. Time and Size of Adopter Categories for Consumer Durable Products.

	Innovators % Adopters	Early adopters		Early majority		Late majority		Laggard	
		Years	% Adopters	Years	% Adopters	Years	% Adopters	Years	% Adopters
Black-and-white TV sets	2.8	3.1	9.5	4.7	32.1	4.7	32.1	12.5	23.5
Home freezers	1.8	4.8	10.9	7.0	32.0	7.0	32.0	18.8	23.3
Steam irons	2.9	3.1	11.3	3.7	31.4	3.7	31.4	10.5	23.0
Water Softeners	1.8	4.8	14.6	4.2	30.6	4.2	30.6	13.2	22.4
Automatic coffee makers	1.7	4.9	15.0	4.1	30.5	4.1	30.5	13.1	22.3
Clothes dryers	1.7	4.6	15.6	3.5	30.3	3.5	30.3	11.6	22.1
Record players	2.5	2.9	15.6	1.9	30.0	1.9	30.0	6.7	21.9
Power lawn-mowers	0.9	6.6	18.1	3.8	29.7	3.8	29.7	14.2	21.7
Room air conditioners	1.0	5.6	18.2	3.0	29.6	3.0	29.6	11.6	21.6
Electric bed coverings	0.6	9.6	18.6	5.3	29.6	5.3	29.6	20.2	21.6
Electric refrigerators	0.2	14.3	20.0	6.0	29.1	6.0	29.1	26.3	21.4

Source: Adapted from Vijay Mahajan, Eitan Muller, and Rajendra K. Srivastava, "Determination of Adopter Categories by Using Innovation Diffusion Models," Journal of Marketing Research, 27 (February 1990). 44. Published by the American Marketing Association.

provided by the normal distribution are in the range of the sizes for the same two groups given by the Bass model. However, the classification based on the Bass model tends to generate a lower percentage of adopters in the Early Majority and Late Majority groups and a higher percentage in the Laggard group. In a related study of personal computer adoptions, the authors found that there were significant differences among the adopter categories in demographic characteristics (age, education, income, and occupation), usage, expertise, magazine reading habits, and advertising focus. Such differences add further weight to the argument that people do differ with respect to their propensity to adopt new products and react differently to innovations of various kinds.

Implementing an Informational Influence Strategy

If informational influence is desired, the most straightforward strategy implication is that the advertiser can attempt to single out the crucial innovator and opinion leadership segments and target promotion and advertising messages to them, using the appropriate credible sources as endorsers. This strategy has not been followed as often as it might seem. Because of the costs of attempting to identify innovators in many product or market situations and the inherent spillover effects of mass media like television, it is often more efficient to segment on the basis of other criteria such as age, income, education, and so on.

There are, however, many ways in which advertising can be designed so as to appeal to innovators and/or otherwise enhance the diffusion and personal influence process. It is possible to *simulate* directly personal influence in the content of the advertisement itself. This is effectively used in "slice-of-life" advertising, which shows a group of people discussing the product. Normally, one of the individuals takes the role of spokesperson for the product and demonstrates or persuades the other or others to use it. Thomas Robertson[24] has argued that the advertiser can essentially seek to "simulate," "stimulate," "monitor," or "retard" personal influence. Concerning simulation, for example, advertising can be used as a replacement for personal influence. An advertising message can show people similar to the viewer who are buying and using the product and, in this sense, act as a "personal influence."

Advertisements can stimulate either information giving or information receiving. The giver of information is most likely to be a recent purchaser. He or she is likely to be in dissonance, and advertising information or direct-mail programs should supply information that can readily be passed along to others. A seeker of information is most likely to be someone considering a purchase. Advertising here should encourage themes like "Ask the man who owns one" to stimulate personal influence. A good example is the advertisement for Advil pain reliever shown in Figure 11–1.

Media can also be chosen to encourage or, in one way or another, take advantage of the flow of personal influence. In some cases, it may be appropriate to single out opinion leaders and, through selective magazines or journals (for example, *Engineering News*, *Golf Digest*) or through direct-mail campaigns, appeal to them directly. This type of strategy is particularly appropriate in industrial mar-

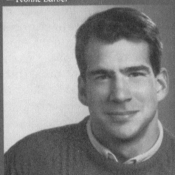

Why more and more muscle ache sufferers are switching to Advil.®

"I was given Advil and it works…It's helped my aches and pains…It's never upset my stomach."—*Derek Green*

Maybe you exercised harder than usual. Maybe you lifted something you shouldn't have. Maybe you just slept in an awkward position.

Well, whatever you did, you're paying for it with muscle aches. Just like these muscle ache sufferers, but they know what to do about it, and so should you.

Take Advil.

These people switched to Advil because it makes their muscle aches go away. They find that one Advil is just as effective as two regular aspirin or two regular-strength Tylenol. Not only that, Advil works just as well on headache, backache, and minor arthritis pain.

Yet as strong as Advil is, it doesn't upset the stomach the way aspirin sometimes can.

1899
1955
TODAY

"Advil has always worked for me, and my doctor recommended it, so I can't go wrong." —*Yvonne Barber*

So don't let those muscle aches make you miserable.

Learn from the experience of others like you. Switch to Advil.

Advil
IBUPROFEN
advanced medicine for pain

ADVANCED MEDICINE FOR PAIN.™
from Whitehall Laboratories

Advil contains a non-prescription strength of ibuprofen. Appearance of the brown Advil tablet and caplet is a trademark of Whitehall. © 1991 Whitehall Laboratories, N.Y., N.Y.

"After a workout sometimes…I hurt all over. I take Advil and that takes the pain away. I can move freely."—*Scott Redford*

Figure 11–1. Stimulating personal influence: Advil.
Courtesy of Whitehall Laboratories.

keting. Direct mail possibly can make the communication more personal and give the recipient a feeling that she or he is part of a select group.

A wide variety of other sales and promotional devices have been used to stimulate word-of-mouth activity and to take advantage of personal influence.[25] Block parties are often used to promote china and silverware sales. In-store demonstrations give the consumer an opportunity to use the product without buying it. House-to-house sampling puts the product physically into the hands of both leaders and nonleaders and can result in source- or recipient-initiated conversations about it. The Ford Motor Company used a number of programs in introducing the Mustang. Disc jockeys, college newspaper editors, and airline stewardesses were loaned Mustangs on the theory that they were likely to influence other people. Upon evaluation, the airline stewardess program was felt to have been unsuccessful since stewardesses were not looked upon as a source of information about automobiles. The other programs were considered successful. Automobile companies, in general, attempt to stimulate adoption and interpersonal information flows through the medium of rental cars. It is a way in which the consumer or potential consumer has the opportunity to use the product without actually purchasing it.

NORMATIVE INFLUENCE: HOW ADS CAN GIVE BRANDS CULTURAL MEANING . . . .

As discussed earlier in this chapter, reference groups can influence consumers not only through the provision of information perceived to be "expert," but also through the provision of norms—standards, values, attitudes, and the like—that are influential with those who belong to, aspire to, or identify with this reference group. As with informational influence, this normative influence of reference groups is also stronger in some situations, and is particularly important and relevant with new products. In many cases, the mere fact that the product is new and other people do not yet have it is the crucial motivation for buying. New products that are significant breakthroughs at the time of their introduction such as television sets, hand-held calculators, home computers, CD players, and so on, are particularly likely to be affected by normative influence.

However, even established products and brands vary in the degree to which normative influence operates, and this variation is due (as discussed earlier in the chapter) to differences in social visibility and conspicuousness. Staples such as salt, sugar, and pepper are not likely to be affected, whereas clothing items, particularly in the area of fashion, will be. Radios are socially very important among teenagers. Furniture and automobiles serve important social as well as functional needs and are much affected by normative influence. It might be argued that whenever the nature of the perceived risk in a product category is primarily functional, a high level of such perceived risk is accompanied by high informational interpersonal influence. In contrast, if the perceived risk is high in a social sense—when there exists uncertainty about how the consumer should act or dress or consume in a socially visible way—the nature of the reference group is likely to be normative.

While the preceding discussion may give the idea that normative reference group influence applies mainly to considerations of socially visible status, this is far from the case. We are talking here not merely of status but of every aspect of what a consumer thinks of as his or her "true self."[26] Perhaps the more inclusive way to conceptualize what is going on here is to think of the *cultural* aspects of the product or brand.

Culture has been defined by the consumer anthropologist Grant McCracken as the "lens" through which all phenomena are seen. It determines how these phenomena will be apprehended and assimilated. Culture is also the "blueprint" of human activity. It determines the coordinates of social activity and productive activity, specifying the behaviors and objects that issue from both. As a lens, culture determines how the world is seen. As a blueprint, it determines how the world will be fashioned by human effort. In short, culture constitutes the world by supplying it with meaning.[27]

According to McCracken, this "meaning" can be characterized in terms of two concepts: cultural categories and cultural principles. *Cultural categories* are the distinctions with which a culture divides up the world—for example, the distinction between leisure and work time or the distinctions of class, status, gender, age, and occupation. These distinctions are made concrete, among other things, through material objects: food and clothing, for instance, can be used to set apart different levels of class and status, or gender and age. The kind of food and clothing that is considered acceptable for one may not be considered acceptable for another, and these differences in acceptability help define these different levels or classes of class and status, or gender and age. *Cultural principles* are the ideas with which this category creation is performed. For example, the clothing differences that are used to show the discrimination between men and women, or between high social classes and low, may do so by communicating the supposed "delicacy" of women and the supposed "strength" of men, the "refinement" of a high social class and the "vulgarity" of a lower one. "Goods are both the creations and the creators of this culturally constituted world," according to McCracken. The science of studying the kinds of cultural symbolism and signs implicit in goods is called *semiotics.*

Where does advertising come into all this? Well, advertising can be used to "transfer" a particular kind of cultural meaning from the outside world to a brand. Later, when the consumer buys the brand, that same meaning is then transferred from the brand to the consumer, through possession, and so on.

How is meaning transferred to a brand? An ad can bring together the brand and some other widely accepted symbol of a particular kind of cultural meaning, in such a way that the ad's viewer or reader sees an essential similarity between the two, so that that particular kind of cultural meaning now becomes a part of the brand. The cultural meaning that is desired to be communicated to the brand (e.g., gender, age, social class, ethnicity), for instance, may be currently associated (in people's minds) with certain kinds of people, places, activities, objects, times of day, and so on, and the ad may cleverly associate them with the brand, using the appropriate tone, pace, camera direction, voice-overs, and so on.

For example, a detergent ad that shows the backyard of a suburban country home, in a weekend afternoon in the summer, with a barbecue going on, then cuts to a family member embracing a small daughter—whose clothes have just been washed by that detergent—while the mother watches with pride, can be interpreted as taking the "family warmth" meaning of the embrace and transferring it to the product, so that when a mother buys and uses it she feels more like a warm, caring mother.[28] Or, think of the transference of masculinity from the cultural symbol of the lone cowboy out on the range in sunset to Marlboro cigarettes and how that masculinity is then felt by every smoker of Marlboro.

From an advertising planning perspective, the planner needs to think about what kind of cultural meaning currently exists for the product category and the brand, then think about what kind of competitively unique cultural meaning is sought for the brand, and then, finally, think about how that desired cultural meaning can be linked to it. Is the product or brand used already, or to be used, as a symbol of social-class position, aspiration, or mobility? Should all social classes or genders or age groups use the product (for example, Coca-Cola) or should its use be largely confined to one social category? Is the product bound to a particular ethnic group such as kosher foods, or does the ethnic background of the consumer play little or no role? Does or should ownership signify membership in a particular subculture, such as teenage punkers (which may exclude it from the more general market)? Finally, the family *life cycle* should be considered.[29] Is the product suitable to the "empty nest" family, the young couple just starting out, or some other stage of the family life?

SUMMARY . . . .

Advertising can take advantage of reference group effects by associating the brand with certain social or reference groups. The important point about reference group effects is that the individual does not have to be a member of the group for influence to occur. In other words, the influence can occur either internally (implicitly) or externally (explicitly), and in the internal case explicit social interaction need not necessarily take place. Another key distinction is between informational influence and normative influence. Informational influence refers to situation in which consumers who don't know much about the product seek information from friends, salespeople, or media personalities. Normative influence refers to situations in which consumers identify with a group to enhance self-image and ego, or comply with a group's norms to gain rewards or avoid punishments.

The major factors that influence the degree of group influence are (1) individual differences in susceptibility, (2) the type of the decision-making unit, (3) the nature of the product category, and (4) the kind of consumption or purchasing situation involved.

Word-of-mouth and diffusion are informational influence processes in which a potential consumer relies on the opinion of others to decide on trying and/or adopting the product. Great advertising campaigns and many otherwise worthwhile products have floundered because of a failure to stimulate diffusion and word-of-mouth communication. And, the reverse is true. Some campaigns have achieved great success because of the effectiveness of diffusion and word-of-mouth. The major factors that determine the rate of diffusion and determine the success or failure of word-of-mouth are motivational characteristics of the audience (including involvement in the product being advertised, self-involvement, and other-involvement) and characteristics of the product or innovation.

Opinion leadership is very important in understanding adoption processes. The basic idea is that certain individuals, called opinion leaders, serve to influence the attitudes and behaviors (such as buying or not buying) of others around them. The concept has been elaborated and the process of diffusion and adoption extended in many ways such as in studies of the motivations for listening to opinion leaders. From a strategies perspective, the advertiser can simulate, stimulate, monitor, or retard reference group influence.

Advertising can give brands cultural meaning through normative influence. Although products take on meaning in the absence of advertising, advertising can create, reinforce, and extend such meanings in a wide variety of ways. McCracken states that meaning can be characterized by either cultural categories or cultural principles. Cultural categories are made concrete through material objects such as food and clothing. Cultural principles are the ideas with which the category creation is performed, for example clothing differences to distinguish men and women. Advertising can be used to transfer a particular kind of cultural meaning to a brand. The advertising planner needs to think about what kinds of cultural meaning currently exists for the product category and brand, and about how a desired cultural meaning can be linked to it.

DISCUSSION QUESTIONS . . . .

1. Identify a "reference group" to which you relate or to which you have related in the past. Trace the situations and instances in which you have been influenced by it and whether the influence was implicit or explicit.

2. What is the difference between informative and normative reference group influence? Which is likely to play a greater role in brand choice?

3. Analyze your own motivations for sending and receiving information regarding purchasing behavior and television commercials. Compare these with the ideas of Dichter given in the chapter.

4. Design an advertisement specifically directed to stimulate a diffusion process. What are its characteristics? Why did you choose particular elements and components?

5. Find a case example of a successful and unsuccessful new product introduction. Analyze the advertising campaigns in each case from the viewpoint of the concepts and ideas given in the chapter.

6. Identify the "opinion leaders" in your class. What are their characteristics? What, if any, influence might they have on buying behavior of other class members?

NOTES. . . . .

1. *Advertising Age*, August 1, 1994, p. 1.
2. V. Parker Lessig and C. Whan Park, "Promotional Perspectives of Reference Group Influence: Advertising Implications," *Journal of Advertising*, 7 (1978), 41–47.
3. For an excellent review of the literature on reference group effects, see William O. Bearden and Michael J. Etzel, "Reference Group Influence on Product and Brand Purchase Decisions," *Journal of Consumer Research*, 9 (September 1982), 183–194.
4. Martin Fishbein, "Attitude and the Prediction of Behavior," in Martin Fishbein, ed., *Readings in Attitude Theory and Measurement* (New York: Wiley, 1967), pp. 477–492.
5. Michael J. Ryan, "Behavioral Intention Formation: The Interdependency of Attitudinal and Social Influence Variables," *Journal of Consumer Research*, 9 (December 1982), 263–278.
6. William O. Bearden, Richard G. Netemeyer, and Jesse E. Teel, "Measurement of Consumer Susceptibility to Interpersonal Influence," *Journal of Consumer Research*, 15 (March 1989), 473–481.
7. Robert B. Settle and Pamela L. Alreck, *Why They Buy* (New York: Wiley, 1989), chap. 7.
8. William Bearden, Richard Netemeyer, and Jesse Teel, "Measurement of Consumer Susceptibility to Interpersonal Influence."
9. C. Whan Park and Parker V. Lessig, "Students and Housewives: Differences in Susceptibility to Reference Group Influence," *Journal of Consumer Research*, 4 (September 1977), 102–110.
10. Thomas S. Robertson, *Innovative Behavior and Communication* (New York: Holt, Rinehart and Winston, 1971).
11. William Bearden and Michael Etzel, "Reference Group Influence on Product and Brand Purchase Decisions."
12. ibid.
13. For articles on diffusion research and opinion leadership, see Hubert Gatignon and Thomas S. Robertson, "A Propositional Inventory of New Diffusion Research," *Journal of Consumer Research*, 11 (March 1985), 849–867, and Dorothy Leonard-Barton, "Experts as Negative Opinion Leaders in Diffusion of a Technological Innovation," *Journal of Consumer Research*, 11 (March 1985), 914–926.
14. Ernest Dichter, "How Word-of-Mouth Advertising Works," *Harvard Business Review*, 44 (November/December 1966), 147–166.
15. The earliest and best known follow-up studies to Katz and Lazarsfeld's *Personal Influence* (see note 18) were done on physician drug adoptions. See Herbert Menzel and Elihu Katz, "Social Relations and Innovations in the Medical Professions: The Epidemiology of a New Drug," *Public Opinion Quarterly*, 19 (Winter 1956), 337–352. For a fully developed treatment of the two-step flow model, see Elihu Katz, "The Two-Step Flow of Communication: An Up-to-Date Report on an Hypothesis," *Public Opinion Quarterly*, 21 (Spring 1957), 61–78.
16. Elihu Katz and Paul F. Lazarsfeld, *Personal Influence* (New York: Free Press, 1955), p. 138.
17. John G. Myers, "Patterns of Interpersonal Influence in the Adoptions of New Products," in Raymond M. Haas, ed., *Proceedings of the American Marketing Association* (Chicago: American Marketing Association, 1966), pp. 750–757.
18. Everett M. Rogers, *Diffusion of Innovations* (New York: Free Press, 1962).
19. Dichter, "How Word-of-Mouth Advertising Works."
20. Hubert Gatignon and Thomas S. Robertson, "A Propositional Inventory for New Diffusion Research," *Journal of Consumer Research*, 11 (March 1985), 849–867, and Hubert Gatignon and Thomas S. Robertson, "Innovative Decision Processes," in Thomas S. Robertson and Harold H. Kassarjian, eds., *Handbook of Consumer Behavior* (Englewood Cliffs, NJ: Prentice Hall, 1991), pp. 316–348.
21. Vijay Mahajan, Eitan Muller, and Frank M. Bass, "New Product Diffusion Models in Mar-

keting: A Review and Directions for Research," *Journal of Marketing*, 54 (January 1990), 1–26.

22. Jehoshua Eliashberg and Thomas S. Robertson, "New Product Preannouncing Behavior: A Market Signaling Study," *Journal of Marketing Research*, 25, no. 3 (August 1988), 282–292.

23. Vijay Mahajan, Eitan Muller, and Rajendra K. Srivastava, "Determination of Adopter Categories by Using Innovation Diffusion Models," *Journal of Marketing Research*, 27 (February 1990), 37–50.

24. Robertson, *Innovative Behavior and Communication,* pp. 210–223.

25. Mancuso, for example, reports on a study in which high school students selected for their opinion leadership potential were given the new product (a new rock-and-roll record) and encouraged to use and develop positive opinions for the record among fellow classmates. See Joseph R. Mancuso, "Why Not Create Opinion Leaders for New Product Introductions?" *Journal of Marketing,* 33 (July 1969), 20–25.

26. Russell W. Belk, "Possessions and the Extended Self," *Journal of Consumer Research*, 15 (September 1988), 131–168.

27. Grant McCracken, *Culture and Consumption* (Bloomington: Indiana University Press, 1988), chap. 5.

28. Grant McCracken, "Advertising from a Cultural Point of View: One Approach to the Gain Ad." Paper presented at the Annual Conference of the Association for Consumer Research, New York, September 1990.

29. William D. Wells and G. Gubar, "Life Cycle Concept in Marketing Research," *Journal of Marketing Research,* 3 (November 1966), 355–363.

SEVEN-UP* . . . .

The 7-Up soft drink was introduced under the name of Bib-Label Lithiated Lemon-Lime Soda in 1929, two weeks prior to the stock market crash. It was promoted as a product "for home and hospital use." Consumers used the product primarily as a mixer and as a cure for hangovers. Demand for the product was modest during the 1930s, primarily because 7-Up faced competition from about 600 other lemon-flavored soft drinks.

In 1942, the Chicago office of J. Walter Thompson was hired as the agency for 7-Up. At that time the name was changed to 7-Up. Sales for 7-Up showed impressive growth over the next two decades, and Seven-Up emerged as the third largest producer of soft drinks behind Coca-Cola and Pepsi.

In the 1960s, sales of the soft drink category grew dramatically. The post–World War II baby boom had caused a significant increase in the 14- to 24-year-old age category, and this category comprised a disproportionate number of the heavy users of soft drinks. However, as Exhibit 1 shows, Seven-Up failed to keep up with industry growth. For example, while industry dollar sales grew 8 percent between 1964 and 1965, Seven-Up experienced no growth in sales. Seven-Up also lagged the industry in 1966 and 1967. Part of the problem appeared to be the introduction of lemon-lime–flavored drinks by competitors. Coca-Cola introduced Sprite and Fresca, PepsiCo marketed Teem, Royal Crown promoted Upper-10, and Canada Dry introduced Wink. Seven-Up management also was concerned that 7-Up was being viewed by consumers as a mixer. This was a concern because the demand for mixers was much smaller than the demand for soft drinks.

EXHIBIT 1	**Percentage Change in Dollar Sales from Previous Years**		
	1965	*1966*	*1967*
Industry	8	13	11
7-Up	0	6	4

To determine how 7-Up might compete effectively, the Seven-Up Company and J. Walter Thompson conducted research. One question posed to consumers

* Source: Professor Brian Sternthal, J. L. Kellogg Graduate School of Management, Northwestern University. Reproduced by permission.

involved naming all the soft drinks they could think of. People named Coke, Pepsi, RC, Tab, Diet Rite. 7-Up was mentioned infrequently. Yet when people were later asked what 7-Up was. almost all respondents knew it was a soft drink. Apparently, people knew what 7-Up was, but had little top-of-mind awareness of the brand when cued with the stimulus soft drink.

Research was also conducted to determine the characteristics people associated with Coke, Pepsi, and 7-Up. People were presented with an attribute and asked whether or not each brand had that attribute. The percentage of those respondents who believed Coke, Pepsi and 7-Up had the attribute inquired about is shown in Exhibit 2.

On the basis of this information, a decision had to be made regarding how to promote 7-Up. One possibility was to emphasize attributes such as 7-Up's value in mixing and for indigestion. This approach would capitalize on the fact that consumers believed 7-Up had these attributes. Another possibility was to stress those attributes consumers associated with Coke and Pepsi, but not 7-Up. This strategy seemed appealing because it would place 7-Up in the mainstream with other soft drinks. Whether one of these strategies or some other one was chosen, it was important that recognition be made of the fact that Seven-Up had relatively limited resources. Coca-Cola was spending about $30 million to advertise this brand, PepsiCo was spending about $20 million, and Seven-Up was allocating approximately $12 million to advertising.

EXHIBIT 2   Consumer's Perception of Soft Drink Brand Attributes

	% INDICATING BRAND HAS ATTRIBUTE		
Attribute	*7-Up*	*Coke*	*Pepsi*
Good for mixing	66	18	4
Good for indigestion	60	17	8
Thirst quenching	60	20	28
Good tasting	58	62	59
Good for snacks	39	62	61
Good for meals	32	47	44
For active, vital people	38	60	66
A drink my friends like	30	55	53
A good buy	28	38	50

CANADA PACKERS: TENDERFLAKE* . . . .

In December 1979, Mr. Brian Burton, brand manager for Canada Packers' Tenderflake lard was writing the annual marketing plan for the fiscal year ending in March 1981. He had been assigned to Tenderflake one year earlier, and his first action had been to initiate a basic attitude and usage study on Tenderflake and its competi-

---

* K. G. Hardy et al., *Canadian Marketing: Cases and Concepts* (Boston: Allyn & Bacon, Inc., 1978).

tors. With these data in hand, Mr. Burton was considering possible changes in brand strategy.

Background

Canada Packers Limited was incorporated in 1927 as a meat-packing company. The company had diversified into a wide variety of products, one of which was Tenderflake lard. Lard is a pork by-product produced by every major meat-packing company in Canada because it offers an opportunity to utilize raw materials fully.

Until 1970, Canada Packer's lard had been distributed in the same manner as the company's meat products. Canada Packers had divided the country into five regions, each of which had been serviced by a separate and autonomous plant. Each plant manager had set prices for his products and had operated a sales force that called on grocery stores in that region. The company had not advertised lard extensively because personal service and low price had been considered the important factors in selling to food wholesalers and supermarkets.

In 1969 top management at Canada Packers had felt that the company's packaged-goods lines were not reaching their profit potential under this decentralized approach. In 1970, they established the Grocery Products Division, and by 1973, this division marketed the company's lines of shortening, margarine, lard, canned meats, cheese, soap, pet food, peanut butter, and salted nuts. Each product had been assigned to a brand manager whose responsibility was to develop strategy and monitor the performance of the brand.

Tenderflake Brand History

Tenderflake lard had never been advertised, but it benefited from the high awareness and reputation of the Tenderflake name, the Maple Leaf family brand name, and the Canada Packers corporate name. Tenderflake lard had achieved sales of 25 million pounds in fiscal 1979, which represented 65 percent of the total lard market. This dominant share had been achieved by Canada Packers' aggressive pricing, which few competitors could match. As a result the brand had generated pretax profits of only 1 cent a pound in fiscal 1978, 1.6 cents a pound in fiscal 1979, and would be fortunate to break even in fiscal 1980.

Tenderflake was distributed across Canada by the 65-person Grocery Products sales force. Each salesperson had a territory that included large and medium-sized grocery outlets and a few wholesalers who serviced the very small grocery stores. Chain retail outlets took a markup of 16 percent on their selling price. In 1979 a standard co-op advertising program was offered to retail outlets whereby Canada Packers put 1 percent of the invoice value of a customer's purchase into a fund used for advertising. Standard volume discounts amounted to another 1 percent variable cost for the brand.

The Market

Mr. Burton knew that shortening and lard were used interchangeably. Company executives estimated that 84 million pounds of lard and shortening would be sold in fiscal 1981. The combined sales of lard and shortening had been declining at about 2 percent per year.

Of the 84 million pounds of lard and shortening to be sold to consumers in fiscal 1981, approximately 60 percent would be shortening. Crisco would sell 55 percent of the shortening poundage, and Tenderflake would sell 65 percent of the lard poundage.

Shortening is white and odorless because it is made from vegetable oil or from a mixture of animal and vegetable fat. Tenderflake is white and odorless (which is not true of all lards) because Canada Packers employed a superior refining process that completely removed all odor and color from the lard. Regardless of color or odor, lard tends to produce a flakier pie crust than shortening because lard creates more layers of pastry, and most experts agreed that lard is easier to use. Major industrial consumers in the quality pastry area specified lard regardless of price.

The price of shortening appeared to influence the sales of lard. Mr. Burton had noted that whenever the price of lard was less than 7 cents below the price per pound of shortening, consumers tended to switch from lard to shortening. Retail prices of lard and shortening had traditionally fluctuated with the price of raw materials. Only Crisco had maintained stable prices and growth in sales and profits despite the general market decline. The prices of competitive products as of December 1979 were as shown in Exhibit 1.

Competition

Crisco shortening was marketed by Procter & Gamble, and it was the only major advertised brand of lard or shortening. Mr. Burton estimated that Procter & Gamble spent approximately $550,000 per year in advertising Crisco. Campaigns had stressed that Crisco was all vegetable, that the product was dependable, and that it was desirable for deep frying and pastry making. Crisco was promoted by the Procter & Gamble sales force, which sold a wide line of paper, food, and soap products to grocery outlets and a few wholesalers. Procter & Gamble's only trade in-

	Retail price per pound
EXHIBIT 1 Prices of Competitive Products, December 1979	
Lards	
Tenderflake	$0.45
Burns	0.44
Schneider	0.44
Swifts	0.45
Shortenings	
Crisco	0.56
Average of cheaper shortenings	0.50
Average of all shortenings	0.53

centive on Crisco was a co-op advertising plan that paid 18 cents on every 36-pound case. Crisco followed a premium price strategy that appeared to produce a profit of 8 cents per pound on the product. Exhibit 2 shows the estimated cost structures of Crisco and Tenderflake as of December 1979.

Crisco and Tenderflake both were packaged in 1-pound and 3-pound containers. Approximately 5 percent of Tenderflake's sales came from the 3-pound container, the majority of these coming from western Canada, while 39 percent of Crisco's sales came from the 3-pound size. Mr. Burton believed that Crisco had higher sales on the 3-pound size because it was priced at a lower cost per pound than the 1-pound size. Because of the low margins and higher per pound packaging cost on the larger size, Canada Packers sold the 3-pound size at a slight premium to the 1-pound package, and Mr. Burton believed that the higher price was responsible for the low proportion of sales in the 3-pound size.

EXHIBIT 2   Estimated Cost Structure of Crisco and Tenderflake

	Crisco per pound	*Tenderflake per pound*
Retail price	$0.56	$0.45
Less: Retail margin	0.09	0.07
Factory price	0.47	0.38
Cost of good sold	0.31	0.31
Gross margin	0.16	0.07
Expenses (including sales force, general administration, freight, distribution, trade allowances, co-op advertising, and volume discounts, but excluding media advertising)	0.06	0.06
Media advertising	0.02	
Profit	0.08	0.01

Consumers

Mr. Burton's first action as a brand manager of Tenderflake had been to commission a consumer study to determine the usage of lard and competing products, a profile of the consumer, and the consumer's attitude toward lard and its competition. A well-known market research company had conducted interviews with a representative sample of 1,647 women across Canada, and this research had been the basis of the "Fats and Oils Study,"[1] that Mr. Burton had received in March 1979.

Women were asked about the time of year when they baked, and this led to the development of the baking seasonality index.

Spring	132
Summer	100
Fall	161
Winter	196

[1] Lard, shortening, cooking oil, butter, and margarine are defined as fats and oils.

The report indicated that lard and shortening were used mainly for baking. Lard was used primarily for pastries, while shortening was used more for cakes and cookies. Exhibit 3 shows how consumers use various fats and oils; Exhibit 4 gives specific data on lard and shortening users.

The attitude toward the product itself seemed to be largely rooted in the usage role of lard and the tradition of passing this role from one generation to the next. Exhibit 5 shows the data on consumer perceptions of lard as a specific product, perceptions of brands, and reasons for using or not using lard.

Crisco and Tenderflake showed uniform strength across the country, but smaller brands of lard and shortening demonstrated some regional strength (Exhibit 6).

In addition to the fats and oils study, Mr. Burton had employed a commercial research firm to conduct several focused group interviews in order to obtain "soft" or qualitative data on Tenderflake and its competitors. Typically, 10 to 15 women gathered and talked freely about baking and oil products under the leadership of a skilled psychologist. Little attempt was made to generalize from these interviews because the samples were small and were not selected randomly. However, the technique produced ideas for marketing strategy and could be verified by the fats and oils study.

EXHIBIT 3   Consumer Use of Fats and Oils[a] (percent)

	Salad cooking oil	Butter	Margarine	Shortening	Lard
Pan frying	43	6	21	13	13
Deep-fat frying	24	1	2	14	11
Salad dressing	25	—	—	—	—
Baking cakes	8	8	20	24	4
Baking cookies	3	10	24	27	13
Baking pastries	1	2	3	49	62
Spreading	—	84	53	—	—
Total ever used	90	89	85	78	58

Users of Lard and Shortening by Application (percent)

			DUAL USERS	
Total (1.565)[b]	Lard only (287)	Shortening Only (609)	Use of Lard (669)	Use of shortening (669)
Pastries	60.6	49.0	61.9	28.0
Cakes	4.9	14.6	4.0	23.1
Cookies	15.0	15.9	12.6	26.0
Pan frying	11.5	10.1	10.6	10.7
Deep-fat frying	8.0	10.3	12.3	11.9

[a] Tables may not sum to 100% because of multiple mentions.
[b] Number of women responding.

EXHIBIT 4   Average Pounds of Lard and Shortening Used per Week

| | Total users | REGION | | | | |
		Maritimes	Quebec	Ontario	Prairies	British Columbia
Lard	0.42	0.45	0.65	0.35	0.42	0.25
Shortening	0.49	0.91	0.60	0.40	0.32	0.37

| | LANGUAGE | |
	French Quebec	Remainder of Canada
Lard	0.70	0.37
Shortening	0.62	0.45

| | CITY SIZE | | | |
	500,000 and over	100,000–499,999	10,000–99,999	Under 10,000
Lard	0.35	0.35	0.40	0.52
Shortening	0.35	0.45	0.47	0.64

| | FAMILY SIZE | | |
	2	3–4	5 and over
Lard	0.35	0.34	0.57
Shortening	0.33	0.44	0.70

| | INCOME | | | |
	Under $4,000	$4,000–6,999	$7,000–9,999	$10,000 and over
Lard	0.57	0.52	0.35	0.27
Shortening	0.59	0.59	0.44	0.36

| | AGE | | | |
	Under 35	35–44	45–54	55 and over
Lard	0.42	0.44	0.39	0.43
Shortening	0.51	0.58	0.45	0.41

| | HEAVINESS OF USE | | | | |
	Total users	Heavy	Heavy medium	Medium light	Light	Non-respondents
Lard						
Users	(956)[a]	(174)	(206)	(209)	(354)	(13)
Usage per week (lb)	0.42	1.41	0.40	0.25	0.05	
Percent consumption	100%	62%	21%	13%	4%	
Shortening						
Users	(1,278)[a]	(300)	(271)	(295)	(364)	(48)
Usage per week (lb)		1–2	1½	1	1	

[a] Number of women responding.

EXHIBIT 5 Perceptions of Brands of Lard[a] (percent)

		Total users (956)
All brands are equally good		55
One brand is better		42
Tenderflake/Maple Leaf	21	
Burns	3	
Schneider	3	
Crisco[a]	8	
Miscellaneous	7	

Volunteered Reasons for Preferring a Particular Brand of Lard (percent)

	Crisco (79)	Tenderflake/ Maple Leaf (199)	Burns (32)
Baking end benefits			
Flaky/better pastry dough	32	34	38
Excellent for pies/cookies/doughnuts	13	13	6
Good/better tasting/baked product	11	13	3
Product benefits			
Easier to handle/blend	14	11	3
Less greasy/not greasy	11	6	—
Better texture	5	11	9
Smells better	4	5	3
Other reasons			
Good result	20	18	34
Always used it	5	18	9
Cheap	4	6	3
Miscellaneous	18	20	22

Perceptions of Lard and Shortening by Users (percent)

Perceived product performance	Lard users said	Shortening users said
Best for pie shells		
Lard	62	25
Shortening	30	68
No difference	8	7
Total	100	100
Produces flakiest pastry		
Lard	54	24
Shortening	38	69
No difference	8	7
Total	100	100
Best for frying		
Lard	38	20
Shortening	35	60
No difference	27	20
Total	100	100
Cheapest		
Lard	74	62

Perceptions of Lard and Shortening by Users (percent) (continued)

Perceived product performance	Lard users said	Shortening users said
Cheapest (continued)		
Shortening	6	14
No difference	20	24
Total	100	100
Most tolerant		
Lard	31	9
Shortening	46	71
No difference	23	20
Total	100	100

Volunteered Reasons for Not Using Lard (percent)

	Total Nonusers (691)
Prefer other product	
Prefer/use shortening/Crisco	26
Prefer/use oil/margarine/butter	12
Health reasons	
Too much fat/animal fat	12
Not good for heart/liver	11
Difficult for digestion/too heavy	6
Too greasy	6
Do not eat fried things/grease	2
Dislike product	
Do not like taste	7
Do not like it	6
Other reasons	
Never tried it	9
Don't see need for it	4
Don't get good results	2
Miscellaneous responses	12

[a] Tables may not add to 100% because of multiple mentions.

The focused group interviews suggested that flakiness and fear of failure were the key areas of consumer concern. For pastries, lard was perceived as a better product than shortening among lard users, and Tenderflake seemed to have a premium-quality image. Among women who used only shortening, there was a strong perception that lard was an oily, cheaper product.

Attack by Crisco

Early in 1979 Crisco aired the television advertisement shown in Exhibit 7. The commercial clearly attacked lard's major product advantage, and Mr. Burton felt that Tenderflake, as the major lard producer, might lose market share to Crisco. He saw this as the same type of approach directed at lard that Procter & Gamble had used previously to pull Crisco ahead of the cheaper shortenings. By December 1979, Mr. Burton had developed several options, and he was about to take action.

EXHIBIT 6 Brand of Shortening Bought Last[a] (percent)

		REGION				
Brand	Total (1,278)	Maritimes (122)	Quebec (345)	Ontario (487)	Prairies (193)	British Columbia (131)
Crisco	52	38	64	47	42	64
Fluffo	12	24	1	15	19	7
Domestic	8	10	9	7	6	6
Others	8	20	2	6	13	11
Don't remember	20	8	24	25	20	12

Brand of Lard Last Bought

						British Columbia
Brand	Total (859)	Maritimes (48)	Quebec (176)	Ontario (308)	Prairies (235)	(92)
Tenderflake	52	69	49	60	51	36
Burns	13	2	2	7	23	30
Swift	7	—	5	5	6	22
Schneider	5	—	1	12	1	—
Crisco	11	4	39	3	4	2
Miscellaneous	18	27	22	14	23	7

[a] Tables may not add to 100% because of multiple mentions or rounding.

Options

Mr. Burton saw an opportunity to raise the price of Tenderflake and to begin advertising. The reasoning was that advertising could help to ensure the stability of Tenderflake volume while improving the gross margin in order to cover advertising and profit. Further decisions would be to define target audiences, brand positioning, and copy strategy for Tenderflake. Mr. Burton thought that the fats and oils study suggested a number of opportunities. In Mr. Burton's judgment an advertising budget of $350,000 probably would receive management approval provided it was well conceived and promised a financial payout.

The sales manager had pointed out that the chain store buyers saw the main competition as other lards and that raising the price of Tenderflake would permit cheaper lards to erode Tenderflake's market share. He strongly advised that Tenderflake maintain its price position with other lards rather than "chasing after Crisco."

EXHIBIT 7 Crisco TV Advertisement

Product:	Crisco
Length:	30 seconds
Monitored:	Toronto
	December 1978

Frame 1:	Scene:	*Young man and woman in kitchen*
	Woman 1:	John, you never have seconds of my pie.
	Man:	Marie, this pie crust is so flaky.
Frame 2:	Scene:	*Close-up of Crisco can on table.*
	Woman 1:	OK, Marie, how'd you make your pie crust?
	Woman 2:	With Crisco.
	Woman 1:	But isn't it lard cheaper?
Frame 3:	Scene:	*Close-up of ingredients being blended in a bowl. Crisco can in background.*
	Woman 2:	Maybe . . . but Crisco's worth the difference. It's softer than lard, so blending's easier.
Frame 4:	Scene:	*Close-up of ingredients being blended in a bowl. Crisco can in background.*
	Woman 2:	Even the bottom crust has such delicate flakes they blow away.
Frame 5:	Scene:	*Two women talking in the kitchen*
	Woman 2:	And Crisco's one hundred percent pure vegetable
	Man:	Mmmm . . . really flaky
Frame 6:	Scene:	*Woman 1 and man in another kitchen*
	Woman 1:	Seconds, John?
	Man:	Mmmm.
	Announcer:	Use all-vegetable Crisco instead of lard. You'll think it's worth the difference.

The most difficult task would be to estimate the probable results of whatever marketing strategy Mr. Burton chose. However, senior marketing managers at Canada Packers would expect the annual marketing plan for Tenderflake to show sales and profit projections for the next five years.

READING . . . .

HIGH-PERFORMANCE MARKETING: AN INTERVIEW WITH NIKE'S PHIL KNIGHT. . . . .

Geraldine E. Willigan

Nike is a champion brand builder. Its advertising slogans—"Bo Knows," "Just Do It," "There Is No Finish Line"—have moved beyond advertising into popular expression. Its athletic footwear and clothing have become a piece of Americana. Its brand name is as well-known around the world as IBM and Coke.

So it may come as a surprise that Nike, the consummate marketer, came to understand the importance of marketing late in its life: after it hit the $1 billion revenue mark. After more than a decade of meteoric growth, Nike misjudged the aerobics market, outgrew its own capacity to manage, and made a disastrous move into casual shoes. All of those problems forced the company into a period of intense self-examination. Ultimately, says founder, chairman, and CEO Phil Knight, the company realized that the way forward was to expand its focus from the design and manufacture of the product, where Nike had always excelled, to the consumer and the brand.

Nike's roots go back to a company called Blue Ribbon Sports, which Knight, a former runner at the University of Oregon, and Bill Bowerman, Knight's former track coach, created in 1962. Blue Ribbon Sports started out distributing running shoes for a Japanese company, then shifted to designing its own shoes and outsourcing them from Asia. Blue Ribbon Sports's performance-oriented product innovations and mastery of low-cost production translated into shoes athletes wanted to wear and could afford. Knight and Bowerman's track connections got the shoes onto the feet of real runners. And then jogging emerged as a new national pastime.

By 1978, the year Blue Ribbon Sports changed its corporate name to Nike, Jon Anderson had won the Boston Marathon wearing Nike shoes, Jimmy Conners had won Wimbledon and the U.S. Open wearing Nike shoes, Henry Rono had set four track and field records in Nikes, and members of the Boston Celtics and Los Angeles Lakers basketball teams were wearing them. Sales and profits were doubling every year.

Then in the mid-1980s, Nike lost its footing, and the company was forced to make a subtle but important shift. Instead of putting the product on center stage, it put the consumer in the spotlight and the brand under a microscope—in short, it learned to be marketing oriented. Since then, Nike has resumed its domination of the athletic shoe industry. It commands 29% of the market, and sales for fiscal 1991 topped $3 billion.

Here Phil Knight explains how Nike discovered the importance of marketing and what difference that discovery has made. This interview was conducted at Nike, Inc.'s Beaverton, Oregon offices by HBR associate editor Geraldine E. Willigan.

HBR: *Nike transformed the athletic shoe industry with technological innovations, but today many people know the company by its flashy ads and sports celebrities. Is Nike a technology company or a marketing company?*

Phil Knight: I'd answer that question very differently today than I would have ten years ago. For years, we thought of ourselves as a production-oriented company, meaning we put all our emphasis on designing and manufacturing the product. But now we understand that the most important thing we do is market the product. We've come around to saying that Nike is a marketing-oriented company, and the product is our most important marketing tool. What I mean is that marketing knits the whole organization together. The design elements and functional characteristics of the product itself are just part of the overall marketing process.

We used to think that everything started in the lab. Now we realize that everything spins off the consumer. And while technology is still important, the consumer has to lead innovation. We have to innovate for a specific reason, and that reason comes from the market. Otherwise, we'll end up making museum pieces.

What made you think the product was everything?

Our success. In the early days, anybody with a glue pot and a pair of scissors could get into the shoe business, so the way to stay ahead was through product innovation. We happened to be great at it. Bill Bowerman, my former track coach at the University of Oregon and cofounder of the company that became Nike, had always customized off-the-shelf shoes for his runners. Over the years, he and some other employees came up with lots of great ideas that we incorporated. One of Bowerman's more legendary innovations is the Waffle outsole, which he discovered by pouring rubber into a waffle iron. The Waffle Trainer later became the best-selling training shoe in the United States.

We were also good at keeping our manufacturing costs down. The big, established players like Puma and adidas were still manufacturing in high-wage European countries. But we knew that wages were lower in Asia, and we knew how to get around in that environment, so we funneled all our most promising managers there to supervise production.

Didn't you do any marketing?

Not formally. We just tried to get our shoes on the feet of runners. And we were able to get a lot of great ones under contract—people like Steve Prefontaine and Alberto Salazar—because we spent a lot of time at track events and had relationships with runners, but mostly because we were doing interesting things with our shoes. Naturally, we thought the world stopped and started in the lab and everything revolved around the product.

When did your thinking change?

When the formulas that got Nike up to $1 billion in sales—being good at innovation and production and being able to sign great athletes—stopped working and we faced a series of problems. For one thing, Reebok came out of nowhere to dominate the aerobics market, which we completely miscalculated. We made an aerobics shoe that was functionally superior to Reebok's, but we missed the styling. Reebok's shoe was sleek and attractive, while ours was sturdy and clunky. We also decided against using garment leather, as Reebok had done, because it wasn't durable. By the time we developed a leather that was both strong and soft, Reebok had established a brand, won a huge chunk of sales, and gained the momentum to go right by us.

We were also having management problems at that time because we really hadn't adjusted to being a big company. And on top of that, we made a disastrous move into casual shoes.

What was the problem with casual shoes?

Practically the same as what happened in aerobics, and at about the same time. We went into casual shoes in the early 1980s when we saw that the running shoe business, which was about one-third of our revenues at the time, was slowing down. We knew that a lot of people were buying our shoes and wearing them to the grocery store and for walking to and from work. Since we happened to be good at shoes, we thought we could be successful with casual shoes. But we got our brains beat out. We came out with a functional shoe we thought the world needed, but it was funny looking and the buying public didn't want it.

By the mid-1980s, the financial signals were coming through loud and clear. Nike had been profitable throughout the 1970s. Then all of a sudden in fiscal year 1985, the company was in the red for two quarters. In fiscal 1987, sales dropped by $200 million and profits headed south again. We were forced to fire 280 people that year—our second layoff ever and a very painful one because it wasn't just an adjustment and trimming of fat. We lost some very good people that year.

How did you know that marketing would solve the problems?

We reasoned it out. The problems forced us to take a hard look at what we were doing, what was going wrong, what we were good at, and where we wanted to go. When we did that, we came to see that focusing solely on the product was a great way for a brand to start, but it just wasn't enough. We had to fill in the blanks. We had to learn to do well all the things involved in getting to the consumer, starting with understanding who the consumer is and what the brand represents.

Didn't Nike understand the consumer right from the start?

In the early days, when we were just a running shoe company and almost all our employees were runners, we understood the consumer very well. There is no shoe school, so where do you recruit people for a company that develops and markets running shoes? The running track. It made sense, and it worked. We and the consumer were one and the same.

When we started making shoes for basketball, tennis, and football, we did essentially the same thing we had done in running. We got to know the players at the top of the game and did everything we could to understand what they needed, both from a technological and a design perspective. Our engineers and designers spent a lot of time talking to the athletes about what they needed both functionally and aesthetically.

It was effective—to a point. But we were missing something. Despite great products and great ad campaigns, sales just stayed flat.

Where did your understanding fall short?

We were missing an immense group. We understood our "core consumers," the athletes who were performing at the highest level of the sport. We saw them as being at the top of a pyramid, with weekend jocks in the middle of the pyramid, and everybody else who wore athletic shoes at the bottom. Even though about 60% of our product is bought by people who don't use it for the actual sport, everything we did was aimed at the top. We said, if we get the people at the top, we'll get the others because they'll know that the shoe can perform.

But that was an oversimplification. Sure, it's important to get the top of the pyramid, but you've also got to speak to the people all the way down. Just take something simple like the color of the shoe. We used to say we don't care what the color is. If a top player like Michael Jordan liked some kind of yellow or orange jobbie, that's what we made—even if nobody else really wanted yellow and orange. One of our great racing shoes, the Sock Racer, failed for exactly that reason: we made it bright bumble-bee yellow, and it turned everybody off.

What's different now?

Whether you're talking about the core consumer or the person on the street, the principle is the same: you have to come up with what the consumer wants, and you need a vehicle to understand it. To understand the rest of the pyramid, we do a lot of work at the grass-roots level. We go to amateur sports events and spent time at gyms and tennis courts talking to people.

We make sure that the product is the same functionally whether it's for Michael Jordan or Joe American Public. We don't just say Michael Jordan is going to wear it so therefore Joe American Public is going to wear it. We have people who tell us what colors are going to be *in* for 1993, for instance, and we incorporate them.

Beyond that, we do some fairly typical kinds of market research, but lots of it—spending time in stores and watching what happens across the counter, getting reports from dealers, doing focus groups, tracking responses to our ads. We just sort of factor all that information into the computer between the ears and come up with conclusions.

What did you learn from the casual shoe failure?

Understanding the consumer is just part of good marketing. You also have to understand the brand. That's really the lesson we learned from casual shoes. That whole experience forced us to define what the Nike brand really meant, and it taught us the importance of focus. Without focus, the whole brand is at risk. Just because you have the best athletes in the world and a stripe everybody recognizes doesn't mean you can take that trademark to the ends of the earth. The ends of the earth might be right off that ledge!

Ultimately, we determined that we wanted Nike to be the world's best sports and fitness company and the Nike brand to represent sports and fitness activities. Once you say that, you have focus, and you can automatically rule out certain options. You don't end up doing loafers and wingtips and sponsoring the next Rolling Stones world tour. And you don't do casual shoes under that brand.

Can you expand a brand without losing focus?

To a point. A brand is something that has a clear-cut identity among consumers, which a company creates by sending out a clear, consistent message over a period of years until it achieves a critical mass of marketing. The thing is, once you hit the critical mass, you can't push it much further. Otherwise the meaning gets fuzzy and confused, and before long, the brand is on the way out.

Look at the Nike brand. From the start, everybody understood that Nike was a running shoe company, and the brand stood for excellence in track and field. It was a very clear message, and Nike was very successful. But casual shoes sent a different message. People got confused, and Nike began to lose its magic. Retailers were unenthusiastic, athletes were looking at the alternatives, and sales slowed. So not only was the casual shoe effort a failure, but it was diluting our trademark and hurting us in running.

How, then, has Nike been able to grow so much?

By breaking things into digestible chunks and creating separate brands or sub-brands to represent them. If you have something that's working, you can try to expand it, but first you have to ask, does this expansion dilute the big effort? Have I taken the thing too far? When you come to the conclusion that you have—through conversations with athletes, your own judgment, what's happening in retail stores or focus groups—then you have to create another category.

How did you make that discovery?

Accidentally. I can't say we had a really smart strategy going forward. We had a strategy, and when it didn't work, we went back and regrouped until finally we hit on something. What we hit on in the mid-1980s was the Air Jordan basketball shoe. Its success showed us that slicing things up into digestible chunks was the wave of the future.

The Air Jordan project was the result of a concerted effort to shake things up. With sales stagnating, we knew we had to do more than produce another great Nike running shoe. So we created a whole new segment within Nike focused on basketball, and we borrowed the air-cushion technology we had used in running shoes to make an air-cushioned basketball shoe.

Basketball, unlike casual shoes, was all about performance, so it fit under the Nike umbrella. And the shoe itself was terrific. It was so colorful that the NBA banned it—which was great! We actually welcome the kind of publicity that pits us against the establishment, as long as we know we're on the right side of the issue. Michael Jordan wore the shoes despite being threatened with fines, and, of course, he played like no one has ever played before. It was everything you could ask for, and sales just took off.

Have you continued to slice up the Nike umbrella since then?

We've created lots of new categories under the Nike brand, everything from cross-training and water sports to outdoors and walking. But what's interesting is that we've sliced up some of the categories themselves.

Take basketball. Air Jordan had two great years, and then it fell on its face. So we started asking ourselves, are we trying to stretch Air Jordan too far? Is Air Jordan 70% of basketball? Or is it 25% of basketball? As we thought about it, we realized that there are different styles of playing basketball. Not every great player has the style of Michael Jordan, and if we tried to make Air Jordan appeal to everyone, it would lose its meaning. We had to slice up basketball itself.

Two new segments came out of that: Force, which is represented by David Robinson and Charles Barkley, and Flight, represented by Scottie Pippin. Force shoes are more stable and better suited to the aggressive, muscular styles of David Robinson and Charles Barkley. Flight shoes, on the other hand, are more flexible and lighter in weight, so they work better for a quick, high-flying style like Scottie Pippin's.

Whenever someone talks about Nike basketball, they think of Air Jordan. But we actually have those three distinct segments, Air Jordan, Flight, and Force, each with its own brand—or sub-brand, really. Each has great athletes representing it, a complete product line, shoes and clothes that are tied together. Instead of one big glop, we have the number one, the number two, and the number four brands of basketball shoes.

What other categories have you sliced up?

Tennis is another good example. We have a very focused category that has been built around the personalities of John McEnroe and Andre Agassi. We created the Challenge Court Collection—very young, very anti-country club, very rebellious—and we became the number one selling tennis category in the world. Nevertheless, we were ignoring 75% of the tennis players out there because most tennis players are a little more conservative than John and Andre. They didn't want those flashy outfits. That loud style isn't even suitable for John anymore. So instead of diluting what Challenge Court stood for, we created a second category within the tennis framework called Supreme Court, which is more toned down. Each of those categories stands for something distinct.

Have you exhausted the list of things that fit under the Nike umbrella?

Actually, we're now pushing the limits of the Nike brand by going into fitness. The core consumer in fitness is a little different from the core consumer in sports. Fitness activities tend to be individual pursuits—things like hiking, bicycling, weight-lifting, and wind surfing. And even within the fitness category, there are important differences. We found that men do fitness activities because they want to be stronger or live longer or get their heart rate or blood pressure down. Their objectives are rather limited. But women do it as sort of a self-actualization thing, as part of the whole package of what they're about.

I'm confident that the brand can encompass both the performance-oriented message and the fitness message over the next year and a half, but we'll have to be careful after that. Given enough time, the messages will probably diverge, and we'll be in danger of blurring Nike's identity. But it won't be the same as casual shoes because this time we'll see it coming and we'll deal with it.

Is Nike's concept of brand building confined to sports and fitness?

The lessons we've learned about brand identity and focus can take us in many directions. The key is to create separate umbrellas for things that aren't part of the Nike brand. Knowing what happened in casual shoes, you probably wouldn't think we'd have anything to do with dress shoes. But in 1988, we acquired Cole-Haan, a maker of dress shoes and accessories. Cole-Haan is part of Nike, Inc., but it's completely separate from the Nike brand.

Actually, we think of Cole-Haan as half a brand because only sophisticated consumers know what it is; it hasn't yet achieved critical mass. That's were we're applying our marketing skill. We bought the brand knowing its potential, and we've simply turned up the marketing volume. We could have created a brand and got it up to $60 million in sales, which is where Cole-Haan was when we bought it, but it would have taken millions of dollars and a minimum of five years. We're further ahead this way. In the four years we've owned Cole-Haan, it's repaid the purchase price and is now at $150 million in sales.

We've been talking about brand building. Isn't TV advertising a big part of that?

Today it's a very important part. In fact, when people talk about Nike, the TV ads are practically all they want to talk about. But we became a billion dollar company without television. For years, we just got the shoes out there on the athletes and ran a limited number of print ads in specialized magazines like *Runner's World.* We didn't complete the advertising spectrum until 1987, when we used TV for the first time.

Our first TV campaign was for Visible Air, which was a line of shoes with transparent material along the midsole so consumers could see the air-cushioning technology. Having gone through the painful experience of laying people off and cutting overhead in the mid-1980s, we wanted the message about our new line of shoes to hit with a punch, and that really dictated TV advertising.

The Visible Air launch was a critical moment for a couple of reasons. Until then, we really didn't know if we could be a big company and still have people work closely together. Visible Air was a hugely complex product whose components were made in three different countries, and nobody knew if it would come together. Production, marketing, and sales were all fighting with each other, and we were using TV advertising for the first time. There was tension all the way around.

We launched the product with the Revolution campaign, using the Beatles song. We wanted to communicate not just a radical departure in shoes but a revolution in the way Americans felt about fitness, exercise, and wellness. The ads were a tremendous hit, and Nike Air became the standard for the industry immediately thereafter.

Did TV change the character or image your company projected?

Not really, because our basic beliefs about advertising didn't change. We've always believed that to succeed with the consumer, you have to wake him up. He's not going to walk in and buy the same stuff he always has or listen to the same thing he's always heard. There are 50 different competitors in the athletic shoe business. If you do the same thing you've done before or that somebody else is doing, you won't last more than one or two seasons.

And from the beginning, we've tried to create an emotional tie with the consumer. Why do people get married—or do anything? Because of emotional ties. That's what builds long-term relationships with the consumer, and that's what our campaigns are about. That approach distinguishes us from a lot of other companies, including Reebok. Their campaigns aren't always bad—their Air-Out Jordan campaign last year worked well—but it's very transaction oriented. Our advertising tries to link consumers to the Nike brand through the emotions of sports and fitness. We show competition, determination, achievement, fun, and even the spiritual rewards of participating in those activities.

How do you wake up the consumer?

By doing new things. Innovation is part of our heritage, but it also happens to be good marketing. You can probably trace it back to the 1960s, when we were selling $100,000 a year instead of $1 billion. We saw the company as having a great competitive advantage because he had a great product at a great price. And it worked a little bit. But what really made things pop was when we innovated with the product. That's when we said, "aha!"

We'd have a hard time stopping innovation in the product area, but we've consciously tried to be innovative in all areas of the business, and right now that means advertising. We need a way of making sure people hear our message through all the clutter. In 24 words or less, that means innovative advertising—but innovative in a way that captures the athletes' true nature. Bo Jackson and Michael Jordan stand for different things. Characterizing them accurately and tying them to products the athletes really use can be very powerful.

Of course, trying to wake people up can be risky, especially since we generally don't pre-test our ads. We test the concepts beforehand, but we believe that the only way to know if an ad works is to run it and gauge the response. So we get nervous when we're ready to go to press, and then we wait and see if the phone rings. If the phone rings, that's usually good. Although some of the calls will be negative, complaints tend to be in the great minority. Besides, we're always prepared for some criticism because somebody will be offended no matter what we do. We don't let that hold us back. Our basic philosophy is the same throughout the business: take a chance and learn from it.

Nike's advertising has been so successful that it's hard to think of it as being risky. What are some of the risks?

The Hare Jordan, Air Jordan commercial that aired during the 1992 Super Bowl represented a big risk from both a financial and a marketing standpoint. It showed Michael Jordan teaming up on the basketball court with Bugs Bunny. We invested in six months' worth of drawings and a million dollars in production costs to show Michael Jordan, probably the most visible representative of Nike, paired with a cartoon character. It could have been too silly or just plain dumb. But we got thousands of positive responses, and *USA Today* ranked it the best Super Bowl ad. The only criticism we got was from the National Stutterers Association for using Porky Pig at the end.

Humor is always a risky business. Take our advertising to women. We produced some ads in 1987 that we thought were very funny but many women found insulting. They were too hard edged. We got so many complaints that we spent three or four years trying to understand what motivates women to participate in sports and fitness. We did numerous focus groups and spent hundreds of hours on tennis courts, in gyms, and at aerobics studios listening to women.

Those efforts paid off in our recent Dialogue campaign, which is a print campaign that is very personal. The text and images try to empathize and inspire. One ad explores a woman's relationship with her mother; another touches on the emotions of a girl in physical education class. Even there it was risky to use such an intimate voice in the ads, but it worked. The newest ads broke in February, and within eight weeks we had received more than 50,000 calls on our "800" number praising the ads and asking for reprints.

But things don't always come together. The campaign to launch the Air 180 running shoe comes to mind. The advertising agency was working with seven directors from around the world and trying to translate words into all those different languages. In the end, we used no words, just images of various kinds. One ad showed a spaceship zooming in on a Waffle Trainer outsole. Another showed cartoon characters bouncing on the shoe to demonstrate the cushioning. When we looked at the ad a month before its Super Bowl launch, it seemed fragmented and almost goofy. Some people thought we could fine-tune it, but others, including me, didn't want to use it at all. It was neither animal nor vegetable. So we ran a Nike general purpose ad, which was safe but somewhat boring. If the competition had had terrific ads, we'd have been hurt quite a bit. We used the Air 180 ads later that spring, but they didn't have the impact we were after.

How do Nike's TV ads create emotional ties with the buying public?

You have to be creative, but what really matters in the long run is that the message means something. That's why you have to start with a good product. You can't create an emotional tie to a bad product because it's not honest. It doesn't have any meaning, and people will find that out eventually. You have to convey what the company is really all about, what it is that Nike is really trying to do.

That's something Wieden & Kennedy, our advertising agency, is very good at. Lots of people say Nike is successful because our ad agency is do good, but isn't it funny that the agency had been around for 20 years and nobody had ever heard of it? It's not just that they're creative. What makes Wieden & Kennedy successful with Nike is that they take the time to grind it out. They spent countless hours trying to figure out what the product is, what the message is, what the theme is, what the athletes are all about, what emotion is involved. They try to extract something that's meaningful, an honest message that is true to who we are. And we're very open to that way of working, so the chemistry is good.

People at Nike believe in the power of emotion because we feel it ourselves. A while ago there was a book published about Nike, and one person who reviewed it said he was amazed that a group of intelligent, talented people could exert so much passion, imagination, and sweat over pieces of plastic and rubber. To me, its amazing that anyone would think it's amazing. I can't say I would be that passionate about cigarettes and beer, but that's why I'm not doing cigarettes and beer.

What's the advantage of using famous athletes in your advertising?

It saves us a lot of time. Sports is at the heart of American culture, so a lot of emotion already exists around it. Emotions are always hard to explain, but there's something inspirational about watching athletes push the limits of performance. You can't explain much in 60 seconds, but when you show Michael Jordan, you don't have to. People already know a lot about him. It's that simple.

The trick is to get athletes who not only can win but can stir up emotion. We want someone the public is going to love or hate, not just the leading scorer. Jack Nicklaus was a better golfer than Arnold Palmer, but Palmer was the better endorsement because of his personality.

To create a lasting emotional tie with consumers, we use the athletes repeatedly throughout their careers and present them as whole people. So consumers feel that they know them. It's not just Charles Barkley saying buy Nike shoes, it's seeing who Charles Barkley is—and knowing that he's going to punch you in the nose. We take the time to understand our athletes, and we have to build long-term relationships with them. Those relationships go beyond any financial transactions. John McEnroe and Joan Benoit wear our shoes everyday, but it's not the contract. We like them and they like us. We win their hearts as well as their feet.

Admittedly, it's a little harder to get the public to identify with athletes in the area of fitness. When you're selling football shoes, you know what your emotion is and who your guys are. When you're selling shoes for hiking and aerobics, it's a different deal. There are no Super Bowl winners, so there are no obvious personalities to represent the activity, which leads to an entirely different type of advertising. We still convey emotion, but we do it on a much more personal level.

What if a Nike athlete does something illegal or socially unacceptable?

There's always a chance that somebody will get into drugs or do something like Mike Tyson did. But if you do your scouting well, you can avoid a lot of those situations. Three or four years ago we were recruiting two very exciting college basketball players, but before we signed them we checked with our network of college coaches. We learned that one of them had a cocaine problem and the other could only play good offensive ball with his back to the basket. Needless to say, we didn't sign either of them, and both of them were a bust in the NBA.

Is social responsibility part of being a marketing-oriented company?

I've always believed that businesses should be good citizens, which has nothing to do with marketing. But the thing I was missing until recently is the issue of visibility—and that is tied to marketing. It's not enough to do good things. You have to let people know what you're doing. And that means having good relations with the press. When it comes to the product, America gets its opinions from advertising. When it comes to Nike as a whole, America gets its opinions from the press.

Our industry, and Nike in particular, gets a lot more press than many others because it's more fun to talk about us than about a company that makes widgets. On the one hand, we don't mind the attention; we like getting our name in the press. But on the other hand, the company usually gets treated in a superficial, lighthearted way, which is not what we're all about. Nike is not about going to a ball game. It's a business. People don't always realize that we take things seriously. So we're learning to explain ourselves better.

We can't make rules that keep drug dealers from wearing our stuff, and we can't solve the problems of the inner city, but we sponsor a lot of sports clinics for youths. And we're underwriting a series called *Ghostwriting* that the Children's Television Workshop is developing to teach kids how to read and write. We're doing it because we think it's the right thing to do, but we also want the visibility.

Is the shift to being marketing oriented an industrywide trend?

We can see now that the entire industry has gone through a major shift. But I'm happy to say that we pretty much led the charge by being first to understand the importance of the brand and the consumer. If we hadn't made that discovery, someone else would have, and we might have been out of business.

SIDEBARS . . . .

INSPIRED DESIGN: HOW NIKE PUTS EMOTION IN ITS SHOES . . . .

Tinker Hatfield

Five years ago, I left my job as Nike's corporate architect to design Nike athletic shoes. The switch was easier than you might think. I learned long ago that a building is not purely functional; it means something to people and evokes an emotional response. It's the same with Nike shoes. A Huarache running shoe or an Air Jordan basketball shoe is not just a combination of price and performance. It has feelings and images associated with it that make people like it better than something else, even when they can't explain why. That gray area, the stuff that no one can really articulate, has to do with the shoe's design.

Inspiration for a design can come from anywhere—from a cartoon, a poster, the environment. But the design process almost always involves the athletes who use our product. Sometimes an athlete tells me what he or she wants in a shoe, but often it's a matter of incorporating the athlete's personality.

Take Bo Jackson. When I was designing the first cross-training shoe for Bo, I watched him play sports, I read about him, I absorbed everything I could about him. Bo reminded me of a cartoon character. Not a goofy one, but a powerful one. His muscles are big, his face is big—he's larger than life. To me, he was like Mighty Mouse. So we designed a shoe called the Air Trainer that embodied characteristics of Bo Jackson and Mighty Mouse. Whenever you see Mighty Mouse, he's moving forward. He's got a slant to him. So the shoe needed to look like it was in motion, it had to be kind of inflated looking and brightly colored, and its features had to be exaggerated. That's how we came up with the larger-than-life, brightly colored Stability Outrigger and the similarly colored, inflated-looking rubber tongue top.

Working with Michael Jordan is a little different. He has his own ideas about how he wants the shoe to look and perform. When we were designing the Air Jordan 7, for instance, he said he wanted a little more support across the forefoot, and he wanted more color. The Air Jordans had been getting more conservative over the years, so what I think he was telling me—without really telling me—is that he wanted to feel a little more youthful and aggressive. Michael has become more mature and contemplative in recent years, but he still plays very exciting basketball, so the shoe had to incorporate those traits as well.

It all came together for me in a poster I had seen advertising an Afro Pop music series on National Public Radio. The imagery in the poster was very exciting and strong and slightly ethnic. I showed Michael the poster, and he thought it elicited the right emotion, so I drew from that. We came up with a shoe that used very rich, sophisticated colors but in a jazzy way.

Sometimes I don't have an athlete to work with. When I was designing our first outdoor cross-training shoe, which was a category we were creating, I didn't have any particular players I could study. So I kept thinking about the outdoors, and that led to Native Americans, who did everything outdoors—from their tribal rituals to their daily chores. What did they wear? Moccasins, which are typically comfortable and pliable. And that led to the idea of a high-tech, high-performance moccasin.

I found a neat old print by Robert Wesley Amick depicting Native Americans in the natural environment, and I painted some high-tech Nike's on their feet so I could visually describe the original inspiration in a humorous but informative scenario. We've built a whole line of shoes around that image. The soles are flexible so you can pad down the trail, the leather is thin and lightweight, the outsole has a low profile, and the colors are earthy.

Stories about how we arrived at particular designs may be entertaining, but the storytelling also helps us explain the shoes to retailers, sales reps, consumers, and other people in the company. You'd be surprised how much information Mighty Mouse, Afro Pop, and a Native American in a Western landscape can convey.

Tinker Hatfield is Nike's director.

TALENT, CHARACTER, AND STYLE: THE NIKE ATHLETE . . . .

Ian Hamilton

To recruit young tennis players and sign them to endorsement contracts to wear and promote Nike tennis shoes and apparel, I scout the junior tennis circuit for athletes with a combination of talent, character, and style. Talent is the most important ingredient for a Nike athlete. To promote our shoes, a player has to have a chance at being one of the best in the game. We're recognized as being the best at what we do and we want to reinforce that message to the consumer by having the world's top athletes wearing Nike.

Character is also important. By getting to know athletes in their early teens, I can tell if they are the type of people who would work well with Nike over the long term. Are they committed to the sport? Do they have a sense of humor? Do they have an attitude that the public will embrace? I meet the parents, coaches, and agents, and we decide if a relationship with Nike is in everyone's best interest. It's important that they want to be part of the Nike family as much as we went them to be.

There are plenty of players who meet the first two requirements, but only Nike athletes meet the third: a distinctive sense of style. People expect Nike to perform to a high standard and to make a statement at the same time. Our athletes do the same thing.

When I started at Nike tennis, John McEnroe was the most visible player in the world, and he was already part of the Nike family. He epitomized the type of player Nike wanted in its shoes—talented, dedicated, and loud. He broke racquets, drew fines, and, most of all, won matches. His success and behavior drew attention on and off the court and put a lot of people in Nikes.

By the end of the 1980s, McEnroe was ready to hand over the angry young man mantle to become more of a tennis elder statesman. And he wanted his Nike image to reflect his new attitude. This coincided perfectly with the emergence of Andre Agassi. When I first saw Andre he was a 15-year-old junior tennis star at Nick Bollettieri's Tennis Academy in Bradenton, Florida. Even then, image was everything to Andre. He had long hair on one side of his head and no hair on the other. His approach to the game was as it is now—"hit the ball as loud as you can." And he was the best player around. From a marketing standpoint, Andre was the perfect vehicle for Nike. Like us, he was anti-tennis establishment and he was different.

To satisfy McEnroe's need for an image change—and to appeal to the huge market of older tennis players who don't want to look like Andre—we segmented the Nike tennis products. Andre became the vehicle for Challenge Court, the "rock and roll tennis" part of the line, while McEnroe and David Wheaton launched Supreme Court, the more subdued part of the line. For as bold and irreverent as Challenge Court is, Supreme Court is tuxedo tennis. It's changed my job from finding players who represent Nike tennis to finding players who represent specific roles within Nike tennis.

We use the players not only to market and design our products but also to set a positive example for the sport. Andre Agassi, for example, has been integral in attracting a lot of young players to the game—and a lot of young players to Nike. Like Michael Jordan in basketball, Andre transcends the sport of tennis. He's got 7,000 members in his fan club—and not all of them are 14-year-old girls.

John McEnroe helped create a program for junior players called the Tournament Tough Player Parent Workshops. Unfortunately, agents and parents pressure today's younger players to turn pro early and make a lot of money. They put them in too many tournaments and, for most kids, burn them out quickly. That gives tennis a bad image and sends the wrong message to kids who might want to take up the game. McEnroe talks with groups of players and their parents and tells them what pro tennis has been like for him and what they should expect. The message is to keep tennis fun and in perspective. Now we're working to get those workshops on television to reach even more people.

Ian Hamilton is Nike's director of tennis sports marketing.

A SENSE OF COOL: NIKE'S THEORY OF ADVERTISING . . . .

Dan Wieden

The people at Nike taught my partner, David Kennedy, and me how to advertise—and how not to advertise. Back in 1980, when David and I first started to work on the account, Nike made it very clear that they hated advertising. They had developed close relationships with athletes, and they didn't want to talk to them in any phony or manipulative way. They were obsessed with authenticity, in terms of both the product and the communication. And they had a sense of what was cool.

Those attitudes have guided all of Nike's advertising. We try to make honest contact with the consumer, to share something that is very hip and very inside. We don't translate the inside jokes because we figure it's OK if the people who are faddish don't understand. Either you get it or you don't. It's more important for us to be true to the athletes by talking to them in a way that respects their intelligence, time, and knowledge of sports.

This approach to advertising seems to be in synch with the times, and I think that's why people respond to Nike ads. Products and services today have to have value and live up to their promise, but a spec sheet approach to marketing won't sell anything. As the world gets more de-humanizing, people want the trust and familiarity of a long-standing relationship. Building that relationship requires a brand with a personality and advertising.

Personality is the difference between the surrogate monkey parent and the real thing: the surrogate might have the nutriment, but everything else is missing, and the relationship never forms. In the business world, brand-building creates the personality that allows people to bond. The Nike brand, for instance, is very complex. Sometimes it's humorous, other times it's very serious—but it's always as if it were coming from the same person.

Advertising creates the environment for the relationship. To me, it takes the place of the human contact we once had as consumers. In the beginning, people had relationships with the shopkeeper, and any advertising simply supplemented that relationship. Today things are so complex that advertising needs to embody that relationship by making contact in more than a superficial way.

The process of creating brands and relationships is also the process by which you create the values our culture operates on, so it has a huge ethical component. The ethical dimension makes our work seem like much more than the movement of goods and services. And it can be scary. I remember sitting here one night with campaigns spread out all over the place getting ready to present to Nike the next morning. I felt we needed to tie things together, so I said, "OK, I'll just do it." That became "Just Do It," a slogan that spread all over the world. I realized then what a big, big stage this is and how important it is to be responsible for what goes on here.

I don't mean to suggest that this is a noncontroversial agency. I don't feel it's our job to produce stuff that doesn't upset people. Being provocative is ultimately more important than be-ing pleasant. But you have to know what you're doing when you walk into the room with broad swords.

Our awareness of the ethical issues is also a factor in the positive response to Nike ads. The general public can sense when something is destructive or at least not very positive. In fact, I think a lot of big ad firms are struggling right now precisely because they've ignored the ethi-cal component of advertising. They've relied on manipulation and cunning, which were effec-tive in the 1980s when greed and self-interest prevailed, and they haven't moved beyond that.

I admit that Nike's product category has made it easier for us to be honest and open. Al-though at one level, all we're really doing is selling sneakers, there's something about athletic shoes and clothes that can inspire enthusiasm or even altruism. There's an honest-to-goodness belief that we're selling something that will help people. It's like an ancient call to a way of life that isn't going to harm the environment or mess you up. It keeps us charged up about what we're doing.

Dan Wieden is creative director at the advertising firm Wieden & Kennedy.

PART IV

MESSAGE

TACTICS

12 CREATIVE APPROACHES

> We despise no source that can pay us a pleasing attention.
> (Mark Twain)
>
> Good advertising is a dialogue with people that lets them bring something to the communication process.
> (Lee Clow, creative director, Chiat/Day)

Suppose you are advertising mutual funds to individual investors. Is it better to use the likable Peanuts characters to talk about your funds (which is what MetLife did for its funds), or quote comparative performance statistics from a fund-rating service like Morningstar (which is what AIM Value Funds did)?

Suppose you want to compare yourself with a competitive brand in your advertising. Is it better to name and show your competitor (as Alfa Romeo did in comparing itself to the BMW), or merely to show (but not name) the comparison brand (which is what BMW did in comparing itself to the Lexus)? In fact, should a leader like BMW compare itself to the newer Lexus at all?

After an advertiser decides on the content of an ad—the "what to say" decision, the task of creating the ad itself is usually handed off to the creative people at the ad agency. Before these writers and art directors proceed to conceptualizing and creating the ad, however, it is usually a good idea to give some thought to the broad framework within which the ad should be created: What kind of appeal should the ad utilize? For instance, should the ad attempt a competitive comparison (a "rational") approach? Or, should it use some type of emotional appeal, such as fear, or humor? Should it use an endorser, and if so, what kind of endorser—an expert in that product category, or a likable celebrity?

While decisions of this sort are not always part of the advertising planning process at either the client or the agency (because of a desire not to limit the flexibility of the creatives, or because of ignorance), the ad creation process could undoubtedly benefit from the accumulated knowledge on when each of these creative approaches is most appropriate, and how each can be implemented most effectively. This chapter will thus present some material on various creative approaches (such as the use of endorsers, or of comparisons), focusing both on *when* each approach is most appropriate, as well as *how* it is best implemented. We will discuss, in turn, the use of comparative and refutational advertising, of emotional advertising (such as advertising that employs fear or humor), and of endorsers.

RATIONAL CREATIVE APPROACHES . . . .

Comparative Advertising

Comparative advertising is a form of advertising in which two or more named or recognizable brands of the same product class are compared and the comparison is made in terms of one or more product attributes.[1] The comparisons can be *implicit* (brands implied but not named), or *explicit* (brands named); the comparisons can be verbal or visual; and the claims can be of complete superiority, of superiority on some attributes but not on others, or of parity; and the advertised brand can have a market share smaller than, roughly equal to, or greater than the comparison brand. Obviously, not all types of comparative ads are equally effective, and we will discuss below what is currently known about which types work best.

Different studies conducted in recent years have found that comparative ads often form about 20 to 30 percent of all the ads being run.[2] It is interesting to note, however, that prior to about 1970, comparative advertising that named the comparison brand was illegal in the U.S. and could not be used. Such ads are now perfectly legal in the U.S., however, and are used quite widely, especially where objective comparisons can be made between brands (e.g, the Ford Taurus advertising that it has more features for the money than competing brands, as in Figure 12–1). Regulations and norms about comparative advertising vary around the world, however, and such ads are still not allowed in several countries. In the U.S., a 1988 provision of the Trademark Revision Act has clarified what can and cannot be said in comparative ads—survey or other research used to back up a comparative claim has to be used very fairly and carefully; claims cannot be misleading or deceptive.[3]

Effectiveness of Comparative Ads

Is a comparative advertisement more effective than a noncomparative one? Much research has focused on this question, and the evidence on greater effectiveness is often equivocal.[4] The results seem to vary not only upon the specific kind of comparative ad used and the brands involved, but also on the measure of effectiveness used (attention/recall, perceived similarity, or persuasion) and even the specific questionnaire scales used to measure effectiveness.

For instance, as is discussed in the copy-testing chapter of this book (Chapter 14), the effectiveness of comparative ads sometimes lies not in raising the preference ratings of the advertised brand, but in lowering the preference ratings of the comparison brands, or even in simply increasing the perceived similarity of the advertised and comparison brands without affecting any preference measures at all.[5] It is thus important, in copy testing or tracking the effectiveness of compar-

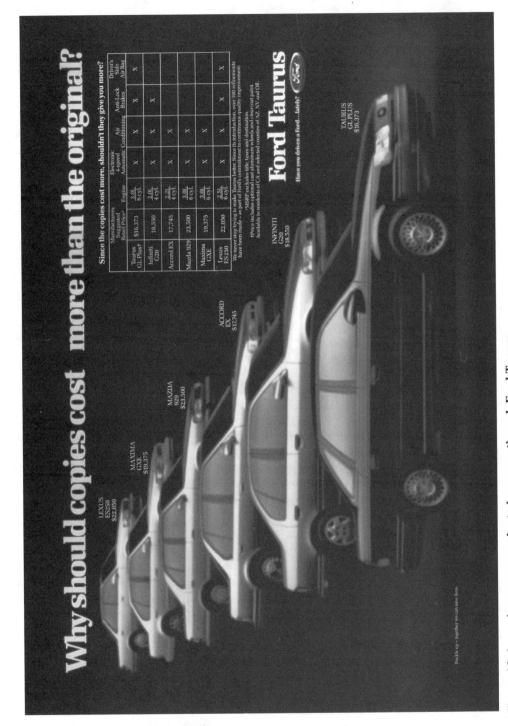

Figure 12-1.   A consumer-oriented comparative ad: Ford Taurus.
Courtesy of Ford Motor Company.

ative ads, to measure beliefs and preferences not only toward the advertised brand but also toward competition, as well as measure perceived similarities among these brands.

If attention and recall are used as the measures of ad effectiveness, various studies have shown that comparative ads do usually get more attention and higher recall than non-comparative ads. Pontiac used comparative advertising for its Grand Am in 1992, comparing it to the Toyota Camry and Honda Accord, because they found focus groups reacted more strongly to comparisons with specific competitors than to unnamed imports.[6] Naveen Donthu found the gain in recall was highest if the comparisons being made were more "intense" (naming explicit competitors, making comparisons on specific attributes, and only making a one-sided claim).[7]

Cornelia Pechmann and David Stewart found that the effects of comparative ads on other measures of effectiveness, such as persuasion, were at least partly due to this increased attention-grabbing ability,[8] and other researchers have noted that because of this interest-evoking ability comparative ads often succeed in increasing the extent to which consumers process the information contained in the ad (see Chapter 5's discussion of how comparative ads promote "central" processing of an ad).

Misidentification

Consumer advocates and the Federal Trade Commission, which legalized comparative advertising in the U.S. in 1971, have argued that the increased (and more "distinctive") information in comparative ads should be beneficial to consumers and increase the chances for better decision making. Many researchers have, however, found that comparative advertising that names competitors can lead to greater consumer confusion about which brand is sponsoring the ad (thus creating awareness and preference for the compared-to brand), especially if the ad is being run on TV or radio, where more confusion is likely.

Indeed, the frequent occurrence of such "sponsor misidentification" is one of the major criticisms against "direct" comparative advertising (where the comparison brand is explicitly named). It is one reason why many companies prefer to run *indirect comparative ads*, in which they do not name comparison brands directly but imply them by showing packaging colors or shapes (such as Folgers coffee not naming Maxwell House but showing the other brand packaged in the latter's blue can).

Leaders versus Followers

Interestingly, research supports the logic that a direct comparative ad from a small-share market follower is least likely to lead to higher awareness for the compared-to market leader (because the market leader already has high awareness), whereas a market-leading high-share brand has the most to lose from a direct comparative ad (by creating "free" awareness for the compared-to smaller brand).[9] This leads to the conclusion that while low-share brands ought to use direct comparative ads, market leaders perhaps ought to use noncomparative or indirectly comparative ads (those that don't name competitors). This suggests that while VISA credit cards might gain by comparing itself to American Express (which has more prestige), American Express might not gain by comparing itself in its ads with VISA. (Both companies ran such comparative ads, comparing themselves with each other, in 1993 and 1994.)[10]

Smaller-share market follower brands also stand to gain more from direct comparative ads in another way: such ads have the effect of getting consumers to put both the advertised and the comparison brand in the same "consideration set," by increasing the degree to which they are perceived as similar to each other. Gerald Gorn and Charles Weinberg[11] point out that a leading brand might therefore not want to engage in comparative advertising, whereas a challenger brand might gain from associating itself with the leader. Their study found that comparative advertising was much more effective than noncomparative advertising in increasing the perceived similarity of the challenger and leader brands, particularly when the leading brand was explicitly named in the ad. Research by Michael Johnson and David Horne also shows that comparative ads promote the consumer perception that the brands being compared are similar to each other.[12]

These studies thus lend support to the idea that comparative advertising by new brands or challenger brands makes sense as an excellent positioning tool. For example, the Subaru ad in Chapter 6, in which Subaru claims a safety record as good as Volvo's, will clearly help to position Subaru as a "safety car" in the same league as Volvo. By the same token, market leaders might be better off not comparing themselves to market followers, for fear of giving them legitimacy. As one senior marketing executive puts it, "Comparative ads are good when you're new, but when you're the standard, it just gives a lot of free publicity to your competitors."[13]

This similarity-increasing effect, however, seems to depend on the nature of the attributes used: one study suggests that direct comparative ads increase the similarity of the advertised and compared-to brand on attributes not featured in the ad. However, they simultaneously differentiate the brands by lowering consumer perceptions of the compared-to brand on the specific attribute used in the comparison.[14]

Effects on Persuasion

Thus far, we have talked about how a comparative ad might help the advertised brand by gaining it "extra" attention and by bringing it perceptually "closer" to the comparison brand. Do these gains necessarily also translate into increased preference for the advertised brand? Not always. Gorn and Weinberg, whose study was cited earlier, found that while while a comparative did bridge the perceived "distance" between the "leader" and the "challenger" brand, it did not significantly raise the attitude toward the advertised brand. Many other studies have also failed to find such attitude-enhancing effects.

These failures could be due, in part, to the fact that these studies often failed to measure (and could not therefore find) possible decreases in consumers' attitudes toward the *comparison* brand. It has also been shown, however, that comparative ads often fail to sway attitudes and preferences because, while people may indeed notice them more, they nonetheless may consider a comparative ad offen-

MCI Math, Part II.

40% = 13%

40% = The discount on calls to MCI customers in your Friends & Family II calling circle.

13% = The average discount that shows up on your MCI Friends & Family II Basic bill.

Friends & Family II. Big claims. Big disappointments.

Friends & Family II advertises 40% off on calls to other MCI customers in your calling circle. But on calls to non-MCI customers in your circle, the savings is only 20%. And on calls to numbers outside your calling circle—that's any number you don't give them in advance—**the savings**

is a nice round 0%. Then there's the small matter of the $36 a year in monthly fees. In the end, the total Friends & Family II discount is a far cry from the 40% you might expect. It's more like 13%.* No wonder 4 out of 5 Friends & Family II Basic customers will save more with...

* Discount off MCI basic rates. AT&T's and MCI's basic rates are about the same.

Figure 12–2.   AT&Ts ad comparing itself to MCI.
Reprinted by permission of AT&T.

sive, less credible, and less informative (especially if they happen to like the brand being shown in a negative light). In fact, there is some evidence that consumers' liking for comparative ads goes up with the "intensity" of the comparative ad, but only up to a point—ads that are "too intense" appear to be disliked.[15] Thus, while AT&T's ad comparing itself to MCI (Figure 12–2) might rate high in persuasion because of its use of specific, persuasive statistics, MCI's response (which was more vitriolic) might to many appear too intense and therefore less persuasive.[16]

AT&T True Math.

20% = 20%

20% = The discount you get on calls to everyone.

20% = The discount you see on your AT&T bill with AT&T True USA℠ Savings.

AT&T True USA℠ Savings. We say 20%. You save 20%.

AT&T *True USA*℠ Savings. Just spend $25 a month on long distance, and we'll subtract 20% off your AT&T bill.** That's 20% off on calls to anyone, anytime, anywhere in the USA. Guaranteed. To sign up, just call *1 800-TRUE-USA.*℠

AT&T. Your True Voice.℠

AT&T

** Discount off AT&T basic residential rates. Available in most areas. Certain exclusions apply.

Figure 12–2.   (continued)

Many studies have shown that comparative ads often evoke such an unfavorable attitudinal reaction because they stimulate more counterarguing by consumers,[17] often because they are perceived as less truthful. Obviously, therefore, comparative ads ought to be designed in ways that try to reduce such counterarguing. Message content that tries to stay as factual and "objective" as possible (as in Figure 12–2 above) can reduce such counterargumentation.[18] It helps to include a credible source, and to get the target audience involved in the ad, so they are motivated to actually make the invited comparison, rather than dismissing it out of hand.[19] It also helps to make the comparison in as "positive" a manner as possible: rather than derogate the comparison brand, it is better to claim superiority over the comparison brand in a nonderogatory manner.[20]

Two-Sided versus One-Sided Comparative Ads

William Swinyard,[21] Michael Etgar and Stephen Goodwin,[22] and others have also argued that there is more counterarguing if the message is one-sided instead of two-sided. (A message is *one-sided* if it presents only positive arguments or attributes and *two-sided* if a few qualifications, usually about relatively minor attributes, are presented.) Two-sided ads are seen as more credible, because they admit that the advertised brands have some shortcomings.

However, not all two-sided ads beat one-sided ads in credibility: research has shown that two-sided ads are especially credible when the attribute on which the weakness is admitted is (a) relatively unimportant, but not trivial, to consumers; (b) perceived to be negatively correlated with the attribute on which superiority is claimed (e.g., "we are more expensive (weakness), but only because we give you higher quality"); (c) one that would not otherwise be known to consumers prior to purchase, so that the advertiser gains some "brownie points" for honesty.[23]

Other research has also shown the general superiority of two-sided appeals, especially with more educated audiences, and with those consumers initially opposed to the brand making the claims, and on attitudes rather than purchase intentions. These results suggest that comparative ads are more likely to be persuasive in changing brand attitudes if they are two-sided rather than one-sided.

Open-Ended versus Close-Ended Comparisons

Another relevant issue is whether conclusions and arguments should be spelled out explicitly in a comparative advertisement or whether the receiver should be left to draw his or her own conclusions about the superiority of the brand sponsoring the comparison. It is often advantageous to leave something out of a message: the closure principle discussed in Chapter 7 comes in here. Leaving something out can stimulate curiosity and motivation to seek additional information about the brand and lead to a consumer-generated belief that is relatively more powerful than a belief created by an explicit statement in the ad. This would argue for not making explicit claims of the sponsoring brand's superiority.

However, there is some risk in assuming that a receiver will "draw his own conclusions." Research suggests that conclusions should be stated explicitly when there is a significant chance that the audience will not be motivated or unable to draw their own conclusions, or when there are real risks of having them draw the wrong conclusions. Alan Sawyer and Daniel Howard found that if the audience is involved in the message, and if the message is one where a conclusion can be easily drawn, an open-ended message (where no explicit conclusion was drawn) led to greater brand attitudes, intentions, and choice than a close-ended message (there was no difference for an uninvolved audience).[24]

Consistent with this finding, Mita Sujan and Christine Dekleva have found that comparative ads gain in relative effectiveness when aimed at more expert consumers and when they make comparisons with specific, well-known brands (rather than types of brands), because the comparative ad can be interpreted more unambiguously under these conditions.[25]

Inoculative Advertising: Building Resistant Attitudes

Can a person be made to resist attempts by competitors or outside influences to change his or her attitudes? How can AT&T prevent residential telephone service consumers from being swayed by a subsequent MCI marketing effort—or vice versa?

A great deal of advertising activity is associated with this goal of "defensive" marketing. Given that we have developed favorable patronage—have a good share of market, for example—how can it be sustained? In attitude theory terms, how can we induce those currently loyal to our brand to remain loyal?

A consumer can be made more resistant to competitive appeals either by attempting to make a brand offering more attractive, or by attempting to train the consumer to withstand the persuasive efforts of competitors. From the first viewpoint, for example, one strategy would be to anchor beliefs about the brand to other beliefs that the consumer values highly. The brand might be shown to be significant in maintaining one's self-esteem or in otherwise enhancing the ego in various ways.

The alternative, of attempting to train a consumer to withstand competitive attacks, has been the subject of some empirical work in marketing. The diffusion of advertising messages can be thought of as similar to the diffusion of germs in the spread of a disease through a population. If individuals are given weakened doses of the germs, they can build defenses to withstand the more potent ones, and thus be made resistant to the disease when exposed to it. The medical or biological analogy is, of course, the notion of inoculating an individual with a weakened dosage, and for this reason it has been called the *inoculation approach*.[26]

In the advertising context, it has been demonstrated that preexposure to weakened forms of counterargument (arguments counter to the position or object being defended) is more effective in building up resistance to strong subsequent attacks than is a simple repetition of supportive arguments.[27] Other research has also shown that a refutational appeal (discussed shortly) provides a greater resistance to attack than a standard supportive appeal.

Back to the telephone service example: A 1990 ad campaign utilizing this inoculation approach was that of AT&T's, warning consumers not to switch to a rival long-distance telephone service on the basis of a telemarketing call promising big savings in monthly phone bills. One newspaper ad said: "Another long distance company might be calling soon. They'll tell how you can save big over AT&T. With quality better than AT&T. How you have nothing to lose by switching now. But you do. If you don't get their pitch in writing. Because there are lots of things they may not tell you. . . . Don't get taken in by big claims. Get the facts."

MCI, in turn, tried its own form of inoculation. In 1993, consumers signing on with MCI were sent a direct-mail warning that "AT&T may call and attempt to switch you from MCI. If they do, we hope you ask AT&T these tough questions . . ."

followed by five questions. The fifth question said, for example: "Why does AT&T declare that MCI's savings are only "a penny per minute"—when those pennies multiplied by many minutes can *really* add up? The fact is, month after month, MCI adds up to real savings." Note here how the MCI customer is being inoculated to AT&T's claim that MCI's savings are only "a penny per minute."

Refutational Advertising

Another term closely related to inoculation is *refutation*. It refers to the process of explicitly or implicitly stating competitive appeals (or consumer beliefs) and then refuting them, instead of dealing exclusively with brand benefits (supportive advertising). Hertz and Avis advertising are examples of both refutational and supportive advertising. For many years, Hertz used a supportive approach, emphasizing the many benefits of renting a Hertz car. Avis, on the other hand, refuted the implicit claim that "No. 1 equals the best" by suggesting that "No. 2 tries harder."

Another example of a refutational automotive ad is the one for Nissan in Figure 12–3, in which Nissan tries to refute the perception that Honda and Toyota are the better-quality Japanese imports. In the headache-remedy market, Bayer refutes the claim that various products are stronger or better than aspirin as follows: "Does buffering it, squaring it, squeezing it, fizzing it, flavoring it, flattening it, gumming it or adding to it improve aspirin?"

Ray cites three reasons why refutational messages appear to work:

1. They are more stimulating than supportive messages. They underline conflict and get people concerned about an area. This motivating factor alone can be quite effective, since refutational defenses can work even if they deal with claims other than those that appear in subsequent attacks.

2. They refute counterclaims and thus make the competitive attacks appear less credible when they appear. This refutation is probably quite satisfying. Statements of counterclaims can arouse dissonance or imbalance. The refutation can restore balance.

3. Refutational messages do contain some supportive information, even though less than supportive messages.[28]

Other research by Michael Kamins and Henry Assael has also shown that refutational ads lead consumers to generate more support-arguments and fewer source derogations (see Chapter 5) than ads with only supportive information.[29] One disadvantage of refutational messages is that they provide a viewer with information about a competitor's product and thus might enhance rather than defend against competitive alternatives. It is, nevertheless, a preferred approach to market situations in which the goal of an advertiser is to build resistance to attitude change and defend against competitive attack.

As mentioned earlier, a refutational approach can be useful not only against a competitive claim but also against a prior consumer belief that is negative. The famous ad for Life cereal that featured the little boy called Mikey is an example of refutational advertising. Here, the challenge was to convince mothers that their kids would actually like Life cereal, despite the fact that it was "healthy" cereal.

Re-Orient your thinking.

If you think Honda or Toyota is at the top of the list of the most trouble-free Asian imports sold in America, maybe you should think again.

According to the 1989 J.D. Power and Associates Initial Quality Survey, Nissan®

rated higher than both of them. And every other Asian import. As well as every domestic nameplate. And all but two of the European imports.

The results were obtained by asking owners to report the number of problems encountered during the first 90 days of ownership. The nameplate with the fewest problems per 100 cars is considered the most trouble-free. Among Asian imports that nameplate is Nissan.

Here's something else to consider. Among individual car models, the

Nissan Maxima® had the fewest problems, making it the most trouble-free car sold in America. And that includes such prestigious stalwarts as the Mercedes-Benz S-Class, the BMW 325 and the Porsche 911.

This kind of owner satisfaction is tremendously satisfying for us.

And something for you to keep in mind when thinking about your next car.

Built for the Human Race.

Figure 12–3.   A refutational ad: Nissan cars.

Courtesy of Nissan.

The TV spot showed two other boys watch Mikey eat Life cereal, betting that he wouldn't like it—and then watching with amazement when he ate it up.

As another application, if a certain segment of American consumers believe that Japanese cars are superior in quality, an ad by an American auto manufacturer aimed at this segment might be more successful in credibly communicating the actually high quality of American cars by first acknowledging this belief about poor quality and then refuting it with evidence (instead of making no reference to that prior belief about lower quality).

A refutational ad in such a situation might gain even more credibility if it were two sided—conceding that quality in prior years was, in fact, poor but then going on to argue that it has since improved substantially. Thus, continuing with the auto example above, General Motors ran a campaign in 1992 headlined "If you've been away from American cars and trucks for a while . . . the people of General Motors have something to show you," following up with quotes from favorable reviews about its new models, and concluding ". . . (in the last six years) 96 percent of our cars and 60 percent of our trucks have been redesigned . . ." A 1993 General Motors campaign in California featured an automotive scrap-yard operator describing how he made a good living over the years scrapping GM vehicles, but then noting that GM's quality now seems to be improving, so that "there's a trend here. It's not good for my business!"[30]

Another example of this creative approach is an ad run by USAir in August 1990 in *The Wall Street Journal*, which highlighted the on-time arrival record of its flights. The ad spanned two bottom half-pages, starting with the headline "It was the worst of times" and ending with "It was the best of times." Under the first headline was a panel of on-time performance statistics from January 1990, showing USAir in sixth place among major airlines. Four other monthly panels followed, showing USAir in second place, followed by the last panel for June 1990 showing that USAir was now number 1. The headline at the bottom of the second page said it all: "USAir now leads the six largest U.S. airlines in on-time arrivals. My, how times have changed."

EMOTIONAL CREATIVE APPROACHES . . . .

The creative approaches discussed thus far are "rational" in the sense that they rely for their persuasive power on arguments, or reasons, about brand attributes. For instance, a comparative approach attempts to show, based on reasons, why the sponsoring brand is superior to competition. There is, of course, the whole category of creative approaches that rely on emotions or feelings for their effectiveness, such as the attempted evocation of warmth and affection, or surgency and excitement, or the use of humor, or of fear.

Since Chapter 8 was devoted completely to the role of feeling responses to advertising, including the use of humor or fear, we will not repeat that material here. Instead, we will only mention once again that emotion-evoking creative approaches are most suitable when the product category is one where, typically, consumers buy the product because of a "feeling" benefit—either the low-involvement "small pleasures" of candy or soda pop or the highly involving feelings associated with fragrances, sports cars, and jewelry. Emotion-evoking creative approaches do not appear to be very successful in "high-involvement, thinking" situations (see Chapter 8 for a fuller discussion).

USING AN ENDORSER . . . .

Advertisers often use endorsers for their products or services—and this makes many endorsers very rich. Basketball star Michael Jordan reportedly earned $36 million per year in endorsement fees when he retired in 1993 ($18 million from Nike, which created its Air Jordan line of basketball shoes around him; $3 million from McDonald's, which created a McJordan hamburger named after him; $2 million from Gatorade, which urged consumers to drink Gatorade to "Be Like Mike;" $3 to $4 million from Sara Lee/Hanes, $2 to $3 million from Wheaties, and others).[31]

Other sports stars, including top golfers like Arnold Palmer, Jack Nicklaus, and Greg Norman, football quarterbacks like Joe Montana, ice hockey star Wayne Gretzky, and tennis champ Andre Agassi also earn millions of dollars every year from advertising endorsements. Star entertainers get rich too: Michael Jackson is reported to have received $5.5 million in 1984 and Madonna $5.0 million in 1989 for appearing in Pepsi's commercials.[32] The question therefore arises: what did these advertisers get in return? When should endorsers be used, and how and when do they help a brand?

In brief, research and commonsense suggest three types of benefits. First, endorsers *enhance advertising readership* (or viewership or listenership) scores.[33] Second, endorsers can *induce positive attitude change* toward a company and its products.[34] In general, the more credible a source, the more persuasive that source is likely to be. Third, the *personality characteristics* of the endorser can get associated with a *brand's imagery*. These benefits are not automatic, however, and obtaining them requires a careful consideration of a brand's marketing or advertising needs, and an endorser's characteristics.

There are two ways of thinking about an endorser's characteristics. The traditional way is to think of an endorser is a "source" of the information in the ad, contributing to the acceptability of the content of (arguments in) the message because of the source's credibility or attractiveness. We shall say more about this way of thinking below. The second, more recent, way is to think of the endorser as possessing some symbolic properties, which are *transferred* from the endorser to the endorsed brand (through advertising) and then from the brand to the consumer (through the acts of purchasing and consuming or owning the brand).

According to this *meaning transfer* model popularized by McCracken, brands benefit from associations with endorsers because endorsers acquire or possess particular configurations of cultural meanings that cannot be found elsewhere.[35] Thus, for instance, the symbolic cultural meanings linked to Michael Jackson and Madonna—presumably their anti-establishment, "bad" images—were what Pepsi wanted and obtained for itself through their endorsements, which then helped Pepsi attract the youths and teenagers who form the crucial part of the soft-drink market. Similarly, Coca-Cola hoped that ads featuring pop star George Michael might improve Coke's image as being "young" and "modern."[36] This meaning transfer model of the value of endorsements is discussed more fully in the chapter on brand personality (Chapter 10) and is thus not repeated here.

A Model of Source Factors in Advertising

Returning to the source model, Figure 12–4 shows various factors of source on which research has focused. The central idea is that consumers view the information in ads as coming from a source, with sources varying in "credibility."[37] (The term *credibility* should not be interpreted literally, and is explained further below.) According to this model, the more credible the source, the more persuasive he or she is likely to be in getting the audience to accept the ad's message.

Shown to the right in Figure 12–4 are various source components of advertising copy. At the center is the object of the advertising, such as the brand, product, service, idea, political candidate, corporation, and so on. The model shows the credibility of this object to depend on the the sponsor, the endorser, the media vehicle, etc.

The sponsor could be the company itself. A famous study by Theodore Levitt,[38] for example, tested whether the effects of salespeople representing a prestigious company (Monsanto Chemical), a medium-credible company (Denver Chemical), and an anonymous company had a differential impact on purchasing agents. It was found that the better the company's reputation, the better were the salespeople's chances of getting a first hearing for a new product and early adoption of the product. Company source effect declined, however, with the riskiness of

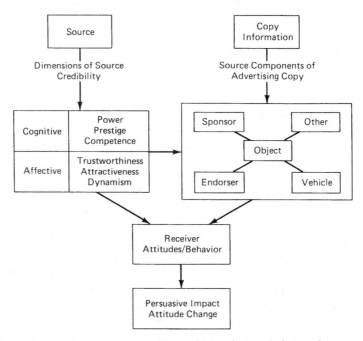

Figure 12–4.   A model of the source dimensions of copy information.

the decision. For high-risk decisions, the nature of the sales presentation and other factors were more important than the *source effect*. Another recent study found that an advertiser could successfully make a more extreme (stronger) claim in an ad if it already had a very positive reputation; a firm with a negative prior reputation could not successfully make the same claims, because it lacked the necessary credibility.[39]

A key source component, our focus here, is the endorser. The *endorser* in an advertisement is the person, celebrity, spokesman, announcer, and so on who endorses or who demonstrates the product. Not all advertisements have an endorser as a copy component, but many of them do. Most of the work on source credibility in advertising has focused on this component, and we shall discuss findings and implications later.

Another aspect is the credibility of the media vehicle itself. The same advertisement appearing in *The Ladies Home Journal*, for example, can have a different impact than if it appeared in *Playboy*. We will discuss this source component further in later chapters dealing with media decisions, but you should recognize here that it is also an important source factor in advertising.

Using Endorsers in Advertising

Dimensions of a Source

What exactly is meant by the *credibility* of a source? As shown on the left of Figure 12–4, researchers have recognized that some judgments about a source concern a cognitive dimension and others an affective dimension. The *cognitive dimension* includes judgments about the power, prestige (from past achievements, reputation, wealth, political power, or visibility), and competence (expertise) of the source. The *affective dimension* includes judgments about trustworthiness, attractiveness, and dynamism.[40]

Other constructs, such as unbiasedness, similarity (between the source and receiver), and physical attractiveness, have also been the focus of research. Similarity is sometimes important because a source that is presented as being similar to the audience member in terms of attitudes, opinions, activities, background, social status, or lifestyle could achieve both liking and identification: there are many situations in which people will tend to like people with whom they have things in common. Some companies (such as the MCI telephone service company) favor using employees in their commercials because they believe the employees are perceived by consumers to be very similar to themselves and, thus, believable.[41] The research on physical attractiveness tends to show that, all other things being equal, the stronger the physical attraction of the source, the greater the liking will be, and the stronger will be the persuasive impact.

All such constructs are considered to be dimensions on which the credibility of a source component can be measured. A source can be high on one dimension and low on another. Consider the competence and unbiasedness dimensions. A doctor could be regarded as very competent (an expert) in recommending a drug product, but he or she would have less persuasive influence if listeners or viewers considered the recommendations to be biased by money payments given the doctor for making the commercial. Similarly, many politicians, although regarded as expert in their field, are also considered biased in their viewpoints.

A research firm, Marketing Evaluations, annually determines a familiarity and likability rating of top male and female personalities (and cartoon characters) based on a mail questionnaire survey of television viewers. The basic rating, called a *Q rating*, is obtained by dividing the number who rated the personality as "one of my favorites" by those who indicated that they were "totally familiar" with the personality. The survey is widely used by marketers and agencies to select celebrity endorsers and is used by TV networks and Hollywood producers to cast their shows and movies. The top personalities overall in August 1992 included Bill Cosby, Jimmy Stewart, Clint Eastwood; Michael Jordan ranked number 1 among teens.[42] According to another company, Video Storyboard Tests, which surveys 3,000 people by phone and mail every year, the TV celebrity endorsers most liked by consumers in 1993 were Candice Bergen, Bill Cosby, and Cher.[43]

Selecting An Endorser

The popularity and Q ratings just discussed presumably get at the prestige and attractiveness dimensions listed earlier. However, the other dimensions listed must also be considered in selecting an endorser from among the four primary endorser types from which a copywriter must usually choose in selecting an endorser: (1) a celebrity, (2) an expert, (3) a typical satisfied customer, and (4) an announcer.

Using a *celebrity* has the advantage of the publicity and attention-getting power of the celebrity virtually regardless of the product type. Large segments of the audience can instantly recognize and identify with the famous person, and the attraction and goodwill associated with the celebrity can be transferred to the product. Local celebrities or actors and actresses who are not so well known can often be used in local or regional market situations to good effect.

On the negative side, celebrities aren't usually considered experts, although celebrities can also be experts in some situations. Thus, Michael Jordan is not just a celebrity but an expert in basketball shoes, and a celebrity like TV talk-show host Oprah Winfrey was also an "expert" when she announced to the world in 1988 that she had lost 67 pounds when using a weight-loss product called Optifast (she had been visibly overweight before). As a result of her endorsement, sales of diet products soared in the following two years.[44] It is very easy, however, to use a celebrity mistakenly for a high-involvement product, a situation in which the consumer is looking for credible information from an expert. For instance, a copier company recently used a basketball and football coach to endorse the reliability of its products.

Furthermore, celebrities not only cost a lot but are hard to get, and if they are already being used by other advertisers, they may be losing credibility at the time they are chosen. Endorsers are usually contractually prohibited from endorsing similar or competing products through exclusivity clauses in contracts, but they may still be overexposed. Very importantly, if some event happens to reduce the popularity of the celebrity with the public, the publicity could backfire on the associated brand as well. Recent examples include the child molestation charges against Michael Jackson, the divorce of Burt Reynolds, Magic Johnson disclosing he had AIDS, the controversy over Madonna's music videos, and the retirement of Michael Jordan.[45]

Research by Michael Kamins suggests that the credibility of celebrity endorsers can be raised if they say things that are not only in favor of the brand but also a few things that are mildly critical of it—that is, a two-sided ad with a celebrity endorser works better than a one-sided ad with a celebrity endorser.[46] And, as noted below, in cases in which the audience is already very supportive of the product, a highly credible source might result in less persuasive impact than an endorser which has lesser power and prestige. There is also the very real danger that while the consumer may find the ad with the celebrity entertaining, very little benefit may actually accrue to the brand being advertised. This distraction effect is discussed further below.

An *expert* is likely to be the best choice when the product is technical or consumers need to be reassured that the product is safe to consume (high-involvement decisions). An expert can allay fears in the audience concerning the product whether those fears arise from not knowing how something works, concern about side effects, concern about fulfilling a role such as father, mother, housewife, and so on, or health-related concerns about product use. Doctors, dentists, lawyers, engineers, and other kinds of experts can be chosen and at considerably less cost than a national celebrity.

A *typical satisfied consumer* is often the best choice when it can be anticipated that there will be strong audience identification with the role involved, the person is "like" many members of the audience, and attributes of sincerity and trustworthiness are likely to come through. To maximize the naturalness of the situation, it is often useful to use a hidden camera and capture the consumer's real-world reactions to using the product in a situation with which the audience can identify. The choice might be a child rather than an adult, or an animal, such as an enthusiastic dog for a dog food commercial.

The national or local talk show in television, and a great deal of local radio advertising, typifies the choice of the *announcer* format. Local radio disk jockeys are classic examples of using an announcer spokesperson as the essential source component. Announcers are more like celebrities than experts, in that they confer some notoriety to the brand, with the likely advantage of some trustworthiness. The actual copy generation process is often less expensive because only the script and, in television, some simple props must be provided. This does not imply that the media buy will be less expensive, but the trade-off is really deciding to put more money into the media buy than into copy production. The addition of props or ways to have the announcer do more than simply sit behind a desk and talk about the product can often enhance the persuasive impact considerably.

As we said earlier, the key criterion in selecting an endorser must be the appropriateness of the "match" or "fit" between the needs of the brand and the characteristics of the endorser. Research shows that the effectiveness of an endorser is related to the type of product being endorsed. In an experiment comparing the impact of using an expert rather than a typical consumer or celebrity in advertising a low-priced but fairly technical product (electronic calculator), it was found that the expert was more effective than either a typical consumer or a celebrity. In contrast, celebrities are often more effective in situations where the product has a high element of psychological and "social" risk (e.g., costume jewelry). Good reviews of the source credibility literature are available.[47]

In general, when the purchase is based most strongly on a brand's awareness and/or likability (such as in many low-involvement purchase decisions), the more appropriate a celebrity endorser is likely to be. A celebrity endorser may also be very useful when the cultural meanings desired for the brand's imagery are linked to the celebrity endorser, and/or when consumers aspire to the lifestyle or reference group associated with that celebrity endorser. Lynn Kahle and Pamela Homer, and Michael Kamins, have also shown that when the product being advertised has improved physical attractiveness as its major benefit, ad effectiveness is usually enhanced to the degree that there is a congruence between the product image and the celebrity image. Thus, an attractive celebrity like Tom Selleck is superior to an unattractive one like Telly Savalas for a luxury car, which promises social appeal, but not for a computer.[48]

In contrast, experts and not celebrities are likely to be more appropriate for more rational and highly involved purchase decisions. If the purchase is driven by logical reasons why a brand is better, then a celebrity may be a waste of money: a noncelebrity might be equally effective, and a lot cheaper.[49] Thus, returning to our chapter-opening example, mutual funds are probably better associated with an expert fund-rating group than with cartoon characters like the Peanuts, however likable they may be. Note that Bill Cosby, despite his top-notch popularity and liking ratings, was a failure when he endorsed the brokerage firm E. F. Hutton in the mid-1980s. Presumably the selection of a brokerage firm requires an expert endorser more than it does a likable entertainer. It has also been shown that consumers are most skeptical of advertising claims and thus might benefit most from a credible and expert endorser, when the claims involved are subjective rather than objective.[50] Considering the large sums of money involved, it is always appropriate to pretest an endorser's attractiveness and expertise ratings before deciding to use one.

Additionally, one other key aspect that should be copy-tested when an advertisement uses endorsers is whether the endorser's presence, while possibly raising awareness of the ad and/or brand, is also detracting from communication of the main copy points. Research shows that this often does happen: an ad with an endorser, compared to an ad without one, often has higher awareness but communicates less about the brand's characteristics or advantages, which can hurt the ability of the ad to create the attitude change or persuasion necessary in many high involvement situations. For instance, though the fictitious endorser Joe Isuzu raised the brand awareness of Isuzu cars, he failed to convince car buyers to visit Isuzu dealerships to check out Isuzu cars in large enough numbers and was subsequently dropped as an endorser. This typically happens because the endorser's presence *distracts* the consumer from the main message in the ad about the brand. Since distraction effects are often of interest in advertising, we will be discussing them more thoroughly later.

It has been suggested that an endorser can be used to attract attention even if there is high risk of the perceived credibility of the source being low. The reason is called the sleeper effect. The *sleeper effect* refers to the case in which the persuasive impact of a message actually increases rather than decreases over time. One hypothesis of why persuasive impact increases is that although the effect of the source is negative (it is not liked or not credible) at the time of viewing or reading, with the passage of time, the association of this negative cue with the message breaks down. The result is an increase in the overall impact of the message over time. Although the idea is intuitively appealing, there are surprisingly few studies that have demonstrated the presence of a sleeper effect, even though dozens of experiments have been done on the subject.[51]

Consistency Theories

Why should a credible source (endorser, company, media vehicle, whatever) raise attitudes toward the advertised brand? The effects of an endorser on the attitudes toward the advertised brand can be understood using *consistency theories of attitude*. This important group of attitude-change theories rests on the assumption that attitude change results by exploiting a person's drive for consistency among the facts associated with an object. For example, an audience member may have a negative opinion about a brand but a positive opinion about a person who is endorsing the brand in an advertisement. This inconsistency should create a tension and a drive to reduce that tension.

There are three obvious routes to the reduction of tension in this context. First, it can be assumed by the consumer that the endorser is not really enthusiastic about the brand. Second, the positive opinion of the endorser can be altered to one less positive. Third, the attitude toward the brand can be changed to one more positive. If the advertising can select an endorser for which audiences have strong positive attitudes and link the endorser strongly to the brand, there will be a tendency to engage in brand-attitude change. To maximize the likelihood of attitude change, it is useful for the source not only to be well liked but also relevant and credible with respect to the product class involved. Otherwise, the audience member can resolve the inconsistency by observing that the endorser's opinion about the product is not relevant because the endorser is not knowledgeable about the product or that the endorser's experience will not apply to others.

There are several types of consistency theories, including *balance theory* (which emphasizes the role of an endorser), *congruity theory* (which predicts the size of attitude change knowing the strengths of existing attitudes and the size of the advocated change), and *dissonance theory* (which considers the drive to make attitudes consistent with behavior). They all focus attention on tension created by cognitive inconsistency that can be resolved by changing beliefs and attitudes.

In the Jell-O campaign, for example, in which Bill Cosby is shown with little children expounding the benefits of Jell-O, the congruity theory explanation is that people who like Cosby may shift their liking for Jell-O because the Jell-O–Cosby link is so strong and positive. Of course, the reverse is true for people who do not like Cosby. The theory offers predictions of the overall attitude effect for conditions such as dislike Cosby–like Jell-O, like Cosby–dislike Jell-O, and so on. However, the proposition that highly credible sources (Cosby) will always lead to an increase in positive attitude for the object (Jell-O) must be qualified somewhat. The theory predicts that although a low-credibility product should gain from the association with a high-credibility source, the source will tend to lose some credibility from the association as well. The predictions of relative gains and losses of each component are functions of the initial credibility positions of each before the association occurs.

Conditions under which the basic proposition that "high-credibility sources lead to higher persuasion" breaks down have been the focus of some studies.[52] There are situations in which a low-credibility source is about equal in effectiveness to a high-credibility source. Even more interesting are those situations in which a low-credibility source is more effective than a high one.

First, it has been found that when receivers feel their behavior is being controlled, negative reactions—such as "this endorser must have been paid to say this"—can be increased if the source is highly credible. According to psychological *theories of attribution*,[53] we are more likely to believe that another person really believes what he says if we cannot easily find another reason (such as financial inducements) why he might have said what have did. That is why so-called "hidden camera" ads that show ordinary people saying nice things about the advertised brand can often be very effective—since the ordinary "people on the street" are not being paid to say what they are saying, they must believe it.

The second case occurs in situations in which receivers have a strong initial positive attitude about the brand or product. Such people tend to generate more support arguments during exposure if the source has low credibility rather than high. The reason is that they are more highly motivated to assure themselves that the position with which they agree is the right one, when the endorser is of low credibility rather than high credibility.

The choice of a source to be included in an advertisement must therefore be done very carefully. If the strategy is to try to increase positive attitudes, high-credibility sources should be used. However, if the strategy is to induce behavior such as product trial directly, it is possible that using a highly credible source can undermine the formation of "real" positive attitudes (internal to the consumer) and thus reduce the incidence of future repeat purchases and brand loyalty.

DISTRACTION EFFECTS . . . .

Probably the most useful research finding supported by numerous studies is that *distraction* (e.g., from elements of the ad execution such as endorsers or music) can affect the number of support arguments and counterarguments evoked by an ad (discussed in Chapter 5). In some situations, this can enhance persuasion: negatively predisposed audience members who would otherwise have generated counterarguments can be distracted from counterarguing, so that the communication will be more effective. For example, in a study by L. Festinger and N. Maccoby, a strong, persuasive tape-recorded message opposing fraternities was more effective at changing attitudes among fraternity men when a silent film on modern painting was shown rather than pictures of fraternity scenes.[54] In general, distractor tasks that involve cognitive activity result in more distraction than do tasks that simply provide visual distraction or manual skills.

An advertiser interested in using distraction to break down resistance to her or his arguments is faced with the delicate task of devising something that will interfere with counterarguing but not, at the same time, interfere with the reception or learning of the message. This is a formidable task that must take into consideration all aspects of the communication and the audience. As David Gardner explains, the critical question in defining distraction seems to be whether the process of counterarguing is interfered with. If attitude change is more apt to be induced due to interference with counterargument, then this is defined as distraction. Based on this definition, distraction takes on many dimensions. If an element in the communication is designed to add support to the message—that is, mood music or artwork—this cannot be defined as distraction because it does not interfere with the counterarguing process; what is support in one communication could be distraction in another due to products, audiences, channels of communication, or a host of unique factors.[55]

A good example of the use of distractors in trying to communicate with a hostile audience is a campaign developed by the Standard Oil Company of California for its Chevron brand.[56] At the time, many consumers were very hostile to oil companies generally; the oil company image as a good corporate citizen was considerably tarnished. One of the first campaigns involved on-the-scene stories, showing tankers being built, explorations, and other activities. Although reasonably successful, the company subsequently developed a whimsical campaign around the theme "We're running out of dinosaurs" to encourage energy conservation. The campaign not only proved effective in educating consumers about the energy situation, but most important, resulted in a significant shift in favorable attitudes for Standard Oil.

SUMMARY . . . .

Before ads are handed off to the advertising agency and actual creative work begins, it is important to consider the broad framework and creative approaches open to copywriters and art directors. This chapter reviews several rational and emotional approaches and some of the research that has been done on each.

The chapter is organized around a discussion of the rational approaches such as comparative advertising, inoculative advertising, and refutational approaches, emotional approaches, using endorsers, and the use of distraction in advertising. Comparative advertising is advertising in which two or more specifically named brands of the same product are compared in terms of one or more attributes. It is now widely used, even though it was illegal prior to 1970. The research on comparative advertising presents a mixed picture of it being more or less effective than noncomparative advertising depending on counterarguing and other information processing mechanisms which come into play. From a strategic viewpoint, comparative advertising is more appropriate for follower brands than for leader brands.

Inoculative advertising utilizes the principles of inoculation in medicine. The objective is to inoculate the audience with small doses of the offending campaign (competitor arguments) so that when the full campaign hits they will be less susceptible and resistant to those arguments. It has been demonstrated that pre-exposure to weakened forms of counterargument is more effective in building resistance than prior presentation of supportive arguments. AT&T's famous campaign to counter MCI inroads is a good example.

Refutational advertising involves explicitly stating competitive claims and then refuting them. It is often contrasted to supportive advertising which focuses on a one-sided presentation of brand benefits only. USAir's "Best of times, Worst of times," campaign is an example.

There is a whole category of approaches that rely on emotions or feelings and pathos as the essential ingredient. Emotion-evoking approaches are most suitable when the product category is one where buying is based on a "feeling" benefit—either the low-involvement small pleasures of candy or soda pop or the highly involving feelings associated with products like perfume, sports cars, or jewelry.

Endorsers are often used in testimonial advertising and are examples of source-oriented approaches. There are many types of sources in advertising and a model of source factors shows the range of source components and the cognitive and affective ways in which the credibility of any of the components can be assessed. Consistency theories encompass a range of theories of attitude change (balance, dissonance, and congruity) that explain endorser and source effects. Research on source credibility has shown that, in some cases, a low-credibility source can be more effective than a high-credibility source. In advertising, three dimensions of course credibility—prestige, similarity, and physical attractiveness—are particularly important.

A final approach is called distraction and involves trying to distract the audience from counterarguing during the viewing or listening process. The Chevron dinosaur campaign, "We're running out of dinosaurs," designed to divert and dissipate some of the audience hostility against oil companies during the energy crisis, is an example.

DISCUSSION QUESTIONS . . . .

1. Using examples of comparative and noncomparative advertisement for the same product category, explain in your own words why or why not you think one is more effective than the other. Consider a modification of the comparative ad that includes more/less explicit attribute comparisons and discuss why the changes would increase (or decrease) effectiveness. Be specific in specifying the criteria you use to evaluate effectiveness.

2. Discuss the desirability of using a doctor instead of a dentist as an endorser in a toothpaste commercial. Assume that the same advertising objectives and the same type of target audience are involved in each case.

3. Choose two testimonial advertisements. Assess their relative persuasiveness using the source factors model given in the chapter.

4. Develop an advertisement for Coors Lite beer that is based on the refutational approach (relative to Bud Lite for example). Discuss the degree to which it

would be likely to build resistant attitudes among current Coors drinkers versus the degree to which it might attract new drinkers to the brand.

5. What exactly is *distraction* in advertising? What is its purpose? What provided the distraction in the Chevron advertisements? Provide other examples of distraction in advertising.

6. Develop a consistency model of attitude change that would predict the changed attitude toward Jell-O knowing the existing attitude on a −5 (strongly dislike) to zero (neutral) to +5 (strongly like) scale; the existing attitude toward Cosby as the source, also on a −5 to +5 scale; and the link between the source and the brand on a 0 (weak link) to +5 (strong link) scale.

7. What is *cognitive tension*? Recall an instance in which you experienced it. How would you measure cognitive tension?

8. Explain why refutational advertising works, and discuss situations in which it would be more (and less) effective.

9. What criteria would you use in choosing an endorser for a new line extension in the "chip" market (potato or corn chips)? Discuss the importance of each in your evaluation of potential candidates and how you would make the final decision.

NOTES. . . . .

1. William L. Wilkie and Paul Farris, "Comparison Advertising: Problems and Potential," *Journal of Marketing*, 39 (October 1975), 7–15.
2. For a review of some studies, see Thomas E. Barry, "Comparative Advertising: What Have we Learned in Two Decades?" *Journal of Advertising Research*, 33, no. 2 (March/April 1993), 19–29.
3. *Adweek's Marketing Week*, June 12, 1989, p. 17.
4. For a review of recent articles on the subject, see Barry (1993), cited above.
5. See, for example, Kathy L. Pettit-O'Malley and Mark S. Johnson, "Differentiative Cpmarative Advertising: Some Positive Results Revealed by Measurement of Simultaneous Effects on the Ad-Sponsoring and Comparison Brands," *Journal of Current Issues and Research in Advertising*, 14, no. 1 (Spring 1992), 35–44.
6. "Comparison Ads Rev Up," *Advertising Age*, January 20, 1992, p. 3.
7. Naveen Donthu, "Comparative Advertising Intensity," *Journal of Advertising Research*, 32, no. 6 (November/December 1992), 53–58.
8. Cornelia Pechmann and David W. Stewart, "How Direct Comparative Ads and Market Share Affect Brand Choice," *Journal of Advertising Research*, 31, no. 6 (December 1991), 47–55.
9. Cornelia Pechmann and David W. Stewart, "The Effects of Comparative Advertising on Attention, Memory, and Purchase Intention," *Journal of Consumer Research*, 17 (September 1990), 180–191.
10. *The Wall Street Journal*, October 18, 1994, p. B1.
11. Gerald J. Gorn and Charles B. Weinberg, "The Impact of Comparative Advertising on Perception and Attitude: Some Positive Findings," *Journal of Consumer Research*, 11 (September 1984), 719–727.
12. Michael D. Johnson and David A. Horne, "The Contrast Model of Similarity and Comparative Advertising," *Psychology and Marketing* (Fall 1988), 211–232.
13. "Creating a Mass Market for Wine," *Business Week*, March 15, 1982, pp. 102–118.
14. Cornelia Pechmann and S. Ratneshwar, "The Use of Comparative Advertising for Brand Positioning: Association versus Differentiation," *Journal of Consumer Research*, 18 (September 1991), 145–160.

15. Donthu (1992), cited earlier.
16. *The Wall Street Journal*, December 20, 1994, p. B7.
17. George E. Belch, "An Examination of Comparative and Noncomparative Television Commercials: The Effects of Claim Variation and Repetition on Cognitive Response and Message Acceptance," *Journal of Marketing Research*, 18 (August 1981), 333–349. For a listing of some other studies, see Barry (1993), cited earlier.
18. Easwar S. Iyer, "The Influence of Verbal Content and Relative Newness on the Effectiveness of Comparative Advertising," *Journal of Advertising*, 17 (3), 1988, 15–21.
19. Jerry B. Gotlieb and Dan Sarel, "Comparative Advertising Effectiveness: The Role of Involvement and Source Credibility," *Journal of Advertising*, 20, no. 1 (1991), 38–45.
20. Shailendra P. Jain, "Positive versus Negative Comparative Advertising," *Marketing Letters*, 4, no. 4 (1993), 309–320.
21. William R. Swinyard, "The Interaction Between Comparative Advertising and Copy Claim Variation," *Journal of Marketing Research*, 18 (May 1981), 175–186.
22. Michael Etgar and Stephen A. Goodwin, "One-Sided Versus Two-Sided Comparative Message Appeals for New Brand Introductions," *Journal of Consumer Research*, 8 (March 1982), 460–465.
23. Cornelia Pechmann, "Predicting When Two-Sided Ads Will Be More Effective Than One-Sided Ads: The Role of Correlational and Correspondent Inferences," *Journal of Marketing Research*, 29 (November 1992), 441–453.
24. Alan G. Sawyer and Daniel J. Howard, "Effects of Omitting Conclusions in Advertisements to Involved and Uninvolved Audiences," *Journal of Marketing Research*, 28 (November 1991), 467–474.
25. Mita Sujan and Christine Dekleva, "Product Categorization and Inference Making: Some Implications for Comparative Advertising," *Journal of Consumer Research*, 14 (December 1987), 372–378.
26. William J. McGuire, "The Nature of Attitude and Attitude Change," in G. Lindzey and E. Aronson, eds., *The Handbook of Social Psychology*, vol. 3 (Reading, MA: Addison-Wesley, 1969), p. 263.
27. Stewart W. Bither, Ira J. Dolich, and Elaine B. Nell, "The Application of Attitude Immunization Techniques in Marketing," *Journal of Marketing Research*, 8 (February 1971), 56–61.
28. Ibid., p. 8.
29. Michael A. Kamins and Henry Assael, "Two-Sided Versus One-Sided Appeals: A Cognitive Perspective on Argumentation, Source Derogation, and the Effect of Disconfirming Trial on Belief Change," *Journal of Marketing Research*, 24 (February 1987), 29–39.
30. "GM Ad Blitz Aima at Californians, Touts a New Image," *The Wall Street Journal*, September 24, 1993, p. B5A.
31. "Is There Life After Basketball? Firms that use Jordan Are About to Find Out," *The Wall Street Journal*, October 7, 1993, p. B1.
32. *The New York Times*, March 27, 1989, p. 30.
33. See W. Freeman, *The Big Name* (New York: Printer's Ink, 1957), and H. Rudolph, *Attention and Interest Factors in Advertising* (New York: Printer's Ink, 1947).
34. R. B. Fireworker and H. H. Friedman, "The Effects of Endorsements on Product Evaluation," *Decision Sciences*, 8 (1977), 576–583, and Joseph M. Kamen et al., "What a Spokesman Does for a Sponsor," *Journal of Advertising Research*, 15 (1975), 17–24.
35. Grant McCracken, "Who Is the Celebrity Endorser? Cultural Foundations of the Endorsement Process," *Journal of Consumer Research*, 16 (December 1989), 310–321.
36. *The New York Times*, p. 30.
37. Joanne M. Klebba and Lynette S. Unger, "The Impact of Negative and Positive Information on Source Credibility in Field Settings," in Richard P. Bagozzi and Alice M. Tybout, eds., *Advances in Consumer Research*, vol. 10 (Ann Arbor, MI: Association for Consumer Research, 1982), pp. 11–16.
38. Theodore Levitt, *Industrial Purchasing Behavior* (Boston: Harvard University Graduate School of Business Administration, 1965).

39. Marvin E. Goldberg and Jon Hartwick, "The Effects of Advertiser Reputation and Extremity of Advertising Claim on Advertising Effectiveness," *Journal of Consumer Research*, 17 (September 1990), 172–179.

40. Galen R. Rarick, "Effects of Two Components of Communicator Prestige." Unpublished doctoral dissertation, Stanford University, Palo Alto, California, 1963.

41. "Candice Bergen Leads the List of Top Celebrity Endorsers," *The Wall Street Journal*, September 17, 1993, p. B1.

42. "Stewart, Cosby Top Q Ratings; Where's Mike?" *Advertising Age*, August 31, 1992, p. 3.

43. See "Candice Bergen," *The Wall Street Journal*, cited earlier.

44. *Business Week*, April 16, 1990, p. 86.

45. "Marketers Tally the Price of Michael Jackson's Fame," *The New York Times*, November 16, 1993, p. C1.

46. Michael A. Kamins, "Celebrity and Non-celebrity Advertising in a Two-Sided Context," *Journal of Advertising Research* (June/July 1989), 34–42.

47. See Hershey H. Friedman and Linda Friedman, "Endorser Effectiveness by Product Type," *Journal of Advertising Research*, 19 (October 1979), 63–71. For reviews of literature, see W. Benoy Joseph, "The Credibility of Physically Attractive Communicators: A Review," *Journal of Advertising*, 11 (1982), 15–24, and Brian Sternthal, Lynn W. Phillips, and Ruby Dholakia, "The Persuasive Effect of Source Credibility: A Situational Analysis," *Public Opinion Quarterly*, 42 (Fall 1978), 285–314.

48. Lynn Kahle and Pamela Homer, "Physical Attractiveness of the Celebrity Endorser: A Social Adaptation Perspective," *Journal of Consumer Research*, 26, no. 1 (1985), 954–960; Michael Kamins, "An Investigation into the "Match-Up" Hypothesis in Celebrity Advertising: When Beauty May be Only Skin Deep," *Journal of Advertising*, 19, no. 1 (1990), 4–13.

49. "Best Ads Don't Rely on Celebrities," *Advertising Age*, May 25, 1992, p. 20.

50. Gary T. Ford, Darlene B. Smith, and John L. Swasy, "Consumer Skepticism of Advertising Claims: Testing Hypotheses from Economics of Information," *Journal of Consumer Research*, 16 (March 1990), 433–441.

51. Darlene B. Hannah and Brian Sternthal, "Detecting and Explaining the Sleeper Effect," *Journal of Consumer Research*, 11 (September 1984), 632–642.

52. Ruby Roy Dholakia and Brian Sternthal, "Highly Credible Sources: Persuasive Facilitators or Persuasive Liabilities?" *Journal of Consumer Research*, 3 (March 1977), 223–232. See also Brian Sternthal, Ruby Dholakia, and Clark Leavitt, "The Persuasive Effect of Source Credibility: Tests of Cognitive Response," *Journal of Consumer Research*, 4 (March 1978), 252–260.

53. See Edward E. Jones and Keith E. Davis, "From Acts to Dispositons," in Leonard Berkowitz, ed., *Advances in Experimental Social Psychology*, 2nd ed. (New York: Academic Press, 1965).

54. L. Festinger and N. Maccoby, "On Resistance to Persuasive Communications," *Journal of Abnormal and Social Psychology*, 68 (1964), 359–367.

55. David M. Gardner, "The Distraction Hypothesis in Marketing," *Journal of Marketing Research*, 10 (December 1970), 25–30.

56. Lewis C. Winters, "Should You Advertise to Hostile Audiences?" *Journal of Advertising Research*, 17 (June 1977), 7–15.

13 THE ART OF COPYWRITING

> "The cat sat on the mat" is not a story. "The cat sat
> on the dog's mat," now that's a story.
> (Gerry Miller, creative director, Dentsu)

> I belong to the school which holds that a good
> advertisement is one which sells the product
> *without drawing attention to itself.* It should rivet the
> reader's attention to the product. Instead of saying,
> "What a clever advertisement," the reader says, "I
> never knew *that* before. I must try this product."
> It is the professional duty of the advertising agent to
> conceal his artifice. When Aeschines spoke, they
> said, "How well he speaks." But when Demosthenes
> spoke, they said, "Let us march against Philip." I'm
> for Demosthenes.
> (David Ogilvy, in *Confessions of an Advertising Man*)

Advertising is both art and science. The science of advertising is the analytical part that we have been looking at up to this point: setting goals, deciding strategy, choosing among different creative styles. Some people call this step *convergent thinking* because the process is to distill lots of information into the core advertising strategy.

But once the message strategy and the broad creative approach have been determined, it is time to create the actual advertising. And, this is a very different process. Here the best approach is *divergent thinking*—letting loose with one's imagination to find the most creative, unexpected way to communicate that core advertising message.

This is not science, but art. We are dealing here not with logical analysis but with the product of raw talent. And, although much advertising, particularly local advertising, is created by someone at the client and media level without the inputs of an advertising agency, most national advertising involves an agency, because that is where this talent usually resides. Of course, such talent is not confined to ad agencies—indeed, clients like Coca-Cola have begun to tap into the pools of talent that create popular entertainment, like Hollywood movies, to the great concern of the ad agency business (see Chapter 1).

It is the job of the creative department of the agency to generate alternative advertising ideas and ultimately to pick one or a few that will go forward into production. The creative department is made up of copywriters who have the main responsibility for creating the advertising, and art directors who are expert at creating or otherwise introducing illustration and pictorial materials. These people are generally under the supervision of a creative director, and a team of such people is involved in developing the advertising to be used on any one campaign.

The creation stage encompasses the creative (*idea generation*) process, the generation of written copy (*copywriting*), artwork of various kinds (*illustrating*), and a preliminary or comprehensive version of the advertisement (*layout*). Obviously, client approval and supplier selection are also important activities that must be done before final production can begin. First, we consider the creative process.

THE CREATIVE PROCESS: COMING UP WITH AN IDEA

The creative process is concerned with taking the baldly stated marketing proposition, usually derived from and couched in terms of marketing research and manufacturing specifications, and turning it into one or more creative ideas that clearly, powerfully, and persuasively convey to the consumer what the brand does for them and why it should matter to them. Such creative processes come into play where research leaves off. It is possible today to use a computer-based *expert system* called ADCAD to specify what kind of advertising appeal and format will work best in what kind of situation[1]—but one still needs a creative process to take such recommendations and turn them into brilliant advertising.

For example, the long-distance company U.S. Sprint wanted to communicate to consumers that its phone lines were made of fiber optics, which led to clearer communications. A noncreative marketing person (or a computer-based expert system) might simply decide to run a commercial in which an announcer simply makes such an announcement, using a "talking head" format. It takes a creative person to come up with the creative idea that the fiber optic lines allow such clear communication that if a pin is dropped in New York, it is heard to fall in Los Angeles when the sound is picked up by a microphone and communicated over U.S. Sprint phone lines. Or, as in another ad, that if a singer in a studio in Los Angeles sings a high note, that note can shatter a wine glass in New York if the sound is carried over U.S. Sprint's fiber optic phone lines.

Consider, as another example, the choice of Bo Jackson—the multisport star athlete—to promote cross-training shoes from Nike. Or consider the campaign from *Rolling Stone* to confront advertiser perceptions that it was a still a "hippie" magazine by juxtaposing people illustrating the "perception" versus the "reality" (see Chapter 10 for an example.) Or, finally, consider the idea to show the exhaustive coverage of the NYNEX Yellow Pages by finding unusual category subheadings and building a pun-filled story around each. A powerful, "big" idea can add immeasurably to the effectiveness of an ad campaign, and the presence or absence of such an idea must be the first thing you look for in evaluating a proposed ad campaign. Two ads with arguably strong "ideas" are presented in Figures 13–1 and 13–2. In Figure 13–1, the "idea" is that Samsonite garment bags have the same convenience and structure as a closet. In Figure 13–2, the "idea" is that each UPS truck is like a complete satellite communications ground station, enabling complete tracking of packages.

How do we come up with such ideas? The creative process has interested many different types of people for some time. One of the pioneers in studying creativity, Alex Osborn, was a founder of Batten, Barton, Durstine & Osborn, one of the largest agencies (now known as BBDO, and part of the Omnicom group). Osborn saw the creative process as starting with the following.[2]

1. **Fact finding**
   a. **Problem definition: picking out and pointing up the problem**
   b. **Preparation: gathering and analyzing the pertinent data**
2. **Idea finding**
   a. **Idea production: thinking up tentative ideas as possible leads**
   b. **Idea development: selecting from resultant ideas, adding others, and reprocessing by means of modification, combination, and so on**

The process begins with fact finding—picking out and identifying the problem and gathering and analyzing pertinent data. The raw material for ideas is information—information from all sources. Leo Burnett once said, "Curiosity about life in all of its aspects, I think, is still the secret of great creative people."[3] Of course, some information is more useful than others. In particular, the creative team should become immersed in as much factual information about the company, the product, competition, and the target audience (their language, needs, motivations, desires) as possible. Obviously, they should have access to the available consumer research.

Sometimes it is worthwhile to get firsthand knowledge of the consumer. Claude Hopkins, whom we met in Chapter 1, would always go out and discuss products with homemakers. One of the top agency executives today still makes it a point to visit supermarkets regularly and ask shoppers why they make certain shopping decisions. Leo Burnett believed in depth interviewing, "where I come realistically face to face with the people *I* am trying to sell. I try to get a picture in my mind of the kind of people they are—how they use this product, and what it is they don't often tell *you* in so many words—but what it is that actually motivates them to buy something or to interest them in something."[4] Focus group interviewing is another approach that tends to generate useful ideas and appropriate words and phrases for use in developing copy.

Fact finding should include a careful discussion of the advertising objectives. The objectives provide the point of departure for the creative process while, at the same time, constraining it. The creative team might properly challenge the constraints implied by the objectives, at least in the early stages of campaign development. In doing so, they might open the way for worthwhile alternatives and provide their own input to formulating objectives. Some solutions to tough problems come only when the focus of the problem is broadened. Thus, the objective need not be viewed as a unilateral, rigid set of constraints, but rather as a flexible,

We Took A Great Idea,

And Made It Fly.

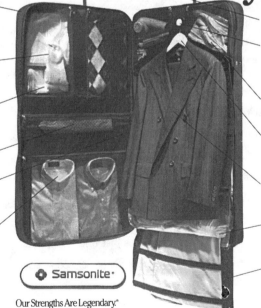

Samsonite's Ultravalet™ Garment Bag is like a closet and chest of drawers in one. And you can carry it on a plane and live right out of it in a hotel room.

With 12 inside pockets, the Ultravalet has a place for everything and keeps everything in its place.

Another nice thing about the pockets is the mesh material that lets you see everything you've packed. You can also get into major pockets from the inside or outside.

There's even a special pocket for ties that helps keep them wrinkle-free.

Unlike most other bags, the Ultravalet opens like a book so you don't have to keep flipping the bag over to pack or unpack.

Thanks to a lot of organized thinking, the Ultravalet is the easiest bag to pack and unpack that we've ever made.

See the Ultravalet at a luggage store soon. And you'll see why it's an idea that's really taking off.

With its special hooks, you can hang the open bag in a closet or on a door and live right out of it.

You'll also appreciate our unique telescoping bar* that pulls out to let you remove suits and dresses without disturbing the ones hanging in front.

Our large, reinforced shoe pockets hold a lot more than shoes.

The bag holds all kinds of hangers so you can pack anything right from the closet.

The Ultravalet folds over backwards,* instead of forwards like other bags, to help keep lapels, sleeves and pockets looking great.

There's also a removable wet pack that keeps wet or soiled items separate from dry ones.

Last but not least, our extended length panel* helps keep longer garments from wrinkling at the bottom.

◆ Samsonite·

Our Strengths Are Legendary.®

For more information and your nearest dealer, call 1-800-262-8282.

*Patent Pending
© 1988 Samsonite Corporation

Figure 13–1.   An ad with a strong creative idea: Samsonite.

Courtesy of Samsonite Corporation.

Introducing TotalTrack. It's like getting live broadcasts from the scene of your package.

Despite what you may have seen on TV, the world's largest staff of on-the-spot reporters isn't at CBS, NBC, ABC, or even CNN. They're at UPS.

Because we've just launched a nationwide cellular tracking system: TotalTrack.

Our 55,000 drivers now carry hand-held computers, while our vehicles are equipped with state-of-the-art cellular technology. So now you can find out the status of any air or designated ground package at any time. We can even confirm delivery in seconds. And only UPS TotalTrack℠ digitally captures the recipient's signature.

Which means that now there's just one thing that travels faster than a UPS package. And that's news of it. **The package delivery company more companies count on.**

Figure 13–2.   An ad with a strong creative idea: UPS.
Courtesy of United Parcel Service.

dynamic guide that is the result of creativity as well as empirical research and managerial experience.

Fact finding should include a digestion and incubation time. The various facts need to be absorbed or "digested," and usually the best ideas emerge only after a period of incubation.

After the information has been digested, *idea generation* is the heart of the creative process. The key is to generate a large quantity of ideas—to avoid inhibiting the process. Evaluating a set of alternatives is a relatively trivial problem next to that of obtaining good alternatives to evaluate. It is somewhat ironic that in refining decision theory very sophisticated methods have been developed to choose among alternatives although we still have only the crudest notion of how to generate alternatives.

Osborn tells of a successful copywriter at BBDO who starts a job by clearing his mind and sitting down at a typewriter and simply writing everything that comes to mind.[5] He even includes silly, worthless phrases with the thought that they will block others if they are not included. In some cases, a piece of copy will be generated on the first try, but, more typically, hundreds of possible ideas will be created before several reasonable alternatives are generated.

There are certain questions that, when posed, can suggest ideas (see Table 13–1).

One of the most fertile is the suggestion to combine various concepts. There have been several systematic approaches proposed to aid the process. One such approach is termed *HIT*, or the *heuristic ideation technique*.[6] Several relevant dimensions of a problem area are identified. For a citrus drink, we might consider the context in which it is used (snack, breakfast, or parties), the benefit it provides (nutrition, preparation ease, color), and the personalities who could endorse it (an athlete, a popular singer, a nutritionist). Then the total set of ideas is the set of all possible combinations of these concepts. Techniques similar to this one have been successful at stimulating new product ideas. One can readily see that products such as toaster waffles, breakfast milkshakes, canned whiskey sours, and aerosol hair sprays could have been conceived with such methods. In a similar vein, some agencies have developed computer-aided name generators. Various words or combinations of letters are systematically combined to provide alternative names for new products.

For some, idea generation comes easier in a group, from which more information and associations are collectively available. The difficulty here is to overcome the inhibiting aspects of group behavior. One technique to encourage the free flow of ideas is *brainstorming*.[7] Developed by Osborn and used regularly at BBDO, it features a group of six to ten people who focus on a problem. The cardinal rule is that criticism is prohibited. All evaluation is withheld until later. The wilder the idea that survives, the better, for it may stimulate a new association that will trigger a more useful idea. The participants are encouraged to build on ideas that appear, combining and improving them. The atmosphere is positive. The objective is quantity. Osborn reported that one such session generated 144 ideas on how to sell blankets.

A related technique, called *synectics,* was developed by William J. J. Gordon.[8]

Table 13–1.   Questions That Spur Ideas for New and Improved Products.

Put to other uses?	New ways to use it? Other uses if modified?
Adapt?	What else is this like? What other ideas does this suggest? Does past offer parallel? What could I emulate?
Modify?	New twist? Changing meaning, color, motion, sound, odor, form, shape? Other changes?
Magnify?	What to add? More time? Greater frequency? Stronger? Higher? Longer? Thicker? Extra value? Plus ingredient? Duplicate? Multiply? Exaggerate?
Minify?	What to subtract? Smaller? Condensed? Miniature? Lower? Shorter? Lighter? Omit? Streamline? Split up? Understate?
Substitute?	Who else instead? What else instead? Other ingredients? Other material? Other process? Other power? Other place? Other approach? Other tone of voice?
Rearrange?	Interchange components? Other pattern? Other layout? Other sequence? Transpose cause and effect? Change pace? Change schedule?
Reverse?	Transpose positive and negative? How about opposites? Turn it backward? Turn it upside down? Reverse roles? Change shoes? Turn tables? Turn other cheek?
Combine?	How about a blend, an alloy, an assortment, an ensemble? Combine units? combine purposes? Combine appeals? Combine ideas?

Source: Philip Kotler, Marketing Management: Analysis, Planning and Control *(Englewood Cliffs, NJ: Prentice Hall, 1967), p. 247, adapted from Alex F. Osborn,* Applied Imagination, *3rd ed. (New York: Scribner's, 1963), pp. 286–287.*

It differs from brainstorming in that it does not focus on a clearly specified problem. Rather, a discussion is stimulated around a general idea that is related to the ultimate specific problem. Instead of being concerned with marketing a citrus beverage, the group might discuss drinking. When a variety of ideas is exposed, the leader starts directing the discussion toward the specific problem. The sessions tend to last longer than the sixty- or ninety-minute brainstorming sessions, based on a belief that fatigue tends to remove inhibitions.

John Keil,[9] in a book on creativity, argues that there are several myths about creativity and creative people, none of which is really supported by the facts. Keil's six myths of creative people are as follows:

1. **Creative people are sophisticated and worldly. They are cultured, well read, and snobbish.**

2. **Creative people are more intelligent than others.**

3. Creative people are disorganized.
4. Creative people are witty and seldom boring.
5. Creative people are more involved with liquor and drugs than others are.
6. Drugs and alcohol stimulate creative thinking.

Like the social stereotypes of any profession, Keil essentially cautions against such stereotyping and argues that creative people have a wide variety of habits, styles, and values. There are boring creative people, as well as witty ones. The incidence of alcoholism and drug abuse in this profession appears no greater than in others such as law or medicine.

The creative process culminates in the specific activities of writing copy, illustrating, and layout. Each of these activities is briefly described in the next sections.

COPYWRITING . . . .

Copywriting, illustrating, and layout are different activities associated with the creative stage of advertising development and are usually done by different people who specialize in one or the other. *Copywriting* in print is the activity of actually putting words to paper, particularly those contained in the main body of the text (the main arguments and appeals used), but also including attendant bylines and headlines. In broadcast, the copywriter is, in effect, a script writer who develops the scenario or script to be used in a radio or television medium; writing a jingle, or the lyrics for music, may also be involved. *Illustrating* is usually the work of an artist in the case of television. *Layout* generally refers to the activity of bringing all the pieces together and, as will be seen, differs in the case of print and broadcast.

How does one write good copy? John Caples is a member of the Advertising Hall of Fame, and his wisdom is worth reading. He retired in 1981 after fifty-four years at Batten, Barton, Durstine & Osborn, the last forty years as vice president. Caples was one of the giants contributing to the success of BBDO. A classic direct-mail advertisement created by Caples is shown in Figure 13–3. Caples states that the best ads are "written from the heart." "Write down every idea that comes into your head, every selling phrase, every key word. Write down the good ideas and the wild ideas. Don't try to edit your ideas at the start. Don't put a brake on your imagination."[10] In his book, he develops a checklist of important guidelines for copywriting:

1. Cash in on your personal experience.
2. Organize your experience.
3. Write from the heart.
4. Learn from the experience of others.
5. Talk with the manufacturer.
6. Study the product.
7. Review previous advertising for the product.
8. Study competitors' ads.
9. Study testimonials from customers.

"Can he really play?" a girl whispered. "Heavens no! Arthur exclaimed. "He never played a note in his life."

They Laughed When I Sat Down At the Piano But When I Started to Play!~

ARTHUR had just played "The Rosary." The room rang with applause. I decided that this would be a dramatic moment for me to make my debut. To the amazement of all my friends, I strode confidently over to the piano and sat down.

"Jack is up to his old tricks," somebody chuckled. The crowd laughed. They were all certain that I couldn't play a single note.

"Can he really play?" I heard a girl whisper to Arthur.

"Heavens, no!" Arthur exclaimed. "He never played a note in all his life. . . But just you watch him. This is going to be good."

I decided to make the most of the situation. With mock dignity I drew out a silk handkerchief and lightly dusted off the piano keys. Then I rose and gave the revolving piano stool a quarter of a turn, just as I had seen an imitator of Paderewski do in a vaudeville sketch.

"What do you think of his execution?" called a voice from the rear.

"We're in favor of it!" came back the answer, and the crowd rocked with laughter.

Then I Started to Play

Instantly a tense silence fell on the guests. The laughter died on their lips as if by magic. I played through the first few bars of Beethoven's immortal Moonlight Sonata. I heard gasps of amazement. My friends sat breathless—spellbound!

I played on and as I played I forgot the people around me. I forgot the hour, the place, the breathless listeners. The little world I lived in seemed to fade—seemed to grow dim—unreal. Only the music was real. Only the music and visions it brought me. Visions as beautiful and as changing as the wind blown clouds and drifting moonlight that long ago inspired the master composer. It seemed as if the master

musician himself were speaking to me—speaking through the medium of music—not in words but in chords. Not in sentences but in exquisite melodies!

A Complete Triumph!

As the last notes of the Moonlight Sonata died away, the room resounded with a sudden roar of applause. I found myself surrounded by excited faces. How my friends carried on! Men shook my hand—wildly congratulated me—pounded me on the back in their enthusiasm! Everybody was exclaiming with delight—plying me with rapid questions. . . . "Jack! Why didn't you tell us you could play like that?". . . "Where did you learn?"—"How long have you studied?"—"Who was your teacher?"

"I have never even seen my teacher," I replied. "And just a short while ago I couldn't play a note."

"Quit your kidding," laughed Arthur, himself an accomplished pianist. "You've been studying for years. I can tell."

"I have been studying only a short while," I insisted. "I decided to keep it a secret so that I could surprise all you folks."

Then I told them the whole story.

"Have you ever heard of the U. S. School of Music?" I asked.

A few of my friends nodded. "That's a correspondence school, isn't it?" they exclaimed.

"Exactly," I replied. "They have a new simplified method that can teach you to play any instrument by mail in just a few months."

How I Learned to Play Without a Teacher

And then I explained how for years I had longed to play the piano.

"A few months ago," I continued, "I saw an interesting ad for the U. S. School of Music—a new method of learning to play which only cost a few cents a day! The ad told how a woman had mastered the piano in her spare time at home—and without a teacher! Best of all, the wonderful new method she used, required no laborious scales—no heartless exercises — no tiresome practising. It sounded so convincing that I filled out the coupon requesting the Free Demonstration Lesson.

"The free book arrived promptly and I started in that very night to study the Demonstration Lesson. I was amazed to see how easy it was to play this new way. Then I sent for the course.

"When the course arrived I found it was just as the ad said — as easy as A.B.C! And, as

the lessons continued they got easier and easier. Before I knew it I was playing all the pieces I liked best. Nothing stopped me. I could play ballads or classical numbers or jazz, all with equal ease! And I never did have any special talent for music!"

Play Any Instrument

You too, can now *teach yourself* to be an accomplished musician—right at home—in half the usual time. You can't go wrong with this simple new method which has already shown 350,000 people how to play their favorite instruments. Forget that old-fashioned idea that you need special "talent." Just read the list of instruments in the panel, decide which one you want to play and the U. S. School will do the rest. And bear in mind no matter which instrument you choose, the cost in each case will be the same—just a few cents a day. No matter whether you are a mere beginner or already a good performer, you will be interested in learning about this new and wonderful method.

Send for Our Free Booklet and Demonstration Lesson

Thousands of successful students never dreamed they possessed musical ability until it was revealed to them by a remarkable "Musical Ability Test" which we send entirely without cost with our interesting free booklet.

If you are in earnest about wanting to play your favorite instrument—if you really want to gain happiness and increase your popularity—send at once for the free booklet and Demonstration Lesson. No cost — no obligation. Right now we are making a Special offer for a limited number of new students. Sign and send the convenient coupon now — before it's too late to gain the benefits of this offer. Instruments supplied when needed, cash or credit. U. S. School of Music, 1631 Brunswick Bldg., New York City.

U. S. School of Music,
1631 Brunswick Bldg., New York City.

Please send me your free book, "Music Lessons in Your Own Home", with introduction by Dr. Frank Crane, Demonstration Lesson and particulars of your Special Offer. I am interested in the following course:

....

Have you above instrument? ....

Name ....
(Please write plainly)

Address ....

City .... State ....

Pick Your Instrument

Piano	'Cello
Organ	Harmony and
Violin	Composition
Drums and	Sight Singing
Traps	Ukulele
Banjo	Guitar
Tenor	Hawaiian
Banjo	Steel Guitar
Mandolin	Harp
Clarinet	Cornet
Flute	Piccolo
Saxophone	Trombone
	Voice and Speech Culture
	Automatic Finger Control
	Piano Accordion

Figure 13–3.   A famous direct-mail advertisement of John Caples.

Source: Advertising Age, *August 1, 1983, p. M50.*

10. **Solve the prospect's problem.**
11. **Put your subconscious mind to work.**
12. **"Ring the changes" on a successful idea.**

Following these rules is good advice in creating copy. The idea of "ring the changes" is particularly useful and interesting. Once a successful idea has been found, it should be used repeatedly with variations on the central theme. For example, an insurance company found that ads featuring retirement annuities brought the most coupon replies. So all the ad headlines featured retirement. However, the appearance of the ads was varied by using different illustrations such as a man fishing . . . a couple sitting on the beach under a palm tree . . . an elderly couple embarking on a cruise ship. As Caples says,

> *Once you have found a winning sales idea, don't change it. Your client may tire of it after a year or two. He sees all the ads from layout stage to proof stage to publication stage. Explain to him that when he is tired of the campaign, it is just beginning to take hold of the public.*[11]

Copywriting obviously becomes more important in the case of long copy and less important in the case where few words are included. Copy should be only as long as necessary to complete the sales job—this means that long copy is often appropriate only for the highly interested reader (such as people contemplating car purchases).

General Copy Principles

While there are no (and should never be any) "rules" for what makes for good copy,[12] it is worthwhile to become familiar with some generally accepted principles. Regardless of the specific ad medium, copy is usually more effective if it is simple, containing only one or two key ideas; contains a benefit or idea unique to the brand being advertised; is *extendible* (can lead to several variations in a campaign); and flows naturally and smoothly from beginning to end.

Good ads are specific, using facts and figures and believable details instead of generalities. An example is the 1993 MCI telephone campaign that offered customers written "proof positive" of the savings they would get every ninety days, compared with those from other phone carriers. Another example is the Toyota ad in Figure 13–4: notice how much more credible the claim about local parts sourcing is because specifics are provided. Another "rule" is to frequently mention the brand name and key consumer benefit; and to conclude the ad by linking back to its beginning, with a strong call to some kind of action.

One overriding rule for developing copy is to keep the format simple, uncluttered, and straightforward. Whether in print or in broadcast, the tendency for including too much information or for complicating the television commercial with too many scene changes, or scenes that are not well integrated, should be avoided. This principle of simplicity extends to the language used as well. Like cluttered format, complicated language is unlikely to induce people to spend the time to "figure it out." The message should always be true to the product. Claims should be sub-

Figure 13–4.   Good use of specifics: Toyota.
Courtesy of Toyota Motor Corporate Services of North America, Inc.

stantiable, and the style should not be radically altered over the life cycle of the product.

Print Copy Principles

For print ads, one of the key elements is the headline, which must flag down the target reader and pull him or her into the body copy, offering a reward for reading on. This is best achieved by headlines that appeal to the reader's self-interest (e.g., by offering free, useful information), are newsy, offer new twists on familiar sayings, and/or evoke curiosity (e.g., by asking a quizlike question).[13] As good examples, see the headlines used in Figures 13–5 and 13–6. It helps if the brand name is mentioned in the headline itself.

Since most people reading print ads never go beyond the headline, it is also extremely important that the headline and visual complement each other so well and "tell the story" so easily, that a reader who only looks at the headline and main visual can "get the message" without having to read a word of the body copy. The choice of the headlines and visuals in the ads in Figures 13–1 and 13–2 earlier have this desirable quality.

As for the body copy itself, it should be detailed and specific (recall Figure 13–4 earlier), support the headline, and be readable and interesting. *Story appeal* is another effective copy device, as can be seen in the Paco Rabanne ad in Figure 13–7 or the John Hancock ad in Figure 13–8. Copy should be only as long as needed to do the selling task (high-involvement purchases may call for detailed copy), but body copy can be made readable by the use of subheads and captions.

As an example of an ad that displays many of these principles, examine the print ad in Figure 13–9. Note that it flags down the target reader (pediatricians), promises them a newsy benefit in the headline, the visual tells the story, specific facts are presented (with a captioned graph), subheads are used, and there is a call-to-action (phone number).

Research by Michael Houston, Terry Childers and Susan Heckler has shown that attribute information is recalled better when it is presented both as a picture and in words (for example, a teddy bear to depict softness in a fabric softener ad) than when it was presented only as words with a different attribute conveyed in the picture. However, this extra recall effect of pictures that exemplify verbal product attribute information appears to occur only when the verbal information is itself of low imagery (does not involve visualization of a concept or relationship).[14] Such imagery or visualization occurs more easily if the ad uses concrete rather than abstract words, if the ad is believable, and if the ad does seem to create more liking for the ad and the brand.[15] The message of the ad is also more memorable if its various parts are consistent rather than inconsistent, for example an ad for ICY vodka from Iceland, showing a bottle apparently made out of ice and using copy reading "Smooth as Ice . . . Icy cold. Icy clear . . ."[16]

Other research has discovered that more imagery is evoked if the picture makes it easy for the consumer to plausibly imagine himself or herself in engaging in that behavior.[17] The effects of an ad's pictures on brand attitudes (liking) seem

Figure 13–5.   A curiosity headline: Turbotax.

Courtesy of Intuit Inc.

Figure 13–6. A newsy, informative headline: Gold Medal Flour.

Reprinted with permission of General Mills, Inc.

Hello:

You snore.

And you stole all the covers. What time did you leave?

Six-thirty. You looked like a toppled Greek statue lying there. Only some tourist had swiped your fig leaf. I was tempted to wake you up.

I miss you already.

You're going to miss something else. Have you looked in the bathroom yet?

Why?

I took your bottle of Paco Rabanne cologne.

What on earth are you going to do with it...give it to a secret lover you've got stashed away in San Francisco?

I'm going to take some and rub it on my body when I go to bed tonight. And then I'm going to remember every little thing about you...and last night.

Do you know what your voice is doing to me?

You aren't the only one with imagination. I've got to go; they're calling my flight. I'll be back Tuesday. Can I bring you anything?

My Paco Rabanne. And a fig leaf.

Paco Rabanne
A cologne for men
What is remembered is up to you

Figure 13–7.   An ad with story appeal: Paco Rabanne.
Courtesy of Paco Rabanne.

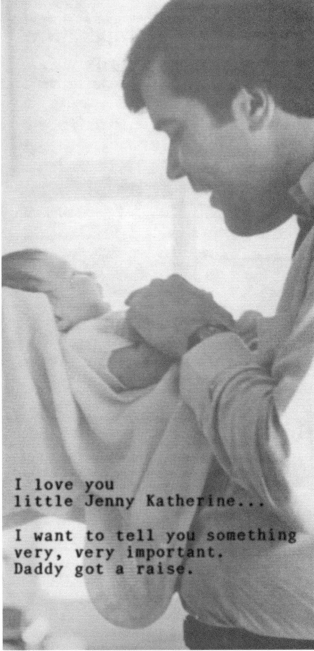

Bill Heater
Age 30
Married, two children

Income
Single Income $35,000

Estimated Expenses
Income tax $8,500
Rent   8,500
Food, Clothing
Insurance   13,000
                 $30,000

Needs
Long-term security
for his family
To build investments

Answer
John Hancock Variable
Life - Insurance with
the following range
of investment options:

Stocks, Bonds,
Money Market,
Aggressive Stocks and
Total Return

Bill Heater is feeling
more at ease about his
family's future since he
invested his raise in
John Hancock Variable
Life. The policy
guarantees Bill a death
benefit while it offers
him the opportunity to
make money through a
variety of investment
options. Plus, he can
change these options as
his needs or market
conditions change.
For more information
about Variable Life,
including charges and
expenses, please contact
your John Hancock
representative for a
prospectus. Read it
carefully before you
invest or send money.

Real life, real answers.

John Hancock
Financial Services

John Hancock Variable Life Insurance Co., Boston, MA 02117

Figure 13–8.   Story appeal: John Hancock.

Courtesy of John Hancock Financial Services.

Technical Breakthrough

Now Take Instant Clinical Temperatures Without Disturbing Your Patients

Say Goodbye to Old-Fashioned Invasive Thermometers

CARLSBAD RESEARCH CENTER, CALIFORNIA—Now you can take temperatures quickly and accurately, with better patient cooperation and no mucous membrane contact, thanks to the latest medical technology.

It's called FirstTemp™: a light, hand-held, all-purpose clinical thermometer from Intelligent Medical Systems.

Fast, Easy to Use and Read

When placed just at the ear's opening, FirstTemp takes an infrared reading from the tympanic membrane in *one second*. This measurement is very accurate, because the tympanic membrane shares the blood

 supply that reaches the hypothalamus (which controls body temperature). The temperature is displayed on a backlit LCD screen.

Reduces Risk of Spreading Orally and Sexually Transmitted Diseases

FirstTemp makes no contagion-spreading contact with mucous membranes. And the probe is covered with a comfortable, disposable speculum that fits adults and infants safely. The covers are applied and ejected without being touched. FirstTemp is a major advance in reducing the risk of spreading orally and sexually transmitted diseases.

Doctors Report Improved Patient Flow, Staff Efficiency

FirstTemp offers new advantages to physicians and hospital personnel: You get the temperature quickly and accurately, while its comfortable, non-invasive nature elicits unprecedented patient compliance.

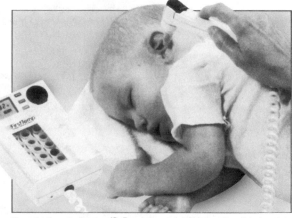

The comfortable, non-invasive nature of FirstTemp elicits unprecedented patient compliance. A sleeping patient—even a baby—can be left undisturbed.   ©1986, Intelligent Medical Systems

Independent Research Supports FirstTemp's Accuracy

In clinical trials at the University of Vermont, FirstTemp was compared to an indwelling Swan-Ganz catheter in the pulmonary artery and to a constant readout rectal thermometer. FirstTemp proved extremely accurate, exhibiting a correlation coefficient of 0.987 and thus upholding the statements of earlier investigators that non-invasive tympanic thermometry will

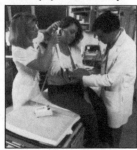

Useful for all ages: In Ambulatory Care, ICU/CCU, ER as well as Pediatrics and NICU.

likely deliver the quickest, most reliable temperature.

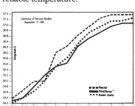

In tests at the University of Vermont, FirstTemp was compared to a Swan-Ganz catheter in the pulmonary artery and an indwelling rectal thermometer. The non-invasive FirstTemp proved extremely accurate, with an overall correlation coefficient of 0.987.

Wide Range Helpful in Hypothermia Cases

FirstTemp's range of 60°F to 110°F (15.5°C to 43.3°C) makes it particularly useful in cases of hypothermia. Both °F and °C readings are available at the flick of a switch.

For more information about First-Temp, call (800) 535-5158 (US) or (800) 628-1414 (California). Clinical references available upon request. □

For More Information, Circle 235 on Quick Response Card.

Figure 13–9.   Good overall print ad: First Temp.

Courtesy of Sherwood Medical.

to increase if they contain product-relevant information, especially for highly involved consumers.[18]

Television Copy Principles

Television scripts (which are discussed further shortly) must usually be written to take advantage of the visual nature of the medium, by using demonstrations, pack close-ups, and the like. The message contained in the pictures is especially important now that many consumers pay only limited attention to advertisements.[19] Since TV ads are fleeting and cannot usually easily communicate much information, simplicity (and frequent and early mention of the brand name and key idea) are strongly recommended. TV ads get higher recall scores if they contain more frequent visual representations of the brand name, package, and key product attributes.

TV ads also get higher persuasion scores if the shots in the ad are more "connected" and better-linked to each other.[20] While there seems to exist a belief that TV ads should use more shots because viewer attention spans are getting shorter—the average number of shots per ad is up from eight in 1978 to thirteen in 1991—research has actually found that as the number of shots per ad goes up, the ad's recall and persuasion scores go down, even among young viewers.[21] Amazingly, it has been found that if the camera angle is such that the product or person appears bigger, stronger or bolder, the ad is evaluated more favorably, though this happens mostly for consumers processing the TV ad in a *low-involvement* fashion (see Chapter 5).[22] It bears repeating, however, that the key factor making for a persuasive TV ad is as simple as the presence of a strong brand-differentiating benefit.[23] While the creative execution is certainly important, if you want a persuasive ad, make sure you've got the right (strong and convincing) message!

Radio Copy Principles

For radio ads, a key principle usually is to write copy that "creates a picture in the mind's eye" of the listener. The radio ad must pull the listener in from whatever is being done when the ad comes on, into an imagined situation, through use of the human voice, sound effects, humor, and music. Research shows that sound effects increase imagery activity and, through that, the evocation of feelings that are not verbally described in the ad. Though it can occasionally be distracting, product-related imagery usually increases the ad's likability and the recall and recognition of ad claims.[24]

It is usually also important in radio to mention the brand name and the key selling benefit early and often. Short words and short sentences are usually easier to understand on the radio. Obviously, radio ads can use various creative tools, and a typology of different kinds of radio ads has been developed.[25] Two examples of humorous award-winning radio ad scripts are presented in Figure 13–10. The ad for Callard and Bowzer illustrates the frequent repetition of the brand name and the use of mnemonic devices, while the ad for the Pork Producers Council illustrates the use of sound effects and dialogue that work on the listener's imagination.

AGENCY: *Lord, Geller, Federico, Einstein, New York*
CLIENT: *Callard & Bowser*
CREATIVE DIRECTOR: *Arthur W. Einstein Jr.*
COPYWRITERS: *Lynn Stiles, John Cleese*
PRODUCERS: *Lynn Stiles, Arthur W. Einstein Jr.*
RECORDING STUDIO: *Molinaire, London*

Plenty of commercials demand attention, but so few of them reward it. With Cleese's absurdly complicated Callard & Bowser spots, you find yourself hanging on every word. Remarkably, in the age of the commercial-zapper, people trust Cleese to make listening worth their while. But the spots are hardly soft-sell. After all, how could you *not* remember the product name after a performance like this?

CLEESE: You know, it's often occurred to me that you're listening to these Callard & Bowser candy commercials while driving the car or doing brain surgery or ironing shirts if you're a man. So how are you going to recall the name Callard & Bowser if you can't write it down? Well, the answer is just remember quack, woof and the letters CB. . . . CB—think of Chicago Bears, or Charlotte Bronte, or even . . . yes, Chauncey Balkin. He's my mother's cousin's uncle's ex-tobacconist—lives in San Diego—don't know whether you know him. If not, perhaps best stick to Charlotte Bronte really. Yes, so you've got quack, woof, Charlotte Bronte. And that's all you need, so off we go, quack, woof, Charlotte Bronte. Quack gives you duck, the duck's a mallard, so the first name starts with a C as in Charlotte and rhymes with mallard—Callard! And the woof gives you dog, the dog's a schnauzer, second name starts with a B as in Bronte and rhymes with schnauzer—Bowser! Callard & Bowser, the name to remember for very special, rather sophisticated English candy. Now if you can't remember quack, woof, Charlotte Bronte, don't rush into candy stores shouting, "Meow, cluck, Louisa May Alcott," . . . just do without.

AGENCY: *Fletcher/Mayo/Associates, Kansas City*
CLIENT: *National Pork Producers Council*
CREATIVE DIRECTOR/AGENCY PRODUCER: *Jeff Wirth*
PRODUCTION COMPANY/COPYWRITERS: *Dick Orkin's Radio Ranch, Hollywood*

Have you noticed that the trade associations for various food commodities have been running some of the cleverest advertising around in recent years? Could be a dissertation topic here for some chow-hound of a marketing student. At any rate, pork is well served by the commercial cited here. The spot will get most of us on its side right away with its reference to that common enemy of dinnertime mankind, the lima bean. (Please—no letters from the Lima Bean Council.) And it goes on from there with a neat interweaving of the sophisticated and the childlike.

ANNOUNCER: Mikey Miller has always been a picky eater.
WOMAN: Mikey, eat your lima beans.
MIKEY: (child's voice) I don't like 'em.
WOMAN: You haven't even tried them.
MIKEY: I don't want to.
WOMAN: Here comes the lima-bean airplane. (airplane noise)
MIKEY: I'm not eating lima beans.
ANNOUNCER: All Mikey wanted to eat was . . .
MIKEY: S'ghetti.
ANNOUNCER: He grew to adulthood, got married, found a job but continued to be just as picky as ever.
MIKEY: (adult voice) What's for dinner?
WIFE: Pork tenderloin with green peppercorn sauce and lima beans.
MIKEY: I hate lima beans.
WIFE: Michael, you haven't even tried them.
MIKEY: I don't like 'em.
WIFE: Here comes the lima-bean choo-choo. Whoo whoo.
MIKEY: (food in his mouth) I don't like lima beans.
WIFE: Well, at least try the pork tenderloin with green peppercorn sauce.
MIKEY: Why can't we have s'ghetti?
WIFE: Mike, you've never even tasted pork tenderloin before, have you?
MIKEY: I don't care.
WIFE: Pork's leaner than ever before. It's juicy. It's tender. Mmmmmmmmm . . .
MIKEY: Then you eat it.
WIFE: Mike, don't you ever get tired of eating the same thing week in and week out? Try the pork tenderloin!
MIKEY: Oh, all right. (takes bite) Oh, this is good.
WIFE: I knew you'd like it.
MIKEY: I'm gonna eat this every day for ever and ever until I die.
WIFE: Which may be very soon.
MIKEY: What?
WIFE: Nothing.

Figure 13–10.   Radio ads using mnemonics and sound effects.

© 1986 ASM Communications, Inc. Used with permission from Adweek.

Outdoor Copy Principles

For outdoor ads, where the message must be communicated in a few seconds, the copy and visual (such as a large pack shot) must be extremely short, simple, strong, and obvious—there is no time for subtlety. Outdoor ads are recalled more if they have fewer words, are about more involving products, are creatively more distinct, and are on the right-hand side of highways than on the left-hand side (from the drivers' perspective).[26]

Retail Copy Principles

Retail ads usually must contain specifics about the merchandise being offered (such as exact sizes, colors, and prices) in order to stimulate immediate buying action. Yet they must also be created in a manner consistent with (and must strive to reinforce) the image of the store. An example of a retail ad was presented earlier, in Chapter 3 (Figure 3–5).

Business-to-Business Ads

Since business-to-business ads are usually written to an audience seeking problem-solving or profit-improving information, they should usually be informative and offer specifics, serious (but not boring), and (ideally) offer case histories of how the advertised brand helped someone else in a similar situation. The software company Lotus, for example, in advertising its Notes product to corporate users, ran ads in September 1993 citing successful adoption by twelve different companies, each named explicitly, with a paragraph describing each specific case. (See Figure 13–11 for another excellent example.)

Long copy ads are good,[27] but they should focus on a single benefit, and it helps if they have a single dramatic image. While the ads need to be factual and informative, they should nonetheless contain some drama or human interest, according to a study by Roper Starch Worldwide.[28] A coupon or phone number can be used to provide more detailed information and generate a lead for a subsequent sales call, either in person or via the telephone.

Advertising on the Internet

As this edition of the book is being written, advertisers are just beginning to advertise on the Internet, the worldwide web of computer networks that promises to become another avenue of electronic commerce. Advertisers set up "home pages" that can be accessed by "web browser" software, and occupy "storefronts" in "on-line malls." It is far too early to tell how advertising will evolve on the Internet, but according to Ogilvy and Mather Direct, one of several agencies venturing in this medium, Internet advertising should not be intrusive, should take place only in designated newsgroups and list servers, should offer full disclosure of what is being sold and under what terms, should only perform consumer research with the consumer's consent, and should not resell consumer data without express user permission.[29]

Figure 13–11. A business-to-business "case history" ad: Digital.

Courtesy of Digital Equipment Corporation.

ILLUSTRATING . . . .

The activity of *illustrating* is of crucial importance for many consumer nondurable products where pictures or photographs are used to convey a central idea, and there is little or no need for long explanations or a recitation of copy points. Normally, an artist will be involved in selecting materials or will actually draw original pictures for the advertising.

Artwork is equally if not more important than writing copy, particularly where the goals of the advertising are attention getting or building awareness. As in writing copy, pictorial materials should be developed that are tied into the self-interest and understanding of the audience, "tell a story" at a glance, are relevant to the product and copy theme, and accurate and plausible in the context of the selling message. Another popular rule is to include pictures of at least some or all of the product.

Illustrating also involves decisions as to what "identification marks" to include. These fall into one of three categories: company or trade name, brand name, and trademarks. In family-branding strategy, the company name, such as Del Monte or Levi Strauss, will obviously play a major role. In other cases, the company name may not even be mentioned or deemphasized, as in many of the detergent brand advertisements of Proctor & Gamble.

The decision regarding brand name will probably have been made prior to actual copywriting, but it may not. A great deal of time and research effort may be required to arrive at the right brand name. Trademarks, service marks, and certification marks like the *Good Housekeeping* seal of approval must also be considered for inclusion in the visual materials. Often a caricature or identifying symbol such as the Pillsbury doughboy, the Green Giant, or Mr. Peanut will be included, and decisions as to how they will be positioned will be required. The visual content, color, artwork, and identification mark decisions are a crucial aspect of print advertising, and choices will heavily determine the effectiveness of the final result.

The United States Trademark Association lists the following as desirable characteristics of a trademark: it is brief, easy to remember, easily readable and speakable, easily adapted to any media, suitable for export, and subtle; has no unpleasant connotations; and lends itself to pictorialization.

Although color ads are assumed to have more impact than black-and-white ads (which usually cost less money to run), Lester Guest provided one of the few studies that examined the differential effect of color.[30] He asked respondents to evaluate companies after being exposed to advertisements. Half the respondents saw a color version of the advertisements and the other half saw a black-and-white version. The ones in color consistently did better across advertisements and years (the study was replicated three times), but the differences were small and usually not statistically significant. Guest concludes that "these studies do not support the contention that companies sponsoring colored advertisements receive a bonus of greater prestige as a consequence of color only."[31]

Many of the same kinds of decisions must be made with respect to the video portion of a television commercial. Here, however, the emphasis is on action and the dynamics of each scene. The director must take into account how one scene will blend into the next, how video materials will serve to enhance and reinforce the audio message, which will be mainly attention-getters, which will carry the copy points, and so on. Chapter 15 has a description of the production of an American Express commercial that illustrates many of these points. The task is further complicated in television by the addition of music or sound effects other than voice.

LAYOUT. . . . .

The *layout* activity involves bringing all the pieces together before the advertising is sent out for production. A layout can be in relatively unfinished form, a *preliminary* layout, or can be a very detailed specification of all aspects of the production requirements, a *comprehensive* layout. (See Chapter 15.) The decision as to how detailed the layout is to be will rest on the agency's trust in the supplier firms. Many agencies choose to send on only preliminary layouts to allow room for a significant amount of creativity in the production process.

Layout involves decisions as to how the various components of headline, illustration, copy, and identification marks are to be arranged and positioned on the page. The size of the advertisement will obviously have an effect on this decision. There are five considerations to take into account in developing print layout:

1. *Balance:* the arrangement of elements to achieve a pleasing distribution or visual impression.
2. *Contrast:* using different sizes, shapes, densities, and colors to enhance attention value and readability.
3. *Proportion:* the relation of objects to the background in which they appear and to each other.
4. *Gaze-motion:* the headline, illustration, copy, and identification marks in that order will usually provide the most logical sequence for gaze-motion (in some cases, however, it may be useful to alter this typical pattern).
5. *Unity:* the qualities of balance, contrast, proportion, and gaze-motion should be combined to develop unity of thought, appearance, and design in the layout. Coupons, for example, should not be placed at the beginning of an advertisement unless the copy theme is built around the idea of clipping the coupon. Unity is best achieved by keeping the layout simple and uncluttered and to ease the reader's task in comprehending the advertisement. Simplicity can be carried forward in many instances by judicious use of "white space" in which most of a large part of the advertisement shows nothing.

Concerning layout, Stephen Baker, an art director, draws a distinction between "arranging elements on a page" and "visualizing an idea." He states

> The former is a designer's (or layout man's) feat; his innate sense of composition, balance, color is brought fully into play. On the other hand, presenting the clearest visual interpretation requires a strong desire to communicate with the audience, a flair for the dramatic, the ability to think in pictorial terms (usually referred to as "visual sense") and, probably most significant, a firm understanding of the advertiser's goal.[32]

Various classifications have been developed for print ad layout styles.[33] These include:

1. *Picture window* (also called Ayer #1): a large picture or illustration with tightly edited copy fitting into the small space alloted to it.
2. *Mondrian/grid:* named after the Dutch painter, these break out space into a series of severely demarcated rectangles or even-sized boxes.
3. *Type-specimen:* these exhibit large type size with no illustration at all.
4. *Copy-heavy:* no illustration, or only a small visual, rely mostly on words.
5. *Frame:* artwork or illustrative material framing the copy (or vice versa).
6. *Silhouette:* the elements form an overall silhouette, or shape, against the background; for example, white space pushed toward the edges of the ad.
7. *Multipanel:* these look like comic-strips.
8. *Circus:* like multipanel, with even more components (e.g., grocery store ads).
9. *Rebus:* photographs, illustrations or diagrams are inserted into the copy, which is usually quite long.

Some research by Chris Janiszewski has shown that the arrangement of ad elements on a page also determines which of the brain's hemispheres processes which element of the ad. Usually, the right hemisphere is better suited for the processing of pictures, and these are better placed on the left side of the page in order to be processed by the right hemisphere. The opposite applies for words. He recommends that if the key information in the ad consists of certain verbal claims, the ad will be more effective if the pictorial attention-grabbers are placed to the right of those key verbal claims, and verbal attention grabbers are placed to the left of those key verbal claims. Such an arrangement will lead to less interference in the processing of the key verbal claims, because each of the attention-grabbing kind of information will be sent to the inappropriate hemisphere (pictures to the left hemisphere instead of the right, words to the right instead of the left).[34]

The layout of a television commercial is the storyboard; various examples of storyboards have appeared in earlier chapters. Here, again, it can be generated in a relatively primitive form, in which only artist sketches and suggestive copy are included, or in a more comprehensive form that details more precisely what actors are to say, how scenes will blend in, and the precise location of identification marks, background music, special effects, and so on. The copy/art team creating a TV commercial will indicate the nature of the camera shots and camera movements, the level and type of music, and so on. Of course, much will change as the commercial is actually shot and then edited, by the director selected for the commercial (see Chapter 15).[35]

TYPES OF TELEVISION COMMERCIALS . . . .

Audio and visual elements can be combined to produce several types of television commercials, just as a story can be told in many different ways. Emphasis can be placed on the story itself, on the problem to be solved, on the central character such as in a testimonial, or on special human emotions or storytelling techniques such as satire, humor, fantasy, and so on. Albert Book and Norman Cary[36] provide a useful classification of the possible alternatives, based on the point of emphasis, focus, or style adopted. Each is referred to as a particular kind of commercial structure to emphasize that a commercial is other than an unrelated jumble of ideas and techniques. The thirteen types of structure identified by them follow:

1. *Story line:* a commercial that tells a story; a clear, step-by-step unfolding of a message that has a definite beginning, middle, and end.

2. *Problem-solution:* presents the viewer with a problem to be solved and the sponsor's product as the solution to that problem. Probably the most widely used and generally accepted example of a TV commercial.

3. *Chronology:* delivers the message through a series of related scenes, each one growing out of the one before. Facts and events are presented sequentially as they occurred.

4. *Special effects:* no strong structural pattern; strives for and often achieves memorability through the use of some striking device, for example, an unusual musical sound or pictorial technique.

5. *Testimonial:* also called word-of-mouth advertising; it uses well-known figures or an unknown "man in the street" to provide product testimonials.

6. *Satire:* a commercial that uses sophisticated wit to point out human foibles, generally produced in an exaggerated style; parodies on James Bond movies, *Bonnie and Clyde*, *Hair*, and the like.

7. *Spokesperson:* the use of an on-camera announcer who, basically, "talks." Talk may be fast and hard sell or more personal, intimate sell.

8. *Demonstration*: uses some physical apparatus to demonstrate a product's effectiveness. Analgesic, watch, and tire commercials employ this approach heavily.

9. *Suspense:* somewhat similar to story-line or problem-solution structures, but the buildup of curiosity and suspense to the final resolution is given a heightened sense of drama.

10. *Slice-of-life*: a variation on problem solution; begins with a person at the point of, and just before the discovery of, an answer to a problem. This approach is heavily used by detergent manufacturers.

11. *Analogy:* offers an extraneous example, then attempts to relate it to the product message. Instead of delivering a message simply and directly, an analogy uses one example to explain another by comparison or implication: "Just as vitamins tone up your body, our product tones up your car's engine."

12. *Fantasy:* uses caricatures or special effects to create fantasy surrounding product and product use: Jolly Green Giant, White Knight, White Tornado, the washing machine that becomes 10 feet tall.

13. *Personality:* a technical variation of the spokesperson or announcer-on-camera, straight-sell structure. Relies on an actor or actress rather than an announcer to deliver the message. Uses a setting rather than the background of a studio. The actor plays a character who talks about the product, reacts to its use, or demonstrates its use or enjoyment directly to the camera.

These structures are, of course, not mutually exclusive, but rather serve to provide points of focus for analysis, copy production, and research. For example, in testimonials and, perhaps, in spokesperson and demonstration commercials, the credibility of source and/or the mode of presentation are likely to be most important. Customer reactions to source could receive special attention, utilizing the ideas on source credibility given earlier in Chapter 12. In story-line, problem solution, and perhaps the chronology and analogy structures, focus would tend to center more on the type of argument (for example, one- versus two-sided or refutation) or the order of argument (primacy-recency, stating a conclusion) dimensions. Each of these seven types of commercials also tends to be more factual in orientation.

The remaining six types all are more emotional in orientation and can be distinguished on the basis of whether the emotion-arousing capacity or the *characterization* being used relates to source or message. The personality and slice-of-life structures, for example, are likely to be more source oriented. The choice of the personality to be used or the characters who will play the role in the slice-of-life situation are emphasized. The special effects, fantasy, satire, and suspense structures are all fundamentally emotional in orientation. Special effects, for example, might be used to arouse emotions with respect to fear, sex, or status. The principal objective would be emotional arousal, and interest would center on whether the particular emotion was evoked in the target consumer.

A slightly different typology has been developed by Henry Laskey, Ellen Day, and Melvin Crask. They divide TV ads into two main types of Informational versus Transformational (see Chapter 9 for a discussion of these terms). Informational commercials are then subdivided into comparative; those using a unique selling proposition; "preemptive"; generic/product class; and those using hyperbole. Transformational ads are classified as either generic; based on the use-occasion; using brand image; or communicating user image.[37]

CREATIVE STYLES . . . .

As has already been suggested, creating advertising is a little like creating art. Two artists viewing the same scene may paint it quite differently, but both can produce high-quality paintings and "effective" products. In this portion of the chapter, several of the creative giants of advertising and examples of their work are presented. An important factor that tends to distinguish them is the nature of the product or market situation. As will be seen, however, there are points of emphasis and style that tend to characterize the approach and make it recognizable.

Just as an art critic can distinguish a Picasso from a Monet, so an experienced copy director can distinguish the work of a David Ogilvy from that of a Leo Burnett. The styles of creative giants in advertising have, over time, become exaggerated to the point of caricature. Furthermore, right or wrong, their approaches become associated with a considerable amount of advertising of the agency with which they are associated. Thus, any description of their creative style may tend to be exaggerated. Such an exaggeration is useful for our purposes, however, because it helps to illustrate the diversity among creative teams in the advertising profession.

The first set of examples profiles the works of David Ogilvy, William Bernbach, Rosser Reeves, and Leo Burnett. These creative giants have had major impacts on advertising over the years, and it is useful to study their styles and classic examples of their work. This is followed by three copy directors who have achieved prominence and recognition in recent years: Philip Dusenberry, Lee Clow, and Hal Riney. Each has had a major impact on the creative output of the advertising agencies with which they are associated and, in many respects, represent the state of the art in advertising in the 1990s.

David Ogilvy: The Brand Image

David Ogilvy—who, now retired from the business, lives in a chateau in France—is most concerned with the *brand image.* Due in part to the nature of the products with which he works, this usually means that he is concerned with developing and retaining a prestige image. He argues that, in the long run, it pays to protect a favorable image even if some appealing short-run programs are sacrificed in the process. In his words,

> *Every advertisement should be thought of as a contribution to the complex symbol which is the brand image. If you take that long view, a great many day-to-day problems solve themselves. . . . Most of the manufacturers who find it expedient to change the image of their brand want it changed upward. Often it has acquired a bargain-basement image, a useful asset in time of economic scarcity, but a grave embarrassment in boom days, when the majority of consumers are on their way up the social ladder. It isn't easy to perform a face-lifting operation on an old bargain-basement brand. In many cases it would be easier to start again, with a fresh new brand. . . . A steady diet of price-off promotions lowers the esteem in which the consumer holds the product; can anything which is always sold at a discount be desirable?*[38]

Ogilvy goes on to say that the personality of the brand is particularly important if brands are similar:

> *The greater the similarity between brands, the less part reason plays in brand selection. There isn't any significant difference between the various brands of whiskey, or cigarettes, or beer. They are all about the same. And so are the cake mixes and the detergents, and the margarines. The manufacturer who dedicates his advertising to building the most sharply defined personality for his brand will get the largest share of the market at the highest profit. By the same token, the manufacturers who will find themselves up the creek are those shortsighted opportunists who siphon off their advertising funds for promotions.*[39]

When Ogilvy obtained the Puerto Rico account, he indicated that what was needed was to "substitute a lovely image of Puerto Rico for the squalid image which now exists in the minds of most mainlanders."[40]

One of the most distinctive aspects of many of Ogilvy's most well-known campaigns is the use of prestigious individuals to convey the desired image for the product. In two cases he actually used clients to represent their own products: Commander Whitehead for Schweppes Tonic and Helena Rubinstein for her line of cosmetics. One of the original advertisements for the Schweppes campaign is shown in Figure 13–12. Others he "created" or developed from individuals or ideas not explicitly part of the original company. One of the most successful was the

The man from Schweppes is here

MEET Commander Edward White-head, Schweppesman Extraordinary from London, England, where the House of Schweppes has been a great institution since 1794.

The Commander has come to these United States to make sure that every drop of Schweppes Quinine Water bottled over here has the original bittersweet flavor essential for an authentic Gin-and-Tonic.

He imports the original Schweppes elixir and the secret of Schweppes unique carbonation is securely locked in his brief case. "Schwepper-vescence," says the Commander, *"lasts the whole drink through."*

Schweppes Quinine Water makes your favorite drink a truly patrician potion—and Schweppes is now available at popular prices throughout Greater New York.

Figure 13–12.   An early advertisement for Schweppes.

Courtesy of Schweppes U.S.A. Limited.

campaign for Hathaway shirts in which a male character with an eye patch was featured. Ogilvy tells how the campaign evolved, for a product with an initial advertising budget of only $30,000.

> *I concocted eighteen different ways to inject this magic ingredient of "story appeal." The eighteenth was the eye patch. At first we rejected it in favor of a more obvious idea, but on the way to the studio I ducked into a drugstore and bought an eye patch for $1.50. Exactly why it turned out to be so successful, I shall never know. It put Hathaway on the map after 116 years of relative obscurity. Seldom, if ever, has a national brand been created so fast, or at such low cost. . . . As the campaign developed, I showed the model in a series of situations in which I would have liked to find myself: conducting the New York Philharmonic at Carnegie Hall, playing the oboe, copying a Goya at the Metropolitan Museum, driving a tractor, fencing, sailing, buying a Renoir, and so forth.*[41]

Ogilvy will, when possible, obtain testimonials from celebrities. Usually their fee will go to their favorite charity. Thus, Ogilvy has used Queen Elizabeth and Winston Churchill in "Come to Britain" advertisements and Mrs. Franklin Roosevelt saying that Good Luck margarine really tastes delicious. His agency, Ogilvy & Mather (now part of the WPP Group) continued this approach in the 1980s for American Express in a print campaign showing interesting photographs of famous celebrities who were card members, with no copy but for the line "Member since 19xx" (see Chapter 10). A campaign for the *Reader's Digest* featured many national figures explaining that they relied on such a magazine because of their busy schedules.

Ogilvy, in addition to being very creative, is also research-oriented. He looks to the experiences of direct-mail advertisers and the various advertising readership services for possible generalizations. He also looks to his colleagues and competitors for insights. From these sources he puts forth various guides, rules, and commandments for the creation of advertising by his staff. The following are his eleven commandments for creating advertising campaigns.

> 1. *What you say is more important than how you say it. Two hundred years ago Dr. Johnson said, "Promise, large promise is the soul of an advertisement." When he auctioned off the contents of the Anchor Brewery he made the following promise: "We are not here to sell boilers and vats, but the potentiality of growing rich beyond the dreams of avarice."*
> 2. *Unless your campaign is built around a great idea, it will flop.*
> 3. *Give the facts. The consumer isn't a moron; she is your wife. You insult her intelligence if you assume that a mere slogan and a few vapid adjectives will persuade her to buy anything. She wants all the information you can give her.*
> 4. *You cannot bore people into buying. We make advertisements that people want to read. You can't save souls in an empty church.*
> 5. *Be well mannered, but don't clown.*

6. *Make your advertising contemporary.*

7. *Committees can criticize advertisements, but they cannot write them.*

8. *If you are lucky enough to write a good advertisement, repeat it until it stops pulling. Sterling Getchel's famous advertisement for Plymouth ("Look at All Three") appeared only once and was succeeded by a series of inferior variations which were quickly forgotten. But the Sherwin Cody School of English ran the same advertisement ("Do You Make These Mistakes in English?") for 42 years, changing only the typeface and the color of Mr. Cody's beard.*

9. *Never write an advertisement which you wouldn't want your own family to read. Good products can be sold by honest advertising. If you don't think the product is good, you have no business to be advertising it. If you tell lies, or weasel, you do your client a disservice, you increase your load of guilt, and you fan the flames of public resentment against the whole business of advertising.*

10. *The image and the brand: it is the total personality of a brand rather than any trivial product difference which decides its ultimate position in the market.*

11. *Don't be a copy cat. Nobody has ever built a brand by imitating somebody else's advertising. Imitation may be the "sincerest form of plagiarism," but it is also the mark of an inferior person.*[42]

William Bernbach: Execution

Perhaps the most exciting agency in the 1960s and 1970s was the one William Bernbach established in 1949, Doyle Dane Bernbach (now, as DDB Needham, part of the Omnicom group). It has been enormously successful although apparently violating several well-established dictums of the advertising business. One of the most sacred laws in evaluating an advertisement is to determine if it really communicates a persuasive message or if it is merely clever or memorable. The primary job of an advertisement is to sell-to communicate a persuasive message. David Ogilvy's first rule for copywriters is "What you say is more important than how you say it." Bernbach replied that "execution can become content, it can be just as important as what you say . . . a sick guy can utter some words and nothing happens; a healthy vital guy says them and they rock the world."[43] In the Bernbach style, the execution dominates.

To say that Bernbach emphasized execution is, of course, a rather incomplete description of his style. What kind of execution? Although it is difficult to verbalize such an approach because it does not lend itself to rules, there are certain characteristics that can be identified. First, Bernbach did not talk down to an audience. An audience is respected. As Jerry Della Femina, a colorful advertising executive, put it: "Doyle Dane's advertisement has that feeling that the consumer is bright enough to understand what the advertising is saying, that the consumer isn't a lunkhead who has to be treated like a twelve year old."[44] The copy is honest. Puffery is avoided, as are clichés and heavy repetition. The advertising demands attention and has something to say. Second, the approach is clean and direct. Bernbach pointed out that "you must be as simple, and as swift and as penetrating as possible. . . . What you must do, by the most economical and creative means possible, is attract people and sell them."[45] Third, the advertisement should stand out from others. It should have its own character. In Bernbach's words,

> *Why should anyone look at your ad? The reader doesn't buy his magazine or tune in his radio and TV to see and hear what you have to say. . . . What is the use of saying all the right things in the world if nobody is going to read them? And, believe me, nobody is going to read them if they are not said with freshness, originality and imagination . . . If they are not, if you will, different.*[46]

Finally, the often repeated rule that humor does not sell is ignored. Doyle Dane Bernbach frequently uses humor to gain attention and to provide a positive reward to an advertisement reader. Robert Fine, one of Bernbach's copywriters, said

> *We recognize that an advertisement is an intrusion. People don't necessarily like advertisements, and avoid them if possible. Therefore, to do a good advertisement you're obligated, really, to reward the reader for his time and patience in allowing you to interrupt the editorial content, which is what he bought the magazine for in the first place. This is not defensive. It just takes into account the fact that an advertisement pushes its way uninvited into somebody's mind. So entertainment is sort of repayment.*[47]

Doyle Dane Bernbach deemphasizes research, believing that it tends to generate advertisements too similar to those of competitors. The assumptions are that others are doing the same type of research, interpreting it the same way, and generating the same policy implications. In Bernbach's words,

> *One of the disadvantages of doing everything mathematically, by research, is that after a while, everybody does it the same way. . . . If you take the attitude that once you* have *found out what to say, your job is done, then what you're doing is saying it the same way as everybody is saying it, and you've lost your impact completely.*[48]

One of Bernbach's first accounts in 1949 was Levy's bread, a relatively unknown New York bread. Bernbach developed radio spots that featured an unruly child asking his mother for "Wevy's Cimmanon Waison Bwead" and getting his pronunciation corrected. In addition, subway posters were used. One showed three slices of bread, one uneaten, one with a few bites gone, and the third with only the crust remaining. The copy read simply "New York Is Eating It Up! Levy's Real Jewish Rye." Without using a single product claim, Levy's bread reportedly became one of the best known brands in town.[49] An ad from the campaign appears in Figure 13–13.

Doyle Dane Bernbach also generated the now-classic Avis campaign (see Figure 6–10).[50] The "We're Number 2, We Try Harder" campaign was effective for vari-

You don't have to be Jewish

to love Levy's
real Jewish Rye

Figure 13–13.   One of Bernbach's ads for Levy's bread.

Courtesy of Best Foods, Inc.

ous reasons. It dared to admit that a firm was indeed in second place. At the same time, it turned this fact to advantage by indicating that a customer could expect better because Number 2 would naturally tend to try harder. It was the perfect application of two-sided communication: state the opposing position first (Hertz is the largest), and then rebut it (we try harder). The campaign was supported by red "We Try Harder" buttons and by a real effort to improve the Avis service. The service was affected, in part, owing to the impact of the campaign on Avis employees. Ironically, despite the fact that the campaign was directed at the giant Hertz, the impact fell primarily on Avis's other competitors. When the campaign began, Avis and National were neck and neck and Hertz was ahead. The campaign made the rent-a-car industry seem to be a two-firm affair. As a result, National and the other competitors were damaged much more than Hertz. In fact, because primary demand was stimulated, Hertz probably benefited from the Avis advertisements. The campaign received an impetus when Hertz decided to reply directly. This reply, which was a controversial strategy, was perhaps the first time the top dog actually recognized a competitor publicly. The strategy was triggered in part by a need to boost the morale of Hertz employees. This whole situation is a good example of how advertising has an impact on employees, which usually is not considered in campaign planning.

It was the Volkswagen campaign that really established the Bernbach approach. As Jerry Della Femina said, "In the beginning there was Volkswagen."[51] It ushered in a decade of the hot, creative agencies that attempted to duplicate the Doyle Dane Bernbach success. The Volkswagen advertisements, like many Doyle Dane Bernbach advertisements, almost always had a large photograph of the product in a setting with a headline and copy below. The headline was usually provocative and tempted readers to continue to the copy. One advertisement showed steam coming out of a nonexistent radiator with the caption "Impossible." A headline under a picture of a flat tire read "Nobody's Perfect." Several advantages of the car were listed under the headline "Ugly is only skin-deep." The two real classics were the lines "Think Small" and "Lemon."

The Lemon advertisement was particularly noteworthy. (See Figure 13–14.) Many of the advertisements directly disparaged the product, an approach that was frowned on in many circles and never used to the extent it was in the Volkswagen campaign. Even for the Volkswagen campaign, Lemon was extreme and was approved by the Volkswagen management only after some tribulation. The copy went on to identify a defect caught by 1 of 3,389 inspectors and discussed the elaborate quality-assurance program of the firm.

The campaign eventually moved into television. One of the early television advertisements was described as follows:

> *The camera looks through the windshield of a car traveling on a dark, snow-covered country road. Heavy loads of fresh snow bend down pine and fir branches. No announcer's voice is heard; the only sound is that of an engine prosaically purring along. In shot after shot the headlights illuminate the falling snow ahead, piling up deeper on the winding, climbing, untracked road. Robert Frost's haunting lines about the woods on a snowy night are inevitably evoked. Curiosity and a measure of suspense are created: Who is driving and where? What errand has taken him out on such a night? Finally the headlights swing off by a large dark building and are switched off. A high door opens and a powerful snowplow rolls past as the announcer's voice begins, "Have you ever wondered how the man who drives the snowplow drives to the snowplow? This one drives a Volkswagen. So you can stop wondering."*[52]

The Volkswagen advertising was particularly fresh when contrasted with the competition. Most Detroit advertising, for example, tended to use drawings rather than photographs so that the impression of elegance could be enhanced. Their copy tended to be rather predictable and bland. The Volkswagen use of photographs, which very realistically set forth the product in all its commonness, and its copy with a tendency to laugh at itself, had to be refreshing.

The campaign was by any measure a phenomenal success. Sales climbed impressively, even when the domestic compacts were introduced, and other foreign cars were severely hurt. The advertising undoubtedly contributed to sales performance. The advertisements were consistently well read, even, on occasion, sub-

Lemon.

This Volkswagen missed the boat.

The chrome strip on the glove compartment is blemished and must be replaced. Chances are you wouldn't have noticed it; Inspector Kurt Kroner did.

There are 3,389 men at our Wolfsburg factory with only one job: to inspect Volkswagens at each stage of production. (3000 Volkswagens are produced daily; there are more inspectors than cars.)

Every shock absorber is tested (spot checking won't do), every windshield is scanned. VWs have been rejected for surface scratches barely visible to the eye.

Final inspection is really something! VW inspectors run each car off the line onto the Funktionsprüfstand (car test stand), tote up 189 check points, gun ahead to the automatic brake stand, and say "no" to one VW out of fifty.

This preoccupation with details means the VW lasts longer and requires less maintenance, by and large, than other cars. (It also means a used VW depreciates less than any other car.)

We pluck the lemons; you get the plums.

Figure 13–14.   **A classic Volkswagen ad from Bernbach.**

Copyrighted by, and reproduced with the permission of, VW of America, Inc.

stantially outscoring cover stories and editorial features.[53] They were talked about by the man in the street and won all sorts of creative awards in the profession. The Volkswagen story is a good illustration of the Bernbach approach to copywriting.

Rosser Reeves: The USP

Especially under the scrutiny of advertising critics, it is considerably easier to justify or explain advertising that is clever, tasteful, and entertaining than advertising that is not so described. In that regard, the approaches of Ogilvy or Bernbach are somewhat easier to defend than the style attributed to Rosser Reeves of the Ted Bates agency (now part of Backer Spielvogel Bates, itself part of the Saatchi group). Reeves did not, of course, try to produce advertising that is not tasteful, but he did make it clear that he wrote not for esthetic appeal but to create sales. He challenged the "artsy, craftsy crowd" by observing, "I'm not saying that charming, witty and warm copy won't sell. I'm just saying that I've seen thousands of charming, witty campaigns that didn't sell."[54]

His conception of the appropriate role of advertising is illustrated in the following questions he posed:

> *Let's say you have $1,000,000 tied up in your little company and suddenly, for reasons unknown to you, your advertising isn't working and your sales are going down. And everything depends on it, your family's future depends on it, other people's families depend on it. And you walk in this office and talk to me, and you sit in that chair. Now, what do you want out of me? Fine writing? Do you want masterpieces? Do you want glowing things that can be framed by copywriters? Or do you want to see the . . . sales curve stop moving down and start moving up? What do you want?*[55]

Reeves was particularly critical of approaches in which the copy is so clever that it distracts from the message. Reeves proposed that each product develop its own *unique selling proposition (USP)* and use whatever repetition is necessary to communicate the USP to the audience. There are three guidelines to the development of a USP. First, the proposition needs to involve a specific product benefit. Second, it must be unique, one that competing firms are not using. Third, it must sell. It therefore must be important enough to the consumer to influence the decision process. The most successful USPs such as "M&M candies melt in your mouth instead of your hand" result from identifying real inherent product advantages. The determination of a USP generally requires research on the product and on consumer use of the product. When a good USP is found, the development of the actual advertisement is a relatively easy process. Among Ted Bates' USPs are "Colgate cleans your breath as it cleans your teeth," "Viceroys have 20,000 filter traps," and "Better skin from Palmolive."

Reeves relied heavily on product research to support specific claims. This support often took the form of rather elaborate experiments. The research tended to be reliable in the sense that others, if they wished, could replicate it and generate similar conclusions. In one case, Ted Bates and Colgate spent $300,000 to prove that washing the face thoroughly (for a full minute) with Palmolive soap would improve the skin.[56] The concern over support of claims is, of course, a useful precaution to avoid FTC action. Reeves did not obtain the documentation only for legal purposes. The fact is that good research can be used to help make the claim more credible.

Once an effective USP is found, Reeves believed that it should be retained practically indefinitely. Such a philosophy requires vigorous defending, especially when a client gets tired of a campaign, which usually happens before the campaign even starts. One client asked Reeves, "You have seven hundred people in that office of yours, and you've been running the same advertisement for me for the last eleven years. What I want to know is, what are those seven hundred people supposed to be doing?" Reeves replied, "They're keeping your advertising department from changing your advertisement."[57] According to Reeves, Anacin spent over $85 million in a ten-year period on one advertising commercial. Reeves pointed out that the commercial "cost $8,200 to produce and it made more money than *Gone With the Wind*."[58] The psychological learning theories with their emphasis on habit formation via repetition provide some theoretical support for the use of heavy repetition in advertising.

The Reeves approach was undoubtedly successful. However, the approach is highly controversial. People object to the style and to the repetition. The use of a USP is particularly troublesome in political campaigns, when many feel that a more thorough discussion of issues is appropriate. In 1952, the Reeves approach was applied to the Eisenhower campaign.[59] Reeves made a set of twenty-second spot commercials for Eisenhower. They all started with the statement "Eisenhower Answers the Nation." Then an ordinary citizen would ask a question such as, "What about the high cost of living?" Eisenhower would then reply. To the cost-of-living question, he said, "My wife, Mamie, worries about the same thing. I tell her its our job to change that on November fourth." Such advertisements may have been effective, but they created a storm of controversy about the nature of political advertising campaigns that exists to this day.

Leo Burnett: The Common Touch

The Leo Burnett agency differs from other larger agencies in that it is not located in New York but, rather, in Chicago. Perhaps partially because of that, it is associated with the common touch. Burnett often used plain ordinary people in his advertisements. The Schlitz campaign featured a neighborhood bartender. A Maytag advertisement showed a grandmother with thirteen grandchildren and a vintage Maytag. In that respect he contrasts rather vividly with David Ogilvy. Burnett put it this way:

> *As I have observed it, great advertising writing either in print or television, is always deceptively and disarmingly simple. It has the common touch without being or sounding patronizing. If you are writing about baloney, don't try to make it sound like Cornish hen, because that is the worst kind of baloney there is. Just make it darned good baloney.*

Not only is great copy "deceptively simple"—but so are great ideas. And if it takes a rationale to explain an ad or a commercial—then it's too complicated for that "dumb public" to understand.

I'm afraid too many advertising people blame the public's inability to sort out commercial messages or advertisements in magazines on stupidity. What a lousy stupid attitude to have! I believe the public is unable to sort out messages, not just because of the sheer flood of messages assaulting it every day, but because of sheer boredom! *If the public is bored today—then let's blame it on the fact that it is being handed boring messages created by bored advertising people. In a world where nobody seems to know what's going to happen next, the only thing to do to keep from going completely nuts from frustration is plain old-fashioned work! Having worked many, many years for peanuts and in obscurity, I think I know how a lot of writers feel today and I sympathize with them, but I also wonder if a lot of writers aren't downright spoiled.*[60]

Burnett further described his orientation by indicating that the best copywriters have "a flair for expression, putting known and believable things into new relationships. . . . We [the Chicago school of advertising] try to be more straightforward without being flatfooted. We try to be warm without being mawkish."[61] The key words are warm and believable. The approach aims for believability with warmth.

In the spirit of providing a common touch, Burnett looks for the "inherent drama" of a product—the characteristic that made the manufacturer make it, that makes the people buy it. The objective is to capture the inherent drama and make it "arresting itself rather than relying upon tricks."[62] Burnett is impatient with a dull factual recitation or a cleverness with words or a "highfaluting rhapsody of plain bombast."[63] The preferable approach is to dig out the inherent drama and present it in a warm, realistic manner. The inherent drama is "often hard to find, but it is always there, and once found it is the most interesting and believable of all advertising appeals."[64]

The Green Giant Company has been with Burnett since the agency was established in 1935. One early advertisement illustrates the use of the inherent drama concept. Burnett wanted to communicate the fact that Green Giant peas were of good quality and fresh. He used a picture of a night harvest with the caption "Harvested in the Moonlight" and included an insert of the giant holding a pod of peas. As Burnett states, "It would have been easy to say, 'Packed Fresh' in the headline, but 'Harvested in the Moonlight' had both news value and romance, and connoted a special kind of care which was unusual to find in a can of peas."[65] A series of four advertisements that featured paintings by Norman Rockwell also were used in early campaigns. One showed a farm kitchen with a boy enjoying a platter of corn on the cob. Jerry Della Femina comments on the Green Giant campaign:

Burnett even tells people what a corny agency he has, but he's not corny. He is a very brilliant man. . . . That Jolly Green Giant is fantastic. He sells beans, corn, peas, everything. When you watch the Jolly Green Giant, you know it's fantasy and yet you buy the product. Do you know what Libby does? I don't. Most food advertising is like gone by the boards, you don't even see it. But the Jolly Green Giant, it's been automatic success when he's on the screen.[66]

The Pillsbury account arrived in 1945. One series of advertisements was termed the Pillsbury "big cake campaign." A large picture of a cake with several slices removed dominated the advertisements, another example of inherent drama: letting an appetizing picture do the selling. The Marlboro campaign started in the mid-1950s. The Marlboro cowboy, the tattoo, the Marlboro Country approach is still going strong and is probably considered one of the classic campaigns. The country flavor and the use of the tattoo provided the common touch. Another early product that used the common touch was Kellogg's cereal. For example, in the campaign for Kellogg's corn flakes, the headline "the best to you each morning" was used in conjunction with an appealing human interest photo (see Figure 13–15).

In what follows, several creative directors who have achieved prominence in recent years are profiled, and some of their well-known agency styles are discussed. It is interesting and useful to compare and contrast them with David Ogilvy, William Bernbach, Rosser Reeves, and Leo Burnett. We will also provide some insights into their lifestyles, their particular approaches to creating advertising, and the agencies with which they are associated.

Philip Dusenberry: Entertainment and Emotion

Producing television commercials can be dangerous! During the shooting of a commercial for Pepsi-Cola in 1984, the central figure, the well-known rock star Michael Jackson, was injured when his hair caught on fire. Although obviously unplanned, it became a national news event. Philip Dusenberry, vice chairman and executive creative director of Batten, Barton, Durstine & Osborn, was the person responsible for development of this famous campaign. Another Dusenberry–BBDO effort was an eighteen-minute film of President Reagan shown at the Republican Convention in the summer of 1984 before the president's acceptance speech. The film showed people, all presumably Reagan supporters, getting married, eating ice cream cones, delivering newspapers, and generally feeling "proud to be an American." According to Dusenberry, too much mention of issues is simply "boring." The film was intended to appeal to the viewer's sense of pride and the needs for developing feelings of patriotism and loyalty. This film also became national news when the networks refused to air it. The criticism was that it did not address the issues and lacked balance.

Dusenberry advocates flexibility and "shunning of the familiar" as basic tenets for good creative strategy. "Don't get too happy too soon with the first idea that comes into your head." His style is one that tries to make heavy use of emotion and warmth, and to create commercials that are very entertaining, through the use of star endorsers and star commercial directors (such as Bob Giraldi, who directed the Pepsi commercials with Michael Jackson). He uses the latest cine-

"*All us men eat Kellogg's Corn Flakes.*"

"The best to you each morning"

Best liked (*World's favorite*)

...Best flavor (*Kellogg's secret*)

...Worst to run out of

Kellogg's CORN FLAKES

© 1958 by Kellogg Company

Figure 13–15.   A Kellogg's Corn Flakes advertisement.

Courtesy of the Kellogg Company.

matic techniques, including rapid cutting and eye-catching visual images and tries out special effects worthy of Steven Spielberg or George Lucas. One Pepsi commercial, called "Archeology," won the top advertising prize at the International Film Festival at Cannes, the industry's most coveted award, and several others. It shows a twenty-third-century teacher leading a class through the ruins of a twentieth-century home. The class comes across a Coke bottle, and asks what it is. The puzzled teacher doesn't know, as the screen reveals the phrase "Pepsi, the choice of a new generation."[67] Most of his work focuses more on the people who use a product and on the benefits or enjoyments it brings than on the product itself. It is characteristic of this style to "elevate people above the product" and to use people in lively and engaging situations. In the Pepsi campaign, the emphasis is on "Pepsi people," for example. This approach is especially clear in his ads for General Electric, in which warm, homey images are used to say that "GE brings good things to life." This style does have its critics—some in the industry say his work relies too heavily on stars and does little to promote the attributes of the product it is supposed to sell.

Dusenberry has been described as a "rabid baseball fan" and one-time aspiring big league catcher. Among his many other accomplishments is a screenplay he wrote called *The Natural*. It met nothing but rejections before catching the eye of the actor-director Robert Redford. Redford directed and played a starring role in the film, which became a box office hit and a popular videocassette. As we will see, many of the creative giants in advertising have made similar impressive creative contributions outside the field of advertising. The son of a Brooklyn cab driver, Dusenberry left college early and became a professional singer and then a disk jockey before becoming an advertising copywriter.

For many years, BBDO was considered a rather conservative agency and the Pepsi campaign emphasizing "Choice of a New Generation" was a significant break with traditional styles. As stated by one reviewer, "the long Coke versus Pepsi battle over which one could sing a better jingle or portray people having more fun at picnics finally came to an end, or at least entered a lull."[68] The attempt was to reach out to the younger generation in their own language, not just through a single campaign format. In addition to Michael Jackson, takeoffs on popular science fiction movies at the time, such as *E.T.* and *Close Encounters of the Third Kind,* were used. Much of this turnaround in style is attributed to Allen Rosenshine, BBDO's chairman, chief executive officer, and former creative director. According to Rosenshine,

> *When parity products develop creative strategies, they all come out the same. Using line extensions and market segmentation to differentiate only adds to the problem. All aimed to be authoritative, assertive, competitive, and convincing about why one product was better than the other. For BBDO, it became clear that the way to go was to leave the rational sell behind. We are far more devoted now to the concept that advertising is a consumer experience with the brand. We are more sensitive too and careful that the experience is enjoyable, pleasant, human, warm and emotional, while no less relevant from the sales strategy viewpoint.*[69]

Lee Clow: Irreverence

Clow has been identified as "the force behind some of the most remarkable U.S. ad campaigns of recent years."[70] Among his major accomplishments was a sixty-second minimovie for Apple Computer's Macintosh, showing a club-wielding symbol of freedom smashing the 1984 Orwellian nightmare. Although aired only once, it generated enormous publicity. Although its successor, a commercial called "Lemmings," was not as successful, it nevertheless established an irreverent style that has become Apple's trademark in advertising. The creative genius behind these commercials was Lee Clow, executive vice president and creative director of Chiat/Day/Mojo, a Los Angeles-based agency.

Other major campaigns with which he has been associated are for products such as Nike brand sports apparel, PepsiCo's Pizza Hut, and Porsche automobiles. In one famous billboard campaign for Nike, he had unidentified Olympic hopefuls in striking poses, such as clearing hurdles at the track, displayed on massive outdoor billboards and the sides of buildings, with only the smallest mention of the sponsor, Nike. He has been described as having a unique ability to spot an idea and know if it will work. In discussing his creative style, Clow argues for the need to generate confidence and to take the lead in sticking to an idea.

> *If you don't act sure of yourself, it's very easy for other people's faith in your product to get shaky. Apple's 1984 commercial, for example, was an idea that was very easy to get nervous about. If it seems that you have some misgivings or second thoughts about something, it's easy for people who are less tuned into creative communication to get nervous about it. Most ideas are a bit scary, and if an idea isn't scary, it's not an idea at all.*[71]

The adopted son of an aerospace worker in the Los Angeles area, Clow is reported to lead a surprisingly traditional life and to be an avid television watcher. It is interesting that Clow attributes to DDB and Volkswagen advertising much of his inspiration for getting into advertising and has described this campaign as the "single greatest advertising work in the history of the business." Volkswagen advertising was launched during the so-called creative revolution of the 1960s, and Clow acknowledges creative artists such as the Beatles, Andy Warhol, and major events during the period, such as the assassinations of President Kennedy and Martin Luther King, Jr., and going to the moon, as having a major impact, on his creative development. The fact that he works in advertising, the antithesis of many of the values espoused during this period, doesn't seem to bother him.

Although Clow reputedly does not actually draw many ads himself, he is a major force in developing the concepts on which many famous Chiat/Day campaigns are based. His style is designed to create impact and he emphasizes the need for an honest dialogue with the consumer and respect for consumer intelligence.

> *If you think you have a better mousetrap or car, or shirt, or whatever, you've got to tell people, and I don't think that has to be done with trickery, or insults,*

*or by talking down to people. I think it can be an honest dialog with the con-
sumer. Good advertising is a dialog with people. . . . The smartest advertising
is the advertising that communicates the best and respects the consumer's intelligence. It's advertising that lets them bring something to the communication process, as opposed to some of the more validly criticized work in our
profession in which they try to grind the benefits of a soap or cake mix into a
poor housewife's head by repeating it 37 times in 30 seconds.*[72]

Hal Riney: Small-Town Warmth

You may not have heard of Hal Riney, but you have probably seen and chuckled at
Frank Bartles and his none-too-talkative friend Ed Jaymes advertising their Bartles
and Jaymes Premium Wine Cooler (actually made by the Gallo Winery) and "thanking you for your support." One of the most successful ad campaigns of the 1980s,
the characters and the line were the brainchild of ad man Hal Riney, who now runs
the San Francisco ad agency that bears his name. The process of creating these
two folksy characters was actually quite serendipitous: they first decided to give
the new wine cooler initials that could be used to order it in a bar (just like "J&B"
Scotch), settled on B&J, then expanded these initials to the names of Bartles and
Jaymes, by looking at a phone book, and then began to dream up characters to go
with these names. Initially, the characters selected were two down-on-their-heels
Madeira (wine) merchants in London who had to get rid of their wine inventory,
but these became two cattle farmers instead. Riney then procured the services of
an old fraternity brother and fishing buddy to play the silent heavy, Ed, and an actual Oregon cattle farmer to be Frank.[73] The series (that ran to over 100 different
spots) began with Frank explaining that, in order to start their wine cooler business, Ed had "taken out a second mortgage on his house and written to Harvard for
his MBA." Since Ed had a balloon payment coming up on the mortgage, Frank
asked people to start buying their wine cooler-and began thanking people for their
support, which became the standard closing line. The campaign was so successful
that it enabled the brand to jump from 40th to 1st place in wine cooler sales a few
months after being launched in 1985, and even attracted a few checks from people
who wanted to help Ed out with his balloon payment.

In addition to the Bartles and Jaymes wine cooler campaign, Riney's agency
is also responsible for the Gallo Wines campaign in which the ads evoke familial
love, cutting from moment to emotional moment, with cathedral-like music from
Vangelis, with an "All the best" from Gallo. Another campaign is for Perrier, in
which quick-cut scenes of children and nature reassure you that whatever had to
happen to make Perrier just right did indeed happen. And, like Phil Dusenberry,
Riney was part of Ronald Reagan's reelection ad campaign in 1984, showing warm
scenes of small-town American life and coming up with the establishing line, "It's
morning again in America." More recently, Riney's agency created the famous Saturn car campaign, "A different kind of company. A different kind of car." What all
these campaigns share is a sentimental, emotional tone that pulls at the heart-
strings, using a series of evocations, with mellow sequencing, soft voices, small-
town realism, soft wit, and very often Hal Riney's own gravelly narration. Riney's

agency also often eschews market research, often preferring to rely on its own intuition about what feels right in a particular situation.

Riney is known as a perfectionist, who makes complex ads that looks like films-using quick cuts, overlapping dialogue, and other elements that attempt to create emotional nuance. Realistic casting and stage props are another element of his style—for a Henry Weinhard beer commercial, he remodeled an old log cabin, an hour-and-a-half from the nearest highway, into an 1882 saloon, instead of constructing it on a sound stage. (A Henry Weinhard beer storyboard is reproduced in Figure 13–16.) For a beer spot featuring Eskimo traders, he and director Joe Pytka traveled to the Arctic Circle to find faces that looked just right.[74] Such realism is considered crucial because it makes it easier to appeal to genuine human emotions. Riney made good use of such realism in his recent launch campaign for Saturn cars.

Riney grew up in semirural Oregon, son of a schoolteacher mother and an itinerant salesman father who left home when Riney was six. He began working in advertising in San Francisco in the mid-1950s, at BBDO, then with a small agency called Botsford Ketchum, and then with Ogilvy & Mather. In 1976, he started his own agency, with the blessings of Ogilvy. His style, along with that of Chiat/Day in Los Angeles (discussed earlier) and Weiden and Kennedy in Portland, Oregon (which created the very successful "Bo knows" commercials featuring Bo Jackson, for Nike), has led to the emergence of a distinctly high-profile "West Coast" school of advertising that in recent years has emphasized the need to take creative risks in creating memorable and (often, but not always) sales-increasing advertising.

IS EXECUTION MORE IMPORTANT THAN CONTENT? . . . .

There are, of course, many other advertising agencies and many other creative approaches and styles that could be presented and discussed. Those reviewed in this chapter are, however, fairly representative of the range of creative output, at least in the leading agencies. Of course, there are dozens of other creative people associated with highly successful agencies and creative output that could have been reviewed as well.

One way to think of the range of creative styles is to think of a continuum from the "what you say is crucial" camp (such as Reeves' USP style) to the "how you say it is crucial" view (represented by the more freewheeling creative styles of Clow and Riney). To the extent this book is going to advocate a position on who is right, we would suggest that both are necessary—a message must be both on strategy in terms of "what" it is communicating *and* highly creative in "how" it communicates that message. Even though this chapter has focused on the importance of the creative process, we must point out that according to research by David Stewart and David Furse the single most important factor in an ad's impact on persuasion, recall, and message comprehension is the presence of a strong brand differentiating message—which is a content, not an executional variable.[75] But even the most appropriate content will get lost in today's crowded airwaves and pages if it is not said boldly, with the taking-on of creative risk.[76]

"CHUCK WAGON"

:60 Commercial

COOK: Come and get it!
VO: Back when the West was young...

COWBOY: Where'd you have to send to to
get that saddle?
VO: Getting just about anything took a lot of
time and trouble.
2nd COWBOY: Mexico.

VO: Even a good beer was a rarity.
COOK: Anybody want a Henry's?

COWBOY: Henry's?
VO: In fact, to get the West's finest beer...
2nd COWBOY: Henry Weinhard's?

VO: Beer drinkers would sometimes
wait for months...
COOK: Just come into town.

VO: Because it would often have to come from
hundreds of miles away.
COWBOY: Where'd they have to send to
to get that beer?
2nd COWBOY: Oregon.

VO: But while it may seem unusual to have taken
so much time and trouble just for a better beer...
COOK: Now for supper...
VO: It really wasn't.
COOK: There's a few things that's not on the
regular menu...

VO: Even then, Westerners always tried to do
everything in a very special way.

COOK: In addition to the beef, we have a nice
loin of buffalo in a light cream sauce.

COOK: Our fresh fish tonight is
brook trout almondine.

COWBOY: Where'd they have to send to
to get that cook?
2nd COWBOY: Los Angeles.

COOK: There's roast antelope with a peach
brandy glaze, braised jack rabbit on fruit,
rattlesnake fritters with herbed tomatoes...

Figure 13–16.   One of Hal Riney's campaigns: Henry Weinhard beer.

Courtesy of Blitz Weinhard Brewing Company.

Thus, the best advertising combines both meaningful content and brilliant creative execution. While the strategy part of the mixture is amenable to rigorous analysis (such as that developed in this book), the creative part is as much art and genius as it is science, which is what makes the advertising business rely so much on the talents of people like the ones just profiled.

SUMMARY . . . .

The creative process concerns the translation of a marketing proposition into the verbal and visual devices that will communicate the essence of that proposition in ways that are attention getting and persuasive. Working in teams, copywriters, and art directors try to come up with creative ideas that set their advertising apart from the clutter. Such idea generation is an extremely challenging task, and various techniques have been developed to facilitate the idea generation process. The best ideas are those that are "on strategy" as well as executionally very distinctive.

In evaluating proposed advertising, it is important to remember that the riskiest advertising is often that which takes no risks at all—playing it safe can mean advertising that is ineffective. Therefore, the "rules" of advertising copy should not be so venerated that they are never broken: the best ads are sometimes those that break all the rules. However, this does not mean that we should learn from the experience of the great practitioners of the art, or from what copy-testing research can teach us. Such experience and research has taught us much about what makes for good ads in print, radio, television, outdoor, retail, and business to business, and some of this learning was reviewed in this chapter.

As in art, two or more creative people can look at the same problem and develop advertising that is quite different. These differences are differences in the creative style of the individual or agency. Even though different, the advertising and the campaigns that evolve can be "successful." For example, the styles of William Bernbach and Rosser Reeves are very different in terms of philosophy and execution, but each has been associated with highly successful advertising. Seven profiles of leading creative people in advertising and the agencies with which they are associated were presented and discussed. The first four, David Ogilvy, William Bernbach, Rosser Reeves, and Leo Burnett, are notable for setting the standards of creative style in the early 1950s and 1960s. The next three, Philip Dusenberry, Lee Clow, and Hal Riney, represent current leaders in an analogous set of currently leading advertising agencies.

Although descriptions of creative styles are difficult and tend to become exaggerated and stereotypical, it is nevertheless useful to compare and contrast them. In the more recent profiles, some additional information is provided on the background and other activities of the person, to provide insights into who creative people are and where they come from.

DISCUSSION QUESTIONS AND EXERCISES

1. Select two print ads aimed at consumers that have recently run (either in magazine ads or in newspapers), one of which you consider to be a "good" ad and

one a "bad" ad. Then write a one-page assessment on each, justifying your assessment.

2. Repeat the exercise in question 1 for a pair of radio ads, a pair of television ads, a pair of retail ads, and a pair of business-to-business ads.

3. Take a marketing positioning statement, based on a situation analysis for a brand and product category that you may have worked on for some marketing project and attempt to come up with five creative ideas that could be used in creating advertising for the selected brand.

4. Now select one of these creative ideas for further development and create rough or mock ads (a print ad, a television storyboard, and a radio script) that build off that creative idea.

5. Ogilvy, Bernbach, Reeves, and Burnett are all creative giants in advertising who have retired or passed on. Compare and contrast their styles with those of Dusenberry, Clow, and Riney, who are current leaders in the field. Who is more like whom? Why?

6. The creative styles of Bernbach and Reeves are probably two ends of a continuum, yet both are associated with highly successful agencies and campaigns. One could conclude that creative style makes no difference. Do you agree or disagree? Why or why not?

7. Suppose that you were chairperson of a billion-dollar agency and were having to choose among three candidates for the position of creative director. Discuss the qualities you would look for in filling the position. What are the characteristics of a top-quality creative person?

NOTES . . . .

1. Raymond R. Burke, Arvind Rangaswamy, Jerry Wind and Jehoshua Eliashberg, "A Knowledge-Based System for Advertising Design," *Marketing Science*, 9, no. 3 (Summer 1990), 212–229.
2. Alex F. Osborn, *Applied Imagination*, 3rd ed. (New York: Scribner's, 1963), p. 11.
3. Leo Burnett, "Keep Listening to That Wee, Small Voice," in *Communications of an Advertising Man*, © 1961 by Leo Burnett Compnay, Inc.; from a speech given before the Chicago Copywriters Club, October 4, 1960, p. 160.
4. Denis Higgens, ed., *The Art of Writing Advertising* (Chicago: Crain Books, 1965), p. 43.
5. Alex F. Osborn, *Your Creative Power* (New York: Dell, 1948), p. 135.
6. Edward M. Tauber, "HIT: Heuristic Ideation Technique—A Systematic Procedure for New Product Search," *Journal of Marketing*, 36 (January 1972), 58–61.
7. Osborn, *Your Creative Power*, p. 294.
8. Discussed in Philip Kotler, *Marketing Management: Analysis, Planning, and Control* (Englewood Cliffs, NJ: Prentice Hall, 1967), p. 256.
9. John M. Keil, *The Creative Mystique: How to Manage It, Nurture It, and Make It Pay* (New York: John Wiley, 1985). See also "Popular Myths About Creativity Debunked," *Advertising Age*, May 6, 1985, p. 48.
10. John Caples, *How to Make Your Advertising Make Money* (Englewood Cliffs, NJ: Prentice Hall, 1983).
11. John Caples, "A Dozen Ways to Develop Advertising Ideas," *Advertising Age*, November 14, 1983, pp. M-4ff.
12. See, for example, William H. Motes, Chadwick B. Hilton, and John S. Fielden, "Language, Sentence, and Structural Variations in Print Advertising," Journal of *Advertising Research*, 32, no. 5 (Sep/Oct 1992), 63–77.

13. Richard F. Beltramini and Vincent J. Blasko, "An Analysis of Award-Winning Advertising Headlines," *Journal of Advetising Research* (April/May 1986), 48–52.

14. H. Rao Unnava and Robert E. Burnkrant, "An Imagery-Processing View of the Role of Pictures in Print Advertisements," *Journal of Marketing Research*, 28 (May 1991), 226–231; Michael J. Houston, Terry L. Childers, and Susan E. Heckler, "Picture-Word Consistency and the Elaborative Processing of Advertisements," *Journal of Marketing Research*, 1987, 24 (December), 359–369.

15. Alvin C. Burns, Abhijit Biswas and Laurie A. Babin, The Operation of Visual Imagery as a Mediator of Advertising Effects," *Journal of Advertising*, 22, no. 2 (June 1993), 71–85.

16. Bernd H. Schmitt, Nader T. Tavassoli, and Robert T. Millard, "Memory for Print Ads: Understanding Relations Among Brand Name, Copy, and Picture," *Journal of Consumer Psychology*, 2, no. 1 (1993), 55–81.

17. See Paula F. Bone and Pam S. Ellen, "The Generation and Consequences of Communication-evoked Imagery," *Journal of Consumer Research*, 19 (June 1992), 93–104, and Kathleen Debevec and Jean B. Romeo, "Self-Referent Processing in Perceptions of Verbal and Visual Commercial Information," *Journal of Consumer Psychology*, 1, no. 1 (1992), 83–102.

18. Paul W. Miniard et al, "Picture-based Persuasion Processes and the Moderating Role of Involvement," *Journal of Consumer Research*, 18 (June 1991), 92–107.

19. Wendy J. Bryce and Richard F. Yalch, "Hearing versus Seeing: A Comparison of Consumer Learning of Spoken and Piuctorial Information in Television Advertising," *Journal of Current Issues and Research in Advertising*, 15, no. 1 (Spring 1993), 1–20.

20. Charles E. Young and Michael Robinson, "Visual Connectedness and Persuasion," *Journal of Advertising Research*, 32, no. 2 (March/April 1992), 51–55.

21. James MacLachlan and Michael Logan, "Camera Shot Length in TV Commercials and their Memorability and Persuasiveness," *Journal of Advertising Research*, 33, no. 2 (March/April 1992), 57–61.

22. Joan Meyers-Levy and Laura Peracchio, "Getting an Angle in Advertising: The Effect of Camera Angle on Product Evaluations," *Journal of Marketing Research*, 29 (November 1992), 454–461.

23. David W. Stewart and David F. Furse, *Effective Television Advertising: A Study of 1000 Commercials* (Lexington, MA: Lexington Books, 1986).

24. Daryl W. Miller and Lawrence J. Marks, "Mental Imagery and Sound Effects in Radio Commercials," *Journal of Advertising*, 21, no. 4 (December 1992), 83–97.

25. Avery M. Abernathy, James I. Gray, and Herbert J. Rotfield, "Combinations of Creative Elements in Radio Advertising," *Journal of Current Issues and Research in Advertising*, 15, no. 1 (Spring 1993), 87–98.

26. Naveen Donthu, Joseph Cherian, and Mukesh Bhargava, "Factors Influencing Recall of Outdoor Advertising," *Journal of Advertising Research*, 33, no. 3 (May–June 1993), 64–80.

27. Robert Chamblee and Dennis M. Sandler, "Business-to-Business Advertising: Which Layout Style Works Best?" *Journal of Advertising Research*, 32, no. 6 (Nov/Dec 1992), 39–48.

28. *Wall Street Week*, October 1, 1993, p. B6.

29. Martin Nisenholtz, "How to Market on the Net," *Advertising Age*, July 11, 1994, p. 28.

30. Lester Guest, "Status Enhancement as a Function of Color in Advertising," *Journal of Advertising Research*, 6 (June 1966), 40–44.

31. Ibid., p. 44.

32. Stephen Baker, *Advertising Layout and Art Direction* (New York: McGraw-Hill, 1959), p. 3.

33. Florence G. Feasley and Elnora W. Stuart, "Magazine Advertising Layout and Design: 1932–1982," *Journal of Advertising*, 16, no. 2 (1987), 20–25; Chamblee and Sandler, 1992, cited earlier.

34. Chris Janiszewski, "The Influence of Nonattended Material on the Processing of Advertising Claims," *Journal of Marketing Research*, 27 (August 1990), 263–278.

35. For an interesting book on the subject of making television commercials, see Michael J. Arlen, *Thirty Seconds* (New York: Farrar, Straus & Giroux, 1980).

36. Albert C. Book and Norman D. Cary, *The Television Commercial: Creativity and Craftsmanship* (New York: Decker Communication, 1970).
37. Henry A. Laskey, Ellen Day, and Melvin R. Crask, "Typology of Main Message Strategies for Television Commercials," *Journal of Advertising*, 18, no. 1 (1989), 36–41.
38. David Ogilvy, *Confessions of an Advertising Man* (New York: Atheneum, 1964), pp. 100–102.
39. Ibid., p. 102.
40. Ibid., p. 51.
41. Ibid., pp. 116–117.
42. Ibid., pp. 93–103.
43. Martin Mayer, *Madison Avenue, U.S.A.* (New York: Pocket Books, 1958), p. 64.
44. Jerry Della Femina, with Charles Spokin, ed., *From Those Wonderful Folks Who Gave You Pearl Harbor* (New York: Simon & Schuster, 1970), p. 29.
45. Higgens, *The Art of Writing Advertising*, pp. 117–118.
46. Mayer, *Madison Avenue, U.S.A.*, p. 66.
47. Frank Rowsome, Jr., *Think Small* (New York: Ballantine Books, 1970), p. 81.
48. Ibid., p. 12.
49. Mayer, *Madison Avenue, U.S.A.*, p. 65.
50. For an interpretation of this campaign from which these comments were drawn, see della Femina, *From Those Wonderful Folks*, pp. 38–39.
51. Ibid., p. 26.
52. Rowsome, *Think Small*, p. 116.
53. Ibid., p. 117.
54. Higgens, *The Art of Writing Advertising*, p. 120.
55. Ibid., pp. 117–118.
56. Mayer, *Madison Avenue, U.S.A.*, pp. 59–61.
57. Ibid., p. 52.
58. Higgens, *The Art of Writing Advertising*, p. 124.
59. Described in Mayer, *Madison Avenue, U.S.A.*, p. 300.
60. Burnett, "Keep Listening to That Wee, Small Voice."
61. Higgens, *The Art of Writing Advertising*, p. 17.
62. Ibid., p. 44.
63. Burnett, "Keep Listening," p. 154.
64. Mayer, *Madison Avenue, U.S.A.*, p. 70.
65. Higgens, *The Art of Writing Advertising*, p. 45.
66. Della Femina, *From Those Wonderful Folks*, p. 141.
67. *The New York Times*, November 16, 1990, p. F29.
68. Stewart Alter, "Ad Age Honors BBDO as Agency of Year," *Advertising Age*, March 28, 1985, pp. 3ff.
69. Ibid., p. 4.
70. Jennifer Pendleton, "Bringing New Clow-T to Ads, Chiat's Unlikely Creative," *Advertising Age*, February 7, 1985, pp. 1 ff.
71. Ibid., p. 5.
72. Ibid.
73. *Insight*, September 14, 1987, pp. 38–40.
74. *The New York Times Magazine*, December 14, 1986, pp. 52–74.
75. David W. Stewart and David F. Furse, *Effective Television Advertising: A Study of 1000 Commercials* (Lexington, MA: Lexington Books, 1986).
76. See *Advertising Age*, July 5, 1993, p. 27.

14 ADVERTISING COPY TESTING AND DIAGNOSIS

> Think of an ad not as what you put into it, but as what the consumer takes out of it.
> (Rosser Reeves, in *Reality in Advertising*, © 1961 by Alfred A. Knopf, Inc.)

The history of ad campaigns is full of many that "bombed," leading to the expenditures of tens of millions of dollars that were totally wasted. (To protect the guilty, no names will be mentioned here!). Would some kind of ad pretesting have prevented such disasters?

At the more operational level, companies and agencies often have two or more strategies or executions they are considering using. For example, AT&T may wonder if it makes more sense to focus on a "low price" message in marketing long-distance calling, or whether the "human contact" appeal is more powerful. Which one should they pick? How should they test the two?

Let's say you are American Express, wanting to turn around your flat-to-declining trends in the number of charge cards and share of charges in the market. You are now testing various campaigns suggested by the new agencies you are considering. Should you test to see which speculative campaign gets the highest recall scores, or is some other copy-testing criterion more relevant to your situation?

If you have an ad that apparently isn't "working," how can you find out *why* it isn't working?

Such questions, and many others, are addressed in copy testing and diagnostic evaluation (which we will simply call *copy testing* for brevity). A significant industry has evolved in the United States and, increasingly, in other countries made up of companies in the business of supplying this kind of service.[1] But while copy testing can serve many useful purposes, it can also serve to inhibit the creative process, if clients insist on running only those ads that "score well" on various copytests. So the choice of whether or not to copytest, and how to copytest, has to be made with care.

The chapter begins with a section on copy-testing strategy, which addresses these sorts of questions. Four widely-used criteria in copy testing and examples of related services are then presented and discussed. This is followed by a review of other tests. A final section is devoted to evaluating copy tests.

COPY-TESTING STRATEGY . . . .

There are three factors that have to be addressed in copy testing: (1) whether or not to test, (2) what and when to test, and (3) what criteria or test to use. Every advertising manager must consider these factors in the context of the overall advertising plan. Copy testing implies that funds will be allocated to research on consumer reactions to the advertising before the final campaign is launched.

Should You Copy-Test?

The first decision is really whether or not to spend more money on research. It is interesting that in terms of total advertising volume, the usual decision is "no." Most local advertising is not tested, and there are many cases in national advertising where copy is used without formal copy testing of any kind. (A recent survey found that about 18 to 19 percent of the largest advertisers and agencies claimed that they did not pretest their TV commercials.[2]) Not only are there money costs involved in testing, but there are time costs as well. Copy testing can mean weeks or months of delay in launching a campaign.

On the other hand, if you are managing a new product entry involving a $20 million advertising budget, investing in copy testing makes sense. Relying solely on the judgments of a creative team, your own experience, or somebody's intuition is very risky when so much is at stake. What is needed is a test of how potential consumers will react, that is, copy testing.

Having said that, it should be pointed out that several "hot" creative agencies strongly believe that their creative product tends to be more fresh and original because they do not test their ads before running them. Many creative people in agencies (but certainly not all) hold a rather negative view of copy testing, viewing it as a report card, a policeman, something that only tells them what is working or not, but not why. Of course, total creative license (with no copy testing) has also been known to have led to ad campaigns that have "bombed" in the marketplace, so most creatives appreciate the "reality check" it provides. But it is clearly important to select a copy-testing system that the creatives respect and believe in, and find useful, and it is important that ads not be created simply to score well on the copy-testing system being used, in a political, "gaming" fashion.

When and What Should You Test?

What and when to test? Copy testing can be done at (1) the beginning of the creative process, (2) the end of the creative process (at the layout stage), (3) the end of the production stage, and/or (4) after the campaign has been launched. In general, tests at the first three stages are called pretests and those at the final stage are called posttests.[3] Various types of tests can be used at any of the four stages and will differ by whether broadcast or print advertising is involved.

Testing at the beginning of the creative process often involves qualitative research, such as focus group interviews to get reactions to copy ideas. These are better suited to the testing of alternative strategies than to the testing of executional ideas, because the executional ideas may be too "rough" to be really testable.

At stage 2, rough mock-ups of the finished copy or, in television, partially complete commercials are tested because of the lower expenses involved (a fully produced commercial typically costs in excess of $200,000). While these rough ads (called *animatics*, *photomatics*, *livamatics*, etc.) are reasonably good predictors of final effectiveness, they must be used with caution in situations where the success of the ad will eventually depend substantially on the actual casting of characters, the actual and final editing of scenes, and so on.

According to a recent survey of leading advertisers and agencies, most pretesting of TV commercials is currently done using such animatics (a video of drawings of the scenes of the commercials, with audio dubbed on), using consumer focus groups or mall intercepts, with the key tests being the clarity of communication and the believability of key copy points.[4] The trend over the last ten years seems to be more towards such quicker, qualitative research, using such rough test ads. We will discuss such *rough testing* in greater detail below in this chapter.

Stage 3 is often bypassed, particularly in cases where the advertising has been shown or aired several times and the new copy is not radically different. A basic issue is whether to develop and test just one version of the advertising, or whether two or more versions should be developed and tested. It is logical, but also expensive, to have alternatives to test. In general, it is more expensive to test at the third and fourth stages. When there is much at stake, when millions of dollars of media time and expensive creative and production effort are involved, a substantial investment in copy testing at all stages is easily justified.

What Criteria Should Be Used?

What criteria or copy test should be used? Copy-testing services can be distinguished by the nature of the response variable used in the test. Although many other factors enter into the choice of a copy test, the criterion (dependent) variable is probably the most important thing on which to focus. What does a particular test measure? How accurate or valid are these measures? We now review five criteria widely used in copy testing and gives examples of copy-testing services based on them.

There are five basic criteria or categories of response that are widely used in advertising research. The first is advertisement recognition. The second, used heavily in television, is recall of the commercial and its contents. The third is persuasion (or attitude change). Fourth, the criterion of purchase behavior is used. A fifth and newer measure is the testing of effects on brand loyalty or the amount of product or service consumed. Some of these criteria will be seen to be more suitable for post-testing of already running advertisements, and others for pretesting, though most can be adapted to either pre- or posttesting.

The key question in choosing among them is: what is the relevant measure of advertising effectiveness for this brand, for this campaign, in the present marketing context? Chapter 4 showed that every brand usually had an advertising "problem" at one of the "hierarchy" levels of awareness, preference (favorable attitudes), trial, or repurchase, and that "diagnostic" consumer data regarding these levels could be used to identify the specific objectives for any particular ad or ad campaign. Further, as was discussed earlier in Chapter 5, recall (and recognition) are usually more important objectives in low-involvement situations, with persuasion the criterion in more highly-involving situations (such as the American Express example the chapter opened with). Thus, every ad being copy-tested should usually have its effectiveness criteria specified in advance, using the kind of thinking presented in Chapters 4 and 5 earlier in this book.

Even so, it is unlikely that only one single criterion will exist for ad effectiveness; multiple criteria are usually required. For instance, it is often useful to think of an ad's recognition or recall scores as indicative of the "breadth" of that ad's effectiveness, because they tell you "how many" people were "reached" by that ad. In contrast, the ad's persuasion or purchase intent scores can be seen as indicators of how "deeply" the ad influenced those people that it "reached": were they moved enough by it to prefer this brand to others, to want to try it?

Each criterion and the measures and service associated with it will be illustrated and discussed in the following sections.

Recognition

Recognition refers to whether a respondent can recognize an advertisement as one he or she has seen before. An example of recognition testing is the Bruzzone Research Company (BRC) tests of television commercials. These tests are done by mail survey in which questionnaires, such as the one shown in Figure 14–1, are mailed to 1,000 households. The sample is drawn from a specially prepared mailing list of households that have either a registered automobile or a listed telephone number. Interest in the task and a dollar bill enclosed with the questionnaire usually generates a return sample of about 500. The recognition question is shown at the top. At the bottom is the brand association question, a critical dimension of most campaigns. On average, 60 percent will recognize a commercial, and 73 percent of these can correctly select the right brand from a list of three alternatives.[5] Test-retest correlations of 0.98 have been reported.

Communicus is another company that uses recognition measures for either television or radio commercial tests. In television, respondents are shown brief (ten-second) edited portions of the commercial, excluding advertiser identification. They are asked to indicate if they have seen or heard it before, to identify the advertiser, and to play back other identifying copy points. Some research has shown that there is a dropoff in the percentage of people who can identify a sponsor, falling from an average of 59 percent in 1974 to about 50 percent in 1980, perhaps because of increased clutter.[6]

The most widely known service in measuring print advertising recognition is Starch INRA Hooper. This service began in 1923. In a typical Starch test, respondents are taken through a magazine and, for each advertisement, asked if they saw

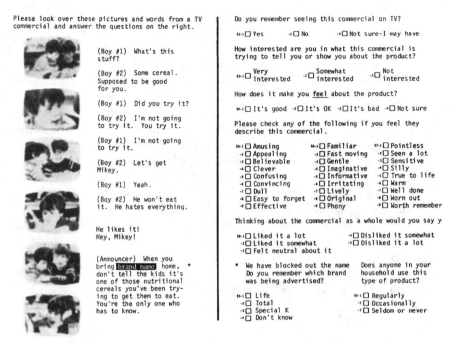

Figure 14–1. Advertising campaign effectiveness survey.

Courtesy of Bruzzone Research Company.

it in the issue. Three measures are generated for each advertisement in the magazine called noted, seen associated, and read most. Each is a percentage derived as follows:

Noted: the percentage of readers of the issue who remember having seen the advertisement.

Seen associated: the percentage who saw any part of the advertisement that clearly indicates the brand, service, or advertisement.

Read most: the percentage who read half or more of the copy.

Studies using Starch data show that recognition depends on the product class, the involvement of the consumer segment in the product class, and on variables such as size, color, position, copy approach, and the nature of the magazine or media. Various reviews of these Starch (and similar) data are available.[7] Although Starch scores are highly reliable in a test-retest sense, there is concern about validity. The respondent can claim readership where none exists to please or impress the interviewer or because of confusion with prior advertising for the brand. Though this bias can be difficult to predict for a particular advertisement, researchers such as Surendra Singh and colleagues have suggested ways to adjust claimed recognition scores to obtain better estimates of actual recognition.[8]

Recognition is a necessary condition for effective advertising. If the advertisement cannot pass this minimal test, it probably will not be effective. In one study of inquiries received by an advertiser of electronic instrumentation, those with low Starch scores were also low in inquiries received. Tatham-Laird and Kudner, a Chicago agency, finds out which specific portions of a TV ad are effective in gaining recall by asking consumers if they recognize photographs of different frames (opening shot, closing shot, etc.) fifteen to twenty minutes after they see the ad. Of course, high recognition does not guarantee effectiveness, but this agency has found a strong relationship between final overall recall and the nature of the opening and closing shots and the amount of product linkage built into the other shots of the ad.[9] There is also some evidence that "emotional" television ads, those that do not feature much verbalizable copy, are better measured for their attention-getting ability on tests of recognition rather than are tests of verbal recall (this issue is discussed further later in the chapter).

It should also be noted that high recognition scores are easier to achieve than are high recall scores, since recognition requires only a judgment about the stimulus and does not require as much retrieval of information from memory as is required by, say, an unaided recall task.[10] Thus recognition can be created by even partly attentive television viewing that does not lead to conscious recall. This may make visually oriented recognition scores a more suitable measure of memory than recall for short (fifteen-second) television ads.[11] Some researchers believe that recognition scores decline more slowly over time than recall scores do, though Surendra Singh, Michael Rothschild, and Gilbert Churchill have shown that a "forced-choice" recognition measure that is "tougher" than a usual yes-no measure does, in fact, decay over time and is a sensitive measure of the memory effect of a commercial.[12]

Finally, some researchers have argued that ads should be pretested using techniques even more sensitive than recognition, such as word fragment or sentence completion, or picture identification. It is argued that such measures of "implicit memory" may apply better to situations when consumers process the ad only very passively. Under such conditions, traditional recognition tests may suggest that an ad had no effect, but (it is argued) consumers who saw the ad and processed it minimally may be able to "fill in" a brand name fragment presented to them (e.g., C__K__ may be filled-in as COKE), better than consumers who didn't see the ad, proving that they did in fact see the ad.[13]

Recall

Recall refers to measures of the proportion of a sample audience that can recall an advertisement. There are two kinds of recall, aided recall and unaided recall. In aided recall, the respondent is prompted by showing a picture of the advertisement with the sponsor or brand name blanked out. In unaided recall, only the product or service name may be given. The best known recall method in television, interviewing viewers within twenty-four to thirty hours after the commercial is aired, is called the day-after-recall method.

Day-After Recall

The *day-after-recall* (*DAR*) measure of a television commercial, first used in the early 1940s by George Gallup, then with Young & Rubicam, is closely associated with Burke Marketing Research, which was recently acquired by ASI.[14] The procedure in most recall tests, which vary by vendor, is to telephone 150 to 300 program viewers twenty-four hours after a television commercial appears. (Some other companies use a different time period, such as seventy-two hours.) They are asked if they can recall any commercials the previous day in a product category (such as soap). If they cannot identify the brand correctly, they are then given the product category and brand and asked if they recalled the commercial. They are then asked for anything they can recall about the commercial, what was said, what was shown, and what the main idea was.

DAR is the percentage of those in the commercial audience (who were watching the show before and after the commercial was shown) who recalled something specific about the commercial, such as the sales message, the story line, the plot, or some visual or audio element. This is called the *percent proven recall*. A less tightly defined measure—of people who have seen something of the ad but maybe don't play back a very specific element—is called *percent related recall*. These recall percentages for the ad being tested are always compared against the *norm*— the historical average for ads of similar length, from similar product categories, from similar (old/new) brands. The tests also provides specific verbatims (transcripts) of what people remember of the ad and analyzes them for the nature of the main message that got communicated.

The DAR is an *on-air* test in that the commercial exposure occurs in a natural, realistic in-home setting. (Sometimes, to save money, the ad is aired on a local cable channel, and viewers are preinvited to watch the program on that channel.) It is well established and has developed extensive norms over the years. The average Burke DAR was 24. One-fourth of all commercials scored under 15 and one-fourth scored over 31. It also provides diagnostic information about which elements of the commercial are having an impact and which are not.

Many copy-testing companies provide a similar recall measure for print media. They may place a magazine with 150 regular readers of that magazine and ask that it be read in a normal manner. The next day readers are asked to describe ads for any brands of interest. Similar tests have also been developed for radio: consumers in a shopping mall fill out a questionnaire in a room while listening to the radio in the background (which plays the radio ad being tested). Twenty-four hours later, they are called back on the telephone and asked questions about recall as well as diagnostic questions on what they like and why.

The Appendix to this chapter provides details on various recall tests as provided by ASI, Gallup and Robinson, and Mapes and Ross, in various media.

Problems with Recall Scores

Recall measures have generated controversy over the years and, as a result, are not as influential as they once were. One concern is that they are an inappropriate measure of emotional commercials. Foote, Cone & Belding measured both masked recognition (where the brand name is blocked out) and DAR for three "feeling" commercials and three "thinking" commercials.[15] The DAR was much lower for the feeling commercials (19 versus 31) whereas the recognition scores were only marginally lower (32 versus 37). The conclusion was that recognition is a better measure of the ability of a feeling commercial's memorability than DAR, which requires the verbalization of the content.

Researchers have also shown that the recall of emotional ads goes up if they are prompted not with the name of the product category of the brand in the ad (the usual method) but, instead, with a description of the opening scene of the ad. It is possible that this increase in recall occurs because this second method (using an "executional prompt") is more consistent with the way in which viewers who are "just watching" ads on TV actually process the ad, and thus with how memory of that ad is stored in their minds.[16]

A more basic concern with DAR is that it simply is not a valid measure of anything useful.[17] First, its reliability is suspect. Extremely low test-retest correlations (below 0.30) have been found when commercials from the same product class have been studied. Second, DAR scores are unduly affected by the liking and nature of the program. For example, DAR scores of commercials in new programs average 25 percent or more below commercials in other shows. Third, the scores vary markedly with the nature of the consumer being tested: if the consumer is a recent purchaser of the product category, scores are higher than if the purchaser is not really in the target market.

Fourth, and most compelling, of eight relevant studies, seven found practically no association between recall and measures of persuasion. Neither is there evidence of a positive association between recall and sales. In contrast, there is substantial evidence linking persuasion measures with sales. As we discussed earlier in Chapter 5, recall and persuasion are conceptually two very different kinds of advertising effects, and one should never be used as an automatic proxy for the other. Thus, ads may need to be tested separately for persuasion.

Persuasion

Forced-Exposure Brand-Preference Change

Theater testing, pioneered by Horace Schwerin and Paul Lazarsfeld in the 1950s, is now done by McCollum/Spielman, ASI, and ARS.[18]

The McCollum/Spielman test uses a 450-person sample spread over four graphically dispersed locations.[19] The respondents are recruited by telephone to come to a central location to preview television programming. Seated in groups of twenty-five in front of television monitors, they respond to a set of demographic and brand-product usage questions that appear on the screen. The respondents view a half-hour variety program featuring four professional performers. In the midpoint, seven commercials, including four test commercials, are shown.

Performer A	Performer B	T 1	C	T 2	C	T 3	C	T 4	Performer C	Performer D

C = Constant Commercials   T = Test Commercial

After audience reactions to the program are obtained, an unaided brand-name recall question is asked that forms the basis of the *clutter-awareness score* (the percentage who recalled that the brand was advertised). The *clutter-awareness (C/A) score* for thirty-second commercials averages 56 percent for established brands and 40 percent for new brands.[20] The four test commercials are then exposed a second time surrounded by program material:

Program Intro.	T 1	Program	T 2	Program	T 3	Program	T 4	Program

T = Test Commercial

An *attitude shift (AS) measure* is obtained. For frequently purchased package goods such as toiletries, the preexposure designation of brand purchased most often is compared with the postexposure brand selection in a market basket award situation. The respondents are asked to select brands they would like included if they were winners of a $25 basket of products. In product fields with multiple-brand usage, such as soft drinks, a constant sum measure (ten points to be allocated to brands proportional to how they are preferred) is employed before and after exposure. For durables and services, the pre- and postpreference is measured by determining

- **The favorite brand.**
- **The next preferred alternative.**
- **Those brands that would not be considered.**
- **Those brands that are neither preferred not rejected.**

An important element of the test is the use of two exposures. McCollum/Spielman and many advertisers argue that fewer than two exposures represents an artificial and invalid test of most advertising. It is especially important that "emotional" ads be tested in a multiple-exposure copy test, because (compared to "rational" ads) such ads "build" (gain in response) more slowly with repetition, and a single-exposure copy test would not accurately gauge the response they would get when frequently exposed in the marketplace.

Finally, diagnostic questions are asked. Some of the areas that are frequently explored include

- **Comprehension of message-slogan.**
- **Communication of secondary copy ideas.**
- **Evaluation of demonstrations, spokesperson, message.**
- **Perception of brand uniqueness/brand differentiation.**
- **Irritating/confusing elements.**
- **Viewer involvement.**

In a rare copy-test validity check, McCollum/Spielman asked advertisers of 412 campaigns (some campaigns consisted of several commercials) that were tested over a three-year period whether the brand had exceeded marketing objectives during the time that the campaign was being aired.[21] These advertising campaigns were then divided into four groups:

- **High AS (attitude shift) and high A/C (awareness/communication).**
- **High AS and low A/C.**
- **Low AS and high A/C.**
- **Low AS and low A/C.**

The results are shown in Figure 14–2. Clearly, the AS persuasion measure was a good predictor of campaign success. The A/C recall measure, on the other hand, may have diagnostic value but it had little relationship to campaign success.

The ARS approach is similar except that their proven recall measure is the percent of respondents that seventy-two hours later claim having seen the advertisement and can give some playback of it.[22] (See the Appendix for details). ARS obtained a correlation of 0.78 with their proven recall measure and the unaided brand awareness level achieved by twenty-four new brands in test markets. Their pre- and postpersuasion measure had a correlation of 0.85 with the trial rate of twenty-six new brands in test markets. Further, the ARS persuasion score correctly predicted which of two commercials would achieve higher test market sales.

ASI (see Appendix for details) relies on a pre- and postmeasure of brand selection in a prize-drawing context. Reliability studies across 100 commercials in fifteen product categories yielded test-retest reliability correlations of from 0.81 to 0.88. Fifteen hundred commercials per year are tested by ASI, so well developed and current norms are available.[23]

The Buy Test design of the Sherman Group does not involve a central location. The respondents are often recruited and exposed to advertising in shopping

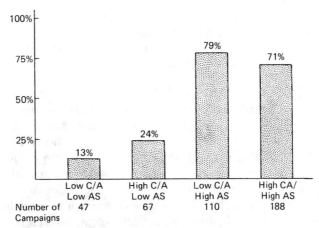

Figure 14–2.   The percentage of campaigns exceeding marketing objectives by their performance in the McCollum/Spielman text.

Source: Adapted from Peter R. Klein and Melvin Tainter, "Copy Research Validation: The Advertiser's Perspective," Journal of Advertising Research, *23, October/November 1982, pp. 9-18. Copyright © 1983 by the Advertising Research Foundation.*

malls.[24] A series of unaided questions on advertisement and copy recall identify those in the *recall/understand* group. The advertising *involvement* group are those who had a favorable emotional response, who believed that the brand positioning fit the execution, and who felt that the advertisement was worth looking at (or reading). The *buying urgency* group is identified in part by intentions to buy, improved product opinion, and the motivation to tell someone something about it. A basic measure, the BUY score, is the percentage of those exposed who become part of all three groups. In 75 percent of fifty cases, the BUY score generated different outcomes from other persuasion measurements. In twenty test-retest contexts, the average difference of the BUY score was within three percentage points.

On-Air Tests: Brand-Preference Change

In a Mapes & Ross test, commercials are aired in a preselected prime-time position on a UHF station in each of three major markets. Prior to the test, a sample of 200 viewers (150 if it is an all-male target audience) are contacted by phone and invited to participate in a survey and cash award drawing that requires viewing the test program. Respondents provide unaided brand-name awareness and are questioned about their brand preferences for a number of different product categories. The day following the commercial exposure, the respondents again answer brand preference as well as DAR questions. The key Mapes & Ross measure is pre- and post-brand-preference change. (The Appendix has details.)

A Mapes & Ross study involved 142 commercials from fifty-five product categories and 2,241 respondents who were recontacted two weeks after participating in a test. Among those who bought the product category, purchases of the test brand were 3.3 times higher among those who changed their preference than among those who did not change.[25]

Purchase Behavior

The fourth criterion is actual brand choice in an in-store, real-world setting. These tests focus on the effects of exposure to shifts in actual *purchase behavior*. Two well-known tests are those using coupons to stimulate purchasing and those involving split-cable testing.

Coupon-Stimulated Purchasing

In the Tele-Research approach, 600 shoppers are intercepted in a shopping center location, usually in Los Angeles, and randomly assigned to test or control groups. The test group is exposed to five television or radio commercials or six print ads. Around 250 subjects in the test group complete a questionnaire on the commercial. Both groups are given a customer code number and packets of coupons, including one for the test brand, which can be redeemed in a nearby cooperating drugstore or supermarket. The *selling effectiveness score* is the ratio of purchases by viewer shoppers divided by the rate of purchases by control shoppers. Purchases are tracked by scanner data. Although the exposure context is highly artificial, the purchase choice is relatively realistic in that real money is spent in a real store.

A similar method is used by General Mills: Two sets of cable households are shown what is ostensibly a new TV pilot program, but only one of these two cells sees an embedded test ad (other noncompetitive ads are also shown). Both sets of consumers are then told "We are going to award you five coupons, each worth $1.00 good for breakfast cereals. You could choose all five coupons for the same breakfast cereal, or you could use the five coupons in any other way you'd like." They are then asked which brand or brands they want their five coupons for, and how many coupons for each brand. The coupon choices are then compared across the two (exposed and nonexposed) cells, and the measure of purchase interest is the percentage of people choosing one or more coupons for the test brand.

Coupon Use or Inquiries: Split-Run Tests

A somewhat different test is often used in the industrial marketing context, in which ads are designed to generate inquiries (often via coupons) that, it is hoped, will eventually be converted into sales via sales calls. Here, it is often possible to conduct a *split-run test*, in which two different versions of an ad are created and placed into one magazine print run in such a way that ad versions A and B are placed into random halves of the print run. Each ad has a coupon or other response device (such as a toll-free telephone number), and each ad has a unique code or "key" number to track which of those pulled each response that come in. Once these logistics are in place, it is easy to test which one of the two ads being tested is the more effective in generating inquiries or leads.

Split-Cable Testing

Split-cable testing by firms such as BehaviorScan will be described in detail in Chapter 16. A panel of around 3,000 households is recruited in test cities. An ID card presented by the panel member to the checkout stand, coupled with a computerized scanner system, allows the purchases of the member to be monitored. The in-store activity is also monitored. Further, panelists have a device connected to their TV set that allows BehaviorScan to monitor what channel is tuned and also to substitute one advertisement for another. Thus, panelists can be divided into matched groups and different advertising directed at each.

In Chapter 16, the use of split-cable testing to conduct advertising weight tests will be discussed. Such split-cable facilities can and are also used to test one set of advertisements against another or to evaluate a host of options, such as the time of day or program in which the ad appears, the commercial length, or the bunching of exposures (versus an even distribution through time). These tests are very expensive, costing in the hundreds of thousands of dollars, and are typically not used to test one ad against another but rather two different creative strategies, each tested as a multiexposure ad campaign lasting several months.

AT&T used the AdTel (Burke) split-cable system to test a new "Cost of Visit" campaign against the established "Reach Out" campaign.[26] Research had determined that a substantial light-user segment had a psychological price barrier to calling and overestimated the cost, particularly at off-peak times.

The campaign objective was to communicate among the light users how inexpensive a twenty-minute telephone visit can be and to stimulate usage during off-peak times. The "Cost of Visit" theme contained surprise (of the low cost), the

Figure 14–3.   AT&T long distance lines residence.

Courtesy of AT&T Communications.

appropriateness of a twenty-minute visit, and the total cost of $3.33 (some believed that it would cost $20.00). One of the ads, "AT&T Long Lines Residence," is shown in Figure 14–3.

Two matched AdTel panel groups of 8,000 were created. During a fifteen-month period the two campaigns were aired, one to each group. Each household received three exposures per week (300 gross rating points per week). Compared to the "Reach Out" campaign, the "Cost of Visit" campaign increased calls during the deep-discount period by 0.6 calls per week among all households and 1.5 calls per week among light-user households. Projections indicated that the campaign would generate $100 million in extra revenue during a five-year period.

Two additional analyses are of interest. During the six months after the test ended, usage fell off but not to the level prior to the test. However, it was clear that reinforcement advertising was needed. The "Cost of Visit" campaign changed two key attitudes more than the "Reach Out" campaign: the attitude toward the value of a long-distance call and the attitude about the rates.

Split-cable testing is the ultimate in testing validity because it allows the advertiser to control experimentally for the effects of the other marketing mix elements and accurately measure the effect of advertising on short-term sales. However, as mentioned, it can cost from twenty to fifty times that of a forced exposure test ($100,000 to $200,000) and take six months to one year or more before the results are known. By that time, new brands or changing consumer preferences could make the results somewhat obsolete. Further, the sales results themselves, when viewed in isolation, offer no clue about the longer-term effect of the advertising on a brand's equity or goodwill. For these reasons, most firms use the split-cable testing method far less than other alternatives.

Measuring Increases in Loyalty and in Consumption Frequency

In recent years, more and more advertisers have begun to create advertising that aims not at creating mere brand preference or favorable attitudes but at deepening already existing favorable attitudes. As discussed earlier in Chapter 4 on "Behavioral Dynamics," in most product categories, consumers are not loyal to just one brand but instead divide their consumption among several well-liked brands. The advertising objective for any one of these well-liked brands is thus to increase its "share of category requirements" for such consumers.

Many copy-testing services have begun to modify their standard methods to capture these "franchise-deepening" effects of an ad. For instance, Mapes and Ross compares data from consumers exposed to an ad versus some not exposed to it, among consumers who already consider the brand as being in their list of favored brands, on both actual postexposure buying patterns as well as on different kinds of attitude statements. They then analyze which specific attitude statements best predict actual increases in units bought, and see which ads best increase these key attitude statements.

Similarly, McCollum-Spielman claims to have developed a system in which the effects of an ad are analyzed separately across consumer segments for that brand that have shown high, medium, or low loyalty to it in the past, so that the loyalty-bolstering effects of the ad sought for the "highly loyals" can be measured separately from the usage-increasing effects sought for the "low loyals."[27]

Researchers Brian Wansink and Michael Ray have also begun to develop copy-testing methods and measures designed to test the extent to which an ad increases the consumer's desire to consume the advertised brand more often, or in newer consumption situations, or to substitute it for a different product category altogether (i.e., its "use-up rate"), instead of simply preferring that brand over others.[28]

Normed versus Customized Measures of Effect

Standardized copy-test measures are useful because they come with norms sometimes based on thousands of past tests. Thus, the interpretation of the test becomes more meaningful. In fact, some copy-test services provide scores that have been adjusted such that the executional impact of the particular ad execution being tested is separated from the impact of the product category itself, the newness of the brand itself, the length (duration) of that ad, and so on. They point out that most—up to 80 percent—of an ad's score on recall and/or persuasion can be a function not of the ad itself but of these background variables. Thus, it is clearly useful to use these standardized, *normed* tests.

However, some objectives, particularly communication objectives, are necessarily unique to a brand and may require questions tailored to that brand. For example, Chevron ran a series of twelve print ads in 1980, such as the one shown in Figure 14–4, mostly telling people that Chevron made a lot less profit than people thought.[29] A posttest sample of 380 respondents were interviewed. Belief change was measured on the item "Chevron makes too much profit" for those aware of the advertising. The ads had a small effect, as those agreeing fell from 81 percent to 72 percent.

Interestingly, however, data from the same study showed that people seeing these print ads and the very positive "Energy Frontier" television campaign actually had less attitude change toward Chevron than did those seeing only the television ads. Thus, the print ads (20 percent of the budget) actually reduced the impact on the attitude toward the firm. Creating a positive attitude obviously had a positive impact on all belief dimensions. Calling attention to a source of irritation—oil company profits—tended to counteract the positive attitude change. The Chevron experience graphically illustrates the risk of measuring a part of a campaign in isolation.

DIAGNOSTIC COPY TESTS . . . .

An entire category of advertising research methods is designed primarily not to test the impact of a total ad but to help creative people understand how the parts of the ad contribute to its impact. Which are the weaker parts of the ad, and how do they interact? Most of these approaches can be applied to mock-ups of proposed ads as well as finished ads.

Qualitative Research

Focus groups research is widely used at the front end of the development of an advertising campaign. In one study of the techniques used by 112 (out of 150 surveyed) of the top advertisers and agencies, focus groups were used 96 percent of the time to generate ideas for advertisements, and 60 percent of the time to test reactions to rough executions.[30] As mentioned near the beginning of this chapter, the

Chevron energy report:

Compared to all U.S. industry—

Chevron's nickel profit makes us just average.

The average profit for all major U.S. industries last year was 5.5¢ on a sales dollar.

By comparison, in 1979 Chevron made about 5.1¢ on each sales dollar of U.S. petroleum sales—a little less than the average of U.S. Industry.

Even on our worldwide sales, we still made less on a sales dollar than the average of all U.S. industries.

Like most companies, we reinvest most of our worldwide profits after dividends plus cash from operations (including depreciation). In 1980, Chevron's reinvestment in energy development in the U.S. will be a record for us—more than twice our '79 U.S. profit.

Investment in U.S. energy development is the best way to help move America toward energy independence. But we must all continue to conserve as much energy as possible.

CHEVRON'S PROFIT ON U.S. PETROLEUM SALES VS. ALL U.S. INDUSTRY
(per dollar of sales in 1979)

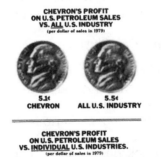

5.1¢ CHEVRON   5.5¢ ALL U.S. INDUSTRY

CHEVRON'S PROFIT ON U.S. PETROLEUM SALES VS. INDIVIDUAL U.S. INDUSTRIES.
(per dollar of sales in 1979)

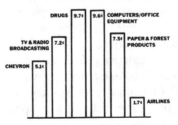

DRUGS 9.7¢   9.6¢ COMPUTERS/OFFICE EQUIPMENT

TV & RADIO BROADCASTING 7.2¢   7.5¢ PAPER & FOREST PRODUCTS

CHEVRON 5.1¢

1.7¢ AIRLINES

JWT Ad No. 100062—
Time, Newsweek, Spts. Ill., U.S. News—4/14, 4/21, 1980

Figure 14–4.   A Chevron "profit" print advertisement.
Courtesy of J. Walter Thompson USA.

use of such qualitative techniques, using "rough" ads, has increased over the last ten years.

Audience Impressions of the Ad

Many copy tests add a set of open-ended questions to the procedures designed to tap the audience's impressions of what the ad was about, what ideas were presented, interest in the ideas, and so on. One goal is to detect potential misperceptions. Another is to uncover unintended associations that may have been created. If too many negative comments are elicited, there may be cause for concern. A Volkswagen commercial showing a Detroit auto worker driving a VW Rabbit because of its superior performance was killed because a substantial part of the audience disliked the company disloyalty portrayed.[31]

Adjective Checklists

The BRC mail questionnaire, shown earlier in Figure 14–1, includes an adjective checklist that allows the advertiser to determine how warm, amusing, irritating, or informative the respondent thinks it to be. Similar checklists are used by ASI, Tele-Research, and other firms and agencies. The agencies Leo Burnett and Young & Rubicam use a similar phrase checklist extensively, often called a VRP (for viewer response profile). Several of their phrases tap an empathy dimension. "I can see myself doing that," "I can relate to that," and so on. Some believe that unless advertisements can achieve a degree of empathy, they will not perform well.

Copy-Testing Emotional Response

Many advertising agencies have begun testing their ads using exhaustive batteries of possible emotional and feeling responses, to gauge whether their ads are evoking the targeted emotions and whether some undesirable negative emotions are being evoked by accident. Various sets of verbal scales have been reported that can be used to gauge such emotional response, and such scales are used by Ayer and McCann-Erickson, among others.[32] Leo Burnett reportedly tests such responses using computer-aided consumer interviewing: the consumer first selects one of a few major emotional categories to describe the feelings evoked by the ad, and then computer then moves to a more finely-grained typology of emotions within that major category, and so on.

BBDO prefers to use a non verbal system, in which consumers who see the ad are presented with fifty-three photographs of peoples' faces, each face carefully chosen to display one of twenty-six particular emotional states from among the universe of emotions. Consumers select the faces that best reflect their own feeling states, and researchers tabulate how often particular photos are chosen. Statistical analysis then places each ad in a two-dimensional emotional space, with the dimensions being *active-passive* and *positive-negative*. (These two dimensions are often found in research on emotions.) When this system was used by BBDO on the Gillette ad called "The Best A Man Can Get," the emotional strategy objective of making men feel better about their shaving experience was apparently met: the ad made men report increased feelings of pride and confidence, as well as joy and happiness.[33]

Physiological Measures

Several kinds of physiological instruments are used to observe reactions to advertisements.[34] In general, they attempt to capture changes in the nervous system or emotional arousal during the exposure sequence. The first two reviewed focus on eye movement.

Eye Camera

This is a device that photographs eye movements, either by photographing a small spot of light reflected from the eye or by taking a motion picture of eye movement. A device records the point on a print advertisement or package, where the eye focuses sixty times each second. Analysis can determine what the reader saw, what he or she "returned to," and what point was "fixed upon." In package research, a respondent can be asked to find a test brand placed on a shelf of competing packages.

Pupillometrics

Pupillometrics deals with eye dilation. Eyes dilate when something interesting or pleasant is seen and constrict when confronted with unpleasant, distasteful, or uninteresting things. One interesting application is its use in screening new television programs.[35] Several related eye-movement devices are used, including the tachistoscope, blur meter, distance meter, illumination meter, and stereo rater.[36]

CONPAAD

Conjugately programmed analysis of advertising (CONPAAD) has a respondent operate either a foot or hand device which controls the intensity of the audio and video channels of a television set. The viewer must exert effort to sustain the signals, which have been programmed to decay in a specific pattern. His or her effort to keep audio and video going is used as a measure of attention and interest in the advertising.[37]

Brain Waves

Some companies test ads by means of the amount, nature, and distribution of the brain waves evoked. Consumers are placed into seats and have electrodes placed on different parts (front, back; left, right) of their scalps. As the ad is shown to them, the brain wave activity in various regions of their brains is recorded through electroencephalography (EEG). These measures cover various frequency ranges and are averaged over time and *normalized* for each individual being tested. Analysis of the frequency and amplitude of this activity can be interpreted to check the attention-getting power of different parts of the commercial, as well as of the ad as a whole. For instance, recognition of parts of the the ad has been shown to be related to increased left hemispheric processing for those parts. The left hemisphere is typically associated with more effortful, analytic, attentional processing, so that an increase in such processing indicates more voluntary information processing.[38]

The possible problems with such data, as with other physiological data (such as galvanic skin response, etc.) are (1) the contaminating effects of "artifacts" (irrelevant instrument or person-related factors that don't really measure the effectiveness of the ad) and (2) the somewhat difficult-to-interpret nature of the data (what does reduced or increased brain wave activity really mean in terms of cognitive processes, for example?).

"On-Line" Monitoring of Commercial Response

A device used by respondents to register interest is part of ASI in-theater tests. It is a dial that can be turned up or down to indicate high or low interest. Data from the dial interest recorder are used to provide diagnostic information on what parts of the commercial were of high or low interest. Market Facts has developed a system in which a respondent presses a button when something in the commercial strikes her or him as especially interesting or irritating. The respondent is then shown the commercial again and asked why the button was punched at each point. The result is a second-by-second understanding of audience reaction. Similar techniques have been used by Linda Alwitt and colleagues to study how soon, and how often, a brand should be shown in a commercial (the answers depend on whether the ad is trying to leverage a brand's existing equity, or to change it).[39]

David Aaker, Douglas Stayman, and Michael Hagerty have used a computer joystick to measure respondent reactions to feelings of warmth while viewing commercials. This procedure can also be used to monitor other feelings, such as irritation, humor, or liking.[40] James MacLachlan and John Myers have used the time it takes the respondent to make a choice between competing brands as a measure of the relative effectiveness of advertising. This is called *response latency* and has several other applications in advertising research.[41] Another potentially useful technique is called *facial action coding*. By observing changes in facial expression during exposure, several kinds of emotional responses can be monitored.[42] G. David Hughes and colleagues have developed dial-turning continuous measurement methods to obtain affective (feeling) and other measures of responses to ads, and have found that the "wearing-out" of an ad can be anticipated via such measures because they show when consumers cease to do any "fresh" processing of such ads.[43]

TRACKING STUDIES . . . .

When a campaign is running, its impact is often monitored via a tracking study. Periodic sampling of the target audience provides a time trend of measures of interest. The purpose is to evaluate and reassess the advertising campaign and perhaps also to understand why it is or is not working. Among the measures that are often tracked are advertisement awareness, awareness of elements of the advertisement, brand awareness, beliefs about brand attributes, brand image ratings, occasions of use, and brand preference. For durables such as cars, consumers are asked what brands they would consider buying on their next purchase, and what brand they are most likely to buy next. Of particular interest is knowing how the

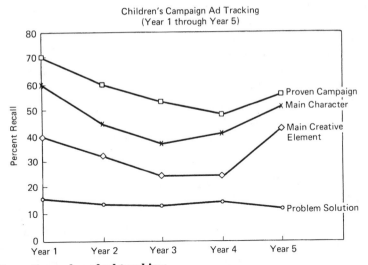

Figure 14–5.   Examples of ad tracking.

Source: Reprinted from the Journal of Advertising Research © *copyright 1985, by the Advertising Research Foundation.*

campaign is affecting the brand, as opposed to how the advertisement is communicating.

Figure 14–5 shows the tracking of an advertising campaign directed at children for a beverage product. Personal interviews were held with children from six to twelve years old. They were shown visual stimuli such as pictures of brand packaging or line drawings of advertising characters. The mostly open-ended questions were consistently coded over five years. The interest was in the "main character," who was the personification of the brand and playback of the "story" of the advertising, the main creative element.[44]

The successful campaign of year 1 was expanded with additional executions which apparently did not have comparable impact. The disappointing results of year 2 led to a fresh round of copy development aimed at making it more "modern" and "relevant" for kids. However, the decline continued in year 3. An analysis of verbatim playback suggested that the predictability of the main character's actions were too predictable and new ads were developed which placed it in a more heroic role, "rescuing" children in adventurous situations. In year 4, the main character measure turned up. For the next season, the campaign used situations from a child's real life to attempt to make the advertising more relevant. The result in year 5 was a dramatic increase in recall of the central creative element and an important increase in two other measures. The tracking program provided in this case actionable information over time, allowing the advertising to be adjusted around the same theme to become more effective.

The Eric Marder firm provides one approach to obtaining tracking data without doing customized studies.[45] They maintain a panel of 3,000 women from 1,000 areas. Each woman keeps a record of all television commercials she sees in the course of one randomly assigned day each month. Before watching television on her assigned day, she records her buying intention for each product category. On the assigned day she watches television normally except that she records the time, the channel, and the brand advertised from every ad she sees, and her buying intention immediately after exposure. The *received messages* (*RMs*) are defined as the total number of commercials recorded per 100 women. The *persuasion rate* (*PR*) is defined as the net percent of the RM that produces a shift in buying intention from some other brand to the advertised brand. Subscribers obtain quarterly reports of the RM and PR from all competing brands in the product class.

SELECTING COPY TESTS: VALIDITY AND RELIABILITY . . . .

A very wide range of copy-testing alternatives has been developed and is available to the advertiser. Beyond the question of whether to test copy at all lies the question of what particular test or tests should be used. The question has occupied the attention of professional and academic researchers since copy testing first began, and a great deal has been written on the subject. Much of the interest lies in assessing the validity and reliability of various types of tests. The subject is also important because considerable stakes are involved by research supplier companies who tend to offer a particular kind of testing service or rely on one testing method. The Advertising Research Foundation maintains a standing committee to monitor and encourage the development of new and better testing methods, and its annual conferences generally relate to questions of the strengths and limitations of particular methods or techniques.

The basic question in test selection is whether or not a test is valid and reliable. Does it really measure the effectiveness of advertising? More specifically, are the particular measures used in any one test true measures of the constructs involved? Is the test reliable and will it measure the same thing each time it is used? Can one test measure everything or are multitests required? These are some of the questions of copy-test selection.

Appropriate Copy-Test Measure(s)

The first problem in assessing copy-test validity is that, if the advertisement is to be tested with respect to a communication objective and a copy test evaluated in that context, there must exist an operational objective—a measurable and useful variable that represents the objective. As Chapter 4 indicated, the development of an operational objective is no simple task. In fact, researchers must often work with a vague or ill-defined set of objectives. Clarity in what is being sought from the ad—and therefore being tested in the copy test—is crucial. One measure cannot generally substitute for another: recall does not measure persuasion, and one must decide which of those is being sought for a particular ad.

Obviously, therefore, the validity of a particular copy test will depend on the advertising response that is desired. A campaign that is designed to gain awareness may not best be measured by a test that focuses on immediate behavioral response. A campaign that attempts to create an image or an association with a feeling such as warmth might require many repetitions and a subtle measurement method, perhaps asking some questions directed at the use experience. A single-exposure test with a coupon-redemption measure may not be appropriate at all. Thus, the usefulness of the various criteria used in testing needs to be evaluated in the context of the advertising objectives involved.

The choice of a copy-test measure should also be guided by the riskiness of the decision involved. To begin a major new campaign involving strategic departure is a high-risk decision that requires a total evaluation of all the constructs mentioned earlier. It is also important to assess whether the copy appears to antagonize respondents in any way. A total evaluation should also involve enough diagnostic information about consumer reactions to the execution so that the decision could be based on all the evaluative and diagnostic measures. It is possible to get high awareness but negative reactions.

Total ad evaluation is not always economically practical or necessary. Extensions of existing campaigns are low-risk decisions requiring only partial evaluation. In particular evaluations, persuasiveness or attitude change will sometimes be the issue and attention will be of little concern. Sometimes clarity of communication will be the issue, and a subjective judgment of its persuasiveness will suffice. Sometimes the major concern will be focused on possible negatives in execution. In each case, the objectives of the copy test will differ.

Best Scales: The ARF Study

Once such objectives have been set, which copy-test measures are most valid for each objective? In a recent study conducted by the Advertising Research Foundation,[46] which involved six copy-testing measures, five pairs of packaged-goods commercials, and sales measures obtained over a year using split-cable testing, it was found that

- **The best (most predictive of sales differences) copy-testing measure for persuasion was a simple poor-to-excellent rating of the brand, obtained after exposure.**
- **The best copy-testing measure for salience was the number of times the brand was mentioned first in unaided awareness for that category.**
- **The best copy-testing measure of communication was "other than to get you to buy the product, what was the main point of the commercial?"**
- **A big predictor of sales was an agree/disagree rating for the statement "this ad is one of the best I've seen recently."**
- **Ads led to sales if they were rated high on either or both of "tells me a lot about how the product works" and "this advertising is funny or clever," but not if they rated high on "I find this ad artistic" or "this ad doesn't give any facts, it just creates an image."**

Competitive Context

Since the ad being tested will eventually run amid competitive clutter, with such clutter decreasing the effectiveness of the tested ad,[47] researchers David Stewart,

Paul Miniard, and others have pointed out that the success or failure of a particular ad campaign can only be assessed completely if the measurements are conducted in a *competitive context*. Further, when copy-testing an ad, measures should be collected not only for the brand in question but also for competitive brands. Thus, though an ad may not show increases in favorable beliefs or overall attitudes for the target brand, it may show effects of leading to declines in the beliefs and attitudes for competitive brands—which will not show up in a copytest unless these competitive measures, too, are collected, including *relative measures* (e.g., "which of these brands is better on this attribute?").

Further, if comparative advertising is being employed, measures of the perceived similarity between the two brands should also be collected, before and after exposure, since one effect of the ad might be to increase the perceived similarity of the brands being compared.[48] Relatedly, since an ad may change certain consumer beliefs about the tested brand (or competitive brands) *other than* those explicitly discussed in the ad, by consumers making their own inferences about those nondiscussed beliefs, copytests should obtain before-and-after measures of such *inferential beliefs* as well, in addition to measuring beliefs explicitly featured in the ad.[49]

Target Market

A second issue here is that, given that a target population can be sensibly defined, the subjects in the test should be representative of the target population. Ideally, they should be selected randomly, and the sample size should be large enough so that the results are statistically valid. Of course, compromises must be made. It is often not feasible economically to obtain large random samples, especially if personal interviews are involved. The bias introduced by nonrespondents is a problem that is particularly crucial in some tests. People differ widely in their propensity to answer questions, to participate in laboratory experiments, to be subjects in physiological tests, and to be members of consumer panels. The danger is that those who refuse to participate may respond differently from those who do. In addition, mall-intercept methods obviously access only mall shoppers, and cable-based tests miss those not connected to a cable. There is also a question as to whether one or even three or four cities can provide a representative sample. Consequently, the results may not represent the population for which the sample was drawn.

Reactivity

Third, and perhaps most significant, is the reaction of the respondents to the test environment and the measuring instruments. Research has shown that consumers expecting to be quizzed on ad recall or recognition performed better on such tests than consumers not expecting those tests.[50] Such reactions can distort the results. When a respondent is in a test situation, he or she tends to act differently. The main problem in any advertising study is the tendency of respondents to act as they should act (called *reactive effect*, *role selection*, the *guinea pig effect*, etc.). There is evidence that this problem is minor in a system such as BehaviorScan when the panel member becomes acclimated to the system. However, it is of greatest concern in systems which demand that the respondent give an attitude response. Is the respondent willing and able to respond accurately?

There are techniques to minimize the reactive effect. One is to divert respondents from the actual purpose of the experiment. Thus, a respondent may be told that she or he is evaluating television programs instead of their accompanying commercials. This technique, however, by no means eliminates all such bias. Furthermore, it has moral and ethical implications. How much deception should a respondent be subjected to without his or her consent? Another approach is to use, wherever possible, nonreactive measures. Thus, one might unobtrusively observe store traffic or sales. Direct-mail tests can usually be conducted with little reactive effect, since a nonreactive response measure to the direct-mail advertisement is usually available.

Rough versus Finished

A fourth issue is whether a rough mock-up can adequately predict the response from the finished ad. Several copy-test firms have reported high correlations with mock-up measures and finished copy measures. The seriousness of the problem will depend on the difference between the mock-up and the finished commercial and the impact of this difference on audience response. For example, it is very difficult to test humor, emotional response, or overall ad likability in rough form.[51] On the other hand, rough ads such as animatics are well-suited to testing copy-point comprehension and can thus be used for strategy testing, although some research shows that animatics may overstate comprehension because they are more static than finished ads.[52]

Number of Exposures

A fifth issue is the frequency of response. To what extent can a copy test predict the response to a campaign that will involve dozens or even hundreds of exposures? Can a single exposure provide meaningful results, or should a minimum of two or three be used? Still another issue is the context in which the test advertisement is embedded. The use of a cluster of advertisements embedded in a program or magazine is the most realistic but adds complexity and is possibly confounding.

Natural versus Forced-Exposure

Finally, such approaches as the theater tests or mall intercept exposure contexts are termed forced exposure tests because the setting is artificial and the respondent is required to watch. The others, such as the BehaviorScan split-cable testing, are termed *on-air tests* because the exposure is a natural home setting in the context of watching a show. Approaches such as the ASI Apex method are on-air but the respondents realize they are in a test and are not watching a show they would watch at a time they would normally watch it. Thus, there is still concern that the exposure context may affect the results.

Thus, running through the validity considerations is a spectrum from artificial to natural. At one extreme would be forced exposure to a commercial mock-up with a paper-and-pencil response using a mall-intercept sample. At the other would be the BehaviorScan system, in which the audience member realizes that he or she is in a panel but otherwise everything is completely natural, including multiple exposures over time.

There are suppliers in each of the three major categories of copy-testing research: laboratory tests, simulated natural environment tests, and market tests. In television, laboratory and simulated natural-environment tests involve forced exposure, whereas market tests tend to be on-air recall tests. A study of advertiser and agency executive opinion on preferences between different versions of on-air and forced-exposure tests[53] revealed the most preferred to be single-exposure, multiple-market tests in the on-air case (rather than single-exposure, single-market; multiple exposure, single market; or multiple exposure, multiple market). In the forced-exposure case, in-theater and laboratory tests were preferred to mobile trailer and in-home forced-exposure tests. These data, of course, indicate overall general preference, and test choices should be made on the basis of the particular situation involved.

Copy-Test Reliability

Copy-test selection must also take into account the reliability of a particular test. Will it measure the same thing each time it is used? Much work has also been done on this question. In a study by Kevin Clancy and Lyman Ostlund, for example, a second measure taken at a later time was developed for 106 on-air recall-tested commercials. The authors report reliability coefficients (the correlation of scores taken at one time with those taken at another time) of 0.67 (and when product category effects were removed) of 0.29.[54] These are comparatively low, and, on this basis, the authors challenge the reliability of on-air recall tests. It has been shown that reliability of preference measures is often even lower than that for recall measures, especially if single-exposure preference measures are being used.[55]

Alvin Silk[56] has pointed out some of the dangers of using the test-retest approach to reliability assessment. It is important that test-retest conditions be equivalent. If, for example, consumers have been exposed to the advertising in different contexts between the two testing occasions or to competitive advertising, the testing conditions may not be equivalent, and a low correlation may not signify low reliability. Research by Jacob Hornik has even shown that the copy-test scores can vary depending on the time of day—immediate recall is highest if the ad is tested at 9 A.M. because people are most alert at that time![57] It is indeed difficult to make straightforward assessments of copy-test reliability using the test-retest procedure because of such factors.

Copy-Test Sensitivity, and Other Considerations

Copy-test selection should take into account several other considerations concerning the nature of a particular test or supplier providing the test. In addition to reliability and validity, for example, Joseph Plummer recommends[58] that tests be assessed on five other criteria:

1. *Sensitivity:* The test should be able to discriminate between different commercials within brand groups.
2. *Independence of measures:* The different test measures should have little interrelationship across many testing experiences.
3. *Comprehensiveness:* The test should provide, in addition to basic evaluative scores, some information that will indicate the reason for the levels of the evaluative scores.
4. *Relationships to other tests:* The test should provide similar results for the same stimuli tested by a similar but different measurement system.
5. *Acceptability:* The test must have some acceptance by those responsible for decisions in terms of a commitment to work with the test findings.

In choosing a supplier, obviously the reputation of the company, such as its service and delivery record, availability of norms, and stature in the industry, will be important. Things like geographic location and costs of the service relative to competitive offerings also come into play.

These are some of the considerations that need to be taken into account in assessing test validity. Figure 14–6 provides an overview of some of the important ways in which copy tests can differ. Each dimension involves validity issues and trade-offs with cost.

The PACT Principles

In 1982, a coalition of twenty-one advertising agencies developed the following principles of copy testing, called *PACT* (*positioning advertising copy testing*), which summarizes much of what we have developed earlier in this chapter and introduces a few others:[59]

1. A good copy-testing system provides measurements which are relevant to the objectives of the advertising.
2. A good copy-testing system is one which requires agreement about how the results will be used in advance of each specific test.
3. A good copy-testing system provides multiple measures because single measurements are generally inadequate to assess the performance of an advertisement.
4. A good copy-testing system is based on a model of human response—the reception of a stimulus, the comprehension of the stimulus and the response to the stimulus.
5. A good copy-testing system allows for consideration of whether the advertising stimulus should be exposed more than once.
6. A good copy-testing system recognizes that the more finished a piece of copy is the more soundly it can be evaluated, requiring, as a minimum, that alternative executions be tested in the same degree of finish.

The Advertisement Used

- Mock-Up
- Finished Advertisement

Frequency of Exposure

- Single exposure test
- Multiple exposure test

How It's Shown

- Isolated
- In a clutter
- In a program or magazine

Where the Exposure Occurs

- In a shopping center facility
- At home on TV
- At home through the mail
- In a theater

How Respondents are Obtained

- Prerecruited forced exposure
- Not prerecruited/natural exposure

Geographic Scope

- One city
- Several cities
- Nationwide

Alternative Measures of Persuasion

- Pre/post measures of attitudes or behavioral that is, pre/post attitude shifts
- Multiple measures that is, recall/involvement/buying commitment
- After only questions to measure persuasion that is, constant sum brand preference
- Test market sales measures that is, using scanner panels

Bases of Comparison and Evaluation

- Comparing test results to norms
- Using a control group

Figure 14–6.   Alternative methods of copy testing.

7. A good copy-testing system provides controls to avoid the biasing effects of the exposure context.

8. A good copy-testing system is one that takes into account basic considerations of sample definition.

9. A good copy-testing system is one that can demonstrate reliability and validity.

EXAMPLE OF A COPY-TEST REPORT. . . . .

An example of the data obtained from a copytest is provided in Figure 14–7, reproduced from *Advertising Age*. Note the use of both persuasion and recall criteria, and the comparison of this ad's test scores—from the target market—with norms.

SUMMARY. . . . .

During and after the creation and production process, the advertiser must decide whether to invest in copy-testing research and what kinds of tests to use. An industry of research supplier companies has evolved to supply copy-testing services. There are hundreds of methods used to test copy. Much advertising is placed without formal copy testing, particularly by local advertisers for whom the investment in advertising does not warrant the extra expense. Certain "creative" agencies also do not believe in pretesting commercials, arguing that it restricts the creativity of their work. Copy testing tends to be done mostly by large national advertisers where the risks and investments are high.

Copy testing can be done at the beginning of the creation process, at the end (layout) stage of the creation process, at the end of the production stage, and after the campaign is launched. Tests at the first three stages are called pretests, whereas those at the fourth stage are posttests.

Criteria used in copy testing can be usefully grouped into five types: recognition, recall, persuasion, behavior, and loyalty. BRC uses mail questionnaires to measure television commercial recognition and brand-name association. Communicus for television, and Starch, for print, uses personal interviews. Day-after recall is widely used but controversial because of its inability to predict persuasion or behavior, especially for emotional appeals. Persuasion has been measured in forced exposure or on-air contexts, by change in brand preference after an exposure to an ad on a UHF station, by change in prize-list brand preference in a theater test, by comparison of the effect on brand preference with a nonexposed control group, by measures of advertising involvement and brand commitment, and by measures tailored to particular advertising objectives. Behavior measures include coupon-stimulated buying after a forced exposure to an ad, split-run tests of ad-generated inquiries, and scanner-based monitoring of panelists in a split-cable testing operation.

Diagnostic testing, to evaluate the advertisement content at all stages of the process, includes qualitative research, audience ad impressions, adjective checklists, checklists of emotions evoked by the ad, eye movement, and the monitoring of audience response during the commercial. Within the laboratory-physiological methods group, measuring devices such as the eye camera, polygraphs, tachisto-

Coke II spot goes flat on persuasion

TV spots supporting Coca-Cola Co.'s test of Coke II, the old "new Coke," deliver a "new name" message that's differentiates the brand from competitors. But Coke II may have a problem in that what's being communicated—a new name—isn't persuading soft-drink purchasers to buy the product.

In tests conducted for *Advertising Age* by Research Systems Corp., 24% of viewers were able to play back the "new name" message. The Coke II spot also contains new product information and competitive comparison, both of which are strategic elements positively related to superior selling commercials.

The commercial features a can of Coke II, with a voice-over informing viewers that "new Coke" is now called Coke II and has real cola taste and the sweetness of Pepsi-Cola. The voice-over suggests that those who've been drinking Pepsi should give Coke II a try. (He also reminds consumers that Coca-Cola Classic *hasn't changed*.)

RSC tested the commercial in four geographically dispersed markets among 832 soft-drink purchasers to assess the commercial's ability to generate a sales/share increase and communicate

its message in a memorable way.

The spot, from McCann-Erickson Worldwide, New York, achieved an ARS Persuasion level of +2.2 among the soft-drink purchaser sample. ARS Persuasion is RSC's measurement of the change in brand preference due to exposure, and the researcher's split-cable validation experience indicates this ARS Persuasion level wouldn't be expected to cause a measurable share increase if the spot alone was aired. The commercial is deemed an average persuader because its ARS Persuasion level isn't significantly different from the +3.0 level expected for an average commercial for this soft drink.

The research company also gauges a commercial's effectiveness by measuring its related recall and key-message communication, through traditional recall interviews 72 hours after the session to get the ARS Persuasion level.

The Recall score for this commercial is 57%, and research conducted by RSC has shown that commercials achieving an adequate level of attention/memorability (23%+ Recall) and communicating a brand-differentiating key message to 16%+ of the

(vs. 13% for all other commercials).

The +2.2 score achieved by Coke II indicates this spot alone couldn't be expected to increase sales/share for the brand. But by using a pool of spots and replacing each when it wears down, RSC said, Coca-Cola can maximize its advertising's Persuasive Rating Point (the combination of ARS Persuasion level and gross rating points) level or sales/share-generating ability for the media budget invested.

Multiple commercials at that ARS Persuasion level and above may have a measurable sales/share effect, the researcher concluded. □

Kimberly Mari

viewers have a 41% chance of | achieving superior selling power |

Figure 14-7. Example of results from a copy test.

Reprinted with permission from Advertising Age, September 7, 1992. © *Crain Communications, Inc. All rights reserved.*

scopes, pupillometers, brain wave measures, and computer-assisted effort measurement are the major alternatives. Recent developments in this area include response latency and face-coding methods. Simulated natural environment tests include those based on intercept research and mobile trailers, fixed facility research, and in-home interviewing. Many of the recognition, rather than the recall, methods fit into this category. Services provided by ARS, ASI, Starch INRA Hooper, and Bruzzone Research are representative of these kinds of tests.

A tracking study provides measures of advertising impact over time by taking periodic (monthly, quarterly, or yearly) surveys of audience response. Awareness of the advertising or of specific claims or elements of the advertising is often included, but any measure relevant to the objectives can be used.

Given the vast array of alternative methods and commercial services for copy testing, the question becomes how to choose sensibly among them. The basic question is whether a particular test is valid and reliable. Three major factors must be considered with respect to validity. First, the test must measure what the campaign seeks to achieve. A test designed to measure one objective (e.g., recall) is different from one that aims to measure another objective (e.g., persuasion). Second, subjects in the test should be representative of the target population. Third, reactions of the subjects to the testing situation that might bias the results should be minimized. Copy-test validity concerns usually focus on the appropriateness of the response measure, the reactive (or guinea pig) effect of being in an experiment (especially when the exposure setting is not natural and when an attitude measure is required), the use of mock-ups, and the representativeness of the sample.

Generally, it has been found that no one test or method is sufficient to satisfy all the needs of copy research, but that tests designed to measure different constructs can indeed do so. Which tests are better, particularly whether recall or persuasion tests are better for testing television commercials, is a continuing debate in the industry. Test reliability must also be considered. Here, again, because of the difficulties of measuring reliability, there are no definitive answers. The norms developed by suppliers over years of testing remain the advertiser's best guide to this question.

Many other practical considerations about the supplier (reputation, service, location, costs, and so on) and the service or test (sensitivity, independence, comprehensiveness, relationships to other tests, and acceptability) should be included in the selection process. The overriding considerations in this decision are that the test or tests chosen should be governed by the objectives of the advertising, the amount of investment involved, and the extent to which there is little or no past experience on which to guide decision making in a particular product or market situation.

DISCUSSION QUESTIONS . . . .

1. Make a list of the factors you would consider in deciding whether to invest in copy-testing research at each of the four stages of testing given in the chapter.

2. Why measure recognition anyway? Why would it ever be of value to have an audience member recognize an ad when he or she could not recall it without being prompted and could not recall its content? Why not just measure recall?

3. Compare the BRC recognition method with the Communicus method. What are the relative strengths and weaknesses?

4. DAR is widely used. Why? Would you use it if you were the product manager for Löwenbräu? For American Express? Under what circumstances would you use it?

5. Review the validity problems inherent in the McCollum/Spielman theater-testing approach. Compare these to
   a. The Mapes & Ross method.
   b. The ASI Apex method.
   c. The Tele-Research approach.
   d. The Behavior Scan approach.

6. Why conduct tracking studies? Why not just observe sales?

7. How will adjective checklists help a creative group? What about eye-movement data?

8. Suppose that the advertising objective is to entice people to try a new brand. Predictive validity is whether recall predicts purchase, whether memorability predicts purchase, whether arousal and interest predict purchase, or whether attitudes predict purchase. From what has been reviewed in previous chapters, discuss the validity question at each of these levels.

9. The various methods of copy research are representative of the various methods of research in social science, particularly psychological and sociological research methods. Give an example in which the methods used by psychoanalytic (Freudian) or clinical psychologists, stimulus-response (behavior) psychologists, multidimensional scalers, attitude researchers, and sociologists are employed in copy research.

10. Laboratory methods are often criticized for their artificiality in copy-testing research. Are there any counterarguments? Discuss.

11. Discuss the advantages and disadvantages of an in-theater method compared to a market test and a recall method versus a recognition method.

12. Design an ideal test of copy effectiveness. Assuming the measures would be made in a natural environment, critically examine the difficulties involved.

NOTES. . . . .

1. One estimate is that as much as $125 million is spent annually on copy testing. Robert Mayer of Young & Rubicam advertising agency suggests that there are "33,000 ways" to test advertising copy. Basal skin response, brain waves, eye movement, pupil dilation, physical effort, aided and unaided noting and recall, copy-point recall, visual and slogan recall, interest and attitude toward the advertisement, knowledge and sales response are some of the measures used. Copy-testing designs include prepost or post-only studies, single versus multiple exposure, projectable versus nonprojectable samples, natural exposure versus forced exposure. Other alternatives include where the exposure should take place (in-home, in-theater, mobile trailer, shopping center intercept, fixed facility), whether the testing is done in groups (such as the family) or in-

dividually, and whether the exposure should attempt to simulate the natural setting by introducing distraction or competitive advertising.

2. Karen W. King, John D. Pehrson, and Leonard N. Reid, "Pretesting TV Commercials: Methods, Measures, and Changing Agency Roles," *Journal of Advertising*, 22, no. 3 (September 1993), 85–97.

3. Readers should refer to the materials in Chapter 15 on the creation and production process for a better understanding of where testing "fits in."

4. Karen W. King, John D. Pehrson, and Leonard N. Reid, "Pretesting TV Commercials: Methods, Measures, and Changing Agency Roles," *Journal of Advertising*, 22, no. 3 (September 1993), 85–97.

5. Donald E. Bruzzone, "The Case for Testing Commercials by Mail." Paper presented at the 25th Annual Conference of the Adertising Research Foundation, New York, October 23, 1979.

6. Lewis C. Winters, "Comparing Pretesting and Posttesting of Corporate Advetising," *Journal of Advertising Research*, 23 (February/March 1983), 25–32.

7. See, for example, Alan D. Fletcher and Paul R. Winn, "An Intermagazine Analysis of Factors in Advertising Readership," *Journalism Quarterly*, 51 (Autumn 1974), 425–430; Kjell Gronhaug, Olav Kvitastein and Sigmund Gronmo, "Factors Moderating Advertising Effectiveness as Reflected in 333 Tested Advertisements," *Journal of Advertising Research*, 31, no. 5 (Oct.–Nov. 1991), 41–50; Dominique M. Hanssens and Barton A. Weitz, "The Effectiveness of Industrial Print Advertisements Across Product Categories," *Journal of Marketing Research*, 17 (August 1980), 294–306; Donald W. Hendon, "How Mechanical Factors Affect Ad Perception," *Journal of Advertising Research*, 13 (August 1973), 39–45; Morris B. Holbrook and Donald R. Lehmann, "Form Versus Content in Predicting Starch Scores," *Journal of Advertising Research*, 20 (August 1980), 53–62; John Rossiter, "Predicting Starch Scores," *Journal of Advertising Research*, 21 (October 1981), 63–68; Lawrence C. Soley and Leonard N. Reid, "Predicting Industrial Ad Readership," *Industrial Marketing Management*, 12 (1983), 201–206; Richard M. Sparkman, Jr., "Cost Effectiveness of Advertising," *International Journal of Advertising*, 4, no. 2 (1985), 131–141; and Rafael Valiente, "Mechanical Correlates of Ad Recognition," *Journal of Advertising Research*, 13 (June 1973), 13–18.

8. Surendra N. Singh and Gilbert A. Churchill, Jr., "Response-Bias-Free Recognition Tests to Measure Advertising Effects," *Journal of Advertising Research* (June/July 1987), 23–36.

9. Charles E. Young and Michael Robinson, "Guideline: Tracking The Commercial Viewer's Wandering Attention," *Journal of Advertising Research* (June/July 1987), 15–22.

10. George M. Zinkhan, William Locander, and James H. Leigh, "Dimensional Relationships of Aided Recall and Recognition," *Journal of Advertising*, 15, no. 1 (1986), 38–46.

11. Herbert E. Krugman, "Low Recall and High Recognition of Advertising," *Journal of Advertising Research* (February/March 1986), 79–86.

12. Surendra N. Singh, Michael L. Rothschild, and Gilbert A. Churchill, Jr., "Recognition Versus Recallas Measures of Television Commercial Forgetting," *Journal of Marketing Research*, 25 (February 1988), 72–80.

13. Charles R. Duke and Les Carlson, "A Conceptual Approach to Alternative Memory Measures for Advertising Effectiveness," *Journal of Current Issues and Research in Advertising*, 15, no. 2 (Fall 1993), 1–14.

14. Benjamin Lipstein, "An Historical Perspective of Copy Research," *Journal of Advertising Research*, 24 (December 1984), 11–15.

15. Hubert A. Zielske, "Does Day-After-Recall Penalize 'Feeling' Ads?" *Journal of Advertising Research*, 22 (February/March 1982), 19–22.

16. Marian Friestad and Esther Thorson, "Remembering Ads: The Effects of Encoding Strategies, Retrieval Cues, and Emotional Response," *Journal of Consumer Psychology*, 2, no. 1 (1993), 1–23.

17. Lawrence D. Gibson, "Not Recall," *Journal of Advertising Research*, 23 (February/March 1983), 39–46.

18. Lipstein, "An Historical Perspective."

19. AC-T Advertising Control for Television, undated publication of McCollum/Spielman Research.
20. Ibid.
21. Lipstein, "An Historical Perspective."
22. "Advertising Quality Deserves More Weight!" Research Systems Corporation, August 1983.
23. ASI Laboratory Methodology, ASI Market Research, Inc., New York, undated.
24. Milton Sherman, "The BUY Test." Paper presented to The Market Research Society, Manchester, England, May 20, 1982.
25. Descriptive material from Mapes & Ross.
26. Alan P. Kuritsky, John D. C. Little, Alvin J. Silk, and Emily S. Bassman, "The Development, Testing, and Execution of a New Marketing Strategy at AT&T Long Lines," *Interfaces*, 12 (December 1982), 22–37.
27. "Preaching to the Converted," talk by Roger Heineman, of Mapes & Ross Inc., at the ARF Brand Equity Research Day, New York, October 27, 1993; and "Measuring Advertising's Effect on Brand Loyalty," talk by Floyd Poling, of McCollum-Spielman Worldwide, at the same conference.
28. Brian Wansink and Michael L. Ray, "Estimating an Ad's Impact on One's Consumption of a Brand," *Journal of Advertising Research* (May–June 1992), 9–16.
29. Winters, "Comparing Pretesting and Posttesting," p. 28.
30. Benjamin Lipstein and James P. Neelankavil, "Television Advertising Copy Research: A Critical Review of the State of the Art," *Journal of Advertising Research*, 24 (April/May 1984) 19–25.
31. "VW Has Some Clinkers Among Classics," *Advertising Age*, September 9, 1985, p. 48.
32. See, for example, Rajeev Batra and Morris Holbrook, "Developing a Typology of Affective Responses to Advertising: A Test of Validity and Reliability," *Psychology and Marketing*, 7, no. 1 (Spring 1990), 11–25, and David M. Zeitlin and Richard A. Westwood, "Measuring Emotional Response," *Journal of Advertising Research* (October/November 1986), 34–44.
33. "Emotion guides BBDO's ad tests," *Advertising Age*, January 29, 1990, p. 12.
34. For a review, see David W. Stewart, "Physiological Measurement of Advertising Effectiveness," *Psychology and Marketing*, 1 (1984), 43–48.
35. Eckhard H. Hess, "Pupillometrics," in F. M. Bass, C. W. King, and E. A. Pessemier, eds., *Applications of the Sciences in Marketing Management* (New York: Wiley, 1968), pp. 431–453.
36. A variation introduced by Haug Associates of Los Angeles utilizes a modified portable tachistoscope devide that is taken into the home and allows testing in the in-home environment. Respondents are shown the first few seconds of a commercial and asked if they know what it is and, if so, to reconstruct the copy points.
37. See, for example, Ogden R. Lindsley, "A Behavioral Measure of Television Viewing," *Journal of Advertising Research*, 2 (September 1962), 2–12, and Lewis C. Winters and Wallace H.Wallace, "On Operant Conditioning Techniques," *Journal of Advertising Research*, 5 (October 1970), 39–45. Associates for Research in Behavior in Philadelphia provides a copy-testing service based on CONPAAD.
38. Michael L. Rothschild, Yong J. Hyun, Byron Reeves, Esther Thorson, and Robert Goldstein, "Hemispherically Lateralized EEG as a Response to Television Commercials," *Journal of Consumer Research*, 15, no. 2 (September 1988), 185–198; Michael L. Rothschild and Yong J. Hyun, "Predicting Memory for Components of TV Commercials from EEG," *Journal of Consumer Research*, 16 (March 1990), 472–478.
39. Linda F. Alwitt, Suzeanne B. Benet and Robert E. Pitts, "Temporal Aspects of TV Commercials Influence Viewers' Online Evaluations," *Journal of Advertising Research*, 33, no. 3 (May/June 1993), 9–21.
40. David A. Aaker, Douglas M. Stayman, and Michael R. Hagerty, "Warmth in Advertising: Measurement, Impact, and Sequence Effects," *Journal of Consumer Research*, 12 (March 1986), 365–381.

41. James M. MacLachlan and John G. Myers, "Using Resonse Latency to Identify Commercials That Motivate," *Journal of Advertising Research*, 23 (October/November 1983), 51–57. For a book on the subject, see James M. MacLachlan, *Response Latency: New Measure of Advertising* (New York: Advertising Research Foundation, 1977).

42. John G. Myers, "Response Latency and Facial Action Coding Research in Advertising," American Marketing Association Doctoral Consortium, University of Chicago, 1978. See also John L. Graham, "A New System for Measuring Nonverbal Responses to Marketing Appeals," American Marketing Association Proceedings, 1980.

43. G. David Hughes, "Realtime Response Measures Redefine Advertising Wearout," *Journal of Advertising Research*, 32, no. 3 (May/June 1992), 61–77; see also his "Diagnosing Continuous Problems with Continuous Measures of Subjects' Responses," *Journal of Current Issues and Research in Advertising* (1990), 175–196.

44. Douglas F. Haley, "Advertising Tracking Studies: Packaged-Goods Case Histories," *Journal of Advertising Research*, 25 (February/March 1985), 45–50.

45. The TEC Audit, TEC Measures, Inc., New York.

46. Russell I. Haley, "ARF Copy Research Validity Study: A Topline Report." Paper presented at the ARF 36th Annual Conference, April 1990, New York; Russell I. Haley and Allan L. Baldinger, "The ARF Copy Research Validity Project," *Journal of Advertising Research* (April/May 1991) 11–32.

47. See Robert J. Kent and Chris T. Allen, "Does Competitive Clutter in Television Advertising "Interfere" with the Recall and Recognition of Brand Names and Ad Claims?" *Marketing Letters*, 4, no. 2 (1993), 175–184.

48. David W. Stewart, "Measures, Methods, and Models in Advertising Research," *Journal of Advertising Research*, (June/July 1989), 54–60; Paul W. Mimiard, Randall L. Rose, Michael J. Barone and Kenneth C. Manning, "On the Need For Relative Measures When Assessing Comparative Advertising Effects," *Journal of Advertising*, 23, no. 3 (September 1993), 41–57.

49. See Sarah Fisher Gardial and Gabriel Biehal, "Evaluative and Factual Ad Claims, Knowledge Level, and Making Inferences," *Marketing Letters*, 2, no. 4 (1991), 349–358.

50. Robert J. Kent and Karen A. Machleit, "The Effects of Postexposure Test Expectation in Advertising Experiments Utilizing Recall and Recognition Measures," *Marketing Letters*, 3, no. 1 (1992), 17–26.

51. "Researchers balk at testing rough ads for likability," *Marketing News*, Sept. 2, 1991, p. 2.

52. Thomas J. Reynolds and Charles Gengler, "A Strategic Framework for Assessing Advertising: The Animatic vs. Finished Issue," *Journal of Advertising Research*, 31, no. 5 (Oct./Nov. 1991), 61–71.

53. Lyman E. Ostlund, Rakesh Sapra, and Kevin Clancy, "Copy Testing Methods and Measures Favored by Top Ad Agency and Advertising Executives." Working paper, Graduate School of Business, University of Arizona, 1978.

54. Kevin J. Clancy and Lyman E. Ostlund, "Commercial Effectiveness Measures," *Journal of Advertising Research*, 16 (February 1976), 29–34. See also Derek Bloom, Andrea Jay, and Tony Twyman, "The Validity of Advertising Pretests," *Journal of Advertising Research*, 17 (April 1977), 7–16, and Richard P. Bagozzi and Alvin J. Silk, "Recall, Recognition, and the Measurement of Memory for Print Advertisements," *Marketing Science*, 2 (Spring 1983), 95–134.

55. Robin A. Higie and Murphy A. Sewall, "Using Recall and Brand Preference to Evaluate Advertising Effectiveness," *Journal of Advertising Research* (Apr/May 1991), 56–63.

56. Alvin J. Silk, "Test-Retest Correlations and the Reliability of Copy Testing," *Journal of Marketing Research*, 14 (November 1977), 476–486.

57. Jacob Hornik, "Diurnal Variation in Consumer Respnses," *Journal of Consumer Research*, 14 (March 1988), 588–590.

58. Joseph T. Plummer, "Evaluating TV Commercial Tests," *Journal of Advertising Research*, 12 (October 1972), 21–27.

59. PACT Agencies, "Positioning Advertising Copy Testing," *Journal of Advertising*, 11, no. 3 (1982), 3–29.

APPENDIX: NOTES ON FOUR COPY-TESTING SERVICES . . . .

ASI Marketing Research Inc.

ASI is one of the U.S.'s largest copy-testing companies. Founded in 1962 as a unit of Columbia Pictures, it initially focused on testing ads for persuasion but expanded to testing ads for recall and purchased the copy-testing business of Burke in 1990, which was the dominant provider of day-after-recall copy tests. ASI has offices in New York, Cincinnati, and Los Angeles. They have strategic alliances with a variety of companies, including the BASES Group (for using copy-test scores in new product introduction models), NFO Research (for copytesting among narrowly defined target markets), Longman-Moran Analytics and Nielsen Household Services (for brand equity measurement), and Infratest Burke (for global copytesting services). They offer a variety of copy-testing services, four of which are described briefly below:

"Recall Plus"

This is an on-air, in-home ad exposure system using cable TV as the exposure medium, providing percentage scores on "related recall" (compared to norms), qualitative verbatims (transcripts) of what ad content was recalled, diagnostic data, and measures of attention and brand linkage. The test TV ad is embedded by ASI in a standardized TV program environment (an unaired, thirty-minute situation comedy), containing four noncompeting test ads and one nontest ad. Tests are conducted in at least two cities, among two hundred respondents in each city (selected according to sex and age quotas) randomly drawn from cable TV households in that city. Respondents are contacted by phone and asked to preview a new TV program, and then reinterviewed after exposure the following day. After confirming program viewership, four product category cues are provided to test for unaided recall. If the respondent cannot correctly identify the advertised brand/company name, more specific prompts are given to get aided recall. The level and depth of recall and communication is probed. Other questions obtain further information on attention, "brand linkage," and consumer demographics. Additional reexposure to the ad can be done to obtain diagnostic data (the ad is re-run on another cable channel while the re-interview is in progress). Ads can be tested in both rough and finished formats. The test has an estimated .87 reliability coefficient.

"Persuasion Plus"

The methodology is essentially the same as that for the recall test above, with the difference being in the measures collected. At the initial phone contact with the respondent, prior to ad exposure, questions are asked on brand preference, and the same questions are then asked on the re-interview following exposure (in the context of a "prize drawing"). The measured change is used to compute a "Tru-share persuasion score," using a mathematical model that adjusts for market-oriented variables such as brand share and brand loyalty, and this is then compared to norms.

"Print Plus"

The test print ad is inserted ("tipped-in") into either a current issue of general distribution magazine (e.g., *People*), or in ASI's propreitary controlled-environment test magazine. Testing is done in at least five geographically dispersed nmarkets, with a sample size of 175 per city. The magazine is personally placed with qualified readers of the magazine, who are asked to be part of a survey, asked preexposure brand preference questions in the context of a "prize drawing," are told to read the magazine normally, and are then called-back the following day. After confirming that the magazine was read, questions are asked to obtain unaided and aided recall, ad content playback, and diagnostics (the respondent is asked to look at the ad while these are asked). Under the guise of having "misplaced" the original brand preference data for the prize drawing, those questions are re-asked to get "postexposure" preference. Demographic classification questions conclude the reinterview. Recall and persuasion scores are provided, relative to norms, as well as qualitative ad content playback verbatim transcripts.

"NFO/ASI Targeted Copy Testing"

To copy-test TV ads among narrow, targeted segments, ASI mails the test TV ads embedded in a thirty-minute program, on videotape, to appropriately selected members of NFO's national consumer mail panel, who play it on their home VCR. Twenty-four hours after exposure, the standard ASI recall phone interview is conducted. ASI claims very good correlation of these related recall scores with their standard-method scores.

"Creative Response Workshop Plus"

Using a system developed by the Leo Burnett ad agency, ASI also conducts shopping mall-intercept interviews in which respondents see a TV ad on a personal computer, answer questions on the computer on how "involving" and "relevant" the ad is to them, answer open-ended diagnostic questions (the answers are recorded digitally on the computer), and finally provide second-by-second reactions to every scene of the ad, using a "dial" methodology developed by ASI.

Mapes & Ross

Mapes & Ross, founded in 1972, pioneered persuasion copy tests under "real-world" conditions. They offer services to copy-test TV, magazine, newspaper, and radio ads, as well as other services to obtain quick reactions to an ad's communication points, to test the effect of ads in retaining the loyalty of existing users, to measure brand and corporate imagery, and tracking studies. Descriptions of some of these follow. Note that the Mapes & Ross magazine copytesting system is very similar to ASI's, described earlier.

"On-Air" TV Commercial Evaluation

Commercials are aired in a preselected prime-time position (usually a movie) on a UHF or independent station, in one or more test cities. Prior to the test, a sample of viewers are contacted by telephone and invited to participate in a survey that requires viewing the test program (a drawing for three cash awards is an incentive). Appointments are set up to interview the respondents the day after the program is aired. Among nonadvertising questions, respondents are questioned about their brand preferences for six different product categories, including the test category. Respondents provide brand names on an unaided basis. The test ad is exposed in a specified time slot, within a standard commercial break during the first half hour of the program.

The day following the airing of the test program those who watched the program are asked—again on an unaided basis—their brand preferences for a number of product categories including the test category. The respondents are then asked on an aided basis (using category and brand prompts) about the recall of six commercials that appeared within the program. Open-ended questions pertaining to what the commercial was about, what ideas were presented, interest in the ideas, and reactions to the commercial are asked of all respondents claiming recall. As an option, respondents can be asked to provide ratings on a ten-point scale on statements about the test brand or test commercial. Demographic and brand bought last questions complete the interview. The scores provided can be compared to norms. Image questions can also be asked and compared to those from a nonexposed control group.

"Newspaper Ad Evaluation"

Regular readers of the newspaper are prerecruited by telephone and invited to read and give reaction to editorial content appearing in the test issue. At the time of recruitment, preexposure brand preference data are collected (in an unaided and masked fashion). After exposure, a phone interview confirms readership and then obtains the postexposure preference data in the same way. Recall questions follow, as do recall content probes. Norms are provided for the pre-post persuasion shifts.

"Radio Ad Evaluation"

Similar to the newspaper method. The test ads are run in a specified time slot within a standard commercial break during the first half of the radio program to which preinvited radio listeners are listening.

"Equimax Measurement of Increased Usership/Loyalty"

Mapes & Ross first develops an attitudinal questionnaire linking attitudes to usage behavior, working jointly with the client. Ads are then tested to see how they affect these predictive attitudinal measures.

Gallup and Robinson

This Princeton-based firm was founded in 1948 by Dr. George Gallup and Dr. Claude Robinson, two of the pioneers in public opinion survey methods. Dr. Gallup, a Journalism Professor at Northwestern University, spent many years working at Young & Rubicam before starting this company. Their copytesting services cover a very wide range, many of which try to measure "Impact," in which consumers who recall test ads seen a day earlier in a real-world exposure environment provide open-ended responses to seven questions on ad content, the thoughts and feelings they had when they saw the ad, changes in buying interest created by the ad, and so on.

Their specific tests include an "In-View" TV ad test, in which the ad is aired on a syndicated program on an independent TV channel, where it is seen by 150 precontacted viewers, who are called back twenty-four hours later to get data on unaided and aided recall (called "Intrusiveness"), persuasion, copy-point communication ("Idea Communication Profile"), persuasion, and so on. Magazine ads can be tested by placing them either naturally or in a tip-in basis into magazine copies that are placed with 200 consumers who are recontacted a day later to collect the recall and "impact" data. An adjustment in scores is made for the magazine's issue size (number of pages). Newspaper and radio ads are tested in a similar fashion to TV ads, by using preinvited respondents. All scores are interpreted relative to norms for 300 different product categories. The magazine tests have a reliability between 0.72 and 0.95 depending on the test used (the same ad tested twice in the same magazine issue, via an A/B split, has the 0.95 figure, for instance).

One of their new services is called "InTeleTest." TV ads are inserted into an hour-long TV pilot program on a videocassette that is personally left with selected respondents for later in-home viewing on their VCR. As an incentive, the respondent's name is entered into a monthly drawing for $300. The respondent fills out some questions immediately before and immediately after viewing the tape, and is called back on the telephone a day later for various questions. The ad is also taped by itself on the videocassette (following the program), for reexposure, after which the respondent provides additional diagnostic and other data.

Research Systems Corporation (ARS)

Research Systems Corporation, based in Evansville, Indiana, is well-known for its *ARS Persuasion* copy-testing system. Data are collected using a laboratory environment to obtain respondent product choices in simulated purchase occasions before and after advertising exposure. The ARS Persuasion measure is simply the percent choosing the advertised product after exposure, minus the percent choosing the advertised product before exposure. The shift measured by RSC must exceed a norm (e.g., a +3.0 percent increase in persuasion for an average soft-drink commercial) before it is predicted to an actual market share increase.

The service also measures a test ad's related recall and key message communication scores, through traditional recall interviews seventy-two hours after the laboratory session that collects the persuasion-shift score. Again, the test ad's attention/memorability score, and ability to deliver a brand-differentiating key message, are compared to norms. It calculates a *Persuasion Rating Points (PRPs) score* for the ad and its media schedule, combining the *ARS persuasion score* with *gross rating points (GRPs)*, which measure media weight. According to RSC, extensive validity and reliability tests have been conducted on the ARS persuasion measure, including relating ARS persuasion scores to split-cable sales tests, supporting its use. In particular, they claim a strong relationship between sales changes and PRPs. While the firm's exact testing methodology is not publicly published, its standard test of persuasion, recall, and diagnostics, conducted among about 200 men and women in each of two cities, costs about $16,000.

15 PRODUCTION AND IMPLEMENTATION

> Once upon a time I was riding on the top of a Fifth Avenue bus, when I heard a mythical housewife say to another, "Molly, my dear, I would have bought that new brand of toilet soap if only they hadn't set the body copy in 10-point Garamond." Don't you believe it.
>
> (David Ogilvy, in *Confessions of an Advertising Man*)

In the previous chapters we have examined how an ad campaign gets planned and have discussed both the strategic and tactical aspects of that planning. Having decided what to say in the ad, and how to say it, the advertiser now has rough copy and art, or a storyboard, or a radio ad script. Perhaps this has been pretested in rough (or even finished) form, as discussed in Chapter 14. Now the ad is ready and approved. It is time to get the ad produced and sent out to the media to be "run": time to move on to actual implementation.

This chapter discusses two aspects of such implementation. First, we discuss the production process for an ad, both print and television. We then move on to a broader discussion of the relationship between the client and agency, looking at that relationship not only at the time of the production of the ad but throughout the advertising process. What do both the client and the agency need to do to maximize the mutual benefits from the relationship, and to get advertising that is both creative, on strategy, and leads to increased sales?

THE ADVERTISING PRODUCTION PROCESS . . . . .

The production of advertising is a process involving many people, much time, and significant expenditures of money. Although the major components of this process can be described, it is very difficult to explain precisely how effective ads are actually created. It is like asking an artist to explain how to create and produce a great painting. Although we might recognize greatness in the final output of the process, it is difficult to set up a creation and production system that will always guarantee such greatness. Behind any print advertisement or television commercial lie hundreds of decisions involving artistic and other judgments by teams of people inside and outside the agency.

Production decisions are important because all the investment on research and development for a new product or maintaining sales levels of an established product is at stake. A produced ad is the means through which advertising objectives are carried out and strategy is executed. All the attention to careful specification of objectives can be ruined by a poor finished ad. And producing ads is expensive. Creating, producing, and conducting the research done on one television commercial, for example, can involve hundreds of thousands of dollars. Although media costs will be even more expensive (on average, media costs represent about 85 percent of a total advertising budget), their success, too, ultimately depends on the nature of the finished ad. The average cost of producing a single national television commercial, without including the ad agency's mark-up, was $222,000 in 1993, according to a survey by the American Association of Advertising Agencies.[1]

This section of this chapter reviews the ad production process. A general model is first presented that traces the various stages and activities involved in the overall process. The creation stage part of the model comes first; this is the part we discussed in Chapter 13, and it is only briefly reviewed here. This is followed by a review of activities at the production stage. Production differs according to whether copy is being produced for print media or for broadcast media. In print media, the important components concern typography and engraving, whereas in broadcast, casting, filming, and editing are of central importance.

What are the basic tasks involved in creating and producing an advertisement? Who does what at which stage? What are the important ways of generating ideas and carrying them forward into final production? What should an advertising manager know about the creation and production process?

A MODEL OF THE CREATION AND PRODUCTION PROCESS. . . . .

Figure 15–1 presents a model of the creation and production process. Note that two basic stages are involved, *creation* and *production.*

The distinction is somewhat artificial because creative activities can take place at any point throughout the entire process, but it is a convenient distinction for several reasons. First, the activities associated with the creation stage take place largely within the confines of the advertising agency. Those associated with production are usually done by outside suppliers to the agency. Second, creation activities are in many ways similar for either print or broadcast advertising.

The *creation stage* involves cases the generation of words (copywriting) and the generation of pictures (illustrating), with copywriters and art directors working as a team, whether the end result is a print advertisement or a broadcast commercial. Rough ads, which may be comprehensive layouts for print ads or detailed storyboards for TV ads, are the output of this stage, which move on to the production stage. (These rough ads are discussed further below.)

The *production stage* activities, usually done by external suppliers, differ in significant respects for print production or broadcast production. Print production involves the graphic arts and specialists in typography, engraving, printing,

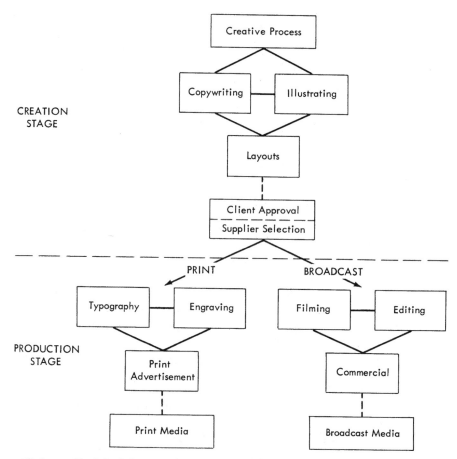

Figure 15–1.   Model of the creation and production process.

and so on. Broadcast production, particularly in television, involves audiovisual studios, production houses, and the basic tasks of filming and editing, which are very similar to the production of a movie. In sum, different types of external suppliers are involved for print and broadcast at the production stage.

The important input to the generation of advertising is referred to as the *creative process* in the model. Much attention has been given to ways of improving this process and generating ideas. Following the generation of copy and a layout, discussed in Chapter 13, the creative director and the agency account executive will next seek the client's approval for the layout and the general nature of the advertising to be produced. Pretest copy research may be sought at this point (using the layout or rough stage, or alternative finished executions) to assist in the decision, following the procedures outlined in the previous chapter.

An important decision at the point of production is the selection of suppliers to actually produce the finished advertisements. These tasks are noted in the model as *client approval* and *supplier selection*.

Following production, the final print advertisements or broadcast commercials are distributed to the appropriate newspapers, magazines, radio, or broadcast stations (media) for printing and airing. This step completes the copy-decision aspects of advertising management insofar as the basic messages are created and produced. Posttest copy-testing research, the subject of Chapter 14, can then be done to see how well the actually does, perhaps through tracking studies.

Creating Rough Print Ads

For print ads, the copywriter and art director may first create a *thumbnail sketch layout*. This is very rough and does not have much drawing detail, and could be in one-half or one-quarter size. Such thumbnail sketches are used to quickly see the effect of variations in the placement and size of the headline, main illustration, and so on, to find the most appealing layout.

After the general location of the ad's elements has been decided on, a full-size *rough layout* or *visual* may be prepared. Here, the headline will be roughed in, and there will be a more detailed (but still not "finished") illustration. Changes can still be made inexpensively at this stage. Some clients are prepared to review concepts at this stage.

Other clients, however, prefer to go on to the next stage of *finished* or *comprehensive layouts* (called *comps*). These require a lot of art time and can be expensive: the pictures may be sketched, the lettering done carefully. Figure 15–2 shows various layout formats.

After this rough print has the approval of all the necessary people, it is worked on by an artist to produce the final art, so such layouts should be good enough to be followed accurately by the commercial artist who will create the final artwork or photograph, and by the outside production people who will do the final printing and engraving. To show the printer exactly where the type should be set, a tissue-paper tracing of the area where the type is to go is attached to the copy that is sent with the artwork, along with specifications of the typeface and size.

It is only after the artwork and set copy are okayed that the ad passes on to the engraver, in the actual production process set out below. Computers and word-processors are used today to speed up the process and lead to camera-ready work being sent to the engraver.

Creating Rough TV Ads

Again, rough TV ads begin by writers and art directors working together to get ideas of what the ad might look like. Once an idea has been found, the copywriter fleshes out the words and/or music while the art director sketches out the visual scenes. These are put together in a *storyboard*, which is a series of small sketches. Twelve small sketches may be used to represent a thirty-second commercial, since key scenes usually last for five or six seconds or more. (The final TV ad will actually have 1,440 frames per minute!).

The first storyboards start out very rough, and the level of detail increases as it moves closer to, and through, the approval process. The initial sketches can be improved by an illustrator. The storyboard may also be supplemented by a script

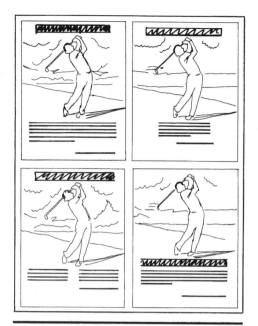

Thumbnail sketches. By executing thumbnails (and even a nonartist can do so), it is possible to experiment quickly with a number of different layout combinations. The art doesn't need to be expert because the purpose is to juggle elements until the best combination is achieved.

Rough layout. After the thumbnail the artist "roughs" up a layout that gives an idea of the finished concept. At this stage changes can be made inexpensively. If the client is sophisticated, he or she can visualize from a rough such as this. Some clients, however, like to work from more finished layouts.

Comprehensive layout. All the elements are presented well enough in the comprehensive to furnish an excellent idea of the printed advertisement. Comprehensives require much art time and can be expensive. Usually, few changes will be made—preferably none.

Figure 15–2.   Types of print layouts.

Source: Philip Ward Burton, Advertising Copywriting, *6th ed. (Lincolnwood, IL: NTC Business Books, 1990). Used with permission.*

sheet, which uses two parallel columns, one for the audio and the other for the video, to describe what the key frames will be like. And the rough TV ad may even be converted into an *animatic*, in which a video camera "pans" across artwork (set on an artstand), with soundtracks and announcer voice-overs added on. Other rough forms are the *photomatic*, using filmed photographs instead of illustrations, the *livomatic*, using inexpensive actors, or the *ripomatic*, using scenes from previous commercials.

Eventually, the storyboard is what is used by the director and the production house to shoot and produce the final commercial (more on that below). Obviously, since the few frames described on the storyboard can only partially capture what the final ad will look like, the director and production house substantially shape the final ad. To give the director more guidance and the agency creatives more control, the storyboard is usually accompanied by a detailed shooting script that suggests camera angles, staging, props, casting considerations (which can be crucial), and music, and these are discussed at pre-production meetings. Yet the creativity and expertise of the director, camera-person, editor, and so on play crucial roles in what actually gets made.

Client Approval and Supplier Selection

Following the creation of the finished layout or comps (for print) and storyboard or animatics (for TV), the creative director and account executive usually get *client approval* of the advertising prior to production. There is always the danger at this point that the client will evaluate it subjectively and get involved in the creative process. When that happens, the result is usually a creative effort that is compromised. Rather, the focus of discussion should be on the advertising objectives and the relationship of the proposed copy to those objectives. The client could, properly, discuss copy testing that has been considered or planned to demonstrate that the advertising will be effective in achieving those objectives. The process of client-agency interaction is discussed further in the next section of this chapter.

Suppliers (typographers, engravers, and printers in the case of print and production houses; sound studios and many others in the case of broadcast) must be selected at this stage. In print, it is usual for an agency to have a group of suppliers that it has come to know and trust and for which print production activities are carried out. In broadcast, particularly television, it is more usual to "put the production out to bid." Often, this involves obtaining bids from three different production studios who will use the storyboard as a basis for bidding. Television commercials in this sense are like other supplies the corporation buys, and getting them produced is treated as a bidding process in much the same way. The production of all ads, whether print or TV or some other medium, requires client approval of production cost estimates.

Production Stage

Production of advertising generally involves a great number of external outside supplier firms and individuals. Although we have not stressed this component of the overall advertising system presented in Chapter 1, it is indeed interesting and represents a "fifth" level or institution that depends heavily on advertising.

Print advertising production differs in significant respects from broadcast production, and we have stressed this fact in the model in Figure 15–1. In print, firms specialized in type and typesetting called typographers will be involved. Others specialized in graphic materials, engravers, may be necessary. Some large printers include these services as part of their offerings. The choice of whether to use specialists or one large printer is another decision facing the creative team.

Concerning broadcast, many other kinds of specialists are needed. These can include a producer, director, set designer, film editor, actors and actresses, composers, musicians, talent scouts, casting directors, music arrangers, camera crews, video and audio equipment supply companies, and many others. Many of these people freelance, and the process of producing a television commercial may require considerable effort in bringing a team together. Often production is channeled through a production house that will contain a sound studio and most of what is necessary to get the job done.

Production is a process that takes a considerable amount of time; from six to eight weeks can be involved. In what follows, we provide a brief sketch of the major activities involved in print and broadcast production. The advertising manager should not hope to become an expert in the graphic arts, but decision making can be enhanced once the basics are known.

Print Production

The rough artwork and copy of the ad must get legal approval before actual production can begin. (This is true of all media, not just print.) The rough artwork is then used by a photographer to take the necessary photographs at a shooting session, or by an illustrator to create the final illustration. The photographs or illustrations may need retouching.

The most important subsequent components of print production deal with the art and science of typography and engraving. Each is a fast-evolving field that has been affected greatly in recent years by computerization.

Typography is done by a specialist in type and typesetting. What the advertiser needs to know is that there are thousands of different type styles and forms from which choices must be made for a specific print advertisement and many ways of composing type. Figure 15–3 provides an example of an ad using different type styles for dramatic effect. Typography is a complex field in itself that takes significant skill and experience to master. It should be appreciated that there is a range of alternatives from which to choose, and the creative director must be prepared to question and oversee those choices. Figure 15–4 gives some valuable lessons on typography from an article by David Ogilvy.

Once the typography has been decided on, the client must approve the retouched photographs or illustrations, and the *mechanical*, which is the guide showing the positioning of the type, artwork, logo, and so on.

The second major activity in producing a print advertisement is engraving. *Engraving* basically deals with the generation and reproduction of pictures, pho-

Figure 15–3. Creative uses of typefaces: Celestial Seasonings.

Courtesy of Celestial Seasonings.

Typography—"the eye is a creature of habit"

Good typography *helps* people read your copy, while bad typography prevents them from doing so.

Advertising agencies usually set their headlines in capital letters. This is a mistake. Professor Tinker of Stanford has established that capitals retard reading. They have no ascenders or descenders to help you recognize words, and tend to be read *letter by letter.*

The eye is a creature of habit. People are accustomed to reading books, magazines and newspapers in *lower case.*

Another way to make headlines hard to read is to superimpose them on your illustration.

Another mistake is to put a period at the end of headlines. Periods are also called full stops, because they stop the reader dead in his tracks. You will find no full stops at the end of headlines in newspapers.

Yet another common mistake is to set copy in a measure too wide or too narrow to be legible. People are accustomed to reading newspapers, which are set about 40 characters wide.

Which typefaces are easiest to read? Those that people are *accustomed* to reading, like the Century family, Caslon, Baskerville and Jenson. The more outlandish the typeface, the harder it is to read. The drama belongs in what you say, not in the typeface.

Sanserif faces like this are particularly difficult to read. Says John Updike, "Serifs exist for a purpose. They help the eye to pick up the shape of the letter. Piquant in little amounts, sanserif in page-size sheets repels readership as wax paper repels water; it has a sleazy, cloudy look."

Some art directors use copy as the raw material for designing queer shapes, thus making it illegible.

In a recent issue of a magazine I found 47 ads with the copy set in *reverse*—white type on a black background. It is almost impossible to read.

If you have to set *very long* copy, there are some typographical devices that increase its readership:

1. A subhead of two lines, between your headline and your body copy, heightens the reader's appetite for the feast to come.

2. If you start your body copy with a drop-initial, you increase readership by an average of 13 percent.

3. Limit your opening paragraph to a maximum of 11 words.

4. After two or three inches of copy, insert a crosshead, and thereafter throughout. Cross-heads keep the reader marching forward. Make some of them interrogative, to excite curiosity in the next run of copy.

5. When I was a boy, it was common practice to *square up* paragraphs. It is now known that widows—short lines—increase readership.

6. Set key paragraphs in bold face or italic.

7. Help the reader into your paragraphs with arrowheads, bullets, asterisks and marginal marks.

8. If you have a lot of unrelated facts to recite, don't use cumbersome connectives. Simply *number* them—as I am doing here.

Figure 15–4.   Some principles of typography.

9. What size type should you use?

This is 5-point, and too small to read.

This is 14-point, and too big.

This is 11-point, and about right.

10. If you use leading (line-spacing) between paragraphs, you increase readership by an average of 12 percent.

You may think that I exaggerate the importance of good typography. You may ask if I have ever heard a housewife say that she bought a new detergent because the ad was set in Caslon. No. But do you think an ad can sell if nobody can read it? You can't save souls in an empty church.

As Mies van der Rohe said of architecture, "God is in the details."

Figure 15–4.   Some principles of typography. (continued)

Source: Adapted from "Ogilvy on Advertising, Wanted: A Renaissance in Print Advertising," Advertising Age, *August 1, 1983, p. M4ff. See also the book,* Olgivy on Advertising *(New York: Crown Publishers, 1983), by the same author.*

tographs, and the visual elements of the advertisement. *Photoengraving* is the process using photography to create a printing surface. Through the photoengraving process, artwork (line charts, drawings, photographs) and paste-up of type can be transferred to a negative photochemically, and the image on the negative transferred to a metal plate for printing. Photoengraving is most commonly used to reproduce artwork, but is also used to reproduce combinations of illustration and type. Engravings can be four-color offset engravings, four color roto engravings, or black-and-white.

Actual printing of the advertisement involves yet another process and more alternatives. Printing can be done by letterpress, gravure, lithography, or silk screening. The first three are processes associated with basic ways of photoengraving. In each case, some type of plate or "mat" is developed from which copies are run. The client will be shown a *proof* before the ad is run; four-color proofs are actually the compilation of four separate engraving plates, one each for red, yellow, blue and black, printed on top of each other. Proofs that show each of the four colors printed separately as well as together are termed *progressive proofs*, or *progressives*.

Broadcast Production

In explaining the basic elements of broadcast production, we focus on television commercial production. Many of the elements of radio commercial production are analogous to the audio portion of television commercials and involve audiotapes rather than videotapes or films. Much radio commercial production is very uncomplicated, consisting of "live commercials" in which written copy is simply provided to a disk jockey or news commentator who reads the copy at the appropriate time slot (with appropriate emphasis, voice delivery, and so on). The studio time may cost a few hundred dollars per hour, and the only other cost is the cost of the talent and the music, etc.

Producing one television commercial can, on the other hand, involve 100 or more people and cost $200,000 or more. The directors that shoot the commercial are often paid princely fees, and every actor appearing in the spot has to be paid a *residual*, or a fee for every time the ad is aired. The two major tasks in television commercial production are filming and editing.

Filming generally is based on a storyboard and a list of specifications supplied by the advertising agency; a production house is the usual type of company involved in television commercial production. These are centered in large metropolitan areas such as New York, Chicago, and Los Angeles, and many specialize in the business of producing television commercials.

Filming begins after all the necessary ingredients have been brought together. A director and/or producer will be assigned. A talent scout may be hired to interface with professional actors or actresses to be included in the commercial. A composer may be hired to develop an original score and musicians and singers to carry it out. The inclusion of a *jingle* in the commercial invariably leads to finding and using this type of talent.

The filming may be done in a fixed location studio. Often, however, it is necessary to move people and equipment to a location site where particular background scenes are called for—a forest, seaside cliffs, and so on. Filming is done in pieces and parts and later is put together and edited at the editing stage. The Green Giant commercial, for example, was made by building a Styrofoam model of a "valley," superimposing animated characters, and then filming the feet and legs of a male model (the giant) standing over the whole thing.

In sum, producing a filmed (or videotaped) television commercial is a major complicated process. Even before filming starts, the producer using the storyboard guide and production notes (announcer preference, set sketches, ideas for props, musical requirements, and so on) gets involved in many activities. These include casting sessions to select the actors and/or announcer, set design sessions to work out exactly how the background will look, location discussions or trips to decide where the commercial will be shot, prop sessions to decide on various articles to be used, and arranging shooting schedules, recording sessions, and completion dates. All this must be done before filming begins, and these meetings are called "preproduction" meetings. Filming of individual scenes is usually not done in the sequence in which they appear in the final commercial. Also visual and sound tracks are usually not recorded at the same time.

Editing is required because much more footage is generated than is finally used. Several different camera angles will be shot, for example, to give the director some choice of the best possible ones to use. After the shooting begins, the film is quickly developed, often overnight, to provide *rushes* or *dailies*, which are hurried prints of inferior quality. These are used by the director to screen the preceding day's work, to select the best shots, and to decide whether further retakes are necessary before the set is torn down and the cast disbanded.

After the sound track is completed and the picture cut and edited, the two are combined into an answer print. There are usually several sound tracks, including the voice and music tracks, and often special sound effects tracks. A sound cutter "lays in" these tracks so they can be mixed. An audio engineer is then brought in to weave the various tracks together. An equally complicated series of editing operations takes place on the picture part of the track. When complete, it is brought together with the master sound track to produce the answer print. The whole process from storyboard to answer print usually takes seven to eight weeks. The answer print is used primarily to get agency and client approval. From it an appropriate number of release prints are generated and shipped to the networks and/or individual stations for broadcast. The release print is what is commonly referred to as the finished commercial. It is not uncommon to produce it in several versions, such as 15 seconds, 30 seconds, or 60 seconds, depending upon the media scheduling decisions. It is the release prints that are shipped to the broadcast media and aired. Recent technological developments allow this "shipment" to occur using satellite transmission.

The following sections discusses the development of a new television commercial for American Express. The issues and complexities of television commercial production are nicely illustrated in this story. Note the importance given to minute details such as what the actor wears, the subtleties required in the father-son relationship, the 43 takes plus "dozens without sound," and the great stakes involved.

Behind the Scenes at an American Express Commercial*

The marketing executives from American Express Co. are unhappy. After months of research, prepreproduction meetings, preproduction meetings, casting sessions, budget audits, and other preparations for this moment, they arrive on location for filming of their television commercial—only to find the leading man wearing the wrong jacket.

In a big national ad campaign, little things like this count. "We believe that advertising is important enough that you want to get it right," says Diane Shaib, vice president for consumer marketing at American Express. For this commercial, getting it right is especially urgent: both the client and its agency, Ogilvy & Mather, have a lot riding on the outcome. American Express is eager to get more men in their twenties and thirties to sign up for its plastic charge card. Ogilvy needs to come up with a successful commercial after the failure of a recent string of American Express ads that the client pulled off the air. Both nervously await reaction to the thirty-second ad, which cost about $100,000 and is now hitting the national airwaves.

Wardrobe Chaos

Just days before the filming, the American Express marketers discuss the wardrobe with the agency. What will look more universal, they wonder—a blue blazer or a corduroy jacket? They are still pondering the question and leaning toward the blazer when they walk onto the set and find the actor wearing a dark cor-

---

* Mark N. Vamos. Reprinted from the May 20, 1985 issue of *Business Week* by special permission. © 1985 by McGraw-Hill, Inc.

duroy jacket. Some of the scenes have already been shot, and the budget clock is ticking. Amid the controlled chaos of a commercial shoot, exasperation is rising behind polite smiles, urgent confabulations are held in corners, and higher authorities are summoned.

For more than ten years, American Express has been running its "Do you know me?" commercials, aimed at its traditional market: successful, older businessmen. Three years ago, however, AmEx decided to pursue the large number of younger women entering the work force and launched its "Interesting Lives" series. The first commercial, its "New Card" spot, showed a young woman taking her husband out to dinner to celebrate the arrival of her card, and it scored big. Women applied in droves. By last year, they held 27 percent of all AmEx green cards, up from 10 percent in the 1970s. The spot won awards and lavish praise for showing a strong, successful woman.

While that reaction startled American Express, subsequent audience research surprised the company even more. Instead of offending young men by showing a woman taking a man out to dinner, the commercial actually attracted them. "We're talking about three years ago—and markets outside of New York," says Shaib. "That's a bit shocking."

That's also when the trouble started. The company and its agency decided to extend the "Interesting Lives" campaign to attract young men by intention rather than by accident—in effect, to turn it into an all-purpose yuppie campaign. "The mission is to tweak their awareness of the card's appropriateness for them," says Shaib. Over the next three years, the company shot six new ads, but the only things they seemed to tweak were noses. One by one, as audience reaction arrived, AmEx pulled the ads. Two were so troublesome that they never even made it past the test-marketing stage. One showed a woman paying for dinner on a first date, the other a husband accompanying his wife on her business trip. Audience reactions included words such as "abrasive" and "castrating"—not exactly the message American Express wanted to convey. "It's very difficult these days to do ads with men and women as equals," sighs Kathleen O'Shaughnessy, a manager of marketing research at AmEx.

Early this year, the client and the agency agreed to try again, and Ogilvy wrote five new commercials. This time, however, AmEx decided to test the spots in rough form before any were produced, something it had not done before. Each ad was translated into color sketches that were transferred onto slides. Actors recorded the accompanying dialogue. With the roughs in hand, AmEx and Ogilvy headed into the field.

One-Way Mirror

At 8 o'clock one evening in late February, nine men and a moderator sit around a gray conference table in midtown Manhattan. They are the targets of the campaign—young men who are eligible for an American Express card but haven't applied. Each will receive $50 for participating in this focus group, the last of eleven such sessions held nationwide. Observing them from a darkened room behind a one-way mirror are eleven staffers from AmEx and Ogilvy, including account managers, researchers, and copywriters. Surprisingly, in a commercial aimed at men, all the observers are women.

Eugene Shore, a psychologist and president of Business Information Analysis Corp., a Pennsylvania research firm, shows the five rough commercials. He asks the focus group for comments and suggestions after each. Some win raves, others are panned. After one rough is shown, someone says, "If I saw this on TV, I'd just say, 'Boy, this is another one of those dumb commercials that make no sense.' "

Working with comments like these, the marketers have already narrowed the choice to two or three strong candidates, one of which is known as "Young Lawyer." It opens with father and son seated at a restaurant table. The dialogue concerns the son's career and how disappointed the father was when he didn't join the family law firm. But now that the son is "Mr. District Attorney," the father is proud of him. The son objects, saying he's only "an assistant to an assistant." He places his American Express card on the tray that the waiter puts on the table with the check. The father laughs, saying: "The pay must be getting better over at City Hall."

The lights come up, and Shore asks for reactions. "I feel this is pointed at the business community, because you have to be successful to have this card," says Stephen, an accountant. Tim, who works for a menswear designer, disagrees: "He says he's an assistant to an assistant. So maybe I can qualify." The women behind the mirror smile at this response. The line is a crucial one. To attract new card-holders, the commercial must convey accessibility—but not too much. The American Express card is prestige plastic. The ad can't make it seem as easy to get as MasterCard or Visa, which AmEx staffers contemptuously refer to as "shoppers' cards." As O'Shaughnessy, the market researcher, later puts it, "It's very difficult to communicate eligibility and at the same time maintain prestige. We're sort of talking out of both sides of our mouth."

"Too Northeast"

Over the next few weeks, Ogilvy staffers begin scouting locations for "Young Lawyer." They also hunt for a director with a flair for filming realistic dialogue. "This ad lives and dies on being able to cast two people who have believable rapport," says Ann Curry Marcato, the Ogilvy vice president responsible for producing the spot. And, Shore warns at the session, the father and son risk "coming across as WASP, bank-club, Harvard."

It is late March when the account management team from Ogilvy and two executives from American Express hold a preproduction meeting to go over the casting, wardrobe, location, and production schedule. That's when the problem of the corduroy jacket first surfaces. "The feedback we've been getting from the research is that the Midwest and West Coast don't respond because they read it as too Northeast," says K. Shelly Porges, director of special markets at AmEx. "Can we do something more cross-country?" Ogilvy's Marcato replies that the agency is aware of the problem, and the discussion moves to other topics.

Ed Bianchi, Marcato's choice for director, who once shot a Dr Pepper extravaganza set on a giant pinball machine, outlines his notion of how the commercial should unfold. He plans to open with a wide shot, showing diners and waiters, and then cut to a close-up of the father and son. "We pick them out through the crowd so you really have the feeling of eavesdropping on them," he says.

Porges objects to opening with a wide shot crowded with fourteen extras. "What makes this an interesting life, anyway? The quality of a relationship. What will a long shot add to that?" she asks. Paul Pracilio, a vice president and associate creative director at Ogilvy, replies: "We have thirty seconds to reach out of that tube and grab someone by the necktie. By cutting in to see them, it's a damn sight more exciting piece of film."

Happy Medium

The discussion moves to the waiter who will bring the check. Since the ad must make the card seem upscale but still accessible, the waiter can't look as if he works at too ritzy a restaurant. "It must be above Brew Burger but below the 21 Club," says Porges. Director Bianchi suggests that the waiter appear early in the commercial, as the son is saying he's only an assistant to an assistant district attorney. "The action of the waiter bringing the check is a subtle hint of what this commercial is going to be about," he says. Porges objects again. "Because of the 'assistant to an assistant' line, the focus groups said, 'Gee, maybe I could get this card,' " she says. "Getting that part garbled would be disastrous to us."

Three days later, the film crew has converted Jerry's Restaurant in Manhattan into a madhouse. The sidewalk is a jumble of cables, reflecting panels, and tripods. In the dining room, twenty-five crew members mill about, carrying equipment and shouting. The father-and-son team sits at a table, repeating their lines. The entire commercial will be shot from several angles, Bianchi explains, to give the editor the option of cutting from one perspective to another.

Representatives from Ogilvy and AmEx are at the back of the room, watching and making suggestions. Still more staffers are in another room, watching a video monitor. Director Bianchi calls for take after take. Frequently, a telephone rings or a bus rumbles past on 23rd Street, ruining the shot. For most of the takes, Bianchi sits next to the camera, his face pressed against the lens so he can see what it is seeing, and grins at the actors.

After forty-three takes involving dialogue—and dozens more without sound—Bianchi is satisfied. But suddenly, he insists on one more close-up of the son pulling the charge card from his wallet. The executives from Ogilvy and American Express are crowded around a video monitor, staring intently as the image of the wallet fills the screen. The son's hand reaches over, pulls out the card, and pauses. It's a VISA card. Everyone laughs and goes home.

Tense Tryout

A week later, the preliminary version of the commercial is ready. A dozen client and agency people sit in red bucket chairs in an eighth-floor screening room at Ogilvy & Mather's New York office. Tension is in the air—not least because, after all the discussion of wide shots and extras, those scenes wound up on the cutting-room floor. "We were thrilled to find so much of the personality of the son and father coming through," Marcato explains as she introduces the commercial. "We thought that it would be strongest to stay up tight." The commercial is run several times. The ad seems a bit choppy, jumping from close-ups of the son to the father to the check to the wallet and, finally, to the card. The Ogilvy team waits for a reaction.

"I think you've captured them just as I always envisioned them," says Shaib, the AmEx marketing vice president. "But because of the number of cuts back and forth, I never feel like I'm intimate with them." She also points out that, with all the close-ups, the commercial never shows the father and son together. After some discussion, the Ogilvy representatives agree to reedit the commercial to include the wide shot that American Express had initially argued against.

AmEx executives say they are pleased with the final version, which includes the wide shot. All the research was worthwhile, they say, because it helped them avoid some pitfalls, such as making the father too stern or the son too wimpy. The father's line about his son's pay getting better, for example, was ultimately given to the son because some viewers saw it as a subtle putdown. Now, the marketers say, the father is distinguished but warm, and the son is the kind of likable but independent character with whom the target market can identify.

The ad, which first appeared on May 6, will run for six to eight weeks, after which American Express will assess its impact. The company thinks it has a winner, but there's one little thing that still bothers it a bit: the son is wearing a corduroy jacket.

THE CLIENT-AGENCY RELATIONSHIP . . . .

Selecting or Changing an Agency

In the single month of October 1993, U.S. marketing clients changed ad agencies, announced agency reviews, or consolidated assignments on accounts with total billings of over $1 billion—including accounts such as Burger King, Diet Coke, IBM PCs, Jeep/Eagle, Subaru cars and TV Guide magazine. This was possibly the biggest set of account changes to occur in one month, but it was not unusual, because clients change their agencies all the time.[2]

Clients usually begin an agency search by putting up their account for a "review," in which both the incumbent agency and invited new agencies could be asked to make presentations to retain or obtain the account. Such a review could be a regular periodic one, or be precipitated by some unhappiness with the quality of the creative work the client thinks it has been receiving from the incumbent agency, or be sparked by an unsolicited contact from one of the "new business" departments of a nonincumbent agency. Agencies often maintain special new business departments, with individuals (nicknamed "rainmakers") charged with the responsibility of getting new business.

Sometimes the source of friction with the current agency could be a change in marketing strategy at the client, with a perception that the current agency is unable or unwilling to implement the new strategy. The dissatisfaction might be caused by poor sales or market share performance, or heightened competitive activity (leading to an agency change as a "quick fix"). Or it might be caused by disputes over agency compensation (sometimes initiated by the agency, which feels it is making too little money on the account). A frequent catalyst for change is the appointment of new marketing or advertising chief at the client, who brings a new perspective (and a different set of agency loyalties and contacts) to his or her new job (the "new broom" syndrome). Such personnel shifts are sometimes caused by a change in ownership of the client, such as merger or acquisition activity.[3] Sometimes it is personnel shifts at the agency that lead to client dissatisfaction, or changes in agency policies.

A recent development has been agency changes caused by changes in client servicing needs, such as the need for global account servicing, the need for specialty advertiser services, or simply the need for wider agency involvement as clients move to creating more integrated communications.[4] A recent example was Reebok's decision in September 1993 to move its account from the small Chiat/Day agency to much-bigger Leo Burnett, ostensibly because Burnett could better serve Reebok's needs to grow internationally. According to Reebok's top marketing executives, "Chiat did not have the global resources."[5]

New agencies making presentations often present speculative (*spec*) campaigns indicating what kind of campaign they would create if they had the account and demonstrating their knowledge and understanding of the client's business. The costs for researching, staffing, and creating these spec campaigns can run in the many hundreds of thousands of dollars; often, but not always, the client inviting the spec campaign will pay for part of these costs.

There are other costs to the client too: the selection of a new agency consumes much management time and attention, as does the creation of a new working relationship. The new agency will require time to get "up to speed" on the client's brands—by one estimate, up to two years. Probably because these nonfinancial costs are larger for more established brands at larger firms, larger firms appear to change agencies less often than smaller firms.[6] On the other hand, it has been found that the stock market does appear to view the news of an agency change positively for the client's stock, at least for a short while.[7]

Clients selecting a new agency are sometimes advised by one of several agency selection consulting firms. A study by James Cagley showed that in making this selection, clients place high weight on the quality and number of people assigned to the account, their creative abilities, a perceived similarity of objectives and operating styles (including personal "chemistry"), the degree of understanding displayed by the agency of the client's business, the agency's reputation for integrity, the agency's reputation for making—and sticking up for—recommendations, and so on. Also important are the agency's size and stability, its servicing, strategic planning, market research and media buying abilities, and the compensation and cost-control aspects.

Of course, the situational importance of these varies across clients and situations.[8] In fact, personal contacts between agency heads and client top management, and positive recommendations from satisfied clients, have been found to be key to agencies' winning new client business.[9] It is important to note at this point that a smart client will not simply select an agency that thinks exactly like the client personnel do, but rather will choose one that provides a complementary perspective.

Account Conflicts

Probably the most important aspect, however, is the absence of account conflicts. Clients will simply not give their account to an agency which already services a competitor—with the notion of a competitor sometimes being defined rather broadly (for example, Hallmark once switched its account from Young & Rubicam because Y&R had a part of the AT&T long-distance service account). The frequency of conflicts increases as the client business undergoes mergers and consolidations—we are rapidly reaching the stage at which a handful of mega-corporations in the consumer packaged-goods fields have brands in almost every product category (e.g., Procter & Gamble/Richardson–Vicks/Noxell, Philip Morris/General Foods/Kraft, Unilever/Chesebrough Pond's/Lipton, Nestlé/Carnation, etc.). This tendency has accelerated as companies introduce more brands, in response to greater consumer segmentation.

The agency response to such client consolidations has been to structure their agencies into "groups," with maximum autonomy: Interpublic, for example, operates as merely a holding company with three autonomous networks: McCann-Erickson, Lintas: Campbell-Ewald and Ammirati and Puris/Lintas, and Lowe and Partners/SMS. The idea is that a client should not object to another agency in the group having the account of a competitor, since there is no opportunity for the transfer of secrets across the agency groups in such a network, and no conflict of interest. Of course, this argument is not always successful.

Building Partnership and Trust

Once an agency has been selected, perhaps the most crucial aspect that can pull them apart is the perception on the client side that the agency is not contributing to the client's business growth. A client should not (and usually does not) hire an agency merely to support what the client thinks: the agency is being hired to bring its own unique talents and perspectives to the client's business, to do the kind of creative thinking that the client simply does not and cannot do in-house. A client who does not expect and reward an agency for fresh thinking is usually going to get terrible advertising.

However, the agency can only make such contributions if both the agency and client work hard to develop the right kind of relationship.[10] Good clients create a sense of partnership with the agency—sharing information, research, and sales data; trusting the agency; being honest with the agency; respecting the expertise of the agency; asking the agency to provide its best thinking and not to settle for safe and mediocre creative. Good clients ask for the agency to get totally immersed in the client's business (such as sales and factory visits) and make it easy and possible for the agency personnel to do so.

The Briefing and Approval Process

The client should brief the agency clearly on what is required and obtain agreement—before creative work is done—on exactly what the ad is expected to shoot for. Consultant Nancy Salz recommends that the client think through the answers to three questions before the briefing: (1) What exactly is the agency being asked to do? (e.g., develop a new TV campaign to defend against a new competitor); (2) What information does the agency need? (e.g., product research, marketing research, etc.); and (3) What questions is the agency likely to ask?[11] It is helpful if the briefing session is attended not only by the agency account personnel but also by the creative and media people working on the account, because this should provide them with greater insight into the marketing context around the ad campaign.

At the briefing session, and in the briefing document, the agency should be given all the information they might need to come up with strategic and creative ideas—product information, competitive information, consumer information, legal information, etc. It is vital that the agency be provided with the problem that the client has, but not with any suggested advertising solution to that problem—because coming up with the solution is what the agency is being hired to do. Any solution-suggestions by the client will only serve to limit and inhibit the agency's creative response. Some of the most famous ad campaign ideas have been born of agency folk asking "way out" questions. Legend has it that Dove soap came up with the claim "contains one-quarter cream" when the agency creative director, at the briefing, asked the scientist what the soap ingredient stearic acid really was, and was told that stearic acids are a main ingredient in face cream. What the client never saw in that fact, the agency creatives did—because they were allowed to let their minds roam freely.

When the agency comes up with its proposed campaigns, the agency account executive should be expected to fight for the agency's recommendations regarding good creative, and not be a passive "yes-man" for the client. A good client does not treat the agency as a superior treats a subordinate, but rather as an equal partner, as a part of the client's own marketing organization. A good client treats the agency people with respect and does not squander the agency's resources through wasted motion. A good client accepts occasional agency mistakes—which will always occur—with good humor; an agency that never makes mistakes is probably not trying hard enough to be fresh in its creative product.

A key element of this relationship has to be the desire and willingness of the client to support creative work that is not simply "safe" but instead is bold and takes risks—as long as it is on strategy. This can happen only if the approval process is kept short and simple, without several layers of management, and without committees, each trying to rewrite the ad and nitpick different creative elements. The approval process needs to use, but not rely exclusively on, research, and the people making the approvals on the client side need to be trained to recognize and approve fresh but on-target creative work. A standard agency complaint is that most MBA brand managers are typically overly analytical, risk-averse, and committee-oriented and have little training in recognizing good creative work.[12]

It is especially important that advertising not be written to please the client's top management only (and their spouses!). Such a process distorts the original vision of the ad and greatly hurts the morale of the creatives. When the agency makes its presentations, criticism should be honest but not brutal; it should be constructive and tactful and depersonalized; it should focus not on the ad's elements but on failures to communicate the agreed-on strategy and message. Praise and reward should be often and plentiful (when it is deserved). The agency should be given the responsibility to take whatever decisions it feels are necessary to achieve its creative vision. While the client should ask for the best creative, the client also needs to stick, over the years, to an idea that is working, instead of asking for change for its own sake.

On the agency side, the agency needs to display a great ability to listen carefully to what the client needs are (including those needs and desires that are not fully articulated) and must appreciate the political ramifications of agency recommendations. Good creative ideas can come from anywhere—including the client—and the agency should be open-minded. The agency needs to take a leadership role in developing and pushing for high quality and bold creative work on the client's account. It is the agency's role to be intellectually honest, to be "of counsel," to offer an outside perspective that the client may not have.

However, in standing up for what it believes is right, the agency should not be arrogant, and should not seek creative awards for their own sake but seek the kind of creative work that is appropriate to the client's strategic objectives. It is also important that the agency not shuffle people—creative, account, and top management—from the client's account simply because it begins to take the client's business for granted. Great attention needs to be placed on creating and maintaining the chemistry and rapport in the day-to-day agency-client relationship.[13] Budgets, details and deadlines must be respected. There should be good communication with the client—clients hate unpleasant surprises!

Costs and Compensation

One major source of friction in client-agency relationships is a client perception that the agency is charging costs unfairly[14] or is making too much money on the client's account. It is important for the agency not to treat the client's money wastefully, but it is equally important for the client not to nitpick on production and other expenses and to ensure that the agency makes adequate profit on the client's account. The key idea, of course, is that an agency's compensation should match its work load.

The basic compensation structures for an agency were discussed in Chapter 1; we will only repeat here that the trend is clearly away from the flat 15-percent commission on billings to a reduced commission, fee-plus-commission, or fee-only arrangements. An agency that creates several campaigns for a client, or has to modify the ads frequently (as in an airline or retail account, whose prices change all the time), or does substantial new work on small-billing brands probably does not make enough money on a flat commission and deserves to negotiate additional fees. On the other hand, an agency that essentially does only maintenance work on long-running campaigns for big-billing brands should probably expect cost-conscious clients to negotiate lower commission rates with it.

Fees and commissions both have advantages and disadvantages—while commissions are not tailored to the amount of work and can lead to agencies making biased recommendations on how much money the client should spend, fees can lead to too much client interference in agency operations, can lead to nitpicking and friction and can create a dangerous "meter-running" mentality in which the quality of work can get hurt. Many clients negotiate the right to inspect the agency's books annually for the client's account to see if it is making too much money on it.

More than the long-term compensation structure, it is the cost-plus expenses that the agency incurs on the client's account that are often the source of friction. Clients are usually accustomed to tight cost controls; many agency people, on the other hand, knowingly or unknowingly treat the client's money as someone else's money (which it is)—money that can be freely spent. In this context, particular mention must be made of commercial production expenses. While it is true that these are usually very small proportions of a brand's overall budget—the brand may be spending $20 million, and three ads in the campaign may cost $450,000 to produce[15]—it is also true that ads are often produced to lavish production budgets, and this can breed resentment and a sense of wasteful spending in the client.

An ad's production costs go up when it requires a distant, high-cost shooting location, a high-priced director, expensive props, an expensive endorser, and when ad hoc "on-location" changes are made in the ad, rather than in "preproduction" meetings. Costs can be reduced by getting multiple bids from different production houses (which charge a 35- to 50-percent markup on their own costs) and by carefully scrutinizing every element of these bids, often with the assistance of consultants.[16] Here, it is important for the agency creatives to remember the cost implications when they *write* a commercial: the same message can often be communicated equally effectively at a much lower production cost (though it is also true that today's video-sophisticated consumers expect expensive, slick "production values" in today's TV commercials).

For example, consider the launch of a new type of motor oil, which (among other advantages) won't freeze at low temperatures. One possible ad in this situation might involve freezing a car in a block of ice, photographing it through time-lapse photography as the ice melts over thirty-six hours, then using special effects to show the motor oil's logo catching fire and the car bursting through an over-sized paper logo, using expensive special-effects photography. A second creative photographic possibility might be simply to open a commercial freezer locker to freeze a rose and an open can of the oil, then show a gloved hand squeezing the rose (which shatters) and then picking up the can of the oil (which pours easily). Clearly, the second ad will cost much less, yet be as effective.

As the commercial production consultant Hooper White writes,[17] "production dollars are typed into the spot by the writer and drawn into it by the art director . . . cost control in production is a before-the-fact exercise . . . the most effective cost control is exercised by agency creative directors, not by outside consultants."

The Ongoing Relationship: Reviews and Audits

It is usually considered a good idea for the client to have a system of regular performance reviews, in which latent sources of dissatisfaction on both sides can be aired and, it is hoped, resolved. This way, if the agency's performance is unsatisfactory, the agency can take early remedial steps, instead of finding out by surprise one day that it has been fired.

For example, if the client is unhappy with the quality of the creative output, the agency can bring a new creative team to work on the client's account or have talent from the agency's other offices contribute ideas. This way, the client can get the fresh creative it wants, without sacrificing the entire, long-term relationship with its present agency. A set of criteria to be used in such audits has been proposed by Paul Michell, consisting of a review of changes in the environment, of changes in organizational and individual relationships (communication, openness, and interpersonal styles, etc.).[18]

SUMMARY . . . .

Following the creative work on an assignment, and any advertising pretesting considered necessary, the ads have to be produced and sent out to the selected media to be "run." This production process involves various people, including many suppliers and vendors outside the advertising agency.

The production process differs by the medium involved. For print production, it involves typographers, engravers, and printing. The rough ad goes through actual typesetting of the verbal copy, photoengraving of the visual elements and the type, and the production of the plate or "mat" from which the actual printed copies will be run. For television production, it includes the casting of actors and actresses, the composing and production of music scores, the actual filming (using a director and support staff), and the editing and mixing of audio and video tracks. Such production usually involves the services of an external production house, selected after competitive bidding. Various "tactical" decisions made at this stage—the choice of exact typeface, the casting of key characters, the choice of musical elements—can have an enormous impact on the success of the actual ad.

Through this production process, and throughout the entire advertising planning and implementation process, the relationship between the advertising agency and the marketing client becomes vitally important. Clients select agencies that they believe have the talent, skills, experience, resources, and insight into their business—as well as the "personal chemistry" to service their needs effectively and to bring in a creative perspective that the clients themselves may lack. Avoiding client conflicts is a major criterion as well. Clients can get more from their agencies if they give them some creative autonomy, share information and objectives with them, treat them as partners in the entire marketing effort, and develop a fair and nondestructive ad approval process. Compensation and cost control are often sources of friction that need to be carefully monitored. The entire agency-client relationship should be carefully reviewed at annual (or other) intervals.

DISCUSSION QUESTIONS . . . .

1. In the American Express example in the chapter, should the client and agency really have been that concerned with the nature of the jacket worn by the actor?

2. Identify a television ad that you have seen recently that apparently required a huge production budget, and discuss ways in which the same creative idea might have been communicated as effectively without such expense.

3. If you were the chief executive officer of a corporation hiring an ad agency, how would you go about selecting one? What would you look for?

4. Why should a marketing company not simply produce all of its ads at an "in-house" agency staffed by company employees, to save money, rather than go to an outside agency that might cost it more money?

5. Describe three different compensation arrangements that might exist between a client and an agency and discuss the pros and cons of each for (a) a large-budget advertiser and (b) a small-budget advertiser.

NOTES. . . . .

1. *Advertising Age*, July 4, 1994, p. 3.
2. *The New York Times*, November 16, 1993, p. C1.
3. Peter Doyle, Marcel Corstjens, and Paul Michell, "Signals of Vulnerability in Agency-Client Relationships," *Journal of Marketing*, 44 (Fall 1980), 18–23.
4. Paul C. N. Michell, Harold Cataquet, and Stephen Hague, "Establishing the Causes of Disaffection in Agency-Client Relations," *Journal of Advertising Research*, 32, no. 2 (March/April 1992), 41–48; Robert M. Viney, "Solving the Agency-Client Mismatch," *Advertising Age*, May 24, 1993, p. 20.
5. *Advertising Age*, Sept 20, 1993, p. 3.
6. Bruce Buchanan and Paul C. Michell, "Using Structural Factors to Assess the Risk of Failure in Agency-Client Relations," *Journal of Advertising Research*, 31, no. 4 (Aug./Sept. 1991), 68–75.
7. Ronald C. Rutherford, Donald L. Thompson, and Robert W. Stone, "The Impact of Changes in Advertising Agencies on Corporate Common Stock Prices," *Journal of Current Issues and Research in Advertising*, 14, no. 1 (Spring 1992), 1.
8. James W. Cagley, "A Comparison of Advertising Agency Selection Factors: Advertiser and Agency Perceptions," *Journal of Advertising Research* (June/July 1986), 39–43.
9. James R. Wills, Jr., "Winning New Business: An Analysis of Advertising Agency Activities," *Journal of Advertising Research*, 32, no. 5 (Sept./Oct. 1992), 10–14.
10. "In Advertising, What Distinguishes a Great Client?" *Adweek*, February 15, 1988, pp. 36–38; and "15 Ways to Use Your Ad Agency More Productively," *Marketing News*, March 18, 1983, pp. 10–11; Jean L. Johnson and Russell N. Laczniak, "Antecedents of Dissatisfaction in Advertiser-Agency Relationships: A Model of Decision-Making and Communication Patterns," *Journal of Current Issues and Research in Advertising* (1990), 45–59.
11. Nancy L. Salz, *How to Get the Best Advertising from Your Agency*, 2nd ed. (Homewood, IL: Dow Jones Irwin, 1988). The Dove soap example below is also taken from Salz.
12. *Advertising Age*, "Product Manager: Adman's Friend or Foe?" August 17, 1981, p. 43.

13. Daniel B. Wackman, Charles T. Salmon, and Caryn C. Salmon, "Developing an Advertising Agency-Client Relationship," *Journal of Advertising Research* (December 1986/January 1987), 21–27.
14. Ibid. p. 25.
15. *Advertising Age*, "Spot Production Costs Drop 4%," October 26, 1987, p. 46.
16. *Advertising Age*, "Marketers Police TV Commercial Costs," April 3, 1989, p. 51.
17. Hooper White, "How to Raise Effectiveness, Lower Costs of TV Spots," *Advertising Age*, September 21, 1981, p. 64.
18. Paul C. N. Michell, "Auditing of Agency-Client Relationships," *Journal of Advertising Research* (December 1986/January 1987), 29–41.

READING. . . . .

IN ADVERTISING, WHAT DISTINGUISHES A GREAT CLIENT?. . . . .

Ten Principles for Building a Better Relationship with Your Agency

Ammirati & Puris, the New York-based ad agency, was asked by its client, Brown-Forman Inc., a simple yet provocative question: What distinguishes a great client?

The question is one that has been tackled before. A great deal has already been written on the subject, from clients and agencies alike. It's interesting to note a remarkable consistency, be it from clients or agencies, from recent documents or those written decades ago. We are not out to reinvent the wheel here; we want to make points that have been made elsewhere. As might be expected, we've added our own perspective.

Here are ten principles that distinguish the great clients:

Inculcate a spirit of partnership.

It is an irony of the business that those clients who pause to ask, "What makes for a great client?" probably already are. That those clients who think to ask, "What can we do to help make better advertising?" often already have very good advertising. And those who ask their agencies for advice in these areas are, by thinking to ask the very question, already practicing the principles that make agency/client relationships work: partnership, honesty and a constant commitment to making things better.

We have observed that there are two kinds of agency/client relationships. There are those in which the client attempts to establish a superior/subordinate relationship and those in which agency and client are equal partners. The former are all to common in our industry—an astonishing fact given that this kind of relationship rarely results in great work.

The "superior/subordinate" relationships are characterized by an atmosphere of mistrust, a lack of respect for the expertise of the agency, and undercurrents of intimidation. It is always clear that the client will make the agency pay if something goes wrong. It is always clear that the client is ready to exercise the option to dismiss the agency.

In some instances, this condition is the sorry result of mismanagement. In others, unfortunately, it is the client's preferred strategy for dealing with the agency, based on the premise that the agency must be pressured and even threatened before it will exert itself sufficiently on the client's behalf. But the irony is that mediocre advertising inevitably results. Threatened peo-

ple seek safe solutions, conventional, tried-and-true approaches that may appear sound, but which go unnoticed amid the overwhelming clutter of other "safe" commercial messages.

In our view, the great agency/client relationships are those based on equal partnership. Fear, intimidation and disrespect have no place. And it is precisely the absence of fear that makes the relationship work. That allows for honesty. That allows agencies to disagree with their clients, to argue, to take the great risks that almost inevitably are required to achieve great results. It also allows agencies to admit when they have failed.

Great advertising is the product of a very real partnership, a joint effort, based on mutual respect of intelligence and expertise.

So, the simplest answer to the question is that great clients insist on a spirit of partnership. What follows are the ways this spirit is most clearly manifest.

Be wary of change for change's sake.

We noted with interest the question: "Who's hot and why?" We encourage a healthy skepticism.

One of the greatest sins an advertising agency can commit is to imitate an advertising trend. The flood of "new wave" commercials of a few years back and the recent rash of "cinema verité," black-and-white footage shot with hand-held cameras, are testaments to how often agencies jump on the bandwagon.

By imitating a trend, the agency fails by definition to achieve its first purpose: to provide a distinctive image for a client. By the time a trend catches on, it is old news. Each new imitation blends in all the more.

We think that success in advertising is achieved by finding a long-term positioning and sticking with it. Advertising must be designed to defy "trends." We are very proud of the fact that our first television commercial for BMW—filmed in 1976—could air today and look thoroughly up to date.

So we would urge our clients to be less concerned with what other advertisers are doing, or with trends in the advertising industry. Instead, we would urge clients to tune into changes in the consumer.

Make sure your agency is making a fair profit on your account.

This is a seemingly self-serving suggestion, to be sure. But there is considerable self-interest to the client, as well. If a client's demands relative to his budget make its account unprofitable, that account will be less important to the agency. It may not get the same attention. In a crisis, it may not get the extra help it needs.

Make the agency totally absorbed in the company's product, the people and the corporate culture.

Great clients totally immerse their agencies in their products. This is hard work for both client and agency. It often costs lots of money to send agency people to operations centers, to salesforce meetings. It involves risks; bringing your agency inside the company so it can witness its weaknesses and know its secrets.

But, it is only in this thorough immersion that agency people can learn facts that become symbols—the parts that stand for the whole. That UPS washes their planes to achieve greater operating efficiency. That Waterford takes "1,120 times longer than necessary" to make a glass. That 400 brand new BMWs are destroyed in tests every year as part of that company's outstanding commitment to quality control. Concrete facts make for terrific claims in a company's advertising campaign.

Yet these facts are simply the most tangible and obvious by-products of a thorough understanding of the product. The far most important part of the "thorough immersion" is that the agency team will have a feel for the client's corporate culture in their fingertips. Client companies are exceedingly different: some are cautious, conservative; others are risky. Some pride themselves on their efficiency; others their commitment to service. But virtually all are proud of their personality.

In our view, the real value of the "total immersion" is that when an agency team thor-

oughly understands a client's "corporate culture," it will be more likely to create campaigns that last. It goes without saying that the advertiser who keeps a single campaign for a decade will have a greater cumulative success than one who changes every year. But the simple fact is that many of great campaigns do not "work" immediately.

If a campaign precisely reflects the advertiser's corporate culture, there's a better chance a client will stick with it. If it evokes a sense of corporate pride or articulates a corporate mission, a client will give it longer to work. That is the real benefit of "total immersion."

Create an environment of experimentation and be prepared to pay for failure.

Probably nothing predicts mediocrity in advertising quite so precisely as an environment of risk-aversion. This form of fear is a very human response to the ever-increasing costs of television production, coupled with the diminishing value of each dollar invested in media. It is natural to want to conform to rules and formulas in the quest for a measure of certainty that the outcome of the development process will be viable advertising. But the sad truth is that very few advertisers have the massive budgets to ensure that a plodding and unobtrusive television commercial will, through omnipresence, ultimately enter the target's mind. Most advertisers spend at a lower level—a level at which you cannot afford to change messages frequently. You have to find a winning campaign: one that will stand out, and last.

Great clients want advertising that stands out. So great clients create an environment of risk-taking, and great clients back up this philosophy with a willingness to pay for experiments that go wrong.

Treat the agency people well.

Agency people enjoy the same movies and sports clients do, and they have the same problems with their kids that clients have. Great clients take the time to get to know their agency people as people. Great clients know that it is human nature for people to work harder for their friends than for business acquaintances. The happy consequence is that the great client gets more effort out of the agency.

Agree on a clearly defined objective for advertising.

We often tell our new business prospects that 80% of advertising has failed before the first word of copy has been written. It's our way of emphasizing the value of thorough, up-front research and attendant analysis.

Similarly, the failure to define or agree upon the precise purpose of advertising dooms the creative process from the start.

It is an irony that creative strategies are often "approved" with an alarming lack of discussion—but creative executions are scrutinized with a fine-tooth comb, often at numerous levels within an organization. Then our creative direction would be precise, our marching orders unambiguous.

It's often in cases of outright failures that truly great clients stand out. We have all experienced big disappointment in our own work. Great clients know these moments are exactly the time to encourage further risk taking.

Keep approvals simple, and disapprovals kind.

Nothing will sap the energy level of an agency more than presenting the same work over and over at succeeding layers of the client's organization, debating the nuances of the copy at every step of the way. The best system for approval of advertising is, frankly, to have as few layers as possible. And yes, this does mean one layer is best.

If there is disagreement, there are these extremely simple axioms. First, be honest. It's very frustrating to be told after the production is complete, "Well, I never really loved this in layout form, but I went along with you because you were so adamant." If clients don't like something, they must say so. Second, be specific. Don't ask for a new execution because this one *"doesn't do it for me." Fight hard to articulate the problem. Only then can it be addressed.*

Third, be kind. It helps to think of commenting on copy as if you are evaluating the person who wrote it—even though, of course, you are not. But that is, somewhat inevitably, the way the writer takes criticism.

So, trite as it may sound, great clients are kind. They find ways to keep the creative person whole, by commenting on what is terrific about the work, or, very simply, by demonstrating that they have listened very carefully to the agency's point of view and respect it.

Make the agency responsible for the advertising and give it the authority it needs to be responsible.

One exceedingly difficult line a great client must walk is that of involvement in the process. On one extreme of the spectrum are clients who would wash their hands of the whole mess, charging the agency with "complete responsibility for the advertising." Often, this lack of involvement is just a way for the client to avoid sharing responsibility for the end results. It is a way to hold the agency and its advertising at arm's length until the outcome is certain.

At the other end of this spectrum are those who say that the advertising is the agency's responsibility, yet consistently deny the approval that empowers the agency to realize its vision.

This takes all forms. The agency recommends a specific headline, a certain director, a particular daypart mix. A client may disagree. But the ideal client does not mandate specific changes. Clients cannot tell an agency that it must achieve its stated goal in a particular television production while mandating that it use a director it does not want to use. Great clients state precisely why they disagree, and then challenge the agency to find a solution that both parties can feel responsible for.

Give the agency a formal evaluation every year.

This sounds more unpleasant than it is. Good agencies rather enjoy the idea that the client will periodically reflect on whether his advertising is better or worse. And, any agency wants to know if there is a major problem before reading about it in the trade press.

Great clients draw up the terms of evaluation—like everything else—in partnership with the agency. And—very importantly—great clients write this evaluation themselves, and they personally review it with agency management. Delegating this function to juniors (often done on the theory that they work most directly with the agency), can make the review too narrow.

PERDUE FOOD* . . . .

"It Takes a Tough Man to Make a Tender Chicken" was the theme of the advertising campaign developed for Perdue Foods, Inc., of Salisbury, Maryland, by its New York–based agency, Scali, McCabe, Sloves, Inc. The campaign often featured Mr. Frank Perdue, president of Perdue Foods, who had become something of a celebrity as a result in the New York market and elsewhere where the print and radio and TV ad campaign had been run. From an obscure position as one of several hundred companies raising broilers in 1968, Perdue Foods had become by the end of 1972 the largest producer of branded broilers in the United States, killing about 1.5 million birds each week, almost twice as many as when the new agency had acquired the account in 1971.

Such visibility attracted competitors as well as customers, and in February of 1973 a major competitor, Maryland Chicken Processors, Inc., launched a direct frontal attack on Perdue Chickens with ads in the New England trade press carrying the headline:

> *Read how Otis Esham's Buddy Boy chicken is going to beat the pants off the other guy's chicken.*

The "other guy," of course, was Frank Perdue, and the Buddy Boy trade ad even featured a back-of-the-head picture of Frank Perdue with the caption "the other guy." It was a no-holds-barred approach which made direct and frequent reference to Perdue chickens. For example, the trade ad began,

> *The other guy has been a friend and neighbor of ours for years, as well as a competitor.*
>
> *To be truthful about it, our hat's off to him. In the past year or so, he's probably done more for the chicken business than any other guy we know.*
>
> *With his help and the help of his fine New York advertising agency, the consumer is now beginning to realize that it's worth paying a few more pennies a pound to get the kind of fine, plump, golden-yellow chicken we produce down here on the Eastern Shore of Maryland.*
>
> *What this means is that the days of footballing the price of chicken all over the lot are probably numbered.*
>
> *The new name of the game is Profits, and that's not just profits for the*

*This case was prepared as a basis for classroom discussion by Frederick E. Webster, Jr. Copyright © 1973 by the Trustees of Dartmouth College.

chicken business but profits for you, too. So, as far as we are concerned, that other guy is doing a real good job.

But he's vulnerable.

The other guy is a spunky little guy (no offense intended, Frank) who loves to go on television and the radio and tell folks about the fine kind of chicken we produce down home.

You think those commercials are going to hurt us?

Uh-uh. They can't do anything but help *us.*

What those commercials are doing is making the consumer aware that a chicken that's good enough to carry the brand name of a proud producer is going to be a better *chicken than the one that is only good enough to be acceptable to the U.S. government.*

Well, the actual truth is, those commercials could just as well be talking about Otis Esham's fresh Buddy Boy chicken. Because Otis's methods of raising and processing chicken are just about identical to the other guy's.

Except for one very important thing and here's where we get to the part about how the other guy is vulnerable.

That was only the first of four columns in a double-page spread. The ad went on to say that "the other guy's" chickens are packed and shipped in ice and that as the ice melts "your chicken is going to begin to get all water-logged," whereas Buddy Boy chickens are quick-chilled to 30°F and shipped in refrigerated trucks. The ad reported that Purity Supreme, a major New England chain, had taken on the Buddy Boy product and that a "hot" Boston-based ad agency, Pearson and Mac-Donald, had been given the Buddy Boy account. The ad also featured pictures of Otis Esham (whose position was not disclosed[1]). Jack Ackerman, head meat buyer for Purity Supreme (with the caption "Jack Ackerman of Purity Supreme, a 'tough bird' "), Pearson and MacDonald, and a crate of dressed broilers showing the "old-fashioned 'ice-packed' method." The ad went on to explain that "By the time you're reading this, Otis Esham will be on the major Boston radio stations telling your customers about how his fresh Buddy Boy chicken is a better chicken because it's a chilled chicken." More information about media plans was given, and readers were given a telephone number to call collect in Parsonburg, Maryland, to talk with "Bubba Shelton, Otis Esham's right-hand man for sales."

An executive at Scali, McCabe, Sloves called this "one of the most blatant frontal assaults I have ever seen in advertising" as the account executive and top agency personnel began to talk about their response. Three classes of action were being considered. Some favored simply ignoring the Buddy Boy campaign because "it can't hurt us, it can only help us." Others wanted to respond directly, with trade and consumer ads, to the charge that ice-packing was an inferior method and that chickens became "water-logged," because this was not true. A third group sug-

---

* In point of fact, Esham was president of Maryland Chicken Processors, a family-owned business. Esham and Perdue had known each other all their lives; at one time they had owned abutting properties.

gested that now was the time for an entirely new Perdue campaign to take the initiative away from Buddy Boy and go after entirely new segments.

Growth of Perdue Foods, Inc.

An article in *Esquire* magazine in April 1973 described chicken farming as "about the last free-enterprise industry in America. Chicken is produced in a no-holds-barred, rags-to-riches, no-control system, at the fascinating confluence of all the commercial strains in the land: the chicken is where the most volatile elements of the assembly line, of the farm and the field, and bid-and-ask all come together." Until 1968, Perdue was raising chickens for resale to other processors. In 1967, sales had been about $35 million, mainly from selling live birds, but the business also included one of the East Coast's largest grain storage and poultry feed milling operations, soybean processing mulch plants, a hatchery, and 600 farmers raising broilers under contract to Perdue.

A buyer's market existed in 1967, which had squeezed chicken profits. More and more processors were lining up their own contract growers and cutting out Perdue and other middlemen. As Frank Perdue noted, "The situation was good for processors. As in all commodities, profit depends on high volume and small margins. A processor's normal profit on chickens runs $\frac{1}{4}$ to $\frac{1}{2}$ cents per pound. But in 1967's market, processors were paying us 10 cents a pound for what cost us 14 cents to produce, and their profits were as much as 7 cents per pound.

As a result of these conditions, Frank Perdue decided to redesign his business to coordinate egg hatching, chick delivery and feeding, broiler processing, and overnight delivery to market and to develop his own brand. The aim was to develop a quality chicken that could demand premium prices. Special attention was devoted to development of exact feeding formulas which would optimize the chickens' growth rate and give the chicken a golden-colored skin preferred by consumers.

Over the next three years, Perdue began consumer advertising on a limited basis. Distribution was concentrated in New York, with a small percentage of other East Coast cities and as far west as Cleveland. The Perdue brand was identified by a tag on the wing of the processed chicken. Distribution was concentrated in butcher shops and smaller chain food outlets.

Perdue Advertising

As the new strategy of integrated production and profit differentiation began to prove itself in the form of increased sales and profit margins, Frank Perdue became increasingly concerned with the quality of his advertising. After a period of intensive reading on the subject and interviews with almost 50 agencies, Perdue selected Scali, McCabe, Sloves, Inc., in April 1971. The agency immediately began to prepare for a major campaign to be launched in New York City in July. Over Frank Perdue's initial objections, the agency developed a campaign featuring him as the spokesman for the product.

The campaign focused on the quality of Perdue's product, often using subtle

EXHIBIT 1   Perdue Foods, Inc.

SCALI, McCABE, SLOVES INC.

CLIENT: PERDUE FOODS INC.

PRODUCT: PERDUE CHICKENS

TITLE: "MY CHICKENS EAT BETTER THAN PEOPLE"

LENGTH: **30 SECONDS**

COMMERCIAL NO.: **TV-PD-30-2C**

1. FRANK PERDUE: A chicken is what it eats. And my chickens eat better than . . .

2. people do. I store my own grain and mix my own feed.

3. And give my Perdue chickens nothing but pure well water to drink.

4. That's why my chickens always have that healthy golden-yellow color.

5. If you want to eat as good as my chickens, you'll just have to eat my chickens.

6. That's really good.

humor to make the point. The direction of the campaign is indicated in Exhibits 1 to 4, photo boards of four TV commercials. Radio and newspaper advertising was also planned. A new wing tax was designed featuring the company name and a money-back guarantee of quality. In an early 60-second TV commercial, Frank Perdue made the following comments:

> When people ask me about my chickens, two questions invariably come up. The first is "Perdue, your chickens have such a great golden-yellow color it's almost unnatural. Do you dye them?" Honestly, there's absolutely nothing artificial about the color of my chickens. If you had a chicken and fed it good yellow corn, alfalfa, corn gluten, and marigold petals, it would just naturally be yellow. You can't go around dyeing chickens. They wouldn't stand for it.
>
> The other question is "Perdue, your chickens are so plump and juicy, do you give them hormone injections?" This one really gets my hackles up. I do nothing of the kind. When chickens eat and live as well as mine do, you don't have to resort to artificial techniques. . . .

In the first year with the new agency, all advertising expenditures were aimed at the consumer. Only after consumer awareness and preference had been created was trade advertising begun. By the end of the first year, Perdue had achieved distribution in more than half of all New York butcher shops and small retail food out-

EXHIBIT 2   Perdue Foods, Inc.

SCALI, McCABE, SLOVES, INC.
CLIENT: PERDUE FARMS
PRODUCT: CHICKEN

TITLE: "BUTCHER SHOP"
LENGTH: 10 SECONDS
COMM'L. NO.: TV-PD-10-9

1. FRANK PERDUE: I don't allow my superior chickens in just any store.

2. That's why you can only buy Perdue chickens in butcher shops and better markets.

3. I don't want to give my name a bad name.

EXHIBIT 3   Perdue Foods, Inc.

SCALI, McCABE, SLOVES INC.

CLIENT: PERDUE FOODS INC.

PRODUCT: PERDUE CHICKENS

TITLE: "CLEAN LIVIN'"

LENGTH: 30 SECONDS

COMMERCIAL NO.: TV-PD-30-3C

1. FRANK PERDUE: Nobody gets near my chickens unless they wear this fancy get-up.

2. This is not to protect people from my chickens.

3. It's to protect my chickens from people.

4. My competitors think I'm nuts to go through all this.

5. But why do you suppose my chickens always have that healthy golden-yellow color . . .

6. instead of a pale one. I'll tell you why. Clean livin'.

7. (SILENT)

EXHIBIT 4   Perdue Foods, Inc.

SCALI, McCABE, SLOVES INC.   TITLE: "COMPETITION"

CLIENT: PERDUE FOODS INC.   LENGTH: 30 SECONDS

PRODUCT: PERDUE CHICKENS   COMMERCIAL NO.: TV-PD-30-5C

1. FRANK PERDUE: Knowing how good my chickens are isn't good enough for me.

2. So every week I have my people go out and buy cases of my competitors' birds.

3. We put them through the same rigid inspection that our own Perdue chickens have to . . .

4. go through. It costs me a lot of money. But it's worth it.

5. It's the only way I have of knowing that I'm ahead of these guys.

6. How're we doing? Did we win yet?

---

lets. Consumer surveys showed well over 50 percent awareness of the Perdue brand. While financial information was not publicly available, Perdue said "you have to assume it paid off." Competitors estimated that Perdue's costs increased between 2 and 4 cents per pound due to promotional expenses. At the retail level, Perdue chickens were able to command a premium of 5 to 10 cents per pound. One out of every six chickens sold in the New York market carried the Perdue brand. Similar campaigns were launched in Hartford, Connecticut (March 1972), and Baltimore (April 1972). Sales in 1972 exceeded $80,000,000.

Perdue advertising attracted a good deal of public attention, partly due to the distinctiveness of Frank Perdue's presentation, which was described by one commentator as having the sincerity and fervor of a Southern preacher. Stories about the company and its advertising appeared in *Business Week* (September 16, 1972), *Newsweek* (October 16, 1972), and *Esquire* (April 1973), among other places.

The Boston Campaign

Perdue's Boston campaign was launched in December 1972, following the basic pattern now established. The Boston market was somewhat different from New York in that a high percentage of chicken sales occurred through chain store supermarkets, whereas in New York the majority was sold through butcher shops and independent food outlets.

Shortly thereafter, Otis Esham publicized his plans to advertise in Boston and even gave the exact dates on which consumer advertising would break. Perdue's immediate response had been to triple Gross Rating Points (GRP) TV and radio coverage and to contract for additional newspaper coverage on heavy food-buying days, in anticipation of Buddy Boy's campaign. Perdue's first radio ads ran on December 18 and TV ads began on January 15.

Now that Buddy Boy's first trade advertising had appeared early in February, executives at Scali, McCabe, Sloves were wondering what steps to take next. Esham was planning radio for the second week of February and TV was scheduled for the beginning of April. It would be possible for Scali, McCabe, Sloves to prepare television ads within 72 hours to refute the points about "water-logged" chickens in the Buddy Boy advertising.

A principal of Buddy Boy's agency, Terry MacDonald, was quoted as saying "We're going to kill them. They have brilliant advertising. But we have the product advantage."

DISCUSSION QUESTION . . . .

1. What action should Scali, McCabe, Sloves recommend to Frank Perdue?

LEVI STRAUSS & CO.* . . . .

Sue Swenson, a member of the research group at Foote, Cone & Belding/Honig, a San Francisco advertising agency, was reviewing four copy-testing techniques described in the appendix to Chapter 14. A meeting was scheduled with the Levi Strauss account group the next day to decide on which copy tests to employ on two new Levi's campaigns. The following week a similar meeting was scheduled involving a campaign for a new bar soap for another client. In each case the task was to determine which testing approach would be used to help make the final selection of which commercials to use in the campaigns. Sue knew that she would be expected to contribute to the discussion by pointing out the strengths and limitations of each test and to make her own recommendation.

Levi Strauss & Co. had grown from a firm serving the needs of miners in the Gold Rush era of the mid-1800s to a large sophisticated clothing company. In 1979 it had sales of over $2 billion drawn from an international and domestic operation. The domestic company, Levi Strauss USA, included six divisions: Jeanswear, Sportswear, Womenswear, Youthwear, Activewear, and Accessories. In 1979, Levi Strauss was among the 100 largest advertisers, with expenditures of $38.5 million, primarily on television.

Concerning the Levi's campaigns, Swenson recognized that two very different campaigns were involved. The first was a corporate image campaign. The overall objective was to build and maintain Levi's brand image. The approach was to build around the concepts of "Quality" and "Heritage," the most meaningful, believable, and universal aspects of the Levi's corporate personality. Unlike competitors who claim quality as a product feature, Levi's 128-year heritage advertisements had an

* Courtesy of Levi Strauss.

important additional dimension. More specifically, the advertising involved the following strategy:

1. *Heritage-quality:* communicate to male and female consumers, ages 12 to 49, that Levi's makes a wide variety of apparel products, all of which share in the company's 128-year commitment to quality.
2. *Variety-quality:* Communicate to male and female consumers, ages 12 to 49, that Levi's makes a wide variety of quality apparel products for the entire family.

Exhibit 1 shows one of the commercials from the pool that was to be tested for the corporate campaign.

The second campaign was for Levi's Action suits. In 1979, the Sportswear division responsible for Action suits spent approximately $6 million on network television commercials and co-op newspaper ads to introduce Actionwear slacks, which topped the sales of both leading brands of men's slacks, Haggar and Farah, in that year. The primary segment was middle-age males who often suffer from middle-age spread. Actionwear slacks, a blend of polyester and other fabrics with a stretchable waistline, were presented as a solution to the problem. The advertising objectives for the new campaign were guided by the following:

Focus: Levi's Action garments are comfortable dress clothes.
Benefits: Primary—comfortable
                Secondary—attractive, good looking, well made, long wearing
Reasons why:
1. Levi's Action slacks are comfortable because they have a hidden stretch waistband and expandable shell fabric.
2. Levi's Action suit jacket is comfortable because it has hidden stretch panels that let you move freely without binding.
3. The Levi's name implies quality and well-made clothes.

Brand character: Levi's Action clothing is sensible, good-value menswear manufactured by Levi Strauss & Co., a company dedicated to quality.

Exhibit 2 shows a commercial from the pool for the Levi Action campaign.

Swenson also knew that previous Levi's commercials had proved exceptionally memorable and effective, owing to their distinctive creative approach. In part, their appeal lies in their ability to challenge the viewer's imagination. The advertising assumes that viewers are thoughtful and appreciate advertising that respects their judgments.

In preparing for the next day's meeting with the Levi account group, she decided to carefully review the notes on four copy-testing services prepared by a staff assistant at FCB/H (see Appendix, Chapter 14). The immediate problem was to decide which of the services to recommend for testing commercials from the two Levi's campaigns. She knew that similar issues would be raised in discussions with another of the agency's clients the following week concerning a national campaign for a bar-soap line extension. Positioning for the bar soap essentially involved a dual cleanliness-fragrance theme and a demonstration commercial focusing on these two copy points.

EXHIBIT 1   A corporate commercial

LEVI'S® "ROUNDUP"

(Music) Yessir, this drive started over a hundred years ago, back in California.

Just a few head of Levi's Blue Jeans, and a lot of hard miles.

Across country that would've killed ordinary pants.

But Levi's? They <u>thrived</u> on it! If anything, the herd got stronger —and bigger.

First there was <u>kid's</u> Levi's. Ornery little critters…seems like nothing stops 'em.

Then there was <u>gal's</u> pants, and tops, and skirts. Purtiest things you ever set eyes on.

And just to prove they could make. it in the big city, the herd bred a new strain called Levi's Sportswear.

Jackets, shirts, slacks… a bit fancy for this job, I reckon, but I do admire the way they're made.

Fact is, pride is why we put our name on everything in this herd.

Tells folks, "This here's <u>ours!</u>" If you like what you got, then c'mon back!

We'll be here. You see, fashions may change…

…but quality <u>never</u> goes out of style!

Courtesy of Levi Strauss & Co., Two Embarcadero Center, San Francisco, California 94106.

EXHIBIT 2   An Action Suit commercial

TV. 30 Sec.
Title: "Action Suit/Bus"

ANNCR: If a man's suit jacket fits
       like a straight jacket . . .
WIFE: Hold on, Joe!
JOE: I can't raise my arms.

ANNCR: If his pants fit their worst
       around his waist,
WIFE: Sit down.
JOE: I can't—these pants are too
     tight.

ANNCR: Then he needs Levi's*
       Action Suit . . . perhaps
       the most comfortable suit
       a man can wear.

ANNCR: The waistband strrrr-
       retches to give more room
       when you need it.

JOE: Comfortable.
ANNCR: The jacket lets you
       move your arms without
       binding.

JOE: I can sit.
OLD LADY: Hmmmmmmph!

JOE: I can stand, too.

ANNCR: Levi's Action Suit from
       Levi's Sportswear.

Courtesy of Levi Strauss & Co., Two Embarcadero Center, San Francisco, California 94106.

DISCUSSION QUESTIONS . . . .

1. What copy-testing service or services should Sue Swenson recommend for testing the two Levi Strauss commercials?
2. What service or services should she recommend for testing the bar-soap commercial?

PART V

MEDIA STRATEGY AND TACTICS

16 MEDIA STRATEGY: SETTING MEDIA BUDGETS

> I know half the money I spend on advertising is wasted, but I can never find out which half.
> (John Wanamaker, founder of a department store)

> In our experience, 49 percent of the time, TV advertising heavy-up plans successfully increased sales relative to a lower or "base" advertising weight level. In other words, [in these cases] brand sales showed a positive relationship to TV advertising spending.
> (George Garrick, of Information Resources, Inc., commenting in 1989 on the results of ten years of experience from BehaviorScan® field tests of TV advertising budgets)

The amount of money spent on advertising varies widely among companies even within the same industry. For example, while Procter & Gamble was spending 11.8 percent of every sales dollar on advertising in the early 1990s, Lever Brothers was spending only 8.1 percent, while Colgate-Palmolive was spending as much as 13.5 percent. Around that same time in the retail industry, while Sears spent 2.7 percent of sales on advertising and Penney's 2.5 percent, K Mart spent only 1.9 percent.[1] (The U.S. average across all industries, by one estimate, is 2.5 percent. Advertising-to-sales ratios for different U.S. industries are given in Table 16–1.) Furthermore, firms often change their advertising expenditures radically from year to year. What generates this wide variation in advertising expenditures among firms within the same industry and over time for the same firm? How do companies go about setting advertising budgets? How should they be setting or establishing their budgets? What set of models and techniques can be employed to improve their decision making? This chapter will be directed to these questions.

Table 16–1.   1994 Advertising-to-Sales Ratios for the 200 Largest Ad Spending Industries

Industry	SIC no.	Ad dollars % of sales	Ad dollars % of margin	Annual ad growth rate (%)
Abrasive, asbestos, misc minrl	3290	1.1	2.5	2.5
Adhesives and sealants	2891	4.8	12.1	7.5
Agriculture chemicals	2870	1.3	7.0	−8.1
Agriculture production-crops	100	2.3	7.1	−1.8
Air cond, heating, refrig eq	3585	1.5	5.9	2.6
Air courier Services	4513	1.4	12.3	0.8
Air transport, scheduled	4512	1.4	14.6	2.6
Apparel & other finished pds	2300	5.6	15.4	9.1
Apparel and accessory stores	5600	2.2	6.3	11.5
Auto and home supply stores	5531	0.9	2.5	2.0
Auto rent & lease, no drivers	7510	2.4	13.3	−1.1
Bakery products	2050	9.9	60.7	−7.5
Beverages	2080	7.5	12.5	6.9
Biological pds, ex diagnstics	2836	1.3	2.3	17.7
Blankbooks, binders, bookbind	2780	3.5	6.9	8.0
Bldg matl, hardwr, garden-retl	5200	3.3	10.2	−0.7
Books: pubg, pubg & printing	2731	3.3	6.0	5.8
Brdwoven fabric mill, cotton	2211	4.0	16.2	9.0
Btld & can soft drinks, water	2086	2.7	5.9	2.4
Cable and other pay TV svcs	4841	1.1	1.7	−1.5
Calculate, acct mach, ex comp	3578	1.8	4.2	13.8
Can Fruit, veg, presrv, jam, jel	2033	0.8	3.1	−16.3
Can, frozn presrv fruit & veg	2030	7.1	18.4	4.4
Carpets and rugs	2273	2.4	8.1	−8.9
Catalog, mail-order houses	5961	6.8	17.2	10.8
Chemicals & allied pds-whsl	5160	3.6	12.9	5.3
Chemicals & allied prods	2800	2.8	6.5	2.5
Cigarettes	2111	4.4	7.9	−2.5
Cmp and cmp software stores	5734	1.5	25.5	23.1
Cmp integrated sys design	7373	1.5	4.1	3.0
Cmp processing, data prep Svc	7374	1.4	3.1	6.4
Communications equip, NEC	3669	1.5	3.8	−3.0
Computer & office equipment	3570	1.2	3.3	1.9
Computer communication equip	3576	1.9	3.4	17.6
Computer peripheral eq, NEC	3577	2.8	7.0	13.8

(continued)

Table 16–1.   1994 Advertising-to-Sales Ratios for the 200 Largest Ad Spending Industries (*Continued*)

Industry	SIC no.	Ad dollars % of sales	Ad dollars % of margin	Annual ad growth rate (%)
Computer storage devices	3572	0.8	3.1	6.4
Computers & software-whsl	5045	0.5	5.9	14.4
Construction machinery & eq	3531	0.2	0.6	−1.1
Convrt papr, paprbrd, ex boxes	2670	5.8	15.7	1.8
Cutlery, hand tools, gen hrdwr	3420	10.2	19.1	9.6
Dairy products	2020	1.4	5.5	9.3
Dental equipment & supplies	3843	2.0	3.9	19.8
Department stores	5311	2.6	10.6	1.8
Dolls and stuffed toys	3942	15.1	28.0	14.0
Drug & proprietary stores	5912	1.4	5.0	4.5
Eating places	5812	3.2	16.2	7.5
Educational services	8200	6.5	16.7	1.6
Elec meas & test instruments	3825	2.7	5.7	3.4
Electr, oth elec eq, ex cmp	3600	2.4	7.3	6.3
Electric housewares and fans	3634	5.1	16.4	5.9
Electric lighting, wiring eq	3640	1.7	4.3	8.5
Electrical IndL apparatus	3620	2.3	6.2	10.7
Electromedical apparatus	3845	1.0	1.6	2.4
Electronic comp, accessories	3670	3.0	18.7	9.4
Electronic components, NEC	3679	0.8	2.7	14.3
Electronic computers	3571	1.7	5.0	10.1
Electronic parts, eq-whsl, NEC	5065	2.9	13.0	14.4
Engines and turbines	3510	1.8	7.2	−7.5
Engr, acc, resh, mgmt, rel svcs	8700	0.7	3.0	3.5
Fabricated rubber pds, NEC	3060	1.5	5.6	3.0
Family clothing stores	5651	2.5	7.9	9.5
Farm machinery and equipment	3523	1.2	4.7	5.2
Finance-services	6199	0.9	5.6	20.1
Food and kindred products	2000	6.3	16.3	4.7
Food stores	5400	4.2	10.3	13.3
Footwear, except rubber	3140	3.8	9.9	3.3
Functions rel to dep bke, NEC	6099	11.5	54.9	11.3
Furniture Stores	5712	6.4	14.8	3.3
Games, toys, chld veh, ex dolls	3944	16.4	30.7	16.4
Gen med & surgical hospitals	8062	0.8	4.0	5.2

(continued)

Table 16–1.   1994 Advertising-to-Sales Ratios for the 200 Largest Ad Spending Industries (*Continued*)

Industry	SIC no.	Ad dollars % of sales	Ad dollars % of margin	Annual ad growth rate (%)
General indl mach & eq, NEC	3569	0.7	2.0	4.2
General industrial mach & Eq	3560	2.2	7.7	4.3
Glass, glasswr-pressed, blown	3220	1.1	2.6	4.9
Grain mill products	2040	9.1	18.3	1.5
Greetings cards	2771	4.9	7.2	10.3
Groceries & related pds-whsl	5140	2.0	16.1	3.3
Grocery stores	5411	1.1	4.5	0.3
Guided missiles & space vehc	3760	0.4	1.7	1.6
Hardwr, plumb, heat eq-whsL	5070	2.3	37.9	8.0
Help supply services	7363	1.0	5.4	−0.4
Hobby, toy, and game shops	5945	1.5	4.9	11.3
Home furniture & equip store	5700	2.9	8.0	10.7
Hospital & medical EVC Plans	6324	0.9	4.0	19.1
Hospitals	8060	4.2	26.8	−5.0
Hotels, motels, tourist courts	7011	3.6	12.2	3.4
Household appliances	3630	3.0	9.6	3.3
Household audio & video eq	3651	3.6	12.2	7.2
Household furniture	2510	4.6	13.6	8.9
Ice cream & frozen desserts	2024	3.6	10.7	−1.1
In vitro, In vivo diagnostics	2835	2.1	5.5	8.2
Indl coml fans, blowrs, oth eq	3564	4.1	14.2	12.9
Indl trucks, tractors, trailrs	3537	1.0	4.5	10.0
Industrial measurement instr	3823	0.8	2.0	−6.2
INdustrial organic chemicals	2860	0.8	2.7	−1.4
Ins agents, brokers, & Service	6411	1.1	4.9	8.3
Investment advice	6282	7.3	19.6	13.5
Jewelry stores	5944	4.3	10.6	−2.4
Jewelry, precious metal	3911	3.0	6.6	3.6
Knit outerwear mills	2253	2.8	7.9	14.5
Knitting mills	2250	3.0	8.9	4.9
Lab analytical instruments	3826	1.8	3.2	2.1
Lumber & oth bldg matl-retl	5211	1.1	4.0	7.3
Lumber and wood pds, ex furn	2400	0.2	1.1	2.6
Magnetc, optic recording media	3695	3.0	8.0	6.9
Malt beverages	2082	5.5	16.1	−0.1

(continued)

Table 16–1. 1994 Advertising-to-Sales Ratios for the 200 Largest Ad Spending Industries (*Continued*)

Industry	SIC no.	Ad dollars % of sales	Ad dollars % of margin	Annual ad growth rate (%)
Management services	8741	1.5	7.0	15.1
Meas & controlling dev, NEC	3829	1.8	4.1	14.8
Meat packing plants	2011	6.0	23.7	5.8
Membership sport & rec clubs	7997	6.5	8.5	−10.1
men, yth, boys frnsh, wrk clthg	2320	3.6	10.7	15.9
Metal forgings and stampings	3460	0.9	2.9	13.1
Metalworking machinery & eq	3540	3.1	8.8	5.2
Millwork, veneer, plywood	2430	1.7	7.5	14.8
Misc amusement & rec service	7990	2.6	6.6	0.6
Misc business services	7380	3.9	7.0	3.6
Misc chemical products	2890	7.2	16.6	5.8
Misc durable goods-whsl	5090	2.0	8.0	12.4
Misc elec machy, eq, supplies	3690	1.5	5.0	3.5
Misc fabricated metal prods	3490	0.7	2.3	−1.8
Misc food preps, kindred pds	2090	2.9	6.5	5.1
Misc general mdse stores	5399	3.6	15.1	3.6
Misc manufacturing industries	3990	2.3	5.8	7.8
Misc nondurable goods-whsl	5190	3.2	11.5	12.3
Misc plastics products	3080	2.1	8.0	0.7
Misc shopping goods stores	5940	2.2	7.2	7.6
Misc transportation equip	3790	4.7	15.1	−0.7
Miscellaneous retail	5900	1.8	6.7	8.7
Mortgage bankers & loan corr	6162	2.2	3.3	14.5
Motion pic, videotape prodtn	7812	12.4	25.8	11.3
Motion pict, videotape distr	7822	6.3	13.8	9.6
Motion picture theaters	7830	3.1	17.3	−6.0
Motor vehicle part, accessory	3714	0.8	3.4	8.1
Motor vehicles & car bodies	3711	2.7	13.2	0.1
Motorcycles, bicycles & parts	3751	1.2	4.8	14.8
Newspaper: pubg, pubg & print	2711	3.4	8.3	0.1
Office machines, NEC	3579	1.2	3.9	−5.0
Offices of medical doctors	8011	1.4	6.7	10.8
Operative Builders	1531	1.1	8.8	0.1
Operators-nonres bldgs	6512	1.6	4.0	−1.3
Ophthalmic goods	3851	8.4	14.6	8.9

(continued)

Table 16–1.   1994 Advertising-to-Sales Ratios for the 200 Largest Ad Spending Industries (*Continued*)

Industry	SIC no.	Ad dollars % of sales	Ad dollars % of margin	Annual ad growth rate (%)
Ortho, prosth, surg appl, suply	3842	2.1	4.1	8.4
Paints, varnishes, lacquers	2851	2.7	6.8	6.1
Paper & paper products-whsl	5110	1.6	6.1	14.7
Paper mills	2621	3.0	12.9	−3.8
Patent owners and lessors	6794	4.3	9.5	15.3
Pens, pencils, oth office matl	3950	4.7	10.5	1.8
Perfume, cosmetic, toilet prep	2844	8.8	15.3	6.8
Periodical: pubg, pubg & Print	2721	5.6	10.4	−3.3
personal credit institutions	6141	0.7	1.5	−0.8
Personal services	7200	7.0	17.9	8.1
Petroleum refining	2911	1.1	8.4	12.1
Pharmaceutical preparations	2834	5.6	7.8	4.8
Phone comm ex radiotelephone	4813	1.9	4.6	10.3
phono recrds, audiotape, disc	3652	11.7	24.2	18.9
photofinishing laboratories	738	3.4	12.0	11.9
Photographic equip & suppl	3861	4.1	10.2	1.7
Plastics matl, synthetic resin	2820	1.2	3.9	1.3
Plastics products, NEC	3089	2.7	7.0	4.3
Plastics, resins, elastomers	2821	0.8	2.5	−1.2
Poultry Slaughter & process	2015	2.5	13.5	10.3
Prepackaged software	7372	3.8	5.2	14.9
Printed circuit boards	3672	1.2	6.5	32.1
Printing trades machy, equip	3555	2.2	5.1	3.9
Prof & coml eq & supply-whsl	5040	2.0	5.8	8.6
Pumps and pumping equipment	3561	1.6	3.9	0.7
Radio broadcasting stations	4832	5.2	13.0	19.8
Radio, TV Broadcast, comm eq	3663	1.2	3.1	13.2
Radio, TV, Cons electr stores	5731	4.1	15.8	3.0
Radiotelephone communication	4812	3.7	6.6	14.3
Real estate investment trust	6798	1.9	3.4	11.4
Refrig & service ind machine	3580	2.1	6.5	−1.5
Retail stores	5990	4.6	11.7	16.3
Rubber and plastic footwear	3021	7.9	19.0	9.5
Sausage, oth prepared meat pd	2013	9.6	24.5	9.5
Security brokers & dealers	6211	1.8	4.5	−17.1

(continued)

Table 16–1.   1994 Advertising-to-Sales Ratios for the 200 Largest Ad Spending Industries (*Continued*)

Industry	SIC no.	Ad dollars % of sales	Ad dollars % of margin	Annual ad growth rate (%)
Semiconductor, related device	3674	2.0	4.1	18.7
Ship & boat bldg & repairing	3730	0.5	2.5	−8.5
Shoe stores	5661	5.4	16.1	12.7
Skilled nursing care facil	8051	1.7	12.7	7.0
Soap, detergent, toilet preps	2840	9.9	22.6	8.3
Spec outpatient facility, NEC	8093	1.0	4.8	15.3
Special clean, polish preps	2842	16.1	26.6	2.5
special industry machinery	3550	4.1	14.4	−8.3
Sporting & athletic gds, NEC	3949	6.4	13.4	17.2
Srch, det, nav, guid, sero sys	3812	4.3	7.7	−0.2
Sugar & confectionery prods	2060	12.7	29.9	6.2
Surgical, med instr, apparatus	3841	1.2	2.5	6.5
Svc to motion picture prodtn	7819	2.0	5.9	9.2
Tele & telegraph apparatus	3661	0.7	2.1	1.3
TV broadcast station	4833	3.2	7.4	6.4
Textile mill products	2200	0.9	3.8	13.3
Tires and inner tubes	3011	1.9	6.5	3.6
Unsupp plastics film & sheet	3081	3.0	9.3	−2.1
Variety stores	5331	1.6	6.6	4.9
Videotape rental	7841	2.0	4.1	13.8
Water transportation	4400	7.3	20.0	−1.1
Wmns, miss, chld, infnt undgrmt	2340	4.2	10.3	9.6
Women's clothing stores	5621	2.6	7.0	1.9
Women's, misses, jrs outerwear	2330	3.1	10.8	6.5
Wood hshld furn, ex upholsrd	2511	2.5	8.0	17.1

Source: Schonfeld & Associates, 1 Sherwood Drive, Lincolnshire, Ill. 60069. (708) 948-8080

SIC = Standard Industrial Classification number. NEC = not elsewhere classified. Ad dollars as percent of sales = ad expenditure/net sales. Ad dollars as percent of margin = advertising expenditures/(net sales − cost of goods sold). Annual ad growth rate (%) = average compound growth in ad spending.

The importance of setting advertising budgets using careful analysis, rather than industry rules of thumb or "gut feel," cannot be overemphasized. Various studies have repeatedly shown that the *average advertising elasticity*—the expected percentage change in volume sales when the amount spent on advertising rises 1 percent—is small, about only 0.22 percent.[2] Clearly, this is only an average across brands, that ignores long-term effects on consumers and effects on the trade, and has various other shortcomings as a measure of the value of advertising spending.

However, it does suggest that at least some brands may be spending too much on advertising (whereas others may need to spend even more than they do now).[3] When you combine this observation with the fact that for many brands, the advertising budget is the single largest discretionary expense, running into tens of millions of dollars, you should realize quickly that "fine-tuning" the advertising budget is an activity that is worth a fair amount of a brand manager's time.

ECONOMIC ANALYSIS IN SETTING AND ALLOCATING BUDGETS . . . .

The theoretical underpinning of an advertising-budget decision is based on *economic marginal analysis* and is easily expressed. A firm should continue to add to the advertising budget for a specific brand or specific geographical market or specific advertising medium as long as the incremental expenditures there are exceeded by the marginal revenue they generate (see Figure 16–1). Similarly, if companies advertising mature industrial products find that the sales potential (and actual sales revenue) per account are increasing, then the budgets for advertising and personal sales calls should go up, too. On the other hand, if very high levels of competitive spending reduce the revenue impact of this company's promotional spending, its budgets should go down.[4] As pointed out in Chapter 2, such an analysis could theoretically be applied to the other components of the marketing mix as well, such as sales promotion, personal selling, distribution, and pricing. A resulting optimal expenditure level could then be obtained for each component, allowing for identification of the optimal budgets for each kind of marketing spending.

If the sum of these expenditures exceeded the available resources, the marketing budget for each would have to be scaled down. Each area would be constrained on the basis of the marginal revenue generated by the last dollar in its

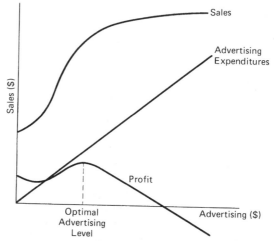

Figure 16–1. **Graph of sales, profit, and advertising curves used in marginal analysis.**

budget. If, for example, the last dollar put into personal selling generated $2 of brand contribution, whereas the last dollar of advertising generated $3 of brand contribution, it would probably be desirable to shift money from personal selling to advertising.

It has been found empirically, for instance, that the elasticity of sales response to price cuts is, on average, about twenty times the elasticity of sales to increases in advertising (this elasticity ratio is higher for mature products than for products early in their life cycles, and for nondurable goods than for durable goods). This suggests that price discounting may be a more appropriate investment of the marketing dollar than an advertising increase, until the point is reached where advertising begins to have the bigger effect.[5] As another example, for the mature industrial product discussed earlier, as the number of sales accounts becomes very large, mass (trade journal) advertising becomes more effective than personalized sales calls, suggesting (at some point) a redeployment of resources away from personal sales into mass advertising.[6] In making allocations across brands, if a dollar of advertising leads to an equal increase in sales revenue for two brands, but one brand had a higher gross margin or contribution ratio than the other, this more profitable brand should be favored with that extra advertising dollar. Of course, personal selling and advertising for individual brands or markets cannot absorb investments in small increments, and spending on one type of promotional vehicle or one brand has "cross-over or spill-over" effects that are very difficult to disentangle,[7] but the principle of "put the money where the bigger payoff is, at the margin" is still valid.

Some Difficulties in Applying Marginal Analysis

There are, unfortunately, some difficulties in applying marginal analysis in practice, as is the case with many other concepts from microeconomic theory. The assumption in the foregoing has been that it is appropriate to consider sales as a function of advertising expenditures, with advertising as the only input and immediate sales as the output. Such an assumption may be reasonable in some direct-response advertising. However, in other situations, it is more tenuous. Even when it does seem reasonable, the determination of the shape and parameters of the response function (of sales, or contribution, responding to advertising) is no easy task. This will be clear when regression estimation techniques are presented in the latter part of this chapter. Furthermore, even when a certain response curve does accurately represent a certain situation, there is no guarantee that it will continue to be valid in the future. The conditions of the market, including the competitive environment, change. As a result, the nature and shape of the response function also can change.

The assumption that sales are determined solely by advertising expenditures is obviously faulty in practically all situations. The nature of the advertising campaign, the copy used, and the media selected will usually influence the shape of the response curve. A strong creative effort will evoke a different response than a tasteless, misdirected campaign, even if the same expenditure levels are involved. Indeed, tests by the Campbell Soup Company and IRI have shown that the biggest sales-response changes can come not from varying how much advertising money you spend, but rather from where you spend it—the selection of target markets and media—and what you say in the ads (the message strategy).[8] Furthermore, it is difficult to sort out the effect of advertising from the effect of other forces that influence sales. Sales are, after all, a result of a company's total marketing and promotional effort as well as a number of environmental conditions, such as competitive actions and a host of economic, climatic, social, and cultural factors. If all factors including competitive activity remained constant except for advertising, it would be reasonable to consider advertising to be the only determinant of sales. The fact is, however, that such conditions do not hold in any real-world situation.

The dependent variable in the response function is sales—by implication, immediate sales. Although there are cases such as direct-mail advertising wherein the use of immediate sales is quite appropriate, in most instances, there is a considerable lag between the time of the advertising and the time of the sales it might have helped stimulate. A consumer buying a car in June could have been affected by advertising for that car the previous fall. People may be affected by the reputation or image of a brand built up through advertising over a considerable period of time. Furthermore, advertising might attract buyers who become loyal customers for several years. Their immediate purchases may be only a small part of the value to the firm that enticed them to try the brand.

Practical Budget-Setting Analysis

There are, in general, two ways in which firms can react to the difficulty of determining the type of marginal analysis recommended by economic theory. They can, essentially, admit that the task is so formidable, at least given their expertise, that it is not worthwhile to pursue it and rely instead on other types of decision rules—or on no rules at all. There are doubtless many companies that base their ad budgets very simply on what they have always spent, historically (possibly adjusted upward with some kind of media cost inflation multiplier). Such inertia is inexcusable, especially in today's extremely competitive environment when it is essential to try very hard to squeeze waste out of smaller marketing budgets. When used, the rules employed may or may not reflect a marginal analysis. Some of these *decision rules* are discussed in the paragraphs that follow. While not necessarily optimal, they have the advantage of simplicity.

A second reaction is to attempt to determine a data-based *response function* (or graphical curve) relating advertising expenditure to sales, despite the difficulties. Once the shape of this curve is known, it can be used to determine the level of advertising that maximizes sales (or the profit contribution from sales). The argument is that, even if the result is imperfect, it might indeed provide some guidance, and the method at least has a theoretical basis. Furthermore, the exercise does not necessarily have to be expensive, so the risk is not excessive. The primary tools used in estimating such a response function are split-cable testing, field experimentation, regression analysis, and laboratory or field studies of the effects of increasing advertising frequency levels. These will be reviewed later in this chapter.

(Another way of developing such a response function is simply to use managerial judgment, perhaps extracted with the assistance of a computer. Such techniques are sometimes labeled *decision calculus techniques* and are not described in this chapter because of their infrequent use).[9]

In the following sections, these two approaches will be more fully explored. Several frequently used decision rules used to set advertising budgets will first be examined. Then various attempts to estimate the response function using experimentation, regression analysis, and optimal repetition frequency analyses will be presented. It should be emphasized here that no method of determining an ad budget is ever perfect, because they are simply too many uncertainties involved in the measurement of advertising effects. Thus several different methods from the ones described below should be tried, and judgment will then have to be applied to come up with a figure that seems warranted from a payout, affordability, brand needs, and competitive standing point of view—all at once. The important thing is to make an effort to do it right.

SIMPLE BUT QUESTIONABLE BUDGETING DECISION RULES. . . . .

There are several decision rules on which many firms draw in making budget decisions.[10] Four such rules will be described. The rules are basically justified by arguing that budgets based on them are unlikely to be far from the actual optimal budget if a marginal analysis could be performed. In many cases, the rules are used in combination, the net budget being a compromise among several of the rules.

Percentage of Sales or of Gross Margin

One rule of thumb used in setting advertising budgets is the *percentage of sales*. Past sales or a forecast of future sales can be used as the base. A brand may have devoted 5 percent of its budget to advertising in the past. Thus, if the plan calls for doing $40 million worth of business next year, a $2 million advertising budget might be proposed. A similar decision could be based upon market share, or unit volume. For example, a brand could allocate $1 million for every share point it holds, or $2 for every case of the product it expects to sell.

The percentage-of-sales guide is the most common approach to setting advertising budgets. A 1981 survey of 55 of the 100 leading consumer advertisers found that over 70 percent reported using some version of the percentage-of-sales method,[11] as did a similar survey of ninety-two British companies.[12]

If a firm or brand has been successful over several years using the percentage-of-sales approach, it might be assumed that the decision rule yielded budgets reasonably close to the optimal, so there is little incentive to change to another approach in setting budgets. The rule does tend to make explicit the marketing mix decision, the allocation of the budget to the various elements of the marketing program. Furthermore, it provides comfort to a prudent financial executive who likes to know that her or his firm can afford the advertising. Finally, if competitors also use such a rule, it leads to a certain stability of advertising within the industry, which may be useful. If there is a ceiling on the size of the market, it is wise to avoid precipitating a war over advertising expenditures.

The major flaw in the method is that it does not rest on the premise that advertising can influence sales. In fact, sales or a sales estimate determine advertising expenditures. It can lead to excessive expenditures for large established brands and for over-the-hill brands that are basically servicing old loyal customers who will very likely continue to buy even if advertising support is withdrawn. It can, conversely, lead to inadequate budgets for promising healthy brands that could potentially become competitive with more advertising muscle.

The second flaw in this method is that it ignores brand profitability, by looking only at brand sales. A more logical rule would be to use a percentage not of sales, but of a brand's gross margin or contribution-to-overhead. This would imply that more profitable brands get more advertising support, compared to less profitable brands, even if their sales revenue figures are identical.

The percentage-of-sales or percentage-of-margin approaches obviously need to be modified in dynamic situations such as the following:

- **When a brand is making a major repositioning move or reacting to one.**
- **When a brand becomes established and dominant.**
- **When a brand is just being introduced.**

Making a Move
When a brand decides to make a move, a substantial increase in advertising might be necessary, an increase that may not be justified by the percentage-of-sales logic. For example, when Philip Morris purchased Miller beer in 1972 and initiated a campaign to reposition it and increase its share, the advertising budget was dramatically increased. Similarly, when the effects of the Miller effort became evident, the other beer companies had to consider breaking out of their percentage-of-sales routine and react to the Miller move.

Established Brand
When a brand becomes established and dominant, it can usually start reducing the percentage of sales allocated to advertising. As brand-name awareness becomes very high and the brand's image becomes very set, it is not usually necessary to advertise as heavily. Conversely, if a smaller brand is struggling to become known and is concerned about advertising at the minimal threshold level, it will often have to spend money at an artificially high percentage-of-sales level.

New Brand
A new product, concept, or brand will have the special task of generating awareness and distribution from a zero level. As a result, it is usually necessary to make heavy investments in advertising during the first year or two of the brand's life. At Colgate-Palmolive, the guide is to base the advertising expenditures on the total gross profit, which is the total sales less the product cost, as follows:[13]

- Advertising in first year equals twice the gross profit.
- Advertising in second year equals half the gross profit.
- Advertising in third and succeeding years equals 30 percent of the gross profit.

All You Can Afford

Firms with limited resources may decide to spend all that they can reasonably allocate to advertising after other unavoidable expenditures have been allocated. This rule usually ensures that they are not advertising too heavily, that advertising monies are not being wasted. It thus does have some logic. Of course, if the value of more advertising could be demonstrated, extra money could usually be raised, so the limitation may be somewhat artificial.

Some larger firms also use this rule. They start with the sales forecast and budget all expenditures, including profit, except advertising. The advertising budget is what is left over. About all that can be said about such a rule, which is actually used in too many situations, is that it generates a financial plan that usually looks neat and attractive in an accounting sense. However, it rests on the assumption that sales are independent of the advertising expenditures. There is no realization that advertising may influence sales. The only reason advertising is included is that its absence would be difficult to justify!

Competitive Parity and Share-of-Voice

Another common guide is to adjust the advertising budget so that it is comparable to those of competitors. The logic is that the collective minds of the firms in the industry will probably generate advertising budgets that are somewhat close to the optimal. Everyone could not be too far from the optimal. Furthermore, any departure from the industry norms could precipitate a spending war.

The problem here is that there is no guarantee that a group of firms is spending at an optimal level. Insofar as their spending habits are constant over time, and assuming that market conditions change over time, they are probably not spending at the optimal level. Even if they are, it is likely that the situations of individual firms are sufficiently unique so that the practices of their competitors should not be followed. In particular, a new small firm in the field might not receive the proportionate amount of impact for its advertising that a large established firm receives. The success of the larger firm may be due to many other factors in addition to advertising. Furthermore, the method does not consider such questions as differences in effectiveness of various campaigns or the efficiency of media placement. Following the competition might offer the satisfaction of knowing you are not taking a big competitive risk, and be politically safe within a company's managerial ranks, but might turn out to be a case of the the blind following the blind. Academic "game theorists" have developed models of how different competitors might end up responding to each other over time.[14]

A very commonly used variant of the competitive parity approach is to set a brand's share of total category advertising (measured over a period such as a year), called *share of voice (SOV)* close to its *share of market (SOM)*. If every brand in the category did this, it would probably ensure that the industry's market share situation stayed at equilibrium, with no changes, assuming all other marketing mix elements were at parity across brands. In practice, market leaders often have a SOV a little less than their SOM, reflecting their advertising *economies of scale*, while market challengers need a SOV higher than their SOM, in order to gain market share. It is often argued that a new brand, being "built up for the future," needs an SOV about twice its targeted SOM, at least for a while. In contrast, an old and established brand being "milked" to support such newer brands might see a SOV substantially below its SOM, and that is very frequently a sure way to lose market share in the long term (the old brand equity may support sales for a while, but equity that is not replenished does get used up!). Market leaders can maintain their leadership by keeping their SOV at much higher levels than those of competitors, while market followers ought to boost their SOV significantly (at least 30 to 40 percent) higher in those geographical markets where the market leader has allowed its SOV to fall dangerously low. Obviously, companies with lower cost structures can more easily afford disproportionately higher SOVs.[15]

Objective and Task

Objective and task, more an *optimal approach* to budgeting than a simple decision rule, is used by two-thirds of the largest advertisers.[16] An advertising objective is first established in specific terms. For example, a firm may decide to attempt to increase the awareness of its brand in a certain population segment to 50 percent. The tasks that are required to accomplish this objective are then detailed. They might involve the development of a particular advertising campaign exposing the relevant audience an average of five times. The cost of obtaining these exposures then becomes the advertising budget. This approach is logical in that it assumes that there is a causal flow from advertising to sales. In effect, it represents an effort to introduce intervening variables such as awareness or attitude, which will presumably be indicators of future sales as well as of immediate sales.

The major problem with this approach is that the link between the objective and immediate and future sales is often not spelled out. Later in this chapter, we will develop a framework for extending it in this direction so that it can indeed provide a logical, defensible basis for setting the advertising budget. Many advertising and new product researchers, however, have managed to develop proprietary estimates of how different levels of ad response objectives (particularly brand awareness) correspond to typical levels of trial for new products and line extensions, and from there to sales volume or share, using their knowledge of historical experience.[17] Another problem is that it is hard to estimate the precise relationship between advertising media exposure and the adjective objective (e.g., brand awareness) itself. Here again, many advertising agencies (such as Foote, Cone & Belding, and others) have built up databases of tracking data results showing how advertising spending (measured in GRPs, discussed in the next chapter, or in ad exposures or frequency) relate to different measures of ad effectiveness (such as ad recall, brand awareness, brand persuasion, etc.).[18] Not surprisingly, these response relationships depend on whether the brand is new or old, the nature of the ad copy itself, the specific ad medium and TV daypart being used, the category growth rate, other marketing actions including promotions, and so on.

MARKET EXPERIMENTATION AND BUDGETING . .

A direct approach to estimating the sales response to advertising is to conduct field market experiments. Advertising expenditure levels are deliberately and systematically varied across areas. Sales changes are monitored through time, sometimes for several years, and related to advertising levels.

One of the best known sets of field experiments was conducted by Budweiser during the 1960s.[19] In one of its experiments seven advertising change treatments were used:

> −100 percent (no advertising)
> −50 percent
> 0 percent (advertising was unchanged)
> +50 percent
> +100 percent (the advertising expenditure was doubled)
> +150 percent
> +200 percent

Six marketing areas were assigned to each advertising treatment. The experiment ran for one year. Not only did "no advertising" result in the same sales level, but a −50 percent level actually resulted in a sales increase. One possible explanation was that there was a light-drinker segment for which reduced repetition was helpful. Other explanations for this "less advertising was better" result have also been offered, such as the idea that if an ad is novel and interesting, it might actually perform better with fewer rather than more exposures, since it then retains its novelty better.[20] Whatever the explanation, this experiment and others in the series resulted in substantial reductions in advertising expenditures, particularly on a per-barrel basis, as Figure 16–2 illustrates.

Other published reports of advertising weight test experiments include a series of studies by the Campbell Soup Company, by Seagrams for their liquor brands, by the Defense Department for its Navy recruitment advertising, by IRI, and by the Advertising Research Foundation for business-to-business advertising. During the period between 1974 and 1979, the Campbell Soup Company conducted a series of advertising weight tests (as well as tests of creative strategy, media mix, and pricing) for V-8 cocktail vegetable juice.[21] It was found that a new creative strategy ("I could'a had a V-8"), when combined with a new media mix and a higher expenditure level, beat the old creative/media mix/spending level in generating higher than the otherwise-forecasted sales levels (as measured by warehouse withdrawal data, a gauge of sales into stores). Other tests, mainly involving Condensed and Chunky soups, Franco-American Pasta, and Swanson Frozen Foods, were also conducted; each lasted less than a year and used a small number of test markets (plus a matched control, no-change market for comparison purposes).[22]

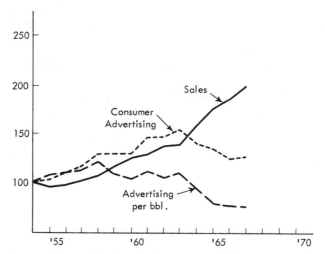

Figure 16–2.   Advertising and sales, Budweiser beer; index 1954 = 100.

Very few of these showed increases in advertising weight to "payout" in extra contribution, even when the advertising budgets were increased by 50 percent. However, once again, changes in creative strategy (such as pushing summer consumption of soups) and in media mix (trying to reach previously unreached consumers) were much more successful.

In trying to generalize from these Campbell Soup results, it is important to remember that these were old, well-established brands, such that it is very likely that their previous levels of advertising and brand awareness were likely to be close to saturation levels. Smaller, newer brands typically show a greater responsiveness to advertising weight increases than older brands, especially if the money is spent in geographical areas where market potentials are high but existing brand penetration is low.[23] However, it is still sobering to note that consumers do not respond swiftly to simply being told the same thing more often—it may be more fruitful to tell them something new and more interesting, and to tell it to people you haven't been telling it to before.

The Defense Department studies (conducted in 1978, over 26 media markets) also showed that Navy enlistments did not vary over a one-year experimental period when national Navy advertising was varied by amounts from −100 percent to +100 percent. However, variations in localized advertising, where copy was tailored to the individual market area, did make a difference.[24] In the Seagrams study, conducted in *Time* and *Sports Illustrated* magazines over 48 weeks in 1981, 21,000 subscribers were sent specially tailored copies of the magazines varying the number of ads seen. Since subscribers were already getting the magazines, they were unaware of the experiment. Weekly questionnaires were sent to subsamples of respondents, tracking the measures of interest. The results showed that higher ad exposure raised per-capita usage and purchase levels of the Seagram brands.[25]

The biggest set of experimental results reported for consumer nondurable products come from a study by Information Resources Inc. (IRI), which generates scanner data from split-cable testing facilities (described further below). In its facilities, brands can test different levels of ad frequency to matched panels of households, and see the sales results at the grocery checkout scanner. In looking at the results of 400 tests conducted between 1982 and 1988, to see "How Advertising Works," IRI and the study's sponsors reported in 1991 that increases in ad weight (budget) only had an effect on sales when they were accompanied by changes in copy or brand strategy, or when a new target audience was being reached through a change in media plans as well. Sales increases occurred more easily for newer and smaller brands than for larger (and older) ones. These sets of results clearly corroborate the results of the Campbell Soup studies mentioned earlier. IRI also reported that sales increases were also greater if the product category was growing, or if the category was large and the number of purchases per buyer were many. Ad-induced sales increases were helped by higher consumer promotions (coupons), but not by higher trade promotions (store displays). A flighting or concentrated ad schedule (in terms of how ads were bunched over time) was more effective than an evenly distributed one. When sales increases did occur, they were large and significant, persisting two years after the ad budget increase (but at declining levels), so that the total increase in sales was double the increase seen in the first year of effect measurement.[26]

Finally, it is important to realize that such weight tests can be done for industrial (business-to-business) products as well. In a study conducted during the period between 1984 and 1986 by the Advertising Research Foundation and the Association of Business Publishers, variations in the number of pages of advertising run for four industrial products were tested over a year.[27] Readers of controlled circulation business magazines in targeted customer companies saw ads for these products at three levels—low weight (under eight pages), medium weight (e.g., fourteen pages), and high weight (e.g., twenty-eight pages). Obviously, these readers did not know of the variation in advertising weight; the sales and inquiries for these products from these companies were then related to the advertising levels. In general, the results confirmed that higher advertising did lead to more sales leads, more sales, and more profits, though the results took a while (four to six months) to emerge and did show a pattern of diminishing returns. (See Figure 16–3.) It also appeared to be useful to increase advertising not only to the end users but also to the intermediary dealers.

Testing Advertising and Other Marketing Mix Elements

Sometimes it is useful to include marketing variables other than advertising in the experiment, particularly when the advertising response will depend on the levels of those other marketing variables. Gerald Eskin reports an experiment involving a new nutritional convenience food in which both advertising and price levels were tested.[28] A sample of thirty stores in each of four test cities was used. Two of the cities received a high advertising weight that was approximately twice that received by the other two cities. In addition, in each city the thirty test stores were split into three panels of ten stores, each matched as to store size and other fac-

First-Year Sales Response among Dealers for Product II

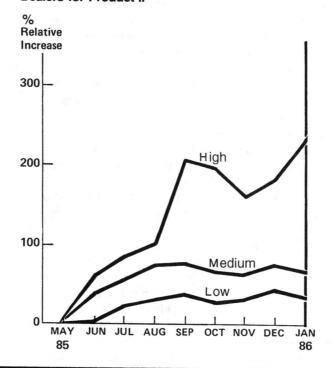

Product I Marginal Returns

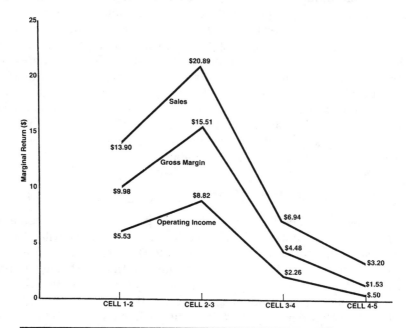

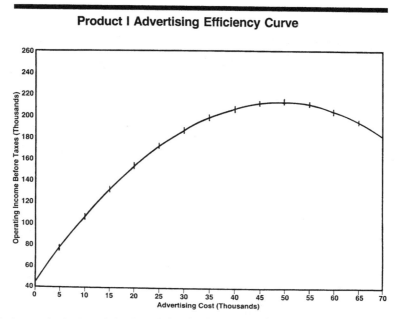

Figure 16–3.   An industrial advertising budget experiment.

Source: Modified from Naples and Wollfsberg, "The Bottom Line: Does Industrial Advertising Sell?" Journal of Advertising Research *(August/September 1987), RC4-RC16. © 1978 by the Advertising Research Foundation.*

tors. Each of these matched panels received one of three price treatments: a base price below 50 cents, a price 10 cents above the base, and a price 20 cents above it. The test ran for six months. Each month the unit sales per store was measured. The experimental design is summarized at the top of Figure 16–4.

The results are summarized at the bottom of Figure 16–4. Clearly, the higher advertising was very effective when the base price was used. In contrast, increased advertising had almost no effect at the highest price. Prior to the test, the belief was that the best candidates for a national program were the combinations of high price and high advertising and low price and low advertising. The logic was that a high price was needed to provide margin to pay for the advertising. The test led to a very different conclusion, however—a low-price and high-advertising program.

In this case, the response to advertising depended on the price level selected. If price had not been included in the experiment, a distorted impression might have emerged as to the advertising response. Inclusion of price, of course, also provided useful information about that marketing decision variable. In general, it is always very useful in an advertising field experiment to also measure the levels of other marketing variables that might impact on the sales results. The sales effects of such variables, called *covariates*, can then be statistically adjusted for in evaluating the effect of advertising weight (*the manipulated variable*) on sales.

Test Design

Advertising:	Low Weight						High Weight					
	Market 1			Market 2			Market 3			Market 4		
Price:	Base	+10c	+20c	Base	+10c	+20c	Base	+10c	+20c	Base	+10c	+20c
N =	(10)	(10)	(10)	(10)	(10)	(10)	(10)	(10)	(10)	(10)	(10)	(10)

Month
1
2
3
4
5
6

Total no. of observations = 720
Measure = total sales/per store/by month

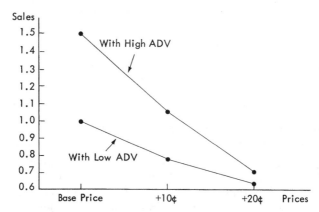

Figure 16–4. **An advertising and price experiment.**

Source: Adapted from Gerald Eskin, "A Case for Test Market Experiments," Journal of Advertising Research, 15, April 1975, pp. 29, 31.

Problems with Market Experimentation

Experimental approaches are indeed useful as direct methods of obtaining information on sales-response curves. However, there are major problems associated with their use.

Experimentation is inherently expensive. There are several types of costs to consider. First, there are the obvious direct costs of setting up the experiment and collecting and analyzing the results. Second is the fact that management decisions are delayed by the research. The researcher is often in a dilemma. On the one hand, validity considerations demand a longer experiment, often covering several repurchase cycles for the product. However, as the length increases, the timeliness of the results suffers. Furthermore, there is the very real likelihood that the situation will change (a major new product will emerge, for example) and the experimental results will not be applicable. Third, there is a security cost, particularly in new product contexts. Competitors will have access to the nature and results of your experiments. Finally, an advertising test will invariably involve excess advertising in some areas and less than optimal in others. The costs of either situation can be very significant.

Market experiments are never "controlled" as well as would be desirable; there are a litany of things that can "go wrong." The company's own sales force can work extra-hard during the test, making it difficult to draw conclusions about whether the source of the sales gain was the advertising weight change or the extra sales effort. The experimental cells can differ in more than just the amount of money being spent—the media mix and/or the creative might also vary, again making interpretation of test results difficult. Retailers can run out of stock because of logistical problems or because they did not anticipate the impact of more advertising. Distributors or retailers in "low-advertising treatment areas" can mount their own advertising or promotion campaign to replace the national advertising being withdrawn. They are more concerned with their marketing position than with any experiment. Competitors' marketing efforts, including new product introductions, can confound the experiment. Further, competitors sometimes deliberately attempt to disrupt the test by radically changing some element of their competitive marketing strategy, such as their price or promotion effort.

Guidelines for Conducting Experiments

A list of guidelines for conducting experiments should include the following:

1. **Use randomly selected control cities, areas, or stores so that the effects of advertising can be separated from all the other influences on sales. If possible, these control groups should be matched with the experimental groups on such dimensions as size, market share, or other sales-influencing variables (such as climate, in the case of soft drinks). For example, it would be useful to compare advertising levels across cities in which the advertised brand had comparable market share positions.**

2. **Use "before" as well as "after" measures. If sales as a result of the experiment can be compared with "last year's sales" or "last month's sales," the results will be much more sensitive. Sometimes it helps to compare sales after the experiment with the level of sales that would have been forecasted to occur if the experiment had not been run, using sophisticated forecasting methods that adjust for random and seasonal influences on sales, and so on.**

3. **Use substantial differences in advertising expenditures. Do not try to compare a 10 or 20 percent change in advertising; rather, look at 50 or 100 percent changes.**

4. **Test reduced advertising as well as increased advertising. The payoff at Budweiser was from the reduced advertising tests.**

5. **Control or at least monitor other variables that might affect the interpretation. For example, price or other marketing variables might be included in the experiment. Or the experiment might be repeated for large stores and small stores. Outside, uncontrollable factors—most notably, competitive behavior—should be monitored.**

6. Make sure that the test is run for an adequate time. A full year is often required when a mature brand is involved. Not only does this provide data on effects on repurchase (not just on initial trial), it also offers data on longer-term, delayed, carryover effects of advertising.

Figure 16–5 illustrates many of these points. This is the *detection table* used by Campbell Soup for its experiments described earlier in this chapter, and addresses the question: what are the chances (probabilities) that experiments will yield a result that is statistically detectible (significant) if (a) the "true" increase in sales caused by the advertising change was either 6 percent or 3 percent (a function of how large the ad increase being tested really is), (b) if the test was conducted in two test and two control markets or four test and four control markets, and (c) if the test was run for three months or six months. As can be seen from the given probabilities, the likelihood of getting a statistically detectible result goes up if the "true" sales effect is larger (6 percent), which implies a larger increase in the ad budget change being tested; if the test is run in more markets (four test and four control); and if the test is run for a longer period of time (six months).

Split-Cable Testing

A relatively new and powerful technique for measuring advertising response is termed split-cable testing. Information Resources, Inc.'s (IRI) BehaviorScan is one of the several split-cable testing operations (Nielsen being another). BehaviorScan maintains a 3,000-member consumer panel (surveyed for demographic information) in each of ten cities (such as Pittsfield, Massachusetts, and Marion, Indiana). All panelists carry ID cards that they present to supermarkets and drugstores when buying. Their purchases are all monitored by IRI, as is in-store activity such as special prices, features, and displays. The panelists have a device connected to their TV sets that allows BehaviorScan to monitor what channel is tuned and also

	Expected Increment			
	6%		3%	
	Probability of reading		Probability of reading	
Number of Markets	In 3 months	In 6 months	In 3 months	In 6 months
2 test, 2 control	0.60	0.75	less than 0.50	less than 0.50
4 test, 4 control	0.87	0.96	less than 0.50	0.6

Figure 16–5.   The Campbell Soup experiment "Detection Table."

Reprinted with permission of Eastlack and Rao, "Advertising Experiments at the Campbell Soup Company," Marketing Science, *8 (Winter 1989). © 1989, the Operations Research Society of America and the Institute of Management Sciences, 290 Westminster Street, Providence, RI 02903.*

to substitute one advertisement for another in what is called a *cut-in*. Panelists are divided into groups of panelists who are indistinguishable except that they are exposed to different advertising. They live in the same neighborhoods and shop at the same stores. The advertising budget test simply involves setting the advertising expenditure (or weight) levels, assigning each to a group of panelists, and monitoring the results.

The ability to control exposure levels and to monitor purchase activity provides the potential to conduct experiments that, unlike field experiments, are tightly controlled. Since the same data source provides information on both advertising exposure and on actual brand purchases, such data are often called *single-source* data, and this is a strong advantage. Further, access to shelf space is guaranteed, so there is little concern about distribution problems. In-store activities that can confound results are at least monitored. The tests are hidden from competitors, which reduces the chance of disruption. The exact number of advertising exposures is known. In a field test, even if the expenditure level were known, the number of exposures could vary enormously. Purchases can be monitored accurately on a daily basis. First (trial) purchases, repeat purchases, coupon redemptions, and the time between purchases are all known.

Split-cable testing is certainly the state of the art and is undoubtedly the most effective way to measure the response function. However, it is not without limitations. First, it is relatively expensive. The test itself will cost at least $100,000 and probably many times more in addition to the in-house cost of the advertiser and the agency.

Second, it is often necessary to run a test for at least six months and perhaps several years. The carryover impact can easily involve six or more purchase cycles, which can extend the test for a year. Further, the need to measure the impact on brand goodwill and loyalty may take longer to determine. In one test of a health care brand with a national budget of $15 million, it took two years before the sales of the low-advertising group, receiving the equivalent of a $10 million budget, declined.[29] After one year it was actually above the other group. With a lengthy test, there is always the danger that conditions may change making the results obsolete and outmoded.

Third, the experiments can actually be overcontrolled.[30] Since distribution is controlled, there is no measure of the ability of the advertising to influence distribution. Thus, effective advertising could easily affect the retailer's initial opinion and decision to stock the brand and the enthusiasm with which it is pushed. The retailers could be exposed to the advertising themselves, or they could be influenced by consumer reaction to it. Yet the split-cable tests really provide little information about such an impact.

Fourth, there is still doubt about the overall representativeness of the markets in which test market scanner data are available. While each service selects its test markets with care, and while tests are done on randomly selected consumers from within each test market panel, the fact remains that extrapolating to the entire United States from results based on a few test markets can be a hazardous undertaking.[31]

Finally, the tools are only now being developed to cope with, and analyze, the huge masses of data that single-source scanner data provide. Remember that every household is monitored for ad exposure every few seconds: a computer tape of data from these panels often contains literally millions of data records. Working with these data requires judgments on how to aggregate the information, across time periods, households, stores, brand varieties and pack sizes, and so on—and the results of the analysis often depend on the often arbitrary decisions on such aggregation. (Many analyses focus on effects on weekly sales at the store level). We are only now learning how to work with such data, and they promise much potential.[32]

Despite these caveats, it is instructive to learn from the database built up from Information Resources, Inc.'s BehaviorScan tests that about half (49 percent) of the 400 tests of increased advertising weight conducted by them between 1979 and 1989 showed a resulting increase in sales—more for new brands (59 percent of tests) than for old brands (46 percent of tests). (See Figure 16–6.) The difference between new and old brands is even more striking when profit impact, rather than sales impact, is considered: 45 percent of the new brand tests "paid out" within a year, while only 20 percent of the established brand tests did so. However, when the cumulative profit effects into the second and third years after the test were also taken into account, the total profit impact almost doubles, and almost all the advertising tests that showed a significant sales effect also showed a significant profit effect.[33]

REGRESSION ANALYSIS FOR BUDGETING . . . . . .

Another approach to estimating the relationship between advertising and sales—the advertising-response curve—is to look at the historical patterns of sales and advertising. When advertising changed in the past, what happened to sales? Or if

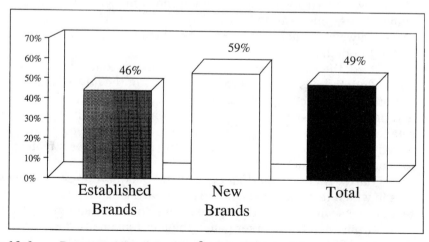

Figure 16–6.   **Percent of BehaviorScan® advertising weight tests showing a significant increase in sales.**

From Information Resources, Inc.

the advertising level differed in different sales areas or by different advertising media, how did sales differ? Such an approach is relatively inexpensive, as it uses data in hand.

A systematic way to analyze such patterns is through the use of a statistical technique called *multiple regression analysis*. A typical regression model could attempt to predict sales in one time period with the following types of explanatory (or independent) variables:

- **Sales in the preceding period.**
- **Advertising in the current period.**
- **Advertising in the previous period.**
- **Advertising two periods back.**
- **Other marketing variables, such as distribution or price, for this brand, as well as for competitive brands.**
- **Some measure of the "quality" of the creative message (e.g., a copy-testing score).**
- **Measures of competitor advertising.**

Sales in the preceding period provide a measure of the existing market position that has probably been caused by the marketing program over a long period. Advertising nearly always has an impact in future periods, representing future purchase cycles. The inclusion of previous advertising expenditures thus provides an attempt to measure this carryover effect of advertising. The advertising response would be the sum of the current impact and the carryover effect. There are many statistical methods that attempt to capture this carryover effect, notably the use of the *Koyck model* (descriptions of which can be found in textbooks of econometric methods). Other methods make current sales depend on current advertising plus some declining percentage of previous spending levels, called a brand's *adstock*.[34] There is considerable controversy, however, on what the carryover or adstock really means: to what extent is it the delayed effect of advertising itself, instead of simply a current purchase reinforcement effect from a satisfactory trial purchase effected by earlier advertising?[35]

To isolate the impact of advertising spending it is necessary to include other marketing variables. First, it is useful (when possible) to try to separate the effect of advertising spending from the effect of copy quality. Second, it is important to include other marketing variables in the predictive model. Suppose, for example, that expenditures for sales promotion and advertising were potential causes of sales change. Unless such promotion was included in the model, the apparent advertising effect might really represent a promotion effect. Third, unless some measure of competitor advertising is also used, the apparent advertising impact may be distorted. Research has clearly shown that competitor advertising reduces the effectiveness of a brand's own advertising.[36] An increase in advertising may have no impact on sales because competitor advertising increased dramatically. Without knowledge of competitor advertising, the advertising response might erroneously be thought to be low. One way of including competitive effects is obtain the actual figure for competitive advertising and include it as another independent (predictive) variable in the regression model. Another is to model this brand's market share as being dependent on its share of total category advertising (called share of voice, as discussed earlier).

One of the key problems facing the regression modeler is how best to model the shape of the relationship between advertising and sales—while typical regression computer programs assume a straight-line relationship between advertising and sales, this relationship is most often a curved, or curvilinear, one. For instance, the responsiveness of sales to advertising may begin to decline after some level of advertising spending. This diminishing-returns phenomenon is then better represented by a downward-sloping curve, in a graph in which advertising levels are related to sales results. Alternatively, some modelers prefer to assume that the relationship is actually S-shaped: in the beginning, when advertising budgets are low, sales do not respond at all to advertising. It supposedly takes time (because it needs several exposures) for advertising to "wear-in." Then we see a point of increasing returns, as sales really begin to respond to increased advertising, as the ad budget exceeds some minimum critical-level threshold. Finally, the curve begins to slope downward again, as once again the diminishing-returns phase appears. Figure 16–7 depicts these three kinds of relationships. Statistical analysts attempt to capture these *nonlinear* (curved) possibilities in their regression models by predicting the log (or some other transformation) of the sales figures by the log (or some other transformation) of the advertising spending figure. Most studies of the shape of the actual advertising-sales relationship conclude that it is one of diminishing returns, although a few claim to find evidence of S-shaped relationships.[37]

Problems with Regression Analysis

Regression analysis is sometimes useful, but on the whole it has been disappointing. There are many problems associated with its use, so that this technique can either not be used at all, or requires the assistance of statistically skilled analysts. Perhaps the most difficult problem is to measure the carryover effect (which is also advertising's contribution to the brand's long-term equity or goodwill). The

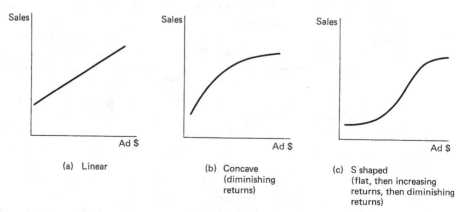

Figure 16–7.   Three views about the advertising-sales relationship.

impact over one, two, or more periods simply gets swamped by all the other sources of sales variation.

There are several other difficulties associated with regression analysis modeling in general and with the problem of measuring the carryover effect in particular. Among them are the following:

1.   There is often little variation in advertising except that due to seasonable factors. Without variation in advertising it is not possible to detect the impact of changes in advertising on sales. This problem is severe when a brand is overadvertising and it is so far out on the advertising response curve that there is no response to any change in advertising. In that case an extreme drop in advertising would be needed to detect any response, and such a variation is simply not in the data.

2.   The data may be faulty. For example, accounting sales data will represent shipments to retailers and not consumer purchases in response to advertising. Syndicated store movement data overcome this problem but are expensive and available only to consumer products firms. Accounting advertising data similarly represent billings by an agency and not exposures to ads. In fact, it is difficult to get any accurate measure of advertising exposures. Note further that any analysis of sales and advertising data covering a time period spanning several years needs somehow to adjust for inflation in media costs over time, as well as the changing population sizes that led to the sales figures. This sometimes leads to regressions in which per capita sales figures are predicted by inflation-adjusted media dollars.

3.   Data describing other marketing variables are often not available or are expensive to obtain. Data describing competitor activities are rarely available.

4.   Annual data really are inadequate since the immediate and carryover effect of advertising usually occurs in months, not years. In fact, statisticians have found that if the product is one that is bought frequently, say, every few weeks, then regressions using annual sales and advertising data can yield very misleading results. It is usually better to perform the analyses on "disaggregated" data, covering small units of time (such as months or quarters) and to do them separately for geographical markets that might show different relationships between advertising and sales.[38] Indeed, if separate response functions can be estimated for separate geographical areas, then this can be very useful in allocating the national ad budget for a brand across those geographical areas.[39]

5.   If a business uses the percentage-of-sales method of establishing a budget, a sales change could cause a change in advertising expenditures instead of the reverse (at least at the annual level). The nature of the causal relationship—advertising causing sales, or anticipated sales causing ad budgets—simply cannot be adequately disentangled by most regression analyses. This suggests that field or split-cable "weight test" experiments may be a better way of understanding how advertising affects sales, since a properly conducted experiment (one with a control group and with random assignment of test and control cells) permits causal conclusions.

Despite these many limitations, such regression analyses have frequently been performed and often found to be quite insightful. As mentioned near the beginning of this chapter, the "average" elasticity of short-term sales response to advertising (the percentage change in sales caused by a one percent change in ad spending) has been found to be low (about 0.1 to 0.3).[40] (See Table 16–2.) The elasticity is higher for consumable food products and in European countries (where overadvertising is presumable less of a problem) than in the United States. Another study found that 90 percent of the effect of advertising for frequently pur-

Table 16–2.   **Results of Meta-Analysis of Regression Studies.**

	Mean[a]	Standard deviation	Available sample Size
Short-term elasticity	.221	.264	128
Carryover	.468	.306	114
R	.783	.214	109

From Gert Assmus, John U. Farley, and Donald R. Lehmann, "How Advertising Affects Sales: Meta-Analysis of Econometric Results," Journal of Marketing Research, 21, no.1 (1984), 66. Published by the American Marketing Association.

[a]*All significantly greater than zero at $p < 0.1$.*

chased branded products could be seen to dissipate somewhere between three and nine months after the advertising.[41]

STUDIES OF OPTIMAL REPETITION FREQUENCY .

Yet another way to arriving at an advertising budget is to figure how many advertising exposures might be required per consumer to achieve the communications or advertising objective (the *frequency* needed per planning period—such as five exposures per four-week cycle). This can then be multiplied by the total number of consumers on whom that objective is sought to be achieved (the *reach* necessary—e.g., 10 million women age twenty-five to fifty-four). The product of these two numbers yields the total number of exposures necessary (in this case, five times 10 million, or 50 million exposures, per four-week cycle). This desired number of exposures can then be "costed out," given a tentative media mix. For example, if it costs $25 to reach 1,000 target women aged twenty-five to fifty-four on prime time network TV (or about 2.5 cents per exposure), and $6 to reach them using daytime television (thus at about 0.6 cents per exposure), then a campaign split evenly between daytime and prime time TV would cost 1.55 cents per target exposure. (The data sources for such costs-per-thousand figures are described in the next chapter). For 50 million exposures every four weeks, this would translate into $775,000 (50 million times 1.55 cents) every four weeks, or a little over $10 million in media costs for a year of thirteen such four-week cycles.

   It should be immediately apparent that this is an extension of the "objectives and task" method of setting advertising budgets outlined earlier in this chapter. In the paragraphs that follow, we will describe further some research that is useful in answering the question of "What should be the appropriate frequency level?" As far as the target reach figures are concerned, these should be derived by working backward from marketing objectives involving incremental sales. For instance, if a packaged-goods company wished to sell another 10 million units of shampoo in the coming year, it might use previous research (or simply management's own judgment) to make the following series of calculations:

Need to sell an additional 10 million units of shampoo.

Every regular customer buys, on average, 10 units a year.

Therefore need to gain 1 million new regular customers.

For every person who becomes a new regular customer, need to get two to try our shampoo (i.e., we have a 50 percent regular repurchase rate among triers).

Therefore need to get 2 million new triers.

For every person who tries our brand, need to get five people to rate it as the brand of shampoo that come first to mind (i.e., we have 20 percent trial among people for whom we are the shampoo brand that comes to mind first).

Therefore, need to make 10 million target consumers have top-of-mind awareness of our shampoo.

The question that we are then faced, of course, is: How many exposures do we need to create (and maintain) such top-of-mind awareness, per four-week cycle or some other time frame, such as the purchasing cycle for that product? (In some other situation, we might be dealing with creating favorable attitudes rather than top-of-mind awareness, but the principle is the same.) We thus need to know something about how many exposures are necessary to lead to creating or maintaining awareness or favorable attitudes.

How Many Exposures?

Michael J. Naples, now president of the Advertising Research Foundation, conducted an extensive review of industry studies of repetition and concluded that, in general, around three exposures within a purchase cycle are about adequate to lead to or maintain the desired level of brand awareness or brand attitudes. Naples found that simply delivering one exposure to a target consumer within a purchase cycle usually was not enough; more than three exposures, on the other hand, usually led to diminishing returns, at least as far as recall was concerned. While this was an average tendency, smaller brands appeared to require (and benefit from) higher frequency more than larger brands did.[42]

Herbert Krugman, a General Electric manager and prominent advertising theorist, also suggests that a level of about three exposures is needed. He suggests that insights into the needed levels of repetition can be gained by considering the difference between the first, second, and third exposures.[43] In his conceptualization, there is no such thing as a fourth exposure.

The first exposure elicits a "What is it?" type of response. The audience member tries to understand the nature of the communication and, if possible, categorizes it as being of no further interest.

The second exposure, if not blocked out, produces several effects. One, particularly in television or radio advertising, is a continuation of the "What is it?" response. The first exposure may not have been adequate to gain an understanding of what it was. (In fact, some television copy-testing systems require at least two exposures for this very reason.) Another response is an evaluative "What of it?" response. The audience member will attempt to determine if it is relevant and convincing. The message will be evaluated. Associated with both responses could be an "Aha, I've seen this before" reaction.

The third exposure is basically a reminder in case the audience member has not yet acted on the message. Any additional exposure is just another third exposure, replicating the third-exposure experience. Thus, Krugman implies that only three exposures are required. However, it is not quite that simple, because some audience segments may, after the first exposure, screen the advertisement out until they are ready to process another exposure. This phenomenon is particularly prevalent in television advertising, where there is low involvement. A potential purchase or a use experience may stimulate an audience member to be receptive to a second-exposure experience. As a result, several actual exposures might be needed before a "second-exposure" experience occurs. The effect of multiple exposures is not to generate a cumulative impact on an individual audience member, but to capture more second- and third-exposure experiences.

As a practical suggestion to General Electric managers, Krugman advised that they start with an objective of exposing two-thirds of their target audience at least twice and not more than four times per month. This advice is compatible with the concept that at least two exposures are needed and that any exposure over four is wasted since the second-exposure experience will have occurred for most of the audience.

A third source for a recommendation of using three or four exposures per planning cycle is the fact that this is the most frequently used level of *effective frequency* used by advertising agencies.[44] The concept of *effective exposure* was put forth in 1977 by advertising researcher Alvin Achenbaum.[45] In essence, the idea is that there is a minimum threshold of necessary exposures, below which the connection between the message and the consumer is simply not established strongly enough. Below this effective-frequency level, therefore, exposures are wasted; people reached with less than this number of exposures—typically, but not always, three or four exposures per purchase cycle—have not been *effectively reached*. Advertising agencies make widespread use of the effective frequency concept.[46]

Wear-Out

While the concept of effective frequency is concerned most about the *minimum* level of exposures necessary, the concept of *wear-out* is concerned with the *maximum* number of exposures that should be used for any particular ad execution in a certain period of time. (*Wear-in,* in contrast, is concerned with how soon a message makes its initial impact.) Wear-out occurs when successive exposures no longer have a positive impact on the audience. Indeed, the marginal impact can turn negative. The determination of the optimal frequency thus involves an understanding and an ability to predict when wear-in and wear-out will occur.

One of the first psychologists to study wear-out empirically was Hermann Ebbinghaus.[47] In a series of experiments reported in 1902, he related retention to repetition. He had a single subject (himself) learn a series of nonsense syllables by oral repetition. He found that diminishing returns set in as the number of repetitions increased. Since that time, wear-out has been documented in a variety of field and laboratory studies by psychologists and advertising researchers. As repetitions build, advertising researchers have found that attention to the commercial, recall of the copy points, awareness of the advertised brand, brand attitude, and purchase intention will build, then level off, and ultimately decline.

One explanation for the wear-out phenomenon is that the audience stops attending to the advertising.[48] They may feel that they have already absorbed the information, or they may become bored. One study found that exposure repetition ultimately generated a significant decline in brand-name recall, but that this decline could be reversed when attention to the advertisement was experimentally induced.[49]

Another explanation of wear-out is that excessive exposure generates irritation. The audience, which accepts advertisements as a necessary part of print or broadcast media, may resent being exposed to the same advertisement many times. Psychologists John Cacioppo and Richard Petty monitored people's verbalized response to a persuasive written communication.[50] They found that the production of support arguments increased and then decreased with exposure. The number of negative thoughts, however, declined after the first few exposures but then increased as repetitions mounted. To combat wear-out, then, it is necessary to attempt to reduce inattention, boredom, and irritation and/or to maximize the degree of "learning" from the ad that continues to occur despite repeated exposure.

One approach to fighting wear-out is to provide advertisements that reward the audience in some way. Information that is valued (features of a personal computer) could be provided. Humor can stimulate attention and liking (but it should be noted that humorous ads can wear-out even faster than straight ads, if consumers get tired of the jokes). Entertainment value can also come from creative approaches using music, dancing, action, or drama, and any of these can forestall wear-out. In fact, there is research to suggest that "emotional" ads wear-out less quickly than more "rational" ads, and that more "complex" ads wear-out more slowly than simpler ads that are "learned" very quickly. If the ad is difficult to process, it can be run for more exposures without wear-out than an easy-to-process ad (which the audience "learns" faster and thus gets bored with faster). An implication of this last statement is that an ad being run frequently ought to be created to be relatively difficult to learn and process (more complex).[51] The exact pattern of wear-out is complex, depending on the measure being tracked (recall? attitudes?), the type of the ad, the spacing (timing and distribution) of the exposures, and so on.[52]

Wear-out can also be combated by spacing commercial exposures over time and by running multiple executions of the same campaign theme. This idea is discussed in more detail in the Chapter on Attention (Chapter 7). Another one of the findings of Ebbinghaus was that spaced repetitions were more effective than the same number massed together.[53] Bobby Calder and Brian Sternthal conducted an experiment involving three commercial exposures embedded in a one-hour adventure show in up to six sessions.[54] The pronounced wear-out found was substantially reduced when the advertising consisted of three commercials rather than a single one. When multiple media are used, variety is naturally introduced, which again will allow a higher level of repetition.

When Is More Frequency Needed?

Clearly, the research-based recommendation just made—that three or four exposures per four-week cycle is often appropriate—is an average; some situations call for more, others for less. The research on wear-in and wear-out provides some insights into the nature of the situations when higher levels of frequency may be justified. Higher levels of frequency may be warranted when the message is more interesting, such as with new brand launches, new messages, new ads; when the message is more complex; and when the message is more reliant on moods or imagery for its effectiveness. The level of frequency should be less when nothing new was being said, when a simple message was being put across, and so on. In particular, advertising that aims to develop associations between the brand and feelings, activities, or people will require more repetition than advertising that is designed to communicate information. Transformational advertising (advertising to transform the use experience, discussed in Chapter 9), for example, can require heavy repetition that continues over years or even decades. Such advertising fortunately is often entertaining and/or well liked, and thus heavy repetition involving multiple campaign executions and variations can be tolerated. Research also shows that messages that are better at generating recall, or more persuasive, are "received" by consumers faster, thus necessitating lower advertising spending.[55]

Batra and Ray, in a laboratory experiment, argued and showed that both wear-in and wear-out occur faster when the consumer has a higher level of involvement in the product category and/or knows more about it. In such situations, the consumer extracts information from the ad in earlier exposures, so that later exposures are essentially waste as far as the advertiser is concerned. More exposure does not lead to more favorable attitudes—in fact, it may even lead to a downturn in such attitudes, since the highly involved consumers, having already learned what the ad has to say, may now find it irritating and tiresome. When the consumer is less involved or less knowledgeable, however, higher levels of repetition are warranted, since they do lead to increasing attitudes and purchase intentions.[56] A graph from their study is presented in Figure 16–8.

The complexity and size of the communication and persuasion task will also affect the repetitions needed. For example, a task that involves establishing a new brand name and communicating a complex new service will undoubtedly require heavy repetition as well as multiple executions. Another of the classic Ebbinghaus findings was that as the number of items to be communicated increased, the number of repetitions necessary to attain a certain level of learning also increased.[57]

Joseph Ostrow, then a senior advertising executive with Young & Rubicam, suggested that heavier repetition would be required when[58]

- **A new brand is involved.**
- **A smaller, less well-known brand is involved. A dominant brand will need less frequency because it will already have a high level of recognition and acceptance.**

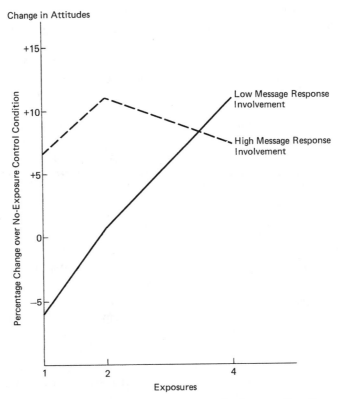

Figure 16–8.   Effect of repetition frequency on attitudes as a function of involvement level.

Source: Batra and Ray, Identifying Opportunities for Repetition Minimization, *Marketing Science Institute, Cambridge, MA, Report No. 84–108, 1984.*

- A low level of brand loyalty has been achieved. A brand with a high level of purchase loyalty and attitude commitment will require less repetition.
- The purchase and use cycle is relatively long. Products with short purchase and use cycles generally need more repetition.
- When the target audience is less involved and less motivated to process the information or when it has less ability to process it (because a lack of background information or because of a lack of mental skills).
- When there exists a great deal of clutter to break through. Of particular importance is the level of competitive advertising. It may be necessary to increase repetition to break through the presence of competitor advertising.

In defining what the optimal frequency level should be for a particular brand, it makes most sense to perform analysis on the sales history for that brand, perhaps using single-source scanner data. One such recent analysis in Britain found, across fifteen frequently purchased packaged goods (such as coffee, tea, detergents, margarine, and cereals) that a frequency of four or more exposures per four weeks seemed to make sense.[59] It should always be remembered in such analyses that if diminishing returns set in after the consumer has *viewed* four exposures, the advertiser may need to actually schedule and run two times that many—many studies have found a 50 percent fall-off between *opportunities-to-see* (what advertisers actually pay for) and *actual viewing* (what the research talks about). Using these guidelines, then, an advertiser can determine what an appropriate level of frequency is, for the brand being considered. When combined with a level of target reach that makes sense from a marketing point of view, this can lead to a "bottom-up" estimate of the advertising budget required. Either this method, or the use of split-cable or field experiments, or of regression, should yield an estimate of an ad budget that makes more logical sense than the other decision rules discussed earlier in the chapter—although the latter are clearly easier to use, and thus are used more frequently.

SUMMARY. . . . .

The theoretical underpinning of the advertising budget is based on economic marginal analysis and is easily expressed. A firm should continue to add to its advertising budget as long as the incremental expenditures are exceeded by the marginal revenue they generate. The determination of the functional relationship between advertising expenditures and sales, which is at the heart of marginal analysis, is most difficult for several reasons. First, the assumption that advertising expenditures affect immediate sales is often faulty. Second, the determination of the shape and parameters of the relationship is no easy task. Finally, the relationship changes through time.

Practical decision makers, in response to the problems of marginal analysis, have used several decision rules. The most widely used approach, which bases the advertising budget on some percentage of sales, can lead to excessive expenditures for well-established brands and inadequate expenditures for new and promising brands.

Setting ad budgets requires determination of the sales response to advertising. One approach is to conduct field experiments by varying advertising levels in different test stores, cities, or areas. Field experiments encouraged Budweiser to reduce advertising in the 1960s. They tend to be costly both in money and time. Further, many factors can confound or mask the results, such as actions of retailers and competitors, the inability to deliver precise levels of advertising to test cities, and the impact of other marketing variables.

Another approach is split-cable testing, wherein advertising seen by matched panels of consumers is controlled and their purchases are monitored via store scanner systems. Split-cable testing scores high on validity and control but is fairly expensive, provides little information of the impact of the advertising on retailers, and can take from six months to two years, depending on the difficulty of measuring long-term effects.

A third approach, regression analysis, works with existing data and is thus inexpensive. However, it, too, has its problems, because of the lack of variability of the advertising data, the lack of data on confounding factors such as competitor actions and other marketing variables, the arbitrariness of the aggregation decisions necessary, the difficulty of measuring the long-term impact of advertising, and others.

Advertising budgets can also be based upon an analysis of how many advertising exposures might be required per consumer to achieve the communications objective—a modified objective-and-task approach to budget setting. The key is to determine how many exposures are needed. A frequent rule of thumb is that three or four exposures per purchase cycle are needed in most contexts. However, this is only an average. In specific situations the maturity of the brand, the involvement level of consumers, the need to avoid wear-out, the complexity of the communication task, and the nature of associations being created, and other factors are needed to decide the optimal frequency. This can then be used, along with a reach target, to determine total budget needs.

DISCUSSION QUESTIONS . . . .

1. At the chapter outset, some large advertising expenditure differences were observed between firms in the same industry. Why?
2. In Figure 16–1, why is the sales curve S-shaped? Explain the gradually accelerating section on the lower half of the curve and the flattening out section on the upper half. Discuss the significance of this shape from the viewpoint of (a) a company, (b) an industry, and (c) the economy as a whole.
3. What is the *percentage-of-sales budgeting approach*? Why is it so widely used? Under what circumstances might it be inappropriate? Why?
4. What assumptions underlie the "all-you-can-afford" and "competitive-parity" approaches to setting advertising budgets?
5. Contact someone in a firm that does a significant amount of advertising. What advertising budget-setting decision rule do they use? To what extent is the budget decision arrived at by a bargaining process?
6. Design a field experiment that would provide input data for the sales response to advertising function for a company selling men's razor blades. How much would the experiment likely cost? Identify other variables that might affect sales in your chosen test markets. What is the role, if any, of *laboratory experimentation* in this context?
7. Repeat question 6 for a company selling technical instruments used in scientific laboratories and hospitals. How would the design differ? Should industrial marketing companies attempt to identify sales-response functions in connection with their advertising activities?
8. Which kinds of firms are likely to invest in advertising and sales experiments? Why are experiments used infrequently? What are the problems and limitations of experiments? Why are experiments involving tests of reduced advertising expenditures so rare?
9. Suppose that you were a brand manager and had developed an experiment involving four Midwest test cities in which four levels of advertising expenditure were used over a six-month period. The resulting sales were compared with the sales during the same six months of the previous year. During your presentation to top management, you run into two challenges. First, the executive

vice president claims that the budget levels suggested by the model will not apply to your campaign in the East because response to advertising is different in that part of the country. Second, the advertising manager claims that the new campaign will have a much higher response than previous advertising and consequently the model output is of no relevance. How would you respond to these questions?

10. What are the two most important attributes of a split-cable test? In what sense might a split-cable test be overcontrolling? Under what circumstances would you worry about such a problem? What are the other disadvantages of split-cable testing?

11. What is the difference between a marginal analysis and a regression analysis?

12. Why might a regression model fit the data better if the log of advertising expenditures is used as the independent variable instead of the advertising expenditures?

13. Why would a regression analysis of a three-year sequence of monthly advertising expenditures and market share of a detergent be a less sensitive and valid way to determine advertising response than an experiment?

14. Suppose that you are attempting to get housewives to try your new gourmet vegetable dish and have divided housewives into two groups—those interested in kitchens and those not so interested. Using your own subjective reasoning, estimate the probability of each group's trying the product after zero, one, three, five, and ten advertising exposures during a three-month period.

15. How might that repetition function in question 14 be affected by whether the ad was in color, whether it used short or long copy, and the vehicle in which the ad appeared?

16. What are the factors that should contribute to wear-out? Illustrate your answer with specific examples of commercials that you can recall. What are some ads that you have not tired of even though might have seen them fifty times? And, which ones have you come to hate when repeated? Why?

NOTES. . . . .

1. *Advertising Age*, September 26, 1990, and later years.
2. See David A. Aaker and James M. Carman, "Are You Overadvertising?" *Journal of Advertising Research*, 22 (August/September 1982), 57–70, and Gert Assmus, John U. Farley, and Donald R. Lehmann, "How Advertising Affects Sales: Meta-analysis of Econometric Results," *Journal of Marketing Research*, 21, no. 1 (1984), 65–74. The 0.22 figure comes from Assmus et al.
3. For a debate on the value of looking at such elasticities, see Simon Broadbent, "What Is a 'Small Advertising Elasticity?'" *Journal of Advertising Research* (August/September 1989), 37–39, and accompanying articles.
4. Srinath Gopalakrishna and Rabikar Chatterjee, "A Communications Response Model for a Mature Industrial Product: Application and Implications," *Journal of Marketing Research*, 29 (May 1992), 189–200.
5. Raj Sethuraman and Gerard J. Tellis, "An Analysis of the Tradeoff between Advertising and Price Discounting," *Journal of Marketing Research*, 28 (May 1991), 160–174.
6. Gopalakrishna and Chatterjee, cited earlier.
7. For a study measuring cross-effects in making allocations across brands, see Peter

Doyle and John Saunders, "Multiproduct Advertising Budgeting," *Marketing Science*, 9, no. 2 (Spring 1990), 97–113. This article also provides other references to the literature on allocating ad budgets across products. See also Amiya Basu and Rajeev Batra, "ADSPLIT: A Multi-Brand Advertising Budget Allocation Model," *Journal of Advertising*, 17, no. 1 (1988), 44–51.

8. J. O. Eastlack, Jr., and Ambar G. Rao, "Advertising Experiments in the Campbell Soup Company," *Marketing Science,* 8, no. 1 (Winter 1989), 57–71; Leonard M. Lodish and Beth Lubetkin, "Key Findings from the 'How Advertising Works' Study." Papers presented at the Marketplace Advertising Research Workshop, New York, November 1991.

9. For descriptions and applications of decision calculus advertising budgeting models, see John D. C. Little, "Models and Managers: The Concept of a Decision Calculus," *Management Science*, 16 (1970), B466–465; John D. C. Little, "BRANDAID: A Marketing Mix Model, Part I: Structure," *Operations Research*, 23 (1975), 628–655; and Amiya Basu and Rajeev Batra, "ADSPLIT: A Multi-Brand Advertising Budget Allocation Model," *Journal of Advertising*, 17, no. 1 (1988), 44–51.

10. For some recent studies of how various advertisers set advertising budgets, see Colin Gilligan, "How British Advertisers Set Budgets," *Journal of Advertising Research*, 17 (February 1977), 47–49; Charles H. Patti and Vincent Blasko, "Budgeting Practices of Big Advertisers," *Journal of Advertising Research*, 21 (December 1981), 23–29; K. M. Lancaster and J. A. Stern, "Computer-Based Advertising Budgeting Practices of Leading U.S. Consumer Advertisers," *Journal of Advertising*, 12, no. 4 (1983), 4–9; and Nigel Peircy, "Advertising Budgeting: Process and Structure as Explanatory Variables," *Journal of Advertising*, 16, no. 2 (1987), 34–40.

11. Patti and Blasko, "Budgeting Practices of Big Advertisers."

12. Gilligan, "How British Advertisers Set Budgets."

13. Barbara Brady, June Connolly, Les Quok, Karen Wachtel, and Peter Weiss, "Bright 'N Soft." Unpublished paper, 1979.

14. See, for example, Pradeep K. Chintagunta and Naufel J. Vilcassim, "An Empirical Investigation of Advertising Strategies in a Dynamic Duopoly," *Management Science*, 38, no. 9 (September 1992), 1230–1244.

15. See John Philip Jones, "Ad Spending: Maintaining Market Share," *Harvard Business Review* (January–February 1990), 38–42, and James C. Schroer, "Ad Spending: Growing Market Share," *Harvard Business Review* (January–February 1990), 44–48, for related analyses.

16. Patti and Blasko, "Budgeting Practices."

17. Joseph Willke, "What New Product Marketers Should Know About Related Recall," *Journal of Advertising Research*, 33, no. 2 (Mar-April 1993), RC-7–RC-12.

18. Frank J. Gromer, "How Much Advertising is Enough?" ANA Media Workshop, New York, February 27, 1985.

19. Russell L. Ackoff and James R. Emshoff, "Advertising Research at Anheuser-Busch, Inc. (1963-68)," *Sloan Management Review* (Winter 1975), 1–15.

20. Minhi Hahn, C. Whan Park, and Deborah J. MacInnis, "The Adaptive Information Processing Hypothesis Accounting for the V-Shaped Advertising Response Function," *Journal of Advertising*, 21, no. 2 (June 1992), 32–46.

21. Joseph O. Eastlack, Jr., and Ambar G. Rao, "Modeling Response to Advertising and Pricing Changes for V-8 Cocktail Vegetable Juice," *Marketing Science*, 5, no. 3 (Summer 1986), 245–259.

22. J. O. Eastlack, Jr., and Ambar G. Rao, "Advertising Experiments in the Campbell Soup Company," *Marketing Science,* 8, no. 1 (Winter 1989), 57–71.

23. Ibid.

24. V. P. Carroll, A. G. Rao, H. L. Lee, A. Shapiro, and B. L. Bayus, "The Navy Enlistment Marketing Experiment," *Marketing Science*, 4, no. 4 (Fall 1985), 352–374.

25. "A Study of the Effectiveness of Advertising Frequency in Magazines," conducted by Time, Inc., in conjunction with Joseph E. Seagram and Sons, Inc., 1982.

26. Leonard M. Lodish and Beth Lubetkin, "Key Findings from the 'How Advertising Works'

Study." Papers presented at the Marketplace Advertising Research Workshop, New York, November 1991.

27. Michael J. Naples and Rolf M. Wulfsberg, "The Bottom Line: Does Industrial Advertising Sell?" *Journal of Advertising Research* (Aug./Sep. 1987), RC4–RC16.

28. Gerald J. Eskin, "A Case for Test Market Experiments," *Journal of Advertising Research*, 15 (April 1975), 27–33.

29. Reg Rhodes, "What AdTel Has Learned." Paper presented to the American Marketing Association's New York Chapter, March 22, 1977.

30. Paul W. Farris and David J. Reibstein, "Overcontrol in Advertising Experiments," *Journal of Advertising Research*, 24 (June/July 1984), 37–44.

31. *Adweek's Marketing Week*, January 23, 1989, p. 24.

32. *Adweek's Marketing Week*, January 23, 1989, p. 24.

33. George Garrick, "Properly Evaluating the Role of TV Advertising." Paper presented at the Advertising Research Foundation 35th Annual Conference, New York, April 1989.

34. Simon Broadbent, "Modeling with Adstock," *Journal of the Market Research Society*, 26, no. 4 (1986), 295–312.

35. Moshe Givon, "Partial Carryover of Advertising," *Marketing Letters*, 4, no. 2 (1993), 165–173.

36. Kevin Lane Keller, "Memory and Evaluation Effects in Competitive Advertising Environments," *Journal of Consumer Research*, 17 (March 1991), 463–476.

37. Julian A. Simon and Johan Arndt, "The Shape of the Advertising Response Function," *Journal of Advertising Research*, 20, no. 4 (1980), 11–28; Robert L. Steiner, "The Paradox of Increasing Returns to Advertising," *Journal of Advertising Research* (February/March 1987), 45–53; and John D. C. Little, "Aggregate Advertising Models: The State of the Art," *Operations Research*, 27 (1979), 629–667.

38. A. G. Rao and P. B. Miller, "Advertising/Sales Response Functions," *Journal of Advertising Research*, 15 (1975), 82–92. For references to the extensive literature on aggregation issues, see Wilfried R. Vanhonacker, "Estimating Dynamic Response Models when the Data are Subject to Different Temporal Aggregation," *Marketing Letters*, 1, no. 2 (1989), 125–137.

39. Laurence N. Gold, "Let's Heavy Up in St. Louis and See What Happens," *Journal of Advertising Research*, 32, no. 6 (Nov./Dec. 1992), 31–38.

40. Gert Assmus, John U. Farley, and Donald R. Lehmann, "How Advertising Affects Sales: Meta-analysis of Econometric Results," *Journal of Marketing Research*, 21, no. 1 (1984), 65–74.

41. Darral G. Clarke, "Econometric Measurement of the Duration of Advertising Effect on Sales," *Journal of Marketing Research*, 13 (November 1976), 345–357.

42. Michael J. Naples, *Effective Frequency: The Relationship Between Frequency and Advertising Effectiveness* (New York: Association of National Advertisers, 1979), p. 79.

43. Herbert E. Krugman, "What Makes Advertising Effective?" *Harvard Business Review* (March/April 1975), 96–103.

44. Kent M. Lancaster, Peggy J. Kreshel, and Joya R. Harris, "Estimating the Impact of Advertising Media Plans: Media Executives Describe Weighting and Timing Factors," *Journal of Advertising*, 15 (September 1986), 21–29, 45; and Peggy J. Kreshel, Kent M. Lancaster, and Margaret A. Toomey, "How Leading Advertisers Perceive Effective Reach and Frequency," *Journal of Advertising*, 14, no. 3 (1985), 32–38, 51.

45. Alvin Achenbaum, "Effective Exposure: A New Way of Evaluating Media." Address before the Association of National Advertisers Media Workshop, New York, 1977.

46. For further references on the effective frequency concept, see Peter B. Turk, "Effective Frequency Report," *Journal of Advertising Research* (April/May 1988), 55–59.

47. Hermann Ebbinghaus, *Grundzuge der Psychologie* (Leipzig: Viet, 1902).

48. Bobby J. Calder and Brian Sternthal, "Television Commercial Wearout: An Information Processing View," *Journal of Marketing Research*, 13 (November 1976), 173–186.

49. Charles S. Craig, Brian Sternthal, and Clark Leavitt, "Advertising Wearout: An Experimental Analysis," *Journal of Marketing Research*, 13 (November 1976), 365–372.

50. John Cacioppo and Richard Petty, "Effects of Message Repetition and Position on Cognitive Response, Recall and Persuasion," *Journal of Personality and Social Psychology*, 37 (January 1979), 97–109.
51. Punam Anand and Brian Sternthal, "Ease of Message Processing as a Moderator of Repetition Effects in Advertising," *Journal of Marketing Research*, 27 (August 1990), 345–353.
52. For a review, see Cornelia Pechmann and David W. Stewart, "Advertising Repetition: A Critical Review of Wearin and Wearout," *Current Issues and Research in Advertising*, 11 (1978), 285–329.
53. Ebbinghaus, *Grundzuge der Psychologie*.
54. Calder and Sternthal, "Television Commercial Wearout."
55. Margaret Henderson Blair, "Situational Effects of Advertising Repetition," *Journal of Advertising Research* (December 1987/January 1988), 45–50.
56. Rajeev Batra and Michael L. Ray, "Situational Effects of Advertising Repetition," *Journal of Consumer Research*, 12 (March 1986), 432–445.
57. Ebbinghaus, *Grundzuge der Psychologie*.
58. Joseph W. Ostrow, "Setting Frequency Levels: An Art or a Science?" *Journal of Advertising Research*, 24 (August/September 1984), I9–I11.
59. Phil Gullen and Hugh Johnson, "Relating Product Purchasing and TV Viewing," *Journal of Advertising Research* (December 1986/January 1987), 9–19.

APPENDIX . . . .

A Model of Adaptive Control

A model that uses experimental data as an explicit input to the budget decision was developed by John D. C. Little, a professor at MIT.* It recognizes that the relationship between advertising and sales changes over time with changing market conditions. As a result, the advertising budget decision should be updated accordingly.

The adaptive-control model starts by assuming a response curve and finding an optimal level of advertising expenditure, as in Exhibit 1. If the decision maker were confident about an estimate of the response function and if he or she believes it would not change over time, the problem would be solved. However, under more realistic conditions, it becomes desirable to obtain more information about the response curve. In particular, it is worthwhile to experiment by advertising at nonoptimal levels in a few test markets to gain such information. The new information from the experiments is added to the existing information on the sales response function to determine the current optimal advertising expenditure rate.

Assume that the advertising sales response function can be described by a specific mathematical function such as the following quadratic function:

$$S(A) = \alpha + \beta A - \gamma A^2 \tag{1}$$

where $S(A)$ = sales

A = advertising expenditures

α, β, γ = parameters

* John D. C. Little, "A Model of Adaptive Control of Promotional Spending," *Operations Research*, 14, November–December 1966, pp. 175–97.

EXHIBIT 1   Sales experiment

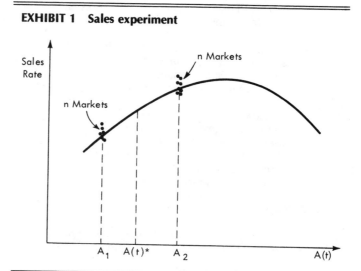

The first two terms in equation (1) represent the familiar straight-line, linear relationship. The third term adds a curvature. An example of equation (1) is the upside-down "U" shown in Exhibit 1.

If M is the gross margin of the product, then profit, P, will be

$$P = MS(A) - A \qquad (2)$$

The value of advertising expenditures, A^*, that will maximize equation (2) can be found graphically or algebraically.[1]

Little has argued that the optimal advertising rate is relatively insensitive to γ as long as the parameter is set within reasonable bounds. Thus, Little assumes that γ is known and constant. He argues, however, that β is not likely to stay constant through time. Changes in competitive activity, product changes, changes in the quality of advertising, or shifts in economic conditions can result in changes in response β.

Exhibit 1 shows the nature of a sales experiment to derive estimates of β. It

---

[1]Substituting equation (1) into equation (2) yields

$$P = M\alpha + M\beta A - M\gamma A^2 - A$$

Taking the derivative of P with respect to A and setting it equal to zero,

$$M\beta - 2M\gamma A - 1 = 0$$

Solving for A.

$$A^* = \frac{M\beta - 1}{2M\gamma}$$

assumes at a particular time, t, the advertising rate $A(t)^*$ is considered to be optimal. All markets with the exception of a set receiving a lower rate, A_1, and a set receiving a higher rate, A_2, are subjected to this level of advertising.[2] The sales rate in the groups of markets at A_1 and A_2 provides information from which a revised estimate of the parameter β can be derived.[3]

Little compared the results of a computer-simulation version of the adaptive-control model with four other modeling alternatives. The model compared particularly well when contrasted with the results of assuming a constant advertising rate. These comparisons can be made by calculating how much the loss in profits would be in each case relative to having perfect information on the respective functions. In one case of assuming a constant rate, for example, losses amounted to 28.7 percent compared with only 1.5 percent for the adaptive-model formulation.

This model illustrates, among other things, the advantages of attempting to make objective measurements of relevant parameter values through experimental procedures and stresses the importance of repeated measurements. It is above all based on a recognition that an advertising manager faces a constantly changing environment and that he or she must adapt both plans and budget to the changing conditions. Many companies in effect are continuously experimenting and engaging in these types of marketing research studies, even though they may not be guided by formal decision rules. Although such research is bound to be costly, the effort is often worthwhile. The adaptive-control model provides an approach to answering the question of how much should be invested in such research, as well as how much to invest in advertising at any particular time.

---

[2]The optimal gap between A_1 and A_2 and optimal number of test markets to use can be calculated. See Little, "Model of Adaptive Control," pp. 128–130.

[3]Letting S_1 and S_2 be the observed mean sales rates in the groups of markets at A_1 and A_2, respectively, the experimental mean for (t) can be calculated as follows:

$$\hat{\beta}(t) = \frac{1}{A_1 - A_2} (\bar{S}_2 + \gamma A_2^2 - \bar{S}_1 - \gamma A_1^2)$$

The β to be used in determining the budget for the next time period, $t + 1$, is termed $\beta(t + 1)$. It is a weighted average of the β used in the current time period $\beta(t)$ and the estimate of β obtained from the experiment, $\hat{\beta}(t)$.

$$\beta(t + 1) = a\beta(t) + (1 - a)\hat{\beta}(t)$$

Thus, the decision rule defining the advertising rate in the next time period, $A(t + 1)^*$, is

$$A(t + 1)^* = \frac{M\beta(t + 1) - 1}{2M\gamma}$$

If the experiment were very accurate, a small value of a could be used and heave reliance placed on the current experiment. If the accuracy of the experiment were low, a large value of a would be appropriate. In this case, the current rate would depend mostly on the rate used in the preceding time period, which in turn represents a summary of all past experience up to that time.

17 MEDIA TACTICS: ALLOCATING MEDIA BUDGETS

> But do the people in Maine have anything to say to
> the people in Texas?
> (Mark Twain, when informed that the telegraph cable had been
> stretched all the way from Maine to Texas)

Let's suppose that, following the methods recommended in the last chapter, you set your brand's budget at $5 million for the upcoming year. Now you are faced with the next set of decisions: Should we spend more of the money in television or in magazines? Within magazines, should we advertise in *Cosmopolitan* or *Vogue*, or both? Should a two-page advertisement be used or would a single-page advertisement be better? Should our television spot be in prime time or during daytime programming? Should it be fifteen seconds or thirty seconds? Such tactical questions need to be addressed in the development of the media plan, the focus of this chapter.

Answering such questions has never been as tough—or as full of opportunity. Today's media environment is not the stable, easy media environment of the 1970s and even 1980s. It used to be, for instance, that if you wanted to advertise to a mass target audience in the United States in 1980, all you had to do was place a prime-time TV spot on the "big three" TV networks (ABC, CBS, and NBC), and you could reach 87 percent of all households in the U.S. By 1990, that had declined to only 62 percent, so the "big three" were no longer enough. One key reason was the increasing penetration of cable TV, which, by 1993, was about 62 percent of U.S. households. Cable TV offered many more channel options (an average of thirty-one by the early 1990s), so viewers began to watch stations other than the big three networks.[1] The age of fragmented media had arrived, allowing for much greater targeting of consumers.

The proliferation of cable TV channels—in a few years, many households in the U.S. will supposedly have access to 500 channels, by recent news reports—has been accompanied by growth in other media too, such as magazines (the number of magazine titles increased from 1,285 in 1977 to 2,230 in 1990). Newer media options have emerged that simply did not exist ten years ago: advertising in stores and on shopping carts, advertising in schools and doctors' waiting rooms, advertising through satellite-based TV channels in Asia, Europe, and the U.S. (see Chapter 20), advertising on the Internet, and even (possibly) advertising on an orbiting illuminated billboard in space![2]

The proliferation of media options has been accompanied by increasing technological means for consumers to avoid advertising messages, should they choose to do so. The number of TV commercial minutes on TV was up from 1,768 in 1978 to 2,046 in 1988, according to research by DDB Needham. However, TV remote controls and videocassette recorders (both now in over 80 percent of U.S. homes) allowed consumers to zap and zip ads with the greatest of ease (Chapter 7 discussed these phenomena).

Alternatively, the new cable technologies hold the promise for advertising to create ads that are much more "interactive," where individually "addressable" consumers can use their cable remote controls to decide which ads to watch, and to request information immediately from ads that interest them, information which can be printed immediately on home color printers.[3] Many large clients (such as Procter & Gamble and Avis), ad agencies (such as Bozell, Jacobs, Kenyon & Eckhardt, and Leo Burnett), and media conglomerates (such as Time Warner, and US West) are experimenting with interactive media and the role of advertising within it, trying to see how ads can be tailored more closely to the interests of each individual viewer and made more enjoyable and entertaining so that the viewer will indeed want to enter into a dialogue with the advertiser. A related development is the growth of home shopping TV channels, such as QVC, which should make consumers more accepting of placing orders immediately after seeing TV ads for products.[4]

Given these changes and challenges, the role of efficiency and creativity in developing media plans has never been greater. The *media plan* identifies and details the media schedule that is to be used. A *media schedule* specifies how the media budget is to be spent. Although the level of detail of a media schedule can vary, it can include the specification of up to four types of media factors:

1. *Media class:* This is the type of medium, such as television, radio, newspapers, magazines, billboards, and direct mail.

2. *Media vehicles:* These provide the immediate environment for the advertisement. For example, within the media class of television, there are various vehicles, such as NBC News and ABC's *Monday Night Football*; and, within the media class of magazines, there are *Esquire*, *Time*, *TV Guide*, and *Vogue*.

3. *Media option:* This is a detailed description of an advertisement's characteristics other than the copy and the artwork used. It specifies, in addition to the media vehicle, such advertisement characteristics as size (full-page or half-page), length (fifteen second, thirty second, or sixty second), color (black-and-white or four-color), or location (inside front cover or interior location).

4. *Scheduling and timing:* These specify how media options are scheduled over time. Among the strategy alternatives are (a) *flighting*, periods of total inactivity; (b) *continuous*, advertising spread evenly through time; and (c) *pulsing*, a continuous base augmented by intermittent bursts of heavy advertising. Timing decisions include the selection of specific issues (the August 17 issue of *Time*) or time slots (the second World Series game).

The media schedule will at a minimum specify the number of planned insertions in each media vehicle. A more detailed media schedule also specifies the other details of a media option, such as size or length and the timing of the advertisement insertions. For example, one media schedule might include ten network commercials on daytime television and two advertisements in *Time, Women's Day,* and *Newsweek,* all in the first quarter of the year. A more detailed media schedule might specify sixty-second commercials and two-page advertisements and that all the advertising was to be placed during the first week in February. (Note that the allocation of media budgets across geographical regions is also something that needs to be decided on. This can be done using the *Brand Development Indices* and *Category Development Indices* for each region or market, calculated in the manner described in Chapter 6 earlier.)

Even for small media budgets, there can be literally thousands, even millions, of possible media schedules from which to choose. The task is to select a media plan from this set that will be relatively effective. In making this selection, the media planner will usually first select a limited set of media possibilities. From this set, the planner will then attempt to develop and evaluate a limited number of media schedules, often using computerized media models as well as judgment. Finally, once the media plan is completely specified, the desired media time (or space) must be bought and prices negotiated with the media owner. This buying process is also briefly discussed at the end of the chapter.

The selection of the most effective media schedule is based in upon both quantitative and qualitative criteria. That is, the media planner attempts first to ensure that, for the available budget, the advertiser is obtaining the maximum number of advertising exposures—to the target segments—at the lowest possible cost. Such analysis requires working with huge masses of data on the audiences of the media vehicles and the costs involved in using these vehicles. Computer programs are often used to assist in such quantitative analyses.

After this number-crunching, however, qualitative judgments have to be applied as well, for a computer cannot completely take into account the qualitative aspects of a particular media buy (for example, the "excitement" value of running a TV ad on the Super Bowl telecast). In addition, judgments also have to be applied in running the computer programs, in determining what these programs should attempt to optimize, such as the desired level of exposures (frequency) and the number of people potentially exposed to the message (reach). These principles, and this process, will be discussed in this chapter, and then illustrated in the context of a media plan of The Broiler.

MEDIA CLASS DECISIONS . . . .

The first media allocation decision, that of allocating the budget over various media, is one that is made on both quantitative and qualitative criteria.

Quantitatively, data are collected on just how many people in the target market can be reached through that media class (such as radio, or newspapers, or daytime television). The source of such data is often a source such as Simmons or MRI (which are both described shortly). Radio, for example, is a terrific medium to reach business commuters through "drive-time" or to reach teenagers. Television's great strength is as a *mass medium*, since it delivers very broad reach at low cost (per thousand people reached, not necessarily per television spot. While a single network prime-time thirty-second spot can cost as much as $350,000, this is actually cheap on a per-person-reached basis, since that one single spot will be potentially exposed to almost 20 million homes.)

While TV reaches mass audiences, magazines and direct mail are excellent in reaching narrowly defined target segments. Radio, too, reaches narrow segments—no single radio station usually has more than 2 to 3 percent of the audience in a market—and, since the listeners of a particular radio station tend to be loyal, a radio campaign is useful in building high levels of frequency against them. Newspapers (and spot television) make geographical targeting possible. One can also target certain types of readers by paying for specific sections of a newspaper, such as business or sports pages for men, or entertainment and food-and-cooking sections for women.[5]

Qualitatively, the most important considerations have to do with the *fit* between the medium and the creative execution. Television, because it can show action using both audio and visual, can make an impact that simply is not possible in other media. For some types of advertising, such as emotional or image advertising, or product demonstrations, this type of impact can be critical to the copy approach. On the other hand, television is a passive medium and is not really suited to copy with high factual content—unless *infomercials* of much longer length are employed. Infomercials were discussed earlier in Chapter 7. Nor is outdoor suited for high information ads: it can only be used for name recognition and "reminder" purposes, since billboards cannot really communicate much information in the few seconds that they are viewed. Billboards are also used heavily by product categories (such as cigarettes and liquor) that are legislatively barred from other media.

Print, especially the magazine medium, is more suitable for long and complex messages. Like magazines, newspapers typically carry ads (especially local ads) containing much more information than do ads on TV or radio.[6] Car advertisers in the U.S. recently have begun to emphasize magazines at the expense of TV, as their ads for new models have begun to offer more product information to technologically more sophisticated consumers.[7] Magazines also generally offer better color reproduction than newspapers. Because of their association with news stories, however, newspapers could have a sense of objectivity and a spirit of being current that could rub off on the advertisements in the right context. Radio can involve the listener by getting him or her to use imagination to visualize stimuli (but radio ads still have much poorer recall than ads in other media, because of the higher clutter).

A second set of qualitative criteria has to do with production logistics. Ads in network TV and magazines often require long *lead times*—they usually have to be submitted to the network or publisher weeks in advance of when they actually appear, making it difficult to use them in situations when the copy might have to be changed on short notice. Radio and newspapers are much more flexible on this score and also have the advantage of lower production costs, so that they are frequently utilized by retailers, banks, airlines, and other businesses where rapid price changes need to be communicated at short notice.

When news has to be communicated rapidly to a target market, broadcast media (TV, radio) and newspapers also have another relevant advantage over magazines or direct mail: while the former will reach their targets almost immediately (called a *fast cume*), the latter will take a while—often a couple of weeks—for their messages to get read and acted upon (a *slow cume*).

A third set of qualitative criteria has to do with the competitive setting. Often, when faced with a high-spending competitor, it makes sense to use another medium than that used by the competitor, to avoid being "swamped" by the competitor's advertising. Alternatively, it may make sense to use the same medium, but to schedule one's own ads at a different time of year. Ultimately, the final choice of media classes involves reconciling these different quantitative and qualitative criteria, using managerial judgment.

Obviously, a good media plan integrates the many different media used. For instance, TV could be the initial medium to generate awareness and interest in a new product, while a follow-up radio campaign using the TV soundtrack could serve as a lower-cost, high-frequency reminder campaign. The radio ads could thus serve as devices to get listeners to replay the imagery of the TV ads mentally, boosting recall of the TV ad and the brand name and brand claims to levels almost as high as would have occurred if the more expensive TV ads had been repeated.[8] Alternatively, a magazine campaign could be used after the TV ads, offering more detailed information, if that was necessary.

MEDIA VEHICLE DECISIONS . . . .

The first consideration in making a media vehicle decision is simply the number of exposures that can be obtained, and for what cost. These quantitative considerations are later supplemented by various qualitative ones, such as the suitability of a particular editorial environment to a particular ad, which we shall discuss later in this section.

Media Terminology

Table 17–1 shows the type of information used by the media planners at the J. Walter Thompson agency in selecting magazines. The first column is the *unit cost* of a full-page color advertisement. The second column shows the total *audience* (also called *readership*), in millions, obtained by the magazine. Note that the total audience is much higher than the *circulation* because of the substantial numbers who read a magazine that someone else bought. The third column is the basic counting statistic, *cost per thousand*, or *CPM*. It is the cost per thousand audience members. Thus, the CPM for *Good Housekeeping* is $1.20, which means that it costs $1.20 to reach 1,000 members of the *Good Housekeeping* audience.

CPM figures are obviously most relevant if they take into account only members of the target audience that are reached, instead of just any reader. The circulation trend figure allows media planners to project the CPM number into the future. As a practical matter, there is a lag of several months and perhaps even a year between the media decision and the placement of the advertisements, so such trends can be significant. However, magazines will often guarantee a certain

Table 17–1. Selecting Magazines

	Unit cost ($1,000s)	Total audience (millions)	Cost per thousand CPM[a]	Percent mag. exposed	Circulation		Target segment			In home		Target concern index	Com-pact. pages	Reader opinions	Other considerations
					Present	trend	%	millions	CPM[a]	% Aud.	CPM[a]				
Good House-keeping	$27.9	23.2	$1.20	62	5.6	+ 1%	21[b]	10.1[c]	2.74	57[d]	4.87[c]	123[f]	14[g]	91	Seal of Approval
Glamour	11.3	5.6	2.02	54	1.7	+ 4	6	2.9	3.88	41	9.46	NA	5	63	Pers. card
Cosmopolitan	13.0	7.5	1.73	63	1.9	+14	7	3.3	3.92	41	9.56	NA	NA	74	Singles aud.
Family Circle	36.0	18.9	1.90	66	8.3	+ 8	18	9.0	4.00	69	5.80	121	4	56	Practical
Woman's Day	34.9	19.2	1.82	67	7.9	+ 5	16	7.9	4.43	63	7.03	118	6	60	Practical
RedBook	26.2	13.7	1.91	66	4.8	−1	11	5.5	4.79	58	8.26	136	0	79	Mommas Aud.
Madamoiselle	7.5	3.0	2.50	58	.8	+ 1	3	1.5	4.95	35	14.14	NA	1	67	Pers. card
Parents	17.4	5.5	3.16	46	2.0	+ 1	5	2.4	7.25	60	12.08	130	10	74	Environment

Adapted from "Numbers Aren't Everything," Media Decisions, 10, June 1975, p. 69.

[a]Cost per thousand

[b]The percent of the target segment covered by the magazine.

[c]The number of the target segment covered by the magazine.

[d]The percent of the magazine's audience exposed in the home.

[e]Cost per thousand considering only the in-home audience.

[f]The extent to which the editorial content reaches out to the target segment.

[g]Compatible pages—the number of editorial pages devoted during the past year to the relevant subject.

circulation level (called a *rate base*) and will refund part of the payment if the circulation does not achieve the guaranteed level.

It is, of course, of no value to obtain audience members if they are not exposed to the advertisements themselves. It is advertisement exposures that are of ultimate interest to the advertiser, not vehicle exposures, but it is the latter that are reported by the media data sources. Thus some adjustments, admittedly imperfect, are necessary. Studies have shown, for example, that in the case of TV programs, somewhere between 40 and 50 percent of the program's audience actually misses seeing the ads that air during the program, either because they are not in the room when the ads come on, or because they are busy doing something else. A similar percentage applies to radio ads listened to while driving a car.[9] If there is reason to believe that advertisement readership among some vehicles is higher than others, the basic CPM figures should be adjusted accordingly.

The fourth column in Table 17–1 is an effort to measure page exposure. It is based upon the survey question, "How many pages out of ten did you open in this particular copy of the magazine?" The result is a crude indicator of *page exposure* as opposed to *vehicle exposure*. Sometimes a subjective opinion as to how seriously audience members look at the advertisements is helpful. Some magazines, for example, are actually bought by some because their advertisements provide information about home decorating, fashion, instrumentation technology, or some other specialized area of interest.

In buying television, the basic unit of counting is the *gross rating point* or *GRP*. A commercial's *rating* is the percentage of the potential audience (such as "all women aged twenty-five to fifty-four") that are tuned in to the commercial. For a national buy, the potential audience could be all U.S. homes with television, whether or not their TV set is on at any particular time. (The number of *homes using television*, or *HUT*, at any given time period is always smaller than the total number of homes with television, and is usually expressed as a percentage of the latter.) However, the concept of ratings will apply for audiences defined by region (the Los Angeles area) or by any other means (for example, adults from eighteen to thirty-five). If the commercial is associated with a program, its rating would be the rating of the program. If it is not associated with a program, it would be the average rating during that time period. The highest rated period is *prime time*, followed by the period just prior to prime time, termed the *early fringe*.

Just as any particular TV program has a rating, it also has a *share* of the total number of households watching any TV program during that time period. Thus, suppose that during the 7:00 to 7:15 time period last Thursday, 60 million TV sets were watching any TV program, of the 100 million TV households that could potentially be actually watching TV. Then the HUT for that time period is 60, or 60 percent. Suppose the TV program *Home Improvement* had, at that time, 20 million households tuned into it. Then the share for *Home Improvement* is 33 (20 million divided by 60 million), but its rating (expressed with respect to households) is 20 (20 million divided by 100 million). Mathematically, a program's rating always equals its share multiplied by the HUT.

To obtain total gross rating points for a media schedule, the ratings of the commercials are summed. For example, the following schedule in which a commercial is run seventeen times in a one-week period yields 142 GRPs:

3 showings in a time slot with a 12 rating = 36 GRP
4 showings in a time slot with a 4 rating = 16 GRP
10 showings in a time slot with a 9 rating = 90 GRP
Total for the week = 142 GRP

GRP figures are often calculated with specific target audiences in mind, and are then sometimes called *T* (for *Target*) *GRPs.*

The number of different people reached through this three-program media schedule depends on the *duplication* between the three programs. If there was absolutely no duplication, then the total ratings achieved would be 12 plus 4 plus 9, or 25, meaning that 25 percent of the target population would have seen the ad at least once. In reality, since we do have duplication, this total number of people exposed to the ad at least once will be somewhat less. If it was 25 percent, however, the average member of the audience will be exposed 5.68 times (142 divided by 25), although many, of course, will not be exposed at all and others will be exposed up to 17 times, since there are 17 potential opportunities to be exposed. (The concept of an *exposure distribution* will be explained shortly.)

One measure of the efficiency of a given program or time slot will be the *cost per rating point* (*CPRP*): cost per rating point = CPRP = cost of a commercial/divided by the rating points delivered by that commercial.

Reach and Frequency

At this stage it is appropriate to introduce the two most basic terms in media planning: *reach* and *frequency*. Reach refers to the number of people or households that will be exposed to an advertising schedule *at least once* over a specified period of time (usually, but not necessarily, a four-week time period). Very important, a person who sees the same ad twice (such as the people in our television example, who could have seen it up to 17 times) is not counted twice (or more), but just once.

Cumulative audience is a more restrictive term, used to designate the reach of two or more issues of the same media vehicle—here the duplication being subtracted out is the *internal overlap* of people who see or read two issues or shows of the same media (such as reading two weekly issues of the same weekly magazine, or watching two weekly episodes of the same TV situation comedy). In such situations, the number of *new* (nonduplicated) readers or viewers picked up by the media vehicle in its second issue or show is called its *accumulation*. When the duplication being subtracted out is one between two or more different media vehicles—what one might call *external overlap*, such as that between one week's issues of *Time* and *Newsweek*—the term *net coverage* is sometimes used as the relevant reach descriptor.

The term *reach* thus almost always refers to *unduplicated reach*, net both of internal and external duplication. However, since in almost every media schedule there are many people who see an ad more than once, frequency refers to the number of times someone sees the ad. *Average frequency* thus refers to the average number of times a person or household is exposed to a schedule. Thus, since GRPs refer to the total number of exposures delivered, and reach is the unduplicated number of people who got those exposures, GRPs equals the average frequency multiplied by the reach (where the reach is measured in terms of rating points).

In our television example earlier, our reach was 25 rating points (for the case of no duplication between the three TV programs), and our average frequency was 5.68, for the total figure of 142 GRPs delivered in that week. For a magazine buy, a schedule that bought one ad each in magazine A (readership of 28 million people) and magazine B (readership of 22 million people) would generate 50 million exposures (sometimes called *opportunities-to-see*, or *OTS*). If 10 million of these people read both magazines A *and* B, we might have 10 million duplicated readers, or a reach of 40 million. Thus our average frequency here is 50 million OTS divided by 40 million reach, or 1.25, over the relevant time period.

Since the number of GRPs or OTS you can buy is directly related to how much money you spend, this brings us to the most basic media planning question: for a given budget, that can buy a given number of GRPs or OTS, do we want to increase reach or increase frequency? For a given budget, there is always a trade-off between increasing reach or increasing frequency. Some criteria for setting the desired frequency levels were discussed in the last chapter. For some campaigns, reach will be critical. For example, a campaign to gain awareness of a new product may need to reach a substantial portion of the market to be successful. Furthermore, a punchy awareness advertisement may not require many repetitions. Another campaign involving a series of advertisements designed to communicate product details may require many exposures, as may an image campaign. In that case the frequency could be a very important characteristic of a proposed media schedule.

Qualifiers on Basic Reach and Frequency

Qualifying Reach

The first refinement of the counting-exposures approach to media vehicle selection is to consider the types of people being exposed. A primary issue in developing advertising objectives is to specify the target segment or segments. It will be of little value to deliver an audience containing people not in a target segment.

In Table 17–1, the seventh column shows the percentage of the target audience that is covered by the magazine. The eighth column is the total target audience reached by the magazine, and the ninth is the CPM, only including the target audience. Such a figure, which includes only the target audience, is sometimes called the *effective audience*. *Good Housekeeping* is still the most efficient magazine, but now *Glamour*'s cost looks better, relative to the other alternatives than it did when the total audience was considered.

Later in this chapter, the available media data will be discussed in more detail. It turns out that data such as product usage and life style profiles of media users are available, but that demographic data on vehicle audiences is much more complete, convenient, and inexpensive. Thus, if a product user target segment can be defined in terms of demographics, the task of matching the target segment to a vehicle audience is much easier. For example, an automobile firm may be targeting on the young adult market or on the senior citizen market. When other segmentation variables are employed, it is usually possible to describe the target segment—for example, heavy users of credit cards—in terms of demographics so that the media demographic information can be employed. The relationship between demographic data sets, media data sets, and product usage data sets, however, is usually not perfect, because they are typically collected by different suppliers, and special techniques to "combine"[10] them have been suggested.

Some studies, however, have shown that such an indirect approach (going through demographics) sacrifices considerable efficiency. It is more direct, and probably more accurate, to evaluate alternative media vehicles in terms of how many target segment consumers they reach, using syndicated media sources that permit such evaluations. For example, Heinz ketchup might select TV programs using data on how many users of its competitor, Hunt's ketchup, were in the audience for each TV program. If this "direct" approach is employed, for instance, TV programs could be evaluated for media cost efficiency on the basis of "cost per exposure per target consumer purchase index," rather than merely "cost per thousand target viewers in the right demographic category."[11]

When several target segments are involved it might be useful to weight each formally as to its relative value. Thus a computer component manufacturer might have as a primary segment design engineers and maintenance engineers, and buyers might represent secondary segments. Weights could then be attached to each group, and a media vehicle's total reach might be evaluated in terms of the weighted sum of the individual groups reached.

Qualifying Frequency

The exposure-counting approach to media decisions implicitly assumes that all exposures to an individual will have equal impact. Thus ten exposures to one individual is as desirable as two exposures to each of five people or one exposure to each of ten people. Clearly, there may be a need to achieve some minimum (*threshold* or *critical mass*) level of frequency against every reached individual, below which that person would not have been effectively reached. Such a frequency level is often called *effective frequency*. Many ad agencies in the U.S. and Canada, for example, use three or four exposures per four-week planning cycle as their effective frequency level for TV; it is often higher (twelve exposures per month) for outdoor and lower (three or four per quarter) for magazines.[12]

At the higher end of the frequency scale, the value of successive exposure will eventually diminish, at least within some time period. If the number of exposures is excessive, the audience can become annoyed, and the impact of future exposures may actually be negative (called wear-out). Because of the need to consider both the minimum threshold exposure levels needed, and the maximum exposure levels that should not be exceeded, the media planner needs not just an average frequency number but an entire *frequency distribution* or *exposure distribution*. Such a frequency distribution specifies the exact number (or percentage) of people exposed once, twice, three times, four times, and so on.

Very often these frequency distributions are statistically estimated using assumptions about the shape of the distribution and carry names such as the *beta binomial distribution*, or *BBD*.[13] The estimation of the frequency distribution is more complex than the estimation of the reach and frequency, but there are still a variety of approaches available. One of the fastest and most inexpensive was first suggested by Richard Metheringham and is usually termed the *Metheringham method*. The inputs required are the reach of each of the vehicles, the duplication between each pair of vehicles, and the duplication between two insertions in the same vehicle. The output is a frequency distribution. The key assumption is essentially that all vehicles are identical with respect to reach and duplication with other vehicles. Thus, the method essentially averages all the input reach data and the duplication data.

The method works quite well when only one vehicle is involved or when, for example, only daytime television spots are involved. However, it works much less well when a more realistic schedule involving several different vehicles is to be evaluated. Other researchers have offered alternative methods, such as *log-linear* and *canonical expansion models*, which work better when exposure distributions within specific target markets are of interest, rather than among the total audiences of the media being considered.[14] Some researchers have even suggested that exposure distributions are not really necessary and that media models using only single-insertion ratings and the number of insertions can perform just as well as models using exposure distributions, in selecting the best schedules.[15]

The following is an example of a frequency distribution for a media insertion schedule involving two insertions in each of three magazines:

Number of Exposures	Frequency Distribution	Audience
0	0.22	198,000
1	0.15	135,000
2	0.25	225,000
3	0.18	162,000
4	0.10	90,000
5	0.02	18,000
6	0.08	72,000
Total	1.00	900,000

The frequency distribution thus provides a much more detailed portrayal than reach and average frequency. The noticeable bulge at 0 and 6 is actually characteristic of many frequency distributions. They essentially reflect those who tend not to read many magazines and those who tend to read many.

A variety of frequency distributions can generate the same reach and average frequency values, which have very different implications. The implicit assumption behind the consideration of frequency distributions is that the number of exposures that an individual receives matters. It is often helpful to make that assumption explicit by specifying the value of successive exposures.

Some illustrative alternatives are shown in Table 17–2. Set A implies that the reach is the only value of a media schedule of interest. It indicates the need is to expose audience members once, and anything more is of no value. Set B implies that all exposures have equal value. Set C suggests that exposures will have equal impact until three exposures are obtained, and then they will have no value. The remaining sets have different assumptions. Clearly, the value given to different exposures matters in the calculations of what the level of reach really is—for instance, if exposure levels below 3 are considered of no value, then our reach should be defined not as the number of people receiving at least one exposure, but as the number of people receiving at least three exposures. Some media people call the level of reach that uses the *effective frequency* as the cutoff level the *effective reach* level.

Measuring Print Vehicle Audiences

Audited circulation data for print media are most easily obtained from the Audit Bureau of Circulations. Such print vehicle circulation data, however, neglect *pass-along* readers both inside and outside the home. Thus, to measure a vehicle's audience (or readership), it is necessary to apply approaches such as *recent reading* and *through-the-book* to a randomly selected probability sample of adults who are personally interviewed. In both approaches, a two-step approach is employed. In the first step, which varies somewhat between the two methods, a large number of magazine title logos are shown to the respondent, and they are are asked to indi-

Table 17–2. Value of Successive Exposures.

| Exposure | Relative Value | | | | | |
	A	B	C	D	E	F
0						
1	1	1	1	0	1	1
2	0	1	1	0	1	0.9
3	0	1	1	1	0.7	0.8
4	0	1	0	1	0.5	0.7
5	0	1	0	1	0.3	0.5
6	0	1	0	1	0	0.5
7	0	1	0	1	0	0.5
8	0	1	0	0	0	0.2
9	0	1	0	0	0	0.2
10	0	1	0	0	0	0

cate whether or not each magazine might have been read or looked into in the past six months.

In *recent reading*, respondents are next asked whether they looked at *any* copy of each title within *that specific past week* (for a weekly publication) or during the *last specific month* (for a monthly publication). One problem is that the survey is unlikely to represent an "average" week, so there is a seasonality factor to consider. And, a reader could read several issues in one week but not in another and so be incorrectly reported as not being a reader in the specific week of the survey. Another concern is the tendency to exaggerate readership of prestige magazines and to minimize readership of vehicles that do not match people's self-image. Still another is the forgetting factor. One study found that 50 of 166 people who were observed reading magazines in a doctor's office said they had never read the magazine they had been observed reading. Companies using this method thus show respondents flash cards with the magazine's logo on them, to aid recall, but it is alleged that respondents often confuse magazine titles (*Home and Garden* with *Better Homes and Gardens*, for instance), which distorts the figures collected.

In the *through-the-book approach*, following the screener question mentioned earlier, respondents are shown a stripped-down copy of a *specific* issue of a magazine that he or she reads and asked whether several articles were read and if they were interesting. The respondent is then asked if he or she read that specific issue. This approach is obviously sensitive to the issue's age. A too-recent issue will miss later readers. A too-old issue risks forgetting.

The two major audience-measuring services are Mediamark (MRI) and Simmons (SMRB). Simmons interviews 19,000 people each year on 140 magazines (called *books* by agency media people) and produces annual reports; MRI interviews 20,000 people on 230 magazines and produces twice-yearly reports. Until 1994, the two services used different methods in estimating readership: Simmons used the through-the-book method, while MRI used the recent-reading method. Because they used different methods, they often yielded different estimates of readership for different magazines, and these differences between the two have sparked sharp controversy through the years.

Table 17–3 shows a comparison of the audience estimates based on the two techniques. MRI's estimates were generally higher—about 10 percent higher for weeklies and as much as 35 percent higher for monthlies. These differences were especially large for small-circulation magazines, which have their readership figures based on very small samples. These differences in readership estimates had major implications for how many ad pages a magazine could sell to advertisers, and ad agencies and clients had to find their own ways to reconcile the two sets of numbers.[16] It has been argued that the major reason why the two sets of numbers varied so much was not the second step of the interview (described earlier), but rather the specific way in which they screen-in readers in the first place.[17] In any event, in September 1994 Simmons announced that it, too, was going to use a modified form of the recent-reading method—one that it claimed would be superior to MRI's.[18]

In addition to media data—including duplication and accumulation data— that cover TV, radio, magazines, newspapers, outdoor, and Yellow Pages, both ser-

Table 17–3.   Total Adult Readers Comparison.

Magazine	Mediamark	Simmons
Time	25,701,000	20,035,000
Newsweek	23,640,000	16,453,000
U.S. News	11,586,000	8,733,000
Family Circle	32,143,000	18,255,000
McCall's	24,641,000	17,287,000
Ladies Home Journal	21,920,000	12,971,000
Harper's Bazaar	3,574,000	3,301,000
Playboy	21,401,000	15,584,000

Source: Adapted from Leah Rozen, "Reader Data Still Don't Jibe," Advertising Age, October 6, 1980, p. 118.

vices also obtain demographic and psychographic data on brand and category users for between 3 and 4,000 brands in over 500 product categories that are analyzed on a national-plus geographic basis. These data are thus used frequently to identify the target markets for ad campaigns (see Chapter 4 on segmentation), and the media reaching those targets. The data are available both in printed volumes and on computer tape (for customized analyses). An example of a page from Simmons is shown in Table 17–4.

For newspapers, readership data—based on telephone interviews—are available from both Simmons and from another service called Birch-Scarborough Research. Both contact over 60,000 adults every year, in over fifty markets nationwide, and provide estimates of the number of adult readers by weekday and for Sunday editions. Demographic breakdowns are provided, as are estimates of cumulative reach.

Measuring Broadcast Vehicle Audience

The principal methods of obtaining audience data for broadcast media are the people-meter and the diary.

The principal source of national television ratings is the Nielsen Television Index, National Audience Demographics (NTI-NAD). The NTI panel consists of approximately 3,000 to 4,000 households, matched according to U.S. national statistics, that agree to have an electronic device called a *people-meter* attached to their TV sets. The people-meter is a small unit placed on top of or beside the television set, recording what channel is viewed at what time, for every half-minute during every twenty-four-hour period. Eight sets of lights on the set are used to indicate which member of the household—including visitors—is watching; these lights can be turned on or off using a remote device, and those watching are meant to turn them on when they start watching and off when they stop. Data from the people-meter are sent periodically by telephone to the Nielsen central offices, where they are related to each person's age, sex, and other parameters that Nielsen collects

Table 17–4. Magazine Readership as Reported by Simmons.

Magazine	Cost per page[b] (1000s)		Audience in 1,000s[a]						Buying style		
	B&W	4-color	Adults	Female	Age 18–34	Household income over 25,000	Brand loyal	Ecologist	Economy minded	Planner	Style conscious
Total Adults (millions)			155.8	81.1	63.1	41.3	40.2	43.5	60.2	67.7	36.0
1. American Baby	$15.7	$21.7	2,308	1,963	1,902	575	636	659	918	880	701
2. Better Homes	51.9	62.8	21,579	16,684	7,815	7,123	6,340	6,439	9,318	10,243	6,399
3. Bon Appetit	11.0	15.7	3,000	2,306	1,206	1,610	941	801	1,074	1,413	1,145
4. Business Week	17.4	26.1	4,147	913	1,770	2,557	1,291	815	1,465	1,878	1,012
5. Car and Driver	13.9	21.3	2,720	539	1,961	1,159	748	767	1,158	1,461	778
6. Ebony	12.9	19.9	6,925	3,639	4,029	1,461	1,716	2,020	2,678	3,036	2,034
7. Family Health	6.2	8.7	3,325	2,281	1,205	1,035	1,016	1,028	1,465	1,690	938
8. Fortune	17.9	27.3	2,190	583	889	1,541	688	425	609	904	486
9. Golf	10.3	15.5	2,283	628	902	1,266	686	568	839	996	794
10. Gourmet	7.0	12.5	2,263	1,573	670	1,126	639	725	773	1,006	773
11. Guns & Ammo	5.3	8.6	2,898	299	1,815	975	797	1,092	1,313	1,478	684
12. House & Garden	14.8	21.8	7,917	6,061	3,071	2,998	2,624	2,374	3,383	3,643	2,792
13. Mademoiselle	8.8	12.8	3,620	3,415	2,180	1,332	1,065	1,111	1,657	1,832	1,656
14. McCall's	42.5	52.2	18,372	16,266	7,143	5,753	5,131	5,577	7,930	8,672	6,023
15. Money Mag.	11.4	17.9	3,691	1,663	1,768	1,927	1,040	958	1,395	1,900	1,001
16. Motor Trend	12.4	19.8	3,358	422	1,926	1,159	823	834	1,303	1,554	721
17. MS.	6.5	8.7	1,375	1,211	991	360	317	486	475	712	425
18. Nat'l Lampoon	6.7	9.9	3,348	759	2,845	1,377	995	912	785	1,225	737
19. Newsweek	33.2	51.7	17,197	6,893	8,827	7,370	5,046	4,422	5,713	7,855	4,582
20. New Yorker	8.3	13.2	3,008	1,412	1,433	1,509	1,078	863	1,099	1,490	855
21. Outdoor Life	14.8	21.4	5,438	1,133	2,784	1,748	1,448	1,937	2,410	2,640	1,236
22. People	23.0	29.5	18,138	10,641	10,992	6,162	4,488	5,296	6,228	8,112	5,230
23. Playboy	36.2	50.6	13,932	2,749	9,596	4,910	3,523	3,729	4,713	5,965	3,334

(Continued)

Table 17-4. Magazine Readership as Reported by Simmons. (Continued)

Magazine	Cost per page[b] (1000s)		Audience in 1,000s[a]				Buying style				
	B&W	4-Color	Adults	Female	Age 18–34	Household income over 25,000	Brand loyal	Ecologist	Economy minded	Planner	Style conscious
24. Playgirl	6.6	8.8	2,110	1,253	1,384	546	526	613	786	1,007	513
25. Reader's Digest	74.6	89.6	39,283	22,303	12,942	12,769	11,360	10,802	15,618	17,937	9,611
26. Road & Track	10.7	16.8	2,454	405	1,761	1,098	589	657	752	1,264	474
27. Rolling Stone	9.1	13.7	2,780	943	2,552	911	663	834	910	1,249	621
28. Seventeen	10.5	15.2	5,259	4,484	3,230	1,573	1,132	1,607	2,266	2,492	1,849
29. Smithsonian	17.5	21.9	4,952	2,404	1,665	2,730	1,630	1,475	1,420	2,321	1,083
30. Sport	13.3	19.4	6,116	1,231	3,816	1,890	1,552	1,488	2,115	2,908	1,722
31. Sports Afield	7.0	10.0	5,318	1,137	2,330	1,982	1,818	1,491	2,193	2,451	1,079
32. Sunset	14.2	19.7	5,227	3,446	1,778	2,317	1,585	1,441	1,827	2,509	1,163
33. Time	45.1	70.3	20,180	8,269	9,854	8,782	5,786	5,192	6,606	9,049	5,032
34. Travel/Holiday	5.9	8.4	1,139	570	299	471	365	397	479	599	332
35. True Story	9.8	12.8	5,925	5,294	3,297	801	1,565	1,946	2,865	2,538	1,665
36. TV Guide	58.8	69.5	42,236	23,389	20,984	11,223	11,130	12,532	16,249	18,818	10,695
37. U.S. News	21.9	34.6	8,635	2,724	3,288	4,112	2,563	2,119	3,310	4,343	2,267
38. Vogue	10.4	15.2	5,755	5,192	2,825	2,194	1,775	1,970	2,495	2,824	2,367
39. Woman's Day	49.9	59.8	18,225	16,606	7,008	5,523	5,121	5,427	7,746	8,876	5,835
40. Working Woman	5.2	7.4	974	941	518	437	756	288	320	597	313

[a]Source: "The 1979 Study of Media and Markets—Multi-Media Audiences: Adult," Simmons Market Research Bureau, 1979.

[b]Source: Consumer Magazine and Farm Publication Rates and Data, Standard Rate & Data Service, November 27, 1980. Shown are the costs of a one-page single-insertion advertisement.

separately and keeps on file. In addition, Nielsen meters New York, Los Angeles, and Chicago to provide local ratings in these areas on a next-day basis. Nielsen also reports HUT, the percentage of all television homes whose set is in use.

People-meters have the advantage, over the previously used television meters called audimeters, of providing information not only about how many people are watching a TV program, but also about who they are, in terms of age, sex, and so on. Before 1987, Nielsen used two samples of people in its national panel: one of people with the *audimeters*, which simply recorded what channel the program was tuned to at different points of time when the set was on, and a second *diary* panel, in which panelists with known age and sex characteristics self-reported their viewing. The data from both sources were then combined. Today, the people-meters provide both kinds of data simultaneously.

However, these people-meters, too, have their problems: people consciously and actively have to turn the meters on and off when they enter or exit the room in which the TV is on, and this can be bothersome. The search is now on for "passive" people-meters, devices that will automatically record who is watching, using sophisticated optics and/or other techniques such as sonar and infrared heat-sensing.[19] Nielsen has also come under criticism for the way in which it selected its people-meter panel, and the way it handles attrition among panel members, and so on. The three major TV networks recently announced a test of an entirely new system, which uses a meter that will not require wires to attach to the TV set but reads a universal program code embedded in each TV show's signal, and actually "talks" and "listens" to the viewer recognizing who they are, using voice recognition and synthesized speech, instead of requiring the viewer to punch in buttons everytime they turn the TV set on.[20]

Scanner data companies such as IRI and Nielsen also provide single-source data on the TV shows actually watched by consumers of different product categories and brands. Nielsen has a 40,000 household panel for such data in a limited number of local markets across the country; these households use paper-and-pencil TV viewing diaries.[21]

Weekly diaries provide the basic data gathering instrument for local television ratings. Nielsen is now the only provider of these data, after Arbitron's exit in 1993. Nielsen monitors over 200 local markets (called *DMAs*, or *designated market areas*). The sample size of the Nielsen effort (called the *Nielsen Station Index*, or *NSI*) ranges from 2,200 households in New York to several hundred in the smallest markets. Monthly reports are provided from four to seven times per year depending on the size of the market. During the three "sweep" months of November, February, and May, over 200 markets are covered by Nielsen. Over the course of a year's time, over 800,000 households will be involved in a television diary panel for one of the two services.

Similarly, diaries are also used by Arbitron to collect quarter-hour estimates of local radio listenership. Arbitron, a national ratings service, asks listeners aged twelve and over to fill out weekly diaries, detailing what stations they listened to, when and where, and their demographic data. Another service called RADAR (for Radio's All-Dimension Audience Research, from a company called Statistical Research) collects listenership data for the national radio networks, interviewing

2,000 prealerted but randomly selected listeners for seven consecutive days to get recall of radio programs listened to the day before. These data for both radio and local TV provide total size and demographic breakdowns for each station and program for every quarter hour, as well as estimates of the relevant cumulative audience, for one-week and beyond. Many services make their data available in printed form, on computer disk, and on-line, for quick reach and frequency estimation of alternative schedules.[22]

The quality of diary data can vary. Some respondents do not fill it out during the day but try to recall viewing activity. Such recall is especially difficult today when there are so many channels or stations, and consumers are often unfamiliar with a station's call letters. As a result, fringe and small-share stations generally do not fare as well from the diary as they do from the electronic meters. Another problem is that the homemaker is often the one who fills it out and is often not conversant with children's shows and lesser-known programs.

Other Media Data

In addition to estimates of the viewership, readership, and listenership of individual media vehicles, various other sources of media information also become useful in developing a media plan. These include estimates of how much your competitive brands are spending, by major medium and by geographical area, obtained through services such as the *Competitive Media Reporting/Leading National Advertisers (CMR/LNA) Reports* (for all media), *Media Records* (for newspapers), the *Rome Report* (for business and trade publications), *Broadcast Advertisers Report* (for television and radio), and so on. Media planners also rely on the *Standard Rate and Data Service (SRDS)* volumes for information on pricing and costs of different media vehicles. Background information on advertisers and advertising agencies is available in the *Standard Directory of Advertisers* and the *Standard Directory of Advertising Agencies*, the so-called "red books," in addition to the annual issues put out by *Advertising Age* magazine. Information about the potential buying power of different geographical areas is provided, among others, by the rankings and "Surveys of Buying Power" put out by *Sales Management* magazine. Many advertising agencies also issue annual guidebooks providing averages of costs and audiences, for use in "quick and dirty" estimation by their clients and internal staff.

Examples of some media data sources are provided in the Appendix to this Chapter.

Using Computerized Media Planning Models

Clearly, making media decisions can be difficult. There are usually a huge number of alternative feasible schedules, and huge masses of cost, audience size, and duplication data. (Chapter 1 provided details of the vast number of media options available and the advertising trends across those media.) Duplication data are usually only available for each pair of media vehicles (such as *Time* with *Newsweek*), and ways have to be found to estimate the total unduplicated reach in schedules with tens or hundreds of media vehicles, not just two. It is no wonder that simple CPM measures are often all that are relied on.

A better way to cope with this complexity, however, is to use a formal *media planning computer model* that will develop estimates of total duplication and then search for the "best" media schedule, given a budget constraint and facts (data) about the vehicles under consideration. Such media selection models have undergone an extensive evolution over the past thirty years, and may be classified into three main types.

The first major category of models use *mathematical optimization techniques*, such as linear, nonlinear, integer, dynamic, or goal programming, and attempt to maximize reach (or some other objective function, such as effective reach) within budget (and other) constraints. The first such widely heralded model was developed in 1961 by the BBDO advertising agency, and there have been various refinements since then. However, these models have all suffered from various severe limitations and are thus not widely used today. Many of these models have room for the user to assign subjective "weights" for each candidate media vehicle that is used in addition to their cost and readership (etc.) numbers, and some use a technique called the *analytic hierarchy process.*[23]

Their demise led to the second major category of models, called *simulation models*. In essence, these operate on real exposure data (obtained from a sample of consumers) and simulate what the reach and frequency exposures would be among these consumers for given media schedules. The frequency exposures obtained are sometimes also combined with a judgment-based response function, and the schedule with the highest response is then judged the most promising. Models in this category include the CAM model developed in Britain in the late 1960s, and various others since then. Their weakness is their inability to evaluate a large number of schedules, which becomes extremely computer-intensive; they are therefore typically used with only a few "candidate" schedules. Companies such as Interactive Marketing Services (IMS) and Telmar use such approaches, through which agencies can evaluate different schedules.

The third type of model is called *heuristic*, which means it develops a reasonably superior, but not necessarily optimal, solution for a media planning problem. An example would be Young & Rubicam's "High Assay" model of 1962, which added vehicles to a schedule based on marginal contribution (in cost per thousand, adjusting for various other factors). Other published models have included Little and Lodish's MEDIAC, Aaker's ADMOD, and so on. Fuller descriptions of these and other computer media models are found in a review by Roland Rust.[24] Very recent models use actual scanner-based, household-level viewing data, which allow estimation of the actual reach and frequency achieved by actual ads for given ad spending levels or GRPs, since individual level ad viewing data are involved. Some of these models try to maximize effective reach, whereas others even try to maximize predicted market share, through their recommended schedules.[25]

It is easily seen why such computer models can be valuable to a media planner, who can quickly see the trade-offs between cost, reach, and frequency for different alternative media schedules under consideration. It is important always to remember, however, that a media planner (or client) should not be seduced by the seeming objectivity of numbers on a computer printout. These numbers have to be modified for various qualitative, judgmental criteria, to which we now turn.

Qualitative Media Vehicle Source Effects

Media vehicle source effects are a measure of the qualitative value of the media vehicle. The concept is that an exposure in one vehicle might have more impact than an exposure of the same advertisement in another vehicle. For example, an advertisement for a women's dress line in *Vogue* might make more of an impact on those exposed than the same advertisement in *National Enquirer,* even if the audiences were the same. Similarly, it is claimed that *Esquire* or *GQ* provide an above-average vehicle for men's fashions because they are an appropriate environment for this type of advertising. The differential impact could be caused by editorial environment, physical reproduction qualities, or audience involvement. Similar source effects can apply to entire media classes, such as television versus newspapers, but these are not discussed here.

Several approaches to the measurement of the vehicle source effect are illustrated in Table 17–1. The target concentration index reflects the degree to which the editorial product reaches out to the target segment—for example, people who have traveled overseas. Each magazine is scored subjectively on this basis. The concept is that if the editorial content is involving, the advertisement will be read with more intensity.

A more objective measure is the number of *compatible pages*, or the number of editorial pages that the magazine has devoted during the last year to the subject in question, such as foreign travel. The reader opinion column is based upon the number of readers who indicate that the magazine is "very important in my life" or is "one of my favorites" or who "find considerable interest in its advertising pages." The in-home columns in Table 17–1 indicate the percentage of the magazine's audience who read the magazine in their home. It is probably believed that the in-home reader is less distracted and more likely to read an advertisement more thoroughly than an out-of-home reader, and so is of "higher quality."

There is general agreement that vehicle source effects do exist. As early as 1962, the Alfred Politz research organization demonstrated that an advertisement in *McCall's* would generate higher "quality" image and brand-preference ratings than identical ads placed in general readership magazines.[26] The kind of vehicle source effect being looked for will obviously depend on the campaign objectives. Thus, an awareness objective will involve different source-effect considerations than will communication or image-oriented objectives. However, there are at least six vehicle attributes that are often relevant considerations: unbiasedness, expertness, editorial "fit," prestige, mood created, and involvement.

Unbiasedness

If advertising concerned with political or social issues is considered, the position of the vehicle may indeed affect the communications. Many advertisers want their ads to be seen in publications that are respected for their objectivity, hoping that it will rub off as some kind of endorsement of their ads. It is also important that advertisers not be seen as attempting to curtail the editorial objectivity of media. In September 1993, Mercedes Benz told thirty U.S. magazines not to run its ads in any issue with articles that may reflect poorly on Germany or the company, but this led to such a public relations flap that the company rescinded the order within a few days.[27]

Expertness

Advertisements can usually be expected to reflect the degree of *expertise* associated with the area of interest of the vehicle in which they appear. Thus, the magazine *Tennis* is seen by its readers as a reliable source of information regarding new product developments in tennis, new playing techniques, new types of tennis court surfaces, and so on. The editors and writers are recognized authorities in competitive and instructive tennis. A reader, therefore, comes to the magazine willing to accept information from this source. The concept is that the reader's mental set does not change when he or she moves from an article in *Tennis* to an advertisement describing a new racket used by Boris Becker.

Obviously, a vehicle's perceived expertise will only rub off on relevant ads. A study found that ads for cooking products using a "reason why" approach benefited from placement in magazines rated as expert regarding cooking issues, but not ads for such products relying on "mood" appeals. Such mood ads benefited instead from placement in "prestige" magazines, while the "reason why" ads did not.[28]

Editorial Fit

A similar argument is made that ads are more effective when they appear near editorial matter that deals with relevant and supportive material. Researchers have argued for a strong *contextual priming effect*. When the editorial matter discusses some attribute, it makes it more likely that an ambiguous ad close by will be interpreted with that same attribute in mind, because the editorial matter makes that attribute more accessible in memory and more likely to be used in subsequent information evaluation. Thus, for an ad that says that a certain car is bigger-sized, if the nearby editorial matter talks about safety in automobiles the reader is more likely to think that the advertised bigger car is safer, instead of thinking that a bigger car must be less economical on fuel.[29] Magazines try to create special sections, or *advertorials*, that maximize the chances of such positive editorial rub-offs, as a sales device to sell more ad pages.

Prestige

A vehicle's *prestige* is another attribute commonly considered to be important for some product. *The New Yorker* has an exclusiveness and aloofness that might be expected to generate a similar feeling toward products advertised in it. Thus, if a product is endeavoring to build a status image, it may well be useful to advertise it in a high-status vehicle. Ads are frequently run in the Super Bowl telecast, at a cost of over $1.2 million for one thirty-second TV ad, more because of the prestige factor and "marquee value" and the attention these spots receive, rather than the

CPM economics of the size of audience being reached. The Super Bowl is, quite simply, the biggest advertising "event" there is in the United States.[30]

A study by Gert Assmus provides an interesting approach toward identifying the components of the vehicle source effect and demonstrates the relevance of the prestige dimension.[31] In his study, 125 people associated with media planning in the medical field rated six medical journals as to the journal's vehicle source effect and as to the extent to which the journals were perceived to have each of sixteen attributes. He found substantial differences in the vehicle source effect ratings. Furthermore, the three attributes that were the strongest predictors of the overall vehicle source effect rating were useful editorial content, prestige, and reference value. A knowledge of these elements could be of value in attempting to assign vehicle source weights in the medical context.

Mood Created

The influence of a vehicle's prestige may be viewed as working through the *mood* it creates among its readers. The concept is that a vehicle-induced mood will affect the impact of a commercial communication. In our context, if we were advertising a Daiquiri mix, we would like to know what mood is associated with a positive attitude toward this product. Then an attempt would be made to determine which vehicles tend to provide such a mood. If any media or vehicles uniquely provided such a mood, they might well also provide more effective exposure than other vehicles. Such an argument could lead to the use of women's glamor magazines for lipsticks, powders, and perfumes, *Self* or *Prevention* for nutrition-oriented advertisements, and *Sports Illustrated* for advertisements that relate to sports and exercise.

It also seems reasonable that vehicles that evoke likable moods are liked more, and that some of this liking gets transferred on the ad and then the brand. Researchers have found that such a transfer of "overall program liking" does indeed occur (at a generally weak level) for TV programs. The specific moods evoked by the TV program do not appear to transfer to the ad or brand, however. The overall liking transfer effect is stronger if the viewer is highly involved in the ad itself, so that the viewer forms an attitude towards the brand right when the ad is being shown, giving an opportunity for program liking at that viewing occasion to bias the brand attitude formed. The effect is weaker for ads that are run at the end of a commercial break or *pod*.[32]

Audience Involvement

According to several researchers and common sense, an involving vehicle should generate a superior commercial exposure than a vehicle that is not very interesting to the audience. Ads that interrupt highly involving programs should benefit because that *involvement* should spillover to the processing of the ad itself. Some researchers have suggested that instead of choosing media vehicles on the basis of the lowest cost-per-thousand exposures, advertisers should instead compute and use cost-per-thousand involved viewers. Their study found that as the level of audience involvement of a program rose, so did an ad's scores on recall, purchase intent, and so on.[33]

In terms of which programs are more involving, some agency executives found that in daytime programming, commercials in serial programs generated more recall and attentiveness than other program types, and situation comedies fared least well. However, it has also been pointed out that involvement in a program doesn't simply mean the level of arousal, active or tension. Involvement can actually be either *cognitive* ("the program makes me think"), *affective* ("it makes me feel deeply"), both, or neither. How people watch programs and how effective ads in those programs will be depends on what kind of involvement is being evoked.[34]

A too-involving program may actually hurt ad effectiveness. One forced-exposure lab setting compared commercials in a low-involvement program (*Brady Bunch*, a situation comedy) with the same commercials in a high-involvement program (*Baretta*, an action program).[35] The low-involvement environment was actually superior with respect to buying intentions and brand and sales message recall. Their findings suggest that a program can be so suspenseful and involving that it detracts from the advertising impact. Another magazine study also found that while readers rated recipe editorial matter less enjoyable and absorbing than they rated fiction and feature articles, readers who read the recipes remembered accompanying ads best while readers of the fiction articles remembered its surrounding ads worst.[36] Ads placed near an emotionally disturbing television news report suffered in recall, in another study.[37] Some other researchers have also argued that an ad that interrupts a very involving program might be the target of feelings of intense dislike.

Thus there seem to be ideas and evidence supporting both the "more involving programs are better" and "less involving programs are better" viewpoints. It has been suggested that which is better may depend on how strong (hard to counterargue) the ad itself is. If the ad is weak (easy to counterargue), a more involving program environment means that the consumer will think more about the program, and thus have fewer negative thoughts about the ad than otherwise, making the ad more effective in more involving programs. But if the ad is strong (harder to counterargue), a less involving program is better for ad effectiveness, since it will distract the consumer less from thinking the positive thoughts the ad is capable of evoking.[38]

MEDIA OPTION DECISIONS . . . .

The media planner is really concerned with advertisement audience size rather than vehicle audience size. Thus, in addition to selecting particular media vehicles, decisions also have to be made about the particular "unit" of advertising that is to be employed—fifteen-second versus thirty-second TV commercial, half-page versus full-page ad, inside-page magazine ad versus back-cover magazine ad, black-and-white versus four-color ad, and so on. A smaller ad costs less, allowing an advertiser to achieve greater reach and/or frequency for the same budget. For instance, fifteen-second TV spots cost 60 to 70 percent of the cost of thirty-second TV spots. But these smaller ads are also presumably less effective than the full-size ads (we present some data below), so some kind of trade-off decision needs to be made to find the optimal size, and so on.

One measurement approach to making such decisions in magazines is to use average *Starch recognition scores* or *Starch ad norms*. In the Starch survey, respondents are taken through a magazine and, for each advertisement, are asked if they saw it in the issue. The *noted* score is the percentage who answer affirmatively. Two companion measures are *seen/associated* (note the name of the advertiser) and *read most* (read more than 50 percent of the copy). The Starch measure dates back to 1923 and has been applied consistently since that early start. One indication of advertisement exposure for a vehicle would be the average Starch noted scores for the full-page advertisements contained in it.

Studies using the Starch data indicate that advertisement exposure will depend on the product class, the involvement of the segment in the product class, and on such media-option variables as the size and color of the advertisement, position, and copy approach.[39]

Advertisement Size and Color

Verling Trohdahl and Robert Jones determined that the size determines 40 percent of the variation in newspaper advertisement readership.[40] Since doubling the advertisement size falls short of doubling the readership, the use of larger advertisements needs to be justified on impact rather than audience-size grounds.

Regarding color, Starch has concluded that readership scores of full-page magazine advertisements using four colors are about 85 percent higher than scores of half-page advertisements using four colors.[41] However, the use of four colors only generates about 50 percent more readership than black-and-white for one-page and two-page advertisements.

Research on recall of TV commercials of different lengths has found that, at least in the short-run, fifteen-second commercials provide 70 or 80 percent of the recall or persuasion effect of thirty-second spots.[42] The difference between fifteen- and thirty-second spots is even less if multiple exposures to each, rather than a single exposure, are considered, and if the ads are "informational" in nature. The total frequency of brand mentions in the ad, rather than the length of the ad itself, is what seems to matter for informational ads. Thirty-second ads seem to have their greatest differential effect for ads that are emotional in executional style, and are exposed just once, on measures of brand name learning and brand attitude.[43]

Advertisement Location

Starch has concluded that advertisements on the back of a magazine will attract about 65 percent more readers than will those toward the middle. Advertisements on the inside front and back covers will attract about 30 percent more readers. Starch "Noted" and "Seen" scores are also higher for ads on the right rather than left page. Similarly, research on TV clutter has shown that TV spots that are at the beginning or the end of a string or pod of commercials—rather than being in the middle of the pod—do better on recall, and are hurt less by increased amounts of advertising clutter.[44]

Copy Execution

Starch found that advertisements very similar to the editorial matter of a magazine suffer somewhat in the noted score but gain 50 percent in terms of the read-most measure. Similarly, the use of comic continuity advertising—the use of panels like a comic strip—receive slightly less noted scores but substantially better read-most scores. Incidentally, larger-sized ad illustrations also help Starch recognition scores.

SCHEDULING AND TIMING DECISIONS . . . .

Decisions on how best to "space out" ads over time are based essentially on assumptions about how the advertising objective being aimed at (e.g., recall, or attitudes) respond to the presence of advertising exposures and decay when such advertising is absent. Based on these assumptions, the advertiser typically chooses from among three patterns of distributing the planned ads over a given time period: (1) *flighting*, or a burst of advertising alternated with periods of total inactivity; (2) *continuous*, or even, advertising spread evenly through the campaign time period; and (3) *pulsing*, a continuous base augmented by intermittent bursts of heavy advertising.

If, for example, it is believed that attitudes require heavy advertising to change (because of a possible S-shaped response function), but that such attitudes do not then decay rapidly once they are changed, such beliefs would suggest the need for flighting if changing attitudes was the advertising objective. Heavy bursts would be needed to change attitudes, and periods of no advertising could be risked because the changed attitudes would not decay rapidly. In contrast, if it was believed that recall both responded easily to advertising, and decayed rapidly if there was no advertising, then a recall-increasing ad campaign would probably need to be continuous. You need to be advertising all the time so as not to see recall drop off dangerously, but such advertising could be at a low frequency level since recall would respond even at these low levels.[45] Of course, such conceptual arguments would need to be modified for several pragmatic considerations: the needs of product seasonality, the need to avoid going head-to-head against a larger competitor, and the need to coordinate advertising pulses with scheduled sales promotion events, for example.

Several studies exist that have empirically examined the shape of the response and decay functions for recall (fewer studies have looked at attitudes). A host of studies, including the Ebbinghaus experiments, have confirmed the commonsense notion that recall declines over time and that this decline is greatest at the outset and diminishes over time. Agency researcher Hubert Zielske conducted a field experiment that is regarded as a classic study of repetition and forgetting.[46] Two groups of women, randomly selected from a telephone directory, were mailed thirteen different advertisements from the same newspaper advertising campaign for an ingredient food. One group received an advertisement weekly for thirteen weeks. The other group received the same thirteen mailings but at intervals of four weeks during the year. Throughout the year, aided only by mention of the product class, recall was measured by telephone interviews. No single person was interviewed in person more than once. A person can become sensitized to the advertisement after an interview; if a person has been interviewed twice, the second interview would usually be biased. The results of the study are shown in Figure 17–1 with the learning and forgetting process graphically displayed.

Zielske's data are usually interpreted to mean that a flight or pulse of ads leads to a higher (temporary) peak in recall, whereas a continuous (evenly spaced) timing strategy would be better for products that required the maximization of average weekly recall (not simply a one-time higher peak in recall). This would imply that if a quick or seasonal peak effect in recall was desired, pulsing policies are superior. Note also that the flighted schedule led to greater and more rapid subsequent fall-of in recall than the even schedule. While the flighting schedule led to a higher one-time peak, it is very important to note that the total number of *recall-weeks* (the number of weeks multiplied by the appropriate recall rate) was higher

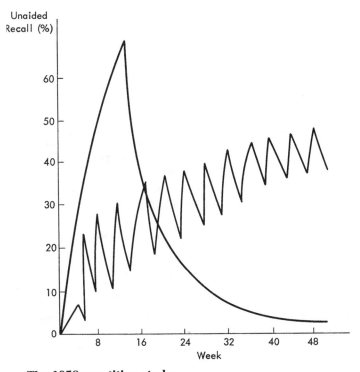

Figure 17–1.   The 1958 repetition study.

Source: Adapted from Hubert A. Zielske, "The Remembering and Forgetting of Advertising," Journal of Marketing, *American Marketing Association, 23, January 1959, pp. 239–243.*

under the even schedule, especially if the data are not *smoothed* (as they have in the graph presented here).[47] Similar results were later found by Edward Strong, who used a computer simulation model (built on data from a two field experiments, including Zielske's original experiment); a flighting schedule led to higher peak recall than a more even schedule.[48]

Leonard Lodish, one of the developers of the MEDIAC media planning model, estimated the forgetting function using data from a study of advertising retention in five magazines by W. R. Simmons.[49] The retention measured was the ability of readers of a specific issue to distinguish among advertisements that appeared in that issue and ones that did not. Lodish found that the retention measure fell by 25 percent each week. Strong, in his simulation, found that recall fell by over 45 percent per week and that the decay over several weeks was proportional to the square root of the number of weeks since last exposure.[50]

Hubert Zielske and Walter Henry later examined seventeen tracking studies involving six established products.[51] A tracking study is a repeated survey over time to track a measure such as awareness. Unaided recall of television advertising copy was the measure in this case. The recall level varied from 10 to 16 percent and the weekly GRP ranged from 40 to 200. A regression analysis yielded the following model:

$$\Delta A_t = 0.30 W_t - 0.10 A_{t-1}$$

where ΔA_t = percentage-point change in unaided recall in week t
W_t = gross rating points received in week t
A_{t-1} = unaided recall level in week $t-1$

The first term indicates, for example, that 100 GRP per week will, on the average, produce three percentage points of unaided recall. The second term in the formula represents the average forgetting rate. For example, if recall in the prior week had been at the 15-percent level, then in the absence of further advertising, recall would be expected to drop to 13.5 percent. Thus, from one week to the next, just 10 percent would be forgotten. That, of course, is less than the 25 or 45 percent found by Lodish and Strong in their studies, demonstrating that these decay functions will be unique to the situation involved.

The point of these efforts to estimate parameters is not so much to indicate specific "universal" parameter values but rather to illustrate approaches that can be taken to estimate functions in given contexts. Further, it is vital to note that the response and decay function parameters are very likely a function also of the measure being modeled—recognition, recall, and attitudes are each likely to behave differently. We know much more about recall than about recognition or attitudes, although it would be reasonable to speculate that the last two would decline more slowly over time than would recall.[52]

It should be noted, in conclusion, that the superiority of flighting or pulsing in maximizing peak levels of recall has been examined not only in the field experiments described earlier, but also in many of the mathematical models built by management scientists, in which an optimal (recall- or profit-maximizing) scheduling strategy is sought. Not surprisingly, the answers obtained depend on the assumptions made about the shape of the decay function, though most of these analyses argue for the superiority of pulsing strategies.[53]

CREATIVITY IN MEDIA PLANNING . . . .

There is a misperception among many students and practitioners of advertising that the entire function of planning, scheduling and buying media is a boring, numbers-oriented task that is not very creative and exciting, certainly compared to the copy and creative function. Reflecting this, the media departments in many agencies are staffed by more junior and less well-paid people; it is certainly more common to find "creative stars" in an agency than "media stars."

Yet this perception is very dangerous, even if it is not entirely untrue. There are many celebrated anecdotes about agencies saving their clients an enormous amount of media money or greatly leveraging the payoff from a small media budget as a result of a creative choice of media vehicles or timing of exposures, and so on. For instance, one magazine aiming its ads at media planners in New York City—convincing them that it was a good media buy—saved money and gathered attention not by placing forgettable ads in the advertising trade journals, but instead by identifying all the bus shelter panels close to the entrances of major New York agencies, and placing its ads on those panels. Another creative use of media timing is that of a certain exercise videotape, which cleverly times its radio ads right on New Years' Day, when consumers make yet another New Years' resolution to shed excess weight. Never forget that media, too, is an area in which tremendous creativity can be used!

MEDIA BUYING AND ORGANIZATION . . . .

Once a final media schedule is determined, using the criteria just discussed, the actual negotiation and buying of the media units (television and radio time, magazine and newspaper space, etc.) have to occur. While the buying of media was traditionally done by the advertising agency that did the creative work on the account, this pattern has recently begun to change. Some clients (such as Chrysler and Nestlé) have begun to consolidate all the media buying for all their accounts (brands) at one agency, rather than spread it over several agencies. In turn, agencies have begun to market their media planning and buying services as stand-alone businesses serving clients that are not that agency's creative clients. Other clients have separated the media-buying task from the creative one and have the media buying done either in-house or through a media-buying service (after modifying the fee structure appropriately for the agency that does the creative work). The media-buying service consolidates buys from multiple clients when it negotiates with the media and can often save clients between 15 and 25 percent on the rates they pay for television and radio ad time.[54]

Such media buying services now place over 30 percent of all U.S. spot television time. The largest U.S. media-buying company, Western International Media, claimed billings of $1 billion in 1994, while its major competitor, SFM Media Corp., was at about $700 million. Western International has offices in thirty U.S. cities and employs nearly 1,100 people. In October 1994, it was acquired by the Interpublic agency group, which can therefore offer cheaper media buys to the clients of its network agencies. Such media buying services are even bigger outside the U.S.: the Paris-based Carat International buys about 15 percent of all European media buys, and in France about 50 to 60 percent of all media buys are done through firms like it.[55]

The underlying reason for these changes has been the negotiating benefit, to the client, of buying a bigger dollar amount of media time or space from each media supplier. The rates for media are rarely fixed in stone, though they may appear to be so when described on a rate card. Broadcast media, and increasingly magazines as well, undertake a negotiation process with agencies and clients taking into account the total size of the media buy as well as the supply-and-demand situation at the time of negotiation. These negotiations determine not just the dollar amounts to be paid but also the particulars of favored page (or time) placement, and so on. As a result of the mergers among media companies (such as Time Warner), large advertisers now negotiate for major cross-media deals with these conglomerates that include magazine ads, direct mail promotions, sales promotions, even product placements in movies.

Since negotiations are involved, the expertise of the agency media buyers obviously matters a lot. For this reason, advertising agencies and media buying services have media buying units in which media buyers specialize according to the medium and the geographical areas involved. Thus, network TV buys are typically made by a different media buyer than one who specializes in local TV stations in, say, Los Angeles. Radio buyers and print buyers are also different people, as are those who perform media research and media planning functions. In dealing with local (nonnational) media, a media buyer typically deals with a "media rep" firm that represents that local station or newspaper nationally rather than with that local media vehicle directly.

These negotiations are complex, and media buys are made at different rates depending on the conditions involved. Network television time, for instance, can either be bought several months ahead by a high-volume buyer wanting a deal covering an entire season (called an *upfront* buy) or bought in the quarter of the year when the ad will air (a *scatter* buy). Of the $9 billion or so that the four major U.S. TV networks earn every year in advertising revenue, about $4.0 billion is sold through upfront deals.[56]

If bought in the upfront market, the advertiser often receives an exposure-size guarantee—the number of people guaranteed to watch the show—but is limited in terms of cancellation flexibility. If the network fails to deliver the promised audience, or if the airing of an ad is somehow botched, the network is typically obliged to "make good" by offering extra time free of charge to make up for the shortfall. If the buy is made in the scatter market, the price paid depends on the supply-and-demand situation at that time: television time, like airline seats and hotel rooms, is a perishable commodity, and prices can move up and down very rapidly, depending on how eager the two sides are to consummate the transaction.

The price paid also varies with the specificity of the schedule: the rates are higher if the advertiser wants his spot to run at a fixed time of day, or fixed-page location, rather than anywhere (the latter is called *run of paper*, or *ROP*, in newspapers, and *run of time* on radio). Further, as if this was not complex enough, the media vehicle reserves the right to yank your spot off the air if all you pay is a lower *preemptible* rate, than a higher *nonpreemptible* rate. This complexity is one reason why media buying is best done by seasoned media buying professionals. The reading at the end of this part of the book describes the process.

THE MEDIA PLAN FOR THE BROILER. . . . .

Now that we have discussed the complete media planning, scheduling, and buying process, it is useful to see what an actual media plan might look like. A simulated television plan for one of the leading fast-food chains, The Broiler, is shown in Figure 17–2. The total advertising and promotional budget is around $250 million, of which well over one-half is earmarked for television. The television plan illustrates a segmentation strategy and several types of scheduling alternatives.

The children segment, including teens, is an important market. The Broiler has always lagged McDonald's with respect to children but has made inroads with the St. Bernard advertising spokesman. The St. Bernard's campaign with additional characters and a "fun" theme is planned. As the figure indicates, national buys of 140 GRP per week will be supported by 300 GRPs per week on local television. Six Saturday morning pulses were planned during the year. In such a pulse, thirty-second commercials would appear every half-hour from 8:30 A.M. to the conclusion of children's Saturday programming.

The young adult market, the eighteen- to thirty-five-year-olds is another important segment for The Broiler. Research showed that within this segment, it was leading on the product quality dimension. For example, in terms of having hot and tasty food, The Broiler received a 88 percent rating, about 20 to 30 points above its rivals. Ratings for "value" were much weaker. The strategy was to lead from strength by focusing upon the product quality dimension. To attract this segment, the media plan suggested 500 to 600 GRPs per week for the adult segment. Five adult pulses were planned, each of which will translate into a thirty-second spot every thirty minutes on each network during prime time.

The plan called for advertising to focus upon certain themes for relatively long periods and to be linked to simple, tested promotions. For example, a hamburger theme was to be used in January and February. In March and April, the emphasis was to be on breakfasts, supported by a breakfast promotion.

Research indicated that The Broiler had not penetrated the heavy user group sufficiently, the group that accounts for 50 percent of the total market. Thus, more attention was focused upon the heavy user segment, especially African Americans, Hispanics, and the ten-to seventeen-year-old set. The prime-time adult schedule included spots featuring African Americans. The effort toward African Americans also included *Ebony* and *Jet* magazines and African American radio. The Hispanic thrust used Spanish television.

Women were to be reached not only by the daytime national media effort, but by a $2 million campaign in *Family Circle*, *Good Housekeeping*, and *People*.[57]

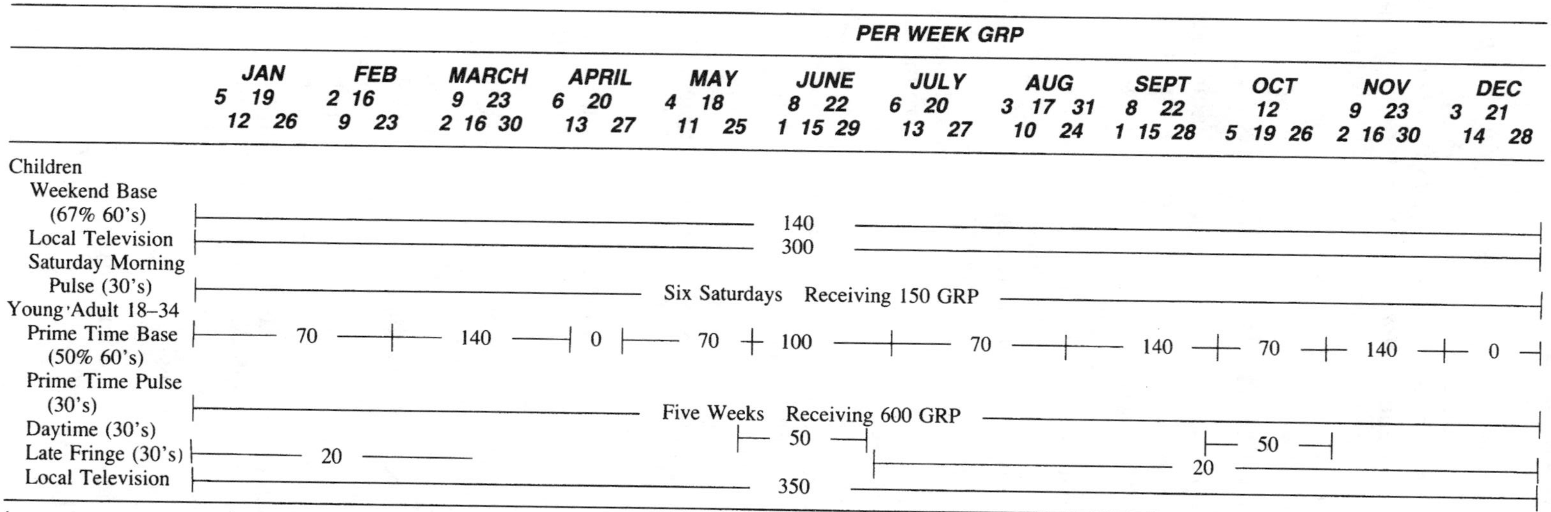

PER WEEK GRP

	JAN	FEB	MARCH	APRIL	MAY	JUNE	JULY	AUG	SEPT	OCT	NOV	DEC
	5 19	2 16	9 23	6 20	4 18	8 22	6 20	3 17 31	8 22	12	9 23	3 21
	12 26	9 23	2 16 30	13 27	11 25	1 15 29	13 27	10 24	1 15 28	5 19 26	2 16 30	14 28

Children
Weekend Base
(67% 60's) 140
Local Television 300
Saturday Morning
Pulse (30's) .... Six Saturdays   Receiving 150 GRP
Young Adult 18-34
Prime Time Base
(50% 60's) 70   140   0   70   100   70   140   70   140   0
Prime Time Pulse
(30's) .... Five Weeks   Receiving 600 GRP   50
Daytime (30's) 50
Late Fringe (30's) 20   20
Local Television 350

[1] Late fringe is the two hour period following prime time.

Figure 17-2.   National television media plan for The Broiler.

612.........

SUMMARY. . . . .

The selection of the type of medium, such as television, radio, or magazines will depend in part upon the number of people in the target audience that the medium can deliver, as well as compatibility with the needs of the creative message, needs regarding timing and flexibility, and so on.

A basic concern in determining which specific media vehicle to select is cost per thousand, or CPM, for print and cost per rating point, or CPRP, for television, both of which are a measure of total exposures per dollar cost. However, it is usually useful also to measure reach (the number of people exposed at least once) and average frequency (the average number of exposures per exposed person). Exposure decisions add precision to an understanding of what the media plan is actually delivering.

Data sources were discussed. One approach to measuring print readership is recent reading, asking people whether they read a magazine last month. The people-meter attaches to TV sets and monitors the stations watched in order to obtain measures of television program viewing. In some contexts, it can be relevant to evaluate vehicles in terms of their expertness, prestige, mood, and audience involvement.

Decisions as to media options, for example, the size and color for print ads and length for TV and radio ads, must also be made as do decisions as to scheduling/timing, the use of flighting, pulsing, or continuous advertising. The actual buying can be done by the advertising agency or by a specialized media buying organization.

DISCUSSION QUESTIONS . . . .

1. A basic component of a media model objective function involves counting exposures generated by an insertion schedule. The remaining components introduced in this chapter attempt to qualify the exposures, the potential worth of the audience member, and so on. How else might you want to qualify exposures? What other components might be added to the list?

2. Comment on the media plan for The Broiler. What would the "value of successive exposure" function look like? How would you go about deciding upon the mix of sixty- and thirty-second commercials?

3. You are an advertising manager for a new line of package marking devices for use by retail food stores. Your advertising is designed to create awareness among chain store managers. Two schedules with equal cost are proposed. One uses many trade journals and will reach 10,000 store managers with a frequency of 1.1. The other reaches fewer journals and will reach 4,000 with a frequency of 5.4. Which of these two alternatives is superior? What other factors should be considered?

4. In a survey of housewives, the readership of *Atlantic Monthly* was exaggerated and the and the readership of *Soap Opera Digest* seemed much less than circulation figures indicated. Why would respondents incorrectly report their read-

ership in this manner? Can you think of any measure, perhaps unobtrusive, to avoid this bias?

5. Of the recent-reading and through-the-book methods, which do you prefer? Why?

6. What are the limitations of the people-meter?

7. Generate vehicle source effect values for a set of magazines or TV programs using your own subjective judgment, assuming a product and an advertising objective. For example, suppose that a product-effectiveness ad was generated for an electric frypan and the magazine alternatives were *Women's Day, TV Guide, Vogue, Elle, McCall's,* and *Time.* Justify your set of values.

8. Under what circumstances would it be effective to pulse advertising rather than spreading it out evenly? Evaluate the strategy of The Broiler to engage in ten or so television pulse campaigns during the year.

9. What are the advantages of using a media buying organization?

10. Given the data in Table 17–4, select media vehicles using CPM figures for (a) all adults and (b) women only.

NOTES

1. For reviews and data on the changing media environment, see Peter B. Turk and Helen Katz, "Making Headlines: An Overview of Key Happenings in Media Planning, Buying, and Research from 1985–1991," *Journal of Current Issues and Research in Advertising,* 14, no. 2 (Fall 1992), 19–34; Dean M. Krugman and Roland T. Rust, "The Impact of Cable and VCR Penetration on Network Viewing: Assessing the Decade," *Journal of Advertising Research,* 33, no. 1 (January/February 1993), 67–73; and "Madison Avenue, Slow to Grasp Interactivity, Could Be Left Behind," *The Wall Street Journal,* December 7, 1993, p. A1.

2. "Blasted Space Ad," *Advertising Age,* June 7, 1993, p. 46.

3. "First Look at Superhighway," Advertising Age, July 26, 1993, p. 8; *The Wall Street Journal,* December 7, 1993, cited earlier.

4. For some news articles on the rapidly-evolving media environment, see the "Interactive Media and Marketing" specials in *Advertising Age.* See also "Advertisers face an Interactive Future" in *Marketing News,* July 4, 1994, p. 10, and the Forum section in *Advertising Age,* May 23, 1994, p. 24.

5. "Newspaper readers get choosier," *Advertising Age,* July 26, 1993, p. 22.

6. Bruce L. Stern and Alan J. Resnick, "Information Content in Television Advertising: A Replication and Extension," *Journal of Advertising Research* (June/July 1991), 36–46; Avery M. Abernathy, "The Information Content of Newspaper Advertising," *Journal of Current Issues and Research in Advertising,* 14, no. 2 (Fall 1992), 63–68.

7. "New Cars Make Magazines Tempting for Detroit," *Advertising Age,* October 19, 1992, p. S-2.

8. Julie A. Edell and Kevin L. Keller, "The Information Processing of Coordinated Media Campaigns," *Journal of Marketing Research,* 26 (May 1989), 149–163; "Radio Study Tells Imagery Potential," *Advertising Age,* September 6, 1993, p. R3.

9. Avery M. Abernathy, "Television Exposure: Programs vs. Advertising," *Journal of Current Issues and Research in Advertising* (1990), 61–77, and "Differences Between Advertising and Program Exposure for Car Radio Listening," *Journal of Advertising Research* (April/May 1991), 33–42.

10. Peter J. Danaher and Roland T. Rust, "Linking Segmentation Studies," *Journal of Advertising Research,* 32, no. 3 (May/June 1992), 18–23.

11. Henry Assael and David F. Poltrack, "Using Single Source Data to Select TV Programs: Part II," *Journal of Advertising Research,* 33, no. 1 (January/February 1993), 48–56.

12. George B. Murray and John R. G. Jenkins, "The Concept of 'Effective Reach' in Advertising," *Journal of Advertising Research*, 32, no. 3 (May/June 1992), 34–42.
13. For an excellent technical review, see Roland Rust, *Advertising Media Models: A Practical Guide* (Lexington, MA: Lexington Books, 1986).
14. Peter J. Danaher and Roland T. Rust, "Media Exposure in Target Markets," *Journal of Current Issues and Research in Advertising*, 15, no. 1 (Spring 1993), 77–86; Peter J. Danaher, "A Canonical Expansion Model for Multivariate Media Exposure Distributions: A Generalization of the 'Duplication of Viewing Law' " *Journal of Marketing Research*, 28 (August 1991), 361–367.
15. Yvan Boivin and Denis Coulombe, "Are Exposure Distributions Really Necessary?" *Journal of Current Issues and Research in Advertising* (1990), 227–238.
16. "Readership Figures for Periodicals Stir Debate in Publishing Industry," *The Wall Street Journal*, September 2, 1987, p. 21.
17. Valentine Appel, "Anatomy of a Magazine Auidence Estimate: The ARF Comparability Study Revisited," *Journal of Advertising Research*, 33, no. 1 (Jan./Feb. 1993), 11–17. See also the article by Daniel T. Mallett, Jr., "The Relationship of Screen-in rates and readership levels in MRI and SMRB," in the same issue, pp. 18–22.
18. *The New York Times*, September 15, 1994, p. C17.
19. *Business Week*, June 18, 1990, p. 27, and Daozheng Lu and David A. Kiewit, "Passive People Meters: A First Step," *Journal of Advertising Research* (June/July 1987), 9–14.
20. *The Wall Street Journal*, February 4, 1994, p. B13.
21. "Nielsen Marketing may bring back TV viewing diaries," *Advertising Age*, October 19, 1992, p. 6.
22. "Agencies hope for Research Standard," *Advertising Age*, September 4, 1991, p. S-10; "Tracking the Networks," *Advertising Age*, September 6, 1993, p. R7.
23. Robert F. Dyer, Ernest H. Forman, and Mohammad A. Mustafa, "Decision Support for Media Selection Using the Analytic Hierarchy Process," *Journal of Advertising*, 21, no. 1 (March 1992), 59–72.
24. Rust, *Advertising Media Models*.
25. James H. Pedrick and Fred S. Zufryden, "Evaluating the Impact of Advertising Media Plans: A Model of Consumer Purchase Dynamics using Single-Source Data," *Marketing Science*, 10, no. 2 (Spring 1991), 111–130; Fred S. Zufryden and James H. Pedrick, "Measuring the Reach and Frequency Elasticities of Advertising Media," *Marketing Letters*, 4, no. 3 (1993), 215–225; C. Samuel Craig and Avijit Ghosh, "Using Household-Level Viewing Data to Maximize Effective Reach," *Journal of Advertising Research*, 33, no. 1 (January/February 1993), 38–47.
26. *A Measurement of Advertising Effectiveness: The Influence of Audience Selectivity and Editorial Environment*. Report by Alfred Politz, Inc., November 1962.
27. "Mercedes in Full Retreat on Ad Placement Order," *Advertising Age*, September 20, 1993, p. 2.
28. David A. Aaker and Philip K. Brown, "Evaluating Vehicle Source Effects," *Journal of Advertising Research*, 12 (August 1972), 11–16.
29. Youjae Yi, "Cognitive and Affective Priming Effects of the Context for Print Advertising," *Journal of Advertising*, 19, no. 2 (1990), 40–48; see also his related articles in the *Journal of Consumer Research* (September 1990), 215–222, and the *Journal of Advertising* (March 1993), 1–10.
30. "Roster for Super Bowl Ads Fills Up Early," *The Wall Street Journal,* December 13, 1993, p. B6.
31. Gert Assmus, "An Empirical Investigation into the Perception of Vehicle Source Effects," *Journal of Advertising* (Winter 1978), 4–10.
32. John P. Murry, Jr., John L. Lastovicka, and Surendra N. Singh, "Feeling and Liking Responses to Television Programs: An Examination of Two Explanations for Media Context Effects," *Journal of Consumer Research*, 18 (March 1992), 441–451.
33. David W. Lloyd and Kevin J. Clancy, "CPMs versus CPMIs: Implications for Media Planning," *Journal of Advertising Research*, 31, no. 4 (Aug./Sept. 1991), 34–44.

34. Donna L. Hoffman and Rajeev Batra, "Viewer Response to Programs: Dimensionality and Concurrent Behavior," *Journal of Advertising Research,* 31, no. 4 (Aug./Sept. 1991), 46–56.

35. Gary F. Soldow and Victor Principe, "Response to Commercials as a Function of Program Context," *Journal of Advertising Research,* 21 (April 1981), 59–64.

36. Claire E. Norris and Andrew M. Colman, "Context Effects on Recall and Recognition of Magazine Advertisements," *Journal of Advertising,* 21, no. 3 (September 1992), 37–46.

37. Norbert Mundorf, Dolf Zillman, and Dan Drew, "Effects of Disturbing Televised Events on the Acquisition of Information from Subsequently Presented Commercials," *Journal of Advertising,* 20, no. 1 (1991), 46–53.

38. Punam Anand and Brian Sternthal, "The Effects of Program Involvement and Ease of Message Counterarguing on Advertising Effectiveness," *Journal of Consumer Psychology,* 1, no. 3 (1992), 225–238.

39. An exhaustive listing of studies that have analyzed Starch scores can be found in Adam Finn, "Print Ad Recognition Readership Scores: An Information Processing Perspective," *Journal of Marketing Research,* 25 (May 1988), 168–177.

40. Verling Trohdahl and Robert Jones, "Predictors of Newspaper Advertising Viewership," *Journal of Advertising Research,* 5 (March 1965), 23–27.

41. Daniel Starch, *Measuring Advertising Readership and Results* (New York: McGraw-Hill, 1966), p. 61.

42. Gordon L. Patzer, "Multiple Dimensions of Performance for 30-second and 15-second Commercials," *Journal of Advertising Research,* 31, no. 4 (Aug./Sept. 1991), 18–25.

43. Surendra N. Singh and Catherine A. Cole, "The Effects of Length, Content, and Repetition on Television Commercial Effectiveness," *Journal of Marketing Research,* 30 (February 1993), 91–104.

44. Peter H. Webb and Michael L. Ray, "Effects of TV Clutter," *Journal of Advertising Research,* 9, no. 3 (1979), 7–12.

45. For a conceptual development of this idea, see Rajeev Batra and Michael L. Ray, "Advertising Situations: The Implications of Differential Involvement and Accompanying Affect Responses," in *Information Processing Research in Advertising,* R. J. Harris, ed. (Hillsdale, NJ: Erlbaum, 1983), pp. 127–151.

46. Hurbert A. Zielske, "The Remembering and Forgetting of Advertising," *Journal of Marketing,* 23 (March 1959), 239–243.

47. Julian L. Simon, "What Do Zielske's Real Data Really Show About Pulsing?" *Journal of Marketing Research,* 16 (August 1979), 415–420.

48. Edward C. Strong, "The Spacing and Timing of Advertising," *Journal of Advertising Research,* 17, no. 6 (December 1977), 25–31.

49. Leonard M. Lodish, "Empirical Studies on Individual Responses to Exposure Patterns," *Journal of Marketing Research,* 8 (May 1971), 214–216.

50. Edward C. Strong, "The Use of Field Experimental Observations in Estimating Advertising Recall," *Journal of Marketing Research,* 11 (November 1974), 369–378.

51. Hubert A. Zielske and Walter A. Henry, "Remembering and Forgetting Television Ads," *Journal of Advertising Research,* 20 (April 1980), 7–13.

52. Regarding the decay and testing of recognition, see Herbert Krugman, "Memory Without Recall, Exposure Without Perception," *Journal of Advertising Research,* 17 (August 1977), 7–12, and Surendra N. Singh and Michael L. Rothschild, "Recognition as a Measure of Learning from Television Commercials," *Journal of Marketing Research,* 20 (August 1983), 235–248.

53. See, for instance, M. W. Sasieni, "Optimal Advertising Strategies," *Marketing Science,* 8, no. 4 (1989), 358–370; H. Simon, "ADPULS: An Advertising Model with Wearout and Pulsation," *Journal of Marketing Research,* 19 (October 1982), 352–363; V. Mahajan and E. Muller, "Advertising Pulsing Policies for Generating Awareness for New Products," *Marketing Science,* 5 (Spring 1986), 89–111; Sehoon Park and Minhi Hahn, "Pulsing in a Discrete Model of Advertising Competition," *Journal of Marketing Research,* 28 (November 1991), 397–405; J. Miguel Villas-Boas, "Predicting Advertising Pulsing Policies in an

Oligopoly: A Model and an Empirical Test," *Marketing Science*, 12, no. 1 (Winter 1993), 88–102.

54. *The New York Times*, October 31, 1994, p. B10.
55. See Turk and Katz, 1992, cited earlier, and the special Media Buying and Planning section in *Advertising Age*, July 26, 1993.
56. Figures from *Advertising Age*, July 26, 1993, p. 38, and *Journal of Advertising*, 21, no. 1 (March 1992), 1.
57. For a similar plan, see "McDonald's 1979 Plan: Beat Back the Competition," *Advertising Age*, February 19, 1979, p. 1.

READING. . . . .

CHECKING IN AT CHECKERBOARD SQUARE. .

Marianne Paskowski and Pam Ellis-Simons

It's late January and the snow is clogging New York's streets, but William Claggett, Ralston Purina's vice president and director of marketing and advertising services, hardly notices. He has May on his mind. That's the time when the network upfront buying season gets underway, and the time when Ralston traditionally leads the pack in committing its dollars. Claggett is making his way to NBC headquarters to learn anything he can—even this early in the game— that might later give Ralston an edge over its competitors.

This early-bird syndrome is only possible because, unlike many other companies, the marketing and media functions at Ralston-Purina cooperate handsomely with each other. Well in advance of the big buy, the two departments have adroitly meshed their needs and squared away their budgets. Ralston knows what it wants.

Ralston's success—its sales and earnings growth rates top the chart in the pet food world—is largely attributable to this unstinting eye for detail. The style at Checkerboard Square is to plot out as completely as possible what courses of action are most appropriate and opportunistic for its stable of brands. While best known for pet products such as its Dog, Cat and Puppy Chows, and its Chex line of cereals, Ralston also houses fast-fooder Jack In The Box, in agriculture division which sells cattle, hog and chicken feed, and, with the acquisition of Continental Bakeries, such all-American classics as Twinkies and Wonder Bread.

Ralston spends heftily to market and advertise this lineup. Last year, it is estimated that the company shelled out more than $200 million in support of some 75 brands, with about 70% targeted towards network TV. These sums are not spent lightly: Ralston has a reputation for being a thorough, "totally inflexible negotiator" who knows just what it wants and what it will pay to get it, in the words of one executive who has sat across from the company as it wrangles its media buys.

Indeed, it is nearly legend that it is well-prepared Ralston who kicks off the annual upfront network tv buying season. While its buttoned-down Claggett denies any "compulsion to be first," he admits the company is never too far back.

Under Claggett's tutelage, the media budgeting and buying season is seen as a supreme challenge and a chance to test one's mettle. Unlike many of its competitors, which keep the marketing and media departments separate, though equal, Ralston gets both groups of specialists working together. Furthermore, even though Ralston has an agency roster that includes some of the largest and best, the company relies heavily on input from its own in-house agency and veteran media group.

Simply put, Ralston is a believer in the theory that the correct use of media can be the crucial key in unlocking a brand's full market potential. As a consequence, Ralston has set out to become more expert than the experts.

For example, Ralston goes through an elaborate drill in preparation for the network tv upfront buy, which usually commences around May or June. Its in-house media team—15 members strong—starts gathering intelligence on the network upfront market in January, early by most standards. It produces an analysis of market conditions in general and forecasts pricing, with input from its agencies and in-house group. Some members of the media team even trek out to Hollywood to get an early fix on new pilots from producers and programers. "Since we are among the first to buy every year, we don't have the luxury of waiting until Variety *covers what they're going to do," says Claggett sarcastically.*

Further into the network cycle, Ralston starts agonizing about share estimates for the networks' fall lineups, culling data from all 10 of its agencies and debating those numbers until everyone is in agreement. "I've been told on good authority that other clients don't get this deeply involved with estimating,"notes Claggett, with more than a hint of pride. (See sidebar, "47 Steps to the Upfront Buy.")

"One agency may say Crazy Like A Fox *is going to do a 22 share, another might say a 32 share, and everyone else will come in at 27–28," relates Claggett. "We then have a little debate where we can change the consensus, and many times do, depending on the reasoning behind it. But we* never *just mathematically average them out," he says with some vehemence.*

Does all this result in a better network deal for Ralston? One network observer, at least, thinks it does. "Ralston, unlike many advertisers, knows exactly what they want when they come to upfront. They say, 'Give me 26 commercials on this show and 38 on that one and how much will it cost.' Most people come in and say 'I have $10 million, I want to reach women 18–35 on Monday, Wednesday and Friday. What do you have?' Ralston, however, picks high-rated shows and winds up buying a schedule that actually runs, which is a rarity these days. Because they are so early, they get what they want, even if they have to pay a little more for it since they're buying per unit cost at that time." He sums up, "They're totally inflexible negotiators. They know what they want and they get it."

NBC's senior vice president of network sales, Robert Blackmore, agrees that Ralston "does an outstanding job in selecting quality shows."

Blackmore points to another Ralston advantage—its longstanding relationship (15 years) with the Paul Schulman media buying service. "One of the advantages to that setup is that Schulman can concentrate on the Ralston package—he has the time to spend on all of the nuances because he's basically concentrating on that one account," Blackmore explains.

While Ralston's attention to detail in network circles is well known, what is less understood is that all media gets put under this high-power microscope. In magazine buys, for example, Ralston's media people call on publishers and editors in New York each September to give each book its yearly report card on the previous year's performance. They also lay out Ralston's expectations for the next year. Big deal, skeptics might say—but the report card has worked for Ralston.

Claggett looks at magazine buys much like he does network TV. Unlike many advertisers which have their agencies buying magazine schedules for specific brands, Ralston buys a corporate package upfront. In addition to this upfront buy, Ralston buys magazines opportunistically. "We are able to take advantage of last minute offers or remnant space right before magazine closings with what we call our opportunistic magazine program because this is all preplanned in advance," he says.

"The challenge is to know as much about a product as the marketing person does," stresses Linda Pavlenko, group media director and a 13-year Ralston veteran. "It's really a team effort, and our relationship with marketing is very good," she reiterates.

And vice versa. Newly recruited brand managers lose little time in learning the world of gross rating points (GRPs). Brand managers are required to attend a series of media seminars and are put into immediate contact with the media department. "In some companies the media department is quite separate from the brand group, but here we discuss things back and forth," Claggett explains, who has spent 18 of his 53 years at Ralston.

For example, at budget time in the early spring, brand managers approach media per-

sonnel to develop final marketing plans for the upcoming year. They base their requests on information that media has been feeding into the brand management funnel throughout the year, not just during the formal budgeting process. That data accommodates the ever-changing needs of brands. When a competitor springs an unpleasant surprise, brand managers have the media data at their fingertips to retaliate. As a result, brand managers, well versed in the ways of media, have a fair idea of what media strategies they should be pursuing.

Media is equally well prepared. "It's not as though media gets involved at the point where approved budgets are coming together," explains Jack Shubert, director of advertising services for Ralston's grocery products division. "Media has been involved with marketing from the very beginning, from the 'blue skies' preplanning sessions and all the way through," he emphasizes.

THE IN-HOUSE ADVANTAGE . . . .

This type of cooperation would not be possible without the presence of an active, in-house media department with clout. Without doubt, Ralston puts a premium on just such an entity.

The best in-house media departments, in Claggett's mind, have had that kind of long-standing, side-by-side relationship with their marketing people. He admires the in-house media operations at corporate giants such as General Foods, Procter & Gamble, General Mills, Colgate, and Nabisco because they are active, smooth partnership operations.

"Somewhere in the corporation you have to be coordinating the whole activity," Claggett advises. And in his universe that translates into an in-house agency shepherding the needs of some 75 brands as well as the efforts of Ralston's 10 advertising agencies. Make no mistake about it, there is also a distinct Ralston culture that must be adhered to. To this end, Continental Baking will move its headquarters from Rye, N.Y., to Checkerboard Square later this year. Claggett is now working with its advertising agencies, Ted Bates and Grey, to indoctrinate the newcomers to the Ralston way of doing business.

"You'll find a lot of companies which have what they call in-house media departments, but quite frankly they spend 99% of their time working on network TV, negotiating and improving the network packages," states corporate media director Don Martin, who's been with Ralston 19 years. "While our people here do that to a great extent, at the same time they might be working on 50 or so brands, and every one has been fully coordinated with a full-service agency media staff or planned in-house. Our people are coordinating plans from the very first meeting with the product managers," he adds.

Because of this hands-on approach to media, Martin believes that the in-house people are in a much better position to review, critique and perhaps alter plans that are being prepared and presented to them by the agencies.

Not that the strong-willed Claggett means to suggest that the entire media function should be brought in-house. "It's not a goal at all, because most of the network action is done in New York," explains Claggett, recognizing that Ralston needs to rely on the resources of agencies close to the heart of Broadcast Row. Furthermore, he adds, "We feel that our system is perfect because we can tap into new media technologies at 10 different agencies and use the best of them. If we did it all ourselves, well, we simply could not," he concedes, his voice trailing off.

While it may not do it all, the in-house agency, in conjunction with the rest of the marketing department, sure does a lot. Checkerboard Advertising is composed of roughly 50 people, or a third of the entire marketing department. Among CA's duties are the handling of outside agency coordination work which involves coordination of agency selection and agency fee systems.

In addition to media, the department's responsibilities include tv and print advertising production, packaging development, audiovisuals for sales meetings, sales analysis, brand publicity, sales promotion, advertising research, media research, corporate market research and even test kitchens.

Checkerboard Advertising works closely with the full agency lineup. "We involve all of our agencies in planning and in share estimates, and we select one of our agencies to work with us on every buy," Claggett explains. However, Ralston usually uses the Paul Schulman Co. to execute its media placement orders. "We have almost a partnership arrangement," says Claggett *of their affiliation with Schulman, a division of one of its agencies, Gardner Advertising. In the past, Ralston has brought Wells, Rich, Greene into the act as well, and this go round, with its CBC buys, they may involve Bates and Grey in the process, reports Claggett.*

From an outsider's perspective, who does what is confusing. "We find it's more effective to do some things ourselves, and let the agencies do other things, and of course, we do some things jointly," says Claggett, trying to shed light on the subject. For example, Ralston handles all network bill/pay, all internal costing, allocation of spots, direct media buying for some brands, and spot TV pool coordination. Some areas are left to agencies, like the bulk of the brand work, creativity and new media and computer uses.

Ralston's media department also handles talent and residuals payments to keep costs down. Most companies leave that cleanup work to their agencies who charge a 17.65% commission for the service. "I defy you to find anywhere in the universe a media department where planners or buyers are aware of how to to T&R," challenges a proud Shubert.

All in all, the in-house operation makes plenty of good business sense for the sprawling St. Louis company. Outside of better control and coordination, there's also substantial cost savings involved. "Generally speaking, our savings are somewhat between two and a half to three times the cost of running the department," confides Claggett. "In terms of eliminating the float, in terms of certain procedures we have, they by far offset the cost of the department." The operation is audited independently by a department which does not report to Claggett.

THE BUDGETING PROCESS . . . .

How does Ralston make all the many pieces come together? By taking a methodical approach. At the first budgeting meeting in early spring, marketing and media sit down to go over brand marketing objectives. The turf is already very familiar to both sides, since they have already worked side-by-side on brands throughout the year.

Basics are reviewed on brand objectives. For network upfront, marketing submits its brand requirements in terms of specific target audience GRPs, weekly weights and planned budgets taken directly from respective media plans. "Out total requirements are the cumulative result of each brand's needs in each specific broadcast daypart," Martin explains. "Our responsibility in media is to then fill those requirements in the most effective way."

Meanwhile marketing already has a pretty good idea about the total budget amount they'll need. "It's based upon the needs of the product, the stage in the life cycle, the R&D investment required, consumer information needs, competitive activity and target audience requirements," tells Martin. Marketing must have its requests in to media so that media can be in position for the upfront network TV buy by May, or whenever the market looks like it's ready to move.

With the basics hashed out, media exits and returns only when it has a prepared plan. A frenzy of activity takes place in the media department. Life is so hectic in the media department during this time that it closes its doors to outside suppliers from March through June.

Media has bolted itself in because it is now under the gun to map out strategy for all media buys as it supervises the information streaming in from its agencies' media departments. "We're getting our act together on everything, network, TV, print, radio," ticks off Pavlenko. For example, agencies are feeding in estimates on a CPM cluster point basis (spot TV), she lists, while analysis of a cable market's subscribing base is also being done. Syndication is far from forgotten. That medium is being studied at the same time newspaper and promotional needs are being evaluated.

Pavlenko points out too that this is the period when the agencies are providing in-depth competitive spending reports of Ralston's competition. "It helps us decide how we're going to split up that money, and it's one thing we rely greatly on the agencies for," she notes.

The topper is that all of Ralston's divisions—pet foods, cereal, industrial feeds, Jack In The Box and now Continental Baking Co.—are being planned simultaneously. Some $200 million plus in expenditures are now being sliced up.

"The push and the crunch starts along as early as February and then is carried on through June or July, when the final documents are put to bed," notes Shubert. "The major push comes

from May to June where we really get into final plans, because a lot of these documents require four or five meetings per brand. It's not just 'one media meeting, go away, bring the plan back, and you're finished,' " he sighs.

When media does finally come back to marketing with its fleshed out media recommendations, both sides review them to make sure that all objectives are fulfilled. The media group, though, already had approved the media plans from its agencies prior to its meeting with marketing staffers. Martin says, "This is a required procedure."

If any differences of opinion between marketing and media surface from this meeting, both sides talk it out. "If we are in complete disagreement we take it to the next higher authority," Martin outlines. The next link in the command chain would be the group marketing director. Although it has happened in the past, "It doesn't happen much now because normally you square those things away in preliminary meetings," Martin adds with relief.

After the meeting between brand managers and media, the budgets go to marketing directors who approve their individual brand budgets. The budget then gets kicked upstairs to the next layer of approval, the director of marketing for grocery products. If all goes well, the next move is up to the president of the grocery products division. From that point on, the budgets travel to a corporate budget committee and ultimately the board of directors.

With approval from the director of marketing and the president of the grocery products group, media can then determine what percentages of the budget for network tv should be spent upfront and opportunistically. While the media budget is still undergoing scrutiny from various layers of approval, the total amount of dollars for media spending has received the nod. "In effect, what we're doing is making forecasts for management of what the situation will be like in the following fiscal year," explains Claggett. "While it's more of a forecast for the coming fiscal year than a tight budget, we do have some parameters to deal with," he clarifies.

The forecasts come in pretty close to what is actually approved, continues Martin. "Normally the variance, from top to bottom, is in the 5% area, and we can live with that," he adds. "We've never really had any major problem in that area," he concludes.

"We're pretty close on the dollars, too, because we have a checkpoint, a last minute reading of conditions right before the market opens, even the day that it's opening," Martin boasts. "This last minute reading prevents us from making any major mistakes in terms of the total dollars that we will be committing on behalf of the company," he notes.

At Ralston, budgets are reviewed at least every quarter. "If need be, we'll do it more often," shrugs Shubert. The budgets are reviewed that often, he explains, "because things are constantly changing, and we want to have an actionable position always."

Martin concurs, adding, "Nowadays, there is no such thing as an annual plan. Anybody who thinks there is lives in the 18th century."

Although Ralston's media department seems to have all the i's dotted and the t's crossed, Claggett, the indefatigable perfectionist, says there's always room for improvement.

He would like to see more creativity in the use of media, especially cable and syndication, as the two forums are likely to take on more importance in future years. Ralston has already taken a giant step in the syndication arena with Nashville, which it developed from scratch. "Initially, we built that to address a problem in a certain section of the country," says Shubert. "Now it is in over a hundred markets and doing very well."

Another area for improvement is personnel. One of the strong points of the media department is that many of the staff have worked together upwards of 15 years. That's one of the keys to the operation's success. But as Ralston continues to grow, the media department will also have to grow to accommodate the influx.

For companies just starting up an in-house media operation, Claggett advises finding the best professionals available. "The other ingredient is making sure they work closely with brand management," he teaches. "Sometimes, it takes years to really develop a rapport and a feeling for working with brand management groups. And when you're starting out, you have to have that," he insists.

As for adversarial relationships that sometimes develop between the media and marketing disciplines, Claggett simply won't allow that to happen. When he walks into NBC's offices, he needs everything he can get from both departments. "The two are working on the same *team, working for the same company," he insists. That team is about to make its plays, and Claggett wants to enter the game knowing he can execute, and score.*

SIDEBARS . . . .

#1—47 STEPS TO THE UPFRONT BUY . . . .

It's not by chance that Ralston Purina is yards ahead of the pack in completing its upfront TV buy each year. "While a lot of people think it's just sitting around in a fancy restaurant discussing millions of dollars," Ralston's Claggett complains, "there is a lot of detail and planning which enters into the buy." At Ralston, the process begins in January with analyses of market conditions. Claggett ticks off those 47 steps.

Preliminary Phase

1. Analyze market conditions and forecast pricing.
2. Notify brand groups and agencies of deadlines for brand needs.
3. Set efficiency goals and objectives.
4. Assemble brand requirements.
5. Estimate total corporate tv budgets by daypart.
6. Assemble overall desired package requirements.
7. Load target audience evaluative data in computer.
8. Establish qualitative evaluation criteria.

Exploratory Phase

9. Discuss new pilot scenarios with major Hollywood producers and network West Coast programers.
10. Discuss available research and reports on new shows.
11. Examine possible fall schedules.
12. Chart past performance shares by time period, by week.
13. Communicate general requirements to each network.
14. Set timetable for negotiations.

Programing Evaluation Phase

15. Attend announcement meetings held by each network.
16. Screen all footage on new pilots.
17. Discuss future storylines on pilots with network programing people.
18. Discuss possible schedule changes.
19. Meet with Ralston's major network agencies to develop corporate share estimates by quarter.
20. Load estimated time period shares and viewer data into computer.
21. Determine best combinations of shows through analysis of all possible or feasible packaging on an anticipated cost basis.

Offer and Bidding Phase

22. Inform networks of specific packages of shows and costs desired.
23. Receive network bids.
24. Determine last minute schedule changes.
25. Perform computer analysis of quantitative/qualitative aspects of each plan.
26. Evaluate packages against original objectives.

Final Negotiation Phase

27. Inform networks of plan weaknesses.
28. Evaluate revised network proposals.
29. Make seasonal and scheduling adjustments in final package desired.
30. Receive final network bids.
31. Discuss different budget level plans at each network.
32. Final evaluation and decision on total corporate package.
33. Determine contract conditions for each network.
34. Negotiate final packages at each network.

Wrap-Up Phase

35. Assign shows to each brand.
36. Set up weekly rotation schedule for all brands.
37. Formalize contract specifics in order letters.
38. Advise brand groups and brand agencies of purchase details.
39. Start "opportunistic" exploration for budget amounts not committed in the upfront buy.

Reevaluation Phase

40. Recalculate audience estimates due to schedule changes.
41. Renegotiate participations due to schedule changes.
42. Shift positions due to competitive and/or marketing considerations.
43. Negotiate make-goods.
44. Negotiate opportunistic packages.

Reporting Phase

45. Compare "goals" vs. "actual" based on A. C. Nielsen research.
46. Police purchase agreements.
47. Report actual achievements vs. goals to product management/agencies.

#2—HOW FOUR OTHER COMPANIES PLAY THE BUDGET GAME . . . .

Marianne Paskowski
Pam Ellis-Simons
While there is always a certain amount of fresh angst involved in developing annual budgets, most of the major companies adhere to a pretty tried and true approach. Oft labeled the "Proc-

ter & Gamble method," this traditional budgeting modus operandi calls for somewhat separate and distinct roles for brand managers and media personnel. Generally, brand managers come up with the product objectives—say the goal is to increase market share by 3% in the Southwest—and then turn the plan over to the media group for coordinated implementation. In this instance, the media department may recommend a certain number of GRPs and suggest various exposures—regional magazines or local radio, perhaps.

At that point, the two camps get together to see if everyone agrees on the objective and solutions. When the answer is "yes," the budget is sent first to higher level marketing executives for approval, then on to the unit's business manager, before it starts laboring its way through layers of bureaucracy for the final okay. At some companies, that go-ahead stamp is given by the president, CEO, or even the board of directors.

Not every company tackles the budgeting process in exactly the same way. Some companies, such as Ralston Purina, Campbell Soup and Clorox, evince a corporate culture that favors well-prepared early bids. This trio already has the budgeting blueprint well underway for the upcoming year. Campbell's started planning its strategy in mid-January to meet an August deadline.

Others, such as Coca-Cola USA and Apple Computers, take their cue from their fiscal calendars. They don't even begin crunching the numbers until late spring or early summer. Coke pulls itself together in three months, tops.

"When you're selling a product which is broadly based, it's not exactly like you're cutting it as close as a gnat's eyelash," quips William Lynn, Coca-Cola's corporate media director.

And, of course, not every brand has the same needs. Some products may be seasonal in nature, necessitating a different budgeting cycle. Other brands may have their plans torn up when a competitor unveils a surprise, or the market itself undergoes an unforeseen change. (These are some of the reasons why formal quarterly budget reviews are fading away. In today's chaotic selling atmosphere, most budgets are under constant review.)

Nor does everyone speak to the same people when affixing spending levels. At many companies, marketing and media executives huddle together to hash out brand objectives and media usage. But at other companies, never the twain shall meet till late in the game. At more egalitarian marketers (at least in theory), middle management plays a much broader role. Apple Computers is a case in point.

The following are brief sketches of how four major marketers view the planning cycle.

CLOROX: THE TEXTBOOK APPROACH . . . .

This Oakland, Calif.–based consumer product specialist has a reputation for being a tough-nosed negotiator. It follows a traditional path that obviously works.

It begins the plans for its household products, which include Clorox Liquid, Softscrub, Tilex and its newly introduced Fresh Step cat box filler, in February in order that they can be put into motion by the start of its fiscal year on July 1. Seasonal products such as charcoal, paint, and salad dressing work on a different schedule and are planned with trade/broker considerations in mind.

The nitty-gritty starts when Clorox brand managers and assistants begin pulling together marketing data from their own media departments as well as from the account servicing departments of the agencies. Needham Harper Worldwide, Young & Rubicam, Foote, Cone & Belding and N. W. Ayer get involved at this early stage.

The marketing data is then presented to the advertising agency management for its review. Later, the documents, along with specific agency recommendations, are forwarded to corporate product management. Once a strategy is agreed upon for a brand, the media departments at Clorox and the agency develop concrete plans. The recipient of this outpouring is the advertising manager. Included in the plan's coverage are promotion, sales and creative strategies. After the ad manager's okay, the budget wends its way to divisional ad managers. Later, the media budget gets wrapped into corporate budgets for the president and chairman to approve.

Clorox is not a proponent of the zero-based budgeting technique. Rather, "We test our way into making significant changes in budgets," tells Robert Bolte, director of media services at Clorox. Even with new products, the development process runs parallel to the existing formula.

Once budgets are signed off, they are rarely formally reviewed. The budget will be reopened "only if significant changes need to be made," Bolte says.

One area of change at the company has been its embrace of computers and in-house software. This technology has speeded, and made more sophisticated, formulation of the budget. Everyone, from assistant brand managers on up, is adept at using this data, notes Bolte.

CAMPBELL SOUP: SEPARATE, BUT PARALLEL . . .

The media budgeting process has changed over the years at Campbell Soup, reports George Mahrlig, director of media services at the Camden, N.J.–based foods company. "It's much more dynamic now because we have decentralized the decision-making process to the business unit level," he says.

After the first year, for example, business unit managers from the soup division will go over these brands' basic directions with the unit's marketing managers. Media personnel are at these meetings, but are not offering input. "At this point, it's just strategic planning," describes Mahrlig. "Advertising and media will be discussed only if they are a substantial part of the brand plan, and then only directionally."

By late April or May, marketing plans have been formulated and presented to management.

The media plan has not been left out. Rather, its development is running separately yet parallel to the marketing overview. Having been in on the objectives meetings, the media group has devised its own very detailed plan. Sometime in May, the media plan is presented to the business unit manager. From that point, the chief financial officer and president of the company put their stamp of approval on the plans.

"This process has its shortcomings," concedes Mahrlig, "but it works well overall." He notes that under this method brands can start their advertising schedules even if they don't have final budgetary approval. "If there was a disagreement about strategy, it would have surfaced and been settled earlier," he points out.

Like Clorox, Campbell's has scrapped its practice of formally reviewing budgets on a quarterly basis. "The responsibility for stewarding the budget falls on the business unit, and it's really a daily, weekly, monthly, ongoing process," says Mahrlig fervently.

COCA-COLA: GETTING IT TOGETHER, FAST. . . . . .

At the soft-drink king, the media budgeting process starts up around June and is finalized around August or early fourth quarter for the following year's spending. Unlike other companies, Coke gathers a slew of corporate and agency players together and pushes them into a room. Coca-Cola's brand directors and media experts sit down with their agencies' account management and media department teams. Coke's Lynn describes this set-up as a "loop," where all four entities are meeting at the same time, arguing and reconciling their views. Soon after, marketing plans are presented and the team addresses the advertising-related portions of the brand's plans.

The media departments at Coke and its agencies then set out to translate these marketing objectives into advertising tactics. For a new product entry, Coke will do "an initial pay-out analysis on share expectations, pretty much the same way as P&G," reports Lynn. The plan goes first to the marketing director for an okay, before heading to the president, for the final okay.

How often do budgets come up for review? "We try to review brand budgets quarterly, but that really depends on the brand's needs," says Lynn. "Some brands may not get reviewed at all, while others will get revised four times."

Since Coke's budgeting process is just getting going around the time the upfront tv market is convening, does the company run into problems by not having an approved and specific spending level in hand? No way, grins Lynn. He reasons that because fourth quarter budgets are already approved, and 50% of the upcoming buy can be cancelled, buying upfront without a firm budget represents no major obstacle. Also, networks will most likely alter a sizable chunk of the buy with second-season programing changes. "It's not a problem at all," shrugs Lynn. "You're just buying a mortgage on someone else's future, so it's not your worry."

APPLE: HIGH-TECH MIGRATION . . . .

This maverick personal computer maker thrives on creativity and individuality, so fittingly, its budget planning process is hardly traditional. Bruce Mowery, advertising, sales promotion and public relations manager for Apple II Division (there is no counterpart for the Macintosh division as yet), says the budgeting process is dictated by the fiscal year beginning October 1.

"Around April," says the former Chiat/Day ad executive, "we begin to think of fiscal 1986—what specific TV shows or miniseries we want to appear on, and what print support there will be." This is about the time when Apple starts its business planning process, so the timing is ideal. The period also coincides with the upfront tv buys of May-June, points out Mowery.

Mowery explains that Apple's media budgeting process is "iterative" and seems to ramble on through October. Financial groups start the business plan for each division at about the time the two divisions' product managers start isolating new product introduction and pinpoint market targets for the upcoming year. Ideas for promotion and exposure are brought to Mowery's attention and he coordinates them for possible "event advertising" opportunities. "Then we migrate to the marketing director as a team and present a plan," outlines Mowery.

"There would probably be changes made and then we'd present the plans to the general manager of the division, along with the marketing director. Marketing is very decentralized and is a team approach," he describes. "We affix a cost to each individual product manager's plan, and then figure out what is needed in advertising support. We then figure out if it's in the ballpark, and cut it if we have to," says Mowery. "It is a zero-based thing. Some items are sacrosanct (such as certain event advertising components), but you've got to build flex into it because the computer world moves so quickly," he believes.

"It is not a classic approach," he admits, "but it works for us. It is representative of middle management playing a broad role, versus a Procter & Gamble with its highly formalized structures for brand managers."

Apple does review its budgets quarterly, because, again, things move so fast in that high-tech world.

While the media budgeting process at Apple may be fairly nontraditional and might not be as cost-effective once done, they feel they get more bang for the buck. Mathematical models and the like, Mowery continues, are useless in a budgeting process which addresses event marketing.

"CPMs are important, but you can't put a mathematical model on a 25% participation in a miniseries. It just doesn't apply to event marketing," he stresses.

Apple, he continues, also keeps its media budget relatively loose so that if a product does not meet expectations, or doesn't appear on time, media sums can be switched. "Because of the high technology of our products, there is always slack," Mowery sums up. "Everything is loosely tied to a product or program so we can quickly untie the knot and reallocate expenditures."

APPENDIX TO PART V . . . .

Sources of Media Data

The advertising media budget allocation process usually begins by background research on the characteristics and market potential of alternative markets. At this stage, sources such as the *Editor and Publisher Market Guide* (source A) or the *Sales and Marketing Management Survey of Buying Power* might be consulted. Competitive activities would also be studied, by consulting sources such as *Leading National Advertisers* (source B), *Leading National Advertisers/Publishers Information Bureau* (source C), *Rome Reports* (source D), or *MediaWatch* (source E), all published by Competitive Media Reporting.

After budgets have been allocated over media classes and markets, audience and cost data on specific media vehicles are usually consulted and used to select those that provide efficient cost-per-thousand means to achieve targeted reach and frequency levels.

For audience (reach) data, sources consulted usually include *Simmons Market Research Bureau's Study of Media and Markets* (see table earlier in chapter 17) or similar *Mediamark Research Inc. (MRI)* reports. In addition, Nielsen reports are usually consulted for television program viewership data, either or a national basis in the *National Television Index National Audience Demographics Report* (sources F and G) or on a local market basis in the *Nielsen Station Index* reports (source H). Radio station data and newspaper readership data are available from sources such as *Scarborough Research* and others.

For cost data, media planners and buyers may turn to sources such as *Standard Rate and Data Service (SRDS)*, which provides cost data in separate volumes for newspapers (source I), magazines (source J), local television stations (source K), and others.

This is only a sampling of media data sources for the U.S. advertising industry, provided to give the reader a feel for the kinds of data available. We are grateful for these companies for allowing us to reproduce these sample pages.

Nearby Shopping Centers

Name (No. of stores)	Miles from Downtown	Principal Stores
Section	5	Foodland
Grant	8	Foodland
Woodville	12	Shop-E-Z Foods
Stevenson	14	Piggly Wiggly, ShopRite
Pisgah	10	Super Valu
Rainsville	18	Lucky, Foodland

Principal Shopping Days-Thur., Fri., Sat.

Stores Open Evenings-Most to 8 nightly and 9 on Fri. & Sat.; Lucky; Piggly Wiggly; Kroger; Foodland except Sun.

13 - RETAIL OUTLETS: Department Stores-Parks; Hammer's; Cato; Sears; Goody's.

Discount Stores-Family Dollar; K mart; Wal-Mart.

Chain Drug Stores-Big B; Hodges.

Chain Supermarkets-Piggly Wiggly; Lucky; Jitney Jungle; ShopRite; Foodland; Food World; Sav-A-Lot.

Other Chain Stores-Goodyear; Goodrich; Lorch Jewelry; Pacific Finance; Radio Shack; Heilig-Meyers; Big Lots.

14 - NEWSPAPERS: SENTINEL (m-tues to fri; S) 6,815; sworn Oct. 1, 1992.

Local Contact for Advertising and Merchandising Data: Anita Bynum, Gen Mgr., SENTINEL, 704 E. Laurel St.; PO Box 220, Scottsboro, AL 35768; Tel. (205) 259-1020.

National Representative: None.

SELMA

1 - LOCATION: Dallas County, E&P Map C-4. County Seat. On Alabama River, center of state. Agric. and cattle area.

2 - TRANSPORTATION: Railroads-Norfolk Southern; Seaboard System.

Waterways-Navigable River to Port of Mobile.

Motor Freight Carriers-4.

Intercity Bus Line-Greyhound.

3 - POPULATION:
Corp. City 90 Cen. 23,755; E&P 94 Est. 22,739
County 90 Cen. 48,130; E&P 94 Est. 46,613

4 - HOUSEHOLDS:
City 90 Cen. 8,371; E&P 94 Est. 8,012
County 90 Cen. 18,130; E&P 94 Est. 17,559

5 - BANKS

	NUMBER	DEPOSITS
Savings & Loan	2	$280,000,000
Commercial	5	$385,000,000

6 - PASSENGER AUTOS: Dallas County 34,314

7 - ELECTRIC METERS: Residence 17,644

8 - GAS METERS: Residence 19,092

9 - PRINCIPAL INDUSTRIES: Industry, No. of Wage Earners-Lumber 808; Cigar Mfg. 282; Lock Mfg. 487; Lawn Mowers 110; Table Mfg. 400; Garment 990; Packaging 254; Bricks 51; Farm Mach. 60; Tractor Mfg. 475; Paper 428; Windshields 180; Glass 180; Candy 350; Aluminum Prods. 285; Air-Craft 500; Apparel 500.

Principal Industrial Pay Days-Fri., Sat.

10 - CLIMATE: Min. & Max. Temp.-Spring 58-79; Summer 70-98; Fall 58-89; Winter 20-60. First killing frost, Nov. 30; last killing frost, Mar. 3.

11 - TAP WATER: Neutral, soft; fluoridated.

12 - RETAILING: Principal Shopping Center-8 blocks on Broad St. (3 blocks E & W).

Neighborhood Shopping Centers-N Broad St. 12; Selmont; E Selma; W Selma; Citizen's Plz.

Nearby Shopping Centers

Name (No. of stores)	Miles from Downtown	Principal Stores
Gastons(6)	NA	IGA
Satterfield(5)	4	Winn-Dixie
Selma Mall(28)	5	JCPenney, Beall-Ladymon
The Market Place(16)		K mart, Winn-Dixie, Harco, Food World
Valley Creek(4)	5	Wal-Mart

Principal Shopping Days-Fri., Sat.

13 - RETAIL OUTLETS: Department Stores-JCPenney; Leon's; Beall's.

Discount Store-Wal-Mart; K mart.

Variety Stores-S.H. Kress; Family Dollar; Top Dollar; Bill's Dollar; Bargain Town.

Chain Drug Stores-Rexall; Harco; Big B; Brown; Swift.

Chain Supermarkets-Winn-Dixie; IGA; Foodland; Big Bear; Food World.

Other Chain Stores-Firestone; Goodrich; Goodyear; Lorch's; Western; Hancock Fabrics; Pic 'N Pay Shoes; Cato; Kenwins Dress For Less; Payless Shoes; Skinner Furn.; Whol. Bedding; Rent-a-Center; Heilig-Meyers Furniture; Radio Shack; Spiller Furniture.

14 - NEWSPAPERS: TIMES-JOURNAL (m-mon to fri; S) 10,300; sworn Sept. 30, 1992.

Local Contact for Advertising and Merchandising Data: David M. Pippin, Pub., TIMES-JOURNAL, 1018 Water Ave., Selma, AL 36701; Tel. (205) 875-2110.

National Representative: Landon Associates.

SHEFFIELD
See FLORENCE

TALLADEGA

1 - LOCATION: Talladega County, E&P Map C-3. County Seat. 54 mi. E of Birmingham. On U.S. Hwys. 231, 280; State Hwys. 21, 77.

2 - TRANSPORTATION: Railroads-Southern; L&N; ACL.

Intercity Bus Line-Continental Trailways.

Motor Freight Carriers-9.

3 - POPULATION:
Corp. City 90 Cen. 18,175; E&P 94 Est. 18,125
County 90 Cen. 74,107; E&P 94 Est. 77,107

4 - HOUSEHOLDS:
City 90 Cen. 5,903; E&P 94 Est. 5,886
County 90 Cen. 27,838; E&P 94 Est. 28,965

5 - BANKS

	NUMBER	DEPOSITS
Savings & Loan	2	N.A.
Commercial	6	N.A.

6 - PASSENGER AUTOS: Talladega County 54,727

7 - ELECTRIC METERS: Residence 21,448

8 - GAS METERS: Residence 10,775

9 - PRINCIPAL INDUSTRIES: Industry, No. of Wage Earners-Textiles & Bags 3,880; Machine Foundry 983; Lumber & Box Mfg. 451; Brooms & Mops 300; Mining 284; Comm. Printing 865; Newsprint 2,000; Misc. 1,520.

10 - CLIMATE: Min. & Max. Temp.-Spring 10-98; Summer 45-109; Fall 14-109; Winter 5-85. First killing frost, Oct. 21; last killing frost, Mar. 21.

11 - TAP WATER: Alkaline, medium hard; fluoridated.

12 - RETAILING:

Nearby Shopping Centers

Name (No. of stores)	Miles from Downtown	Principal Stores
Talladega Commons	NA	Wal-Mart
Marble City(11)	NA	
Ogletree(14)	NA	Bargaintown, Wal-Mart
Sylacauga(5)	NA	Sears, Harco, Family Dollar
Syla. Shopping Square(3)	NA	Winn-Dixie, K mart, Carport
Talladega Plz. (4)	NA	Carport, Family Dollar, Payless, Sears
Talladega(19)	NA	Winn-Dixie, Harco, Belk-Hudson

Principal Shopping Days-Mon., Fri., Sat.

13 - RETAIL OUTLETS: Department Stores-Belk-Hudson; Maudee's; Helen's; Cohen's 2; Kitchens.

Discount Stores-Top Dollar; Bargain Town, USA; Simply 6-21; 6&8 Store; $3.00 Bill Store; Super 10 2; Lee's; K mart 2; Wal-Mart 2; Family Dollar 2; Bud's.

Chain Drug Stores-Harco 2; Buy Wise; Big B 3.

Chain Supermarkets-Winn-Dixie 3; Food World 2; 3-B Warehouse, 5; Consumer Foods.

Other Chain Stores-Goodyear; Dress For Less 2; Sherwin-Williams 2; Cato 2; Braswell Furn.; Marvin's; Foote Bros.; Shoe City 2; Pic 'N Pay; Farmer's Furn.

14 - NEWSPAPERS: HOME (m-mon to sat) 8,861; sworn Oct. 1, 1992.

Local Contact for Advertising and Merchandising Data: Ed Fowler, Gen. Mgr., HOME, PO Box 977, Talladega, AL 35160; Tel. (205) 362-1000; FAX (205) 249-4315.

National Representative: None.

TROY

1 - LOCATION: Pike County, E&P Map C-4. County Seat. Agriculture, cattle, hog, broiler, mining & industrial area. Timber & pulpwood, miscellaneous manufacturing, wholesale grocery, drug, insecticide distributing center. Distribution Headquarters (14 Counties) State Hwy. Department. Central SE part of state. 44 mi. from Montgomery; 140 mi. from Birmingham.

2 - TRANSPORTATION: Railroads-Seaboard-Coastline; Southern.

Motor Freight Carriers-4.

Intercity Bus Line-Greyhound.

3 - POPULATION:
Corp. City 90 Cen. 13,051; E&P 94 Est. 13,508
County 90 Cen. 27,595; E&P 94 Est. 28,276

4 - HOUSEHOLDS:
City 90 Cen. 4,479; E&P 94 Est. 4,636
County 90 Cen. 9,083; E&P 94 Est. 9,307

5 - BANKS

	NUMBER	EST. DEP.
Commercial	3	$56,395,000

6 - PASSENGER AUTOS: Pike County 21,004

7 - ELECTRIC METERS: Residence 3,963

8 - GAS METERS: Residence 2,080

9 - PRINCIPAL INDUSTRIES: Industry, No. of Wage Earners-Woodworking 497; Textiles 511; Fertilizer/Insecticides 116; Truck Body 115; College/State University 795.

Principal Pay Day-Fri.

10 - CLIMATE: Av. Mean Temp. 63; Jan. 43; July 79. Av. rainfall 47 in.

11 - TAP WATER: Alkaline, slightly hard; fluoridated.

12 - RETAILING: Principal Shopping Centers-10 blocks on 4 Sts.; Troy Plz.; Park Lane.

Nearby Shopping Centers

Name (No. of stores)	Miles from Downtown	Principal Stores
Parklane(6)	NA	Piggly Wiggly, Sears, Fred's Dollar Store
Troy Plz.(8)	NA	Winn-Dixie
Southland Vlg.	NA	Piggly Wiggly, TG&Y

Principal Shopping Days-Mon. through Sat.

13 - RETAIL OUTLETS: Department Stores-Rosenberg's; Leon's; Stanton's; Wal-Mart; Town Sq.; Kitchens.

Variety Store-Fred's.

Discount Stores-Bargain Town, USA; Top Dollar.

Chain Drug Stores-SupeRx; Harco.

Chain Supermarkets-Piggly Wiggly; IGA; Winn-Dixie; Junior Foods; Food World.

Other Chain Stores-Diana Shops; Goodyear; Sears; Kenwin; Eleanor Shops; Baxter Shoes; Firestone; Withit Shoes.

14 - NEWSPAPERS: MESSENGER (m-tues to fri) 4,000; (S) 4,200; sworn Oct. 1, 1992.

Local Contact for Advertising and Merchandising Data: Deedie Carter, Adv. Dir., MESSENGER, 918 S. Brundidge St.; PO Box 727, Troy, AL 36081; Tel. (205) 566-4270.

National Representative: Landon Associates.

A. Sample page from *Editor and Publisher Market Guide*. Reprinted with permission from the *Editor and Publisher Market Guide,* 1994 edition, published by *Editor and Publisher,* 11 W. 19th Street, New York, NY 10011.

LEADING NATIONAL ADVERTISERS
ISSUE TABLE
JANUARY - DECEMBER 1994/1993

PAGE 1

NUMBER OF ISSUES IN EACH MONTH

MAGAZINE	JAN 94	JAN 93	FEB 94	FEB 93	MAR 94	MAR 93	APR 94	APR 93	MAY 94	MAY 93	JUN 94	JUN 93	JUL 94	JUL 93	AUG 94	AUG 93	SEP 94	SEP 93	OCT 94	OCT 93	NOV 94	NOV 93	DEC 94	DEC 93	YTD 94	YTD 93
ALLURE	1	1	1	1	1	1	1	1	1	1	1	1	1	1	1	1	1	1	1	1	1	1	1	1	12	12
AMERICAN BABY	1	1	1	1	1	1	1	1	1	1	1	1	1	1	1	1	1	1	1	1	1	1	1	1	12	12
AMERICAN HEALTH	1	1	0	0	1	1	1	1	1	1	1	1	1	1	0	0	1	1	1	1	1	1	1	1	10	10
AMERICAN HERITAGE	0	0	1	1	0	0	1	1	1	1	0	0	0	0	1	1	1	1	1	1	1	1	1	1	8	8
AMERICAN HOMESTYLE	1	0	0	1	1	1	0	0	1	1	1	1	0	0	1	1	0	0	1	1	1	1	1	1	8	8
AMERICAN PHOTO	1	1	0	0	1	1	0	0	1	1	0	0	1	1	0	0	1	1	0	0	1	1	0	0	6	6
AMERICAN WAY	2	2	2	2	2	2	2	2	2	2	2	2	2	2	2	2	2	2	2	2	2	2	2	2	24	24
ARCHITECTURAL DIGEST	1	1	1	1	1	1	1	1	1	1	1	1	1	1	1	1	1	1	1	1	1	1	1	1	12	12
ART & ANTIQUES	1	1	1	1	1	1	1	1	1	1	1	1	0	0	0	0	1	1	1	1	1	1	1	1	10	10
ATLANTIC MONTHLY THE	1	1	1	1	1	1	1	1	1	1	1	1	1	1	1	1	1	1	1	1	1	1	1	1	12	12
AUDUBON	1	1	0	0	1	1	0	0	1	1	0	0	1	1	0	0	1	1	0	0	1	1	0	0	6	6
AUTOMOBILE MAGAZINE	1	1	1	1	1	1	1	1	1	1	1	1	1	1	1	1	1	1	1	1	1	1	1	1	12	12
AUTOWEEK	5	4	4	4	4	5	4	4	5	5	4	4	4	4	5	5	4	4	5	4	5	6	4	4	53	53
BABY TALK	1	1	1	1	1	1	1	1	1	1	1	1	1	1	1	1	1	1	1	1	1	1	1	1	12	12
BACKPACKER	0	0	1	1	1	1	1	1	1	1	1	1	0	0	1	1	1	1	1	1	0	0	1	1	9	9
BASSMASTER	1	1	1	1	1	1	1	1	1	1	1	1	1	1	0	0	1	1	0	0	1	1	1	1	10	10
BETTER HOMES & GARDENS	1	1	1	1	1	1	1	1	1	1	1	1	1	1	1	1	1	1	1	1	1	1	1	1	12	12
BICYCLING	1	1	1	1	1	1	1	1	1	1	1	1	1	1	1	1	0	0	1	1	1	1	1	1	11	11
BLACK ENTERPRISE	1	1	1	1	1	1	1	1	1	1	1	1	1	1	1	1	1	1	1	1	1	1	1	1	12	12
BON APPETIT	1	1	1	1	1	1	1	1	1	1	1	1	1	1	1	1	1	1	1	1	1	1	1	1	12	12
BOYS' LIFE	1	1	1	1	1	1	1	1	1	1	1	1	1	1	1	1	1	1	1	1	1	1	1	1	12	12
BRIDAL GUIDE	1	1	0	0	1	1	0	0	1	1	0	0	1	1	0	0	1	1	0	0	1	1	0	0	6	6
BRIDE'S	0	0	1	1	0	0	1	1	0	0	1	1	0	0	1	1	0	0	1	1	0	0	1	1	6	6
BUSINESS WEEK	4	3	4	4	4	5	4	5	6	5	4	4	4	4	5	5	4	4	5	5	5	5	4	4	53	53
CABLE GUIDE PLUS TOTAL TV	1	1	1	1	1	1	1	1	1	1	1	1	1	1	1	1	1	1	1	1	1	1	1	1	12	12
CAR AND DRIVER	1	1	1	1	1	1	1	1	1	1	1	1	1	1	1	1	1	1	1	1	1	1	1	1	12	12
CHILD	0	0	1	1	1	1	1	1	1	1	1	1	0	0	1	1	1	1	1	1	1	1	1	1	10	10
COLONIAL HOMES	0	0	1	1	0	0	1	1	0	0	1	1	0	0	1	1	0	0	1	1	0	0	1	1	6	6
COMPUTE	1	1	1	1	1	1	1	1	1	1	1	1	1	1	1	1	1	1	0	1	0	1	0	1	9	12
CONDE NAST TRAVELER	1	1	1	1	1	1	1	1	1	1	1	1	1	1	1	1	1	1	1	1	1	1	1	1	12	12
CONSUMERS DIGEST	1	1	0	0	1	1	0	0	1	1	0	0	1	1	0	0	1	1	0	0	1	1	0	0	6	6
COOKING LIGHT	1	1	0	0	1	1	1	1	1	1	1	0	1	1	0	0	1	1	1	1	0	0	0	0	8	7
COSMOPOLITAN	1	1	1	1	1	1	1	1	1	1	1	1	1	1	1	1	1	1	1	1	1	1	1	1	12	12
COUNTRY AMERICA	1	1	1	1	1	1	1	1	1	1	1	1	1	0	0	1	1	1	1	1	1	1	1	0	11	10
COUNTRY HOME	0	0	1	1	0	0	1	1	0	0	1	1	0	0	1	1	0	0	1	1	0	0	1	1	6	6
COUNTRY LIVING	1	1	1	1	1	1	1	1	1	1	1	1	1	1	1	1	1	1	1	1	1	1	1	1	12	12
CRUISING WORLD	1	1	1	1	1	1	1	1	1	1	1	1	1	1	1	1	1	1	1	1	1	1	1	1	12	12
DELTA SKY	1	1	1	1	1	1	1	1	1	1	1	1	1	1	1	1	1	1	1	1	1	1	1	1	12	12
DETAILS	1	1	1	1	1	1	1	1	1	1	1	1	1	1	1	1	1	1	1	1	1	1	1	1	12	12
DISCOVER	1	1	1	1	1	1	1	1	1	1	1	1	1	1	1	1	1	1	1	1	1	1	1	1	12	12
EATING WELL	1	1	0	0	1	1	0	0	1	1	0	0	1	1	0	0	1	1	0	0	1	1	0	0	6	6
EBONY	1	1	1	1	1	1	1	1	1	1	1	1	1	1	1	1	1	1	1	1	1	1	1	1	12	12
ECONOMIST	4	4	4	4	4	4	5	4	4	5	4	4	5	5	4	4	4	4	5	5	4	4	4	4	51	51
ELLE	1	1	1	1	1	1	1	1	1	1	1	1	1	1	1	1	1	1	1	1	1	1	1	1	12	12
ELLE DECOR	0	0	1	1	0	0	1	1	0	0	1	1	0	0	1	1	0	0	1	1	0	0	1	1	6	6
ENDLESS VACATION	1	1	0	0	1	1	0	0	1	1	0	0	1	1	0	0	1	1	0	0	1	1	0	0	6	6
ENTERTAINMENT WEEKLY	3	4	3	4	4	4	5	5	4	4	4	4	4	4	4	4	4	3	5	5	4	4	5	5	49	50
ENTREPRENEUR	1	1	1	1	1	1	1	1	1	1	1	1	1	1	1	1	1	1	2	1	1	1	1	1	13	12
ESQUIRE	1	1	1	1	1	1	1	1	1	1	1	1	1	1	1	1	1	1	1	1	1	1	1	1	12	12
ESSENCE	1	1	1	1	1	1	1	1	1	1	1	1	1	1	1	1	1	1	1	1	1	1	1	1	12	12
FAMILY CIRCLE	1	1	2	2	1	1	2	2	1	1	2	2	1	1	1	1	2	2	1	1	2	2	1	1	17	17
FAMILY FUN	0	0	1	1	1	1	1	0	1	1	1	0	0	0	1	1	1	1	1	0	1	1	1	1	10	7
FAMILY HANDYMAN	1	1	1	1	1	1	1	1	1	1	1	1	0	0	1	1	0	0	1	1	1	1	1	1	10	10
FAMILY LIFE	0	0	0	0	1	0	0	0	1	0	0	0	1	0	0	0	1	0	0	0	0	1	1	1	5	2
FIELD & STREAM	1	1	1	1	1	1	1	1	1	1	1	1	1	1	1	1	1	1	1	1	1	1	1	1	12	12
FINANCIAL WORLD	2	2	2	2	3	3	2	2	2	2	2	2	2	2	2	2	3	3	2	2	2	2	1	1	25	24
FITNESS	1	1	0	0	1	1	0	0	1	1	0	0	1	1	0	0	1	1	0	0	1	1	0	0	6	6
FOOD & WINE	1	1	1	1	1	1	1	1	1	1	1	1	1	1	1	1	1	1	1	1	1	1	1	1	12	12
FORBES	3	2	2	2	2	3	2	2	2	2	2	2	2	2	3	3	2	2	3	3	2	2	2	2	27	27
FORTUNE	2	2	2	2	2	2	2	2	3	3	2	2	2	2	2	2	2	3	3	3	2	4	2	2	26	29
FOUR WHEELER	1	1	1	1	1	1	1	1	1	1	1	1	1	1	1	1	1	1	1	1	1	1	1	1	12	12
GENTLEMEN'S QUARTERLY	1	1	1	1	1	1	1	1	1	1	1	1	1	1	1	1	1	1	1	1	1	1	1	1	12	12
GLAMOUR	1	1	1	1	1	1	1	1	1	1	1	1	1	1	1	1	1	1	1	1	1	1	1	1	12	12
GOLF	1	1	1	1	1	1	1	1	1	1	1	1	1	1	1	1	1	1	1	1	1	1	1	1	12	12
GOLF DIGEST	1	1	1	1	1	1	1	1	1	1	1	1	1	1	1	1	1	1	1	1	1	1	1	1	12	12

B. Sample page from *Leading National Advertisers*. Courtesy of *Competitive Media Reporting*.

LEADING NATIONAL ADVERTISERS
MAGAZINE TOTALS BY PARENT COMPANY
January - December 1994

COMPANY/MAGAZINE	PAGES	% OF CO.	DOLLARS	% OF CO.	# OF INS.
1000 ISLANDS INT COUNCIL..............	1.12	100.0	24.970	100.0	5
BETTER HOMES & GARDENS	0.05	4.5	10.480	42.0	2
LADIES' HOME JOURNAL	0.07	6.3	8.290	33.2	2
NEW YORK MAGAZINE	1.00	89.3	6.200	24.8	1
1001 RUGS....................	0.81	100.0	13.250	100.0	5
SOUTHERN ACCENTS	0.81	100.0	13.250	100.0	5
1928 JEWELRY CO....................	8.61	100.0	500.898	100.0	9
ELLE	4.65	54.0	198.877	39.7	5
REDBOOK	3.96	46.0	302.021	60.3	4
2 HULLS....................	6.25	100.0	19.740	100.0	10
CRUISING WORLD	6.25	100.0	19.740	100.0	10
20/21 SOFTWARE INC....................	0.83	100.0	24.286	100.0	5
SUCCESS	0.83	100.0	24.286	100.0	5
21ST CENTURY COMMUNICATIONS............	0.17	100.0	1.260	100.0	1
INCOME OPPORTUNITIES	0.17	100.0	1.260	100.0	1
24 FIFTH AVENUE RESTAURANT............	2.30	100.0	23.767	100.0	5
NEW YORK MAGAZINE	2.30	100.0	23.767	100.0	5
26 RED....................	0.33	100.0	6.450	100.0	1
DETAILS	0.33	100.0	6.450	100.0	1
2XIST INC....................	5.00	100.0	123.677	100.0	5
DETAILS	2.00	40.0	33.879	27.4	2
MENS HEALTH	2.00	40.0	53.550	43.3	2
VANITY FAIR	1.00	20.0	36.248	29.3	1
315 E62 ST ANTIQUE DEALERS............	0.28	100.0	8.395	100.0	1
ARCHITECTURAL DIGEST	0.28	100.0	8.395	100.0	1
3D POLITICS....................	0.07	100.0	1.280	100.0	2
NEW YORKER	0.07	100.0	1.280	100.0	2
4 DAY TIRE STORES....................	18.17	100.0	381.330	100.0	29
AUTOWEEK	0.83	4.6	6.300	1.7	5
CAR AND DRIVER	8.67	47.7	222.960	58.5	12
ROAD & TRACK	8.67	47.7	152.070	39.9	12
4 WEST....................	8.67	100.0	55.611	100.0	12
FOUR WHEELER	8.67	100.0	55.611	100.0	12
40TH ST TRIM & FABRIC CORP...........	3.14	100.0	56.350	100.0	3
BRIDE'S	1.14	36.3	21.870	38.8	2
MODERN BRIDE	2.00	63.7	34.480	61.2	1
47 STREET PHOTO....................	64.00	100.0	1.338.080	100.0	12
POPULAR PHOTOGRAPHY	64.00	100.0	1.338.080	100.0	12
4WD HARDWARE INC....................	0.50	100.0	3.195	100.0	1
FOUR WHEELER	0.50	100.0	3.195	100.0	1
5 & 10 NO EXAGGERATION RESTAURANT......	0.31	100.0	2.140	100.0	1
NEW YORK MAGAZINE	0.31	100.0	2.140	100.0	1
6TH AVE ELECTRONICS CITY INC..........	4.00	100.0	140.296	100.0	4
CAR AND DRIVER	1.00	25.0	40.458	28.8	1
ELLE	1.00	25.0	37.910	27.0	1
POPULAR PHOTOGRAPHY	1.00	25.0	34.340	24.5	1
ROAD & TRACK	1.00	25.0	27.588	19.7	1
70 WEST MARINA....................	2.00	100.0	6.780	100.0	12
SALT WATER SPORTSMAN	2.00	100.0	6.780	100.0	12
72 MARINE SALES....................	0.49	100.0	14.190	100.0	8
BASSMASTER	0.49	100.0	14.190	100.0	8
77 MAIDEN LANE SALON....................	0.25	100.0	8.140	100.0	1
W	0.25	100.0	8.140	100.0	1
7TH LEVEL INC....................	3.00	100.0	32.145	100.0	3
COMPUTE	3.00	100.0	32.145	100.0	3
800 LOOSGRV....................	0.33	100.0	10.256	100.0	1
SASSY	0.33	100.0	10.256	100.0	1
800 MARKETING INC....................	0.49	100.0	87.778	100.0	6
PEOPLE WEEKLY	0.49	100.0	87.778	100.0	6
800-DENTIST PHONE SERVICE.............	1.00	100.0	12.680	100.0	1
TEXAS MONTHLY	1.00	100.0	12.680	100.0	1
800-FLOWERS....................	3.29	100.0	94.291	100.0	4
FAMILY HANDYMAN	1.00	30.4	34.535	36.6	1
NEW YORK MAGAZINE	0.29	8.8	5.570	5.9	1
TRAVEL HOLIDAY	2.00	60.8	54.186	57.5	2
800-LUGGAGE....................	0.33	100.0	9.192	100.0	1
DELTA SKY	0.33	100.0	9.192	100.0	1
900 NUMBERS....................	1.00	100.0	12.925	100.0	1
ENTREPRENEUR	1.00	100.0	12.925	100.0	1
A & B INDUSTRIES INC....................	0.50	100.0	2.070	100.0	1
CRUISING WORLD	0.50	100.0	2.070	100.0	1
A & E APPAREL INC....................	2.00	100.0	30.690	100.0	6
ENTREPRENEUR	2.00	100.0	30.690	100.0	6
A & G PRODUCTS INC....................	0.67	100.0	8.600	100.0	2
NATURAL HISTORY	0.67	100.0	8.600	100.0	2
A CHRISTMAS CAROL....................	0.50	100.0	10.460	100.0	1
NEW YORKER	0.50	100.0	10.460	100.0	1
A CHRISTMAS PLACE....................	0.17	100.0	3.919	100.0	1
AMERICAN WAY	0.17	100.0	3.919	100.0	1
A DAY AT THE MOVIES....................	1.50	100.0	58.732	100.0	2
ENTERTAINMENT WEEKLY	1.00	66.7	52.532	89.4	1
NEW YORK MAGAZINE	0.50	33.3	6.200	10.6	1
A F SCHMALZIRED COMPANY....................	0.44	100.0	6.460	100.0	3
SOUTHERN ACCENTS	0.44	100.0	6.460	100.0	3
A JAMAIS....................	0.17	100.0	7.700	100.0	1
WORKING WOMAN	0.17	100.0	7.700	100.0	1

C. Sample page from *Leading National Advertisers/Publishers Information Bureau.* Courtesy of *Competitive Media Reporting.*

THE CMR ROME REPORTS ADVERTISING REPORT JAN-DEC 1994

SERENA LODGES & HOTELS

PUBLICATION	INS	PGS	DOL
TRAVEL WORLD NEWS	3	0.75	4500
			4,500

1-800-CRUISES INC — LAKE WORTH FL

PUBLICATION	INS	PGS	DOL
TRAVEL TRADE NEWS ED	19	2.28	17123
TRAVEL WEEKLY	27	7.18	110029
			127,152

100 OAKS — NASHVILLE TN

PUBLICATION	INS	PGS	DOL
CHAIN STORE AGE EXEC	1	1.00	8840
			8,840

100VG-ANYLAN FORUM — NORTH HIGHLANDS CA

PUBLICATION	INS	PGS	DOL
COMMUNICATIONSWEEK	4	2.00	45360
			45,360

1220 EXHIBITS

PUBLICATION	INS	PGS	DOL
EXHIBITOR	4	2.00	5352
			5,352

168 CLUB

PUBLICATION	INS	PGS	DOL
COMPUTER SHOPPER	1	0.25	5366
			5,366

1ST AMER MGMT CO INC — IN

PUBLICATION	INS	PGS	DOL
AMERICAN METAL MARKE	2	0.83	3270
MODERN METALS	1	0.33	1885
PLANTS SITES & PARKS	1	0.33	2425
			7,580

20/20 SOFTWARE — OLD GREENWICH CT

PUBLICATION	INS	PGS	DOL
LAN TIMES	1	0.50	6897
			6,897

20TH CENTURY FOX FILM CORP — LOS ANGELES CA

PUBLICATION	INS	PGS	DOL
ADVERTISING AGE - NA	1	2.00	30130
ADWEEK/EAST	1	2.00	12365
BRANDWEEK	2	3.00	28715
BROADCASTING & CABLE	5	28.00	144460
CHAIN DRUG REVIEW	1	0.60	9509
DISCOUNT STORE NEWS	4	3.67	49360
ELECTRONIC MEDIA	6	13.40	77554
HFN	1	1.00	12830
MEDIA WEEK	1	1.00	14200
MULTICHANNEL NEWS	1	3.00	16664
SUPERMARKET NEWS	2	1.80	37000
VIDEO BUSINESS	10	1150.00	1227430
VIDEO SOFTWARE	4	8.00	62600
VIDEO STORE	25	38.25	409139
			2,131,956

20TH CENTURY FOX FILM CORP — NEW YORK NY

PUBLICATION	INS	PGS	DOL
ADWEEK/EAST	1	2.00	12365
HFN	1	1.00	12830
INSIDE MEDIA	1	2.00	18426
SUPERMARKET NEWS	1	1.00	17000
VIDEO SOFTWARE	1	2.00	15170
VIDEO STORE	3	5.00	53345
			129,136

21ST CENTURY AUTOMOTIVE MKTG ASSO — OMAHA NE

PUBLICATION	INS	PGS	DOL
DEALER BUSINESS	2	1.67	11248
			11,248

21ST CENTURY CONTAINERS LTD — ATLANTA GA

PUBLICATION	INS	PGS	DOL
CHEMICAL EQUIPMENT	1	0.17	2603
CHEMICAL WEEK	1	0.33	4430
CPI PURCHASING	1	0.33	2290
ENVIRONMENT TODAY	2	0.85	8543
MATERIAL HANDLING PR	1	0.17	2545
POLLUTION ENGINEERIN	1	0.33	2075
WATER & WASTES DIGES	2	0.33	3754
			26,240

21ST CENTURY METALS INC — BENSENVILLE IL

PUBLICATION	INS	PGS	DOL
WHOLESALER	4	2.40	16600
			16,600

21ST CENTURY MKTG — FARMINGDALE NY

PUBLICATION	INS	PGS	DOL
DIRECT	11	5.50	43190
SALES & MARKETING ST	1	1.00	7600
			50,790

225 THE INTL SHOWCASE — NEW YORK NY

PUBLICATION	INS	PGS	DOL
HFN	13	7.80	139672
			139,672

230 FIFTH AVE — NY

PUBLICATION	INS	PGS	DOL
HFN	2	1.20	16688
			16,688

2500 AD SOFTWARE INC — BUENA VISTA CO

PUBLICATION	INS	PGS	DOL
EDN/EDN P & C	2	0.22	4950
EMBEDDED SYSTEMS PRO	3	2.11	9919
			14,869

2CD-ROM LLC — DALLAS TX

PUBLICATION	INS	PGS	DOL
BYTE	3	0.38	21540
			21,540

2ND SOURCE CELLULAR — FT THOMAS KY

PUBLICATION	INS	PGS	DOL
CELLULAR BUSINESS	4	4.00	17396
			17,396

3 SIGMA — COVINGTON OH

PUBLICATION	INS	PGS	DOL
CONVERTING MAGAZINE	2	2.00	9990
			9,990

3-6 COMPUTERS — HOLLYWOOD CA

PUBLICATION	INS	PGS	DOL
INFOWORLD	5	0.56	46950
			46,950

3-G VIDEOCASSETTE CORP — CANOGA PARK CA

PUBLICATION	INS	PGS	DOL
NON-FOODS MERCHANDIS	1	1.00	8035
SUPERMARKET BUSINESS	1	0.60	11920
			19,955

3-STRIKES CUSTOM DESIGN INC — STAMFORD CT

PUBLICATION	INS	PGS	DOL
BRANDWEEK	4	1.33	23110
INCENTIVE	1	0.17	1150
POTENTIALS IN MARKET	11	1.33	17305
SALES & MARKETING ST	1	0.25	3025
			44,590

360 SYSTEMS — WESTLAKE VILLAGE CA

PUBLICATION	INS	PGS	DOL
BROADCAST ENGINEERIN	6	5.25	30990
RADIO WORLD	9	9.00	31050
SOUND & VIDEO CONTRA	8	2.50	12982
TV TECHNOLOGY	4	4.00	21600
			96,622

3C RESEARCH — LEONIA NJ

PUBLICATION	INS	PGS	DOL
SURFACE MOUNT TECHNO	4	1.33	9716
			9,716

3COM CORP — FOXBOROUGH MA

PUBLICATION	INS	PGS	DOL
DATA COMMUNICATIONS	1	2.00	21500
			21,500

3COM CORP — WASHINGTON DC

PUBLICATION	INS	PGS	DOL
COMPUTER RESELLER NE	2	2.00	28470
DATA COMMUNICATIONS	2	3.00	37900
INFORMATIONWEEK	1	2.00	44638
LAN TIMES	1	1.00	13695
NETWORKWORLD	7	9.33	197860
PC	1	2.00	82005
PC WEEK	2	4.00	106150
VARBUSINESS	2	2.00	28380
			539,098

3COM CORP — SANTA CLARA CA

PUBLICATION	INS	PGS	DOL
COMMUNICATIONSWEEK	33	60.00	1107940
COMPUTER RESELLER NE	48	52.00	729920
COMPUTERWORLD	7	14.00	362250
DATA COMMUNICATIONS	13	22.00	250300
INFORMATIONWEEK	2	4.00	89276
LAN TIMES	27	41.00	530695
NETWORK COMPUTING	17	28.67	591895
NETWORKWORLD	33	56.34	1187962
PC	19	33.00	1373395
PC WEEK	41	78.20	2102260
RESELLER MANAGEMENT	1	1.00	8465
VARBUSINESS	12	14.00	190890
			8,525,248

3COM CORP — GA

PUBLICATION	INS	PGS	DOL
COMPUTER RESELLER NE	5	5.00	71175
DATA COMMUNICATIONS	3	6.00	64500
LAN TIMES	1	2.00	25190
NETWORK COMPUTING	1	2.00	41135
NETWORKWORLD	1	2.00	41500
			243,500

3COM CORP FULFILLMENT CNTR — AUSTIN TX

PUBLICATION	INS	PGS	DOL
COMMUNICATIONSWEEK	2	1.34	22124
COMPUTERWORLD	1	1.20	38000
DATA COMMUNICATIONS	3	3.34	31730
LAN TIMES	1	2.00	25190
NETWORK COMPUTING	2	2.67	50450
NETWORKWORLD	5	8.20	165980
VARBUSINESS	1	0.67	7772
			341,246

3D SYSTEMS INC — VALENCIA CA

PUBLICATION	INS	PGS	DOL
MACHINE DESIGN	7	4.50	54665
			54,665

3D1 PRODUCTIONS INC

PUBLICATION	INS	PGS	DOL
WINDOWS	2	2.00	33190
			33,190

3DBM FACTORY DIRECT SALES — DALLAS TX

PUBLICATION	INS	PGS	DOL
TV TECHNOLOGY	10	1.92	15068
			15,068

3DX

PUBLICATION	INS	PGS	DOL
SATELLITE ORBIT	1	0.50	8636
			8,636

3G GRAPHICS — KIRKLAND WA

PUBLICATION	INS	PGS	DOL
WINDOWS	3	0.75	12255
			12,255

3L GLOBAL ELECTRONICS — ST PETERSBURG FL

PUBLICATION	INS	PGS	DOL
ECN	3	0.75	5880
EE PRODUCT NEWS	2	0.50	6870
ELECTRONIC ENGINEERI	1	0.33	5252
			18,002

3M CO — SALT LAKE CITY UT

PUBLICATION	INS	PGS	DOL
HEALTH MANAGEMENT TE	1	1.00	5030
NEW STEEL	1	1.00	4560
			9,590

3M CO — AUSTIN TX

PUBLICATION	INS	PGS	DOL
AMERICAS NETWORK	1	1.00	5127
			5,127

3M CO — ST PAUL * MN

PUBLICATION	INS	PGS	DOL
33 METAL PRODUCING	1	1.00	4045
ADVERTISING AGE - NA	5	3.00	69835
AMERICAN LABORATORY	3	2.60	27428
AUTOMOTIVE BODY REPA	1	1.00	8695
AUTOMOTIVE ENGINEERI	1	1.00	8090
AUTOMOTIVE MARKETING	1	0.25	2664
AV VIDEO	2	1.50	11210
BUILDING DESIGN & CO	2	2.00	19490
BUILDING OPERATING M	8	9.00	61760
BUILDING SUPPLY HOME	15	16.25	107328
CEE NEWS	6	12.00	121050
CHEMICAL & ENGINEERI	1	1.00	12600
CHEMICAL PROCESSING	3	3.00	24094
CLEANING MANAGEMENT	1	1.00	3875
COMMERCIAL CARRIER J	1	2.00	17230
COMPUTER DESIGN	5	7.00	71765
COMPUTER PICTURES	2	1.50	10829
COMPUTER RESELLER NE	9	9.00	128115
COMPUTER TECHNOLOGY	5	4.20	56175
COMPUTERWORLD	14	14.00	392000
CONSULTING/SPECIFYIN	2	2.00	13290
DESIGN NEWS	39	35.61	358521
DISCOUNT MERCHANDISE	7	7.00	73500
DISCOUNT STORE NEWS	7	7.20	94285
DO-IT-YOURSELF RETAI	6	6.00	50125
DRUG STORE NEWS	4	1.97	31580
ECN	1	1.00	8000
EDN/EDN P & C	2	2.00	17390
ELECTRICAL WHOLESALI	3	3.00	15725
ELECTRONIC PACKAGING	8	8.25	43600
ELECTRONICS NOW	3	0.83	8825
ENVIRONMENTAL LAB	5	3.25	14387
ENVIRONMENTAL SOLUTI	2	2.00	8712
ESD TECHNOLOGY	1	1.00	2550
EVALUATION ENGINEERI	6	6.33	35190
FLEET OWNER	1	2.00	19205
FLEXO	1	1.00	2881
FOLIO	1	1.00	5170
FOOD PROCESSING	1	1.00	6395
FURNITURE TODAY	1	1.00	8900
GOVERNING	3	3.00	27200
GOVERNMENT EXECUTIVE	1	0.50	5950
GRAPHIC ARTS MONTHLY	3	6.00	53430
HFN	4	4.00	48200
HOSPITAL PURCHASING	6	6.00	30240
HOSPITALS & HEALTH N	1	1.00	7860
HYDROCARBON PROCESSI	3	3.00	16695
INDUSTRIAL HEATING	3	3.00	12630
INDUSTRIAL MAINTNC &	3	1.93	25720
INDUSTRIAL PRODUCT B	1	0.50	11072
INDUSTRIAL SAFETY &	3	1.10	12227
INFOWORLD	10	10.00	285500
LABORATORY EQUIPMENT	1	1.00	13220

D. Sample page from *Rome Reports.* Courtesy of *Competitive Media Reporting.*

SECTION 2 BRAND DETAIL WITHIN PARENT COMPANY

PARENT COMPANY BRAND/PRODUCT NETWORK NY TIME & PROGRAM NAME	DAYPART	WEEKLY TOTALS NO. OF COMM	MINUTES AND SECONDS	MON MAY 29	TUE MAY 30	WED MAY 31	THU JUN 1	FRI JUN 2	SAT JUN 3	SUN JUN 4
AMR CORP										
AMERICAN AIRLINES-DOMESTIC										
C 2:30P NCAA WORLD SERIES GAME	S/S	2	1:00						1:00	
ANHEUSER-BUSCH COMPANIES INC ********										
ANHEUSER BUSCH-CORP PSA										
N 9:00A MEET THE PRESS	S/S	2	1:00							1:00
BUD ICE BEER										
N 7:00P NBA PLAYOFF NITE	P/T	3	1:30					1:00		1:00
F 3:00P STANLEY CUP PLYFFS	S/S	3	1:30							1:30
PRODUCT TOTALS		6	3:00					1:00		1:30
BUD ICE BEER-BUD ICE LIGHT BEER										
F 3:00P STANLEY CUP PLYFFS	S/S	3	1:30							1:30
BUD LIGHT BEER										
N 7:00P NBA PLAYOFF NITE	P/T	9	4:30		1:30		1:30	1:00		:30
C 12:37X LATE LATE/TOM SNYDER	E/L	1	:30		:30					
C 11:35P LATE SHOW/DAVID LTTRMN	E/L	1	:30	:30						
N 11:30P SATURDAY NIGHT	E/L	1	:30						:30	
E/L FRINGES TOTALS		3	1:30	:30	:30				:30	
PRODUCT TOTALS		12	6:00	:30	2:00		1:30	1:00	:30	:30
BUDWEISER BEER										
N 7:00P NBA PLAYOFF NITE	P/T	6	3:00			1:30	:30			1:00
N 3:25P NBA PLAYOFF GAME-DAY	M-F	4	2:00	2:00						
F 3:00P STANLEY CUP PLYFFS	S/S	2	1:00							1:00
C 12:37X LATE LATE/TOM SNYDER	E/L	3	1:30							
C 11:35P LATE SHOW/DAVID LTTRMN	E/L	5	2:30	:30		:30	:30	1:00	:30	
N 1:35X LATE NT/CONAN OBRIEN	E/L	5	2:30			:30	:30	:30		
N 2:24X LATER	E/L	1	:30			:30				
N 11:30P SATURDAY NIGHT	E/L	1	:30			:30				
N 11:35P TONIGHT SHOW	E/L	1	:30						:30	
E/L FRINGES TOTALS		14	7:00	:30		2:00	1:00	1:00	1:00	
PRODUCT TOTALS		26	13:00	3:00	2:00	2:30	1:30	1:30	:30	2:00
BUDWEISER BEER-CORP PSA										
A 11:30A THIS WEEK	S/S	1	:30							:30
C 9:00A SUNDAY MORNING	S/S	1	:30							:30
PRODUCT & S/S DAYTIME TOTALS		2	1:00							1:00
SEA WORLD PARK-&BUSCH GARDENS										
A 7:30P AMERICA'S/HOME VIDEOS	P/T	1	:30							:30
A 8:30P BRINGING UP JACK	P/T	1	:30						:30	
A 8:00P SISTER SISTER	P/T	1	:30				:30			
A 9:00P STEP BY STEP	P/T	1	:30					:30		
N 10:00P EARTH 2	P/T	1	:30				:30			:30
PRODUCT & PRIME TIME TOTALS		5	2:30				:30	:30	:30	1:00
PARENT CO. PRIME TIME TOTALS		23	11:30		1:30	1:30	2:00	2:00		3:00
PARENT CO. M-F DAYTIME TOTALS		4	2:00	2:00						
PARENT CO. S/S DAYTIME TOTALS		12	6:00							6:00
PARENT CO. E/L FRINGES TOTALS		17	8:30	1:30	2:30	1:00	1:00	1:30	1:00	
PARENT COMPANY WEEKLY TOTALS		56	28:00	3:30	4:00	3:00	3:00	3:00	1:30	9:00
...RG RESIDENTIAL...										
A 9:00P ABC FAMILY MOVIE	P/T	2	1:00						1:00	
A 10:11P ABC MONDAY NIGHT MOVIE	P/T	1	:30		:30					
A 9:00P ABC SUNDAY NIGHT MV	P/T	1	:30							:30
A 9:30P HANGIN WITH MR COOPER	P/T	1	:30					:30		
C 9:00P WORLD MUSIC AWARDS	P/T	4	2:00		2:00					
C 9:30P CYBILL	P/T	2	1:00	1:00						
C 9:00P INTRUDERS	P/T	1	:30				:30			
C 9:00P TONY AWARDS	P/T	1	:30							:30
F 8:18P COLD HARD FACTS	P/T	1	:30							:30
F 8:51P FOX NIGHT AT THE MOVIE	P/T	1	:30		:30					
F 8:31P LIVING SINGLE	P/T	1	:30				:30			
F 9:01P MEDICINE BALL	P/T	1	:30							
F 9:30P MY WILDEST DREAMS	P/T	1	:30		:30					
N 7:00P NBA PLAYOFF NITE	P/T	3	1:30			:30	:30			:30
PRIME TIME TOTALS		21	10:30	2:00	3:00	:30	1:00	:30	1:00	2:30
A 6:00A ABC NEWS THIS MORNING	M-F	8	4:00		1:00	1:00	1:00	1:00		
A 1:00P ALL MY CHILDREN	M-F	2	1:00	:30	:30					
A 3:00P GENERAL HOSPITAL	M-F	4	2:00			:30	:30	:30		
A 7:00A GOOD MORNING, AMERICA	M-F	2	1:00			:30	:30			
A 11:00A MIKE & MATY SHOW	M-F	1	:30				:30	:30		
A 2:00P ONE LIFE TO LIVE	M-F	4	2:00	:30		:30	:30			
C 2:00P AS THE WORLD TURNS	M-F	4	2:00		:30	:30		:30	:30	
C 1:30P BOLD AND THE BEAUTIFUL	M-F	3	1:30			:30	:30	:30		
C 6:00A CBS MORNING NEWS	M-F	3	1:30		:30	:30	:30			
C 7:00A CBS THIS MORNING	M-F	2	1:30				:30	:30		
C 3:00P GUIDING LIGHT	M-F	2	1:00	:30	:30					
C 11:00A PRICE IS RIGHT	M-F	3	1:30		:30		:30			
C 12:00N YOUNG AND THE RESTLESS	M-F	3	1:30					1:00		
N 1:00P DAYS OF OUR LIVES	M-F	4	2:00			:30	:30	:30		
N 10:00A LEEZA-MORNING	M-F	6	3:00	:30	:30	1:00	:30	:30		
N 6:00A NBC NEWS AT SUNRISE	M-F	5	2:30	:30	:30	:30	:30	:30		
N 11:00A OTHER SIDE/NBC	M-F	1	:30	:30						
N 7:00A TODAY SHOW	M-F	7	3:30				:30	:30		
M-F DAYTIME TOTALS		59	29:30	6:00	6:00	5:30	7:00	5:00		
N 4:00P HOOP IT UP	S/S	3	1:30							1:30
A 12:06X IN CONCERT	E/L	2	1:00					1:00		
C 12:37X LATE LATE/TOM SNYDER	E/L	2	1:00		:30	:30				
C 11:35P LATE SHOW/DAVID LTTRMN	E/L	1	:30					:30		
N 2:11X FRIDAY NIGHT VIDEOS	E/L	2	1:00					1:00		
N 12:36X LATE NGT/CONAN OBRIEN	E/L	2	1:00	1:00						
N 1:24X LATE NT/CONAN OBRIEN	E/L	4	2:00		1:30	:30				
N 2:34X LATER	E/L	1	:30				:30			
N 11:35P TONIGHT SHOW	E/L	4	2:00					:30		
E/L FRINGES TOTALS		18	9:00	1:00	2:30	1:00	:30	:30		
PRODUCT TOTALS		101	50:30	10:30	11:30	7:00	8:30	8:00	1:00	4:00

NETWORK TV REPORT MONITORED DURING WEEK ENDING JUNE 4, 1995

E. Sample page from *Media Watch.* Courtesy of *Competitive Media Reporting.*

60 MINUTES
WEEKS 1234 MINS 240
SUN 7.00PM - 8.00PM   DN   CBS

NTI NAD REPORT — NOVEMBER 1994
TABLE 10A -- EVENING
AUDIENCE BY MARKET SECTION
INDIVIDUAL NETWORK PROGRAMS (TOTAL DURATION)

RATINGS(%)	HOUSE-HOLDS	WRK WOM 18+	WOMEN 18+	18-34	18-49	25-54	35-64	55+	MEN 18+	18-34	18-49	25-54	35-64	55+	TEENS TOTAL 12-17	FEMALE 12-17	CHILDREN 2-11	6-11
TOTAL U.S.	18.4	10.7	14.2	5.0	7.0	9.1	13.5	28.9	11.9	4.3	6.2	8.2	12.1	25.7	2.2	2.6	1.9	2.0
TERRITORY																		
NORTHEAST	21.0	11.4	15.7	5.8	7.8	9.7	13.8	32.6	13.0	5.6	8.7	8.8	12.2	28.7	2.0∧	IFR	2.2∧	1.9∧
EAST CENTRAL	17.7	9.3	13.1	5.1	6.8	8.5	12.1	25.1	12.8	4.8	7.2	9.4	13.1	24.8	.9v	IFR	3.0∧	2.8∧
WEST CENTRAL	19.7	11.8	15.5	5.9	7.1	9.5	14.5	31.7	12.5	5.4	7.0	8.5	12.6	27.5	2.7∧	IFR	2.0∧	2.2∧
SOUTHEAST	18.9	11.3	15.2	5.6	7.7	10.1	14.5	28.4	12.4	3.9	6.3	8.7	12.6	25.1	2.8∧	IFR	1.8∧	2.4∧
SOUTHWEST	15.4	9.5	11.1	3.9∧	6.1	7.8	10.9	22.9	10.9	2.8∧	5.8	9.2	13.5	21.3	4.1∧	IFR	2.4∧	2.5∧
PACIFIC	16.1	9.8	13.0	3.4	6.1	8.2	14.0	28.6	9.7	3.0	4.6	5.6	9.5	24.6	1.5∧	1.3v	.8∧	.9v
COUNTY SIZE																		
A	17.9	9.7	13.0	4.3	6.4	8.1	12.4	28.5	11.3	4.2	6.4	8.2	11.9	25.0	1.9∧	1.0v	1.7	1.7∧
B	18.1	11.3	14.5	5.8	7.5	9.9	14.6	28.1	11.5	4.3	5.8	8.0	12.3	25.2	2.3∧	3.3∧	2.3	2.5∧
C & D	19.5	11.6	15.6	5.1	7.4	9.7	14.0	30.1	13.0	4.5	6.4	8.6	12.1	27.1	2.6∧	3.7∧	1.9	2.1∧
CABLE/VCR STATUS																		
ANY CABLE	17.2	10.6	13.2	5.2	6.9	8.9	12.8	27.1	10.9	3.7	5.8	7.7	11.5	24.2	1.7	1.7∧	2.0	2.1
PAY CABLE	14.2	8.4	10.0	4.8	5.6	7.3	10.2	24.0	8.7	2.9	5.1	6.6	9.4	21.4	1.2∧	.9v	1.5	1.6∧
NO CABLE	20.6	10.9	16.0	4.7	7.2	9.5	15.0	31.6	13.8	5.5	6.9	9.3	13.2	28.3	3.1	4.1∧	1.9	2.0∧
VCR OWNERSHIP	17.5	10.8	13.2	5.2	7.1	9.2	13.5	28.5	11.5	4.4	6.3	8.3	11.9	25.9	1.9	2.3	1.6	1.6
HHLD SIZE																		
1	23.5	19.6	29.7	IFR	13.5	17.8	24.3	36.3	16.0	IFR	9.6	11.7	15.0	26.4	IFR	IFR	IFR	IFR
2	24.1	14.3	20.3	8.6	11.2	13.9	19.3	29.5	19.6	6.5	9.0	12.0	18.6	28.8	IFR	IFR	IFR	IFR
3+	11.6	7.2	6.9	3.5	5.1	6.4	8.5	17.1	7.0	3.3	5.0	6.5	8.6	18.7	2.2	2.4	1.9	2.0
4+	10.0	6.3	5.6	3.3	4.8	5.9	7.2	11.0	5.6	2.7	4.6	5.8	7.3	13.0	1.9	2.6	1.9	2.1
PRESENCE OF NON-ADULTS																		
ANY UNDER 18	9.2	6.3	5.4	3.7	4.8	5.5	6.6	IFR	5.7	3.2	5.0	6.0	7.2	IFR	2.2	2.6	1.9	2.0
ANY UNDER 12	8.6	5.7	5.0	3.8	4.4	5.0	6.2	IFR	5.7	3.6	5.2	5.8	7.1	IFR	2.1	3.0∧	1.9	2.0
ANY UNDER 6	8.0	5.7	4.8	4.2	4.4	4.9	5.8	IFR	4.9	3.7	4.6	5.0	6.1	IFR	2.1∧	IFR	1.8	1.7∧
ANY 6-11	8.4	5.4	4.9	3.3	4.2	4.7	6.2	IFR	5.9	2.7∧	5.3	5.7	7.1	IFR	2.2∧	2.8∧	1.9	2.0
ANY 12-17	9.7	6.9	5.8	2.8∧	5.4	6.1	6.6	IFR	5.8	1.8∧	4.8	6.5	7.2	IFR	2.2	2.6	2.5	2.8
HOUSEHOLD INCOME																		
$20-29,999	17.7	9.0	13.9	3.3∧	5.2	7.6	13.9	27.8	11.9	3.6∧	5.3	7.6	10.7	24.2	2.7∧	IFR	1.9∧	2.5∧
$30-39,999	18.2	11.2	13.9	5.6	7.5	9.4	14.2	29.2	11.7	3.6∧	5.6	7.3	11.5	27.3	1.9v	IFR	1.6∧	1.4v
$40-59,999	16.5	10.5	11.6	4.7	7.0	8.9	13.1	26.1	10.0	3.9	5.1	7.1	11.1	26.1	1.7∧	1.9v	1.5∧	1.3∧
$60,000+	18.7	12.3	12.6	6.4	8.6	10.5	13.9	28.6	12.2	6.0	8.0	10.1	12.9	27.8	1.6∧	IFR	1.4∧	1.1∧
SELECTED UPPER DEMOS																		
$40,000+ WITH NON-ADULTS	11.0	7.0	5.9	3.8	5.5	6.0	7.1	IFR	6.3	3.5	5.2	6.4	7.4	IFR	1.7∧	1.5∧	1.5	1.2∧
$40,000+ & HOH POM	15.6	11.5	10.9	6.4	7.7	9.7	12.7	25.0	10.4	5.5	6.8	9.0	11.5	25.6	2.0∧	1.1v	1.5∧	.9v
$40,000+ & HOH 1+ YRS. COLLEGE	18.7	13.0	12.7	7.2	8.6	10.3	13.8	29.6	12.6	6.0	8.0	10.2	13.5	29.9	2.0∧	1.4v	1.5∧	1.1∧
EDUCATION OF HEAD OF HOUSE																		
NO COLLEGE	18.1	9.0	14.0	3.5	5.6	7.7	12.4	26.3	10.9	3.4	4.8	6.7	10.5	22.4	2.4	3.1∧	2.0	2.1
4+ YEARS OF COLLEGE	19.5	14.1	14.3	7.8	9.5	11.1	15.3	29.6	13.9	7.9	8.8	10.6	13.7	30.4	2.1∧	1.7v	2.3	1.8∧
RACE																		
BLACK	14.8	8.8	10.8	6.2	6.5	7.8	10.0	23.8	7.7	2.8∧	4.6	6.7	9.1	IFR	4.2∧	IFR	3.0∧	3.4∧

VIEWERS PER 1000 TOTAL U.S. VIEWING HOUSEHOLDS--REFERENCED TO 17.58 MILLION HOUSEHOLDS TUNED TO THIS PROGRAM

	HOUSE-HOLDS	WRK WOM 18+	WOMEN 18+	18-34	18-49	25-54	35-64	55+	MEN 18+	18-34	18-49	25-54	35-64	55+	TEENS TOTAL 12-17	FEMALE 12-17	CHILDREN 2-11	6-11
TOTAL U.S.	268		792	91	246	293	366	476	602	78	212	256	307	331	27	15	42	26
TERRITORY																		
NORTHEAST	65		195	24	61	70	83	122	144	22	50	60	68	81	5∧	IFR	9∧	5∧
EAST CENTRAL	30		99	12	32	36	44	58	85	11	32	38	45	44	1v	IFR	9∧	5∧
WEST CENTRAL	47		133	16	38	47	60	82	99	15	37	41	50	56	5∧	IFR	7∧	5∧
SOUTHEAST	54		162	19	50	60	74	95	117	13	39	50	59	65	6∧	IFR	7∧	6∧
SOUTHWEST	26		68	8∧	25	28	33	39	62	6∧	23	32	38	28	6∧	IFR	7∧	4∧
PACIFIC	45		135	12	41	51	71	80	96	11	32	35	46	56	3∧	1v	3∧	2v
COUNTY SIZE																		
A	103		297	34	94	111	138	180	235	33	92	107	124	122	9∧	2v	15	8∧
B	86		244	32	81	97	120	138	176	23	61	76	94	96	8∧	6∧	15	10∧
C & D	79		251	25	71	86	109	158	191	22	60	73	89	114	10∧	7∧	13	8∧
CABLE/VCR STATUS																		
ANY CABLE	181		469	60	156	190	229	267	358	43	129	155	190	195	13	6∧	26	16
PAY CABLE	73		163	28	65	80	93	77	138	17	58	69	83	67	5∧	2v	11	7∧
NO CABLE	86		323	31	90	104	137	209	244	35	83	101	117	136	14	9∧	16	10∧
VCR OWNERSHIP	240		598	82	219	261	318	319	490	68	186	226	263	252	20	12	30	18
HHLD SIZE																		
1	50		221	IFR	28	40	62	179	85	IFR	30	37	38	46	IFR	IFR	IFR	IFR
2	113		361	36	90	114	172	237	309	25	61	83	133	220	IFR	IFR	IFR	IFR
3+	104		211	46	129	140	132	60	209	42	121	136	136	64	25	14	39	25
4+	53		104	28	79	82	68	17	105	21	75	81	75	19	18	12	33	22
PRESENCE OF NON-ADULTS																		
ANY UNDER 18	70		123	41	102	102	77	IFR	114	27	89	97	81	IFR	27	15	42	26
ANY UNDER 12	46		87	37	73	72	47	IFR	85	25	72	73	55	IFR	12	8∧	42	26
ANY UNDER 6	27		54	31	47	43	20	IFR	46	20	40	39	24	IFR	4∧	IFR	25	9∧
ANY 6-11	27		53	16	43	46	35	IFR	55	9∧	45	47	41	IFR	10∧	7∧	32	26
ANY 12-17	37		61	8∧	51	52	49	IFR	55	5∧	39	47	48	IFR	27	15	15	12
HOUSEHOLD INCOME																		
$20-29,999	31		111	9∧	25	32	48	77	87	10∧	25	30	31	55	4∧	IFR	6∧	4∧
$30-39,999	41		101	15	37	42	50	55	83	10∧	28	33	39	48	3v	IFR	5∧	2v
$40-59,999	68		132	19	58	70	82	58	117	17	44	58	72	57	5∧	3v	8∧	4∧
$60,000+	100		167	26	83	100	116	61	176	28	82	98	115	74	5∧	IFR	6∧	3∧
SELECTED UPPER DEMOS																		
$40,000+ WITH NON-ADULTS	46		67	17	57	58	48	IFR	72	14	53	62	54	IFR	10∧	5∧	14	7∧
$40,000+ & HOH POM	66		100	19	56	70	75	27	100	17	50	64	72	34	5∧	1v	6∧	2v
$40,000+ & HOH 1+ YRS. COLLEGE	118		197	37	101	117	128	72	205	32	96	118	133	82	8∧	3v	10∧	4∧
EDUCATION OF HEAD OF HOUSE																		
NO COLLEGE	104		426	33	95	118	170	298	289	32	80	99	128	184	16	10∧	23	14
4+ YEARS OF COLLEGE	94		176	32	85	95	106	73	171	32	77	90	97	77	5∧	2v	11	5∧
RACE																		
BLACK	26		71	16	29	31	31	36	40	6∧	17	21	22	IFR	8∧	IFR	10∧	6∧

N.B. SEE LEAD PAGE OF THIS SECTION FOR EXPLANATIONS OF SYMBOLS.
Copyright 1994 Nielsen Media Research—Printed in U.S.A.

298

F. Sample page from the *National Television Index (NTI) National Audience Demographics Report.* Courtesy of *Nielsen Media Research.*

NTI NATIONAL AUDIENCE DEMOGRAPHICS REPORT
NOVEMBER 1994
TABLE 6A -- AUDIENCE BY RESPONDENT CHARACTERISTICS: ESTIMATES OF INDIVIDUAL NETWORK PROGRAMS (TOTAL DURATION)
EVENING

Each demographic cell lists three stacked values: rating (%) / audience (000) / index. △ denotes a symbol flag (see lead page).

PROGRAM NAME / DAY / START	DUR	NTWK	TYPE	WEEKS·MINS	KEY	HOUSE-HOLDS	WORKING WOMEN 18+	WW 18-49	WW 25-54	WW 35+	(18-49) W/ CHILD <3	<12	<18	PART TIME 18+	PT 18-49	LOH 18-49 W/CH <3	WOMEN W/ CHILD<3 18+	18-34	18-49	TWO INC FAM W 18+	W 18-49	W 25-54	MEN 18+	MEN 18-49	MEN 25-54
SIMPSONS TWO(P-->) SUN VARIOUS	30	FOX	EA	12 4 / 90	A/B	10.4 / 9.89	6.0/2.66/268	7.1/2.50/252	5.7/1.98/200	3.3/.91/92	7.8/.34/35	7.4/1.00/101	6.7/1.23/125	4.5/.42/43	5.8/.42/42	7.5/.72/73	7.2/.86/87	7.9/.69/69	7.4/.83/84	5.1/1.00/101	5.7/.93/95	5.6/.87/88	6.7/1.38/139	7.8/1.27/129	6.9/1.08/109
SINATRA DUETS(S) FRI 10.00PM	60	CBS	PC	4 / 60	A/B	7.6 / 7.25	5.6/2.46/339	4.1/1.46/201	5.1/1.78/246	7.2/1.97/272	4.5△/.20△/27△	2.9/.39/54	3.6/.67/93	3.3△/.31△/43△	1.7△/.12△/17△	2.4△/.23△/32△	2.3△/.37△/37△	2.1△/.19△/26△	2.3△/.26△/36△	7.3/1.42/196	6.0/.98/136	7.0/1.08/149	4.4/.92/127	3.3/.54/75	5.0/.78/107
SISTER, SISTER(P-->) WED 8.00PM	30	ABC	CS	34 / 60	A/B	9.2 / 8.78	5.6/2.48/283	5.6/1.99/227	6.0/2.08/237	5.8/1.58/180	5.9/.26/30	6.7/.91/104	6.9/1.28/146	5.5/.52/59	5.1/.36/42	5.7/.55/63	6.3/.74/85	8.1/.55/62	6.2/.70/79	5.3/1.03/118	5.5/.90/103	5.9/.91/104	3.3/.69/78	3.3/.54/62	3.7/.58/66
SISTERS SAT 10.00PM	60	NBC	GD	123 / 180	A/B	8.9 / 8.46	7.8/3.42/405	7.9/2.80/331	8.2/2.86/338	8.0/2.20/260	8.4/.37/44	7.0/.94/111	6.9/1.29/152	8.9/.84/99	8.8/.63/74	8.5/.82/97	8.2/.98/116	8.1/.71/84	8.3/.94/111	7.0/1.37/162	7.2/1.18/139	7.9/1.23/146	3.6/.74/87	3.1/.51/61	4.0/.62/74
60 MINUTES SUN 7.00PM	60	CBS	DN	1234 / 240	A/B	18.4 / 17.58	10.7/4.71/268	8.4/2.97/169	9.9/3.43/195	13.4/3.68/210	4.2/.19/11	5.5/.74/42	6.1/1.12/64	9.8/.92/52	4.6/.33/19	4.1/.39/22	4.0/.47/27	3.3/.29/16	3.7/.41/24	10.3/2.01/114	8.9/1.45/82	10.3/1.60/91	9.5/1.96/112	6.7/1.10/62	8.9/1.39/79
STEP BY STEP FRI 9.00PM	30	ABC	CS	1234 / 120	A/B	11.9 / 11.33	7.9/3.46/305	7.9/2.81/248	7.7/2.68/237	7.6/2.10/186	10.1/.45/39	9.9/1.34/118	9.5/1.76/155	8.3/.77/77	10.1/.72/64	11.4/1.10/97	10.6/1.26/111	10.1/.88/78	10.6/1.20/105	7.7/1.50/132	8.2/1.33/118	7.5/1.16/102	4.3/.89/67	4.6/.76/67	4.8/.75/66
SWEET JUSTICE SAT 8.00PM	120	NBC	GD	2 / 120	A/B	7.4 / 7.06	5.4/2.37/335	4.8/1.69/239	5.3/1.83/260	6.6/1.82/258	3.8△/.17△/24△	2.7/.37/52	3.5/.64/91	5.5/.51/73	4.3△/.31△/44△	3.3△/.32△/46△	3.3/.40/56	2.8△/.24△/35△	3.2△/.36△/50△	3.7/.72/102	3.5/.57/80	4.4/.68/96	2.4/.50/71	1.9△/.31△/44△	2.5/.39/55
THUNDER ALLEY WED 8.00PM	30	ABC	CS	1 / 30	A/B	10.6 / 10.11	5.9/2.58/255	5.8/2.05/203	6.0/2.07/204	5.4/1.47/146	10.6/.47/46	7.6/1.02/101	7.1/1.32/130	8.3/.78/77	8.3/.59/58	9.4/.90/89	7.9/.94/93	8.4/.73/72	8.3/.94/93	6.6/1.29/127	6.3/1.04/102	6.8/1.06/105	5.1/1.05/104	5.5/.91/90	5.7/.89/88
TOUCHED BY AN ANGEL WED 9.00PM	60	CBS	GD	1 / 60	A/B	9.0 / 8.59	5.6/2.45/286	4.5/1.60/186	5.5/1.92/224	7.0/1.92/224	2.2△/.10△/11△	4.1/.55/64	4.7/.87/102	4.7/.44/52	2.2△/.16△/19△	2.6△/.29△/29△	2.6△/.32△/37△	2.4△/.21△/24△	2.4△/.27△/32△	4.2/.82/95	3.2/.52/61	4.7/.73/85	3.5/.72/84	2.7/.44/52	4.1/.64/75
TRIBUTE-TV FUNNST FAMILIES(S) SAT 10.00PM	60	NBC	CV	4 / 60	A/B	12.1 / 11.54	9.2/4.06/352	9.6/3.40/295	9.6/3.34/289	9.4/2.57/223	10.5/.46/40	9.6/1.30/112	9.7/1.80/156	12.5/1.17/101	12.3/.87/76	1.00/87	9.9/1.18/102	9.9/.86/75	10.1/1.13/98	10.0/1.96/170	9.8/1.60/139	9.7/1.51/130	6.2/1.29/111	6.4/1.04/90	6.5/1.02/88
TURNING POINT WED 10.00PM	60	ABC	DN	1 34 / 180	A/B	11.3 / 10.81	8.3/3.66/338	7.8/2.75/254	8.6/2.98/276	9.3/2.57/237	6.0/.27/25	7.3/.98/91	7.6/1.41/130	8.1/.76/70	7.3/.52/48	7.8/.75/75	7.2/.86/79	7.8/.68/63	7.4/.83/77	7.8/1.53/142	7.8/1.27/117	8.3/1.74/132	7.1/1.46/135	7.0/1.14/106	7.8/1.22/112
20/20 FRI 10.00PM	60	ABC	DN	1234 / 240	A/B	13.8 / 13.14	10.2/4.50/343	9.5/3.36/255	10.5/3.63/276	11.9/3.27/249	10.6/.47/36	10.0/1.35/103	10.4/1.93/147	11.0/1.04/79	9.4/.67/51	11.6/1.12/85	10.3/1.22/93	9.7/.84/64	10.4/1.18/89	10.5/2.05/156	10.3/1.68/128	11.2/1.74/132	6.7/1.38/105	5.8/.95/72	7.1/1.12/85
UNDER SUSPICION FRI 9.00PM	60	CBS	GD	123 / 180	A/B	9.1 / 8.65	5.6/2.46/284	4.1/1.43/166	4.9/1.68/194	7.0/1.93/223	4.6△/.20△/23△	2.7/.37/43	3.5/.64/74	5.8/.55/63	2.6△/.19△/22△	3.3/.31/36	3.0/.36/41	2.6/.23/26	3.0/.34/39	4.4/.86/100	3.6/.59/68	4.8/.75/87	3.3/.69/80	2.3/.37/43	3.5/.55/63

N.B. SEE LEAD PAGE OF THIS SECTION FOR EXPLANATIONS OF SYMBOLS.

G. Sample page from the *National Television Index (NTI) National Audience Demographics Report.* Courtesy of *Nielsen Media Research.*

METRO HH	STATION DAY PROGRAM	DMA HOUSEHOLD RATINGS WEEKS				MULTI-WEEK AVG	H U T	DMA RATINGS PERSONS											WOMEN								MEN						TNS	CHILD
R T G / S H R		1	2	3	4	R T G / S H R		2+	18+	12-24	12-34	18-34	18-49	21-49	25-54	35+	35-64	50+	18+	12-24	18-34	18-49	21-49	25-49	25-54	50+	W K G	18+	18-34	18-49	21-49	25-49	25-54	12-17	2-11	6-11
1 / 2		3	4	5	6	7 / 8	14	15	16	17	18	19	20	21	22	23	24	25	26	27	28	29	30	31	32	33	34	35	36	37	38	39	40	41	42	43
1 / LT	R.S.E. THRESHOLDS 25+% (1 S.E.) 4 WK AVG 50+%	2 / LT	2 / LT	2 / LT	2 / LT	1 / LT	1	1 / LT	1 / LT	3 / 1	2 / LT	2 / LT	1 / LT	1 / LT	1 / LT	1 / LT	1 / LT	1 / LT	5 / 1	3 / 1	2 / LT	2 / LT	2 / 1	1 / LT	2 / 1	1 / LT	4 / 1	2 / LT	2 / LT	2 / LT	2 / 1	6 / 2	4 / 1	6 / 1
	3:00PM																																			
9 / 29	WLS MON INSIDE EDITION	10	9	11	9	10	30	32	4	5		2		3	3	4	7	5	9	6		3	4	4	4	5	12	3	3	1	2	3	3		1	1
10 / 30	TUE INSIDE EDITION	9	10	10	10	10	31	31	4	5	2	2	2	2	3	7	4	11	7	3	4	4	4	5	14	3	2				1	2		1	1
8 / 25	WED INSIDE EDITION	9	7	8	9	8	26	31	3	4	1	1	2	2	3	6	4	9	6	1	3	3	4	4	12	4	2		1	1	1	1		1	1
8 / 24	THU INSIDE EDITION	7	7	9		8	24	32	3	4	1		2	3	3	5	4	7	6	2	4	4	4	5	9	3	2	1	1	1	1	1		1	1
5 / 14	THU INSIDE EDTN TK			5		5	14	35	2	2			1	1	4	4	6	2			1	1	1	1	4		2	3					2			
10 / 30	FRI INSIDE EDITION	12	8	10		10	30	33	5	6	3	3	3	4	4	7	5	9	9	6	7	7	7	7	8	13	5	2		1	1	1	1	3	1	
9 / 28	AV5 INSIDE EDITION	9	8	9	9	9	28	32	4	5	1	2	2	3	3	6	4	9	7	2	4	4	4	5	12	4	2		1	1	1	1	1	1	1
4 / 8	SUN KAPALUA-GLF SU	4				4	8	50	2	2	1	1			1	3	2	5	1						1	3	1	3		1	1	2	2			
2 / 4	SUN MRLL LYNCH-GLF		2				4	52	1	1						1	1	2									2	1	1	1	1	1	1			
7 / 13	SUN SKATE AMER2ABC			7		7	13	52	3	4		1	1	2	2	3	6	3	8	6		1	3	3	4	5	12	4	2	1							
4 / 7	SUN SUN AFTRNN MV2				4	4	7	59	2	2			1		2	2	3	2				1	2	2	2		2	3	3	4	2	2	4	5	
6 / 18	WMAQ MON DONAHUE	7	7	6	5	6	18	34	3	3	2	2	2	2	2	3	2	5	4	2	3	3	3	3	6	3	2	1	1	1	1	1		1	1
5 / 16	TUE DONAHUE	5	6	5	5	5	16	34	2	2	2	2	2	2	2	3	2	4	4	3	3	3	3	3	5	3	2	1	1	1	1	1		1	
5 / 15	WED DONAHUE	3	5	6	5	5	15	34	2	2	2	2	2	2	2	3	2	4	4	3	3	3	3	3	5	3	1		1	1	1	1			
6 / 19	THU DONAHUE	7	6	5		6	19	34	3	3	2	2	2	2	3	3	2	4	5	4	3	3	3	3	9	3	2	1	1	1	1	1			
5 / 16	THU DONAHUE TK				5	5	15	35	3	4	3	3	4	3	3	3	2	3	4	2	1	1	1	1	4	1	4	7	5	4	3	3			
6 / 16	FRI DONAHUE	5	6	5	7	6	16	36	2	3	1	1	1	2	2	2	2	4	3	3	1	1	1	1	7	3	2	1	1	1	1	1			
6 / 17	AV5 DONAHUE	6	6	5	6	6	17	34	2	3	2	2	2	2	2	2	2	5	4	3	3	3	3	3	6	3	2	1	1	1	1	1			
2 / 5	SAT WRLD CP GLF-SA		2				5	43					1	1			3						1	1	1	1		2	1	1	1	1	1			
11 / 20	SUN NBC NFL FTBL 2	14	7	17	4	11	19	55	6	7	3	6	7	7	7	8	7	7	8	4	2	4	4	4	5	4	11	10	10	11	12	12	3	2	2
2 / 5	WPWR MON GOOF TROOP	1	2	1	1	1	5	32	1		1		1						1			1			1								2	3	2
2 / 7	TUE GOOF TROOP	2	2	1	3	2	6	31	1		1	1	1	1					1		3	2	1	3	2	1								3	3	3
2 / 6	WED GOOF TROOP	3	1	2	1	2	5	32			1		1	1	1	1			1		2	1	1	1	1									3	3	3
2 / 5	THU GOOF TROOP	1	2	1		1	5	32	1			2	1						1		1	1	1	1									3	4	4
2 / 6	THU GOOF TROOP TK				2	2	6	35	3	1	2	2	1	2	2	1	2		1		2	2	2	2			1			1	2	2	9	5	7
2 / 5	FRI GOOF TROOP	1	2	2		1	5	34	1		1								1		1	1	1	1						1	1	1		2	3	
2 / 5	AV5 GOOF TROOP	2	2	2	2	2	5	32	1		1	1	1	1	1	1			1		1	1	1	1							1	1		2	3	4
2 / 5	SAT HEAVEN HELP US	1	3	2	3	2	5	41	1	1	1	1	1		1		1		1		1	1	2	2	2	1	1							1	6	2
4 / 8	SUN SUN 50 FEATURE	3	5	4	4	4	7	53	2	2	5	4	3	3	2	2	2	1	1	3	7	4	4	4	3	1	2	2	1	1	1	1	1	6	2	2
1 / 3	WTTW MON WILD AMERICA	1	1	1	1	1	3	32									1	1															1		
1 / 3	TUE WILD AMERICA	1	1	1	1	1	3	31	1	1			1	1	1	1	1			1	1	1	1				1	1		1		1			
1 / 4	WED WILD AMERICA	1	1	2	1	1	4	32	1	1						1	1							1	1									
1 / 3	THU MOV 2				1	1	3	35	1	1				1				1						2	1									
1 / 3	THU WILD AMERICA	1	1			1	2	32										1				1	1	1				1							
1 / 3	FRI WILD AMERICA	2	1	2		1	4	33	1	1												1		1			1							1	
1 / 3	AV5 WILD AMERICA	1	1	1	1	1	3	32	1					1	1	1	1	1				1		1			1								
4 / 10	SAT J WILSON-COOKN	4	3	5		4	10	40	2	2			2	2	2	3	3	3	1	2	3	2	4	2	2	2	2	2	2	2	2	2	1			
	3:15PM																																			
<<	WCIU THU MARKET COMMNTY	<<	<<	<<		<<	33																													
15 / 31	WFLD SUN FOX NFL-PSTGM1	15				15	30	49	9	10	7	9	10	10	10	10	10	10	2			2	2	3	3	2		5	14	14	14	15	15	15	8	3	
3 / 8	WTTW SAT PLEDGE			3	3	3	7	40	1	1				1	1	2	2	3	1		2	2	2	3	3	3		1	1	1	1	1	1			
1 / 2	SUN PLEDGE			1	1		2	58	1	1			1	1	2	2	3	1						2	3		1									
	3:30PM																																			
4 / 10	WBBM MON AMERCN JOURNAL	3	2	5	4	4	10	36	2	2			1	1	1	3	2	4	3		1	1	1	1	2	6	1	1						1		
4 / 11	TUE AMERCN JOURNAL	3	3	4	4	3	10	36	2	2		1	1	1	1	3	2	4	3	1	2	2	2	2	5	1	1	1								
4 / 11	WED AMERCN JOURNAL	4	4	3		4	11	36	2	2		1	1	1	1	2	2	5	3	1	1	1	1	1	5	2	1	2	1	1	1	1	1		2	1	1
3 / 9	THU AMERCN JOURNAL	4	3	3		3	9	35	2	2		1	2	1	1	1	2	2	3	1			1		5	2	1	1								
2 / 6	THU AMERCN JRNL TK				2	2	6	35	1	1	2		1	1	1	2	2	3	1			1			3	1		1							1	2	
4 / 12	FRI AMERCN JOURNAL	6	3	4		4	12	37	2	3		1	1	1	1	2	4	2	6	3	2	2	2	2	3	7	2	2			1	1	1			
5 / 12	FRI AMRCN JOURNL H			5	5	5	12	40	2	2		1	1	1	1	2	2	3	4	2	3	3	2	3	2	6										
4 / 11	AV5 AMERCN JOURNAL	4	3	4	4	4	10	36	2	2		1	1	1	1	1	3	2	5	3	1	2	2	2	2	6	1	2	1	1	1	1	1			
1 / 3	SAT EYE-SPORTS-SAT	2	<<			1	3	45		1			1		1	1				1					1		1	2	1	1	1	1	1			
1 / 2	WCFC SAT SIMPLY FISHNG	1	<<	1	<<	1	2	41								1								1						1		1	1			
<<	SUN JEWISH JEWELS	1	1	<<	<<	<<		52																												
<<	WCIU MON CHESPIRITO	<<	<<	<<	<<	<<		39																												
<<	TUE CHESPIRITO	<<	1	<<	<<	<<		38		1							1																			
<<	WED CHESPIRITO		1	<<	<<	<<		38		1							1														1	1	1			
<<	THU CHESPIRITO	<<	<<	<<	<<	<<		37																												
<<	FRI CHESPIRITO	<<	<<	<<	<<	<<		39																												
<<	AV5 CHESPIRITO	<<	<<	<<	<<	<<		38																												
<<	SAT PAID PROGRAM	<<	<<	<<	<<	<<		44																												
<<	SUN NATNL GREEK TV	<<	<<	<<	<<	<<		53																												
4 / 10	WFLD MON TAZMNA M-F-FOX	3	4	3	4	4	10	36	2		2	1								1								1						4	9	8
3 / 10	TUE TAZMNA M-F-FOX	3	4	3	4	3	10	36	2		1	1							1	2								1				1		1	10	6
4 / 11	WED TAZMNA M-F-FOX	5	4	4	3	4	11	36	2	1	2	1	1	1					1	2	1	1	1				1	1	1			1		3	8	6
3 / 9	THU TAZMNA M-F-FOX	4	3	2		3	9	35	2		2	1	1	1					2	1	1	1						1			1			4	8	7
3 / 9	FRI TAZMNA M-F-FOX	4	3	3	3	3	9	38	2		2	1							2	1														3	7	7
4 / 10	AV5 TAZMNA M-F-FOX	4	4	3	3	4	10	36	2		2	1	1	1					2	1	1							1	1	1				3	9	7
8 / 16	SUN BEARS LV PSTGM	7				7	15	49	4	5	4	4	4	5	5	5	5	5	2		1	2	2	2	2	3	8	7	7	7	7	8	4			
8 / 15	SUN FOX NW CH POST	6		8		7	14	50	4	5		5	5	5	5	5	4	4	2	3		2	2	2	2	1	8	10	8	8	8	8	5	2	3
1 / 3	WGBO FRI UP ON-HOUSETOP			1	1	1	3	40	1	1				1	1	1	2	1						2	4	2										

| | | 3 | 4 | 5 | 6 | 7 / 8 | 14 | 15 | 16 | 17 | 18 | 19 | 20 | 21 | 22 | 23 | 24 | 25 | 26 | 27 | 28 | 29 | 30 | 31 | 32 | 33 | 34 | 35 | 36 | 37 | 38 | 39 | 40 | 41 | 42 | 43 |

See Program Index for complete details of program start time, duration and weeks of telecast.

Nielsen has been advised that a station(s) conducted a special promotional activity. See page 3.

H. Sample page from the *Nielsen Station Index* report. Courtesy of *Nielsen Media Research.*

St. Petersburg

Pinellas County—Map Location F-4

TIMES

490 First Ave., South, St. Petersburg, FL 33701-4204.
Phone 813-893-8554, Classif, 813-893-8363. Fax 813-893-8981

ABC

Location ID: 1 NSNL FL **Mid 016331-000**
Member: NAA; ABC Coupon Distribution Verification Service; ACB, Inc.
MORNING AND SUNDAY.

1. PERSONNEL
VP/Mktg—Al Corey.
Adv Dir—Richard Reeves.
Gen Adv Mgr—Bruce E. Karlson.
Retail Adv Mgr—Ralph Scaglione.

2. REPRESENTATIVES and/or BRANCH OFFICES
Cresmer, Woodward, O'Mara & Ormsbee.
Towmar, Inc.—Mexico.
RJR Media Sales, Inc. (Hotel & Resort).
American Publishers' Representatives LTD. (Canada)
The Leonard Company.

3. COMMISSION AND CASH DISCOUNT
15% to agencies; 15th following month. No cash discount.

4. POLICY-ALL CLASSIFICATIONS
30-day notice given of any rate revision.
Alcoholic beverage advertising accepted daily and Sunday—except in comics.

ADVERTISING RATES
Effective January 1, 1995 (card #95G).
Received February 28, 1995.

5. BLACK/WHITE RATES

	Morn.	Sun.
SAU open, per inch	212.00	275.00

Inches charged full depth: col. 21.5; pg. 129; dbl truck 279.5.

VOLUME DISCOUNTS

Inches:	% Discount	Morn.	Sun.
375"	3	205.64	266.75
750"	6	199.28	258.50
1,200"	10	190.80	247.50
1,600"	12	186.56	242.00
2,000"	14	182.32	236.50
3,200"	18	173.84	225.50
6,500"	24	161.12	209.00
9,000"	26	156.88	203.50
12,500"	28	152.64	198.00

5a. ZONE EDITIONS

	Per inch, per day Morn.	Sun.
City South*	32.34	46.41
City East*	48.08	64.08
City West*	41.80	56.69
Siminole*	23.96	30.49
Largo*	30.51	41.19
Clearwater*	44.20	55.42
North Pinellas*	17.88	22.57
Pasco SW*	27.92	37.20
Pasco NW*	27.92	38.32
Hernando**	14.34	18.74
Citrus**	10.51	13.95
Tampa (Hillsborough)***	10.60	14.10

(*) Regional editions on Wednesday in the three City zones, Seminole, Largo, Clearwater, North Pinellas and two Pasco zones include non-subscribers.
(**) Regional editions on Thursday in the Hernando and Citrus Times includ non-subscribers.
(***) Regional edition on Friday in Tampa (Hillsborough) includes non-subscribers.

DISCOUNTS

When purchased in combination, regional editions or City Times (excluding Tampa) earn the following discounts: any 2 zones 5%; any 3 zones 6%; any 4 or more zones 7%.

NON-SUBSCRIBER RATES

Edit. (Day)	Per inch
City South (Wed)	41.93
City East (Wed)	61.80
City West (Wed)	53.71
Seminole (Wed)	30.88
Largo (Wed)	39.33
Clearwater (Wed)	55.27
North Pinellas (Wed)	23.16
South Pasco (Wed)	34.65
North Pasco (Wed)	34.65
Hernando (Thur)	22.16
Citrus (Thur)	18.19
Tampa (Fri)	21.20

Circulation not received since 9-30-89.
Minimum 3/4 column inch.

6. GROUP COMBINATION RATES-B/W & COLOR
Total Market Coverage (TMC) and Alternate Delivery available for both R.O.P. and Preprints.
Geographical and targeted zoning also available.
Details and rates available upon request.
Circulation not received since 3-31-90.

7. COLOR RATES AND DATA

National ROP

Cost per edition	b/w 1 c	b/w 2 c	b/w 3 c
St. Petersburg Times Daily or Sun	940.00	1,260.00	1,575.00
City South	395.00	555.00	705.00
City East	395.00	555.00	705.00
City West	395.00	555.00	705.00
Seminole	160.00	240.00	320.00
Largo	395.00	555.00	705.00
Clearwater	395.00	555.00	705.00
North Pinellas	160.00	240.00	320.00
North & South Pasco*	395.00	555.00	705.00
Hernando	160.00	240.00	320.00
Citrus	160.00	240.00	320.00
Tampa (Hillsborough)	160.00	240.00	320.00

(*) Color ad must run in both Pasco zones.

Double-Trucks or Companion Pages

Cost per edition	b/w 1 c	b/w 2 c	b/w 3 c
St. Petersburg Times Daily or Sun	1,425.00	1,730.00	2,060.00
City South	555.00	705.00	870.00
City East	555.00	705.00	870.00
City West	555.00	705.00	870.00
Seminole	240.00	320.00	395.00
Largo	555.00	705.00	870.00
Clearwater	555.00	705.00	870.00
North Pinellas	240.00	320.00	395.00
North & South Pasco*	555.00	705.00	870.00
Hernando	240.00	320.00	395.00
Citrus	240.00	320.00	395.00
Tampa (Hillsborough)	240.00	320.00	395.00

Minimum 3/4 column inch.
Closing dates: Reservations 6 days in advance: for all given zone editions. Daily issues 4 days; Sunday 6 days prior to publication date. Cancellation date 9:30 a.m. 4 days prior to publication.

8a. INSERTS
PREPRINTED INSERTS

Cost/M	Std*	Tab*	Flexee*
2 pgs	54.00	45.00	38.00
4 pgs	64.00	54.00	45.00
6 pgs	78.00	58.00	51.00
8 pgs	85.00	64.00	58.00
10 pgs	92.00	70.00	65.00
12 pgs	98.00	78.00	71.00
14 pgs	101.00	83.00	76.00
16 pgs	105.00	85.00	80.00
18 pgs	107.00	89.00	82.00
20 pgs	109.00	92.00	85.00
22 pgs	111.00	96.00	87.00
24 pgs	113.00	98.00	88.00
28 pgs	114.00	101.00	90.00
32 pgs	116.00	105.00	91.00
36 pgs	117.00	107.00	97.00
40 pgs	118.00	109.00	101.00
44 pgs	119.00	111.00	105.00
48 pgs	120.00	113.00	109.00

(*)Std. 210+ sq. inches per pg; Tab 106-210 sq. inches per pg.; Flexee up to 105 sq. inches per pg. add 1.00 per/M for 48+ pg.
500.00 minimum.

FREQUENCY DISCOUNTS

Inserts per year:	Discount	Inserts per year:	Discount
6 to 11	4%	36 to 47	14%
12 to 23	6%	48 to 59	18%
24 to 35	10%	60 or more	22%

9. SPLIT RUN
Minimum 3/4 col. inches. Times, 4-way split accepted.
Basic rate plus 142.00 per split service charge in each newspaper for each makeover. Color is an additional: 106.00 per color plate.

11. SPECIAL DAYS/PAGES/FEATURES
Best Food Day: Thursday.
Travel Day, Sunday.

12. R.O.P. DEPTH REQUIREMENTS
Ads over 18 inches deep charged full col.

13. CONTRACT AND COPY REGULATIONS
See Contents page for location of regulations—items 1, 2, 4, 6, 7, 8, 9, 10, 11, 12, 13, 13, 15, 16, 17, 18, 19, 20.

14. CLOSING TIME
Published Morning and Sunday.

Day	Time	Closes	Day	Time	Closes
Mon	5 pm	Fri	Fri	5 pm	Tue
Tue	5 pm	Fri	Sat	5 pm	Wed
Wed	12 n	Mon	Sun	5 pm	Thu
Thu	5 pm	Mon			

SPECIAL SECTIONS

Day	Time	Closes
Food (Thu)	12 n	Mon
Religion (Sat)	12 n	Tue
Travel/Floridian (Sun)	5 pm	Tue
At Home (Sat)	5 pm	Tue

15. MECHANICAL MEASUREMENTS
PRINTING PROCESS: Offset.
6 col; ea 2-1/16"; 1/8" betw col.
Inches charged full depth: col. 21.5; pg. 129; dbl truck 279.5.

16. SPECIAL CLASSIFICATIONS/RATES
Travel, Tour Operator and Transportion:

	Morn.	Sun.
Per inch	212.00	275.00

Travel Advertising: Hotels, Resorts, Tourist Boards, (Florida State Only):

	Daily	Sun.
Per Inch	119.00	156.00

ROP EMPLOYMENT RATES:

	Daily	Sun.
Per inch	228.00	301.00

17. CLASSIFIED RATES
For complete data refer to classified rate section.

18. COMICS
POLICY—ALL CLASSIFICATIONS
When orders are placed through Metro-Puck Comic Network—see that listing.
Effective January 1, 1995. (Card No. 94G)
Received October 31, 1994.

Unit size	Inch equiv.	Unit rate
1/6 page	22-1/2	5,556.00
1/4 page	32-1/4	7,247.00
1/3 page	43	8,087.00
1/2 page	64-1/2	10,629.00
2/3 page	86	14,141.00
1 page	129	21,680.00

CLOSING TIMES
Friday, 16 days prior to publication.
MECHANICAL MEASUREMENTS
PRINTING PROCESS: Rotary Offset.
Standard page size: 13" wide x 21-3/8" deep.
For ad sizes see Metro-Puck Comic Network listing.
Colors available: ANPA/AAAA: 3 plus black; comic blue, red, yellow.

19. MAGAZINES

TV Dial

SUNDAY.
Effective January 1, 1995. (Card No. 94G)
Received February 28, 1995.

BLACK/WHITE RATES

MONOTONE	Full Run	MONOTONE	Full Run
7 x 10	19,250.00	2 x 3	1,650.00
3 x 10	8,250.00	1 x 5	1,375.00
3 x 7	5,775.00	2 x 2-1/2	1,375.00
2 x 10	5,500.00	3 x 1-1/2	1,238.00
3 x 5	4,125.00	2 x 2	1,100.00
2 x 7	3,850.00	1 x 3	825.00
3 x 4	3,300.00	1 x 2-1/2	688.00
2 x 6	3,300.00	1 x 2	550.00
2 x 5	2,750.00	1 x 1-1/2	413.00
3 x 3	2,475.00	1 x 1	275.00
2 x 3-1/2	1,925.00	1 x 3/4	206.00

COLOR RATES AND DATA
Minimum 3/4 inches.
Use b/w rate plus the following applicable cost:

	b/w 1 c	b/w 2 c	b/w 3 c
Extra, per page or less	415.00	640.00	850.00
Double truck	495.00	765.00	1,020.00

CLOSING TIMES
12 days before publication date.
MECHANICAL MEASUREMENTS
PRINTING PROCESS: Offset.
Full page 3 cols. wide x 10" deep.
SPECIAL CLASSIFICATION/RATES
Coated Stock Cover Rates

	Black & 3 colors
Back Cover	11,685.00
Inside Front Cover	10,674.00
Inside Back Cover	10,815.00
Centerfold page	8,570.00
3-page gatefold	28,989.00

20. CIRCULATION
Established 1884. Per copy daily .25; Sunday 1.00.
Net Paid—A.B.C. 9-30-94 (Newspaper Form)

	Total	NDM	Outside
	NEWSPAPER DESIGNATED MARKET		
Morn	329,604	289,750	39,854
Sun	423,691	364,949	58,742

Unpaid distribution (not included above):
Morn Total 3,508; Sun Total 743.
A.B.C. Zip Code Analysis available from publisher.
For county, MSA & DMA data, see CIRCULATION 95.

Sanford

Seminole County—Map Location G-3

HERALD

P.O. Box: 1667, 300 N. French Ave., Sanford, FL 32771-1667.
Phone 407-322-2611. Fax 407-323-9408

Location ID: 1 NSNL FL **Mid 016332-000**
Member: NAA.
EVENING AND SUNDAY MORNING (except Saturday).

1. PERSONNEL
Bus Mgr—Odessa Pugh.
Adv Dir—Tracy Schneider.

2. REPRESENTATIVES and/or BRANCH OFFICES
Landon Associates, Inc.

3. COMMISSION AND CASH DISCOUNT
15% to agencies; 2% 10th following month.

4. POLICY-ALL CLASSIFICATIONS
30-day notice given on any rate revision.
Alcoholic beverage advertising accepted.
Insertion orders or contracts containing liability disclaimers are not accepted. Agencies are held responsible for payment of invoices for advertising placed by them on their own behalf or on behalf of their clients. In lieu of agency liability, written documentation must be provided by the advertiser assuming responsibility for payment.

ADVERTISING RATES
Effective January 1, 1992.
Received November 5, 1991.

5. BLACK/WHITE RATES
SAU flat, per inch 8.43
Inches charged full depth: col. 21.5; pg. 129; dbl truck 279.5.

6. GROUP COMBINATION RATES-B/W & COLOR
Also sold in combination with Herald Advertiser (Thurs.), comb. per inch 13.52.
Circulation not received since 9-30-91.

7. COLOR RATES AND DATA
Available daily.
Use b/w rate plus the following applicable net costs:

	b/w 1 c	b/w 2 c	b/w 3 c
Extra	75.00	140.00	210.00

4-color process, extra 285.00.

11. SPECIAL DAYS/PAGES/FEATURES
Best Food Days: Wednesday & Sunday.
Church, TV Magazine, Friday; Business Health, Education, Sunday.

12. R.O.P. DEPTH REQUIREMENTS
Ads over 18-1/2 inches deep charged full column.

14. CLOSING TIME
Published Evening (ex. Sat) and Sunday Morning.

Day	Time	Closes	Day	Time	Closes
Mon	12 n	Fri	Thu	3 pm	Tue
Tue	3 pm	Fri	Fri	3 pm	Wed
Wed	3 pm	Mon	Sun	3 pm	Thu

SPECIAL SECTIONS

Day	Time	Closes
Sunday People	12 n	Thu

15. MECHANICAL MEASUREMENTS
PRINTING PROCESS: Offset.
6 col; ea 2-1/6"; 1/8" betw col.
Inches charged full depth: col. 21.5; pg. 129; dbl truck 279.5.

16. SPECIAL CLASSIFICATIONS/RATES
Legal, Political, Automotive and all other—general rates apply. Cash with order unless placed by recognized agency.

17. CLASSIFIED RATES
For complete data refer to classified rate section.

20. CIRCULATION
Established 1908. Per copy .30, .75 Sunday.
Net Paid—Sworn 9-30-94

	Total	CZ	TrZ	Other
ExSat	6,685	5,123	589	973
Sun	6,605	5,031	541	1,033

For county, MSA & DMA data, see CIRCULATION 95.

Sarasota

Sarasota County—Map Location F-5

HERALD-TRIBUNE

801 S. Tamiami Trail, Sarasota, FL 34236.
Phone 813-957-5126. Fax 813-957-5235

ABC

Location ID: 1 NSNL FL **Mid 016333-000**
Member: ACB, Inc., NAA.
MORNING, SATURDAY AND SUNDAY.

April, 1995 **Newspaper Advertising Source**

I. Sample page from *Standard Rate and Data Service Newspaper Advertising Source.* Courtesy of *Standard Rate and Data Service.*

49 Women's

GLAMOUR®

A Conde Nast Publications, Inc. Publication

ABC MPA

Location ID: 8 MLST 49 **Mid 001296-000**
Published monthly by Conde Nast Publications, Inc., Conde Nast Bldg., 350 Madison Ave., 10th Fl., New York, NY 10017. Phone 212-880-8800. Fax 212-880-8336

For shipping info., see Print Media Production Source.

PUBLISHER'S EDITORIAL PROFILE

GLAMOUR is edited for the contemporary American woman. It informs her of the trends, recommends how she can adapt them to her needs, and motivates her to take action. Over half of Glamour's editorial content focuses on fashion, beauty and health, as well as coverage of personal relationships, career, travel, food and entertainment. Rec'd 11/12/91.

1. PERSONNEL
Pub—Charles Townsend, 880-8653
Adv Prod—Paula Hayden. 880-8462.
Adv Dir—Debbi Fine, 880-8697.
Adv Mgr—Stephanie Britton, 880-7822.

2. REPRESENTATIVES and/or BRANCH OFFICES
Chicago 60611—Greg Clements, 875 N. Michigan Ave. Phone 312-649-3527.
Beverly Hills, CA 90212—Nina Rosenblatt, Art Bartholomew, 9100 Wilshire Blvd. Phone 213-205-7600.
San Francisco 94111—Anne Sortwell, Robin McKnight, 50 Francisco St. Phone 415-955-8230.
Marblehead, MA 01945—Harle Wehde, 44 Pickwick Rd. Phone 617-639-1662.
Troy, MI 48084—Larry Wallace, 3250 W. Big Beaver Rd, Ste 233. Phone 810-643-8728.
Atlanta—Coleman & Bentz, Inc.
Dallas, TX—Carol Orr & Co.
Odessa, FL—Swain & Eversole.

3. COMMISSION AND CASH DISCOUNT
15% to recognized agencies. No cash discount. Invoices are payable 30 days from date of invoice.

4. GENERAL RATE POLICY
Announcement of any change in rate will be made at least 2 months in advance of black and white closing date for the issue affected. Orders for issues thereafter at rates then prevailing.

ADVERTISING RATES
Effective January 1, 1995. (Issue)
Rates received January 18, 1995.

5. BLACK/WHITE RATES

1 page	53,260.
2/3 page	39,420.
1/2 page or Digest	33,600.
1/3 page	20,830.
1/6 page	10,790.

VOLUME DISCOUNT
Based upon the number of pages run in a 12 month period, advertisers are entitled to discounts off the open page rate. To qualify, you must place a minimu of 3 pages of advertising in Glamour within a 12 month period.

FREQUENCY DISCOUNT

3 pages	4%	18 pages	14%
6 pages	6%	24 pages	16%
9 pages	9%	36 pages	18%
12 pages	12%	48 pages	20%

5a. COMBINATION RATES
Also sold in combination—see listing for Conde Nast Select in class 22.

6. COLOR RATES

2-Color:	
1 page	65,920.
2/3 page	48,240.
1/2 page or Digest	43,950.
1/3 page	30,300.
1/6 page	19,510.
4-Color:	
1 page	75,050.
2/3 page	57,600.
1/2 page or Digest	50,610.
1/3 page	39,610.
1/6 page	20,520.

7. COVERS
2nd cover 90,090. 4th cover 93,830.
3rd cover 78,810.
Non-cancellable.

8. INSERTS
Available.

9. BLEED
Extra 15%
Full page or less.
No charge for gutter bleed.

11. CLASSIFIED/MAIL ORDER/SPECIALTY RATES
DISPLAY CLASSIFICATIONS:
TRAVEL
All travel and resort advertisers (country and state tourist offices, carriers, hotels, tour operators) appearing in the travel section qualify for the following rates:
BLACK AND WHITE RATES:

	1 ti	3 ti	6 ti	12 ti
1 page	43,530.	40,829.	39,978.	37,426.
2/3 page	31,080.	29,837.	29,215.	27,350.
1/2 page	26,800.	25,728.	25,192.	23,584.
1/3 page	16,230.	15,581.	15,256.	14,282.
1/6 page	8,150.	7,824.	7,661.	7,172.
56 lines	6,450.	6,192.	6,063.	5,676.
42 lines	4,830.	4,637.	4,540.	4,250.
35 lines (1/12 page)	4,070.	3,907.	3,826.	3,582.
28 lines	3,340.	3,206.	3,140.	2,939.
21 lines	2,480.	2,381.	2,331.	2,182.
14 lines (1 in.)	1,660.	1,594.	1,560.	1,461.

COLOR RATES:

	1 ti	3 ti	6 ti	12 ti
2-Color:				
1 page	52,690.	50,582.	49,529.	46,367.
2/3 page	38,560.	37,018.	36,246.	33,933.
1/2 page	35,180.	33,773.	33,069.	30,958.
1/3 page	21,170.	20,323.	19,900.	18,630.
4-Color:				
1 page	59,960.	57,562.	56,362.	52,765.
2/3 page	46,580.	44,717.	43,785.	40,990.
1/2 page	42,920.	41,203.	40,345.	37,770.
1/3 page	33,240.	31,910.	31,246.	29,251.

Frequency rates are based on the use of any combination of standard units in 3, 6, or 12 separate issues within a 12-month period. Frequency rates are allowed in advance only after credit has been established with The Conde Nast Publications Inc. Such contracts must specify units of space and issues to be used; otherwise, frequency rates allowed as earned. If any portion of a contract is cancelled, the advertiser will automatically be short-rated at the rate earned. Frequency rate refunds will be credited (or paid in cash, if requested) as earned during each advertiser's contract year.

SHOP BY MAIL
BLACK AND WHITE RATES:

	1 ti	3 ti	6 ti	12 ti
1 page	45,020.	43,219.	42,319.	39,618.
2/3 page	32,470.	31,171.	30,522.	28,574.
1/2 page	24,170.	23,203.	22,720.	21,270.
1/3 page	16,170.	15,523.	15,200.	14,230.
1/6 page	8,110.	7,786.	7,623.	7,137.
42 lines	4,890.	4,694.	4,597.	4,303.
35 lines	4,070.	3,907.	3,826.	3,582.
Catalogue	4,910.	4,714.	4,615.	4,321.

COLOR RATES:

	1 ti	3 ti	6 ti	12 ti
2-Color:				
1 page	58,550.	56,206.	55,037.	51,524.
2/3 page	42,170.	40,483.	39,640.	37,110.
1/2 page	31,440.	30,182.	29,554.	27,667.
1/3 page	20,960.	20,122.	19,702.	18,445.
1/6 page	10,540.	10,118.	9,908.	9,275.
4-Color:				
1 page	63,250.	60,720.	59,455.	55,660.
2/3 page	47,880.	45,965.	45,007.	42,134.

SCHOOLS
BLACK AND WHITE RATES:

	1 ti	3 ti	6 ti	12 ti
1 page	38,180.	36,653.	35,889.	33,598.
2/3 page	25,620.	24,595.	24,083.	22,546.
1/2 page	19,170.	18,403.	18,020.	16,870.
1/3 page	12,770.	12,259.	12,004.	11,238.
98 lines	9,320.	8,947.	8,761.	8,202.
93 lines	8,860.	8,506.	8,328.	7,797.
92 lines	8,770.	8,419.	8,244.	7,718.
84 lines	7,520.	7,219.	7m069.	6,618.
71 lines	6,410.	6,154.	6,025.	5,641.
60 lines	5,710.	5,482.	5,367.	5,025.
59 lines	5,360.	5,146.	5,038.	4,717.
56 lines	5,100.	4,896.	4,794.	4,488.
49 lines	4,450.	4,272.	4,183.	3,916.
46 lines	4,390.	4,214.	4,127.	3,863.
42 lines	3,840.	3,686.	3,810.	3,379.
35 lines	3,210.	3,082.	3,017.	2,825.
28 lines	2,580.	2,477.	2,425.	2,270.
21 lines	1,950.	1,872.	1,833.	1,716.
14 lines	1,340.	1,286.	1,260.	1,179.
Agate line	95.	...	...	...

COLOR RATES:

	1 ti	3 ti	6 ti	12 ti
2-Color:				
1 page	47,270.	45,379.	44,434.	41,598.
2/3 page	34,570.	33,187.	32,496.	30,422.
1/2 page	31,500.	30,240.	29,610.	27,720.
1/3 page	21,740.	20,870.	20,436.	19,131.
4-Color:				
1 page	56,850.	54,576.	53,439.	50,028.
2/3 page	43,680.	41,933.	41,059.	38,438.
1/2 page	40,280.	38,669.	37,853.	35,446.
1/3 page	30,030.	28,829.	28,228.	26,426.

Minimum space for schools; 14 agate lines (1 inch). On repeat order, unless new copy is received by closing date, last copy run will be inserted. Frequency rates are based on the use of 3, 6, or 12 separate issues within a 12-month period.

RETAIL RATES
CONDITIONS: Retail rates are available to department stores, specialty stores, and businesses primarily in the retailing of merchandise to consumers in limited trading areas. Not available to chain stores. To qualify 1 to 3 retailers' names per ad. Store names acceptable, but must be the same size as the largest logo of the manufacturer. Manufacturers logos as well as fiber and fabric symbols, trademarks and trade names, may appear in the ad and travel carriers, hotels and resort areas may be used as backgrounds and described in copy. Eligibility for the retail rate requires approval from the publisher in addition to meeting the retail requirements listed above. General rates apply if certain products of a non-fashion nature are advertised in conjuction with the retail store.

BLACK AND WHITE RATES:

1 page	42,610.	1/3 page	16,700.
2/3 page	31,500.	1/6 page	8,650.
1/2 page	26,920.		

COLOR RATES:

2-Color:			
1 page	52,710.	1/2 page	35,100.
2/3 page	38,560.	1/3 page	24,180.
4-Color:			
1 page	60,010.	1/3 page	31,660.
2/3 page	46,040.	1/6 page	16,390.
1/2 page	42,450.		

MASS RETAIL
BLACK/WHITE RATES:

1 page	47,920.	1/3 page	18,750.
2/3 page	35,470.	1/6 page	9,720.
1/2 page	30,260.		

COLOR RATES:

2-color:			
1 page	59,300.	1/2 page	39,560.
2/3 page	43,410.	1/3 page	27,280.
4-color:			
1 page	67,540.	1/2 page	47,620.
2/3 page	51,870.	1/3 page	35,680.

12. SPLIT-RUN
Available only in full page, 2/3 page, 1/2 page units, or a vertical column unit when run in combination with a full page, subject to following conditions: Offset material required: Entire magazine distribution must be purchased; changes may be made in any or all of the 9 specified geographic areas.
Split-run flexibility is available for net (non-commissionable) (service charges) on each changing unit of advertising as follows:
Per black change—1,630.
Per black spread change—2,080.
Per change of all film of 4 color page—2,930.
Per change of all film of 4 color spread—4,360.
Supplied inserts for geographic copy splits, per stop—800.
Areas are always printed, bound and shipped in the same numerical sequence from 1 through 9 and the number of changes are counted and charged for in accordance with this sequence.
4-color advertising: Advertiser may change all 4-color film in each area or may change the black film only.
Black and white advertising: Advertiser may change entire page in each area, or may furnish a master film with white area for changes in store logos or lists. Separate film required for each store list. Publisher will not set type. All material to be delivered complete before closing date. No extensions granted. Advise publisher 14 days prior to closing date of intention to split run.
Copy splits, regional ads, and pre-printed inserts will be delivered to their proper areas subject to an allowable variation of 5% due to mechanical error and local distribution patterns.

TRUE ALTERNATE SPLIT
(Every Other Copy)

BLACK AND WHITE RATES:	
1st page	2,470.
Spread	3,170.
COLOR RATES:	
2 color:	
1st page	3,330.
Spread	4,680.
4 color:	
1st page	4,080.
Spread	5,850.
Supplied inserts (not pre-mixed)	2,170.

CLUSTER SPLIT
(Every 50/75 Copies)
BLACK AND WHITE RATES:
1st page 1,630. Spread 2,080.
COLOR RATES:
2-Color:
Spread 2,930. 1 page 1,900.
4-Color:
Spread 4,360. 1 page 2,930.
INSERTS
Supplied inserts (not pre-mixed) 800.

13a. GEOGRAPHIC and/or DEMOGRAPHIC EDITIONS

AREA 1
Includes Maine, New Hampshire, Vermont, Massachusetts, Rhode Island.
BLACK AND WHITE RATES:
1 page 14,345.
COLOR RATES:
2-Color:
1 page 14,575.
4-Color:
1 page 15,135.
CIRCULATION:
Sworn 6-30-94—102,630

AREA 2
Includes New York, New Jersey, Connecticut, Foreign, Canada.
BLACK AND WHITE RATES:
1 page 37,970.
COLOR RATES:
2-Color:
1 page 38,040.
4-Color:
1 page 39,350.
CIRCULATION:
Sworn 6-30-94—580,075

NEW YORK METRO
BLACK AND WHITE RATES:
1 page 19,420.
COLOR RATES:
2-Color:
1 page 19,700.
4-Color:
1 page 20,280.
CIRCULATION:
Sworn 6-30-94—190,938

AREA 3
Includes Pennsylvania, Delaware, Maryland, Washington, D.C., Virginia, W. Virginia.
BLACK AND WHITE RATES:
1 page 19,420.
COLOR RATES:
2-Color:
1 page 19,700.
4-Color:
1 page 20,280.
CIRCULATION:
Sworn 6-30-94—214,833

AREA 4
Includes Tennessee, N. Carolina, S. Carolina, Georgia, Florida, Alabama, Mississippi
BLACK AND WHITE RATES:
1 page 25,550.
COLOR RAYES:
2-Color:
1 page 25,830.
4-Color:
1 page 26,560.
CIRCULATION:
Sworn 6-30-94—314,339

AREA 5
Includes Texas, Oklahoma, Arkansas, Louisiana.
BLACK AND WHITE RATES:
1 page 19,420.
COLOR RATES:
2-Color:
1 page 19,700.
4-Color:
1 page 20,280.
CIRCULATION:
Sworn 6-30-94—182,920

AREA 6
Includes Hawaii, S. California, Arizona, New Mexico.
BLACK AND WHITE RATES:
1 page 19,420.
COLOR RATES:
2-Color:
1 page 19,700.
4-Color:
1 page 20,280.
CIRCULATION:
Sworn 6-30-94—209,147

AREA 7
Includes Washington, Oregon, N. California, Idaho, Nevada, Alaska.
BLACK AND WHITE RATES:
1 page 19,420.
COLOR RATES:
2-Color:
1 page 19,700.
4-Color:
1 page 20,280.
CIRCULATION:
Sworn 6-30-94—182,571

AREA 8
Includes Montana, Wyoming, Utah, Colorado, N. Dakota, S. Dakota, Nebraska, Kansas, Minnesota, Iowa, Missouri.
BLACK AND WHITE RATES:
1 page 19,420.
COLOR RATES:
2-Color:
1 page 19,700.
4-Color:
1 page 20,280.
CIRCULATION:
Sworn 6-30-94—195,254

AREA 9
Includes Wisconsin, Illinois, Michigan, Ohio, Indiana, Kentucky.
BLACK AND WHITE RATES:
1 page 31,800.
COLOR RATES:
2-Color:
1 page 31,830.
4-Color:
1 page 32,950.
CIRCULATION:
Sworn 6-30-94—369,318

14. CONTRACT AND COPY REGULATIONS
See Contents page for location—items 1, 2, 3, 7, 10, 18, 19, 24, 30, 35.

15. GENERAL REQUIREMENTS
Also see SRDS Print Media Production Source.
Printing Process: Offset Full Run Regional Cover
Trim Size: 8 x 10-7/8; No./Cols. 3.
Binding Method: Perfect.
Colors Available: 4-color process; GAA/SWOP; 5th cylinder.
Covers: 4-color process.

AD PAGE DIMENSIONS

1 pg	7	x	10-3/16
1/2 v	3-1/2	x	10-3/16
1/2 h	7	x	5-1/16
1/12 v	2-1/4	x	2-1/2
1 col	2-1/4	x	10-3/16
2 col	4-5/8	x	10-3/16
1 Col. SQ	4-5/8	x	5-1/16
1/2 Col.	2-1/4	x	5-1/16
Digest	4-5/8	x	7-3/16

16. ISSUE AND CLOSING DATES

Issue:	On sale	Closing	Issue:	On sale	Closing
Jan '95	12/13	10/20	Jul	6/13	4/20
Feb	1/17	11/18	Aug	7/11	5/19
Mar	2/14	12/20	Sep	8/15	6/20
Apr	3/14	1/20	Oct	9/12	7/20
May	4/11	2/17	Nov	10/17	8/18
Jun	5/16	3/20	Dec	11/14	9/20

Supplied inserts non-cancellable the lst of the 4th month preceding date of issue. Orders for cover pages are non-cancellable. Options on cover positions must be exercised at least 30 days prior to Four-Color closing date. If order is not received by such date, cover option automatically lapses. Inside 4 color, 2 color and black and white order cancellation dates 15 days prior to closing date.

SPECIAL FEATURE ISSUES
Jan/95—Finally! Fashion You Can Afford.
Feb/95—Your Sexiest Outfit.
Mar/95—Spring Fashion Newsmakers.
Apr/95—20 Ways to Wear Pink.
May/95—Bold Strokes: The Best Swimwear for 1995.
Jun/95—Activewear for Style and Performance.
Jul/95—Sportswear: When the Livin' is Easy.
Aug/95—First Look At Fall Fashion and Accessories.
Sep/95—The Best Fall Looks: What's Worth It, What's Not.
Oct/95—Fall in Step: Shoe Report.
Nov/95—Your Holiday Fashion Survival Guide: Fun Party Clothes to Get You Through the Season.
Dec/95—Cozy Days, Sexy Nights.

17. SPECIAL SERVICES
A.B.C. Supplemental Data Report released September 1990 issue.

18. CIRCULATION
Established 1939. Single copy 2.50; per year 15.00.
Summary data—for detail see Publisher's Statement.

A.B.C. 6-30-94 (6 mos. aver.—Magazine Form)

Tot. Pd.	(Subs.)	(Single)	(Assoc.)	(Bulk)
2,186,214	1,123,233	1,062,981		

Average Non-Analyzed Non-Paid Circulation (not incl. above):
Total 52,050

TERRITORIAL DISTRIBUTION 2/94—2,178,465

N.Eng.	Mid.Atl.	E.N.Cen.	W.N.Cen.	S.Atl.
135,387	349,801	341,864	145,107	351,284
E.S.Cen.	W.S.Cen.	Mtn.St.	Pac.St.	Canada
106,905	182,920	106,799	312,161	114,627
Foreign	Other			
21,076	10,534			

Publisher states: "Effective with January 1992, rates based on a circulation average of 2,000,000."

(C-C)

734 **Consumer Magazine and Agri-Media Source** **May, 1995**

J. Sample page from *Standard Rate and Data Service Magazine and Agri-Media Source.* Courtesy of *Standard Rate and Data Service.*

Commercial Television Stations | **Cleveland, OH**

Clarksburg-Weston, WV—Continued

Affiliation
CBS

Personnel
Smith, Michael A.   Gen/Sales Mgr
Gamblin, Deborah   Adv/Promotion Dir
Brady, Cheryl   Traffic Mgr
Calcagni, Tom   News Editor
Weaver, Phil   Assign Editor
Pellegrin, Nick E.   Prog Dir

Corporate Ownership
Not reported

Representatives
Katz-TV

Facilities
Video 100,000w; Audio 20,000w
Antenna Height: 884 ft. above avg. terrain
Operating schedule: 20 hours daily
Time zone: Eastern
Airdate: June 22, 1960

Special Features
Mono
Billboards: 5 sec
Infomercials: 30min
Dayparts available: Daytime

Production Specifications
VHS, 3/4in. U-Matic

Programming
             MON-FRI
 7:00-9:00a CBS This Morning
 9:00-10:00a Phil Donahue
10:00-11:00a Family Feud
11:00-12:00n The Price Is Right
12:00-12:30p News 5 Alive-12
12:30-1:30p The Young and The Restless
 1:30-2:00p The Bold and The Beautiful
 2:00-3:00p As The World Turns
 3:00-4:00p Guiding Light
 4:00-5:00p Vickil
 5:00-6:00p Entertainment Tonight/News 5 Alive
 6:00-7:00p News 5 Alive/CBS Evening News
 7:00-8:00p Rescue 911/Wheel Of Fortune
             MON   PRIME
 8:00-9:00p Evening Shade/Dave's World
 9:00-10:00p Murphy Brown/Love & War
10:00-11:00p Northern Exposure
             TUES
 8:00-9:00p Rescue 911
 9:00-11:00p CBS Tuesday Movie
             WED
 8:00-9:00p The Nanny/Hearts Afire
 9:00-10:00p In The Heat Of The Night
10:00-11:00p 48 Hours
             THU
 8:00-9:00p How'd They Do That?
 9:00-10:00p Eye To Eye w/Connie Chung
10:00-11:00p Second Chance
             FRI
 8:00-9:00p Diagnosis: Murder
 9:00-10:00p Burke's Law
10:00-11:00p Picket Fences
             SAT
 8:00-9:00p Dr. Quinn, Medicine Woman
 9:00-10:00p Harts Of The West
10:00-11:00p Walker, Texas Ranger
             SUN
 7:00-8:00p 60 Minutes
 8:00-9:00p Murder, She Wrote
 9:00-11:00p CBS Sunday Movie

Location ID: 30 3TAD 43   Mid 088115-000

WLYJ-TV ch 46
PHONE: 304-623-5784
775 W. Pike St.
Clarksburg, WV 26301

Mailing Address
P.O. Box 2544
Clarksburg, WV 26302-2544

Affiliation
Independent

Personnel
Kincaid, Jack L   Gen Mgr
Huff, Marilyn   Prog Dir

Corporate Ownership
Christian Communications Center, Inc.

Representatives
Not Applicable

Facilities
Video 156,000w; Audio 15,600w
Antenna Height: 796 ft. above avg. terrain
Time zone: Eastern
Airdate: February 8, 1981

Special Features
Mono

Production Specifications
3/4in. U-Matic

Location ID: 30 3TAD 43   Mid 087428-000

Cleveland, OH

WAKC-TV ch 23
PHONE: 216-535-7831 | **FAX: 216-535-6300**
853 Copley Rd.
Akron, OH 44320

Affiliation
ABC

Personnel
Berk, Jr., Roger   Pres
Berk, Robert C   VP
Fox, Chip   Gen Sales Mgr
O'Neil, Bill   Prog Dir
Bacher, Eric   Adv/Promotion Dir
Thornton, Eldrea   Traffic Mgr
Williamson, Mark   News Dir.

Corporate Ownership
Group One Broadcasting, L.P.

Representatives
Broadcast Spot Sales Inc

Facilities
Video 1,290,000w; Audio 175,000w
Antenna Height: 1,000 ft. above avg. terrain
Operating schedule: 24 hours daily
Time zone: Eastern
Airdate: July 19, 1953

Special Features
Stereo, Closed Caption
Billboards: 5 sec, 10 sec
Infomercials: 30min
Dayparts available: Early Morning, Late Night, Weekend

Production Specifications
1in. Reel, 2in. Reel

Location ID: 30 3TAD 44   Mid 087372-000

WBNX-TV ch 55
PHONE: 216-922-5500 | **FAX: 216-929-2410**
2890 State Rd.
Cuyahoga Falls, OH 44223

Mailing Address
P.O. Box 91660
Cleveland, OH 44101

Affiliation
Independent
Fox Kids Network

Personnel
Spangler, Lou   Gen Mgr
Keith, Anne Catherine   Stat Mgr/Prog Dir
Metheney, Colleen   Traffic Mgr
Brown, Eddie   Gen Sales Mgr
Stone, Debbie   Adv/Promotion Dir
Parrett, Dick   Natl Sales Mgr

Corporate Ownership
Winston Broadcasting Network, Inc.

Representatives
Not Applicable

Facilities
Video 5,000,000w; Audio 250,000w
Operating schedule: 21 hours daily
Time zone: Eastern
Airdate: December 1, 1985

Special Features
Billboards: 5 sec, 10 sec
Infomercials: 30min
Dayparts available: Various

Production Specifications
VHS, 3/4in. U-Matic, 1in. Reel, 1/2in. M2

Sports Programming
Ohio State Basketball
Big Ten Basketball

Location ID: 30 3TAD 44   Mid 085283-000

WEWS-TV ch 5
PHONE: 216-431-5555 | **FAX: 216-431-3640**
3001 Euclid Ave
Cleveland, OH 44115

Affiliation
ABC

Personnel
Robinson, Gary   VP/Gen Mgr
Sherwin, Jane   Gen Sales Mgr
Olevitch, Larry   Natl Sales Mgr
Chirdon, Robert   Local Sales Mgr
Stark, Gary   Prog Dir
Cheplowitz, Terri Moir Local Prog/Mktg Mgr
Cerveny, George   Traffic Mgr

Corporate Ownership
Scripps Howard Broadcasting

Representatives
Blair

Facilities
Antenna Height: 1,020 ft. above avg. terrain
Operating schedule: 24 hours daily
Time zone: Eastern
Airdate: December 17, 1947

Special Features
Stereo, Closed Caption
Infomercials: 30min
Dayparts available: Daytime, Weekend

Production Specifications
3/4in. U-Matic, 1in. Reel, 1/2in. M2

Location ID: 30 3TAD 44   Mid 086579-000

WGGN-TV ch 52
PHONE: 419-684-5311
3809 Maple Ave.
Castalia, OH 44824

Mailing Address
P.O. Box 247
Castalia, OH 44824

Affiliation
Independent

Personnel
Yost, Rusty   Gen Mgr
Jordon, Virginia   Traffic Mgr

Corporate Ownership
Christian Faith Broadcast, Inc.

Representatives
Not Applicable

Facilities
Video 1,482,000w; Audio 148,200w
Antenna Height: 774 ft. above avg. terrain
Operating schedule: 17 hours daily
Time zone: Eastern
Airdate: December 5, 1982

Special Features
Mono

Production Specifications
1in. Reel

Programming
             MON-FRI
 8:30-10:00a Beverly Exercise/Life Anew
10:00-1:00p Praise the Lord
 1:00-2:00p Action Sixties
 2:00-3:00p John Hagee/Steve Brock (Mon)
 2:00-3:00p John Hagee/Nancy Harmon (Tue)
 2:00-3:00p John Hagee/Dr. Cherry (Wed)
 2:00-3:00p John Hagee/Pat Boone (Thu)
 2:00-3:00p John Hagee/Jay Sekulow (Fri)
 3:00-4:00p Rod Parsley/Jewish Voice (Mon)
 3:00-4:00p Rod Parsley/Roy Harless (Tue)
 3:00-4:00p Rod Parsley/Calvin Evans (Wed)
 3:00-4:00p Rod Parsley/Leonard Repass (Thu)
 3:00-4:00p Rod Parsley/Carson Fraley(Fri)
 4:00-5:00p Superbook/Sunshine Factory(Mon)
 4:00-5:00p Superbook/Kid's Club (Tue)
 4:00-5:00p Superbook/Sunshine Factory(Wed)
 4:00-5:00p Superbook/Joy Junction (Thu)
 4:00-5:00p Superbook/Sunshine Factory(Fri)
 5:00-6:00p 700 Club
 6:00-7:00p American Times Nws/Real McCoys
10:00-11:00p Praise the Lord
             MON   PRIMETIME
 7:00-8:00p Specials
 8:00-9:00p Life Anew
 9:00-10:00p Rejoice
             TUE
 7:00-8:00p Armour Baptist
 8:00-9:00p Life Anew
 9:00-10:00p Adrian Rodgers
             WED
 7:00-8:00p CBM Worship Service
 8:00-9:00p Life Anew
 9:00-10:00p God's News/Central Message
             THU
 7:00-8:00p Wall of Fire/Betty J Robinson
 8:00-9:00p Life Anew
 9:00-10:00p Jack Hayford
             FRI
 7:00-8:00p Dr. D. James Kennedy
 8:00-9:00p Life Anew
 9:00-10:00p Armour Baptist
             SAT
 7:00-8:00p In Touch
 8:00-9:00p Day of Dscvry/Voice of Salvatn
10:00-10:00p Fred Price
             SUN
 6:00-7:00p Dr. D. James Kennedy
 7:00-8:00p CBM
 8:00-9:00p Lloyd Oglivie/E.V. Hill
 9:00-10:00p Day of Dscvry/Jewish Voice

Location ID: 30 3TAD 44   Mid 087615-000

K. Sample page from *Standard Rate and Data Service TV and Cable Source.* Courtesy of *Standard Rate and Data Service.*

PART VI

THE BROADER ENVIRONMENT

18 ADVERTISING REGULATION

> Consumers have a considerable tolerance for
> exaggeration and puffery in advertising. . . . They
> undoubtedly expect advertisements to be biased
> and to present merchandise in an attractive light.
> (Neil Borden, 1942, professor of advertising, Harvard University)

A good measure of the importance of advertising regulation and the issues associated with regulating advertising content is the launching of a new journal called the *Journal of Public Policy and Marketing*. Many of the articles and book reviews published in this new journal are devoted to advertising regulation in one form or another.[1] Advertising has a responsibility within our economic system to provide information on new and existing products and services. Most of what is purchased is advertised. Thus, the economic health of both buyers and competitors is affected if the advertising system is injected with false or misleading claims. The result can be a misallocation of resources, disappointed or even injured buyers and damaged competitors.

Advertising regulation is a fascinating subject, and it is heavily determined by political attitudes. Those who believe in less government and think that business should be left alone to regulate itself tend to favor less advertising regulation. Others who believe government has a role to play tend to want more legislation and government regulation. One manifestation of this principle is the cycles of power and authority of the Federal Trade Commission, the government agency most responsible for advertising regulation. For example, Jef Richards notes, "President Reagan entered office with a commitment to a "New Federalism," which meant, in part, liberating business from excessive federal regulation. . . . As a result, the FTC staff was cut by 43 percent over the next eight years . . . and it experienced an infusion of 'Chicago School' free-market economists dedicated to a cost-benefit approach to trade regulation."[2] In response to such criticism, FTC Chairman Janet D. Steiger, speaking to the Consumer Federation of America in the spring of 1990, declared that the Commission's staff was aggressively pursuing cases against national advertising. In her speech, she highlighted the following areas for FTC attention: (1) promotional practices of the tobacco and alcohol industries, (2) health claims in food advertising, (3) children's advertising, including toy advertising and "900" telephone services to "Dial-A-Santa," (4) advertising to the elderly concerning health, safety, and financial security, and (5) environmental "green claims" such as those asserting a product is "biodegradable," or "environmentally safe." She reported that nearly fifty cases had resulted in almost $100 million in judgments and more than $6.5 million in redress awards to consumers.[3] In the early 1990s, these topics have indeed been major thrusts of advertising regulation activity at the FTC.

To understand advertising regulation, a host of issues need to be addressed. One central issue is *definitional*—what is deception? When Blatz claims that it is "Milwaukee's finest beer," is deception involved when many (particularly other Milwaukee brewers) argue that other beers are superior? What does "finest" mean? One advertisement claimed that a hair dye would color hair permanently. If someone exposed to the advertisement believed that the dye would hold for hair not yet grown and thus a single dye would last for decades, is the claim deceptive?

There are other issues as well. How many people need to misunderstand before deception is involved? When there is disagreement about what is deception, who should decide? How can dishonest and careless advertisers be detected, prosecuted, and punished? To what extent can self-regulation be relied upon? What are appropriate remedies? These questions and others make the issue of deception a complex area for an advertiser, the media, and the government.

In the following sections, the history of regulation will be briefly sketched. The concept of deception will then be considered. The role of advertising research will then be examined followed by a discussion of the remedies available to the FTC when deception is found. Finally, the matter of lawsuits and self-regulation will be considered.

HISTORY OF FEDERAL REGULATION OF ADVERTISING · · · · · · · · · · · · · · · ·

In 1914, the Federal Trade Commission Act was passed, which created the federal agency that has had the primary responsibility for the regulation of advertising. Section 5 of the FTC Act contained this prohibition: "Unfair methods of competition in commerce are hereby declared unlawful." The aim was to provide an agency that could deal with restraints of trade more effectively than had the Sherman antitrust law. The problem of deceptive advertising was not a target of the FTC Act. Ira Millstein, a legal scholar, observes: "The most important development in the long history of the FTC's prohibition of false advertising was that the FTC concerned itself with the problem in the first place."[4] In many respects it was a fortuitous accident.

The FTC first became concerned with deceptive advertising because of its effect upon competition and not because of a concern for consumer protection. In the first test case in 1919, the FTC moved against Sears, Roebuck.[5] Sears had advertised that their prices for sugar and tea were lower than those of competitors because of their larger buying power. The claim was found to be false, but the FTC action was upheld, not because of subsequent damage caused the consumer but by the fact that smaller competitors could be injured. Thus, for many years, advertising regulation was largely concentrated on the need to protect small firms and competitors rather than consumers themselves.

In 1931, in the landmark *FTC* v. *Raladam* case, the Supreme Court specifically held that the FTC could not prohibit false advertising if there is no evidence of injury to a competitor.[6] The ruling struck a decisive blow in that it stopped any movement in the direction of protecting the consuming public directly. However, it was a blessing in disguise, for it helped to mobilize support for redefining the powers of the FTC. The ultimate result was the Wheeler-Lea Amendment passed in 1938, which amended Section 5 of the FTC Act to read as follows: "Unfair methods of competition in commerce and unfair or deceptive actions or practices in commerce are hereby declared unlawful." Thus the obligation to demonstrate that injury to competition occurred was removed. The issue then was not a jurisdictional one but rather how to move forward against deceptive advertising.

In addition to the FTC and Wheeler-Lea Acts, many cases of advertising regulation in federal courts are based on the Lanham Trademark Act.[7] A recent development is the increasingly important role of state attorneys general. The historical preeminence of the Federal Trade Commission as the chief regulator of American advertising has been challenged by the National Association of Attorneys General (NAAG). Multistate regulator efforts have raised questions about the legality of state restrictions on national advertising. Richards[8] analyzes the history of this development and concludes that state attorney generals will continue to be an important arm of advertising regulation and that all parties involved must adjust to this new reality.

A basic issue in the enforcement of these laws against deceptive advertising, to which we now turn, is how to define and identify deception.

WHAT IS DECEPTIVE ADVERTISING? . . . .

Conceptually, deception exists when an advertisement is introduced into the perceptual process of some audience and the output of that perceptual process (1) differs from the reality of the situation and (2) affects buying behavior to the detriment of the consumer. The input itself may be determined to contain falsehoods. The more difficult and perhaps more common case, however, is when the input, the advertisement, is not obviously false, but the perceptual process generates an impression that is deceptive. A disclaimer may not pass through the attention filter or the message may be misinterpreted.

Legally, the definition of deception has evolved over the years since the Wheeler-Lea Amendment was passed. Refinements have been caused by the FTC in its decisions in individual cases and in its Trade Regulation Rules, which cover unlawful trade practices of entire industries. The FTC positions can be appealed to the courts, which ultimately provide the legal definition of deceptive advertising.

To provide guidance in the face of a history of sometimes conflicting decisions regarding deception, the FTC in 1983 decided to go on record with a formal position. Although somewhat controversial (it was passed on a three-to-two vote), it does represent an important effort to define deception. Dividing the definition into its three major components, it states that deception will be found if

1.   There is a misrepresentation, omission, or practice that is likely to mislead.
2.   The consumer is acting responsibly (or reasonably) in the circumstances.
3.   The practice is material and consumer injury is possible because consumers are likely to have chosen differently if there was no deception.[9]

Although some argue that this definition only codifies the body of law that preceded it, most observers suggest that the definition involves two major changes from prior positions that make it harder for an ad to quality as deceptive.[10] First, the deception must be likely to mislead, whereas the prior understanding was that it need only have a tendency or capacity to mislead. Second, the deception must occur in consumers acting responsibly or reasonably in the circumstances rather than simply occuring in a substantial number of consumers (even if they are naive and unthinking). Thus, the consumer is charged with at least some minimal responsibility in interpreting the advertising.

Petty[11] shows that an important distinction in defining deceptive advertising is between commercial speech which is partially protected by the First Amendment and political speech which is fully protected. He presents an audience impact model as a practical solution to the problem. Commercial speech is speech which potentially influences people as consumers whereas political or other forms of speech potentially influences people in some other role.

In the following discussion, we will look more closely at the three dimensions of deceptive advertising discussed above.

A Misrepresentation or Omission

There are a variety of ways in which misrepresentations or omissions can occur:

1. *Suggesting that a small difference is important.* A Lorillard ad that correctly claimed that its cigarette was the lowest level of tar and nicotine in a cigarette test reported in *Reader's Digest* was ruled deceptive because the differences between Lorillard's Kent and several other brands was insignificant and meaningless.[12]

2. *Artificial product demonstrations.* Firms or their advertising agencies that misrepresent any advertised demonstration, picture, experiment, or test designed to prove any material feature of a product, or prove its superiority to another product may be subject to FTC orders prohibiting such future representations. A television commercial for a car wax used flaming gasoline on an automobile to demonstrate that the wax could withstand intense heat.[13] However, because the gasoline was only burning for a few seconds, no significant heat was generated and the test really proved nothing. Campbell Soup and its agency, in producing commercials, used marbles to make soup ingredients rise to the surface which was found to be deceptive.[14] In a "Bear Foot" campaign for Volvo cars, a "monster truck" was depicted running over a row of cars and crushing all of them but a Volvo 240 station wagon. The FTC charged both Volvo and Scali, its ad agency, with falsely depicting the comparative performance of cars. The FTC alleged that some of the Volvos used in the demo had been structurally reinforced and subjected to less-severe monster-truck treatment than competing vehicles and that structural supports in some of the competing cars had been severed. The case was settled by

consent order and both Volvo and Scali were required to pay $150,000 each to the U.S. Treasury.[15]

3. *Using an ambiguous or easily confused phrase.* The use of the phrase "government-supported" could be interpreted as "government-approved" and was therefore challenged.[16] In another case the FTC held that a toothpaste claim that it "fights decay" could be interpreted as a claim that it provides complete protection and was therefore deceptive.[17] The FTC alleged that commercials claiming that a Nestlé product, Carnation Coffee-Mate Liquid nondairy coffee creamer, was "low in fat" falsely implied that the product was low in fat—a half-cup serving of the liquid had nearly twice the fat of an identical serving of whole milk and nearly four times the fat of 2-percent milk.[18]

An Illinois state bar association rule imposed a blanket ban on attorneys advertising themselves as "certified" or "specialists." The implication was that the state of Illinois had formally authorized certification or specialists in trial advocacy which was not true.[19] Advertising by professionals like lawyers, doctors, dentists, and so on has been under careful scrutiny by regulators in recent years because they have been allowed to advertise for the first time and because of the potential for consumer harm.

4. *Implying a benefit that does not fully or partially exist.* An aspirin substitute, Efficen, was truthfully advertised as containing no aspirin. However, the FTC charged that the no aspirin claim implied incorrectly that the product would not have Aspirin's side effects.[20] General Electric was charged with misrepresenting the amount of light that its lower wattage, cost-saving replacement bulbs produce. In addition to the consent order, GE was required to inform its customers that the bulbs provide less light than the bulbs to which they were compared.[21] Stouffer Food was charged with making deceptive claims that its Lean Cuisine frozen entrees were low in sodium by claiming that the products "make sense," "skimp," on sodium, and were formulated to contain less than "1 gram" of sodium per entree. The advertising failed to disclose adequately that 1 gram is equivalent to 1,000 milligrams, the commonly used unit of measurement for sodium. The Commission charged that this failure could lead consumers to underestimate the sodium content of the product.[22]

5. *Implying that a product benefit is unique to a brand.* An FTC complaint against Wonder Bread argued that Wonder Bread's claim that its brand built bodies twelve ways falsely implied that Wonder Bread was unique with respect to such a claim. Although this charge was subsequently dropped, it does illustrate one possible way in which the definition of deception could be broadened.[23] Interestingly, Hunt-Wesson Foods, soon after the Wonder Bread complaint was filed, developed a policy of avoiding advertising brands that are virtually similar to their competitors. Another example concerns low-alcohol beer. Anheuser-Busch began to market a beer with a low alcohol content that it called "LA" defined by the Bureau of Alcohol, Tobacco and Firearms (BATF), the agency that regulates labeling of alcoholic malt beverages, as a beer containing less than 2.5 percent alcohol by volume and less than 2 percent alcohol by weight. Both Heilman and Miller planned to use the LA name, and in response to A-B's request to cease and desist, sued A-B for antitrust and attempting to monopolize the low-alcohol beer market.

A-B filed a counterclaim for trademark infringement, unfair competition, and trademark dilution.[24]

6. *Implying that a benefit is needed or that a product will fulfill a benefit when it will not.* Gainesburgers once advertised that its product contained all the milk protein your dog needs. It was true that the product had milk protein and that competitors' products did not. But it was also true that dogs need little or no milk protein. The FTC argued that the line "Every BODY Needs Milk" incorrectly implied that good health required regular milk consumption.

In the search for ways to differentiate their products, many companies have turned to the environment and the use of environmental appeals. Many cases have come before the FTC concerning claims that a particular product will aid or improve the environment. According to FTC Commissioner Deborah K. Own, the FTC's "overriding goals in investigating environmental marketing claims are preventing consumer deception and ensuring that objective environmental performance claims are adequately substantiated." As environmental marketing has mushroomed, so have the number of cases brought before the FTC. Companies are prohibited from making any general environmental benefit claims—such as "environmentally friendly" or "safe to the environment"—unless the company can substantiate the claim and discloses exactly what it means by such terms.[25] Jerome Russell Cosmetics was charged with making false and unsubstantiated environmental claims in marketing its cosmetics products as "ozone safe" and "ozone friendly," when, in fact, they contained a harmful ozone-depleting substance. In another case, American Enviro Products was charged with making unsubstantiated claims that its "Bunnies" disposable diapers, when disposed of in a landfill, would decompose and return to nature "within three to five years" or "before your child grows up," and that its product offered a significant environmental benefit compared with other disposable diapers. Under a consent agreement, the company was prohibited from making similar misrepresentations and was required to support future environmental claims with reliable scientific evidence.[26]

7. *Incorrectly implying that an endorser uses and advocates the brand.* Advertisements implied that an acne medication was superior and had cured Pat Boone's daughter's acne when neither claim was true.[27] Pat Boone, the endorser, was ordered to return his remuneration to users. An endorser in general only need inform the audience that payment is involved when there is an implication that no payment is involved. Procter & Gamble, however, was found guilty of implying incorrectly that washing machine manufacturers distributed P&G detergents with their machines because they endorsed P&G brands rather than because they were paid to do so. The FTC has developed a set of guidelines called *FTC Guides Concerning Use of Endorsements and Testimonials in Advertising*, which were used in a case involving Diamond Mortgage Corporation and A. J. Obie Associates. These companies developed television advertising campaigns designed to encourage investors to secure shares in what turned out to be nonexistent mortgages. In a classic Ponzi scheme, most of the investors' money went to paying previous investors. Both companies filed for bankruptcy, but because huge amounts of money had been siphoned off, investors lost significantly and some of the companies' executives went to jail. In an effort to recoup some of their investments, several Obie in-

vestors sued actors Lloyd Bridges and George Hamilton for endorsing the companies in ads. The actors claimed they were spokespersons, who were not required
to substantiate the truthfulness of endorsements, rather than endorsers, who have
that duty. The court decided the actors were endorsers because the *Guides* provide that "an 'endorsement' means any advertising message ... which ... consumers are likely to believe reflects the opinions, beliefs, findings or experience of
a party other than the sponsoring advertiser...." The court also declared that
there is no requirement that the endorser be an expert and that an endorser does
not have to have a financial interest in the sale of the product to establish liability.
It was also held irrelevant that the actors were not active participants in the preparation of the commercials. Finally, it was found that the advertising agency could
not escape liability even though the agency did not film the commercials but only
arranged their airing, and neither the agency nor the producer could escape liability by blaming the other. The fact that the producer had not been sued was also
deemed to be irrelevant.[28]

In a similar case, Black & Decker was found to have misrepresented that its
iron with a shut-off feature had the exclusive endorsement of The National Fire
Safety Council (NFSC), an organization with expertise in appliance fire safety. The
FTC argued that the NFSC did not have expertise in evaluating or testing appliance
fire safety and did not grant its exclusive endorsement to Black & Decker on the basis of a valid test or evaluation.[29]

8. *Omitting a needed qualification.* The FTC can require that a more complete
disclosure be made to correct a misconception. Thus, Geritol was required to indicate that the "tired feeling" it was supposed to help was possibly caused by factors that the product could not treat effectively.[30] Similarly, baldness cures have
been required to indicate that baldness usually is hereditary and untreatable. Toys
are usually assumed to be safe. Therefore, toy manufacturers have a special responsibility to point out possible unsafe aspects of their toys. Clorox settled FTC
charges that its television commercials referred to its Take Heart salad dressing as
"fat free" and "no fat" while, in fact, there were one or two grams of fat per two ta-
blespoonfuls of the dressing. The agreement did not prohibit any claims about fat,
saturated fat, cholesterol, or sodium that were specifically permitted in labeling
for the advertised serving size by the FDA.[31]

A Kraft company ad claiming Kraft Singles cheese product slices contained
the same amount of calcium as 5 ounces of milk and more calcium than most imitation cheese slices was found deceptive. Although the cheese slices were made
from 5 ounces of milk, it was not revealed that much of the calcium is lost in processing. One defense was that the claim was not material to consumers. The FTC
found that consumers placed great importance on calcium consumption and that
a 30 percent exaggeration of calcium content was a numerically significant claim
that would affect consumer purchasing decisions.[32]

In 1989, the FTC issued a complaint charging Campbell Soup, which controls
about two-thirds of the more than $2 billion retail soup market in the United States,
with making deceptive and unsubstantiated claims for its soups. Campbell's ads
that were part of its "Soup is Good Food" campaign, linked the low fat and cholesterol content of its soup with a reduced risk of heart disease. However, it failed to

disclose that the soups were high in sodium and that diets high in sodium may increase the risk of heart disease.[33]

It is interesting to consider how far pressure from the FTC for complete disclosure could go. There are a wide variety of advertised brands that differ little in substance from competitors. It is a common practice to associate a brand with an attribute of the product class. Should the brand be required to state in its advertisement that all brands are virtually identical in this respect? For example, an aspirin advertisement may emphasize the product's pain-relieving quality without mentioning that all aspirin-based brands will have a similar effect.

9. *Making a claim without substantiation.* The FTC can require advertisers to substantiate claims made with respect to safety, performance, efficacy, quality, or comparative price when such claims will be relied on by a consumer who lacks the ability or knowledge to independently judge their validity. Firestone was ordered to stop advertising that its tires "stop 25 percent faster," and Fedders was told to stop calling its reserve cooling system "unique" because they were unable to support these claims with valid test or survey data. Inadequate substantiation is considered an *unfair* (as opposed to *deceptive*) *action* by the FTC. Removatron was ordered to cease and desist from making claims that any of its hair-removal devices, products, or treatments would achieve permanent hair removal unless it relies on "competent and reliable scientific" evidence defined as "adequate and well-controlled, double-blind clinical testing." The company also had to send a copy of the order to each purchaser of the Removatron device.[34]

10. *Bait and switch.* Companies that solicit business on one basis and than switch consumers to other products can be charged with unfair and deceptive practices. Many cases have involved the use of 900 telephone numbers. For example, US Sales advertised its automobile auction information service on radio and television. The ads encouraged consumers to call a 900 number (1-900-HOT-CARS) for information about government auctions of automobiles. Callers to the 900 number were charged $2 per minute for a twelve-minute call, at the end of which they were given an 800 number to call. Those who called were solicited to purchase lifetime memberships in US Sales service for $99.95, which entitled them to receive information about additional automobile auctions. The impression from the ads was that callers would receive information about buying excellent cars at extremely low prices. Instead, callers were informed of sales at which cars in poor condition were sold at relatively low prices and cars in good condition were sold at approximately fair market value. Although the defendants pleaded that the ads consisted merely of *puffing* (which we review in the next section), and that a reasonable consumer would not be misled by such typical advertising hyperbole, the courts declared that the ads went beyond mere puffing. The FTC need only show that a reasonable consumer, upon hearing the advertisement, is likely to be mislead to his or her detriment. In fact, the Commission is required only to show that it is likely, not that it is certain, that a reasonable consumer would be mislead. Ads are illegal if they have a "tendency" or "capacity" to deceive; actual deception of particular consumers need not be proven. The court ordered US Sales and Dean Vlahos to pay consumer redress of over $9 million and granted a permanent in-

junction that required the defendants to obtain a performance bond for any future sales. Other cases involving 900 numbers are *FTC* v. *Starlink*, a service offering employment opportunity information, and *FTC* v. *M.D.M. Interests*, a company that represented falsely to consumers that they could obtain Visa or Mastercards regardless of credit history by making a $50 call to a 900 number. The company failed to disclose that substantial deposits in the issuing banks were required, and that a substantial fee was often charged.[35]

11. *Identifying the advertising.* The FTC reached a consent order agreement with Nu-Day enterprises that would permanently prohibit false advertising that a diet program could cause weight loss without exercising. The advertising appeared in a thirty-second show called "The Perfect Diet," which appeared to be an independent consumer news program airing interviews to report on the discovery of the Nu-Day diet. The FTC charged the TV show was an infomercial containing false and misleading metabolism and weight-loss claims for the diet program. In addition to a consent order banning the false metabolism claims, the advertising required a disclosure within the first thirty seconds, and every fifteen minutes thereafter as follows: "The program you are watching is a paid advertisement for (the product or service)."[36]

12. *Telemarketing.* Many cases have come before the Commission that involve deception arising from telemarketing practices. The largest telemarketing fraud settlement ever revealed by the FTC involved an oil and gas lease scheme that bilked investors out of more than $51 million. Defendants were charged with falsely representing their ability to "eliminate the risk" of participating in an oil and gas lottery. In about a year, customers filed more than 66,000 applications but won only sixty leases. The court froze $12 million of the assets of the companies and the personal assets of the individuals named in the case. Victimized customers got back more than 90 cents on the dollar in this case.[37]

13. *Intellectual property.* The problems of copyright have emerged as a new and important issue to advertisers. A legal copyright protects the description of the results of research; it does not protect the investment required to attain those results. Nor are "facts" protected under the Copyright Act of 1976. Compilations of facts are protected only to the degree that the materials represent original effort. The work or effort involved in compiling the facts is not subject to copyright protection. Hence, Apple Computer was not allowed to exclude Microsoft and Hewlett-Packard from using the Macintosh improvements for an electronic interface with Microsoft's Windows 3.0 and H-Ps New Wave graphic user's interfaces (GUIs) despite Apple's substantial research investment. Similarly, Lotus was not allowed to force Borland to stop using the Lotus 1-2-3 interface in Borland's Quattro Pro. Another example is Consumer Reports. Comparative evaluations reported in a product survey by Consumer Reports may be copied with or without attribution to CR as the source. The expense and research incurred by Consumers Union in discovering such "facts" does not give those "facts" copyright protection. The description of those facts is copyrightable. Constants, formulae, and computer algorithms are not protected, whereas manuals and programs utilizing or describing the constants, formulae, and algorithms are protected.[38]

These are some of the ways in which misrepresentations or omissions can occur. In an interesting test of first amendment rights, Todd Fox and several students at the State University of New York sued the university for prohibiting "commercial enterprise" from operating on the SUNY campus. A saleswoman from American Futures Systems, a company that sells housewares, conducted a "Tupperware-like" party demonstrating the company's products in the student dorm. She was arrested by campus police and charged with trespass and soliciting without a permit. This case went all the way to the Supreme Court and illustrates the difficulties of separating commercial and noncommercial speech. It is an example of yet another dimension of the issues involved in misrepresentations and omissions.[39] We turn now to a look at the question of puffery.

Puffery

A rather well-established rule of law is that *trade puffing* is permissible. *Puffing* takes two general forms. The first is a subjective statement of opinion about a product's quality, using such terms as "best or greatest." Nearly all advertisements contain some measure of puffery. "You can't get any closer" (Norelco), "Try something better" (J&B Scotch), "Gas gives you a better deal" (American Gas Association), "Live better electrically" (Edison Electric Institution), "State Farm is all you need to know about insurance," and "Super Shell" are examples. None of these statements has been proved to be true, but neither have they been proved false. They all involve some measure of exaggeration.

In 1946, the court set aside the FTC ruling in the *Carlay* case that a weight-reduction plan involving Ayds candy, which claimed to be "easy" to follow, was deceptive. The court noted that "what was said was clearly justifiable . . . under those cases recognizing that such words as 'easy,' 'perfect,' 'amazing,' 'prime,' 'wonderful,' 'excellent,' are regarded in law as mere puffing or dealer's talk upon which no charge of misrepresentation can be based."[40]

The second form of puffery is an exaggeration extended to the point of outright spoof that is obviously not true. A Green Giant is obviously fictitious, and even if he were real, he wouldn't be talking the way he does. In the 1927 Ostermoor case, the court pointed to the puffery argument in denying that a mattress company was deceptive in using an illustration appearing to depict that the inner filling of a mattress would expand to 35 inches when in fact it would expand only 3 to 6 inches.[41]

Ivan Preston and Ralph Johnson and, later, Preston examined the puffery issue and declared that although it is well established in law, it is at the same time somewhat vulnerable and has often been denied.[42] For example, in the *Tanners Shoe Company* case, the FTC denied the puffery defense, declaring that it was stipulated that it is not literally true that respondents' shoes will assure comfort or a perfect fit to all individuals. The Commission argued that such a representation was false because it attributed to the product a quality which it did not possess rather than exaggerating a quality which it did possess.[43]

Jef Richards, in an article titled "A 'New and Improved' View of Puffery," cited the considerable amount of literature on puffery written in the late 1970s and 1980s and provided a penetrating analysis of definitions ranging from the very broad to the very narrow. He argued that marketing researchers who generally accept the argument that puffery is frequently deceptive are basing this conclusion on a much broader definition than has been adopted by regulators. Based on stated definitions and policy, puffing has been narrowed to the point where no deceptive claim can properly be termed puffery. Many claims labeled puffs could be proved deceptive if better evidence was presented and "by this logic it is inappropriate to criticize the FTC for retaining the puffing defense, but the FTC staff is certainly vulnerable to criticism for failing its obligation to prove deceptive claims to be deceptive. . . . For marketing managers, this means that many claims commonly presumed to be puffery are no longer shielded by the legal 'puffery doctrine.' There is no safe harbor when using traditional magic words like 'the best,' 'wonderful,' or 'excellent,' If proved deceptive, even a trade name like 'Wonder Bread' could be regulated . . . sellers should take care not to cling to a false sense of security when using exaggerated claims."[44]

Alexander Simonson and Morris Holbrook analyzed the concept of permissible puffery by examining the communications content of sellers' claims and the circumstances underlying buyer-seller transactions. The study included warranty cases as well. A basic question studied was whether permissible puffery can be identified with reference only to the communications at hand or whether the identification requires consideration of other underlying factors. The authors argue strongly for the latter conclusion. Based upon an empirical study of hundreds of warranty cases, they challenge the existence of an applicable determination of puffery derived solely from the content of the communications. For example, an index of communications subjectivity does *not* contribute significantly to determining puffery or warranty outcomes. The determination must be made in connection with the situational circumstances of the case. The results mirror Preston's concern that the FTC's message-response views are perhaps not useful if they do not concomitantly view the circumstances of a communication. In sum, the application of the puffery defense in warranty cases is an interactive circumstance-related concept. This calls into question the usability of a "definition" of puffery that includes a "reasonable person" standard but does not account for numerous situation-specific factors.[45] We turn now to the issue of the reasonable consumer.

Who Is Deceived—The Reasonable Consumer?

Who is it that needs to be protected? The FTC has historically taken the extreme position that essentially all are to be protected, in particular those who are naive, trusting, and of low intelligence.

In 1944, this position was graphically illustrated by two cases. In the *Charles of the Ritz* case, the FTC found that the trademark "Rejuvenescence" was associated with a foundation makeup cream in a manner that promised the restoration of a youthful complexion.[46] Some, including those ignorant, unthinking, and credulous, might believe that the product could actually cause youth to be restored. In

Gelb v. *FTC*, the FTC prohibited the claim that a hair-coloring product could color hair permanently.[47] Its position was that some might believe that even new hair would have the desired new color.

The 1955 *Kirchner* case provided some relief to the charge that no deception can exist.[48] It involved a swimming aid, and the claim that when the device was worn under a swimming suit it was "thin and invisible." The commission decided that buyers who were not "foolish or feebleminded" would be unlikely to take this claim literally, noting

> *Perhaps a few misguided would believe, for example, that all "Danish pastry" is made in Denmark. Is it, therefore, an actual deception to advertise "Danish pastry" when it is made in this country? Of course not. A representation does not become "false and deceptive" merely because it will be unreasonably misunderstood by an insignificant and unrepresentative segment of the class of persons to whom the representation is addressed.*[49]

The *Kirchner* case also indicated that advertising aimed at particularity susceptible groups will be evaluated with respect to that group. Thus, when children are the target, deception will be evaluated with respect to them. One case was decided on the basis of the advertising impact on a "busy businessman." This refinement is interesting because it recognizes that people may perceive stimuli differently, depending on the situational context.

In 1983, the FTC narrowed its definition of deception in an important way. Previously, an advertisement was held to be deceptive if it "has the tendency or capacity to deceive a substantial number of consumers in a material way." However, in the *Cliffdale* case, the proper test for finding deception was whether the claim is "material and likely to mislead consumers acting 'reasonably' under the circumstances." The key word is "reasonably." A mail-order company, Cliffdale Associates, had advertised an automobile fuel economy device, the $12.95 BallMatic Valve, which made deceptive performance claims. The FTC concluded that consumers acting reasonably would not be materially affected.

Russell Laczniak and Sanford Grossbart[50] conducted an empirical study of whether reasonable consumers might also be deceived under various circumstances. Adult consumers were exposed to subjective claims, objective claims, and a combination of subjective and objective claims as well as high and low message involvement manipulations of camera advertising. The authors also collected data on expertise. It was found that expertise was related to positive message-related cognitive responses and appeared to be independent of the level of objective claim content. In other words, experts were influenced by subjective claim advertising. More involved receivers have been found to engage in more critical message analysis and greater cognitive elaboration than less-involved receivers which in turn leads to the generation of more positive cognitive responses. Whereas judicial and regulatory authorities seem to assume that reasonable consumers have defenses against deceptive advertising because of higher message involvement and greater product-class expertise, the results do not support this assumption. Expert and more involved consumers may actually be more vulnerable to deception.

Materiality of the Falsehood

For an advertisement to be deceptive, it must contain a *material untruth*; that is, one capable of affecting purchase decisions. It should be likely that the advertisement will cause public injury. Millstein explains:

> *"Public injury" does not mean that a consumer must actually suffer damage, or that it must be shown that goods purchased are unequal to the value expended. Rather, "public injury" results if the advertisement has a tendency to induce action (such as the purchase itself) detrimental to the consumer that might not otherwise have been taken. If such action could not have been induced by the claim (even though false), there is no "public injury." This requirement comports with the express provision of Section 15 of the FTC Act, as amended, that the advertisement must be misleading in a material respect to be actionable.*[51]

Courts and the FTC have ruled that only mock-ups and props that were intended to demonstrate visually a quality that was material to the sale of a product would be prohibited. If the demonstration would not affect consumer's decisions, then, even if it were misrepresented, it would not be deceptive. Thus, mashed potatoes could be used in television commercials in scenes depicting ice cream consumption (ice cream will melt too rapidly under lights) if the texture and color of the prop were not emphasized as selling points of the product.

The materiality question is nevertheless one in which advertisers are often in a no-win situation. In the *Kraft* case,[52] the Commission staff judged the ads to imply that Kraft Singles cheese contained as much calcium as 5 ounces of whole milk, whereas the slices contained only about 70 percent as much calcium. To provide evidence for a defense resting on the assumption that the claims were essentially "immaterial," Kraft commissioned Professor Jacob Jacoby of New York University to conduct a survey of consumer reactions to the claim. After some introductory questions, respondents in this telephone survey were told that "although each slice of Kraft Singles is made from 5 ounces of whole milk, it does not contain as much calcium as 5 ounces of milk. One slice actually contains 70 percent of the calcium in 5 ounces of milk." Then they were asked whether they would continue buying or stop buying Kraft Singles in light of that information. Ninety-six percent said they would continue buying. Thus, the survey provided support for Kraft's position that the claim was unlikely to affect consumers' choice. In spite of this evidence, the FTC declared it "insufficiently probative to rebut the evidence in support of the materiality of the milk equivalency claim."

Richards and Preston[53] argue that the Commission has, through it presumptions in the *Kraft* case, created a nearly impossible situation for advertisers. Advertisers must prove a negative: that their claim was not important to any significant number of reasonable consumers in any way relevant to any conduct related to the product. To reject such evidence, the Commission need only argue that some group of reasonable consumers was overlooked or that some conduct or relevance was ignored. Much relates to how materiality should be tested. The authors suggest comparing the importance of the implied falsity with that of the truth. However, the focus needs to be shifted from whether the claim is likely to affect consumer behavior to whether it is *more likely* than a true claim to have such an effect. As they state, "If consumers will take the same action (e.g., purchase) whether the claim is true or false, that claim can hardly be considered important to their 'choice of, or conduct regarding, the product.' "

A related issue is the dissemination of nutrition information. The Nutrition Labeling and Education Act of 1990 required the Food and Drug Administration to implement sweeping changes in the regulations governing food labeling. Pauline Ippolito and Alan Mathios[54] summarize the major features of the labeling requirements and analyze the likely impacts on the flow of nutrition information to consumers. They concluded that although much in the new rules was likely to improve consumer information, there were serious concerns. In the attempt to prevent deceptive claims, the new rules also eliminated the potential for many types of truthful, nonmisleading claims that could generate unnecessary losses for consumers. The authors argue that use of health claims in advertising and labeling plays an important role in educating the public about diet and health and in improving food choices. Good consumer policy should focus as much on increasing the flow of truthful information as it does on stopping deceptive claims.

In a similar vein, David Stewart and Ingrid Martin[55] examined the question of the intended and unintended consequences of warning messages and labels. They concluded that warnings tend to inform rather than persuade consumers and consumers selectively attend to warning messages. Because of multiple effects of warnings and the varying responses of different groups of consumers, warning messages should be carefully designed and should be designed using empirical research rather than just expert opinion or judgment.

DETERMINING DECEPTION USING ADVERTISING RESEARCH . . . .

The crucial issue in deceptive advertising is often the determination of how the advertising claims are perceived by consumers and what impact such perceptions have on consumer behavior. Since these issues are also central to copy testing and to the evaluation of an advertising campaign, it would be natural for the FTC and the courts to avail themselves of the methodologies of advertising research. Until the late 1960s, however, there was actually little consumer research employed in this context. Several factors inhibited the use of consumer research on perceptions.

1. The FTC simply was not required by the courts to develop evidence—subjective judgment was held as adequate.

2. The use of independently commissioned survey research is somewhat inconsistent with the traditional adversary system of justice wherein each side submits arguments and evidence to support a position. To an attorney, agreeing to a carefully conceived and conducted survey might be too much like calling a prestigious witness without knowing which side his or her testimony will support.

3. There are methodological difficulties and pitfalls in any study. The population must be defined, a defensible sampling plan created, and questions designed to pass tests of unbiasedness and validity. Additional pressures on any research design are created in the legal context by opposing lawyers and experts who will try to discredit it. Some early survey efforts were badly flawed by using small, unrepresentative samples and naive questionnaires.

4. Defendants have lacked motivation to introduce survey evidence because it could be used against them. In the 1963 *Benrus Watch* case, a survey showed that 86 percent correctly interpreted an ad, but the FTC used the fact that 14 percent had been deceived as evidence against Benrus.[56]

Over the years, the reluctance to use consumer research to determine how advertising is perceived and how it impacts consumers has gradually declined for two reasons. First, the consumer research community has both advanced their methods and worked to apply them in the legal setting. Several prominent consumer researchers have worked for the FTC, for example, and thereby have helped show how research methods can be applied to determine the impact of deception upon perceptions, beliefs, and behavior. Second, the courts, seeing the power of consumer evidence, especially concerning perceptions, have begun to look for such evidence and be suspicious when it is missing or flawed.

FTC Commissioner Deborah Owen and Attorney Joyce E. Plyler[57] reviewed the role of empirical evidence in regulation cases. They argued that objectivity is best achieved through the use of empiricism and that copy tests are the most scientific method of measuring actual consumer perceptions. However, disputes over methodological flaws may undermine the empirical evidence and the Commission may have no choice but to rely on a more subjective interpretation of the ad. It is important that the Commission understand what flaws in methodology are fatal and what flaws do not significantly affect the accuracy of survey findings. And, copy tests may not be feasible or other kinds of marketing research and expert testimony may be more useful. The basic question remains of whether it is possible for the Commission to establish a coherent set of guidelines for the use of extrinsic evidence in support of its standards as to what constitutes "reason to believe." There is a set of guidelines on claims substantiation and they might be used in developing reason to believe guidelines. In determining the degree of substantiation necessary for an objective product claim, the Commission considers:

1. The type of claim.
2. The type of product.
3. The benefits of a truthful claim.
4. The consequences of a false claim.
5. The cost of developing substantiation.
6. The amount of substantiation experts in the field believe is reasonable.

Preston[58] reported on a content analysis of evidence introduced in deceptive advertising cases. The focus was on evidence that was rejected because it was unable to establish the factual finding it was introduced to support. It was found that a very significant amount of such "erroneous evidence" was submitted and that the invalidity and consequent rejection were predictable in advance based on the professional knowledge of lawyers and researchers. One reason is the nature of legal action and the nature of the interaction between lawyers and researchers. The result is considerable waste. Preston suggests that the FTC should develop guidelines by having legal writers analyze and synthesize all relevant decisions into brief expressions that summarize points as usable rules.

Richards[59] has proposed a method for gathering empirical evidence that goes beyond the typical Burke in-home, day-after recall tests or in-theater recall tests done by Audience Studies, Inc. It uses a modified semantic differential measured not only for the test ad but also for a control condition and "true" and "false" communications presented as memo text, not ad copy or layout. The communications are presented to sampled subjects in a laboratory "without editorial or programming context." Subjects also rate product attributes on a materiality scale such as "would or would not affect my decision." There are five treatments for each ad, separately measuring ad belief, ad comprehension, a true and false memo, and a control treatment for separate sets of subjects. The method is called *RPI*, or *Relative Proximity Index*.

What Is an Acceptable Level of Misperception?

A key lingering issue had been the determination of the "acceptable" level of misperception. What percent of an audience needs to be mislead for deception to occur? In general, levels under 5 percent are considered to be irrelevant and are ignored. However, as the *Benrus Watch* case illustrates, levels as low as 15 to 20 percent have been deemed high enough to support a finding that deception exists. In the 1972 *Firestone Tire* case, the FTC concluded that if 10 percent of the audience perceived the claim that the Safety Champion tire was free of any defects and safe under any conditions, that level was substantial.[60]

To develop a guideline as to what level of miscomprehension should be expected in an average ad, the American Association of Advertising Agencies sponsored a study. Respondents were exposed to a set sixty television ads and were asked six true/false questions about each (and a series of editorial messages). A remarkably consistent finding (both using ads and the editorial messages) was that about 30 percent of the content was miscomprehended. The implication is that any baseline under 30 percent is unfair and unrealistic.

Others have concluded that a close examination of the study suggests that any baseline measure should be less than 30 percent. First, the study involved a single exposure to a broad audience in an artificial situation, whereas most advertising involves multiple exposures in natural settings and a target audience.[61] Second, some of the questions were ambiguous, poorly worded, or immaterial. Third, the measure used may not be appropriate. Other measures, based upon unaided recall, for example, might generate much lower levels. In addition, there is a concern that the study focused on literal miscomprehension, whereas much of deception involves claims that are literally true.

Preston and Richards also make the case that some miscomprehension is eradicable and should not be considered a baseline.[62] For example, "I don't have no bananas" is ambiguous but could be easily revised to remove the ambiguity.

There is no question that miscomprehension does occur. The question is: What should the "baseline" level be in a particular context? The standard will surely depend on the context. If health and safety are involved, only very low or even zero levels of misperception might be tolerated. However, if the "danger" in buying the wrong soap or toothpaste is modest, higher levels can be tolerated.

REMEDIES . . . .

The FTC has a variety of remedies at its disposal and must select the remedy most appropriate to the situation. Among the remedies are the cease-and-desist order, restitution, affirmative disclosure, and corrective advertising.

Cease-and-Desist Orders

The *cease-and-desist order*, which prohibits the respondent from engaging further in the deceptive practice, is actually the only formal procedure established by the FTC Act for enforcing its prohibition of "deceptive acts and practices." It has been criticized as being a command to "go and sin no more," which has little practical effect. Due to procedural delays, it is not uncommon for several years to elapse between the filing of the complaint and the issuance of the order. In one extreme case, it took sixteen years for the commission to get the "Liver" out of Carter's Little Liver Pills.[63] During the delay, the advertising can go on. By the time the cease-and-desist order is issued, the advertising may have served its purpose and another campaign may be underway anyway.

Restitution

Restitution means that the consumer is compensated for any damage. For example, the FTC required a mail-order company to make restitution in the form of full refunds for its skin cream, diet plans, vitamin supplements, and other products that had advertised claims not adequately substantiated.[64] Restitution is rarely considered because of its severity.

Affirmative Disclosures

If an advertisement has provided insufficient information to the consumer, an *affirmative disclosure* might be issued.[65] Affirmative disclosures require "clear and conspicuous" disclosure of the omitted information. Often the involved information relates to deficiencies or limitations of the product or service relating to matters of health or safety. Kenrec Sports, Inc., was ordered to disclose certain limitations to its swimming aid, such as adding a statement that the device was not a life preserver and should always be used in shallow water.[66] Medi-Hair International was required to devote at least 15 percent of each advertisement for its baldness concealment system to the limitations and drawbacks of the system for one year.

Corrective Advertising

Corrective advertising requires advertisers to rectify past deception by making suitable statements in future commercials.[67] The concept is illustrated by the 1971 Profile Bread case, the first case for which corrective advertising was a part of the remedy.[68] The consent order agreed to by Continental Baking specified that 25 percent of the next year's Profile Bread advertising had to include a FTC-approved message, such as the following:

> *Hi, I'm Julia Meade for Profile Bread. Like all mothers, I'm concerned about nutrition and balanced meals. So, I'd like to clear up any misunderstanding you may have about Profile Bread from its advertising or even its name. Does Profile have fewer calories than any other brands? No. Profile has about the same per ounce as other brands. To be exact, Profile has seven fewer calories per slice. That's because Profile is sliced thinner. But eating Profile will not cause you to lose weight. A reduction of seven calories is insignificant. It's total calories and balanced nutrition that count. And Profile can help you achieve a balanced meal because . . .*[69]

There was some evidence that the sales of Profile Bread suffered as a result of the corrective advertising.

The 1975 FTC corrective advertising order against Warner-Lambert's Listerine is important because it was appealed all the way to the Supreme Court.[70] Listerine had advertised for over fifty years that gargling with Listerine mouthwash helped prevent colds and sore throats by killing germs. The order required them to include the statement, "Listerine will not help prevent colds or sore throats or lessen their severity" in $10 million of advertising, which was equal to the average annual Listerine expenditure during the prior ten-year period.

Listerine implemented the order by embedding the statement in a commercial featuring two couples, each with a husband finding himself having "onion breath." One couple used Scope and the other Listerine. The wife using Scope sniffed her husband's breath and said that she didn't know that "clinical tests prove Listerine fights onion breath better than Scope." The other replied, "We always knew." The corrective disclosure appeared midway in the thirty-second spot as follows: "While Listerine will not help prevent colds or sore throats or lessen their severity, breath tests prove Listerine fights onion breath better than Scope."

Three field studies basically found that the corrective advertising had a modest impact. In day-after recall tests, only 5 percent mentioned the corrective message when asked to describe the ad; it was the fourth most recalled message in the ad.[71] Two studies focused on before-after changes in beliefs about Listerine. One, using four waves of telephone interviews, found a reduction of about 20 percent in overall deceptive beliefs about Listerine's effectiveness.[72] The other, an FTC study, consisted of seven waves of questionnaire mailings which garnered 10,000 returned questionnaires (a 70 percent response rate) from the Market Facts consumer panel.[73] Beliefs that Listerine is effective for colds and sore throats fell about 11 percent (14 percent for Listerine users). The amount of mouthwash used for colds and sore throats dropped 40 percent, but a substantial level of misperception about Listerine effectiveness remained after the campaign.

The Listerine case clearly established the FTC's authority to order corrective advertising, but it also served to raise some important issues. Any remedy should be nonpunitive in nature and should not be burdensome. How do you determine whether the corrective advertising is generating damage to sales or image? Any remedy should preserve First Amendment rights to express ideas. What about those ideas that are counter to the corrective message's claims? Can an advertiser simply decide to stop advertising, thereby avoiding corrective advertising?

One problem with corrective advertising is that it has usually resulted in lawyers writing copy and insisting that it be run some arbitrary length of time. William Wilkie has observed that the much more sensible approach would be to give the advertisers a communication task and let them achieve it any way that they can.[74]

Such an approach was partially applied in the *Hawaiian Punch* case.[75] Hawaiian Punch used a catchy jingle, "Seven Natural Fruit Juices in Hawaiian Punch," together with fruit photos even though it contains only 11 to 15 percent fruit juice. Hawaiian Punch agreed to disclose the actual fruit juice content of the product ("contains not less than 11 percent natural fruit juice"). The disclosure was to run until a specified survey found that 67 percent of fruit drink purchasers are aware that Hawaiian Punch contained less than 20 percent natural fruit juice. A series of seventeen semiannual telephone surveys indicated that relevant perceptions were slow to change.[76] Over the period between 1974 and 1982, the proportion of consumers who believed that Hawaiian Punch had 20 percent or less fruit juice increased from 20 percent (1974) to 40 percent (1975) to 50 percent (1982). The target was reached only after nine years of advertising.

The implementation of the communication objective approach to corrective advertising will always face difficulties. The problem of ascertaining how misperception and its effect are to be measured and the appropriate target level of misperception that should be obtained reappears in this context. Judgments on such questions are required to set communication objectives. Obviously, a zero misperception level is not generally feasible. Yet regulators and the general public to which they must answer have difficulty accepting realistic standards. A key is to know whether the advertiser is making a good faith effort toward the objective. Copy testing could logically be used to address this point, but the parties would have to agree in advance on relevant and suitable tests, a difficult prospect. Another problem is the cost of measuring deception over time. The tracking required to measure the impact of the commercials—no problem for large advertisers, who do that anyway—could be costly for smaller advertisers and may require the government to share some of the costs.

Corrective advertising has only rarely been considered since the Listerine case, largely because of the difficulties in deciding on the target objective. However, it remains an important option and serves to focus attention on the central issues in deception cases.

COMPETITOR LAWSUITS. . . . .

Another mechanism that inhibits deceptive advertising is the possibility of *competitor lawsuits*, in which firms charge that false advertising has caused them damage. In one case, a suit was successfully brought by Honeywell against a competitor who supplied replacement parts to Honeywell's safety control systems and had incorrectly claimed that its products had comparable quality and ease of replacement to that of Honeywell.

During the last decade, the 1946 Lanham Trademark Act has been broadened to provide the basis for suits in which a competitor has been disparaged in a comparative ad. In one visible case, an automatic rental firm, Jartran, ran a series of ads that were judged to have damaged U-Haul.[77] In one ad, a special introductory Jartran price was compared to U-Haul's usual price, implying a price difference that did not exist. In another, older, smaller U-Haul trucks were compared to new larger Jartran trucks, incorrectly implying a difference between the average truck in the two fleets.

In most cases, the relief is an injunction to stop the offending practice. However, a wide range of remedies exit. In the Jartran case, the firm was ordered to replace $6 million in lost U-Haul profits and another $13.6 million to compensate for U-Haul's corrective advertising outlay. Another $20 million was assessed because the action was judged to be willful and malicious.

SELF-REGULATION . . . .

Self-regulation is another vehicle to combat deceptive advertising by national advertisers. In place in the United States since 1971, it is intended to provide a fast, flexible alternative to FTC and the courts. Complaints from consumers or competitors are investigated by the National Advertising Division (NAD), an arm of the Council of Better Business Bureaus (CBBB). In evaluating a complaint, NAD normally requests that the advertiser submit substantiation for the claims made in the challenged advertisements. If the complaint is judged to be justified and substantiation found to be inadequate, the advertiser is requested to modify or withdraw the challenged advertising. The finding can be appealed to a panel drawn mostly from the advertising industry.

The self-regulation process does provide remedies in a meaningful number of cases—perhaps 100 cases each year are brought before the NAD. Although the penalties are relatively minor—a case can generate negative publicity, or bring in the FTC, or suggest to major media that they deny access to the offender—as a practical matter nearly all advertisers comply with NAD findings. The biggest value, however, is probably to provide a forum to establish standards for advertisers and to make visible issues regarding deception in advertising.[78]

In one series of eleven rulings by the NAD, three involved claims that were substantiated.[79] For example, Revlon supplied independent research to support its claim that Colorsilk, a hair-coloring product, promises color that is rich, true, and lasting and hair that feels silkier and looks healthier.

The other eight companies either modified or discontinued their advertising. Curtis Mathes failed to mention that labor charges were not included when advertising its four-year limited warranty on its television sets. Hall of Music in television advertisements offered over eighty of the world's greatest masterpieces in a two-album collection. The NAD was concerned that the consumer might believe that he or she was getting the entire selection instead of excerpts. Louis Marx in television advertisements for Big Wheel, a ride-on toy, used the disclaimer, "assembly required." The children's unit of NAD felt that simpler wording is needed for child-directed advertisements. E. J. Brach advertised that "We still use fresh, natural ingredients, so Brach's tastes better than other candy." The NAD indicated that some clarification was required, since some artificial coloring and flavoring is used.

A useful review and critique of self-regulation programs is given by Herbert Rotfeld.[80] He argues that self-regulation is not sufficient to protect the consumer interest fully, and it is not valid to assert that self-regulation alone makes government programs unnecessary. Because government is the motivating force for business cooperation with self-regulation, the power of self-regulation declines as government enforcement activity is cut back. Without the threat of government action, Rotfeld argues, only the most altruistic of firms would ever pay heed to self-regulation directives. In sum, if you are for stronger self-regulation you must also be for vigilant government activity![81]

SUMMARY . . . .

Conceptually, deception exists when an advertisement is input to the perceptual process of some audience and the output of that perceptual process (1) differs from the reality of the situation and (2) affects buying behavior to the detriment of the consumer. The legal definition has been influenced by a formal 1983 FTC position which stated that deception will be found if there is a misrepresentation or omission that is likely to mislead a consumer acting responsibly to the consumers detriment.

A misrepresentation or omission can occur in at least nine situations:

1. Suggesting that a small difference is important.
2. Artificial product demonstrations.
3. Using an ambiguous or easily confused phrase.
4. Implying a benefit that does not fully or partially exist.
5. Implying that a product benefit is unique to a brand.
6. Implying that a benefit is needed or that a product will fulfill a benefit when it will not.

7. Incorrectly implying that an endorser uses or advocates the brand.
8. Omitting a needed qualification.
9. Making a claim without substantiation.

Puffing, the subjective statement of opinion concerning a product's quality, using terms such as "best," is permissible. However, the definition of what is puffery and deception has been narrowed over time. The 1983 FTC statement narrowed the definition of deception from "having the capacity to deceive a substantial number of consumers in a material way" to "material and likely to mislead consumers acting 'reasonably' under the circumstances." Thus the "unthinking and credulous" seem no longer to be protected.

Consumer research was rarely used in deception cases until the 1970s for several reasons. The FTC's subjective judgment was deemed adequate, legal adversaries were not comfortable using advertising research as evidence, there were methodological difficulties and defendants feared that consumer research would be used against them. A key issue is to determine the acceptable level of misperception. The AAAA study based upon single exposures to ads found that around 30 percent of claims made in commercials are misperceived, about the same level found in other television programming. The appropriate level will clearly be a function of the situation and the measure used.

The FTC has several available remedies. Cease-and-desist orders prohibit the defendant from engaging further in the deceptive practice. Restitution provides compensation to those deceived. Affirmative disclosure requires that missing information be disclosed in a clear and conspicuous manner. Corrective advertising seeks to eliminate the effects of prior misleading advertising. Efforts to employ corrective advertising by requiring the insertion of some phrase in the ads generally has had little impact. A more useful remedy would be to demand corrective advertising aimed at some communication objective. The difficulty is to establish that objective.

Deception in advertising can also be controlled by competitor lawsuits and by self-regulation. The Lanham Trademark Act has been used as a vehicle to combat damage when a competitor is disparaged unfairly in a comparative ad. The advertising industry has developed an ambitious program of self-regulation, which rests largely on the support of industry itself. It has provided relatively fast and effective results in comparison to action using the FTC or the courts.

DISCUSSION QUESTIONS . . . .

1. In your judgment, are the following deceptive?
   a. Geritol (tired blood).
   b. Wonder Bread (the implied uniqueness issue).
   c. Colgate-Palmolive (the use of simulated sandpaper).
   d. Efficen (implying a benefit that doesn't exist).
2. For the advertisements of the products in question 1, how would you use advertising research to help determine whether deception is present?

3. All advertisements have the capacity to deceive some audience members. For example, if an ad merely showed a picture of a glass of milk, some people would believe that the advertisement was falsely implying that everyone must drink at least one glass of milk a day because that belief has been ingrained in them. Comment.

4. Evaluate the following proposals:
   a. Advertising for brands that are, for all practical purposes, identical to competitors' should be eliminated.
   b. The use of live models or spokespeople should be eliminated.
   c. Only the product itself, with no background scenes, can be shown in an advertisement.

5. The FTC is concerned about the use of endorsements by celebrities or experts (as opposed to the use of ordinary people or a "slice-of-life" dramatization). What guidelines would you suggest that would help ensure that such advertisements would not be deceptive? Illustrate how your guidelines would apply by considering examples.

6. If a brand is not substantially different from its competitors, should its advertisements state that fact? What would be the effect of such a rule?

7. Pornography, which is protected by free speech guarantees, is judged by whether the average person applying contemporary community standards believes the dominant theme appeals to prurient interests. What is the standard applied to advertising? Is that appropriate? Should the rights of business to inform be specified by the FTC? What guidelines should be used in interpreting surveys designed to measure deception?

8. If the FTC holds that inadequate substantiation exists for an advertising claim, it has held responsible not only the manufacturer but also the agency preparing the advertising, the media running it, and the celebrity used in the advertisement to endorse the product. Comment on this policy.

9. Identify three advertisements that contain claims that should have prior substantiation.

10. In some corrective advertising proposals, a one-year period and 25 percent of advertising budgets were suggested as the extent of the corrective advertising effort. How should the percentage and the time period be determined? How should it vary with products and situation? Give examples.

11. How would you determine if the National Advertising Review Board is effective at resolving complaints concerning deceptive advertising? If its concern is broadened to include issues of taste, how do you think it will perform in that regard? How would you then measure performance?

12. In a survey of 200 people, 90 percent recognized the *Good Housekeeping* Seal, 50 percent relied upon it for purchasing decisions, and 29 percent believed that the product met federal quality and safety standards, but no one interviewed recognized that the seal was given only to advertisers. Should such a seal be continued? What role does it have in consumer decision making?

13. Develop four or five central ideas of an advertising code for children.

14. Some argue that comparative advertisements in which one or more competitors are explicitly named are unfair to competitors and tend to be deceptive

and therefore should be illegal. Such advertisements are, in fact, illegal in France, Belgium, Spain, and Italy. Comment.

15. Comment on the AAAA study of miscomprehension levels. Does 30 percent provide a benchmark level of miscomprehension that should be used in deceptive advertising cases?

NOTES. . . . .

1. For a review which includes other relevant journals, see Debra A. Laverie and Patrick E. Murphy, "The Marketing and Public Policy Literature: A Look at the Past Ten Years," *Journal of Public Policy and Marketing*, 12, no. 2 (Fall 1993), 258–267.
2. Jef I. Richards, "FTC or NAAG: Who Will Win the Territorial Battle?" *Journal of Public Policy and Marketing*, 10, no. 1 (Spring 1991), 118.
3. *Enforcement of National Advertising Regulations*, CCH Trade Regulation Report No. 97, March 20, 1990, p. 1.
4. Ira N. Millstein, "The Federal Trade Commission and False Advertising," *Columbia Law Review*, 64 (March 1964), 439.
5. *Sears, Roebuck & Co. v. FTC*, 258 Fed. 307 (7th Cir. 1919).
6. *FTC v. Raladam Co.*, 258 U.S. 643 (1931).
7. Dennis A. Yao and Christa Van Anh Veechi, "Information and Decisionmaking at the Federal Trade Commission," *Journal of Public Policy and Marketing*, 11, no. 2 (Fall 1992), 1–11. For a book-length treatment of advertising legislation, see Ross D. Petty, *The Impact of Advertising Law on Business and Public Policy* (Westport, CT: Quorum Books, 1992).
8. Jef I. Richards, "FTC or NAAG: Who Will Win the Territorial Battle?" *Journal of Public Policy and Marketing*, 10, no. 1 (Spring 1991), 118–132.
9. FTC (1983) at 689–690. For an analysis of this definition, see Gary T. Ford and John E. Calfee, "Recent Developments in FTC Policy on Deception," *Journal of Marketing*, 50 (July 1986), 82–103 and David M. Gardner and Nancy H. Leonard, "Research in Deceptive and Corrective Advertising: Progress to Date and Impact on Public Policy," in *Current Issues and Research in Advertising*, ed., James H. Leigh and Claude R. Martin, Jr. vol. 12, no. 2 (Ann Arbor: University of Michigan Graduate School of Business, 1989), 275–309.
10. Thomas C. Kinnear and Ann R. Root, "The FTC and Deceptive Advertising in the 1980s: Are Consumers Being Adequately Protected?" *Journal of Public Policy & Marketing* (1988), 40–48.
11. Ross D. Petty, "Advertising and the First Amendment: A Practical Test for Distinguishing Commercial Speech from Fully Protected Speech," *Journal of Public Policy & Marketing*, 12, no. 2 (Fall 1993), 170–177.
12. *P. Lorillard Co. v. FTC*, 186 F.2d 52 (4th Cir. 1950).
13. *Hutchinson Chem. Corp.*, 55 FTC 1942 (1959).
14. This is a classic case in which product demonstrations were found deceptive and which introduced the term "corrective advertising" into marketing. See "Marbles in the Soup," *Advertising Age*, October 17, 1994, p. 25ff.
15. *Volvo North America Corp. et al., and Scali, McCabe, Sloves, Inc.*, CCH #23,041 (Aug. 1991): BNA ATRR No. 1530 (Aug. 22, 1991), 244.
16. *FTC v. Sterling Drug, Inc.*, 215 F.Supp. 327, 330 (S.D.N.Y.) aff'd 317 F.2d 699 (2d Cir. 1963).
17. *Bristol-Myers Co.*, 46 FTC 162 (1949), aff'd 185 F.2d 58 (4th Cir. 1950).
18. *Nestlé Food Co.*, CCH #23,091, FTC File No. 9123160 (Oct. 1991); BNA ATRR No. 1540 (Nov. 7, 1991), 577.
19. *Gary E. Peel v. Attorney Registration and Disciplinary Commission of Illinois*, CCH #69,046 (S. Ct., June 1990); BNA ATRR No. 1469 (June 7, 1990), 883.

20. Ivan L. Preston, "Communication Research in the Prosecution of Deceptive Advertising." Lecture given at the University of Texas, May, 1986.
21. *General Electric Co.*, CCH #23,279, FTC Fole No. 912 3366 (Nov. 1992); BNA ATRR No. 1590 (Nov. 12, 1992), 587.
22. *Stouffer Food Corp.*, FTC Dkt. 9250, CCH #23,082 (Oct. 1991).
23. "FTC to Issue Consent in Wonder Case," *Advertising Age*, November 5, 1973, p. 1.
24. *Miller Brewing Co.* v. *Anheuser-Busch, Inc.*; *G. Heilman Brewing Co., Inc.* v. *Anheuser-Busch, Inc.*, CCH #67,881 (DC E WI, Dec. 1987); BNA ATRR No. 1349 (Jan. 21, 1988), 89.
25. *FTC Member's Views on Environmental Claims*, CCH #50,777 (Mar. 1992); *American Enviro Products, Inc., et al.*, CCH #23,048, FTC File No. 902 3110 (Mar. 1992); *RMED International, Inc., et al.*, CCH #23,149, FTC File No. 902 3112 (May 1992).
26. *Jerome Russell Cosmetics U.S.A., Inc. et al.*, FTC File No. 902 3365, CCH #23,001 (June 1991) and *American Enviro Products, Inc., et al.*, FTC File No. 902 3110 CCH #23,048 (Aug. 1991); BNA ATRR No. 1532 (Sept. 12, 1991), 301.
27. Amy Freedland, "Truth or Consequences: Deceptive Advertising Laws and Policies of the Twentieth Century." Unpublished paper, University of Michigan, Ann Arbor, 1990.
28. *Diamond Mortgage Corp. of Illinois dba Diamond Financial Services, Inc.*, ID No. 36-3244958, *Debtor John Aramowicz et al.* v. *Lloyd Bridges et al.*, CCH #69,190; CCH #69,191 (July 1990); CCH #69,192 (Sep. 1990), (U.S. Bankrupcy Ct., N IL).
29. *Black & Decker (U.S.) Inc.*, CCH #22,755, FTC File No. 892 3061 (Nov. 1989); BNA ATRR No. 1440 (Nov. 9, 1989), 651.
30. *J. B. Williams Co.*, 3 Trade Reg. Rep. 17. 339 (FTC Dkt. No. 8547, 1965), appeal docketed, No. 16, 969 (6th Cir. 1965).
31. *The Clorox Co.*, CCH #23,269, FTC File No. 912 3337 (Oct. 1992): BNA ATRR No. 1587 (Oct. 22, 1992), 501.
32. *Kraft, Inc.* v. *Federal Trade Commission*, CCH #69,911 (CA-7, July 31, 1992): BAN ATRR No. 1579 (Aug. 13, 1992) 189, 209.
33. *Campbell Soup Co.*, CCH #22,967, FTC Dkt 9233 (Apr. 8, 1991); BNA ATRR No. 1511 (Apr. 11, 1911), 509.
34. *Removatron International Corp. and Frederick E. Goodman* v. *FTC*, CCH #68,749 (CA-1, Sep. 1989).
35. *Federal Trade Commission* v. *US Sales Corp. also dba Data Resource Systems and Dean S. Vlahos, individually and as an officer and director of US Sales Corp.*, CCH #69,702 (DC N IL, Jan. 1991); BNA ATRR No. 1554 (Feb. 27, 1992), 280; *Federal Trade Commission* v. *Starlink, Inc., and Frank Fioravanti, aka Frank Avanti*, CCH #69,715 (DC E PA, Feb. 1992); BNA ATRR No. 1552 (Feb. 13, 1992), 199; *M.D.M. Interests, Inc., et al.*, CCH #23,150 (Feb. 1992); BAN ATRR No. 1554 (Feb. 27, 1992), 256; *Service Consumer Protection Act of 1991*—H.R. 3490 (Feb. 1992); BNA ATRR No. 1554 (Feb. 27, 1992); 256.
36. *Nu-Day Enterprises, Inc. et al.*, CCH #23,089, FTC File No. 882 3156 (Oct. 1991); BNA ATRR No. 1539 (Oct. 31, 1991), 546.
37. *U.S. Oil and Gas Co., et al.*, CCH #22,985, FTC File No. 812 3232 (Apr. 1991); BNA ATRR No. 1514 (May 2, 1991), 627.
38. *Feist* v. *Rural Telephone*, CCH #26,702 (S. Ct. 111, S. Ct. 1282, Mar. 1991).
39. *Board of Trustees of the State University of New York, et al.* v. *Todd Fox, et al.*, CCH #68,637 (S. Ct., June 1989).
40. *Carlay* v. *FTC*, 153 F.2d 493, 496 (1946).
41. *Ostermoor & Co.* v. *FTC*, 16 F.2d 962 (2d Cir. 1927).
42. Ivan L. Preston and Ralph H. Johnson, "Puffery: A Vulnerable (?) Feature of Advertising." Paper presented at the annual convention of the Association for Education in Journalism, University of South Carolina, August 1971, Ivan L. Preston, "The FTC's Handling of Puffery and Other Selling Claims Made `By Implication,' " *Journal of Business Research* (June 1977), 155–181, and Ivan L. Preston, *The Great American Blow-Up: Puffery in Advertising and Selling* (Madison, WI: University of Wisconsin Press, 1975).
43. *Tanners Shoe Company*, 53 FTC Decisions 1137 (1957).

44. Jef I. Richards, "A 'New and Improved' View of Puffery," *Journal of Public Policy and Marketing*, 9 (1990), 82. Richard cites Aaker and Myers, 1987 as an example of an advertising textbook that repeats the allegation that puffery may be deceptive and admonishes educators to make students understand that the law no longer recognizes puffed claims as immune to regulation.

45. Alexander Simonson and Morris B. Holbrook, "Permissible Puffery Versus Actionable Warranty in Advertising and Salestalk: An Empirical Investigation," *Journal of Public Policy and Marketing*, 12, no. 2 (Fall 1993), 216–233.

46. *Charles of the Ritz Dist. Corp.* v. *FTC*, 143 F.2d 676 (2d Cir. 1944).

47. *Gelb* v. *FTC*, 144 F.2d 580 (2d Cir. 1944).

48. *Trade Reg. Rep.* 16664 (FTC, November 7, 1963).

49. Ibid., at 21539-40.

50. Russell N. Laczniak and Sanford Grossbart, "An Assessment of Assumptions Underlying the Reasonable Consumer Element in Deceptive Advertising Policy," *Journal of Public Policy and Marketing*, 9 (1990), 85–99.

51. Millstein, "False Advertising," p. 438.

52. *Kraft, Inc.* (1991), Docket No. 9208 , Jan. 30, 1991, FTC Lexis 38.

53. Jef I. Richards and Ivan L. Preston, "Proving and Disproving Materiality of Deceptive Advertising Claims," *Journal of Public Policy and Marketing*, 11, no. 2 (Fall 1992), 45–56.

54. Pauline M. Ippolito and Alan D. Mathios, "New Food Labeling Regulations and the Flow of Nutrition Information to Consumers," *Journal of Public Policy and Marketing*, 12, no. 2 (Fall 1993), 188–205.

55. David W. Stewart and Ingrid M. Martin, "Intended and Unintended Consequences of Warning Messages: A Review and Synthesis of Empirical Research," *Journal of Public Policy and Marketing*, 13, no. 1 (Spring 1994), 1–19.

56. *Benrus Watch Co.*, 3 Trade Reg. Rep. 16541 (FTC, July 31, 1963).

57. Deborah K. Owen and Joyce E. Plyler, "The Role of Empirical Evidence in the Federal Regulation of Advertising," *Journal of Public Policy and Marketing*, 10, no. 1 (Spring 1991), 1–14.

58. Ivan L. Preston, "The Scandalous Record of Avoidable Errors in Expert Evidence Offered in FTC and Lanham Act Deceptiveness Cases," *Journal of Public Policy and Marketing*, 11, no. 2 (Fall 1992), 57–67.

59. Jef I. Richards, *Deceptive Advertising: Behavioral Study of a Legal Concept,* (Hillsdale, NJ: Erlbaum, 1990). See also, Thomas J. Maronick, "Copy Tests in FTC Deception Cases: Guidelines for Researchers," *Journal of Advertising Research*, 31, no. 6 (December 1991), 9–19 and Fred W. Morgan, "Judical Standards for Survey Research: An Update and Guidelines," *Journal of Marketing*, 54 (January 1990), 59–70.

60. *Firestone Tire*, 81 FTC Decisions 298, 1972.

61. Gary T. Ford and Richard Yalch, "Viewer Miscomprehension of Televised Communication—A Comment," *Journal of Marketing*, 46 (Fall 1982), 27–31.

62. Ivan L. Preston and Jef I. Richards, "Consumer Miscomprehension as a Challenge to FTC Prosecutions of Deceptive Advertising," *The John Marshall Law Review* (Spring 1986), 605–635.

63. *Carter Products, Inc.* v. *FTC*, 186 F.2d 821 (7th Cir. 1951).

64. Dorothy Cohen, "The FTC's Advertising Substantiation Program," *Journal of Marketing* (Winter 1980), 26–35.

65. Robert F. Wilkes and James B. Wilcox, "Recent FTC Actions: Implications for the Advertising Strategists," *Journal of Marketing*, 38 (January 1974).

66. *Kenrec Sports, Inc., et al.*, 3 Trade Reg Rep. 19. 971 (1972).

67. For an excellent review of corrective advertising from which much of this section draws, see William L. Wilkie, Dennis L. McNeill, and Michael B. Mazis, "Marketing's `Scarlet Letter': The Theory and Practice of Corrective Advertising," *Journal of Marketing*, 48 (Spring 1984), 11–31.

68. *ITT Continental Baking Co.* (1973), 8860, 83 FTC 865.

69. Ibid.

70. *Warner-Lambert* (1975), 8891, 86 FTC 1398.
71. Michael B. Mazis, Dennis L. McNeill and Kenneth Bernhardt, "Day After Recall of Listerine Corrective Commercials." Working paper, American University, Washington, DC, 1981.
72. Gary M. Armstrong, Metin N. Gurol, and Frederick A. Russ, "Detecting and Correcting Deceptive Advertising," *Journal of Consumer Research*, 6 (December 1979), 237–246.
73. Michael B. Mazis, *The Effects of FTC's Listerine Corrective Advertising Order*. Report to the FTC, Washington, DC, 1981.
74. William L. Wilkie, *Consumer Research and Corrective Advertising*, (Cambridge, MA: Marketing Science Institute, 1973).
75. *RJR Foods, Inc.* (1973), C2424 (July 13).
76. Thomas C. Kinnear, James Taylor, and Odee Gur-Arie, "Affirmative Disclosure: Long-Term Monitoring of Residual Effects," *Journal of Business Policy and Marketing*, 2, forthcoming.
77. *U-Haul Int'l, Inc.* v. *Jartran, Inc.*, 601 F.Supp. 1140 (1984), aff'd 793 F.2d 1034 (9th Cir. 1986).
78. Jean J. Boddewyn, "Advertising Self-regulation: True Purpose and Limits," *Journal of Advertising*, 18, no. 2 (1989), 19–27.
79. "Pillsbury Loses Some Brownie Points at NAD," *Advertising Age*, March 17, 1980, p. 10.
80. Herbert J. Rotfeld, "Power and Limitations of Media Clearance Practices and Advertising Self-Regulation," *Journal of Public Policy and Marketing*, 11, no. 1, (Spring 1992), 87–95.
81. For a book on self-regulation, see Jean J. Boddewyn, *Global Perspectives on Advertising Self-Regulation: Principles and Practices in Thirty-eight Countries* (Westport, CT: Quorum Books, 1992).

19 ADVERTISING AND SOCIETY

> Nine-tenths and more of advertising is largely
> competitive wrangling as to the relative merits of
> two undistinguishable compounds. In a truly
> functional society, 90 percent of people employed
> by advertising would be able to engage in
> "productive occupations."
> (Stuart Chase, *Tragedy of Waste*, 1925)
>
> Advertising is more than advertisements alone. It is
> an institutional part of our society, a social force
> affecting and affected by our style of life.
> (Raymond Bauer and Stephen Greyser, *Advertising in America*)

For decades, indeed centuries, broad social and economic issues have been raised concerning the role of advertising in society. In 1759, Dr. Samuel Johnson suggested that advertisers had moral and social questions to consider:

The trade of advertising is now so near to perfection, it is not easy to propose any improvement. But as every art ought to be exercised in due subordination to the publick good, I cannot but propose it as a moral question to these matters of the publick ear. Whether they do not sometimes play too wantonly with our passions.[1]

Since then, advertising has been studied, analyzed, defended, and attacked by individuals representing a wide spectrum of professional interests, including economists, sociologists, politicians, businessmen, novelists, and historians.

A STRUCTURING OF THE ISSUES . . . .

The central issues of advertising and society can be divided into three categories, as depicted in Figure 19–1. The first category represents the nature and content of the advertising to which people are exposed. Is the practice of advertising inherently unethical? Are appeals used that manipulate consumers against their will? There are a variety of issues associated with taste. Is advertising too repetitious, too silly, too preoccupied with sex? Does it irritate or offend the audience member? Finally, there are questions about the fairness of advertising to children, es-

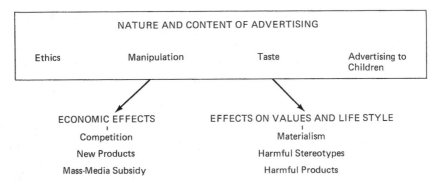

Figure 19–1. Structuring the issues.

pecially when the sugar products involved could adversely affect their health. In essence, this category, the nature and content of advertising, considers the means rather than the ends of advertising, the means being the copy and media tactics used.

The remaining two categories represent the aggregate effects of advertising on society as a whole. These are often called secondary consequences or effects. One of these is the effect on society's values and lifestyles. There are those who believe that advertising competes with or dominates such other socialization agents as literature, plays, music, the church, the home, and the school; that it fosters materialism at the expense of other basic values; that it may serve to reinforce sexual or racial discrimination; or that it promotes harmful products. The second is the effect of advertising on society's economic well-being and on the efficiency of the operation of the economic system. To what extent can the power of advertising lead to the control of the market by a few firms, which will weaken competition and raise consumer prices? What is the economic value of advertising as an efficient mechanism for communicating the existence of new products? To what extent does it subsidize mass media?

NATURE AND CONTENT OF ADVERTISING . . . . . .

Ethics

Is it ethical to advertise cigarettes or to engage in alcohol advertising, which might persuade young people to start smoking and drinking? These and other questions of advertising and marketing *ethics* have become subjects of heated debate in recent years. Two new book-length treatments of marketing ethics have appeared in the early 1990s.[2] Gene Laczniak[3] notes that literature on marketing ethics has moved from nonmainstream into mainstream publications and that a much wider range of ethical issues and concerns are now being addressed such as packaging, professional services advertising by physicians, attorneys, and accountants, and emerging social issues about environmental or "green marketing." In other words, advertising and marketing ethics is being legitimized as a regular subject for teaching and research. There are now various normative and descriptive models of ethics. Normative models attempt to assemble the factors that ought to be weighed in reaching ethical decisions. Descriptive models focus on describing the processes marketers use in adjudicating a marketing issue. And, efforts are being made to test empirically some of the propositions from these models.

Donald Robin and R. Eric Reidenbach[4] argue that the direct adaptation of moral philosophy principles to marketing is unsuitable. Marketing must develop its own philosophy of ethics. Time, history, and context are important considerations that constrain the appropriateness of traditional moral theories. Moral philosophies are designed to prescribe how humans should behave, not how business organizations should behave. Three important constraints on marketing are imposed by society, capitalistic objectives, and human capacities and limitations. The degree to which any of the basic marketing functions are ethical or unethical must be measured within our understanding of their history, the times and context in which they are applied, the expectations of society, the requirements of capitalism, and our best understanding of human nature. For example, it is not appropriate to claim that marketing is unethical because it is profit-oriented or because it distributes utility according to merit rather than some other way. And persuasion should not be considered ethical or unethical until we understand the setting in which it is applied—it could be ethical in a sophisticated advanced society and unethical in a developing country. Puffery is another good example of where the situation is of particular importance in understanding ethical and unethical marketing behavior. Alan Dubinsky and Barbara Loken[5] have developed a model which addresses some of these issues.

Ethics has received increased attention in recent years because of business and government practices which have aroused public ire and indignation such as stock market scandals, insider trading on Wall Street, the collapse of savings and loan associations resulting from unethical (but not necessarily illegal) behavior, junk bonds, defense procurement, and crooked politicians. John Kenneth Galbraith, a famous economist, argues that we are undergoing an economic hangover from a "Binge of Greed " in the 1980s.[6] Donald Kanter[7] argues that events such as these have produced a nation of cynics and that this cynicism spills over into people's views toward advertising. Many are challenging the ethics of agency executives who accept commissions for developing advertising to sell cigarettes, for example. S. D. Hunt and L. B. Chonko[8] found that agency executives are not as concerned about the ethics of their behavior as they are about agency/client/vendor relations and about the effectiveness of the advertising message. Many corporations are making ethical issues a proactive part of the planning process and are creating the position of ethics officer.[9] Martin Marietta created a board game called Gray Matters to alert employees to ethical dilemmas and to teach the company's ethical standards.[10] In response to the increasing attention and concern, many of the nation's leading business schools have incorporated ethics courses into the curriculum.

There is considerable overlap between what many consider to be ethical issues in advertising and the issues of manipulation, taste, and advertising's effects on values and lifestyles reviewed in this chapter. In what follows, we will therefore consider ethics from these various viewpoints. In the next section, for example, we review motivation research in the context of the manipulation issue. Although the motivation research user may not have absolute power over consumers, there are still ethical questions associated with its use. Is the practice of conducting depth interviews to attempt to isolate hidden motives acceptable? It is one thing to probe in an analyst's office for medical reasons but another to do so in the home or laboratory for commercial reasons. Can interviewers be sure that such an experience will not do psychological harm? And, what about the common situation wherein a respondent is not told the actual purpose of the interview? These issues really focus on the research effort itself.

Does Advertising Manipulate?

Perhaps the essence of a free marketplace and a free society is the freedom to make decisions of various kinds, or in this context, the freedom to select or not select a particular brand. There are those who fear that this freedom is circumscribed by the "power" of advertising—that advertising is so effective it can manipulate a buyer into making a decision against his or her will or at least against his or her best interests in allocating his financial resources.

The argument takes several forms. First, there is concern with the use of motivation research, the appeal to motives at the subconscious level. Second, there is the use of indirect emotional appeals. Finally, there is the more general claim of the power of scientific advertising to persuade—to make people believe things and behave in ways that are not in their own or society's best interests.

Motivation Research

Motivation research is an approach that draws on the Freudian psychoanalytic model of consumer decision making. It assumes that important buying motives are subconscious, in that a respondent cannot elucidate them when asked an opinion of a brand or a product class. Thus, a person may dislike prunes because of a subconscious association of prunes with old age or parental authority but may not consciously realize the existence of this association and its relevance to purchasing decisions. A consumer may actually prefer a cake mix that requires the addition of an egg because it subconsciously satisfies the need to contribute to the baking process, although she or he consciously believes that the only reason is that a fresh egg adds quality.

Motivation research made a strong impact on marketing in the 1950s; many saw it as a decisive and powerful marketing tool. Furthermore, it received widespread attention beyond marketing professionals by such books as Vance Packard's The *Hidden Persuaders*.[11] The result was a feeling that advertising could indeed identify subconscious motives and, by playing on these motives, influence an unsuspecting public. The result was an Orwellian specter of the consumer's subconscious being exposed and manipulated without his or her knowledge.

The concept of the consumer being manipulated at the subconscious level reached its zenith with a subliminal 1956 advertising experiment by James Vicary. In a movie theater, he flashed the phrases, "Drink Coke" and "Hungry, Eat popcorn" on the screen every five seconds.[12] The phrases were exposed for 1/3,000th of a second, well below threshold levels. The tests, which covered a six-week period, were reported to have increased cola sales by 57 percent and popcorn sales by 18 percent. The concept of subliminal advertising operating at the subconscious level really suggested manipulation. However, this test lacked even rudimentary controls and has not been replicated. Furthermore, many other tests of subliminal communication in an advertising context have had negative results. There is, therefore, an overwhelming consensus among the advertising professional community that subliminal perception simply does not work.

Joel Saegert,[13] however, has suggested that perhaps this conclusion might be premature. One marketing study did generate significantly greater "thirst ratings" by subjects exposed subliminally to the word *Coke* than other subjects exposed to a nonsense syllable word. Furthermore, psychologists have been able to increase indications of existing traits such as depression, homosexuality, and stuttering by subliminal stimuli, but only where these traits already existed in the subjects.[14] Clearly, these studies only raise the possibility that subliminal communication might be able to bring unconscious motives to the surface, not that it could create or change motives.

We now know that motivation research, for better or worse, was oversold, and that motivation research knowledge does not give an advertiser anything approaching total control over an audience. Motivation research does have a role to play in developing effective advertisements, however. It has been particularly useful in providing insight, in suggesting copy alternatives, and in helping creative people avoid approaches that will precipitate undesirable reactions. Most people probably make choices most of the time for reasons they are aware of, particularly in situations in which real economic risk is involved. Unlike the situation of having the receiver totally under the control of the persuader, popularized in brainwashing experiments, advertising does not control a receiver's options. Although marketing professionals have accepted the reduced scope of motivation research, the layperson is still haunted by the specter of the "hidden persuaders."

Emotional Appeals

The communication of factual information about a product's primary function is usually accepted as being of value to the consumer. However, when advertising utilizes appeals or associations that go beyond such a basic communication task, the charge of manipulation via *emotional appeals* is raised. Tibor Scitovsky declared

> To the extent that it (advertising) provides information about the existence of available (buyer) alternatives, advertising always renders the market more perfect. If advertising is mainly suggestive and confined to emotional appeal, however, it is likely to impede rational comparison and choice, thus rendering the market less perfect.[15]

The implication is that consumers will be led to make less than optimal decisions by such emotional appeals. The FTC reviewed several hundred proposed television commercials. FTC Commissioner Mary Gardiner Jones observed that "a typical theme running through these commercials is to hold the product out as the pathway to success and happiness and the antidote to what is otherwise a drab, boring, or lonely life. Thus, dishwashing liquids are advertised as sweeping away the dullness of life. They are the housewife's pathroad to beauty and romantic excitement. Their use will make the whole world soft and gentle. Bath soaps have a similar rejuvenating capacity. Use of these products is associated with cool sophistication, weddings, traveling, entertainment and enjoyment of life at its unhampered best. . . .[16]

These observations are related to issues of deception. The line between artistic license and deception is something hard to draw. Is an advertisement an innocent, entertaining exaggeration that few will take seriously, or is it really capable of deceiving? Jones's observations also involve some definitional issues. How should such basic concepts as product, needs, rationality, and information be defined? Raymond Bauer and Stephen Greyser have noted that different people writing about advertising have radically different perceptions of these key concepts.[17]

Consider the word *product*. The critic views a product as an entity with only one primary identifiable function. Thus, an automobile is a transportation device. The businessperson is concerned with a product's secondary function, because it may represent the dimensions upon which the product differentiation rests. The automobile's appearance might provide a mechanism by which the individual can express his or her personality. High horsepower and superior handling may provide an outlet for an individual's desire for excitement.

Another key concept is *need*. The critic sees consumer needs as corresponding to a product's primary function. Thus, there is a need for transportation, nutrition, and recreation. The businessperson, on the other hand, takes a much broader view of consumer needs, considering any product attribute or appeal on which real product differentiation can be based as reflecting legitimate needs—needs that are strong enough to affect purchase decisions.

Two other central concepts are *rationality* and *information*. The critic sees any decision that results in an efficient matching of product to needs, as he or she defines these terms, as rational. Information that serves to enhance rational decision making is good information. The businessperson contends that any decision a consumer makes to serve his or her own perceived self-interest is rational. Information, then, is any data or argument that will truthfully put forth the attractiveness of a product in the context of a consumer's own buying criteria.

In part, the resolution of these different perspectives will inevitably involve value judgments and honest differences in premises. To some extent, however, they involve assumptions about consumer decision making and utility theory that should be amenable to research. The challenge is to identify clearly, using a common vocabulary, the value judgments that are required and to isolate precisely the empirical questions.

Power of Modern Advertising

There also exists a somewhat more general claim that advertisers have the raw power to manipulate consumers. Many companies have the capacity to generate large numbers of advertisement exposures. Furthermore, some observers believe that these companies can utilize highly sophisticated, scientific techniques to make such advertising effective.

This book has, in fact, attempted to marshal scientific knowledge from theory and practice. The reader should by now be painfully aware of the limitations of the most sophisticated approaches available. The fact is that consumer-choice behavior is determined by many factors in addition to advertising—the advice of friends, decisions and lifestyles of family members, news stories, prices, distribution variables, and on and on. Advertising is but one of many variables, and it has a limited role. It can communicate the existence of a new automobile and perhaps induce a visit to a dealer, but it can rarely make the final sale. It can explain the advantages of a toothpaste and perhaps be influential in getting some people to try the brand, but it has little impact on their decision to repurchase it. There is an inexhaustible number of examples of huge promotional efforts for products that failed. If advertising had the power that some attribute to it, many of these products would still be with us.

Taste

Some critics feel that advertising is objectionable because the creative effort behind it is not in good taste. This type of objection was explored in a massive study conducted in the mid-1960s.[18] More than 1,500 people were asked to list those advertisements that they found annoying, enjoyable, informative, or offensive. Of the more than 9,000 advertisements involved, 23 percent were labeled as annoying and 5 percent as offensive. Although a portion of these advertisements irritated respondents because they were considered deceptive, the majority were so categorized for reasons related to questions of taste.

Advertising may not be omnipotent, but many contend that it is too omnipresent or intrusive. More than 42 percent of the annoying advertisements in the foregoing study were considered too loud, too long, too repetitious, or involved unpleasant voices, music, or people. Another 31 percent had content that was considered silly, unreal, boring, or depressing. Nearly one-fourth of the offensive advertisements were considered inappropriate for children. More than one-fourth of the offensive advertisements involved such products as liquor or cigarettes. A study by David Aaker and Donald Bruzzone found that of 524 prime-time television commercials, the top 8 most irritating commercials were the 8 commercials for feminine hygiene products like tampons.[19] Commercials for women's undergarments and hemorrhoid products were close behind. Clearly there is a strong product-class effect with respect to irritation with television advertising.

The Appeal

In an open letter to the *Detroit News* entitled, "You Dirty Old Ad Men Make Me Sick," a reader took issue with the use of sex in advertising. In making her case, she described several advertisements:

> *A love goddess runs down the beach, waves nibbling at her toes, her blond streaked hair sweeping back behind wide, expectant eyes. A flimsy garment clings to every supple curve. She runs faster, arms open, until finally she*

throws herself breathlessly into HIS arms. . . . Where's this scene? Right in your living room, that's where. Wild and passionately aroused, she can't stop herself. She runs her fingers through his hair, knocks his glasses off, and kisses him and kisses him again. . . . Who's watching? Your nine-year-old daughter as she sits on her stuffed panda bear and wipes jelly off her face.[20]

The letter received considerable response from advertising professionals. Some argued that advertisements, as long as they are not obscene, reflect society and its collective lifestyles. They observed that nudity and the risqué are part of the contemporary world in which advertising is embedded. Others agreed that sex is overused and suggested that effective advertising can be created without titillating.

One problem is that television commercials have to create attention and communicate a message—and accomplish all this in thirty or even fifteen seconds—a demanding task, indeed. Another problem is that television reaches large, broad audiences. It is one thing to use a risqué approach in *Playboy* magazine and quite another to use it on prime-time television when the likelihood of offending is much greater.

Fear appeals have also been criticized. The intent of the fear appeal is to create anxiety that can supposedly be alleviated by an available product (insurance against a fire or a safe tire to prevent accidents) or action (stop smoking). There exists the possibility that such appeals may create emotional disturbances or a long-run anxiety condition in some audience members. The cumulative effects of such advertising may be highly undesirable to some, although it can also be argued that they quickly cease to have any significant degree of emotional impact and that the audience soon becomes immune to the messages.

Intrusiveness

To some people, advertising, especially television advertising, is often like a visitor who has overstayed his welcome. It becomes an intrusion. Greyser postulates a life cycle wherein an advertising campaign moves with repetition from a period of effectiveness, and presumably audience acceptance, to a period of irritation.[21] The cycle contains the following stages:

1. **Exposure to the message on several occasions prior to serious attention (given some basic interest in the product).**
2. **Interest in the advertisement on either substantive (informative) or stimulus (enjoyment) grounds.**
3. **Continued but declining attention to the advertisement on such grounds.**
4. **Mental tune-out of the advertisement on grounds of familiarity.**
5. **Increasing reawareness of the advertisement, now as a negative stimulus (an irritant).**
6. **Growing irritation.**

The number of exposures between the start of a campaign and the stage of growing irritation is obviously a key variable. On what factors will it depend? An important factor, of course, is the intensity of the campaign itself. Bursts of advertising that generate many exposures over a short time period will undoubtedly run a high risk of irritation. A second factor involves other advertising to which the audience is exposed. The cycle will be shorter if different brands and even different product classes use similar approaches. Advertisements involving similar demonstrations, spokespeople, jingles, or animation may be difficult to separate in the mind of an audience member. Campaigns for beer, soda, and menthol cigarettes, for example, have been perceived as being highly similar. Product usage and brand preferences are two additional factors affecting the cycle time period. Greyser noted that:

> Consumers dislike only 21 percent of the advertisements for products used (19 percent annoying, 2 percent offensive), whereas they dislike 37 percent of advertisements for products they don't use (29 percent annoying, 8 percent offensive). For brand preferrers the tendency is even more marked: only 7 percent of advertisements for one's favorite brand are disliked compared with 76 percent of the advertisements for "brands wouldn't buy" (only product users included).[22]

Still another factor is the entertainment value of the advertisement. Campaigns using advertisements with high entertainment value have demonstrated their ability to survive heavy repetition. An important issue is the determination of the link between liking and effectiveness. There is some evidence that the very pleasant and the very unpleasant advertisements are more effective than those in between. A disliked commercial may attract attention and communicate better than a bland commercial. Further, the negative feeling toward the ad may not get attached to the brand. The nature of the relationship will undoubtedly depend on the audience, the product, and other variables. Furthermore, there are several definitional and measurement problems involved.

The result is a decrease in the long-run effectiveness of advertising. It is in the best interests of advertisers to be concerned not only with the irritation caused by specific campaigns, but also with that caused by the impression of advertising in general. Twenty- or thirty-second television spots may be cost-effective for the brand but less so when the total impression of a cluttered media is considered.

Political advertising associated with elections to government offices has become increasingly vitriolic and the focus of much consumer and voter criticism. It is characterized by advertising in which one opponent launches a vicious and degrading attack on the ethics, morals, or law-breaking behavior of the other, followed by a counterattack by his or her opponent of a similar kind. This type of political advertising is often used as a very visible example of bad taste in mass communications, almost analogous to pornography, and adding further to the general cynicsm of voter attitudes towards politicians and government. The problem, of course, is that advocates of the negative advertising strategy have shown that in many instances it works and wins votes. As we have discussed in other parts of the book, negative advertising can be very effective in accomplishing a primary objective like wining an election, but can also result in undesireable secondary side-effects such as increasing cynical attitudes about politics and politicians.

Advertising to Children

Advertising to children has been a major focus of public policy and concern for many years. Groups such as ACT (Action for Children's Television) and CARU (Children's Advertising Review Unit) have been particularly active. CARU was established in 1974 by the National Advertising Division of the Council of Better Business Bureaus for the purpose of: (1) monitoring children's advertising for truth and accuracy, (2) evaluating proposed children's advertising, (3) promoting research into children's advertising, and (4) disseminating information to the public.[23]

In 1977, an FTC staff report recommended that: (1) all television advertising be banned for any product that is directed to or seen by audiences composed of a significant proportion of children who are too young to understand the selling purpose of the advertising, and (2) either balance televised advertising for sugared food products directed to or seen by audiences composed of a significant proportion of older children with nutritional and or health disclosures funded by advertisers or ban it completely. These proposals, which were intensely debated, were ultimately defeated in part because of changes in the political environment in the early 1980s.[24]

The proposals were based upon several facts and judgments. First, children between the ages of two and eleven spend about 25 hours per week watching television and see approximately 20,000 ads per year. About 7,000 of these ads are for highly sugared products. Second, there is evidence that some preschool children cannot differentiate between commercials and programming, cannot understand the selling intent of commercials, and cannot distinguish between fantasy and reality. Third, children between the ages of seven and twelve have difficulty balancing appeals of highly sugared products with long-term health risks—by age two, about one-half of children have diseased gums and decayed teeth. Fourth, there are no counterads for fruit and vegetables. Fifth, much of children's advertising is deceptive in that it omits significant information, such as the complexity and safety of operating toys.

Opponents of the proposals marshaled their own facts and judgments. First, banning television advertising to protect those children who do not understand the selling intent of commercials will deny advertisers the right of free speech to communicate with other audience members, who, in fact, constitute the great majority of the audience for most children's programs. Second, the FTC does not have the professional competence to serve as a "national nanny" deciding what children should be exposed to. Parents are generally both more competent and involved to help children interpret information and make decisions. Third, there is no evidence of a relationship between television exposure and the incidence of tooth decay. Further, there is very little evidence that eating the most heavily advertised products will cause tooth decay. Fourth, there is evidence that children are aware that fruits and vegetables are more nutritious than highly sugared foods. David Boush et al.,[25] in an experiment with middle schoolers, found that adolescents showed discernible patterns of beliefs about advertising tactics by grade 6.

Advertising skepticism appeared to be multidimensional, with components of disbelief in advertiser claims and mistrust of advertiser motives. Higher levels of knowledge about advertising tactics were positively related to increased skepticism of advertising.

In 1984, the decision of the Federal Communicaitons Commission (FCC) to lift guidelines limiting commercial time for children's advertising on TV was met with much criticism from public interest groups, and legislators. Later, in 1987, the Commission launched a review on whether limits should be reimposed and whether "children's programs based on toys are actually program-length commercials and, if so, whether they should be banned." Before the Commission acts against such programs, opponents have to prove that they cause more harm to children than good. The major issues are whether TV advertising to children is inherently unfair, whether it causes children to make poor product decisions, whether it increases parent-child conflict, and whether it results in undesirable socialization of children. The broader issues, particularly associated with toys and games that involve violence, are whether advertising of such games, or the games themselves, should be disallowed. A related question is whether advertising, even though it does not contain violent material, should be sponsoring television programs that do depict violent scenes that can be seen by children.

The controversy has generated an ongoing stream of research on the effects of children's advertising. Marvin Goldberg and Gerald Gorn[26] in a series of experiments generally confirm that advertising can influence children to select the advertised product (highly sugared cereals, candy, etc.) over more nutritious products. In one experiment,[27] for example, children who viewed candy commercials picked significantly more candy over fruit as snacks. Eliminating the candy commercials proved as effective in encouraging selection of fruit as did exposing the children to fruit commercials or nutritional public service announcements. M. Carole Macklin,[28] in studies of preschoolers, found in contrast to some widely held beliefs, that some were able to comprehend the informational role of TV advertising. Merrie Brucks, Gary Armstrong, and Marvin Goldberg[29] had nine- to ten-year-olds verbalize their thoughts while watching commercials, reasoning that the number of counterarguments produced would indicate the child's use of cognitive defenses. It was found that counterarguing occurred, but only when a cue was present to activate the process.

Deborah Roedder[30] identified three types of child information processing: (1) *strategic*—for ages ten to eleven years old and older, (2) *cued*—six to ten years old, and (3) *limited*—under six years old. Strategic processors can evaluate a product's appeal with greater sophistication because they can store information about the selling intent, other products, and past experiences. Prompts can be used to encourage use of storage and retrieval strategies by cued processors but would not benefit limited processors very much. Thomas Barry[31] developed the following set of guidelines for determining when children's advertising can be considered deceptive: (1) preexamination of questioned advertisements, (2) sample selection to obtain relevant and representative children, (3) determination of the understanding level of the children, (4) measurement of appropriate responses, (5) determination of whether deception does exist, (6) determination of the impact of the deception, (7) making a final decision concerning continuation of the ad campaign or a cease and desist order with or without corrective advertising. The Children's TV Act of 1990 requires broadcasters to provide programming that serves the educational and informational needs of children and must limit the amount of advertising for any programming aimed at children.[32] One criticism is that the Act is to general in specifying what content is "educational and informational." Some stations have attempted to use public service announcements and programs such as the Flintstones and G.I. Joe to satisfy the regulations. In Europe, a Broadcast Commission Directive on advertising was adopted in 1989 that banned subliminal techniques, banned tobacco and prescription medicine ads, and set conditions for advertising alcohol and ads aimed at children.[33]

EFFECTS ON VALUES AND LIFESTYLES . . . .

Advertising by its very nature receives wide exposure. Furthermore, it presumably has an effect on what people buy and thus on their activities. Because of this exposure and because of its role as a persuasive vehicle, it is argued that it has an impact on the values and lifestyles of society and that this impact has its negative as well as positive side. Richard Pollay,[34] in an article titled, "Quality of Life in the Padded Sell . . . ," for example, states that appeals to mass markets tend to promote conformity; appeals to status promote envy, pride and social competitiveness; appeals to fears promote anxiety; appeals to newness promote disrespect for tradition, durability, experience, or history; appeals to youth promote reduced family authority; and appeals to sexuality promote promiscuity.[35]

The key issues are which values and lifestyles are to be encouraged as healthy, which are to be avoided, and what relative impact or influence advertising has on them. Despite their difficulty and their relationship to deep philosophical questions, they are well worth addressing to illuminate judgments and assumptions about our market system and society that are too often glossed over.[36]

It is interesting that the issues are hotly debated at the international level, and that countries, particularly third world countries, are vitally interested in them. The United Nations' UNESCO organization, for example, put together a sixteen-member commission to study the "totality of communication problems in modern society."[37] The commission's report, which became known as the *MacBride Report* (named after the Irish diplomat Sean MacBride who headed the commission), produced eighty-two recommendations directed largely at the potential dangers of advertising and the needs for controls on advertising practices. As might be expected, reactions to the report were highly polarized with support largely coming from third world countries and opposition coming from industry representatives in developed countries.

Three issues that have attracted particular attention are (1) the relationship of advertising to materialism, (2) the role that advertising has played in creating harmful stereotypes of women and ethnic minorities, and (3) the possible contribution of advertising in promoting harmful products.

Materialism

Materialism is defined as the tendency to give undue importance to material interests. Presumably, there is a corresponding lessening of importance to nonmaterial interests such as love, freedom, and intellectual pursuits.

Bauer and Greyser argue, however, that although people do spend their resources on material things, they do so in the pursuit of nonmaterial goals.[38] They buy camping equipment to achieve a communion with nature, music systems to understand the classic composers, and an automobile for social status. The distinctive aspect of our society is not the possession of material goods, but the extent to which material goods are used to attain nonmaterial goals. Bauer and Greyser thus raise the issue of whether material goods are a means to an end rather than an end in themselves. In making such an evaluation it is useful to consider how people in other cultures fulfill nonmaterial goals. The leader in a primitive culture may satisfy a need for status in a different way from someone in our culture, but is the means used really that relevant? Russell Belk and others[39] have begun a systematic series of studies into materialism in American society showing its manifestations in advertising, comic books, television programming, swap meets, and the role of consuming and consumption in many facets of life generally. Belk has developed a materialism scale based on measures of possessiveness, nongenerosity, and envy. It was tested using three generations of family members. Middle-generation members showed the highest acceptance of materialism values. Materialism tends to be negatively related to happiness.

Does advertising create or foster materialism or merely reflect values and attitudes that are created by more significant sociological forces? Mary Gardiner Jones develops the argument that advertising, especially television advertising, is a contributing force:

> *The conscious appeal in the television commercial . . . is essentially materialistic. Central to the message of the television commercial is the premise that it is the acquisition of things which will gratify our basic and inner needs and aspirations. It is the message of the commercial that all of the major problems confronting an individual can be instantly eliminated by the application of some external force—the use of a product. Externally derived solutions are thus made the prescription for life's difficulties. . . . In the world of the television commercial all of life's problems and difficulties, all of our individual yearnings, hopes—and fears—can yield instantly to a material solution and one which can work instantly without any effort, skill or trouble on our part.[40]*

Associating advertising with materialism, of course, does not demonstrate a causal link, as Commissioner Jones would be the first to recognize. In fact, such a link is impossible to prove or disprove. It is true that advertising and the products advertised are a part of our culture and thus contribute to it in some way. It is also true, however, that advertising does not have the power to dominate other forces (family, church, literature, and so on) that contribute to the values of society.

Rebecca Quarles and Leo Jeffres,[41] in a study of fifty-three countries found little support for John Kenneth Galbraith's view that advertising is a pervasive force in altering consumer spending and savings habits. The authors conclude that income appears to lead to consumption, which, in turn, leads to advertising. Susan Spiggle,[42] in a content-analysis study of underground comics, found that, contrary to expectations, even counterculturists adopt materialistic values. Underground comics were dominated by materialistic concerns and more positively depicted materialistic pursuits than Sunday comic strips. Counterculturalists do not reject materialism but simply adapt it to their lifestyles.

Thomas Lipscomb,[43] in a study of boys and girls in the first, third, fifth, and seventh grades, found that materialism tends to develop earlier in boys than girls and that older children talk about consumer products to a substantially greater degree than younger children. Michael Jacobson founded a Washington nonprofit organization called the Center for the Study of Commercialism to "oppose the excess of marketing messages that crowd out socially beneficial messages."[44] Jacobson believes that advertising, even if scrupulously honest, promotes materialism, envy, insecurity, greed, and selfishness, and that marketing expenses should be taxed to reduce the volume of ad messages. Kim Corfman, Donald Lehmann, and Sunder Narayanan,[45] in a study of 735 adults and their purchases of consumer durables, found that the most important values determining the utility for durables were social values, stimulation, and materialism. Self-oriented values and warm relations with others had smaller effects. Materialism significantly increased the utility of 79 percent of the durables studied. Richard Pollay and Bonwari Mittal,[46] in a study of 188 students and 195 heads of households, found that most experienced conflict in evaluating advertising—a conflict between its personal uses and economic value and its potential for cultural degradation.

The issues to which we now turn concern the role of advertising in creating harmful stereotypes and in promoting harmful products.

Promoting Stereotypes

The accusation that advertising has contributed to the role stereotyping of women and ethnic minorities has been supported by several studies. In 729 advertisements appearing in 1970, none showed women in a professional capacity, whereas 35 of them so portrayed men.[47] The authors concluded that the advertisements reflected the stereotype that women do not do important things, are dependent on men, are regarded by men primarily as sex objects, and should be in the home. Harold Kassarjian, a UCLA psychologist, examined print advertising in 1946, 1956, and 1965 and found that only one-third of 1 percent of the advertisements contained African Americans, that the African Americans in the ads of the 1940s were in low-status roles, that the African Americans of the 1960s tended to be entertainers, and that the appearance of African Americans as true peers was sparse.[48]

A host of questions are raised. Does role stereotyping continue in advertising? What negative impact does advertising have in creating stereotypes, or what positive force does it have in breaking them down? In the absence of definitive answers to these questions, what should the advertisers' position be? Should countering role stereotypes be one objective of advertising? It is known that role portrayals of women in advertising which are consistent with the roles played by women in the viewing audience is more effective than when the roles are inconsistent. Thus, advertising showing women in traditional roles is less effective with an audience of professional women, and vice versa.[49]

Promoting Harmful Products

There is a national concern with the problems of alcohol and cigarettes. Local legislators have increased taxes to around 45 percent of total alcohol sales and toughened drunk-driving laws. Happy Hours have been banned in several states. Twenty-three states have complied with a federal law to increase the drinking age to twenty-one or lose highway funds. The Surgeon General's report on tobacco and lung cancer has led to a wave of calls for increased legislation and proposals to ban cigarette advertising.

Concerning alcohol, a group calling itself SMART (Stop Merchandising Alcohol on Radio and Television) has proposed a ban on wine and beer advertising. There have been other less severe proposals as well. Some have suggested counterads which would dramatically "advertise" the health disadvantages of drinking. Similar movements against cigarettes were effective and led to the banning of cigarette advertising on television. Others have proposed that beer advertising (like wine advertising) stop using sports figures in their advertising. There is already a ban on the use of active athletes and actual drinking in beer commercials.

The basic argument is that alcohol, like cigarettes, is a "harmful" product. Alcohol is unhealthy for the individual and is indirectly responsible for injuries and deaths resulting from drunk drivers. Why encourage people to use alcohol via advertising? The use of sports stars whom kids admire suggests that alcohol is not only harmless but that it is associated with fun-loving, healthy people.

There are a variety of counterarguments. First, there is no evidence that advertising, which is geared toward brand choice rather than increasing consumption, affects total alcohol consumption.[50] Multicountry studies do not indicate that those countries, such as Finland and Norway, which already ban alcohol advertising on television, have lower consumption than other countries, such as the United Kingdom, which do not. Over time, observations are similar. Beer advertising has increased substantially in the first half of the 1980s, while sales dropped around 12 percent during the same period. On the other hand, per capita alcohol consumption has risen during the past thirty years at the same rate as in western Europe, without, of course, any advertising. In addition to this basic counterargument, there is also the suggestion that

- A ban of advertising would prohibit product innovation that may be helpful. For example, firms have introduced products such as the wine coolers and the low-alcohol beers.
- The real goal is to return to alcohol prohibition, which did not work—it only created a revenue source for gangsters and made lawbreakers of the rank and file of America.
- Many other products could be criticized on similar grounds. Should advertising for automobiles be banned when high performance and sportiness is stressed since that could contribute to reckless driving?

An interesting study by Camille Schuster and Christine Powell[51] showed that the Sloan-Kettering Report linking cancer and smoking, warning labels on cigarettes, and implementation of the Fairness Doctrine, which gave equal time to antismoking messages in the 1950s and 1960s, all resulted in declines in cigarette consumption. However, in all cases, the declines were short-lived and consumption would generally recover and continue upward a year or so after the announcements. In contrast, the outright banning of cigarette advertising on radio and television in 1970 had little negative impact on cigarette consumption. In fact, consumption increased after the ban was put into effect. Thus, outlawing advertising in the case of either cigarettes or alcohol may not be the most effective way of handling the problem.

The Special Case of Cigarettes

There is little question that health and cigarette industry officials disagree on the effects of cigarette smoking on public health and that there is a significant battle going on in the United States surrounding the issue of cigarettes and smoking. It is a battle of gargantuan proportions, involving what appears to be the decline of a huge tobacco products industry, many government departments, a large and newly aggressive health care industry, and all forms of mass media. It is in reality an enormous social science experiment involving competitive forces attempting to influence a specific kind of consumer behavior. On one side, there are dozens of government and nonprofit organization agencies and groups trying to stop smoking behavior, and on the other giant corporations trying to maintain and encourage it. This section briefly reviews some of the claims and counterclaims and the forces at work in this interesting national debate. In particular, the focus is on the tools and strategies that have been used in the fight to reduce or eliminate smoking in the United States.

Actually, the fight over tobacco and cigarette advertising has been going on in one form or another for many years. An array of tools and strategies, arrayed on a contiuum of regulatory severity ranging from minor to major impact, have been used in attempting to decrease tobacco consumption. They include: (1) legislation prohibiting use of the product in public places, (2) antismoking campaigns, (3) taxation, (4) lawsuits against tobacco companies, (5) warning labels in packaging and advertising, and (6) legislation prohibiting various forms of cigarette advertising and promotion. All may be considered factors contributing to a decrease in, or cessation of, consumption. Not included is the industry that has evolved to serve those who want to quit smoking using products such as nicotine patches, gums, candies, and prescription drugs as well as organizations and clinics engaged in the business of smoking cessation.

Tobacco companies obviously want to maintain or increase cigarette consumption. Apart from their normal use of advertising to promote specific cigarette brands (there is very little primary demand advertising in the cigarette industry per se), the industry has invested heavily in lobbying efforts and educational and promotional campaigns to counter the tide of negative publicity. In an article titled, "Tobacco Money Lights Up Congress," Dan Coughlin maintains that African

Americans are a particularly important segment for tobacco companies and that African American delegations continue to take money from the companies. He also cites an example of a congressman who was able to earmark $200 million from federal cigarette taxes to prop up the tobacco price-support system while, at the same time, strongly opposing excise taxes.[52] William Beaver[53] maintains that as the domestic market continues to shrink, tobacco companies will increase overseas operations, particularly in western Europe and the former Soviet Union. Whereas the old socialist regimes severely restricted marketing U.S. tobacco products, that is not the case today. Thomas Hopkins, an economist at the Rochester Institute of Technology, claims that regulation (not just tobacco regulation) is costing business nearly $400 billion per year, and there is certainly much antiregulation sentiment both in business and among the population generally.[54]

The beginnings of the decline of the tobacco industry have been traced to the 1964 Surgeon General's report linking smoking to lung cancer. Warning labels on cigarette packages followed, and, by the early 1970s, cigarette advertising was banned from broadcast media. Although 47 percent of the adult population smoked in 1967, by the late 1980s, it has declined to 32 percent. Many companies have begun to limit or ban smoking on the job as more and more attention is directed to the harmful effects of "secondhand" smoke. Corporate costs attributed to smoking have been identified as associated with sick leave, higher insurance premiums, greater legal liability, and worker morale. A new industry has developed to help smokers kick the habit. One estimate is that smokers spent about $250 million in efforts to quit smoking in 1991.[55] The evidence that smoking is addictive and causes serious health problems is very strong, although industry executives have publically denied these allegations. Lonnie Bristow[56] maintains that smoking kills nearly one-half million Americans each year, more than all the other preventable causes of death combined. A large portion of the $4 billion spent on tobacco advertising in 1994 was directed to children, and some 3,000 children start smoking every day. Smoking has been implicated in heart disease, lung and other cancers, miscarriage, and numerous other types of ailments. Based on a National Center for Health Statistics Report of adolescent smokers, boys are more likely to smoke than girls, white teenagers more likely than minorities, and teens from troubled families smoke the most.[57]

Perhaps the most significant factor in decreasing the incidence of smoking has been state legislation which bans smoking in public places. Industries such as the airlines have taken the lead in creating smoke-free airplane flights, but the most significant actions have occurred via legislation which bans smoking in government buildings and eating establishments, airports, and so on. Much legislative activity also focuses on restricting smoking in workplaces and whether companies have the right to deny employment to workers who smoke. Peter Jacobson et al.,[58] in a study of tobacco control initiatives in New York, Minnesota, Florida, Illinois, Texas, and Arizona, concluded that it is very difficult to enact strong statewide tobacco control legislation because of the manner in which the legislative debate is framed, the relative dearth of leadership by medical and health organizations and the complex interaction between statewide antismoking legislation and local smoking ordinances.

Bruce Samuels et al.[59] report on the campaign for passage and implementation of Pittsburgh's Smoking Control Ordinance, in which proponents at first sought to keep it noncontroversial. The tobacco industry attempted to defeat the ordinance by generating controversy. After a year of implementation, each side tried exactly the opposite tactic! As of 1991, James Coil and Charles Rice[60] reported that although most states have statutes governing the practice of smoking in public or private workplaces, none imposes an absolute ban on smoking while at work. However, some employers have adopted a policy of employing a smoke-free workforce. In response, fifteen states have enacted statutes protecting workers from being hired or discharged based on their off-the-job use of tobacco. David Ludington[61] argues that businesses that permit smoking in the workplace are acting unethically because tobacco is the number one cause of premature death. And, nonsmokers who are exposed to tobacco smoke are adversely affected. He states that 36 percent of all organizations have a restrictive smoking policy but that the majority of businesses do not ban smoking. William Weis[62] reported that consumer surveys have shown that a majority of employees, including a majority of smokers, want stronger smoking restrictions at work. The tobacco companies have fought the efforts by commissioning studies to ridicule companies that have chosen to implement clean-air policies.

In recent years, national, regional, and local antismoking advertising campaigns have been mounted by a variety of public health and medical groups such as the American Medical Association, The American Heart Association, the American Lung Association, The American Cancer Society, and many others. Former Surgeon General C. Everett Koop and Attorney General Janet Reno have been vocal antismoking advocates. Senator Edward Kennedy introduced the Tobacco Product Education and Health Protection Act in November 1989. The bill would have established a Center for Tobacco Products to organize federal education efforts aimed at convincing people to stop smoking. The bill would have also granted authority to states, counties, and cities to regulate tobacco ads or warning statements on cigarette packages.[63] The heightened amount of antismoking advertising and publicity has probably contributed significantly to a decrease in smoking, but relatively little well-designed empirical research has been done on this important question. In terms of resources, it is not clear how much has been spent by antismoking agencies to decrease smoking demand. On the other hand, we know fairly well what industry spends on advertising cigarette brands. We turn to this next.

Table 19–1 shows sales and earnings data on leading cigarette manufacturers for 1992 and 1993. Sales and earnings are shown for the parent companies to provide perspective. Philip Morris, the parent of Philip Morris USA tobacco, had sales of almost $61 billion in 1993 and about $26 billion of this total was generated by its tobacco subsidiary, Philip Morris USA. Philip Morris also owns Kraft General Foods, and food sales make up most of the remainder. Unlike all of the other major tobacco manufacturers, Philip Morris USA actually increased sales by 1.2 percent from 1992 to 1993. Marlboro, PM's flagship brand, holds about 23 percent of the market and dominates all others.[64] Much of the 1993 sales increase was the result of the success of the low-priced brand, Basic, which had gained a 5.3 percent market share by 1993. Table 19–2 shows advertising expenditures for brands of five

Table 19–1. Sales and Earnings of Leading Tobacco Companies, 1992–1993 (millions of dollars).

Parent		1992	1993	% Change	Tobacco subsidiary	1992	1993	% Change
Philip Morris Cos.					**Philip Morris USA**			
Sales	Worldwide	59,131	60,901	3.0	Sales	25,677	25,973	1.2
	U.S.	39,101	38,387	−1.8	**Brands:**			
Earnings	Worldwide	4,939	3,091	−37.4	Bristol, Cartier, Parliament,			
	U.S.	8,146	5,695	−30.1	Basic, Alpine, Benson & Hedges,			
					Bucks, Cambridge, Marlboro,			
					Merit, Virginia Slims			
RJR Nabisco					**R.J. Reynolds Tobacco Co.**			
Sales	Worldwide	15,734	15,104	−4.0	Sales	9,027	8,079	−10.5
	U.S.	13,182	11,570	−12.2	**Brands:**			
Earnings	Worldwide	299	−145	−148.5	Winston, More, Now,			
	U.S.	2,634	1,284	−51.3	Salem, Vantage, Camel,			
					Best Value, Doral, Magna,			
					Sterling, Century			
Loews					**Lorillard, Inc.**			
Sales		13,691	13,687	0.0	Sales	2,185	1,909	−12.7
Earnings		123	594	384.5	**Brands:**			
					Newport, Old Gold, Kent,			
					Kent III, Kent Golden Light,			
					Lorillard			

Table 19–2.   Advertising Expenditures of Leading Cigarette Brands, 1992–1993 (thousands of dollars).

	1992	1993	% Change
Phillip Morris USA			
Marlboro	85,899	75,650	−11.9
Virginia Slims	19,025	17,388	−8.6
Merit	31,233	10,159	−67.5
Basic	0	7,817	NA
R J. Reynolds Tobacco Co.			
Camel	22,987	42,912	86.7
Winston	14,279	17,604	23.3
Now	0	5,919	NA
Lorillard, Inc.			
Newport	35,948	34,536	−3.9
Kent	5,320	8,353	57.0
Lorillard	3,465	7,060	103.8
Brown & Williamson Tobacco Co.			
Kool	5,712	20,532	259.4
Capri	13,698	15,175	10.8
Viceroy	12	10,576	NA
Raleigh	4,827	5,418	12.2
American Tobacco Co.			
Misty	14,887	8,974	−39.7
Carlton	18,359	8,632	−53.0

Adapted from Advertising Age, *September 19, 1994.*

companies. About $75.7 million was spent on Marlboro advertising in 1993, down from about $85.9 million in 1992. Philip Morris also reduced advertising for Virginia Slims and Merit, as did American Tobacco for its Misty and Carlton brands. In contrast, R. J. Reynolds, Lorillard, and Brown & Williamson increased their advertising expenditures for most of their brands. The ad investment in Kool jumped 259 percent, to over $20 million, and Camel was increased 86.7 percent, to about $43 million.[65]

Another antismoking tool has been taxation and so-called "sin taxes." A tobacco tax, Proposition 99, for example was approved in California and tobacco taxation has been proposed as a major source of revenue in redesigning the nation's health care system. Congressman Fortney Stark proposed two bills, one to make tobacco growers repay $7.2 billion Stark claims they cost Medicare and Medicaid each year for treatment of lung cancer and emphysema, and the other to eliminate the deductibility of advertising expenses for tobacco products. Neither bill made it out of the House Ways and Means Committee.[66]

Lawsuits in which private citizens or government bodies bring suits against tobacco companies have been another antismoking force. Maria Mallory[67] reports that tobacco cases are now attracting well-heeled plaintiffs' lawyers who are bringing class action lawsuits alleging that millions of people have been hurt by addiction and that states are now becoming involved. In early 1994, Florida Governor Lawton Chiles successfully introduced legislation described as the toughest ever aimed at the tobacco industry. The law authorized the state of Florida to sue cigarette makers for reimbursement of about $300 million a year in Medicaid expenses for smoking-related illnesses.

An interesting case concerns "Joe Camel," a cartoon character used by R. J. Reynolds in advertising Camel cigarettes. The issue was whether the character would entice minors to smoke. Even though the Camel campaign did not feature children and did not run in media that were oriented to children under eighteen, the Federal Trade Commission expressed concern over the possibility of "spillover" exposure that would reach young children. The case raised fundamental issues of how the FTC should attempt to prove whether the Joe Camel advertising did target minors. R. J. Reynolds admitted trying to appeal to younger smokers, but only those of legal age. Many of the issues reviewed in the last chapter about the meaning of deception, materiality, and numbers of consumers deceived were raised in this case.[68] New nonprofit organizations in the business of opposing the cigarette industry have proliferated. For example, an organization called Stop Teenage Addiction to Tobacco (STAT) publishes a quarterly called *Tobacco and Youth Reporter*, which chronicles industry techniques for targeting children.[69]

One of the most striking antismoking ideas is to regulate tobacco as a controlled substance like marijuana and bring it under the purview of the Federal Drug Administration. It implies virtual prohibition of tobacco products if the regulations make it illegal to smoke cigarettes under normal circumstances.

Rising cigarette prices pushed by increases in federal, state, and local taxes can be considered another antismoking factor. Very little published research appears to have been done on the topic; for example, is there a price at which smokers would reduce smoking drastically or "disadopt" the product by breaking the habit altogether?

Warning labels pointing out the health risks of smoking have been included on cigarette packages and in cigarette advertising since the Federal Cigarette Labeling and Advertising Act of 1965 and the Public Health Cigarette Smoking Act of 1969. The effects of warning labels are difficult to trace and the growing literature on the topic tends to show mixed results. Stewart and Martin[70] reviewed the large literature on warning messages (over 130 articles on the subject were cited) and concluded that warnings inform rather than persuade consumers and that consumers selectively attend to them. Like advertisements, warning labels can experience wear-out and possible negative consumer reactions. Caution is needed in designing warning labels because of the multiple effects and because of varying responses from different groups of consumers. Michael Hilton[71] focused on alcohol warning labels and concluded that awareness of the warning label was only moderately high. Consumers knew the hazards described by the label but the evidence that labels changed perceptions of risk is mixed. There is little or no evidence that risk-related behaviors such as heavy drinking were changed by labels. However, label designs can probably be significantly improved.

Banning cigarette advertising rather than banning the product is a final strategy that characterizes antismoking efforts. Cigarette advertising is prohibited over broadcast media (television and radio) but is permitted in print media (magazines and newspapers). Lester Johnson and Robert McAuliffe[72] reviewed the subject. As early as 1986, prominent health organizations and a professional medical association were calling for a ban on all types of tobacco product promotion. But opponents of a ban argued as follows. First, there is a failure to show a link between advertising and aggregate cigarette demand. Second, there is a possible violation of First Amendment rights in not being allowed to advertise a legal product. Third, there is protection afforded commercial speech. On the other hand, ban proponents argued that the consequences of tobacco's use may persuade some legislators to focus on the ethics of promoting the nation's leading cause of avoidable premature death.[73] Whether you are a dedicated smoker more interested in living for the day than in extending your lifespan or a nonsmoker worried about your own lungs or those of a loved one, this debate is one of the most interesting and important in recent advertising and marketing history. How it plays out will affect many people and organizations over the coming decade.

Green Marketing

The environmental movement has spawned a number of new issues about advertising and its effects on values and lifestyles that are briefly reviewed in this section. Advertising has been a part of the Environmental Protection Agency (EPA) and other profit and nonprofit organization efforts to encourage recycling, energy conservation, and many ecologically positive behaviors. It has been the vehicle through which the nation has received a great deal of information and education from cleaning up waste dumps to preserving spotted owls. Many corporations have recognized the importance of social responsibility and have taken appropriate steps to become more environmentally responsible. A recent trend has been for corporations to begin using environment appeals in marketing regular products. This so-called *green marketing* has been challenged on a number of grounds.

Thomas Hemphill[74] reports that by 1995, consumers will spend $8.8 billion on environmentally friendly, "green" products, nearly five times more than the $1.8 billion spent in 1990. One problem is that advertisers have seized on environmental advertising claims as an effective way to sell products and services. In addition, puffery and exaggeration are often considered appropriate strategies. Such strategies have lead to a rise in regulatory attention and activity. For example, the Environmental Protection Agency has attempted to establish environmental labeling standards and has supplied voluntary guidelines on the use of terms such as "recycled" and "recyclable." Companies such as Procter & Gamble have developed product and packaging labeling programs to increase consistency and make it easier for consumers to locate and understand environmental information. Many of the issues are definitional. What does *natural* mean? Harold Takooshian and Richard Tashjian[75] point out that natural products appeal to consumers who equate terms such as *synthetic* and *artificial* with bad, unhealthy, and undesirable. The result is the danger of rejection of important new products and scientific discoveries, new forms of plastics for example, that might be viewed as "unnatural."

A comprehensive review of legal standards for environmental marketing claims was done by Jason Gray-Lee, Debra Scammon, and Robert Mayer.[76] Environmental claims such as shaving creams that "contain no CFCs", laundry detergents that are "biodegradable," and disposable diapers that are "degradable," require special scrutiny because they are especially likely to confuse consumers. How could a consumer verify that a brand's packaging contained recycled materials? A seller may not be able to control recycling in a particular community for which recycling claims are being made. What does "environmentally friendly" really mean? One result is that, in 1992, the FTC published a set of guidelines, *Guides for the Use of Environmental Marketing Claims*, to address some of the definition problems. Between 1990 and 1992, forty-eight cases were brought against marketers making environmental claims. In the first ten months of 1993, the FTC issued an additional sixteen consent orders relating to environmental claims. The claims that have been the focus of attention are: general claims such as "safe" pesticides or "environmental" formula, solid waste claims—Hefty trash bags are "degradable," ozone-related claims such as "ozone-friendly" and "ozone-safe," recyclability claims, and others. Independent organizations such as Scientific Certification Systems and Green Seal grant environmental seals of approval and evaluate products on attributes such as recycled content. One reaction is that advertisers have become much more cautious in using environmental appeals. California has proposed stringent definitions of terms such as *ozone-friendly*, *biodegradable*, *photodegradable*, *recycled*, and *recyclable*.[77] Use of the terms outside the boundaries of the state-written definitions carries criminal sanctions. If the ruling stays in effect, national advertisers must either fashion separate environmental appeals for California, ignore California, or let the California statute dictate the advertising to be used in all other states. What happens in this case may well determine much about the future of green marketing.

Health Claims and Food Marketing

Another area of controversy that has stirred much attention and national debate about advertising and marketing practices is the use of *health claims*, particularly in food advertising. Americans have become much more health-conscious, and companies have moved forcefully to produce food and other products that can lead to healthier lives. As in the case of green marketing, the public policy problem is that some claims may be considered deceptive and mislead consumers.

Special attention has been given to the use of seals of approval for food[78] and of in-ad disclosure of health warnings.[79] Pauline Ippolito and Alan Mathios[80] studied the ready-to-eat cereal market when producers were prohibited from advertising cereals' health benefits but were later permitted to make health claims. Results showed that health claims led to significant increases in consumer knowledge of the fiber-cancer relationship, in fiber-cereal consumption, and in product innovation. In contrast, government and general information sources had limited impact on fiber-cereal choices. The authors conclude that policies governing producer use of health claims should be evaluated not only on how well they control deceptive or misleading claims, but also on how well they encourage producers to disseminate evolving health information to consumers.[81] The Nutrition Labeling and Education Act (NLEA) was passed in 1990 and requires the Food and Drug Administration to implement major changes in regulations governing food labeling. For example, with some exceptions for small firms and raw produce and fish products, all product labels must contain a nutrition panel showing the nutritional values of the contents.[82]

All the foregoing issues in one way or another deal with the nature and content of advertising and its effects on values and lifestyles. We turn now to a look at advertising and society from the viewpoint of advertising's economic effects.

ECONOMIC EFFECTS OF ADVERTISING . . . .

It is unreasonable to separate the economic and social impact of advertising. The social issues, by themselves, tend to focus on the negative aspects of advertising—its intrusiveness, content that is in bad taste, and the possibly undesirable impact on values and lifestyles. If advertising were regarded solely on these grounds, it would be difficult to defend, despite the fact that much advertising is entertaining, some may even be of real artistic value, and some is directed toward supporting causes that are universally praised. Advertising is basically an economic institution. It performs an economic function for an advertiser, affects economic decisions of the audience, and is an integral part of the whole economic system. Thus an economic evaluation should accompany other types of appraisal of advertising. Here are some of the economic benefits of advertising:

1. **Advertising provides informational utility.**
2. **Maintains or enhances brand equity.**
3. **Supports the media.**
4. **Provides employment.**
5. **Reduces distribution costs.**
6. **Provides product utility.**
7. **Stimulates introduction of new products.**

Advertising provides information to consumers and can help them make better economic decisions than they would otherwise. The other side of the coin in many nutrition-related deceptive advertising cases is that banning the advertising would eliminate the increased awareness of nutrition issues that such advertising generates.

A study by David Aaker and Donald Norris of 524 prime-time television commercials suggests that even television advertising is perceived as informative by substantial groups of people.[83] On the average 18.1 percent of respondents (approximately 500 per commercial) checked the word *informative* from a list of twenty adjectives when asked to describe a commercial. The percentage was over 20 when snack and beverage items were excluded.

Advertising plays an important role in establishing and maintaining brand names.[84] A brand name identifies the source of a product and provides a construct by which a buyer can store information about that source. A buyer can reasonably assume that a manufacturer willing to risk large sums of money to tell about a product is not likely to let poor product quality damage the investment. The concept of *brand equity* was introduced in Chapter 10 to highlight the value of branding and brand names. Brand equity implies that brand names can add value to a product independent of any other production or marketing activities. Just adding the name Coca-Cola, for example, to a new soda drink adds value to the drink. The measurement of the value of the equity in a brand name is a challenging task which has become of particular importance for corporate mergers and acquisitions.

Advertising provides more than 60 percent of the cost of magazines, more than 70 percent of the cost of newspapers, and nearly 100 percent of the cost of radio and television.[85] For their support of the commercial television stations, advertisers receive approximately 15 percent of the airtime.[86] Although some broadcast media such as cable or pay television are, like magazines and newspapers, subscriber-supported, financial support from advertising is still dominant. Public radio and television is an alternative which is supported by donations and/or taxation.

In his 1925 book on the tragedy of waste, Stuart Chase stated that, in a truly functional society, 90 percent of the people employed by advertising would be able to engage in "productive occupations." There are many who would disagree. The proposition assumes that only *production* (or form utility) and not *marketing* (time, place, and possession utility) is productive. There are few in today's world that would argue that marketing has no role to play or does not add value. Advertising provides employment for significant numbers of people in both the United States and in other advanced industrialized countries. A million or more jobs are probably associated with the creation, production, and delivery of advertising in the United States alone.

As noted in Chapter 3, advertising is part of a total marketing program. Without advertising, the communication function would still remain but would probably have to be accomplished in some other way by retailers, salespeople, and so on. The alternative in many situations could cost significantly more. In 1964, cookie companies spent only 2.2 percent of sales on advertising, whereas cereal companies spent 14.9 percent.[87] However, the cookie companies spent 22.1 percent of sales on other selling and distribution costs, compared with 12.1 percent of sales for cereal companies. Cookie companies employed routemen to deliver goods and service the shelves. Cereal companies, however, had created sufficient consumer demand so that the retailer found it worthwhile to monitor the stock and the firms were relieved of this marketing expense. Cookie companies in effect shifted marketing cost from advertising to other marketing activities.

Advertising, by generating associations between products and moods, lifestyles, and activities, can add to the utility a buyer receives from the product. Most people do not buy cars solely to move from one point to another, but to achieve a feeling of independence, to express a personality, or to establish a certain mood or feeling. Evaluating the amount of utility, if any, that advertising adds to a product returns us to the fundamental issue raised earlier of the definition of such terms as "need" and "product." In a recent study of the contributions of advertising to productivity, the American Association of Advertising Agencies argues that innovation and high technology, as a primary source of productivity, should not be focused solely on cost reduction, but rather on "innovation for higher value."[88] The focus is on considering the total product. The argument is that the consumer's conceptual perception of the product is as significant as the physical characteristics and should be considered a product ingredient.

Advertising encourages new product development by providing an economical way to inform potential buyers of the resulting new products or product improvements. In many situations, innovation requires large research and development expenditures and substantial investments in production facilities. Advertising contributes by informing consumers about the existence of the innovation and encourages competition.

The development of new products and the improvement of existing products can mean an expanding economy with more jobs and investment opportunities and a product selection that is continually improving in breadth and quality.

Effect on Business Cycles

Advertising could theoretically be a tool to alleviate the economic pain arising from extreme swings in the business cycle. A knowledgeable businessperson, anticipating a booming economy and capacity production, should reduce advertising expenditures. Conversely, when the economy is weak and orders are needed, many firms should increase their advertising. Since the extremes of a business cycle cause inflation or unemployment, any mechanism to stabilize conditions would be an economic benefit. The problem is that many advertisers, especially those who tend to set their advertising budgets at a fixed percentage of sales, actually increase advertising when times are good and decrease it when sales are weak. These firms may thus actually increase the extremes of the business cycle instead of decreasing them. Julian Simon concluded that this tendency actually dominates and advertising expenditures generally follow the same course as the business cycle.[89] He also concluded that the potential of advertising to affect the business cycle is small, since decisions such as inventory investment are much stronger determinants of the nature of economic cycles. The evidence to date is that advertising has a negative though small impact in reducing the extremes of the business cycle.

ADVERTISING AND COMPETITION . . . .

The existence of vigorous competition is important to a market economy. Competitive forces lead to real product innovation, the efficient distribution of goods, and the absence of inflated prices. The question is: What impact does advertising have on competition?[90] There have been hypotheses put forth indicating that advertising can actually decrease the level of competition. For example, it is argued that heavy advertising expenditures in many industries generate strong brand loyalty that tends to create barriers to potential competitors. The hypothesized result is fewer competitors, less competition, and higher prices.

One measure of competition within an industry is the degree to which the sales of the industry are concentrated in the hands of a few firms. The specific construct is the concentration ratio; that is, the share of industry sales held by the four largest firms. When the concentration ratio exceeds 50 percent, price competition is theorized to be less vigorous and high prices result. Among the many industries that would qualify under this criterion are automobiles, aircraft, electric lamps, flat glass, primary aluminum, and household refrigerators and freezers.[91]

The concentration ratio as an indicator of market concentration and competition has intuitive appeal and is convenient, but there are conceptual and theoretical problems. The main problem is in defining the industry meaningfully. Theoretically, an industry should include all brands from which buyer choice is made. Does the cereal industry include instant breakfast, breakfast squares, and "pop tarts"? Do aluminum companies compete only with one another, or do they also compete with copper and steel companies? Should import competition be included? Another problem is that it does not reflect the distribution of market shares among firms. It is thus now largely replaced with HHI (the Herfindahl-Hirschman Index), which is the sum of the squares of the market shares of all the competitors. For example, the HHI of a four-firm industry would be 2,500 if all had 25 percent shares but would be twice as much if one firm had a 70 percent market share. George Milne[92] has developed a marketing approach to the measurement of industry concentration.

A Causal Model

Figure 19–2 provides a simplified causal model that summarizes various hypotheses suggesting that advertising contributes to a reduction of competition in the marketplace. The model introduces several crucial constructs such as market concentration, barriers to entry, and product differentiation. The arrows represent hypothesized causal relationships among these constructs. After presenting these hypotheses, some counterarguments will be raised and several relevant empirical studies will be examined.

The central construct in the model is market concentration. The basic argument is that when concentration exists, there is little incentive to engage in vigorous price competition and higher prices and profits are generated. With price competition inhibited, there is a hypothesized incentive to engage in heavy, non-informative advertising, the cost of which is passed on to the buyer in the form of higher prices. The reduced price of private-label brands is cited as evidence of such higher prices.

Another hypothesized effect is the attempt to differentiate products that are essentially identical with respect to their primary function. Differentiated products can generate brand loyalty and thus escape vigorous price competition. The

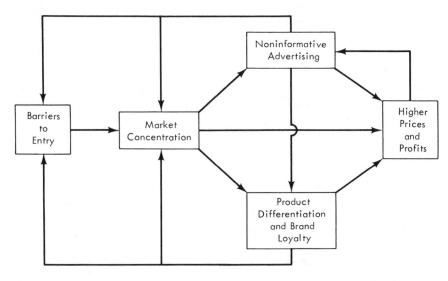

Figure 19–2.   Market concentration: some hypothesized causes and effects.

result is another link to higher prices and profits. The higher profits are not considered earned rewards of product innovation but the result of market power. The issue of the definition of a product is, of course, central (recall the earlier discussion on the definition of product and related terms).

Concentration is said to be perpetuated and increased by the existence of barriers to entry. Advertising is thought by some to generate entry barriers directly and through the product differentiation it generates. The purpose of product differentiation is presumably to develop a reason for a buyer to buy one brand over another and generate brand loyalty. This brand loyalty is hypothesized to be a barrier to entry.[93]

Advertising is also hypothesized to give larger advertisers two kinds of advantages. First, the large advertiser is thought to receive preferential treatment by the media with respect to the cost and selection of advertising space. Second, a threshold level of advertising is hypothesized to exist, below which advertising would be ineffective. When this threshold level is high, the cost of entering a market and the attendant risk becomes excessive.[94]

One additional feature of Figure 19–2 should be emphasized. The existence of higher prices and margins tends to generate advertising since it "pays" to advertise high-margin products. Thus, the feedback from higher prices to advertising. The result is an ever-increasing cycle of concentration-profitability-advertising-concentration.

J. N. Kessides,[95] in a cross-industry study of the entry-deterring effects of advertising concludes that there are two countervailing effects of advertising on entry. On the one hand, advertising impedes entry because it gives rise to a sunk cost barrier. On the other hand, it reduces the perceived risk of entry. Industries with high advertising intensities are more prone to entry than lower-intensity industries. The reduction in perceived risk of entry with advertising present appears to outweigh the other effects. Advertising promotes entry in the large majority of industries, but can retard it in a few.

The advertising of physician services has become the focus of studies of advertising and entry in recent years. Advertising in this industry was banned prior to 1982. The FTC played the major role in forbidding the ban on advertising by the American Medical Association. The result has been that advertising of physician services has increased from about 5 percent in 1982 to about 20 percent by 1987. John Rizzo and Richard Zeckhauser[96] surveyed almost 2,000 physicians who answered questions about their advertising policies and concluded that advertising inhibited entry into the physician market. However, it was also found that experienced physicians for which advertising would have the greatest benefit advertised less. In general, they were reluctant to have themselves or their practices associated with advertising. Thus, to this point in the evolution of the industry, advertising may have facilitated entry. The authors conclude that advertising will be more of a barrier to entry when advertising acceptance increases among well-established physicians.

The Cereal Industry

The cereal industry provides a good vehicle to illustrate the argument. Paul Scanlon[97] pointed out that the three largest firms in the industry—Kellogg, General Foods, and General Mills—account for about 85 percent of industry sales, and all but about 2 percent of the balance is held by the next three largest firms. Thus, the concentration level is indeed high. Scanlon further suggested that the concentration is caused by advertising levels that have operated at approximately 15 percent of sales for the three largest firms. Turning to market performance, he observed that the industry profits are high and that product quality is low, as evidenced by the nutritional shortcomings of breakfast cereal, particularly of the more popular, heavily advertised brands. Scanlon estimated that cereal prices were 25 percent higher than they would be if the industry were not concentrated.

These arguments have not gone unchallenged. Stern and Dunfee found that the four largest cereal brands (as opposed to firms) controlled only 29.7 percent of the market in 1964, down from 37.5 percent in 1954.[98] And, two other indexes of competition had increased over time. One, total cereal consumption, increased 10 percent between 1960 and 1970, despite rises in cereal prices that exceeded the inflation rate. The other was new product introductions. Of course, a question arises whether the new brands represented real consumer benefits or whether they were instead only minor variations of existing products designed to replace competitive brands.[99]

Ippolito and Mathios[100] focused on the cereal market in a period in which information developed about the health benefits of fiber. Advertising of fiber health claims was banned until Kellogg succeeded in challenging the restrictions in 1984 even though the health effect of fiber were well known from about the mid-1970s. The authors argued that advertising should contribute a large portion to the public stock of information about the relations between fiber and health. They conclude that consumers react to new relevant information, but that there are considerable costs in acquiring and processing the information. Advertising plays a role in both providing relevant information and in reducing costs to the consumer of acquiring and processing it.

A viable level of competition and relatively low prices might exist with high levels of concentration in at least two situations. The first is when it is feasible to enter the market on a local or regional scale. Brands that dominate the market nationally may be vulnerable in a local market where buyer tastes and needs may be somewhat unique. Furthermore, while the cost of a national entry may be large, the cost of reaching a small geographic segment may be more modest.

The second type of situation is where there exists what Galbraith termed countervailing power on the industrial buyer side.[101] If concentration exists on the buyer side, it can counter the market power of a few sellers. Thus, Sears Roebuck, Montgomery Ward, and the major automobile companies can extract price concessions from the tire companies. A&P, Safeway, and the other large grocery chains are in a position to gain price reductions from grocery manufacturers.

Empirical Studies

Several of the hypotheses imbedded in the model represented in Figure 19–2 have been explored empirically. Some associations have been found, but the associations often have alternative explanations.

Advertising and Prices

A very basic question is what impact advertising has upon prices. Robert Buzzell and Paul Farris found that firms with higher relative prices advertise their products more intensively than do those with lower prices.[102] They controlled for product quality by using judgments of perceived quality made by the managers of the involved products. Paul Farris and Mark Albion review this study and several others and conclude that there is a relationship between advertising and pricing.[103] However, they caution that several factors need to be considered in making interpretations. First, a higher price could simply reflect higher quality, and the controls for quality are difficult to make. Second, consumers would probably demand lower prices for a nonadvertised product as it is not obvious how unadvertised products could compete in the same market with a lack of advertising being their sole distinguishing feature. Finally, the relative prices of advertised and unadvertised brands are less important than the absolute or average price level of a product category that would prevail in the absence of advertising. It is by no means clear that the average price is higher when some brands are heavily advertised. The argument that advertising can support the entry of new low-cost brands is supported by research on eyeglass retailing. Lee Benham found that eyeglass prices were 25 to 30 percent higher in states with total advertising bans presumably because the entry of high-volume, low-priced retailers is inhibited.[104] Lakshman Krishnamurthi and S. P. Raj using data from a split-cable AdTel television test concluded that increased advertising lowers price sensitivity. Effects were examined by segment. The effect was stronger in the high price sensitivity segment than in the low-price segment.[105]

The relation between price advertising and product quality has also been studied. W. P. Rogersen[106] developed a model of the welfare implications of price advertising of professional services. Professional services have a high content of intangible attributes, one of which is quality. Price advertising of professional services may thus increase welfare by giving firms incentives to differentiate through choosing different qualities and providing consumers with a signal of product quality.[107]

Advertising and Profitability

The evidence of an association between advertising and profitability is stronger. Economists William Comanor and Thomas Wilson, in an influential study, attempted to explain interindustry differences in profit rates.[108] They examined the return on equity after taxes of forty-one consumer-goods industries, using both the advertising-sales (A/S) ratio and the average advertising expenditures of the major firms as indicators of advertising intensity. Although they did not find high correlation (only 0.10) between four-firm concentration ratios and the A/S ratio, they did determine, using a regression model, that both advertising measures were significantly related to profitability. They concluded that industries with high advertising outlays earned approximately 50 percent more than other industries. They further attributed much of the profitability differential to entry barriers created by advertising expenditures, arguing that such a cross-sectional study (as contrasted with a time-series study) tends to emphasize the long-run difference among industries and thus should reflect basic structural characteristics like concentration. At least for manufacturing industries, this basic finding has been consistently found in several studies using different samples and measures.[109] L. G. Thomas argues that there are three bases for large, above-normal profits of firms in industries with heavy advertising: advertising durability, economies of scale, and heterogeneity (best selling brands have lower per unit marketing costs). Heterogeneity is found to be the most important explanation of supranormal profits, whereas both durability of advertising and economies of scale were found to have little effect. Thomas thus suggests that high profits constitute rent to brands of high quality.[110]

However, such speculation on causal explanations for the association is less than definitive. There are industry characteristics that could jointly cause profits and a tendency to rely on advertising. Or, it may be that advertising in some industries is often a more economically efficient means of marketing than any other marketing alternative. From this perspective, the finding that firms in an industry who use advertising compared with those that do not (or use it less) are more profitable is not surprising. In such instances, the nature of the causal link might be quite different from what is implied by Comanor and Wilson.

Advertising and Brand Stability

Brand loyalty, created in part by advertising, is hypothesized to be a barrier to entry and thus to competition.[111] If such a hypothesis holds, relatively stable brand shares might be expected in industries with extensive advertising. In an early study, Lester Telser examined the leading brands of various product categories in 1948 and 1959 and found an inverse relationship between product class advertising intensity and the stability of the market share of the leading brands.[112] He suggested that the advertising helped to encourage new brand introductions, which, in turn, contributed to the lack of brand stability. New brand introductions, of course, are far different from the entry of new competitors.

REMEDIES

If the argument represented by Figure 19–2 is accepted, what should be done about it? In particular, are additional restrictions on advertising appropriate? Assume, for example, that some advertising actually does encourage concentration and results in anticompetitive effects and that therefore some restraints could be justified. The problem is: Which part of whose advertising results in anticompetitive effects? Should restrictions be placed on the cereal industry or only on its largest firms? Or should any restraints apply to the entire food industry? What kinds of restraints? Should advertising actually be banned in some industries? What impact would that have on new product development?

There are restraints on some advertising now. Certain services like legal and medical services are restricted in the way they can be advertised. In most states, the prices of prescription drugs cannot be advertised. There are restraints with respect to certain media. Liquor and cigarettes cannot be advertised on television. It is instructive to review these situations and to consider whether the reasons for the restrictions are defensible and whether they have had undesirable, unanticipated consequences. B. J. Sheldon and K. Doroodian[113] studied the effects of cigarette advertising on demand and the reaction of consumers and industry to government health warnings during the 1952–1984 period. It was concluded that industry advertising increased consumption, that the cigarette industry increased advertising in response to health warnings, and that when an advertising medium is removed (through a ban) total industry advertising is reduced. Susan Holak and Srinivas Reddy,[114] using the cigarette industry's advertising ban of 1970 as a natural experiment, found substantial differences in elasticity and inertia between pre- and postban periods. Demand becomes more inelastic with respect to advertising fluctuations if television and radio can no longer be used as media vehicles. Thus, a ban on advertising can have both positive and negative effects. The consumption of products such as cigarettes may be reduced overall or for certain segments (even this conclusion, however, is controversial[115]). But because brand loyalty levels increase after a ban is imposed, a ban may serve as a barrier to entry. In other words, simply banning advertising in an attempt to reduce demand for products like cigarettes may be ineffective.

It might be possible for the government to restrict advertising levels in certain industries. Restrictions could take the form of mandatory controls on the rates at which firms could increase their advertising budgets. It could even include a provision for firms to decrease their level of advertising. A problem with any such proposal is that it would work to the disadvantage of the small, vigorous firm that is trying to compete with larger organizations and of the innovative firm that must announce new product developments. If the absolute level of advertising were controlled, the smaller firms would not be inhibited, but the large firms would be penalized simply because of their size. Furthermore, there is the sticky issue of determining the exact level of advertising expenditures that would be desirable in any given context. There is precedent for such a move, however. In 1966, the Monopolies Commission in Great Britain recommended a 40 percent cut in advertising expenditures of the leading detergent companies and a 20 percent reduction in wholesale prices. However, partly because of threats to move some of their operations to the European continent, an alternative proposal was adopted. The two involved companies agreed to introduce new, less promoted detergents, priced 20 percent below existing brands.[116]

There have been proposals made to place a tax on advertising or to reduce the tax deduction allowed for advertising over a certain amount.[117] It presumably would not affect the small competitor who would not be advertising at the affected level. Of course, the determination of the amount of reduction and the level at which the reduction would be applicable would be difficult to fix. Furthermore, companies could alter their marketing mix in ways to shift the advertising dollar to other forms of promotion that might have an impact similar to that of advertising. And, any such plan would discriminate against those companies that tend to rely on advertising in favor of companies like Avon, for example, that rely mainly on direct selling.

SUMMARY. . . . .

Advertising plays a very important role in society, particularly in industrialized countries that have well developed mass communications infastructures. There are three categories of issues concerning advertising and society. Two of them represent the aggregate effects of advertising on society's value and lifestyles and on society's economic well-being. The third focuses on the nature and content of advertising. It involves issues of ethics, manipulation, taste, advertising to children, cigarette and environmental, or green, marketing, and health claims in food marketing.

There has been considerable interest in the question of advertising and ethics in the past decade because of many questionable business and government practices which have been brought to public attention generally. Whether it is ethical to participate in advertising cigarettes in view of new medical findings on the link between cigarette smoking and cancer is an example. It is clear that advertising ethics and other social and economic issues of advertising are heavily intertwined. Consider the argument that advertising manipulates consumers. First, there is concern that advertisers, using subconscious motives uncovered by motivation research, can manipulate an unwilling consumer. Although it is now recognized by professionals that the power of motivation research is limited, some ethical questions about its use still remain. Second, there is a concern with the use of emotional appeals. The key issue is the definition of a product. Is a product an entity with one or more primary functions or does it involve any dimension relevant to the consumer when she or he makes a purchase decision? Finally, there is the more general concern with the power represented by the volume of advertising and the skill of the people who create it. Some advertising is criticized on the basis of taste—that it uses appeals that are offensive, that the content is annoying, or that it is simply too intrusive. Some critics object to the use of sex appeals, especially when children may be exposed to the advertising. Others are concerned with the use of fear appeals. The irritation life cycle is conceptualized to help understand the intrusive quality of advertising. An FTC proposal to ban all television advertising to preschool children and all sugar product television advertising to older children was seriously and vigorously debated.

It is unreasonable to separate the economic and social effects of advertising. Advertising is basically an economic institution, and any overall appraisal of advertising should include an analysis of its economic impact. Advertising provides economic value to society in many ways. It enhances buyer decision making by providing information and by supporting brand names. It provides an efficient means for firms to communicate with their customers. Such a function is particularly important in the introduction of new products. By generating various product associations, advertising can add to the utility a buyer receives from a product. It provides employment, supports the various media, and has the potential to reduce extremes in the levels of consumer buying.

A central issue is the impact that advertising has on competition. It is argued that heavy advertising expenditures in some industries generate product differentiation among products that are essentially identical. This product differentiation provides the basis for brand loyalties that represent a significant barrier to potential competitors. It is also hypothesized that in these industries, heavy advertising expenditures are needed for successful competition. Such large expenditure levels represent another barrier to entry of new competitors. With the entry of new competitors inhibited, there is a tendency for industries to become more concentrated over time—to have fewer competitors. The result is a reduction in vigorous competition, higher prices, and excessive profits. Advertising in such industries is regarded as noninformative; its role is to shift buyers around among "identical" products and is thus largely an economic waste.

The implications of these hypotheses have been studied by economists. They have found evidence of association between advertising and concentration, but, on balance, the association is weaker than might be expected. The evidence of association between advertising and profitability is somewhat stronger. There is considerable controversy concerning the macroeconomic effects of advertising, and scholars can be found who vigorously defend one side or the other. Issues are both theoretical, concerning questions of causation and inference, and methodological involving measurement of difficult constructs such as concentration and market boundaries.

The practical question is what remedies are appropriate? Among the proposed remedies are that advertising in some industries be limited or prohibited or that a tax be applied to advertising. Remedies that are defensible and will not cause more problems than they solve are not easy to develop. Many studies have been done on the effects of eliminating cigarette advertising without a definitive conclusion being reached that such a public policy will result in more harm or more good.

DISCUSSION QUESTIONS . . . .

1. Suppose that a motivation research study found that homemakers disliked a certain transparent, clinging, wrapping material because of their basic dislike of cooking, which was subconsciously transferred to the material. As a result, nonkitchen uses were emphasized in the advertising. Is this manipulation? In the research, the housewives were told only that the aim of the study was to determine their attitudes toward housekeeping in general. Was such a guise ethical?

2. Define the terms *need*, *product*, *information*, and *rationality*. Does a commercial showing a group of people enjoying a cola drink communicate information? Is it an appropriate appeal? Consider other examples. Is manipulation involved?

3. Richard Avedon, a photographer and consultant to agencies and clients, helped develop for Calvin Klein jeans a very controversial set of television commercials. They featured the fifteen-year-old actress-model Brooke Shields in a variety of sultry, sophisticated, suggestive commercials. In one, Brooke Shields says in a suggestive manner, "Nothing comes between me and my Calvins." In another controversial television commercial for a men's fragrance, a man wearing a pajama bottom is seen getting out of bed and discussing the previous night by phone with a woman who had slept with him.
   a. Do you feel that such advertising is effective? In what way?
   b. Would you run such advertising on network television if you felt it was effective if you were an advertiser? If you were an agency whose client had insisted on it?
   c. If you were a CBS censor, would you allow it on your network?

4. Suppose you are the president of a major consumer food company. A church group claiming to represent 2.5 million members is attempting to reduce the "excessive violence, sex, and profanity" on television. The members have informed you that they are boycotting all products advertised on eight programs, including *Miami Vice* and *Dallas*, and expect that their boycott will cost you $20 million in sales. What would your response be? Do you feel that you should have a policy concerning such programming? Would you screen episodes of such programs and selectively avoid episodes that are particularly objectionable?

5. Take a position on the FTC proposals regarding television advertising to children. What about banning the advertising of sugar products directed at children under twelve? Would you prefer that food advertisers to children fund "counterads" geared to promote nutrition? What about cutting back Saturday morning kids' advertising to four minutes per hour? Would you alter or add to

the following partial listing of the provisions of a Canadian broadcasting code for children?

a. Product characteristics should not be exaggerated.

b. Results from a craft or kit that an average child could not obtain should not be shown.

c. Undue pressure to buy or to urge parents to buy should be avoided.

d. A commercial should not be repeated during a program.

e. Program personalities will not do commercials on their own programs.

f. Well-known persons other than actors will not endorse products.

g. Price information should be clear and complete.

h. Messages must not reflect disdain for parents or casually portray undesirable family living habits.

i. Advertising must not imply that product possession makes the owner superior.

j. The media should contribute directly or indirectly to sound and safe habits.

6. Should there be similar codes for other society groups such as senior citizens or ethnic minorities?

7. What is materialism? It has been said that our society emphasizes the use of material goods to attain nonmaterial goals. Comment. Is America too materialistic? What is advertising's role in establishing values and lifestyles? How does a nation go about changing its values?

8. Should advertisers be concerned about minority stereotypes developed in advertisements? Why? If you were an agency president, how would you develop a policy and set of procedures in this regard?

9. In your view, should beer advertisers be banned from using sports figures in their ads? What about the use of image advertising in general? Should beer and wine advertising be banned from television and radio advertising? From all advertising? What about the use of "power/sportiness" appeals in automobile advertising? Should beer advertisers stop all college and sports promotions?

10. In an open letter to the makers of Alka-Seltzer, the following questions were posed by Ries, Cappiello, Colwell, a New York advertising agency: Why did you spend $23 million to promote a product that everyone knows about? Why did you spend $23 million to promote a product that is mostly bicarbonate and aspirin? Why not put some of that money into your laboratories? Why not develop new products that are worth advertising? Comment.

11. What would be the economic effect of a ban on all advertising? Of a ban on radio and television advertising?

12. What is the definition of a market? What is the distinction between the compact car market and the automobile market? Campbell had 8 percent of the dry-soup market in 1962 versus 57 percent for Lipton and 16 percent for Wyler's. Should an analyst focus on the soup market or the dry-soup market?

13. The concentration ratio in the beer industry went from 21 percent in 1947 to 34 percent in 1963. Yet the fact that Pabst was third in 1952, ninth in 1957, and third again in 1962 indicates that the industry was far from stable. Furthermore, regional brands like Lone-Star and Pearl, two Texas brands that forced a

national brand out of their market, compete very effectively with national brands and require only a regional advertising budget. Comment.

14. What is the economic impact of advertising? When will it generate lower prices? Under what conditions will it increase prices? Evaluate the causal model represented in Figure 19–2.

15. If you were the chairman of an advertising agency with a cigarette account would you drop the account after hearing the Surgeon General's report on smoking and health?

16. It has been proposed by Ralph Nader that a 100 percent tax be applied on all advertising expenditures in excess of a percentage specified for different companies by the FTC. Evaluate this proposal. How else might large advertising expenditures be reduced? What would be the effect of a law outlawing advertising in the cigarette industry? In the detergent industry (in which 11 percent of sales is spent on advertising)?

NOTES. . . . .

1. *The Works of Samuel Johnson*, LL.D., IV (Oxford: Talboys and Wheeler, 1825), p. 269. For a contemporary book, see Roxanne Hovland and Gary B. Wilcox, eds., *Advertising in Society: Classic and Contemporary Readings on Advertising's Role in Society* (Chicago, NTC Business Books, 1989).

2. Gene R. Laczniak and Patrick E. Murphy, *Ethical Marketing Decisions: The Higher Road* (Boston: Allyn and Bacon, 1993), and N. Craig Smith and John A. Quelch, *Ethics in Marketing* (Homewood, Il.: Irwin, 1993). For an earlier book, see F.P. Bishop, *The Ethics of Advertising* (London: Robert Hale, 1949).

3. Gene R. Laczniak, "Marketing Ethics: Onward Toward Greater Expectations," *Journal of Public Policy and Marketing*, 12, no. 1 (Spring 1993), 91–96.

4. Donald P. Robin and R. Eric Reidenbach, "Searching for a Place to Stand: Toward a Workable Ethical Philosophy for Marketing," *Journal of Public Policy and Marketing*, 12, no. 1 (Spring 1993), 97–105.

5. Alan J. Dubinsky, and Barbara Loken, "Analyzing Ethical Decision Making in Marketing," *Journal of Business Research*, 19 (1989), 83–107.

6. John Kenneth Galbraith, "The Economic Hangover from a Binge of Greed," *Business and Society Review*, 81 (Spring 1992), 6–7.

7. Donald L. Kanter, "Cynical Marketers at Work," *Journal of Advertising Research*, v28, n6 (Dec 1988/Jan 1989), 28–34.

8. S. D. Hunt and L. B. Chonko, *Journal of Advertising*. See also, L. B. Chonko and S. D. Hunt, "Ethics and Marketing Management: An Empirical Examination," *Journal of Business Research,* 13 (August 1985), 339–359; O. C. Ferrell and L. G. Gresham, "A Contingency Framework for Understanding Ethical Decision Making in Marketing," *Journal of Marketing* 29 (Summer 1985), 87–96; and D. M. Krugman and O. C. Ferrell, "The Organizational Ethics of Advertising: Corporate and Agency Views," *Journal of Advertising*, 10, no. 1 (1981), 21–30ff.

9. Edward S. Petry, Jr., and Fred Tietz, "Can Ethics Officers Improve Office Ethics?" *Business and Society Review*, 82 (Summer 1992), 21–25.

10. Jeffrey Zack, "Playing Ethics at Martin Marietta," *Business and Society Review*, 84 (Winter 1993), 48–49.

11. Vance Packard, *The Hidden Persuaders* (New York: Pocket Books, 1957).

12. William L. Wilke, *Consumer Research* (New York: Wiley, 1986), p. 377.

13. Joel Saegert, "Another Look at Subliminal Perception," *Journal of Advertising Research*, 19 (February 1979), 55–57.

14. Del Hawkens, "The Effects of Subliminal Stimulation on Drive Level and Brand Preference," *Journal of Marketing Research*, 7 (August 1970), 322–326.
15. Tibor Scitovsky, *Welfare and Competition* (Homewood, IL: Irwin, 1951), pp. 401–402.
16. Mary Gardiner Jones, "The Cultural and Social Impact of Advertising on American Society," *Arizona State Law Journal*, 3 (1970).
17. Raymond A. Bauer and Stephen A. Greyser, "The Dialogue That Never Happens," *Harvard Business Review*, 50 (January–February 1969), 122–128.
18. Raymond A. Bauer and Stephen A. Greyser, *Advertising in America: The Consumer View* (Boston: Division of Research, Graduate School of Business Administration, Harvard University, 1968).
19. David A. Aaker and Donald E. Bruzzone, "Causes of Irritation in Advertising," *Journal of Marketing*, v49, n2 (Spring 1985), 47–57.
20. Kathy McMeel, "You Dirty Old Ad Men Make Me Sick," *Advertising Age*, December 1, 1969, p. 28.
21. Stephen A. Greyser, "Irritation in Advertising," *Journal of Advertising Research*, 13 (February 1973), 8.
22. Ibid., p. 6.
23. Gary M. Armstrong, "An Evaluation of the Children's Advertising Review Unit," *Journal of Public Policy and Marketing*, 3 (1984), 38–55.
24. Gary M. Armstrong and Merrie Brucks, "Dealing With Children's Advertising: Public Policy Issues and Alternatives," *Journal of Public Policy and Marketing*, 7 (1988), 98–113.
25. David M. Boush, Marian Friestad, and Gregory M. Rose, "Adolescent Skepticism Toward TV Advertising and Knowledge of Advertising Tactics," *Journal of Consumer Research*, 21, no. 1 (June 1994), 165–175.
26. See for example, Marvin E. Goldberg and Gerald J. Gorn, "Children's Reactions to Television Advertising: An Experimental Approach," *Journal of Consumer Research*, 1 (September 1977), 69–75, and "Some Unintended Consequences of TV Advertising to Children," *Journal of Consumer Research*, 5 (June 1978), 22–29 by the same authors.
27. Gerald J. Gorn and Marvin E. Goldberg, "Behavioral Evidence of the Effects of Televised Food Messages on Children," *Journal of Consumer Research*, 9 (September 1982), 200–205.
28. M. Carole Macklin, "Preschoolers' Understanding of the Informational Function of Television Advertising," *Journal of Consumer Research*, 14 (September 1987), 229–239.
29. Merrie Brucks, Gary M. Armstrong, and Marvin E. Goldberg, "Children's Use of Cognitive Defenses Against Television Advertising: A Cognitive Response Approach," *Journal of Consumer Research*, 14 (March 1988), 471–482.
30. Deborah L. Roedder, "Age Differences in Children's Responses to Television Advertising: An Information-Processing Approach," *Journal of Consumer Research*, 8, no. 2 (September 1981), 144–153.
31. Thomas E. Barry, "A Framework for Ascertaining Deception in Children's Advertising," *Journal of Advertising*, 9, no. 1 (Winter 1980), 11–18.
32. Kim McAvoy, "FCC Gets Into the Children's Act," *Broadcasting and Cable*, 123, no. 30 (July 26, 1993), 42–43.
33. "EC Reviewing Policy on Advertising," *Business Europe*, 33, no. 14 (April 12–18, 1993), 1–3.
34. Richard M. Pollay, "Quality of Life in the Padded Sell: Common Criticism of Advertising's Cultural Character and International Public Policies, in James H. Leigh and Claude R. Martin, Jr., eds., *Current Issues and Research in Advertising* (Ann Arbor, MI: University of Michigan, 1986), pp. 173–250.
35. ibid., p. 196. See also, Richard W. Pollay, "The Distorted Mirror: Reflections on the Unintended Consequences of Advertising," *Journal of Marketing*, 50 (April 1986), 18–36, and Morris B. Holbrook, "Mirror, Mirror, on the Wall, What's Unfair in the Reflections of Advertising?" *Journal of Marketing*, 51 (July 1987), 95–103.
36. John G. Myers, *Social Issues in Advertising* (New York: American Association of Advertising Agencies Educational Foundation), 1972.

37. Kusum Singh and Bertram Gross, " 'MacBride': The Report and the Response," *Journal of Communications*, 31 (October 1981), 104–117.
38. Bauer and Greyser, "The Dialogue That Never Happens."
39. Russell W. Belk, "Materialism: Trait Aspects of Living in the Material World," *Journal of Consumer Research*, 12 (December 1985), 265–280; and Morris B. Holbrook and Elizabeth C. Hirschman, "The Experiential Aspects of Consumption: Consumer Fantasies, Feelings, and Fun," *Journal of Consumer Research*, 9 (September 1982), 132–140.
40. Jones, "The Cultural and Social Impact of Advertising on American Society." Presented to the Trade Regulation Roundtable of the Association of American Law Schools, San Francisco, December 1969, pp. 13–14.
41. Rebecca C. Quarles and Leo W. Jeffres, "Advertisng and National Consumption: A Path Analytic Re-examination of the Galbraithian Argument," *Journal of Advertising*, 12, no. 2 (1983), 4–13, 33.
42. Susan Spiggle, "Measuring Social Values: A Content Analysis of Sunday Comics and Underground Comix," *Journal of Consumer Research*, 13, no. 1 (June 1986), 100–113.
43. Thomas J. Lipscomb, "Indicators of Materialism in Children's Free Speech: Age and Gender Comparisons," *Journal of Consumer Marketing*, 5, no. 4 (Fall 1988), 41–46.
44. As quoted in Steven W. Colford, "Jacobson: Battling 'Excess of Marketing,' " *Advertising Age*, 62, no. 24 (June 10, 1991), 12.
45. Kim P. Corfman, Donald R. Lehmann, and Sunder Narayanan, "Values, Utility, and Ownership: Modeling the Relationship for Consumer Durables," *Journal of Retailing*, 67, no. 2 (Summer 1991), 184–204.
46. Richard W. Pollay and Banwari Mittal, "Here's the Beef: Factors, Determinants, and Segments in Consumer Criticism of Advertising," *Journal of Marketing*, 57, no. 3 (July 1993), 99–114.
47. Alice E. Courtney and Sarah Wemick Lockeretz, "A Woman's Place: An Analysis of the Roles Portrayed by Women in Magazine Advertisements," *Journal of Marketing Research*, 8 (February 1971), 92–95.
48. Harold H. Kassarjian, "The Negro and American Advertising, 1946–65," *Journal of Marketing Research*, 6 (February 1969), 29–39.
49. Thomas W. Leigh, Arno J. Rethans, and Tamatha R. Whitney, "Role Portrayals of Women in Advertising: Cognitive Responses and Advertising Effectiveness," *Journal of Advertising Research*, (October–November 1987), 54–63.
50. "Whole World Is Watching U.S. Alcohol Ad Debate," *Advertising Age*, February 11, 1985, p. 70.
51. Camille P. Schuster and Christine P. Powell, "Comparison of Cigarette and Alcohol Advertising Controversies," *Journal of Advertising*, 16, no. 2 (1987), 26–33. See also, Avery M. Abernethy and Jesse E. Teel, "Advertising Regulation's Effect Upon Demand for Cigarettes," *Journal of Advertising*, 15, no. 4 (1986), 51–55, and George P. Moschis, "Point of View: Cigarette Advertising and Young Smokers," *Journal of Advertising Research*, (April–May 1989), 51–60.
52. Dan Coughlin, "Tobacco Money Lights Up Congress," *Business and Society Review*, 83 (Fall 1992), 19–21. See also, Roger Rosenblatt, "How Tobacco Executives Live With Themselves," *Business and Society Review*, 89 (Spring 1994), 22–34; Myron Levin, "How the Building Doctor Inhales Tobacco Money," *Business and Society Review*, 87 (Fall 1993), 44–48; and Bob Herbert, "Tobacco Hush Money for Black Leaders," *Business and Society Review*, 88 (Winter 1994), 62–63.
53. William Beaver, "The Marlboro Man Rides into the Eastern Bloc," *Business and Society Review*, 88 (Winter 1994), 19–23.
54. Excerpted from Doug Bandow, "Is Business Drowning in a New Regulatory Tide?" *Business and Society Review*, 82 (Summer 1992), 45–49.
55. See articles entitled "No Smoking Sweeps America," "A Sign of the Times: Smokers Need Not Apply," and "There's a Whole Industry Out There to Help You Kick the Habit," by Joan C. Hamilton, Emily T. Smith, Paul Angiolillo, and Reginald Rhein, Jr., *Business Week*, 3009, Industrial/Technology Edition, July 27, 1987, pp. 40–46. For a book on smoking

behavior, see W. Kip Viscusi, *Smoking: Making the Risky Decision* (New York: Oxford University Press, 1992).

56. Lonnie R. Bristow, "Protecting Youth from the Tobacco Industry," *Vital Speeches of the Day*, 60, no. 11 (March 15, 1994), 333–336. Greenhalgh states that smoking kills one-fifth of all smokers in middle age, twenty-five years before the end of their expected lifespan. Women smokers have a higher incidence of miscarriage and premature labor. See Trisha Greenhalgh, "Never Too Late to Stop Smoking," *Accountancy*, 110, no. 1192 (December 1992), 64.

57. Excerpted from Susan Krafft, "The Marlboro Man is Really a Troubled Teen," *American Demographics*, 15, no. 12 (December 1993), 12–13.

58. Peter D. Jacobson, Jeffrey Wasserman and Kristiana Raube, "The Politics of Antismoking Legislation," *Journal of Health Politics, Policy and Law*, 18, no. 4 (Winter 1993), 787–819.

59. Bruce E. Samuels, Michael E. Begay, Annua R. Hazan, and Stanton A. Glantz, "Philip Morris's Failed Experiment in Pittsburgh," *Journal of Health Politics, Policy and Law*, 17, no. 2 (Summer 1992), 329–351.

60. James H. Coil and Charles M. Rice, "State Regulatory Update: Smoker-Protection Statutes: Fifteen States Now Protect Smokers from Discrimination Based on Their Off-The-Job Tobacco Use," *Employment Relations Today*, 18, no. 3 (Autumn 1991), 383–390.

61. David M. Ludington, "Smoking in Public: A Moral Imperative for the Most Toxic of Environmental Wastes," *Journal of Business Ethics*, 10, no. 1 (January 1991), 23–27.

62. William L. Weis, "A Smoke Cloud Over Tobacco's Future," *Business and Society Review*, 52 (Winter 1985), 37–40.

63. See Stephen Barlas, "Bill Poses Threat to Cigarette Ads," *Marketing News*, 24, no. 4 (February 19, 1990), 1–2.

64. The second and third place brands are Winston (R. J. Reynolds) with 6.7 percent and Basic (Philip Morris) with 5.3 percent. See "Marlboro Friday, Sullen Sunday for Smokes," *Advertising Age*, September 28, 1994, p. 28.

65. Advertising-to-sales (A/S) ratios for cigarettes tend to be in the 1–3 percent range. For example, in 1993, American Brands A/S ratio was 2.6 percent and B.A.T. Industries 1.5 percent. The reciprocal idea of sales per advertising dollar for these two companies were $38.43 and $66.68, respectively in 1993. See "100 Leading National Advertisers by Most-Advertised Segment," *Advertising Age*, September 28, 1994, p. 53.

66. See "Health Issues Percolating in Calif.," *National Underwriter*, 95, no. 33 (August 19, 1991), 8; and Alan P. Crawford, "Stark Raving Mad," *Adweek (Easter Edition)*, 33, no. 48 (November 30, 1992), 16.

67. Maria Mallory, "These Days Where There's Smoke, There's A Lawsuit," *Business Week*, 3375, June 6, 1994, p. 36. and Maria Mallory, "Florida May Kick the Tar Out of Tobacco," *Business Week*, 3379, July 4, 1994, p. 29.

68. For a review, see Ross D. Petty, "Joe Camel and the Commission: The Real Legal Issues," *Journal of Public Policy and Marketing*, 12, no. 2 (Fall 1993), 276–281.

69. Morton Mintz, "The Tobacco Pushers' Marketing Smokescreen," *Business and Society Review*, 79 (Fall 1991), 49–54.

70. David W. Stewart and Ingrid M. Martin, "Intended and Unintended Consequences of Warning Messages: A Review and Synthesis of Empirical Research," *Journal of Public Policy and Marketing*, 13, no. 1 (Spring 1994), 1–19.

71. Michael E. Hilton, "An Overview of Recent Findings on Alcoholic Beverage Warning Labels," *Journal of Public Policy and Marketing*, 12, no. 1 (Spring 1993), 1–9.

72. Lester W. Johnson, "Cigarette Advertising and Public Policy," *International Journal of Social Economics*, 15, no. 7 (1988), 76–80 and Robert McAuliffe, "The FTC and the Effectiveness of Cigarette Advertising Regulations," *Journal of Public Policy and Marketing*, 7 (1988), 49–64.

73. See Michael J. Garrison, "Should All Cigarette Advertising Be Banned?" *American Business Law Journal*, 25, no. 2 (Summer 1987), 169–205 and Kenneth E. Warner, Virginia L. Ernster, John H. Holbrok, and Eugene M. Lewit, "Promotion of Tobacco Products: Issues

and Policy Options," *Journal of Health Politics, Policy and Law*, 11, no. 3 (Fall 1986), 367–392.

74. Thomas A. Hemphill, "Marketer's New Motto: It's Keen To Be Green," *Business and Society Review*, 78 (Summer 1991), 39–44.

75. Harold Takooshian and Richard H. Tashjian, "The Unnatural Use of Natural Advertising," *Business and Society Review*, 76 (Winter 1991), 43–47. See also, Norman Kangun, Les Carlson, and Stephen J. Grove, "Environmental Advertising Claims: A Preliminary Investigation," *Journal of Public Policy and Marketing*, 10, no. 2 (Fall 1991), 47–58; Jerry Taylor, "The Greening of the First Amendment," *Regulation*, 14, no. 4 (Fall 1991), 35–39, and Roger D. Wynne, "Defining "Green": Toward Regulation of Environmental Marketing Claims, *University of Michigan Journal of Law Reform* (Spring–Summer 1991), 785–820.

76. Jason W. Gray-Lee, Debra L. Scammon, and Robert N. Mayer, "Review of Legal Standards for Environmental Marketing Claims," *Journal of Public Policy and Marketing*, 13, no. 1 (Spring 1994), 155–167.

77. Steven W. Colford, "Fade-Out for Green?" *Advertising Age*, December 5, 1994, p. 1ff.

78. James T. Bennett, Kevin F. McCrohan, Public Policy Issues in the Marketing of Seals of Approval for Food," *Journal of Consumer Affairs*, 27, no. 2 (Winter 1993), 397–415; Richard F. Beltramini and Edwin R. Stafford, "Comprehension and Perceived Believability of Seals of Approval Information in Advertising," *Journal of Advertising*, 22, no. 3 (September 1993), 3–13.

79. Edward T. Popper and Keith B. Murray, "Communication Effectiveness and Format Effects on In-Ad Disclosure of Health Warnings," *Journal of Public Policy and Marketing*, 8 (1989), 109–123.

80. Pauline M. Ippolito and Alan D. Mathios, "Health Claims in Food Marketing: Evidence on Knowledge and Behavior in the Cereal Market," *Journal of Public Policy and Marketing*, 10, no. 1 (Spring 1991), 15–32.

81. For an interesting review of the public policy issues surrounding the use of the term "healthy" see Linda F. Golodner, "Healthy Confusion for Consumers," and Peter B. Hutt, "FDA Regulation of Product Claims in Food Labeling," *Journal of Public Policy and Marketing*, 12, no. 1 (Spring 1993), 130–134.

82. For a review, see Pauline M. Ippolito and Alan D. Mathios, "New Food Labeling Regulations and the Flow of Nutrition Information to Consumers," *Journal of Public Policy and Marketing*, 12, no. 2 (Fall 1993), 188–205. The authors warn that although there is much in the new labeling that is likely to improve consumer information, there are problems in determining the most appropriate kinds of information to improve food choices.

83. David A. Aaker and Donald Norris, "Characteristics of Television Commercials Perceived as Informative," *Journal of Advertising Research* (February 1982).

84. Phillip Nelson, "Advertising as Information," *Journal of Political Economy*, 82 (July/August 1974), 729–754.

85. Fritz Machlup, *The Production and Distribution of Knowledge in the United States* (Princeton, NJ: Princeton University Press, 1962), p. 265.

86. Julian L. Simon, *Issues in the Economics of Advertising* (Urbana, IL: University of Illinois Press, 1970), p. 276.

87. "Grocery Manufacturing." Technical Study No. 6, National Commission on Food Marketing, June 1966, p. 147.

88. *The Value Side of Productivity: A Key to Competitive Survival in the 1990s* (New York: Committee on the Value of Advertising, American Association of Advertising Agencies, 1990).

89. Simon, *Issues in the Economics of Advertising*.

90. For a recent book-length treatment of the subject see, Robert E. McAuliffe, *Advertising, Competition, and Public Policy: Theories and New Evidence* (Lexington, MA: Lexington Books, 1987). McAuliffe addresses advertising as a barrier to entry, questions of correlation and causality, measurement issues, and implications for public policy.

91. Frederic M. Scherer, *Industrial Market Structure and Economic Performance* (Boston: Houghton-Mifflin), 1980, p. 62.

92. George R. Milne, "A Marketing Approach for Measuring Product Market Differentiation and Concentration in Antitrust Cases," *Journal of Public Policy and Marketing*, 11, no. 2 (Fall 1992), 90–100.

93. For a model of advertising and entry see, Richard Schmalensee, "Advertising and Entry Deterrence: An Exploratory Model" (Cambridge: Massachusetts Institute of Technology, 1982).

94. Paul D. Scanlon, "Oligopoly and 'Deceptive' Advertising: The Cereal Industry Affair," *Antitrust Law & Economics Review*, 3 (Spring 1970), 101.

95. J. N. Kessides, "Advertising, Sunk Cost, and Barriers to Entry," *The Review of Economics and Statistics* (February 1986).

96. John A. Rizzo and Richard J. Zeckhauser, "Advertising and Entry: The Case of Physician Services," *Journal of Political Economy*, 98 (June 1990), 476–500.

97. Scanlon, pp. 99–110.

98. Louis W. Stern and Thomas W. Dunfee, "Public Policy Implications of Non-price Marketing and De-Oligopolization in the Cereal Industry," in Fred C. Allvine, ed., *Public Policy and Marketing Practices* (Chicago: American Marketing Association, 1973), pp. 271–287.

99. See also Paul N. Bloom, "The Cereal Companies: Monopolists or Super Marketers'?" *MSU Business Topics* (Summer 1978), 41–49.

100. P. M. Ippolito and A. D. Mathios, "Information, Advertising, and Health Choice: A Study of the Cereal Market," *Rand Journal of Economics*, 21 (Autumn 1990).

101. John K. Galbraith, *American Capitalism: The Concept of Countervailing Power* (Boston: Houghton-Mifflin, 1956).

102. Robert D. Buzzell and Paul W. Farris, *Marketing Costs in Consumer Goods Industries,* Marketing Science Institute, Report N. 76-111, August 1976.

103. Paul W. Farris and Mark S. Albion, "The Impact of Advertising on the Price of Consumer Products," *Journal of Marketing*, 44 (Summer 1980), 17–35, 57; Lee Benham, "The Effect of Advertising on the Price of Consumer Products, *Journal of Marketing*, 44 (Summer 1980), 17–35.

104. Lee Benham, "The Effect of Advertising on the Price of Eyeglasses," *The Journal of Law and Economics*, 15 (October 1972), 337–352.

105. Lakshman Krishnamurthi and S. P. Raj, "The Effect of Advertising on Consumer Price Sensitivity," *Journal of Marketing Research*, 22 (May 1985), 119–129.

106. W. P. Rogersen, "Price Advertising and the Deterioration of Product Quality," *Review of Economic Studies*, LV (1988), 215–229.

107. For other studies on price-related questions, see Mary Jane Sheffet, "The Supreme Court and Predatory Pricing," *Journal of Public Policy and Marketing*, 13, no. 1 (Spring 1994), 163–167; and Joseph P. Cannon and Paul N. Bloom, "Are Slotting Allowances Legal Under Antitrust Laws?" *Journal of Public Policy and Marketing*, 10, no. 1 (Spring 1991), 167–186.

108. William S. Comanor and Thomas A. Wilson, "Advertising, Market Structure and Performance," *Review of Economics and Statistics*, 49 (November 1967), 423–440.

109. Scherer, *Industrial Market Structure and Economic Performance*, p. 286.

110. L. G. Thomas, "Advertising in Consumer Goods Industries: Durability, Economies of Scale, and Heterogeneity," *The Journal of Law and Economics* (April 1989).

111. Richard Schmalensee, "Brand Loyalty and Barriers to Entry," *Southern Economic Journal*, 40 (April 1974), 579–588.

112. Lester G. Telser, "Advertising and Competition," *Journal of Political Economy* (December 1964), 537–562.

113. B. J. Sheldon and K. Doroodian, "A Simultaneous Model of Cigarette Advertising: Effects on Demand and Industry Response to Public Policy," *The Review of Economics and Statistics* (November 1989).

114. Susan L. Holak and Srinivas K. Reddy, "Effects of a Television and Radio Advertising Ban: A Study of the Cigarette Industry," *Journal of Marketing*, 50 (October 1986), 219–227.

115. James L. Hamilton, "The Demand for Cigarettes: Advertising, the Health Scare and the

Cigarette Advertising Ban," *Review of Economics and Statistics*, 54 (1972), 401–411; Lynne Schneider, Benjamin Klein, and Kevin M. Murphy, "Governmental Regulation of Cigarette Health Information," *Journal of Law and Economics*, 24 (December 1981), 575–612.

116. Scherer, *Industrial Market Structure*, p. 404.

117. Robert C. Pace, "The Story of the Florida Tax on Advertising," *International Journal of Advertising*, 7 (1988), 283–292.

20 GLOBAL MARKETING AND ADVERTISING

"Midtown Manhattan and the 7th Arrondisement of
Paris have more in common than midtown
Manhattan and the Bronx."
(from a 1985 advertisement by Saatchi & Saatchi, declaring itself
a "global agency.")

"There are about two products that lend themselves
to global marketing—and one of them is Coca-Cola"
(Carl Spielvogel, chairman and CEO of Backer Spielvogel Bates
Worldwide interview in *The Wall Street Journal*, May 12, 1988).

With brands like Coca-Cola, Swatch, and Benetton now marketed the same way in many countries of the world, *Global Marketing* has become quite a buzzword in the 1990s, and this is so for many good reasons.

THE GLOBALIZATION OF MARKETS . . . .

First, the consumer and business markets in North America, western Europe, and Japan—while still very big in size—have begun to show signs of slower growth, as their rates of annual population and household growth slow down to 2 or 3 percentage points per year. Companies with most of their sales in these markets have thus realized the need to look to other markets for growth. The consumer goods giant Procter & Gamble, for instance, already has over $4 billion in sales coming from 130 markets outside the U.S., and sees such non–U.S. sales as its main source of future growth. In particular, many countries in Asia have annual growth rates for their economies that are much higher: China's economy, for instance, grew at over 9 percent per year for the ten years prior to 1994 (and shows no signs of slowing down).

Second, while the mature markets of North America, western Europe, and Japan are becoming ever more price-competitive (and less profitable) for major brands, with an increasing number of consumers preferring to buy cheaper private (store) label brands, consumers in the rapidly developing markets of Asia (and elsewhere) are showing a voracious appetite for branded goods, which often serve a need to reflect rapidly changing social aspirations.[1] Thus, Western companies are finding sales in the newly growing markets of the world to be both easier and more profitable.

Third, the crumbling of political, economic, and customs barriers in the last few years has made it much easier for companies to operate in a truly global manner, instead of merely multinationally or in a *multidomestic* manner. For instance, the increasing integration of western European economies at the end of 1992, and the opening up of the eastern European markets to the West, means that companies can now more easily consolidate their production facilities for Europe in one country instead of producing locally in every European country, thus realizing economies of scale. This has led to the increased attention to the need to create truly global brands that can take advantage of such economies. Relatedly, many of the retailing customers to which manufacturing companies sell their products are themselves becoming transnational (especially in Europe), and manufacturers have to deal with them on a multicountry basis.

Fourth, the growth of global media has led both to the increasing homogenization of consumer tastes across the world, and to the increasing use of standardized or global advertising campaigns which can be seen simultaneously in many different countries. Of course, this is an incomplete and still-evolving phenomenon, and some consumer segments (such as teenagers or young business professionals) are more likely to be part of the "global village" than are other consumers. Nevertheless, with the growth of satellite- and cable-based TV channels across the world, global brands such as Nike and Canon have increasingly begun to strengthen their global brands through the use of standardized global ad campaigns.

The argument for such global commonality of tastes was made very strongly by Harvard Marketing Professor Ted Levitt, who wrote in 1983 that nothing confirmed such globalization more than "the success of McDonald's from the Champs Élysées to the Ginza, of Coca-Cola in Bahrain and Pepsi-Cola in Moscow, and of rock music, Greek salad, Hollywood movies, Revlon cosmetics, Sony televisions, and Levi jeans everywhere."[2] Levitt argued that such homogenization of tastes allowed perceptive global marketers to market very similar products worldwide at lower cost than smaller-scale local producers. We shall see later that Levitt's arguments, while provocative and insightful, somewhat overstate the case for such homogenization, and most global marketers in fact combine or blend local variation with global standardization.[3]

In any event, there is no doubt that global marketing and advertising are becoming very important today because major companies and brands have begun to see the need to grow in countries outside their traditional domestic bases, and because the globalization of markets, media, and consumer tastes is beginning to allow for the production, marketing and advertising of brands on a truly global basis. Finally, advertising agencies (such as Saatchi & Saatchi, the WPP group, and the Interpublic group) themselves have, since the early 1980s, begun to form global networks and alliances (see Chapter 1). They did this in part because their increasingly global clients began to seek global servicing capabilities, and in part because they wished to gain a larger share of the fast growth in advertising revenues outside the United States and western Europe. This growth in the ability of advertising agency networks to create and implement global advertising campaigns will be discussed more fully in a later section of this chapter.

GLOBAL PRODUCTION AND MARKETING: THE ARGUMENT FOR GLOBALIZATION . . . . .

A key business advantage enjoyed by companies that operate with a global strategy is that they can enjoy operating economies of scale. This means that by having larger volumes of the same product manufactured and sold over a larger market area, such a global company can produce and market them at a lower cost per unit than a smaller-scale competitor. These economies of scale can come in production and packaging costs, in research and development costs, and in marketing costs, among others. Packaging costs can often be cut by having one standardized package carrying multilingual packaging information: this is often done for products sold in western Europe.

In addition, because it sells essentially the same product in multiple countries, a global company can invest far more resources in research and development than smaller local competitors, because its R&D expenses can be amortized over its much larger global sales volume. Thus while a local camera manufacturer selling only in Thailand cannot spend much on R&D to improve its product, a Japanese camera manufacturer like Nikon sells its cameras worldwide and thus can invest much more in basic technology development than that Thai competitor, giving its product a technological advantage in the marketplace.

Finally, if the same product can be marketed in the same way in many countries, a global company can potentially leverage the same investment in packaging, market research, and advertising development and production costs over all of these markets, instead of incurring these expenses afresh in each of these markets. This source of marketing cost savings can be another source of pricing advantage, and is one reason why the idea of building global brands—those with the same name, packaging, formulation, and advertising in multiple countries—is so appealing. (Another reason is simply that consumers in each of these markets may all be so similar that they all respond best to that unified brand proposition.) Colgate-Palmolive, for instance, introduced its Colgate tartar-control toothpaste nearly simultaneously in over forty countries, each of which was allowed to choose one of two ads—saving the global giant an estimated $1 million in ad production costs alone, per country.[4]

PERSISTING CULTURAL DIFFERENCES: THE ARGUMENT FOR LOCALIZATION . . . . . .

Counteracting these potential savings, of course, is the reality that consumers in every country are still somewhat different from each other, with different habits, tastes, and preferences, so that the product or brand that works in one market may not work in another. For example, while Americans like to drink orange juice for breakfast, French consumers don't, and while Middle Easterners prefer toothpaste that tastes spicy, this taste may not work well in other markets! Global marketer McDonald's finds it has to vary its menu in different countries—serving beer in Germany, wine in France, and milkshakes flavored with local fruits in Singapore and Malaysia, for example.[5] The business literature is full of stories of disastrous mistakes made by international marketers who failed to understand local consumer differences—such as Pepsodent toothpaste trying to use a teeth-whitening appeal in parts of Asia, where dark-stained teeth were considered prestigious.[6]

More generally, people living in different countries often belong to different cultures, and cultures may even vary widely within a large and multiethnic country (such as India). Every culture is a complex web of social relations, religious beliefs, languages, and consumption attitudes and habits, all of which will obviously impact on how communications are delivered and received.[7] It is a basic principle in communication theory that, for any communication to be successful, the sender of the message must understand the frame of reference of the receiver of the message.[8] Obviously, therefore, a multinational advertiser must understand the cultural nuances of a local market in order to be successful, because it may differ substantially from the culture of the "home" market.

There are numerous ways to contrast cultures, such as their degree of *traditionalism* versus *secularization*,[9] the degree to which they rely on explicit and verbal information (so-called *low-context cultures*) versus implicit and nonverbal information (called *high-context cultures*),[10] and the degree to which they are *individual-oriented* versus *interdependent* or *relational*.[11] For instance, many researchers classify North American and west European cultures as relatively more secular, low-context and individual-oriented, compared to Asian cultures, with Hispanic cultures falling somewhere in between.[12] Given the demonstrated differences across cultures on these and other dimensions—including level of economic development—it seems entirely logical that consumers in different countries may have different ways of deciding which brands to buy, different levels of involvement toward the same product categories,[13] different attitudes towards advertising, and so on.[14]

It is commonly accepted that certain product categories, such as food and beverages, have a very high degree of *cultural grounding*, where such cultural differences make global standardization more difficult than in other categories.[15] Even if the product category is not so culturally grounded, such as personal computers or industrial products, various types of differences still persist across markets. Media availability and distribution arrangements are often very different. Government regulations vary. Consumers have different expectations and preferences concerning colors used in packaging (purple is a death color in Brazil, whereas white is the color for funerals in Hong Kong).[16] And, the competitive environment for a particular brand may vary dramatically: it may be the leader in one market but a minor brand in another—it may even be seen as a niche, import brand, rather than one of the major brands. It may face brands that follow very different positioning strategies across these many markets. It may even be at different stages of the life cycle in different markets: new in one, mature in another, so that having a standardized advertising approach makes little sense.

Finally, marketing and advertising campaigns that are standardized so that they can be used in multiple markets, if not the whole world, have the obvious disadvantage that they may be aimed at the lowest common denominator and may end up not appealing strongly enough to any particular market. As Laurance Ha-gan, the London-based Director of Marketing Development for J. Walter Thompson put it, "The greater the audience for any message the more bland and general, the less specific and compelling, that message will be."[17]

CROSS-NATIONAL DIFFERENCES IN CULTURE AND CONSUMER BEHAVIOR . . . .

Since advertising attempts to communicate the literal and symbolic meaning attached to a brand, and since cultures differ in the ways in which they construe and communicate meaning, successful advertising obviously requires a thorough understanding of the culture within which that advertising message is communicated. Thus, even if a foreign advertiser were to create an advertising message for a local market entirely from scratch—a strategy of *localizing* the advertising message—the task would be hard, and it would be easy to make cultural blunders. Obviously, the task of "standardizing" the advertising message so that it can be used unchanged worldwide is even harder, for now one has to find a message that is equally effective in all these multiple cultures at the same time.

Just how similar or different are consumers across the world? As the quotes that opened this chapter illustrate, there are many different viewpoints. Ted Levitt's view that the world was moving toward greater cultural convergence was discussed earlier, and it is certainly true that with political and customs barriers crumbling, with television channels like MTV and CNN and STAR-TV being bounced off satellites into homes across the globe, with more people traveling and vacationing in other countries, and with global fast-food franchises such as McDonald's appearing at streetcorners from Beijing to Buenos Aires, it often appears that we are indeed all moving toward one homogenized global community.

Such tendencies toward globalization of tastes, and of trends, are especially apparent when one looks at particular demographic subcategories. Teenagers the world over, for example, are more exposed than most to cultural influences from other countries, through fashions in music, clothing, food, personal appearance, and sports. While regional and national differences still persist, teenagers the world over increasingly watch the same TV channels and movies, listen to the same music, idolize the same music and sports stars, and play the same videogames. Their lives and aspirations are shaped worldwide by the same global trends of increasing divorce among their parents, a fear of AIDS, and environmental concerns. Teens typically travel abroad more than their parents and are more likely to know a foreign language, especially English. Not surprisingly, teenagers are less likely to be parochial and nationalistic, and more likely to identify with pan-national organizations (such as a feeling of being an "European" and not simply "German" or "French.")[18] Given such commonality in how teens view the world, it is not surprising that brands that market to teens (such as videogame maker Nintendo) try to use common advertising approaches across multiple countries.

Similarly, women the world over are seeking more actively to participate in workplace success and identify less closely than before with the traditional female roles of mother/nurturer and wife/homemaker. Thus, although very important differences still undoubtedly persist, there can be no doubt that consumers the world over are becoming more alike each other. Global marketers and ad agencies—such as Coca-Cola or McCann-Erickson—seek to monitor and understand these global trends very closely, in order to better market and advertise their brands on a global basis.

It should be noted, by way of warning, that it is entirely possible that the trend towards more homogenous brand preferences we are seeing is not one of true globalization but rather simply one of the increasing popularity in the rapidly developing parts of the world (such as China, India, South America, and Eastern Europe) of the brands and cultural symbols that imply a larger-than-life "western" or even "American" lifestyle—such as Coca-Cola, Marlboro cigarettes (with its Marlboro man cowboy imagery), Levi jeans, Nike athletic shoes, and so on.[19] The popularity of American endorsers and foreign-sounding brand names in Japanese advertising may also be attributed to a desire among Japanese consumers to appear cosmopolitan and westernized.[20] Thus, it is possible that the apparent increase in demand across the world for certain well-known brands such as Coca-Cola and Levi's is largely because they are seen by consumers in many newly opened markets as symbols of the freedom and affluent lifestyles of the West, and not because they are seen as global brands per se. Simply being a global brand may not always be important; what is more likely to be important is what the brand stands for around the globe, such as high technology (examples: Sony, Kodak), or prestige (Rolex, Mercedes, Gucci, Lacoste). There are a few exceptions, such as Benetton, whose "United Colors of Benetton" concept trumpets the very idea of a global village (and that brand's part in it). Generally, however, some of the strongest global brands are not seen by local customers as being global at all, but as home-grown and local (such as Heinz or Kellogg's in the U.K.).

Indeed, one of the clear determinants of a brand's imagery in many countries is the image of its country of origin (such as Japan, the United States, France, Italy, Germany, Korea, etc.).[21] Research has shown that particular countries are consistently associated with certain qualities or imagery. For instance, France—and therefore a brand associated with France, such as Perrier mineral water—could be widely perceived to be linked to qualities such as aesthetic sensitivity, refined taste, sensory pleasure, elegance, flair, and sophistication.[22] Successful brands that have taken advantage of such imagery include Heineken beer, which is a mass-market beer in Europe but chose a premium positioning in the U.S. because Dutch beers are "supposed" to be superior, and Häagen-Dazs and Crabtree and Evelyn, whose names suggest an entirely fabricated European origin. (The name Häagen-Dazs suggests that this ice-cream is made in Scandinavia, but its true origins are 100 percent New Jersey, U.S.)

It seems paradoxical that at the same time that consumer preferences are supposedly becoming homogenized, we also find a widely reported trend to micromarketing and direct marketing. Consumers are also supposedly becoming more differentiated in their wants and needs (see Chapter 3 on database marketing). How are we to reconcile these apparently divergent trends?

One way of reconciling these is to understand that while consumer segments do indeed exist across the world, these segments are increasingly defined not by geographical and national boundaries, but instead by universal consumer wants and needs. Thus, as our chapter-opening quote from Saatchi & Saatchi said, an affluent, college-educated, white-collar, dual-income American couple in midtown Manhattan may indeed have more in common with one in the 7th arrondisement in Paris than with one in the Bronx. We will now investigate this idea in more detail.

GLOBAL CONSUMER SEGMENTS . . . .

There are clearly cases when the same consumer segment exists in many countries across the world, though obviously to differing degrees. Thus, the very rich in Korea, China, the Netherlands, or Brazil may all want to buy luxury cars such as a Mercedes, and that car can be positioned as such worldwide to this segment. Cross-cultural anthropologists talk about *cross-cultural cohorts*, groups of people who belong to different cultures or nationalities but nevertheless share common sets of needs, values, and attitudes.[23] Thus, no matter where they live, consumer groups such as new mothers, computer users, international business travelers, audiophiles, high-end photographers, and so on represent groups with similar needs and wants. Because babies' bottoms are the same everywhere, diapers such as Pampers can use the same marketing and advertising strategies worldwide.

Many researchers, companies and advertising agencies have conducted research to find out if such *global segments* can be identified using psychographic research (Chapter 6 discusses psychographics). Alfred Boote, a psychographic researcher, studied the comparative value structures of 500 women each in Germany, the United Kingdom, and France in 1978, and found both similarities and differences. In terms of similarities, it appeared through statistical analyses that all three countries had four types, or segments, of women, labeled "traditional homemaker," "contemporary homemaker," "appearance-conscious," and "spontaneous." However, while the "traditional homemakers" accounted for about one-third of the sample from each country, the proportions for the other three segments varied dramatically across countries. The "contemporary homemakers" were found more often in the U.K. than in the other two countries, the "appearance-conscious" group was made up almost entirely of Germans, while the "spontaneous" group was mostly French. Boote's conclusion was that while a common advertising strategy might be possible for these three European countries, thematic variations across countries, to accomodate country-specific differences, were also advisable.[24]

Not surprisingly, many other researchers and ad agencies have also attempted to find common "Euro-Consumer" segments, given the recent (1992) integration of much of western Europe into one big market of 320 million consumers. The ad agency of D'arcy, Masius, Benton and Bowles found four lifestyle groups common across western Europe (called "Successful Idealists," "Affluent Materialists," "Comfortable Belongers," and "Disaffected Strivers"), and one prevalent only in southern Europe ("Optimistic Strivers."). The first group, which is materialistically successful but still believes in socially responsible ideals, is especially prevalent in Germany and Scandinavia.

An even larger-scale study is that conducted by the Backer Spielvogel and Bates (BSB) ad agency, conducted since the late 1980s in at least different eighteen countries from all over the world. Called *Global-Scan*, about 1,000 consumers in each country are asked not just questions on values and attitudes, but also on brand and product usage, and media use. The analysis focuses on those attitudes and values that appear to be predictive of actual consumer behavior (product and brand use). According to the agency, the data suggest that 95 percent of the population surveyed can be put into one of the five global segments below, with the remaining 5 percent "unassignable:"

Strivers (26 percent of the U.S., also high in France and Spain). Young, success-seeking, leading time-pressured lives. Materialistic, pleasure-oriented, seek instant gratification and convenience. These are mostly "baby-boomers" in the U.S., but are older in other countries such as Germany.

Achievers (22 percent of the U.S., also high in Spain). Slightly older, already successful, affluent. Opinion-leaders, status-conscious. Seek to buy quality.

Pressured (13 percent of the U.S.). Mostly women, facing financial or familial pressure. Highly stressed.

Adapters (18 percent of the U.S., higher in Germany). Older, with somewhat traditional values but open-minded, living comfortably in their golden years.

Traditionals (16 percent of the U.S., higher in Germany). Most traditional and conservative, prefer to stick to the familiar and established in their personal lives and their consumption patterns.

The BSB survey finds many other very interesting differences and patterns both within and across countries. Within Japan, for instance, there appear to be major differences in value-orientation between men and women, and between younger and older consumers. Men believe more in traditional family roles than women, and younger Japanese are more materialistic and consumption-oriented than older Japanese. These data suggest that values and attitudes might shift dramatically in Japan with the changes in generations. Across the U.S. and Japan, meanwhile, the research showed that while U.S. strivers sought cars that were fun, stylish, and fast, Japanese strivers were most interested in extra features such as expensive stereo systems and lace curtains—they considered their car an extra room of their home![25] Other research also exists on consumer segments within Japan, including a major new segmentation scheme developed by SRI, who created VALS and VALS II in the United States (see Chapter 6).

Finally, the Young & Rubicam ad agency has its own theory-based global segmentation scheme, called Cross Cultural Consumer Characterizations (4Cs), in which consumers in twenty countries have been placed into seven segments based on data on their goals, motivations, and values. These seven segments include two are characterized by financial insecurity, three that comprise the "middle majority" (seeking success and achievement but also security and conformity), and two that are more driven by either internal values or social betterment.

In sum, many of the global segmentation schemes discussed above—and the many others not discussed here—find (not surprisingly) between five to seven groups of consumers, varying chiefly on the dimensions of income, desire for material success and social acceptance, and personal or social idealism. Put rather crudely, every country has its rich, middle-class, and poor, those who live their lives "keeping up with the Joneses" and those who instead are dreamers and rebels. Since human nature and circumstance are essentially the same no matter where you live, this should not come as a surprise. The challenge facing a global marketer and advertiser is in not only knowing the global segment to which your target consumer belongs, but also the local differences that make that same consumer different in one country than in another. The following section discusses the need to focus on both simultaneously.

SEEKING A BALANCE: PLANNING GLOBALLY BUT ACTING LOCALLY . . . .

Not surprisingly, the solution to this global-versus-local dilemma is to modify products just enough in local markets to make them strong competitors in those local markets, but to maintain whatever uniformity is possible across multiple markets to allow for some of the potential global economies of scale to be realized. This is often called a strategy of *glocalization*, or "planning globally but acting locally." In essence, companies try to centralize and coordinate as much as possible, to save money and cut costs—such as research and development expenditures, the shooting of footage or photographs for ad commercials, certain key-account sales and service activities, and so on. At the same time, they localize those marketing activities that are most effective in differentiating the brand from a local perspective, such as the choice of "add-on" accessories or service packages offered to the local customer.[26]

A frequently-used compromise between complete standardization and complete localization is one of regional or "country cluster/segment" standardization, in which the product is varied to match regional or country segment/cluster tastes, but uniformity is maintained within that region or segment. Thus Polaroid markets a Spectra System of cameras and accessories in the United States, but the same line is called its Image System in Europe—and marketed on the same pan-European basis by its European headquarters.[27] Apart from using geographical convenience, the clusters or segments used might also be based on common needs (such as new mothers, international business travelers, etc.), demographics (such as teenagers), or psychographics (such as the different global value segments discussed in the previous section).

No matter what the exact strategy followed, it is vital that the global marketing program make sufficient use of prior research about the acceptability in other countries of marketing practices in another, and allow the local subsidiary managers adequate input into the tailoring of marketing programs for their countries.[28] It is the local P&G manager in Venezuela, for instance, and not someone based in Cincinnati, who must decide if the commercial positioning developed for Pro-V formula Pantene shampoo in Taiwan—that it strengthens the hair and makes it shine—will also work in Venezuela (which it did).[29] Global companies, such as Nestlé, have elaborate "cross-pollination" mechanisms and systems to ensure that marketing ideas and practices used in one market are known and made available to managers in other countries, such as newsletters and conferences. But the decision of whether and when to use a particular idea is usually left to local managers, though there is often strong central prodding to reuse an existing idea than to start from scratch, in order to save money.

GLOBAL BRANDING AND POSITIONING . . . .

As just discussed, because a global marketing strategy attempts both to standardize (in order to conserve resources) and to localize (in order to be maximizally responsive to local market needs), a *global brand* is rarely the same identical combination of product, package, name, positioning, and advertising execution all over the world. Instead, the brand is more likely to appear in each of those countries using one of a few alternative formulations, packages, names and ad campaigns, with the exact "mix" varying by country or region. For instance, the same Palmolive soap can appear worldwide in three different shapes, seven fragrances, one core packaging design, and two related positionings, one each for the developed and developing countries.[30]

Given the apparent advantages of global branding and the many factors arguing for such brands, just how widespread is the practice of *global branding*? The consulting company Interbrand claims that seven of the world's top ten brands are American: Coca-Cola, Kellogg's, McDonald's, Kodak, Marlboro, IBM, and American Express.[31] One research study has shown, however, at least as far as brands originating in the United States are concerned, the international diffusion of such brands is actually rather limited. With the exception of a few "star" brands (presumably brands like Coca-Cola), most of these U.S.–based international brands still obtained the vast majority of their sales from the U.S. and Canada. When brands do expand into other markets, they tend to expand first into culturally similar markets (such as the U.K., for a brand from the U.S.), and they tend to use the same brand name. It also did not appear, in this research study, that standardized brands were either "younger" or "older" in age than nonstandardized brands: local brands do not necessarily "mature" into global brands.[32]

Building a global brand is obviously an extremely challenging task. Obviously, the general principles of brand-building in any one country apply, such as creating strong brand awareness and strong, positive, and consistent brand associations, and a strong visual brand identity, such as an logo or symbol (see Chapter 8 for some details). Advertising plays a major (but not exclusive) role in these, as it does in establishing the brand's reputation for high and consistent quality, another key component of building a brand's equity. For a brand that seeks to be global, however, an additional requirement is a certain core consistency of brand imagery worldwide—but one that still works locally in each market. Alvin Schechter, chairman and chief executive of the Schechter Group, a New York design consultancy, points out that "it may be global marketing, but it's (still) *received* locally."[33]

Brands strong in one country (such as the U.S.) that seek to become global must first find out what equities the brand has in its home country, determine through research which of these are transferable to the new target countries, and then find out how they can best be leveraged and communicated in that new market. Many discover that not all the equities that are strong in the home country can be leveraged in other markets: Ford, Chrysler, Kraft, and American Airlines, for example, have much stronger brand equity in the U.S. than in the U.K.[34] Brands going global also face the special challenges of obtaining access to distribution and to raw materials and other resources, access taken for granted in the home market.[35] Indeed, many global marketers seeking to enter new markets choose acquisitions of existing local brands, or joint ventures with them, as the most efficient ways to gain such access, instead of simply extending their existing brands into the new market.

Once such a strong brand identity has been established, great care has to be taken to protect the brand against trade mark infringement of all of the brand's various equities (name, logo, packaging design and colors, etc.). Such *intellectual property rights* are not legislated and/or enforced with equal vigor in different parts of the world, and a global marketer must be especially vigilant to protect these rights, for they form the essence of the asset we have called the global brand.

GLOBAL ADVERTISING . . . .

Given the background above on the forces making for global marketing and branding, it should come as no surprise that there are many marketers who see an inexorable drive to more global advertising as well. Obviously, there are many others who see such globalization as impossible, given the many differences that exist across countries, cultures, and markets. But this global-versus-local debate is really pointless, because, in reality, the issue is not one of whether an ad campaign for a brand can be completely *globalized*, but rather of the extent or degree to which a global brand's campaign can be *standardized* across the world.

According to Sandra Moriarty and Thomas Duncan, such advertising standardization can vary on a continuum, if one breaks up an ad into its *message strategy* and *tactical execution* components. At one extreme, an advertiser could totally standardize both the advertising message strategy and the tactical message executions. Next on the continuum would be a standardized strategy with *translated executions*, followed by standardized strategy with *modified executions*, to *totally localized strategy and executions* on the other extreme.[36] Taken literally, the extreme of having the same strategy and identical execution in every country implies a nonverbal presentation (to get around language barriers). While this happens occasionally, it is rare. Thus, the options are usually ones of having the same strategy or modifying it and, if the same strategy is retained, of merely translating the tactical execution or modifying it more substantially.

Research shows that most global marketers still tend to use the *substantial modification* or *complete localization* approaches more than *complete standardization*. One recent survey of international advertisers found that only 9 percent claimed to use totally standardized advertising in all markets, 37 percent used completed localized advertising, while a majority (54 percent) used local agencies to tailor an umbrella strategy theme to the customs, values and lifestyles of their local markets.[37] Another survey of major U.S.–based multinationals found that advertising standardized themes and creative contexts (i.e., executional elements) were both used about 40 percent of the time, with *larger* multinationals, with *larger local operations*, in *more affluent local markets*, tending to do more localization.[38]

Standardization appears to be more common for television advertisements than for print advertisements; among business-to-business and high-tech product categories (e.g. computers, audio and video equipment, cars); and among emotion-, image-, and fashion-oriented (so-called *high-touch*) product categories (e.g. fragrances, clothing, jewelry).[39] Standardized strategies and campaigns appear most appropriate and effective when the product is utilitarian and the message is informational, or when a brand's identity and desirability are integrally linked to a specific national character (e.g., Coca-Cola or McDonald's), according to the copy-testing firm of McCullom-Spielman.[40] Ad campaigns for food and beverage products are often the hardest to standardize, since eating and drinking habits and beliefs are often very culture-bound. It is easier to standardize advertising for a new brand than it is for an old, established, brand, which may already have multiple and hard-to-reconcile images in different local regions of the world, and may be at different life-cycle stages in different markets, thus facing incompatible marketing challenges. It is also easier to standardize campaigns across Western markets (e.g., the U.S. and Germany) than across Western and Eastern markets (e.g. the U.S. and Japan).

While the fully standardized approach is rarely used, there did appear for a time to be a trend to moving towards more standardization,[41] although some very recent data suggests this trend may now be reversing back to a preference for localization.[42] A trend toward standardization would be in accordance with the many forces discussed earlier in this chapter: the increasing globalization of markets and of media, the increasing degree of cultural convergence among consumers of various countries, and the possibility for cost savings in market research and advertising production costs. To this must be added the desire of companies to fully leverage creative ideas and concepts that are successful in one market and have the potential to be successful elsewhere. Powerful creative ideas are scarce (see Chapter 13), and one business advantage enjoyed by large global enterprises is this ability to tap a pool of powerful creative ideas and concepts from across the world. Some other research finds that when agencies and clients attempt to standardize, media research, scheduling and buying were found to be comparatively the hardest to standardize.[43]

We can discuss the possibilities of creating standardized ad campaigns at each of the four levels used as the organizing theme in this book: *message strategy*, *message tactics*, *media strategy*, and *media tactics*.

MESSAGE STRATEGY . . . .

Message strategy has to do with the choice of the benefit to be conveyed, as well as the positioning and segmentation choices. It is often easiest, in developing a global brand, to standardize on the core positioning platform for the brand, while allowing for local executional variations in other brand elements. If the basic need being met is common the world over, the same message strategy can likely be employed.

Thus, Oil of Olay uses the same positioning—a moisturizing cream for mature women—even though the name, formulation, and packaging can vary slightly across markets. Procter & Gamble sells its Pert Plus Shampoo-and-Conditioner product with the same "BC-18" formula under different names in different countries, but in all markets still uses the basic message of time-saving ("wash-and-go") convenience.[44] Chanel and other fragrances can appeal worldwide to the same human need (to look beautiful), and Swatch watches to the same universal need to have fun.

On the other hand, the same product or service may sometimes need to be positioned very differently in different markets, if the market is at different levels of economic development or product life cycle, or if the habits and attitudes toward that product category are culturally influenced, or if the competitive position of the brand is very different.

Economic Differences

Citibank positions its automated, twenty-four-hour, globally networked consumer banking facilities using a "convenience" positioning in Hong Kong and Germany, but as a high-status, lifestyle aspirational symbol in Greece and certain economically less developed countries. Similarly, the Honda Accord car is a mid-market sedan in the affluent United States market but occupies a more upscale, premium position in the car markets of various less economically developed Asian and eastern European countries.

Consumer Behavior Differences

General Foods found that its orange drink Tang had to be sold in France as an "anytime" cold refreshing beverage, rather than as a breakfast drink, because orange juice is not a breakfast tradition in France. Other research has shown that, in the 1970s, while car advertisers in the U.S. found it best to emphasize leisure and get-to-the-wilderness benefits of car ownership, consumers in Brazil were apparently more responsive to the benefits of being able to use cars to travel to urban culture.[45]

Competitive Resource Differences

These are illustrated by the Heineken beer example cited earlier, which developed historically as a mass-market beer in Europe, but decided it would be more feasible to aim at an upscale target in the U.S., with a premium positioning, rather than fight the likes of Budweiser for the mass-market there.

Even if the same target market and same core positioning proposition are used in many different markets in the world, important variations may be necessary across these markets. For instance, Johnny Walker Black Label, the world's largest scotch whisky brand, has a very strong and premium brand image across the world. Research showed that its equities everywhere included its square-sided bottle, the black and gold coloring on the diagonally-centered label, and so on. However, this research also showed that while the brand was perceived everywhere as being a premium, luxury brand, it varied across countries in the extent to which it was seen as old-fashioned and traditional, versus modern and elegant—and consumers in different countries varied in which of those two kinds of luxury scotch whiskies they preferred. The advertising brief for the different countries thus varied in whether it emphasized the "old-fashioned, genuine, traditional" angle or the "more modern, sophisticated, elegant" angle, while keeping to the common core positioning of "luxury, premium" positioning.[46]

MESSAGE TACTICS . . . .

Message tactics have to do with the tone and format of the advertising message selected: the choice of relying on an image-oriented, rational, emotional, humor-based, fear-based, comparative (etc.) approach. Many studies have shown that advertisers in different countries vary in the preference for creating advertising that uses a rational or informative approach, versus a "softer-sell" emotional or image-based approach. This presumably has to do with cultural differences across consumers in these countries, although it is also possible that advertisers in some countries use a common advertising style or approach simply because that's what every other local advertiser seems to have always used (in other words, out of habit and ignorance rather than out of carefully considered choice). Another reason for such differences may be laws or traditions concerning the acceptability of comparative advertising, which are not allowed or shunned in many countries (see Chapter 18).

Much research, has shown, for example that Japanese ads tend to be more "indirect," less "pushy," more laden with symbolism, less copy-intensive, more emotional, more humorous, more status-oriented, more aimed at building company image, and less comparative, than ads in the United States.[47] British TV ads tend to be more soft-sell in approach and more entertaining than U.S. TV ads, for a variety of cultural, historical, and advertising practice reasons.[48] French print ads tend to use less information and more sex appeals (and more humor and emotion), than print ads in the U.S.[49] German ads tend to be relatively more direct and factual, using more information,[50] as do ads in the People's Republic of China (though this may soon change).[51]

Rational ads tend to be less attention-getting and less persuasive than emotional and humorous ads in the U.K. and France, according to copy-testing research. This research also suggests that Europeans are relatively more likely than Americans to view their local ads as entertaining, but also more likely to have trouble understanding those ads![52] A great deal of other research has attempted to measure the information content of ads in various countries and concludes that, in general, U.S. advertising is less informative than that in Asia, but is more so than that in Europe. U.S. ads are also more likely to use a "lecture" fomat than are ads in Taiwan and France, which are more likely to be "drama"-oriented.[53] ("Dramas" versus "Lectures" are discussed in Chapter 9).

Such differences arise for a complex variety of cultural reasons (e.g., the historical importance of imagery and symbolism in Japanese literature, or the German preference for stressing concrete and tangible concepts over fantasy).[54] In addition, they are also influenced by the presence or absence of laws about comparative advertising or advertising substantiation and deceptiveness, and so on. One research study found that ads in France and Taiwan tend to "overpromise" about what the product can deliver, compared to U.S. ads.[55] Such differences could also be caused by media cost and availability: Japanese ads may be less copy-intensive in part because they are mostly fifteen-second spots, to allow for higher repetition and smaller budgets.[56] But just because ads in a certain country tend to be of a certain kind doesn't mean they should always be that way. A study conducted in the UK, France, and Germany by the copy-testing company GfK found that in all three countries, consumers wished that their local ads would be more informative, easier to understand, more believable—and less emotional.[57] Japanese consumers have been exposed to comparative advertising only since 1987, and some advertisers believe that Japanese ads are now becoming more "hard-sell," although the empirical evidence on this is not clear.[58]

It could be argued (and debated) that such differences in national character and preferences might diminish over time as we move toward greater cultural homogeneity in the world. Given these current differences in local advertising practice and preference—and in differences in media and production costs—however, it is not surprising that most global companies tend to modify their local advertising to suit these local needs.[59] A study found, for example, that Japan-based and German-based companies advertising in Indonesia, Spain, and the U.S. all tended to adapt their advertising approaches to these markets.[60]

Even if the same creative approach is used across countries, the specific executional elements may need to be varied. For example, humor needs special care when used in multiple markets, because there are well-documented differences in what consumers in different countries find to be funny (see Chapters 9 and 12). The use of an emotional appeal must recognize the fact that while some societies are highly emotionally demonstrative, others prefer more sedate and private behaviors. If the creative tactic is the use of logic and reasoned argument, the level and nature of the arguments used may need to be adapted to the education and product-category knowledge levels of the target consumer. A consumer in India doesn't have to be told about the quality of a brand of tea, for example, but a European consumer might. A fear appeal may work better if it uses local variations in what people find most threatening and anxiety-provoking. The choice of expert or celebrity endorser may also need to vary across countries, although a few endorsers may have an appeal that transcends national boundaries (such as Michael Jackson for Pepsi, or Arnold Palmer for Rolex).

Research has also shown that Europeans are, in general, more skeptical of advertising than are Americans, and like their ads less.[61] The copytesting company McCollum-Spielman has also found, in developing copy-test norms for recall and persuasion across twenty-four countries, that consumers in different countries vary tremendously in the degree to which they pay attention to ads and/or are persuaded by them. For instance, Japanese consumers are very unlikely to pay attention to ads (the average level of awareness created by ads is apparently low) but are, in contrast, very likely to be persuaded (the average level of persuasion, as measured by copy tests, is very high). They also report that the same standardized ad execution is very likely to get very different recall and/or persuasion scores in different countries.[62]

As a result of such differences in what kinds of advertising "works best" in each country, many global advertisers use the same positioning or theme or creative idea across local markets, but then give the advertising execution a local twist. For instance, Snuggle fabric softener uses the same creative idea of a cuddly animal but varies which animal it uses in different markets. Impulse deodorant spray uses the same idea of a romantic outcome emerging after the consumer "acts on impulse" but varies the local settings and casting. Obviously, product shots have to match the local packaging, and this can sometimes be changed through the use of computer graphics techniques. If fresh local production is not required, the same centrally produced television footage or print photographs or art can simply be dubbed or overlaid with the local language. The other extreme is to produce the local ad entirely from scratch, in which case there are obviously few, if any, savings in production costs. In a few cases local regulations may even mandate the use of locally shot footage.

Obviously, the more the standardization, the more the potential savings in time and cost. Ads that rely largely on visuals and music are more easy to use in multiple markets than those that are copy-heavy or use slogans (which often do not translate well). Gillette used the same emotional images of the link between father and son for its Sensor brand of razor across European markets after tests showed they were interpreted the same way. Global companies attempt to create campaigns that they think have the best chances of succeeding worldwide (or in as many markets as possible) and then ask their local subsidiaries to try to use that global campaign unless local modifications are proven to be essential. Many create the photography, television shooting, and music-track recording in one central location (often called the *lead agency*) and then urge or require local agencies to use them whenever possible, following specified use guidelines or standards. (Local voice tracks can easily be added on.) Local modifications and extensions are often subjected to a central approval process. Gilbey's gin, for instance, which is sold in 150 countries, developed a campaign in New York and then offered it to the various ad agencies that handled the account in various markets. They were offered the options of running it unchanged, adapting it for local use, or running their own locally created ads—if they scored at least as well as the New York campaign in local copy tests.[63]

MEDIA STRATEGY . . . .

Media strategy refers to the setting and allocation of advertising budgets. Logic would suggest that there are more factors that argue for differences across countries than for similarities. Ad budgets would be likely similar across countries if purchase cycles for that product category are similar, since the frequency of exposure often depends on the length of the purchase cycle. On the other hand, there are many more factors that most likely will be different across countries: the absolute and relative costs of various media, the number of target consumers reached by these media, the spending levels and patterns of competitive brands, the product life cycle stage and household penetration percentages for the product category, and so on.

For example, the cost-per-thousand people (for adults 15 and older) in 1993 for a thirty-second prime-time TV spot ranged from about $5 in Japan to almost $24 in Switzerland (and about $7 in the U.S. and U.K., and $12–13 in much of Western Europe).[64] Thus, it is very likely that a multinational might need to have widely varying ad budgets (on a pro rata basis) in many markets. Further, the allocations of a given budget across media categories might need to be different too. For example, although cinema advertising is extremely minor in the U.S., it is a major advertising medium in many parts of Asia. Research has confirmed that advertisers in different countries follow very divergent methods to determine their advertising budgets and vary widely in how their budgets are allocated across media.[65]

MEDIA TACTICS . . . .

Media tactics refers to the allocation of advertising budgets across specific media vehicles. Since by far the bulk of the media options available in any market are local or regional—specific to that country—the media planning and buying almost always have to be done at a local or regional level.[66] Countries also vary dramatically in the degree to which various media reach different audiences, and in the availability of advertising time and space in those media. For instance, databased direct marketing is still quite small in most markets outside the United States, because the availability of lists is very limited (although this is changing slowly, especially in Europe).

This need for local decision making is made even stronger by the absence in many markets of the kinds of syndicated media data we discussed in Chapter 17, so that unless the media planner is physically in the local market there is almost no way of knowing the relative costs and efficiencies of local media options. Usually, therefore, the media planning and buying are done locally, but the core elements of media strategy—such as the target audience definition, the reach and frequency goals, and so on—may still be decided centrally, or at least be made subject to central approval.

While such local media buying is therefore usually necessary, it must be noted that the late 1980s and early 1990s have seen a dramatic increase in the number of global or regional media channels, such as satellite-based TV channels that are either received directly at home via satellite-receiving dishes, or via cable. These include Star TV in Asia (which by 1993 was reaching over 45 million viewers in thirty-eight countries), SuperChannel in Europe (reaching over 55 million households), Telemundo and Univision in Latin America, and MTV (237 million households) and Cable News Network (CNN) the world over. Experts have put the growth rate of such media at between 10 to 15 percent per year.[67]

It is thus becoming possible to make centralized (and thus cost-efficient) cross-country media buys using some of these media channels, and large global advertisers are in a position to obtain lower prices from such channels by virtue of the size of their media buys. For example, Unilever would deal in a centralized manner with Star TV in Hong Kong to buy satellite coverage for many of the Asian markets reached by Star TV in which local Unilever subsidiaries operate (such as India, Indonesia, etc.), and would obtain lower prices because these media buys are several times bigger than those of local Indian or Indonesian competitors. It should be noted that such media buys are still mostly made for ad campaigns that vary by country. Truly global media buys—using absolutely standardized campaigns placed in media with multinational reach—is still very small, and aimed mostly at English-speaking business executives or key national elites.[68]

Finally, it should also be noted that media institutional arrangements also vary greatly across countries. Much more media buying is done via huge media organizations in Europe (e.g., Carat in France) than is currently done in the United States, for instance, although there have recently been legislative restrictions restricting it in Europe.[69] And, while agency compensation is still mostly commission-based in the U.S., it is fee-based or calculated on a cost-plus basis in many other parts of the world.[70]

ORGANIZING FOR GLOBAL ADVERTISING. . . . . . .

International advertising networks have existed since 1899, when J. Walter Thompson first went international. McCann-Erickson opened its London office in the 1920s, to handle Standard Oil, one of the first truly global brands. Since then, most larger agencies and agency holding companies have greatly expanded their international networks, through full- or part-ownerships of local agencies, joint ventures, strategic alliances, etc. Today, at least thirteen ad agency networks have operations or affiliates in more than thirty-nine countries each. These thirteen include Backer Spielvogel Bates, BBDO, Leo Burnett, D'arcy Masius Benton and Bowles, DDB Needham, FCB Publicis, GGK, Grey, Lintas/Ammirati, Ogilvy and Mather, Saatchi & Saatchi, J. Walter Thompson, Young & Rubicam, and McCann-Erickson.[71] As discussed in Chapter 1, several of these belong to one agency holding group (e.g., Lintas/Ammirati and McCann-Erickson are both part of Interpublic).

Much of this growth in international agency networks occurred during the late 1980s. There are at least two reasons for this growth. First, global clients (such as Procter & Gamble, Unilever, Johnson & Johnson, S. C. Johnson, Nestlé, Philip Morris, etc.) are greatly expanding their operations outside their home markets and have increasingly begun to consolidate their accounts at one or two global agencies that can service that accounts' needs in most or all of the countries in which that brand is marketed. For example, in 1991, BBDO serviced the Pepsi account in forty countries over the world.[72] Such consolidation can lead to reduced production costs, enhanced coordination, and a greater chance that a consistent brand image is projected worldwide. While the trend toward such consolidation seems strong, some research has shown that in most cases client companies still use different agencies for their home markets (e.g. the U.S.) and for overseas.[73]

The other reason is simply that the rate of growth in advertising spending has recently become very high outside North America and western Europe, so that ad agencies based in those regions have been driven to expand into other markets to take advantage of that advertising billings potential. In the late 1980s, Japan was the second biggest advertising market outside the U.S., followed by the U.K., Germany, Canada, France, Italy, Spain, Australia, Brazil, Netherlands, Switzerland, Finland, Sweden, and Denmark.[74]

As part of these global servicing requirements, global clients have begun to demand centralized account servicing structures from agencies so that the global headquarters personnel of the client can deal with just one account team at the agency that is reponsible for the creation, coordination, and implementation of the global ad campaign for that client. (It should be remembered here that by a *global ad campaign*, we do not mean one that is used unchanged in every local market, but rather one that is modified by locally affiliated agencies on an as-needed basis.). In response, most global agencies now have a few key account personnel (in New York, London, etc.) that serve as the global account managers who deal with the headquarters personnel of these global companies. These global account managers, in turn, then deal with the local account managers for that account in the various networked local agencies. The local account managers then deal with the local client personnel in either adapting the global ad campaign or in creating the local campaign, and in planning and implementing the local media buys.

Obviously, one of the key barriers or problems to creating global ad campaigns is the possible resistance of local ad agency and/or client personnel to campaigns "not invented there" but imposed centrally from elsewhere. To help overcome this, many global campaigns are created with advance input from the personnel of local operations (both client and agency) and may even use multinational account and creative teams at the central location (e.g., McCann-Erickson reportedly has a creative team in New York working on Coca-Cola's global campaigns that consists of people of various nationalities). Such multinational teams may be permanent, or temporary (assembled for a particular campaign and then dissolved, with the members returning to their home countries). In addition, the advertising concept developed centrally is almost always tested locally, to see if it will work well there. Even the Marlboro (cigarette) Man and Tony the Tiger (for Kellogg's cereals) symbols have had to be carefully tested around the world, and were by Leo Burnett. When such local tests reveal that fine-tuning is needed, this gives the agency an opportunity to get local creatives to help improve the ad with their changes. Not only does this make the ad work better in that local market, it also gives the local creatives a sense of co-authorship—the "not invented here" resistance gives way to an "we improved it here" enthusiasm.[75]

Another reason for such centralized campaign creation is that creative talent (such as creative directors) is often scarce in certain parts of the world.[76] It is hard for Citibank's ad agency in Belgium, for instance, to create a satisfactory campaign from scratch, because the best creative talent in Belgium often prefers to work in Paris, with its bigger opportunities, rather than in Brussels. Even when creative talent is easily available locally, centralized campaign creation has the advantage of making sure that the creative product produced locally is not different from the kind desired merely because the creative style and philosophy of the local agency differed from that of the central agency (instead of a difference in marketing circumstances).[77]

SUMMARY. . . . .

A few key conclusions can be drawn that will serve to summarize this chapter. First, there are many potential advantages to creating globally coordinated brands and ad campaigns, but, in most cases, there are enough variations in local consumer, competitive, cultural, and economic conditions to make complete standardization impossible or infeasible. Despite the increasing convergence of markets, consumers and media across the world, vast differences remain. Thus, most companies try to balance global and local needs as best they can, often by creating strategies and creative ideas centrally but allowing local tactical and executional variations. In doing so, they seek to use ad agencies with global resources and networks, and both clients and agencies are modifying their structures and systems to implement global ad campaigns.

DISCUSSION QUESTIONS . . . .

1. If you have traveled or lived overseas, write down some differences in consumer attitudes or behavior that you noticed while outside your home country. How do you think these differences might affect the marketing and advertising of products?
2. Do you agree that North American and western European cultures are relatively more "secular," "low-context," and "individual-oriented," compared to Asian cultures? Why or why not?
3. Which brands do you think are truly global brands? What do you think gives them this global appeal?
4. Can you think of some examples of ads that you have seen recently that might have some problems if they ran unchanged in some other countries? In which countries would they have a problem, and why? How might they need to be modified to run in those countries?

NOTES. . . . .

1. See the article "Brands: It's Thrive or Die" in *Fortune*, August 23, 1993, pp. 32–36, including the box on "Asia, Where the Big Brands are Blooming."
2. Theodore Levitt, "The Globalization of Markets," *Harvard Business Review*, 61, no. 3 (May–June 1983), 92–102.
3. See, for example, Joanne Lipman, "Marketers Turn Sour on Global Sales Pitch Harvard Guru Makes," *The Wall Street Journal*, May 12, 1988, p. A1.
4. See Lipman's article in the *The Wall Street Journal*, op. cit., for these and other examples.
5. See Lipman's article in the *Wall Street Journal*, op. cit., for these and other examples.
6. David A. Ricks, *Big Business Blunders: Mistakes in Multinational Marketing*, (Columbus, OH: Grid, 1983).
7. See, for example, David K. Tse, Russell W. Belk, and Nan Zhou, "Becoming a Consumer Society: A Longitudinal and Cross-Cultural Content Analysis of Print Ads from Hong Kong, the People's Republic of China, and Taiwan," *Journal of Consumer Research*, 15 (March 1989), 457–472.
8. Wilbur Schramm, *The Process and Effects of Mass Communication* (Urbana, IL: University of Illinois Press, 1954).

9. Max Weber, *The Sociology of Religion* (Boston: Beacon Press, 1964).

10. Edward T. Hall, *Beyond Culture* (Garden City, NY: Doubleday, 1976).

11. Hazel Rose Markus and Shinobu Kitayama, "Culture and the Self: Implications for Cognition, Emotion, and Motivation," *Psychological Review*, 98, no. 2 (1991), 224–253; Harry C. Triandis, "The Self and Social Behavior in Differing Cultural Contexts," *Psychological Review*, 96, no. 3 (1989), 506–520.

12. Rita Martenson, "International Advertising in Cross-Cultural Environments," *Journal of International Consumer Marketing*, 2, no. 1 (1989), 7–18.

13. Judith L. Zaichkowsky and James H. Sood, "A Global Look at Consumer Involvement and Use of Products," *International Marketing Review*, 6, no. 1 (1989), 20–34.

14. See, for instance, Srinivas Durvasala, J. Craig Andrews, Steven Lysonski, and Richard G. Netemeyer, "Assessing the Cross-National Applicability of Consumer Behavior Models: A Model of Attitude toward Advertising in General," *Journal of Consumer Research*, 19 (March 1993), 626–636.

15. John A. Quelch and Edward J. Hoff, "Customizing Global Marketing," *Harvard Business Review*, 64, no. 3 (May–June 1986), 59–68, and Barry N. Rosen, Jean J. Boddewyn, and Ernst A. Louis, "U.S. Brands Abroad: An Empirical Study of Global Branding," *International Marketing Review*, 6, no. 1 (1988), 7–19.

16. For these and other examples see Hirotake Takeuchi and Michael E. Porter, "Three Roles of International Marketing in Global Strategy," in Michael E. Porter, *Competition in Global Industries* (Cambridge, MA: Harvard Business School Press, 1986).

17. "Global Ads: Fashion, Fact, or Fantasy?", *Campaign*, November 28, 1986, pp. 67–69.

18. See, for example, the "EuroBarometer" report on "Young Europeans in 1990" by the Commission of the European Communities, Brussels/Luxembourg, May 1991.

19. See Charles F. Frazer, "Issues and Evidence in International Advertising," *Current Issues and Research in Advertising*, James H. Leigh and Claude R. Martin, Jr., eds. (Ann Arbor: University of Michigan School of Business Administration, 1989).

20. Barbara Mueller, "Standardization vs. Specialization: An Examination of Westernization in Japanese Advertising," *Journal of Advertising Research*, 32, no. 1 (1992), 15–24.

21. Some references on such country-of-origin effects include Gary M. Erickson, Johny K. Johansson and Paul Chao, "Image Variables in Multi-Attribute Product Evaluations: Country of Origin Effects," *Journal of Consumer Research*, 11 (September, 1984), 694–699; C. Min Han, "Country Image: Halo or Summary Construct?" *Journal of Marketing Research*, 26 (May 1989), 222–229; and Sung-Tai Hong and Robert S. Wyer, Jr., "Effects of Country-of-Origin and Product Attribute Information on Product Evaluation: An Information Processing Perspective," *Journal of Consumer Research*, 16 (September 1989), 175–187.

22. D. Peabody, *National Characteristics* (New York: Cambridge University Press, 1985).

23. For a discussion of cross-cultural psychology, see M. H. Segall, *Cross-Cultural Psychology: Human Behavior in Global Perspective* (Monterey, CA: Brooks/Cole, 1989), and H. Knepler and M. Knepler, *Crossing Cultures* (New York: Macmillan, 1983).

24. Alfred S. Boote, "Psychographic Segmentation in Europe," *Journal of Advertising Research*, 22, no. 6 (December 1982/January 1983), 19–25.

25. Many of these details about the BSB Global Scan survey and some of the other global segmentation schemes briefly reported here are taken from the chapter on "Going Global: International Psychographics," in Rebecca Piirto, *Beyond Mind Games* (Ithaca, NY: American Demographics Books, 1991). The interested reader should consult this excellent book for more details.

26. Takeuchi and Porter, op. cit.

27. Cited in Kamran Kashani and John A. Quelch, "Can Sales Promotion Go Global," *Business Horizons* (May–June 1993), 37–43.

28. Kamran Kashani, "Beware the Pitfalls of Global Marketing," *Harvard Business Review* (September–October 1989), 91–98.

29. "P&G sees success in policy of transplanting ad ideas," *Advertising Age*, July 19, 1993, p. I-2.

30. Maureen R. Marston, "Transferring Equity Across Borders," *Journal of Advertising Research* (May–June 1992), RC-3–5.

31. "Things Go Better with Brands," *Industry Week,* September 21, 1992, p. 11.

32. Rosen, Boddewyn, and Louis, op. cit.

33. "How Big Is Your Umbrella?" *BrandWeek*, December 6, 1993, pp. 22–23.

34. *BrandWeek*, December 1993, op. cit.

35. Clay Edmunds, "Evaluating the Equities in Your American Brand: Will they Translate in the E.C.?", *Journal of European Business* (March/April 1991), 11–16. See also Christine Restall, "Multinational Brand Marketing" in *Understanding Brands*, Don Cowley, ed. (London: Kogan Page, 1991).

36. Sandra E. Moriarty and Thomas R. Duncan, "Global Advertising: Issues and Practices," *Journal of Current Issues and Research in Advertising* (1990), 313–341.

37. Robert E. Hite and Cynthia Fraser, "International Advertising Strategies of Multinational Corporations," *Journal of Advertising Research* (August/September 1988), 9–17.

38. William L. James and John S. Hill, "International Advertising Messages: To Adapt or Not to Adapt," *Journal of Advertising Research* (June/July 1991), 65–71.

39. The evidence for this and some of the points below can be found in Moriarty and Duncan, op. cit.

40. "Global Advertising: Standardized or Multi-Cultural?" *Topline*, McCollum-Spielman Worldwide, no. 37 (June 1992).

41. Cited in Moriarty and Duncan, op. cit.

42. Ali Kanso, "International Advertising Strategies," *Journal of Advertising Research*, 32, no. 1 (January/February 1992), 10–14.

43. Heribert Meffert, and Jurgen Althans, "Global Advertising: Multi-National vs. International," *International Advertiser*, (February 1986), 34–37.

44. Wolfgang Breur and Richard Kohler, "Procter & Gamble in Europe: A roll-out launch," in *Marketing in Europe: Case Studies*, Jordi Montana, ed. (London: Sage Publications, 1994), 121–134.

45. Richard Tansey, Michael R. Hyman, and George M. Zinkhan, "Cultural Themes in Brazilian and U.S. Auto Ads: A Cross-Cultural Comparison," *Journal of Advertising*, 19, no. 2 (1990), 30–39.

46. See the case study on this brand in David Arnold, *The Handbook of Brand Management* (London: *The Economist* Books, 1992), pp. 231–236.

47. Many of these studies are reviewed by Moriarty and Duncan, cited earlier. See also C. Anthony Di Benedetto, Mariko Tamate and Rajan Chandran, "Developing Creative Advertising Strategy for the Japanese Marketplace," *Journal of Advertising Research*, 32, no. 1 (1992), 39–48, and Jyotika Ramaprasad and Kazumi Hasegawa, "Creative Strategies in American and Japanese TV Commercials: A Comparison," same issue, pp. 59–67.

48. Terence Nevett, "Differences Between American and British Television Advertising: Explanations and Implications", *Journal of Advertising*, 21, no. 4 (1992), 61–71.

49. Abhijit Biswas, Janeen E. Olsen and Valerie Carlet, "A Comparison of Print Advertisements from the United States and France," *Journal of Advertising*, 21, no. 4 (1992), 73–81.

50. John L. Graham, Michael L. Kamins and Djoko S. Oetome, "Content Analysis of German and Japanese Advertising in Print Media from Indonesia, Spain, and the United States," *Journal of Advertising*, 22, no. 2 (1993), 5–15.

51. Marshall D. Rice and Zaiming Lu, "A Content Analysis of Chinese Magazine Advertisements," *Journal of Advertising*, 17, no. 4 (1988), 43–48.

52. *Topline*, no. 37, op. cit.

53. See the review in Fred Zandpour, Cypress Chang, and Joelle Catalano, "Stories, Symbols, and Straight Talk: A Comparative Analysis of French, Taiwanese, and U.S. TV Commercials," *Journal of Advertising Research*, 32, no. 1 (1992), 25–38.

54. Graham, Kamins and Oetome, op. cit.

55. Zandpour et al., op. cit.

56. Di Benedetto, op. cit.

57. *Topline*, no. 37, op. cit.
58. "Advertising in Japan: Land of the Hardening Sell," *The Economist*, September 10, 1988; Mueller (1992), op. cit.
59. Nicolaos Synodinos, Charles Keown, and Laurence Jacobs, "Transnational Advertising Practices: A Survey of Leading Brand Advertisers," *Journal of Advertising Research*, 29, no. 2 (1989), 43–50.
60. Graham, Kamins and Oetome, op. cit.
61. "U.S. likes print; U.K. doesn't," *Advertising Age*, May 31, 1993, p. 12.
62. Topline, no. 37, op. cit.
63. See the Advertising column in the *The New York Times*, June 7, 1994, p. C4, for more details.
64. "TV is advertisers' big pick in Europe," *Advertising Age*, June 21, 1993, p. I-19.
65. Nicolaes E. Synodinos, Charles F. Keown, and Lawrence W. Jacobs, "Transnational Advertising Practices," *Journal of Advertising Research* (April/May 1989), 43–50.
66. David W. Stewart and Kevin J. McAuliffe, "Determinants of International Media Purchasing: A Survey of Media Buyers," *Journal of Advertising*, 17, no. 3 (1988), 22–26.
67. W. P. Dizard, Jr., *The Coming Information Age* (New York and London: Longman, 1989).
68. David W. Stewart and Kevin J. McAuliffe, "Determinants of International Media Purchasing: A Survey of Media Buyers," *Journal of Advertising*, 17, no. 3 (1988), 22–26.
69. "French Media Law prompts mergers," *Advertising Age*, October 25, 1993, p. 6.
70. Synodinos, Keown and Jacobs (1989), op. cit.
71. See the annual World Brands report in *Advertising Age*, September 2, 1991, p. 25, and later years.
72. *Advertising Age*, September 1991, op. cit.
73. Barry N. Rosen, Jean J. Boddewyn, and Ernst A. Louis, "Participation by U.S. Agencies in International Brand Advertising: An Empirical Study," *Journal of Advertising*, 17, no. 4 (1988), 14–22.
74. Survey by Starch INRA Hooper, 1987.
75. *Advertising Age*, September 1991, op. cit.
76. Alan T. Shao and John S. Hill, "Executing Transnational Campaigns: Do U.S. Agencies Have the Overseas Talent?" *Journal of Advertising Research*, 32, no. 1 (1992), 49–58.
77. Douglas C. West, "Cross-National Creative Personalities, Processes, and Agency Philosophies," *Journal of Advertising Research* (September/October 1993), 53.

READING . . . .

A BLUEPRINT FOR CAMPAIGNS THAT TRAVEL AROUND THE WORLD . . . .

Noreen O'Leary

After the Supreme Court broke up Standard Oil in 1911, the man running its advertising department was invited by John Rockefeller to create an agency to handle its disparate new operations. In taking the Standard Oil accounts into Europe in the '20s and Latin America in the '30s, Harrison McCann's new shop became a pioneering force in creating the modern global agency.

Today, that head start on international expansion has led to an agency that generates 73% of its $6.7 billings overseas. Longtime McCann-Erickson Worldwide clients such as Coca-

Source: © 1994 ASM Communications, Inc. Used with permission from *Adweek* Magazine.

Cola, Unilever, General Motors and Standard Oil's off-spring, Exxon/Esso, require work to be done in 50 or more countries each.

Such far-flung assignments dictate a nimble yet consistent approach to the creative product. Given its decades of experience, McCann has firm ideas about how to execute ads across international boundaries. For instance, it distanced itself from the trendy "same execution everywhere" theories that took hold in the merger-happy '80s. Rather, McCann sees global clients as existing on a continuum, along which they can move fluidly as their corporate needs change.

"You can't treat brands like precious icons," says Bruce Nelson, who was named executive vice president/director of worldwide accounts last month. "They're running like broncing bulls in a constantly changing marketplace. You have to know how to ride them."

A longtime McCann copywriter, Nelson is the agency's first chief strategist to come out of the creative side. For six years, he was McCann's executive vice president/director of strategic creative development; in March 1993, he was tapped as executive vice president/creative director, worldwide accounts. To Nelson, that mix is not an insignificant detail about his view of the business.

"As a creative person, it's easy for me to explain strategy to a client in concrete terms," he notes. "You can bring to the account side of the job a certain amount of dynamism and nuance from the creative side."

With his strategist's hat on, Nelson outlines two points on the global account axis. On one end are pure international brands like Martini & Rossi vermouth that use "one sight, one sound, one sell" campaigns. At the other end are clients such as Nabisco, which favor decentralized product positioning for goods sold under different names based on the marketing needs of a particular country.

In between those extremes are two main styles of advertising. One stresses a consistent product positioning regardless of where a product is sold and under whatever brand name is adopted. For a McCann client like Nescafé and its well-publicized serial romance campaign, the product positioning or product demonstration is the same, whether it's applied to Nestlés Gold Blend in Britain or Taster's Choice in America. The rest of the message may be specific to satisfy the needs of each country's culture.

A client like Black & Decker may opt instead for a consistent brand positioning. What the brand stands for remains the same and the advertising fits a pattern. The campaign imagery is then adjusted on a country-to-country basis to reflect local tastes.

"A product occupies functional territory, while a brand occupies mental territory," Nelson explains. "Because a product seeks to persuade by its features, it is fundamentally rational. Because a brand seeks to persuade by the magnetic pull of what it stands for—in addition to its performance—it is fundamentally emotional."

This duality can be seen in the agency's work for United Parcel Service. Six years ago, UPS wanted to expand into Europe and Asia, but its longtime U.S. agency, Ammirati & Puris, had no overseas offices. McCann pitched the business in April 1988, and, by October of that year, UPS was launched into 15 countries simultaneously.

Starting from scratch, UPS now claims annual revenues of more than $1 billion in Europe and $300 million in Asia. Last month, the International Advertising Association cited McCann's UPS work as the year's best global television campaign. "The difficulty of achieving consistency while still appealing to target audiences across several continents makes this a tough category," the IAA judges noted. "UPS managed this easily."

"We were moving rapidly to deploy our services overseas. We didn't have a group of seasoned marketing people internationally," relates Peter Fredo, UPS' vice president for advertising and public relations. "So we couldn't afford not to have a partner who was already there with a strong overseas network. We needed an agency like McCann who has been there as long as they have and could execute our strategy as effectively and quickly as possible."

To compete in a crowded market, UPS first had to establish its brand identity. "UPS was coming into the market late. It was the fourth or fifth player in Europe," Nelson says. "No one over there knew UPS. It wasn't like the U.S., where everyone has warm memories of being a kid and seeing a big brown truck delivering presents at Christmas time. So we had to create an immediate level of respect with the consumer. We didn't want to come across as the arrogant American. The strategy became, 'We're not in the business of delivery. We're in the business of trust.' "

Once that emotional bond was formed, McCann and UPS moved to increase brand awareness through product performance. The global television spots developed last year took two forms: one that showed UPS delivering packages for a smartly attired young executive, and the other depicting a merchant "guaranteeing" the shipment of critical goods for an anxious business woman. Both use the themeline "As sure as taking it there yourself."

The European delivery spots track a package's whereabouts en route to Hong Kong. In a reedited version for use in Asia, which was shot with a different cast, the package moves from Hong Kong to London, with the Hong Kong harbor and rickshaws replacing the Houses of Parliament and black London cabs. Footage of shiny UPS fleets is shared by all spots.

Most of the creative work on UPS is produced out of McCann, New York, headed by creative director Louis Popp. But three overseas creative directors are also assigned to the account, in London, Milan, and Tokyo.

"Developing a campaign is a highly controlled process," Nelson explains. "All the main work is done in a centralized fashion out of a particular office. But we will send around storyboards so our people in the field can check cultural variables."

Adds Jerry Green, the executive creative director of McCann, London, who works on UPS: "It's all based on the principle of 'What goes around, comes around.' We don't suffer from the 'not invented here' syndrome. We pool our experiences. That's what makes it work."

For McCann's packaged-goods clients, the creative issues are often more complex, given the nuances involved for appropriate cultural interpretation in speaking to consumers. But business-to-business advertising brings its own set of positioning challenges.

"It's true that in packaged goods, the consumer has more of an emotional relationship with a brand. In business-to-business marketing, the transactions occur much less frequently, but they cost so much," Nelson says. "Someone may be spending millions of dollars on a decision. So that tends to balance out the emotional aspect of frequency."

There are some general rules that cross over either category. "In developing any global campaign, you first have to identify which approach to use, then figure out how to best express that in a way that it can travel across borders," says Nelson. "If you focus on the eccentricity of a product, your ideas won't travel. And you can't focus on the eccentricity of a market—tapping into something like British humor—because then the idea won't travel, either."

Nelson describes himself as the point man for any number of teams around the world that develop such strategies, working by faxes, phones and videoconferences. "I become a conscience, catalyst or compass in the process," says Nelson. "Is the client thinking too narrowly about the strategy? Or too expansively? Are we playing it too safe? Or too loose? There is a profound difference between image and reputation: Image is what you say about you. Reputation is what others say about you. Certain reputations have great elasticity. Others need more focus."

McCann bases its worldwide account coordinators wherever clients center their own operations. For UPS, that means Atlanta and London. For L'Oréal, it's Paris; AT&T is in Brussels.

"McCann is a culture of cooperation and coordination," Nelson says of the way the agency has established its international presence. "We've become a learning organization. We view the whole world as a giant marketing laboratory where we're dealing with clients of varying degrees, with centralized and decentralized organizations. We're constantly learning from this experience. Everything is a test market for us."

In chasing new business, Nelson may go anywhere to cherry-pick talent for creative proposals. In late 1991, McCann pitched Hitachi's corporate branding assignment. The effort was coordinated out of New York, but it drew on creative teams in London, Seattle, Hong Kong and Tokyo.

"You can use time as your friend, not your enemy," says Nelson. "Thanks to time differences, we had people in various parts of the world working on Hitachi 24 hours a day." That around-the-clock cooperation led to success. "Relatively speaking, Hitachi is not a huge account for us in New York," Nelson admits. "But while it was a wonderful practical victory for us here, it was a large symbolic victory for Tokyo. Next time it might be Tokyo helping New York out on a big pitch."

The goal is to allow good ideas to bubble up from any office around the world. The popular soap-opera romance campaign for Taster's Choice in the U.S. originated in Britain, for example. And for Johnson & Johnson's oral care products advertising, McCann's Australian creatives came up with an animated Mr. Reach toothbrush character, which has since been exported for European and U.S. campaigns.

To Nelson, the ability to spot important trends and successful work around the world is critical. In this instance, size and experience are claimed as significant advantages.

"When you're on your third generation of doing this, you know how to manage cross-border clients," Nelson says. "There have been other people before us at McCann who have made enough mistakes and perfected the system. We can stand on their shoulders. It's become the institutionalized sensibility of this organization."

INDEX

INDEX